British Archives

fourth edition

British Archives

fourth edition

A Guide to Archive Resources in the United Kingdom

Editors
Janet Foster and Julia Sheppard

Consultant Editor
Richard Storey

palgrave

First published 2002 by
PALGRAVE
Houndmills, Basingstoke, Hampshire RG21 6XS and
175 Fifth Avenue, New York, N. Y. 10010
Companies and representatives throughout the world

PALGRAVE is the new global academic imprint of
St. Martin's Press LLC Scholarly and Reference Division and
Palgrave Publishers Ltd (formerly Macmillan Press Ltd).

ISBN 0–333–73536–6 hardcover

This book is printed on paper suitable for recycling and made from fully managed and sustained forest sources.

Cataloguing-in-publication data

A catalogue record for this book is available from the British Library.

Cataloguing-in-publication data is available from the Library of Congress

10   9   8   7   6   5   4   3   2   1
11   10   09   08   07   06   05   04   03   02

Printed and bound in Great Britain by
Creative Print & Design (Wales), Ebbw Vale

Contents

Acknowledgements

We are again indebted to our many colleagues and friends for their support and assistance during the compilation of this edition. Their encouragement has helped us immensely.

For this edition we enjoyed the benefit of Richard Storey's 'retirement', which enabled him to join us as consulting editor providing an extensive knowledge of the archive scene, important assistance with checking copy and proofs, and a constant source of sound advice.

Revision of the Useful Publications section was considerably helped by suggestions and contributions from the following: Sally Brown, Heather Creaton, Simon Fowler, Jenny Haynes, Serena Kelly, David Lee, Alexandra Nicol, Richard Olney, Jonathan Pepler, Lesley Richmond, Anthony Richards and Rosemary Seton.

The Wellcome Trust has again made this work possible through generously allowing us the use of its facilities and services. Tracy Tillotson patiently dealt with the endless correspondence and revisions and thus we owe her a huge debt of gratitude. Other staff at the Wellcome Library have been very tolerant of the effects of the burdens imposed, particularly during the latter stages of production. Michael Clark, of the IT Department, resolved a number of problems with the original database. The Librarian, David Pearson, has always recognised the importance of the book and took practical measures to enable its completion.

Assistance with the database was given by Christine Kane and, at Alpha Index, Stuart Martin and Philip Meldrum. Anna Lloyd, Sophie Lucas and Christi Daugherty undertook the laborious data entry corrections at proof stage. Ruth Austin gave careful attention to the final proofreading. Excellent copy-editing and advice was supplied by Caroline Richmond, whose knowledge of the book and attention to detail have, yet again, proved invaluable. Chris Boulter worked hard as our production manager at Macmillan during the early stages, while latterly, with the change to Palgrave, we have been fortunate to work with Alison Jones, who pulled out all the stops to help us in the final stages.

Finally, for their amazing and never-failing support, Janet would particularly like to thank her life partner Jessamy Harvey, in addition to Margaret Crockett, her business partner and friend of us both, and Julia would like to thank John Orbell and her friends.

Foreword

British Archives was first published in 1982. It remains the only book providing a general guide to archives throughout the United Kingdom and is recognised as the principal reference work in its field.

For this fourth edition the book has again expanded. It now has 1,231 entries and a total of 478 institutions were contacted for possible inclusion as new entries. There has been a large amount of revision within existing entries – partly this involved introducing details of e-mail and website addresses. Even more time-consuming has been the keeping track of changes consequent upon yet another round of local authority reorganisation in addition to the funding initiatives for special collections within the higher education sector. A major development has been the decision, reached in agreement with the Business Archives Council, to include business archives for the first time, which are if anything even more prone to constant change than the local authority repositories.

The archive scene in the United Kingdom, as elsewhere, has been transformed by the explosion in electronic access to information. A huge number of projects have made possible access to catalogues, lists and guides on the Internet. In addition, the archival networking projects provide alternative subject and regional access for researchers, and these are included in the list of Useful Organisations and Websites. *British Archives*, as stated in all editions, is not a comprehensive listing of all collections, but a first step to locating the whereabouts of archives, and readers are advised to use Internet resources as well as this reference work. The Useful Publications list has been expanded and revised into sections arranged by topic and type of material to facilitate searching.

In response to comments indicating that there was confusion about which index to use, for this edition we have merged the former Alphabetical Listing and Collections Index to provide a consolidated Main Index which appears at the back of the book. Also, in view of the changing status of counties and the expansion of unitary authorities, we have decided, following consultation with the profession, that the List of Entries by County was no longer viable.

Work on this fourth edition took far longer than anticipated, partly as a result of the wide spread of new approaches, partly as a result of problems with our new database, and also as a result of the huge amount of revision required for most of the entries. This was exacerbated by the number of poor-quality or illegible returns. The editors have done their utmost to ensure that the information presented is as correct as possible, but inevitably a published work of this scale, which includes contact details that are changing daily, cannot help but be out of date in some instances.

Nevertheless, we are confident that this fourth edition continues to give a useful overall view of the archives distributed throughout the United Kingdom, and thus information will be collected towards a fifth edition, whatever format that may have. We would therefore welcome any additions or suggestions and invite comments to be sent to us c/o the Wellcome Library, 183 Euston Road, London NW1 2BE.

Janet Foster and Julia Sheppard

Introduction

Archives: What they are and how to use them

Strictly speaking, archives are the documents created in the normal course of the life of an institution or individual in order for them to function, and as such provide a historical record. Thus an archive is a cohesive body of original documents emanating from one source. However, the term is now used much more loosely to cover any primary source material in a variety of media and format whatever its origin (hence including documents, photographs, audio-visual, electronic records and even printed material). Also it can be used to describe the physical place where records are held. Although the title of this book is *British Archives*, we are taking the wider definition and including 'artificial' collections, so called because they have been consciously put together, usually around a subject area or a type of material, and have not accumulated naturally over the course of time.

In many cases, archives will remain in the institution that has created them, and increasingly professional archivists are involved in their preservation. Many such bodies, however, have decided that they are neither able satisfactorily to house their old records nor adequately to make them available for historians to consult, hence there is also a steady transfer of such archives to established collecting repositories.

Researchers should be aware that consulting archives is not the same as looking up information in a book. Archives are unique: the reader cannot assume that they are freely available or easily accessible, or even that the originals can be consulted. They are never 'loaned', and copies are not necessarily obtainable. Finding aids – catalogues, lists and indexes – vary greatly in style and detail. The emergence of standards in archival description is leading to greater consistency in cataloguing although there is no single archive classification system, and in some places finding aids may not exist although, at the least, guides to overall holdings may increasingly be found on the web. A great deal depends greatly on the type of institution – the facilities and services of, for example, a large and well-staffed county record office cannot be expected everywhere, even in other local authority repositories. However, there is a general commitment to raise standards within the profession, assisted by a variety of organisations and publications noted in the relevant sections of this book.

It will be obvious from consulting the entries in this book that a number of the archives are administered by librarians, clerks, secretaries, honorary archivists or other individuals whose chief priorities or duties may be elsewhere. Moreover, the archives are frequently not stored readily to hand, or may be in use by others or being filmed or repaired. Increasingly, too, certain categories of records, e.g. parish registers, particularly in local authority record offices, may only be consulted on microfilm/fiche, and there may be heavy demand for use of the film/fiche reader. For all these reasons it is therefore always advisable to contact the repository in advance and/or check the website to confirm access arrangements and to make a prior appointment. Background preparation and reading are also essential if the reader is to grasp the significance of the archives and the types of documentation likely to be encountered. It must be remembered that records were not normally created with the needs of historical research in mind. It is easy to fall into the trap of assuming that records will directly answer a specific query; rather it is necessary to understand how and why they were created before embarking on any research into them. Although archivists are not necessarily authorities on all that their holdings contain, they will do everything possible to direct the researcher towards the relevant material. If any enquiry is lengthy and a personal visit to the archive is impossible, some offices now offer a paid research service or may be able to give details of a professional researcher in the area. See Useful Organisations and Websites for relevant organisations.

Methodology

British Archives is not a commercial directory and no charge is made for an entry. Inevitably, it cannot be comprehensive, since any organisation holding its own non-current records selected for preservation can claim to have an archive. Our approach has been to cover as many places as possible where archives, in the widest sense of the word, are held and are relatively accessible.

As with the third edition, restrictions on time and finance made it impossible to visit repositories. Therefore we have again relied mainly on questionnaires, which were sent out accompanied by sample entries and a slightly revised key subject word list. We are indebted to all those who so kindly took the time and trouble to complete and return the questionnaires.

Sources

We have drawn on a number of reference works in order to locate archives, in addition to monitoring professional archival publications and historical and other general works where primary sources were quoted. Approaches were also made to organisations which had advertised for archivists or whose existence was drawn to our attention by historians and colleagues. In addition, a number of organisations requested to be included and the Historical Manuscript Commission's ARCHON web pages were consulted.

Additions and exclusions

Following discussions with the Business Archives Council, businesses have been included for the first time although we have concentrated on those previously covered by the Business Archive Council's *Directory of Corporate Archives* rather than attempting to contact every major business in the United Kingdom. We have also made a concerted effort to contact all new universities and more voluntary organisations including charities and religious organisations.

Privately held collections of estate and family papers have not been extensively covered, although we have included several of the most well-known collections, particularly if an archivist is employed. Further information about these collections is available from the Historical Manuscripts Commission (see p.xxi) and in their two-volume guide *Principal Family and Estate Collections* (see Useful Publications, p.xxxiii).

National museums and a limited number of other museums are included. However, no comprehensive coverage of all the museums in Britain has been attempted, although most will have maintained some records of their administration and collections, management and some have accepted collections of archives and manuscripts.

Similarly, the many local history, archaeological, literary and philosophical societies have not been systematically listed, both because of the numbers involved and because information about them is normally available from the relevant local authority record offices. The latter may indeed hold these archives or have an agreement to administer them on behalf of the societies. Borough records outside of established repositories have also not been systematically covered; local authority record offices should be able to advise on their whereabouts if they have not been deposited.

Information collection

On the whole we have relied on questionnaires, supplemented by telephone calls, e-mails, and website consultations, to clarify queries or to confirm the current situation with those repositories which failed to respond. In 1998 we started to send our questionnaires and key subject lists for new entries. This was followed in 1999 by circulating those institutions having existing entries with their third edition entry, annotated where we considered more information could helpfully be forthcoming. We tried to encourage fuller responses where appropriate, and many organisations took the opportunity to revise their existing entry completely. For the first time, information was requested about e-mail and website addresses.

Updating has been a continuous process up to proof stage (October 2001). Contact details, particularly for electronic communication, are continually changing, and where our information is no longer accurate we apologise for any inconvenience caused.

It will be appreciated that the quality and details of returns is not consistent. Although editorial persistence and research achieve a substantial measure of improvement in many cases, the guide is primarily based on information received and there is still considerable variation in the entries. Inevitably, returns from some of the larger repositories will be more general and in these cases the reader is particularly advised to consult the published and electronic finding aids available.

Information was sought under the headings detailed below. Where any section is not included in an entry, this indicates that no information of relevance was supplied. In some instances, where it was impossible or inappropriate to have a full entry, information about the institution and its holdings were summarised into a brief statement or minimal entry.

Entry headings

Name of repository: In some cases related repositories under one parent body have been given the same entry number with subsections 'A', 'B' etc, e.g. entry 561 British Library.

Parent Organisation: This is included if applicable, although the historical background section may also yield relevant information.

Address: In a few cases the postal address is different from the address at which the archives are stored.

Telephone: New telephone codes continue to be introduced and British Telecom is liable to change codes yet again, so if a number is unobtainable for long periods it is worth checking that the code and/or number remain correct.

Fax: These numbers have been included where supplied.

E-mail: These may be general enquiry addresses or the personal address of the archivist/custodian.

Website: Many repositories already have a web presence but many are in the process of being mounted; in addition, we have not always included those sites which did not have relevant information.

Enquiries: Both title and name were requested but were not always given. Qualifications have not been included. A contact address is given if different from the main address.

Open: This normally states opening arrangements, i.e. days and hours of opening and any regular annual closures apart from bank and other public holidays. Academic institutions are normally closed for longer periods over Easter and Christmas. Many smaller places are closed for lunch. Some places are open by arrangement only.

Access: This gives information about persons who may consult the records and whether there are restrictions such as closure periods. Where an appointment is necessary this is also indicated. A very few repositories charge for access: rates of charges are liable to change and have not been included. Some local authority record offices operate the County Archives Research Network (CARN) system of issuing readers' tickets. Information about availability of a paid research service is included here.

Historical background: An outline administrative history of the organisation is supplied, including details of predecessor bodies where appropriate and, if relevant, the development of the repository and/or collections. It is also noted if the repository gives assistance to local societies and landed estates, and whether it is a Diocesan Record Office and/or recognised as a place of deposit for public records.

Acquisitions policy: The aims of the collecting policy and/or major subject areas may be given.

Archives of organisation: Outline details are provided, including dates if known. Where the formula 'usual local authority record holdings' has been used for local authority record offices, see the fuller description below (p.xii)

Major collections: This category usually covers material acquired by the organisation as gifts or on deposit, and names significant collections, with covering dates where possible. In some instances, the formula 'deposited local collections' has been used by local authority record offices and local studies libraries; for the fuller description see below.

Non-manuscript material: This lists any other materials, e.g. plans, drawings, photographs, maps, sound archives, films and supporting printed material.

Finding aids: Unpublished catalogues, lists and indexes, etc, available in the offices or online are mentioned here. In some cases, it is stated whether lists are sent to the National Register of Archives (NRA) or the renamed National Register of Archives for Scotland (NRAS), and relevant list reference numbers may be given.

Facilities: Provisions for readers are given, usually specifying availability of reprographic facilities, e.g. photocopying, photography, microfilm/fiche reader/printer etc. Reading aids have not normally been included. Specific charges for these services are not given.

Conservation: This notes where in-house facilities for paper conservation are available or whether work is contracted out. In some cases, it is indicated if outside work is undertaken by the conservation staff.

Publications: Details are listed of published guides or other relevant works about the repository or its holdings, although they are not necessarily still in print.

Local authority record offices and local study libraries

Local authority record offices, i.e. county, city and some borough record offices, provide a comprehensive record service to the general public, collecting material both official and unofficial which is of relevance to the history of the locality. For these reasons, entries for local authority record offices may use the formulae 'usual local authority record holdings' and 'deposited local collections' to avoid repetition of similar information.

'Usual local authority record holdings' can be described as follows:

Local government and related records: archives of the local authorities, which may range from charters of a medieval burgh to recent committee records of an urban district or county council. Quarter session records are also frequently held. Hence all aspects of local government – poor law, health, education, etc – are likely to be covered.

'Deposited local collections' comprise the following main categories:

Ecclesiastical records: these may include parish records (all such records over 100 years old are now held at designed Diocesan Record Offices unless the parish itself provides special storage), as well as tithe, probate and non-conformist records, e.g. the non-current records of Methodists, Baptists and Quakers.

Estate and family archives, including manorial records: many of these archives are held and include leases, deeds, maps and other documents relating to property, in addition to the personal correspondence and other papers of local families and individuals.

Solicitors' and estate agents' papers: including records of former clients' businesses or estates, auction and sale details.

Business and industrial records: records of local businesses, manufacturers and branches of national firms, in addition to records from small family retail concerns. Such records may include accounts, correspondence, plans, photographs and publicity.

Voluntary organisations: records of charitable bodies, local societies, associates, clubs and branches of national bodies, mostly 19th century onwards.

Antiquarian collections: manuscripts, transcripts of documents, etc, assembled by an individual and usually relating to a specific area.

Local studies libraries may contain a miscellany of items relating to the locality and its history, primarily non-manuscript, consisting (apart from the books) of some or all of the following: census returns; Ordnance Survey and other maps; illustrative material including postcards and photographs; drawings; newspapers and cuttings; directory details of local functions; material assembled by local historians; and printed ephemera, including programmes, theatre bills, advertising etc. Where manuscript material is held this might include rate books, local business records, papers of local residents and celebrities, written and oral memoirs, journals and correspondence.

Appendices

These are used to provide information about institutions which, for various reasons, do not have an entry.

How to Use this Book

The entries are arranged alphabetically by town and running heads of town names are given on each page. London is the area of postal districts only.

All listings and indexes refer to entry number and not page number unless specifically indicated otherwise.

There are two principal ways into the information in the book: the Main Index and the Guide to Key Subjects. The Main Index comprises a consolidated list of entry titles (indicated by bold type); predecessor names; parent organisations, where relevant; personal names; and collection names. The Guide to Key Subjects is intended to give an indication of subject strengths rather than providing a comprehensive subject index. There are limitations to both and the introductory remarks to both of them should be read.

The Useful Organisations and Websites section provides information about the increasing number of national and specialist organisations concerned with archives, in addition to details of the main UK archival gateways on the Internet.

The Useful Publications section comprises works of general reference, including directories and surveys, as well as guides to specific topics and subjects.

Readers are encouraged to read the Introduction for an understanding of the rationale for the content of this book.

Useful Organisations and Websites

Access to Archives (A2A)

Public Record Office, Kew, Richmond, Surrey TW9 4DU Tel: 020 8392 5328
Fax: 020 8392 5281 E-mail: a2a@pro.gov.uk Web: www.a2a.pro.gov.uk
Access to Archives (A2A) is the English strand of a virtual national archives catalogue for the UK, with funding from the Heritage Lottery Fund. It aims to bring together a critical mass of information about the rich national archival heritage and making that information available globally from one source via the web. Initially concentrating on retrospective conversion of catalogues, it has now expanded to provide for new cataloguing projects. At present it consists of various local initiatives – local, either geographically or conceptually, in that they relate to archives in the same subject specialism. The A2A website carries a constantly updated searchable database of all the catalogues that have been converted.

AIM25

Project Co-ordinator: Robert Baxter, College Archives, King's College London, Strand, London WC2R 2LS Tel: 020 7848 2011 E-mail: robert.baxter@kcl.ac.uk Web: www.aim25.ac.uk
AIM25 is a project funded by the Research Support Libraries Programme (RSLP) to provide a single point of networked access to collection-level descriptions of the archives and manuscript collections of the principal colleges and schools of the University of London, of other higher education institutions and their constituents in the area bounded by the M25 London orbital motorway. Also included are some of the principal royal colleges and societies of medicine and science based in London. The archives of more than 50 institutions will be covered. A second round of funding has extended the participating institutions to include the main medical colleges.

Archives Council Wales (ACW)

Co-ordinator: Gwyn Jenkins, National Library of Wales, Aberystwyth, Ceredigion SY23 3BU. Web: www.llgc.org.uk/cac
The Archives Council Wales (ACW) was established in 1995 and represents institutions and organisations from all parts of Wales involved in the administration of archives. It has produced guidelines and these, with its minutes and annual reports, are available on its web page.

Archives Hub

Project Manager: Amanda Hill, Archives Hub, Manchester Computing, University of Manchester, Oxford Road, Manchester M13 9PL Tel: 0161 275 6055 E-mail: amanda.hill@man.ac.uk
Web: www.archiveshub.ac.uk
The Archives Hub provides another strand of the National Archives Network and is a single point of access to descriptions of archives held in UK universities and colleges. At present these are primarily at collection level, although where possible they are linked to complete catalogue descriptions. A steering group which includes representatives of the Public Record Office, the Historical Manuscripts Commission and the other archive networks guides the progress of the project. The service is hosted by Manchester Computing at the University of Manchester on behalf of the Consortium of University Research Libraries (CURL) and is funded by the Joint Information Systems Committee (JISC).

ARCHON see Historical Manuscripts Commission (HMC)

Army Museums Ogilby Trust

Director: Antony Makepeace-Warne, 58 The Close, Salisbury, Wiltshire SP1 2EX
Tel: 01722 332188 Fax: 01722 334211 E-mail: dir@amot.demon.co.uk
Web: www.armymuseums.org.uk

The Trust was established in 1954 to promote a wider interest in military history. The Trust's work now concentrates on supporting the development of regimental museums in the UK and raising standards of access and display.

Artists' Papers Register

Chair: Rupert Shepherd, 80A Fentiman Road, London SW8 1LA Tel: 020 7820 0200 Web: www.hmc.gov.uk/artists
The Artists' Papers Register is a long-term project of the Association of Art Historians, supported by the Getty Grant Program, the Henry Moore Foundation and the Universities of Birmingham and Leeds, where two project officers have been based. The Register covers, irrespective of status, not only painters and sculptors, but also designers and design groups, craft-workers, and other art and design-related organisations. The existing database is currently made accessible on the web.

Association for Manuscripts and Archives in Research Collections (AMARC)

Membership Secretary: Dr C. Breay, Department of Manuscripts, The British Library, 96 Euston Road, London NW1 2DB E-mail: claire.breay@bl.uk
AMARC promotes the accessibility, preservation and study of manuscripts and archives in libraries and other research collections in Great Britain and Ireland. It brings together curators, researchers and all who share a scholarly interest in this field. AMARC is the successor to the SCONUL Manuscripts Group, and continues its activities in collaboration with other like-minded groups. Membership is open to both individuals and institutions.

The Association of Genealogists and Researchers in Archives (AGRA)

Joint Secretaries, 29 Badgers Close, Horsham, West Sussex RH12 5RU Web: www.agra.org.uk
AGRA was founded in 1968 as the Association of Genealogists and Record Agents to promote and maintain high standards of professional conduct and expertise in genealogy, heraldry and record searching and to safeguard the interests of members and clients. It does not undertake research but publishes a booklet listing members and their interests.

Association of Independent Museums (AIM)

Secretary: Diane Lees E-mail: d.lees@vam.ac.uk Web: www.museums.org.uk/aim
The Association of Independent Museums (AIM) aims to assist all independent museums with advice and liaison with other bodies and to raise standards in the museums, many of which hold archives. Membership is open to any group or individual interested in the future of independent museums. AIM runs events and produces a series of focus papers.

British Association for Local History (BALH)

PO Box 1576, Salisbury, Wilts SP21 8EY Tel: 01722 413242 Web: www.balh.co.uk
Established in 1982 to supersede the Standing Conference for Local History, BALH is a national charity which promotes local history and services local historians. A quarterly journal, *The Local Historian*, plus *Local History News* and other books and pamphlets are published. Visits and conferences are organised; there is a mail base for local history; and an insurance service for local societies is operated.

British Association of Picture Libraries and Agencies (BAPLA)

Chief Executive: Linda Royle, 18 Vine Hill, London EC1R 5DZ E-mail: enquiries@bapla.org.uk
Web: www.bapla.org.uk
BAPLA is a professional trade association which provides an information service for the location of images. It addresses issues of interest to its members on a local, national and international level and works to ensure that picture library users and suppliers enjoy an efficient service of the highest standard. It has over 400 member companies and publishes an annual *Directory*, with a full listing of its members.

British Records Association (BRA)

40 Northampton Road, London EC1R 0HB Tel: 020 7833 0428 Fax: 020 7833 0416 E-mail: archivez@charityvfree.com Web: www.hmc.gov.uk/bra
The British Records Association (BRA) was founded in 1932 as a national organisation to assist with the preservation, care, use and publication of historical records. It has an annual conference and publishes a twice-yearly *Journal*, a *Newsletter* and guidelines. It also runs a Records Preservation Section, which rescues and advises on the deposit of papers, deeds and documents of all kinds.

British Universities Film & Video Council (BUFVC)

77 Wells Street, London W1T 3QJ Tel: 020 7393 1500 Fax: 020 7393 1555
E-mail: bufvc@open.ac.uk Web: www.bufvc.ac.uk
The BUFVC was founded in 1948 and exists to support and promote the use of moving images in UK higher and further education, and the use of moving images in research generally. It achieves this through a variety of services, databases, publications and other activities. Membership is open to organisations with an interest in higher education, teaching and research. It maintains a reference library and a film and video library with viewing and editing facilities. BUFVC events organised annually include conferences and courses. The Council also produces various publications, including *Viewfinder* (thrice-yearly).

Business Archives Council (BAC)

Office Manager: Mrs Sharon Quinn-Robinson, 101 Whitechapel High Street, London E1 7RE
Tel: 020 7422 Fax: 020 7422 0026 E-mail: bac@archives.gla.ac.uk Web: www.archives.gla.ac.uk/bac
A registered charity, the BAC was established in 1934. Its objectives are: to encourage the preservation of British business records; to advise on the administration and management of archives and current records: and to promote the use of business records. Membership comprises businesses and professional associations; libraries, universities and record offices; and individual archivists, business people, enthusiasts, historians and records managers. The Council publishes the *Business Archives* journal (biannually).

Business Archives Council of Scotland (BACS)

BACS Surveying Officer, Archives & Business Records Centre, University of Glasgow, 7-87 Dumbarton Road, Glasgow G11 6PW Tel: 0141 330 4159 Fax: 0141 330 4158 E-mail: bacs@archives.gla.ac.uk Web: www.archives.gla.ac.uk/bacs
The Business Archives Council of Scotland (BACS) was established in 1960 as an independent archive body concerned with the active preservation of Scottish Business Records. It is a registered charity funded by donations from Scottish businesses and a grant-in-aid from the Scottish Record Office. The Council employs one full-time Surveying Officer who operates out of the University of Glasgow Archives & Business Records Centre.

The Catholic Archives Society

Hon. Secretary, Innyngs House, Hatfield Park, Hatfield, Hertfordshire AL9 5PL Web: www.catholic-history.org.uk/catharch
The Catholic Archives Society was founded in 1979. It does not hold archives but promotes the care and preservation of the records of the dioceses, religious foundations, institutions and societies of the Roman Catholic Church in the United Kingdom and Eire. The Society seeks to obtain these objectives by promoting the identification and listing of Catholic records, by providing those with responsibility for these records with information, technical advice and training opportunities, by arranging an annual conference, by publishing a yearly periodical, *Catholic Archives*, and by circulating a *Bulletin* to members.

Centre for Metropolitan History

Institute of Historical Research, Senate House, Malet Street, London WC1E 7HU Tel: 020 7862 8790 Fax: 020 7862 8793 E-mail: ihrcmh@sas.ac.uk Web: www.ihrinfo.ac.uk/cmh/cmh.main.html
Established in 1988 in collaboration with the Museum of London and other organisations, the

Centre for Metropolitan History promotes the study and wide appreciation of London's character and development from its beginnings to the present day, and is concerned to set the history of London in the wider context provided by knowledge of other metropolises. It runs conferences and meetings and is part of the Institute of Historical Research (see entry below)

Charity Archivists and Records Managers Group (CHARM)
Annie Lindsay, The Wellcome Library, 183 Euston Road, London NW1 2BE E-mail: a.lindsay@wellcome.ac.uk Web: www.archives.org.uk
CHARM provides a forum and support network for archivists, records managers and others responsible for the management of charity records and archives. It aims to promote the importance of charity records and archives and to raise the profile of the role of archivists and records managers within the charity sector as well as the archive, records management and information professions as a whole. CHARM is affiliated to the Society of Archivist's Specialist Repositories Group.

Ephemera Society
8 Galveston Road, London SW15 2SA Tel: 01923 829079 Fax: 01923 825207 Web: www.ephemera-society.org.uk
Founded in 1975, the Ephemera Society is concerned to promote the preservation and study of printed and MS ephemera of all types and subjects. It organises exhibitions, lectures and collectors' fairs, and acts as an information forum for members through its quarterly publication, *The Ephemerist*.

Family Records Centre (see also entry 608)
1 Myddleton Street, London EC1 1UW Tel: 01704 569824/020 8392 5300 Web: www.familyrecords.gov.uk
The Family Records Centre, which opened in 1997, replaced the St Catherine's House Public Searchroom of the Office of National Statistics and the Chancery Lane Census and Wills Microfilm Reading Rooms of the Public Record Office. It provides expert advice on birth, adoption, marriage and death certificates, as well as an information point selling family history publications and a family history reference area.

Federation of Family History Societies (FFHS)
Administrator, Benson Room, Birmingham and Midland Institute, Margaret Street, Birmingham B3 3BS Web: www.ffhs.org.uk
The FFHS is an international organisation based in the UK which represents, advises and supports over 220 family history societies and genealogical organisations worldwide, with a total membership of over 180,000. Its principal aims are: to co-ordinate and assist the work of societies or other bodies interested in family history, genealogy and heraldry; and to foster the spirit of mutual co-operation by sponsoring projects in these fields. The FFHS offers a forum for constituent societies in addition to offering training and an international information service. Publications, aimed mainly at the genealogist, include many on different source materials.

Friends of the National Libraries
The Secretary, c/o Dept of Manuscripts, The British Library, 96 Euston Road, London NW1 2DB Tel: 020 7412 7559 Web: www.bl.uk/information/friends2.html
The Friends of the National Libraries, a voluntary organisation consisting mainly of private individuals, was founded in 1931 in order to help acquire for the nation printed books, manuscripts and archives, in particular those that might otherwise leave the country. The Friends operate by making grants towards purchase, by eliciting and channelling benefactions, and by organising appeals and publicity.

Gateway to the Archives of Scottish Higher Education (GASHE)
Project Manager: Victoria Peters, GASHE, Archives & Business Records Centre, University of

Glasgow, 77-87 Dumbarton Road, Glasgow G11 6PW Tel: 0141 330 2992 Fax: 0141 330 4158
E-mail: gashe@archives.gla.ac.uk Web: www.gashe.ac.uk
GASHE is the Scottish counterpart to AIM25 and is similarly funded by the Research Support
Libraries Programme (RSLP). It intends to provide an integrated gateway to higher education
institutions' records, the primary resources for Scotland's educational, intellectual and cultural history. The project provides collection- and lower-level descriptions of archives and related materials in differing media, covering a vast chronological breadth and across a diverse range of higher
educational institutions. The online resource will enable subject and functional guided navigation
in addition to providing value-added biographical and institutional access points.

Great Britain Philatelic Society (GBPS)
Membership Secretary: Andrew Lajer, The Old Post Office, Hurst, Berkshire RG10 0TR Tel: 0118
934 4151 Fax: 0118 934 4947 E-mail: andrewlajer@compuserve.com Web: ww.gbps.org.uk
The GBPS was founded in 1955 by a small but enthusiastic group of collectors, and since that time
has grown steadily both in this country and abroad to over 700 members. The Society's primary
aim is to promote, encourage and contribute to the advancement of the philately of Great Britain.
The GBPS now covers all aspects of GB philately: stamps, postal history, postal stationery, booklets, college stamps, revenues, telegraphs, and philatelic conservation. Its consultants can be contacted for advice. Meetings are held regularly, normally at the British Philatelic Centre, London,
and a *Newsletter* and *Journal* are published.

Greater London Archive Network (GLAN)
Chairman: David Mander, Hackney Archives Department, 43 De Beauvoir Road, London N1
5SQ Tel: 020 7241 2886 Fax: 020 7241 6688 Web: www.hmc.gov.uk/glan
GLAN was founded in 1982, with the aim of improving communications between those responsible for London local authority archives. In recent years GLAN has attracted many members from
a wider constancy, and our membership is now open to all those engaged in the care of archives and
local studies collections in the Greater London area. It organises visits to various repositories and
libraries and training meetings on various subjects, which have attracted an increasing number of
associate members. It produces a number of publications including *London Local Archives* (a
directory), *Film archives in London* and *Greater London History Sources* (vol 1 covering the City
of London).

Higher Education Digitisation Services (HEDS)
University of Hertfordshire, College Lane, Hatfield, Hertfordshire AL10 9AB Tel: 01707 286078
Fax: 01707 286079 E-mail: heds@herts.ac.uk Web: http://heds.herts.ac.uk
HEDS was established in 1996 and provides an advice and consultancy service for digitisation projects. HEDS will support project development from the first feasibility assessment through to final
delivery of digitised material. It serves not only the higher education sector, but also public libraries, museums and other non-profit-making organisations

Historical Manuscripts Commission (HMC)
Secretary: Dr C.J. Kitching, Quality House, Quality Court, Chancery Lane, London WC2A 1HP
Tel: 020 7242 1198 Fax: 020 7831 3550 E-mail: nra@hmc.gov.uk Web: www.hmc.gov.uk
Search Room: Mon-Fri 9.30-5.00.
Established in 1869 by Royal Warrant, its terms of reference were extended in 1959. The HMC's
primary purpose is to provide information about the existence, location and nature of manuscripts
and records for the study of British history. They also give advice on matters relating to their preservation, care, cataloguing and accessibility for research, and produces reports and publications.
The HMC maintains the Manorial Documents Register (MDR), an index to surviving manorial
records in England and Wales, which is currently being revised and computerised: the sections for
Wales, Yorkshire and Hampshire and the Isle of Wight are now available online. It also maintains
the National Register of Archives (NRA), an information bank recording the nature and whereabouts of archives and manuscripts outside the public records. The NRA contains over 43,000

unpublished lists of historical papers, together with published catalogues, guides and other finding aids. The NRA lists are now available to search online. The HMC website also carries ARCHON – Archives on Line – which is the principal online information gateway for UK archivists and users of manuscript sources for British history. It has details of UK record repositories and repositories throughout the world which have collections of manuscripts of British interest. It also provides information for archivists on archival organisations and initiatives including the various standards.

Historic Houses Archivists Group
Chairman: Ann Mitchell, Woburn Abbey, Woburn, Bedfordshire MK43 0YP Tel: 01525 290666 Fax: 01525 290271 Web: www.archives.org.uk/groups
The Historic Houses Archivists Group was formed in 1986 and its current membership includes archivists working in country houses and landed estates throughout the United Kingdom. It aims to encourage the best possible maintenance and administration of privately owned archives, and to enable those responsible for the care of private archives to meet to discuss matters of common interest and concern. To this end the Group meets twice a year and maintains active links with other interested organisations within the UK and Europe. It circulates a biannual *Newsletter* to its members and publicises training courses of relevance to members' interests.

The Historical Association
Secretary: 59a Kennington Park Road, London SE11 4JH Tel: 020 7735 3901 Fax: 020 7582 4989 Web: www.history.org.uk/HTML/aboutHA.htm
Founded in 1906, the Historical Association aims to develop public interest in history and to advance its study at all levels. Members may be amateurs or professional historians. It has a network of 60 local branches, which allows those with interests in history and the past, especially history education, to meet and exchange views. The Association also produces numerous publications.

Institute of Historical Research (IHR)
Academic Secretary, School of Advanced Study, University of London, Senate House, Malet Street, London WC1E 7HU Tel: 020 7862 8740 Fax: 020 7862 8745 E-mail: ihr@sas.ac.uk Web: www.ihrinfo.ac.uk/ihr/bbs.ihr.html
Founded in 1921 as a postgraduate institute of the University of London, the IHR provides extensive resources for bona fide historical students. Its substantial open access library of printed editions of historical sources includes extensive collections of guides and inventories of British and foreign archives, both national and local. It also publishes works of reference and administers research projects.

Institute of Paper Conservation
Leigh Lodge, Leigh, Worcester WR6 5LB Tel: 01886 832323 Fax: 01886 833688 E-mail: information@ipc.org.uk Web: www.ipc.org.uk/introframe.htm
The Institute of Paper Conservation is an international specialist organisation concerned with the conservation of paper and related materials. It aims to increase professional awareness by co-ordinating the exchange of information and facilitating contacts between its members through meetings, seminars and publications (a quarterly newsletter and an annual journal, *The Paper Conservator* (1976-)).

International Council on Archives (ICA)
Executive Secretary: 60 rue des Francs-Bourgeois, 75003 Paris, France
Web: www.ica.org/ong/ica/eng/intro.html
The ICA was founded in 1948 as the professional organisation for the world archival community, dedicated to promoting the preservation, development and use of the world's archival heritage. It brings together national archive administrations, professional associations of archivists, regional and local archives, and archives of other organisations as well as individual archivists. The ICA has over 1,500 members in over 170 countries and territories. A non-governmental organisation, it

works closely with intergovernmental organisations such as UNESCO and the Council of Europe. An international congress is held every four years, and various publications are produced.

Library Association (LA)

Chief Executive, Dr Bob McKee, 7 Ridgmount Street, London WC1E 7AE Tel: 020 7255 0500 Fax: 020 7255 0501 E-mail: info@la-hq.org.uk Web: www.la-hq.org.uk

The Library Association (LA) was established in 1877 and is the leading professional body for librarians and information managers. It is committed to enabling its members to achieve and maintain the highest professional standards, and encouraging them in the delivery and promotion of high-quality library and information services responsive to the needs of users. Members come from all sectors, including business and industry, further and higher education, schools, local and central government departments and agencies, the health service, the voluntary sector and national public libraries. It produces a monthly *Library Association Record* and numerous publications including indexes, abstracts and subject bibliographies.

The London Archive Users Forum

Secretary: Isobel Watson, 29 Stepney Green, London E1 3JX Fax: 020 7265 8236

Founded in 1987, the Forum provides for the exchange of views between users and archivists concerning records in and of the London area, organises a range of meetings and publishes a regular *Newsletter*.

Map Curators' Group (MCG)

Group Convener: Mrs A M Sutherland, Map Collection, Edinburgh University Library, 43 George Square, Edinburgh, EH8 9LJ Tel: 0131 650 3969 Fax: 0131 667 9780 E-mail: ann_sutherland@ed.ac.uk Web: www.cartography.org.uk

The MCG was founded in 1966 as an integral part of the British Cartographic Society to promote the professional development of map curatorship. In 1982 the Group became an organisation in liaison with the Library Association (LA) through which it is recognised as the authoritative body on map librarianship matters in this country. Members of the Group and participation in its activities are open to any BCS member. The Group arranges lectures, as a part of the Society's programme, and visits to established map collections. It organises training programmes in map librarianship and holds an open forum at least once each year at which members can discuss mutual problems, pool resources and consider future activities. The MCG produces a quarterly newsletter, *Cartographiti*, in addition to a lively email list *lis-maps*.

Museums Association (MA)

Director: Mark Taylor, 24 Calvin Street, London E1 6NW Tel: 020 7426 6940 Fax: 020 7426 6961 E-mail: info@museumsassociation.org Web: www.museumsassociation.org

The Museums Association (MA) was founded in 1889 as a non-governmental organisation to represent the interests of museum and gallery employees, museums and galleries as institutions and their collections. It aims to promote professional standards in museums and art galleries by campaigning, training and publications, and is also concerned with archives and affiliated issues, e.g. copyright. Its publications include *Museums Journal* (monthly) and *Museums Yearbook*. The MA has over 5,000 members, both individuals and institutions, drawn from museums, art galleries, museum suppliers, overseas associations and museum studies courses.

National Cataloguing Unit for the Archives of Contemporary Scientists (NCUACS)

Director: Peter Harper, University of Bath, Claverton Down, Bath BA2 7AY Tel: 01225 323522 Fax: 01225 826229 E-mail: ncuacs@bath.ac.uk Web: www.bath.ac.uk/Centres/NCUACS

The NCUACS is a small unit funded by various charitable and other grants. It was set up in 1987 and is the successor body of the Contemporary Scientific Archives Centre. It is not an archive, but locates and catalogues papers of distinguished contemporary British scientists and engineers prior to placing them in appropriate repositories. The Unit produces a short booklet, *Preserving*

Scientific Source Materials, which is a guide for owners of scientific archives advising them on the type of material they might find.

National Council for Conservation and Restoration (NCCR)

c/o UKIC, 106 The Chandlery, 50 Westminster Bridge Road, London SE1 7QY Tel: 020 7721 8721 Fax: 020 7721 8722 Web: www.nccr.org.uk

The NCCR is the body that represents the interests of conservators and restorers in the United Kingdom and Ireland, speaking for the sector with one voice. Participating organisations include the Society of Archivists and Institute of Paper Conservation. It aims to encourage the conservation and public access to cultural heritage items and collections held in the United Kingdom and Ireland. It assists all those with responsibility for the care of heritage collections to understand how best to conserve or restore them, promoting public access to heritage and public awareness of the need to preserve our cultural heritage from neglect and decay.

National Council on Archives (NCA)

Secretary: Margaret Turner, 26 Cruise Road, Sheffield S11 7EF Tel: 0114 230 4772

E-mail: turnermargaret@hotmail.com Web: http://nca.archives.org.uk

The NCA was established in 1988 to bring together major bodies and organisations concerned with the care, custody and use of archives, and to provide a forum for the regular exchange of views between them. It provides a regular forum for the exchange of views and acts as a channel through which current concerns in the field of archives can be brought to the attention of the public, government or relevant institutions or organisations. It also assists the work of the Historical Manuscripts Commission and the Advisory Council on Public Records in such ways as those bodies deem appropriate. It has published a number of reports including *Archives On-line* and *British Archives: The Way Forward*, which outlined a possible National Archives Network.

National Manuscripts Conservation Trust (NMCT)

The Secretary, c/o National Preservation Office (see below) Tel: 020 7412 7048 Fax: 020 7412 7796 E-mail: npo@bl.uk Web: www.bl.uk/services/preservation/nmct.html

The NMCT was established in 1990 by the British Library and the Historical Manuscripts Commission, with funding from the Office of Arts and Libraries and from private benefactors, to provide financial assistance to owners and custodians in the United Kingdom in preserving the nation's written heritage. Since 1999 the awards have been administered by the National Preservation Office (NPO) on behalf of the trustees. The NPO can advise applicants to NMCT on matters relating to specific preservation policies and strategies and to best practice in preservation, and provides *Guidelines for Applicants* downloadable from its website.

National Preservation Office (NPO)

Director, Dr Vanessa Marshall, The British Library, 96 Euston Road, London NW1 2DB

Tel: 020 7412 7612 Fax: 020 7412 7796 E-mail: npo@bl.uk Web: www.bl.uk/services/preservation

The NPO was founded in 1984 and provides an independent focus for ensuring the preservation and continued accessibility of library and archive materials in the United Kingdom and Ireland. It provides an advisory service and produces a number of publications and videos. A series of preservation guidance leaflets is available free of charge or can be downloaded from the NPO website.

National Register of Archives (NRA) see Historical Manuscripts Commission (HMC)

National Register of Archives for Scotland (NRAS)

The Registrar, HM General Register House, 2 Princes Street, Edinburgh EH1 3YY

Tel: 0131 535 1403 Fax: 0131 535 1430 E-mail: john.mclintock@nas.gov.uk Web: www.nas.gov.uk

Like the Royal Commission on Historical Manuscripts, the NRAS also has the role, through the National Archives of Scotland (see entry 329) of advising government departments, institutions, businesses and private individuals on the care and preservation of their records. In addition, it also maintains a register of lists received.

Oral History Society

The Secretary, c/o Department of Sociology, Essex University, Colchester CO4 3SQ Tel: 020 7412 7405 E-mail: rob.perks@bl.uk Web: www.oralhistory.org.uk

The Oral History Society is a national and international organisation dedicated to the collection and preservation of oral history. It encourages people of all ages to tape, video or write down their own and other people's life stories. It offers practical support and advice about how to get started, what equipment to use, what techniques are best, how to look after tapes, and how to make use of what has been collected. In conjunction with the British Library National Sound Archive (entry **5.61D**), it also holds one-day oral history training courses. The journal *Oral History* is published biannually.

Press Association (PA) News Library

Library Supervisor, Richard Peacock, PA News Ltd, PA News Centre, 292 Vauxhall Bridge Road, London SW1 1AE Tel: 020 7963 7011 Fax: 020 7963 7065 (cuttings library) E-mail: newslibrary@pa.press.net Web: www palib.press.net

PA News is the national news agency of the United Kingdom and Republic of Ireland. It dates back to 1928 and maintains an archive of more than 14 million cuttings from national newspapers over the last 100 years and which is updated daily. Apart from being called upon for the national and regional press and international news agencies, the agency also supplies information upon request from TV companies, lawyers, PR companies, publishers, industries and government departments. Customers may either visit the PA news library in person, or commission one of the library's expert team to do it on their behalf. PA Photos, a picture library service, is also run from this address.

Records Management Society

Admin. Secretary: Ms Jude Awdry, Woodside, Coleheath Bottom, Speen, Princes Risborough, Buckinghamshire HP27 0SZ Tel: 01494 488599 Fax: 01494 488590 E-mail: rms@rms-b.org.uk Web: www.rms-gb.org.uk

The Records Management Society was established in 1983 to encourage the highest professional standards in the fields of records and information management. Membership is open to all concerned with records and information, regardless of their professional or organisational status or qualifications, and the Society provides regular contact for members through its bi-monthly meetings and *Bulletin*.

Re:source The Council for Museums, Archives and Libraries

Chief Executive: Neville Mackay, 16 Queen Anne's Gate, London SW1H 9AA Tel: 020 7273 1444 Fax: 020 7273 1404 E-mail: info@resource.gov.uk Web: www.resource.gov.uk

Re:source was launched in 2000 in order to work with and for museums, archives and libraries within the United Kingdom, tapping the potential for collaboration between sectors. It replaced the Museums and Galleries Commission and the Library and Information Commission, and for the first time the archives sector was included in a nationally funded body. A major initiative has been the establishment of Regional Archive Councils, which have received funding to develop Regional Archive Strategies and to employ Archive Development Officers.

Royal Commission on Historical Manuscripts see Historial Manuscripts Commission (HMC)

Scots Ancestry Research Society

Mrs Jean Brodie, 8 York Road, Edinburgh EH5 3EH Tel/Fax: 0131 552 2028 E-mail: scotsanc@aol.com Web: www.royalmile.com/scotsancestry

The Society was established in 1945. It is a non-profit-making society for research into sources for tracing ancestry in Scotland. Since its inception it has carried out research for clients all over the world and has massed a wealth of experience and knowledge.

Scottish Archive Network (SCAN)
Web: www.scan.org.uk
The Scottish Archive Network (SCAN) is based at the National Archives for Scotland in Edinburgh (entry **329**) and is supported by the Heritage Lottery Fund (HLF) and the Genealogical Society of Utah (GSU). It is a three-year project to open up Scotland's rich archival heritage to all by revolutionising access to Scottish Archives, their catalogues and contents. The main aims are to link archives large and small, public and private, throughout Scotland; to create a unique knowledge base on Scottish history and culture; to make a major historical resource, the wills, available to researchers worldwide; and to be accessible to everyone across the web.

Scottish Conservation Bureau
Bureau Manager: Carol E. Brown, Longmore House, Salisbury Place, Edinburgh EH9 1SH
Tel: 0131 6688668 Web: www.sscr.demon.co.uk
The Scottish Conservation Bureau, founded in 1980, is a branch of Historic Scotland's Technical Conservation, Research and Education Division (TCRE). The Bureau promotes registers of conservation professionals, helps develop training and effectiveness and provides a public enquiry service for all those seeking conservation advice.

Scottish Genealogy Society
Family History Centre, 15 Victoria Terrace, Edinburgh EH1 2JL Tel: 0131 220 3677
Web: www.sol.co.uk/s/scotgensoc
Open: Tues: 10.30-5.30; Wed: 10.30-8.30; Sat: 10.00-5.00.
This is a learned society linked with other major Scottish family history societies. It has a library and publications programme covering all aspects of Scottish genealogy.

Scottish Records Association
c/o National Archives of Scotland, Thomas Thomson House, 99 Bankhead Crossway North, Edinburgh EH11 4DX Web: www.scan.org.uk/bookshop/scotrecordsassociation.htm
The Scottish Records Association is a charity which acts as a forum where users, owners and administrators of records can discuss matters concerning the custody, conservation and accessibility of records. The Association publishes the annual journal, *Scottish Archives*, a palaeography self-help pack and other publications.

Society of Archivists
Office Administrator: Mary Fox, 40 Northampton Road, London EC1R 0HB Tel: 020 7239 9280
Fax: 020 7278 2107 E-mail: societyofarchivists@archives.org.uk Web: www.archives.org.uk
Originally founded in 1947 as the Society of Local Archivists and renamed in 1954, the Society of Archivists is the recognised professional body for archivists, archive conservators and record managers in the British Isles. It promotes the care and administration of archives and the better administration of archive repositories, advances the training of its members, and encourages relevant research and publication. Membership is over 1,700. The Society maintains a voluntary register based on qualification, holds regular meetings and runs an in-service training scheme for archive conservators in Britain as well as a programme of continuing professional development training events. Various publications are produced, including a *Journal*, a monthly *Newsletter* and *Career Opportunities*.

Society of Genealogists (see also entry 812)
14 Charterhouse Buildings, London EC1M 7BA Tel: 020 7251 8799 Fax: 020 7250 1800
E-mail: genealogy@sog.org.uk Web: www.sog.org.uk
Administrative Centre: 9 Dallington Street, London EC1V 0BQ

The Society of Genealogists offers a unique combination of research material, guidance and support for those interested in family history and the lives of earlier generations. It is a charity whose objects are to promote, encourage and foster the study, science and knowledge of genealogy. It maintains a reference library and an extensive document collection open to non-members on payment of a fee.

Society of Indexers

Globe Centre, Penistone Road, Sheffield S6 3AE Tel: 0114 281 3060 Fax: 0114 281 3061
E-mail: admin@socind.demon.co.uk Web: www.socind.demon.co.uk
The Society of Indexers exists to promote indexing, the quality of indexes and the profession of indexing.

Standing Conference on Archives and Museums (SCAM)

Secretary: Louise Hampson, York Minster Archives, Dean's Park, York Tel: 01904 557239
Fax: 01904 557215 E-mail: louiseh@yorkminster.org Web: www.hmc.gov.uk/scam
SCAM is a partnership of representatives from the Museums Association (MA), the Society of Archivists, and the Association for Independent Museums (AIM). It promotes understanding and fosters ways of working together among members of the three groups. The aim is to benefit the care of archives and their public use by giving practical advice, sharing problems common among museum curators and archivists, and publishing information useful to all who have archives in their care.

UK Film Archive Forum

c/o British Universities Film & Video Council (see above) E-mail: faf@bufvc.ac.uk Web: www.bufvc.ac.uk/faf
The UK Film Archive Forum was established in 1987 and represents all the public sector film and television archives. It has particular interests in the preservation of nitrate film, acetate film and videotape, the training of archivists, acquisitions policy, standards for archives, copyright, co-operation with film laboratories, and contacts with foreign archives.

Ulster Historical Foundation (UHF)

Research Director: Brian Trainor, 12 College Square East, Belfast BT1 6DD Tel: 028 90 332288
Fax: 028 90 239885 Web: www.uhf.org.uk
The Ulster Historical Foundation (UHF) is a genealogical research agency which provides a full research service for the historic province of Ulster and maintains a large collection of completed searches on Ulster families. It runs the Guild, a membership club, which can be joined by family historians who wish to publicise their research interests. The UHF has a wide range of publications and hosts annual genealogical conferences.

Useful Publications

General

Chadwyck-Healey: *Index of Manuscripts in the British Library*, 10 vols (Cambridge: Chadwyck-Healey, 1984-6).

——: *National Inventory of Documentary Sources in the United Kingdom and Ireland* (Cambridge: Chadwyck-Healey, 1985-) [microfiches of lists of MSS and archives held by a variety of repositories nationally, with union index. Index on CD-Rom with User manual, 1994].

Davies, I. and Webb, C.: *Using Documents* (English Heritage, 1996) [aimed at schoolchildren and based on themes from national curriculum].

Glanville, P.G.: *Councils, Committees and Boards: a Handbook of Advisory, Consultative, Executive and Similar Bodies in British Public Life* (Beckenham: CBD Research, 8/1993).

Historical Manuscripts Commission: *Lists of Accessions to Repositories* (1956 onwards) (HMSO, 1957-72) [annually].

——: *Accessions to Repositories and Reports added to the National Register of Archives* (1972-91 annually) (HMSO, 1975-91) [*Major Accessions to Repositories* is now published electronically only. See www.hmc.gov.uk].

——: *A Guide to the Reports on Collections of Manuscripts of Private Families, Corporations and Institutions in Great Britain and Ireland*, 7 vols (HMSO, 1914-73).

Institute of Historical Research, University of London: *Historical Research for Higher Degrees in the UK*, comp. J.M. Horn, Part I: Theses Completed [in the previous year]; Part II: Theses in progress [in the current year] (London: IHR, annually).

——: *History Theses, 1901-70*, comp. P.M. Jacobs (London, IHR, 1976).

——: *History Theses, 1971-80*, comp. J.M. Horn (London, IHR, 1984).

——: *History Theses, 1981-90*, comp. J.M. Horn (London, IHR, 1994).

International Council on Archives: *International Bibliography of Directories and Guides to Archival Repositories* (London: K.G. Saur, 1990).

Martin, G. and McIntyre, S.: *A Bibliography of British and Irish Municipal History. Vol. 1: General Works* (Welwyn Garden City: Leicester University Press, 1972).

Munro, D.J. (comp.): *Microforms for Historians: a Finding-List of Research Collections in London Libraries* (London: University of London, 1994).

National Council on Archives: *British Archives: the way forward* (London: NCA, 2000).

National Library of Ireland: Manuscript Sources for the History of Irish Civilisation, 11 vols (Boston: Hall, 1965); First Supplement, 1965-1975, 3 vols (Boston: Hall, 1979).

Olney, R.J.: *Manuscript Sources for British History: their nature, location and use* (London: IHR, 1995).

Roberts, S. et al.: *Research Libraries and Collections in the United Kingdom* (London: Clive Bingley, 1978).

Storey, R.A. and Madden, J.L.: *Primary Sources for Victorian Studies: a Guide to the Location and Use of Unpublished Materials* (London: Phillimore, 1977; updated, Leicester, 1987).

Walford, A.J.: *Walford's Guide to Reference Material*, 3 vols (London: Library Association, 7/1996-8) [online from 2000].

Watson, A.G.: *Catalogue of Dated and Dateable Manuscripts, c 435-1600, in Oxford Libraries*, 2 vols (Oxford: Clarendon Press, 1984).

Archive Practice and Conservation

Bass, R: 'Computerisation of the Manorial Documents Registered, *J.S.A.*, vol 20, no. 2 (Oct 1999), pp. 201-7.

British Standards Institution: *Repair and Allied Processes for the Conservation of Documents*, BS4971 (London, rev.edn, draft 1999).

——: *Recommendations for the Storage and Exhibition of Archival Documents*, BS5454 (London, 2000).

——: *Information and documentation. Records management. General*, BS ISO 15489-1 (2001)

——: *Information and documentation. Records management. Guidelines*, PS ISO/TR 15489-2 (2001)

Cook, M: *The Management of Information from Archives* (Aldershot: Gower, 1999).

Cornish, G.P.: *Copyright: Interpreting the Law for Libraries, Archives and Information Services* (London; Library Association, 3/1999).

Ellis, J. (ed.): *Keeping Archives* (Port Melbourne: D.W. Thorpe in association with the Australian Society of Archivists, 2/1993).

Forbes, H. (comp.): *Local Authority Archive Services, 1992: a Survey Commissioned by the Royal Commission on Historical Manuscripts and National Council on Archives* (London: British Library R and D Report 6090, HMSO, 1993).

Historical Manuscripts Commission: *Archives at the Millennium* (London: HMC, 28th Report of the Royal Commission on Historical Manuscripts, 1999).

——: *A Standard for Record Repositories* (London: HMC, 3/2001) [also available on HMC website].

Kitching, C.J.: *Archive Buildings in the United Kingdom, 1977-1992* (London: HMSO, 1993).

——: *Archives. The Very Essence of our Heritage* (Chichester: Phillimore, 1996).

Knightbridge, A.: *Archive Legislation in the United Kingdom* (Society of Archivists Information Leaflet No. 3, 1986).

McKay, Peter H.: *A Guide to the Retention of Modern Records on Landed Estates* (Letchworth: Hall-McCartney for the Historic Houses Archivists Group, 1992).

National Preservation Office: *A National Preservation Strategy for Library and Archive Collections in the United Kingdom and Ireland: principles and prospects* (BL, 2001 – www.bl.uk.npo).

——: NPO publishes a series of guidance leaflets to advise on preservation issues generally (see their website).

Post, J.B. and Foster, M.R.: *Copyright: a Handbook for Archivists* (London: Society of Archivists, 1992).

The Public Records Acts (London: HMSO, 1958, 1967).

Rickards, M: *Collecting Printed Ephemera* (Oxford: Phaidon-Christie's Ltd, 1988).

Sargent, D. (ed.): *The National Register of Archives: an International Perspective* (London: Institute of Historical Research, 1995).

Society of Archivists: *Directory of Suppliers* (5/1999)

Walne, P: *Dictionary of archival terminology Dictionnaire de terminologie archivistique*

Mu'jam al-mustalahat al- arshifiyah: English, French and Arabic with equivalents in Dutch, German, Italian, Russian and Spanish (Beirut: Arab Scientific Publishers, 1990).

Williamson, B.: *Using Archives at National Trust Properties: a Practical Guide* (London: National Trust, 1985).

Arts, Architecture & Design

Bailey, R.M. (comp.): *Scottish Architects' Papers. A Source Book.* (Edinburgh: Rutland, 1996).

Franchi, F: *Directory of Performing Art Resources* (3/1998).

Kamen, R.H.: *British and Irish Architectural History: a Bibliography and Guide to Sources of Information* (New York: Nichols, 1981).

Pinhorn, M.: *Historical, Archaeological and Kindred Societies: a List* (Newport: Pinhorns, 1985).

Lambert, D.: *Record of Documentary Sources for British Gardens, Gardening and Landscape Design: Report on the Pilot Study 1989-90* (York: Publication No. 4, Centre for the Conservation of Historic Parks and Gardens, Institute of Advanced Architectural Studies, University of York, 1991).

Varley, G. (comp. & ed.): *Art and Design Documentation in the UK and Ireland: a Directory of Resources* (Bromsgrove: ARLIS, 1993).

Business Records

Armstrong, J. and Jones, S.: *Business Documents: their Origins, Sources and Uses in Historical Research* (London: Mansell, 1987).

Cockerell, H.A.L. and Green, E.: *The British Insurance Business, 1547-1970: an Introduction and Guide to its History and Records in the United Kingdom* (Sheffield: Sheffield Academic Press, 1994).

Fowler, S: *Sources for Labour History* (London, PRO, Users Guide No. 12, 1995).

Habgood, W. (ed.): *Chartered Accountants in England and Wales: a Guide to Historical Records* (Manchester: MUP, 1994).

Historical Manuscripts Commission: *Records of British Business and Industry, 1760-1914: Textiles and Leather* (London: HMSO, Guide to Sources for British History, 1990).

——: *Records of British Business and Industry, 1760-1914: Metal Processing and Engineering* (London: HMSO, Guide to Sources for British History, 1994).

Jones, C.A.: *Britain and the Dominions: a Guide to Business and Related Records in the United Kingdom concerning Australia, Canada, New Zealand and South Africa* (Boston: Hall, 1978).

Orbell, J.: *A Guide to Tracing the History of a Business* (Aldershot: Gower, for the Business Archives Council, 1987).

Orbell, J and Turton, A. (comps.): *British Banking: A Guide to Historical Records* (Aldershot: Ashgate for the Business Archives Council, 2001).

Richmond, L.M. and Stockford, B.: *Company Archives: a Survey of the Records of 1000 of the First Registered Companies in England and Wales* (Aldershot: Gower, 1986).

Richmond, L.M. and Turton, A. (eds): *The Brewing Industry: a Guide to Historical Records* (Manchester: Manchester University Press, 1990).

——: *Directory of Corporate Archives* (London: Business Archives Council, 4/1997).

Ritchie, L.A. (ed.): *The Shipbuilding Industry: a Guide to Historical Records* (Manchester: Manchester University Press, 1992).

Smallbone, L. (comp.) and Storey, R. (ed.): *Employers' and Trade Associations' History* (Coventry: University of Warwick, 1992).

Turton, A. (ed.): *Managing Business Archives* (Oxford: Butterworth/Heinemann in association with the Business Archives Council, 1991).

Directories

Abraham, B. (ed.) and Aldridge, T.M. (consultant ed.): *Directory of Registers and Records* (London: Longman, 5/1993).

Barbour, S.: *Museums Yearbook, including a Directory of Museums and Galleries of the British Isles* (London: Museums Association, annual).

Bloomfield, B.C. (ed.) with the assistance of Potts, K.: *A Directory of Rare Books and Special Collections in the United Kingdom and the Republic of Ireland* (London: Library Association 2/1997).

Chadwyck-Healey [Know UK]: *National Inventory of Documentary Sources 1992-98* (NIDS) (Cambridge, Chadwyck-Healey, CD-ROM 1994-). [Reproduces archive and manuscripts finding aids on microfiche. Published in 8 units p.a. with cumulative com index. Index also on CD-ROM.]

Committee of London Research Libraries in History: *A Guide to History Libraries and Collections in London* (London: ULL, 14/1999).

Cotton, C: *London Local Archives: a directory of local authority and other record offices and libraries in London* (London: Greater London Archives Network, 4/1999).

Cox, M. (ed.): *Exploring Scottish History: a directory of resource centres in Scottish local and national history in Scotland* (Edinburgh: Scottish Library Association, 1992).

Cox, Richard W: *History of Sport: A Guide to the Literature and Sources of Information* (Sports History Publishing, Frodsham, Cheshire, 1994).

Dale, P. (ed.), British Library: *Guide to Libraries and Information Units in Government Departments and other Organisations* (London: British Library Science Reference and Information Service, 1990-) (33/1998).

Dale, P. (ed.); *Directory of museums and special collections in the UK* (Colchester, Portland press with Museums Association, 2/1996).

Ferguson, J.P.S.: *Directory of Scottish Newspapers* (Edinburgh: National Library of Scotland, 1984).

Franchi, F. (comp.): *Directory of Performing Art Resources* (London, 3/1998).

Gibson, J.S.W. and Peskett, P.: *Record Offices: How to Find Them* (Birmingham: FFHS, 8/1998) [gives helpful maps of locations].

Harrold, A.: *Academic Libraries in the United Kingdom and the Republic of Ireland* (London: Library Association, 3/1994).

Helferty, S. and Refausse, R. (eds): *Directory of Irish Archives* (Dublin: Blackrock, Irish Academic Press, 3/1999).

Henderson, G.P. and Henderson, S.P.A. (eds): *Directory of British Associations and Associations in Ireland* (Beckenham: CBD Research, 14/1998).

Historical Manuscripts Commission: *Guides to Sources for British History* (details on HMC website).

Library Association: *Libraries in the United Kingdom and the Republic of Ireland 2001* (London, Library Association, 2001).

The Libraries Directory (Cambridge: James Clarke, 1991-) [biennial]. Also CD Reference Edition (2001) [includes addresses for archives and local history].

The London Museums Guide (London: South Eastern Museums Service, 1999-).

Mortimer, I: *Record Repositories in Great Britain* (Kew: PRO, 11/1999).

Pickering, O.: *A Guide to the Research Collections of Member Libraries* (Leeds: Consortium of University Research Libraries, 1996).

Reynard, K.W. (ed.): *ASLIB Directory of Literary and Historical Collections in the UK* (London: ASLIB, 1993).

Reynard, K.W. and J.M.E. (eds): *The ASLIB Directory of Information Sources in the United Kingdom* (London: ASLIB, 10/1998).

Richard, S. (comp.): *Directory of British Official Publications: a guide to sources* (London: Mansell, 2/1984).

Rickards, M: *The Encyclopaedia of Ephemera*: a guide to the fragmentary documents of everyday life for the collector, curator and historian (London, British Library, 2000).

Shaw, G. and Tipper, A.: *British Directories: a bibliography and guide to directories published in England and Wales (1850-1950) and Scotland (1773-1950)* (Leicester: Leicester University Press, 1988).

Vaurie, A. (ed.): 'International Directory of Archives', *Archivum*, Vol. XXXIII (Munich and London: Saur, ICA, 1988).

Watt, I.: *A Directory of UK Map Collections* (London: Map Curators Group Publication No. 3, 4/2000).

Education

Allan, A.R.: *University bodies: a survey of intra- and supra-university bodies and their records* (Liverpool: Archives Unit, University of Liverpool, 1990).

Stephens, W.B. and Unwin, R.W.: *Materials for the Local and Regional Study of Schooling, 1700-1900* (London: British Records Association, Archives and the User No. 7, 1987).

Thompson, K.: *The Use of Archives in Education: a bibliography* (Leicester: Society of Archivists. 1982).

Family History

Blatchford, R. And Heslop, G. (eds.): *The Genealogical Services Directory* (York: GR Specialist Information Services, 2000).

Camp, A.J.: *Wills and their Whereabouts* (London: A.J. Camp, 4/1974).

Cory, K.B.: *Tracing your Scottish Ancestry* (Edinburgh: Polygon, 2/1996).

Cox, J. and Colwell, S: *Never Been Here Before? A Genealogist's Guide to the Family Records Centre* (London: PRO, 1997).

Cox, J. and Padfield, T.: *Tracing your Ancestors in the Public Record Office*, ed. A. Bevan

(Kew: PRO, 5/1999).

Foot, W.: *Maps for Family Historians* (London: Public Record Office Readers Guide no. 6, 1994).

Fowler, S. and Spencer, W.: *Army Records for Family Historians* (London: PRO, 2/1998).

Gibson, J.S.W. et al (eds.): *Census Returns, 1841-1891, in microform: a directory to local holdings* (Birmingham: FFHS, 6/1997).

——: *Coroners' Records in England and Wales* (Birmingham: FFHS, 2/1997).

——: *Local Census Listings, 1522-1930: holdings in the British Isles* (Birmingham: FFHS, 3/1997).

——: *Marriage, Census and other Indexes for Family Historians* (Birmingham: FFHS, 7/1998).

——: *Poll Books c1696-1872: a Directory to Holdings in Great Britain* (Birmingham: FFHS, 1994).

——: *Poor Law Union records.* 1 South-East England and East Anglia (Birmingham: FFHS, 2/1997); 2 The Midlands and Northern England (Birmingham: FFHS, 2/1997); 3 South-West England, The Marches and Wales (Bury: FFHS, 2/2000); 4 Gazetteer of England and Wales (Birmingham: FFHS, 2/1997)

——: *Probate Jurisdictions: Where to Look for Wills* (Birmingham: FFHS, 4/1994).

——: *Quarter Sessions Records for Family Historians: a Select List* (Birmingham: FFHS, 4/1995).

——: *A Simplified Guide to Probate Jurisdictions: Where to Look for Wills* (Birmingham: FFHS, 4/1997).

——: *Specialist Indexes for Family Historians* (Birmingham: FFHS, 4/1997).

Grenham, J.: *Tracing your Irish Ancestors: the complete guide* (Dublin: Gill and Macmillan, 1992).

Hawkings, D.T.: *Criminal Ancestors: a guide to historical criminal records in England and Wales* (Stroud: Sutton, 1993).

Herber, M. D.: *Ancestral Trails: The Complete Guide to British Genealogy and Family History* (Stroud: Sutton, 1997).

Hey, D.: *The Oxford Guide to Family History* (Oxford: OUP, 1996).

Higgs, E.: *Making Sense of the Census: the Manuscript Returns for England and Wales, 1801-1901* (London: HMSO, 1989).

Historical Manuscripts Commission: *Principal Family and Estate Collections: family names A-K* (HMC: Guides to Sources for British History, 1996).

—— *Principal Family and Estate Collections: family names L-W* (HMC: Guides to Sources for British History, 1999)

Logan, R.: *Friendly Society Records* (Birmingham: FFHS, 2000)

Maxwell, I, G. McGrath (ed.): *Tracing Your Ancestors in Northern Ireland. A Guide to Ancestry Research in the Public Record Office of Northern Ireland* (Belfast: Stationery Office, 1997).

Moulton, J.W.: *Genealogical Resources in English Repositories* (Columbus, Ohio: Hampton House, 1988).

Rodger, N.A.M.: *Naval Records for Genealogists* (Kew: PRO, 2/1998).

Rogers, C.D.: *Tracing Missing Persons: an Introduction to Agencies, Methods and Sources in England and Wales* (Manchester: MUP, 1986).

Rowlands, J. (ed.): *Welsh Family History: a Guide to Research* (FFHS, 2/1998).

Sinclair, C.: *Tracing your Scottish Ancestors: a Guide to Ancestry Research in the Scottish Record Office* (Edinburgh: 2/1997).

Smith, K. et al: *Records of Merchant Shipping and Seamen* (Kew: PRO, 1998).

Society of Genealogists: *National Index of Parish Registers* (London, 1968-).

——: 'Original Parish Registers in Record Offices and Libraries', *Local Population Studies*, supplements (1974, 1976, 1978, 1982).

Williams, C.J. and Watts-Williams, S.J. (comps): *Cofrestri Plwyf Cymru/Parish Registers of Wales* (Aberystwyth: National Library of Wales, 1986).

Yeo, G. (comp.): *The British Overseas: a Guide to Records of their Births, Baptisms, Marriages, Deaths and Burials available in the United Kingdom* (London: Guildhall Library, 3/1995).

Labour History

Bennett, J. and Tough, A. (comps) and Storey, R. (ed.): *Trade Union and Related Records* (Coventry: University of Warwick, Occasional Publication No. 5, 6/1991).

Fowler, S.: *Sources for Labour History* (London: PRO, 1995).

MacDougall, I. (comp. and ed.): *A Catalogue of some Labour Records in Scotland and some Scots Records outside Scotland* (Edinburgh: Scottish Labour History Society, 1978).

Marsh, A. and Ryan, V.: *Historical Directory of Trade Unions*, 4 vols (Farnborough/Aldershot: Gower, 1980-88) [includes the survival and location of records].

Thompson, K.: *The Use of Archives in Education: a Bibliography* (Leicester: Society of Archivists, 1982).

Literature

Index of English Literary Manuscripts (London: Mansell, 1980-):

Vol. I: 1450-1625, ed. P. Beal (1980).

Vol. II: 1625-1700, ed. P. Beal (1987-93).

Vol. III: 1700-1800, ed. M.M. Smith (1986-92).

Vol. IV: 1800-1900, eds B. Rosenbaum and P. White (1982-90).

Ringler, W.A.: *Bibliography and Index of English Verse in Manuscript, 1501-1558* (London: Mansell, 1992).

Sutton, D.C. (ed.): *Location Register of Twentieth-Century English Literary Manuscripts and Letters: a Union List of Modern English, Irish, Scottish and Welsh Authors in the British Isles*, 2 vols (London: British Library, 1988).

——: *Location Register of English Literary Manuscripts and Letters: eighteenth and nineteenth centuries* (London: British Library, 1995-).

Local History

Alcock, N.W.: *Old Title Deeds. A Guide for Local and Family Historians* (Chichester: Phillimore, 1986).

Ellis, M.: *Using Manorial Records* (London: PRO Reader's Guide No. 6, rev. edn, 1997).

Gibson, J.S.W.: *Local Newspapers 1750-1920: a Select Location List* (Birmingham: FFHS, 1987).

Harvey, J.H.: *Sources for the History of Houses* (London: British Records Association, Archives and the User No. 3, 1974).

Harvey, P: 'Manorial Records' (London: British Records Association, Archives and the User No. 5, rev/1999).

Hindle, P.: *Maps for Local History* (London: Batsford, 1988).

——: *Maps for Historians* (Chichester, 1998).

Humphery-Smith, C. (ed.): *The Phillimore Atlas and Index of Parish Registers* (Chichester: Phillimore, 1984).

Iredale, D.: *Local History Research and Writing* (Chichester: Phillimore, 1980) [rev. edn. of *Enjoying Archives* (Newton Abbott: David and Charles, 1973)]

Iredale, D. & Barrett, J.: *Discovering Local History* (Princes Risborough: Shire, 1999).

Humphery-Smith, C. (ed.): *The Phillimore Atlas and Index of Parish Registers* (Chichester: Phillimore, 1984).

Moody, D: *Scottish Towns: Sources for Local Historians* (London: Batsford, 1986).

——: *Scottish Local History: an Introductory Guide* (Batsford: London, 1986).

Morton, A. and Donaldson, G.: *British National Archives and the Local Historian: a Guide to Official Record Publications* (London: Historical Association, 1980).

Richardson, J.: *The Local Historian's Encyclopedia* (New Barnet: Historical Publications, 2/1986).

Riden, P.: *Record Sources for Local History* (London: Batsford, 1987).

Sinclair, C: *Tracing Scottish Local History: a Guide to Local History Research in the Scottish Record Office* (Edinburgh: HMSO, 1994).

Stephens, W.B.: *Sources for English Local History* (Cambridge: Cambridge University Press, 2/1981).

Stuart, D.: *Manorial Records: an Introduction to their Transcription and Translation* (Chichester: Phillimore, 1992).

Tate, W.E.: *The Parish Chest: a Study of the Records of Parochial Administration in England* (Cambridge: CUP, 3/1969).

Victoria County History (1900-; now published by Oxford University Press for the Institute of Historical Research) [c200 vols for counties in England].

West, J.: *Village Records* (London: Macmillan, 1962).
——: *Town Records* (Chichester: Phillimore, 1983).

Military/Naval History

Bryon, R.V. and Bryon, T.V. (eds): *Maritime Information: A Guide to Libraries and Sources of Information in the UK* (Chichester, Maritime Information Publications, 1994).

Cantwell, J.D.: *The Second World War: a Guide to Documents in the Public Record Office* (London: PRO, 1998).

Fowler, S., Elliott, P., Conyers Nesbit, R. and Goulter, C: *RAF Records in the PRO* (London: PRO, 1994).

Holding, N.: *The Location of British Army Records* (Bury, Lancashire: Federation of Family History Society (4/1999).

Mayer, S.L. and Koenig, W.J.: *The Two World Wars: a Guide to Manuscript Collections in the United Kingdom* (London: Bowker, 1976).

Roper, M.: *The Records of the War Office and Related Departments, 1660-1964* (London: PRO, 3/1998).

Spencer, W.: *Records of the Militia and Volunteer Forces, 1757-1945* (London: PRO, 1997).

Wise, T. and Wise, S.: *A Guide to Military Museums and other Places of Military Interest* (Knighton: Imperial Press, 9/1999).

Other Media

Alban, J: *Film and Sound Archive Sourcebook* (London: SoA, 1999).

Ballantyne, J. (ed.): *Researcher's Guide to British Newsreels*, 3 vols (London: British Universities Film and Video Council, 1983-93).

——: *Researcher's Guide to British Film & Television Collections* (London: British Universities Film and Video Council, 6/2001).

British Association of Picture Libraries: *BAPLA Directory* (1995).

British Film Institute: *National Film Archive Catalogue*, Vol. 1: Non-Fiction Films; Vol. 2: Feature Films; Vol. 3: Newsreels (London: British Film Institute, 1980-).

Eakins, R. (ed.): *Picture Sources UK* (London: Macdonald, 1985).

Evans, H. and Evans, M. (comps): *Picture Researcher's Handbook: an International Guide to Picture Sources and How to Use Them* (London: Chapman & Hall 5/1992).

Houston, P.: *Keepers of the Frame: the Film Archives* (London: British Film Institute, 1994).

Wall, J. (comp.): *Directory of British Photographic Collections* (London: Heinemann, 1977).

Ward, A.: *A Manual of Sound Archive Administration* (Gower: Aldershot, 1990).

Wilson, D: *The Care and Storage of Photographs: Recommendations for Good Practice* (London for National Aerial Photographic Libraries, 1997).

Overseas

Baldock, R.W.: 'A Survey of Southern African Manuscripts in the United Kingdom', *Communications from the Basel Africa Bibliography*, Vol. 16 (1976), 3-27.

Burdett, A.L.P.: *Summary Guide to Archive and Manuscript Collections relevant to the Former British Colonial Territories in the United Kingdom* (London: Commonwealth Archivists Association, 1988).

Davison, S. (ed.): *Northern Ireland and Canada: a Guide to Northern Ireland Sources for the Study of Canadian History, c1705-1992* (Belfast: Queen's University/PRONI, 1994)

Gunasingam, S. (ed.): *Directory of South Asian Library Resources in the UK and the Republic of Ireland* (London: South Asian Library Group, 1987).

Hartley, J.M.: *Guide to Documents and Manuscripts in the United Kingdom relating to Russia and the Soviet Union* (London: Mansell, 1987).

Hewitt, A.R.: *Guide to Resources for Commonwealth Studies in London, Oxford and Cambridge, with Bibliographical and other Information* (London: Athlone, 1957).

Ingram, K.E.: *Sources for West Indian Studies: a Supplementary Listing, with Particular Reference to Manuscript Sources* (Zug: Inter Documentation, 1993).

International Council on Archives: *Guide to the Sources of Asian History* [A series of volumes covering Pakistan, Indonesia, India, Korea and Singapore].

Jones, P.: *Britain and Palestine, 1914-1948: Archival Sources for the History of the British Mandate* (Oxford: OUP for the British Academy, 1979).

Kurucz, G.: *Guide to Documents and Manuscripts in Great Britain relating to the Kingdom of Hungary from the Earliest Times to 1800* (London: Mansell, 1992).

Mander-Jones, P.: *Manuscripts in the British Isles relating to Australia, New Zealand and the Pacific* (Canberra: Australian National University, 1972).

Matthews, N.: *Materials for West African History in the Archives of the United Kingdom* (London: Athlone Press, 1973).

Matthews, N. and Wainwright, M.D. (eds): *A Guide to Manuscripts and Documents in the British Isles relating to the Far East* (Oxford: OUP, 1977).

——: *A Guide to Manuscripts and Documents in the British Isles relating to the Middle East and North Africa* (Oxford: OUP, 1980).

Morriss, R. (ed.): *A Guide to British naval papers in North America* (London, Mansell for National Maritime, 1994).

Pearson, J.D.: (comp.): *A Guide to Manuscripts and Documents in the British Isles relating to South and South-East Asia*, Vol. 1: London, Vol. 2: British Isles (London: Mansell, 1989, 1990).

——: *A Guide to Manuscripts and Documents in the British Isles relating to Africa*, Vol. 1: London; Vol. 2: British Isles (London: Mansell 1993, 1994).

Prochaska, A.: *Irish History from 1700: a Guide to Sources in the Public Record Office* (London: British Records Association, Archives and the User No. 6, 1986).

Raimo, J.W. (ed.): *A Guide to Manuscripts relating to America in Great Britain and Ireland* (London: Mansell, 1979).

Thurston, A.: *Guide to Archives and Manuscripts relating to Kenya and East Africa in the United Kingdom, Vol. 1: Official Records; Vol. 2: Non-Official Archives and Manuscripts* (London: Hans Zell, 1991).

——: *Sources for Colonial Studies in the Public Record Office*, Vol. I (London: Institute of Commonwealth Studies, University of London and PRO, HMSO, 1995).

Twining, W. and Varnden, E.: *Legal Records in the Commonwealth* (Aldershot: Dartmouth, c.1994).

Walne, P. (ed.): *A Guide to Manuscript Sources for the History of Latin America and the Caribbean in the British Isles* (London: Oxford University Press, 1973).

Wilson, B.G. (ed.) and Burdett, A. (comp.): *Manuscripts and Government Records in the United Kingdom and Ireland relating to Canada* (Ottawa: National Archives of Canada, 1992).

Politics

Cook, C. (ed.): *Sources in British Political History, 1900-1951* (London: Macmillan, 1975-):
    Vol. 1: *A Guide to the Archives of Selected Organizations and Societies* (1975).
    Vol. 2: *A Guide to the Papers of Selected Public Servants* (1975).
    Vol. 3: *A Guide to the Private Papers of Members of Parliament, A-K* (1977).
    Vol. 4: *A Guide to the Private Papers of Members of Parliament, L-Z* (1977).
    Vol. 5 (with Weekes, J.): *A Guide to the Private Papers of Selected Writers, Intellectuals and Publicists* (1978).
    Vol. 6: *First Consolidated Supplement* (1985).

Hazlehurst, C. and Woodland, C.: *Guide to the Papers of British Cabinet Ministers, 1900-1964* (London: Royal Historical Society Guides and Handbooks Series No. 19, 1996)

Historical Manuscripts Commission: *Papers of British Cabinet Ministers, 1782-1900* (Guide to Sources for British History, 1982).

——: *Private Papers of British Diplomats, 1782-1900* (Guide to Sources for British History, 1985).

——: *Private Papers of British Colonial Governors, 1782-1900* (Guide to Sources for British History, 1986).

——: *Papers of British Politicians, 1782-1900* (Guide to Sources for British History, 1989).

Religion

Donahue, C. (ed.): *The Records of the Medieval Ecclesiastical Courts, part II: England* (Berlin: Report of the Working Group on Church Court Records, Duncker and Humblot, 1994).

Historical Manuscripts Commission: *Papers of British Churchmen, 1780-1940*, Guide to Sources for British History no. 6 (1987).

Kitching, C.J.: *The Central Records of the Church of England: a Report and Survey presented to the Pilgrim and Radcliffe Trustees* (London: Church Information Office, 1976).

Marchant, L.: *A Guide to the Archives and Record of Protestant and Christian Missions from the British Isles to China, 1796-1914* (Nedlands: University of Western Australia Press, 1966).

Mullett, M.: *Sources for the History of English Nonconformity, 1660-1830*, (London: British Records Association, Archives and the User No.8, 1991).

Owen, D.M., *Records of the Established Church in England excluding parochial records* (London: British Records Association, Archives and the User No. 1, rev/1997).

Seton, R. and Naish, E. (comps): *A Preliminary Guide to the Archives of British Missionary Societies* (London: School of Oriental and African Studies, 1992).

Smith, C.J: *Directory of Catholic Archives in the United Kingdom and Eire* (Newcastle upon Tyne: Catholic Archives Society, 4/1997).

Smith, D.M.: *Guide to Bishops' Registers of England and Wales: a Survey from the Middle Ages to the Abolition of Episcopacy in 1646* (London: Royal Historical Society, 1981).

Williams, J.A.: 'Sources for Recusant History (1559-1791) in English Official Archives', *Recusant History* (journal of the Catholic Records Society), Vol. 16, No. 4 (Oct 1983).

Science and Medicine

Bearman, D. and Edsall, J.T. (eds): *Archival Sources for the History of Biochemistry and Molecular Biology: a Reference Guide and Report* (Philadelphia: American Philosophical Society, 1980).

Bridson, G.D.R., Phillips, V.C. and Harvey, A.P.: *Natural History Manuscript Resources in the British Isles* (London: Mansell, 1980).

Harper, P.: *Guide to the Manuscript Papers of British Scientists Catalogued by the Contemporary Scientific Archives Centre and the National Cataloguing Unit for the Archives of Contemporary Scientists, 1973-1993* (Bath: NCUACS, University of Bath, 1993).

Historical Manuscripts Commission: *The Manuscript Papers of British Scientists, 1600-1942* (Guide to Sources for British History, 1982).

Linnean Society: *Preserving the archives of nature: a guide for the owners of papers in nature conservation* (Linnean Society: London, 1994).

MacLeod, R.M. and Friday, J.R.: *Archives of British Men of Science: Introduction and Index to the Publication in Microfiche of a Survey of Private and Institutional Holdings* (London: Mansell, 1972).

McBurney, V. *British Library: Science, Technology and Industry. Guide to Libraries in London* (London, British Library, 1995)

Morris, P.J.T. and Russell, C.A.: *Archives of the British Chemical Industry, 1750-1914: a Handlist* (Faringdon: British Society for the History of Science, 1988).

Summers, A.: *How to find source materials: British Library collections on the history and culture of science technology and medicine* (London, British Library, 1996).

Social History and Social Science

Barrow, M.: *Women, 1870-1928: a Select Guide to Printed and Archival Sources in the United Kingdom* (London: Mansell, 1981).

Batts, J.S.: *British Manuscript Diaries of the Nineteenth Century: an Annotated Listing* (London: Centaur, 1976).

Bridgeman, I. and Emsley, C.: *A Guide to the Archives of the Police Forces of England and Wales* (Leigh-on-Sea: Police History Society, 1989).

Carter, S: *Women's Studies: A Guide to Information Sources* (London: Cassell, 1990).

Cox, A.: *Sources for the Study of Public Housing* (London: Guildhall Library and the London Archive Users' Forum, 1993).

Cox, R.: *History of Sport: a Guide to the Literature and Sources of Information* (Cheshire: British Society of Sport History in association with Sports History Publishing, 1994).

Foster, J: *Aids Archives* (London: London School of Hygiene and Tropical Medicine, 1990).

Ker, N.R.: *Medieval Manuscripts in British Libraries*, Vols 1-4 (Oxford: Clarendon Press, 1969-92).

Lumas, S.: *Making Use of the Census* (London: HMSO, 2/1993).

Matthews, W. (comp.): *British Diaries: an Annotated Bibliography of British Diaries Written between 1442 and 1942* (Gloucester, Mass.: Peter Smith, 1967).

Swann, B. and Turnbull, M.: *Records of Interest to Social Scientists, 1919 to 1939I*, 3 vols (London: HMSO, 1971-78).

Surveys

Cook, C. and Waller, D.: *Sources in Contemporary British History*, Vol. 1: *Organisations and Societies* (London: Longman, 1994).

Cook, C., Leonard, J. and Leese, P.: *Sources in Contemporary British History*, Vol. 2: *Individuals* (London: Longman, 1994).

Cornish, G.P.: *Archival Collections of Non-Book Materials: a Listing and Brief Description of Major National Collections* (London: British Library Information Guide No. 3, 1986).

Coxe, H.O.: *Catalogue of the Manuscripts in the Oxford Colleges* (Oxford: Oxford University Press, 1852; repr. E.P. Publishing, 1972).

Creaton, H.: *Sources for the History of London 1939-45. A Guide and Bibliography* (London: British Records Association, Archives and the User No. 9, 1998).

Historical Manuscripts Commission: *A Guide to the Reports on Collections of Manuscripts of Private Families, Corporations and Institutions in Great Britain and Ireland*, 7 vols (HMSO, 1914-73).

——: *Guide to the Location of Collections described in the Reports and Calendars Series, 1870-1980* (1982).

——: *Surveys of Historical Manuscripts in the United Kingdom in Select Bibliography* (3rd ed., 1997) [Now online]

Keene, D. and Harding, V.: *A Survey of Documentary Sources for Property Holding in London before the Great Fire* (London: London Record Society, 1985).

Macdonald, B.: *Broadcasting in the United Kingdom: a Guide to Information Sources* (London: Mansell, rev. 2/1994).

Morgan, P. (comp.): *Oxford Libraries outside the Bodleian: a Guide* (Oxford: Bodleian Library, 2/1980).

——: *Select Index of Manuscript Collections in Oxford Libraries outside the Bodleian* (Oxford: Bodleian Library, 1991).

Percival, J. (ed.): *A Guide to Archives and Manuscripts in the University of London*, Vol. 1 (London: University of London, LRCC, 1984).

Sturges, R.P.: *Economists' Papers, 1750-1950: a Guide to Archive and other Manuscript Sources for the History of British and Irish Economic Thought* (London: Macmillan, 1975).

Transport

Bryon, R.V. and Bryon, T.N. (eds): *Maritime Information: a Guide to Libraries and Sources of Information in the United Kingdom* (London: Maritime Information Association, 3/1993).

Clinker, C.R.: *Railway History Sources: a Handlist of the Principal Sources of Original Material with Notes and Guidance on its Use* (Bristol: Avon-Anglia, 1976).

Mathias, P. and Pearsall, A.W.H. (eds): *Shipping: a Survey of Historical Records* (Newton Abbot: David & Charles, 1971).

Ottley, G.: *Railway History: a Guide to Sixty-One Collections in Libraries and Archives in Great Britain* (London: Library Association Subject Guide to Library Resources No. 1, 1973).

Riden, P.: *How to Trace the History of Your Car* (Cardiff: Meston Press, 1998).

1 Aberdare Library

Parent organisation: Rhondda-Cynon-Taff County Borough Council (Education Department)

Address: Central Library, Green Street, Aberdare, Mid Glamorgan CF44 7AG

Telephone: (01685) 885318

Fax: (01685) 881181

Enquiries: Mr A.R. Prescott

Open: Mon, Wed: 9.00–7.00; Tues: 9.00–6.00; Thurs: 9.00–5.00; Sat 9.00–1.00.

Access: Generally open to the public. Appointments advisable for microform sources.

Historical background: The Public Library Act was adopted in 1904. Cynon Valley Borough Council was formed from Aberdare and Llandwdano urban district councils (and Rhigosa/Penderyn) in 1974. The local collection has been greatly expanded from the 1970s onwards. Cynon Valley Libraries became Rhondda-Cynon-Taff County Borough Council in 1996, when the present name was adopted. A local history collection for Pontypridd and Taff Ely is maintained at Pontypridd Library (Library Road, Pontypridd CF37 2BY).

Acquisitions policy: To collect any available material appertaining to the history of the Cynon Valley.

Archives of organisation: Council minutes, correspondence, etc, 1904– .

Non-manuscript material: Collections of local historians: W. W. Price Collection (1873–1967), mainly notes and pamphlets, c1920–1967, and Rev Ivor Parry Collection (1908–75), mainly notes and articles from local newspapers, c1950–1970.
Extensive photographic collection, especially on Cynon Valley (c7000).
Aberdare Times, 1861–1902; *Aberdare Leader*, 1902– , and other local newspapers (on microfilm), 1833– .
Census returns, 1841–91 (on microfilm).
Maps and newspaper cuttings. Small collection of videos and films.
Sketches by Bacon sisters, 1827–8.

Finding aids: Newspaper indexes; document schedules; keys to maps; guide to photograph classification; list of videos and films.

Facilities: Photocopying. Photography by arrangement. Microfilm/fiche readers.

Conservation: Contracted out.

Publications: D.L. Davies: *A Guide to Local Genealogical Sources.*

2 Aberdeen Central Library

Parent organisation: Aberdeen City Council: Arts and Recreation Department

Address: Reference and Local Studies Department, Central Library, Rosemount Viaduct, Aberdeen AB25 1GW

Telephone: (01224) 652512

Fax: (01224) 624118

E-mail: refloc@arts-rec.aberdeen.net.uk

Website: www.aberdeencity.gov.uk

Enquiries: The Reference and Local Studies Librarian, Mrs Susan Bell

Open: Mon–Thurs: 9.00–8.00; Fri–Sat: 9.00–5.00.
Prior notice is necessary as some material is stored elsewhere.

Access: Generally open, except where depositors have stipulated otherwise.

Historical background: The Public Library Acts were adopted for Aberdeen in 1884, and the library service began in 1886 in the Mechanics' Institute building, Market Street. The present central library was opened in 1892, with extensions in 1905 and 1981–2. The library includes a well-stocked reference library and local studies department.

Acquisitions policy: Items relating to Aberdeen and the surrounding area are considered for acquisition by donation or purchase. Archive deposits by local societies are welcomed.

Major collections: Aberdeen Airport, aircraft movement log-books, 1972–88.
Aberdeen Mechanics' Institute, reports, rules and regulations, library catalogues, handbills, late 19th century.
Papers relating to the Bruce family of Heatherwick Farm, Inverurie.
Journals and letter-books of George Sim (1835–1908), naturalist.
William Watson (1796–1878), Sheriff-Substitute of Aberdeenshire, writings on industrial schools.

Non-manuscript material: Aberdeen city plans, 1661– .

George Washington Wilson Photographic Collection.

Photographs of places, people and events in Aberdeen.

Local newspapers, 1747– .

Ordnance Survey maps, various dates and scales, for Aberdeen, Aberdeenshire, Banffshire and Kincardineshire.

Finding aids: Manuscript lists and card catalogues.

Facilities: Photocopying. Microfilm/fiche readers/printers.

Conservation: Contracted out.

3 Aberdeen City Archives

Parent organisation: Aberdeen City Council

Address: Aberdeen

A Town House

Address: Town House, Broad Street, Aberdeen AB10 1AQ

Telephone: (01224) 522513

Fax: (01224) 638556

E-mail: archives@legal.aberdeen.net.uk

Website: www.aberdeencity.gov.uk/archivists.htm

Enquiries: The City Archivist, Miss J.A. Cripps

Open: Wed–Fri: 9.30–4.30. Closed for a fortnight in December.

Access: Generally open to the public, by appointment. Non-core records are outstored.

Historical background: Established in 1980 by the City of Aberdeen District Council. Since 1996 the archives service has been responsible for administering the holdings of the former Grampian Regional Archives.

Acquisitions policy: To maintain the local authority archives for Aberdeen City Council and to acquire, by gift, loan and purchase, records in all formats relevant to the history of Aberdeen and its locality.

Archives of organisation: Royal Burgh of Aberdeen, 12th century–1975; Burgh of Old Aberdeen, 1603–1891; Burgh of Woodside,

1868–91; Aberdeen Harbour Board, 1801–1935 (incomplete).

Major collections: Records of Hall Russell Shipbuilders, 19th–20th centuries; Aberdeen Association for Prevention of Cruelty to Animals, 1872–1970; Aberdeen Congregational Churches, 1798–1971; Northern Cooperative Society, 1861–1993; Aberdeen Chamber of Commerce, 1856–1980; Voluntary Service Aberdeen, 19th–20th centuries.

Non-manuscript material: Town Clerk's library of local books and pamphlets, 18th–20th centuries.

Finding aids: Survey list, 1970. Detailed listing in progress.

Facilities: Photocopying. Photography by arrangement.

Conservation: Contracted out.

B Old Aberdeen House

Address: Old Aberdeen House, Dunbar Street, Aberdeen AB24 3UJ

Telephone: (01224) 481775

Fax: (01224) 495830

Enquiries: The Duty Archivist

Open: Mon–Wed: 10.00–1.00, 2.00–4.00.
Closed for a fortnight in December.

Access: Generally open to the public. Appointment recommended.

Historical background: The repository was opened in 1986 for the records of Grampian Regional Council and its predecessors. At local government reorganisation in 1996 the premises were inherited by Aberdeen City Council, which currently maintains the archives for itself and on behalf of the other constituent authorities of Aberdeenshire and the Moray councils and the Grampian Joint Valuation Board.

Acquisitions policy: To maintain local authority archives for Aberdeen City Council and to acquire, by gift, loan and purchase, records in all formats relevant to the history of Aberdeenshire.

Archives of organisation: Grampian Regional Council and Grampian Joint Valuation Board; county councils of Aberdeen, Banff, Kincardine and Moray (education and poor law records also for Aberdeen Town Council);

burgh and (pre-1975) district councils (except Moray and Upper Banffshire); recent transfers from Aberdeen City Council (principally planning and architects' departments).

Major collections: Robert Gordon University and Aberdeen Educational Trust, 1730–1990.

Finding aids: Lists.

Facilities: Photocopying. Photography by arrangement.

4 Aberdeen City Gallery and Museums
James McBey Reference Library

Parent organisation: Aberdeen City Council

Address: Schoolhill, Aberdeen AB9 1PQ

Telephone: (01224) 523700

Fax: (01224) 632133

E-mail: info@aagm.co.uk

Website: www.aagm.co.uk

Enquiries: the Registrar, Mr J. Wilson

Open: Mon–Fri: 10.00–12.30, 2.00–4.30.

Access: Generally open to the public.

Historical background: The original art gallery was built in 1885. The James McBey Print Room and Art Library, opened in 1961 as a memorial to James McBey (1883–1959), etcher and painter, was endowed by his widow.

Acquisitions policy: Accepts donations of local artists' papers.

Major collections: Sir George Reid RSA (1841–1913), letters and papers.
William Dyce, RSA (1806–64), papers.
Records of Messrs Berry and Mackay, marine opticians of Aberdeen, are held in the museum.

Non-manuscript material: Collection of James McBey's books and memorabilia.
Hall Russell shipbuilding plans.
Slide collection.

Finding aids: Berry and Mackay: NRA 14969.

Facilities: Photocopying by arrangement. Microfiche reader.

5 Aberdeen University
Special Collections & Archives

Parent organisation: University of Aberdeen, Directorate of Information System & Services, Heritage Division

Address: King's College, Aberdeen AB24 3SW

Telephone: (01224) 272598

Fax: (01224) 273891

E-mail: speclib@abdn.ac.uk

Website: www.abdn.ac.uk/diss/historic/

Enquiries: The Manager, Heritage Division, Dr. A.G. Knox
The Senior Curatorial Assistant, Mrs J. Pirie

Open: Mon–Fri: 9.30–4.30. Advance notice of visits is desirable.

Access: Approved readers. Written application preferred.

Historical background: For over 200 years there were two separate universities in Aberdeen, each with its own statutory rights and degree-granting privileges. The first, King's College, was founded in Old Aberdeen in 1495. The second, Marischal College, was founded in New Aberdeen by George Keith, 4th Earl Marischal of Scotland, in 1593. The two colleges remained rival institutions until 1860, when a royal ordinance united them under the title of the University of Aberdeen. The Manuscripts and Archives Section of the university library was established in its present form in 1969.

MSS and books formerly belonging to scholars of the north-east from the 16th century onwards now form part of the university library. Material has been transferred from the library of Christ's College. The archives of St Machar's Cathedral, which are stored in the cathedral charter room, and of National Trust for Scotland properties in the vicinity are made available for study in the library reading room.

Acquisitions policy: The principal function of the section is the systematic accumulation and preservation of the university's archives. Non-archival material relating to the university is acquired as often as possible. Until 1976 the university acted as a repository for local historical material in the absence of a local authority record office in the region, under the terms of the agreement reached between the Scottish universities and the NRAS. Since 1976 it has shared this activity with the local council archives offices.

Archives of organisation: Archives of King's College, Marischal College and the University of Aberdeen.

Major collections: Individual MSS and archival collections bought by the library, given to it, or deposited in it on loan (*c*4000 separate items and collections).

Greig-Duncan collection of texts and music of ballads and folksongs of the North-East, 1876–1917.

Collections of papyri, ostraca and non-European MSS.

Non-manuscript material: An oral history archive of the university is being built up.

George Washington Wilson Photographic Collection: glass-plate negatives of views in UK, South Africa, Australia (*c*40,000).

Finding aids: All collections are catalogued briefly by title and entered in the university library on-line catalogue accessible via the Internet. Standardised descriptive or summary lists are circulated via the NRAS.

All descriptive and summary lists are being mounted in a searchable database on the website.

Facilities: Photocopying. Photography. Microfilm/fiche reader/printer.

Conservation: Presently contracted out. It is planned to extend the conservation service at Marischal Museum to cover paper conservation.

Publications: Guide to Sources of Information: Manuscripts and Archives (Aberdeen, 1979).

M.R. James: *A Catalogue of the Medieval Manuscripts in the University Library Aberdeen* (Cambridge, 1932).

E.G. Turner: *Catalogue of Greek and Latin Papyri and Ostraca in the Possession of the University Library, Aberdeen,* Aberdeen University Studies, no.116 (Aberdeen, 1939).

L. Macfarlane: 'William Elphinstone's Library', *Aberdeen University Review,* xxxvii (1957–8), 253.

——: 'William Elphinstone's Library Revisited', *The Renaissance in Scotland in Literature, Religion, History and Culture* (Leiden, 1994).

C. Roth: *The Aberdeen Codex of the Hebrew Bible,* Aberdeen University Studies, no.138 (Edinburgh, 1958).

N.R. Ker: *Medieval Manuscripts in British Libraries,* ii (Oxford, 1977), 2.

J. Carter and C. McLaren: *Crown and Gown: an Illustrated History of the University of Aberdeen, 1495–1995* (Aberdeen University Press, 1994).

Other descriptions can be found in *Aberdeen University Library Bulletin, Aberdeen University Review* and *Northern Scotland,* passim.

6 Gordon Highlanders Museum

Address: St Lukes, Viewfield Road, Aberdeen AB15 7XH

Telephone: (01224) 311200

Fax: (01224) 319323

E-mail: museum@gordonhighlanders.com

Website: www.gordonhighlanders.com/museum.html

Enquiries: The Curator, Miss Melanie Brooker

Open: April–Oct: Tues–Sat: 10.30–4.30; Sun: 1.30–4.30.
Nov–March: by appointment only.

Access: Generally open to the public, by prior appointment and after payment of the normal entry charge to museum.

The Gordon Highlanders Museum opened in 1997. It holds archives of the Gordon Highlanders 75th and 92nd Regiments, 1784–1994, and collections of papers, including photographs and scrapbooks, have been acquired. There are catalogues and indexes and photocopying is available.

7 Northern Health Services Archives

Parent organisation: Grampian Health Board

Address: ARI Woolmanhill, Aberdeen AB25 1LD

Telephone: (01224) 555562

E-mail: archives@grampian.scot.nhs.uk

Enquiries: The Archivist, Miss F.R. Watson

Open: Mon– Fri: 9.00–5.00.

Access: Generally open to the public, by appointment, subject to 30-, 75- and 100-year closure periods on certain records.

Historical background: Grampian Health Board was set up in 1974, the successor authority to the North Eastern Regional Hospital Board, itself established in 1947 under the National Health Service (Scotland) Act. The board is accountable to the Secretary of State for Scotland and to local people to improve health and ensure that appropriate services are available for the residents of Grampian. The archives department, formed in 1980, holds the records of hospitals, community services, NHS authorities and many other health-related predecessor authorities in the north-east of Scotland.

Acquisitions policy: To acquire by deposit or donation material relevant to health care and health-care institutions and organisations currently or formerly in existence in the Grampian area.

Archives of organisation: Archives of Grampian Health Board and North Eastern Regional Hospital Board and their constituents.

Major collections: Records of Aberdeen Royal Infirmary (f. 1739), including 18th-century case notes and estate papers of Kinnadie and Towie (Aberdeenshire); Royal Cornhill Hospital, Aberdeen (f. 1800); Royal Aberdeen Children's Hospital (f. 1877); district lunatic asylums in Aberdeen, Banff and Elgin; medical, surgical, obstetric and TB case notes, 1920s–1950s; ophthalmology notes, 1890s–1950s.

Non-manuscript material: Photographs of hospitals in north-east Scotland, exteriors and interiors.

Finding aids: TS lists, copies of which are held in the National Archives of Scotland (entry 329). Index of north-east doctors, midwives, druggists, dentists, etc, mainly mid-18th to mid-19th centuries, in preparation.

Facilities: Photocopying. Photography by arrangement.

Publications: D. Campbell & F. Watson: *The Hospitals of Peterhead and District* (1994).

F. Watson: *Westburn Medical Group 1896–1996: A Practice Centenary* (1996);

——: *Sickness and in Health: North East Health Records as a Source for Family History* (1988).

8 Cardiganshire Record Office/ Archifdy Ceredigion Archives

Parent organisation: Ceredigion County Council

Address: Swyddfa'r Sir, Marine Terrace, Aberystwyth, Ceredigion SY23 2DE

Telephone: (01970) 633697/8

E-mail: archives@ceredigion.gov.uk

Enquiries: The Archivist, Helen Palmer

Open: Mon–Fri: 10.00–1.00, 2.00–4.00.

Access: Generally open to the public.

Historical background: The office was established in 1974. Previously records for the area had been collected by the National Library of Wales (entry 9). The office acts as a Diocesan Record Office for St Davids but holds only microfilm copies of parish registers. It is recognised as a place of deposit for public records.

Acquisitions policy: Archives, manuscripts and ephemera relating to the old county of Cardiganshire, now known as Ceredigion.

Archives of organisation: Usual local authority record holdings.

Major collections: Deposited local collections.

Finding aids: Lists sent to NRA.

Facilities: Photocopying. Microfilm readers.

Conservation: Contracted out.

Publications: Short guide available from office.

9 National Library of Wales
Manuscripts and Records

Address: Aberystwyth, Ceredigion SY23 3BU

Telephone: (01970) 632880

Fax: (01970) 632883

E-mail: ymh.lc@llgc.org.uk

Website: www.llgc.org.uk

Enquiries: The Keeper of Manuscripts and Records, Mr G. Jenkins

Open: Mon–Fri: 9.30–6.00; Sat: 9.30–5.00. Closed first full week in October.

Access: By reader's ticket; over 18 years of age.

Historical background: The library was established by Royal Charter in 1907 and is a copyright library. It is recognised as a place of deposit for public records. The library is now responsible for the National Screen and Sound Archive of Wales (entry 11).

Acquisitions policy: MS and archival material relating to Wales.

Archives of organisation: Complete organisational archive, 1907– .

Major collections: General Series of the National Library of Wales MSS.

Records of the Court of Great Sessions in Wales, 1542–1830.

Pre-1858 probate records.

Archives of the Anglican Church in Wales and of many parish churches.

Archives of the Welsh Calvinistic Methodist Church and other nonconformist denominations.

Archives of landed estates, families, institutions and individuals.

Welsh Political Archive: archives of parties, pressure groups and politicians; election ephemera.

University of Wales research dissertations, 1899– .

Non-manuscript material: Census returns, 1841–91, and indexes of births, deaths and marriages, 1837–1992 (microfilm).

Department of Pictures and Maps: pictorial, cartographic, photographic, audio-visual and multimedia collections.

Department of Printed Books: printed material, including newspapers and periodicals.

Finding aids: Calendars, schedules and lists (*c*1000 vols, mostly TS); associated card indexes; conversion from paper to disk in progress. Computerised cataloguing and indexing from 1999.

Facilities: Photocopying and photographic unit. Microform readers. Printing unit.

Conservation: Preservation and conservation unit.

Publications: Annual Report [includes list of accessions].

National Library of Wales Journal (1939–) [articles on the library's holdings].

Guide to the Department of Manuscripts and Records, the National Library of Wales (Aberystwyth, 1994).

10 National Monuments Record of Wales

Parent organisation: The Royal Commission on the Ancient and Historical Monuments of Wales

Address: Crown Building, Plas Crug, Aberystwyth, Ceredigion SY23 1NJ

Telephone: (01970) 621200

Fax: (01970) 627701

E-mail: nmr.wales@rcahmw.org.uk

Website: www.rcahmw.org.uk

Enquiries: The Head of Library and Archive, Mrs Hilary Malaws

Open: Mon–Fri: 9.30–4.00; restricted service 1.00–2.00.

Access: Generally open to the public. An appointment is not normally necessary but advance notice is advisable.

Historical background: The Royal Commission was established in 1908 to make an inventory of the ancient and historical monuments of Wales and Monmouthshire. It is currently empowered by a royal warrant of 1992 to survey, record, publish and maintain a database of ancient and historical sites, structures and landscapes in Wales. It is responsible for the National Monuments Record (NMR) of Wales, for the supply of archaeological information to the Ordnance Survey for mapping purposes, for the coordination of archaeological aerial photography in Wales, and for the sponsorship of the regional Sites and Monuments Records.

Acquisitions policy: To collect, maintain and make available a comprehensive record of the archaeological, architectural and historical monuments of Wales (including its territorial waters) from the earliest times to the present day. The NMR collects records created or held by the Royal Commission, other organisations such as Cadw and the Welsh Archaeological Trusts, and private sources. Generally these consist of modern records. Indexes and descriptions of records and archives held in other repositories and organisations are also acquired. A copy of the Collecting Policy is available on request.

Archives of organisation: Archive of Royal Commission fieldwork and research, including reports, notes, drawings, plans, photographs, 1908– .

National Buildings Record (NMR since 1964), Welsh section, photographs, drawings, surveys, documents, 1941– .

Major collections: Cadw: notices of 'listing' and associated photographs of buildings, notices of 'scheduling' of ancient monuments, field monument warden reports and photographs.

Ministry of Works: photographs of monuments in state care.

National Trust: North Wales Vernacular Buildings Survey, Welsh archaeological surveys of NT property.

Regional Archaeological Trusts: excavation records.

Ordnance Survey Archaeology Division: records, photographs and maps.

Property Services Agency: plans and drawings of government and public buildings.

Numerous private collections.

Non-manuscript material: Major national collection of photographs (c1 million) of ancient sites and historic buildings, including vertical and oblique air photographs, 1850s– .

Large-scale OS maps (c30,000), including incomplete set of original OS 25-inch second edition annotated plans. A few of these plans were never published at this scale.

Plans and drawings (originals or copies) from various sources, including architects (c25,000).

Finding aids: Card indexes currently in process of computerisation (mostly site-based); computerised accession register and embryonic catalogue.

Facilities: Photocopying. Photography. Microfiche reader.

Conservation: Contracted out.

Publications: Annual Report (for Royal Commission including NMR). NMR leaflet.
Various thematic or area-based publications from the Royal Commission available.

11   National Screen and Sound Archive of Wales

Parent organisation: National Library of Wales

Address: Unit 1, Science Park, Cefn Llan, Aberystwyth, Ceredigion SY23 3AH

Telephone: (01970) 626007

Fax: (01970) 626008

E-mail: wftva@aol.com

Website: www.llgc.org.uk

Enquiries: The Access Officer, Mr Iestyn Hughes

Open: Mon–Thurs: 9.00–5.30; Fri: 9.00–5.00.

Access: The Archive's records are open to anyone with a genuine interest in the collection. An appointment is necessary. Intending researchers should apply to the Archive for research charges and use of footage costs.

Historical background: The Wales Film and Television Archive was set up as a pilot project in 1989. During the next three years, two permanent staff (with the help of a part-time technician) were employed to research the feasibility of establishing a permanent film and video archive for Wales. In 1992 an increase in funding allowed the Archive to move into its own independent premises in Aberystwyth.

Acquisitions policy: The collection of film and television material reflecting the people, history and culture of Wales, and the contribution of amateurs and professionals alike to its development.

Non-manuscript material: Lord Tenby Collection: including the long-lost feature *The Life Story of David Lloyd George* (1918), *Hepworth Cinema Interviews* (1916), interviews with British leaders and home movies of David Lloyd George.

Jack Howells Collection: including *Dylan Thomas* (1962).

S4C Collection: includes television programmes such as *Lleifior* and *Tair Chwaer*, Animated series such as *Superted* and the *Animated Shakespeare Tales*, and feature films, e.g. *Coming Up Roses* (1986), *Un Nos Ola Leuad* (1991) and *Cwm Hyfryd* (1992).

Wales Arts Council Collection: large collection of shorts and documentaries made by amateur film-makers with the help of Wales Arts Council funding.

Kenneth Griffith Collection: television programmes and documentaries made by the independent film director.

Teliesyn Collection: programmes and filmed dramas made for television by the prolific Welsh production house.

National Library of Wales Collection (c50% of holdings), including films of A.J. Sylvester and Sir Ifan ab Owen Edwards, Welsh Office films, amateur films, e.g. of National Eisteddfod, 1951.

Welsh Film Board fictional and educational films, 1970s.

Finding aids: A bilingual computerised system integrates all information about the collection (e.g. title, reel, accession, depositor details), and titles are catalogued with subject, people and place indexes.

Facilities: Best light teleciné facilities for Super 8mm, Standard 8mm and 16mm film to Betacam, VHS and SVHS videotape.

Conservation: Film conservation undertaken in-house; film copying contracted out.

Publications: Wales Film and Television Archive Catalogue, Volume 1 [bi-lingual catalogue of 150 titles within the Archive's collection].
David Lloyd George: The Movie Mystery.

12 University of Wales

Address: Hugh Owen Library, Penglais, Aberystwyth, Ceredigion SY23 3DZ

Telephone: (01970) 622391

Fax: (01970) 622404

E-mail: lib@aber.ac.uk

Enquiries: The Director of Information Services, Dr Mike Hopkins

Open: Term: Mon–Fri: 9.00–10.00; Sat: 9.00–5.00; Sun: 11.00–6.00.
Vacation: Mon–Fri: 9.00–1.00.

Access: Visiting scholars and others engaged in serious research. They should supply a suitable testimonial and obtain the written permission of the Director before they can use the library.

Historical background: The library has deposited in the National Library of Wales (entry 9) various materials from the Powell Collection and a collection of papers formed by E. R. G. Salisbury (1819–90), including some MS material on Welsh local history and a large accumulation of press cuttings on the history and topography of Wales and the Welsh border and on contemporary political events. These may be consulted there but may not be reproduced without the permission of the registrar and director. In 1989 the College of Librarianship Wales amalgamated with the university and is now the Thomas Parry Library. It is located on a separate campus at Llanbadarn Fawr, Aberystwyth, Ceredigion, SY23 3AS, tel. (01970) 622417, where a collection of films,

sound recordings, photographs and architectural plans relating to libraries and librarianship is maintained.

Acquisitions policy: The library acquires papers of those associated with the university.

Archives of organisation: The registrar's office holds some internal records. The library has the University of Wales MSS Collection: chiefly early library records, including stockbooks, accessions, donations, binding etc, and some MSS relating to the foundation of the university; also minute books of a number of student societies.

Major collections: George Powell Collection: George Powell of Nanteos near Aberystwyth, bequest includes *c*200 MSS, including music MSS, 17th–mid-19th century, and many autograph letters of writers, artists and musicians of the 19th century.

Thomas Webster MSS: letters to Thomas Webster (1773–1844), first professor of geology at University College London, 1818–44.

Richard Ellis (1865–1928 MSS: notebooks and correspondence *re* unfinished study of antiquarian Edward Lloyd.

David De Lloyd MSS: Professor of Music at the college, 1926–48, scores and notes on Welsh music and musical history and theory.

Thomas Francis Roberts MSS: Principal of the college, 1891–1919, correspondence relating to all university matters.

J.O.Francis Archive: TS and acting copies of his plays and broadcast talks.

Lily Newton Archives: *re* her work on river pollution in mid-Wales, mid–20th century.

Finding aids: On-line catalogues.

Facilities: Photocopying. Photography. Microform readers.

Conservation: In-house provision for basic repairs and rebinding.

Publications: J. Challinor (ed.): 'Some correspondence of Thomas Webster, geologist (1773–1844)', *Annals of Science,* xvii/3 (1961), 175–95; xviii/3 (1962), 147–75; xix/1 (1963), 59–79; xix/4 (1963), 285–97; xx/1 (1964), 59–80; xx/2 (1964), 143–64.

B.F. Roberts: *The Richard Ellis Papers: Handbook and Schedule* (Aberystwyth, 1983).

13   Abingdon School Archive

Address: Park Road, Abingdon, Oxfordshire OX14 1DE

Telephone: (01235) 521563

Fax: (01235) 534596

E-mail: hm.sec@abingdon.org.uk

Website: www.abingdon.org.uk

Enquiries: The Archivist

Open: Term: Mon–Fri: 9.00–1.00.

Access: Generally open to the public, by written appointment only.

Historical background: Founded by the Benedictine monks of Abingdon Abbey some-time before the 12th century, the school survived the dissolution of the monasteries and was re-endowed in 1563 by John Roysse, an old boy and a member of the Mercers' Company. It remained an endowed grammar school until it came under the direct grant system in 1947. In 1975 it reverted to full independence. The archives date from the 18th century.

Acquisitions policy: The archive purchases books, documents and other items associated with the school. It encourages donations and deposits from pupils, masters, old boys and governors.

Archives of organisation: Admissions registers, 1844– ; school magazine, *The Abingdonian*, 1890– ; Roysse's charity account books, 1777–1878 and minute books, 1862–78.
Governor's minute books, 1878– ; headmasters report, 1878– ; letter files, 1878– ; ledgers, cashbooks, accounts, 1878– .

Non-manuscript material: Building plans, 1870s– .
Photographs of buildings, pupils, masters, teams, governors, headmasters and distinguished alumni. Cine film, 1950–1960s, of school plays and sporting activities. Programmes of concerts, plays, prize-giving.

Finding aids: Lists.

Facilities: Photocopying.

Conservation: Contracted out.

Publications: A. Preston: *The Church and Parish of St Nicholas, Abingdon* (OUP, 1929).
T. Hinde and M. St John Parker: *An Illustrated History of Abingdon School* (James & James, 1997).

14   Christ's Hospital

Address: 1 Old Station Yard, Abingdon, Oxfordshire OX14 3LQ

Enquiries: The Clerk to the Governors

Christ's Hospital is a charity with a private archive, holding records of the Fraternity of the Holy Cross and the Guild of Our Lady, 1165–1547; records of Christ's Hospital, 1533–1918; and records (minutes and accounts) of other charities, deriving from 17th-century benefactors, administered by the governors. Access is strictly at the discretion of the governors.

15   Radley College Archives

Address: Abingdon, Oxfordshire OX14 2HR

Telephone: (01235) 543078

Fax: (01235) 543106

E-mail: aem@radley.org.uk

Website: www.radley.org.uk

Enquiries: The Archivist, Mr A.E. Money

Open: Term time only, by arrangement.

Access: Generally open to the public, by appointment.

Historical background: Radley College was founded as St Peter's College in 1847 by the high churchmen Rev. William Sewell of Exeter College, Oxford, and Rev. Robert Singleton, late headmaster of St Columba's College, Ireland. The college has had an archivist since 1945.

Acquisitions policy: Anything to do with the school is welcomed. Mainly written or photo-graphic material, memoirs, diaries and letters.

Archives of organisation: Archives of the college, including minutes of council meetings, 1860s– , and minutes of Radleian Society (f. 1887), 1911– .

Major collections: Diary of Rev. Robert Singleton, first warden (*d*.1881), 1847–8.
TS copies of the following papers:
Diary of Rev. William Wood, assistant master and later warden (*d*.1919), 1855–67.
Letters home of John A. Godley, later Lord Kilbracken (1847–1932), 1857–61.
Talbot letters: letters from the two sons of Hon. Gerald Talbot, Private Secretary to Lord Canning, Governor-General in India, 1856–7.

Non-manuscript material: Photographs of buildings, groups, individual boys and masters, 1850s–1860s. Some film material.

Facilities: Photocopying.

Publications: C. Hibbert: *No Ordinary Place: Radley College and the Public School System 1847–1997* (1997).
A.E. Money: *Manly and Muscular Diversions: Public Schools and the Nineteenth Century Sporting Revival* (1997).

16   Britten–Pears Library

Parent organisation: The Britten–Pears Foundation

Address: The Red House, Aldeburgh, Suffolk IP15 5PZ

Telephone: (01728) 452615

Fax: (01728) 453076

E-mail: bpl@britten-pears.co.uk

Website: www.britten-pears.co.uk

Enquiries: The Director, Dr Jenny Doctor

Open: Mon–Fri: 10.00–1.00, 2.15–5.15, by appointment only.

Access: Bona fide researchers, at the discretion of the Librarian and Trustees.

Historical background: The Britten–Pears Library was set up in 1973 to house the working collection of printed and MS music, books and personal papers of Benjamin Britten (1913–76) and Peter Pears (1910–86). The main public access area is the library built by Britten and Pears in the early 1960s; the rest of the collection is housed in converted farm buildings, and a purpose-built extension opened in 1993.

Acquisitions policy: To acquire any major Britten MSS remaining at large. Book acquisition in the areas of 20th-century music, music printing and publishing, politics, art and literature. Also local history.

Major collections: Music and literary MSS, letters and diaries of Benjamin Britten and Peter Pears.
MSS of other composers, including Gustav Holst (1874–1934), Frank Bridge (1879–1941), Sir Michael Tippett (1905–98) and Cecil Armstrong Gibbs (1889–1960).
Archives of the English Opera Group/English Music Theatre.

A few literary MSS, including drafts for the libretti to Britten's operas.

Non-manuscript material: Annotated poetry and drama texts. Proof and other interim music material.

Finding aids: In-house lists and computer catalogue.

Facilities: Photocopying. Microfilm/fiche readers.

Publications: J. Evans, P. Reed and P. Wilson (comps): *A Britten Source Book* (Aldeburgh, 1987).
P. Reed (ed.): *The Travel Diaries of Peter Pears*, Aldeburgh Studies in Music 2 (Woodbridge: Boydell & Brewer/The Britten–Pears Library, 1995).
P. Banks and others (comp): *Benjamin Britten: a Catalogue of the Published Works* (Aldeburgh: The Britten–Pears Library, 1999).

17   Alderney Society Museum

Address: Alderney, Channel Islands GY9 3TG

Telephone: (01481) 823222

Fax: (01481) 824979

E-mail: alderney.museum@virgin.net

Enquiries: The Administrator, Mr Peter Arnold

Open: Easter–end of Oct: Mon–Fri: 10.00–12.00, 2.00–4.00; Sat, Sun: 10.00–12.00.

Access: Generally open to the public.

The society museum was established in 1966. It is maintained on a voluntary basis and holds local history collections relating to the history of Alderney, including materials on occupations, folk history and records of iron age archaeological excavations. Photocopying facilities are available.

18   Queen Alexandra's Royal Army Nursing Corps Museum (QARANC)

Address: Army Medical Services Museums, DMSTC, Keogh Barracks, Ash Vale, Aldershot, Hampshire GU12 5RQ

Telephone: (01252) 340212

Fax: (01252) 340224

Enquiries: The Curator, Capt. (retd) P.H. Starling

Open: Mon–Fri: 8.30–3.30. Other times by arrangement.

Access: Generally open to the public. No charge, but donations appreciated.

Historical background: The museum was established to give a pictorial history of army nursing from the Crimea to the modern day. In 1995 it moved from the Royal Pavilion, Aldershot (its location since 1966), to join the Royal Army Medical Corps Museum at the address shown above.

Acquisitions policy: To acquire, by purchase, gift, bequest, exchange or loan, items relevant to QARANC, QAMFNS, QAIMNS, TANS, Almeric Paget Massage Corps, PCANSR, ANS, Florence Nightingale and the nurses who accompanied her to the Crimea.

Major collections: Reports and papers of Dame Maud McCarthy (1858–1949), Matron-in-Chief, British Expeditionary Force, France, 1914–19.
Letters of Dame Katharine Jones, Matron-in-Chief, 1940–44.
Other MS collections relating to army nursing experience in war and peace.

Non-manuscript material: Photographic library.

Facilities: Photocopying.

Publications: J. Piggott: *History of QARANC* (Trowbridge, 1990).

19 Roman Catholic Records Office

Parent organisation: Ministry of Defence (Army)

Address: RC Bishopric of the Forces, AGPDO, Middle Hill, Aldershot, Hampshire GU11 1PP

Telephone: (01252) 349007

Fax: (01252) 349006

Enquiries: The Senior Chaplain (RC) or The Notary

Access: Generally open to the public, by appointment only.

In 1952, a policy decision at the HQ of the Royal Army Chaplain's Department (RAChD)

decreed that all sacramental records of marriages, baptisms, confirmations etc which had taken place in service RC churches worldwide for the tri-services should be housed centrally at Aldershot. Consequently, all chaplains sent the registers to St Michael's House, where they were collated by date into other registers, then card-indexed by surname. Some records date back to 1856. Since 1989, the records have been computerised as they come in, and it is hoped that in time the bulk of the 200,000 records will be on computer. The office is recognised as a place of deposit for public records. See also Royal Army Chaplain's Department Museum and Archives (entry 24).

20 Alnwick Castle
Duke of Northumberland's Estate Office

Address: Estates Office, Alnwick Castle, Alnwick, Northumberland NE66 1NQ

Telephone: (01665) 510777

Fax: (01665) 510876

Enquiries: The Archivist, Colin Shrimpton

Open: Strictly by arrangement.

Access: Bona fide scholars, by appointment only.

The substantial archives and MS collections dating from 12th to 19th centuries are fully described in HMC Third Report, xii and App 45 125 (Alnwick Castle) (2); Fifth Report, xi (4); Sixth Report, xi and App 221 33 (Syon House) (5); and NRA 0836. The archives comprise the following: estate and manorial records; legal papers; household records; official and professional correspondence; family papers and personal correspondence; miscellanea (including MS items, notes, catalogues, cuttings, photographs etc); borough records; business records; ecclesiastical records; forestry papers; lord lieutenancy, military and naval records; royal correspondence, late 14th century– .

21 Fusiliers of Northumberland Archives

Address: The Abbot's Tower, Alnwick Castle, Alnwick, Northumberland NE66 1NG

Telephone: (01665) 602152 or 510211

Fax: (01665) 603320

E-mail: fusnorthld@aol.com

Enquiries: The Hon. Curator, Capt. (retd) P.H.D. Marr

Open: By arrangement.

Access: Generally open to the public. An appointment is necessary.

The regiment maintains its own archives, including records of service, 1688- , courts martial books, daily order books, regimental and battalion orders and letter-books, plus war diaries, World War I and World War II. Personal papers and diaries of former members are also accepted and there are large collections of these and of photograph albums. NRA 20951.

22 Armitt Library

Parent organisation: The Armitt Trust

Address: The Armitt Library and Museum, Rydal Road, Ambleside, Cumbria LA22 9DL

Telephone: (01539) 431212

Fax: (01539) 431313

E-mail: almc@armitt.com

Website: http://fp.armitt.plus.com/ armitt_collection.htm

Enquiries: The Library Manager

Open: Mon–Fri: 10.00–12.30, 1.30–4.00.

Access: Freely available to all students and scholars.

Historical background: The Armitt Library is a charitable institution founded in 1912 under the terms of the will of Mary Armitt (1851–1911), a scholar and local historian who collected books and artefacts which became the archives of the library. The Armitt Trust Library incorporated the Ambleside Book Club (f.1828), of which William Wordsworth (1770–1850) was a member, and the Ambleside Ruskin Society (f.1882) in association with John Ruskin (1819–1900). The library has acted as a repository for documents, especially of local history interest, from its origin. It moved to new, purpose-built accommodation in 1997.

Acquisitions policy: Collects material relevant to the literary and social history of the Lake District.

Archives of organisation: Minutes and other records relating to the administration of the trust and library, 1828- .

Major collections: Personal papers of the Armitt sisters, Mary, Annie and Sophia, authors and naturalists.
Documents relating to Harriet Martineau (1802–76), John Ruskin, William Wordsworth, W.G. Collingwood (1854–1932), Thomas Alcock Beck (1795–1846), Arthur Ransome (1884–1967), Hugh Walpole (1884–1941), Charlotte Mason, educationalist, and the Arnold family of Fox How.

Non-manuscript material: Topographical books on the Lake District. Prints and drawings of Lake District by William Green, early 19th century.
Beatrix Potter (1866–1943) watercolours (*c*400). Works of art by Kurt Schwitters (1887–1948), Barbara Crystal Collingwood (1887–1961) and many others.
Herbert Bell photograph albums.
Ruskin books and memorabilia.

Finding aids: TS lists of collections. Computer database which currently lists books and MSS.

Facilities: Photocopying.

23 R. Twining & Co. Ltd

Address: Southway, Andover, Hampshire SP10 5AQ

Telephone: (01264) 334477

Fax: (01264) 348318

E-mail: sam.twining@twinings.com

Website: www.twinings.com

Enquiries: The Director

Open: Mon–Fri: 8.30–4.30, by appointment only.

Access: Bona fide researchers, at the discretion of the company, by written application to the Director.

Historical background: The company was founded in 1706 by Thomas Twining in Devereux Court, Temple Bar, London. It expanded and in 1825 started Twinings Bank, which was taken over by Lloyds Bank in 1829. It received its first royal warrant in 1837 and acquired the business of Edmund Antrobus, tea and coffee merchant, in 1872. In 1904 it registered as a limited company. Ibex Coffee Co. Ltd. was acquired in 1939 and in 1964 the company became part of Associated British Foods Group. Since then it has expanded rapidly with its own factories. Records of Twinings Bank are in Lloyds TSB Group Archives (see entry 683) and letters of Rev. Thomas Twining (1734–1804) have been given to the British Library (see entry 561).

Acquisitions policy: Maintains archives of the company and acquires objects of particular interest to tea. There is a museum at the Twinings shop at 216 Strand, London, and at Norwich Castle Museum (see entry 940).

Archives of organisation: Records of firm, 1706– , including company accounts, correspondence, family trees.

Non-manuscript material: Photographs, family portraits.
Unique collection of books on tea.

Facilities: Photocopying.

Publications: The Twinings in Three Centuries (1910).
E.E. Newton: *Twinings in the Strand* (1922).
S.H. Twining: *225 Years in the Strand, 1706–1931* (1931).
———: *The House of Twinings, 1706–1956* (1956).

24 Royal Army Chaplain's Department
Museum and Archives

Parent organisation: Ministry of Defence (Army)

Address: Armed Forces Chaplaincy Centre, Amport House, Amport, Andover, Hampshire SP11 8BG

Telephone: (01264) 773144

Fax: (01264) 771042

Enquiries: Maj. (retd) M.A. Easey

Open: Mon Fri: 10.00–12.00, 2.00–4.00, by appointment.

Access: Military personnel and members of the public, by arrangement only.

Historical background: The present department was formed, by royal warrant, in 1796. The museum, in its present form, dates from 1968, although there was a departmental collection of memorabilia before that. It is recognised as a place of deposit for public records. For the department's Roman Catholic records see Roman Catholic Records Office (entry 19).

Acquisitions policy: Actively acquires material from chaplains by loan or gift.

Archives of organisation: Church services registers and precedent books.
Records of Protestant marriages, baptisms and deaths. Registers of military cemeteries overseas.

Major collections: Letters of Field Marshal Montgomery.
Personal papers and memorabilia, including POW material of various chaplains over the years.

Non-manuscript material: Many photographs, some drawings and prints. Medal collections and uniforms.

Finding aids: Partial card index.

Facilities: Photocopying. Photography.

25 Scottish Fisheries Museum

Parent organisation: Scottish Fisheries Museum Trust Ltd

Address: St Ayles, Harbourhead, Anstruther, Fife KY10 3AB

Telephone: (01333) 310628

Fax: (01333) 310628

E-mail: andrew@scottish-fisheries-museum.org

Website: www.scottish-fisheries-museum.org

Enquiries: The Curator, Linda McGowan

Open: April–Sept: Mon–Sat: 10.00–5.30; Sun: 11.00–5.00;
Oct–March: Mon–Sat: 10.00–4.30;
Sun: 12.00–4.30.

Access: Bona fide researchers, with proof of identity. An appointment is necessary.

The museum was opened in 1969, and virtually all its collections have been donated. These cover fisheries and cognate industries (e.g. boat building) in Scotland over the last 200 years and some local material relating to Anstruther. Apart from documents there are films, paintings and artefacts, drawings and plans (*c*5,000), and photographs (*c*16,000) and slides (*c*5,000). There are photocopying and photography facilities and catalogued indexes.

26 Arbroath Signal Tower Museum

Address: Ladyloan, Arbroath, Angus DD11 1PU

Telephone: (01241) 875598

E-mail: signal.tower@angus.gov.uk

Enquiries: The Curator, Ms Fiona Guest

Open: Mon–Sat: 10.00–5.00;
July and Aug: Sun: 2.00–5.00.

Access: Generally open to the public, on written application.

Historical background: The museum was opened in 1974 by Arbroath Town Council; since 1975 it has been part of Angus Council Cultural Services.

Acquisitions policy: Any local material.

Major collections: Arbroath Museum Society, 1843–1918.
Miscellaneous local private records, 18th–20th centuries.
Alex Shanks Dens Ironworks: engineers' catalogues of boilers, steam engines and lawn-mowers, and papers, 1859-c1950.
William Sharpey (1802–80), physiologist: letter-book, diplomas and certificates, 1821–74.
Bell Rock Lighthouse visitor books.

Non-manuscript material: Plans, photographs, maps and sound archives.

Finding aids: Archive list. Sharpey: NRA 24032.

Facilities: Photocopying.

27 Ayrshire Archives: North Ayrshire Council

Parent organisation: North Ayrshire Council

Address: Library Headquarters, 39/41 Princes Street, Ardrossan, Ayrshire KA22 8BT

Telephone: (01294) 469137

Fax: (01294) 604236

E-mail: reference@naclibhq.prestel.co.uk

Enquiries: The Local History Librarian, Mrs Jill McColl
The Archivist, Ayrshire Archives, Mr Kevin Wilbraham (see entry 39)

Open: Mon, Tues, Thurs, Fri: 9.30–5.00;
Sat: 10.00–1.00, 2.00–5.00.

Access: Generally open to the public.

Historical background: Ayrshire Archives is a joint service sponsored by the three local authorities in Ayrshire — East, North and South Ayrshire councils. The service was established in 1996 as a result of local government reorganisation and is responsible for all archival and records management issues relating to the three authorities. While the main office is located at the Ayrshire Archives Centre in Ayr (see entry 39), access to records in North Ayrshire is through the Local History Library at Library Headquarters in Ardrossan.

Acquisitions policy: To acquire all possible material relating to the history of the area.

Archives of organisation: Records of North Ayrshire Council and predecessor bodies, including Cunninghame District Council (1975–96) and the Royal Burgh of Irvine (1306–1975).

Major collections: Alexander Wood Memorial Library: collection of local primary and secondary source material, 18th–19th centuries.
Cunninghame of Auchenharvie papers (1586–1946).

Non-manuscript material: Local maps, postcards, photographs and drawings.
Ardrossan and Saltcoats Herald, 1857– .
Microfilms of parish registers and census returns.

Finding aids: Catalogues and lists. Lists are sent to NRAS.

Facilities: Photocopying. Microfilm/fiche readers.

Publications: Various information leaflets and local publications.

28 Clan Donald Centre Library

Parent organisation: Clan Donald Lands Trust

Address: Armadale, Ardvasar, Isle of Skye IV45 8RS

Telephone: (01471) 844389

Fax: (01471) 844275

E-mail: library@cland.demon.co.uk

Website: www.highlandconnection.org/clandonaldcentre.htm

Enquiries: The Curator/Archivist, Ms Maggie Macdonald

Open: Easter–Oct: Mon–Sun: 9.30–5.30 Oct–Easter: Mon–Fri: 9.30 5.30, by appointment.

Access: Generally open to the public by day ticket to the centre or by annual membership season ticket. A charge is made.

Historical background: The Clan Donald Lands Trust was founded in 1971, when it purchased part of the Macdonald estate on the Isle of Skye. As well as developing a visitor centre with museum and historic gardens, the trust has built up a major collection of books and MSS relating to Clan Donald and the history of the Highlands and Islands. A study centre was opened in 1990.

Acquisitions policy: MSS, objects and other materials relating to the cultural heritage of the Lords of the Isles; the several clans within Clan Donald; the geographic areas from which those clans originated; the lives and careers of individual clansmen; the history of the trust's Skye estates.

Major collections: Macdonald Estate Papers, Skye and North Uist, mainly 18th and 19th century.
Macdonald of Glenalladale and Borrodale papers, 1759–1910.
Macdonald of Inchkenneth papers, 1825–60.
Papers of Hector Macdonald-Buchanan (*d* c1831) as factor to Mrs Anne Campbell or MacLeod of Strond, 1804–31.

Non-manuscript material: Reference library (7000 books), photographs, maps and plans, microfilms of censuses and parish records for Western Highlands and Islands; genealogical collections.

Finding aids: Detailed catalogue Macdonald Estate Papers (microfiche at NRAS); relevant indexes are in preparation. Catalogue, handlists and indexes of other MSS collections.

Facilities: Photocopying. Microfilm/fiche readers. Photography by arrangement. Paid research service available.

Conservation: Contracted out.

29 Armagh County Museum

Parent organisation: National Museums and Galleries of Northern Ireland (NMGNI)

Address: The Mall East, Armagh BT61 9BE

Telephone: (028) 37523070

Fax: (028) 37522631

E-mail: acm.um@nics.gov.uk

Enquiries: The Curator, Mrs Catherine McCullough

Open: Library/Archives: Mon–Fri: 10.00–5.00; Sat: 10.00–1.00, 2.00–5.00.

Access: Generally open to the public.

Historical background: Around 1839 the Armagh Natural and Philosophical Society started a museum, which moved to the present address in 1857. Armagh County Council took over the building and collections in 1931 and opened Armagh County Museum in 1935. The museum was rebuilt and enlarged in 1962 and transferred to the Ulster Museum trustees as a regional branch on local government reorganisation in 1973.

Acquisitions policy: To increase the collections selectively, so as to illustrate the history of Co. Armagh, and to build up a supporting library and archive for student reference.

Major collections: Armagh militia records, 1793– .
Charlemont estate papers, 19th century.
T.G.F. Paterson collection of MSS and TS on genealogy and local history.
Correspondence of George Russell 'AE' (1867–1935).
Sundry items of MSS, TS annotated published pamphlets etc relating to Co. Armagh.

Non-manuscript material: Photographic archive collection.
Books and pamphlets forming a reference collection to assist the study of museum collections in the fields of history, local history, prehistory, social history, art, genealogy etc.

Finding aids: Card index.

Facilities: Photocopying and photography may be arranged subject to management discretion.

Conservation: Access to the services of a full conservation department as a branch of the Ulster Museum and part of NMGNI.

Publications: 'Armagh County Museum: the Reference Library', *Irish Booklore*, ii/1 (1972).
D.R.M. Weatherup: 'The published writings of T.G.F. Paterson', *Seanchas Ardmacha*, vi/2 (1972).
——: 'Armagh Public Library', *Irish Booklore*, ii/2 (1976).

30 Armagh Observatory

Address: College Hill, Armagh BT61 9DG

Telephone: (028) 37522928

Fax: (028) 37527174

E-mail: jmf@star.arm.ac.uk

Website: www.arm.ac.uk

Enquiries: The Librarian, John McFarland

Open: Mon–Fri: 9.00–5.00.

Access: Normally research workers only; an appointment is necessary.

Historical background: The Armagh Observatory was founded in 1790 by Richard Robinson (1709–94), Archbishop of Armagh.

Acquisitions policy: To maintain the observatory archives.

Archives of organisation: Archives of the observatory, c1790– .

Major collections: Papers of members of staff, including correspondence and MSS of E.J. Opik; MSS by J.L.E. Dreyer (1852–1926), director of the observatory.

Non-manuscript material: Photographic material: Palomar sky survey; SRC sky survey; ESO sky survey; Boyden photographs (ADH telescope), South Africa.

Facilities: Photocopying. Microfiche reader.

Publications: P. Moore: *Armagh Observatory, 1790–1967* (Armagh, 1967).

J. Butler and M. Hoskin: 'The Archives of Armagh Observatory', *Journal for the History of Astronomy*, 18 (1987), 295.

J.A. Bennett: *Church, State and Astronomy in Ireland: 200 years of Armagh Observatory* (Belfast, 1990).

The Irish Astronomical Journal is produced from the observatory and includes annual reports.

J. McFarland: 'The Rare and Antiquarian Book Collection of the Armagh Observatory', *Irish Astronomical Journal*, 18 (1987), 102.

——: 'The Historical Instruments of Armagh Observatory', *Vistas in Astronomy*, 33 (1990), 149.

31 Armagh Public Library

Robinson Library

Address: The Library, Abbey Street, Armagh BT61 7DY

Telephone: (028) 37523142

Fax: (028) 37524177

E-mail: armroblib@aol.com

Enquiries: The Keeper, the Very Rev. H. Cassidy

Open: Mon– Fri: 9.00–1.00, 2.00–4.00.

Access: Generally open to the public. An appointment is desirable.

Historical background: The library was founded in 1771 by Archbishop Robinson by Act of Parliament. He wanted a university for the northern part of the island of Ireland and decided the first requirement was a public library. Governors and guardians of the library are the Archbishop of Armagh (Chairman), the Dean and Chapter of the Cathedral and two lay members.

Acquisitions policy: Strengthening of the collection of Church of Ireland material, local history, material on St Patrick and Jonathan Swift and some theology.

Archives of organisation: Minute books, 1796– .
Registers of borrowers and books borrowed, 1796–1828, 1828–1916.
Property rental books, 1840–90.

Major collections: Papers of Anthony Dopping, Bishop of Meath (1682–97), and William Reeves, Bishop of Down (1882–96).
Correspondence of Lord John George Beresford, Archbishop of Armagh (1822–62).
Episcopal visitation records, 17th and 18th century.

Non-manuscript material: Large collection of 18th-century pamphlets.
Rokeby Collection of prints, including a 'Piranesi' set, 17th and 18th century.

Finding aids: Handwritten author catalogue, card catalogue; computerised cataloguing in progress.

Facilities: Photocopying.

Conservation: Contracted out.

Publications: Catalogue of Manuscripts in the Public Library of Armagh (1928).

32 Cardinal Tomás Ó Fiaich Memorial Library and Archive

Parent organisation: Armagh Diocesan Historical Society

Address: 15 Moy Road, Armagh BT61 7LY

Telephone: (028) 37522981

Fax: (028) 37511944

E-mail: ofiaichlibrary@btinternet.com

Enquiries: The Librarian, Mr Crônan O'Dôibhlan

Open: Mon–Fri: 2.00–5.00 (until further notice).

Access: Generally open to the public.

Historical background: Following the death of Cardinal Ó Fiaich, his library and papers were left in the care of the Armagh Diocesan Historical Society which has also taken over the RC Diocesan Archives. The society decided that a building should be erected in which these materials, as well as the archives of the archdiocese of Armagh, would be accommodated and made available for researchers. The archives are housed in a new building funded by the Heritage Lottery Fund and opened in 1999.

Acquisitions policy: To acquire material relating to the history of the archdiocese of Armagh and its parishes; topics in which Cardinal Ó Fiaich was particularly interested, e.g. Irish church history, the Irish language and Irish games and Irish European links.

Major collections: Correspondence and other papers of the archbishops of Armagh, 1787–1963.
Papers of Cardinal Tomás Ó Fiaich (1923–90).
Papers of Micheline Kerney Walsh, former director of Overseas Archive, University College Dublin.

Non-manuscript material: Albums of photographs relating to careers of various archbishops.
O'Kane collection of audio-tapes containing interviews with northern participants in the Irish war of independence.
News-cuttings relating to careers of archbishops.

Finding aids: Calendars for the papers and correspondence of the archbishops. Card index to Ó Fiaich papers.

Facilities: Photocopying.

33 Irish Studies Library

Parent organisation: Southern Education and Library Board

Address: Library Headquarters, 1 Markethill Road, Armagh BT60 1NR

Telephone: (028) 37520705

Fax: (028) 37526879

E-mail: irishandlocal@hotmail.com

Enquiries: The Irish Studies Librarian, Mr Joe Canning

Open: Mon, Weds and Fri 9.30–5.00; Tues, Thurs: 9.30–7.15.

Access: Generally open to the public.

Historical background: The board was established in 1973 following the reorganisation of local government in Northern Ireland. The major part of the library's archives was inherited from Newry Public Library.

Acquisitions policy: To acquire material relating to the board's area and material by local writers.

Archives of organisation: Annual reports and minutes of Library Committee, 1973– .

Major collections: Usual local history collection, including Crosslé, papers relating to history of Newry and district and of local families.

Finding aids: Lists.

Facilities: Photocopying. Microfilm/fiche reader/printers.

Conservation: Contracted out.

34 Arundel Castle
Duke of Norfolk's Library and Archives

Parent organisation: Arundel Castle Trustees Ltd

Address: Arundel, West Sussex BN18 9AB

Telephone: (01903) 882173

Fax: (01903) 884581

Website: www.arundelcastle.org

Enquiries: The Librarian to the Duke of Norfolk, Dr J.M. Robinson

Open: Tues–Wed: 10.00–1.00, 2.00–5.00.

Access: To all accredited scholars. A daily research fee is charged. Personal papers less than 100 years old are not normally available.

Historical background: The Duke of Norfolk's archives form one of the largest and most complete family collections in England and have a unique importance for the study of English Catholic history. Assistance is received from West Sussex Record Office (entry 241).

Acquisitions policy: Archives of the Howards and related families; modern records of Arundel Castle Trustees and of estates owned by the Duke.

Archives of organisation: Records and papers of the Fitzalan-Howard family and their family estates in various counties, 13th century– .
Northern estate papers deposited at Sheffield Archives (entry 1107), Carlton Towers and Herries (Everingham) papers deposited at the University of Hull (entry 458).

Major collections: Collection of illuminated MSS held in the library.

Non-manuscript material: Recusant collection: a large series of 17th-century printed pamphlets.

Finding aids: Ongoing new cataloguing of title deeds and estate records; lists are available at Arundel Castle and will be sent to NRA.

Facilities: Limited photocopying.

Conservation: Contracted out.

Publications: F.W. Steer (ed.): *Catalogue of the Earl Marshal's Papers at Arundel Castle* (1963–4).
——: *Arundel Castle Archives* (Chichester, 1968–80) [4 vols].

35 Leonard Cheshire Archive

Parent organisation: Leonard Cheshire and Ryder Cheshire

Address: Staunton Harold Hall, Melbourne Road, Ashby de la Zouch, Leicestershire LE65 1RT

Telephone: (01332) 863660

Fax: (01332) 863660

E-mail: j.roberts@national.leonard-cheshire.org.uk

Website: www.leonard-cheshire.org

Enquiries: The Archivist, Jill Roberts

Open: Mon–Fri: 9.30–5.00, by appointment.

Access: Bona fide researchers.

Historical background: Leonard Cheshire (formerly the Leonard Cheshire Foundation) is a voluntary organisation founded in 1948 by Group Captain Lord Cheshire (1917–1992). At the time best known as a World War II RAF hero, Cheshire opened his own home to care for a colleague who was dying of cancer. From this beginning, the charity has developed to offer more than 250 services to disabled people in 55 countries worldwide.

Ryder Cheshire is a smaller charity which develops disability and health projects, currently in the UK and the Far East. It was co-founded in 1959 by Leonard Cheshire and his wife Sue Ryder (1923–2000), and was formerly known first as the Ryder–Cheshire Mission for the Relief of Suffering and then as the Ryder–Cheshire Foundation.

Their joint archive was established in the late 1980s and has employed a full-time archivist since 1993.

Acquisitions policy: To maintain the central archives. Records generated by individual LC services or projects are not actively acquired, although some of this material has been kept on an ad hoc basis.

Archives of organisation: Archives of Leonard Cheshire UK (subdivided into central office and regional office structural levels), Leonard Cheshire International, and Ryder Cheshire.

Leonard Cheshire's own working records, with a very small amount of more personal records, eg family photographs.

Major collections: Collections of personal papers of trustees and others connected with the organisation.

Research papers generated by Andrew Boyle and Richard Morris, biographers of Leonard Cheshire.

Non-manuscript material: Photos, VHS videos, audio tapes and slides. 16mm films deposited with the National Film and Television Archive (see entry 556 B).

Finding aids: Guides to most collections. Subject index.

Publications: Archive leaflet.

36 Veteran Car Club of Great Britain

Address: Jessamine Court, 15 High Street, Ashwell, Hertfordshire SG7 5NL

Telephone: (01462) 742818

Fax: (01462) 742997

E-mail: hq@vccofgb.co.uk

Website: www.vccofgb.co.uk

Enquiries: The Secretary

Open: Mon–Fri: 10.00–4.30, by appointment only

Access: The library is for the benefit of club members. Non-members may apply to the Secretary in writing, stating the basis for their research and their background.

Historical background: The club was founded in 1930 to encourage and foster the preservation of pre-1919 vehicles. In order to enter events, vehicles have to be dated by the Dating Committee of the Club. There is a substantial library of period motoring literature supporting this research.

Acquisitions policy: Period motoring literature bearing upon pre-1919 vehicles is continually being added to the library collection.

Archives of organisation: Minutes of committee meetings relative to administration, event organisation and the dating of pre-1919 vehicles.

Major collections: F.R. Simms (1863–1944), automotive inventor, entrepreneur and organiser: minutes and correspondence of the Daimler Motor Syndicate Ltd, 1893–5; correspondence and papers deriving from Simms's role as consulting engineer to H.J. Lawson's enterprise; correspondence with Robert Bosch *re* magneto ignition.

John Pollitt, motor engineer and historian: research correspondence, mainly 1940s–1950s, about the history of the motor industry and trade; Pollitt's summarising of his findings; also some 150 letters to the Yorkshire Motor Car Mfg. Co., 1899.

Miscellaneous collections, including cuttings-books of S.F. Edge (1868–1940), racing cyclist and motor entrepreneur; and of Charles Jarrott and J.W. Stocks, racing driver.

Non-manuscript material: Small non-catalogued photographic archive. *Veteran Car,* the club magazine, period sales literature and vehicle handbooks in the library.

Finding aids: Pollitt and Simms papers and club records listed by NRA, 1960s.

Facilities: Photocopies can be taken of a small number of pages; larger quantities by negotiation.

Publications: E. Nagle: *Veterans of the Road* (1955).
Bulletin of the National Register of Archives, no. 13 (1964), pp.16–20; no.14 (1967), pp.14–17.
Royal Commission on Historical Manuscripts: *Report of the Secretary to the Commissioners, 1968–9* (1969), p.60.

37 Buckinghamshire Records and Local Studies Service

Parent organisation: Buckinghamshire County Council

Address: County Hall, Walton Street, Aylesbury, Buckinghamshire HP20 1UU

Telephone: Record Office: (01296) 382587 (enquiries) 382771 (bookings) Local Studies Library: (01296) 382250

Fax: (01296) 382274

E-mail: record office: archives@buckscc.gov.uk local studies: localstudies@buckscc.gov.uk

Website: www.buckscc.gov.uk/archives

Enquiries: The County Archivist, Mr Roger Bettridge. All postal enquiries should be accompanied by an SAE or international reply coupon from overseas.

Open: Record Office: Mon–Thurs: 9.00–5.15; Fri: 9.00–4.45; late opening 1st Thurs in month 5.15–7.45, by appointment only.
Local Studies Library: Mon, Wed, Fri: 9.00–5.30; Tues, Thurs: 9.00–8.00; Sat: 9.00–4.00.

Access: Generally open to the public. The office operates the CARN reader's ticket system. Prior notice of a visit is advisable to reserve a seat. Booking is required for microfilm/fiche readers (now in the Local Studies Library). A paid research service is available (prepayment required).

Historical background: The record office was established in 1938 with the appointment of the first county archivist by Buckinghamshire County Council and moved into its present purpose-built premises in the New County Offices in 1966. In 1997 it was merged with the Local Studies Library to form the Buckinghamshire Records and Local Studies Service. However, the Record Office and Local Studies Library continue at present to operate as two separate service points. Since the establishment of Milton Keynes Council as a unitary authority in 1997, the office continues to provide the archive service for that area under a joint agreement. The Record Office acts as the Diocesan Record Office for Oxford (Archdeaconry of Buckingham). Buckinghamshire Archaeological Society (f.1847) has transferred its collections of deeds, maps, manorial and estate records and monumental inscriptions, while retaining its own archives, papers of local historians, transcripts of documents and printed items. Contact: Hon. Archivist, County Museum, Church Street, Aylesbury, Buckinghamshire, HP20 2QP.

Acquisitions policy: Records of Buckinghamshire County Council and of other public bodies, organisations, families and individuals directly or indirectly relevant to the historic county of Buckinghamshire.

Archives of organisation: Usual local authority record holdings, including records of the county Quarter Sessions, 1678–1971.

Major collections: Deposited local collections, of which the following contain papers of wider significance:
Hobart-Hampden MSS, including papers of Robert, 4th Baron Trevor and 1st Viscount Hampden, as diplomat at The Hague, 1736–46; Robert, Lord Hobart, as governor of Madras, 1794–8, and secretary of state for war and the colonies, 1801–4; Lord Vere Henry Hobart, as director-general of the Ottoman Bank, 1861–72, and governor and president of Madras, 1872–5; F.J. Robinson, Viscount Goderich and 1st Earl of Ripon, 1796–1835.
Fremantle MSS, including private and naval papers of Admiral Sir T.F. Fremantle (1765–1819), and Capt S.G. Fremantle (1810–60); papers of Sir W.H. Fremantle relating to Ireland and as deputy ranger of Windsor Great Park, 1830–50, and Sir T.F. Fremantle (1798–1890), 1st Baron Cottesloe, as a Conservative minister, 1834, 1841–6, and deputy chairman/chairman of the Board of Customs, 1846–73.
Bulstrode MSS, including correspondence of Lord Webb Seymour (1777–1819); the 11th and 12th Dukes of Somerset, including official correspondence of the latter as First Lord of the

Admiralty, 1859–66; papers of Sir John Ramsden (1831–1914), 5th Bart; miscellaneous papers, diary and note-books of Edward Horsman (1807–76), MP.
Spencer Bernard MSS, including official correspondence of Scrope Bernard (1758–1830) *re* Ireland and the Home Department; banking papers of Morlands Bank (and predecessors), c1780–1832.
Howard–Vyse MSS, including official papers of FM Sir George Howard (1720–96) and Gen. Richard Vyse (1746–1825).
Hartwell MSS, including miscellaneous legal papers of Sir William Lee (1688–1754), as chief justice of King's Bench, and of Sir George Lee (1700–53), as Dean of Arches; correspondence of Dr John Lee (1783–1866).
Clayton MSS, including papers of Sir Robert Clayton (1629–1707), scrivener of London; official papers of George, Baron Jeffreys of Wem, as Lord Chancellor, 1685–8.
Carrington MSS, including letters of the 2nd Baron Carrington (1796–1868) to his family.
Grenville MSS, including correspondence of William Wyndham, Baron Grenville, (1759–1834), and Thomas Grenville (1755–1846).
Correspondence of Lydia Catherine, Dowager Duchess of Chandos, c1728–50.
Papers of William Henry Grenfell, Baron Desborough (1855–1945) including papers *re* British Olympics Association.
Literary papers of Thomas Wright (1859–1936), author and popular biographer, and Theodora Roscoe (*d*1962), author and poet.
Letters from George Church, convict transported to Tasmania, 1845–54.
Business records of E. Gomme Ltd, furniture manufacturers (G-Plan), and related firms, 1881–1980, including pattern books and catalogues; Hazell, Watson and Viney Ltd, printers, 1866–1993; and Wycombe Marsh Paper Mills, 1920–c1990.

Finding aids: Catalogues sent to NRA; draft guide with subject index; personal and place-name indexes; consolidated personal and place-name and subject indexes to annual lists of accessions, 1976–95.

Facilities: Photocopying. Photography and microfilming by arrangement. Microfilm/fiche readers/printers.

Conservation: In-house conservation unit.

Publications: Annual Reports and Lists of accessions (1976–) [detailed].

Consolidated Indexes to Lists of Accessions, 1976–85, 1986–95.
House History: a Short Guide to Sources (1987).
Wartime Buckinghamshire 1939–45 (rev. 1995).
The Buckinghamshire Sheriffs, 992–1992 (1992).
Archive Teaching Units: *Parliamentary Enclosure; Elections in Buckinghamshire, 1740–1832; Buckinghamshire in the French Revolutionary and Napoleonic Wars, 1792–1815.*

38 Aylsham Town Council Archives

Address: Town Hall, Market Place, Aylsham, Norfolk NR11 6EL

Telephone: (01263) 733354

Fax: (01263) 733354

Enquiries: The Town Clerk, Mrs Maureen Reynolds
The Hon. Archivist, Ron Peabody (01263) 733230

Open: By appointment.

Access: Bona fide researchers.

Historical background: The collection was started by the second parish clerk, who was in office from 1897 to 1937, and has been continually augmented since then.

Acquisitions policy: Material relating to the history of Aylsham, mainly by donation or deposit, but a small purchase fund is available.

Archives of organisation: Minutes of the Parish Council; Poor Law records; material relating to the Aylsham Navigation Company and the Turnpike Trustees.

Major collections: Town Crier's books, 1899–1923.
Papers relating to royal celebrations, 1897 and 1902, 'Aylsham Derby' papers.

Non-manuscript material: Posters, photographs, slide collection, oral history collection, artefacts.

39 Ayrshire Archives

Parent organisation: South Ayrshire Council

Address: Ayrshire Archives Centre, Craigie Estate, Ayr KA8 0SS

Telephone: (01292) 287584

Fax: (01292) 284918

E-mail: archives@south-ayrshire.gov.uk

Website: www.south-ayrshire.gov.uk/archives/default.htm

Enquiries: The Archivist, Mr Kevin Wilbraham

Open: Tues–Thurs: 10.00–4.00.

Access: Generally open to the public, by appointment.

Historical background: Ayrshire Archives is a joint service sponsored by the three local authorities in Ayrshire — East, North and South Ayrshire Councils. The service was established in 1996 as a result of local government reorganisation and is responsible for all archival and records management issues relating to the three authorities. While the service is peripatetic, the main office is located at the Ayrshire Archives Centre in Ayr, which also serves as the principal repository for the archival and non-current records of South Ayrshire.

Acquisitions policy: To preserve and collect the evidential and historically significant records of the three Ayrshire authorities and their predecessor bodies and any other historically significant records relating to Ayrshire.

Archives of organisation: Records of South Ayrshire Council and predecessor bodies, including the Commissioners of Supply, 1713–1929; highway authorities, 1767–1883; school boards and trusts, 1767–1919; poor relief authorities, 1845–1930; Ayr County Council, 1890–1975; Kyle and Carrick District Council, 1975–96; various burgh and parish records.

Major collections: Local estate and family papers, including Kennedy of Kirchmichael, 1453–1832; Wellbeck Estates Ltd, 1798–1900; Hamiltons of Rozelle and Carcluie, 1734–1926; Woodburn Family of Monckton, 1795–1903; and the Holms Estate, 1860–1931.
Local solicitors' records, including David Shaw & Co., Ayr, 1892–1918, and Jamieson and Beattie, Galston, 1841–1931.
Ayrshire and Arran Health Board, including the records of Ailsa Hospital, 1869–1971, and Ravenspark Hospital, 1858–1966.
Kirk session records for the Church of Scotland and dissenting Presbyterian congregations within the Presbytery of Ayr, 1615–1983.

Non-manuscript material: Portland Estate plans, c1760–1928.

Finding aids: Computerised index and lists. Catalogue lists are sent to the NRAS.

Facilities: Photocopying. Microfiche readers.

Conservation: In-house conservation unit at Glasgow City Archives (see entry 387).

Publications: Various information leaflets and *A Guide to the Ayrshire Archives Centre.*

40 Ayrshire Sound Archive

Address: University of Paisley, Craigie Campus in Ayr, Beech Grove, Ayr KA8 0SR

Telephone: (01292) 886265

Fax: (01292) 886006

E-mail: archives@south-ayrshire.gov.uk

Enquiries: The Ayr Campus Librarian, Ms A. Goodwin
The Ayrshire Sound Archive Vice-Chairman, Mr Kevin Wilbraham, Ayrshire Archives (see entry 39)

Open: Ayr Campus Library: Term: Mon–Fri: 9.00–9.00; Sat: 9.00–5.00.
Vacation: Mon–Fri: 9.00–5.00

Access: Anyone may consult the recordings on request at Ayr Campus Library. Recordings may be borrowed only by those who join the library; there is a modest annual charge for library membership.

Historical background: The Ayrshire Sound Archive was formerly part of the Ayrshire Federation of Historical Societies. It was reconstructed in 1998 as a separate organisation dedicated to the preservation and promotion of Ayrshire's oral heritage.

Acquisitions policy: To record information relevant to Ayrshire and its inhabitants.

Non-manuscript material: A wide range of recordings covering topics including: coal mining; textiles; rural life; schooling; social and economic conditions; and World War I.

Finding aids: Catalogue.

Facilities: Listening facilities are available at Ayr Campus Library. It is also intended that listening facilities are made available at the Ayrshire Archives Centre and various local libraries.

41 Burns' Cottage and Museum

Parent organisation: Trustees of Burns' Monument

Address: Alloway, Ayr KA7 4PY

Telephone: (01292) 441215

Fax: (01292) 441750

Website: www.robertburns.org

Enquiries: The Curator, Mr John Manson

Open: By appointment.

Access: Generally open to the public by application in writing to the curator.

Historical background: The Trustees of Burns' Monument were formed in 1814 to build a monument in memory of Robert Burns (1759–96). This monument was built in 1823, and in 1881 the trustees acquired Burns' Cottage, the poet's birthplace. The trustees remain responsible for the upkeep of the two properties. Since 1881 the trustees have acquired a unique collection of Burns' MSS, an extensive library and authentic items which belonged to the poet.

Acquisitions policy: To add to existing collections.

Archives of organisation: Records of the Burns' monument and cottage, 1814– .

Major collections: Extensive collection of Robert Burns' MSS and correspondence, including the Graham of Fintry Collection and the Cunningham Collection.

Non-manuscript material: Memorabilia, pictures, statues, photographs, books.

Finding aids: Catalogue.

Facilities: Photography by arrangement.

Conservation: Contracted out.

42 Carnegie Library

Parent organisation: South Ayrshire Council

Address: 12 Main Street, Ayr KA8 8ED

Telephone: (01292) 282109

Fax: (01292) 611593

E-mail: carnegie.lib@south-ayrshire.go.uk

Website: www.south-ayrshire.gov.uk

Enquiries: The Principal Officer, Libraries and Galleries

Open: Mon, Tues, Thurs, Fri: 9.00–7.30; Wed, Sat: 9.00–5.00.

Access: Generally open to the public.

Historical background: The collection originally covered the whole of Ayrshire, but since local government reorganisation in 1974 has been restricted to Kyle and Carrick.

Acquisitions policy: To obtain, when possible, further material on Kyle and Carrick and Robert Burns.

Major collections: Kyle and Carrick Collection: minute books of various local societies, committees, etc.
Robert Burns (1759–96) Collection: the only original MS is the Visitors' Book for Burns' Cottage.
Other MS items are still being processed.

Non-manuscript material: Robert Burns Collection: c1200 books by and about Burns.
Kyle and Carrick Collection: photographs, slides, cassette recordings; newspapers, 1803– , some on microfilm/fiche.

Finding aids: Catalogue to Robert Burns Collection. Newspaper index being completed. Local collection being catalogued. NRA 18760.

Facilities: Photocopying. Microfilm reader/printer.

43 Badminton Muniments

Address: Badminton House, Badminton, Gloucestershire GL9 1DB

Telephone: (01454) 218202/3

Fax: (01454) 218221

Enquiries: The Archivist, Mrs M. Richards: family and household records and general enquiries
The County Archivist, Gloucestershire Record Office (GRO) (see entry 406): estate records (Glos and Wilts)
National Library of Wales (NLW) (see entry 9): Welsh estate records

Open: By appointment. It is possible to make temporary deposits of material for removal at GRO to overcome the difficulties of limited access.

Access: Badminton: His Grace's permission is needed for access, and requests should be addressed to the Duke. An appointment is necessary.

GRO and NLW generally open to the public.

Historical background: Badminton has been the family seat since it was inherited in 1655 by the future 1st Duke of Beaufort. The present muniment room was built to a design prepared by James Gibbs for the 3rd Duke. The interior of the 'evidence room' was completed in 1758 to working drawings made by Stephen Wright, who advised the 4th Duchess that the shelving should be lined with wood to preserve the papers from damp. Successive duchesses played an important part in preserving the papers now in the Badminton muniment room. An archivist was first appointed in 1940.

Acquisitions policy: To maintain the collections.

Archives of organisation: Somerset family wills and settlements with related papers, 16th–20th centuries; Berkeley of Stoke Gifford family wills and settlements, 16th–18th centuries; Coventry family wills and settlements 1699–1737; Ormonde family settlements, 1715–16.
Somerset family papers and correspondence, 17th–20th centuries, including Capel and Seymour families, 17th century.
Berkeley of Stoke Gifford family papers and correspondence, 15th–18th centuries, including Sir Richard Berkeley's 'Discourse of the Felicity of Man'.
Coventry family papers and correspondence, 17th–18th centuries, including 'Meditations and Reflections Moral and Divine', dedicated to Anne, Countess of Coventry.
Ormonde family papers, 1712–16.
Culling Smith family papers, 1758–1851.
Wellesley family correspondence, 1800–52.
Political and official papers of the Dukes of Beaufort, 17th–20th centuries.
Berkeley of Stoke Gifford political and official papers, 16th–18th centuries, including the Virginia governorship of Lord Botetourt, 1768–70.
Household inventories, accounts and papers: Badminton (including horticultural papers), 17th–20th centuries; Raglan Castle, early 17th century; Worcester House, London, 1622–82; Troy House, 17th–20th centuries; Stoke Park (Berkeley), 18th–20th centuries; Croome Court and Snitterfield (Coventry), 1698–1745; Ormonde establishment, London and Richmond, 1712–15.

Non-manuscript material: Architectural plans relating to Badminton House, 17th–19th centuries; Stoke Park, 18th–20th centuries; Netheravon House, 18th century.

Maps (mainly at GRO), 17th–20th centuries.

Finding aids: HMC Report XII, appendix IX, 'The manuscripts of His Grace the Duke of Beaufort' (1891). Provisional catalogue of architectural plans. Glos. and Wilts. estate, family and household records fully catalogued and indexed. Copies of the catalogue (comp. 1989) can be consulted at the NRA, Bodleian Library, NLW or GRO, as well as at Badminton.
NLW: Catalogues of Welsh manorial records (6 vols), Badminton deeds and documents (2 vols), 1941, 6; 'Preliminary Schedule' of more recent deposits, 1965 (NRA).

Facilities: Photocopying. Photography, if own equipment is provided or by arrangement with a commercial photographer.

Conservation: Contracted out.

Publications: A. Gomme: 'Badminton Revisited', *Architectural History*, 27 (1984) [architectural plans and drawings].
R. Duthie: 'The Planting Plans of Some Seventeenth-Century Flower Gardens', *Garden History*, 18/2 (1990).

44 Devonshire Collection

Parent organisation: The Trustees of the Chatsworth Settlement

Address: Chatsworth, Bakewell, Derbyshire DE45 1PP

Telephone: (01246) 582204

Fax: (01246) 565375

Website: www.chatsworth-house.co.uk

Enquiries: The Librarian and Keeper of Collections, Mr P.J. Day

Open: April–Dec: Mon–Fri: 9.00–5.00, by written appointment.

Access: Accredited postgraduate students or scholars only; reading fees and search fees payable.

Historical background: There are now concentrated at Chatsworth the collections of art, books, estate archives and political and personal correspondence of the Cavendish family, Earls of Devonshire from 1618 to 1694, and Dukes of Devonshire from 1694 onwards. The family fortune and estates were founded in the mid–16th century by Sir William Cavendish and his wife Bess of Hardwick, who built the first

Chatsworth. The house was rebuilt by the 1st Duke of Devonshire (1640–1707), a strong supporter of William of Orange, and the collections of art were founded by his son the 2nd Duke, a celebrated connoisseur. The 3rd and 4th Dukes served as Lords Lieutenant of Ireland, and the 4th Duke was briefly Prime Minister of England. The 6th Duke greatly extended the house and collections at Chatsworth, and the 8th Duke, as the Marquis of Hartington, was a prominent Liberal politician.

Acquisitions policy: To acquire works of art, books or archives that help to document the history of the family, their houses and collections.

Archives of organisation: MSS of the philosopher Thomas Hobbes (1588–1679), tutor to the Earls of Devonshire.
MSS of the scientist Henry Cavendish (1731–1810).
Political correspondence of the 3rd (1698–1755), 4th (1720–64) and 8th (1833–1908) Dukes of Devonshire.
Correspondence of Sir Joseph Paxton (1803–65), gardener to the 6th Duke of Devonshire.
Building and household accounts for Chatsworth, Hardwick, Chiswick and Devonshire houses.
Estate archives for present and former family estates in England and Ireland.

Non-manuscript material: Old Master drawings (c2000) and prints (c14,000), 15th–17th centuries.
Designs for court masques by Inigo Jones (c400).
Rare printed books, 15th–19th centuries (c50,000).
Paintings (c1,000).

Finding aids: Calendars of MSS and correspondence copied by NRA. Paintings, sculpture and drawings listed by Photographic Survey of the Courtauld Institute of Art.

Facilities: Photocopying. Photography.

Conservation: Contracted out.

Publications: International Exhibition Foundation: *Treasures from Chatsworth: the Devonshire Inheritance* (Washington, DC, 1978–9).
Royal Commission on Historical Manuscripts: *Principal Family and Estate Collections: Family Names A–K* (Guide to Sources for British History 10, 1996): Cavendish entry.

45 South Eastern Education and Library Board

Irish and Local Studies Section

Address: Library Headquarters, Windmill Hill, Ballynahinch, Co. Down BT24 8DH

Telephone: (028) 97566400

Fax: (028) 97565072

E-mail: ref@bhinchlibhq.demon.co.uk

Enquiries: The Irish and Local Studies Librarian, Deirdre Armstrong

Open: Mon–Fri: 9.00–5.15. Closed 12 and 13 July.

Access: Generally open to the public; an appointment is preferred.

Historical background: Originally the Down County Library Service, the SEELB came into being after local government reorganisation in 1973. The present service covers most of Co. Down, parts of south-western Antrim and the southern and eastern suburbs of Belfast.

Acquisitions policy: All material relevant to Ulster studies collected, particularly material on the SEELB area, including ephemera.

Archives of organisation: Minutes of the Down County Library Service and the SEELB, 1973– .

Major collections: Usual local history collection, with special emphasis on Co. Down and South Antrim.

Finding aids: Various indexes, lists, catalogues.

Facilities: Photocopying, Microfilm/fiche reader/printers.

Conservation: Contracted out.

Publications: Local history source lists for: The Ards, Castlereagh and Donaghadee (1980); The Mournes (1982); Comber (1984).

Newspaper index series: *Co. Down Spectator,* 1904–64; *Downpatrick Recorder,* 1836–86; *Mourne Observer,* 1949–80; *Newtownards Chronicle,* 1873–1939; *Northern Herald,* 1833–6; *Northern Star,* 1792–7; Newtonards Chronicles 1901–39.

The Spirit of the North is High [source list for 1798 rebellion in Co. Down].

46 North Down Heritage Centre

Parent organisation: North Down Borough Council

Address: Town Hall, Bangor, Co. Down BT20 4BT

Telephone: (028) 91270371

Fax: (028) 91271370

E-mail: enquiries@northdown.gov.uk

Website: www.northdown.gov.uk

Enquiries: The Manager, Mr I.A. Wilson

Open: Mon–Fri: 10.30–4.30.

Access: Bona fide researchers, by appointment only.

Historical background: The council was formed in 1973 and inherited the records of Bangor Borough Council from 1927.

Acquisitions policy: Records relevant to the northern part of Co. Down, excluding material *re* textiles, folk life and agriculture.

Archives of organisation: Council records *re* public health, gas and the harbour, early 20th century.
Burial records of municipally-owned cemeteries, 1895– .

Non-manuscript material: Extensive photographic archive.
Folio of maps by Thomas Raven, 17th century.
Cine film archive of the area, 1950s–1960s.

Facilities: Photocopying. Photography.

Conservation: Contracted out.

47 University of Wales, Bangor

Department of Manuscripts

Address: The Library, University of Wales, Bangor, Gwynedd LL57 2DG

Telephone: (01248) 382966

Fax: (01248) 370576

E-mail: iss075@bangor.ac.uk
iss177@bangor.ac.uk

Website: www.bangor.ac.uk

Enquiries: The Archivist and Keeper of Manuscripts, Mr Tomos Roberts

Open: Term: Mon, Tues, Thurs, Fri: 9.00–5.00; Wed: 9.00–9.00.
Vacation: Mon–Fri: 9.00–5.00.

Access: Generally open to the public; prior arrangement preferred.

Historical background: The library of the University of Wales, Bangor, previously University College of North Wales, has been an approved repository since 1927. It was therefore the first record office in North Wales (the Caernarvonshire Record Office opened in 1947, and the Flintshire Record Office in 1952). It is recognised as a place of deposit for public records.

Acquisitions policy: Deposits and donations are not solicited, but are gratefully accepted. Papers relating to all aspects of life in North Wales, past and present, are particularly welcome.

Archives of organisation: Records of UCNW, Bangor, 1883– , including student registers, 1884–1944.

Major collections: Holdings run to some 500,000 items, and include family and estate papers; mine and quarry papers; quarter sessions records (Borough of Beaumaris, acquired by purchase during World War II); literary MSS in Welsh and English; personal papers; deposits by solicitors etc.

Bangor (General) MSS; Baron Hill MSS; Beaumaris and Anglesey MSS; Bodorgan MSS; Bodrhyddan MSS; Carter Vincent MSS; Kinmel MSS; Lligwy MSS; Maesyneuadd MSS; Maenan MSS; Mostyn MSS; Nannau MSS; Penrhyn Castle MSS; Plas Coch MSS; Plas Newydd MSS; Porth yr Aur MSS.

Non-manuscript material: Printed ephemera, all topics.

OS maps, 2½ and 6 inch: Wales and borders.

Finding aids: Catalogues and indexes (Bangor MSS catalogue is continually in progress). Provisional Guide to Special Collections, 1962 (TS).

Facilities: Photocopying. Photography. Microfilm/fiche reader.

Conservation: In-house department.

48 Middlesex University

Address: Cat Hill Campus, Barnet, Hertfordshire EN4 8HT

A Hall–Carpenter Archives

Enquiries: The Hon. Secretary, Oliver Merrington

Historical background: The Hall–Carpenter Archives were founded in 1982 as the national UK Lesbian and Gay Archives from the Campaign for Homosexual Equality's media monitoring service. From 1984 to 1986 it received funding from the Greater London Council and was housed in the London Lesbian and Gay Centre (now closed). Some of its collections were dispersed as follows: the British Library of Political and Economic Science (entry 560) received the organisational archives, including Albany Trust; Campaign for Homosexual Equality; Gay Liberation Front; Gay News Ltd; Lesbian and Gay Christian Movement and Scottish Homosexual Rights Group; papers of gay rights campaigners e.g. Peter Tatchell; and periodicals (c250 titles); and the National Sound Archive (entry 561 D) received a major oral history project investigating the lives of lesbians and gay men in the London area over the last 60 years, with transcripts. Remaining collections were moved to Middlesex University.

Acquisitions policy: Material in any format that relates to the history, social and personal experiences of lesbians and gay men. Priority is given to material from the UK and Eire and relating to women and people from ethnic minorities.

Non-manuscript material: Press cuttings, 1950s–1990s.
Gay ephemera, including banners, badges, leaflets and posters.

Finding aids: List of press cuttings in preparation. Computer catalogue of BLPES and handlist at NSA.

Facilities: Photocopying. Photography.

Publications: Inventing Ourselves: Lesbian Life Stories (Routledge, 1989).
Walking After Midnight: Gay Men's Life Stories (Routledge, 1989).

B Library of Historic Advertising

Telephone: (020) 8362 6687

E-mail: j.vaknin@mdx.ac.uk

Enquiries: The Assistant Librarian, Judy Vaknin

Open: Term: Mon–Fri: 1.00–3.00.

Access: Open to researchers, by arrangement.

The library consists of a large collection of advertisements from a wide range of magazines, focussing primarily on major British and American companies (c50,000). The adverts were previously the stock of a commercial picture business called Half-Brick Images, run by Colin McArthur. The images are currently organised by company, in broad categories such as cosmetics, travel, food, late 19th century–1970s. There are some basic lists. Photocopying is available.

C Museum of Domestic Design & Architecture

Telephone: (020) 8411 5244

Fax: (020) 8411 6639

E-mail: moda@mdx.ac.uk

Website: www.moda.mdx.ac.uk

Enquiries: The Curator, Lesley Hoskins

Open: Tues–Sat: 10.00–5.00.

Access: Generally open to scholars and the public, by appointment.

Historical background: The Silver Studio Collection was acquired in 1967 by Hornsey College of Art, which was incorporated into Middlesex Polytechnic in 1974. The polytechnic became a university in 1992. It moved to purpose-built premises on the Cat Hill campus in 2000.

Acquisitions policy: The main effort is concentrated on the conservation, cataloguing and exhibiting of the existing collection, but examples of Silver Studio designs are added as discovered and the library's holdings are being enlarged.

Major collections: Silver Studio Collection: records of Arthur Silver (1852–96) and Rex Silver (1879–1965), wallpaper and textile designers of London, including business and personal correspondence from manufacturers and others, e.g. Walter Crane (1845–1915) (c2000 letters), day books, diaries (30 vols), 1880–1960.

Peggy Angus Archive: papers, and tile and wallpaper designs.
British and American Domestic Design Archive.
Crown Wallpaper Archive.

Non-manuscript material: Silver Studio Collection; Photographic record albums (60); designs for textiles and wallpapers (c40,000); textile samples (c5000); wallpaper samples (c3000); postcards (c500). Newspapers cuttings, scrapbookss, ephemera.
Library of Sir J.M. Richards (1907–92), architectural writer and critic.
Peggy Angus Library.
Charles Haslar Collection of typography and printed ephemera, 1800–1960s.

Finding aids: Letters preliminarily sorted but not fully catalogued. Typed catalogue.

Facilities: Photocopying.

Conservation: In-house facilities for paper conservation.

Publications: Catalogue of Museum of London Exhibition of Silver Studio Work (1980).
Silver Studio Collection Textile Design, 1850–1960 (1983).
Art Nouveau Designs from the Silver Studio Collection, 1885–1910 (1986).
A Popular Art: British Wallpapers, 1920–1960 (1989).

49 Barnoldswick Library

Parent organisation: Lancashire County Council

Address: Fern Lea Avenue, Barnoldswick, Lancashire BB18 5DW

Telephone: (01282) 812147

Fax: (01282) 850971

Enquiries: The Local Studies Assistant, Ms Karen Hill

Open: Mon: 10.00–7.00; Wed–Fri: 10.00–5.00; Sat: 10.00–4.00.

Access: Generally open to the public; an appointment is not always necessary.

Historical background: Barnoldswick New Library was opened in 1989, and the Craven and Yorkshire collections of local history material previously housed at Colne Library (entry 254) were added to Barnoldswick Library stock. The Barnoldswick Local History Society Collection was added in 1991.

Acquisitions policy: Local history material relating to Barnoldswick, Earby, Salterforth and Kelbrook areas and West Yorkshire in general.

Major collections: Barnoldswick UDC minutes, 1938–71, and abstract of accounts, 1919–70; Earby UDC minutes, 1915–42, and yearbooks, 1955–74.
Earby Co-operative Society Book, 1911–32.
Salterforth Water Company correspondence.
Barnoldswick Local History Society Collection.

Non-manuscript material: OS maps and photographic collections for West Craven area (Barnoldswick, Salterforth, Kelbrook, Earby, Thornton, Bracewell and Brogden).
Plans for Barnoldswick and West Craven area.
Craven Herald, 1929–66.

Finding aids: Catalogue of Barnoldswick Local History Collection. Index to newspapers, maps, and censuses.

Facilities: Photocopying. Microfilm/fiche reader.

Publications: K.A. Green: *Barnoldswick & District Maps.*
S. Byrne: *Barnoldswick Jottings.*
E. Gregson: *Barnoldswick New Library Brief History.*

50 Barnsley Archive Service

Address: Central Library, Shambles Street, Barnsley, South Yorkshire S70 2JF

Telephone: (01226) 773950/773938

Fax: (01226) 773955

E-mail: archives@barnsley.ac.uk

Enquiries: The Archivist and Local Studies Officer, Mrs L. Whitworth-Cox

Open: Mon, Wed: 9.30–1.00, 2.00–6.00; Tues, Fri: 9.30–1.00, 2.00–5.30; Thurs: 9.30–1.00.

Access: Generally open to the public; advance notice preferred.

Historical background: The service was founded within the library in 1986. It inherited material relating to the Barnsley area, including records of Barnsley Borough and predecessor authorities which came into Barnsley in 1974.

Acquisitions policy: Material relating to the area covered by Barnsley Metropolitan District.

Archives of organisation: Borough minutes, with rate books and papers, early 19th century– ; UDC and RDC minutes and papers.

Major collections: Deposited local collections, including records of Barnsley British Co-operative Society and West Riding Miners' Permanent Relief Fund Friendly Society.
Local Methodist and Congregational records.
Records of local societies and businesses, including Lancasters, estate agents, with valuation books, c1829–1963.
Papers of Lord Mason.

Non-manuscript material: Collection of illustrations, including photographs from Barnsley Borough engineers, 1950s–1960s (c1000), and the Biltcliff collection of postcards (c200).

Finding aids: Lists of some collections; other lists in progress. Lists sent to NRA.

Facilities: Photocopying. Photography. Microfilm/fiche reader/printer.

Publications: Information leaflet and family history handbook available on request.

51 National Union of Mineworkers

Address: 2 Huddersfield Road, Barnsley, South Yorkshire S70 2LS

Telephone: (01226) 215555

Fax: (01226) 215561

Enquiries: The President

Open: Mon–Fri: 9.00–12.00, 1.30–5.00.

Access: Bona fide researchers, by prior appointment.

Historical background: The union was established in 1944 by a number of regional coal-mining unions who had previously been affiliated to the Miners' Federation of Great Britain (set up in 1889). Few pre-1944 records survive due to loss and war damage. Areas frequently retain their own organisation and relief fund records.

Acquisitions policy: To maintain archives in conjunction with the regional organisations, which also retain their records.

Archives of organisation: MFGB: annual proceedings, 1889–1944; circulars and financial statements.

NUM: annual reports and minutes, 1944– ; reports and minutes of area organisations, some correspondence and press cuttings.

Major collections: Papers of W.E. Jones (president, 1951–60) are at The Brynmor Jones Library, at the University of Hull (entry 458).

Non-manuscript material: Bound journals.

Publications: See C. Cook: *Sources in British Political History, 1900–1951*, vol. 1, pp. 195–7, vol. 5, pp. 75–7.

52 North Devon Record Office

Parent organisation: Devon Record Office

Address: North Devon Library and Record Office, Tuly Street, Barnstaple, Devon EX31 1EL

Telephone: (01271) 388608/388607 (Local Studies Centre/microform bookings); 388611 (Beaford Photographic Archive)

Fax: (01271) 388608

E-mail: ndevrec@devon.gov.uk

Website: www.devon.gov.uk

Enquiries: The Senior Archivist, Mr T. Wormleighton

Open: Mon, Tues, Thurs, Fri: 9.30–5.00; Wed: 9.30–1.00; two Sats each month: 9.30–4.00.

Access: Generally open to the public. Admission charge (season and exemption tickets available). Documents required between 12.00 and 2.00, and on the Saturdays on which the record office is open, should be ordered in advance. A paid research service is available.

Historical background: The office forms part of the North Devon Local Studies Centre, in cooperation with a branch local history library and the North Devon Athenaeum, a private free library. The centre opened in 1988, at which time records relating to north Devon were transferred from Devon Record Office, Exeter (entry 365).

Acquisitions policy: Records of the North Devon area.

Archives of organisation: Usual local authority record holdings, including parish records for Archdeaconry of Barnstaple; records of North Devon and Torridge District Councils and

their predecessor authorities; North Devon area school, school board, Poor Law Union and hospital records.

Major collections: Deposited collections for North Devon area.
Archives of Chichester family of Arlington Court.

Non-manuscript material: Beaford Photographic Archive of historical and modern images of rural life.

Finding aids: Catalogues and indexes. Lists sent to NRA.

Facilities: Photocopying. Microfilm/fiche readers/printer.

Conservation: Provided by Devon Record Office, Exeter.

Publications: List of collections, 1988–1997.

53 Cumbria Archive Service
Cumbria Record Office, Barrow

Address: 140 Duke Street, Barrow-in-Furness, Cumbria LA14 1XW

Telephone: (01229) 894363

Fax: (01229) 894371

E-mail:
barrow.record.office@cumbriacc.gov.uk

Website: www.cumbria.gov.uk/archives/barec.asp

Enquiries: The Area Archivist, Mr A.C.J. Jones

Open: Mon–Fri: 9.30–5.00; Wed: 5.00–7.00; Sat: 9.30–4.00, by appointment
Local Studies Library material:
Mon–Wed, Fri: 9.30–7.00; Thurs: 9.30–5.00; Sat: 9.30–4.00.

Access: Generally open to the public. The office operates the CARN reader's ticket system.

Historical background: The record office at Barrow opened in 1979, although archives had been collected locally in temporary premises since 1975. The office also absorbed records from the Furness Collection gathered from 1948 onwards by the Central Library, Barrow. It acts as a Diocesan Record Office for Carlisle (south-western parishes) and is recognised as a place of deposit for public records. It is part of the Cumbria Archive Service, with other offices at Carlisle (entry 223) and Kendal (entry 480). Following building extensions, the office joined the Local Studies Library in 1998 to provide a unified service within a new joint search room.

Acquisitions policy: Official and unofficial records for the former area of Lancashire North of the Sands and the county borough of Barrow-in-Furness.

Archives of organisation: Usual local authority record holdings, including significant collections from Barrow Borough Council and from some neighbouring authorities.

Certain records from parishes and businesses within the Millom area of South Cumberland.

Major collections: Deposited local collections, including the following which have a wider significance:

Duke of Buccleuch's Furness estate records reflecting the iron-ore trade, *c*1854–1963.

Vickers Shipbuilding and Engineering Ltd, Barrow-in-Furness: naval gun mounting drawings, *c*1890–1950; photographs and printed ephemera from the shipbuilding industry.

Ellen Rose Fieldhouse Collection: papers of a local enthusiast, covering local history and dialect, and relating chiefly to the parish of Kirby Ireleth.

Non-manuscript material: Soulby Collection of posters, handbills, etc, generally mostly by J. Soulby, Ulverston printer, early 19th century.

Finding aids: Catalogues and indexes. Some collections are unlisted. Selected catalogues sent to NRA.

Facilities: Photocopying. Photography. Microfilming. Microfilm/fiche reader. Research Service.

Conservation: Shared facilities; none on site.

Publications: The Ellen Rose Fieldhouse Collection (Cumbria Archive Service, 1992).
Cumbrian Ancestors: Notes for Genealogical Searches (3/1998).

54 Automobile Association

Address: AA Archives, Stenson Cooke Centre, Priestley Road, Basingstoke, Hampshire RG24 9NY

Telephone: (01256) 492392

Enquiries: The Archivist, Michael Passmore

Open: By arrangement only.

Access: Bona fide researchers only, strictly by appointment. Application should be made in writing to the archivist.

Historical background: The Automobile Association was founded in 1905. It is technically a club, although it now has several businesses related to it. The current records of the association are not under the archivist's control and the 'archives' are rather the historic holdings, some of which are the prewar records.

Acquisitions policy: To maintain the archival holdings which have been built up over the years and to add memorabilia.

Archives of organisation: Some minutes of committees, including Motor Legislation Committee, 1919–43.

Files *re* organisation of AGMs, motoring organisations, petrol rationing, AA vehicles and telephone boxes. Copies of all AA publications, including handbooks.

Major collections: Miscellaneous historical and associated material, including early correspondence.

Non-manuscript material: Photographs, badges, vehicles, press cuttings. Large collection of AA motoring memorabilia.

Finding aids: NRA 12322.

Publications: S. Cooke: *This Motoring* (1930).
D. Kier (ed.): *Golden Milestone* (1955).
H. Barty-King: *The AA: History of the first 75 years of the Automobile Association, 1905–1980* (1980).

55 American Museum in Britain

Address: The Library, Claverton Manor, Bath BA2 7BD

Telephone: (01225) 460503

Fax: (01225) 480726

E-mail: amibbath@aol.com

Enquiries: The Curator, Miss Judith Elsdon

Open: Mon–Fri: 9.30–5.30.

Access: Bona fide researchers only, by invitation, arising from telephone or postal enquiry. An appointment is necessary.

The museum was opened in 1961 and has acquired by donation material relevant to the American decorative arts from the 17th to the mid–19th centuries. The collection is very limited, but includes correspondence, wills, bills of sale and documents of slave hire and emancipation, as well as 19th-century US newspapers, 20th-century topographical postcards and fashion plates.

56   Bath and North-East Somerset Record Office

Parent organisation: Bath and North-East Somerset Council

Address: Guildhall, High Street, Bath BA1 5AW

Telephone: (01225) 477421, 477420

Fax: (01225) 477439

E-mail: colin_johnston@bathnes.gov.uk

Enquiries: The Archivist, Mr C. A. Johnston

Open: Mon: 9.00–1.00, 2.00–8.00; Tues–Thurs: 9.00–1.00, 2.00–5.00; Fri: 9.00–1.00, 2.00–4.30.

Access: Generally open to the public.

Historical background: The office was established by the Bath City Council in 1967 and is recognised as a place of deposit for public records. Records of Bath Municipal Charities and St John's Hospital, 17th–20th centuries, are housed at the hospital but made available at the Record Office, which also has a catalogue of the records. Applications for access should be made to: The Clerk to the Trustees, Bath Municipal Charities and St John's Hospital, Thrings and Long, Midland Bridge Road, Bath; tel. (01225) 448494.

Acquisitions policy: Records relating to Bath and North-East Somerset.

Archives of organisation: Records of Bath City Council, 12th century–1996, and successor authority, 1996– .

Major collections: Local deposited collections, including hospital records.
Records of Royal Bath and West of England Society, 1777– .

Non-manuscript material: Maps, plans, photographs, microfiches of parish registers.

Finding aids: Catalogues, indexes and lists.

Facilities: Photocopying. Microfilm/fiche readers/printer.

Conservation: Contracted out.

57   Bath Central Library

Parent organisation: Bath and North-East Somerset Council

Address: 19 The Podium, Northgate Street, Bath BA1 5AN

Telephone: (01225) 787400

Fax: (01225) 787426

E-mail: libraries@bathnes.gov.uk

Website: www.bathnes.gov.uk

Enquiries: The Librarian-in-Charge

Open: Mon: 10.00–6.00; Tues–Thurs: 10.00–7.00; Fri, Sat: 9.30–5.00.

Access: Generally open to the public. Identification is required for some material. Advance notice may be necessary for material kept on a different site.

Historical background: The reference library was built in 1900 in conjunction with the Victoria Art Gallery to commemorate Queen Victoria's jubilee. It received local collections previously held at the Guildhall and continued to build on these. In 1990 the reference and lending libraries were amalgamated to form the current central library in purpose-built accommodation.

Acquisitions policy: To expand and strengthen the existing collections, especially those relating to local history, by purchase and donation.

Major collections: Papers of the Walcot Estate, 17th–18th centuries, and Pulteney Estate, 18th–19th centuries.
James Thomas Irvine's papers relating to Bath, especially the Abbey restoration and Roman Bath excavations.
Napoleonic Collection relating to the French Revolution and Napoleonic newspapers (800 vols).
Some records of local societies, 19th and 20th centuries, including Bath Field Club correspondence.
Boodle Collection of scrapbooks relating to Bath and Somerset (39 vols).

Non-manuscript material: Extensive collections on the history of Bath, comprising pamphlets, maps, plans, prints, photographs and slides, including the following:
Buxton Collection of pamphlets of the Civil War period, most with Somerset interest.
Chapman Collection of books, maps and pamphlets.

Hunt Collection of scrapbooks containing original drawings, watercolours, maps and autograph letters relating to Bath and the surrounding area (6 vols).

Finding aids: Full card catalogues and (since 1986) some material included on computerised catalogue. Indexes to maps, plans and all illustrations. NRA 25737.

Facilities: Photocopying. Microfilm/fiche readers/printers. Photography by arrangement.

Conservation: In-house binding; other work contracted out.

58   Crafts Study Centre

Parent organisation: Holburne Museum of Art

Address: Great Pulteney Street, Bath BA2 4DB

Telephone: (01225) 466669

Fax: (01225) 333121

E-mail: holburne@bath.ac.uk

Website: www.bath.ac.uk/holburne

Enquiries: The Curator, Barley Roscoe

Open: Tues–Sat: 10.00–5.00; Sun: 2.30–5.30.

Access: Bona fide students and researchers, by appointment only (2–3 weeks' notice preferred).

Historical background: The Crafts Study Centre opened at the Holburne Museum in 1977 for the purpose of making a permanent collection of work by the finest British artist-craftspeople of the 20th century.

Acquisitions policy: To acquire, mainly by donation, photographs, books, documents and working notes pertaining to crafts and crafts people.

Major collections: Papers of leading artist-craftsmen and women, including Bernard Leach, Michael Cardew, Katharine Pleydell-Bouverie, William Staite Murray, Ethel Mairet, Edward Johnston and Irene Wellington. Records of the Red Rose Guild.

Finding aids: Leach catalogue in progress. Lists of other material in preparation.

Facilities: Photocopying. Photography.

Publications: J. Howes: *Edward Johnston: a Catalogue of the Crafts Study Centre Collection and Archive* (Bath, 1987).

59   Downside Abbey Archives

Parent organisation: English Benedictine Congregation

Address: Downside Abbey, Stratton-on-the-Fosse, Radstock, Bath, Somerset BA3 4RH

Telephone: (01761) 235148

Fax: (01761) 235124

Enquiries: The Archivist, Dom Philip Jebb

Open: Open on most days, including weekends, except the first Sunday of Lent, by prior arrangement only.

Access: Serious students, by appointment only. Application should be made in the first instance in writing to the Archivist. Applicants need to indicate the nature of their research and to supply a reference. Personal papers of individuals (apart from strictly academic papers) are not normally available until 50 years after death.

Historical background: The Benedictine community of St Gregory the Great, now at Downside, has a history going back to 1605, when some English monks in Spanish and Italian monasteries came together to start a monastery in Douai, then part of the Spanish Netherlands. The community ran a school for English Catholics and sent priests (illegally) into England to support the recusants. In 1794, driven out of France by the Revolution, they came to England and settled in Downside in 1814. The community has run a school for English boys since the early 17th century, and been involved from the foundation in pastoral care of Catholics in England and Wales and engaged in historical and theological work. All these activities are reflected in the archives, although much material was lost during the French Revolution.

Acquisitions policy: English Benedictine history, but also histories of other religious communities which have ceased to exist and individuals in some way connected with the monastery or school. Also 19th- and 20th-century Catholic Australia, because the first two Archbishops of Sydney were monks of Downside.

Archives of organisation: Official papers and correspondence of the English Benedictine Congregation, 1617– , including minutes of General Chapters, constitutions and declarations, correspondence, records of Congregation officials and of individual houses (St Gregory's and others), bursar's, parish and other accounts, mainly mid-17th century– .

Records of Downside Weather Station and of St Gregory's Press.

Correspondence and official decisions of Presidents' General of the EBC, mainly 1790s– .

Records and financial accounts of pastoral work in England and Wales, 1640s– , and Australia, 1830–81.

Major collections: Annals and biographies, 1600–1850.

Collection of pamphlets, correspondence and diaries concerning the constitutional controversy, 1880–1900.

Personal papers of monks, mid-17th century, including Cardinal Gasquet, Archbishop Polding of Sydney, Abbot Cuthbert Butler and Abbot Christopher Butler and of lay men and women (*c*100).

Correspondence of Edmund Bishop, James Weale, F.J. Baigent, Adrian Fortescue, Archbishop David Mathew, St Oliver Plunkett.

Papers of J. Harting, ornithologist and naturalist, 19th century.

World War I and II chaplains' correspondence.

Accounts of escapes from France, late 18th century, and voyages to Australia, 19th century.

Non-manuscript material: Postcards of European architectural and topographical interest, late 19th century– (*c* 40,000).

Extensive collection of photographs and portraits, mainly of monks and nuns, other ecclesiastics, old boys of the school, 1850s– .

Architectural plans and drawings for Downside and churches elsewhere, including work by Pugin, Hanson, Cowper and Giles, Gilbert Scott, 19th and 20th centuries.

Copies of documents from continental archives in Spain, France and Italy relating to EBC history.

Finding aids: Card indexes and lists in progress. NRA 19936.

Facilities: Photocopying. Microfilm/fiche readers.

Publications: Dom Philip Jebb: 'Archives of the English Benedictine Congregation kept at St Gregory's, Downside', *Downside Review* , cxciii/312 (1975) [an updated version is in the *Bulletin* of the Catholic Archives Society, 14 (1994), 20–36].

Various articles by Dom Aidan Bellenger in *Catholic Archives*.

Early editions of *Downside Review*, late 19th century, included a series of articles 'Among the Archives'.

60 Fashion Research Centre
Museum of Costume

Parent organisation: Bath and North-East Somerset Council

Address: 4 Circus, Bath BA1 2EW

Telephone: (01225) 477754/477752

Fax: (01225) 444793

E-mail: costume_enquiries@bathnes.gov.uk

Website: www.museumofcostume.co.uk

Enquiries: The Assistant Keeper of Collections (Costumes), Mrs R. James

Open: Study Collection: Mon–Wed: 10.30–12.30, 2.30–4.30.
Library: Thurs–Fri: 10.00–12.30, 2.00–4.30.

Access: By appointment only.

Historical background: The centre was opened in 1974 as an extension to the Museum of Costume in Bath to make available study facilities in the history of dress. The aim is to provide a centre for reference and research from both documentary material and actual specimens of costume maintained in a study collection. The collections at both the museum and research centre deal mainly with fashionable dress in Europe for men, women and children from the late 16th century to the present day.

Acquisitions policy: To expand and strengthen existing primary and secondary collections in the history of costume and related subjects by donations and occasional purchases.

Major collections: Archives of costume historians, including Nancy Bradfield and Geoffrey Squire.

Non-manuscript material: Fashion periodicals: 1802– (*c*100 titles).

Trade catalogues from British firms, *c*1900– (*c*600).

Sunday Times Fashion Archive: fashion photographs, 1957–72 (*c*2000).

Worth/Paquin Archives: designs, photographs and press cuttings from house records of both firms, 1902–56.

Fashion plates, late 18th-century–1920 (*c*2000).

Photographs: 19th- and 20th-century cartes-de-visite and photograph albums; fashion photographs; photographs of works of art from the medieval period to the 20th century (c10,000).

Paper dressmaking patterns, 1875–1990, (c1500).

Knitting patterns and related material, 1920– (c2000).

Embroidery patterns, 1875–1970 (c500).

Finding aids: Catalogues and indexes (e.g. to fashion designers represented in Sunday Times Fashion Archive or *Vogue* magazine, 1930–).

Facilities: Photography by arrangement.

61 Provincial Archives of La Sainte Union Religious Congregation

Parent organisation: International Congregation of La Sainte Union, Rome

Address: La Sainte Union Convent, 29 Pulteney Road, Bath BA2 4EY

Telephone: (01225) 461984

Enquiries: The Archivist, Sr Margaret Joseph Lythgoe, 18 Titmuss Avenue, Thamesmead, London SE28 8DH; tel (020) 8310 0018.

Open: By advance appointment.

Access: All Sisters of the Congregation and to bona fide researchers. Restricted access to documents less than 50 years old.

Historical background: The Congregation of La Sainte Union was founded in Douai, France, in 1826, with special emphasis on work for the Christian education of youth. The Sisters were expelled by the French government at the end of the 19th century. The foundations of the Anglo-Hibernian province (UK and Ireland) were laid in 1858. The present provincial repository was formally established in Bath in 1980. It contains some valuable material on other LSU provinces founded from England, particularly the USA, Argentina and West Indies.

Acquisitions policy: Archives of the Congregation, with special reference to foundation years, the life of the founder, the spread of the Congregation overseas, and, in particular, the establishment of new communities and schools in the UK and Ireland. Also material illustrating the lives and works of members of La Sainte Union.

Archives of organisation: Documents and reports received from general and provincial administration, including six-year General Chapters, general and provincial councils, regional meetings, education conferences. Records of spiritual formation and profession ceremonies.

Major collections: Letters and conferences of Fr Jean Baptise Debrabant, the founder, to the Sisters, 1828–76.

Collections of letters from Sisters who established the first houses of the Congregation in North and South America and later in the West Indies and Africa, early 20th century– .

Non-manuscript material: Photographs of the first LSU Mother House in Douai.

Biographies of the founder.

Histories of LSU schools and of the various pastoral and charitable works of the Congregation.

School journals.

Finding aids: Catalogues, lists and indexes.

Facilities: Photocopying.

62 Royal Photographic Society Collection

Address: The Octagon, Milsom Street, Bath BA1 1DN

Telephone: (01225) 462841 ext. 217, 218, 219, 220

Fax: (01225) 448688/469880 (with ansaphone)

E-mail: pam@collections.rps.org pam@rps.org

Website: www.rps.org

Enquiries: The Curator, Ms Pam Roberts

Open: Enquiries: Mon–Fri: 10.00–5.00.
Visits by appointment only:
Tues–Thurs: 10.00–1.00, 2.00–5.00.

Access: Generally open to the public, by appointment. Non-members will be charged a research fee on a daily basis, depending on requirements.

Historical background: The Royal Photographic Society came into existence in 1853. The collection of photographs was not established until the 1920s, when J. Dudley Johnston was simultaneously president, secretary and curator. It was formed from the gifts of photographers of their own work and their personal collections. The material is mainly 19th century but also extends into the 20th century, with the emphasis on pictorialism.

Acquisitions policy: Material is acquired mainly by donation, although some purchases are made. There is an updated acquisitions policy aimed at contemporary British photography. Coverage includes collections of medical photography and nature photography.

Archives of organisation: Archives of RPS, including early minute books, records of group meetings, 1853– ; correspondence and catalogues, 1850s– .

Non-manuscript material: Principally photographs on a variety of media, glass, paper, metal etc (250,000), including the work of Julia Margaret Cameron (1815–79); Roger Fenton (1819–69), first secretary; D.O. Hill (1802–70) and Robert Adamson (1820–47); W.H. Fox Talbot (1800–77); Horace Nicholls (1867–1941); Samuel Bourne (1834–1912); Francis Frith (1822–98); O.G. Rejlander (1813–75); Linnaeus Tripe (1822–1902); H.P. Robinson (1830–1901); Frederick Evans (1852–1943); Alvin Langdon Coburn (1882–1966); Edward Steichen (1879–1973); Alfred Stieglitz (1864–1946); Clarence White (1871–1925); Alexander Keighley (1861–1947); Horsley Hinton (1863–1908); Nicéphore Niépce (1765–1833); J.D. Llewelyn (1810–82); Oxley Grabham (1865–1939); Frank M. Sutcliffe (1853–1941).

Kodak and other cameras and items of photographic equipment, including light meters (6000), 1838– .

Fox Talbot: *The Pencil of Nature, Sun Pictures of Scotland.*

Du Mont Collection of books illustrated by photography.

Photographic periodicals and books, 1850s– (24,000).

Finding aids: Computerised catalogue for equipment. Card catalogue for books and photographs.

Facilities: Photocopying. Photography.

Conservation: Contracted out.

Publications: The Treasures of the RPS (Heinemann/RPS, 1980) [covers contents of photographic collection up to 1915].
P. Roberts: *The Royal Photographic Society Collection* (RPS, 1994).
——: *Alfred Stieglitz: Camera Work: the Complete Illustrations, 1903–1917* (1997).
CD-Rom on 'Camera work' produced with University of Westminster.
CD-Rom on WHF Talbot holdings (*c*700 items).

Items about collection appear regularly in the *Photographic Journal*, published by the RPS, and the *British Association of Picture Libraries and Agencies Journal.*
Various publications on individual photographers.

63   University of Bath Library

Address: Claverton Down, Bath BA2 7AY

Telephone: (01225) 826826 ext. 3464

Fax: (01225) 826229

E-mail: e.richmond@bath.ac.uk

Enquiries: The University Archivist, Lizzie Richmond

Open: Mon–Fri: 9.00–5.00, by appointment.

Access: Approved readers. Some of the university archives are subject to extended closure periods.

Historical background: The University of Bath received its charter in 1966, having developed from the Bristol College of Science and Technology. A professional archive post was established in 1998. Since 1987 the library has housed the National Cataloguing Unit for the Archives of Contemporary Scientists (see entry xxiii).

Acquisitions policy: To build and maintain a collection in support of the university's teaching and research interests.

Archives of organisation: Archives of the University of Bath, *c*1960– .

Major collections: Papers of Sir Isaac Pitman (1813–97), inventor of the Pitman shorthand system, and Sir (Isaac) James Pitman (1901–85), Conservative MP for Bath, educationalist and inventor of the initial teaching alphabet.
Watkins Collection of documents and photographs relating to the role of steam power in the British economy, 1850–1914.

Non-manuscript material: Large collection of books in and about shorthand.
Library of the Initial Teaching Alphabet Foundation.
Small collection of printed material and original sound recordings relating to the Independent Commission for World Wide Telecommunications Development, 1983–5.

Finding aids: List of Pitman Initial Teaching Alphabet Foundation material.

Facilities: Photocopying.

Conservation: Contracted out.

64 The Divine Healing Mission

Parent organisation: Crowhurst Christian Healing Centre

Address: The Old Rectory, Crowhurst, Battle, East Sussex TN33 9AD

Telephone: (01424) 830204

Fax: (01424) 830053

E-mail: divine@theway.co.uk

Enquiries: The Archivist, Miss Daphne Higginson

Open: Mon–Fri: 9.30–4.00, by arrangement only.

Access: Bona fide researchers, by appointment. A general ten-year closure rule applies but this can be relaxed in certain cases.

Historical background: The Society of Emmanuel was founded by J.M. Hickson in 1905 to revive the healing ministry in the Anglican Church; it and became the Divine Healing Mission in 1933. Crowhurst Home of Healing was founded by Howard Cobb in 1930. The two organisations amalgamated in 1958 under the present name. Development of the archive began in 1991, and the records are now stored in a purpose-built room.

Acquisitions policy: Maintaining the archives of the mission with an archive records management policy and outside material relating to the work of the DHM.

Archives of organisation: Minutes of committees, 1933–88, with some administrative and finance papers.

Major collections: Letters of J.M. Hickson from his overseas missions, 1867–1933.
Unpublished books and sermons of E. Howard Cobb, 1878–1950.
Prayer letters and papers of Godfrey Mowatt.

Non-manuscript material: Copies of *The Healer* magazine, first published by the Society of Emmanuel, 1908–70; continued under the titles *Abundant Life* and, later, *Crowhurst*, 1972–98.
Photographs, 1905–80.

Finding aids: Catalogues and indexes in preparation.

Facilities: Limited photocopying.

65 Beaulieu Archive

Parent organisation: Montagu Ventures Ltd

Address: John Montagu Building, Beaulieu, Brockenhurst, Hampshire SO42 7ZN

Telephone: (01590) 612345 exts 259, 283

Fax: (01590) 612624

E-mail: info@beaulieu.co.uk

Website: www.beaulieu.co.uk

Enquiries: The Archivist, Miss Susan Tomkins

Open: Mon–Fri: 10.00–5.00.

Access: Generally open to the public, by appointment.

Historical background: Originally family papers of the Lord Montagu of Beaulieu and papers of the Beaulieu Estate, now expanded to include material relating to the Beaulieu leisure complex. See also National Motor Museum (entry 66).

Acquisitions policy: Multimedia material relating to the Beaulieu Estate and Montagu family.

Archives of organisation: The Beaulieu Estate records, late 18th–19th century.
Poor House records, late 18th century–early 19th century.
Papers of Henry, 1st Lord Montagu of Beaulieu (1832–1905).
Records of Montagu Ventures Ltd.
Some records of Ditton Park Estate, Berkshire.

Non-manuscript material: Oral history collection.
Photographs.

Finding aids: Catalogue. Some lists and indexes.

Facilities: Photocopying. Photography.

Conservation: Contracted out.

Publications: H.E.R. Widnell: *The Beaulieu Record* (1973).
F. Hockey: *Beaulieu: King John's Abbey* (1976).
A.J. Holland: *Buckler's Hard: a Shipbuilding Village* (1985).
C. Cunningham: *The Beaulieu River Goes to War* (1994).
——: *Beaulieu: the Finishing School for Secret Agents* (1998).

66 National Motor Museum Libraries

Parent organisation: National Motor Museum Trust

Address: Trust Centre, Beaulieu, Brockenhurst, Hampshire SO42 7ZN

Telephone: (01590) 612345

Fax: (01590) 612655

E-mail: nmmt@beaulieu.co.uk

Website: www.beaulieu.co.uk/motormuseum

Enquiries: The Reference Librarian

Open: Mon–Sun: 10.00–12.30, 2.00–5.00.

Access: Generally open to the public for reference; a reading room is provided.

The reference library was formed in 1961 and moved to its present position in 1972. The bulk of the collection is printed material, including sales catalogues and owners' handbooks, although there is some material from the motor industry and sporting personalities, including photo archives of Bedford; Commer; Cranes of Dereham, trailer manufacturers; Ford; Scammell; Sparshatts of Portsmouth, distributors and coachbuilders (including ledgers); and Thornycroft. There is a photographic library and sound archive. The museum also houses the Shell Art Collection of posters and postcards, including original artwork, 1914–1980s. Charges for researchers were introduced in 1999. (See also Beaulieu Archives, entry 65.)

67 Bethlem Royal Hospital Archives and Museum

Parent organisation: South London and Maudsley NHS Trust (hospital's own archives) The Bethlem Art and History Collections Trust (other historical and art collections)

Address: The Bethlem Royal Hospital, Monks Orchard Road, Beckenham, Kent BR3 3BX

Telephone: (020) 8776 4307 (general enquiries); 8776 4053 (Archivist)

Fax: (020) 8776 4045

E-mail: museum@bethlem.freeserve.co.uk

Enquiries: The Deputy Archivist

Open: Mon–Fri: 9.30–5.00, by appointment.

Access: Open to the public by appointment. 100-year closure on medical and other records relating to individual patients; 30-year closure on other public records.

Historical background: The Bethlem Royal Hospital (the original 'Bedlam') was founded in 1247 as the Priory of St Mary of Bethlehem. By 1400 it was a hospital for the insane. It has occupied sites in Bishopsgate (1247–1676); Moorfields (1676–1815); St George's Fields, Southwark (1815–1930); and the present location (since 1930). It came under the control of the City of London in 1547, and was administered jointly with Bridewell Hospital from 1557 to 1948. Between 1816 and 1864, Bethlem housed the first State Criminal Lunatic Asylum (replaced by Broadmoor Hospital). Under the National Health Service (NHS) in 1948 Bethlem was united with the Maudsley Hospital, Denmark Hill. The Maudsley was opened in 1923 as a London County Council mental hospital and became the postgraduate Institute of Psychiatry in 1946. The joint hospital has been administered by a Board of Governors (1948–82), a Special Health Authority (1982–94), and an NHS trust (since 1994). In 1995 Warlingham Park Hospital (formerly the Croydon Mental Hospital) came under the Bethlem and Maudsley NHS Trust, which was changed in 1999 to the South London and Maudsley NHS Trust. The archives department was set up in 1967, and is recognised as a place of deposit for public records.

Acquisitions policy: Archives of Bethlem and Maudsley hospitals. Reference books and other material relating more generally to the history of psychiatry and to art and psychiatry are also collected. Works by artists who have suffered mental disorders.

Archives of organisation: Bethlem Hospital: minutes of the Court of Governors of Bridewell and Bethlem, 1559–1948, and of the General Committee of Bridewell and Bethlem, 1737–1948 (on microfilm).
Patients admission registers, 1683– , casebooks, 1816–1948; various administrative and financial records, 18th century– ; records of the State Criminal Lunatic Asylum 1816–64; title deeds, maps, plans and surveys relating to endowment estates; miscellaneous records, including photographs.
Maudsley Hospital: minute books and files transferred from LCC, 1923–48.
Records of the joint hospital, 1948– .

Croydon Mental Hospital (later Warlingham Park Hospital) casebooks, 1903–13.

Non-manuscript material: Museum holdings include a collection of work by artists who have suffered from mental disorder, notably Richard Dadd, Louis Wain and Jonathan Martin.

Finding aids: NRA lists, 1958/9 (in process of revision). Indexes to Court and General Committee books, casebooks and admission registers.

Facilities: Photocopying.

Conservation: Full in-house service.

Publications: P. Allderidge: *The Bethlem Royal Hospital: an Illustrated History* (1995).

68 Raymond Mander and Joe Mitchenson Theatre Collection

Address: The Mansion, Beckenham Place Park, Beckenham, Kent BR3 2BP

Telephone: (020) 8658 7725

Fax: (020) 8663 0313

Enquiries: The Director, Mr Richard Mangan

Open: Mon–Fri: 10.30–4.30.

Access: Bona fide researchers, by appointment only. An hourly charge is made.

Historical background: The collection was begun by Raymond Mander and Joe Mitchenson in the 1930s. Subsequently a charitable trust was formed with the two founders as directors.

Acquisitions policy: Anything and everything to do with the theatre and allied arts.

Non-manuscript material: Programmes, cuttings, photographs, posters, paintings, designs, books, pottery relating mainly, but not exclusively, to London theatre. Also material on actors, actresses, playwrights, designers, composers, singers, dancers, music hall and variety. Library (7000 books).

Finding aids: Indexes of pottery and designs. Book catalogue.

Facilities: Photocopying.

69 Bedford Central Library
Reference and Local Studies Library

Parent organisation: Bedfordshire County Council

Address: Harpur Street, Bedford MK40 1PG

Telephone: (01234) 350931/270102 (direct line)

Fax: (01234) 342163

E-mail: stephensonb@bedfordshire.co.uk

Enquiries: The Local Studies Librarian, Barry Stephenson

Open: Mon, Wed: 9.30–7.00; Tues, Thurs, Fri: 9.30–5.30; Sat: 9.30–5.00.

Access: Generally open to the public.

Historical background: The present collection is the result of the merger in 1985 of the Bedfordshire County Local Studies Collection, which started in 1925, with the Local Studies Collection of Bedford Central Library.

Acquisitions policy: To collect all published and pictorial material covering Bedfordshire, past and present.

Major collections: Material relating to John Bunyan (1628–88) and Mark Rutherford (1831–1913).

Non-manuscript material: Usual local history collection, including newspapers, 1842– ; photographs, 1880– ; illustrations, 1700– ; maps, 1765– ; handbills and posters, 1800– ; microfilms of parish registers, 1532–1812; census returns, 1841–91 (microfilm).
Census index for English and Welsh counties; index of births, marriages and deaths, 1837–1992 (both fiche).

Finding aids: Catalogues and indexes. NRA 19222.

Facilities: Photocopying. Microfilm/fiche reader/printer.

70 Bedford Museum

Parent organisation: Bedford Borough Council

Address: Castle Lane, Bedford MK40 3XD

Telephone: (01234) 353323

Fax: (01234) 273401

E-mail: bmuseum@bedford.gov.uk

Website: www.bedford.gov.uk/bedford/tic/museums.htm

Enquiries: The Curator, Miss R. Brind

Open: Tues–Sat: 11.00–5.00; Sun and bank holiday Mon: 2.00–5.00.

Access: By appointment.

The museum maintains and collects archives relevant to its main collecting areas of recent local history, archaeology and natural history of the north Bedfordshire area (NRA 0560).

71 Bedford School Archive

Address: Bedford School, De Parys Avenue, Bedford MK40 2TU

Telephone: (01234) 362200

Fax: (01234) 362283

E-mail: rmiller@bedfordschool.beds.sch.uk

Enquiries: The Archivist, R.G. Miller

Open: School hours, by arrangement.

Access: Generally open to the public via the archivist, by appointment.

Historical background: The school is a Tudor foundation with extensive archive material. The main body of pre-1800 material is held at the offices of The Harpur Trust, Princeton Court, Pilgrim Centre, Brickhill Drive, Bedford MK41 7P2. The school archive consists of post–1800 material collected in recent years and housed in three rooms in the school.

Acquisitions policy: To consolidate and extend the school's archive; material relating to Old Bedfordians is always accepted.

Archives of organisation: Administrative material concerning the school, its pupils and staff, finance, estates and architects, including G.F. Bodley (1827–1907) and Oswald Milne (188–1968).

Major collections: Papers and memorabilia of old boys, including Sir Thomas Erskine May (1815–86) and Frederick Burnaby (1842–85); also extensive numbers of trench diaries, World War I.

Finding aids: Catalogued in part.

Facilities: Photocopying.

Publications: Sargeaunt and Hockliffe: *History of Bedford School* (1924).
Barlen, Stambach and Stileman: *Bedford School* (1983).

72 Bedfordshire and Luton Records Service

Parent organisation: Bedfordshire County Council in partnership with Luton Borough Council

Address: County Hall, Cauldwell Street, Bedford MK42 9AP

Telephone: (01234) 228833/363222 ext. 2833

Fax: (01234) 228854

E-mail: archive@csd.bedfordshire.gov.uk

Website: www.bedfordshire.gov.uk

Enquiries: The County Archivist, Mr K.T. Ward

Open: Mon–Fri: 9.00–1.00, 2.00–5.00.

Access: Open to the public without appointment or reader's ticket and without charge. Access information is given in the Service Charter, Code of Conduct for Searchroom Users, Access Guide for Disabled Visitors, Guides to Copying and Photographic Orders, and Enquiry Service for family and local historians (free leaflets available on request).

Historical background: Bedfordshire Record Office was established in 1913 under the auspices of the Records Committee formed by Bedfordshire County Council in 1898 and is the only officially designated archive repository in the county. Bedfordshire was one of the pioneers of the local repository network and is the oldest county archives service. The record office moved to purpose-built premises in 1969, and in 1993 earned a charter mark award for excellence in public services. A full records management service for the authority was established in 1989. The office is recognised as a place of deposit for public records and designated as the Diocesan Record Office for St Albans (Archdeaconry of Bedford). From 1997 the service has been jointly funded by Bedfordshire County Council and Luton Borough Council.

Acquisitions policy: Documents recording or illustrating the topography, ownership, occupation and use of land in the historic county, and human activity — the social, economic, religious, cultural, political, administrative life and history of the county's inhabitants, communities, organisations and government at all levels.

Archives of organisation: Usual local authority archive holdings, including Quarter Sessions records, 1651– ; Poor Law Union records, 1834– ; county council archives, 1889– ; and district and parish council records.

Major collections: Deposited local collections from businesses, landed estates, Anglican and non-conformist churches, public services, including hospitals, and papers of private individuals.

Non-manuscript material: Substantial collections of maps and plans, architectural drawings, and illustrations. There is a collection of local printed material on open access in the Record Office searchroom.

Finding aids: Most collections catalogued, with detailed subject index on cards. Holdings generally well indexed and many conspectus finding aids available e.g. glebe terriers, monumental inscriptions, cemetery registers and rate books. Catalogues sent to NRA.

Facilities: Photocopying generally on demand. Plan printing, colour copying and photography by arrangement. Microfilm/fiche readers/printers. Lap-top computers and tape-recorders permitted (subject to clearance with duty staff).

Conservation: In-house facilities with limited scope for outside work.

Publications: Guide to the Bedfordshire Record Office (1957).
Guide Supplement (1966).
Guide to the Russell Estate Collections for Bedfordshire and Devon to 1910 (1966).
The Bedfordshire Parish Registers Series [80 vols, 1931–92; indexed transcripts of all Bedfordshire parish registers up to 1812]; also available on fiche.
Newsletter [thrice-yearly, 1986–].
National Inventory of Documentary Sources (Chadwyck-Healey, microfiche, 1984–).
Leaflets and short guides on a range of subjects.
Sources for Records relating to Ethnic Minorities (1995); *Sources for Women's History* (1997).

73 Cranfield University
Information and Library Service

Parent organisation: Kings Norton Library

Address: Cranfield, Bedford MK43 0AL

Telephone: (01234) 750111 ext. 3722

Fax: (01234) 752391

E-mail: j.harrington@cranfield.ac.uk

Website: www.cranfield.ac.uk/cils/library/

Enquiries: The Information Services Manager, Mr John Harrington

Open: Mon–Fri: 8.30–9.00; Sat: 9.30–6.00.

Access: Generally open to the public.

Historical background: Founded in 1946 as the College of Aeronautics, for the education of aeronautical engineers, the university became Cranfield Institute of Technology in 1970 with the power to award degrees; it now deals with many aspects of applied science. It changed its name to Cranfield University in 1993.

Acquisitions policy: To acquire books, periodicals and published material (e.g. reports) on those subjects taught at Cranfield. There is no formal acquisitions policy on historical material.

Archives of organisation: Small collection of official records.

Major collections: Reports on aerodynamics, aeronautical engineering and related engineering subjects (*c*100,000).

Non-manuscript material: The institute has acquired the library of the Aeronautical Research Council.

Facilities: Photocopying. Microfiche readers/printer.

74 Belfast Central Library
Irish and Local Studies Department

Parent organisation: Belfast Education and Library Board

Address: Royal Avenue, Belfast BT1 1EA

Telephone: (028) 90509150

E-mail: info@libraries.belfast-elb.gov.uk

Website: www.belb.org.uk

Enquiries: The Senior Librarian, Mrs. Linda Huston

Open: Mon, Thurs: 9.30–8.00; Tues, Wed, Fri: 9.30–5.30; Sat: 9.30–1.00.

Access: Generally open to the public.

Historical background: Since the 1920s the library has acquired the papers of local antiquarians and literary figures.

Acquisitions policy: To acquire material relating to the work of local historians and writers.

Major collections: Irish antiquarian and bibliographical studies: F.J. Bigger (1863–1926), 40,000 items; J.S. Crone (1858–1945), 10,000 items; A.S. Moore (1870–1961), 1000 items; A. Riddell (1874–1958), 5000 items.
Gaelic MSS: Bryson MacAdam Collection of Ulster Gaelic writings, 17th–18th centuries (44 MS vols).
MSS, TSS and/or correspondence of the following: Lynn Doyle (1873–1961); Alexander Irvine (1863–1941); Amanda McKittrick Ros, 1897–1939; Forrest Reid (1876–1947); Sam Thompson, 1956–65.

Non-manuscript material: Theatre and cinema posters and programmes relating mainly to Belfast (c5000).
Photographs, political ephemera, postcards relating to Ireland.

Finding aids: Various lists and indexes.

Facilities: Photocopying. Limited photography. Microfilm/fiche reader/printer.

Publications: B. O'Buachalla: *Clar na Lamhscribhinni Gaeilge: 1 Leabharlainn Phoibli Bheal Feirste* (Baile Atha Cliath: An Chead Chlo, 1962).
Guide to Irish and Local Studies Department (1980).

75 Belfast Climate Office

Parent organisation: Meteorological Office

Address: Progressive House, 32 College Street, Belfast BT1 6BQ

Telephone: (028) 90328457

Fax: (028) 90328457

E-mail: dcampbell@meto.gov.uk

Enquiries: The Senior Meteorological Officer

Open: Mon–Thurs: 8.30–5.00; Fri: 8.30–4.30.

Access: Generally open to the public, preferably by appointment. Meteorological records in the Public Record Office of Northern Ireland (see entry 81) may be consulted only on application to Belfast Climate Office.

Historical background: The Meteorological Office originated as a department of the Board of Trade in 1855. Under Public Records Acts the office is authorised to select technical meteorological records for retention and maintain approved places of deposit at Belfast, Bracknell (entry 120) and Edinburgh (entry 327).

Acquisitions policy: Responsible for original meteorological and climatological records from any source in Northern Ireland. Donations are welcomed.

Major collections: Comprehensive collection of weather observation registers and climatological returns for locations in Northern Ireland. Records older than ten years are deposited in the Public Record Office of Northern Ireland.

Finding aids: Full catalogue in the Public Record Office of Northern Ireland.

Facilities: Photocopying by arrangement.

76 Belfast Harbour Commissioners' Library

Address: Harbour Office, Corporation Square, Belfast BT1 3AL

Telephone: (028) 90554422

Fax: (028) 90554411

E-mail: info@belfast-harbour.co.uk

Enquiries: The Senior Administrative Officer, R. Yeates

Open: By arrangement only.

Access: Bona fide students, by appointment only.

Belfast Harbour Commissioners was set up by Act of Parliament in 1847. The library has acquired archival material from various bodies, and its collections relate largely to Belfast and its port from 1600 onwards. The collection was catalogued in 1999 and a list of the contents of the library is available to interested parties.

77 Campbell College

Address: Belmont Road, Belfast BT4 2ND

Telephone: (028) 90763076

Fax: (028) 90761894

E-mail: hmoffice@campbellcollege.co.uk

Website: www.info-links.com/schools/ccb

Enquiries: The Archivist, Mr C.F. Gailey

Open: Term: Mon–Fri: 9.30–1.00.

Access: Old Campbellians and others with suitable references, by appointment.

The college was opened in 1894 under the terms of the will of Henry James Campbell (1813–89) with the stated purpose of giving 'a superior liberal Protestant education' for boys. Although much of the early material was unfortunately destroyed, there remains a collection of Old Campbellians' historical reminiscences and photographs, which is being actively augmented. The register of the college is published in five volumes. A history of the school, *Neither Rogues nor Fools*, is available on application.

78 General Register Office, Northern Ireland

Address: Oxford House, 49–55 Chichester Street, Belfast BT1 4HL

Telephone: (028) 90252021/2/3/4

Fax: (028) 90252120

E-mail: gro.nisra@dfpni.gov.uk

Website: www.nisra.gov.uk/gro/

Enquiries: The Registrar General

Open: Mon–Fri: 9.30–4.00.

Access: Open to the public; fees vary.

Historical background: The Registrar General's Office was set up for the whole of Ireland and at the date of partition (1921) divided into General Register Office (Northern Ireland) and General Register Office (Republic of Ireland). Since 1973 the registrars of births, deaths and marriages have been local authority staff, paid for by the Department of Finance and Personnel, Northern Ireland.

Acquisitions policy: The Registrar General is required by statute to arrange for the registration of all births, marriages and deaths in Northern Ireland, and for the storage and safe keeping of all such records.

Major collections: Marriage records (Northern Ireland), 1845– .
Birth and death records (Northern Ireland), 1863– .

Non-manuscript material: Some pre-1921 birth and death indexes on microfilm. Post-1973 birth and death records on microfiche.
Computerised historic indexes: births, deaths and marriages, 1922– .

Finding aids: Indexes to all records available.

Facilities: Index search facilities. Microfilm/fiche readers.

Publications: Registrar General's annual reports, quarterly reports.

79 Linen Hall Library

Address: 17 Donegall Square North, Belfast BT1 5GD

Telephone: (028) 90321707

Fax: (028) 90438586

E-mail: info@linenhall.com

Website: www.linenhall.com

Enquiries: Mr John Gray

Open: Mon–Fri: 9.30–6.00; Sat: 9.30–4.00.

Access: Generally open to public; a prior application and a letter of reference are desirable.

Historical background: The library was founded in 1788 as the Belfast Reading Society and subsequently named the Belfast Library & Society for Promoting Knowledge. Its stated aim was the 'collection of an extensive library, philosophical apparatus, and such productions of nature and art as tend to improve the mind and excite a spirit of general inquiry'. The library has particular strengths in Irish and local studies, history, travel and genealogy.

Acquisitions policy: To strengthen existing collections of Irish material.

Archives of organisation: Minute books, 1788– .

Major collections: Minute books of Belfast local societies, including Anacreontic Society; Burns Society; Harp Society; Natural History and Philosophical Society.
Minute books of Belfast Trades Council.
Northern Ireland Political Collection, including archives of Northern Ireland Civil Rights Movement and the Northern Ireland Women's Movement.
Manuscript collections, including Henry Joy collection, 1780–1820, and Blackwood collection of local genealogies of Co. Down families.

Non-manuscript material: Northern Ireland Political Collection ephemera.
Theatre & Performing Arts archive.

Facilities: Photocopying.

80 Presbyterian Historical Society of Ireland

Parent organisation: The Presbyterian Church in Ireland

Address: Room 220, Church House, Fisherwick Place, Belfast BT1 6DW

Telephone: (028) 90248377

Fax: (028) 90248377

E-mail: info@presbyterianireland.org

Website: www.presbyterianireland.org

Enquiries: The Hon. Secretary, Rev. Dr W. J. H. McKee
The Assistant Secretary, Mr Alan McMillan

Open: Mon, Tues, Thurs, Fri: 10.00–12.30; Wed: 10.00–1.00, 2.00–4.00.
Closed 12 and 13 July.

Access: Generally open to the public; an appointment is not normally necessary, but a telephone call is advisable. Presbytery records require the consent of the Clerks of Presbytery.

Historical background: The Presbyterian Historical Society was founded in 1907. Its constitution states, 'the object of this Society shall be to collect and preserve the materials, and to promote the knowledge of the history, of the Churches of the Presbyterian order in Ireland.'

Acquisitions policy: The society's policy is to acquire, mostly by donation or deposit, material relevant to the history of the congregations in the Presbyterian Church in Ireland and their ministers.

Archives of organisation: Records of the General Synod of Ulster and the Seceders and, since 1840, of the General Assembly of the Presbyterian Church in Ireland.
Records relating to some presbyteries and congregations.
Files detailing records held by congregations; histories of congregations.

Major collections: Baptismal and marriage registers.
Writings by Presbyterian ministers.
Tenison Groves census records.
Fasti of the Irish Presbyterian Church, 1613–1840, by Rev. James McConnell.

Non-manuscript material: Witness newspaper files; other publications of Presbyterian interest, e.g. *The Irish Presbyterian* and McComb's *Almanac*.
Some portraits and photographs and other artefacts of Presbyterian interest, e.g. communion vessels, hour glasses, offering ladles and communion tokens.
Collection of pamphlets on religious topics.

Finding aids: Indexes of ministers, congregations and church records. Computerised library list.

Facilities: Photocopying. Photography by arrangement.

Publications: Annual Bulletin
A History of Congregations in the Presbyterian Church in Ireland, 1610–1982.
J.M. Barkley: *Fasti of the General Assembly, 1840–1910* [in three parts].

81 Public Record Office of Northern Ireland

Parent organisation: Department of the Environment (NI)

Address: 66 Balmoral Avenue, Belfast BT9 6NY

Telephone: (028) 90251318

Fax: (028) 90255999

E-mail: proni@nics.gov.uk

Website: proni.nics.gov.uk/index.htm

Enquiries: The Chief Executive

Open: Mon–Wed, Fri: 9.15–4.45; Thurs: 9.15–8.45. Documents are not produced after 4.15 (Mon–Wed, Fri) and 8.15 (Thurs).
Closed last week of November and first week of December.

Access: Generally open to the public. There is a 30-year closure on offical records and an annual inspection fee to commerical researchers only.

Historical background: The Public Record Office of Northern Ireland was set up by the Public Records Act (Northern Ireland) 1923 to be responsible for the custody of official records of government departments, courts of law, statutory bodies etc. Provision was also made for the deposit of imperial records, i.e. those relating to Northern Ireland created by government at Westminster, and for the record office to accept records from private depositors.

PRONI is currently involved in reviewing and cataloguing records of the 26 district councils, including those of Belfast City Council.

Acquisitions policy: Official records are transferred to the Public Record Office of Northern Ireland under the terms of the 1923 Act. The office seeks to acquire a wide range of private records, in particular family, estate and business archives; ecclesiastical records; papers of clubs and societies; and emigrant letters.

Archives of organisation: Official records, mainly 1922– , but also significant series from the 1830s, including OS maps, education records, and board of guardian records.

Major collections: Private archives, mainly 16th century–, including estate and family archives of the major landholding families in Northern Ireland.
Large collection of business records, especially the linen industry.

Non-manuscript material: Very small collection of tapes and films.
Several large collections of photographic glass plate negatives.

Finding aids: Computerised and manual catalogues. Indexes. Deputy Keeper's reports, 1954–89.

Facilities: Photocopying. Photographic copies. Microfilm readers. Self-service microfilm reading room for church records and 1901 census.

Conservation: Full in-house service; no outside work is undertaken.

Publications: A large number of publications, some published by HMSO, others by the Public Record Office; these include education facsimile packs, calendars, lists of selected papers, guides to various types of records. A publications list is available.

82 Queen's University Archives

Address: Main Library, Queen's University, Belfast BT7 1LS

Telephone: (028) 90273607

Fax: (028) 90323340

E-mail: m.smallman@qub.ac.uk

Website: www.qub.ac.uk

Enquiries: The Librarian, Special Collections

Open: Term: Mon–Fri: 9.00–9.30. Vacation: Mon–Fri: 9.00–5.00. Summer vacation: Sat: 9.00–12.30.

Access: Approved readers, by written application; an appointment is necessary. Certain categories of archives are not available to outside readers.

Historical background: Queen's College, Belfast, was founded in 1845, first opened in 1849, and formed a constituent college of Queen's University in Ireland from 1850. In 1882 Queen's University in Ireland was dissolved and Queen's College became part of the Royal University of Ireland. In 1908 Queen's College was elevated to university status as Queen's University of Belfast. It is hoped that when fully listed the historical archives will be transferred to PRONI (see entry 81).

Acquisitions policy: To augment existing records with relevant material.

Archives of organisation: Minutes of Senate, Academic Council and other university committees. Calendars of Queen's College and University. Sets of examination papers.

Major collections: Personal and official papers of former senior officers.

Non-manuscript material: Plans and photographs of university property; photographs of former staff members.

Finding aids: Handlist.

Facilities: Photocopying.

83 Royal Ulster Rifles Regimental Museum

Address: 5 Waring Street, Belfast BT1 2EW

Telephone: (028) 90247279/90232086

Fax: (028) 90232086

E-mail: rurmuseum@yahoo.co.uk

Website: www.rurmuseum.tripod.com

Enquiries: Maj. (retd) M. B. Murphy

Open: Mon–Thurs: 10.00–12.30, 2.00–4.30; Fri: 10.00–12.30, 2.00–3.00.

Access: Generally open to the public; an appointment is recommended.

The museum was first established at the regimental depot, Armagh, in 1932 and transferred to purpose-built premises in Belfast in 1962.

Artefacts and papers connected with the Royal Ulster Rifles, the Royal Irish Rifles, the 83rd and the 86th Regimental and associated units are acquired. The holdings include personal papers, war diaries, record books, medal rolls, casualty lists, photograph albums and histories. A computerised listing is in progress and photocopying is available.

84　St Malachy's College

Address: 36 Antrim Road, Belfast BT15 2AE

Telephone: (028) 90748285

Website: www.stmalachyscollege.com

Enquiries: The Archivist, Dr Eamon Phoenix

Open: Term time, by appointment.

Access: Bona fide researchers.

Historical background: St Malachy's College was founded in 1833 as a Roman Catholic diocesan seminary. It is also the oldest Catholic grammar school in the north of Ireland. The archives were formally opened to researchers in 1987 and are housed in the associated library of Monsignor J. O'Laverty, PP (1828–1906), historian of the RC Diocese of Down and Connor, containing a unique collection of volumes on Irish history.

Acquisitions policy: Papers, photographs and memorabilia relating to the college and its alumni are welcomed.

Archives of organisation: Archives of the college, including lists of former students, c1856–1926, and account books, c1844– .

Major collections: Memoirs and diaries relating to the college and its alumni.
O'Laverty MSS: 16 Gaelic MSS.
Donellan MSS: two Gaelic MSS from the South Armagh/North Louth region, collected by Rev. L. Donnellan (c1900–1960), Co. Armagh.
Correspondence of Muiris ó Droiguneáin (Maurice Drinan), Gaelic scholar (1900–79), relating to Gaelic literature.

Non-manuscript material: Cuttings books of Laurence O'Neill, Lord Mayor of Dublin, c1918–24.
Photographs of students and college.

Finding aids: Catalogue.

Facilities: Photocopying.

Conservation: In-house.

Publications: C. O'Dochartaigh: 'Guide to O'Laverty Manuscripts', in *St Malachy's College Sesquicentennial Record* (Belfast, 1983).

85　Ulster Museum

Address: Botanic Gardens, Belfast BT9 5AB

Telephone: (028) 90383000

Fax: (028) 90383003

Website: www.ulstermuseum.org.uk

Enquiries: The Librarian, Department of History

Open: Mon–Fri: 10.00–12.45, 2.00–5.00.

Access: Bona fide enquirers, by appointment and by prior application in writing, by telephone or in person at the museum.

Historical background: The Ulster Museum has its roots in the Museum of the Belfast Natural History and Philosophical Society (f. 1831) and the Belfast Municipal Art Gallery and Museum (f. 1890), whose collections were amalgamated in 1910. In 1929 the Belfast Museum and Art Gallery was opened on the present site, and in 1962 it was transferred to a statutory board of trustees as the Ulster Museum.

Acquisitions policy: To build up comprehensive collections relating to the north of Ireland and, where appropriate, to Ireland as a whole, in the fields of antiquities, art, botany and zoology, geology, industrial archaeology, local history and numismatics.

Major collections: Antiquities Department: Aztec MS; four Tamil books.
Botany and Zoology Department: Templeton MSS: MSS of John Templeton (1766–1825), botanist, including his journal, 1806–25 (microfiche), Irish flora illustrated by himself, records of mosses and ferns and a list of Irish shells (c25 vols).
Hyndman MSS: numerous notes by George C. Hyndman (1796–1868), Belfast marine biologist and entomologist; also dredging papers, British Association Belfast Dredging Committee, 1844–57.
Thompson MSS: notes and correspondence of William Thompson (1805–52), Belfast naturalist and author of *Natural History of Ireland*.
Other small but important collections: notebooks of P.H. Grierson (1859–1952) on non-marine mollusca, and a checklist of Irish insects by Alexander Henry Haliday (1806–70).

Local History Department: Welch MSS: personal and excursion diaries, natural history notes, memoranda and lists of negatives of Robert J. Welch (1859–1936), photographer and amateur naturalist (c20 vols).

Barber MSS: MSS of Rev. Samuel Barber of Rathfriland, United Irishman.

Non-manuscript material: Local History Department: maps (c300); topographical drawings, paintings and prints (c1000); portraits (c250); posters, including playbills (c900); theatre programmes (c450); newspapers (c400); greetings cards (c2500).

Belfast and other locally printed books, pamphlets, chapbooks and broadsides (c500).

Welch Collection: glass plate negatives by R.J. Welch of Irish subjects (c600).

Hogg Collection: glass plate negatives (c550), lantern slides (c1500) and original prints by Alexander R. Hogg (1870–1939), of Irish (chiefly Belfast and Ulster) subjects, c1900–40.

Historical and Topographical Collection negatives (c3000); a few small and medium-sized collections, c1890-c1965 (c4000). Slides made in the field and from specimens.

Departments other than Local History keep their own specialised collections of negatives and slides.

Antiquities Department: Victorian sketch books of monuments and antiquities; watercolours of Indian temples and South African costume.

Art Department: topographical and portrait specimens (c2000).

Botany and Zoology Department: drawings and watercolours, including watercolours of shells and butterflies by Robert Templeton (1802–92) (c1000).

Geology Department: British Association for the Advancement of Science: Irish Collection photographs (c800).

Finding aids: Art and local history pictorial collections: computerised topographical index. Hogg Collection: classified card catalogue with subject index. Thompson MSS being catalogued.

Facilities: Photocopying. Photography. Microfiche reader.

Publications: A.W. Stelfox: 'John Templeton's Notes on Irish Land and Freshwater Mollusca', *Irish Naturalist*, xxiii (1914), 29.

N. Fisher: 'George Crawford Hyndman's MSS', *Journal of Conchology*, xix (1931), 164.

E.E. Evans and B.S. Turner: *Ireland's Eye: the Photography of Robert John Welch* (Belfast, 1977).

A List of the Photographs in the R.J. Welch Collection in the Ulster Museum, 1: Topography and History (Belfast, 1979); *2: Botany, Geology and Zoology* (Belfast, 1983).

R. Nash and H.C.G. Ross: *Dr Robert Templeton (1802–1892), Naturalist and Artist* (Belfast, 1980).

Concise Catalogue of the Drawings, Paintings and Sculptures in the Ulster Museum (Belfast, 1986).

W.A. Maquire: *Caught in Time: the Photographs of Alexander Hogg of Belfast, 1870–1939* (Belfast, 1986).

86 Jenner Museum

Address: The Chantry, Church Lane, Berkeley, Gloucestershire GL13 9BH

Telephone: (01453) 810631

Fax: (01453) 811690

E-mail: manager@jennermuseum.com

Website: www.dursley-cotswolds-uk.com

Enquiries: The Museum Manager, Dr M. Beeson

Open: By prior arrangement only.

Access: Bona fide researchers, by written appointment.

Historical background: The Jenner Museum was founded in 1967. It collects and displays material relevant to Edward Jenner (1749–1823) and smallpox vaccination.

Acquisitions policy: Material relating to Jenner, smallpox and vaccination from around the world.

Major collections: Prof R.A. Shooter Archive Collection of material on smallpox and vaccination worldwide.

Non-manuscript material: Photographs of smallpox patients, late 19th century–1970s.

Finding aids: Computer catalogue.

Facilities: Photocopying.

Conservation: Contracted out.

87 Berwick upon Tweed Record Office

Parent organisation: Northumberland Archives Service

Address: Berwick upon Tweed Borough Council Offices, Wallace Green, Berwick upon Tweed, Northumberland TD15 1ED

Telephone: (01289) 330044 ext. 230

Fax: (01289) 330540

E-mail: archives@berwickc.demon.co.uk

Website: http://swinhope.demon.co.uk/ genuki/nbl/northumberlandro/berwick.html

Enquiries: The Borough Archivist, Mrs Linda Bankier

Open: Wed, Thurs: 9.30–1.00, 2.00–5.00.

Access: Generally open to the public. Advance notice required for use of microfilm.

Historical background: A branch repository of the Northumberland Archive Service (see entry 920) was opened in 1980 to provide access to the archives of the ancient borough of Berwick upon Tweed. Purpose-converted premises on the same site were opened in 1990, and the office now provides a comprehensive service for North Northumberland.

Acquisitions policy: Documentary sources relating to the history of Berwick upon Tweed and North Northumberland comprising the area covered by the present Berwick upon Tweed Borough Council.

Archives of organisation: Usual local authority record holdings, including Berwick borough archives: guild minute books, 1505–1837; borough accounts, 1603–1841; freeman's records, 16th–20th centuries; Tweedmouth and Spittal manorial records, 1658–1926; borough court records, 17th–19th centuries; quarter sessions records, 1694–1951.

Major collections: Deposited local collections, including business records of Berwick Salmon Fisheries Company, 18th–20th centuries.
Family and estate records of Ford and Etal, Haggerston and Blake (Tillmouth and Twizell) and Crossman (Holy Island).
Non-conformist church records.

Finding aids: Lists of collections.

Facilities: Photocopying by arrangement. Microfilm/fiche readers.

Conservation: Contracted out.

Publications: Berwick-on-Tweed Illustrated 1894–1994.
Leaflets on Family History Resources in office and microfiche for sale.

88 King's Own Scottish Borderers
Regimental Museum and Archives

Address: Regimental Headquarters, The King's Own Scottish Borderers, The Barracks, Berwick upon Tweed, Northumberland TD15 1DG

Fax: (01289) 331928

Website: www.army.mod.uk/infantry/kosb/

Enquiries: Lt. Col. C.G.O. Hogg, DL

Open: By appointment only.

Access: Generally open to the public; an appointment is necessary. There is no charge, but donations are welcomed.

Regimental records are held, 1689– . There are lists and regimental histories. Photocopying is available.

89 Beverley Local Studies Library

Parent organisation: East Riding of Yorkshire Council

Address: Champney Road, Beverley, East Yorkshire HU17 9BG

Telephone: (01482) 885358

Fax: (01482) 881861

E-mail: user@bevlib.yahoo.co.uk

Enquiries: The Team Leader, Reference and Information, Miss Pamela J. Martin

Open: Mon, Wed: 9.30–5.00; Tues, Thurs, Fri: 9.30–7.00; Sat: 9.00–12.00, 1.00–4.00.

Access: Generally open to the public; material available for consultation on request; an appointment is necessary for census microfilms and IGI fiche. A research service is provided and charged for after the first half hour.

Historical background: Beverley Borough Library Local History Department was started in 1906, collecting standard material on all the Yorkshire Ridings, to which was added the former East Riding County Library Yorkshire collection. The library was taken over by Humberside Leisure Services in 1974 and subsequently by the East Riding of Yorkshire Council in 1996.

Acquisitions policy: Purchase, donation and deposit of all types of material. All subject areas are covered, more particularly in relation to Beverley and the East Riding of Yorkshire, but also including other regions of Yorkshire.

Major collections: J.E. Champney Collection of Yorkshire material, donated in 1929.
A small collection of scrapbooks compiled by Gillyatt Sumner containing original MSS and copies of documents, chiefly on history of Beverley and immediate area, c1800–1850.
Small set of MS poll-books for Beverley parliamentary elections, c1800–1820.

Non-manuscript material: Census microfilms, East Riding, 1841–91 (includes some Hull reels, 1841–81, and complete 1891).
Newspaper microfilms.
Large collection of ephemera on Beverley parliamentary elections, c1790–1868; also some for East Riding county elections.
Substantial collection of Beverley playbills, 1817–21.
Stan Owen Collection: photographs, scrapbooks and ephemera relating to Hessle.
W. Stuart Witly photograph and slide collection (c 1000 of each) mainly covering Beverley with some East Riding.

Facilities: Photocopying. Microfilm/fiche reader/printers.

90   East Riding Archive Office

Parent organisation: East Yorkshire Council

Address: County Hall, Beverley, East Yorkshire HU17 9BA

Telephone: (01482) 885007

Fax: (01482) 885463

E-mail: mike.rogers@east-riding-of-yorkshire.gov.uk

Enquiries: The East Riding Archivist, Mr Ian Mason

Open: Mon: 2.00–4.45; Tues: 9.30–8.00; Wed, Thurs: 9.30–4.45, Fri: 9.30–6.00.
Closed last full week in January.

Access: Generally open to the public, by appointment.

Historical background: The office was founded as the East Riding County Record Office in 1953. Following reorganisation in 1974 it became Humberside County Record Office and held the same material, with the exception of some private deposits placed in University of Hull Library (entry 458) and one in the North Yorkshire County Record Office (entry 929). The office acts as the Diocesan Archive Office for York (parish records of the Archdeaconry of the East Riding) and is recognised as a place of deposit for manorial, tithe and public records. Following reoganisation in 1996 it became East Riding Archive Office, holding the same material.

Acquisitions policy: All records relating to the area of the present East Riding or complementing existing collections.

Archives of organisation: East Riding of Yorkshire Council archives, 1996– , and those of all predecessor function authorities, including Humberside County Council, 1974–96, East Riding County Council, 1889–1974, East Riding Quarter Sessions, 1706–1971, urban district and rural district councils, 1894–1974, district/borough councils, 1974–96, and borough councils, including Beverley Corporation, 12th–20th centuries, and Hedon Corporation 14th–20th centuries.
East Riding Register of Deeds, 1708–1976.

Major collections: Family and estate collections, including:
Beaumont family of Beverley and South Cave, 15th–19th centuries; Bethell family of Rise, 12th–20th centuries; Chichester-Constable family of Burton Constable, 12th–20th centuries; Grimston family of Kilnwick and Grimston Garth, 14th–20th centuries, including naval papers of Vice-Admiral Henry Medley (d1747); Harrison Broadley family of Hull and Welton, 16th–20th centuries; Hildyard family of Winestead, 14th–20th centuries; Howard Vyse family of Langton, 13th–19th centuries; Howden Manor estates (Bishopric of Durham), 15th–20th centuries; Kilnwick Percy estates, 16th–19th centuries; Londesborough settled estates, 16th–20th centuries; Osbaldeston and Mitford families of Hunmanby, 13th–20th centuries; Saltmarshe family of Saltmarshe, 16th–20th centuries; Scholfield family of Sand Hall, 16th- 20th centuries; Sotheran Estcourt family, 15th–20th centuries.
Solicitors' records of Clark & Co., Snaith, 14th–20th centuries; MacTurk & Co., South

Cave, 16th–20th centuries; Powell and Young, Pocklington, 15th–20th centuries; Taylor Bromer & Co., Howden, 17th–20th centuries.
Ecclesiastical records: Anglican, Methodist, Baptist, non-conformist and Society of Friends records.
Public records, including shipping registers, Bridlington, 1786–1847, Goole, 1828–94.
Coroners' records, Hull, 1853– .
East Riding and Scunthorpe AHAs, including Goole and Rawcliffe hospitals, 19th–20th centuries.

Non-manuscript material: Microfilms of non-parochial and Friends registers for the area.

Finding aids: Catalogues, indexes and lists. Lists sent to NRA.

Facilities: Photocopying. Photography. Microfilming. Microfilm/fiche readers.

Conservation: Contracted out.

Publications: Handlists and guides for sale/free: list of publications available.

91 Bexley Local Studies & Archives Centre

Parent organisation: Bexley Council

Address: Central Library, Townley Road, Bexley Heath, Kent DA6 7HJ

Telephone: (020) 8301 1545

E-mail: archives.els@bexleycouncil.gov.uk

Website: www.bexley.gov.uk/service/lib-localstudies.html

Enquiries: The Local Studies Manager, Mr Stuart Bligh
The Archivist, Oliver Wooller

Open: Mon–Sat: 9.00–5.00; winter: 9.00–dusk. Annual stock-taking closure early December.

Access: Generally open to the public. Microfilm machines should be booked in advance.

Historical background: Bexley was part of the administrative county of Kent until 1965. The centre was established in 1972 to preserve the records of former local and semi-official authorities in the area and to collect documentary material relevant to local studies. It combines a local studies library and archive repository, and acts as a Diocesan Record Office for Rochester and Southwark.

Acquisitions policy: To increase holdings of material of local relevance.

Major collections: Usual local authority record holdings and deposited collections, including archives of Belvedere, Danson, Footscray Place and Hall Place estates.

Non-manuscript material: OS maps. Large collection of local photographs and prints.

Finding aids: Catalogues and indexes; lists sent to NRA.

Facilities: Photocopying. Microfilm/fiche reader/printers.

Conservation: Contracted out.

Publications: Guide to family history resources and large range of local history publications.

92 Albion Archive

Parent organisation: Biggar Museum Trust

Address: 9 Edinburgh Road, Biggar, Lanarkshire ML12 6AX

Telephone: (01899) 221497

Fax: (01899) 221497

E-mail: sprocketlambie@aol.com

Website: www.biggar-net.co.uk/museums

Enquiries: Mr Brian Lambie

Open: Mon–Fri: 10.00–5.00; weekends by appointment.

Access: Generally open to the public.

Historical background: Biggar Museum Trust was founded in 1972 and controls a number of museums. The archive was previously at Moat Park Heritage Centre (see entry 94).

Acquisitions policy: Albion Motors archives and vehicles; Scottish motoring history in general.

Major collections: Albion Motor Car Company, later Albion Motors Ltd (still later part of British Leyland Motor Corporation): minute-books, documents, photographs, job sheets (164,000) and other memorabilia, 1899–1972.

Non-manuscript material: Job sheets on microfilm. Photograph albums, loose photographs (c8000).

Facilities: Photocopying. Photography. Microfilm readers.

Conservation: Films currently being transferred to CD-Rom.

93 Leadhills Miners' Reading Society Library

Parent organisation: Leadhill Heritage Trust

Address: 69 Main Street, Leadhills, Biggar, Lanarkshire ML12 6XP

Enquiries: The Secretary, the Library Committee, Ms Alison White, 21 Main Street, Leadhills; tel: (01659) 74414

Open: Easter–Oct: Sat, Sun: 2.30–4.00; other times by appointment.

Access: Generally open to the public. The library is run by a committee of voluntary workers; there is a yearly subscription and donations are welcomed.

Historical background: The Leadhills Miners' Reading Society was founded in 1741 and is the oldest subscription library in the British Isles. Allan Ramsay, poet, was born in Leadhills in 1686, and the library commemorates his name. Members included a number of celebrated men, notably William Symington (1763–1831), mining engineer; Dr John Brown (1786–1854), Edinburgh author; and Dr James Braid (?1795–1860), surgeon. The lead mines in the village closed in the 1930s and the membership of the Reading Society declined. In 1940 the Lanarkshire County Council took over the building, but by 1965 the local authority withdrew financial support. In 1969, with the help of grants, the restoration of the building was started and the library reopened in 1972. The library also has a small exhibition of relics.

Acquisitions policy: The library does not purchase, but from time to time receives gifts of books, photographs etc.

Archives of organisation: Library records, including MS 'Members' Roll', 1741–1903; minute-books, 1821– ; ledgers of book loans, 1903– .

Major collections: Mining records, 1738 (Leadhills).
Minute books of the local curling club, early 19th century.

Non-manuscript material: Photographs. Maps of mining grounds.

Finding aids: New catalogue as part of the Scottish Cultural Resources Access Network (SCRAN).

Facilities: Photography permitted on written application to the committee.

Publications: Information leaflets on the library are available.

94 Moat Park Heritage Centre

Parent organisation: Biggar Museum Trust

Address: Moat Park, Biggar, Lanarkshire ML12 6DT

Telephone: (01899) 221050

Fax: (01899) 221050

Website: www.biggar-net.co.uk/museums

Enquiries: The Managers, Margaret Brown and Anne Matheson

Open: Easter–Oct: Mon–Sat: 10.00–5.00; Sun: 2.00–5.00.
Nov–Easter: Mon–Fri: 9.30–5.00;
Sat and Sun by appointment.

Access: Generally open to the public. A charge is made for genealogical research.

Historical background: Biggar Museum Trust was founded in 1972 and controls a number of museums. Local archives have been collected during the past 30 years. The Albion Archive has now been transferred (see entry 92).

Acquisitions policy: Local history material from the Upper Clyde and Tweed valleys.

Major collections: Miscellaneous day books and ledgers of local businesses, 1797– .
School exercise books, 1807–47, and later.
Young family papers (farming), c1800–60.
Biggar Gaslight Co., miscellaneous papers.
Biggar Horticultural Society, 1861– .
Curling Club minutes, 1887–1901.
Architects' plans of local farms and houses, 1838– (mostly 1898–1910).
Rental books/farm accounts books, 18th and 19th centuries.

Non-manuscript material: Photographs and slide collection covering Scotland and Europe, including that of Rev. G. Allan (23,000 negatives and 8000 transparencies), c 1935– c1970.
Transcripts of local MSS in museum.

Finding aids: NRA 13035; NRAS 0419.

Facilities: Photocopying. Microfilm reader.

Conservation: Contracted out.

95 Wanlockhead Miners' Library

Parent organisation: Wanlockhead Museum Trust

Address: Goldscaur Row, Wanlockhead, Biggar, Lanarkshire ML12 6UJ

Telephone: (01659) 74387

Fax: (01659) 74481

Enquiries: Manager, Mr Gerard Godfrey

Open: Apr–Oct: Sun–Sat: 10.00–5.00

Access: Bona fide researchers, by appointment only.

Historical background: A library founded in 1756 by the Miners' Reading Society was taken over by Wanlockhead Museum Trust in 1974 with the intention of preserving the collection and developing an archive of Scottish lead-mining.

Acquisitions policy: The archive is being enlarged, mainly by copies of historical documents and results of mine surveying and industrial archaeology.

Archives of organisation: Records of the library and museum trust.

Major collections: Records of economic and social aspects of the lead-mining industry in Wanlockhead, Leadhills and Strontian.
Records of village institutions, including Curling Society, village band and village council.

Non-manuscript material: Maps and photographs.

Finding aids: Catalogue and list.

Facilities: Photocopying.

96 Shrewsbury RC Diocesan Archive

Parent organisation: Diocese of Shrewsbury

Address: c/o The Curial Offices, 2 Park Road South, Birkenhead L43 4UX

Telephone: (0151) 653 5172

Fax: (0151) 652 9855

E-mail: curia@dioceseofshrewsbury.org

Website: www.dioceseofshrewsbury.org/trustees_pages/main_trustees.htm

Enquiries: Canon John Marmion

Open: By arrangement.

Access: Bona fide researchers, by appointment only.

The Diocese of Shrewsbury was established in 1850 and covers the old geographical counties of Cheshire and Shropshire. The diocesan archives are maintained on a parish- and subject-themed basis, and include parish and school plans. Material on the Catholic families of the diocese is accepted.

97 Wirral Archives

Address: Wirral Museum, Town Hall, Hamilton Street, Birkenhead, Merseyside CH41 5BR

Telephone: (0151) 652 6106/7/8

Fax: (0151) 653 7320

E-mail: archives@wirral-libraries.net

Website: www.wirral.libraries.net

Enquiries: The Archivist

Open: Thurs, Fri: 10.00–5.00; Sat: 10.00–1.00. These hours will be expanded in due course and visitors are recommended to check before visiting.

Access: Generally open to the public; an appointment is advisable.

Historical background: The archives department was established at the time of local government reorganisation in 1974 to administer the records inherited by the Wirral Metropolitan Borough Council. The service is, however, based at a reference library which has been collecting material of local interest (including manuscripts, 1856–), and which had gradually been given custody of the former Birkenhead Borough Council's archives in the 1960s. The library is recognised as a place of deposit for public records. In 2001 the new record office and local history museum opened at the former Birkenhead Town Hall.

Acquisitions policy: To collect, by means of deposit, gift or purchase, records of all kinds relating to the locality.

Archives of organisation: Usual local authority record holdings, late 18th century– , including material relating to Birkenhead Park (designed in 1843–7 by Sir Joseph Paxton and the first municipal park to be laid out at public expense)

and to the Birkenhead Street Railway (the first street tramway in Britain, 1860).

Major collections: Many deposited business and private records, including the following which have wider significance: archives of Unichema Chemicals Ltd, formerly the Bromborough (Wirral) branch of the Price's Patent Candle Co. Ltd; this has material relating to Price's Village, a model village built for the company's workforce at Bromborough Pool in 1853.

Archives, including plans, of Cammell Laird Shipbuilders Ltd of Birkenhead, a major contractor to the Royal Navy, c1810–1993.

Archives of local hospitals, including administrative and clinical records, mid-19th century–.

Some antiquarian collections, including that of John Stafford, a mid-18th century Macclesfield attorney, which relates to Macclesfield Borough and School and to villages throughout Cheshire, 15th–18th centuries.

Finding aids: Handlists and catalogues; sent to NRA.

Facilities: Photocopying. Photography. Microfilm reader/printer.

Publications: Copies of lists available on request.

98 Birmingham and Midland Institute

Address: 9 Margaret Street, Birmingham B3 3BS

Telephone: (0121) 236 3591

Fax: (0121) 212 4577

E-mail: admin@bmi.org.uk

Website: www.bmi.org.uk

Enquiries: The Administrator and General Secretary, Philip St J. Fisher

Open: Mon–Fri: by appointment.

Access: Members of the institute (a small annual fee is charged); others at the discretion of the administrator.

The Birmingham Library was founded in 1779 and amalgamated in 1965 with the Birmingham and Midland Institute, which had been established in 1854. Records of the institute including minutes, are maintained from its foundation. See J. Hunt's *History of Birmingham and Midland Institute* (1954).

Library holdings relate to the Midland counties (literary, topographical and biographical).

99 Birmingham Archdiocesan Archives

Parent organisation: Birmingham Roman Catholic Archdiocese

Address: Cathedral House, St Chad's Queensway, Birmingham, West Midlands B4 6EU

Telephone: (0121) 236 2251

Fax: (0121) 233 9266

Enquiries: The Archivist, Rev. Dr J. Sharp

Open: Mon–Fri: 9.00–5.00, by prior appointment.

Access: Bona fide scholars, on written application.

Historical background: The records of the Vicars Apostolic of the Midland district are one of the best sources for the history of the Roman Catholic body in England in the 18th century. In 1685, at the request of James II, episcopal government was re-established by the Vicars Apostolic, whose aim throughout the 18th century was to ensure the subordination of the regular clergy to episcopal authority. With the exception of the Bishop of the Western Vicariate they were chosen from the secular clergy and were delegates of the Pope, depending on Rome for faculties to govern their districts. There are some gaps in the archive, notably documents lost in the early 19th century when Bishop Milner, 1806–26, moved to Wolverhampton, and when Dr Kirk abstracted papers for his *Church History.* Many of the records were received from Oscott College (see entry 1152).

Archives of organisation: Records of the Vicars Apostolic of the Midland district, 1700–1850, and of the Bishops of Birmingham, 1850–1900, including correspondence with agents of the Vicars Apostolic in Rome, late 18th, early 19th centuries; Bishops' and Archbishops' Papers 1900–65.

Records of the daily administration of the diocese and parishes, 1830–1954.

Deeds of the Manor of Erdington, and of the Coyney family properties in north Staffordshire, 13th–17th centuries.

Archives, including annals, ledgers, correspondence and memoirs, of Sedgley Park School,

1763– , and St Wilfrid's College, Cotton, 1873– ; Besford Court School, 1917–95.
Papers of Canon F.W. Drinkwater and of Monsignor A.F. Davis (1903–86).

Finding aids: Lists at NRA.

Facilities: Photocopying. Scanning.

100 Birmingham Central Library

Address: Chamberlain Square, Birmingham B3 3HQ

Telephone: (0121) 303 2751/2614/2615

Fax: (0121) 233 4458

E-mail: bham.socialsciences@dial.pipex.com

Website: www.birmingham.gov.uk

Enquiries: The Head of Service (Social Sciences), Ms R. Neylin
The Head of Music Services, Mr J. Gough
The Head of Service (Local Studies & History), Mr. P. Drake

Open: Mon–Fri: 9.00–8.00; Sat: 9.00–5.00.

Access: Generally open to the public. Archives are unrestricted, except where controlled by specific agreement with the record owner.

Historical background: The library first opened in 1866 but was completely destroyed by fire in 1879. It reopened later that year and moved into new premises which it occupied until 1973, when it moved into its present building. It is particularly noted for its unique Shakespeare Library (perhaps second only in the world to the Folger Library) and for a number of special collections of printed books.

Acquisitions policy: Generally, archive materials are collected by the Birmingham City Archives (entry 101), but the Social Sciences Service Area has acquired significant archives relating to political, labour and trade-union movements in Birmingham and, where appropriate, wider afield. It is also the official repository for records from the Co-operative Union. In addition, significant material relating to transport, railways in particular, is acquired.

Major collections: Social Sciences: trade and statistical returns from Co-operative Union member societies; Co-operative Wholesale Society Wage Negotiations Archive; archives of the Birmingham Labour Party and the Birmingham Conservative Party; various local

branch records of trade unions; records of the Birmingham Co-operative Movement and the Workers Educational Association; minutes and records of the General Strike in Birmingham; archives of individual Labour activists.
Railway Collection: Hayden diaries of Swindon works, George Bradshaw letters, 19th century; Railway & Canal Historical Society Collection, 1825– .

Non-manuscript material: Railway Collection: plans, architectural drawings and a large collection of photographs; also Wingate Bett Transport Ticket Collection, 1840– (*c*1 million).
Local Studies and History of Birmingham: photographic archives, including Francis Frith archive, 1860s–1960s; Sir Benjamin Stone Collection; Warwickshire Photographic Survey; Dyche Collection: 20th-century portraits of black Birmingham people; Francis Bedford Collection.
Collection of newspapers, pamphlets, seals and maps.
London, Midland & Scottish Railway and British Rail (Residual) Law Libraries.

Finding aids: Handlists, copies sent to NRA; index to Local Studies Collection; partial index to photographic collection.

Facilities: Photocopying. Photography. Microfilm/fiche readers/printers.

Conservation: Conservation workshop with two staff on site. Some additional routine work contracted out to commercial binders.

Publications: Birmingham Public Libraries: *Catalogue of the Birmingham Collection* (1918; suppl., 1931).
M. Large: 'Sources of Labour History: Primary Material in the Social Sciences Department of Birmingham Library', in A. Wright and R. Shackleton: *Worlds of Labour: Essays in Birmingham Labour History* (Birmingham, 1983).
P. James: *Coming to Light: Birmingham's Photographic Collections* (1998).

101 Birmingham City Archives

Parent organisation: Birmingham City Council

Address: Central Library, Chamberlain Square, Birmingham B3 3HQ

Telephone: (0121) 303 4217

Fax: (0121) 464 1176

E-mail: archives@birmingham.gov.uk

Website: www.birmingham.gov.uk

Enquiries: The Senior Archivist, Public Services, Siân Roberts

Open: Mon, Tues, Fri, Sat: 9.00–5.00; Thurs: 9.00–8.00.

Access: Generally open to the public. Records are closed for 50 years, except where legislation or agreements with owners provide otherwise. A paid genealogical research service is available.

Historical background: The City Archives originated as the manuscript collections of Birmingham Central Library (entry 100). They were separately administered from 1932 to 1968 and then reintegrated with the library collections until 1984, when they again became independent. The title Birmingham City Archives was adopted in 1994. It acts as the Diocesan Record Office for Birmingham (parish records) and is recognised as a place of deposit for public records.

Acquisitions policy: To collect and preserve archival material relating to the City of Birmingham, its people, businesses and institutions. Records of some regional and national organisations based in the city are also held. The collections include deeds and estate and family papers relating to the surrounding area acquired before the present network of county record offices was established. Among the places within the present collecting area are the ancient parishes of Birmingham: Aston, Edgbaston, Frankley, Handsworth, Harborne, Kings Norton, Northfield, Sheldon, Sutton Coldfield and Yardley.

Archives of organisation: Official records, including West Midlands County Council, 1974–86; Birmingham City Council archives, 1736– ; quarter sessions records, 1839– ; Magistrates' court records, 1860– ; coroners' records, 1875– ; school records, 1722– ; and hospital records, 1756– .

Major collections: Anglican diocesan and parish records for the diocese of Birmingham and parish records for the part of the diocese within the city boundary, 16th–20th centuries; nonconformist church records, 18th–20th centuries.

Business archives include the records of Boulton & Watt, steam engine manufacturers, with the personal, scientific and business correspondence of James Watt and Matthew Boulton; John Hardman & Co., stained glass and metalwork manufacturers, 1839–1970; Boulton & Fothergill, metalwork and silver manufacturers; Soho Mint Ltd, 18th–19th centuries; Metropolitan Cammell Ltd, railway/rolling stock manufacturers, 1860–1940; BSA Ltd, motor-cycle and gun manufacturers, 1880–1960; IMI plc, ammunition and metalwork manufacturers, 1860–1940; Albright & Wilson, phosphorus manufacturers, 1840–1940; Birmingham Battery & Metal Co., 1836–1991.

British Organ Archive: accounts, drawings and correspondence of British organ-building firms, 19th–20th centuries, collected by the British Institute of Organ Studies, and formerly deposited at the University of Keele Library (see entry 476).

Records of authorities and associations include those of West Midlands Regional Health Authority, 1948– ; National Association of Health Authorities; British Jewellery & Giftware Federation and its predecessors, 1850– ; Birmingham Botanical Gardens, 1820– ; Birmingham Royal Institution for the Blind, 1848– ; Middlemore Homes, 1870– ; Birmingham Triennial Music Festival, c1806–1912.

Family and estate papers include those of Quakers such as the Albright, Cadbury, Hutton and Russell families, as well as records of the Calthorpe, Colmore, Gooch, Holte, Ryland and Taylor estates, which substantially controlled the development of the city, and records of the Hagley Hall, Hams Hall, Westwood Park, Coleshill Park and Elford Hall estates outside the city.

Finding aids: Catalogues are available for about 60 per cent of the collections. Indexes by personal name, place, name and subject. Special indexes for apprenticeships and maps. Lists are sent to the NRA.

Facilities: Photocopying. Photography.

Conservation: Conservation facilities on site.

Publications: Birmingham Public Libraries: *Catalogue of the Birmingham Collection* (1918; suppl., 1931).

A. Andrews: 'The Birmingham Reference Library', *Archives*, v (1951).

U. Rayska: 'The Archives Section of Birmingham Reference Library', *Archives*, liv (1978).

N.W. Kingsley: *Guide to the Birmingham City Archives* (on web page).

102 Birmingham Museum and Art Gallery

Parent organisation: Birmingham City Council

Address: Chamberlain Square, Birmingham B3 3DH

Telephone: (0121) 303 2834

Fax: (0121) 303 1394

Website: www.bmag.org.uk

Enquiries: The Principal Curator, Jane Farrington

Open: By arrangement only.

Access: Bona fide researchers, strictly by prior appointment.

Historical background: Birmingham Museum and Art Gallery officially opened in 1885, although a Corporation Gallery had opened in 1867. Many of the collections had been acquired by the corporation before that date.

Acquisitions policy: Material relevant to items in the collection and collection history, artists' papers acquired with items, museum records and historical material.

Archives of organisation: Documentation of the collections, 1885– , including museum day-books.

Major collections: Artists' papers of A.J. Gaskin, (1862–1928), and Joseph Southall (1861–1944).
Business records of Hardman Co. (stained glass), 1840s–1948.

Non-manuscript material: Photographs of Morris, Marshall, Faulkener & Co. (stained glass).

Publications: S. Davies: *By the Games of Industry: Birmingham Museums and Art Galleries, 1885–1985* (1985).

103 Birmingham Oratory

Address: 141 Hagley Road, Edgbaston, Birmingham B16 8UE

Telephone: (0121) 454 0496

Fax: (0121) 455 8160

E-mail: oratory@globalnet.co.uk

Enquiries: The Librarian and Archivist, Mr Gerard Tracey

Open: Mon–Fri, by arrangement only.

Access: Bona fide researchers or enquirers who have previously contacted the archivist. Records relating to domestic affairs of the oratory may be closed.

Historical background: The oratory was founded in 1847 by John Henry Newman (1801–90), who subsequently founded the Brompton Oratory (entry 570). He left his extensive collection of papers to the oratory, and soon after his death it began to collect together the letters that he had sent out. In the past there has not been a clear distinction made between archives of the oratory and collections of papers given by those connected with it.

Acquisitions policy: Letters by Newman and complementary material are acquired.

Archives of organisation: Records of projects and foundations connected with the oratory, e.g. Catholic University of Ireland, Oratory Public School and other minor educational foundations. Records relating to domestic affairs of the oratory.

Major collections: Documents relating to Newman (c120,000): personal papers, theological memoranda, administrative notes, correspondence, 1808–90 (420 files divided into four main subject divisions), also authenticated copies of his letters. These include correspondence of his companions, e.g. Edward Caswall (1814–78), hymn-writer, Ignatius Ryder and Ambrose St John, and those connected with him, e.g. Thomas Mosley and William Palmer (1811–79). A large collection of papers about Newman, assembled since his death.
Papers of members of the oratory, including literary MSS.

Finding aids: Newman letters, indexed by date and correspondents. Description of collection and catalogue of other materials (by type): NRA 27809.

Facilities: Photocopying. Photography.

104 King Edward VI Schools in Birmingham

Address: Foundation Office, Schools of King Edward VI in Birmingham, Edgbaston Park Road, Birmingham B15 2UD

Telephone: (0121) 472 1147 ext. 220

Fax: (0121) 415 6000

Enquiries: The Resources Librarian, Kerry York

Open: Mon–Wed: 9.15–5.00; Thurs: 9.00–5.00; Fri: 9.00–4.30.

Access: Generally open to the public; an appointment is advisable.

Historical background: King Edward's School was founded in 1552. More schools were established in the 18th and 19th centuries. Today seven schools exist under one administrative umbrella also known as King Edward VI Foundation. Since 1552, the foundation has also been a significant local landowner. The Foundation Archive was established in 1980.

See also King Edward VI College (entry 1144).

Acquisitions policy: No formal acquisitions policy; records are accepted from former pupils, teachers and governors if relevant to schools.

Archives of organisation: Records of governing body and individual schools, 1552– .

Major collections: Few surviving records of the Guild of the Holy Cross in Birmingham, 14th century.

Non-manuscript material: Architectural plans, including Sir Charles Barry's plans of King Edward's School, New Street, 1833; estate surveys; photographs.

Finding aids: MS list at Foundation Office; no external copy.

Facilities: Photocopying at the discretion of the librarian.

Conservation: Contracted out.

Publications: Dugdale Society, iv (ed. W.F. Carter); vii (ed. W.F. Carter and E.A.B. Barnard); xx (ed. P.B. Chatwin); xxv (ed. P.B. Chatwin); xxx (ed. J. Izon).

T.W. Hutton: *King Edward's School, Birmingham 1552–1952* (1952).

W.I. Candlet et al: *King Edward VI High School for Girls, Birmingham* (1971).

C. Boardman: *Foundation and City Governors of the Schools of King Edward VI, Birmingham* (1985)

A. Trott: *No Place for Fop or Idler. Story of King Edward's School, Birmingham* (1992).

105 Newman College Library and Information Services

Parent organisation: Newman College of Higher Education

Address: Bartley Green, Birmingham B32 3NT

Telephone: (0121) 476 1181 ext. 208

Fax: (0121) 476 1196

E-mail: library@newman.ac.uk

Website: www.newman.ac.uk

Enquiries: The College Librarian, Mrs C. Rock

Open: Mon–Fri: 9.00–5.00.

Access: Generally open to the public.

Historical background: Founded in 1968 by the Catholic Education Council, Newman College is a Catholic college of higher education.

Acquisitions policy: To strengthen existing research collections.

Major collections: Collection on life and works of John Henry Newman (1801–90) (c500 items).
West Midlands Local History Collection (c4000 items).

Non-manuscript material: WMLH Collection includes maps, photographs and oral history interviews.

Finding aids: Integrated library catalogue available on-line at www.libweb.newman.ac.uk.

Facilities: Photocopying. Microfilm/fiche reader/printer.

Conservation: Contracted out.

106 St Paul's Convent Archive

Parent organisation: Sisters of St Paul Apostle

Address: St Paul's Convent, Selly Park, Birmingham B29 7LL

Telephone: (0121) 415 6100

Fax: (0121) 414 1063

Enquiries: The Archivist, Sr Phyllis Brady

Open: By prior arrangement.

Access: Bona fide researchers, with a suitable recommendation.

Historical background: The congregation was established in 1847. It now runs St Paul's College of Education and other schools.

Acquisitions policy: To maintain and consolidate the archives.

Archives of organisation: Correspondence relating to the foundation and life of the congregation, 1847– .
Data concerning apostolates' property, 1847– .
Administrative records of the congregation, including constitutions, acts of chapters, council meetings, registers of members, legal documents, baptismal, birth and death certificates, wills, contracts, journals, diaries, annals, circular letters.
Correspondence with Rome, bishops and other ecclesiastics.
St Paul's College of Education archive and administrative records of other second-level schools owned by the congregation.

Non-manuscript material: Photographs, slides, tapes, videos and artefacts relating to the history and work of the convent. Theses.

Finding aids: Listing in progress.

Facilities: Photocopying.

107 University of Birmingham Information Services

Address: Birmingham, West Midlands

A Special Collections Department

Address: Heslop Room, Main Library, Edgbaston, Birmingham B15 2TT

Telephone: (0121) 414 5838

Fax: (0121) 471 4691

E-mail: special-collections@bham.ac.uk

Website: www.is.bham.ac.uk/specialcoll/

Enquiries: The University Archivist, Miss Christine Penney

Open: Mon–Fri: 9.00–5.00; Sat: 10.00–2.00 (1.00 in vacation).
Closed for one week in the summer vacation.

Access: Open to bona fide researchers. All new readers should apply in advance to the University Archivist and must provide a letter of introduction from a person of recognised status.

Historical background: The University of Birmingham, which received its royal charter in 1900, originated in Mason Science College, which was founded in 1880 and incorporated as Mason University College in 1897. In 1999 Westhill College, which had previously amalgamated with Selly Oak College, became part of the university. The Special Collections Department is now part of the Collection Management Division of Information Services at the University of Birmingham, a service which was formed in 1995 following a convergence of the University Library, the Academic Computing Service, Film & Television Services and the Centre for Computer Based Learning. The department is housed in the Main Library, which has its origins in the library of Mason Science College, and archives and manuscripts have been acquired from the late 1950s. It is a recognised place of deposit for public records.

Acquisitions policy: To build and strengthen existing collections and to collect in the fields where active academic research is taking place in the university, by purchase, deposit or donation.

Archives of organisation: Historical records of the University of Birmingham (f.1900) and of its predecessor institutions, Mason College (f.1880) and Queen's College (f.1828 as the Birmingham School of Medicine and Surgery, and transferred to Mason College in 1892).

Major collections: Correspondence and papers of political and diplomatic figures including Sir John Elijah Blunt (1832–1916); Austen Chamberlain (1863–1937); Joseph Chamberlain (1836–1914); Neville Chamberlain (1869–1940); William Harbutt Dawson (1860–1948); Anthony Eden (1897–1977), 1st Earl of Avon; Charles Masterman (1873–1927); Sir Oswald Mosley (1896–1980); Nikolai Shishkin.
Literary and music manuscripts, including papers of Sir Granville Bantock (1868–1946); Martin Booth (b.1944); Noel Coward (1899–1973); Sir Edward Elgar (1857–1934); John Galsworthy (1867–1933); David Lodge (b.1935); Harriet Martineau (1802–76); Henry Reed (1914–86); Frances Brett Young (1884–1954); and the Shaw Hellier Collection of contemporary copies of Handel and Purcell scores.
Papers of present and former members of the university and its predecessor institutions, including Professors Lancelot T. Hogben (1895–1975); Maurice Stacey (1907–94); Edward Arbert (1836–1912); and Sir Oliver Lodge (1851–1940).
Missionary archives, including records of the Church Missionary Society, 1799– , and Church of England Zenana Missionary Society,

1880–1957, and personal papers of more than 300 missionaries connected with these societies. Institutional archives and personal papers of individuals relating to sport, principally athletics, including records of the Amateur Athletic Association (f.1880) and of the Midland, Northern and Southern Counties Athletic Association and papers of Harold Abrahams (1899–1978) and Joe Binks (1874–1966).

Records of other organisations and institutions include British Cotton Growing Association; Church Pastoral Aid Society; Monumental Brass Society, 20th century, including many original brass rubbings; Royal Institute of Public Administration (f.1922); St John's College, Nottingham (formerly London College of Divinity); Young Men's Christian Association, c1850–1998; various local government associations, including the Association of Metropolitan Authorities, Association of County Councils and Association of District Councils and their predecessors.

Other personal, family and local history collections, including papers of Bishop E.W. Barnes (1874–1953), Bishop of Birmingham; Leonard Jay (1888–1963), printer; Leslie Weatherhead (1893–1976), Methodist minister and author; Vassili Alexandrovich Pashkov (1870–1901), Russian army officer and Baptist convert; Cadbury family, relating to the cocoa trade in West Africa, 19th–20th centuries; letters of Jerningham and Bedingfeld families of Norfolk, 1780–1843; family and antiquarian collections relating to Shropshire; personal travel diaries, 18th–20th centuries.

Small collection of MSS of medical interest.

Non-manuscript material: Photographs (164 portfolios) taken by or for Sir Lawrence Alma-Tadema (1836–1912), with some of his drawings and a few prints, 19th century.

Finding aids: Computerised catalogue. Handlists for most collections. Lists sent to NRA.

Facilities: Photocopying. Photography. Microfilming/fiching. Microfilm/fiche readers/printers.

Conservation: In-house service provided by the Bindery and Conservation Department.

Publications: B.S. Benedikz: *The Chamberlain Collection Introduction and Guide* (1978).
C.L. Penney: 'The Manuscript Collections of the University of Birmingham', *Archives*, XVII (1986).

B.S. Benedikz: 'The Political Archives of Birmingham University', *Diplomacy and Statecraft*, 2 (1991).
R. Keen: 'The Church Missionary Society Archives', *Catholic Archives*, 12 (1992).
C.L. Penney: 'Mission archives', in Lynne Price, Juan Sepulveda and Graeme Smith (eds), *Mission Matters* (1997).
University of Birmingham: *Research Libraries Bulletin*, 1– (Winter 1994–).

B Selly Oak Campus: Orchard Learning Resources Centre

Address: Hamilton Drive, Weoley Park Road,, Birmingham B29 6QW

Telephone: (0121) 415 2255

Fax: (0121) 415 2273

E-mail: olrc@bham.ac.uk

Website: www.is.bham.ac.uk/olrc/special.htm

Enquiries: The Deputy Director, Meline E. Nielsen

Open: Term: Mon–Fri: 9.00–5.00.
Vacation: Mon–Fri: 9.00–4.30.

Access: Bona fide researchers.

Historical background: Selly Oak Colleges were a loose confederation of 20th-century inter-denominational training and mission colleges, the earliest of which was Woodbrooke College (see entry 108). In 1997 Selly Oak College integrated with Westhill College which has since become part of the University of Birmingham. The organisational archives remain with the administrative departments and are not administered by OLRC.

Acquisitions policy: Archives of missionary and mission history relevance.

Major collections: Mingana Collection of Syriac and Arabic manuscripts from the Christian and Muslim traditions (c3000).
Harold Turner Collection relating to new religious movements comprising documents from journals, books, unpublished papers, newspapers, original material from the movements themselves, and dissertations.
Archives of the Student Christian Movement (including the Church Education Movement), 1890– ; also records of the Indian Church Aid Association; Churches of Christ; Korea Mission; Institute of Rural Life, all 20th century.

Papers of individual missionaries, e.g. James Edward Leslie Newbigin, David Paton, William Paton (1886–1943) and W.C. Willoughby.

Finding aids: On-line catalogues. Indexes.

Facilities: Photocopying. Microfiche reader.

C Shakespeare Institute Library

Address: Stratford-upon-Avon, Warwickshire

E-mail: j.a.shaw@bham.ac.uk

Website: www.is.bham.ac.uk/specialcoll/ sites_sha.htm

Enquiries: The Librarian, Jim Shaw

Open: Mon–Thurs: 9.30–8.00; Fri–Sat: 9.00–5.00

Access: Bona fide researchers.

Historical background: The Shakespeare Institute was founded in 1951 by Allardyce Nicol, Professor of Drama at the University of Birmingham.

Acquisitions policy: Theatre archives with relevance to the work of the Institute.

Major collections: Archives of the New Shakespeare Company, 1962-, relating to the Open Air Theatre productions in Regent's Park and tours.
Prompt books and scripts of the Renaissance Theatre Company, 1986– .

Finding aids: On-line collection-level descriptions.

108 Woodbrooke Quaker Study Centre

Address: 1046 Bristol Road, Birmingham B29 6LJ

Telephone: (0121) 472 5171

Fax: (0121) 472 5173

E-mail: enquiries@woodbrooke.org.uk

Website: www.woodbrooke.org.uk

Enquiries: The Librarian, Mary Jo Clogg

Open: Mon–Fri: 9.00–5.00 (subject to alteration).

Access: Generally open to the public; an appointment is necessary.

Historical background: The college, one of the Selly Oak Colleges, was founded in 1903. It is a Quaker centre for religious, social, peace and international studies.

Acquisitions policy: Archives accepted of Woodbrooke connections only.

Archives of organisation: Archives of the college, including minutes of committees, students' lists, timetables and publicity, 1903– .

Major collections: Papers of James Rendel Harris (1852–1941), biblical scholar and director of Woodbrooke, 1903–18.

Non-manuscript material: Photograph collection.
Bevan-Naish collection of 17th-century tracts.
Mingana Collection of Syriac MSS (c60 boxes of microfilm; originals at University of Birmingham, Selly Oak Campus, see entry107B).

Finding aids: Lists.

Facilities: Photocopying.

Publications: R. Davis (ed.): *Woodbrooke, 1923–1953* (London, 1953).
R. Ralph Barlow: *Woodbrooke, 1953–1978: a Documentary Account*, ed. D.B. Gray (York, 1982).

109 Blackburn Central Library Local Studies Department

Parent organisation: Blackburn with Darwen Borough Council

Address: Town Hall Street, Blackburn, Lancashire BB2 1AG

Telephone: (01254) 661221

Fax: (01254) 690539

Website: www.blackburn.gov.uk/library

Enquiries: The Head of Cultural Services, Mrs N.L. Monks

Open: Mon–Wed: 9.30–7.00; Thur, Fri 9.30–5.00; Sat: 9.30–4.30; Sun: 11.00–3.00.

Access: Generally open to the public; a prior appointment is desirable for some of the material, e.g. Wolstenholme Collection, Lees Hall Collection.

Historical background: Blackburn Public Library was formed in 1860. From 1974–98, it formed part of Lancashire County Library. Unitary status was regained in 1998, when the new Borough of Blackburn with Darwen was formed.

Acquisitions policy: Collections which relate to the history, topography, geology, natural history and current state of the geographic area of Blackburn with Darwen and immediate surrounding environs (where appropriate), by purchase and donation.

Major collections: General local history collection for the Blackburn area, including Wolstenholme Collection relating to William Wolstenholme, blind organist, and Lees Hall Collection of temperance material.

Non-manuscript material: Photograph collection (c6000 items).

Finding aids: Newspaper index, 1793–1829, 1837–85, 1887–8, 1891–6. Index to photographs and map index.

Facilities: Photocopying. Photography by arrangement. Microfilm reader/printer.

Conservation: Contracted out.

Publications: Section in *Local Studies in Lancashire.*

110 Blackburn Museum and Art Gallery

Parent organisation: Blackburn with Darwen Borough Council

Address: Museum Street, Blackburn, Lancashire BB1 7AJ

Telephone: (01254) 667130

Fax: (01254) 695370

E-mail: stephen.whittle@blackburn.gov.uk

Website: www.blackburn.gov.uk/museum/due.htm

Enquiries: The Curator

Open: Tues–Sat: 10.00–4.45.

Access: Bona fide scholars.

Historical background: The Blackburn Museum was founded in 1862 and has been in its present premises since 1874. The museum maintains the collections of the East Lancashire Regimental Museum, founded in 1934, and Lewis Textile Museum, founded in 1938. The Feilden Papers are now with Lancashire Record Office (see entry 1044).

Acquisitions policy: Local history, regimental history and the textile trade.

Major collections: The Regimental Museum Collection includes records of the East Lancashire Regiment.
The Hait Collection of Western and Islamic MSS.

Non-manuscript material: Local history collection includes some films and cassette recordings. Textile history collection includes a number of 19th-century pattern books.

Finding aids: Handlists and database.

Facilities: Photocopying. Photography and microfilming by arrangement.

Publications: J. Horrocks: *My Dear Parents: an Englishman's Letters Home from the American Civil War* (London, 1982).
J. Aytoun: *Redcoats in the Caribbean* (Blackburn, 1984).

111 West Lothian Council Local History Library

Parent organisation: West Lothian Council

Address: Hopefield Road, Blackburn, West Lothian EH47 7HZ

Telephone: (01506) 776331

Fax: (01506) 776345

E-mail: sybil.cavanagh@westlothian.gov.uk

Website: www.westlothian.gov.uk/libraries/

Enquiries: The Local Collection Librarian, Mrs M.S. Cavanagh

Open: Mon–Thurs: 8.30–5.00; Fri: 8.30–4.00; Sat (1st of each month): 9.00–1.00.

Access: Generally open to the public.

Historical background: The library service was started in 1924, and local material has been collected since 1975.

Acquisitions policy: To improve existing collections relating to local history of West Lothian.

Major collections: Council minutes for Armadale Town, Bathgate Town, Linlithgow Town, Whitburn Town, and West Lothian County, 19th and 20th centuries.
District council minutes for Torphichen and Bathgate, East Calder, West Calder, Uphall and Whitburn, 19th and 20th centuries.

Some parochial board and parish council minutes.

Non-manuscript material: Photographs (*c*10,000), maps, videos.
Local newspapers, 1873– .
Old parish records and census returns, 1841–91 (microfilm).

Finding aids: Catalogue of all holdings. Various lists and indexes.

Facilities: Photocopying. Microfilm/fiche reader/printer.

Conservation: Contracted out.

*Publications: Guide to the Collection.
Guide to Family History Resources in the Collection.*

112   Blackpool Reference Library

Parent organisation: Blackpool Borough Council

Address: Queen Street, Blackpool, Lancashire FY1 1PX

Telephone: (01253) 478090

Fax: (01253) 478071

Enquiries: The Head of Cultural Services, Mrs P. Hansell.
The Reference and Local Studies Librarian, Miss G.H. Marsland

Open: Mon, Fri: 9.00–5.00; Wed, Sat: 10.00–5.00; Tues, Thur: 9.00–7.00.

Access: Generally open to the public. It is advisable to book in advance to use the microfilm and microfiche readers and essential for reader printers.

Historical background: The collection concentrates mostly on the town of Blackpool and its history. Material about neighbouring areas has been purchased only in recent years.

Acquisitions policy: Documents relating to Blackpool and its history are purchased. Relevant donations are willingly accepted.

Major collections: Local history collection, principally of non-MS material.

Non-manuscript material: Local newspaper, 1873– (on microfilm).
Photographs and postcards relating to local subjects (*c*5000).

Finding aids: Bibliography of family history resources (regularly updated).

Facilities: Photocopying. Photography with permission only. Microfilm/fiche readers/printers.

113   Royal Signals Museum

Parent organisation: Royal Signals Museum Trust

Address: Blandford Camp, Blandford Forum, Dorset DT11 8RH

Telephone: (01285) 482413

Fax: (01258) 482084

E-mail: royalsignalsmuseum@mail.army.org.uk

Website: www.royalsignals.army.org.uk/museum/

Enquiries: The Assistant Archivist, Mr T. A. Stankus

Open: Mon–Fri: 10.00–5.00.

Access: Bona fide researchers; as space is limited, an appointment is necessary.

Historical background: The library and archives were formed in 1967, when the Royal Signals Museum was opened at Blandford Camp. The collection covers the history of army communications from the Crimean War to the present time. It also covers the history of the Royal Engineer Telegraph Battalions, the Royal Engineer Signal Service and the Royal Corps of Signals, which was formed in 1920. Records of the Uxbridge and Middlesex Yeomanry Cavalry, previously held by the Middlesex Yeomanry and Signals Historical Trust, Harrow-on-the-Hill, have been transferred to the museum for safekeeping.

Acquisitions policy: To collect and preserve all relevant material relating to the history of military communications by all means, i.e. radio, line, despatch rider service, pigeons. Purchases of relevant material are made.

Major collections: Diaries, journals and letters of officers and soldiers who have served in the RE Telegraph Battalions, the Signal Service and the Royal Signals, 19th and 20th centuries.
Details of Royal Signals units, which include a number of historical records.
Uxbridge and Middlesex Yeomanry Cavalry (1797 and 1830 respectively): archives, plus

those of subsequent units and other yeomanry companies and signals regiments.

Non-manuscript material: Personal photographic collections donated by ex-members of the corps.
Technical manuals dealing with military radio and line equipment.

Finding aids: General index to all collections. Index to photographic collection.

Facilities: Photocopying and photography by prior appointment.

114 Bodmin Town Museum

Parent organisation: Bodmin Town Council

Address: Mount Folly, Bodmin, Cornwall PL31 2HQ

Telephone: (01208) 77067

Fax: (01208) 76616

E-mail: bodmin.museum@ukonline.co.uk

Website: www.chain.org.uk/bodmin-museum/

Enquiries: The Chairman, E.J. Chapman

Open: Easter to end October, by arrangement.

Access: Generally open to the public, by written appointment.

The museum was started by a local historian, Mr Les Long, and taken over by the council in its present location in 1986. It holds Bodmin borough records, 1702–1974, and the Mayor's Coal Fund account books, 1922–54, as well as a photograph collection. Indexes are available. See NRA 38716.

115 Bolton Archive and Local Studies Service

Parent organisation: Bolton Metropolitan Borough Council

Address: Central Library, Civic Centre, Le Mans Crescent, Bolton, Lancashire BL1 1SE

Telephone: office hours (weekdays): (01204) 333333. Tues & Thurs evenings and Sats: (01204) 391591

Fax: (01204) 332225

E-mail: archives.library@bolton.gov.uk

Website: http://bold.bolton.gov.uk/library

Enquiries: The Archivist: Ms Samantha Collenette
The Local Studies Librarian, Mr B.D. Mills

Open: Tues, Thurs: 9.30–7.30; Wed, Fri: 9.30–5.30; Sat: 9.30–5.00.

Access: Generally open to the public; prior notice is appreciated, but not essential. Advance booking is advisable for access to microform holdings. Archives are not produced from storage between 12.00 and 2.00 on Saturdays.

Historical background: The service was established in 1990 by the amalgamation of the Archive Service (f. 1974) and the Local Studies Section of the Central Reference Library (f. 1853). It is recognised as a place of deposit for public records.

Acquisitions policy: To collect and preserve archives, printed, audio-visual and other material relating to the area administered by Bolton Metropolitan Borough Council.

Archives of organisation: Bolton Borough quarter sessions records, 1839–1971.
Bolton Borough Magistrates' Court records, 1839–1989.
Records of Bolton MBC and eight predecessor local authorities (Bolton CB, Farnworth MB, Blackrod UD, Horwich UD, Kearsley UD, Little Lever UD, Turton UD and Westhoughton UD), with inherited archives, including, townships and civil parishes, 1640– ; Great Bolton and Little Bolton Improvement Trustees, 1792–1850; Turton and Entwistle Reservoir Commissioners, 1832–66; Irwell Valley Water Board, 1853–1963; Bolton Poor Law Union, 1837–1929; Bolton and Heaton School Boards, 1883–98; Bolton Rural District Council, 1872–98.

Major collections: Archives of Non-conformist and Methodist churches, 18th–20th centuries.
Records of local estates, families and individuals, including Ainsworth of Smithills, Crompton of Hall i'th'Wood (including papers of Samuel Crompton, inventor of the spinning mule), Heywood of Bolton, 16th–20th centuries.
Business records, including cotton spinning and manufacture, bleaching and finishing; engineering; coal-mining; papermaking; brewing; tanning and leather manufacture, architecture, 17th–20th centuries.
Records of local charities, societies, trade unions and employers' organisations, 19th–20th centuries.

Archives of the Bolton Whitman Fellowship, including correspondence of the American poet Walt Whitman, 1819–92.

MSS maps and plans of estates, enclosure, turnpike roads, railways, canals, bleachworks, coal mines and other industrial premises, waterworks, 1620–1950.

Non-manuscript material: Local history collection, including books and publications of local authors; biographical newspaper cuttings; newspaper indexes.

Microfilms of local newspapers, 1823– ; local census returns, 1841–91; local parish registers, 16th–20th centuries; public cemetery burial registers, 1856–1998.

Microfiche of the General Register Office Index (England and Wales), 1837–1947, IGI (United Kingdom and Ireland), 1881.

Census indexes (England and Wales).

Large scale local OS maps and town plans, 1847– .

Oral history collection of tapes, with summaries and indexes.

Collection of local photographs and illustrations.

Finding aids: Detailed lists, calendars and catalogues with indexes of places, personal names and subjects. Lists sent to NRA.

Facilities: Photocopying. Photography by arrangement. Microfilm/fiche readers/printers.

Conservation: Work undertaken by Greater Manchester County Record Office (see entry 874).

Publications: Guide to Archive Service (1999). *Handlist of Registers* (5/1999).

116   Warburtons Ltd

Address: Back O'th' Bank House, Hereford Street, Bolton, Lancashire BL1 8HJ

Telephone: (01204) 531004

Fax: (01204) 523361

Enquiries: The Corporate Affairs Manager, Mrs Jill Kippax

Open: Mon–Fri: 9.00–5.00.

Access: By prior arrangement only, at the discretion of the company.

Historical background: Warburtons began as a family baking business in 1876. It was incorporated in 1921 and grew by acquisitions between then and 1992. It is owned by the fifth generation of the family.

Acquisitions policy: To maintain the archives.

Archives of organisation: Family and business papers, early 1900s– .

Non-manuscript material: Marketing videos, mid 1980s– .

Finding aids: Descriptive lists.

Facilities: Photocopying.

Publications: T. Bond: *100 Years of Good Baking* (1976).
Warburtons, Family Bakers since 1876 (1995).

117   Alliance and Leicester Group Archives

Parent organisation: Alliance and Leicester plc

Address: Girobank plc Paperstore, Dunnings Bridge Road, Bootle, Merseyside L30 6UT

Telephone: (0151) 966 2822

Fax: (0151) 966 2831

Enquiries: The Group Archivist, Mr N. Hardman

Open: Mon–Fri: 9.30–4.30.

Access: Bona fide researchers, strictly by appointment. Written arrangement only. 30-year closure on Girobank plc archives.

Historical background: The Alliance and Leicester Building Society has three main constituent parts: the Leicester Permanent Building Society (f. 1853), the Brighton and Sussex Equitable Permanent Benefit Building Society (f. 1863), and the Leicester Temperance and General Permanent Building Society (f. 1875). The Leicester-based societies grew generically, and the Brighton and Sussex decided in 1929 to expand through acquisition. This strategy culminated in its change of name to the Alliance Building Society in 1945, to reflect the fact that it had by then merged with 13 other building societies. In 1974 the two Leicester societies merged to form the Leicester Building Society. This merged with the Alliance Building Society in 1985 to form the Alliance and Leicester Building Society. In 1990, with its acquisition of Girobank plc from the Post Office Corporation, the building society became the first ever to purchase a UK bank. Girobank had been created between 1965 and 1968, under the auspices of the Post Office, as a national giro system. Throughout the 1970s it provided more banking facilities, and in 1975 the Post Office (Banking Services) Act enhanced this role. In 1978 it became the National Girobank to reflect these changes, and in 1981 it became a clearing bank. In 1985 it became plc within the Post Office and between 1988 and 1990 it was sold off to the society. In 1994 the personal bank was merged, following an Act of Parliament, with the building society's mortgage, lending and savings business to form Personal Financial Services. Girobank plc now deals purely with the group's banking services to corporate customers. In 1997 the society converted to the Alliance and Leicester plc. The archives are recognised as a place of deposit for public records.

Acquisitions policy: Records of the company and its predecessors. National coverage, with all types of business records, except customer records, operational records and records of individual members of staff.

Archives of organisation: Archives of parent company (excluding customer accounts and personnel records), 1853– .
Girobank plc archives, 1965– .
Records of 15 building societies merged with the Alliance and its predecessor (incomplete).

Non-manuscript material: Large collection of photographs, films and videos dealing with the company and various activities of staff.

Finding aids: Guide to records open to the public and computer database.

Facilities: Photocopying.

118 Russell-Cotes Art Gallery and Museum

Parent organisation: Bournemouth Borough Council

Address: East Cliff, Bournemouth, Hampshire BH1 3AA

Telephone: (01202) 451800

Fax: (01202) 451851

Website: www.russell-cotes.bournemouth. gov.uk

Enquiries: The Museums Department

Open: Tues–Sun: 10.00–5.00.

Access: Generally open to the public.

Historical background: In 1908 Sir Morton Russell-Cotes (1835–1921) and his wife, Lady Annie (1835–1920), gifted their home, East Cliff Hall, and its contents to the Borough of Bournemouth; it was opened as a museum in 1922.
The Bournemouth Symphony Orchestra archive was transferred from Poole Museum Services in 1993.

Acquisitions policy: To maintain supporting documentation of the collections.

Major collections: Archives of the Bournemouth Symphony Orchestra.

Non-manuscript material: Photographs, drawings and cartoons.
Concert programmes.
Memorabilia of Henry Irving (1838–1905) and Sarah Bernhardt (1844–1923).

Finding aids: Computer index.

Facilities: Photocopying by arrangement.

Conservation: Contracted out.

119 Tank Museum

Address: Bovington, Dorset BH20 6JG

Telephone: (01929) 405070/405096

Fax: (01929) 405360

E-mail: davidf@tankmuseum.co.uk

Website: www.tankmuseum.org.uk

Enquiries: The Curator, Mr David Fletcher
The Director, Col. (retd) John Woodward

Open: Mon–Fri: 10.00–4.45

Access: Generally open to the public, by appointment; normal museum entrance charges apply.

Historical background: Founded after World War I as the Royal Tank Corps Museum, the current museum embraces all regiments of the Royal Armoured Corps. It exists as an independent registered charity as a corps and a regimental museum. Exhibits and archives are the property of the trustees.

Acquisitions policy: To collect and preserve material connected with the history and development of mechanised armoured warfare on land, covering all nationalities but with particular emphasis on the UK.

Archives of organisation: Tank Museum archives, 1920s– .

Major collections: A comprehensive collection of handbooks and other documents associated with the development of armoured fighting vehicles, 1914– .

War diaries and histories of many British armoured regiments and the papers of numerous individuals associated with the development of tank warfare.

Non-manuscript material: Photographs, films, technical drawings and maps relating to armoured fighting vehicles and their use, 1914– .

Finding aids: Detailed card index system; a computer index is ongoing.

Facilities: Photocopying. Photography.

120 National Meteorological Library and Archive

Parent organisation: The Meteorological Office

Address: Library: London Road, Bracknell, Berkshire RG12 2SZ
Archive: The Scott Building, Sterling Centre, Eastern Road, Bracknell RG12 2PW

Telephone: (01344) 854841 (library); 855960 (archive)

Fax: (01344) 854849 (library); 855961 (archive)

E-mail: metlib@meto.gov.uk

Enquiries: The Library and Archive Services Manager

Open: Mon–Fri: 8.30–1.00, 2.00–4.30.

Access: Open to the public, preferably by appointment.

Historical background: The Meteorological Office originated as a department of the Board of Trade in 1855. It is now an agency within the Ministry of Defence. Under Public Records Acts the office is authorised to select technical meteorological records for retention and maintain recognised places of deposit for public records at Bracknell, Edinburgh (see entry 327) and Belfast (see entry 75). The office also holds archives of the Royal Meteorological Society, which was founded in 1850 as the British Meteorological Society and succeeded the Meteorological Society of London (1823–41). In 1921 the RMS amalgamated with the Scottish Meteorological Society.

Acquisitions policy: Responsible for original meteorological and climatological records and

reports from sources in England, Wales and various overseas stations. Donations are welcomed.

Archives of organisation: Published and unpublished reports and scientific papers of the Meteorological Office.

Released administrative records of the Meteorological Office are transferred to the Public Record Office (entry 1058).

Major collections: Systematic collections since the formation of the Meteorological Office include meteorological observation registers for England, Wales and overseas stations; weather charts from the Central Forecast Office; ships' weather logs; climatological returns; private weather diaries, mid–18th century– .

Royal Meteorological Society archives, c1791– , mainly 1850– , including papers of George Symons, founder of the British Rainfall Association, 1851.

Non-manuscript material: The National Meteorological Library includes rare books and a photographic collection.

Royal Meteorological Society: rare books and pamphlets.

Finding aids: Index cards and computer-based lists. NRA 9962/37105.

Facilities: Photocopying. Microfilming.

121 Bradford Cathedral
Archives and Library

Address: 1 Stott Hill, Bradford, West Yorkshire BD1 4EH

Telephone: (01274) 777720

Fax: (01274) 777730

Enquiries: The Hon. Librarian, Miss Connie Priestley, c/o The Cathedral
The Hon. Archivist, Mrs Astrid Hansen, 37 Manor House Road, Wilsden, Bradford BD15 0EB

Open: Mon–Fri: by arrangement.

Access: Bona fide researchers; a prior appointment is necessary. Access to the archives is very limited, but the Hon. Archivist will answer postal enquiries; the fee is dependent on the work involved. Please note availability of registers on microfiche at West Yorkshire Archive Service, Bradford (entry 125).

Historical background: The Cathedral Church of St Peter, Bradford, founded in 1919, is based on the Parish Church of St Peter, which had a muniments room from the 16th century. There are some more recent archival resources in the Cathedral Library, which was begun in 1979.

Acquisitions policy: Continued deposit of registers and records.

Archives of organisation: Baptism, marriage and burial registers of the Parish Church of St Peter, Bradford, 1599– ; vestry minutes, 1686– ; churchwardens' accounts, 1667– . The registers and their indexes prior to 1837 are held on microfilm by the West Yorkshire Archive Service, Bradford (see entry 125) and the library of the University of Bradford (see entry 124).

Major collections: Records of Bradford charities and day and Sunday schools, 19th century.

Non-manuscript material: Parish church and cathedral magazines, 1897– ; the *Bradford Antiquary*, 1888– .
Architects' plans for extension, 20th century.

Finding aids: NRA 17769. The baptism and marriage registers are well indexed.

122   The Colour Museum

Parent organisation: Society of Dyers and Colourists

Address: Perkin House, PO Box 244, Gratten Road, Bradford, West Yorkshire BD1 2JB

Telephone: (01274) 390955

Fax: (01274) 392888

E-mail: colour.museum@sok.org.uk

Website: www.sok.org.uk

Enquiries: The Curator, Miss S. Burge

Open: By appointment only.

Access: Generally open to the public, by prior arrangement.

Conservation: Contracted out.

The society was formed in 1884. Collection began in 1948, partly records relating to the society and partly material relating to the textile coloration industry generally. The museum opened in 1978. It holds archives of the Society of Dyers and Colourists and donations to the society from the industry it services of items relating to the coloration of textiles, which includes dyeing and textile printing. There are also a number of items which relate to other colour users, such as paint manufacturers and paper printers, mostly post-1884. There is a partial card index and computer system. Photocopying and photography may be arranged. See *The Colour Museum Visitors Guide.*

123   National Museum of Photography, Film & Television

Parent organisation: The National Museum of Science & Industry

Address: Pictureville,   Bradford,   West Yorkshire BD1 1NQ

Telephone: (01274) 202030

Fax: (01274) 723155

E-mail: enquiries@nmpft@nmsi.ac.uk

Website: www.nmpft.org.uk

Enquiries: The Duty Enquiry Officer

Open: By appointment.

Access: Generally open to the public, by appointment. Restrictions according to condition of material.

Historical background: The National Museum of Photography, Film and Television is part of the National Museum of Science & Industry. Originally opened in 1983, the museum reopened in 1999 with enhanced facilities. The Photographs Collection selectively traces the aesthetic and technical developments of photography from the early experiments by William Henry Fox Talbot (1800–77) and Sir John Herschel (1792–1871) in the 1830s to examples of contemporary practice across the many genres and uses of the medium. It is particularly strong in the early history of photography, the documentary and fine art genres, and applied, advertising and amateur practices.

Acquisitions policy: The museum collects equipment, images and printed ephemera connected with photography, film and television. Acquisition policies for individual collections appear on the museum website.

Non-manuscript material: Photographs Collection, includes Fox Talbot images (c6500) and many examples of significant 20th-century work; recent examples of documentary and fine art photography.

Daily Herald news photograph archive, 1914–1960s (strongest section covers 1929–44), and the Focal Press and Zoltan Glass collections.
The Kodak Museum Collection of photographs (*c*50,000) plus equipment, 1840– .
Cinematography Collection, including Buckingham Movie Museum, Indian Film Posters and the Roy Ashton and Phil Leakey Hammer Horror collections.
Television Collection, including the Commercial Heaven collection of television advertising, 1955–1980s.

Finding aids: Subject index to *Daily Herald* archive. Other items are listed on the museum computer.

Facilities: Photocopying. Photography. Microfilm reader.

Conservation: Contracted out.

Publications: See the Science Museum website: www.sciencemuseum.org.uk/publications/photo.html.

124 University of Bradford

Address: J.B. Priestley Library, Bradford, West Yorkshire BD7 1DP

Telephone: (01274) 233400

Fax: (01274) 233398

E-mail: library@bradford.ac.uk

Website: www.bradford.ac.uk

Enquiries: The Librarian, Dr M.B. Stevenson
The Commonweal Librarian, Karen Spencer

Open: Mon–Fri: 8.45–5.30;
Sat, Sun: 8.45–1.00 (term– time only).

Access: Bona fide researchers, on application

Historical background: The original Bradford Technical College grew out of schools of weaving, design and building in the 1860s. Established as the Bradford Institute of Technology in 1882, it became a College of Advanced Technology in 1957 and received its Royal Charter as the University of Bradford in 1966.
The Commonweal Collection developed from the collection begun by David Hoggett in the 1950s and bequeathed to the university library in 1975. It became a registered charity in 1997 and since 1993 has been associated with the Gandhi Foundation.

Acquisitions policy: Acquires material relating to peace and war-resistance movements, mainly by gift.

Archives of organisation: Archives of the university and of its predecessors, 1860s– .

Major collections: Commonweal Collection consists of various organisations, including Direct Action Committee, 1950s–60s; Committee of One Hundred; International Voluntary Service; International Confederation for Disarmament and Peace; United Farm Workers; and Molesworth Peace Camp.
Research archives of scholars of peace action and peace movements, especially Geoffrey Ostergaard's papers *re* the Gandhian Sarvodaya movement, India.
J.B. Priestley (1894–1984): substantial archives *re* his life and works, including MSS, publishers' agreements, photographs and personalia.

Non-manuscript material: Photographs, drawings, posters, videos, pamphlets and ephemera *re* peace movements.

Finding aids: Some outline lists.

Facilities: Photocopying.

125 West Yorkshire Archive Service: Bradford District Archives

Parent organisation: West Yorkshire Joint Services

Address: 15 Canal Road, Bradford, West Yorkshire BD1 4AT

Telephone: (01274) 731931

Fax: (01274) 734013

E-mail: bradford@wyasbrad.org.uk

Website: www.archives.wyjs.org.uk

Enquiries: The Principal District Archivist
The County Archivist, Mrs S. Thomas

Open: Mon–Thurs: 9.30–1.00, 2.00–5.00; alternate Thurs to 8.00.
Closed one week in February and one week in November for stock–taking.

Access: Generally open to the public, by appointment. A paid research service is available.

Historical background: An archive department was established in Bradford Central Library in 1974 by the metropolitan district council; in

1982 it joined the West Yorkshire Archive Service and in 1985 it moved from the library to separate premises. Bradford library's manuscript collection initially formed the core of the department's holdings, now considerably increased from official and other sources. It also acts as the Diocesan Record Office for Bradford and is recognised as a place of deposit for public records.

Acquisitions policy: To acquire archive material relating to the history of the area covered by Bradford Metropolitan District.

Archives of organisation: Records of Bradford Metropolitan District Council and superseded authorities: Bradford County Borough, Keighley Municipal Borough; urban district councils of Baildon, Bingley, Denholme, Ilkley, Queensbury, Shipley and Silsden; townships and school boards.

Major collections: Deposited local collections include significant textile, iron and engineering archives, also those of textile trade unions, Independent Labour Party and Yorkshire Co-operatives Ltd.
Family and estate collections include those of Sir Francis Sharp Powell, MP, of Horton Hall (late 19th century), Ferrand of Bingley, Tempest of Tong and Spencer-Stanhope of Horsforth and Cawthorne.
Leeds and Liverpool Canal Company records.

Non-manuscript material: Yorkshire Television Video History Archive.

Finding aids: The majority of collections are catalogued and also accessible through item-level indexes. Links to West Yorkshire Archive Service computerised database and to NRA computer. Catalogues are sent to NRA.

Facilities: Photocopying. Microfiche reader/printer.

Conservation: Undertaken by West Yorkshire Archive Service Headquarters, Wakefield (entry 1184).

Publications: I. Mason (comp.): *Bradford Archives 1974–1995: an Illustrated Guide to Bradford District Archives* (1996).

126 Brecknock Museum

Parent organisation: Powys County Council

Address: Captain's Walk, Brecon, Powys LD3 7DW

Telephone: (01874) 624121

Fax: (01874) 611281 (please mark FAO museum)

E-mail: brecknock.museum@powys.gov.uk

Enquiries: The Curator, David Moore

Open: Mon–Fri: 10.00–5.00 (throughout year); Sat: 10.00–4.00 (Nov–Feb); Sun: 12.00–5.00 (April–Sept).

Access: Bona fide researchers, by appointment.

Historical background: The museum was founded in 1928 by the local historical society, the Brecknock Society. The society handed the museum and its collections to Breconshire County Council in 1950, and since 1974 it has been administered by the county of Powys. The archive was begun in 1928 and contains research papers and other documents collected by members of the Brecknock Society. Brecon Assizes quarter and petty sessions records are now with Powys County Archives (entry 531).

Acquisitions policy: All archives are now collected and acquired by Powys County Archives.

Archives of organisation: Minute books and other documents of the museum and Brecknock Society, 1928– .

Major collections: Papers of Sir John Conway Lloyd (1878–1954).

Non-manuscript material: Photographs of Breconshire interest.

Finding aids: General index to all of the collection. Schedules of major collections.

Facilities: Photocopying. Photography by arrangement.

127 South Wales Borderers and Monmouthshire
Regimental Museum of the Royal Regiment of Wales

Address: The Barracks, Brecon, Powys LD3 7EB

Telephone: (01874) 613311

Fax: (01874) 613275

E-mail: rrw@ukonline.co.uk

Website: www.ukonline.co.uk/rrw/index.htm

Enquiries: The Curator, Martin Everett

Open: 1 Oct–31 March: Mon–Fri: 9.00–1.00, 2.00–5.00.
1 April–30 Sept: Mon–Sat: 9.00–1.00, 2.00–5.00.

Access: Bona fide scholars, by prior arrangement. Military family history research is charged for.

Historical background: The regiment was raised in 1689 and in 1969 amalgamated with the Welch Regiment to become the Royal Regiment of Wales. See also the Welch Regiment Museum of the Royal Regiment of Wales (entry 220). In 1934 the first display was opened in a room in the Brecknock County Museum; later it moved to the keep in the barracks, and in 1959 it opened in its present location. The museum is registered, and is recognised as a place of deposit for public records.

Acquisitions policy: Any items which in any way relate to the history of any unit connected to the South Wales Borderers, the Monmouthshire Regiment and the Royal Regiment of Wales (24th/41st Foot).

Archives of organisation: Records of South Wales Borderers, 24th Foot, Monmouthshire Regiment and the Royal Regiment of Wales, 1689– , including letters, pay-books, citations, battle reports and officers' records.

Major collections: Usual military museum collection, including war diaries and personal papers.
MS diaries, letters, journals, scrapbooks, especially of the Anglo-Zulu War (1879), Tsingtao (1914), Norway (1940) and Malaya (1955–6).

Non-manuscript material: Photographs (8000), medal collection (2000), arms, uniforms and artefacts.

Finding aids: Computerised catalogue. Indexes. NRA 20951.

Facilities: Photocopying. Photography.

128 Generalate Archives of the Poor Servants of the Mother of God

Parent organisation: Congregation of the Poor Servants of the Mother of God (SMG)

Address: St Mary's Convent, The Butts, Brentford, Middlesex TW8 8BQ

Telephone: (020) 8847 4800 ext. 226

Fax: (020) 8847 4155

Enquiries: The Archivist, Mr Paul Shaw

Open: Strictly by arrangement.

Access: By appointment only, on application to the Archivist and subject to the approval of the generalate of the congregation. Access to the public is at present limited while the archives are reorganised.

The order was founded in London in 1869, with the primary aim of serving the urban poor, by Frances Margaret Taylor (1832–1900). She was a Roman Catholic convert from Anglicanism who served as a nurse in the Crimean War and published her experiences as *Eastern Hospital and English Nurses* (1856), which established her reputation as a journalist and author. She was also the founder editor of the Catholic periodical *The Month* in 1864–5. By 1900 the order administered more than 20 houses and institutions, including the Providence Free Hospital, St Helens. The order was focused upon work in England and Ireland, but also had houses in Italy and France; more recently it has extended its charitable work to the USA, Africa and South America. Houses were acquired in Roehampton in 1876 and 1927, and the generalate continues to be based there. Archives of the order from its foundation are currently being reorganised, catalogued and relocated. See R.G. Wells: *A Woman of Her Time and Ours: Mary Magdalene Taylor, SMG* (Charlotte, NC, USA, 2/1994).

129 Leprosy Mission International

Address: 80 Windmill Road, Brentford, Middlesex TW8 0QH

Telephone: (020) 8569 7292

Fax: (020) 8569 7808

E-mail: friends@tlmint.org

Website: www.leprosymission.org

Enquiries: The International General Director, Trevor Durston

Open: Mon–Fri: 9.00–5.00

Access: By written request, giving background for consultation; an appointment is necessary.

Historical background: The Leprosy Mission is a medical missionary society founded in 1874. The principal object of the organisation is 'to minister in the name of Jesus Christ to the physical, mental and spiritual needs of sufferers from leprosy, to assist in their rehabilitation and to work towards the eradication of leprosy'.

Acquisitions policy: To maintain the archive of the society.

Archives of organisation: Minutes of council and various committees, 1878–1987.
Reports, 1894– .
Correspondence file series and papers received from more than 50 countries, c1905–c1988.
Personnel files.

Non-manuscript material: Large photographic and film collection; tape-recordings.
Library has various histories, pamphlets, journals and publications of the mission.
Property plans.

Finding aids: Various interim lists and card index.

Facilities: Photocopying.

130 Bridgend Library and Information Service

Parent organisation: Bridgend County Borough Council

Address: Coed Parc, Park Street, Bridgend, West Glamorgan CF31 4BA

Telephone: (01656) 767451

Fax: (01656) 645719

E-mail: blis@bridgendlib.gov.uk

Enquiries: The County Borough Librarian, John Woods

Open: Mon, Wed, Thurs: 9.00–6.00; Tues, Fri: 9.00–7.00; Sat: 9.00–5.00.

Access: Generally open to the public.

Bridgend Library and Information Service was formed in 1996. Previously it was part of Mid Glamorgan County Council. It holds material relating to the history and culture of the historical county of Glamorgan but with special emphasis on the Bridgend County Borough area, including papers of local historians. There are also photographs (c2000), newspaper cuttings, oral history tapes, ephemera and maps.

131 Brighton College

Address: Eastern Road, Brighton, East Sussex BN2 2AL

Telephone: (01273) 704200

Fax: (01273) 704204

Website: www.brightoncollege.org.uk

Enquiries: The Archivist, Richard Brightwell

Open: Term only: Mon–Fri: 9.30–1.00.

Access: Generally open to the public, on written application and by appointment only.

Historical background: Brighton College was founded in 1845 by William Aldwin Soames. It obtained charitable tax status for schools in the 1927 Finance Act. The college archives were established in 1950 by G.P. Burstow.

Acquisitions policy: Anything to do with the history of the school and its former pupils.

Archives of organisation: Corporate and financial records; pupil records; correspondence and papers of various headmasters, bursars and other officers of the college; magazines, 19th and 20th centuries.

Non-manuscript material: Photographs; uniforms past and present; ephemera; architectural drawings of college buildings; books by or about former pupils.

Finding aids: Card index and typescript catalogue.

Facilities: Photocopying by arrangement.

Publications: G.P. Burstow and M. Whittaker: *A History of Brighton College*, ed. Sir Sydney Roberts (Brighton, 1957).
M.D.W. Jones: 'Brighton College v Marriott: Schools, Charity Law & Taxation', *History of Education*, xii/2 (1983), 121–32.
M.D.W Jones: *A Short History of Brighton College* (Brighton, 1986).
——: *Brighton College 1845–1995* (Chichester, 1995).

132 Brighton Reference Library

Parent organisation: East Sussex County Libraries

Address: Vantage Point, New England Street, Brighton, East Sussex BN1 2GW

Telephone: (01273) 296969

Fax: (01273) 296965

Website: www.brighton-hove.gov.uk/bhc/libraries/

Enquiries: The Reference Library Manager, Mrs E. Jewell

Open: Mon, Tues, Thurs, Fri: 10.00–7.00; Sat: 10.00–4.00.

Access: Generally open to the public.

Historical background: Brighton's public library was established when the Royal Literary and Scientific Institution closed in 1869 and presented its large collection of books to the town. With some other bequeathed collections, the institution's books formed the basis of a reference library which opened in some of the upper rooms of the Pavilion in 1869. The reference library is particularly rich in local material on both East and West Sussex. However, in recent years a good deal has been transferred to East and West Sussex Record Offices (see entries 513 and 241).

Acquisitions policy: Donations and deposits are accepted in close co-operation with East Sussex County Record Office.

Archives of organisation: Minutes and other records relating to East Sussex County Library.

Major collections: Brighton rate books, 1791–1894.
Minutes and accounts of trade union groups, Brighton and Sussex, 19th–20th centuries.
Minutes of Brighton Labour Party and Friendly Societies.
Working notes and correspondence of Brighton Community Publishing Group, Queenspark.

Non-manuscript material: Sussex newspapers and journals, 18th–20th centuries.
Drawings, prints, photographs, magic-lantern slides, glass negatives, postcards, slides of Brighton and Sussex.
Census returns, East and West Sussex, 1841–81, and Brighton Manor court rolls (on microfilm).

Finding aids: Booklet listing trade union, Friendly Society and Labour Party material. Local history catalogue.

Facilities: Photocopying. Photography by arrangement. Microfilm/fiche reader/printer.

Publications: *A-Z of Special Collections.*
T. Carder: *The Encyclopaedia of Brighton.*

133   Design Council Archive

Parent organisation: University of Brighton

Address: Design History Research Centre, Grand Parade, Brighton, East Sussex BN2 2JY

Telephone: (01273) 643219/643209

Fax: (01273) 643217

E-mail: dhrc@brighton.ac.uk

Website: www.brighton.ac.uk/descoarchive/

Enquiries: The Curator, Dr Catherine Moriarty

Open: Mon–Fri: 9.30–4.30.

Access: Approved external readers, on application. An appointment is always necessary.

Historical background: The Design History Research Centre was established in 1993. The Design Council was founded as the Council of Industrial Design in 1944 and given its present name in 1972. It was restructured in 1994 when the Archive moved to the centre, where it provides significant opportunities for postgraduate research into various aspects of design practice and policy and its economic and cultural significance in the 20th century. The slide collection is now housed at Manchester Metropolitan University (see entry 881).

Acquisitions policy: Ongoing deposits from the current Design Council.
To develop holdings pertaining to design and the state in Britain, including papers of individual designers, critics and promoters.

Archives of organisation: Design Council archive, including extensive correspondence, documents, publications, posters, photographs and ephemera, 1944– , plus records *re* landmark exhibitions, regional events and international shows.

Non-manuscript material: Photographic library of the Council of Industrial Design (100,000 prints; 60,000 negatives).

Finding aids: Database for documents, publications, posters and some photographic material.

Facilities: Photocopying.

Publications: A leaflet about the archive is available.
J. Maguire and J.M. Woodham: *Design and Cultural Politics in Postwar Britain* (Leicester University Press, 1997).

134 Preston Manor

Parent organisation: Royal Pavilion Libraries and Museums

Address: Preston Manor, Brighton, East Sussex BN1 6SD

Telephone: (01273) 292772

Fax: (01273) 292771

Enquiries: The Keeper, David Beevers

Open: Closed until 1.00 Mon; rest of Mon–Fri, by arrangement.

Access: Generally open to the public, but no children under 16 unless accompanied by an adult. An appointment is always necessary.

Historical background: Collection of documents relating to Sussex, the property of Sir Charles Thomas Stanford (1858–1932), who bequeathed Preston Manor and its estate to Brighton Corporation (now Brighton Borough Council).

Acquisitions policy: To maintain the archives relating to the families who owned Preston Manor.

Archives of organisation: Family papers of the Stanfords, who held Preston Manor from 1795, including manorial court rolls, indentures and agreements relating to land holdings and building conveyances.

Major collections: Large collection of deeds and documents relating to East and West Sussex, arranged by parish.
Letters by Sussex authors.

Non-manuscript material: Photographs of Preston Manor.
Collection of Sussex family bookplates; books by Rudyard Kipling and Sussex authors.

Finding aids: Card index. East and West Sussex collections: NRA 1296.

Facilities: Photocopying by arrangement.

135 Roedean School Archives

Address: Roedean Way, Brighton, East Sussex BN2 5RQ

Telephone: (01273) 603181

Fax: (01273) 680791

Website: www.roedean.co.uk

Enquiries: The Archivist

Open: Term: Mon–Fri: 9.30–4.30, by appointment.

Access: Generally open for research, by written application.

Historical background: Wimbledon House School was opened by the Lawrence sisters in Sussex Square, Brighton, in 1885. Roedean School was purpose-built to accommodate the expanding roll and opened in 1898.

Acquisitions policy: Material, including photographs and correspondence, is gratefully received from old pupils, staff and other interested persons.

Archives of organisation: School archives, including council minutes, register of admissions, 1885– , and records of staff.
School magazine, 1885– .
Documentation of war years at Keswick, 1939–45.

Non-manuscript material: Photographs including pupils and staff, 1885– .
Plans, especially of Lawrence House and Keswick House.
Drawings and paintings, notably by Dorothy Martin.

Facilities: Photocopying.

136 University of Sussex

Address: Falmer, Brighton, East Sussex BN1 9QL

A Library

Telephone: (01273) 606755 ext. 3489

Fax: (01273) 678441

E-mail: library@sussex.ac.uk

Website: www.susx.ac.uk/library/manuscripts

Enquiries: The assistant Librarian with responsibility for manuscripts

Open: By arrangement.

Access: Academic researchers, on written application.

Historical background: The university library was opened to readers in 1964. In 1970 a section was created within the library to handle the special materials acquired to support research projects that had arisen from the curriculum. In 1973 these special collections were divided into two groups, official published papers and manuscripts. Since then the Manuscripts Section has maintained and serviced the manuscript collections, together with small supporting collections of printed books. In 2000 the German-Jewish Studies Centre archive was officially opened.

Acquisitions policy: To collect papers which support research and teaching in the university, especially literary, political, sociological, and scientific papers of the late 19th and 20th centuries.

Major collections: Collections include the following: Benn Levy, MP, c1930–70; Charles W. Gibson, MP, c1910–70; James Gerald Crowther, papers on scientific journalism and politics; Sir Richard Gregory, c1880–1952; John Hilton Bureau papers: *News of the World* readers' problems, 1945–68; Kenneth Allsop, 1940–68; Kingsley Martin, 1910–69; Rudyard Kipling and family, 1860–1940; Leonard and Virginia Woolf, 1890–1969; Rosey Pool: American negro literature, 1945–70; Sir Lawrence Dudley Stamp, 1910–65.

Common Wealth Party papers, 1940– .

Matusow papers on 20th-century US politics and culture, 1940–74.

Wartime Social Survey papers, 1940–41.

Maurice Reckitt papers on religion, politics and society, 1915–50.

Geoffrey Gorer papers, c1920–1981.

New Statesman archive, 1944–88.

Nicolson Papers, 1970s: correspondence of Nigel Nicolson while editing the letters of Virginia Woolf.

German-Jewish collection, including diaries, letters, testimony survival narratives and other biographical sources recording the experiences and achievements of refugees 18th century– .

Non-manuscript material: Printed books associated with individual collections, e.g. works and studies of Virginia Woolf, Leonard Woolf, Rudyard Kipling.

Finding aids: Descriptive handlists to each collection. Handlists are lodged with the NRA. All handlists available on web pages.

Conservation: Contracted out.

Publications: T. Graves and E. Inglis (comp.): *University of Sussex Library, Special Collections* (1998).

email: library@sussex.ac.uk
website: htpp:www.susx.ac.uk/library/manuscript

B Mass-Observation Archive

Telephone: (01273) 678157

Fax: (01273) 678441

E-mail: moa@sussex.ac.uk

Website: www.susx.ac.uk/library/massobs

Enquiries: The Archivist, Ms Dorothy E. Sheridan

Open: By arrangement.

Access: Bona fide researchers, on written application; reference/sponsorship required. No postal research is undertaken.

Historical background: Mass-Observation was a social science research organisation set up in 1937 by Tom Harrisson and Charles Madge. They aimed to create what they called an 'anthropology of ourselves', using two main approaches: (a) the recruiting of a panel of volunteer 'observers' to record their everyday lives in diaries and to respond to detailed monthly questionnaires; and (b) the establishment of a core of full-time investigators based in London. During World War II Mass-Observation was used by the Ministry of Information for a short period to monitor civilian morale. The papers generated by this work (which continued into the 1950s) were brought to the University of Sussex in 1970. The archive was officially opened in 1975, when it became a charitable trust.

Acquisitions policy: The original Mass-Observation collection is virtually complete, but a small amount of complementary material (private papers, letters, diaries, scrapbooks and personal material donated by individuals), dating from 1937 to the present day, continues to be accepted. In addition, the archive itself is the centre for a nationwide contemporary writing project, 'Mass-Observation in the 1980s and 1990s', begun in 1981 and still in operation, and regularly receives contributions from volunteer writers willing to record their lives in response to thematic open-ended questionnaires sent to them by the archivist.

Major collections: Mass-Observation records: personal diaries, 1937–63; detailed questionnaire replies, 1937–53; papers resulting from a wide range of investigations into British social life before, during and immediately after World War II.

Papers resulting from the contemporary Mass-Observation project (2500 writers since 1981), arranged thematically and chronologically on aspects on everyday life in Britain.

Non-manuscript material: Photographs taken by Humphrey Spender of Bolton and Blackpool, 1937–8, for Mass-Observation's 'Worktown Project' (c400).

The library includes *Mass-Observation* and related publications; these may not be borrowed.

Newspaper cuttings relating to Mass-Observation's history.

Ephemera, including posters, pamphlets, leaflets etc, which are related to topics investigated by Mass-Observation.

Finding aids: Lists and indexes. Sections of the collection are still being catalogued.

Facilities: Photocopying. Microfilm reader. Educational materials for schools. Special facilities for increasing access to disabled readers.

Conservation: Contracted out.

Publications: D. Sheridan: *Mass-Observation Archive: Guide for Researchers* [pamphlet available for sale from the archive].

A. Calder and D. Sheridan (eds): *Speak for Yourself: a Mass-Observation Anthology* (1984).

——: 'Ordinary Hardworking Folk: Volunteer Writers in Mass-Observation 1939–50 and 1981–91', *Feminist Praxis*, nos. 36/7 (1993) [special issue on Mass-Observation].

—— : 'Reading Mass-Observation Writing: Theoretical and Methodological Issues in Researching the Mass-Observation Archive', *Auto/Biography*, the Bulletin of the BSA Auto/Biography Group, 2/2; also pubd as Mass-Observation Archive Occasional Paper no.1, University of Sussex Library (1993).

'Writing to the Archive: Mass-Observation as Autobiography', *Sociology*, 21/1 (1993), 27–40.

'Using the Mass-Observation Archive as a Source for Women's Studies', *Women's History Review*, 3/1 (1994), 101–13.

D. Sheridan, B.V. Street and D. Bloome: *Writing Ourselves: Mass-Observation and Literacy Practices* (1999).

The Mass-Observation Archives produces an Occasional Paper Series, details on request.

137　Bristol Central Library Reference Department

Parent organisation: Bristol City Council

Address:　County Central Library, College Green, Bristol BS1 5TL

Telephone: (0117) 929 9147 (Reference Enquiry Desk)

Enquiries: The Local Studies Librarian

Open: Mon, Tues, Thurs: 9.30–7.30; Wed, Fri, Sat: 9.30–5.00.

Access: Generally open to the public, but advance notice is required for the use of MSS, early printed material and some other valuable items. A research service is available, charged for after the first half hour.

Historical background: The City Library of Bristol has been in existence since 1613. Much of the early stock survives in the Reference Library, which also contains the books of the Bristol Library Society, founded in 1772. Most MS material relevant to the history of Bristol is housed in the Bristol Record Office (entry 139).

Acquisitions policy: To strengthen the existing collections, especially those relating to local history and local literary figures, by purchase and donation.

Major collections: MS and printed material relating to Thomas Chatterton (1752–70) and Samuel Taylor Coleridge (1772–1834).

Richard Smith Collection: MS and printed material relating to the history of the theatre in Bristol, 1672–1843.

Letters and papers relating to the Southwell family, 1655–1777.

Small collection of documents relating to slavery in the West Indies and the slave trade generally, 1723–36.

The Ellacombe Collection: MSS and other material relating to the history and topography of south-east Gloucestershire.

Non-manuscript material: Extensive collections on the history of Bristol and its environs, including books, pamphlets, pictorial material, colour and monochrome transparencies, sound archives.

Braikenridge Collection: c9000 items on the history of the city, including engravings, ephemera and other pre-1850 material.

Emanuel Green Collection of books on the history of Somerset.

Finding aids: Catalogues, lists and indexes.

Facilities: Photocopying. Microfilm/fiche readers.

Conservation: Contracted out.

138 Bristol Museums Service

Parent organisation: Bristol City Council

Address: City Museum & Art Gallery, Queen's Road, Bristol BS8 1RL

Telephone: (0117) 922 3571

Fax: (0117) 922 2047

E-mail: general@brmuseum.demon.co.uk

Enquiries: The Collections Manager, Mr Ray Barnett

Open: Mon–Fri: 10.00–5.00, by appointment.

Access: Generally open to the public, by prior arrangement.

The museum dates from the 1820s. It holds archives relating to its history and acquires only archives complementing objects held: others are referred to the local record office. There are considerable collections of non-manuscript holdings, including photographs of shipping. At present there is no catalogue of MSS, but photocopying and photography are available.

139 Bristol Record Office

Parent organisation: Bristol City Council

Address: 'B' Bond Warehouse, Smeaton Road, Bristol BS1 6XN

Telephone: (0117) 922 4224

Fax: (0117) 922 4236

E-mail: bro@bristol-city.gov.uk

Enquiries: The City Archivist, John S. Williams

Open: Mon–Thurs: 9.30–4.45; first Thurs of each month to 8.00, by appointment.
Closed last two weeks of January.

Access: Generally open to the public. Appointments are welcomed but are not essential. A paid research service is available.

Historical background: The record office was established in 1924. Newly converted premises were opened in 1992. The office also acts as the Diocesan Record Office for Bristol (parish records for the Archdeaconry of Bristol) and is recognised as a place of deposit for public, manorial and tithe records.

Acquisitions policy: The office is interested in all records relating to the city and county of Bristol. Acquisitions are mainly by donation or deposit, occasionally by purchase.

Archives of organisation: Usual local authority record holdings, 12th century– .

Major collections: Deposited collections including the following which have a wider significance:
Records of J.S. Fry and Sons Ltd, chocolate manufacturers, 1693–1966.
Records of Imperial Tobacco Ltd, formerly W.D. and H.O. Wills, tobacco manufacturers, late 18th–20th centuries.
Papers of Sir George White, transport pioneer, c1874–1935.
Records of P. and A. Campbell Ltd, paddle-steamer company, 1893–1971.

Non-manuscript material: Large number of plans, drawings and photographs relating to the area.
Over 200 films, 1902– (VHS viewing copies available of some).

Finding aids: Place, subject and personal names indexes compiled from lists of holdings. Various specialist indexes available. Lists sent to NRA.

Facilities: Photocopying. Microfilm/fiche readers/printer. Photography and microfilming by arrangement.

Conservation: Occasional work undertaken by another repository.

Publications: I. Kirby: *Diocese of Bristol: a Catalogue of the Records* (1970).
E. Ralph: *Guide to the Bristol Archives Office* (1971).
Various guides to records, posters, maps and postcards; full list available.

140 Clerical Medical Investment Group Ltd

Parent organisation: Halifax Group

Address: Narrow Plain, Bristol BS2 0JH

Telephone: (01275) 555960

Fax: (01275) 555961

Enquiries: The Archivist

Open: Mon–Fri: 8.00–5.00, by appointment.

Access: Generally open to the public, at the discretion of the Archivist.

Historical background: The company originated as the Medical, Clerical and General Life Assurance Society in 1824. It was acquired by Employers' Liability Assurance Company in 1920, but continued to operate independently and regained complete independence when the latter merged with Northern Assurance Company in 1960. Clerical Medical became a mutual office by Act of Parliament in 1961 and merged with the Halifax Group in 1997. The archive was started in 1979 and an archivist was appointed in 1981.

Acquisitions policy: Material related to Clerical Medical Investment Group Ltd and associated companies, by gift, transfer or purchase.

Archives of organisation: Archives, including minute books, policy-holders' ledgers, copy policy books and registers, of Clerical Medical Investment Group, 1824– ; General Reversionary and Investment Co., 1835– ; Lands Improvement Co., 1853– ; PEG Investment Co., 1925– .

Finding aids: Lists and computerised indexes. Finding aids published in *National Inventory of Documentary Sources.*

Facilities: Photocopying. Photography by arrangement. Microfilm/fiche readers.

Conservation: Contracted out.

Publications: Lichfield House, No. 15 St James's Square (1983).

141 Clifton Diocesan Archives

Parent organisation: Roman Catholic Diocese of Clifton

Address: St Ambrose, North Road, Leigh Woods, Bristol BS8 3PW

Telephone: (0117) 973 3072

Fax: (0117) 973 5913

Enquiries: The Diocesan Archivist, Rev. Dr. J.A. Harding tel. (01275) 833699

Open: By private arrangement with the Archivist.

Access: Only serious students, by appointment with the Archivist.

The diocese covers Gloucestershire, Somerset and Wiltshire, and the archives contain the records, mainly episcopal correspondence, of the western district, 1780–1850, and of the diocese of Clifton, 1850– . These include plans, drawings and photographs of churches.

142 Courage Archives

Parent organisation: Scottish Courage Ltd

Address: PO Box 85, Bristol BS99 7BT

Telephone: (0117) 929 7222 ext. 2347

Fax: (0117) 925 7959

E-mail: kenneth.thomas@we.ac.uk

Enquiries: The Company Archivist, Ken Thomas

Open: By appointment only.

Access: Bona fide researchers. There is a 30-year closure rule on some records.

Historical background: John Courage founded the firm in London in 1787. After incorporation in 1888, Courage grew by acquisition and takeover to be one of the largest breweries in England. The Courage group includes the following larger brewers: Barclay Perkins & Co. (acquired 1955), H. & G. Simonds Ltd (1960), John Smith's (1970), Watneys (1991) and Trumans (1991). In turn Courage has had a succession of parent companies, among them Imperial Tobacco, Hanson Trust, and the Fosters Brewing Group, and it is presently owned by Scottish Courage Ltd, a division of Scottish & Newcastle plc.

Archives of related breweries are also held at a large number of local authority record offices, mostly London Metropolitan Archives (entry 688)

Acquisitions policy: Maintains the archives of the company only.

Archives of organisation: Archives of the parent company and *c* 100 subsidiary companies, late 18th century– .

Non-manuscript material: Large photograph collection.

Finding aids: Computer-generated lists, searchable database.

Facilities: Photocopying.

Conservation: Contracted out.

Publications: J. Pudney: *A Draught of Contentment: the Story of the Courage Group* (London, 1971).

H. Janes: *The Red Barrel: a History of Watney Mann* (London, 1963).

143 Feminist Archive

Address: Trinity Road Library, St Philips, Bristol BS2 0NW

Telephone: (0117) 935 0025

E-mail: femarch@mcmail.com

Website: www.femarch.mcmail.com

Enquiries: The Archivist

Open: Wed: 2.00–5.00.

Access: Women; men are restricted to published matter. General enquiries will be answered if an SAE is enclosed, but no prolonged research can be undertaken. Access to some collections may be restricted by the donors.

Historical background: The archive is a charity which was started in 1978 and expanded and outgrew various premises, including a room in Bath University; it moved to its present location in 1988. It is run by a collective of volunteers. The northern branch of the Feminist Archive is at the Violence, Abuse and Gender Relations Unit at Leeds Metropolitan University, Leeds LS1 3HE.

Acquisitions policy: To collect and preserve donated material, including audio cassettes, from the 1960s to the present pertaining to the women's movement and feminist issues.

Major collections: Dora Russell Collection: records of the journey through Europe of the Women's Peace Caravan, 1958. Also some of Dora Russell's own papers.
Greenham Peace Camp Collection, including papers of Carole Harwood.
Letters to *Spare Rib* magazine.

Non-manuscript material: Photographs, drawings, posters, records, stickers, calendars, conference papers, periodicals and various ephemera. Audio cassettes of interviews.

Finding aids: Cataloguing is underway.

Facilities: Photocopying.

Conservation: Contracted out.

Publications: Newsletters and various leaflets available.

144 John Wesley's Chapel
The New Room in the Horsefair

Parent organisation: The Methodist Church

Address: 36 The Horsefair, Bristol BS1 3JE

Telephone: (0117) 926 4740

Enquiries: The Hon. Archivist

Open: By arrangement.

Access: Bona fide researchers, on written application.

The manuscript collection at the New Room (which is the oldest Methodist building in the world, 1739) is built around three collections of letters made by the Rev. Dr William L. Watkinson, president of the Wesleyan Conference in 1897. These were brought together early in the 20th century. Added to these collections are a number of gifts of letters and journals, making a total of some 1200 items, of which most are 19th century. The collections contain letters of John Wesley (1703–91) and all the major figures of 19th-century Wesleyan Methodism. There is a catalogue available.

145 Society of Merchant Venturers of Bristol

Address: Merchants' Hall, The Promenade, Clifton, Bristol BS8 3NH

Telephone: (0117) 973 8058/3104

Fax: (0117) 973 5884

E-mail: smv.bristol@btinternet.com

Enquiries: The Hon. Archivist

Open: Mon Fri: 10.00–12.30, 2.00–5.00.

Access: Bona fide scholars, with the consent of the society and strictly by appointment only.

Historical background: The society was incorporated by Royal Charter in 1552. Microfilms of books of proceedings, 1605–1900, are at Bristol University (entry 146).

Acquisitions policy: Acquisitions are mainly by donation or deposit.

Archives of organisation: Archives cover records of trade, shipping and docks, 17th century– , as well as records relating to the society's administration of almshouses, independent schools and other charities.

Finding aids: Lists sent to NRA.

Facilities: Photocopying. Photography allowed.

Conservation: Contracted out.

Publications: E. Ralph: *A Guide to the Archives of the Society of Merchant Venturers of Bristol* (1988).

146 University of Bristol Library
Special Collections Department

Address: Tyndall Avenue, Bristol BS8 1TJ

Telephone: (0117) 925 5334

Fax: (0117) 925 5334

E-mail: library@bristol.ac.uk

Website: www.bris.ac.uk/depts/library

Enquiries: The Special Collections Librarian, Michael Richardson
The Archivist, Hannah Lowery

Open: Mon–Fri: 9.15–4.45; an appointment is preferred

Access: Members of the University of Bristol; others on application.

Historical background: University College Bristol was founded in 1876 and became a university on grant of a charter in 1909. The Gladstone Library of the National Liberal Club was purchased by the library in 1976. The University Library is a repository for archives relating to the West Indies.

Acquisitions policy: Acquisitions are by donation, deposit and purchase.

Archives of organisation: Bristol University College and University of Bristol: archives of the institution, 1876– .
Papers relating to individuals connected with the university, including Arthur Roderick Collar (1935–82), Prof. Sir (Frederick) Charles Frank (1935–98), Dr Heinz London (1886–1972), Prof. Conwy Lloyd Morgan (1875–1938), Sir Philip Robert Morris (1942–80), Prof. Cecil Frank Powell (1916–69), Arthur Mannering Tyndall (1921–84). Also papers of John Beddoe (1854–1907), Cecil Reginald Burch (1901–83), Charles Hubert Sisson, and Philip John Worsley.

Major collections: Bateman Collection: resources for the history of the Labour movement, 20th century.

Bristol Moravian Church: diaries, minute books, memoirs and other items of church history, 1760–1893.

Henry Marc Brunel: letter books, sketchbooks, diaries, accounts, etc, 1860–1903.

Isambard Kingdom Brunel (1806–59): letter books, sketchbooks, calculation books, accounts, correspondence, diaries, etc. 1824–59.

Sir Marc Isambard Brunel (1769–1849): letter books and journals.

Edward Conze: correspondence, papers, notes, publications relating to oriental theology.

Clifton suspension Bridge Trust: accounts, minute books, plans, 1829–1939.

European Parliament election addresses, 1979– .

Joan and Victor Eyles: working papers and books relating to the history of geology, including Sowery family letters relating to geology, c1679–1892.

General election addresses, 1892.

Hamish Hamilton, publisher: editorial files and correspondence.

Hinkley Pont 'C' Inquiry, 1988–9.

Philip Napier Miles: autograph scores and correspondence, 1884–1951.

National Liberal Club: including papers relating to the Liberal Party.

Sir George H. Oatley (1863–1950): architectural drawings and letters, including work of people with whom he co-operated, c1850–c1980.

Paget family: accounts, correspondence, family and estate papers, relating mainly to Somerset and Staffordshire, 1270–1920.

Penguin Books Ltd, historical and editorial files, 1935–70; includes papers of Eunice Frost (1914–98), Sir Allen Lane (1902–70) and Betty Radice.

Pinney Family: accounts, letter books, family and estate papers, relating mainly to Dorset, the West Indies, and the Bristol sugar trade, 1650–1986.

Sizewell 'B' Inquiry, 1986.

Somerset Miners' Association: minutes, accounts, correspondence, etc, 1864–1964.

John Addington Symonds: correspondence and family papers, 1884–1980.

Women's Liberal Federation: minutes, accounts, correspondence, 1888–1988.

Jane Cobden Unwin: letters to her on Irish independence and anti-slavery, 1880–1939.

Non-manuscript material: Recordings, cassettes, photographs, films, plans, drawings and printed books referring to the history of Bristol

University College and Bristol University, 1876– .
Fry Collection of printed portraits.

Finding aids: Indexes, lists, catalogues, calendars. Lists sent to the NRA.

Facilities: Photocopying. Photography. Microfilm/fiche reader/printer.

Conservation: Contracted out.

Publications: Guide to Special Collections. The Brunel Collection (1997).

147 University of Bristol Theatre Collection

Address: 21 Park Row, Bristol BS8 5LT

Telephone: (0117) 928 7836/954 5464

Fax: (0117) 928 7832

E-mail: s.j.morris@bris.ac.uk

Website: www.bris.ac.uk/depts/drama/

Enquiries: The Keeper, Sarah Morris
The Assistant Keeper, Miss Frances Carlyon

Open: Mon–Fri: 9.15–4.45; an appointment is recommended.

Access: Bona fide researchers and students. Groups by appointment only. A paid research service is available.

Historical background: The Theatre Collection was founded in 1951, funded by the Rockefeller Foundation. It was originally conceived as a working collection of graphic material illustrating the development of theatre, based on the earliest acquisitions (the Robinson Collection and the Landstone Bequest). It has grown significantly since the 1970s, with an increase in archive material and original designs. The holdings cover the period from the 18th century to the 1990s.

Acquisitions policy: Primary and secondary source material, books, original and printed artworks, models, photographs and other visual material covering all aspects of drama and theatre history. Costumes, props and printed plays are not actively collected unless they are contained within a collection. The main emphases are on British Victorian and 20th-century theatre, theatre design, and women's theatre.

Archives of organisation: Some administrative papers of the Department of Drama and the Theatre Collection, 1947–98.

Major collections: Old Vic Archive: administrative business papers and production records, 1818-, including photographs, prompt books, playbills, personal papers, financial records, minute books, etc.
Bristol Old Vic Archive: administrative papers and production records, 1946–93.
Herbert Beerbohm Tree Collection: personal papers of Herbert Beerbohm Tree (1853–1917), actor-manager and builder of Her Majesty's Theatre, London; business records of the theatre and material covering all aspects of productions, including press cuttings and photographs, 1880–1917; also personal papers, mainly correspondence, of his wife Maud, 1880–1937.
Eric Jones-Evans (1899–1989), theatre historian's collection of scripts, photographs, prompt books and personal papers, 19th and 20th centuries.
Kathleen Barker, theatre historian's personal research papers, with particular strengths in Bristol theatre history.
Women's Theatre Collection: scripts, books, personal papers of women playwrights and actors, 1890s– .
Collections of John Moody, director; Robert Donat, actor; John Clements, actor; Ernest Thesiger, actor.

Non-manuscript material: Robinson Collection: playbills for West Country theatres, 18th and 19th centuries.
Landstone Bequest: London theatre programmes, 1944–69, plus additions up to 1990s.
Richard Southern (theatre historian) Collection: prints of theatre architecture, costume and scene design; engravings, playbills, designs, paintings, books, 18th–20th centuries.
Alan Tagg Collection: models and designs for productions, 1950s–1980s.
Extensive collections (mainly British) of programmes and periodicals; slides and photographs; costumes and props; prints and original artwork of costumes and set designs; portraits and other paintings.

Finding aids: Card index system supplemented by computerised database (in progress — can be used on site). Books are catalogued on the university's on-line library catalogue.

Facilities: Photocopying. Photography. Microfiche reader.

Conservation: Contracted out.

Publications: C. Robinson: 'British Theatre Collection', *Theatrephile*, 1 (Dec 1983).

148 Wesley College

Address: College Park Drive, Henbury Road, Bristol BS10 7QD

Telephone: (0117) 959 1200

Fax: (0117) 950 1277

E-mail: librarian@wescage.demon.co.uk

Website: www.wescoll.demon.co.uk

Enquiries: The Librarian, Mrs Janet Henderson

Open: By arrangement.

Access: Bona fide researchers, on written application.

Historical background: Three colleges have amalgamated to create the Bristol college: Didsbury College, Manchester (f. 1842), Wesley College, Headingley (f. 1868), and Richmond College, London (1843–1972).

Acquisitions policy: To maintain and consolidate the archives and collections relating to Methodism.

Archives of organisation: Archives of the three constituent colleges, Wesley, Didsbury and Richmond, 19th and 20th centuries.

Major collections: Antiquarian collections, including papers of Rev. George Morley (d1843) and his son, George Morley, surgeon of Leeds; Dr Adam Clarke (?1762–1832), theologian, and his family.
Correspondence of Methodist worthies, c1790-c1840; letters and papers relevant to the Wesleys, c1700-c1850 (3 vols); letters and newspaper cuttings re troubles in Tonga, 1883–7.

Non-manuscript material: Pamphlet collections on church controversy, particularly Methodism, c1680–1850 (153 vols).
Hymnals, 1640–1900.

Finding aids: TS catalogue: NRA 27644.

Facilities: Photocopying. Microfilm/fiche readers.

Publications: D. MacCulloch: 'Manuscript Collections at Wesley College, Bristol: a Handlist', *Proceedings of the Wesley Historical Society*, xliii, 95.

149 Brixham Museum & History Society

Address: Bolton Cross, Brixham, Devon TQ5 8LZ

Telephone: (01803) 856267

E-mail: mail@brixhamheritage.org.uk

Website: www.brixhamheritage.org.uk

Enquiries: The Curator, Dr Philip Armitage

Open: By arrangement.

Access: Generally open to the public, by appointment only; a research fee is charged.

Historical background: The Brixham Museum & History Society (a registered charity) was founded in 1958 for the purpose of recording, saving and displaying the heritage of the town and fishing port. The museum moved to its present site in 1976.

Acquisitions policy: Passive and selective collection of archival material to illustrate the history and locality of Brixham and environs, with special reference to material of a maritime nature.

Major collections: Documents associated with the trawling industry, including fishermen's apprenticeships and skippers' certificates, late 19th century.
Blueprints and specifications from Simpson, Strickland & Co. Ltd, Kingswear, engineers, yacht and steam launch builders, late 19th century–1930 (c225).
Local land deeds and legal records.

Non-manuscript material: Photographs relating to the history of the town, its people, and maritime activites (c1700).
Brixham Urban District Council Medical Officers of Health annual reports, 1897–1967.
Brixham *Western Guardian* (weekly newspaper), 1902–68 (53 vols).

Finding aids: Accession register. Computer-based index to photographic archive.

Facilities: Microfilm reader.

Conservation: Contracted out.

150 Isle of Arran Heritage Museum

Address: Rosaburn, Brodick, Isle of Arran KA27 8DP

Telephone: (01770) 302636

Website: tom.k.mccloud@btinternet.com

Enquiries: The Archivist, Stuart Gough

Open: Weds: 10.30–4.30

Access: Generally open to the public, a donation is welcomed. Genealogical research work will be carried out by members of the museum on request, for agreed charges.

The museum was established in 1979 and it acquires items with an Arran connection. It holds material relating to land tenure, genealogy, emigration, archaeology, music, poetry, geology, shipping, the fishing industry, horticulture, local industries, and most aspects of life on the island. There are also photographic collections, especially those of MacFee and Anderson, *c*1900–1912. Museum documentation record cards are available as well as photocopying and microfiche reader finding aids. The museum has issued two publications by A. Fairhurst, *Arran Heritage Museum Guide* and *Exploring Arran's Past.*

151   Bromley Public Library
Archive Section

Parent organisation: London Borough of Bromley

Address: Central Library, High Street, Bromley, Kent BR1 1EX

Telephone: (020) 8460 9955 ext 261

Fax: (020) 8313 9975

E-mail: bromley.cen.lib@cityscape.co.uk

Enquiries: The Archivist, Miss E. Silverthorne

Open: Mon, Wed, Fri: 9.30–6.00; Tues, Thurs: 9.30–8.00; Sat: 9.30–5.00; appointments recommended.

Access: Generally open to the public.

Historical background: The Greater London borough of Bromley was formed in 1965 by the amalgamation of Bromley, Beckenham, Penge, Orpington and Chislehurst, all of which had previously been part of Kent; Penge had been in Surrey until 1889, then in London until 1900. The first archivist was appointed in 1970. Previously there had been haphazard collection of material at all libraries, with the largest at Bromley, the result of the activities of a committee of local historians in the 1920s. There is close liaison with the Centre for Kentish Studies (entry 868), which has transferred some

local material, including Anglican parish records (diocese of Rochester: Beckenham, Bromley and Orpington deaneries). The library is recognised as a place of deposit for public records.

Acquisitions policy: Records of all kinds relating to the area of the borough.

Archives of organisation: Records of predecessor authorities, late 19th century– .

Major collections: Usual local authority record holdings and deposited collections.

Finding aids: Lists sent to NRA.

Facilities: Photocopying. Photography by arrangement. Microfilm/fiche reader/printers. CD-Rom.

Conservation: Contracted out.

152   Bromsgrove Library

Parent organisation: Worcestershire County Council

Address: Stratford   Road,   Bromsgrove, Worcestershire B60 1AP

Telephone: (01905) 765024

Fax: (01527) 575855/6

E-mail: bromsgrovelib@worcestershire.gov.uk

Enquiries: The Bromsgrove Librarian

Open: Mon, Fri: 9.30–7.00; Tues, Wed: 9.30–5.00; Sat: 9.30–4.00.
Closed on bank holidays and usually on the following day.

Access: Generally open to the public. Some notice is necessary if manuscripts are to be consulted.

Historical background: The library first acquired the Housman collection because of the family's connection with the town.

Acquisitions policy: Donations of relevant material on the Housman family are accepted.

Major   collections: Letters   of   Laurence Housman (1865–1959), pacifist and brother of A.E. Housman, 1927–58 (approx 1200 sheets); and of his sister, Clemence Housman (approx 20 sheets).

Non-manuscript material: Small collection of background material on the Housman family.
Bromsgrove Messenger, 1860– .

Facilities: Photocopying. Microfilm/fiche readers.

153 St Mary's Convent, Buckfast

Parent organisation: St Scholastica's Abbey, Teignmouth

Address: St Mary's Convent, 7 Buckfast Road, Buckfast, Devon TQ11 0EA

Telephone: (01364) 643280

Enquiries: The Archivist, Dame Mildred Murray-Sinclair

Open: By arrangement.

Access: Researchers, and those genuinely interested in monastic history. An appointment is necessary.

The community was founded in 1662 at Dunkirk for English Benedictine nuns on the continent. It also represented a similar monastery founded at Pontoise. During the French Revolution the nuns were imprisoned, and on release they settled at Hammersmith until 1863, when the community removed to Teignmouth. When St Scholastica's Abbey closed in 1987, the recusant library, primarily of pre-18th century books, was transferred to Downside Abbey (entry 59). Four of St Scholastica's community (including the archivist) have started a small community at Buckfast and hold the archives there. The archives of St Scholastica's date back to its foundation, although little remains for the early years in Dunkirk. No lists or catalogues are yet available.

154 Buckfast Abbey

Address: Buckfastleigh, Devon TQ11 0EE

Telephone: (01364) 645500

Fax: (01364) 643891

Website: www.buckfast.org.uk

Enquiries: The Archivist

Open: Not open to the public, but enquiries about the history of the abbey and the monastic life may be answered.

Access: By appointment.

Historical background: The abbey was originally founded in 1018 but, like other abbeys, was suppressed in 1539. In the following centuries the church and monastery became a ruin. The abbey was refounded in 1882 by a group of exiled monks from France, and the monastery was subsequently rebuilt on the medieval foundations.

Acquisitions policy: To maintain the archive of the abbey.

Archives of organisation: Records of the abbey, 1882– . The only notable documentary record of the medieval abbey is a part of the cartulary which the abbey was able to acquire in later years.

Non-manuscript material: A collection of architects' drawings for the rebuilding of the abbey and more recent restorations.

Facilities: Photocopying at the discretion of the archivist.

Publications: R Clutterbuck: *Buckfast Abbey: a History* (1994).

155 Salford RC Diocesan Archives

Parent organisation: Salford Roman Catholic Diocesan Trustees

Address: St Mary's Presbytery, 3 Todmorden Road, Burnley, Lancashire BB10 4AU

Telephone: (01282) 422007

Fax: (01282) 424622

E-mail: davelannon@aol.com

Enquiries: Fr David Lannon

Open: By arrangement only.

Access: Bona fide scholars, by appointment.

Acquisitions policy: Relevant diocesan and local RC history material acquired, by donation and purchase.

Archives of organisation: Diocese, parish and related societies records, 1850– .
NB Parish registers are either in individual parishes or the Lancashire Record Office (see entry 1044).

Major collections: Bishops' official Acta.
Bishop Casartelli papers, 1852–1925.
Education and Catholic schools material.

Non-manuscript material: Deed plans and photographs.
Directories and diocesan almanacs.

The *Harvest*, 1887–1969; *Catholic Federationist*, 1910–23.

Finding aids: Lists and subject index.

Facilities: Photocopying.

Publications: The Acta of Bishop Vaughan, Second Bishop of Salford, 1872–1892.
The Acta of Bishop Bilsborrow, Third Bishop of Salford, 1892–1903.

156 Staffordshire and Stoke-on-Trent Archive Service
Burton on Trent Archives

Parent organisation: Staffordshire County Council and Stoke-on-Trent City Council

Address: Riverside, High Street, Burton on Trent, Staffordshire DE14 1AH

Telephone: (01283) 239556

Fax: (01283) 239571

E-mail: burton.library@staffordshire.gov.uk

Website: www.staffordshire.gov.uk

Enquiries: The Group Librarian
The Lichfield Archivist-in-Charge (01543 510720)

Open: Mon, Tues, Fri: 9.15–6.00; Wed, Sat: 9.15–1.00; Thurs: 9.15–7.00.

Access: Generally open to the public; previous notification of a visit to the Archive Collection is essential.

Historical background: The present building was opened in 1976 to house archives from the Burton area, principally Burton borough records.

Acquisitions policy: Local archives are accepted on deposit or as gifts.

Major collections: Records of Burton borough, and board of guardians, 1830s– .
Burton Methodist archives, 19th century– .
Education records from the former County Borough of Burton, 1870s– .

Facilities: Photocopying. Microfilm/fiche readers.

157 Bury Archives Service

Parent organisation: Bury Metropolitan Borough Council

Address: 1st Floor, Derby Hall Annexe, Edwin Street (off Crompton Street), Bury BL9 0AS

Telephone: (0161) 797 6697

Fax: (0161) 253 5915

E-mail: information@bury.gov.uk

Website: www.bury.gov.uk

Enquiries: The Archivist, Mr K. J. Mulley

Open: Mon–Fri: 10.00–1.00, 2.00–5.00; Sat (1st of each month): 10.00–1.00. Appointments are essential, except on Tuesdays.

Access: Generally open to the public. The service operates the CARN reader's ticket system.

Historical background: Bury Metropolitan Borough Council was formed in 1974 by the amalgamation of Bury County Borough with Prestwich and Radcliffe boroughs, and Ramsbottom, Tottington and Whitefield urban districts. The archive service was established in 1986 to administer large backlogs of council records created by the local government reorganisation, and scattered private records previously deposited with the borough museum and libraries. In 1992 it moved to new premises in Edwin Street, and certain local authority records previously deposited with Lancashire Record Office were transferred back to Bury. Other records for the locality are held by Lancashire Record Office (see entry 1044) (including Bury and Prestwich manorial), Manchester Archives and Local Study (entry 877) (parish records), and Greater Manchester County Record Office (entry 874) (Wilton estate and some public records).

Acquisitions policy: Archives of organisations and individuals based in, or primarily relating to, the area of the borough, including local branches of national or regional bodies. Records on certain media (film, sound recordings) have been transferred to the North West Film Archive (see entry 886) and the North West Sound Archive (entry 245).

Archives of organisation: Local authority records, 1675– .

Major collections: Usual deposited local records, including non-conformist churches, 1789–1992; schools, 1851–1985; tithe maps, Bury and Prestwich parishes, 1838–42; businesses, 1782– , including Richard Bealey & Co., bleachers and chemical manufacturers, 1750–1935; Woodcock & Sons, solicitors, 1780–1980;

trade unions and co-op societies, 1858– ; local social, recreational and political groups, 1839– ; personal and family papers, including Hutchinson family of Bury, 1727–1950.

Non-manuscript material: Plans, drawings, photographs and maps are included in many of the archives listed above; building regulation plans (*c*12,000) for Bury, 1866–1948, Whitefield, 1866–1927, and Ramsbottom, 1877–1948; tithe maps, Bury and Prestwich parishes (schedules Prestwich only).
Photograph collection (*c*14,000; accessed through digitised copies).

Finding aids: Lists; name and place indexes to deeds and plans. Lists sent to NRA.

Facilities: Photocopying. Microfilm/fiche reader.

Conservation: Provided by agreement with Greater Manchester Record Office.

Publications: 'Routes' guide to family history; *Newsletter* (quarterly).
Guide (1995).

158 Suffolk Record Office
Bury St Edmunds Branch

Parent organisation: Suffolk County Council

Address: 77 Raingate Street, Bury St Edmunds, Suffolk IP33 2AR

Telephone: (01284) 352350

Fax: (01284) 352355

E-mail: bury.ro@libher.suffolkcc.gov.uk

Website: www.suffolkcc.gov.uk/sro/index.html

Enquiries: The Public Service Manager, Mrs Sheila Reed

Open: Mon–Sat: 9.00–5.00.

Access: Generally open to the public. The office operates the CARN reader's ticket system. A paid research service is available.

Historical background: The office was established as Bury St Edmunds Borough Record Office in 1938 and was known as Bury St Edmunds and West Suffolk Record Office from 1950 to 1974. It became the Bury St Edmunds Branch of the Suffolk Record Office in 1974. It is the Diocesan Record Office for St Edmundsbury and Ipswich (Archdeaconry of Sudbury) and a recognised place of deposit for public records.

Acquisitions policy: Archival and printed material relating to the former administrative county of West Suffolk.

Archives of organisation: Usual local authority record holdings.

Major collections: Deposited local collections, including estate and family papers of the Dukes of Grafton (the 3rd Duke was Prime Minister, 1768–70); papers of Hervey family, Marquisses of Bristol, in Lincolnshire, Essex and Sussex, 14th–20th centuries; records of Robert Boby, engineers, 1866–1909; Suffolk Regiment archives, 17th–20th centuries.

Non-manuscript material: Local studies library as integral part of record office.

Finding aids: Catalogues and indexes; catalogues sent to NRA; annual summary of accessions published.

Facilities: Photocopying. Photography. Microfilm/fiche readers/printers (some self-service). Microfilming by arrangement.

Conservation: Available in-house.

Publications: Guide to Genealogical Sources (5/1998).

159 Royal Caledonian Schools Trust

Address: 80A High Street, Bushey, Hertfordshire WD2 3DE

Telephone: (020) 8421 8845

Fax: (020) 8421 8845

E-mail: rcet@caleybushey.demon.co.uk

Website: www.caritasdata.co.uk/charity6/ch005236.htm

Enquiries: The Chief Executive, Mr John Horsfield

Open: Term: Mon–Fri: 9.00–3.30.
Closed during all state school holidays.

Access: Bona fide researchers, by appointment only. A substantial part of the archives are deposited at the Bushey Museum; an appointment to view can be made via the trust's office.

The Royal Caledonian Schools were founded in 1815 by the Highland Society of London under the presidency of Queen Victoria's father, the

Duke of Kent and Strathearn. The aim was to care for children of Scotsmen lost in the Napoleonic wars. At the turn of the century the schools moved to Bushey, where they have continued to care for children of Scottish parentage. Today most of the children are the sons and daughters of men serving in the Scottish regiments and of needy Scots living in the London area. The archives consist of minute books, registers and other records of the day-to-day running of the trust and schools since 1815; also files on the majority of children who attended the schools, which can only be accessed by them or their legal successors. The trust also has a fine collection of photographs of school events, late 19th and 20th centuries.

160 Gwynedd Archives and Museums Service
Caernarfon Area Record Office

Parent organisation: Gwynedd Council

Address: Victoria Dock, Caernarfon, Gwynedd LL55 1SH

Telephone: (01286) 679095

Fax: (01286) 679637

E-mail: annrhydderch@gwynedd.gov.uk

Enquiries: The Principal Archivist and Heritage Officer, Ann Rhydderch, County Offices, Shirehall Street, Caernarfon, Gwynedd LL55 1SH

Open: Tues, Thurs, Fri: 9.30–12.30, 1.30–5.00; Wed: 9.30–12.30, 1.30–7.00.
Closed second full week in October.

Access: Generally open to the public. The office operates the CARN reader's ticket system. Day tickets are also available.

Historical background: The County Record Office was founded in 1947 and Gwynedd Archive Service was established in 1974, incorporating Anglesey and Merioneth record offices. It became the Gwynedd Archives and Museums Service in 1985. The office also acts as the Diocesan Record Office for Bangor and St Asaph (parish records). There is a Gwynedd Archives Service Record Office at Dolgellau (see entry 280). The office is recognised as a place of deposit for public records.

Acquisitions policy: The office collects material relating to the historic county of Caernarfonshire. It acquires the authority's own records and those of its predecessors, public records, parish records and any other records germane to the history of the county.

Archives of organisation: Usual local authority record holdings.

Major collections: Deposited local collections, including the following which have a wider significance: records of the slate quarrying industry; shipping and other maritime history collections; Ffestiniog Railway archives; estate records, notably those of Boduan, Cefnamlwch, Glynllifon, Rug (Denbighshire) and Vaynol.

Non-manuscript material: Major collections of topographical prints, photographs, local newspapers and Welsh-language periodicals.
Oral history recordings (*c*600).

Finding aids: Catalogues, lists and indexes of people, place and subject. Catalogues sent to the NRA.

Facilities: Photocopying. Photography. Microfilm/fiche readers.

Conservation: In-house. Some outside work undertaken.

Publications: No up-to-date guide, but the Gwynedd Archives Service has a large number of publications on its holdings.

161 Royal Logistic Corps Museum

Address: The Princess Royal Barracks, Deepcut, Camberley, Surrey GU16 6RW

Telephone: (01252) 340871

Fax: (01252) 340875

E-mail: query@rlcmuseum.freeserve.co.uk

Enquiries: The Curator, Mr F.G. O'Connell
The Archivist, Dr A.R. Morton

Open: Mon–Fri: 10.00–4.00; Sat: 10.00–3.00.

Access: Bona fide researchers. Some personal collections are restricted. Appointments are necessary.

Historical background: The museum opened in 1993 and has combined the collections of the corps detailed below. Most material dates from 1850 onwards; the collections complement but do not include personnel records and unit war diaries.

Acquisitions policy: To acquire material relating to the history, personnel and equipment of the corps listed below and their predecessors.

Archives of organisation: Archives of the Royal Corps of Transport, the Royal Army Ordnance Corps, the Royal Pioneer Corps, the Army Catering Corps and the Royal Engineers Postal and Courier Service.

Major collections: Documents, publications, personal recollections and photographs donated by individuals who have served with corps supporting the army.
Examples of official documentation.

Non-manuscript material: Photographic collections, corps journals, training manuals.

Finding aids: Individual collection listings.

Facilities: Photocopying. Photography.

Conservation: Contracted out.

162 Royal Military Academy Sandhurst
Sandhurst Collection

Address: Camberley, Surrey GU15 4PQ

Telephone: (01276) 412503

Fax: (01276) 412595

Enquiries: The Curator

Open: Mon–Fri: 10.00–5.00.

Access: Approved readers, on written application (normally 48 hours' notice is required) and by prior appointment only.

Historical background: The Royal Military Academy Sandhurst, established in 1947, is an amalgamation of the Royal Military Academy (Woolwich) (f. 1741) and the Royal Military College (Sandhurst) (f. 1800). The archive section was set up in 1986, and is recognised as a place of deposit for public records.

Acquisitions policy: To collect material relating to the history of the RMAS and its predecessors.

Archives of organisation: Archives of the three constituent organisations, including correspondence, letter-books, files and publications, 18th century– .

Major collections: Papers of Gen. Sir J.G. Le Marchant (1766–1812), first Lieutenant-Governor of the Royal Military College.

Non-manuscript material: Large quantity of ephemera.

Finding aids: Some holdings are listed in the Public Record Office (see entry 1058) and the rest are in the process of being listed. Le Marchant: NRA 0184.

163 Addenbrooke's Hospital
Archives Office

Parent organisation: Addenbrooke's NHS Trust

Address: c/o Administration, Box 146, Addenbrooke's Hospital, Hills Road, Cambridge CB2 2QQ

Telephone: (01223) 245151 ext. 6737

Fax: (01223) 216502

Enquiries: The Hon. Archivist, Mr P. Rundle

Open: Mon–Fri: a.m.

Access: Bona fide researchers. An appointment is necessary.

Historical background: The hospital is named after Dr John Addenbrooke (1620–1719), who left a sum of money to build 'a small physical hospital for poor people of any Parish or any County'. This bequest gave John Addenbrooke the distinction of being the first Englishman to bequeath his private wealth to found a voluntary hospital. The original hospital was in Trumpington Street, Cambridge, but the new hospital was completed in 1984. Addenbrooke's is the district general and teaching hospital for Cambridge. It is recognised as a place of deposit for public records.

Archives of organisation: Records of the hospital, including: minute books, 1766–1939; rules and orders, 1778–1908; annual reports, 1863– ; accounts, 1740–67, 1923–41; clinical records, 1878–1947.

Non-manuscript material: Portraits and photographs of medical staff and governors, 1800– .
Small collection of surgical instruments and ward equipment.

Finding aids: Lists

Facilities: Photocopying.

164 British Antarctic Survey Archives Service

Parent organisation: Natural Environment Research Council

Address: High Cross, Madingley Road, Cambridge CB3 0ET

Telephone: (01223) 221531

Fax: (01223) 362616

E-mail: mjvi@bas.ac.uk

Enquiries: The Archivist and Registrar, Mr M.J. Vine

Open: Mon–Fri: 9.30–1.00, 2.00–5.00.

Access: By appointment only. A means of identification may be required.

Historical background: The survey originated as Operation *Tabarin*, an expedition organised during World War II primarily to maintain a British presence in Antarctica, although the opportunity was taken to carry out scientific work. At the end of the war the operation was transferred to the Colonial Office and renamed the Falkland Islands Dependencies Survey, with scientific research as its main purpose. A scientific office was established in London in 1950 and specialist units at various universities from 1956. The organisation was renamed the British Antarctic Survey in 1962 and became a constituent institute of the Natural Environment Research Council in 1967. Most of the survey's activities in the UK were centralised at a new headquarters in Cambridge in 1976. Some 20 Antarctic stations have been established at various times, four of which are currently operational and involved in a wide spectrum of research. The Archives Service was established in 1979 and is recognised as a place of deposit for public records.

Acquisitions policy: Internal transfers of scientific, logistical and administrative records. Loans and gifts are accepted from closely related organisations and from individuals connected in some way with the survey.

Archives of organisation: Specimen registers, maps, air photographs, original observations (e.g. field and laboratory notes) and derived data of scientific staff in the fields of atmospheric, earth and life sciences, 1943– .
Internal reports on building and maintaining stations in Antarctica and South Georgia, and on the scientific work carried out from them, 1943– .

Administrative and logistical records, the latter dealing with shipping, aviation and dog travel, from the former London and Port Stanley (Falkland Islands) offices and from the present headquarters in Cambridge.

Major collections: Whaling inspectors' records, 1924–66, deposited by the Sea Mammal Research Unit.

Non-manuscript material: Plans of Antarctic stations. Hand-drawn and printed maps.
Photographs and cine film/video material relating to all aspects of British Antarctic Survey activities.
A limited selection of historical books and an extensive collection of relevant scientific publications in the library.

Finding aids: Archival lists produced from computer database with on-line indexes.

Facilities: Photocopying. Photography.

Conservation: Contracted out.

Publications: V. Fuchs: *Of Ice and Men: the Story of the British Antarctic Survey, 1943–1973* (Oswestry, 1982).
J. Rae and G.J. Smith: *BAS Archives: Guide to Holdings* (Cambridge, 1987).
S. Robertson: *Operation Tabarin* (Cambridge, 1993).

165 Cambridge University Library

Parent organisation: University of Cambridge

Address: West Road, Cambridge CB3 9DR

Open: Manuscripts Room: Mon–Fri: 9.30–6.45; Sat: 9.00–12.30.
Closed one week in September and certain other days around public holidays.

Facilities: Photocopying. Photography. Microfilming. Microfilm readers. Ultra-violet light.

Conservation: Full in-house facilities.

A Manuscripts Department

Telephone: (01223) 333000/333143

Fax: (01223) 333160

E-mail: mss@ula.cam.ac.uk

Website: www.lib.cam.ac.uk/mss

Enquiries: The Keeper of Manuscripts and University Archives, Dr P.N.R. Zutshi

Access: Bona fide researchers, on production of satisfactory references in accordance with the Library Syndicate's regulations. A charge may be made and intending readers are advised to write in advance.

The Admissions Office (for first visit) is open Mon-Fri: 9.30–12.30, 2.00–4.15; Sat: 9.30–12.30.

Historical background: Cambridge University is known to have possessed a library since the second decade of the 14th century. It retains few MSS from its pre-Reformation holdings, but since 1574 the MS collections have been continuously enlarged. The present library building was opened in 1934. An extension was added in 1972, when the University Archives, until then separately housed, were brought into the library. It is a recognised place of deposit for public records.

Acquisitions policy: MSS of all types are acquired, with the emphasis on strengthening existing collections.

Major collections: The older collections, both Western and oriental, are mainly of a literary character.

The Taylor-Schechter Genizah Collection of Hebraica.

Western MSS acquired over the past 100 years include records of the Diocese and Dean and Chapter of Ely; several East Anglian family and estate archives; private papers of Cambridge men, e.g. Adam Sedgwick (1785–1873) and Charles Darwin (1809–82); records of the Bible Society (formerly the British and Foreign Bible Society), 19th–20th centuries, Society for Promoting Christian Knowledge (SPCK), 1699–1970, and other national and university societies.

Commercial records, including Phoenix Assurance, 1782–20th century; Jardine Matheson & Co 19th century; Vickers plc, 19th–20th centuries.

Queens' College Archives.

Medieval MSS of Pembroke College and Peterhouse.

Non-manuscript material: Microfilms of MSS in other locations, e.g. the papers of Field Marshal J.C. Smuts (1870–1950).

Finding aids: Lists and indexes.

Publications: Catalogue of the (Western) Manuscripts Preserved in the Library of the University of Cambridge (Cambridge, 1856–

67/R 1980) [the preface to the reprint contains details of the principal catalogues of both Western and oriental MS collections published to 1979].

P. de Brun and M. Herbert: *Catalogue of Irish Manuscripts in Cambridge Libraries* (Cambridge, 1986).

J.H. Baker: *Catalogue of English Legal Manuscripts in Cambridge University Library* (Woodbridge, 1996).

Various published handlists and indexes.

B University Archives

Telephone: (01223) 333147/333148

Fax: (01223) 333160

E-mail: archives@ula.cam.ac.uk

Website: www.lib.cam.ac.uk/handbook/d5.html

Enquiries: The Keeper of Manuscripts and University Archives, Dr P.N.R. Zutshi

Historical background: From at least the 14th century the university kept its muniments in a chest in the tower of the University Church. It was from here that they were allegedly removed and destroyed in the 1381 rising. In fact more than 50 items, the earliest dated 1266, survive from before this date. By 1420, when Rysley compiled the first catalogue, the chest had been transferred to the New Chapel above the newly built Divinity Schools. During the Civil War the archives may have been hidden in private houses before being returned, in 1662, to a custom-built muniment room next to the Registry office in the Old Schools, the Registry being recognised henceforth as their keeper. In 1836 the Registry's office and the archives were moved into the new Pitt Press building and they remained there until 1934, when the building of the new University Library enabled their return to the Old Schools. In 1972 the archives were transferred physically into the university library and in 1977 came under the librarian's authority. Some of the university's departments and libraries hold papers.

Acquisitions policy: Acquisitions are restricted to records of the administration of the university and its departments.

Archives of organisation: Charters, grants of privilege, title deeds; university statutes; records of the university's legislative and executive bodies and of the chancellor's and commissary's jurisdiction; financial records; syndicate minutes; departmental records; matriculation and degree records; records of charitable foundations and other endowments.

Records of University Press; Board of Extra-Mural Studies; Course on Overseas Development; Botanic Garden; Appointments Board; Department of Geology.

Institute of Astronomy archives and collections, including records of Cambridge observatories, 1823– .

Non-manuscript material: Estate maps and plans. Architectural plans and drawings. Photographs. Items of academic dress (few).

Finding aids: Card index. Typescript lists of many collections, some sent to NRA.

Publications: Statutes, 1785– .
H.R. Luard: 'A List of Documents in the University Registry from the Year 1266 to the year 1544', *Proceedings of the Cambridge Antiquarian Society* (o.s.), iii (1864–76), 385–403.
A Chronological List of the Graces, Documents and other Papers in the University Registry which Concern the University Library (Cambridge, 1870).
Grace Books, Alpha to Delta (Cambridge 1897–1910) [*Beta* in two parts].
E.S. Leedham-Green: 'University Press Records in the University Archives: an Account and a Checklist', *Transactions of the Cambridge Bibliographical Society,* viii (1984), 398–418.
H.E. Peek and C.P. Hall: *The Archives of the University of Cambridge: a Historical Introduction* .
D.M. Owen: *Cambridge University Archives: a Classified List* (Cambridge, 1989).

C Royal Commonwealth Society Collections

Telephone: (01223) 333000/333198

Fax: (01223) 333160

Enquiries: Miss T.A. Barringer

Historical background: The organisation, founded as the Colonial Society in 1868 and known successively as the Royal Colonial Institute, the Royal Empire Society and the Royal Commonwealth Society, built up a library from its earliest days. The society had its headquarters in Northumberland Avenue, London WC2, from 1885. In the early 1990s the library was threatened with piecemeal sale and dispersal as a result of the society's financial difficulties, but a successful international appeal succeeded in buying the entire collection for the University of Cambridge, and it was transferred to the University Library in the summer of 1993.

Acquisitions policy: Newly published material is no longer added to the collection but donations of relevant manuscripts and photographs are welcome.

Archives of organisation: Archives of the Royal Commonwealth Society: substantial collection of minute books of the council of the society and varied committees; correspondence; memoranda; miscellaneous items.

Major collections: Papers of Sir George Arthur (1784–1854) as Superintendent of British Honduras, 1814–24.
Some official correspondence and private papers of Hugh Childers (1827–96), cabinet minister.
Diaries and notebooks of Cuthbert Christy (1863–1932), doctor and traveller.
Correspondence and diaries of Sir John Glover (1829–85), administrator in West Africa.
Papers of Colonel Henry Burney (1792–1845), diplomat in Siam and Burma.
British Association of Malaya:'diaries, letters, reminiscences (20 boxes).
Charts and documents relating to the North West Company, the fur trade and Canadian exploration.

Non-manuscript material: Photographs (70,000), including c3000 photographs of members of the society, 1880–1925.
Smaller collection of negatives and some slides.
Several collections of paintings and prints, notably paintings by A.H. Fisher, Gen. Edward Frome, A.A. Anderson, and the Gifford Collection of prints and drawings of St Helena.

Finding aids: Updated typescript catalogue to Manuscript Collection available on request. Detailed handlist to major collections.

Publications: D.H. Simpson: *Manuscript Catalogue of the Royal Commonwealth Society* (1975).
National Inventory of Documentary Sources (Chadwyck-Healey microfiche, 1984–).
Library Notes, nos. 1–306 (1957–91).

D Royal Greenwich Observatory Archives

Telephone: (01223) 333000, 333056 (direct line)

Fax: (01223) 333160

E-mail: ajp@ula.cam.ac.uk

Website: www.lib.cam.ac.uk/handbook/d12.html

Enquiries: The Royal Greenwich Observatory Archivist, Mr A.J. Perkins

Historical background: The Royal Observatory, Greenwich, was founded in 1675 by Charles II for the improvement of navigation. It became the Royal Greenwich Observatory in 1948. In 1988 the collection was moved from Herstmonceux Castle, East Sussex, to Cambridge University Library. The archives were developed largely under Sir George Biddell Airy (1801–92), 7th Astronomer Royal, who also acquired the records of the Board of Longitude. The archives of the RGO are public records. The records reflect the role of the RGO in navigational astronomy, astrometry and astrophysical research, and in the construction of major astronomical telescopes. The Royal Greenwich Observatory closed on 31st October 1998.

Acquisitions policy: Modern records of the RGO accrue to the collection in accordance with the Public Records Act 1958. The personal papers of the Astronomers Royal, members of staff, and associated astronomers and scientists are accepted on deposit, as are collections of papers related to the RGO and astronomy.

Archives of organisation: Papers of the Astronomers Royal, 1675–1971, and directors of the RGO, 1972–98.
Papers and records of HM Nautical Almanac Office, 1937–98.
Administrative papers, 1911–98.
Departmental and project papers, 20th century, including records of the Anglo-Australian Telescope Project, 1963–74, and the Northern Hemisphere Observatory (La Palma), 1970–98.

Major collections: Records of the Board of Longitude, 1737–1828; Royal Observatory, Cape of Good Hope, 1820–1978, and Radcliffe Observatory, 1929–67.
Kew Observatory papers, solar observations and records, 1858–93.
Stonyhurst College Observatory sunspot drawings, 1880–1947.
Papers of John Guy Porter (1900–81); Roderick Oliver Redman (1905–75); and Donald Harry Sadler (1908–87).
Letters of David Kinnebrook (c 1775–1802); papers of Michael V. Penston (1943–90).

Non-manuscript material: Plans of the observatory buildings and grounds at Greenwich and Herstmonceux, and of observing sites.
Astronomical drawings and drawings of places with astronomical associations.
Photographs of astronomical subjects, and people and places with astronomical associations.
Maps concerned with the move of the Royal Observatory, c1944.
Some films and videos concerned with telescopes and astronomy.
Sound recordings by working astronomers (oral history of the Royal Observatory).
Microfilms of the earlier papers.

Finding aids: Handlists to the major classes. Catalogue and index to the papers of John Flamsteed (also in machine-readable form). Index to photographs and records of Royal Observatory, Cape of Good Hope. Index to Airy papers. Lists of papers of the earlier Astronomers Royal sent to NRA.

Publications: Archives of the Royal Greenwich Observatory, Cambridge University Library Handbook D12.

166 Cambridgeshire Archives Service
County Record Office, Cambridge

Parent organisation: Cambridgeshire County Council

Address: Shire Hall, Castle Hill, Cambridge CB3 0AP

Telephone: (01223) 717281

Fax: (01223) 717201

E-mail: county.records.cambridge @cambridgeshire.gov.uk

Website: www.camcnty.gov.uk

Enquiries: The County Archivist, Mrs E.A. Stazicker
The Deputy County Archivist, Dr Philip Saunders

Open: Tues–Thurs: 9.00–12.45, 1.45–5.15; Fri 9.00–12.00, 1.45–4.15; Tues to 9.00, by appointment.

Access: Generally open to the public. The office operates the CARN reader's ticket system.

Historical background: The office was established for receipt of records in 1930, but had no staff until 1948. Before 1930, Cambridge University Library (entry 165) acted as a local repository. The office also acts as Diocesan Record office for Ely (parish records) and for the Archdeaconry of Ely and the deaneries of Ely and March in Wisbech Archdeaconry, and holds probate records for the Diocesan Archdeaconry. Other diocesan and archdeanconry records are at Cambridge University Library (see entry 165); parish records for other deaneries are at Wisbech Museum (entry 1207) and Norfolk Record Office (entry 939). There is a Branch Office at Huntingdon (entry 459).

Acquisitions policy: The service seeks to acquire records of all sorts relating to the area of the present administrative county. This comprises, with some minor adjustments, the historic counties of Cambridgeshire, the Isle of Ely and Huntingdonshire. Records for the Cambridgeshire and Isle of Ely area are held mainly at Cambridge Record Office.

Archives of organisation: Usual local authority record holdings.

Major collections: Deposited local collections, including records of Bedford Level Corporation, 1663–1920 (with some earlier records); nearly complete series relating to land drainage of fens and adjoining counties; records of various women's groups, of which Cambridge was particularly prolific, 1884–1984.

Non-manuscript material: Aerial photographs, 1949–69; Cambridge Antiquarian Society glass lantern slides, 1920s and 1930s.

Finding aids: Hard-copy lists and indexes, and some computer-assisted indexing, available in-house only at present. Limited subject-based information available on web-site.

Facilities: Photocopying. Photography by arrangement. Microfilming. Microfilm/fiche readers.

Conservation: Paper, parchment and book-binding in-house; advice relating to record care always available; outside work undertaken occasionally.

Publications: Annual Reports (1965–) [include lists of accessions].

A. Black: *Guide to Education Records* (1972).

M. Farrar: *Genealogical Sources in Cambridgeshire* (2/1994).

167 Cambridgeshire Collection

Parent organisation: Cambridgeshire Libraries

Address: Central Library, 7 Lion Yard, Cambridge CB2 3QD

Telephone: (01223) 712000

Fax: (01223) 712018

Website: www.camcnty.gov.uk/library

Enquiries: The Local Studies Librarian, Mr Christopher Jakes

Open: Mon–Fri: 9.30–7.00; Sat: 9.00–5.30.

Access: Generally open to the public.

Historical background: Cambridge Free Library opened in 1855 and from that date collected material relating to Cambridge and Cambridgeshire, both current and retrospective. In 1974 material from the local collection of Cambridgeshire and Isle of Ely County Library was incorporated with the city library collection to form the current collection.

Acquisitions policy: To collect material, principally published, relating to the City of Cambridge and the former county of Cambridgeshire and Isle of Ely, past, present and future.

Non-manuscript material: Photographic record of the Cambridge Antiquarian Society.
Industrial archaeological record of the Cambridge Society for Industrial Archaeology.
Various photographic collections.
Books, articles, annual reports, periodicals and associated monograph material.
Handbills and posters, 1734– ; illustrations, 1688– (c400,000).
Maps, principally printed, 1574– .
Newspapers, 1764– ; printed ephemera.
Tape-recordings and gramophone records relating to Cambridgeshire.

Finding aids: Catalogues. Indexes. Computer link to County Record Office. Listed buildings and county council minutes.

Facilities: Photocopying. Photography. Microfilm reader/printer. Tape play-back facilities.

Publications: Guide for Users.
Guide to Catalogues and Indexes.
Cambridgeshire Newspapers and the Local Researcher.
Village Projects: a Guide for Users.

An annotated Catalogue of Books and Articles, Pamphlets and Periodicals Acquired, 1855-1983 [on microfiche].

M.J. Petty: '"The Albatross Inheritance": Local Studies Libraries', *Library Management*, vi/1 (1985).

168 Centre of South Asian Studies

Parent organisation: University of Cambridge

Address: Laundress Lane, Cambridge CB2 1SD

Telephone: (01223) 338094

Fax: (01223) 316913

E-mail: ljc10@cam.ac.uk

Website: www.s-asian.cam.ac.uk

Enquiries: The Secretary/Librarian, Dr L.J. Carter

Open: Term: Mon–Fri: 9.30–5.30.
Vacation: Mon–Fri: 9.30–5.00.
Closed August.

Access: By appointment; written application required two weeks in advance, with references and statement of study.

Historical background: The archive was begun in 1966 to collect papers relating to economic, social and political conditions during the period of British rule in India, Burma and Ceylon. Contact was made with persons whose papers would not otherwise have found their way into a collection. This was done through the Indian Civil Service Pensioners' Association, and later all recipients of a pension from the former Indian Empire were contacted. Funding has come from various sources.

Acquisitions policy: Contacts made by word of mouth are the main source of material, which is personally collected by the librarian.

Major collections: Papers of Sir Edward Benthall (1893–1961); Sir Malcolm Darling (1880–1969); J.T. Gwynn (1881–1956) and J.P.L. Gwynn, Indian Civil Service, Madras; P.T. Mansfield (1892–1975), ICS Bihar and Orissa; Sir Reginald (1882–1927) and Lady Maxwell, ICS Madras etc.
Collection of writings (memoirs, letters, etc) by British women who lived and worked in India, and a series of answers to questionnaires.

Non-manuscript material: Tape-recordings made in India of people who knew Gandhi and were connected with the early days of the Independence movement; the conditions in Delhi and Punjab in 1947; Anglo-Indians; Roman Catholic missionaries and those who remained in India after 1947.
Tape-recordings made in England of wives and widows of Indian civil servants, and other government officers (forestry etc), missionaries and educationalists.
More than 80,000 photographs, including negatives and glass slides.
Cine films: home movies (16mm, 9.5mm and 8mm) covering aspects of domestic and social life, ceremonial, engineering, indigenous village life, people, crafts, tribals.
Maps on South and South-East Asia (300); Indian newspaper collection (3350 reels of microfilm).

Finding aids: Typescript lists of unpublished material. Handlists of photographic collections. Shotlists for cine films.

Facilities: Microfilm/fiche readers. Editing table for films. On-line terminals to the Internet.

Publications: M. Thatcher and L. Carter (eds): *Cambridge South Asian Archive* (1973, 1980, 1983, 1995) [5 vols], reproduced in (Chadwyck-Healey) *National Inventory of Documentary Sources in the United Kingdom.*
D. Boyes: *Principal Collections of Photographic Material in the Cambridge South Asian Archive* (1984).
L. Carter and D. Bateson: *Principal Collections of Papers in the Cambridge South Asian Archive* (3/1995).
L. Carter: *Brief Guide to Original Memoirs held in the Cambridge South Asian Archive* (1989).
Annual Reports of the Centre of South Asian Studies, University of Cambridge.

169 Cheshunt Foundation Archives

Address: Westminster College, Madingley Road, Cambridge CB3 0AA

Telephone: (01223) 741084

Fax: (01223) 300765

E-mail: jet40@cam.ac.uk

Enquiries: The Director, The Cheshunt Foundation, Rev. J.E. Tollington

Open: By special arrangement only.

Access: Any person with reasonable grounds; an appointment is necessary.

Historical background: The Cheshunt Foundation is the legal continuation of the former Cheshunt College, originally founded at Trevecca in 1767 by Selina, Countess of Huntingdon (1707–91), an aristocratic patron of the Wesleys. Cheshunt effectively ceased to operate as a theological college after the early 1970s.

Acquisitions policy: No acquisitions are sought; there is a small inflow of items of new relevant material given by individuals.

Archives of organisation: Records of Cheshunt College, 1767–1970s.
Correspondence of Selina, Countess of Huntingdon (several thousand items).

Finding aids: Catalogue, well indexed. Cheshunt Collection: NRA 12352.

Facilities: Photocopying. Microfiche reader.

Publications: E. Welch: *Calendar and Index of Cheshunt College Archives,* List and Index Society Special Series 14 (1981).
—— (ed.): *Cheshunt College: the Early Years* (Herts Records Society, 1991).

170 Christ's College

Parent organisation: University of Cambridge

Address: Cambridge CB2 3BU

A Muniments

Telephone: (01223) 334900

Fax: (10223) 339557

Enquiries: Hon Keeper of Muniments, Prof. G.T. Martin

Open: Mon–Fri by arrangement.
NB The Keeper is normally away between January and March

Access: Bona fide researchers by appointment, subject to approval of the Governing body of the College.

Historical background: The college was founded in 1439 as God's House, licensed by Henry VI, and was refounded and richly endowed as Christ's College in 1505 by the Lady Margaret Beaufort.

Acquisitions policy: To collect and preserve material concerned with all aspects of the history of the College.

Archives of organisation: Archives include deeds, grants, manorial rolls, confirmations, conveyances, terriers, grants of advowsons, college account books, student admission books and other administrative records, 11th century– .

Non-manuscript material: Maps and plans of present and former college estates; architectural plans and drawings of college buildings.
Photographs of sporting events, late 19th century– , and of undergraduates, 20th century– .
Tape recordings. Photographic albums of *HMS Challenger* voyage.

Finding aids: List of documents.

Facilities: Photocopying.

Publications: J. Peile: *Biographical Register of Christ's College, 1505–1905, and of the earlier foundation of God's House, 1448–1505* 2 vols (Cambridge, 1910–13).
H. Rackham: *Early Statutes of Christ's College* (Cambridge, 1927).

B Old Library

Telephone: (01223) 334951

Fax: (01223) 339557

E-mail: mycc2@cus.cam.ac.uk

Enquiries: Assistant to the Librarian, Mrs M. Courtney

Open: By arrangement.

Access: Bona fide scholars on written application.

Historical background: The Old Library, which is an extension by G.F. Bodley of the original 16th century College Library, contains material given by benefactors throughout the College's history.

Acquisitions policy: To receive gifts and bequests of MSS and photographic material from Fellows and others.

Major collections: Western MSS collections.
Papers of Charles Stuart Calverley (1831–1884), poet; Charles Darwin (1809–1882), naturalist; Douglas Rayner Hartree (1897–1958), mathematical physicist; John Stevens Henslow (1796–1861), botanist; Henry More (1614–1687), theologian; William Henry Denham

Rouse (1863–1950), classical scholar; Charles Lesingham Smith (1806–78) mathematician.

Finding aids: Catalogues for Western and Oriental mss in process of computerisation

Facilities: Photocopying.

Publications: M.R. James: *A Descriptive Catalogue of the Western Manuscripts in the Library of Christ's College Cambridge* (Cambridge, 1905).

171 Churchill College

Parent organisation: University of Cambridge

Address: Storey's Way, Cambridge CB3 0DS

A Churchill College Archives

Address: Storey's Way, Cambridge CB3 0DS

Telephone: (01223) 336168

Fax: (01223) 336177

E-mail: jb210@chu.cam.ac.uk

Website: www.chu.cam.ac.uk

Enquiries: The College Archivist, Ms Joan Bullock-Anderson.

Open: Mon–Tues: by arrangement.

Access: Bona fide researchers, by appointment only. There are restrictions on personal papers and all records under 30 years old.

Historical background: Churchill College was founded in 1960 as the national memorial to Sir Winston Churchill. By statute, 70 per cent of its junior members are admitted to study science, engineering and mathematics because of Sir Winston's wish to increase the number of highly trained technologists in the UK and forge closer links between industry and the universities. Originally for men, the college became co-educational in 1972. The development of the college's archives has been actively pursued since about 1987, and they have been administered separately from the Churchilll Archives Centre (see below) since 1992.

Acquisitions policy: Records of the college's administration and of student bodies. Papers of fellows and alumni. Papers from external sources relating to the college's foundation and development.

Archives of organisation: Charter, 1960; statutes, 1960– ; minutes and papers of governing body, college council and committees, 1959– ; administrative papers of most college departments relating to fellows, students, finance, property, academic matters, building etc; records of the college trustees relating to the foundation and early administration of the college, 1958– c1966; records of clubs and societies.

Finding aids: Guide to the Archives of Churchill College, indexed and continuously updated. Brief outline of holdings sent to NRA.

Facilities: Photocopying.

B Churchill Archives Centre

Address: Churchill College, Cambridge, Cambridgeshire CB3 0DS

Telephone: (01223) 336087 (Search Room)

Fax: (01223) 336135

E-mail: archives@chu.cam.ac.uk

Website: www.chu.cam.ac.uk/archives

Enquiries: The Archivist and Keeper

Open: Mon–Fri: 9.00–5.00.

Access: Bona fide researchers, by appointment only. Special conditions apply to a number of collections. In all cases the Archivist should be consulted in writing.

Historical background: The Archives Centre, opened in 1973, constitutes an American tribute to Sir Winston, since the cost of construction and endowment was met by a group of prominent US citizens.

The building of an extension to the Archives Centre is taking place until Spring 2002. This will inevitably cause disruption, and full details of anticipated closure periods are available at: www.chu.cam.ac.uk/archives/visiting.

Acquisitions policy: The centre was built to house Sir Winston's own papers, and to establish and make available a wide-ranging archive of the 'Churchill Era' and after, covering all those fields in which Churchill played a personal role or took a personal interest.

Major collections: Papers of Sir Winston Churchill and of more than 400 other political, military, naval, diplomatic and scientific figures, including Lord Alexander of Hillsborough, Lord Attlee, Ernest Bevin, Sir Alexander Cadogan, Sir James Chadwick, Sir John Cockcroft, Lord Duncan-Sandys,

Admiral of the Fleet Lord Fisher of Kilverstone, Lord Hailsham, Lord Hankey, Lt.-Gen. Sir Ian Jacob, Neil Kinnock, Reginald McKenna, Lise Meitner, Lord Noel-Baker, Sir Eric Phipps, FM Lord Slim, Sir Edward Spears, Lady Thatcher, Lord Vansittart and Sir Frank Whittle.

Non-manuscript material: Numerous photographs, mainly on the life and career of Churchill; microfilms; video and audiotapes.

Finding aids: TS catalogues of all major collections. Computerised catalogue and index of Churchill papers in preparation. Catalogues sent to NRA. Guides available on website.

Facilities: Photocopying. Photography and microfilming by arrangement. Accommodation in college usually available during university vacation.

Conservation: In-house paper conservation workshop.

Publications: A Guide to the Holdings of Churchill Archives Centre (1994) [a complete list of collections, reprinted annually].

172 Clare College Archives

Parent organisation: University of Cambridge

Address: Clare College Memorial Court, Queens Road, Cambridge CB3 9AJ

Telephone: (01223) 333228

Fax: (01223) 333219

E-mail: rss1@cam.ac.uk

Enquiries: The College Archivist, Dr R. Schofield

Open: Mon–Fri: 9.00–5.00, strictly by arrangement.

Access: Bona fide enquirers, by prior appointment. Restrictions are applied to personal records and all documents under 30 years old.

Historical background: Clare College was founded as University Hall by Richard de Badew in 1326 and refounded and endowed by Elizabeth de Clare between 1338 and 1359. Subsequent benefactions include the college properties. In 1521 a fire destroyed almost all records. The archives were formerly administered by the bursar; an archivist was appointed in 1985 and new accommodation was converted in 1999.

Acquisitions policy: Records relating to the college's administration, properties and affairs, and to related bodies. Papers of alumni and student organisations.

Archives of organisation: Statutes, 1359–1989; minutes of governing body and subsidiaries, 1644– ; accounts, including main college accounts, 1549–1977; registers of property transactions, 1354–1950; letter-books and files, 1628– .

Student records, including admission registers, 1631–1979, and tutorial accounts, 1658–1948.

Estate records for college properties in Cambridgeshire and many parts of England, 1298– .

Records of college benefices, 1539–1990.

Records of benefactions and trusts, 1525–1971.

Major collections: Papers of alumni, including Samuel Blithe (1636–1713), Edward Atkinson (1819–1915), Cecil Sharp (1859–1924), John Reynolds Wardale (1859–1931), W.C. Denis Browne (1888–1915), Mansfield Forbes (1889–1936) and Sir Harry Godwin (1901–85).

Records of student association, 1940– .

Minutes and accounts etc of various student clubs, notably Boat Club, 19th–20th centuries.

Non-manuscript material: Maps and plans, 1634– .

Photographs and engravings of benefactors, alumni and buildings.

Series of student and alumni magazines, 1889– .

Finding aids: Preliminary lists. Computerised catalogue in progress. Classification scheme and handlists. Brief lists sent to NRA.

Facilities: Photocopying.

Conservation: Contracted out to two private organisations.

Publications: J.R. Wardale: *Clare College* (London, 1899).

—— : *Clare College Letters and Documents* (Cambridge, 1903).

M.D. Forbes: *Clare College, 1326–1926* (Cambridge, 1927, 1930) [2 vols].

W.J. Harrison: *Notes on the Masters, Fellows, Scholars and Exhibitioners of Clare College, Cambridge* (Cambridge, 1953).

—— : *Life in Clare Hall* (Cambridge, 1958).

H. Godwin: *Cambridge and Clare* (Cambridge, 1985).

173 Corpus Christi College

Parent organisation: University of Cambridge

Address: Trumpington Street, Cambridge CB2 1RH

Telephone: (01223) 338030 (Early Archives); (01223) 338046 (Modern Archives); (01223) 338000 (Porters Lodge)

E-mail: rm248@cam.ac.uk

Enquiries: The Archivists, Miss Robin Myers (Modern Archives) or Mrs C. Hall (Early Archives)

Open: College records: by arrangement (may be closed during vacation periods).
Older administrative records are kept in the college's Parker Library and are available for readers in that library only.

Access: College records: open to those having sent a letter of request/reference, subject to the discretion of the keeper of the records. Recent personal and administrative records are not yet on open access. For material in the Parker Library apply to the assistant librarian readmissions procedure to become a reader.

Historical background: The College of Corpus Christi and the Blessed Virgin Mary was founded in 1352, uniting two town guilds of those names, under the patronage of Henry, Duke of Lancaster. The small medieval college was enlarged, reorganised and generously endowed by Matthew Parker, Queen Elizabeth's first Archbishop of Canterbury, who had been Master of the College under King Edward VI. The MS collection he bequeathed to the college is enshrined in the college's Parker Library, a separate entity within the college with its own librarian.

Acquisitions policy: Acquisitions are restricted to material relevant to the history of the college and the corporate activities of its members. Donations of MSS or papers by old members are housed in the Parker Library.

Archives of organisation: The college muniments proper comprise predominantly bursarial material; there is an incomplete series of college accounts, 1376– . Medieval charters, especially relating to property in Cambridge, and registers covering the careers of fellows.
Incomplete series of more recent administrative records with their supplementary ephemera.

Major collections: College library: papers of Arthur Boutwood (1864–1924), philosopher and theologian; correspondence of the Postlethwayt, Rogerson and Kerrich families, 1633–1828.

Parker Collection: bequest of Archbishop Matthew Parker (*d* 1575) of medieval and Reformation MSS; also material relating to Parker and his associates.

Non-manuscript material: Photographs and ephemera relating to the collegiate activities of old members.
Old prints and drawings of the college.

Finding aids: Typescript catalogue. Card catalogue of estate deeds. Handlists of maps.

Facilities: Photocopying. Photography by arrangement.

Publications: M.R. James: *A Descriptive Catalogue of the MSS in the Library of Corpus Christi College Cambridge* (Cambridge, 1912) [2 vols].
R. Vaughan and J. Fines: 'A Handlist of MSS in the Library of Corpus Christi College Cambridge not Described by M.R. James', *Transactions of the Cambridge Bibliographical Society*, iii (1960).

174 Department of Plant Sciences Library

Parent organisation: University of Cambridge

Address: Downing Street, Cambridge CB2 3EA

Telephone: (01223) 333930

Fax: (01223) 33953

E-mail: rs10018@cus.cam.ac.uk

Enquiries: The Assistant Librarian, Mr R. Savage

Open: Term: Mon–Fri: 8.30–5.15.
Vacation: Mon–Fri: 8.30–5.15.

Access: Members of the university; others with an interest in plant sciences.

Historical background: The Department of Plant Sciences was formerly the Botany School. The library was established in 1762 in association with the Botanic Garden; it has been in its present building since 1903.

Acquisitions policy: The library accepts donations of relevant botanical papers.

Major collections: Notes and some correspondence of eminent botanists, including Charles

Cardale Babington (1808–95), founder of the Entomological Society; John Stevens Henslow (1796–1861); William Border (1781–1862); A.G. Tansley (1871–1955); and G.C. Evans.

Finding aids: NRA 9541.

Facilities: Photocopying. Microfiche reader.

Conservation: Undertaken by Cambridge University Library (entry 165).

175 Downing College

Parent organisation: University of Cambridge

Address: Maitland Robinson Library, Cambridge CB2 1DQ

Telephone: (01223) 334800 (Porter's Lodge; Archivist); (01223) 334829 (Library)

Enquiries: The Fellow Archivist

Open: By arrangement only.

Access: Application must be made to the librarian to consult the Bowtell Collection. Consultation of archives is by appointment only, application to be made to the Fellow Archivist or Assistant.

Historical background: The college was founded in 1800 following years of litigation over the will of the founder, Sir George Downing (?1684–1749). Acquisition of land for the college site, development of the domus, and the development of the college within the university are reflected in the collection.

Acquisitions policy: Maintenance of archives and addition of modern college records (administrative and academic), where relevant.

Archives of organisation: Records of the college, including Downing family and estate papers; opinions and petitions *re* legal contest over foundation; college statutes; minute and account books; residence books.

Major collections: Library: Collection of John Bowtell (1753–1813), Cambridge antiquarian: includes Borough of Cambridge records; deeds, 16th–18th centuries; medieval fragments; MSS on bell ringing.

Non-manuscript material: Wilkins Plans: architectural plans for the college; farm plans of Downing estates in Cambridgeshire, mid–19th century.

Finding aids: Bowtell Collection: NRA 22707. Full lists and indexes to be compiled for archives.

Facilities: Photocopying.

Publications: C.M. Sicca: *Committed to Classicism: the Building of Downing College Cambridge.*
S. French: *The History of Downing College Cambridge.*
—— (ed.): *Aspects of Downing History.*

176 East Asian History of Science Library

Parent organisation: Needham Research Institute

Address: 8 Sylvester Road, Cambridge CB3 9AF

Telephone: (01223) 311545/369252

Fax: (01223) 362703

Enquiries: The Librarian, Mr J.P.C. Moffett

Open: Mon–Fri: 9.30–5.00.

Access: Bona fide scholars and research workers, by appointment only.

Historical background: The personal collection of Dr Joseph Needham (1900–95) forms the nucleus round which the library is developing. Dr Needham worked, with a number of collaborators, for more than 40 years on the history of Chinese science, technology and medicine. The library, as part of the Science and Civilization in China Project, became a recognised educational charity in 1963. It belongs to, and is governed by, the East Asian History of Science Trust.

Acquisitions policy: Chinese material of all periods connected with the history of science, technology and medicine is constantly being added, with Japanese and Western material on the same subjects.

Major collections: Archival and photographic material, 1940– , including a quantity of MSS in European and Asian languages, especially Chinese and Japanese, comprising principally notes and maps.

Non-manuscript material: Printed books (including many rare Chinese editions), periodicals and offprints.
Microfilm/fiche collections of Chinese material not widely available in the West.

Finding aids: Card catalogues.

Facilities: Photocopying. Microfilm/fiche reader.

Publications: J. Needham and others: *Science and Civilization in China* (Cambridge, 1954–) [18 vols to date].

177 Emmanuel College

Parent organisation: University of Cambridge

Address: Cambridge CB2 3AP

Telephone: (01223) 334292/334200

Fax: (01223) 334426

E-mail: jm215@emma.cam.ac.uk

Enquiries: The Archivist

Open: Mon–Fri: 9.00–5.30, by arrangement.

Access: Bona fide researchers, by appointment.

Historical background: Emmanuel College was founded in 1584 by Sir Walter Mildmay. The archives were first assembled in 1955 by H.S. Bennett.

Acquisitions policy: Consolidation of the college archives by receipt of non-current records from the various college offices.

Archives of organisation: Foundation deeds and statutes; estate deeds and records, 1584– , including a few medieval deeds and manorial court rolls; administrative records, including order books, 1588– , and minute books, 1895– ; financial records, 1584– ; admission registers, 1584– ; records of undergraduate societies, 19th and 20th centuries; chapel records, including accounts and inventories, 1599– .

Major collections: Letters, papers and photographs of past members of the college, including Henry Melville Gwatkin (1844–1916), historian and theologian; Edward Woodall Naylor (1867–1934), composer and musical historian; and Cyril Northcote Parkinson (1910–93), author and historian. Also a collection of letters of F.R. Leavis (1895–1978), English scholar and critic.

Non-manuscript material: Plans of college buildings, maps of college estates, photographs of the college and people connected with it.

Finding aids: Handlists and indexes in the College Archives. Not generally sent to NRA. Gwatkin: NRA 27206.

Facilities: Photocopying and photography by arrangement.

Conservation: Contracted out.

Publications: M.R. James: *The Western MSS in the Library of Emmanuel College* (Cambridge, 1904).
P. Hunter Blair: 'The College Archive', *Emmanuel College Magazine*, lxi (1978–9), 14–18.

178 Fitzwilliam College

Parent organisation: University of Cambridge

Address: Huntingdon Road, Cambridge CB3 0DG

Telephone: (01223) 332000

Website: www.fitz.cam.ac.uk

Enquiries: The Archivist

Open: By arrangement.

Access: Bona fide researchers only.

Historical background: The college was founded in 1869 as a non-collegiate organisation catering for students unable to afford college fees and college life. It developed into an identifiable foundation known firstly as Fitzwilliam Hall and then as Fitzwilliam House until 1966, when it received collegiate status. Board meeting minutes are housed in Cambridge University Library (entry 165), but copies are in the collection at the college.

Acquisitions policy: To maintain the archives of the college.

Archives of organisation: Records of the non-collegiate foundation from its inception, growth and final achievement of collegiate status, 1869– .

Non-manuscript material: Photographs.

Finding aids: Catalogue.

Publications: W.W. Grave: *Fitzwilliam College Cambridge, 1869–1969* (Fitzwilliam Society, 1983).

179 Fitzwilliam Museum
Department of Manuscripts and Printed Books

Parent organisation: University of Cambridge

Address: Trumpington Street, Cambridge CB2 1RB

Telephone: (01223) 332900

Fax: (01223) 332923

E-mail: fwml@ula.cam.ac.uk

Website: www.fitzmuseum.cam.ac.uk

Enquiries: The Keeper

Open: Tues–Fri: 10.00–12.30, 1.30–4.30.

Access: Museum staff, members of the University of Cambridge; others with special research enquiries on written application. The archives of the museum are not open to the public.

Historical background: The museum was founded in 1816 by Richard, seventh Viscount Fitzwilliam of Merrion, when he bequeathed to the University of Cambridge, in which he took his MA in 1764, his fine art collections, his library, and the sum of £100,000 to build a museum. The museum now has five curatorial departments: Antiquities, Applied Arts, Coins and Medals, Manuscripts and Printed Books, and Paintings, Drawings and Prints.

Acquisitions policy: To strengthen the collection by purchase, gifts, bequests and loans.

Major collections: Illuminated MSS (Western and oriental).
MS and printed music.
Literary and historical MSS.
Autograph letters.
McClean Collection of illuminated MSS and incunabula.

Non-manuscript material: Lord Fitzwilliam's Library. Exhibition catalogues. Dealers' catalogues. Sale catalogues. Incunabula. Private press books.

Finding aids: Card and slip catalogues.

Facilities: Photocopying. Photography. Microfilm/fiche reader/printer.

Publications: J.A. Fuller-Maitland and A.H. Mann: *Catalogue of the Music in the Fitzwilliam Museum* (London, 1893).
M.R. James: *A Descriptive Catalogue of the Manuscripts in the Fitzwilliam Museum* (Cambridge, 1895).
—— : *A Descriptive Catalogue of the McClean Collection of Manuscripts in the Fitzwilliam Museum* (Cambridge, 1912).
F. Wormald and P.M. Giles: *A Descriptive Catalogue of the Additional Illuminated Manuscripts in the Fitzwilliam Museum Acquired between 1895 and 1979* (Cambridge, 1982).

180 French Resistance Archive

Parent organisation: Anglia Polytechnic University

Address: East Road, Cambridge CB1 1PT

Telephone: (01223) 363271 ext. 2303

Fax: (01223) 352973

E-mail: j.f.mccarren@anglia.ac.uk

Website: libweb.anglia.ac.uk/useliby/specials.htm

Enquiries: The Academic Liaison Librarian, Jane McCarren

Open: Term: Mon–Thurs: 9.00–8.30; Fri: 9.00–4.30.
Vacation: Mon–Fri: 10.00–4.30.

Access: Access by non-members of the university is by appointment only. Users are advised to apply as far in advance as possible.

Historical background: The collection was started in the 1970s when the university was the Cambridgeshire College of Arts and Technology. Dr Hilary Footitt and Dr J.C. Simmonds gathered the material. The collection was used to develop teaching materials as well as to provide users with a selection of important primary and secondary sources. The material represents as many different social, economic and political groups as possible. Originally a print collection, the archive now holds audiotapes, videotapes, photographs and slides as well. For Anglia Polytechnic University Chelmsford campus see entry 227.

Non-manuscript material: Copies of unpublished material concerned with the Resistance in World War II; Resistance journals; photographs and postcards; slides; audio and videotape interviews with former members of different movements and Allied services, e.g. Special Operations Executive (SOE).
Microfilms of Resistance journals.

Finding aids: Computer-generated catalogue.

Facilities: Photocopying. Audio and videotape facilities. Microfilm reader/printer.

Publications: H. Footitt and J.C. Simmonds: *The Resistance Experience: Teaching & Resources.*
J. Holford-Miettinen: *The French Resistance Archive: a Brief Introduction.*
—— : *Two Sticks and TNT: the French Resistance Archive.*

181 Girton College

Parent organisation: University of Cambridge

Address: Cambridge CB3 0JG

Telephone: (01223) 338897

Fax: (01223) 339890

E-mail: kp10011@cus.cam.ac.uk

Enquiries: The Archivist, Ms Kate Perry

Open: Mon–Fri: 9.00–5.00, by appointment.

Access: Bona fide scholars and research workers.

Historical background: The college, originally for women, was founded in 1869.

Acquisitions policy: To strengthen the collection by purchase, gifts and bequests.

Archives of organisation: Documents and photographs relating to the college's internal administration, 1869– .

Major collections: Papers relating to the higher education of women and the inception of an organised women's movement, 19th century, including those of Barbara Bodichon (1827–91); Emily Davies (1830–1921), founder; Bessie Rayner Parkes (1828–1925), writer, publisher and editor.
Papers of the Society for Promoting the Training of Women (SPTW), 1859–1990.
Papers of alumni, including Dorothy Moyle Needham (1896–1987), Barbara Wootton (1897–1988), Eugenie Sellers Strong (1860–1943) and Ethel Fegan (1897–1975).

Non-manuscript material: Blackburn Collection: pamphlets and books collected by Helen Blackburn (1842–1903), suffragist.

Finding aids: Catalogues and lists.

Facilities: Photocopying.

182 Gonville and Caius College

Parent organisation: University of Cambridge

Address: Trinity Street, Cambridge CB2 1TA

A College Archive

Telephone: (01223) 332446

Fax: (01223) 332456

E-mail: ellie@cai.cam.ac.uk

Website: www.cai.cam.ac.uk/archive/source.html

Enquiries: The College Archivist and Deputy Curator of Portraits, Miss Ellie Clewlow

Open: Mon–Fri: 9.30–12.30, 2.30–4.30, by appointment only.

Access: Members of the college and other bona fide researchers by appointment only. Letter of introduction or agreed form of identification required.

Historical background: The Gonville and Caius College Archive is the intended repository for the preservation of records which reflect or illustrate the history of the college and its members. It developed from the undifferentiated muniments of the ancient treasury, which held all older records dating from the foundation of Gonville Hall in 1348 to the building of the new treasury in 1879. Since the late 19th century these older records of governance, estates and finance have been augmented by the administrative records of college officers and some student societies. The archive moved to a new facility in 1996.

Acquisitions policy: The archive accepts records which reflect or illustrate the history of the college and its members. These include records of estates, manors and livings, administration of the college and its related student and alumni bodies, the personal papers of Caians, and collections of ephemeral and photographic materials.

Archives of organisation: Admission register, 1560– ; reports of college meetings, 1651– ; records of scholarships and fellowships, 1581– ; bursars' books, 1423–1523, 1608– ; bursars' indentures, 1490–c1640. Archives of the master, bursar, registrary, chapel, precentor, library and senior tutor. Estate records, including deeds; lease books, 1348– ; maps and architectural plans.

Non-manuscript material: Substantial photographic collection, including photographs of college buildings and estates, clubs and members of the college. Maps, plans and drawings of college buildings and estates.

Finding aids: Historical registers of oldest muniments, 1657–1970. Computerised catalogue of estate deeds, maps and architectural drawings in progress.

Facilities: Photography and microfilm only, by arrangement.

Conservation: Contracted out.

Publications: J. Venn (comp.): *Biographical History of Gonville and Caius College*, iii (1901) [contains a summary of some of the more important older muniments]; iv, part 2 (1912) [contains an Estates Chronicle to 1901]. C.N.L. Brooke: *A History of Gonville and Caius College* (Boydell, 2/1996). A. Neary: 'Bare Bones and Living History: the College Archives', *The Caian* (Nov 1990).

B Library

Telephone: (01223) 332419

Fax: (01223) 332430

E-mail: library@cai.cam.ac.uk

Website: www.cai.cam.ac.uk/library/lib_source.html

Enquiries: The Librarian, Mr J.H. Prynne

Open: Mon–Fri: 9.00–5.00, by appointment.

Access: Approved readers, on written application. A letter of introduction is required.

Historical background: The college has possessed a collection of books since 1349 and has housed them in a library since 1441; some 350 volumes survive from this medieval library. The collection has been augmented by the acquisition of printed books and some MSS, while continuing as a working collection for undergraduates.

Acquisitions policy: The library normally acquires MSS only by donation or bequest.

Major collections: Papers of certain members or former members of the college, principally those of C.M. Doughty (1843–1926), poet and traveller; John Venn (1834–1923), logician and historian of the college; Charles Clayton (1821–83); and Charles Wood (1866–1926), composer.

Non-manuscript material: Collections relating to the Old Catholic movement, including newspaper cuttings, with some correspondence.

Finding aids: Holdings are partially listed. Annotated copy of M.R. James' *Catalogue* (see *Publications* below).

Facilities: Photocopying, photography and microfilm (university library facilities). Microfilm/fiche reader by arrangement.

Publications: M.R. James: *A Descriptive Catalogue of the Manuscripts in the Library of*

Gonville and Caius College (Cambridge, 1907, 1911) [2 vols].
Supplement to the Catalogue (Cambridge, 1914).

183   Jesus College
Old Library and Archives

Parent organisation: University of Cambridge

Address: Cambridge CB5 8BL

Telephone: (01223) 339414 (Keeper); 339439 (Archivist)

Fax: (01223) 339407

Enquiries: The Keeper

Open: By arrangement.

Access: Approved readers, on written application.

Historical background: The college succeeded to the buildings and property of St Radegund's Priory, Cambridge, in 1496. The contents of the library reflect the scholarly interests of the fellows of the college since its foundation.

Acquisitions policy: Materials relating to the college and its old members.

Archives of organisation: Royal and episcopal charters, deeds, etc relating to the priory of St Radegund and the college, 12th and 13th centuries; records relating mainly to property and accounts, 1496– .

Major collections: Archives: biographical material relating to college members.
Library: medieval MSS, including a large group from Durham priory and other northern monasteries (*c*80 items).

Non-manuscript material: Political tracts of the Civil War period.
Malthus family library including books of Thomas Robert Malthus (1766–1834), political economist (*c*2300 vols).

Finding aids: Catalogue of archives. Catalogues and card indexes in library.

Facilities: Photocopying and photography by arrangement.

Conservation: Contracted out.

Publications: M.R. James: *A Descriptive Catalogue of the Manuscripts in the Library of Jesus College, Cambridge* (Cambridge, 1895).

A. Gray: *The Priory of St Radegund, Cambridge* (Cambridge Antiquarian Society, 1898).
J. Harrison et al: *The Malthus Library Catalogue* (New York, 1983).

184 Kettle's Yard

Parent organisation: University of Cambridge

Address: Castle Street, Cambridge CB3 0AQ

Telephone: (01223) 352124

Fax: (01223) 324377

E-mail: kettles-yard-gen@lists.cam.ac.uk

Website: www.kettlesyard.co.uk

Enquiries: The Director, Mr Michael Harrison

Open: Mon–Fri: 2.00–4.00.

Access: Generally open to the public, but a letter of application, stating interest, is essential.

Historical background: Kettle's Yard was the home of Jim and Helen Ede from 1957 until 1973, during which time their collection of 20th-century art, and furniture, textiles and ceramics from a wide historical period, was formed; it was given to the university in 1966.

Acquisitions policy: To maintain the Ede Collection.

Major collections: Correspondence of Jim Ede (1895–1990) with artists, including Alfred Wallis (1885–1942), Ben Nicholson (1894–1982), Winifred Nicholson (1893–1981), David Jones (1895–1974), T.E. Lawrence (1888–1935), William Congdon (1912–98), and Helen Sutherland; also his lectures, various diaries, unpublished writings on art, administrative correspondence with the University of Cambridge, and material relating to the publication of his book *Savage Messiah*.
Material and sketchbooks of Henri Gaudier-Brzeska (1891–1915) and Christopher Wood (1901–30).

Non-manuscript material: Microfilm of Sophie Brzeska's diaries held by Cambridge University Library (entry 165).
Personal library (art, literature, religion) of Jim Ede; Jan and Zoe Ellison bequest of literature on pottery and crafts.
Art periodicals, catalogues and publications from major art galleries.

Finding aids: Card index. Detailed computer list in progress.

Facilities: Photocopying.

Conservation: Paper conservation contracted out.

Publications: J. Lewison: *Kettle's Yard: an Illustrated Guide* (Cambridge, 1980).
J. Ede: *Kettle's Yard: a Way of Life* (Cambridge, 1995 (reprint)).
Kettle's Yard and its Artists (Cambridge, 1995).

185 King's College
Library and Archive Centre

Address: Cambridge CB2 1ST

Telephone: (01223) 331337 (Librarian); (01223) 331444 (Archivist)

Fax: (01223) 331891

E-mail: librarian@kings.cam.ac.uk
archivist@kings.cam.ac.uk

Website: http://bear.kings.cam.ac.uk/library/html

Enquiries: The Librarian, Mr Peter Jones (for medieval MSS)
The Archivist, Ms Jacqueline Cox (for College and Modern Archives)

Open: Mon–Fri: 9.30–12.30, 1.30–5.15.
Closed for six weeks May–June.

Access: Bona fide researchers, with a letter of introduction and by appointment with the Librarian or Archivist.

Historical background: The archives of the college are of two kinds. The College Archives contain records of King's since its foundation in 1441 and of its estates. The Modern Archives comprise the personal paper collections of former members of college and associated individuals. The archives were given separate accommodation within the library in 1983.

Acquisitions policy: Administrative records of the college, by transfer; personal papers of members of the college, by gift or deposit.

Archives of organisation: Records of the internal administration of the college and its estate, c1200– , including some monastic records.

Major collections: Modern Archive Collections: MSS of Isaac Newton (1642–1727) [in Keynes Library]; Rupert Brooke (1887–1915); T.S. Eliot (1888–1964); Richard Kahn (1905–89); Nicholas Kaldor (1909–86); John Maynard Keynes (1883–1946); Joan Robinson (1902–82); Oscar Browning (1837–1923); Le Fanu family,

18th–19th century; E.M. Forster (1879–1970); C.R. Ashbee (1863–1942); Roger Fry (1866–1934); Alan Turing (1912–54).

Finding aids: Catalogues, copies sent to NRA. Integrated name index to Modern Archive collections. Catalogues of several Modern Archive collections available on-line as part of website.

Facilities: Photocopying. Photography. Microfilming.

Publications: M.R. James: *A Descriptive Catalogue of the Manuscripts in the Library of King's College, Cambridge* (Cambridge, 1895). J. Saltmarsh: 'The Muniments of King's College', *Proceedings of the Cambridge Antiquarian Society*, xxxiii (1931–2), 83–4. ——: 'Handlist of the Estates of King's College, Cambridge', *Bulletin of the Institute of Historical Research*, xii (1934), 32–8. A. Doig: *The Architectural Drawings Collection of King's College* (Cambridge, 1979). *A Catalogue of the Papers of John Maynard Keynes in King's College Library* (Cambridge, 1995).

186 Lucy Cavendish College

Parent organisation: University of Cambridge

Address: Lady Margaret Road, Cambridge CB3 0BU

Telephone: (01223) 339009

Fax: (01223) 332178

E-mail: kld27@cam.ac.uk

Website: www.lucy-cav.ac.uk

Enquiries: The Archivist, Karen Davies

Open: By special arrangement only.

Access: Bona fide researchers, by appointment. There are restrictions on personal papers and all records under 30 years old.

Historical background: Lucy Cavendish College was founded in 1965 as the fourth Cambridge college for women. It received its royal charter in 1997 and is now a fully self-governing college of the University of Cambridge. The college admits mature women only, having developed out of a 1950s movement (the 'Dining Group') which provided a focus for women academics who were not members of a college. It was named after Lucy, Lady Frederick Cavendish (1841–1925),

because of her life-long concern with education, particularly that of women.

Acquisitions policy: Records of the 1950s Dining Group, college administration and student bodies. Papers of fellows and alumni and of 'women leaders' (in conjunction with the college's Centre for Women Leaders).

Archives of organisation: Minutes and papers of governing body and committees 1965– ; administration papers of college departments relating to fellows, students, finance, property, academic matters, buildings, etc 1965– .

Major collections: Papers of Lucy Cavendish: chiefly correspondence with her siblings, 1840s–1920s.
Papers of Joyce Grenfell (journalist, actress and honorary fellow); chiefly correspondence with her friend Virginia Graham, 1930s–1970s, and of Jane Kenrick, who was active in womens' issues in the 1960s and 1970s.

Non-manuscript material: Photographs of fellows, students, buildings and events, 1965– .
Student magazines and college newsletters, 1972– .
Presscuttings, 1964– .

Finding aids: Guide to the Archives of Lucy Cavendish College (1996).

Facilities: Photocopying.

Publications: J. Bailey (ed.): *The Diary of Lady Frederick Cavendish* (London, 1927) (2 vols).
C. Kate Bertram: *Lucy Cavendish College, Cambridge: a History of the Early Years* (Cambridge, 1989).
J. Hampton (ed.): *Joyce and Ginnie: the Letters of Joyce Grenfell and Virginia Graham* (1997).

187 Magdalene College

Parent organisation: University of Cambridge

Address: Cambridge CB3 0AG

A Old Library and Archives

Telephone: (01223) 332100

Enquiries: The Keeper of the Old Library

Open: Term: Thurs: 12.00–1.00.

Access: Qualified scholars; an appointment is necessary. Some modern collections are accessible only with the permission of the governing body or are closed under a time restriction.

Historical background: The college was originally a Benedictine hostel founded in 1428. In c1480 it became known as Buckingham College, which was refounded in 1542 as the College of St Mary Magdalene. The archives commence with the foundation of Buckingham College and continue to the present, but they are comparatively sparse before 1660.

Acquisitions policy: Material relating to former members of the college.

Archives of organisation: College records: a varied collection of administrative and estate records, 12th–20th centuries.

Major collections: Personal and literary papers of those connected with the college, including Charles Kingsley (1819–75), author; A.C. Benson (1862–1925), master; George Mallory (1886–1924), mountaineer; William R. Inge (1860–1954), Dean of St Paul's; I.A. Richards (1892–1979), philosopher and literary critic.
Papers of the Ferrar family, of London, Little Gidding and Huntingdon, c1590–1790.

Finding aids: Comprehensive handlists.

Facilities: Photocopying. Photography.

Publications: M.R. James: *A Descriptive Catalogue of the Manuscripts in the College Library of Magdalene College, Cambridge* (Cambridge, 1909).
D. Ransom (ed.): *The Ferrar Papers 1590–1790.*

B Pepys Library

Telephone: (01223) 332100

Fax: (01223) 332187

Enquiries: The Pepys Librarian

Open: Michaelmas and Lent terms: Mon–Sat: 2.30–3.30.
Easter term and summer extension (to Aug 31st). Mon–Sat: 11.30–12.30, 2.30–3.30.

Access: Qualified scholars; a letter of reference is always required and an appointment is necessary.

Historical background: Samuel Pepys's private library, comprising his entire personal collection made between 1649 and 1703, was conveyed to the college by the terms of his will in 1724. These terms forbid either subtraction from or addition to the collection. The books stand in the original presses as he ordained them to be left at his death.

Major collections: Medieval, music and naval MSS.
Pepys's private and state papers, including his diary and original library catalogues.

Facilities: Photography.

Publications: HMC: Report on the Pepys Manuscripts (1911).
R.C. Latham (ed.): *Catalogue of the Pepys Library* (Woodbridge, 1978–94) [11 vols].

188 Marshall Library of Economics

Parent organisation: University of Cambridge

Address: Sidgwick Avenue, Cambridge CB3 9DB

Telephone: (01223) 335214/335217

Fax: (01223) 335475

E-mail: marshlib@econ.cam.ac.uk

Website: www.econ.cam.ac.uk/marshlib/archives/archives.htm

Enquiries: The Archivist, Ms Alex Saunders

Open: Mon–Fri: 9.00–5.00.

Access: Bona fide researchers, by appointment.

Historical background: The library was established in 1925. The nucleus of the original department library was collected by Alfred Marshall for the use of students from 1909 onwards. After Marshall's death in 1924 the greater part of his private library was merged with the departmental library. John Maynard Keynes, the first official librarian, took an active part in the acquisition of manuscript material relating to economists from the 1930s onwards.

Acquisitions policy: Material relevant to economics, particularly personal papers of Cambridge economists.

Archives of organisation: Papers on new library building, c1960– .

Major collections: Correspondence and papers of Alfred Marshall (1842–1924), Herbert Somerton Foxwell (1849–1936), John Neville Keynes (1852–1949), James Bonar (1852–1941), Arthur Cecil Pigou (1877–1959), Charles Ryle Fay (1884–1961), Gerald Frank Shove (1887–1947), Austin Robinson (1897–1993). Letters of Jean Gustave Courcelle-Seneuil (1813–92),

Henry Fawcett (1833–84), Millicent Garrett Fawcett (1847–1929), Clara Collet (1860–1948). Family papers of John Hilton (1880–1943). Minute books of Marshall Society, 1927– .

Non-manuscript material: Newspaper cuttings, photographs, maps.
Economics exam paper collection.
Papers read to Cambridge Economics Club.
Watercolours by Mary Paley Marshall.
Video and printed material on Phillips Machine of the Economy.

Finding aids: Computerised catalogues and indexes.

Facilities: Photocopying at archivist's discretion. Photography by arrangement.

Conservation: Contracted out.

189 Museum of Zoology

Parent organisation: University of Cambridge

Address: Downing Street, Cambridge CB2 3EJ

Telephone: (01223) 336650

Fax: (01223) 336679

E-mail: umzc@zoo.cam.ac.uk

Website: www.zoo.cam.ac.uk/museum/museum.htm

Enquiries: The Administrator, Beatrice Willis

Open: Term: Mon–Fri: 2.00–4.45.
Vacation: Mon–Fri: 10.00–1.00, 2.00–4.45.

Access: Generally open to the public.

Historical background: The museum's collections date from the purchase of the Harwood Collection of Comparative Anatomy by the university in 1814. The museum moved into a new building in 1865 and the bulk of existing collections was accumulated between then and 1915. The museum was integrated with the Department of Zoology in 1938 and moved into its present purpose-built accommodation, linked with the department, between 1968 and 1970. Manuscript material, including correspondence of Alfred Newton (1829–1907), Professor of Zoology, is housed in the University Library (see entry 165).

Acquisitions policy: Material relevant to the collections.

Archives of organisation: Museum collections are documented by field notes and letters from collectors.

Major collections: Leonard Blomefield (1800–93), naturalist: research notes and papers, c1826–58.
Correspondence of John Henry Gurney (1819–90), MP, and John Henry Gurney (1848–1922), ornithologist, with Alfred Newton, zoologist, 1853–90.
James Edward Hepburn (1811–69), ornithologist: notebooks and catalogues, 1850–69.
Oliver Janson (1850–1926), entomologist: journal, 1864–1925.
John Wolley (1823–59), ornithologist: notebooks (12 vols).
Cambridge Natural History Society minutes, 1857-c1969.

Non-manuscript material: Specimen collections, including bird skins, fish, fossil vertebrates, insects, are of international significance. Most were made in the 19th century, but an active collecting policy is also pursued, for example of fossil vertebrates.

Finding aids: Accession register.

190 Newnham College Archives

Parent organisation: University of Cambridge

Address: Sidgwick Avenue, Cambridge CB3 9DF

Telephone: (01223) 335738/40

E-mail: ab280@hermes.cam.ac.uk

Enquiries: The Clerk to the Archives, Anne Thomson

Open: By arrangement.

Access: Bona fide scholars, by appointment.

Historical background: The college was founded in 1871 for the higher education of women. It remains a college for women only.

Acquisitions policy: To maintain college records and receive relevant material by gift or bequest.

Archives of organisation: College records, 1870s– , mainly official papers, including minutes of council, governing body, committees; records of students; estate and finance records; Balfour Laboratory minutes and correspondence.
Papers of Eleanor Mildred Sidgwick (1845–1936), principal, 1892–1910, and sister of A.J. Balfour, including correspondence, addresses and photographs.

Major collections: Papers of Jane Ellen Harrison (1850–1928), classical scholar.
Some papers of Graham Wallas (1858–1932), political psychologist.
A small collection of material relating to Lord John Russell's family.

Non-manuscript material: Women's degrees: press cuttings, 1896 and 1919.
Photographs of members and buildings, 19th and 20th centuries.

Finding aids: Lists and card index.

Facilities: Photocopying. Photography by arrangement.

191 Pembroke College Archives and Library

Parent organisation: University of Cambridge

Address: Cambridge CB2 1RF

Telephone: (01223) 338121

Fax: (01223) 338163

Enquiries: The Librarian, Mr T.R.S. Allan

Open: By arrangement.

Access: Bona fide scholars, by appointment.

The college was founded in 1347. The library was designed by Alfred Waterhouse and built in 1875. It houses the college archives, which comprise a large collection of medieval property deeds and various registers containing lists of fellows etc, but no medieval accounts pre-1557. A list of the archives is available. The library also holds papers of those associated with the college, including musical MSS of John Dunstable (*d* 1543), mathematician and composer; commonplace books, note-books and correspondence of Thomas Gray (1716–71), poet; and an MS of Sir George Stokes (1819–1903), mathematician and physicist. The medieval MSS are deposited in Cambridge University Library (entry 165). See M.R. James: *A Descriptive Catalogue of the Manuscripts in the Library of Pembroke College, Cambridge* (Cambridge, 1905).

192 Peterhouse

Parent organisation: University of Cambridge

Address: Cambridge CB2 1RD

Telephone: (01223) 338200

Fax: (01223) 337578

Enquiries: The College Archivist, Dr R.W. Lovatt

Open: By arrangement, preferably during term time.

Access: Approved scholars (references may be required), by appointment in writing.

Historical background: In *c*1200 a hospital was founded on the present site of St John's College, and a community of scholars was also established there, first references being in 1280. Differences between the two communities led to a deed of separation of 1284 (taken to be the foundation date of the college). The college's collection of medieval MSS has been placed on deposit in Cambridge University Library (entry 165).

Archives of organisation: The medieval holdings are substantial, including charters and deeds *re* property of the college, 12th century–(*c*2000); statutes, 1344– ; bursar's account rolls, 1374– [incomplete series]; old registers, 1401–1660s; records of gifts and inventories; accounts and resignations of fellows, 1420– ; bakehouse books, 1542– ; governing body minutes, 1650– .

Major collections: The library holds some papers of Matthew Wren (1585–1667), theologian; Joseph Beaumont (1616–99), theologian and poet; James Clerk Maxwell (1831–79), physicist; Peter Guthrie Tait (1831–1901), mathematician and physicist; Edward John Routh (1831–1907), mathematician; Adolphus Ward (1837–1924), historian; and Harold Temperley (1879–1939), historian.

Finding aids: Lists are available in the college. Maxwell: NRA 9500.

Facilities: Photocopying by permission.

Publications: HMC First Report, App. 77-82 (1)

M.R. James: *Descriptive Catalogue of Manuscripts in the Library of Peterhouse, Cambridge* (Cambridge, 1899).

T.A. Walker: *Bibliographical Registers of Peterhouse Men, 1284–1616* (Cambridge, 1927, 1930) [2 parts].

Dom Anselm Hughes (comp.): *Catalogue of the Musical Manuscripts at Peterhouse, Cambridge* (Cambridge, 1953).

R. Lovatt: 'The Early Archives of Peterhouse', *Peterhouse Record* (1975–6), 26–38.

193 Queens' College

Parent organisation: University of Cambridge

Address: Queens' Lane, Cambridge CB3 9ET

Telephone: (01223) 335549 (direct line to College Library); (01233) 335511 (enquiries)

Fax: (01223) 335522

Enquiries: The Archivist

Open: Mon–Fri: 10.00–5.00, by prior arrangement only.

Access: Bona fide scholars, by written appointment.

The college was founded in 1448. Administrative and estate archives pre-1800 are housed and administered by Cambridge University Library (entry 165). Post-1800 archives are held in college and include restricted access materials. The college is a member of Cambridge Colleges Conservation Consortium. *See* J.F. Williams: 'The Muniments of Queens' College', *Proceedings of the Cambridge Antiquarian Society*, xxvii (1924–5), 43–8; and J. Twigg: *The History of Queens' College, Cambridge, 1448–1986* (1987).

194 Ridley Hall Library

Address: Cambridge CB3 9HG

Telephone: (01223) 741080 (Secretary's office)

Fax: (01223) 741081

E-mail: jb215@cam.ac.uk

Enquiries: The Librarian, Rev. Dr J. Begbie

Open: College hours. Closed during vacations.

Access: Bona fide researchers, by permission of the librarian only.

The hall was founded in 1877 and is a member of the Cambridge Federation of Theological Colleges. Apart from theological pamphlets and the library, it houses the papers of Charles Simeon (1759–1836), founder of the Church Missionary Society. There are lists available in the library. See F.W.B. Bullock: *History of Ridley Hall* (2 vols) (1941–53).

195 St Catharine's College

Parent organisation: University of Cambridge

Address: Cambridge CB2 1RL

Telephone: (01223) 338317

Fax: (01223) 338340

Enquiries: The Keeper of Muniments, Professor J.H. Baker

Open: Mon–Fri: a.m., by prior arrangement only.

Access: Approved researchers, on written application; an appointment is necessary. Some classes of records are restricted.

Historical background: The college was founded as St Catharine's Hall in 1473 and incorporated by charter in 1475. The founder made provision for a record tower, but this has long since disappeared and there are no administrative records before the 17th century. The college was very small until the present century, and there are few personal records other than admissions.

Acquisitions policy: Documents of college interest only (mostly transfers from the college office).

Archives of organisation: College archives, including muniments of title, 13th century– ; a few court rolls; correspondence, 17th century–, including tutorial correspondence of G.E. Corrie, 1819–43; lease books, 1598– ; audit books, 1623– ; stewards' accounts, 1622– ; admission books, 1642– ; order books, 1640– ; pupils' accounts, 1670–83, 1748–75, 1849–1940; estate accounts, 18th century– ; papers of college societies, 1871– ; minutes of governing body, 1873– .

Non-manuscript material: Photographs, mainly sporting; ephemera.

Finding aids: Typescript shelf-lists. Partial card index. See also E.A.B. Barnard: Catalogue of Documents in the Muniment Room, the Master's Lodge and the College Library [TS, 1930; addenda, 1934–5; copy in Cambridge University Library].

Facilities: Photocopying (flat documents only).

Publications: H. Philpott: *Documents Relating to St Catharine's College in the University of Cambridge* (Cambridge, 1861).
Some of the older records are summarised in W.H.S. Jones: *A History of St Catharine's College, Cambridge* (1936), 279–89.

196 St Edmund's College

Parent organisation: University of Cambridge

Address: Mount Pleasant, Cambridge CB3 0BN

Telephone: (01223) 336250

Fax: (01223) 336111

Website: www.st-edmunds.cam.ac.uk/

Enquiries: The Archivist, Rev. Dr C. Moss

Open: By arrangement.

Access: Bona fide researchers only.

Historical background: The college was founded in 1896 by the 15th Duke of Norfolk as a house of residence for Roman Catholic priests who were taking degrees at the university. It is now a college and an approved foundation of the University of Cambridge, maintaining its Roman Catholic tradition. Its MS collections are held by Cambridge University Library (entry 165).

Acquisitions policy: To maintain the archives of the college.

Archives of organisation: Records of the college, including correspondence relating to the foundation and recognition by the university, 1895– .

Major collections: Papers of founders and other ecclesiastics, including the 15th Duke of Norfolk (1847–1917) and Baron Anatole von Hügel (1854–1928), president of St Edmund's House.

Non-manuscript material: Photographs.

Finding aids: Catalogue in preparation.

Publications: G. Sweeney: *St Edmund's House: the First Eighty Years.*

197 St John's College

Parent organisation: University of Cambridge

Address: Cambridge CB2 1TP

A Archives

Telephone: (01223) 338631

Fax: (01223) 337035

E-mail: mgul@cus.cam.ac.uk

Enquiries: The Archivist, Mr M. Underwood

Open: Mon–Fri: 10.00–1.00, 2.15–5.30, by appointment.

Access: Open to those having a letter of reference, subject to the discretion of the archivist and the College Council.

Historical background: The college was founded in 1511 by the executors of Lady Margaret Beaufort, mother of Henry VII, as successor to, and on the site of, the hospital of St John the Evangelist. Statutes made for its government by Bishop Fisher from 1516 to 1530 were all superseded by new ones given by the crown in 1545, and these in turn by others in 1580, until the 19th-century commissions ushered in a period of frequent reform and reorganization. The college is now governed by statutes made in 1926–7 (under powers given to the Universities Commission in 1923), as subsequently amended by the governing body of the college.

Acquisitions policy: Acquisitions are restricted to records relating directly to the college and to members of it.

Archives of organisation: Administrative and financial records of the college from its foundation, including accounts and correspondence of college officers and records of admissions of members (regularly from 1545). Title deeds of college estates and those of the hospital of St John, the hospital of Ospringe, Kent, the priory of Higham, Kent, and the priory of Broomhall, Berkshire. Some household accounts of Lady Margaret Beaufort (1443–1509), 1498–1509.

Major collections: Medieval MSS.

Non-manuscript material: Printed bills and Acts of Parliament relating to college properties.
Printed material relating to the university's affairs in the late 18th and 19th centuries.
Numerous maps, plans and surveys; architectural drawings relating to the college site.
A few photographs of the college buildings and certain properties.
OS 6 inch and 25 inch maps of Cambridge city and areas in which the college holds property; a few other printed maps.

Finding aids: Calendar with supplementary card index. Computer-based lists and keyword indexes.

Facilities: Photocopying, subject to the discretion of the Archivist.

Publications: T. Baker: *History of St John's College, Cambridge,* ed. J.E.B. Mayor (Cambridge, 1868) [calendars of College Registers, c1545–1671].

J.E.B. Mayor and R.F. Scott: *Admissions to the College of St John the Evangelist, Cambridge,* i–iv (Cambridge, 1882–1931).

Records of R.F. Scott in *Notes from the College Records* [extracts from *The Eagle,* 1889–1915, college magazine].

A.C. Crook: *From the Foundation to Gilbert Scott: a History of the Buildings of St John's College, 1511–1885* (Cambridge, 1980).

——: *Penrose to Cripps:* [A history of the buildings, 1885–1970] (Cambridge, 1978).

B Library

Telephone: (01233) 339393

Fax: (01233) 337035

E-mail: jah63@cam.ac.uk

Website: www.joh.cam.ac.uk/library

Enquiries: The Special Collections Librarian, Mr Jonathan Harrison

Open: Mon–Fri: 9.00–5.00

Access: Members of St John's College, and others by appointment.

Acquisitions policy: Material relating to the college and/or its members, and material by and/or belonging to members of the college, by donation, bequest or purchase.

Major collections: Medieval MSS (*c*270), and a substantial collection of later MSS. A small collection of oriental MSS and musical MSS.
Modern MSS include papers of John Couch Adams (1819–92), astronomer; Sir Cecil W.H. Beaton (1904–80), photographer, artist, writer, and designer; Miles Bland (1786–1867), mathematician; Samuel Butler (1835–1902), writer, artist, photographer, and musician; Terrot R. Glover (1869–1943), classicist; Sir Joseph Larmor (1857–1942), physicist; James B. Mullinger (1834–1917), historian; Robert Peirson (1821–91), astronomer; Charles W. Previté-Orton (1877–1947), historian; Cyril B. Rootham (1875–1938), musician; James J. Sylvester (1814–97), mathematician; Joseph R. Tanner (1860–1931), historian; Isaac Todhunter (1820–84), mathematician.

Non-manuscript material: A small collection of maps, including some early OS maps. Photographs, drawings, engravings and lithographs, etc of the college and its members.
The Samuel Butler Collection: includes many drawings and pictures, a large collection of photographs and glass negatives, and a number of Butler's personal effects.

Finding aids: Annotated copies of M.R. James's *Descriptive Catalogue* and the other catalogues listed under *Publications* below.
Card indexes to modern MSS, 19th and 20th centuries; and drawings and photographs of the college and its members.
Database for the photographs and negatives and to the papers of John Couch Adams, together with printed lists.
Card index to the Samuel Butler collection and a database of the photographs and negatives.
Larmor: NRA 22852; Previté-Orton: NRA 10633; Scientific MSS: NRA 9502.

Facilities: Photocopying at the discretion of the Special Collections Library.
Photography by arrangement. Microfilm/fiche readers.

Conservation: Part-time in-house provision.

Publications: M. Crowe: *A Description of the Manuscripts and Scarce Books in the Library of St John's College, Cambridge* (Cambridge, 1842).
M.R. James: *A Descriptive Catalogue of the Manuscripts in the Library of St John's College, Cambridge* (Cambridge, 1913).
H.F. Jones and A.T. Bartholomew: *The Samuel Butler Collection: a catalogue and commentary* (Cambridge, 1921).
G. Browne: *A Supplementary Hand-list of the Muhammadan Manuscripts Preserved in the Libraries of the University and College of Cambridge* (Cambridge, 1922).

198 Scientific Periodicals Library

Parent organisation: Cambridge University Library

Address: Bene't Street, Cambridge CB2 3PY

Telephone: (01223) 334744

Fax: (01223) 334748

Enquiries: The Librarian of the Scientific Periodicals Library, Michael L. Wilson

Open: Mon–Fri: 9.00–6.00; Sat: 9.00–1.00.

Access: Bona fide researchers, by appointment.

Historical background: The library was founded in 1820 by the Cambridge Philosophical Society. It was jointly administered by society and university between 1881 and 1976, since when it has been administered by Cambridge University Library (entry 165) where papers and notes of Charles Babbage (1792–1871), mathematician, 1808–c1866, have been transferred.

Acquisitions policy: No active collections policy.

Archives of organisation: Records of the Cambridge Philosophical Society, 1819– .

Major collections: Miscellaneous note-books of Vernon Harcourt (1789–1871), chemist; T.R. Robinson (1792–1882), astronomer; J.T. Desaguliers (1683–1744), natural philosopher.

Small collections of records of Natural Science Club; Cambridge Graduate Science Club; Cambridge University Wireless Society.

Facilities: Photocopying. Photography by arrangement with university library. Microform reader/printer.

Conservation: Undertaken by Cambridge University Library.

199 Scott Polar Research Institute

Parent organisation: University of Cambridge

Address: Lensfield Road, Cambridge CB2 1ER

Telephone: (01223) 336555

Fax: (01223) 336549

E-mail: rkh10@cam.ac.uk

Enquiries: The Archivist, R.K. Headland

Open: Mon–Fri: 10.00–12.30, 2.30–5.00.

Access: Bona fide students, by appointment.

Historical background: The Scott Polar Research Institute was founded in 1920 as a memorial to Captain Robert Falcon Scott and his four companions, who died returning from the South Pole in 1912. The MS collection was started in the same year with a deposit of papers relating to Scott's two Antarctic expeditions, and has continued to expand ever since with the acquisition of documents relating to all aspects of Arctic and Antarctic exploration and research, particularly expedition diaries and correspondence. The institute is recognised as a place of deposit for public records.

Acquisitions policy: To continue to extend the collection by donations, deposits, and occasional purchases.

Major collections: Records of Captain Scott's Antarctic expeditions, 1901–4 and 1910–13, and of numerous other expeditions in the heroic era of Antarctic exploration, 1900–20.

Records of the search for the North-West Passage in the 19th century, notably the personal papers of Sir John Franklin (1786–1847), Lady Jane Franklin (1792–1875), Sir George Back (1796–1878), Sir William Parry (1790–1855), Sir John Ross (1777–1856), Sir James Clark Ross (1800–62) and Sir John Richardson (1787–1865).

Antarctic Treaty papers.

South Georgia whaling and administrative papers, 1904–66.

Non-manuscript material: Extensive collections of watercolours, drawings and prints, photographs, films, sound recordings, press cuttings.

Finding aids: Author/biographical catalogue. Indices of expeditions and voyages.

Facilities: Photocopying. Photography and microfilming by arrangement. Microfilm/fiche reader.

Publications: C. Holland: *Manuscripts in the Scott Polar Research Institute, Cambridge, England: a Catalogue* (London and New York, 1982).

200 Sedgwick Museum of Earth Sciences

Parent organisation: University of Cambridge

Address: Downing Street, Cambridge CB2 3EQ

Telephone: (01223) 333456

Fax: (01223) 333450

E-mail: mdg2@esc.cam.ac.uk

Website: www.esc.cam.ac.uk

Enquiries: The Chief Assistant, Mr M.G. Dorling

Open: Mon–Fri: 9.00–1.00, 2.00–5.00; Sat: 10.00–1.00.

Access: Generally open to the public.

Historical background: The museum was founded in 1728 and rededicated in 1904.

Acquisitions policy: Acquires material relating to the earth sciences and including archival materials.

Archives of organisation: Geological collections archive, 1728– .

Major collections: Papers and or notebooks of Edward Alexander Newell Arber (1870–1918), botanist; Thomas George Bonney (1833–1923), geologist; Charles Darwin (1809–82); Gertrude Lilian Elles (1872–1960); Sir Vivian Ernest Fuchs (1908–99), explorer; Thomas McKenney Hughes (1823–1917), geologist; Edward King (1735–1807), antiquary; John Edward Marr (1857–1933), geologist; Adam Sedgwick (1785–1873), geologist; John Strange (1732–99), author; Edward Tawney (1841–82); John Woodward (1665–1728), physician.

Finding aids: Electronic and manual catalogue.

Facilities: Photocopying. Photography. Microfilm/fiche readers.

Conservation: Contracted out.

201 Seeley Historical Library

Parent organisation: University of Cambridge

Address: Faculty of History, West Road, Cambridge CB3 9EF

Telephone: (01223) 335340

Fax: (01223) 335968

E-mail: hisl@ula.cam.ac.uk

Enquiries: The Seeley Librarian, Dr L. Washington

Open: Term: Mon–Fri: 9.00–7.15; Sat: 9.00–6.00.
Vacation: Mon Fri: 9.00–5.00.
Closed for three weeks in September.

Access: Bona fide students, by appointment.

Historical background: The library was established in 1807 and renamed in 1897 to commemorate Sir John Seeley's services to the empire and the university.

Non-manuscript material: Microfilms of Kenya National Archives; British cabinet papers, 20th century; US national archives, mainly consular reports; and papers of Sir John Colborne (1778–1863).

Finding aids: Participating member of the university's union catalogue. Colborne: NRA 5288.

Facilities: Photocopying. Microfilm readers.

202 Selwyn College

Parent organisation: University of Cambridge

Address: Grange Road, Cambridge CB3 9DQ

Telephone: (01223) 335880

Fax: (01223) 335837

Website: www.sel.cam.ac.uk

Enquiries: The Librarian

Open: By arrangement.

Access: Bona fide researchers, by appointment.

Historical background: The college was founded in 1882 as an approved foundation. It became a full college of the university in 1957. The papers of Brooke Foss Westcott are now held by the library of Westcott House Theological College, Jesus Lane, Cambridge CB5 8BP; tel. (01223) 350074. Contact the librarian for an appointment.

Acquisitions policy: College archives and any material relating to Bishop Selwyn.

Archives of organisation: College archives, 1882– .

Major collections: Papers of George Augustus Selwyn (1809–78), Primate of New Zealand.

Non-manuscript material: Microfilms of the Selwyn sermons, of some of the papers, and of 11 volumes of Bishop Cotton's journals.

Finding aids: Selwyn: NRA 24352.

Facilities: Photocopying (permission of governing body may be required). Microfilm reader only at the university library.

Conservation: Member of the Cambridge Colleges Conservation Consortium.

Publications: A short history of the college was published in 1973.
W.R. Brock and P.H.M. Cooper: *Selwyn College: a History* (Edinburgh, 1994).

203 Sidney Sussex College

Parent organisation: University of Cambridge

Address: Sidney Street, Cambridge CB2 3HU

Telephone: (01223) 338800/338824 (Muniment Room)

Fax: (01223) 338884

Enquiries: The Archivist, Mr N.J. Rogers

Open: Mon–Thurs: 9.00–12.55, 2.00–5.15; Fri: 9.00–12.55; 2.00–4.15.

Access: Bona fide researchers; an appointment is necessary. There is restricted access to some college papers.

Historical background: The college was founded in 1596 by the executors of Lady Frances Sidney, Countess of Sussex. The Muniment Room, established in 1938, houses MSS and early printed books, formerly kept in the Old Library, and the archives, previously housed in the Master's Lodge.

Acquisitions policy: Any material relating to the history of the college and its members.

Archives of organisation: Masters' records, records of college administration, tutorial and bursarial records. Also material relating to college estates.

Major collections: Manuscript collection, mainly Western medieval (119 MSS).
Papers of Richard Allin (?1675–1747), John Hey (1734–1815), George Ralph Mines (1886–1914), David Thomson (1912–70) and Samuel Ward (1572–1643).

Non-manuscript material: Estate maps, architectural drawings.

Finding aids: Various typescript calendars.

Facilities: Photocopying and photography by arrangement.

Conservation: Member of the Cambridge Colleges Conservation Consortium.

Publications: Some of the muniments are described in HMC Third Report, xx and App. 327–29 (2) (1872).
For MSS 1–106, *see* M.R. James: *A Descriptive Catalogue of the Manuscripts in the Library of Sidney Sussex College, Cambridge* (Cambridge, 1895).
The Ward papers are listed by M. Todd in *Transactions of the Cambridge Bibliographical Society*, 8 (1985), 582–92.

204 Trinity College Library

Parent organisation: University of Cambridge

Address: Cambridge CB2 1TQ

Telephone: (01223) 338488

Fax: (01223) 338532

E-mail: trin-lib@lists.cam.ac.uk

Website: http://rabbit.trin.cam.ac.uk

Enquiries: The Librarian

Open: Mon–Fri: 9.00–5.00.

Access: Members of the college; others by appointment.

Historical background: The college was founded by King Henry VIII in 1546. He amalgamated two existing colleges, the King's Hall (f. 1317) and Michaelhouse (f. 1324), with various small hostels, and added to their revenues substantial endowments from the dissolved monasteries.

Acquisitions policy: Records relating directly to the college, and personal and professional papers of past and present members of the college.

Archives of organisation: A few property deeds and 'Black Book' of Michaelhouse, and a large number of records from King's Hall, including Seneschal's accounts, 1337– .
Administrative and financial records of the college, 1546– .
Title deeds and other records relating to the acquisition and administration of college estates, 12th–20th centuries.
Records of college clubs and societies, 19th–20th centuries.

Major collections: Medieval MSS (1500) and a substantial collection of oriental MSS.
Modern MSS include papers of Sir Isaac Newton (1642–1727); Dawson Turner (1775–1858), banker and botanist; William Whewell (1794–1866); Thomas, Lord Macaulay (1800–59); Lord Houghton (1809–85); Alfred, Lord Tennyson (1809–92); A.J. Munby (1828–1910); Henry Sidgwick (1838–1900), philosopher; J.G. Frazer (1854–1941), social anthropologist; A.E. Housman (1859–1936); G.H. Hardy (1877–1947), mathematician; Rose Macaulay (1881–1958), author; A.A. Milne (1882–1956); Sir George Pine Thomson (1887–1965), rear-admiral and chief press censor; Ludwig Wittgenstein (1889–1951); Piero Sraffa (1898–1983), economist; Lord (R.A.) Butler (1902–82); Otto Frisch (1904–79), physicist; and many other distinguished members of the college.

Non-manuscript material: Printed books (c220,000), including 750 incunabula; Sir Isaac Newton's Library; the Capell Collection of Shakespeariana; and the Rothschild Collection of 18th-century literature.

Photographs and portraits, maps and plans.

Finding aids: Typescript catalogues and card index of college archives and modern manuscripts. Catalogues sent to NRA.

Facilities: Photocopying, photography and microfilming by arrangement. Microfilm/fiche readers.

Publications: E.H. Palmer: *Catalogue of the Arabic, Persian and Turkish MSS in the Library of Trinity College, Cambridge* (Cambridge, 1870).
M.R. James: *Catalogue of the Western Manuscripts in the Library of Trinity College, Cambridge* (Cambridge, 1900–04) [4 vols].
H.M.J. Loewe: *Catalogue of the Hebrew MSS in the Library of Trinity College, Cambridge* (Cambridge, 1926).
P. Gaskell: *Trinity College Library: the first 150 years* (Cambridge, 1980).
D. McKitterick, ed.: *The Making of the Wren Library* (Cambridge, 1995).

205 Trinity Hall

Parent organisation: University of Cambridge

Address: Trinity Lane, Cambridge CB2 1TJ

Telephone: (01223) 332500

Fax: (01223) 332537

Website: www.trinhall.cam.ac.uk/

Enquiries: The Librarian or the Archivist

The college was founded in 1350. Virtually none of its medieval records survive, although there is a small collection of charters. Apart from M.R. James: *A Descriptive Catalogue of Manuscripts.* (1907), there is A.W.W. Dale (ed.): *Warren's Book: Documents etc relating to Trinity Hall, Cambridge* (1911), and a typescript list, by A.L. Pink, of Trinity Hall documents to 1600.

206 Tyndale House Library

Parent organisation: University and Colleges Christian Fellowship

Address: 36 Selwyn Gardens, Cambridge CB3 9BA

Telephone: (01223) 566601

Fax: (01223) 566608

E-mail: librarian@tyndale.cam.ac.uk

Website: www.tyndale.cam.ac.uk

Enquiries: The Librarian, Dr David Instone Brewer

Open: Mon–Fri: 9.00–5.30

Access: Any scholar, by appointment. Monthly charge for reader's ticket.

Historical background: Founded in 1944 to provide research facilities in biblical studies in a spirit of loyalty to the historic Christian faith.

Acquisitions policy: Collects all published material relevant to academic biblical studies, and non-published material as it becomes available.

Non-manuscript material: Unpublished OS maps of Palestine during the British protectorate, mostly 1920–45.

Finding aids: Full MARC catalogue kept internally and shared with Cambridge University Library, and published on the website.

Facilities: Photocopying. High definition microfiche readers, network and internal access of every desk.

Publications: Tyndale Bulletin (twice-yearly).

207 United Reformed Church History Society

Parent organisation: United Reformed Church

Address: Westminster College, 7 Sherlock Road, Cambridge CB3 0HR

Telephone: (01223) 741084

Website: www.lib.cam.ac.uk/university/libraries/westminstercollege.html

Enquiries: Mrs M.M. Thompson

Open: By appointment only.

Access: Members of the society or the United Reformed Church; other enquirers by arrangement.

Historical background: The original collection was assembled by the Presbyterian Historical Society and relates to the history of English Presbyterianism from the 16th century. Since 1972 some material from Congregationalism (other than local church records) has been acquired, as well as material from the United Reform Church itself. The library and archive were moved to Westminster College in 1998.

Acquisitions policy: Material relating to persons, including ministers, is acquired but local churches are encouraged to deposit archives locally. The library acquires basic reference material for the three constituent traditions of the United Reformed Church and other Free churches.

Archives of organisation: Archives relating to ministers and missionaries and the records of the General Assembly and Presbyteries of the Presbyterian Church of England.

Major collections: Material relating to ministers and missionaries of the Congregational Union/ Church and Churches of Christ.
Biographical information about former Presbyterian, Congregational and United Reformed Church ministers.

Non-manuscript material: Collection of 17th-century pamphlets and books.

Finding aids: Author index for books and pamphlets and some MSS. Lists of other items.

Facilities: Limited photocopying service.

Conservation: Assistance sought from Cambridge University Library, (entry 165).

Publications: United Reformed Church History Society Journal.

208 University Museum of Archaeology and Anthropology

Parent organisation: University of Cambridge

Address: Downing Street, Cambridge CB2 3DZ

Telephone: (01223) 333516

Fax: (01223) 333517

Website: http://cumaa.archanth.cam.ac.uk

Enquiries: The Director

Open: Tues–Sat: 2.00–4.30.

Access: Bona fide researchers may have access free of charge; a prior written appointment is essential.

The museum was established in 1884. The archives date from then and relate exclusively to the growth and documentation of the collections, focusing primarily on associated research. There is also an extensive archive of photographs, currently being catalogued.

209 Canterbury Cathedral Archives

Address: The Precincts, Canterbury, Kent CT1 2EH

Telephone: (01227) 865330

Fax: (01227) 865222

E-mail: archives@canterbury-cathedral.org

Website: www.canterbury-cathedral.org/ archives.html

Enquiries: The Cathedral Archivist, Miss Heather Forbes

Open: Mon–Thurs: 9.00–5.00; 1st and 3rd Sat of each month: 9.00–1.00.
Annual stock–taking closure two weeks in January.

Access: Generally open to the public, by appointment.

Historical background: Cathedral records have been kept here since the foundation of the cathedral in 597. From 1884 to 1915 and from 1956 to 1970 the office acted as the City Record Office, and from 1970 it was run as the joint City and Chapter Record Office. It became the Diocesan Record Office in 1959, and the Archive Filing Unit for Canterbury City Council was opened in 1981. The service has been administered by Kent County Council since 1989. It is recognised as a place of deposit for public records.

Acquisitions policy: Normal statutory acquisitions from all three authorities; deposits or gifts are accepted.

Archives of organisation: Records of Dean and Chapter of Canterbury, 742– ; City of Canterbury 1200– ; Diocese of Canterbury 1364– .

Major collections: Parish records for the Archdeaconry of Canterbury; private deposits.

Finding aids: Catalogues. On-line computer index to most of the catalogues of the Dean and Chapter records and private deposits can be consulted by staff.

Facilities: Photocopying. Photography. Microfilming. Microfilm/fiche reader/printer.

Conservation: Full range of paper and parchment conservation and binding. Facilities for map repair are limited. Limited outside work undertaken.

Publications: Quarterly newsletter incorporating finding aid additions.

210 Institute of Heraldic and Genealogical Studies

Address: Northgate, Canterbury, Kent CT1 1BA

Telephone: (01227) 768664

Fax: (01227) 765617

E-mail: ihgs@ihgs.ac.uk

Website: www.ihgs.ac.uk

Enquiries: The Registrar, Jeremy Palmer

Open: Mon, Wed, Fri: 10.00–4.30.

Access: By appointment with the librarian.

Historical background: A school for the study of the history and structure of the family was founded by Cecil Humphery-Smith on the suggestion of the late Canon K.J.F. Bickersteth in 1957. The institute opened in Canterbury in 1961 and was established as an educational trust. Subsequently it moved into its present premises (which date from 1283 with 16th-century and later additions). Full-time and other courses of instruction are held to train and qualify members of the genealogical profession and provide researchers into the applications of family history studies.

Acquisitions policy: To build a corpus of original material for the study of social, economic and environmental changes and historical structures of family life.

Major collections: Family History: unpublished MSS collections relating to some 15,000 family groups.
Case histories and genealogical tracings.
Estate maps, collections of deeds and related documentation, manorial incidences and papers, 13th–20th centuries.
Tyler Collection: extracts from Kentish parish records, wills, marriage settlements, local history material; several hundred MS note-books by eminent antiquary and family historian, and related documents.
Hackman Collection: similar material for Hampshire.
Humphery-Smith Collection: extensive MS notes on Sussex families, records of coats of arms in all churches of Sussex county, in Canterbury Cathedral and elsewhere, with related research notes; very large British and European armorial indexes; transcripts of rolls of arms and heraldic treatises with related notes; several original heralds' note-books; painted and blazoned armorials (16th and 17th centuries).
Culleton Papers: four large bound MS books of working papers of 19th-century genealogical and heraldic practice.
MS indexes: the Augmented Pallot Index to several million London marriages; Andrew's Index to British overseas.
Lang Collection of Gretna Green Marriages, 1795–1895.

Non-manuscript material: Pamphlets relating to parish and local histories (c5000).
A collection of European heraldic works unique in the UK.
An extensive library of secondary source material for genealogical research.

Finding aids: Lists, indexes and guides. A comprehensive classified catalogue is in preparation.

Facilities: Photocopying. Microfilm/fiche reader. Palaeographic aids.

Publications: Family History (1962–) [journal of the institute].
Guide to Pallot Index (1986).
Maps of the parishes and probate jurisdictions of the UK and other research aids.

211 King's School
Archives and Walpole Library

Address: Canterbury, Kent CT1 2ES

Telephone: (01227) 595501

Fax: (01227) 595595

E-mail: headmaster@kings-school.co.uk

Website: www.kings-school.co.uk

Enquiries: The School Archivist, Mr P. Pollak

Open: By arrangement.

Access: Bona fide students, by appointment.

Historical background: A school has been attached to the cathedral since 600 ad; however, pre-1750 material is kept in the Canterbury Cathedral Archives (entry 209). The Walpole Library is based on the collection accumulated by Sir Hugh Walpole between the wars.

Acquisitions policy: Material relating to the school is acquired as limited resources permit.

Additions to the Walpole Library collection of literary MSS are by gift.

Archives of organisation: Records of pupils, 1750– ; lists of King's Scholars, 1541– (incomplete); usual school material: academic, sporting, administrative, 1750– . School magazine *The Cantuarian*, 1882– .

Major collections: Sir Hugh Seymour Walpole (1884–1941), novelist, collection of literary MSS.

Non-manuscript material: Collection of topographical prints and drawings relating to Canterbury premises and the King's School, mainly 18th and 19th centuries.
The Walpole and Somerset Maugham libraries.

Finding aids: MS indexes.

Facilities: Photocopying by arrangement.

Publications: Printed catalogues of Walpole and Maugham libraries.

212 Royal Museum and Art Gallery with Buffs Regimental Museum

Address: High Street, Canterbury, Kent CT1 2RA

Telephone: (01227) 452747

Fax: (01227) 455047

Website: www.canterbury.gov.uk

Enquiries: The Assistant Curator

Buffs Museum holds records of the Buffs (later Buffs Royal East Kent Regiment), 1803–1953, including records of service, order books, journals and diaries. See NRA 20951 Regimental Museums survey of manuscript collections.

213 University of Kent at Canterbury

Address: Canterbury, Kent CT2 7NU

A Templeman Library

Telephone: (01227) 764000 ext. 7609

Fax: (01227) 823984

E-mail: sac1@ukc.ac.uk

Website: www.ukc.ac.uk/library/special/html/specoll/homepg.htm

Enquiries: The Special Collections Librarian, Mrs S. Crabtree

Open: Mon–Fri: 9.30–4.30, and occasionally at other times, but in all cases by prior arrangement.

Access: Approved readers, on written application, by phone or e-mail.

Historical background: The university was founded in 1963. University archives are not under the jurisdiction of the library.

Acquisitions policy: Selected acquisitions of material related to existing collections.

Major collections: Frank Pettingell (1891–1966): collection of 19th-century drama: includes 1000 plays and 350 pantomimes in MS or TS, only 36 of which are known to have been published; several hundred MSS related to productions at the Britannia Theatre, Hoxton; playbills and programmes.
Melville family (late 19th to mid-20th century): records relating to provincial and London theatres run by the Melvilles; plays in MS and TS; playbills.
C.P. Davies Wind- and Water-Mill Collection: press cuttings, MS notes, photographs; archives of millers and mill construction firms.
John Holman Collection of mill memorabilia.
John Crow (1904–69): papers and correspondence.
Catherine Crowe (1790–1872): material gathered by a researcher for an intended biography.
Hewlett Johnson (Dean of Canterbury, 1931–63): papers and correspondence.
R.E.W. Maddison (1901–93): papers and correspondence.
Alan Reeve-Jones: screenplays in TS and MS.
E.M. Tenison (1880–1962): papers and correspondence.
Lord Bernard Weatherill (Speaker of the House of Commons, 1983–92): papers and correspondence.

Non-manuscript material: Frank Pettingell Collection: printed play texts, separately bound (with many prompt books and actors' copies) (*c*3000); printed texts in composite volumes (1800); pantomime libretti (331); playbills (*c*300).
Fawkes/Boucicault Collection: playbills, programmes, cuttings.
Collection of popular literature, chiefly ballads and popular poetry, with some chapbooks.

Grace Pettman Collection, including her writings in 20th-century popular magazines and religious tracts.

Kingsley Wood Press Cuttings: 25 large press cutting books covering the career of the politician and cabinet minister, 1903–40.

Muggeridge Collections: photographs of English windmills, 1905– .

Finding aids: Catalogue to the Frank Pettingell Collection. Other materials are in the process of being catalogued; available on website.

Facilities: Photocopying. Photography. Microfilm/fiche printer.

Conservation: Only minor repairs carried out in-house.

Publications: G.S. Darlow: 'A Brief Description of the Frank Pettingell Collection of Plays in the University Library, Canterbury, Kent', *Theatre Notebook*, xxxi/3 (1977), 2.

B Centre for the Study of Cartoons and Caricature

Telephone: (01227) 823127

Fax: (01227) 823127

E-mail: j.m.newton@ukc.ac.uk

Website: library.ukc.ac.uk/cartoons

Enquiries: The Curator, Mrs Jane Newton

Open: Mon–Fri: 9.00–5.00.

Access: By appointment. A paid research service is available.

Historical background: The Cartoon Study Centre was established in 1973 with initial funding from the Nuffield Foundation, and cataloguing and research work has been funded by an additional grant from the Leverhulme Trust.

Acquisitions policy: There is no purchasing budget; long-term loans and donations/bequests are accepted relating to the field of study and existing collections of original cartoon drawings.

Major collections: Original cartoon drawings from British newspapers and journals, 1900– , including political-humorous, wartime and social comment cartoons (c85,000). Artists represented include Low, Strube, Vicky, Cummings, Lee, Zec, Haselden, Smythe, Jensen, Garland, Dyson, Trog, Horner, Mac and Illingworth.

Non-manuscript material: Library comprising volumes on cartoons and caricature and associated graphic and illustrative books. Newspaper cuttings.

Finding aids: An on-line computerised database (search by artist, date, persons and keywords) exists for half the collection and is constantly being added to.

Facilities: Photocopying. Photography.

Conservation: Contracted out.

Publications: Numerous exhibition and other publications.

214 Cardiff Central Library

Parent organisation: Cardiff County Library Service

Address: St David's Link, Frederick Street, Cardiff CF10 2DU

Telephone: (02920) 382116

Fax: (02920) 871599

E-mail: enquiry@libraries.gov.uk

Website: www.libraries.cardiff.gov.uk

Enquiries: The County Librarian, Mr Paul Sawyer

Open: Mon–Wed, Fri: 9.00–6.00; Thurs: 9.00–7.00; Sat: 9.00–5.30 (MS material not available after 4.30).

Access: Generally open to the public; advance notice of a visit is preferred.

Historical background: The library was founded in 1862 as the Cardiff Free Library with the following foundation collections: (a) MSS acquired with the Tonn Library, purchased from the Rees family of Llandovery in 1891; (b) literary and historical MSS and deeds of Welsh interest, purchased from the collection of Sir Thomas Phillipps in 1896. Subsequent additions by purchase (especially in the 1920s–1950s) and gift from a variety of sources. The majority of deeds and manorial documents (which relate to Wales and the bordering counties of England) have been transferred to the Glamorgan Record Office, Cardiff (entry 217). The Mackworth Collection of early music has been placed in Cardiff University (see entry 215).

Acquisitions policy: Material is no longer acquired.

Major collections: Welsh literary MSS, mostly poetry, medieval–18th century (*c*100 vols).
Non-Welsh medieval MSS, mostly religious (*c*50 vols).
Historical MSS, relating mostly to Wales and including 19th- and 20th-century literary MSS (*c*4300 groups).
Papers of the Marquesses of Bute, mainly 19th century.

Non-manuscript material: Large collection of maps, photographs, prints, original drawings etc, relating mainly to South Glamorgan and adjacent counties.

Finding aids: Card index and shelf list.

Facilities: Photocopying. Microfilm/fiche readers.

Publications: MSS are described in various library reprints, and brief details of acquisitions are in *Morgannwg*, ii–xv (1958–71).
N.R. Ker: 'Cardiff Public Library', *Medieval Manuscripts in British Libraries*, ii (1977), xx, 331–77.

215 Cardiff University
The Library/Information Services

Address: PO Box 430, Cardiff CF1 3XT

Telephone: (02920) 874000

Fax: (02920) 371921

E-mail: asslilby@cf.ac.uk

Website: www.cardiff.ac.uk/uwcc/infos

Enquiries: The Director, Information Services

Open: Mon–Fri: 9.00–5.00; an appointment is preferred; and at other times when the library is open a prior appointment is essential.

Access: Members of the college; others on written application.

Historical background: Cardiff University came into existence in 1988 as a result of the merger of University College, Cardiff (f. 1883) and the University of Wales Institute of Science and Technology (UWIST). During the century of its existence the library of University College, Cardiff, accumulated a substantial collection of MSS and archives. The Department of Music holds the Mackworth Collection of music. The Youth Movement Archive has been transferred to the British Library of Political and Economic Science (see entry 560).

Acquisitions policy: There is no acquisitions policy, but collections offered are accepted where appropriate.

Major collections: Edward Thomas (1878–1917), poet: MSS, papers, letters, scrapbooks, photographs, first editions.
E.G.R. Salisbury (1819–90): papers and printed ephemera.
Lower Swansea Valley Project: papers of K.J. Hilton, director, 1960–65.
Educational Settlements: papers of Sir J.F. Rees, 1929–42, especially the Merthyr Settlement.
Cardiff Trades Council: records, 1941–82.
Papers of deceased members of the college, including Cyril Brett, professor of English (*d* 1936); B.J. Morse, lecturer in Italian (*d* 1977); C.M. Thompson, professor of chemistry (*d* 1932); S.B. Chrimes, professor of history (*d* 1984); D.E. Evans, tutor in charge of extramural studies (*d* 1951); E.J. Jones, lecturer in education and professor at University College Swansea (*d* 1977); H.J.W. Tillyard, professor of Greek (*d* 1968); T.H. Robinson, professor of Semitic languages (*d* 1964).
Welsh medium teachers' union, 'UCAC' (Undeb Cenedlaethol Athrawon Cymru), 1940–*c*1990.

Non-manuscript material: Ifor B. Powell Pamphlet Collection: mainly printed pamphlets and press cuttings on the League of Nations and Far East between the world wars.
TSS handlists of Salisbury MSS, miscellaneous MSS, Cardiff Trades Council records, Edward Thomas Collection.

Facilities: Photocopying. Microfilm/fiche readers.

Publications: *The Ifor B. Powell Pamphlet Collection in the Library of University College, Cardiff: a Checklist* (Cardiff, 1972).
S.Y. McCleave (comp.): *A Catalogue of Manuscript Music in the Mackworth Collection* (Cardiff, 2000).

216 Central Register of Air Photography for Wales

Parent organisation: Welsh Office

Address: Planning Division, Room G–003, Crown Offices, Cathays Park, Cardiff CF1 3NQ

Telephone: (02920) 823819

Fax: (02920) 823080

E-mail: air_photo_officer@wales.gsi.gov.uk

Enquiries: The Air Photographs Officer

Open: Mon–Fri, by appointment.

Access: Generally open to the public by arrangement: for a cover search, a map or OS national grid reference of the area of interest will be required.

Historical background: The National Air Survey, flown 1945–52 by the RAF, was used to plan post-war development and forms the basis of the collection. Subsequent surveys have been added. The Central Register of Air Photography for Wales was formed in 1975 and is operated by the Air Photography Unit: it is the only comprehensive source of information about air photos of Wales.

Acquisitions policy: Continued updating of the collection.

Non-manuscript material: Extensive collection (over 200,000) of air photographs of different scales covering Wales at various dates, including the National Air Survey (1:10,000) flown 1945–52 by the RAF.
Other RAF photographs, including small-scale national surveys, 1969, 1981; pre–1979. OS air photographs; extensive colour photographs, 1983–92; oblique and infra-red photos of Welsh coastline.
Meridian Airmaps Ltd Collection of photos, 1963–83.
Original films of RAF, pre–1979.

Facilities: Photography. Photostats (map information superimposed). Reference and loan of library prints.

217 Glamorgan Record Office

Parent organisation: Glamorgan Archives Joint Committee

Address: Glamorgan Building, King Edward VII Avenue, Cathays Park, Cardiff CF10 3NE

Telephone: (02920) 780282

Fax: (02920) 780284

E-mail: glamro@cardiff.ac.uk

Website: www.llgc.org.uk/cac/cac0026.htm

Enquiries: The Glamorgan Archivist, Miss Susan Edwards

Open: Tues, Thurs: 9.30–5.00; Wed: 9.30–7.00; Fri: 9.30–4.30, an appointment is necessary to consult microforms.

Access: Generally open to the public. A paid research service is available.

Historical background: The office was established in 1939 to serve the county of Glamorgan, which was divided into the counties of Mid-, South and West Glamorgan on local government reorganization in 1974. Initially, these three counties combined to provide a joint archives service, but in 1992 West Glamorgan withdrew from this arrangement. Further local government reorganisation in 1996 abolished the counties of Mid- and South Glamorgan, and the Glamorgan Record Office now provides a joint service for the six authorities of Bridgend, Caerphilly, Cardiff, Merthyr Tydfil, Rhondda Cynon Taff and the Vale of Glamorgan. After local government reorganization in 1974, most of the archive collection of the former Cardiff City Library was transferred to the Glamorgan Record Office. It also holds ecclesiastical parish records from the whole of the Diocese of Llandaff. It is recognised as a place of deposit for public and manorial records.

Acquisitions policy: The office accepts archival material for the geographical area which it serves in the former counties of Mid- and South Glamorgan and the Diocese of Llandaff.

Archives of organisation: Glamorgan County Council, 1889–1974, and other local authority record holdings.

Major collections: Deposited collections, including the following which have a wider significance: South Wales Coalfield, pre–1947 records received from the National Coal Board.
Dowlais Iron Company Collection, containing extensive correspondence, 1792– .
Society of Friends records relating to the whole of Wales, 1650– .
Bruce Collection, containing correspondence received by the first Lord Aberdare (1815–95).
Papers of John Singleton Copley, Baron Lyndhurst (1772–1863), Lord Chancellor.

Finding aids: Lists and indexes.

Facilities: Photocopying. Photography and microfilming by arrangement. Family History Room: microfilm/fiche readers/printer centralising sources for family history.

Conservation: In-house facilities.

Publications: Dowlais Iron Company: Calendar of the London House Letter-book Series, 1837–1867 [42 schedules; reproduced TS].

On the Parish: an Illustrated Source Book on the Care of the Poor under the Old Poor Law (1988).
A Catalogue of Glamorgan Estate Maps (1992).
Hughesovka: a Welsh Enterprise in Imperial Russia (1992).
Poor Relief in Merthyr Tydfil Union in Victorian Times (1992).
The Bridges of Merthyr Tydfil (1992).

218 National Museums & Galleries of Wales

A Library

Address: Cathays Park, Cardiff CF1 3NP

Telephone: (02920) 573202

Fax: (02920) 373214

Website: www.nmgw.ac.uk

Enquiries: The Librarian, Mr John R. Kenyon

Open: Tues–Fri: 10.00–5.00.

Access: Bona fide researchers, preferably by prior arrangement.

Historical background: The National Museum of Wales received its charter of incorporation in 1907. Besides various outstations (see B and C below), there are four departments in Cathays Park: Archaeology and Numismatics, Art, Biodiversity & Systematic Biology, and Geology. There is no archivist in Cathays Park; archives are handled by curatorial staff within the relevant departments and central records are held by the Resource Management Division.

Acquisitions policy: No formal policy; the majority of archives are acquired by donation.

Major collections: John Ward papers (archaeology, local history) in main library.
Files on artists in Department of Art.
Natural history MSS.

Non-manuscript material: Early photographs of Welsh buildings etc in main library.
Collection of maps in Department of Geology.

Finding aids: No formal overall catalogue or list.

Facilities: Photocopying. Photography. Microfilm/fiche readers.

Conservation: Generally contracted out.

Publications: Natural History MSS listed in G.D.R. Bridson and others: *Natural History Manuscript Resources in the British Isles* (1980), 53–6.
A. Lloyd Hughes: 'G.B. Sowerby Letters in Cardiff', *Archives of Natural History*, x/1 (1981), 172.
J.R. Kenyon: 'Some Glamorgan Documents in the National Museum of Wales Library', *Morgannwg*, 37 (1993), 100–02.

B Museum of Welsh Life

Address: St Fagans, Cardiff CF5 6XB

Telephone: (02920) 573500 ext. 437

Fax: (02920) 573490

Website: www.nmgw.ac.uk/mwl/index.en.shtml

Enquiries: The Archivist, Mr A. Lloyd Hughes

Open: Mon–Fri: 9.30–1.00, 1.45–4.30.

Access: Bona fide researchers, preferably by prior arrangement.

Historical background: In 1946 the Earl of Plymouth offered St Fagans Castle, with its gardens and grounds, to the National Museum of Wales as a centre for a folk museum. It was opened to the public in 1948.

Acquisitions policy: To complement existing collections in the fields of Welsh ethnology by donations or deposits, in co-operation with other archival institutions in Wales.

Major collections: Ty'n-y-pant MSS: *c*800 MSS in the Welsh language relating to the history and folklore of Cantref Buallt, Breconshire.
T.C. Evans and T.H. Thomas MSS, relating to Glamorgan folklore and dialect, the National Eisteddfod, Gorsedd of Bards, heraldry etc.
W. Meredith Morris MSS, relating to the folklore and dialect of Pembrokeshire, musicology etc.
Farmers' and craftsmen's account books, diaries, eisteddfodic essays etc.
Questionnaires on aspects of Welsh folk culture, dialects, farming etc.

Non-manuscript material: Pamphlets and broadsides.
Photographs (*c*150,000); cine-films (*c*200); videos (*c*300); sound archives (*c*9000 tapes).
The library houses a unique collection of books (*c*45,000) and periodicals of historical and

ethnological interest, with special emphasis on Wales.

Finding aids: Catalogue of Welsh Folk Museum MSS 1–3000 (1979, 1981) [3 vols to date]. Copies sent to NRA.

Facilities: Photocopying. Photography. Microfilm/fiche reader. Tape-recorders.

Publications: A. Lloyd Hughes: 'The Welsh Folk Museum Manuscripts', *Folk Life*, xvii (1979), 68–70.

C Welsh Industrial and Maritime Museum

Address: 126 Bute Street, Cardiff CF1 6AE

Telephone: (02920) 480755

Fax: (02920) 487252

Website: www.nmgw.ac.uk/wimm/ index.en.shtml

Enquiries: Dr David Jenkins

Open: Tues–Fri: 10.00–5.00.

Access: Generally open to the public, by appointment.

The museum collects relevant MSS, artefacts and photographs relating to industrial and mar-itime Wales, and holds an extensive collection of photographs, prints and drawings relating to Wales. A card index is available.

219 St Michael's College

Address: Llandaff, Cardiff CF5 2YJ

Telephone: (029) 20563379

Fax: (029) 20576377

Enquiries: The Rev. Librarian

Open: By arrangement with the Librarian.

Access: Generally open to the public, by appointment.

The Cathedral Library at Llandaff was estab-lished during the episcopate of Bishop Alfred Ollivant (1798–1882) DD, Lord Bishop of Llandaff, 1849–82. Owing to reorganisation in the cathedral, the whole library was moved to the Ollivant Room at St Michael's College in 1986. The library holds sermon notes and let-ters and diaries of Ollivant and Bishop Edward Copleston (1776–1849). *See* M. Tallone: *Cathedral Libraries of Wales* (Athlone Press, 1962).

220 Welch Regiment Museum of the Royal Regiment of Wales (42nd/41st Foot)

Address: The Black and Barbican Towers, The Castle, Cardiff CF10 2RB

Telephone: (02920) 229367

E-mail: rrw@ukonline.co.uk

Website: www.rrw.org.uk

Enquiries: The Curator, Mr John Dart
The Museum Assistant, Mr John Rees

Open: By appointment.

Access: A charge is made.

Historical background: The museum developed from a collection displayed in the late 1920s in the old Regimental Depot, Cardiff, for the ben-efit of recruits under training. During the 1950s that collection formed the basis for a small regi-mental museum on the same site. In 1964 the museum became a charitable trust by a declara-tion of trust drawn up under the guidance of the Army Museums Ogilby Trust, and in 1978 it opened in its present location. The museum was one of the first in Wales to be registered under the Museums and Galleries Commission Registration and is recognised as an approved place of deposit for public records. See also the South Wales Borderers and Monmouthshire Regimental Museum of the Royal Regiment of Wales (entry 127).

Acquisitions policy: Archival material and artefacts relating to the history and services of the 41st and 69th Regiments of Foot (later 1st and 2nd Battalions) and of the Welch Regiment, which includes also its Territorial Force and Territorial Army Battalions and wartime Service and Reserve Battalions. Also material relating to the Militia Volunteers, local militia and other affiliated auxiliary units raised within the old 41st Regimental District of South Wales, and the services of all battalions of the Royal Regiment of Wales (24th/41st Foot) from 1969.

Archives of organisation: War diaries, 1914–18, 1941–5, court-martial books, letter-books.
Various order books, 1806– ; Digests of Service, 1719– .
The archives do not include the personal service records of ex-members of the regiment.

Non-manuscript material: Prints, drawings, and a large collection of photographs and albums.

[handwritten: ✳ transferred to SWANSEA Opening mid 2005 Tel: 01792 459 640]

Finding aids: Photo albums and MS books (NRA 20951).

Conservation: Contracted out.

221 Welsh Historic Monuments: Cardiff

Parent organisation: National Assembly for Wales

Address: Cathays Park, Cardiff CF10 3NQ

Telephone: (02920) 500200

Fax: (02920) 826375

E-mail: cadw@wales.gsi.gov.uk

Website: www.cadw.wales.gov.uk

Welsh Historic Monuments was established as a new archive in 1996, based in Cardiff, to maintain and extend the photographic and drawing collections. For National Monuments Record of Wales see entry 10.

222 Welsh Music Information Centre

Address: Ty Cerydd, 15 Mount Stuart Square, Cardiff CF10 5DP

Telephone: (02920) 465700

Fax: (02920) 462733

Enquiries: The Director

Open: Mon–Fri: 9.30–5.00, by appointment only.

The Welsh Music Archive was founded in 1976 and re-established in 1983 as the Welsh Music Information Centre, funded principally by the Arts Council of Wales at Cardiff University. It moved in 1999 to its present address, and opened with new staff in 2001. Original manuscripts and scores have been transferred to the National Library of Wales (see entry 9), but the centre holds copies of performance scores as part of its policy of promoting contemporary Welsh music. A new catalogue is in the course of preparation.

223 Cumbria Archive Service
Cumbria Record Office, Carlisle

Parent organisation: Cumbria County Council

Address: The Castle, Carlisle, Cumbria CA3 8UR

Telephone: (01228) 607285

Fax: (01288) 607274

E-mail: carlisle.record.office@cumbriacc.gov.uk

Enquiries: The County Archivist, Mr Jim Grisenthwaite (service-wide enquiries)
The Assistant County Archivist, Mr David Bowcock (office enquiries)

Open: Mon–Fri: 9.00–5.00.

Access: Generally open to the public. The office operates the CARN reader's ticket system.

Historical background: The office was officially opened in 1962, although archives had been collected before then and staff were appointed from c1944. It also acts as the Diocesan Record Office for Carlisle, and is recognised as a place of deposit for public records. Administrative assistance is given to the Egremont Estate Office, Cockermouth Castle. Cumbria Archive Service has other offices at Kendal (see entry 480), Barrow-in-Furness (see entry 53).

Acquisitions policy: Official and unofficial records for the historic county of Cumberland and the City of Carlisle.

Archives of organisation: Usual local authority record holdings.

Major collections: Deposited local collections, of which the following have a wider significance: political and other personal and family papers of Sir Esme Howard (Lord Howard of Penrith), diplomat, 1780–1961. Papers of Catherine Marshall, suffragist and pacifist, of Hawse End, Keswick, c1880–1956. Estate and family records of Earl of Lonsdale, c1100–1950, including West Cumberland coal-mining, 17th–20th centuries.

Finding aids: Catalogues and indexes. Some collections are unlisted. Selected catalogues sent to NRA.

Facilities: Photocopying. Photography. Microfilming. Microfilm/fiche readers/printer.

Conservation: In-house facilities.

Publications: R.C. Jarvis: *The Jacobite Rising of 1715 and 1745*, Cumberland County Council Record Series, i (Carlisle, 1954).
E. Hughes (ed.): *The Fleming Senhouse Papers*, Cumberland County Council Record Series, ii (Carlisle, 1961).

B.C. Jones: 'Cumberland, Westmorland and Carlisle Record Office, 1960–65', *Archives*, vii/34 (1965), 80.

——: 'Cumberland and Westmorland Record Offices, 1968', *Northern History*, iii (1968), 162.

H.W. Hodgson: *A Bibliography of the History and Topography of Cumberland and Westmorland* (Carlisle, 1968).

Cumbrian Ancestors: Notes for Genealogical Searchers (3/1998).

224 Carmarthenshire Archives Service

Address: Parc Myrddin, Richmond Terrace, Carmarthen SA31 1JP

Telephone: (01267) 228232

Fax: (01267) 228237

E-mail: archives@carmarthenshire.gov.uk

Website: www.carmarthenshire.gov.uk

Enquiries: The County Archivist, Mr J. Davies

Open: Mon–Thurs: 9.00–4.45; Fri: 9.00–4.15.

Access: Generally open to the public. Booking is necessary for the use of microforms.

Historical background: The office was established as Carmarthenshire Record Office in 1959. It also acts as a Diocesan Record Office for St David's (parish registers) and is recognised as a place of deposit for public records.

Acquisitions policy: Historical documents from within the boundaries of the county of Carmarthen.

Archives of organisation: Usual local authority record holdings.

Major collections: Deposited local collections, including the following which has a wider significance: Cawdor Collection, containing the Golden Grove Book, an 18th-century collection of pedigrees relating to the whole of Wales.

Finding aids: Catalogues and indexes. Sent to NRA.

Facilities: Photocopying.

Publications: S.G. Beckley: *Carmarthen Record Office Survey of Archive Holdings* (1980).

Tracing Your Family History in the Carmarthenshire Record Office (1992).

225 Castle Ashby Archives

Parent organisation: Compton Estates

Address: Estate Office, Castle Ashby, Northamptonshire NN7 1LJ

Enquiries: The Agent

Open: By arrangement.

Access: Bona fide researchers, by appointment only.

The archives of the Comptons, Earls and Marquesses of Northampton since 1618, including principally estate records for Northamptonshire and Warwickshire as well as some family documents, mostly 19th century. There is a catalogue available, which is also held at Northamptonshire Record Office (see entry 931) and at the NRA.

226 Royal Engineers Corps Library

Parent organisation: Institution of Royal Engineers

Address: Brompton Barracks, Chatham, Kent ME4 4UG

Telephone: (01634) 822416

Fax: (01634) 822419

Website: www.army.mod.uk/royalengineers/museum.htm

Enquiries: The Librarian

Open: Mon, Wed, Fri: 9.00–5.00.

Access: Members of the institution and serving members of the armed forces. Generally open to the public, by appointment.

Historical background: A Royal Engineers Library was formed at Chatham in 1813. A corps library was established in London in 1847 and branch libraries were set up at selected stations as funds permitted; by 1862 there were 16 home station and 19 overseas libraries, excluding India. Between 1924 and 1928 all home station libraries except those at Chatham and Aldershot were abolished and only nine remained abroad. The corps library was moved from London to Chatham in 1939. The present library is now the only RE library, having inherited the best of the items of all the other libraries as they closed down. The Institution of Royal Engineers was founded in 1875. The original libraries were set up to hold technical books relevant to the work of the corps in all its varied aspects.

Acquisitions policy: Items on military engineering worldwide, with particular emphasis on the work and history of the Corps of Royal Engineers.

Archives of organisation: RE reports, documents, letters, construction plans etc.

Major collections: Connolly papers: biographical notes on RE officers to 1860.

Non-manuscript material: Photograph albums of Royal Engineers and of their life, work and play, c1855– .

Finding aids: Computer database/card index system. NRA 36689.

Facilities: Photocopying. Photography. Microfilm/fiche readers.

227 Anglia Polytechnic University
Chelmsford Campus

Address: Rivermead Library, Bishop Hall Lane, Chelmsford, Essex CM1 1SQ

Telephone: (01245) 493131 ext. 3757

Fax: (01245) 495920

Website: www.libweb.anglia.ac.uk/useliby/specials.htm

Enquiries: The Campus Librarian

Open: By appointment.

Archive of Industrial Archaeology, comprising company documents, slides, newsletters, photographs and tape-recorded interviews with former employees relating to industries in and around Chelmsford, including the world's first radio factory, Marconi, Hall Street, Chelmsford, and the Bromfield Ironworks and Paxmans of Colchester, diesel engine manufacturer. There is also a local studies collection including documents, maps, videos and books. The Cambridge campus holds the French Resistance Archive (see entry 180).

228 Essex Record Office

Parent organisation: Essex County Council

Address: Wharf Road, Chelmsford, Essex CM2 6YT

Telephone: (01245) 244644

Fax: (01245) 244655

E-mail: ero.enquiry@essexcc.gov.uk

Website: www.essexcc.gov.uk/ero

Enquiries: The County Archivist, Mr Ken Hall

Open: Mon: 10.00–8.45; Tues–Thurs: 9.15–5.15; Fri, Sat: 9.15–4.15.

Access: Generally open to the public; an appointment is advisable. The office operates the CARN reader's ticket system. A paid research service is available.

Historical background: The Record Office opened formally in 1938, although parish and other records had been collected from 1936. Before the reorganisation of London in 1964 the office covered old Essex, which included the boroughs of Havering, Barking and Dagenham, Waltham Forest, Newham and Redbridge. The office also acts as the Diocesan Record Office for Chelmsford, and is responsible for the cathedral archives. It is recognised as a place of deposit for public records. There are branch offices at Southend and Colchester (entries 1123 and 250 respectively).

Acquisitions policy: Archival and printed material relating to the county of Essex.

Archives of organisation: Usual local authority record holdings.

Major collections: Deposited local collections, including the following which have a wider significance:

Papers of Sir Thomas Smith relating to the colonisation of the Ards in Ulster, 1572–7.

Correspondence of the Cornwallis and Bacon families, 1622–80.

Record book and papers of William Holcroft as JP, verderer and captain of militia, 1661–8.

Journals and correspondence of James Paroissien, relating to South America, 1806–27.

Non-manuscript material: The Essex Sound Archive.

Extensive photographic and pictorial collections.

Collection of local history printed material in the Essex Record Office Library.

Finding aids: Catalogues. Lists. Indexes. Lists sent to NRA.

Facilities: Photocopying. Photography. Microfilming. Self-service microfilm/fiche readers.

Conservation: In-house facilities for paper conservation. Outside work undertaken for institutions and private individuals.

Publications: F.G. Emmison: *Guide to the Essex Record Office* (1969).
Essex Family History: a Genealogist's Guide to the Essex Record Office.
Publications catalogue available.

229 Marconi Archives

Parent organisation: Marconi plc

Address: Marconi Archives, West Hanningfield Road, Great Baddow, Chelmsford, Essex CM2 8HN

Telephone: (01245) 242390

Fax: (01245) 242384

E-mail: marconi.archives@marconi.com

Website: www.marconi.com

Enquiries: The Archivist

Open: Mon–Fri: 9.00–5.00, by appointment only.

Access: At present restricted.

Historical background: GEC was founded in 1886 in London and became a limited company in 1900. It took over AEI in 1967 and merged with English Electric in 1968. Many famous names, such as Gugielmo Marconi (1874–1937), James Watt (1736–1819) and Robert Stephenson (1803–59), contributed to the early history of the company. GEC Archives began as the Hugo Hirst (joint founder and chairman 1910–43) Collection, and were officially formed in 1993. In 1999 GEC became Marconi plc and the GEC Collection was merged into the Marconi Archives.

Acquisitions policy: The archives collect any material on the history of Marconi, GEC and associated companies, without geographical boundaries.

Archives of organisation: Archives of GEC, 1886–1999; Marconi Company, 1889– .
Archives of amalgamated companies, notably AEI, 1927–69 (includes Metropolitan-Vickers Siemens, BTH, Edison Swann, Hotpoint and W.T. Henley); English Electric, 1917–68 (includes Elliot Bros., Marconi, Ruston & Hornsby, Stephenson, Hawthorn & Vulcan Foundry, Willans & Robinson, Dick Kerr); VSEL, Ferranti and Plessey.

Major collections: Guglielmo Marconi Collection, 1880–1937.
Hugo Hirst Collection, 1863–1943.
Hirst Research Centre Collection, 1919–95.
Weinstock Collection, 1963–97.

Non-manuscript material: Photographs, technical reports, film, video and sound recordings. Marconi artefacts.

Finding aids: Database.

Facilities: Photocopying. Photography.

Conservation: Limited.

Publications: J. Dummdow: *1899–1949 Metropolitan Vickers Electric Co. Ltd* (Metropolitan Vickers Ltd. 1949).
W.J. Baker: *History of the Marconi Company* (London, 1969).
R. Jones & O. Marriott: *Anatomy of a Merger: a History of GEC, AEI and English Electric* (London, 1970).
B. Ritchie: *Into the Sunrise: a History of Plessey 1917–198* (James & James, 1989).
R.P. Bradley: *GEC Traction and its Predecessors, 1823–Present Day* (1993).

230 Cheltenham & Gloucester College of Higher Education

Address: Francis Close Hall Campus, Swindon Road, Cheltenham, Gloucestershire GL50 4AZ

Telephone: (01242) 543496

Fax: (01242) 543283

Website: www.chelt.ac.uk/lis.archives

Enquiries: The Team Leader, Archives and Record Management

Open: Mon–Fri: 9.00–4.45; access at other times may be possible by appointment.

Access: Any serious student or researcher.

Historical background: The college was founded in 1847 as the Church of England Training Colleges at Cheltenham, to train both men and women as teachers. It adopted the names St Paul and St Mary in the late 19th century. It was renamed in 1990. From 1921 to 1979 separate principals were appointed to the constituent male and female departments, but they remained under the control of one college council. The colleges merged in 1979 to form a college of higher education. Recently the college has established the Dymock Poets Archive and Study Centre.

Acquisitions policy: Deposits from former students are welcomed and material relating to the Dymock Poets and other Georgian poets is collected.

Archives of organisation: St Paul & St Mary College Archive: full documentation of the development of an important teacher-training establishment.

Major collections: Deposited papers of former students and staff.

Dymock Poets Archive: a collection of manuscripts, printed works, and critical and biographical material relating to Lascelles Abercrombie (1881–1938), Wilfrid Wilson Gibson (1878–1962), Rupert Brooke (1887–1915), John Drinkwater (1882–1937), Edward Thomas (1878–1917) and Robert Frost (1874–1964).

Finding aids: Database.

Facilities: Photocopying.

Conservation: Contracted out.

Publications: Occasional Papers series.

231 Cheltenham College

Address: Bath Road, Cheltenham, Gloucestershire GL53 7LD

Telephone: (01242) 513540

Fax: (01242) 265630

Enquiries: The Librarian, Mrs C.E. Cawley

Open: Term: normal school hours.
Vacation: by arrangement only.

Access: Generally open to the public, by appointment.

Cheltenham College was founded as an educational establishment for boys in 1841. The archives are in process of collection and arrangement and old Cheltonians are actively encouraged to deposit material. There are scrapbooks and school magazines, 1841– , as well as school registers and photographs. A computer catalogue is in progress.

232 Cheltenham Ladies' College Archive

Address: Bayshill Road, Cheltenham, Gloucestershire GL50 3EP

Telephone: (01242) 520691 ext. 250

Fax: (01242) 227882

E-mail: archives@cheltladiescollege.org

Website: www.cheltladiescollege.org

Enquiries: The Archivist

Open: Term: Mon–Fri: 9.30–4.00, by appointment.

Access: Open for research on written application. Free to ex-students and staff of CLC. A moderate charge may be made to cover costs such as research, postage and photocopying.

Historical background: The college was founded in 1853 and moved to its present site in 1873. Dorothea Beale (1831–1906), principal 1858–1906, developed the college to be in the forefront of women's education. The Guild (college's association of ex-pupils) previously held much of the college archive. There is now a permanent archive display room showing the history of college and an archive storeroom for documents and books.

Acquisitions policy: Actively encourages deposits from ex-students and staff.

Archives of organisation: School magazines, 1880– ; school registers, 1908– ; admission books, 1882– ; lists of early pupils, 1853– ; prospectus, 1858– ; CLC programmes, 1877– .

Major collections: Arris breviary of four gospels MSS, given by John Ruskin.
Autograph collection, major part given by Lord Askwith.

Non-manuscript material: Photographs, 1863– ; plans; film and audio newspaper cuttings; postcard collection; botanical drawings by Dorothy Herman.

Finding aids: A computerised database is being prepared.

Facilities: Photocopying.

Conservation: Liaises with Cheltenham Museum and Gloucestershire Record Office (see entry 406) for advice on conservation matters.

Publications: A Brief History and Guide.

Autograph letter collection included in University of Reading Literary MSS Survey.

233 Planned Environment Therapy Trust
Archive and Study Centre

Address: Church Lane, Toddington, Cheltenham, Gloucestershire GL54 5DQ

Telephone: (01242) 620125

Fax: (01242) 620125

E-mail: archive@pettarchiv.org.uk

Website: www.pettarchiv.org.uk

Enquiries: The Archivist

Open: Mon–Fri: 9.00–4.00, by prior arrangement.

Access: Open to any bona fide researcher, by written application to the Archivist and by appointment; much of the material is restricted.

Historical background: The PETT was founded in 1966 by Dr Marjorie Franklin, a pioneering psychiatrist/psychoanalyst, using private monies and funds from Q-Camps Committee (1935–c1966) and Children's Social Adjustment Ltd (1948–69), which had earlier founded and run Alresford Place School. Founding Trustees with Dr Franklin were W. David Wills and Arthur T. Barron, both of whom had extensive experience in therapeutic community work with children and young people. The Archive and Study Centre was established in 1989 to fulfil one of the trust's founding aspirations. It aims to encourage and promote research and discussion in the fields covered by the archive through an active oral history recording project, seminars and publication, and the projected compilation of a comprehensive research directory and guide to published and archival sources.

Acquisitions policy: Papers of individuals, institutions and organisations involved in planned environment therapy, milieu therapy and therapeutic community.

Archives of organisation: Archives of PETT, 1966– .

Major collections: Marjorie Franklin (1877–1975) Collection and Arthur T. Barron (1919–93) Collection.

Personal and professional papers of W. David Wills (1903–81), Christopher Beedell (*b* 1925) and Kenneth Barnes (1903–98).

Materials related to Otto Shaw, and the archives of the Red Hill School, 1934–92; Peper Harow Therapeutic Community, 1970–93; A.S. Neill (1883–1973) and George Lyward (1894–1974); Association of Workers for Maladjusted Children, 1951– ; and the Cotswold Community, 1967– .

Dr David Clark's papers re the founding and early years of the Association of Therapeutic Communities, 1970–82.

Archives of the Sussex Youth Trust, Chalvington Trust and School, 1980–92; Westhope Manor/Shotton Hall School, 1949–94; Q-Camps Committee, 1935–c1966, including Hawkspur Camp for Men, one of the earliest therapeutic communities in England, 1936–40; Barns School in Scotland, 1940–5; Homer Lane Society, 1964– ; New Barns School, 1965–92; Messenger House Trust, 1970–87 and Hutchinson Settlement, 1977–87; the Arbours Association of Therapeutic Communities, 1970– ; Hengrove School (Tring), 1947–97.

Non-manuscript material: Growing oral history collection. Expanding collection of films, photographs, videotapes and sound recordings.

Finding aids: Catalogues and lists, to be sent to NRA.

Facilities: Limited photocopying. Photography. Audio and video playback and copying facilities.

Conservation: Contracted out.

234 Zurich Financial Services (UKISA) Ltd

Address: Eagle Star Centre, Montpellier Drive, Cheltenham, Gloucestershire GL53 7LQ

Telephone: (01242) 221311 ext. 22856

Fax: (01242) 250046

E-mail: isabel.syed@zurich.co.uk

Enquiries: The Group Archivist, Mrs Isabel Syed

Open: By arrangement only.

Access: Bona fide researchers, by appointment following application in writing to the Group Archivist. There are some restrictions on some classes of records.

Historical background: Eagle Star was founded in 1904 as British Dominions Marine; there followed expansion into general business and a name change in 1911 to British Dominions General. Life insurance started in 1916 by acquisition of Eagle (1916), Sceptre (1917) Star (1917) and there were further changes 1917 to Eagle and British Dominions, then to Eagle, Star and British Dominions; and to Eagle Star in 1937. Many other acquisitions followed. Eagle Star became part of BAT Industries in 1984, but was demerged and became part of the Zurich Financial Services Group in 1998. The archives department was set up in 1986.

Acquisitions policy: Material relating to Eagle Star and its constituent companies and to Zurich UK.

Archives of organisation: Archives of Eagle Star, 1904– , and of constituent companies, including Eagle, 1807–1916; Star, 1843–1917; Sceptre, 1864–1917; English & Scottish Law, 1839–1918; Midland Employers' Mutual, 1898–1959.
Part of archives of Zurich UK (f. 1922).

Non-manuscript material: Advertising and staff films and videos, including 'The Magic Scroll', 1930.
Museum of memorabilia at Eagle Star Centre.

Finding aids: Database indexes.

Facilities: Photocopying. Photography.

Conservation: Contracted out.

Publications: A.F. Shepherd: *Links with the Past* (Eagle Star, 1917).
I. Syed: *Eagle Star: a Guide to its History and Archives* (1997).
K. Lüönd: *Inspired by Tomorrow* (1998) [history of the Zurich Insurance Company, 1872–1997].

235 Chertsey Museum

Parent organisation: Runnymede Borough Council

Address: The Cedars, 33 Windsor Street, Chertsey, Surrey KT16 8AT

Telephone: (01932) 565764

Fax: (01932) 571118

E-mail: amandale@tons.co.uk

Enquiries: Stephen Nicholls

Open: Wed–Thurs: 12.30–4.30; Sat: 11.00–4.00.

Access: Generally open to the public.

Historical background: The museum was founded in 1965 and a research room was opened in 1993.

Acquisitions policy: Items relating to the history of the Borough of Runnymede, within resource restrictions.

Major collections: Registers and records of Chertsey Congregational Church, 1757–1911.
Accounts of Egham charities, 1838–84.
Minutes of Chertsey and District Emergency Relief Committee, 1914–40.
Records of Chilsey Green Farm and Dairy, 1925–60.
Chertsey rate books, 20th century.
Chertseyana Collection on Chertsey Town (3 vols).

Non-manuscript material: Photograph collection (3000); maps; drawings and prints; directories; small collection of oral history tapes.

Finding aids: Catalogues and indexes. NRA 36480.

Facilities: Photcopying. Photography by arrangement.

236 Cheshire and Chester Archives and Local Studies Service

Parent organisation: Cheshire County Council

Address: Cheshire Record Office, Duke Street, Chester, Cheshire CH1 1RL

Telephone: (01244) 602574 (enquiries)

Fax: (01244) 603812

E-mail: recordoffice@cheshire.gov.uk

Website: www.cheshire.gov.uk/recoff/default.htm

Enquiries: The County Archivist, Mr Jonathan Pepler

Open: Mon: 1.30–5.00; Tues, Wed, Fri: 9.00–5.00; Thurs: 9.00–6.00; Sat (3rd in month): 9.00–4.00.

Access: Generally open to the public. A paid research service is available.

Historical background: The service was formed in 2000 by joining the County Archives and Local Studies with the core archive services of Chester Archives to provide a comprehensive archive service for the whole geographical county of Cheshire. The two services had co-existed for more than 50 years. The City Record Office was established in 1948 and the first professional county archivist was appointed in 1949, though the listing of the county muniments had commenced in 1933. The office is the Chester Diocesan Record Office (since 1961) and acts for the Dean and Chapter of Chester. It is also recognised as Liverpool Diocesan Record Office for the deposit of parish registers and records from parts of the diocese included in Cheshire in 1974. The office is recognised as a place of deposit for public records. It houses the manuscripts (but not the library) of Chester Archaeological Society. Access is given to the archives of the Duke of Westminster by arrangement with the estate office. The office provides archives and local studies services to Warrington and Halton under a three-year agreement from 1998.

Chester Community History & Heritage Service, Town Hall, Chester CH1 2HJ; tel: (01244) 402110; houses a local history library and the image bank of digitised historical photographs, provides a postal enquiry service and produces a range of local and family history leaflets.

Acquisitions policy: To acquire records of administrative or historical significance for the county of Cheshire and the diocese of Chester.

Archives of organisation: Usual diocesan and local authority holdings including Chester city charters, mayors' and sheriffs' records, 12th century– .

Major collections: Archives of 21 Chester city guilds, 15th–20th centuries; Chester Bluecoat Hospital, 1700–1948; Chester College, 1839–1987; Chester Royal Infirmary, 1755–1956.

Large range of family and estate collections, including Arderne, Cholmondeley, Crewe, Egerton of Oulton, Egerton of Tatton, Leicester of Tabley, Shakerly, Stanley of Alderley, Tollemache, Vernon/Venables and Wilbraham.

Business collections, including Fodens, lorry manufacturers, and ICI, Mond Division.

Manuscripts of J.P. Earwaker, antiquarian, c1200–1897.

Non-manuscript material: Maps, including excellent OS coverage of the county at all scales. Prints, photographs and lantern slides.

Newspapers, including *Chester Courant*, 1747–1982; *Chester Chronicle*, 1775– ; *Cheshire Observer*, 1856–1989.

Finding aids: Catalogues, lists and indexes in various formats. Lists sent to NRA.

Facilities: Photocopying. Microfilm reader/printer. Photography and microfilming by arrangement.

Conservation: Full in-house facilities.

Publications: A.M. Kennett: *Chester Schools: a Guide to the School Archives* (1973).
——: *Archives and Records of the City of Chester* (1985).
F.I. Dunn: *The Ancient Parishes, Townships and Chapelries of Cheshire* (1987) [with map].
C.M. Williams (ed.): *Cheshire Record Office Guide* (1991).
Various leaflets on sources.

237 Cheshire Military Museum

Address: The Castle, Chester, Cheshire CH1 2DN

Telephone: (01244) 327617

Fax: (01244) 327617

Website: www.chester.ac.uk/militarymuseum

Enquiries: Maj. (retd) J.E. Ellis

Open: Tues, Thurs: 9.00–5.00, by appointment.

Access: Bona fide researchers. A small charge is made.

Historical background: The museum opened in its present location in 1972 and was refurbished in 2001. It houses the records of the 22nd (Cheshire) Regiment and the Cheshire (Earl of Chester's) Yeomanry. The former was raised in 1689 and the latter in 1797.

Acquisitions policy: Documents, photographs and associated material relating to the above regiments; also general military involvement in Cheshire.

Archives of organisation: Records of 22nd (Cheshire) Regiment, late 18th century– , including regimental journals, documents, letters and photographs.
Records of Cheshire (Earl of Chester's) Yeomanry, including orders and correspondence, mainly late 19th century.

Major collections: Small collection of correspondence of General Sir Charles Napier (1782–1853).

Non-manuscript material: Photographs and maps; printed books; some video archives.

Finding aids: Index.

Facilities: Photocopying.

Conservation: Consultation with Cheshire and Chester Archives and Local Studies Service (see entry above), and North West Museum Service Conservation Department.

238 Eaton Estate Office

Parent organisation: The Grosvenor Estate

Address: The Eaton Estate Office, Eccleston, Chester, Cheshire CH4 9ET

Telephone: (01244) 684400

Fax: (01244) 671838

Enquiries: The Archivist, Eileen Simpson

Open: Not open to the public. Archives can be made available for consultation at Cheshire and Chester Archives and Local Studies Service (see entry 236)

Access: Access by permission only. Forms of application obtainable from relevant record office by arrangement.

Historical background: The Grosvenors of Eaton are descended from the Grosvenors of Hulme in central Cheshire and acquired Eaton through marriage in the 15th century. The titles Earl Grosvenor, Marquess of Westminster and Duke of Westminster were conferred in 1784, 1831 and 1874. The agricultural estates of the Grosvenor Estate are administered from the Eaton Estate Office.

Acquisitions policy: Maintains the estate archive.

Archives of organisation: Estate records (deeds, rentals, accounts, maps, etc) of the Eaton and Chester estates of the Grosvenors, 12th–20th centuries; deeds and papers relating to Denbighshire and Flintshire estates, 15th–20th centuries. Accounts and papers relating to Eaton Hall building and household, 17th–20th centuries; family and personal papers, 16th–20th centuries.

Non-manuscript material: Photographs of former Hall of Eaton and other estate buildings.

Finding aids: NRA 13470, updating in progress.

Conservation: Contracted out.

Publications: A Calendar of Ancient Charters Preserved at Eaton Hall, Cheshire (1862).
Schedules of Deeds and Documents in the Muniment Room at Eaton (1898).
Principal Family and Estate Collections: Family Names A-K, HMC Guide to Sources for British History, no. 10 (1996,; 74–6.

239 Derbyshire Library Service
Local Studies Department

Address: Chesterfield Library, New Beetwell Street, Chesterfield, Derbyshire S40 1QN

Telephone: (01246) 209292 ext. 38

Fax: (01246) 209304

E-mail: chesterfield.library@derbyshire.gov.uk

Enquiries: The Central Librarian, Mrs A. Ainsworth

Open: Mon–Fri: 9.30–7.00; Sat: 9.30–1.00.

Access: Generally open to the public, but since some archives are housed in a basement store it is advisable to write in advance. A paid family history research service is available.

Historical background: The library was established in 1879 with a strong engineering background due to George Stephenson's influence. It has gradually accumulated archival material over the years. The library came under Derbyshire County Council with reorganisation in 1974 and moved into a new central library in 1985.

Acquisitions policy: While the library retains the existing archive collections, all offers of archival material are now referred to Derbyshire Record Office (entry 896).

Archives of organisation: Annual reports, stock, issue and cash records, reports, correspondence, 1885–1992.

Major collections: Collections of family papers, notably: Barnes family, landowners and owners of Grassmoor colliery, including bills and accounts, 18th–19th centuries (c1000 items); Twigg family from Ashover area, some material relating to local mining, mostly 18th century (c500 items).
Records of local businesses, including Plowrights Brothers Ltd, engineering firm; Greaves, chemist shop, mid-19th century– .

Unitarian church records, 1692–1968.
Methodist records for Chesterfield area: church records, 1828–1974; circuit records, 1912–57.
Education records, 1863–1970.
Handford local history collection.
Oakley Collection: deeds (c300) and other documents on north-east and west Derbyshire, c1571–1875, collected by R.H. Oakley, local historian.
Arkwright Cotton Mill, Bakewell: wage books, 1786–1811.

Non-manuscript material: Substantial collection of photographs and slides of the Chesterfield area, c1880– .
Stephenson Collection of books, pamphlets etc, showing contribution of George Stephenson to railway history.
Census returns, 1841–91.
Derbyshire Times, 1854– ; *Derbyshire Courier,* 1828–1922; *Derby and Chesterfield Reporter,* 1823–1930; *Derby Mercury,* 1732–1800.
Maps, historical and current, of various scales covering Chesterfield area.

Finding aids: Various lists and indexes. Card catalogue.

Facilities: Photocopying. Microfilm/fiche readers/printer.

Conservation: Binding, photograph and map encapsulation undertaken at Derby City Library Bindery.

Publications: Local Studies in Derbyshire: a Guide to Library Resources (1996).
Family History in Derbyshire: a Guide to Library Reseources (1994)
Microfilms in Derbyshire Libraries (1997).
Monumental Inscriptions: a List of Transcripts and Indexes in the Local Studies Library, County Hall, Matlock (1998).

240 Robinson Museum

Parent organisation: Robinson & Sons Ltd

Address: Wheatbridge, Chesterfield, Derbyshire S40 1YE

Telephone: (01246) 505158

Fax: (01246) 208164

Enquiries: The Company Historian, Peter White

Open: Mon–Fri: 8.30–5.00, by appointment.

Access: Access by prior arrangement only and at the discretion of the company.

Historical background: The company was founded in 1839 by John Bradbury Robinson to manufacture packaging. It later expanded to the production of surgical dressings and hygiene products. By 1939 it employed 3500; its highest employment was 5000 in 1960 (including overseas subsidiaries).

Acquisitions policy: The archive grows out of company record-keeping. Currently it is also attempting to bring back artefacts such as samples of products. Its archive and collection trace the company's history and its involvement with its home town.

Archives of organisation: Records of Robinson & Sons Ltd, 1839– , and of subsidiary companies in Britain and New Zealand/Canada.

Major collections: Personal papers of company founder, John Bradbury Robinson (1802–69), and his son, William Bradbury Robinson (1826–1911).

Non-manuscript material: Samples of packaging, including pillboxes, rigid card boxes, round boxes and cartons, 1839– , and surgical dressings, sanitary towels and diapers, 1855– .
Large collection of Brampton Brown ware pottery.

Finding aids: Home-grown system orginated by grandson of founder.

Facilities: Photocopying.

Publications: P.M. Robinson and A.L. Spence: *The Robinsons of Chesterfield* (Robinson & Sons Ltd, Chesterfield, 1937).
C. Porteous: *Pillboxes & Bandages* (1960).
Chesterfield and District Local History Society: *Robinson & Sons Ltd, 1839–1989* (1989).

241 West Sussex Record Office

Parent organisation: West Sussex County Council

Address: County Hall, Chichester, West Sussex PO19 1RN

Telephone: (01243) 753600

Fax: (01243) 533959

E-mail: records.office@westsussex.gov.uk

Website: www.westsussex.gov.uk/cs/ro/rohome.htm

Enquiries: The County and Diocesan Archivist, Mr Richard Childs

Open: Mon–Fri: 9.15–4.45; Sat: 9.15–12.30, 1.30–4.30.

Access: Generally open to the public. Closed first week in December. The office operates the CARN readers' ticket system. A paid research service is available.

Historical background: The Records Committee was set up in 1939 and took in records from that date, although an archivist was not appointed until 1946. Since reorganisation in 1974 the office has covered the old West Sussex area and part of what was East Sussex. The office also acts as the Diocesan Record Office for Chichester and is recognised as a place of deposit for public records. It is the repository and conservation centre for the South East Film and Video Archive.

Acquisitions policy: MSS, photographic, film, audio and newspaper material relating to West Sussex.

Archives of organisation: Usual local authority record holdings.

Major collections: Deposited local collections, including the following which have a wider significance: Wilfred Scawen Blunt MSS: Irish and Middle Eastern politics, and literary, 19th and 20th centuries.
Cobden MSS: political, 19th century.
Eric Gill Collection: works of art, 20th century.
Goodwood MSS: political and cultural, 18th and 19th centuries.
Hussey MSS: visual art and music, 20th century.
Maxse MSS: political, 20th century.
Petworth House Archives: Thomas Harriott astronomical papers, 17th century.
Royal Sussex Regiment MSS: military, 18th–20th centuries.

Non-manuscript material: Crookshank Collection: William Blake.
Ronald Shephard Railway Collection.
Local newspaper files, 19th–20th centuries.

Facilities: Photocopying. Photography. Microfilming. Microfilm/fiche reader/printers. Scanning. Film video transfer.

Conservation: In-house facilities.

Publications: Official Guide and Report on the East and West Sussex Record Offices (1954).
F.W. Steer and I.M. Kirby: *Catalogue of the Records of the Bishop, Archdeacons and Former Exempt Jurisdictions*(1966).

P.M. Wilkinson: *Genealogists' Guide to the West Sussex Record Office* (1994).
K.C. Leslie and T.J. McCann: *Local History in West Sussex: a Guide to Sources* (1975)
Local History Mini Guides to Sources (nos. 1–9 published to date).
Over 70 publications [list available].
See also *Publications* under East Sussex Record Office (entry 513)

242   Guild of Handicraft Trust

Address: The Old Silk Mill, Sheep Street, Chipping   Campden,   Gloucestershire GL55 6DS

Telephone: (01386) 841417

E-mail: gofhtrust@ukonline.co.uk

Enquiries: The Secretary, Frank Johnson

Open: By appointment only.

Access: Generally   open   to   the   public. Wheelchair access.

Historical background: The Guild of Handicraft Trust held its inaugural meeting in 1990 and was granted registered charitable status in 1992. It was established to focus attention on the artists and craftspeople of the North Cotswolds. The trust does not have a permanent base but is actively looking for one in Chipping Campden. The material available at the start was limited, but since the trust's foundation more has been, and continues to be, added.

Acquisitions policy: The trust does not have a clearly defined policy at present other than to collect all relevant archival material that may be offered. Security and environmental conditions govern the nature and extent of what can be accepted. The subject areas relate to the North Cotswolds and cover the Arts and Crafts movement, current arts, crafts and design practice. Materials are in the form of drawings, photographs, publications, models and maquettes.

Major collections: Records of Guild of Handicraft founded by C.R. Ashbee (1863–1942), 1902– .

Non-manuscript material: Drawings by C.R. Ashbee of architectural work in and around Campden, executed and unexecuted designs (c450).
Alec Miller, guildsman, woodcarver and sculptor: models and plaster casts; photographs;

sketchbook and drawings; published and other articles.

Sidney Reeve, silversmith, collection of drawings (*c*500) and photographs of silverwork and jewellery.

Jesse Taylor/William Greening collection of photographs, *c*1895–1930s (*c*450).

Hart workshop, Ashbee's silversmith's workshop, drawings (*c*4000), photographs, models and patterns, Essex House Press material, Guild of Handicraft visitors book, 1903– .

Paul Woodroffe (1875–1954), illustrator, book designer and stained glass artist, book collection (*c*160).

Roland Dyer (1924–74), photographer, collection of photographs, 1950s (*c*900)

Robert Welch, sketches and general arrangement drawings, prototypes, samples, production pieces, trade catalogues and other related material, 1955– .

Finding aids: Catalogues in preparation.

Conservation: Contracted out.

243   Vintage Sports Car Club Library

Address: The Old Post Office, West Street, Chipping Norton, Oxfordshire OX7 5EL

Telephone: (01608) 644777

Fax: (01608) 644888

E-mail: info@vscc.co.uk

Website: www.vscc.co.uk

Enquiries: The Librarian, Nick Walker

Open: Tues–Fri: 9.00–5.00.

Access: Normally members only; other bona fide researchers, by arrangement.

Historical background: The VSCC was founded in 1934. Its library has developed by bequests and purchases.

Acquisitions policy: Material relating to motor cars, particularly sports cars, mainly of the period 1914–39.

Archives of organisation: Club minutes and *Bulletins*, 1934– ; *Newsletters* and membership lists, 1946– ; some subject files on major issues.

Non-manuscript material: Photo, film and video collection covering VSCC sporting events; complete collection of programmes and race records for these events, 1948– ; Library collection of relevant printed works.

Facilities: Photocopying.

244   Royal Agricultural College

Address: Stroud Road, Cirencester, Gloucestershire GL7 6JS

Telephone: (01285) 652531 ext. 2274

Fax: (01285) 889844

E-mail: sarah.howie@royagcol.ac.uk

Website: www.royagcol.ac.uk

Enquiries: The Librarian, Sarah Howie

Open: Term: Mon–Thurs: 9.00–8.00; Fri: 9.00–6.00; Sat: 9.00–12.30, 1.00–4.00.
Vacation: Mon–Fri: 9.00–12.00, 1.00–5.00, by prior appointment.

Access: Generally open to the public by arrangement. There is a day charge or annual membership subscription.

Historical background: The college was founded in 1845 and is an independent college in the university sector. Special collections were built up mainly in the 1930s.

Acquisitions policy: To maintain its own archives and receive donations in the subject areas of agriculture, rural estate management, land management and rural economy.

Archives of organisation: Archives, including examination papers, course photographs and RACA *Journal*, 1875– .

Non-manuscript material: Publications by or about RAC staff and students.

Facilities: Photocopying.

245   North West Sound Archive

Address: Old Steward's Office, Clitheroe Castle, Clitheroe, Lancashire BB7 1AZ

Telephone: (01200) 427897

Fax: (01200) 427897

E-mail: nwsa@ed.lancscc.gov.uk

Enquiries: Andrew Schofield

Open: Mon–Fri: 9.00–5.00.

Access: Generally open to the public; an appointment is preferred. Charges are made for loan services.

Historical background: The archive was founded in 1979 in Manchester and was transferred in 1981 under the auspices of Lancashire Record Office, although it is still independent and has a separate committee.

Acquisitions policy: To record and preserve the recordings of the life, language, traditions and culture of north-west England, i.e. Lancashire, Greater Manchester and the Peak District.

Non-manuscript material: General oral history collections relating to the region.
Solidarity recordings (Granada TV).
Jodrell Bank Radio Astronomy collections.
BBC Radio Manchester and Lancashire collections.
Surveys of English dialects (Leeds University) and children's playsongs.
Oral history collections: Bolton, Manchester Jewish Museum, Manchester Ship Canal, Salford Quays, Strangeways, Oldham Local Studies.

Finding aids: Computer catalogue.

Facilities: Photocopying.

Publications: Various compilation packs from the collections.

246 Stonyhurst College

Address: Clitheroe, Lancashire BB7 9PZ

Telephone: (01254) 826345

Fax: (01254) 826732

Enquiries: The Librarian, Mr David Knight

Access: On personal application, normally with a letter of introduction, to the Librarian.

Historical background: Stonyhurst College dates from the reign of Queen Elizabeth I, when English Catholics wishing to educate their children in their own religion had to send them abroad. A number of institutions were established on the continent, one of the earliest being the English College at St Omer in 1593. Subsequent colleges were set up in Bruges and Liège and, in 1794, in Stonyhurst.

Major collections: A large number of MSS relating to English Catholicism, 1570–1850 (the period known as recusancy), consisting of deeds, returns of recusants, transcripts of various letters, account books, manorial documents and estate papers, including letters *re* the English College at Liège, 1780–1814 (3 vols).

Collection of annual letters on the Scottish Mission, 1562–1752.

Finding aids: MS Collection: NRA 22957.

Facilities: Photocopying.

Publications: HMC Second Report, xiii and App. 143–46 (1); Third Report, xxi, and App. 334–41 (2); Tenth Report, xxv and App. IV 176–99 (13).

247 Clogher Diocesan Archives

Address: St Macartan's Cathedral, Clogher, Co. Tyrone BT76 0AD

Telephone: (028) 85548235

Enquiries: The Dean
The Secretary of the Friends of Clogher Cathedral, Mr Jack Johnston

Open: By appointment.

Access: Generally open to the public. There is no charge for reasonable requests.

Historical background: The Diocesan Archives room was set up in 1972 as a memorial to Rt Rev. S.J. Heaslett, the first Anglican bishop of Tokyo (who was later Primate of the Japanese Church). Bishop Heaslett was born in Tedarnet parish in Clogher diocese. A former diocesan library had existed in Clones.

Acquisitions policy: Archives relating to Clogher diocese (Church of Ireland).

Archives of organisation: Diocesan visitation books, 1661– (100 vols).
Chapter lease book, 18th–19th centuries.
Chapter minutes.
Rural deans' reports and cathedral preachers' books, c1800– .

Major collections: Clogher Corporation Book, 1783–1800.
Seal and letters patent of Bishop John Porter, 1798.

Non-manuscript material: Maps, including a set of the first OS series for the Clogher Valley and maps of all the parishes in the diocese (4 vols).

Publications: *Clogher Cathedral Graveyard* (1972) [list of tombstone inscriptions].

248 Order of the Company of Mary Our Lady

Address: Convent of Notre Dame, Burwood House, Cobham, Surrey KT11 1HA

Telephone: (01932) 868331

Fax: (01932) 867454

Enquiries: The Sr Archivist

Open: Mon–Fri: 9.00–12.00.
Closed during school holidays.

Access: Open to members of the Company of Mary. All others by appointment.

The Company of Mary is a Roman Catholic religious order of apostolic religious women founded in 1607 by Saint Jeanne de Lestonnac in Bordeaux with the approval of Pope Paul V. It was the first order dedicated to the education of youth, with Ignatian spirituality, and spread over Europe, North and South America, Asia and Africa. The union of all the houses and the establishment of central government took place in 1921 with the Generalate in Rome. The General Archivist, resident in Rome, oversees the collections and issues guidelines to ensure the safe-keeping of archival material in the designated repositories. The archives at Cobham form a small collection concerned mainly with the internal affairs of the convent. A catalogue and classification list for the collections worldwide, 1607–1921, can be found in Pilar Foz y Foz ODN, *Primary Sources for the History of the Education of Women in Europe and America: Historical Archives Company of Mary our Lady, 1607–1921* (Rome, 1985).

249 Data Archive

Parent organisation: Economic and Social Research Council

Address: University of Essex, Wivenhoe Park, Colchester, Essex CO4 3SQ

Telephone: (01206) 872001

Fax: (01206) 872003

E-mail: archive@essex.ac.uk

Website: www.data-archive.ac.uk

Enquiries: The Senior Administrator, Rowan Currie
The Assistant Director (Information), Bridget Winstanley

Open: Mon–Fri: 9.00–5.15.

Access: Data are available at cost to the academic (HEFC-funded) community. Administrative charges and royalties apply for non-academic use. Appointments are necessary.

Historical background: The Data Archive was founded in 1967. It is a national, multi-disciplinary research facility with a brief to acquire, store and disseminate computer-readable copies of social science and humanities datasets for further analyses by the research community. The archive also provides information on the location and availability of social science data and sponsors various activities, including workshops, user groups and regular newsletters, designed to improve the quality of data and their secondary analysis.

Acquisitions policy: To obtain computer-readable files from all areas of the social sciences from academic, governmental and commercial sources, to store them and to disseminate copies for further analyses.

Non-manuscript material: Historical and contemporary research data on a variety of magnetic media (c5000 datasets). Major holdings include Labour Force Surveys, General Household Surveys, Family Expenditure Surveys, ONS Macro-Economic Data, British Crime Surveys, British Household Panel Study, Election Studies, computerised historical records, including 19th-century censuses.

Finding aids: BIRON, the archive's on-line catalogue and index, is available from the Data Archives web site.

Publications: The Data Archive Bulletin [published three times a year].
A list of other publications is available on request.

250 Essex Record Office
Colchester and North-East Essex Branch

Parent organisation: Essex Record Office, Chelmsford

Address: Stanwell House, Stanwell Street, Colchester, Essex CO2 7DL

Telephone: (01206) 572099

Fax: (01206) 574541

Website: www.essexcc.gov.uk/heritage/fs_recof.htm

Enquiries: The Branch Archivist, Mr P.R.J. Coverley

Open: Mon: 10.00–5.15; Tues–Thurs: 9.15–5.15; Fri: 9.15–4.15.
Mon (2nd of the month): 10.00–8.45.

Access: Generally open to the public; an appointment is advisable. The office operates the CARN reader's ticket system. A paid research service is provided at the Essex Record Office in Chelmsford (see entry 228).

Historical background: This branch office of Essex Record Office was established in 1985. It is recognised as a place of deposit for manorial and tithe documents as well as public records.

Acquisitions policy: Collections of interest for the county of Essex. The main catchment area consists of the current Colchester and Tendring local authority areas.

Archives of organisation: Usual local authority record holdings.

Major collections: Deposited local collections.

Finding aids: Indexes (place, subject, name), catalogues. Lists sent to NRA.

Facilities: Photocopying. Photography, microfilming: in-house facility at ERO, Chelmsford.

Conservation: In-house facility at ERO, Chelmsford.

Publications: See ERO Chelmsford.

251 Society of Engineers

Address: Guinea Wiggs, Nayland, Colchester, Essex CO6 4NF

Telephone: (01206) 263332

Fax: (01206) 262624

E-mail: secretary@society-of-engineers.org.uk

Enquiries: Mrs L.C.A. Wright

Open: Mon–Fri: 9.00–5.30.

Access: By appointment only.

The Society of Engineers was established in 1854 and in 1910 incorporated the Civil and Mechanical Engineers Society (f. 1859). It is the third oldest engineering society in the UK, and uniquely represents the interests of civil, electrical, mechanical, chemical and aeronautical engineers. The library maintains the society's archives as well as collections of memorabilia and photographs relating to members.

252 University of Essex

Address: The Albert Sloman Library, Wivenhoe Park, Colchester, Essex CO4 3SQ

Telephone: (01206) 873333

Fax: (01206) 872289

E-mail: nigel@essex.ac.uk

Website: www.libwww.essex.ac.uk/speccol.htm

Enquiries: The Librarian

Open: Term: Mon–Fri: 9.00–10.00; Sat: 9.00–6.00; Sun: 2.00–7.00.
Vacation: Mon–Fri: 9.00– 5.30.

Access: On written application to the librarian.

Historical background: The University of Essex was founded in 1963. In 1996 the National Archive of Social Policy and Social Change was established as part of the library. The Data Archive (see entry 249) is separately administered by the university.

Acquisitions policy: Donation or deposit of records either relevant to the teaching and research at the university or of local interest.

Major collections: Archives of the Colchester and Coggeshall meetings of the Society of Friends, including correspondence of Steven Crisp.
Papers of the Rowhedge Iron Works.
Archives of the Social Democratic Party (SDP) and the Tawney Society, 1981–8.
Papers and reports of the Scientific Committee on Problems of the Environment (SCOPE), International Council of Scientific Unions, 1982–8.
Papers of the National Viewers' and Listeners' Association.
Paul Sieghart (1927–89): Human Rights Archive.
Sir Vincent Evans Collection: papers of the European Court of Human Rights.
Letters and papers of Henri and Sophie Gaudier-Brzeska.
Diaries, papers and work-ledger of John Hassall, poster artist and book illustrator.
Diaries of Samuel Levi Bensusan (1872–1958), author.
Papers of Professor Donald Davie (*b* 1922), author.
Papers of Lord Alport, MP, Deputy Speaker, House of Lords (1971–94).
Papers of K.F. Bowden *re* computerisation of medical records.

Sigmund Freud Collection: mainly photocopies and typescripts.

Charter88 Archives, including committee papers and publications concerning constitutional reform in the UK, 1988–96.

National Archive of Social Policy and Social Change [QUALIDATA] contemporary archive collections in the social sciences, including the papers of Peter Townsend (*b* 1928).

Finding aids: Handlists to many collections. Bowden: NRA 2778.

Facilities: Photocopying.

Conservation: Contracted out.

Publications: S.H.G. Fitch: *Colchester Quakers* (Colchester, 1962).

253 University of Ulster at Coleraine Library

Address: Coleraine, Co. Londonderry BT52 1SA

Telephone: (028) 70324345/70324346 (direct line)

Fax: (028) 70324928

E-mail: cp.ballantine@ulst.ac.uk

Website: www.ulst.ac.uk/library/craine/hewitt

Enquiries: The Sub-Librarian, Ms C.P. Ballantine

Open: Term: Mon–Fri: 9.00–10.00; Sat: 10.00–5.00.
Vacation: Mon–Fri: 9.00–5.00.
Special collections available only up to 5.00, or by arrangement.

Access: Anyone establishing a serious interest.

Historical background: The University of Ulster was established in 1984 by merging the former New University of Ulster with Ulster Polytechnic. There are four campuses, at Belfast, Coleraine, Jordanstown and Magee College, Londonderry.

Acquisitions policy: To strengthen relevant research areas.

Major collections: Papers of: George Shiels (1886–1949), playwright; Denis Johnston (1901–84), playwright and author; George Stelfox (1884–1972), naturalist; E. Norman Carrothers (1898–1977), botanist and railway engineer; Francis Stuart (1902–2000), novelist. Headlam–Morley correspondence.

Paul Ricard Collection of World War II material.

MSS of John Hewitt (1907–87), poet.

Non-manuscript material: Library of John Hewitt, including rural Ulster poets of the 19th century.

E.N. Carrothers bookplates.

Considerable runs of newspapers and other material in microtext form.

European Documentation Centre.

Co-operative Documentation Centre.

Facilities: Photocopying. Photography by arrangement.

254 Colne Library

Parent organisation: Lancashire County Council

Address: Market Street, Colne, Lancashire BB8 0AP

Telephone: (01282) 871155

Fax: (01282) 865227

Enquiries: The Assistant Librarian, Reference, Mrs Christine Bradley

Open: Mon: 9.30–7.00; Tues: 9.30–12.00; Wed, Thurs, Fri: 9.30–5.00; Sat: 9.30–4.00.

Access: Generally open to the public. Booking is advisable for the use of microfilm.

Historical background: The collection relates specifically to the present area of Pendle District, with emphasis on Colne, Trawden and Foulridge. Records relating to the area which was in the West Riding of Yorkshire before local government reorganisation in 1974 are now housed at Barnoldswick Library (see entry 49). See also Nelson Library (entry 913).

Acquisitions policy: Material collected relevant to Colne and surrounding area only.

Major collections: Parish registers, 1599– (on microfilm); overseers of poor accounts, 1767–87; surveyors' accounts and minute books, 1767–1876; rate books and tax returns, 1523– . Council minutes, 1893– ; census enumerators' returns, 1841–81.

Methodist Church minutes, 1815– ; Co-operative Society minute books, 1882–1964.

Friends of Wycoller Collection; Colne Literary and Scientific Society minute books, 1898–1957; records of Colne, Earby and Barnoldswick Amalgamated Association of Beamers and Twisters and Weavers, 1905–71.

Non-manuscript material: Maps, plans and posters covering the Colne area, 1610– (c1000).
Photographic material (7800 items).
Local newspapers, 1854– .
Oral history of Foulridge.
Slide lectures on Colne, Trawden and Wycoller.
Films of royal visits, 1913, 1938; Festival of Britain; Pageant of Colne.
Pendle and Burnley Family History Society Library (in local studies department) records of genealogical research covering Pendle, Burnley, Lancashire and parts of Yorkshire (200 vols and 2000 microfiche).

Finding aids: Lancashire Record Office: guide to material relating to Pendle District (photo-copies of relevant pages of full catalogue).
Lancashire County Library Local Studies in Lancashire: guide to resources.

Facilities: Photocopying. Microfilm reader/printer.

Conservation: Contracted out.

Publications: The Wills of Colne & District, 1545–1830.
Colne and its Times: an Index to the Local Newspaper, 1874–1974 (1974–).
Maps of Colne & District: a Catalogue.
Photographic Source Material for Pendle District: a Catalogue.
The Ernest Spivey Collection of Photographic Negatives.
The Local Wotwegot: a Catalogue of Colne Local History Collection.

255 BP Archive

Parent organisation: BP plc

Address: University of Warwick, Coventry, Warwickshire CV4 7AL

Telephone: (024) 76524521

Fax: (024) 76524523

E-mail: bparchive@bp.com

Website: www.bp.com

Enquiries: The Group Archivist, Michael Gasson

Open: Mon–Thurs: 9.00–5.00; Fri: 9.00–4.00.

Access: Bona fide researchers. An appointment is usually necessary. In general there is a 30-year closure period. Special permission is required from owners for access to records of Iraq Petroleum Company.

Historical background: Incorporated in 1909 as Anglo-Persian Oil Co. Ltd. to develop the oil resources of Iran, the company pioneered the oil industry in the Middle East. The British Government held a majority shareholding from 1914 to 1967, selling its shareholding in 1987. British Petroleum Co. Ltd. was acquired in 1917 as its UK marketing subsidiary, its activi-ties being superseded in 1932 by the joint mar-keting company, Shell-Mex and BP Ltd., which operated until 1975. The company is a share-holder in Iraq Petroleum Co. Ltd. (formed 1911) and an equal partner in Kuwait Oil Co. Ltd. (formed 1933). The company name was changed to Anglo-Iranian Oil Co. Ltd. in 1935; and to The British Petroleum Co. Ltd. in 1954 following the Iranian oil nationalisation crisis. It developed a significant exploration and mar-keting presence in the US from 1969 when oil was discovered in Alaska; acquiring an interest in The Standard Oil Co. in 1970, wholly acquired in 1987; merging with Amoco Corporation in 1998; and taking over Atlantic Richfield Co. (ARCO) in 2000. In 1998 the Company was renamed BP Amoco plc, and in 2001 BP plc. It acquired Burmah Castrol in 2000.

Acquisitions policy: Records created by the BP group in the course of business.

Archives of organisation: Archives of BP (including a small amount of records relating to its founder, W.K. D'Arcy, and to events leading to the incorporation of the company) covering all aspects of the group's activities worldwide from late 19th century– .

Also, the archive groups of some major jointly held subsidiaries including Kuwaiti Oil Co Ltd., Iraq Petroleum Co. Ltd., and Shell-Mex and BP Ltd.

Non-manuscript material: Maps, plans, large photographic collection.

Shell-Mex and BP Advertising Archive con-tains photographs, advertisements, posters, original artwork and booklets.

The Shell Art Collection of posters and post-cards is at the National Motor Museum (entry 66).

Finding aids: Electronic catalogue for the main BP Archive. Hard copy catalogues exist for other collections.

Facilities: Limited photocopying; colour photocopying and photography also by arrangement. Microfilm/fiche readers.

Conservation: Contracted out.

Publications: H. Longhurst: *Adventure in Oil: the Story of British Petroleum* (London, 1959). R.W. Ferrier: *The History of BP, Vol. 1: The Developing Years 1901–1932* (Cambridge, 1982). J.H. Bamberg: *The History of BP, Vol. 2: The Anglo-Iranian Years 1928–1956* (Cambridge, 1994). ——: *British Petroleum and Global Oil, 1950–1975: the Challenge of Nationalism* (Cambridge, 2000). B. Ritchie: *A Portrait in Oil: an Illustrated History of BP* (London, 1995).

256 Camping and Caravanning Club Archive

Parent organisation: The Camping and Caravanning Club Limited

Address: Greenfields House, Westwood Way, Coventry CV4 8JH

Telephone: (024) 76694995

Fax: (024) 76694886

Website: www.campingandcaravanningclub.co.uk

Enquiries: The Director General, Mr D. J. R. Welsford

Open: Mon–Fri: by appointment only.

Access: Club members and bona fide researchers, by prior appointment only.

Historical background: Founded as the Association of Cycle Campers in 1901, the organisation changed its name to The Camping Club of Great Britain and Ireland in 1919.

Acquisitions policy: To acquire any material relevant to the history of the club and the development of camping and caravanning.

Archives of organisation: Minutes of AGMs, annual reports, yearbooks, handbooks and sites lists, 1906– . Magazines, 1906– .

Major collections: Historical material relating to the founder of the original club, T. H. Holding.

Non-manuscript material: Films, photographs and sound records.

Collections of pennons, early tents and other equipment.

Finding aids: In-house indexed database in preparation.

Conservation: Some conservation work contracted out.

257 Coventry Central Library

Parent organisation: Coventry City Council

Address: Smithford Way, Coventry CV1 1FY

Telephone: (024) 76832336 (Library); 76832329 (Tom Mann Centre)

Fax: (024) 76832440

E-mail: covinfo@discover.co.uk

Enquiries: The Local Studies Librarian

Open: Mon, Tues, Thurs: 9.00–8.00; Fri: 9.00–5.00; Sat: 9.00–4.30.

Access: Generally open to the public. An appointment is preferred for manuscript material.

Historical background: The George Eliot Collection was founded in 1919 to mark the centenary of the author's birth, and the Angela Brazil Collection was presented by her sister in 1947. MS material of the Tom Mann Centre, previously held in the library, is now at the Modern Records Centre at the University of Warwick (entry 261) but trade union books, pamphlets and periodicals remain.

Acquisitions policy: To acquire further material relating to the collections already held.

Archives of organisation: Minute books and other records of the Coventry Library Society, the predecessor of Coventry City Libraries, and of the Coventry Book Club, the former subscription department of the Central Library.

Major collections: Letters and other MS records relating to George Eliot (1819–80), her friends and relatives, especially those with Coventry connections. Scrapbooks, photographs and other personal possessions of Angela Brazil (1868–1947), writer of children's stories.

Non-manuscript material: Usual local studies collection covering Coventry and Warwickshire, including newspapers, maps, photographs and recordings.

Facilities: Photocopying. Photography. Microfilm/fiche readers.

Conservation: Access to facilities at Coventry City Archives (see entry 258).

258 Coventry City Archives

Parent organisation: Coventry City Council

Address: Mandela House, Bayley Lane, Coventry CV1 5RG

Telephone: (024) 76832418

Fax: (024) 76832421

E-mail: coventryarchives@discover.co.uk

Enquiries: The City Archivist, Susan Worrall

Open: Mon: 9.30–8.00; Tues–Fri: 9.30–4.45. Appointments are needed after 4.45 on Mondays.

Access: Generally open to the public. Advance notice is welcomed for some classes of documents.

Historical background: The St Mary's Hall Muniment Room was constructed in 1892 and the city appointed its first archivist in 1938. The City Archives now forms part of the Cultural Services section of the Leisure Services Department of Coventry City Council. It is recognised as a place of deposit for public records.

Acquisitions policy: To encourage, by donation or deposit, records produced by organisations and individuals presently or formerly connected with Coventry.

Archives of organisation: Records of Coventry City Council, 12th century– , including minutes, financial records, property deeds, apprenticeship enrolments, 1781– , admissions of freemen, 1714– ; also the records of superseded local authorities such as the boards of guardians, school boards, and parish councils.

Major collections: Local public records, including quarter sessions, magistrates court, coroner's court and hospital records.
Medieval records of the city, 12th century– , including minutes of the Court Leet, 1421– , and records of Coventry's trading companies (gilds).
Records of the Blitz and the post-war reconstruction of the city.
Deposited and donated collections also include local and district trade union records; business records, notably Rootes (and constituent companies, e.g. Singer Motors), Armstrong Siddeley, Armstrong Whitworth, Daimler and Clarke Cluley; records of non-conformist churches, clubs, societies, schools and other local organisations.

Non-manuscript material: Collection of oral history tapes (with some transcripts) covering most aspects of Coventry's recent history, especially the motor car and allied trades.
Microfilms of Church of England and Roman Catholic registers for Coventry and environs and local cemetery records.
Detailed 1851 map of Coventry prepared for the local Board of Health.
Plans for the reconstruction of Coventry after the Second World War.

Finding aids: Catalogues of the borough archive, private accessions and city council records are gradually being computerised, and direct customer access, both onsite and remotely, is planned. Card indexes for Coventry freemen (women included from 1930s) and microfiche indexes of apprenticeship enrolments, 1781–1841. Catalogues sent to NRA.

Facilities: Photocopying. Photography. Microform readers/printer.

Conservation: In-house unit undertaking full range of paper and parchment conservation. Very limited amounts of outside work undertaken.

Publications: E. Castle: *People to Coventry* (1996).
——: *Coventry at School* (1997).
A. Munden: *Coventry Martyrs* (1997).
A. Gooder (ed. T. John): *Criminals, Courts and Conflict: a Study of Crime and Litigation in 14th century Coventry* (1999).

259 Coventry University
Lanchester Library

Address: Frederick Lanchester Building, Gosford Street, Coventry, West Midlands CV1 5DD

Telephone: (024) 76887516

Fax: (024) 76887525

E-mail: c.rock@coventry.ac.uk

Website: www.library.coventry.ac.uk

Enquiries: The University Librarian, Mr P. Noon

The Deputy Librarian, Caroline Rock

Open: Term: Mon–Thurs: 9.00–8.45; Fri: 9.00–5.15; Sat: 10.00–12.45.
Vacation: Mon–Fri: 9.00–5.15.

Access: Approved readers, on application to the University Librarian.

Historical background: The family of F.W. Lanchester, aeronautical and automotive engineer, presented books and papers to the college (later Coventry Polytechnic, now Coventry University) in 1960. Since then, the archive has been added to considerably by purchase of his sketchbooks and other materials. The Lanchester Library is named in his honour. The original papers were microfilmed with the aid of a British Library grant. The library was relocated in 2000.

Acquisitions policy: To receive, by gift or purchase, any relevant material offered.

Major collections: Papers, publications and sketchbooks of F.W. Lanchester.

Non-manuscript material: Archive of photographs of Lanchester cars.
Richardson Coventry history tapes project.

Finding aids: Catalogue of F.W. Lanchester papers (1966). Indexing in progress.

Facilities: Photocopying. Microfilm/fiche readers/printers.

Publications: E.G. Baxter: *Catalogue of the private papers of F.W. Lanchester....*
C.S. Clark and J. Fletcher: *The Lanchester Legacy — a Trilogy of Lanchester Works* (Coventry, 1995–6).

260 Herbert Art Gallery and Museum

Parent organisation: Coventry City Council Museums Service

Address: Jordan Well, Coventry, West Midlands CV1 5QP

Telephone: (024) 76832381

Fax: (024) 76832410

E-mail: coventry.museums@dial.pipex.com

Enquiries: The Collections Research and Development Manager, Margaret Rylatt

Open: Mon–Fri: 10.00–5.30.

Access: Generally open to the public; an appointment is necessary.

Historical background: The Herbert Art Gallery and Museum opened in 1960. Its collections cover the natural and social history of the area as well as visual arts. The Museum is a biological records centre.

Acquisitions policy: Archives have been created and kept for the purpose of running the museum service.

Archives of organisation: Museum archives, 1960– , including accession books, other collection information and catalogues. Files of local information.

Major collections: Archaeological archives from excavated sites in Coventry.
Dr W.T. Elliott letters *re* conchological and microbiological research (25 vols).
H.W. Daltry papers and miscellaneous documents *re* entomological collection.

Non-manuscript material: Photographs of Coventry places, people and events.
Oral history recordings.
Printed ephemera including posters, leaflets and booklets.

Finding aids: Card and computer indexes.
Complete handlist of visual arts permanent collection.

Facilities: Photocopying. Photography by arrangement.

Conservation: In-house paper conservation.

261 Modern Records Centre

Parent organisation: University of Warwick

Address: University of Warwick Library, Coventry, West Midlands CV4 7AL

Telephone: (024) 76524219

Fax: (024) 76572988

E-mail: archives@warwick.ac.uk

Website: www.warwick.ac.uk/services/library/mrc/mrc

Enquiries: The Archivist, Mrs Christine Woodland

Open: Mon–Tues: 9.00–5.00; Wed–Thurs: 9.00–7.00; Fri: 9.00–4.00.

Access: All serious researchers; a few days' notice of a visit is advisable. Some accessions are subject to restricted access.

Historical background: The centre was established in 1973 on the initiative of a group of academics at the University of Warwick and with the aid of a grant from the Leverhulme Trust Fund. Its objects are to ensure the preservation (where necessary by collecting) of original sources for British political, social and economic history, with particular reference to labour history, industrial relations and industrial politics, and to make such sources available for research.

The archives of BP International are now housed in the same building as the centre, but are administered separately (see entry 255).

Acquisitions policy: To build on existing strengths, especially in industrial relations and industrial politics.

Archives of organisation: Archives of the university, including records of the former Coventry College of Education, established as an emergency training college in 1946 and merged with the University of Warwick in 1978, are held in the centre, but are closed.

Major collections: Confederation of British Industry Predecessor Archive; also some other trade and employers' association records, including Engineering Employers' Federation.
Trades Union Congress records, pre-1988.
Trade union archives, including constituents of Manufacturing, Science, Finance Union, Rail, Maritime and Transport Workers Union, Transport and General Workers' Union, Union of Construction, Allied Trades and Technicians; also unions in the fields of education, the printing industry, public service (UNISON constituents) and the Post Office and telecommunications, as well as in a variety of other occupations.
Political records, including a significant concentration of records of British Trotskyism.
Pressure groups, including Campaign for Nuclear Disarmament, Howard League and NACRO; also comprehensive holdings of public documents of Amnesty International and Anti-Concorde Project.
Charities: Young Women's Christian Association records, mainly pre-1960, including minutes, serials and other publications, and ephemera, and some files.
Individuals' papers, including those of Lady Allen of Hurtwood (1897–1976); Sir Ernest Benn (1875–1954), publisher and individualist (personal papers); Frank Cousins (1904–86); R.H.S. Crossman (1907–74), full transcripts of published diaries; R.A. Etheridge, convenor at

Austin Motor Company, Longbridge; Sir Victor Gollancz (1893–1967), publisher and humanitarian (personal papers); Reg Groves, socialist activist and historian.
Some business records, mostly motor industry under an agreement with British Motor Industry Heritage Trust (see entry 377).
National Cycle Archive.
Rubery Owen Holdings archives.
Some publishing records of Victor Gollancz Ltd.

Non-manuscript material: Numerous accessions include printed reports, journals and pamphlets, individual items and small groups of ephemera over a wide range of political, social and economic activity.
The University Library has an extensive collection of journals, reports and pamphlets of trade unions and employers' and trade associations which may be consulted in the centre. This collection includes part of the former Board of Trade Library.
Historical Library of the Howard League (owned by the University Library).

Finding aids: Typescript catalogues or interim finding aids exist for many accessions; searchroom card indexes are based on these. Lists sent to NRA. The Summary Guide and selected catalogues are available on the website.

Facilities: Photocopying (limited). Microfilm/fiche reader. Listening facilities for tapes (limited). Provision for use of lap-top computer.

Publications: R.A. Storey and J. Druker: *Guide to the Modern Records Centre* (1977).
C. Woodland and R.A. Storey: *The Taff Vale Case: a Guide to the ASRS Records* (1978).
——— : *The Osborne Case Papers and other Records of the Amalgamated Society of Railway Servants* (1979).
R.A. Storey and S. Edwards: *Supplement to the Guide to the Modern Records Centre* (1981).
J. Bennett and R.A. Storey: *The First Labour Correspondent and the Board of Trade Library* (1983).
N. Baldwin and R.A. Storey: *The International Transport Workers' Federation Archive* (1985).
R.A. Storey and A. Tough: *Consolidated Guide to the Modern Records Centre* (1986).
J. Bennett and R.A. Storey: *Trade Union and Related Records* (6/1991).
C. Wightman and R.A. Storey: *Women at Work and in Society* (2/1991).
L. Smallbone and R.A. Storey: *Employers' & Trade Associations' History* (1992).

S. Duffield and R.A. Storey: *The Trades Union Congress Archive 1920–60* (1992).

R.A. Storey, A. Tough and C. Woodland: *Supplement to the Consolidated Guide* (1992).

J. Bennett et al: *Tom Mann: a bibliography* (1993).

R. Storey: *Automotive History Sources in Coventry Archives* (1996).

——: *The Personal Papers of Sir Victor Gollancz (1893–1967)* (1997).

L. McDonald et al: *Rubery Owen Holdings Ltd Archive* (1997).

A. Crookham et al *The Confederation of British Industry and Predecessor Archives* (1997).

——: *The Trades Union Congress Archive 1960–70* (1998).

Also Information Bulletin, Annual Report and Information Leaflet series, and lists reproduced in the *National Inventory of Documentary Sources*, (Chadwyck-Healey microfiche 1984).

262 University of Warwick
Centre for Research in Ethnic Relations

Address: Ramphal Building, University of Warwick, Coventry, West Midlands CV4 7AL

Telephone: (024) 76523607 (enquiries); (024) 76523605 (Librarian)

Fax: (024) 76524324

Website: www.warwick.ac.uk/fac/soc/crer_rc

Enquiries: The Director, Prof. D. Joly

Open: Mon–Fri: 9.00–4.00.

Access: Bona fide researchers, by prior appointment.

The CRER was set up with a grant from ESRC in 1984 to continue the work of the Research Unit on Ethnic Relations at the University of Aston. It has a unique collection of non-book materials, primarily British, covering a wide range of issues in ethnic relations, including periodicals, newspapers, press cuttings and videos. A database of the centre's resources is accessible on the website.

263 Cranbrook Museum

Parent organisation: Cranbrook and District Local History Society

Address: Carriers Road, Cranbrook, Kent TN17 3JX

Telephone: (01580) 712069

Enquiries: The Archivist, Ms B. Carman

Open: Tues, Thurs–Sat: 2.00–4.30; Wed: 10.00–4.00

Access: Generally open to the public.

The Museum opened in 1973 and the Archive Room has been developed since 1975. It acquires local history material, including deeds, maps and other documents, plus oral history tape recordings, on Kent and Cranbrook and its families. A database on the families and an automated subject index are being developed.

264 Innerpeffray Library

Address: Crieff, Tayside PH7 3RS

Telephone: (01764) 652819

E-mail: library@innerpeffray.ss.net.co.uk

Enquiries: Mr E.W. Powell

Open: Mon Wed, Fri, Sat: 10.00–1.00; 2.00–4.00 Sun: 2.00–4.00

Access: Generally open to the public. It is advisable to ring in winter, when opening times may change.

The library dates from 1680 and is probably the oldest public library in Scotland. Its own archives include MS borrowing ledgers, 1747–1968, and visitors books, early 19th century– . There are a few family MSS, e.g. commonplace books, held among the library collections. See NRAS 824; NRA 17568.

265 Cromarty Courthouse

Address: Church Street, Cromarty, Highland IV11 8KA

Telephone: (01381) 600418

E-mail: courthouse@mail.calis.co.uk

Enquiries: The Curator, David Alston

Open: April–Oct: Mon–Sun: 10.00–5.00; Oct–March: Mon–Sun: 12.00–4.00, by appointment.

Access: Generally open to the public; an appointment is necessary.

The courthouse holds miscellaneous papers relating to the burgh of Cromarty and court case papers, mostly 19th century, (*c*1500). The latter are held with permission of the National Archive of Scotland (see entry 329) pending completion of cataloguing. There is also a small archive of oral history recordings and some photographs of the area, early 20th century.

266 Wellington College

Address: Crowthorne, Berkshire RG45 7PU

Telephone: (01344) 772262

Fax: (01344) 771725

E-mail: mps@wellington-college.berks.sch.uk

Enquiries: The Archivist, Mr N.B. Ritchie
The Bursar

Open: Most Weds–Thurs: 9.00–12.30, 1.30–5.30.

Access: Generally at the Archivist's discretion and by appointment, giving a week's notice. Some material is restricted. Unsuitable for school or group search. Research provided for a nominal fee to cover costs.

Historical background: The college, which opened in 1859, is a 'royal and religious foundation'. Foundationers of either sex are children of serving officers killed on active service, but the school is very largely a fee-paying, independent boarding school.

Acquisitions policy: To maintain the college archive and acquire letters, diaries and artefacts.

Archives of organisation: Administrative, domestic, academic and estate records (incomplete).

Major collections: Deposits from old boys and governors, including letters of the Duke of Wellington; E.F. Benson (1867–1940) letters and notebooks, *c*1859–73.
Correspondence relating to the education of the Princes Adolphus and Francis of Teck, 1883–1910.

Non-manuscript material: Plans and drawings showing the architectural development of the college.

Finding aids: Card index. NRA 21772.

Facilities: Photocopying. Photography.

Conservation: Contracted out.

Publications: D.H. Newsome: *A History of Wellington College* (1959).

Registers of Wellington College 1859–1996 (11/1997).

267 Croydon Archives Service

Parent organisation: London Borough of Croydon

Address: Central Library, Croydon Clocktower, Katharine Street, Croydon CR9 1ET

Telephone: (020) 8760 5400 ext. 1112

Fax: (020) 8253 1012

E-mail: localstudies@croydononline.org

Website: www.croydon.gov.uk

Enquiries: The Archivist, Steve Griffiths

Open: Mon: 9.00–7.00; Tues, Wed, Fri: 9.00–6.00, Thurs: 9.30–6.00; Sat: 9.00–5.00; Sun: 2.00–5.00

Access: Generally open to the public. Notification of visits is advised.

Historical background: The present London Borough of Croydon was created in 1965 from the former County Borough of Croydon (originally incorporated as a municipal borough in 1883) and the Urban District of Coulsdon and Purley. Croydon Public Library opened in 1890 and began a local collection, including manuscript material, soon afterwards. A distinct local history library was formed in 1973. An archivist was appointed in 1990 and the Archives Service was formally constituted in 1993. The library is recognised as a place of deposit for public records.

Acquisitions policy: To acquire non-current records of Croydon Council and its predecessor authorities, and other archival material relating to the area of the present borough and its inhabitants.

Archives of organisation: Records of Croydon Vestry, 1741–1899; Croydon Local Board of Health, 1849–83; Borough and County Borough of Croydon, 1883–1965; London Borough of Croydon, 1965– ; Croydon Rural District, 1896–1915; Coulsdon and Purley UDC, 1915–65; Croydon Board of Guardians, 1842–1930; Croydon Quarter Sessions, 1889–1965.

Major collections: Records of Croydon Literary and Scientific Institution, *c*1839–1930.

Estate records of Delmé-Radcliffe family re Addiscombe etc, 1329–1799; Eldon familyreShirley, 1698–1867.

Archives of Gillett and Johnston, bellfounders, 1877–1985; Mission of Hope maternity home/adoption agency/children's home, c1900–c1970; South Suburban Co-operative Society, 1887–1961; Women's International League (Croydon and District Branch), 1918–76. Items re the East India Company's Military Seminary/Addiscombe College, c1740–c1909.

Personal and family papers of F.G. Creed (1871–1957), inventor, c1890–c1980; antiquarian papers of C.W. Johnson (1799–1878), C.G. Paget (d 1952) and W.H. Mills (1870–1951).

Non-manuscript material: The Archives Service is housed with the Local Studies Library, which holds a large collection of books, pamphlets, periodicals, sale particulars, published maps, photographs, audio-visual material etc.

Finding aids: Various lists and indexes. Lists sent to NRA.

Facilities: Photocopying. Microfilm/fiche reader/printers.

Conservation: Contracted out.

268 Whitgift Foundation Archives

Parent organisation: The Whitgift Foundation

Address: Whitgift School, Haling Park, Croydon, Surrey CR2 6YT

Telephone: (020) 8688 9222, ext. 2143

Fax: (020) 8760 0682

E-mail: archives@whitgift.co.uk

Website: www.whitgift.co.uk

Enquiries: The Archivist, Mr F.H.G. Percy

Open: Term: Mon, Wed, Thurs: 10.00–4.30 by appointment only; other times by arrangement.

Access: Approved readers, on application by letter or telephone; an appointment is always advisable. Certain information about former pupils and living persons is restricted at the discretion of the Archivist.

Historical background: The Whitgift Foundation of a hospital for aged poor and a grammar school in Croydon was established by John Whitgift, Archbishop of Canterbury, in 1596.

Acquisitions policy: To continue to receive material relevant to the history and development of the foundation, the school and the Old Whitgiftian Association, as well as biographical details relating to old boys, staff and governors.

Archives of organisation: Ancient muniments, foundation deeds and account books, 15th century– ; leases of property, 17th century– . Administrative records of the hospital and school, including minutes of the Court of Governors, 1871– (incomplete records prior to this); school rolls, 1871– ; school magazines, 1879– ; research papers relating to the history of Whitgift School.

Records of former pupils.

Non-manuscript material: Maps, plans, architectural drawings, photographs and engravings of buildings and antiquities.Press-cuttings.

Some microfilm of records held elsewhere.

Finding aids: Lists and catalogues. Card indexes in progress.

Facilities: Photocopying. Photography by arrangement. Microfilm reader.

Conservation: Contracted out.

Publications: History of Whitgift Grammar School (Croydon, 1892).

Abstracts of the Ancient Muniments of the Whitgift Foundation (Croydon, 1934).

F.H.G. Percy: *History of Whitgift School* (Batsford, 1976).

—— : *Whitgift School: a History* (Whitgift Foundation, 1991).

269 North Lanarkshire Archives

Parent organisation: North Lanarkshire Council

Address: 10 Kelvin Road, Lenziemill, Cumbernauld, Lanarkshire G67 2BD

Telephone: (01236) 737114

Fax: (01236) 781762

Enquiries: The Archivist, John Mackenzie

Open: Mon–Fri: 9.00–5.00.

Access: Generally open to the public, preferably by prior arrangement.

Historical background: North Lanarkshire Archives was formed in 1996 by an amalgamation of the holdings of Motherwell, Monklands and Cumbernauld district councils.

Acquisitions policy: Archives within the North Lanarkshire boundaries or relating to North Lanarkshire.

Archives of organisation: Records of the burghs of Airdrie, Kilsyth, Wishaw, Motherwell, Coatbridge and Cumbernauld; also of Cumbernauld New Town.

Major collections: Estate papers of Drumpellier, 1560–1961, and Dalzell, 1413–1940.

Non-manuscript material: Significant collections of maps and plans; photographs and postcards.

Finding aids: Handlists for most collections.

Facilities: Photocopying. Plan-copier.

Conservation: Contracted out.

270 Ayrshire Archives: East Ayrshire Council

Baird Institute Local History Centre

Parent organisation: East Ayrshire Council, Library and Information Services

Address: Baird Institute, 3 Lugar Street, Cumnock, Ayrshire KA18 1AD

Telephone: (01290) 421701

Fax: (01290) 421701

Enquiries: The Heritage Services Librarian, Mrs Anne Geddes
The Archivist, Ayrshire Archives, Mr Kevin Wilbraham (see entry 39).

Open: Mon, Tues, Thurs, Fri: 10.00–1.00, 1.30–4.30.

Access: Generally open to the public.

Historical background: Ayrshire Archives is a joint service sponsored by the three local authorities in Ayrshire — East, North and South Ayrshire councils. The service is peripatetic and responsible for all archival and records management issues relating to the three authorities. While the main office is located at the Ayrshire Archives Centre in South Ayrshire (see entry 39), access to records in East Ayrshire is through the Libraries and Information Service at the Baird Institute Local History Centre.

Acquisitions policy: To build up the archival collection for the district.

Archives of organisation: Records of East Ayrshire Council and predecessor bodies, including Kilmarnock and Loudon District Council, 1975–96; Cumnock and Doon Valley District Council, 1975–96; and the Burgh of Kilmarnock, 1686–1975.

Major collections: Usual deposited local collections.

Non-manuscript material: Pamphlets, photographs, glass negatives.
Microfilms of parish records and census returns.

Finding aids: Catalogues and lists. Lists sent to NRAS.

Facilities: Photocopying. Microfilm/fiche readers.

Publications: Various information leaflets and details of microfilm holdings.

271 Fife Council Museums East

Address: County Buildings, St. Catherine Street, Cupar, Fife KY15 4TA

Telephone: (01334) 412933/4

Fax: (01334) 413214

Enquiries: The Assistant Museum Curator, Ms Marion Wood

Open: Mon–Fri: 9.00–5.00.

Access: Bona fide researchers, by appointment.

Historical background: The District Museum Service was founded in 1983.

Acquisitions policy: Archaeology and social history of north-east Fife.

Archives of organisation: Records relating to museum collections and collectors.

Major collections: Records of Tayside Floorcloth Co., Newburgh, and Newburgh Friendly Society.
Personal papers of Alexander Laing (1808–92), local antiquarian and collector; Rev. John Anderson (1796–1864), geologist; and Martin Anderson ['Cynicus'] (1854–1932), artist.

Non-manuscript material: Local maps, photographs, postcards.

Finding aids: Card indexes.

Facilities: Photocopying. Photography.

272 Gwent County Record Office

Address: County Hall, Cwmbran NP44 2XH

Telephone: (01633) 644886

Fax: (01633) 648382

E-mail: gwentrecords@torfean.gov.uk

Website: www.llge.org.uk/cac/cac00004.html

Enquiries: The County Archivist, Mr David Rimmer

Open: Tues–Thurs: 9.30–5.00; Fri: 9.30–4.00.

Access: Generally open to the public, preferably by appointment. A paid research service is available.

Historical background: Monmouthshire Record Office was founded in 1938 and Gwent Record Office was established following local government reorganisation in 1974. It also acts as the Diocesan Record Office for Monmouth, Swansea and Brecon (parish records), and is recognised as a place of deposit for public records.

Acquisitions policy: Accepts collections of archives, by gift or deposit, relating to the county of Gwent and the historic county of Monmouthshire.

Archives of organisation: Usual local authority record holdings, including quarter sessions of the County of Monmouth, 18th–20th centuries; Monmouthshire County Council, 1889–1974; Gwent County Council, 1974– .

Major collections: Cwmbran Development Corporation records, 20th century.
1st Baron Raglan and descendants papers, including those relating to the Napoleonic and Crimean War, 18th–19th centuries.
Lewis of St Pierre: estate papers and deeds, 14th– 20th centuries.
Lord Llangattock of the Hendre (Rolls) family and estate papers and deeds, 15th–20th centuries.
Marquis of Abergavenny estate papers and deeds, 16th–20th centuries.
Hanbury of Pontypool Park business records and deeds, 16th–20th centuries.

Non-manuscript material: OS maps of Monmouthshire, 1878–1920.

Finding aids: Catalogue and indexes. Lists sent to NRA.

Facilities: Photocopying. Microfilm/fiche reader.

Conservation: Full conservation facilities.

Publications: W.H. Baker: *Guide to the Monmouthshire Record Office* (1959).

273 Barking and Dagenham Archives

Parent organisation: London Borough of Barking and Dagenham

Address: Valence House Museum, Becontree Avenue, Dagenham RM8 3HT

Telephone: (020) 8227 5293

Fax: (020) 8227 5296

E-mail: valencehousemuseum@hotmail.com
scurtis@bardaglea.org.uk

Website: www.barking-dagenham.gov.uk/4-heritage/heritage/menu.html

Enquiries: The Heritage Services Manager, Ms Susan Curtis

Open: Tues–Fri: 9.30–1.00, 2.00–4.30;
Sat: 10.00–4.00.

Access: Bona fide researchers, by appointment only.

Historical background: Dagenham Public Libraries acquired certain parish and urban district records and in 1963 were given the family papers of the late Captain A.B. Fanshawe, RN. In 1974 a curator/archivist, who administers the borough archives from the local history museum, was appointed.

Acquisitions policy: Non-current records of the London Borough of Barking and Dagenham and its predecessors, and of local firms and organizations etc, by donation or deposit.

Major collections: Local government records: Barking, 1666– ; Dagenham, 1838– .
Local property title deeds, 15th–19th centuries.
Business archives of Lawes Chemical Co. Ltd, 1872–1969.
Fanshawe family MSS, including genealogical papers and pedigree, and correspondence and papers of Sir Richard Fanshawe (1600–66), mainly as ambassador to Portugal, 1662–3, and Spain, 1664–6.

Non-manuscript material: Photographs, drawings, paintings and prints. Maps and plans.

Finding aids: Local history collection: NRA 1293.

Facilities: Photocopying. Microfilm reader/printer.

Conservation: Contracted out.

Publications: Guide to Local History Resources.

274 Bergman Österberg Archives

Parent organisation: University of Greenwich

Address: The Library, Dartford Campus, Oakfield Lane, Dartford, Kent DA1 2SZ

Telephone: (020) 8331 9271

Fax: (020) 8331 9275

E-mail: r.m.moon@gre.ac.uk

Enquiries: The Campus Librarian, Ms Rosemary Moon

Open: Term: Mon–Thurs: 9.00–9.00; Fri: 9.00–7.00; Sat: 10.00–5.00.

Access: Generally open to the public, by appointment.

Historical background: The Bergman Österberg Physical Training College was founded in 1885 by Madame Bergman Österberg, who pioneered physical education as a new profession for women. Training continued on the Dartford Heath site until 1986, and, although courses had become more general and male students were eventually accepted for certain of them, physical education was still the major specialism when training ceased. Latterly the courses were run by the Dartford Faculty of Education and Movement Studies of Greenwich University.

Acquisitions policy: Donations from old students and their relatives of all types of memorabilia, including uniforms, games equipment and badges.

Archives of organisation: Documents and photographs covering the history of the college, 1885– .

Major collections: Madame Bergman Österberg biographical material.

Non-manuscript material: One of the early gymslips, a garment invented at Madame Bergman Österberg's Physical Training College in about 1893; physical education equipment.

Finding aids: Lists and a card index.

Facilities: Photocopying.

275 Dartford Central Library

Parent organisation: Kent County Council Arts and Libraries Department

Address: Central Park, Dartford, Kent DA1 1EU

Telephone: (01322) 221133

Fax: (01322) 278271

Enquiries: The Team Librarian, Reference, Information and Local Studies, Mr C. Bull

Open: Mon: 9.30–5.30; Tues, Fri: 9.15–5.30; Sat: 9.00–5.00

Access: Generally open to the public.

Historical background: Since it was established in 1916, the library has collected material on the local area.

Acquisitions policy: Local history material is acquired, but archival material is at the Centre for Kentish Studies (see entry 868).

Archives of organisation: Library reports, minutes, cuttings, photographs, statistics and ledgers, 1916– .

Non-manuscript material: Usual local history collection, including glass negatives of Ernest Youens, and drawings of Clement Youens, late 19th-early 20th centuries.
Large collections of maps and photographs.

Finding aids: Card catalogue and database.

Facilities: Photocopying. Photography. Microfilm/fiche readers.

Publications: Guide to the Local Studies Collection [pamphlet].

276 Corus Group Records Centre (formerly British Steel)

Address: Shotton Works, Deeside, Flintshire RH5 2NH

Telephone: (01244) 892135/6

Fax: (01244) 892137

E-mail: record.centre@corusgroup.com

Enquiries: The Records Centre Manager, Mr Rolf M. Holthöfer

Open: Mon–Fri: 8.00–3.45.

Access: Bona fide researchers, at the discretion of the Records Centre Manager.

Historical background: The Records Centre was set up in 1978 to look after the archival records of the constituent companies of British Steel on its formation in 1967 and to provide a records management service to all its inter-departmental customers. Certain non-statutory records have been transferred to local authority record offices. Most of the records were transferred from three regional record centres to Deeside in 1999.

Acquisitions policy: Restricted to records relating to British Steel plc, its constituent companies and related bodies.

Archives of organisation: Records of the pre-nationalised steel companies: Colvilles Ltd, Dorman Long & Co., Richard Thomas & Baldwin Ltd, Stewarts & Lloyds, United Steel Companies Ltd.

Non-manuscript material: Film archive.
Small collections of publications relating to the history of the iron and steel industry.

Finding aids: Records transmittal lists. Computer indexes.

Facilities: Photocopying. Microfiche readers.

277 Derby Cathedral

Address: The Cathedral Office, St Michael's House, Queen Street, Derby DE1 3DT

Telephone: (01332) 341201

Fax: (01332) 203991

Website: www.derbycathedral.org

Enquiries: The Archivist, Miss K.M. Bunting

Open: By arrangement only.

Access: Bona fide researchers, strictly by appointment.

The cathedral was the parish church of All Saints until 1927. The nearby bridge chapel, one of very few remaining in this country, is now under the same administration. It holds a small collection of miscellaneous records, mainly late 19th–early 20th centuries. Parish registers are now in Derbyshire Record Office (see entry 896).

278 Derby Local Studies Library

Parent organisation: Derby City Council, Derby City Libraries

Address: 25B Irongate, Derby DE1 3GL

Telephone: (01332) 255393

Enquiries: The Local Studies Librarian, Mrs L.G. Owen

Open: Mon, Tues: 10.00–7.00; Wed–Fri: 10.00–5.00; Sat: 10.00–1.00.

Access: Generally open to the public. Readers should make prior arrangements to book use of microfilm/fiche readers. A paid research service is available.

Historical background: The collection is based on two family libraries, the Devonshire and Bemrose libraries, acquired in 1878 and 1914 respectively. The Devonshire Collection consisted of books, pamphlets, prints, election addresses and MSS; the Bemrose Library included some MS items and early editions of the works of Derbyshire authors. There were subsequently a number of deposits, some quite large, before the establishment of the local record office.

Acquisitions policy: To strengthen and enlarge existing primary and secondary collections on the history of Derby and Derbyshire and environmental studies within the county.

Major collections: Derby Corporation deeds, 17th–19th centuries (10,000).
Borough court records.
Derby Union Board of Guardians records, 1837–1915.
Various collections of family papers, notably of the Pares family.
Duesbury Collection of records of Derby China Factory, 1780–1800.
Wyatt Collection relating to lead-mining, 1810–50.
Derby Canal Company records, 1793–1974.

Non-manuscript material: Large collections of illustrative material, including photographs (c8000), broadsides, tapes and maps.
Newspapers: *Derby Mercury,* 1732–1933; *Derby and Chesterfield Reporter,* 1828–1930; *Derbyshire Advertiser,* 1876–1976; *Derby Evening Telegraph,* 1879– .
Census returns, 1841–91, for Derbyshire and some small portion of surrounding counties.

Finding aids: Various lists and indexes.

Facilities: Photocopying. Microfilm/fiche readers/printer.

Publications: Local Studies Collections Guide (1997).

279 Wiltshire Heritage Museum and Library

Parent organisation: Devizes Museum

Address: 41 Long Street, Devizes, Wiltshire SN10 1NS

Telephone: (01380) 727369

Fax: (01380) 722150

E-mail: wanhs@wiltheritage.org.uk

Enquiries: The Librarian, Mrs Lorna Haycock

Open: Tues–Sat: 10.00–5.00, by appointment.

Access: Generally open to the public and members. A paid research service is provided.

Historical background: The Archaeological and Natural History Society was formed in 1853 to collect information on the history of Wiltshire, and the library contains large and expanding collections relating to all aspects of Wiltshire life, especially archaeology, local history and genealogy of the county.

Acquisitions policy: Collections illustrating the archaeology, natural history and local history of Wiltshire and Wessex.

Archives of organisation: Annual reports/minutes etc, 1853– .

Major collections: Notes, working papers and correspondence of many local historians, including Correspondence of Sir Richard Colt Hoare with William Cunnington and other contemporary antiquaries, William Stukeley's Commonplace Book, Edward Kite's collection of pedigrees, and T.H. Baker's collection of transcripts of monumental inscriptions (23 vols).

Non-manuscript material: John Buckler watercolours of churches and major houses, 1805–10 (10 vols).
Plans, drawings, photographs and maps (c10,000).
An extensive pamphlet collection, 1853– .
Press-cutting collection, 1853– .

Finding aids: Catalogues, lists and indexes. Lists sent to NRA.

Facilities: Photocopying. Photography. Microfilm/fiche readers.

Conservation: Contracted out.

Publications: Wiltshire Archaeological and Natural History Magazine, 1854– [annually].

280 Gwynedd Archives and Museums Service
Archifdy Meirion Record Office

Parent organisation: Cyngor Gwynedd Council

Address: Cae Penarlag, Dolgellau, LL40 2YB

Telephone: (01341) 424444

Fax: (01341) 424505

E-mail: archives.dolgellau@gwynedd.gov.uk

Website: www.gwynedd.gov.uk/archives/archivesframeset.htm

Enquiries: The Area Archivist and Museums Officer, Mr E.W. Thomas

Open: Mon, Wed–Fri: 9.00–1.00, 2.00–5.00. Closed for first full week in November.

Access: Generally open to the public. An appointment is desirable for the use of microfilm/fiche readers.

Historical background: The office was set up in 1952 as the record office for the county of Meirioneth. It is recognised as a place of deposit for public records.

Acquisitions policy: Documentary evidence relating to the old County of Meirioneth.

Archives of organisation: Usual local authority record holdings.

Major collections: Deposited local collections.

Non-manuscript material: Slate quarry plans.

Finding aids: Catalogues, indexes. Catalogues sent to NRA.

Facilities: Photocopying. Photography. Microfilm/fiche readers.

Conservation: In-house.

Publications: K. Williams Jones: *Calendars of the Meirioneth Quarter Session Rolls* (1965).

281 Dollar Museum

Parent organisation: Dollar Museum Trust

Address: Castle Campbell Hall, High Street, Dollar, Clackmanannshire FK14 7AY

Telephone: (01259) 742895

Fax: (01259) 742895

Enquiries: The Hon. Curator, Mrs Janet Carolan.

Open: Easter to Christmas, by arrangement with the Curator.

Access: An appointment is recommended.

Historical background: The museum was founded in 1987 and inherited material from the defunct Dollar Town Council.

Acquisitions policy: Material relevant to Dollar and the immediate vicinity is collected.

Major collections: Minute books of societies and clubs, 19th century.
Miscellaneous papers relating to the locality.

Non-manuscript material: Large photographic collection, including Devon Valley Railway.
Dollar Magazine, 1902– .
Early guide books; published reminiscences, 19th century; local cemetery inscriptions; scrapbooks.

Finding aids: Catalogue.

282 Doncaster Archives

Parent organisation: Doncaster Metropolitan Borough Council

Address: King Edward Road, Balby, Doncaster, South Yorkshire DN4 0NA

Telephone: (01302) 859811

E-mail: doncasterarchives@hotmail.com

Website: www.doncaster.gov.uk/education/document.asp?wsdocid=413

Enquiries: The Principal Archivist, Dr B.J. Barber

Open: Mon–Fri: 9.00–12.45, 2.00–4.45.

Access: Open to the public, with the customary 30-year restriction on access and, in addition, any restrictions imposed in respect of public records. An appointment is advisable for use of the microfilm/fiche readers. A paid research service is available.

Historical background: The borough of Doncaster had a series of honorary archivists (including P.G. Bales, later first county archivist of Cambridgeshire) before the appointment of a professional archivist in 1973. In the following year the department took responsibility for the new metropolitan district. In 1979 it became the Diocesan Record Office for the Archdeaconry of Doncaster (Diocese of Sheffield); it is also a recognised place of deposit for public records. The office has received archival holdings transferred from Doncaster Central Library.

Acquisitions policy: To locate, collect and preserve records of all kinds relating to the Doncaster Metropolitan District and make them available to the public in accordance with a policy notified to the Historical Manuscripts Commission.

Archives of organisation: Records of superseded rural and urban district councils; and the borough of Doncaster, 1194– ; quarter sessions and manorial records.

Major collections: Family and estate archives include Cooke-Yarborough of Campsmount (microfilm); Copley of Sprotbrough; Davies Cooke of Owston, 15th century– ; and Warde-Aldam of Frickley, notably papers of William Aldam, MP, 1840–90.
Records of the manor of Conisbrough, 1265–1935.
Records of 85 parishes in the Archdeaconry of Doncaster.
Records of Bridon plc (formerly British Ropes), 1751–1974.
Records of Great Northern Railway Locomotive Friendly Society, 1867–1981.

Non-manuscript material: Building control plans for the superseded county borough and rural and urban district councils, 1860–1974.

Finding aids: Lists of holdings of this department and other South Yorkshire archive departments. Lists sent to the NRA. Place and subject card indexes. Names card index to a large proportion of the parish records and some other classes of records.

Facilities: Photocopying. Microfilm/fiche readers.

Conservation: Undertaken by the Conservation Department of Sheffield Archives (see entry 1107) under the South Yorkshire Joint Agreement on Archives.

Publications: Doncaster Archives: a Guide to Sources for Local and Family History (1999).

283 Dorchester Reference Library
Local Studies Collection

Address: Colliton Park, Dorchester, Dorset DT1 1XJ

Telephone: (01305) 224442/224448/224501

Fax: (01305) 266120

Enquiries: The Reference Librarian, Mr N.G. Lawrence

Open: Mon: 10.00–7.00; Tues, Wed, Fri: 9.30–7.00; Thurs: 9.30–5.00; Sat: 9.00–4.00.

Access: Generally open to the public.

Historical background: Much material was acquired in the 1960s on the building of the new library. The Thomas Hardy Society Library is housed here. The T.E. Lawrence material is now at Wareham Library, tel. (01929) 556146.

Acquisitions policy: Any material relating to Dorset and the existing collections, in particular to Thomas Hardy (1840–1928).

Major collections: Lock Collection (deposited by Henry Lock of the solicitors who dealt with the Hardy family): includes correspondence of the Hardy and Hand families; letters from literary figures, 1868–1940; press cuttings; photographs; play programmes.
Ralph Wightman Collection: scripts with MS annotations of BBC Radio programme 'Country Magazine', 1942–53.

Non-manuscript material: Maps; illustrations; audio and video cassettes; records; films.
PhD theses relating to the collection (microtext).
Microfilms of census returns and of local newspapers, 1737– .
Printed material and cuttings relating to Rev. William Barnes
Typescripts, taken mainly from MSS, connected with the Powys family, primarily T.F. Powys (1875–1953), but also John Cowper Powys (1872–1963).

Facilities: Photocopying. Microfilm/fiche reader/printer.

Conservation: Contracted out.

Publications: C.P.C. Pettit: *A Catalogue of the Works of Thomas Hardy in Dorchester Reference Library* (1984).
J.C. Ward: *A Catalogue of Works by and about William Barnes (1801–1886) in Dorchester Reference Library* (1986).
L.A. Mudway: *A Catalogue of Work by and about T.E. Lawrence ('Lawrence of Arabia') (1888–1935) in Wareham Library* (1998).

284 Dorset County Museum

Parent organisation: Dorset Natural History and Archaeological Society

Address: High West Street, Dorchester, Dorset DT1 1XA

Telephone: (01305) 262735

Fax: (01305) 257180

E-mail: dorsetcountymuseum@dormus.demon.co.uk

Website: www.dorset.museum.clara.net

Enquiries: Mr Richard de Peyer

Open: Mon–Sat: 10.00–5.00; Sun (July and Aug): 10.00–5.00.

Access: Generally open to the public, by appointment. There is a daily admission fee for research.

Historical background: The Dorset County Museum was founded in 1846 as a private institution, which it still is. The Dorset Natural History and Antiquarian Field Club was founded in 1875. The two bodies joined in 1928 as the Dorset Natural History and Archaeological Society.

Acquisitions policy: The archive collections centre on the geology, archaeology, natural history, local history, literature and fine arts of the county of Dorset.

Archives of organisation: Archives of the museum and predecessor bodies, 1846– .

Major collections: Thomas Hardy (1840–1928) Memorial Collection: MSS, notebooks, diaries, letters, books from Hardy's library, watercolours, photographs and personalia.
Rev. William Barnes (1801–86), poet and grammarian: a large collection of MSS, diaries, letters, scrapbooks, notebooks and personalia.
Sylvia Townsend Warner (1893–1978) and Valentine Ackland: a large collection of MSS,

diaries, notebooks, letters, personal items and books.
Natural History MS collections of notebooks, diaries, etc.
Archaeological archives relating to all principal Dorset excavations.
John Cowper, Llewellyn and Theodore Powys letters, short story, novel, and poetry MSS.

Non-manuscript material: Printed material relating to each of the authors noted above.
Photographic archive (140,000 images).
Archive of ephemera relating to Dorset places, people and subjects.

Finding aids: Card indexes.

Facilities: Photocopying. Photography.

Conservation: Contracted out to Dorset Record Office (see entry 285) or Area Museums Council.

Publications: Proceedings of the society [annual].
Archaeological Society [monograph series].
County Record Society series.

285 Dorset Record Office

Parent organisation: Dorset County Council, Bournemouth Borough Council and Borough of Poole

Address: 9 Bridport Road, Dorchester, Dorset DT1 1RP

Telephone: (01305) 250550

Fax: (01305) 224839 (County Council Offices)

E-mail: archives@dorset-cc.gov.uk

Website: www.dorset-cc.gov.uk/archives

Enquiries: The County Archivist, Mr H. Jaques

Open: Mon–Fri: 9.00–5.00; Sat: 9.30–12.30.

Access: Generally open to the public; an appointment is advised to be assured of a place, particularly in the microfilm search room. Usual closure periods on archives; persons using documents for legal purposes must have the owner's permission.

Historical background: Dorset Record Office was founded in 1955 and in 1957 it received the collections of the Dorset Natural History and Archaeological Society from the Dorset County Museum. The office serves as the Diocesan Record Office for parish records within the Diocese of Salisbury (Archdeaconries of Dorset and Sherborne) in the county of Dorset, and is recognised as a place of deposit for public records. In 1974 Bournemouth and Christchurch came into Dorset from Hampshire. Since 1997 the Dorset Archives Service, based at the Record Office, operates as a combined service for the administrative areas of Dorset County Council, Bournemouth Borough Council and the Borough of Poole under a joint agreement between the three authorities.

Acquisitions policy: All archives relating to the county of Dorset concerning all aspects of the history and life of the county.

Archives of organisation: Usual local authority holdings, including Dorset County Council minutes, 1889– ; older departmental records and modern legal documents (the latter are not available for research).

Major collections: Deposited local collections, including the following which have a wider significance:
State papers of Sir John Trenchard, Chief Secretary of State, 1693–5.
Accounts and other papers of Sir Stephen Fox and others as paymasters of the forces and in other public offices, 1638–1712.
War Office letter-books of Sir W. Yonge, 1741–5, and Henry Fox, Lord Holland, 1746–55; Army Agent's accounts, 1755–64; court of enquiry relating to Gibraltar, 1749–50.
Correspondence and papers of William Bankes, 1803–55.

Non-manuscript material: Photographic, film and sound archive.
Plans and drawings of Ernest Wamsley-Lewis of Weymouth (1889–1978), architect, 1928–71.

Finding aids: Catalogues. Lists. General indexes. Most catalogues sent to NRA.

Facilities: Photocopying. Photography by arrangement. Microfilm/fiche readers/printer. Record-searching service.

Conservation: In-house service and outside work undertaken.

Publications: A.C. Cox: *Index to the Dorset County Records* (1938).
M.E. Holmes: 'The Dorset Record Office', *Archives,* vii (1966), 207.
Dorset Motor Taxation Records: a Short Guide (1994).
Railway Records in the Dorset Record Office (1997).

Guide to the Location of the Parish Registers of Dorset (1998).

Guide to the Transcripts held in the Dorset Record Office (1998).

A Guide to theLocation of Non-Conformist and Roman Catholic Registers of Dorset.

List of Diaries and Memoirs in the Dorset Record Office.

H. Jaques (ed.): *The Archives of Dorset: a Catalogue of an Exhibition to Mark the First 30 Years of the Dorset Record Office.*

286 Isle of Man Civil Registry

Parent organisation: Isle of Man Government

Address: The Registries, Deemsters Walk, Bucks Road, Douglas, Isle of Man IM1 3AR

Telephone: (01624) 687038/9

Fax: (01624) 687039

E-mail: civil@registry.gov.im

Enquiries: The Registrar, Mrs S.K. Cain
The Deputy Registrar, Mrs P.A. Birch

Open: Mon–Fri: 9.00–1.00, 2.00–5.00.

Access: Generally open to the public. While there is no charge to inspect indexes, there is a search fee to consult volumes.

Historical background: By the General Registry Act 1965 the General Registry was constituted to carry out the functions of the Rolls Office, the Registry of Deeds and the Registrar General's Department, and the statutory posts of Chief Clerk Rolls Office, the Registrar of Deeds and Registrar General were amalgamated into the one post of Chief Registrar. The General Registry is the office of the High Court and incorporates the Companies Registry, the Probate Registry, the Business Names Registry and the Industrial and Building Societies Registry. Its functions include the issue of summonses and processes for all divisions of the High Court; the making of Grants of Probate, Administration and other Grants of Representation; and the registration of all deeds and documents leading to title to real estate in the island.

Archives of organisation: Wills, 1911– .
Statutory records of registered births, 1878– .
Church of England baptisms, 1611–1878.
Marriage records: Church of England, 1629–1849; Church of England and dissenters, 1849–83; statutory records, 1884– .
Statutory records of death, 1878– .

Church of England burial records, 1610–1878.
Records of legal adoptions registered in the Isle of Man, 1928– .
Deeds of property, 1911– .
Company registration records, 1865– .
High Court Records, original Acts and Resolutions of Tynwald; Grants of Representation to the estates of descendants; original plans and valuations of Manx estates; many other documents relating to the history and development of the Isle of Man.

Finding aids: Indexes on microfiche.

Facilities: Photocopying. Microfilming. Microfilm reader. Certified copies of entry can be purchased.

Conservation: Contracted out.

287 Isle of Man Public Record Office

Parent organisation: Isle of Man Government

Address: Unit 3, Spring Valley Industrial Estate, Braddan, Douglas, Isle of Man IM2 2QR

Telephone: (01624) 613383

Fax: (01624) 613384

E-mail: public.records@registry.gov.im

Website: www.gov.im/deptindex/reginfo.html

Enquiries: The Public Records Officer, Miss M.J. Critchlow

Open: Mon–Thurs: 8.30–5.30; Fri: 8.30–5.00, by appointment.

Historical background: Established in 1992 to develop a statutory framework for Manx public records and records management in the public sector, the Isle of Man Public Record Office is currently in temporary premises. Assistance can be given in locating government records still held by departments; for pre-20th-century public records and all private Manx records the Manx National Heritage Library (entry 288) should be consulted in the first instance.

Acquisitions policy: Records of Manx public administration.

Archives of organisation: Board and departmental records, predominantly 20th century.

Finding aids: In preparation.

Facilities: Photocopying. Microfilm/fiche reader.

288 Manx National Heritage Library

Parent organisation: Manx Museum

Address: Kingswood Grove, Douglas, Isle of Man IM1 3LY

Telephone: (01624) 648000

Fax: (01624) 648001

E-mail: enquiries@mrh.gov.im

Website: www.gov.im/mnh

Enquiries: The Librarian-Archivist, Mr R.M.C. Sims

Open: Mon–Sat: 10.00–5.00.
Closed for the last week of January.

Access: Generally open to the public. No appointment is necessary, but notification of an intended visit is appreciated.

Historical background: The Manx Museum Trustees have pursued a policy of collecting Manx books and MS material since their institution in the 1880s. The library, open to the public since 1922, holds certain classes of Manx public records as well as literary papers and the records of Manx families, societies and businesses.

Acquisitions policy: Public and private records relating to the Isle of Man.

Major collections: Isle of Man Government: court records; registered deeds, 1600–1910.
Wills: ecclesiastical and civil, 1629–1910.
Papers of the Derby family, 17th–18th centuries.
Papers of the Atholl family, 18th–19th centuries.
Records of the Isle of Man Steam Packet Co. Ltd, 1822–1980.

Non-manuscript material: Printed ephemera and a large collection of Manx books, pamphlets and newspapers, plans, prints, photographs and film.
Microfilms of census returns, 1841–91, parish registers to 1883, and other genealogical sources.
Microfilm of majority of Manx newspaper collection, 1793–.

Finding aids: Various lists and indexes. New lists are sent to NRA.

Facilities: Photocopying. Photography. Microfilm/fiche readers.

Conservation: The library has its own archives conservator and workshop.

Publications: Early Maps of the Isle of Man (1974).
100 Years of Heritage: the Work of the Manx Museum and National Trust (1986) [describes history and scope of library].
Various information sheets are available.

289 East Kent Archives Centre

Parent organisation: Kent County Council Arts & Libraries

Address: Enterprise Business Park, Honeywood Road, Whitfield, Dover, Kent CT16 3EH

Telephone: (01304) 829306

Fax: (01304) 829306

E-mail: eastkentarchives@kent.gov.uk

Enquiries: The Senior Archivist, Ms Alison Cable

Open: Tues–Fri: 9.00–5.00; appointments are advised.

Access: Generally open to the public. The centre operates the CARN reader's ticket system. A paid research service is available.

Historical background: The centre opened in 2000 to house collections formerly held by Thanet Branch Archives, Folkestone Library, Hythe Town Archives and Lydd Town Council. Some records relating to the area served by the centre have been transferred from the Centre for Kentish Studies (entry 868).

Acquisitions policy: Archives relating to the Thanet, Dover and Shepway district council areas, except Church of England records.

Archives of organisation: Records of the boroughs of Dover; Ramsgate; Margate; Hythe, c1278–1974; Sandwich; Deal and Lydd, c1400–.
Records of the Liberty of Romney Marsh; and Confederation of Cinque Ports and Lord Warden.
Records of local urban and rural district councils, and boards of guardians.

Major collections: Archives of Dover Harbour Board; National Coal Board, Kent, 1677–1980s; Broadstairs and Margate Pier and Harbour Commissions; Margate Seabathing Hospital, 1791–1998; East Kent Mental Asylum, 1875–1993.

Local non-conformist, school and hospital records.

Personal papers of the Cobb family of Margate, brewers, bankers and shipping agents, 1615–1927.

Non-manuscript material: Photographs. Maps. Plans.

Finding aids: Catalogues and lists. Sent to NRA.

Facilities: Photocopying. Photography. Microfilm readers.

290 Down County Museum

Address: The Mall, Downpatrick, Co. Down BT30 6AH

Telephone: (02844) 615218

Fax: (02844) 615590

Enquiries: The Keeper of Collections, Ms Lesley Simpson

Open: Tues–Fri: 10.00–5.00; Sat, Sun: 2.00–5.00 Additional opening June–Aug: Mon: 10.00–5.00. Sun: 2.00–5.00.

Access: Generally open to the public.

The museum maintains collections illustrative of the history of County Down from the earliest times, with documentation relating to the collections, including minute books, certificates, maps and plans. There is also a photograph collection. Photocopying and photography are available.

291 Black Country Living Museum

Parent organisation: Black Country Museum Trust Ltd

Address: Tipton Road, Dudley, West Midlands DY1 4SQ

Telephone: (0121) 557 9643

Fax: (0121) 557 4242

E-mail: walden@bclm.co.uk

Website: www.bclm.co.uk

Enquiries: The Curatorial Department

Open: March–Oct: Mon–Fri: 10.00–5.00. Nov–Feb: Wed–Fri: 10.00–4.00, by appointment.

Access: Generally open to the public, by arrangement.

Historical background: It was originally set up in 1966 by Dudley Metropolitan Borough Council as a section within the museum department. Since 1976 the Museum has been run as a charity by the Black Country Museum Trust Ltd.

Acquisitions policy: Printed and pictorial information, archives and published ephemera which relate to the history of the region, or which assist in the understanding and interpretation of other objects in the collection. Material which would be more appropriate elsewhere is not collected.

Major collections: Archives of Kenrick, hollowware manufacturers, West Bromwich, 1790s–1960s, and Braith & Kirk, metal fabricators, 1890–1950s.

Documents and catalogues of James Smellie Ltd, Dudley, art metal workers.

Non-manuscript material: Black Country Society photographic collection.

Finding aids: Lists, accessions register and database.

Facilities: Photocopying by arrangement.

292 Dudley Archives and Local History Service

Parent organisation: Dudley Metropolitan Borough Council

Address: Mount Pleasant Street, Coseley, Dudley, West Midlands WV14 9JR

Telephone: (01384) 812770

Fax: (01384) 812770

E-mail: archives.pls@mbc.dudley.gov.uk

Website: www.dudley.gov.uk/council/library/archives

Enquiries: The Archivist, Mrs K.H. Atkins

Open: Tues, Wed, Fri: 9.00–5.00; Thurs: 9.30–7.00; Sat (1st and 3rd of each month): 9.30–12.30, by appointment. Limited service, 1.00–2.00.

Access: Generally open to the public. A paid genealogical research service is available.

Historical background: Archives have been collected since 1947 and the first qualified archivist was appointed in 1972. The service also acts as the Diocesan Record Office for Worcester (Deaneries of Dudley, Himley and Stourbridge parish records). It is recognised as a place of deposit for public records.

Acquisitions policy: Records relating to the area of the present metropolitan borough.

Archives of organisation: Usual local authority record holdings.

Major collections: Deposited local collections, of which the following is of wider significance: archive of the Earls of Dudley, 12th–20th centuries.

Non-manuscript material: The Local History Library includes newspapers, cuttings, and local photographs (c17,000).
Local history collections can also be found at the following area libraries: Brierley Hill, Halesowen and Stourbridge.

Finding aids: Lists and handlists. Some lists sent to NRA.

Facilities: Photocopying. Photography. Microfilm/fiche readers/printer.

Conservation: Some contracting out.

Publications: Checklist of Sources for Genealogical Enquirers.
List of Principal Holdings of Archives (being revised).
Various handlists. Full publications list available.

293 West Dunbartonshire Libraries

Parent organisation: West Dunbartonshire Council

Address: Dumbarton Library, Strathleven Place, Dumbarton G82 1BD

Telephone: (01389) 733273/763129

Fax: (01389) 607302

E-mail: arthur.jones@west-dunbarton-gov.uk

Enquiries: The Senior Information Services Librarian, Arthur F. Jones
The Information Services Librarian, Graham N. Hopner

Open: Mon–Thurs: 9.30–8.00; Fri: 9.30–5.00; Sat: 10.00–5.00.
Closed first three working days of January.

Access: Open to all. Charged research can also be undertaken.

Historical background: After the reorganisation of local government in 1975 Dumbarton Library became a recognised repository for archives within the newly created Dumbarton District, and it acquired the records of the various local authorities which had been in existence up to that time. After 1981 it carried out a policy of also acquiring the records of organisations and individuals active in the district. Since the subsequent reorganisation of local government in 1996 it has continued doing this for the western part of West Dunbartonshire (Dumbarton and the Vale of Leven), while Clydebank Library (see entry 383) carries out a similar function for the eastern section.

Acquisitions policy: To collect records relating to the Dumbarton and Vale of Leven areas of West Dunbartonshire.

Archives of organisation: West Dunbartonshire Council records, 1996– .

Major collections: Dumbarton Burgh records, 1599–1975.
Collection of charters, documents and letters pertaining to the town of Dumbarton, 15th century– .
Dumbarton District records, 1975–96.
Census returns for Dumbartonshire and West Stirlingshire, 19th century.
Parish registers for Dumbartonshire and West Stirlingshire.

Non-manuscript material: Maps and plans of the western part of West Dunbartonshire (c1000).
Drawings, paintings and prints (c300).
Photographic prints (c15,000), negatives (c8000) and slides (c2000).
Local newspapers, 1851– .
Audio-visual material (c300).

Finding aids: Various lists and indexes. Important additions are reported to NRAS.

Facilities: Photocopying. Photography. Microfilm/fiche readers/printers.

Conservation: Contracted out.

Publications: Catalogue of local publications available.

294 Dumfries and Galloway Archives

Parent organisation: Libraries, Information and Archives Service, Department of Community Resources, Dumfries and Galloway Council

Address: The Archive Centre, 33 Burns Street, Dumfries, Dumfries and Galloway DG1 2PS

Telephone: (01387) 269254

Fax: (01387) 264126

E-mail: marionst@dumgal.gov.uk

Website: www.dumgal.gov.uk/services/depts/comres/library/archives.htm

Enquiries: The Archivist, Miss Marion M. Stewart

Open: Tues, Wed, Fri: 11.00–1.00, 2.00–5.00; Thurs: 6.00–9.00.

Access: Generally open without pre-booking, but prior notice is prudent for a visit to the Archive Centre.

Historical background: The archive services provided for Nithsdale District Council (as part of the Museum Service) by Dumfries Archive Centre and for Dumfries and Galloway Regional Council by the Regional Library Service were amalgamated in 1996 when Dumfries and Galloway Council replaced the previous local authorities. The county archives, described below, are still accessed at the Ewart Library (Catherine Street, Dumfries DG1 1JB; tel: (01387) 253820/260285, Reference & Local Studies Librarian: Mrs Ruth Airley). However, the service is run as an integrated part of the Libraries, Information and Archives Service.

Acquisitions policy: Active collecting policy for all records pertaining to Dumfries and Galloway or to individuals native to this area.

Archives of organisation: Burgh records of Dumfries, covering council and court 1506– , treasurers and chamberlains, 1640– , dean of guild, 1777– , parish churches, 1648– , general administration and miscellaneous including titles, rentals, rating, taxation, shipping and voting, c1450–c1990; records of the parochial board and police commissioners, 19th century; burgh records of Sanquhar, 1714–1974, including council and court, valuation rolls, planning, accounts, education and parochial boards and heritors' records; burgh records of Moffat, 1864–1974, including council and committees, housing, planning trusts and other administrative records; records of Nithsdale District Council, 1975–96, including council committees, accounts, and miscellaneous; Dumfriesshire building control and planning authority records, 1940s–1975.

County records of Dumfriesshire, 1667–1974, Kirkcudbrightshire, 1728–1974, and Wigtownshire, 1736–1974, including county council and committees; commissioners of supply and highway authorities; valuation and voting rolls; education and parochial boards (not burghs or Wigtownshire); Dumfries and Galloway Regional Council and the district councils of Annandale and Eskdale, Nithsdale, Stewartry and Wigtown council and committees, 1975–96.

Major collections: Records of the Seven Incorporated Trades of Dumfries, 1612–1890. Deposited family papers, including those of Grierson of Lag, 1518–1761, Stewart of Shambellie, 1590–1961, McCartney of Halketleaths, 1560s–1830s, Maxwells of Munches, of Barncleuch, of Elshieshields, and of Terregles, 1450–1898, Copland of Collieston, 1555–1928, Hunter-Arundell of Barjarg, 1800s, Arnott of Kirkconnel Hall, 1647–1876, McClellan of Chapeltown and Borness, 1667–1804, Thomson of Ingleston, 1646–1824, Clerk Maxwell of Middlebie, 1640s–1850s.

Beattock writs, 1703–1859; Culvennan charters, 1400s–1800s; correspondence of explorer Sir John Richardson, 1832–64; marriage registers of Gretna Hall, 1829–55, and of Sark Toll Bar, 1832–45.

Kirk Session records of Dumfries, 1648–1960; of Troqueer and Maxwelltown, 1698–1975; of Kirkbean, 1714–1876; and of Morton, Glencairn and Penpont, 1714–1978.

Records of Dumfries Presbytery, 1647–1885; Dumfries Wesleyan Methodists, 1796–1968; St John's and St Mary's Episcopalian churches, Dumfries 1762–1957.

Records of Dumfries, Industrial School, 1750–1973; the Mechanics Institutes at Annan 1850–1905; and Dumfries, 1920–37; Dumfriesshire Regiment of Militia, 1798–1817; Dumfries Volunteers, 1795–1802; the Police Forces of Dumfries, Dumfriesshire, Kirkcudbrightshire, Wigtownshire and of Dumfries and Galloway, 1849–1973; Customs records and shipping registers at Dumfries, 1824–1973; Kirkcudbright, 1824–41; Stranraer, 1824–1908; and Wigtown, 1836–1920.

Architectural plans and drawings of Walter Newall, 1809–60.

Records of local firms, clubs and organisations, 1700s–1900.

Miscellaneous estate and other maps and architectural drawings, 1700s–1900s.

Non-manuscript material: Local newspapers 1777– (on microfiche) with index.
Local photographic collections, 1880s and *Galloway News* photographic archive, 1947–80; OS maps, 1846– .
Monumental inscriptions for graveyards throughout Dumfries and Galloway.
Abridgements and indexes to the sasine registers for Dumfriesshire, Kirkcudbrightshire and Wigtownshire, 1617–1970.
Extensive local studies library of printed books, pamphlets, notes and other supporting reference material.

Finding aids: Detailed, indexed holdings guide for contents of Archive Centre (available for searching on-line) and shelf lists for archives in Ewart Library; calendars for several collections and transcripts available for early council minutes and some other classes of records; source lists available by subject and by place.

Facilities: Photocopying. Photography. Microfilm/fiche reader/printers.

Publications: Ancestor Hunting in Dumfries Archive Centre.
Publications list available.

295 Dumfries and Galloway Health Board Archives

Address: Crichton Royal Hospital, Easterbrook Hall, Bankend Road, Dumfries, Dumfries and Galloway DG1 4TG

Telephone: (01387) 244228

Fax: (01387) 269696

Enquiries: The Archivist, Mrs Morag Williams

Open: Tues–Fri: 9.00–5.00.

Access: Bona fide researchers, by appointment only. Searches undertaken by the Archivist for a charge.

Historical background: The parent body, the Dumfries and Galloway Health Board, has been fully operational since 1974. Archive work has been pursued since 1983.

Acquisitions policy: All material relating to health care in south-west Scotland in Wigtownshire, Kirkcudbrightshire, Dumfriesshire, now known as Dumfries and Galloway Region.

Archives of organisation: Dumfries and Galloway Royal Infirmary: minute books and annual reports, 1777– ; cash books, ledgers, letter-books and staff registers.
Crichton Royal Hospital: trust documents, 1820s– , minute books, annual reports, case notes, registers of admission, obligants books, staff registers, 1839– ; house magazine, 1844– ; registers of restraint and seclusion, accident, death, sheriff's warrants, 1858– .
Cottage hospital material relating to Stranraer (Garrick), Kirkcudbright, Castle Douglas, Moffat, Langholm (Thomas Hope), including minutes, annual reports (incomplete), some letter-books, patients' registers, 1892– .
Infectious diseases hospitals, including patients' registers for Newton Stewart, Castle Douglas and Thornhill, 1898– .
Cresswell Maternity Hospital material, 1939– .
Area Health Board minutes, 1973– .

Non-manuscript material: Architectural plans, art therapy material, 1839– ; extensive collection of (psychiatric) artefacts for Crichton Royal; photographs for all hospitals; limited oral archive.

Finding aids: Computer database in preparation.

Facilities: Photocopying. Photography.

Conservation: Contracted out.

Publications: M. Williams and A. C. Morrell: *The History of Kirkcudbright Hospital* (1984).
M. Williams: *The History of Thomas Hope Hospital* (1989).
Geals, Gordon, Paterson, Train and Williams: *Cresswell Maternity Hospital, 1939–1989* (1989).
M. Williams: *History of Crichton Royal Hospital 1839- 1989.*
——: *The History of Lochmaben Hospital 1908–1986* (1986).
—— : *The History of Garrick Hospital, 1892–1992* (1992).
——: *The History of Newton Stewart Hospital 1897–1997* (1997).
T. Baillie: *The Dumfries Ether Diary* (1996).

296 Dumfries Museum

Parent organisation: Dumfries and Galloway Council

Address: The Observatory, Dumfries, Dumfries and Galloway DG2 7SW

Telephone: (01387) 253374

Fax: (01387) 265081

E-mail: dumfriesmuseum.demon.co.uk

Website: www.dumfriesmuseum.demon.co.uk

Enquiries: The Museums Officer, Siobhan Ratchford

Open: April–Sept: Mon–Sat: 10.00–5.00; Sun: 2.00–5.00.
Oct–March: Tues–Sat: 10.00–1.00, 2.00–5.00.

Access: Generally open to the public; an appointment is essential.

Historical background: The museum was established by Dumfries Astronomical Society and began collecting in the 1860s, but the Dumfries Archives Centre (entry 294) is now the repository for all archival material.

Acquisitions policy: Archival material is not now collected.

Archives of organisation: Dumfries Astronomical Society minute books, 19th century.

Major collections: William Grierson (1773–1852), diaries, 1794–1809.
School scrapbook, produced partly by J.M. Barrie.
Documents relating to witchcraft in Dumfries.

Non-manuscript material: Local photographs, estate maps and plans, OS maps.
Small local history library.

Finding aids: Subject catalogues.

Facilities: Photocopying. Photography. Microfiche reader.

Conservation: Paper conservation is contracted out.

297 Dunblane Museum

Parent organisation: The Trustees of the Dunblane Museum

Address: The Square, Dunblane FK15 OAQ

Telephone: (01786) 825691

Enquiries: The Hon. Curator, Mrs M.P. Davies, 22 Argyle Way, Dunblane, FK15 9DX

Open: Early May–early Oct: Mon–Sat: 10.00–1.00, 2.00–4.30.

Access: Access by arrangement; a donation is requested.

Acquisitions policy: Documents, books etc relating to Dunblane, primarily religious, but also social and economic.

Archives of organisation: Archives, MSS, books and artefacts concerned with the cathedral.

Major collections: Diaries, letters, newspaper cuttings of Dr W. Blair (1830–1916), minister, 1856–1916, and Dr Hutchison Cockburn, (1882–1973), minister, 1918–45.

Non-manuscript material: Plans and drawings of cathedral restoration, 1817; 1891–3. Photographs.

Finding aids: Catalogues, lists, indexes.

Conservation: Contracted out.

Publications: Journal of the Friends of Dunblane Cathedral (annually).

298 Leighton Library, Dunblane

Telephone: (01786) 822850

Enquiries: The Hon. Custodian, Bill Moore, 'Cranford', Smithy Loan, Dunblane FK15 0HQ

Open: May–Oct: Mon–Fri: 10.00–12.30, 2.00–4.30.
At other times by arrangement with the Hon. Custodian.
Items required for prolonged study may be consulted at Stirling University (entry 1134).

Access: Generally open to all, preferably with advanced notice. There is no charge but donations are welcome.

Historical background: The library, which is the oldest private library in Scotland, was built between 1684 and 1687 to hold the books of Robert Leighton, Bishop of Dunblane, 1660–71, and Archbishop of Glasgow, 1671–4. It operated as a subscription library from the early 1700s–1840. The contents lay undisturbed until 1989, when money was raised for restoration of the building and treatment of the books. The library opened to the general public in 1990. It is run by the Leighton Library Trustees, members of whom are descendants of the original trustees. Papers of the trustees are retained by Tho. & J.W. Batty, Solicitors, 61 High Street, Dunblane FK15 0EH.

Archives of organisation: Minutes and papers relating to the library.

Major collections: Various MSS relating to Scottish history, especially religious history; also literary MSS.

Some MSS may also be seen at Dunblane Museum (entry 297).

Non-manuscript material: Books, 1500–1840 (*c*4500).

Facilities: None at the Leighton Library. Photocopying and photography by arrangement. Microfilm/fiche readers at Stirling University Library.

Publications: G.W. Willis: *The Leighton Library, Dunblane: Catalogue of Manuscripts* (Stirling, 1981).

—— : 'The Leighton Library, Dunblane: its History and Contents', *The Bibliothek*, x/6 (1981), 139–57.

299 Dundee Art Galleries & Museums
McManus Galleries

Parent organisation: Dundee City Council

Address: Albert Square, Dundee DD1 1DA

Telephone: (01382) 432020

Fax: (01382) 432078

E-mail: arts.heritage@dundeecity.gov.uk

Enquiries: The Facility Manager, Janice Murray

Open: Mon–Wed, Fri, Sat: 10.00–5.00; Thurs: 10.00–7.00.

Access: Bona fide researchers, by appointment.

Historical background: Formerly the Albert Institute, the McManus Galleries opened as a free library in 1867. The Art Galleries and Museum were formed in 1873. Some collections formerly held by Broughty Castle Museum have been transferred.

Acquisitions policy: Ephemera only; other archival collections will be directed to the appropriate archive centre, either Dundee Central Library (entry 300) or Dundee City Archives (entry 301).

Archives of organisation: Acquisition registers and some supporting documentation, 1872– . Annual museum reports, 1958–73 (incomplete) and correspondence.

Major collections: Whaling journals, log-books, certificates, seamen's papers, note-books etc, early 19th–20th centuries.
Correspondence and photographs of Mary Slessor, Church of Scotland missionary in West Africa, *c*1877–1913.

Chalmers Publishing House Collection, including ink recipes, and correspondence between James Chalmers (1782–1853) and Rowland Hill (1795–1879) concerning the postal service, early 19th- mid-20th century.

Non-manuscript material: Textile industry: ephemera, machine plans, specifications and technical films, late 19th–20th centuries.
Rail transport: ephemera and plans, especially relating to North British line and the Tay rail bridges, mainly late 19th century.
Shipbuilding: ephemera and plans, particularly of the Caledon and Gourlay shipping yards, 19th–20th centuries.
Friendly societies and trade unions: collection of certificates and rule books etc, late 19th–20th centuries.
Supporting photographic archives, particularly strong for textiles; local topography; whaling; education, including the Tay training ship *Mars*, retail trades.
Sound Archives, 20th century (*c*100).

Finding aids: Card index. Lists sent to NRA.

Facilities: Photocopying. Photography, by arrangement only.

Conservation: Paper conservation contracted out.

300 Dundee Central Library
Local Studies Department

Parent organisation: Dundee City Council, Neighbourhood Resources and Development Department

Address: The Wellgate, Dundee DD1 1DB

Telephone: (01382) 434377

Fax: (01382) 434642

E-mail: central.library@dundeecity.gov.uk

Website: dundeecity.gov.uk/dcchtml/nrd/centlib/loc_stud.htm

Enquiries: The Local Studies Librarian, Eileen Moran

Open: Mon, Tues, Fri, Sat: 9.30–5.00; Wed. 10.00–7.00; Thurs: 9.30–7.00.

Access: Generally open to the public; proof of identity and 24 hours' notice are required. Some material available only in surrogate format.

Historical background: The library was established in 1869 and its collections were founded on significant donations and bequests by contemporary benefactors. Certain archive materials of the former Dundee District Libraries and the Art Galleries and Museums, and their predecessors, 1880– , are housed in the Central Library.

Acquisitions policy: Donations of suitable local material welcomed.

Major collections: The Compt Book of David Wedderburne, 1587–1630.
MS and other material concerning local persons including Edwin Scrymgeour (1866–1947), Prohibitionist and MP; William McGonagall (*d* 1902) 'poet'; Mary Slessor (1848–1914), missionary.
Dundee Trades Council Collection, MS and printed material, to *c*1960.
Miscellaneous MS material relating to local authors and organisations, including Thomas Hood, poet, letters to his aunt, 1815–45; James Bowman Lindsay (1799–1862), scientist and philologist, MS notebooks and printed works; Glover Trade records, 1566–1797.
Collection of whaling log-books.

Non-manuscript material: Dundee Photographic Surveys, 1915 and 1992.
Wilson Collection of photographs, *c*1888–*c*1910 (*c*4000).
Lamb Collection of 19th-century ephemera.
Ower Collection of architectural drawings, late 19th century–early 20th century.
Cynicus (Martin Anderson), satirist, drawings and printed works, early 20th century.

Finding aids: Catalogues and indexes. The following databases and descriptive pages are available on the website.
Wighton Collection (also at wighton.sol.-co.uk); Wilson Photographic Collection; Sir James Ivory; Mary Slessor; William McGonagall; James Bowman Lindsay; Rare Books and Manuscripts, forthcoming).

Facilities: Photocopying. Photography. Microfilm/fiche readers/printer.

Conservation: Contracted out.

Publications: J. MacLauchlan: *A Brief Guide to the Old Dundee Historical Collection* (Dundee, 1901).

301 Dundee City Archives

Parent organisation: Dundee City Council

Address: 21 City Square (callers should use 1 Shore Terrace), Dundee DD1 3BY

Telephone: (01382) 434494

Fax: (01382) 434666

E-mail: archives@dundeecity.gov.uk

Website: www.dundeecity.gov.uk/dcchtml/sservices/archives.html

Enquiries: The City Archivist, Mr Iain Flett

Open: Mon–Fri: 9.15–1.00, 2.00–4.45.

Access: Generally open to the public, by appointment.

Historical background: The archive was a district office from 1975 to 1996 and acted on an agency basis for Tayside Regional Council. It became Dundee City Archives again in 1996. Perth & Kinross and Angus county records have been transferred to their relevant archives.

Archives of organisation: Usual local authority record holdings; retransmitted records from the National Archives of Scotland include Dundee Presbytery, Custom & Excise, and Agriculture & Fishery series.

Major collections: Deposited collections, including the following which have a wider significance:
Dundee Chamber of Commerce, formerly Forfarshire Chamber of Commerce, and Baltic Coffee House and Chamber of Commerce, records, 1819–1960.
Dundee Harbour Trustees and various shipping company records, 19th–20th centuries.
Dundee Jute and Flax Union records, 1906–71, including references to jute industry in India.
Loyal Order of Friendly Shepherds Friendly Society records, 1871–1989.
Records of First Scottish American Trust Co. Ltd, and those of subsequent investment companies, 1873–1970.
Geekie family, Keillor, Angus correspondence etc, 1646–1850, includes letters from Alexander Geekie, surgeon in London, *c*1678–1724.
Papers of David Greig, FRCSEd (*fl* 1850s), including copies of his letters written while serving as assistant surgeon in the Crimea.
Papers of Dr Thomas Dick, LLD, FRAS (1774–1857), 1814–1908.
Account books covering voyages of the brigantines *Flora* and *Tagus* of Dundee, 18th century.
Jas. Scott & Sons, merchants, spinners and jute manufacturers, records (including India and South America), 1861–1969.

Williamson Memorial Unitarian Church records, 1832–1979.

Wedderburn of Pearsie family papers (including service in East India Company), 1483–1918.

Earl of Northesk papers, 13th–20th centuries.

Non-manuscript material: James Collie contour survey of Dundee, 1851.

OS maps for Dundee, 1871 and 1901.

Finding aids: Handlists.

Facilities: Photocopying.

Publications: W. Hay (ed.): *Charters, Writs and Public Documents of the Royal Burgh of Dundee, 1292–1880* (Dundee, 1880).

Archives Argus [newsletter of the Friends of Dundee City Archives].

302 Dundee University Archives

Address: Tower Building, Dundee DD1 4HN

Telephone: (01382) 344095

Fax: (01382) 345523

E-mail: archives@dundee.ac.uk

Website: www.dundee.ac.uk/archives

Enquiries: The University Archivist, Ms P. Whatley

Open: Mon–Wed, Fri: 9.00–1.00, 2.00–5.00 (closes 6.00 during term)

Access: Generally open to the public. Appointments are advisable.

Historical background: The university has its origins in University College, Dundee, founded in 1881. The college became part of St Andrews University in 1897, was renamed Queens College in 1954, and was granted its charter as a university in 1967. In 1994 Duncan of Jordanstone College of Art, formerly an independent institution, became a faculty of the university. The Archives Department is also responsible for the Kinnear Local Collection (local books and newspapers) and the Joan Auld Memorial Collection (19th- and 20th-century British labour history), which complement the MSS holdings.

Acquisitions policy: To identify and collect the records of the university and its predecessor and associated institutions; as well as business records, particularly those of the textile and related industries; other records relating to Dundee and Tayside; health care records, and

records relating to religion, in the Tayside area, are collected. Research in all these areas is actively promoted.

Archives of organisation: University archives: records of the university, 1967– , and of its predecessors, University College and Queens College, c1875–1966, including Dundee School of Economics, Dundee Medical School (University of St Andrews), and Duncan of Jordanstone Art College, c1899– .

Major collections: Records of the textile industry and its links with India and Pakistan, particularly relating to jute and linen, and including engineering, 1795–c1985.

Shiell and Small, solicitors, Dundee: records of the firm and of principal clients, particularly railway companies and prominent Dundee businessmen, 1826–c1935.

Records of local medical associations, 1864–1927, and Dundee Medical Library, 1880–1903; papers relating to the history of medicine in Angus, 16th century–1936; papers of R.C. Alexander (1884–1968), surgeon, c1899–1950, including RAMC field service notebooks, 1917–18; R.P. Cook (1906–89), biochemist, papers, including correspondence with Alexander Fleming, Ernst Chain and Howard Florey.

Glasite church sermons and correspondence, 1728–1885; papers relating to the College and Collegiate Church of the Holy Spirit, Isle of Cumbrae, c1850–1929.

MSS and correspondence of Thomas Campbell (1777–1844), poet, 1797–1854; papers of Joseph Lee (1876–1949), journalist and poet, 1898–1948, including illustrated journals while prisoner of war in Germany, 1916–18, and correspondence with Robert Bridges (1844–1930), poet, 1914.

Correspondence of Alexander Scott (1853–1947), chemist, 1851–1935, including letters to William J. Russell; papers of Alexander Mackenzie (1869–1951), chemist, c1896–1936; Sir Robert Robertson (1869–1948), chemist, 1894–1949; A.D. Walsh (1916–71), chemist, c1930–1970; James Ballantyne Hannay (1855–1931), chemist and innovator, including papers *re* diamond research, 1842–1987, and Prince of Wales Theatre, Glasgow, 1871–87; John Berry (*b* 1907), biologist and ornithologist, papers relating to the North of Scotland Hydro-Electric Board, and to nature conservancy, 1932–89, including correspondence with Sir Peter Scott (1909–89); McClean Hydrometric Data Collection, c1900–1950s.

Records of Dundee Stock Exchange Association, 1876–1964; papers relating to east of Scotland shipping, including whaling, 1767–1980; papers of Wilson family of Alva, mainly woollen manufacturers, 1771–1976, including letters from America, 1815–29, letters and photographs relating to service in the French and British Red Cross, 1916–18 and letters *re* Anschluss and the German occupation, 1938–45; James Dalyell (1798–1870), naval officer and coastguard, papers, *c*1817–73, including service in West Indies, *c*1817–27, and the Pacific, 1841–5, and journals of walking tours in France, 1828–34; Michael Peto (1908–70), photographer, correspondence, including letters from A.S. Neill (1883–1973), 1943–5; Catherine Kinnear (1912–88), bibliophile and antiquary, papers, 1845–1955; Peter Carmichael of Arthurstone, engineer, biographical writings and papers, 1837–90.

Tayside Health Board: records of Dundee hospitals and boards of management, including the Dental Hospital, 1820–1974.

Brechin Diocesan Library MSS: correspondence of Bishop Alexander Penrose Forbes, 1844–74; transcripts of episcopal registers, *c*1681–1890; records of the Diocese of Brechin and some congregations, *c*1744–1970; William Drummond of Hawthornden (1585–1649), diary and commonplace book; Psalter, Book of Hours, sermons, 15th century.

Bett Bros. Ltd, house building and property development records, *c*1930s–1980s.

Cox Brothers Ltd, jute spinners and manufacturers, Dundee, *c*1819–1950, records including Cox family papers.

Grimmond family, merchants, papers relating to J. & A.D. Grimmond Ltd, jute spinners and manufacturers, Dundee, 1797–1902.

Grampian Club, Tayside hill-walking and mountaineering club, books, journals and original material.

Non-manuscript material: Maps and plans, particularly Tayside and Fife and including railway plans, 1746–*c*1970 (*c*3500); technical drawings, particularly textile machinery, *c*1850–1960.

Ruggles Bequest: contemporary drawings of American Civil War, 1863–4; David Waterson (*c*1870–1954), artist, watercolour studies; Neil Stewart (*c*1820–*c*1890), medical illustrations; miscellaneous pathological lithographs, *c*1815–*c*1890.

Photographs, particularly the university and its predecessors, including staff and students, *c*1882– , industry in Tayside, jute industry in India, and medical conditions (13,500).

Torrance Collection of photographs of Middle East, *c*1880–1970.

George H. Bell (1905–86), physiologist, collection of photographs of the medical profession, and of Scotland, Italy and Africa.

Hugh S. Stannus (1877–1957), specialist in tropical medicine, glass negatives of Central Africa, *c*1905–1918.

Alexander Burn Murdoch (*c*1880–1954), stereoscopic negatives of trans-Canada rail journey, 1912, and stereoscopic glass slides, including Scotland, French and Swiss Alps, 1924–53.

Michael Peto photographs of international figures in politics, especially Hungary, and arts, especially ballet, plus people and social conditions in London, South Wales, Dundee, Europe, India, and the Far and Middle East, *c*1946 (*c*120,000).

Local glass plate negative collection.

Glass plate negatives taken in the north-east of Scotland, 1900–30.

Finding aids: Descriptive lists, card indexes, databases of photographs, maps and plans, source lists on various subjects. Lists sent to NRAS.

Fonds-level descriptions of all collections will shortly be available on the HE Hub service.

Facilities: Photocopying. Photography. Microfilm/fiche readers.

Conservation: Contracted out.

303 Andrew Carnegie Birthplace Museum

Parent organisation: The Carnegie Dunfermline Trust

Address: Moodie Street, Dunfermline, Fife KY12 7PL

Telephone: (01383) 724302

Fax: (01383) 729002

E-mail: info@carnegiemuseum.co.uk

Website: www.carnegiemuseum.co.uk

Enquiries: The Curator, Mr D. Barclay

Open: Nov–March: Mon–Sun: 2.00–4.00.
Apr–Oct: Mon–Sat: 11.00–5.00; Sun: 2.00–5.00.

Access: Accredited scholars or reseachers, by appointment only. A standard search fee is charged for access to the archives.

Historical background: The main collection of personalia and memorabilia of Andrew Carnegie (1835–1919), manufacturer and philanthropist, was presented by his widow between 1926 and 1928, and there have been occasional subsequent additions. See also Carnegie Dunfermline and Hero Fund Trusts (entry 304).

Acquisitions policy: Items connected with Andrew Carnegie.

Archives of organisation: Annual reports and publications of the Carnegie trusts and institutions.

Major collections: Carnegie Collection includes MSS and typescripts of his publications.

Non-manuscript material: Extensive collection of photographs of Andrew Carnegie, Carnegie Steel Company, Carnegie's family, friends and others, taken at ceremonies throughout the UK.
Newspaper cuttings *re* Carnegie's death and centenary (13 vols).
Full set of Carnegie first editions.

Finding aids: Catalogue; some indexes available.

Facilities: Photocopying and photography can be arranged.

Conservation: Contracted out.

304 Carnegie Dunfermline and Hero Fund Trusts

Address: Abbey Park House, Abbey Park Place, Dunfermline, Fife KY12 7PB

Telephone: (01383) 723638

Fax: (01383) 721862

E-mail: admin@carnegietrust.com

Enquiries: The Secretary and Treasurer, Mr W.C. Runciman

Open: Mon–Fri: 9.00–5.00.

Access: Access is normally given to accredited scholars or researchers; appointments should generally be made.

Historical background: The Carnegie Dunfermline Trust was established in 1903 to improve the social, recreational and cultural amenities of the native town of Andrew Carnegie (1835–1919). The Carnegie Hero Fund Trust was established in 1908 to provide financial assistance if necessary to people who have been injured or sustained financial loss, or to the families of people who have been killed in heroic endeavour to save human life in peaceful pursuits throughout the British Isles. See also Andrew Carnegie Birthplace Museum (entry 303).

Acquisitions policy: Consolidation of the trusts' archives.

Archives of organisation: Records of the Carnegie Dunfermline Trust and the Carnegie Hero Fund Trust, including reports, minutes, correspondence files, title deeds, newspaper cuttings, photographs, tape and video recordings and plans.

Finding aids: List of archives, 1977.

Facilities: Photocopying.

305 Dunfermline Central Library

Parent organisation: Fife Council

Address: Abbot Street, Dunfermline, Fife KY12 7NL

Telephone: (01383) 312600/312994 (direct)

Fax: (01383) 312608

Enquiries: The Local History Librarian, Anne Rodwell

Open: Mon, Tues, Thurs, Fri: 10.00–7.00; Wed, Sat: 10.00–5.00.

Access: Generally open to the public; no appointment is necessary, but a preliminary letter or telephone call is welcome.

Historical background: The library, the first Carnegie Free Library in the world, was established in 1883, and the local history collection is based on a collection gifted in 1920.

Acquisitions policy: Local records covering West Fife, previously Dunfermline District.

Archives of organisation: Records of Tradesmen and Mechanics Library, 1826–30; Dunfermline Subscription Library, 1789–1828; and Dunfermline Public Library, 1880– .

Major collections: Usual local history collection, including records of Dunfermline Abbey and non-conformist churches, 19th–20th centuries; turnpike records and papers, 1809–79; Dunfermline Co-operative Society minutes and papers, 1861–1967; Dunfermline Naturalists Society records, 1861–1967; Incorporation of Weavers entry and minute books, 1596–1863.

Erskine Beveridge (1851–1920) Collection: notes on local churchyards.

Finding aids: Card catalogues incorporating subject index in process of being automated on OPAC. See NRAS 1834.

Facilities: Photocopying. Microfilm/fiche reader.

306 Scottish Horse Regimental Museum

Parent organisation: Scottish Horse Trust

Address: The Cross, Dunkeld, Perthshire PH8 0AN

Enquiries: Miss M. McInnes

Open: Easter–beginning of Oct: Mon–Wed: 10.00–12.00, 1.30–5.00.

Access: Generally open to the public during the season. Research is undertaken and a donation is required.

Historical background: Raised by the Marquis of Tullibardine (the 8th Duke of Atholl) in South Africa in 1900, the regiment served in the South African Campaign and World Wars I and II.

Archives of organisation: Correspondence and telegrams, diaries and courts martial.
Registers of animals and reports on operations, 1899–1902.
Registers of Scottish Horses, 1901– .
Scottish Horse casualties in Gallipoli, 1915–17.

Major collections: Correspondence and papers, 1902–18, including letters from Viscount Haldane, Secretary of State for War, 1905–12. Miscellaneous files and narratives *re* World War II.

Publications: The Scottish Horse, 1900–1956.

307 Strict Baptist Historical Society Library

Address: Dunstable Baptist Chapel, St Mary's Gate, off West Street, Dunstable, Bedfordshire

Website: www.strictbaptisthistory.org.uk

Enquiries: The Chairman and Hon. Secretary, Kenneth Dix, 38 Frenchs Avenue, Dunstable, Beds LU6 1BH; tel. 01582 696962; e-mail: secretary@sbhs.org.uk
The Hon. Librarian David J. Woodruff, 10 Priory Road, Dunstable, Beds LU5 4HR; tel. 01582 602242; e-mail: librarian@sbhs.org.uk

Open: By arrangement only.

Access: Generally open to the public, by appointment.

The Strict Baptist Historical Society was formed in 1960 to promote an interest in the history and stand for Scriptural truth maintained by Strict Baptists, and also to bring into being a central repository where material of historical interest connected with the rise and growth of Strict Baptists can be preserved. The society's library contains a considerable number of documents of historical interest. A catalogue and photocopying are available. An *Annual Bulletin* and *Newsletter* of the Society are published.

308 Durham Cathedral Dean and Chapter Library

Address: The College, Durham DH1 3E

Telephone: (0191) 386 2489

E-mail: r.c.norris@durham.ac.uk

Enquiries: The Deputy Librarian, Mr Roger Norris

Open: Mon–Fri: 9.00–1.00, 2.15–5.00. Closed for the whole of August.

Access: Bona fide students; references are required, with means of identification.

Historical background: The cathedral library of the Dean and Chapter of Durham descends in direct historic continuity from the library of the Benedictine house (f. 10th century in Durham), which was dissolved in 1540 and then changed into a capitular foundation of a dean and 12 residentiaries. The cathedral archives are held by the University of Durham (see entry 311), which also supplies professional assistance to the library.

Major collections: Extensive collection of medieval MSS (see 'Publications' below).
Papers include those of the following: I.T. Ramsey, Bishop of Durham, 1966–72; General Synod, i.e. Liturgical Commission, 1960s–

1970s; J.B. Lightfoot, Bishop of Durham, 1879–89; H.H. Henson, Bishop of Durham, 1920–39. Parochial clergy correspondence, c1895–1910.
Antiquarian collections of the following: Christopher Hunter (1675–1757); Thomas Randall, headmaster, Durham School, 1761–8; George Allan (1736–1800); Robert Surtees (1779–1834); Sir Cuthbert Sharp (1781–1849); James Raine (1791–1858).
Music MSS, early 17th–19th centuries.

Non-manuscript material: Extensive iconographic material, including photographs, negatives and engravings.

Finding aids: Card indexes. Henson: NRA 28047.

Facilities: Photography by arrangement.

Conservation: Contracted out.

Publications: Sir Roger Mynors: *Durham Cathedral Manuscripts* (1939).
N.R. Ker: *Monastic Libraries in Great Britain* (1964; supplement, 1987).

309 Durham County Record Office

Parent organisation: Durham County Council

Address: County Hall, Durham DH1 5UL

Telephone: (0191) 383 3253/3474

Fax: (0191) 383 4500

E-mail: record.office@durham.gov.uk

Website: www.durham.gov.uk

Enquiries: The County Archivist, Miss J. Gill

Open: Mon, Tues, Thurs: 8.45–4.45; Wed: 8.45–8.00; Fri: 8.45–4.15.

Access: Generally open to the public, by appointment. Documents required for Wednesday evening and Saturday morning must be ordered by the previous day.

Historical background: The office was established in 1961 to cover the whole county; no archive service had existed previously. The department moved to its new building in 1964. It also acts as the Diocesan Record Office for Durham (parish records), and is recognised as a place of deposit for public records. The Darlington branch office was closed in 1991.

Acquisitions policy: Records of institutions and individuals in the areas administered by

Durham County Council and Darlington Borough Council.

Archives of organisation: Records of Durham County Council, 1889– , and its predecessors, 16th century– .

Major collections: Deposited local collections, including the following which have a wider significance:
Londonderry records: estate and business papers, including those relating to Seaham Harbour and coal interests in east Durham, family and personal papers.
Strathmore records: estate records and records relating to 'Grand Allies' and the development of the Durham coalfield in the 18th century.
National Coal Board records: pre- and post-nationalisation records.

Non-manuscript material: OS plans for pre-1974 county, 1856–1939; photographs (c30,000).

Finding aids: Typescript catalogues, all sent to NRA; database of total holdings of the Office.

Facilities: Photocopying. Self-service photocopying from microfilm. Colour-photocopying and photography by arrangement. Microfilm/fiche readers. Microfilming in-house.

Conservation: Facilities for conservation available in-house; outside work undertaken on a limited basis.

Publications: W.A.L. Seaman: *Durham County Reecord Office* (1969).
Londonderry Papers: Catalogue of Documents … (1969).
Free handlists, and guides for certain classes of records; list available on request.

310 St John's College Archives

Address: 3 South Bailey, Durham DH1 3RJ

Telephone: (0191) 374 3579

Fax: (0191) 374 3573

Website: www.dur.ac.uk

Enquiries: The Librarian, Dr M. Bonnington

Open: By prior arrangement.

Access: Approved readers, on written application; an appointment is necessary.

St John's College was founded in 1909 as an independent but constituent college of the

University of Durham. The college archives have grown, almost accidentally, with the collection of various documents, including MSS and photographs, associated with the college and with members of staff. Among these are a collection of sermons by Canon Gouldsmith and dissertations of the Bernard Gilpin Society. There is a TS list available.

311 University of Durham Library
Archives and Special Collections

Address: Palace Green, Durham DH1 3RN

Telephone: (0191) 374 3202/3003; (0191) 374 3610 (Durham Cathedral Muniments)

Fax: (0191) 374 3002

E-mail: pg.library@durham.ac.uk

Website: www.dur.ac.uk/library/asc

Enquiries: The Sub-Librarian (Special Collections), Miss E.M. Rainey

Open: Term: Mon, Fri: 9.00–5.00; Tues–Thurs: 9.00–6.00; Sat: 10.00–1.00.
Vacation: Mon–Fri: 9.00–5.00.
Advance notice is advisable for all collections, and essential for Durham Cathedral Muniments and associated collections, which are located in a separate building nearby, access to which is by prior arrangement only.

Access: Generally open to the public. Proof of identity is essential.

Historical background: The University Library, founded in 1833, incorporates Bishop Cosin's Library, founded in 1668. Until 1963 it was the only official archive repository in County Durham apart from Gateshead Borough Library. Its department of Archives and Special Collections was founded in 1990 by a merger of its Special Collections with the Department of Palaeography and Diplomatic. The latter had been established in 1948 under a joint scheme of Durham University and the Dean and Chapter of Durham Cathedral for the care of archives, mainly from the northern counties, and for the promotion of the study of MS material. It is recognised as a place of deposit for public records. Russian Research Collection materials, reflecting Russian history and society of the late 19th and early 20th centuries, have been transferred to the library.

Acquisitions policy: Material relating to the library's existing collections or relevant to the university's research interests and teaching. Material relating to North-East England or connected with the Palatinate, Diocese, Cathedral, County, City and University of Durham, co-ordinating policy in this area with Durham Cathedral Dean and Chapter Library and Durham County Record Office (entry 309); political papers of national and international significance but with a local connection; the Sudan during the Condominium period, 1899–1955; modern literary MSS; hymnology.

Archives of organisation: Some central administrative records of the university, and some records of its colleges and student societies, 19th–20th centuries. Records and correspondence of the University Observatory (astronomical, meteorological and seismological), 1838–c1957.

Major collections: Archives of institutions and jurisdictions, solicitors' accumulations, and deeds groups.
Durham Cathedral Dean and Chapter Muniments: archives of Durham Cathedral, monastic to 1539, and its estate, and associated collections, including Church Commission deposits, 11th–20th centuries.
Durham diocesan records and associated collections; central administrative archives, 15th–20th centuries.
Durham diocesan probate records, 1540–1857, and registered copies of wills for Co. Durham only, 1858–1940.
Church Commission deposits of Durham Bishopric financial and estate records, 15th–20th centuries.
Durham Bishopric Halmote Court (copyhold) records, 16th–20th centuries, and other manorial records, including Chester Deanery, 16th–20th centuries, chiefly 20th century; and Weardale Chest Papers (Forest of Weardale and Stanhope Park, Co. Durham), 16th–17th centuries.
Durham Palatinate Records: some enclosure records, 17th–19th centuries, and other records of the Durham Chancery court, chiefly c1880–1920; and Durham Prothonotary records, chiefly writs and other legal and financial papers, 17th–19th centuries. (Most Durham Palatinate records are in the Public Record Office, entry 1058).
Durham City Guild records, 16th–20th centuries, and a few Freemen's records, 1754–1813.

Land tax records: Co. Durham townships, 1780s–20th century.

Solicitors' papers, and deed groups, including Booth and Lazenby papers, chiefly 19th–early 20th centuries; Clayton and Gibson papers, including Marquess of Bute and Clavering deeds, 16th–19th centuries; Dixon-Johnson deeds, 17th–19th centuries; Eden papers, 13th–20th centuries; Greenslade deeds, mainly Co. Durham, 15th–19th centuries; Spennymore Settlement papers, 1930–62.

Antiquarian collections, especially Durham Palatinate and its courts, 13th–20th centuries, including Mickleton & Spearman MSS; Old University MSS; Surtees Raine MSS; Hogg MS including papers of Thomas Hogg (d 1776) of Norton, Co. Durham, land agent; and papers of Robert Blair (1845–1923); Clifton William Gibby (1902–89); and Christophe Roy Hudleston (1905–92).

Family, estate and political papers including: Backhouse Papers: personal and business papers of a Quaker banking family, and of related families, including the Gurneys of Norwich, chiefly 18th–20th centuries.

Baker Baker Papers: family, estate, and business papers of the Baker family of Crook Hall, Durham City, and Elemore Hall, Pittington, Co. Durham, including material on the Boulby alum works near Saltburn, North Yorks, 16th–20th centuries.

Clavering family of Greencroft, letters and papers, 15th–19th centuries, including papers on the 1715 Jacobite rebellion in the North-East.

Cookson family papers, particularly illustrating their business and industrial interests on Tyneside, 18th–20th centuries.

Duff family papers, chiefly papers of Sir James Fitzjames Duff (1898–1970).

Earl Grey Papers: political, private and estate papers of the Greys of Howick, 18th–20th centuries, including papers of John, Viscount Ponsonby (c1770–1855), Evelyn Baring, 1st Earl of Cromer (1841–1917), and Evelyn Baring, 1st Baron Howick of Glendale (1903–73).

Headlam and Headlam-Morley family papers, 18th–20th centuries.

Howard of Naworth Papers: Cumbrian and Northumberland estate records of the Howard of Naworth family (Earls of Carlisle), including some records of their Dacre predecessors, and papers of Lady Aurea Macleod (1884–1972), 12th–20th centuries.

Lawson Papers: literary drafts and some political papers of John James (Jack) Lawson, Baron Lawson (1881–1965), miners' leader and cabinet minster.

Ord of Sandys Hall, Sedgefield, deeds and estate papers, 1606–1858.

Shafto (Beamish) Papers: deeds, estate papers and colliery accounts of estates successively owned by the Davison, Eden and Shafto families, 15th–20th centuries.

Shipperdson Papers: personal and estate papers and colliery accounts of the Hopper and Shipperdson families of Murton and Pittington, Co. Durham.

Thorp Correspondence, 1831–62: letters and papers of Charles Thorp (1783–1862), first Warden of the university.

Wharton of Old Park papers, letters and diaries, including Grand Tour correspondence, 18th–19th centuries.

Ecclesiastical papers:

Cosin Letter-Books: correspondence, 1593–1686, of John Cosin (1594–1672), Bishop of Durham, Isaac Basire (1607–76), Archdeacon of Northumberland, and other northern churchmen.

Jabez Bunting (1779–1858), Methodist minister: 20th-century transcripts of his correspondence, 1799–1858.

Middle and Far East Collections:

Abbas Hilmi II Papers: official, personal and estate papers, 1892–1944, of Abbas Hilmi II (1874–1944), Khedive of Egypt, 1892–1914; also includes letters of Ibrahim Pasha (1789–1848), eldest son of Muhammad Ali Pasha, Viceroy of Egypt, relating to his military campaigns in Syria in the 1830s and 1840s.

Papers of Sir Donald Hawley (b 1921), barrister and diplomat, covering his career in the Sudan Political Service and later postings in Gulf states, Cairo, Lago, Baghdad and Malaysia.

Working papers of Thomas Muir Johnstone (1924–83) on modern South Arabian languages, with sound recordings of a number, including Mehri, Socotri, Harusi and Jibbali.

Papers of Malcolm John MacDonald (1901–81), cabinet minister, colonial governor and diplomat, covering all periods of his life, including his service in Canada, Africa and the Far East.

Sudan Archive: official, semi-official and private papers of officials, soldiers, businessmen, missionaries, and many others who served or lived in the Sudan, 1899–1956. Also includes some material of the Mahdist period and substantial quantities of papers relating to countries bordering on the Sudan. Includes papers of

Sir Reginald Wingate (1861–1953), Sir Rudolf Baron Slatin (1875–1932), Sir Gilbert Clayton (1875–1929), Sir Harold MacMichael (1882–1969), Sir James Robertson (1899–1983), and the papers of the Gordon Memorial College Trust Fund and more than 300 smaller collections. Working papers of Eric Watkins, foreign correspondent, on the Yemen, 1990–94.

Oriental MSS: miscellaneous MSS of oriental interest (literary, linguistic, travel, etc), principal languages Arabic, Persian, Turkish, Pali, Chinese, Japanese and English.

Literary and musical collections:

Abbott Literary MSS and Papers, including MSS of John Wolcot (Peter Pindar), George Darley, the Rossetti family, letters of G.M. Hopkins to Coventry Patmore, MSS and correspondence of Edward Thomas, and letters of Gordon Bottomley.

Basil Bunting (1900–85), poet, multi-media archive.

Cosin MSS, theological, liturgical, historical, medical, scientific and culinary MSS books, 11th–19th centuries, but predominantly medieval.

Papers of William Plomer (1903–74), novelist, poet and librettist, with much literary correspondence, including letters from Benjamin Britten, E.M. Forster, Christopher Isherwood, Edith and Osbert Sitwell, Stephen Spender.

Porter Correspondence: literary papers and letters of William Ogilvie, Jane, Anna Maria, and Sir Robert Ker Porter, 1790s–1847.

Pratt Green MSS, 18th–20th centuries: hymns, tunes, papers of hymnologists and hymn writers, including John Wilson (1905–92) and H.C.A. Gaunt (1902–30).

Autograph scores of three early chamber works of Dame Ethel Smyth (1858–1944).

Scientific papers: astronomical papers of Thomas Wright (1711–80) of Byers Green, Co. Durham.

Records of learned societies: Architectural and Archaeological Society of Durham & Northumberland, 19th–20th centuries; Cremation Society of Great Britain, 19th–20th centuries; Surtees Society, 19th–20th centuries.

Scholars' papers, including papers of Louis Allen (1922–91), military historian and Japanologist; Karl William Britton (1909–83), philosopher; Frank Byron Jevons (1858–1936), philosopher; Wilhelm Levison (1876–1947), historian; Peter Willis (b 1933), architectural and landscape historian.

Non-manuscript material: Sudan Archive: photographs (c40,000), maps, cine films, museum objects, and a large quantity of related printed material.

Plans, photographs and slides of the restoration of Durham Castle, 1920–39.

Edis and Gibby collections of negatives, lantern slides and photographic prints, principally of buildings, places and people in Co. Durham, 19th–20th centuries.

Extensive collections of early and rare printed books.

Durham County parliamentary election poll-books and contest literature in pamphlet and broadside form, with some MS material, 1675–1874.

Playbills for City of Durham theatres, 1769–1859.

Maps of Co. Durham and towns and areas within it, 16th–20th centuries.

Local Collection (covering Co. Durham, Northumberland, Cumbria, North Yorks) of periodicals, pamphlets, directories and books.

Coins of the Durham mint, Henry II–Bishop Tunstall (Bishop of Durham, 1530–59).

Finding aids: Various lists, indexes, catalogues and calendars. Lists sent to NRA. Collection-level descriptions and numerous detailed finding aids available on the website.

Facilities: Photocopying. Photostat camera. Photography. Microfilming. Beta-radiography. Microform readers. Ultra-violet lamp. Video-spectral comparator. Cold light source. Video and audio playback facilities.

Conservation: In-house conservation workshop. Outside work not normally undertaken.

Publications: Durham University Library Archives and Special Collections Introductory Guide [free].

Muniments of the Dean and Chapter of Durham Cathedral: an Introductory Guide [free].

Sudanese Studies at Durham: a Guide to Resources [free]

Summary Guide to the Sudan Archive.

Numerous lists of individual collections. A list of publications is available.

312 Ushaw College Library

Address: Ushaw College, Durham DH7 9RH

Website: www.dur.ac.uk/ushaw/about_ushaw/research.htm

Enquiries: The Librarian, Dr A.J. MacGregor

Open: By arrangement.

Access: Bona fide scholars, by prior written appointment only.

Historical background: Ushaw College is a direct descendant of the English College in Douai, France (1568–1793), and its archives cover the Roman Catholic history of Northern England from c1700. In 1971, when the English College in Lisbon closed, its archives and MSS were moved to Ushaw College.

Acquisitions policy: Acquires, by gift or loan, documents relevant to English Roman Catholic history.

Archives of organisation: College archives, including MSS from Douai, 1794– .

Major collections: Lisbon Collection: extensive archives of the English College in Lisbon, 1628–1973, and its MSS collections, including correspondence of Bishop Richard Russell (1630–93) and papers of the Jorge and Donovan families relating to Anglo-Portuguese trade, 19th century.

Letters of John Lingard (1781–1851), historian, 1840s; and Cardinal Nicholas Wiseman (1802–65).

Smaller collections of 19th-century letters, including those of Cardinal John Newman (1801- 90).

44 medieval MSS.

Non-manuscript material: Books and pamphlets, particularly strong on Roman Catholic theology, church history and English recusancy (50,000).

Finding aids: Card catalogues. Lisbon College archives: NRA 29239. Ushaw College, archives and MSS: NRA 13674. Other lists in preparation.

Publications: M. Sharratt: 'The Lisbon Collection at Ushaw', *Northern Catholic History*, 8 (1973), 30–34.

——: 'Lisbon College Register 1628–1813', *Catholic Record Society*, 72 (1991).

Articles, principally in the *Ushaw Magazine*, 1891–1994.

313 South Lanarkshire Archives & Information Management Service

Parent organisation: South Lanarkshire Council

Address: 30 Hawbank Road, College Milton North, East Kilbride, Lanarkshire G74 5EX

Telephone: (01355) 239193

Fax: (01355) 242365

Website: www.southlanarkshire.gov.uk/gateway.htm

Enquiries: The Archivist, Mr Francis A. Rankin

Open: Mon–Thurs: 9.00–12.30, 1.30–4.45; Fri: 9.00–12.30, 1.30–4.15. An appointment is essential.

Access: Generally open to the public.

Historical background: South Lanarkshire Council was vested in 1996 under the Local Government (Scotland) Act 1994. The new authority covers the area previously administered by Hamilton District Council, East Kilbride District Council, Clydesdale District Council and a part of what was formerly Glasgow District. The Archives & Information Management Service developed out of a records management section established by the East Kilbride Development Corporation. The first appointment of a professional archivist was in 1997. The service currently operates from the Record Centre pending the development of an archival repository. Some council archives are currently managed by South Lanarkshire Council Libraries at Hamilton Central Library (entry 423). The archives of Lanark County Council, 1720–1975, and Rutherglen Burgh Council, 1323–1975, remain for the time being at Glasgow City Archives (entry 387) .

Acquisitions policy: To select, acquire and preserve the archives of South Lanarkshire Council and its predecessors, and companies, organisations and individuals within the community of South Lanarkshire.

Archives of organisation: Records of South Lanarkshire Council, 1996– ; Hamilton, East Kilbride and Clydesdale District Councils, 1974–96; East Kilbride Development Corporation, 1947–95; East Kilbride Burgh Council, 1963–75; Hamilton Burgh Council (part), (1943–75).

Major collections: Lawrie & Symington, live-stock and agricultural auctioneers; Lanark Keith & Patrick, solicitors, Hamilton.

Non-manuscript material: Architectural drawings and photographic library of East Kilbride Development Corporation, 1947–95.

Finding aids: Full lists available in the search room. Copies sent to NRAS.

Facilities: Photocopying. Photography and colour photocopying by arrangement. Microfilm readers.

Conservation: Contracted out.

314   North London Collegiate School

Parent organisation: Frances Mary Buss Foundation

Address: Canons, Edgware, Middlesex HA8 7RJ

Telephone: (020) 8952 0912

Fax: (020) 8951 1391

E-mail: office@nlcs.harrow.sch.uk

Website: www.nlcs.harrow.sch.uk

Enquiries: The School Archivist, Mrs Karen Morgan

Open: Term: by arrangement only.

Access: Bona fide researchers, and pupils and ex-pupils of the school, by appointment.

Historical background: The school was founded in 1850 by Frances Mary Buss (1827–94), with the assistance of her parents and brothers, in the family house in Camden Town. From the beginning it aimed to give girls an education that would fit them for professional life, with a strong academic bias. The school was later divided into an upper and lower school, the latter eventually becoming the Camden School for Girls, now separately run by the local authority. NLCS moved gradually to Edgware from 1929, and in 1938 it became a direct grant school. Today it still occupies Canons, the 18th-century home of James Brydges, Duke of Chandos, and is an independent school.

Acquisitions policy: To maintain the archive.

Archives of organisation: Admissions registers, 1870– ; governors' minutes; headmistresses' reports; and school magazine, 1876– .

Major collections: Letter-book of Cassandra, wife of James Brydges, 18th century.
Correspondence of Frances Mary Buss and contemporaries.
Records of the early progress of women's education.

Non-manuscript material: Photographs, paintings and sketchbooks of R.W. Buss, artist.
Works by Old North Londoners and past headmistresses.

Finding aids: Database in progress.

Facilities: Photocopying.

Publications: The North London Collegiate School 1850–1950: Essays in Honour of the Centenary of the Mary Buss Foundation (Oxford, 1950).
North London Collegiate School 1850–2000 (forthcoming).
M. Keightley: *Canons* (1985).
School magazine (annual).

315   Bank of Scotland Archives

Address: 12 Bankhead, Crossway South, Sighthill, Edinburgh EH11 4EN

Telephone: (0131) 529 1288/1305

Fax: (0131) 529 1307

E-mail: archives@bankofscotland.co.uk

Website: www.bankofscotland.co.uk

Enquiries: The Deputy Archivist, Helen Redmond-Cooper
The Assistant Archivist, Seonaid McDonald

Open: By appointment only.

Access: No access to customer records less than 100 years old or to others less than 50 years old without special permission. The bank reserves the right to refuse access.

Historical background: The Bank of Scotland was founded by Act of Parliament of Scotland in 1695. It absorbed the Caledonian Bank in 1907, the Union Bank of Scotland in 1955 and the British Linen Bank in 1971. The Bank has an extensive branch network in Scotland and the right to issue its own bank notes.

Acquisitions policy: Main acquisitions arise as part of the records management programme: only identified strays or items which are directly relevant to the bank's history. Material outside these areas will be acquired only after consultation with NRAS and the National Library of Scotland (entry 331).

Archives of organisation: Archives of the Bank of Scotland, 1695– , and of all banks that are part of the group and its predecessors, including Union Bank of Scotland, 1830–1954; and British Linen Bank, 1746–1971.

Non-manuscript material: Pictures, silver coins, bank-notes, firearms and banking memorabilia housed in the bank museum.

Finding aids: NRAS 945 and 1110 (in process of recataloguing).

Facilities: Photocopying. Photography. Microfilm reader by arrangement.

Conservation: Contracted out.

Publications: R.S. Rait: *The History of the Union Bank of Scotland* (Glasgow, 1930).
C.A. Malcolm: *The Bank of Scotland, 1695–1945* (1946).
——: *The British Linen Bank* (1950).
C.S. Checkland: *Scottish Banking: a History, 1695–1975* (Glasgow, 1975).
C.W. Munn: *The Scottish Provincial Banking Companies* (Edinburgh, 1981).
N. Tamaki: *The Life Cycle of the Union Bank of Scotland 1830–1954* (1983).
R.S. Saville: *The Bank of Scotland, 1695–1996* (Edinburgh, 1995).
A. Cameron: *Scotland's First Bank: an Illustrated History* (Mainstream, 1995).
A. Cameron: *Bank of Scotland 1695–1995: a Very Singular Institution* (Edinburgh, 1995).
R. Saville: *Bank of Scotland: a History, 1695–1995* (Edinburgh, 1996).

Historical background: The Geological Survey Office in Scotland was set up in 1867, although mapping had started in 1854. It holds MS, graphic and photographic material of the British Geological Survey and its predecessors, the Geological Survey of Great Britain and the Institute of Geological Sciences, relating to the geological land survey of Scotland. The archival material, comprising some 25,000 items, is included as part of the wider national geoscience record collection available for reference at BGS Edinburgh. See also British Geological Survey Library Keyworth, Nottingham (entry 483), for central administrative archives.

Acquisitions policy: To add to the existing collection in pursuance of the survey's role as a repository for national geological archives.

Archives of organisation: The survey's own archives, which include correspondence, registered files, papers, photographs and field observations, notably official notebooks of Geological Survey staff.

Major collections: Plans of abandoned mines (other than coal and oil shale), c1872– , held on behalf of the Health and Safety Executive, and non-coal mine plans and company borehole journal books, c1800-c1950, deposited by NCB/British Coal.

Non-manuscript material: Photographs (c10,000) and mine plans (c2000).

Finding aids: Lists of holdings and on-line database index.

Facilities: Photocopying. Photography.

Conservation: Contracted out.

316 British Geological Survey
National Geological Records Centre

Address: Murchison House, West Mains Road, Edinburgh EH9 3LA

Telephone: (0131) 650 0307

Fax: (0131) 667 2785

E-mail: r.gillanders@bgs.ac.uk

Enquiries: The Records Officer, Mr Richard Gillanders

Open: Mon–Thurs: 9.00–5.00; Fri: 9.00–4.30.

Access: Generally open to the public, by appointment only.

317 Chartered Institute of Bankers in Scotland

Address: 38B Drumshau, Edinburgh EH3 7SW

Telephone: (0131) 473 7777

Fax: (0131) 473 7788

Website: www.ciobs.org

Enquiries: The Chief Executive, Dr C.W. Munn

Open: Mon–Fri: 9.00–1.00; 2.00–5.00.

Access: Bona fide researchers, by appointment.

The institute was founded in 1875 and maintains a collection of Scottish banking documents. The library has a special collection of banking histories.

318 Edinburgh Central Library

Parent organisation: Edinburgh City Libraries and Information Services

Address: George IV Bridge, Edinburgh EH1 1EG

Telephone: (0131) 225 5584

Fax: (0131) 242 8009

Enquiries: Edinburgh Room: The Principal Library Officer, Ann Nix
Fine Art Library: The Principal Library Officer, Hil Williamson
Music Library: The Principal Library Officer, Martina McChrystal
Scottish Library: The Principal Library Officer, Fiona Myles

Open: Mon–Thurs: 10.00–8.00, Fri: 10.00–5.00; Sat: 9.00–1.00.

Access: Generally open to the public. Restrictions on certain categories of fragile materials.

Historical background: Edinburgh Public Libraries opened in 1890 with a reference library, newsroom and home reading library serving the City of Edinburgh. The Edinburgh Room, Fine Art Library and Music Library were opened in the 1930s and the Scottish Library in 1960.

Acquisitions policy: Edinburgh Room: maintains a comprehensive collection of printed material on the city past and present. This is supplemented by manuscripts, illustrative material etc as appropriate.
Scottish Library: print and non-print material covering the life, history and culture of Scotland.
Music Library: items with local and regional interest, including recordings.

Archives of organisation: Substantial collection of material relating to Edinburgh City Library, including correspondence, minutes, publications, catalogues, 1890– .

Major collections: Edinburgh Room: records of local organisations, including school logbooks, school board minutes and correspondence, account books, minutes (c1000 items).
Music Library: Edinburgh Music Society minutes, 1728–95, and index to music.

Non-manuscript material: Edinburgh Room: broadsides, including playbills, political broadsides, acts and proclamations, ballads (c2200). Microfilm copies of census returns and parish registers.
Large collection of press cuttings.
Maps and plans, 16th century– (c2800).
Prints and drawings, excellent for costume and architecture (c10,000).
Photographs, including large callotype collection from the 1840s of the work of D.O. Hill and Robert Adamson, and Dr Thomas Keith (c12,000).
Films and tapes.
Scottish Library: large collection of press cuttings. Significant collection of family history material, including more than 1000 published family histories.
Extensive map and print collections, 17th century– .
Parish registers and census returns for the Lothians, Borders, Dumfries and Galloway, Ayrshire, Stirlingshire, Clackmannanshire, Kinrosshire, Shetland, Orkney, Caithness and Sutherland.
Photographs (c1000), negatives (c950), and lantern slides (c1700), including Dr I.F. Grant's Highland Folklife Collection, and the Dr Thomas Keith Collection, 1855–6
Fine Art Library: Dyer Collection of Japanese watercolour paintings, prints, photographs and books.
Press cuttings on Scottish art, architecture and design.
Music Library: extensive collection of programmes relating to local musical events, early 19th century– ; Scottish music, late 18th century– .

Finding aids: Edinburgh Room: most MSS and older material accessible only through card catalogue and manual indexes; more recent acquisitions included in computerised catalogue. Separate indexes of press cuttings, illustrations, broadsides.
Scottish Library: Various catalogues and indexes available.

Facilities: Photocopying. Photography available. Microfilm/fiche readers/printers. Laser copying.

Conservation: Contracted out.

319 Edinburgh City Archives

Parent organisation: The City of Edinburgh Council

Address: Department of Corporate Services, City Chambers, 247 High Street, Edinburgh EH1 1YJ

Telephone: (0131) 529 4616

Fax: (0131) 529 4957

Enquiries: The City Archivist, Mr Richard Hunter

Open: Mon–Thurs: 9.00–1.00, 2.00–4.30; Fri: phone enquiries only.

Access: Generally open to the public; prior consultation is advisable.

Historical background: The City Archives, as the official local repository for the City of Edinburgh, house the bulk of the historic and administrative records of the burgh.

Acquisitions policy: Primary official and non-official records relating to the area of the present authority, its predecessor bodies and all associated organisations.

Archives of organisation: Usual local authority record holdings, 14th century– , with the major part of the holdings relating to the period after 1700.
Edinburgh Town Council minutes, 1551–1975; City of Edinburgh District Council minutes, 1975– ; Edinburgh Dean of Guild plans, 1762–1975; building control plans, 1975– ; register of Burgesses and Guildbrethren, 1487–1955; Edinburgh Valuation Roll survey books, c1850–1975; Burgh Court records, 1900–74; Edinburgh Police Commissioners minutes, 1805–60; Edinburgh Parochial Board, 1845–1900; Edinburgh Parish Council, 1893–1930; Leith Dean of Guild Court, 1870–1920; Edinburgh and Leith Police, c1840–1970; Incorporation of Hammermen of Edinburgh, 1494–1963; Edinburgh Extent and Annuity Rolls, 1580–1833; Canongate Jail records, 1750–1840; Incorporation of Bakers of Edinburgh, 1522–1947; Incorporation of United and Incorporated Trades of St Mary's Chapel, 1669–1910; Edinburgh Chamber of Commerce, 1785–1971.

Major collections: Substantial records relating to other bodies, principally those closely associated with the civic authorities, such as the Burgh of the Canongate, Trinity Hospital, the Convention of Royal Burghs of Scotland, Lothian Region Transport and the Royal High School, but also including the Scottish Modern Art Association, several Episcopal congregations, Bell and Bradfute (booksellers) and early administrative records of Edinburgh University.

Non-manuscript material: Significant holdings of architectural plans and drawings, from the Dean of Guild to the surviving records of the City Archivist and City Engineer, 18th–20th centuries.

Finding aids: Survey lists of some 40 per cent of the holdings now available. Lists sent to NRAS.

Facilities: Photocopying.

Conservation: Contracted out.

320 Edinburgh College of Art

Address: Lauriston Place, Edinburgh EH3 9DF

Telephone: (0131) 221 6040 (Secretary); 451 3219 (Archivist)

Fax: (0131) 221 6041 (Secretary); 451 3164 (Archivist)

E-mail: m.wood@geordi.eca.ac.uk; a.e.jones@hw.ac.uk

Website: www.eca.ac.uk

Enquiries: The Secretary, Mr Michael Wood
The Archivist, Ms Ann Jones

Open: By arrangement with the Archivist.

Access: Bona fide researchers, by appointment. Access is currently provided by the Archivist at Heriot-Watt University (see entry 325).

Historical background: Prior to the establishment of Edinburgh College of Art, art education in Edinburgh was divided between four institutions. The Board of Manufacturers Drawing Academy, founded in 1760 to promote the art of drawing for the use of manufacture; the School of Applied Art, founded in 1892 under the direction of Sir Rowand Anderson; the Royal Scottish Academy Life School, which opened in 1859; and the Art Department of Heriot-Watt College, founded in 1877 to provide artistic training for technical education. In 1906 the Town Council of Edinburgh was invited by the Scottish Education Department to establish and maintain a School of Art to take over responsibility for the higher art education in Edinburgh, and to serve as a central institution for the south-east of Scotland. The resulting institution was Edinburgh College of Art, founded in 1907, which is now an associated college of Heriot-Watt University.

Cataloguing of the archive has been supported by a project of the Scottish Higher Education Funding Council under the Non-Formula Funding Specialised Research Collections in the Humanities Initiative, 1995–99. Some archives of the Board of Manufacturers Drawing Academy and the School of Applied Art will be found in the National Archives of Scotland (see entry 329).

Acquisitions policy: To strengthen collections relating to the history and development of the institution and its predecessors, and the artists, staff and students associated with them.

Archives of organisation: Records relating to governance, administration, finance, teaching, research and the staff and students of Edinburgh College of Art, 1907– ; some records of the College's predecessors: Board of Manufacturers School of Art, 1869–1908; and the School of Applied Arts, 1892–1904.

Major collections: Collections relating to past staff and students of the college, including records of Charles J. McCall and Kenneth and Elizabeth Balmain.

Non-manuscript material: Edinburgh College of Art Photographic Collection, 1880s–1980s. The School of Drawing and Painting Collection of student art works (c3000 items).

Finding aids: Full descriptive catalogue.

Facilities: Photocopying. Microfilm readers.

Publications: Guide to the Collections (1999).

321 Fettes College

Address: Carrington Road, Edinburgh, Lothian EH4 1QX

Telephone: (0131) 332 2281

Fax: (0131) 332 3081

E-mail: enquiries@fettes.com

Website: www.fettes.com

Enquiries: The Hon. Archivist

Open: By arrangement only.

Access: Bona fide researchers, by appointment.

Historical background: The college was founded in 1870 under the terms of the will of Sir William Fettes, Bart., of Comely Bank and Redcastle (1750–1836): 'It is my intention that the residue of my whole Estate should form an Endowment for the maintenance, education and outfit of young people whose parents have either died without leaving sufficient funds for that purpose, or who from innocent misfortune during their lives, are unable to give suitable education to their children.' The college is a co-educational boarding school.

Acquisitions policy: Records relating directly to the history of the college and to prominent Old Fettesians.

Archives of organisation: School records.
Minutes of meetings of Governors of the Fettes Trust.

Non-manuscript material: Photographs, plans, maps.
Portraits.
Selwyn-Lloyd Memorial Library.

Publications: A Hundred Years of Fettes (1970).
R. Philip: *A Keen Wind Blows: the Story of Fettes College* (1998).

322 Free Church College

Address: The Mound, Edinburgh EH1 2LS

Telephone: (0131) 226 4978

Fax: (0131) 220 0597

Website: www.freechurch.org

Enquiries: The Hon. Librarian

Open: Mon–Fri: 8.45–4.45.

Access: Approved readers, on written application.

Historical background: The college became the Free Church College in continuity from New College, subsequent to the reorganisation of the Free Church College and Offices by the Executive Commission after the emergence of the United Free Church in 1900. The building originally comprised luxury flats occupied by leading notables of Edinburgh society. Kirk Session and Presbytery records are deposited in the National Archives of Scotland (entry 329); finance papers, 1848–1910, are deposited in the National Library of Scotland (entry 331).

Major collections: Many documents of historical and antiquarian significance, relating mainly to the Scottish Church.

Non-manuscript material: Portraits of leading Scottish churchmen; D.O. Hill's famous painting 'The First Free Church General Assembly', 1843.
Celtic library, housed in Senate Hall.

Finding aids: Lists of archives. NRA 23336.

Facilities: Photocopying by arrangement.

323 General Register Office for Scotland

Address: New Register House, Edinburgh EH1 3YT

Telephone: (0131) 334 0380

Fax: (0131) 314 4400

E-mail: records@gro-scotland.gov.uk

Website: www.open.gov.uk/gros/groshome.htm

Enquiries: The Registrar General, Mr James Meldrum

Open: Mon–Fri: 9.00–4.30.

Access: Records are available in microform to the public on payment of a fee (list of charges available). Advance booking recommended. Pay-per-view searching of historical indexes over 100 years old is available on-line at www.origins.net.

Historical background: The office was established in 1855 on the introduction of compulsory registration of births, deaths and marriages in Scotland. New Register House was designed by Robert Mathieson, an assistant surveyor of HM Office of Works. The office provides a facility for record searching thought to be unique in the UK, housing under one roof the old parochial registers, the statutory registers and open census records.

Acquisitions policy: Intake of statutory or closely allied material only.

Archives of organisation: Statutory registers of births, deaths and marriages, 1855– .
Open census records, 1841–91.
Minor records of births, deaths and marriages registered abroad, 1855– (Scottish nationals only).

Major collections: Parish records of Church of Scotland, 1553–1854 (incomplete).
Miscellaneous records relating to pre-1855 events, including some irregular border marriages.

Non-manuscript material: Microfilm/fiche of records.
Registrar General's published weekly, monthly, quarterly and annual reports, 1855– .
Published census reports, 1841–1991.

Finding aids: Statutory registers: computer indexes. Parochial registers: computer indexes to births and baptisms; marriages and proclamations of marriages; a few paper death indexes. Open census records: street indexes for larger towns; computer indexes for census years 1881 and 1891. Minor records: index. Miscellaneous privately-produced publications for 1841 to 1871 census years.

Facilities: 100 search places, each with computer terminal and microfiche reader.

Conservation: Contracted out.

Publications: Registrar General's Annual Report.
Information leaflets (including guidance for family historians).
List of Registration Districts.
Family tree chart of Scotland, 1855– .
Guide to using the computer indexes.
Parish map guide.

324 Grand Lodge of Scotland

Address: Freemasons' Hall, 96 George Street, Edinburgh EH2 3DH

Telephone: (0131) 225 5304

Fax: (0131) 225 3953

E-mail: gsec@grandlodgescotland.org

Website: www.grandlodgescotland.org

Enquiries: The Grand Secretary

Open: Mon–Fri: 9.00–5.00, by arrangement.

Access: Bona fide scholars and anyone genuinely interested in freemasonry, by appointment.

Historical background: The Grand Lodge of Scotland of Ancient, Free and Accepted Masons was established in 1736.

Acquisitions policy: To maintain its own archives and those of other Scottish lodges, as appropriate.

Archives of organisation: Minutes, 1736–1893; cartulary and lists of lodges and members, 1736– ; registration books, 1799– ; statutes and ordnances of the masons of Scotland, 1598–9;

records of Aitcheson's Haven Lodge, 1598, 1738–1851.

Major collections: Miscellaneous lodge minutes, including Lodge of Scotland. Freemasons in Rome, 1735–7.

Non-manuscript material: Collection of masonic certificates.

Finding aids: NRAS 2612 (NRA 27749).

325 Heriot-Watt University Archive

A Riccarton Campus

Address: Riccarton, Edinburgh EH14 4AS

Telephone: (0131) 451 3218/3219

Fax: (0131) 451 3164

E-mail: a.e.jones@hw.ac.uk

Website: www.hw.ac.uk/archive

Enquiries: The University Archivist, Ms Ann Jones

Open: Mon–Fri: 9.30–4.45, by appointment. Other times by arrangement.

Access: Generally open to the public by appointment. Some institutional record series are closed for 30 years or longer at the discretion of the Archivist.

Historical background: The university's origins date from the Edinburgh School of Arts, founded in 1821 as the first Mechanics Institute set up to provide evening classes for skilled workers. In 1852 it incorporated the proceeds of a fund set up to provide an Edinburgh memorial to James Watt and thus became the Watt Institution and School of Arts. In 1885 it merged with the charitable trust founded by George Heriot in 1623 to become the Heriot-Watt College. From 1928 to 1966 it was an autonomous Scottish Central Institution, and in 1966 it became Heriot-Watt University. The University Archive was established as an administrative department in 1984 and is part of the University's Corporate Communication Division. The Scottish Brewing Archive (entry 398) formerly administered by Heriot-Watt University, is now in Glasgow.

Acquisitions policy: To strengthen existing collections on the history of the Heriot-Watt University and its Scottish Borders Campus, and the working lives of staff, students and other key individuals connected with the institution. The collection documents links with industry and the university's contribution to Scottish higher education, culture and the economy.

Archives of organisation: Records relating to governance, administration, finance, teaching, research, and the staff and students of the university, 1966– , and its predecessors: the Edinburgh School of Arts, 1821–52; the Watt Institution and School of Arts, 1852–85; Heriot-Watt College, 1885–1966.

Major collections: Gibson-Craig family and estate records of the Riccarton Estate and its owners, 15th–19th centuries.
James Watt Collection: records relating to James Watt, 1705–1990; business records of James Brown (employee of James Watt), 1817–63; Subscription Fund for the erection of a monument to James Watt in Edinburgh, 1824–54; the Watt Club (student organisation, now the University's Graduate Association), 1854– .
Papers of Sir Robert Blair (1859–1935), first Chief Education Officer of London County Council, 1904–24.
Leith Nautical College records, 1855–1987.
John Tweedie Collection: local history collection relating to Riccarton and the surrounding districts.

Non-manuscript material: Photographs, films, medals and awards, maps and plans, publications of the University and its predecessors (some maps form part of the Gibson-Craig papers).
The University Archive also manages the university's collection of works of art and historical artefacts.

Finding aids: Fonds, series and item-level descriptions. Index to calendars. Database access for Gibson-Craig, Sir Robert Blair and Leith Nautical College collections, some available on website.

Facilities: Photocopying. Photography by arrangement.

Conservation: Contracted out.

Publications: Heriot-Watt University: from Mechanics Institute to Technology University, 1821–1973 (1973).
L.A. Wallace: 1821–1992: Physics at Heriot-Watt University, Edinburgh (1993).
A. Anderson and B.G. Gowenlock: Chemistry in Heriot-Watt, 1821–1991 (1998).

Guide to the Collections (1999).
History of Heriot-Watt (forthcoming).
Various pamphlets.

B Scottish Borders Campus

Address: Nether Road, Galashiels TD1 3HF

Website: www.hw.ac.uk/sbc/archive/
archive.html

Open: By arrangement.

Historical background: Heriot-Watt University's Scottish Borders Campus traces its origins to technical classes organised by the Galashiels Manufacturers Corporation in textile design and the chemistry of dyeing, culminating in the establishment of the Galashiels Combined Technical School in 1883. In 1906 the school was renamed the South of Scotland Central Technical College. In 1922 the college was granted Central Institution status, and again was renamed as the Scottish Woollen Technical College. In 1965 the college moved to its site in Netherdale, Galashiels, and became the Scottish College of Textiles (SCOT). From 1989 SCOT constituted the Faculty of Textiles of Heriot-Watt University, and in 1998 SCOT merged with the university and became the Scottish Borders Campus of Heriot-Watt University.
The archive was initially established by members of the Design Department of SCOT. As a result the collection specialises in design records, detailing the Scottish Borders textile industry. The collection was first surveyed by the Business Archives Council (Scotland) in 1988. From 1995 the archive came under the management of Heriot-Watt University Archive through a Scottish Higher Education Funding Council Non-Formula Funding of Specialised Research Collections in the Humanities Project grant. In 1998 the archive formally became the responsibility of Heriot-Watt University Archive (see entry A above).

Acquisitions policy: To collect records relating to the campus and its predecessors, and, where appropriate, to strengthen existing business collections, and to acquire archives relating to the Scottish textile industry, especially within the Scottish Borders region.

Archives of organisation: Records relating to governance, administration, finance, teaching, research, and the staff and students of the Scottish Borders Campus, 1998– , and its predecessors: Galashiels Combined Technical School

1889–1900; South of Scotland Central Technical College, 1906–22; Scottish Woollen Technical College, 1922–65; Scottish College of Textiles, 1965–98.

Major collections: Business records, which contain a substantial body of fabric samples, and pattern books, including:
P. & L. Anderson, Galashiels, tweed manufacturer (mainly men's wear), 1874–1946; Blenkhorn Richardson, Hawick, woollen manufacturer, 1883–1967; The Clayton Aniline Co. Ltd, Manchester, dyes and pigment catalogues, 1930–56; Donald Brothers Ltd., Dundee, furnishing fabrics, 1896–1964; Gibson and Lumgair, Selkirk and Galashiels, woollen manufacturer, 1939–61; Hopes of Stow, Galashiels, drapers, 1918–66; R. & A. Sanderson, Galashiels, tweed manufacturer (men's wear), 1852–1956; Robert Stocks & Co. Ltd, Kirkcaldy, linen merchant and manufacturer, 1811–1956.
Robert Miles Collection: printed books, papers, correspondence and photographs relating to the textile industries, 1763–1975.

Non-manuscript material: Newspaper cuttings; early cuttings relate to the textile industry in general, later ones also relate to fashion, 1921–63.

Finding aids: Fonds, series and item-level description. Catalogue available on the website.

Facilities: Photocopying. Photography by arrangement.

Conservation: Contracted out.

Publications: Guide to the Collections (1999).

326 Huntly House Museum

Parent organisation: Edinburgh City Museums and Galleries

Address: 142 Canongate, Edinburgh EH8 8DD

Telephone: (0131) 529 4143

Fax: (0131) 557 3346

Website: www.ebs.hw.ac.uk/edc/cac/venues/
huntly_house.htm

Enquiries: The Keeper of Applied Art

Open: Mon–Sat: 10.00–5.00.

Access: Generally open to the public, by appointment.

Acquisitions policy: It is not general policy to acquire archives, but the holdings of taped interviews, personalia and political/trade union material will be developed.

Major collections: Business records, including, Ford Rankin Glass Works; Norton Park Glass Works (Edinburgh and Leith Flint Glass Works), c1791–c1917; A.W. Buchan & Co., Thistle Potteries, 1867–1972.
Collections of local history material relating to Edinburgh.

Non-manuscript material: Memorabilia of FM Earl Haig (1861–1928); Sir Walter Scott (1771–1832); Robert Burns (1759–96); R.L. Stevenson (1850–94).
Taped interviews.
Photographs of Edwardian interiors at Laurieston Castle.
Photographic collections of life and work of Edinburgh's people.
NB Photographs and associated documentary material relating to South Queensferry and Dalmeny and the Forth road and rail bridges is also held at the Queensferry Museum, 53 High Street, South Queensferry EH30 9HN; tel. (031) 331 5545.

Finding aids: NRAS 17572 (NRA 19065).

Facilities: Photocopying. Photography by arrangement.

Conservation: Contracted out.

327 Meteorological Office Edinburgh

Parent organisation: Meteorological Office

Address: Saughton House, Broomhouse Drive, Edinburgh EH11 3XG

Telephone: (0131) 244 8358/244 8368

Fax: (0131) 244 8389

E-mail: ekerr@meto.gov.uk

Enquiries: The Superintendent, Mr M.R. Porter

Open: Mon–Fri: 9.00–4.00.

Access: Generally open to the public, preferably by appointment.

Historical background: The Meteorological Office originated as a department of the Board of Trade in 1854. Under the Public Records Acts the office is authorised to select technical meteorological records for retention and maintain approved places of deposit in Edinburgh, Bracknell (entry 120) and Belfast (entry 75). In 1920 the Meteorological Office took over

responsibility for climatological observations in Scotland from the Scottish Meteorological Society and agreed to maintain an office in Edinburgh for the records.

Acquisitions policy: Responsible for original meteorological and climatological records from any source in Scotland. Donations are welcomed.

Archives of organisation: Minute books of the Scottish Meteorological Society, 1859–81.
Daily, and some hourly, climatological data for locations in Scotland; extensive coverage since 1857 plus some earlier data.
Complete hourly data and log-books from meterological observatories on Ben Nevis, 1883– 1904, and at Fort William, 1890–1904.

Non-manuscript material: Library collection of the Scottish Meteorological Society, including some rare books.

Finding aids: Index of contents of archives. Work has started on a computer-based catalogue of the climatological records.

Facilities: Photocopying by arrangement. Microfilm/fiche reader.

Conservation: Contracted out.

328 Napier University

Address: Sighthill Court, Sighthill, Edinburgh EH11 4BN

Telephone: (0131) 455 3432

Fax: (0131) 455 3566

E-mail: c.morgan@napier.ac.uk

Website: www.napier.ac.uk

Enquiries: The Archivist, Ms C. Morgan

Open: Limited hours, by arrangement.

Access: Bona fide researchers, by appointment.

The university was founded in 1964 and holds only its own administrative records from then, including student records. Accession lists are available as well as photocopying and micro-film/fiche readers.

329 National Archives of Scotland

Address: HM General Register House, Princes Street, Edinburgh EH1 3YY

Telephone: (0131) 535 1314

Fax: (0131) 557 9569

E-mail: enquiries@nas.gov.uk wsr@nas.gov.uk

Website: www.nas.gov.uk

Enquiries: The Keeper of the Records of Scotland, Mr George MacKenzie

Open: Historical and West Search Rooms: Mon–Fri: 9.00–4.45.
Legal Search Room: Mon–Fri: 9.30–4.30.

Access: Legal Search Room, HM General Register House: searches of a legal or commercial nature; a fee is charged.
Historical Search Room, HM General Register House, and West Search Room, West Register House: readers' tickets are issued on personal application (not by post). Tickets are valid for three years; personal identification is necessary before issue. Advance notification is strongly advised as 50 per cent of records are outhoused.

Historical background: The department originated in the office of the Clerk of the Rolls (13th century), who was responsible for the custody of the non-current records of government and whose successors, the Lord Clerk Register and Deputy-Clerk Register, were also responsible for supervising the framing of the public legal registers and their safe-keeping. The General Register House (f. 1774) was designed by Robert Adam as the earliest purpose-built record repository in the British Isles, in order to centralise most of the public and legal records and facilitate access to them. In 1847 the Antiquarian Room, now the Historical Search Room, was opened to the public for the purposes of historical and literary research free of charge. The office of Keeper of the Records of Scotland and the modern development of the National Archives of Scotland (until 1999 the Scottish Record Office) date from the Public Registers and Records (Scotland) Act, 1948. In 1971 the West Register House, an internal conversion of the former St George's Church, Charlotte Square (f. 1811), was opened as a branch repository, mainly for modern records. In 1994 Thomas Thompson House was opened to store c50 per cent of the records of the NAS.

Acquisitions policy: The NAS is the repository for the public (government and legal) records of Scotland and also assists in preserving Scotland's archival heritage by accepting custody of records for which it is the most suitable repository.

Archives of organisation: The archives of the National Archives of Scotland, 1579– , mainly mid-18th century– , when plans for the building of General Register House got under way. Registers of readers' permits and historical research, 1847– .

Major collections: The surviving legislative and administrative records of the kingdom of Scotland prior to the parliamentary union with England in 1707, thereafter the records of the various government agencies and departments in Scotland until the present, with regular transmissions of records from the departments of the Secretary of State for Scotland and nationalised industries.
Records of the Scottish central courts (Court of Session and High Court of Justiciary) and many local courts.
Public registers of sasines and deeds relating to property and private rights.
Records of local authorities and churches.
More than 450 separate collections of private archives, family papers, records of institutions, businesses and industrial firms.
Much of the material in private archives, and even in certain public record groups, relates to overseas.
Details of records not in official custody are contained in surveys carried out by the NRAS, which is a branch of the NAS.

Non-manuscript material: Large collection of maps and plans, many hand-drawn, 18th century– .
Photographs in certain record groups; microfilm holdings of records held both within and outside the NAS; modern records in microfiche (e.g. valuation rolls).
Early printed material, including books, in private archive deposits.
Printed books reference library (limited access), mainly legal, topographical, biographical and general Scottish history, as well as many standard reference works and historical clubs' publications.

Finding aids: Catalogue or reference rooms in both repositories (readers are advised on how to use the repertories, inventories and handlists); indexes in the reference rooms for some record groups. Computerised database of Scottish Office department files now being compiled in West Search Room (interrogated by staff on request). Source lists, prepared and distributed to certain interested bodies and institutions, on major themes, e.g. overseas countries, communications, industry, education, medicine, maritime history etc.

Facilities: Photocopying. Photography. Microfilming. The West Search Room is also equipped for map and plan consultation and the use of tape-recorders and portable computers. Computer and Microfilm Search Room with facilities for on-line searches of Gift and Deposit (GD) on CLIO text base (General Register House).

Conservation: In-house provision.

Publications: Information on accessions and surveys can be found in *The Annual Report of the Keeper of the Records of Scotland* (1996); *Tracing Your Scottish Ancestors* (2/1997) and *Tracing Scottish Local History* (1994); *History at Source*, a range of educational publications based on NAS exhibitions; Military, Jacobite and Rob Roy source lists.
Free information leaflets.
Catalogue of NAS publications available on request.

330 National Gallery of Scotland Library

Parent organisation: National Galleries of Scotland

Address: The Mound, Edinburgh EH2 2EL

Telephone: (0131) 624 6501

Fax: (0131) 220 0917

E-mail: nglibrarian@galscot.ac.uk

Enquiries: The Librarian, Penelope Carter

Open: Mon–Fri: 10.00–12.30, 2.00–4.30, by prior arrangement only.

Access: Bona fide researchers, by appointment.

The National Gallery of Scotland was founded in 1850 and opened in 1859. It maintains research files on all items in its paintings, drawings and sculpture collections, with related catalogues. There is also a collection of photographs and slides with miscellaneous notes on artists. Archives, 1856–1906, are deposited at the National Archives of Scotland (entry 329), where there are indexes. See also the Scottish National Portrait Gallery (entry 349) and Scottish National Gallery of Modern Art (entry 348). The gallery produces the following publications: annual reports of the

National Gallery of Scotland, catalogues of gallery collections and exhibition catalogues.

331 National Library of Scotland
Manuscripts Division

Address: George IV Bridge, Edinburgh EH1 1EW

Telephone: (0131) 466 2812

Fax: (0131) 466 2811

E-mail: mss@nls.uk

Website: www.nls.uk

Enquiries: The Head of the Manuscripts Division, Mr I.F. Maciver

Open: Mon, Tues, Thurs, Fri: 9.30–8.30; Wed: 10.00–8.30; Sat: 9.30–1.00.
Manuscripts for evening use must be ordered by 4.00.
Annual closure for stock–taking: 1st week of October.

Access: The great majority of holdings are available for consultation by serious researchers; a library reader's ticket, temporary or long term, which is issued on completion of the register and production of identification, is necessary. A few items or collections are restricted by date or require the permission of the owner.

Historical background: The National Library of Scotland was created by Act of Parliament in 1925, on the basis of the gift to the nation of the non-legal collections of the Advocates' Library. The Faculty of Advocates had collected a wide range of MS material since the 1680s, and the National Library has continued and expanded this activity.

Acquisitions policy: All MS material relating to Scotland and the activities of Scots worldwide. All subject areas are covered and there are few geographical restrictions. Medieval MSS, literary MSS and papers of all periods, historical documents, family papers and archives of organisations (cultural, political, commercial) are all represented. A detailed acquisitions policy statement is available.

Non-manuscript material: Some architectural and engineering plans. Important MS maps and estate plans (mostly stored and consulted in the Map Library, Salisbury Place, Edinburgh). Oral history tapes.

Finding aids: Inventories of large uncatalogued accessions available in typescript (sent to NRA and included in the *National Inventory of Documentary Sources*); various subject lists also available. Collections and named manuscripts index available on the library's website.

Facilities: Photocopying. Photography. Microfilm/fiche readers.

Conservation: Paper and vellum repair and all aspects of binding in-house.

Publications: National Library of Scotland: Catalogue of Manuscripts acquired since 1925, vols 1–8 (HMSO, 1938–92); later vols available in typescript.
Summary Catalogue of the Advocates' MSS (HMSO, 1971).
A variety of leaflets on library services.

332 National Monuments Record of Scotland

Parent organisation: Royal Commission on the Ancient and Historical Monuments of Scotland

Address: John Sinclair House, 16 Bernard Terrace, Edinburgh EH8 9NX

Telephone: (0131) 662 1456

Fax: (0131) 662 1477/1499

E-mail: nmrs@rcahms.gov.uk

Website: www.rcahms.gov.uk

Enquiries: The Curator

Open: Mon–Thurs: 9.30–4.30; Fri: 9.30–4.00.

Access: Generally open to the public. An appointment is preferable for complex enquiries.

Historical background: The RCAHMS is an independent non-departmental government body financed by Parliament through the Scottish Office under the sponsorship of Historic Scotland. The amalgamation in 1966 of the Royal Commission on the Ancient and Historical Monuments of Scotland, founded in 1908 to make an inventory of all ancient and historical monuments in Scotland, and the Scottish National Buildings Record, set up in 1941 to make and preserve records of buildings in anticipation of their possible destruction by enemy action, enabled the two largest collections of photographs and drawings of ancient monuments and historic buildings in Scotland to be combined in a single archive, known as the National Monuments Record of Scotland (NMRS). In 1976 an aerial survey component was added to its recording programme, and in 1983 it became responsible for providing information on archaeological and historical sites to Ordnance Survey for mapping purposes.

Acquisitions policy: Records of archaeological sites, built environment and design for all of Scotland and Scotland's architects. The NMRS adds to the existing collection of drawings, prints, photographs, slides and MSS by purchase, donation and deposit, and by making photographic copies of relevant material in other public and private muniments.

Major collections: Principally non-MS material (see below).
Society of Antiquaries of Scotland collection, MSS and drawings, 19th century.
Ordnance Survey record cards of archaeological sites.
Air photographic cover of Scotland (RAF, OS, All Scotland Survey), 1940s–1980s.

Non-manuscript material: Extensive collection of plans, drawings, photographs and maps, including the following:
Burn Collection: architectural drawings from the London office of William Burn (1789–1870).
Lorimer Collection: office drawings of the architectural practice of Sir Robert Lorimer (1864–1929) and engineering drawings of the Northern Lighthouse Board.
Erskine Beveridge collection of photographs of archaeological sites and buildings in the West Highlands and Fife.
Royal Commission on the Ancient and Historical Monuments of Scotland: aerial photographs of archaeological and architectural sites.
Library of more than 11,000 books and pamphlets.

Finding aids: Computer index to the collections in NMRS Library and on website. Relevant information sent annually to NRAS.

Facilities: Photocopying. Photography. Microfilm/fiche reader/printer. Scanned images, data downloads.

Conservation: In-house and contracted out.

Publications: Inventories of ancient and historical monuments, lists of archaeological sites and monuments, catalogues of aerial photographs, monograph, and annual reviews. A detailed list of publications is available.

RCAHM (Scotland): *National Monuments Record of Scotland Jubilee: a Guide to the Collections* (HMSO, 1991).
Monuments on Record [CD-ROM celebrating 90 years of the Royal Commissions on Historical Monuments].

333 National Museums of Scotland Library

Address: Chambers Street, Edinburgh EH2 1JF

Telephone: (0131) 247 4153

Fax: (0131) 247 4311

E-mail: library@nms.ac.uk

Website: www.nms.ac.uk

Enquiries: The Head of the Library, Elize Rowan

Open: Mon–Fri: 10.00–12.30, 2.00–5.00.

Access: Bona fide researchers, by prior appointment only.

Historical background: The National Museums of Scotland came into being with the passing of the National Heritage (Scotland) Act 1985. The present National Museums of Scotland Library was formed from the libraries of the three national museums in the group which were formerly the Royal Scottish Museum, the National Museum of Antiquities of Scotland and the Scottish United Services Museum. It functions now as a unified service on two sites. The Chambers Street Library, originally founded with the Royal Scottish Museum in 1854, covers the decorative arts, the history of science and technology and natural history. The curatorial departments have their own archives relating to objects in the collections. The library archives cover the history of the museum and its building, material relating to the Edinburgh University Natural History Museum and the papers of natural historians. Some listing of the collection has been made but the latter is not actively curated or developed.
The Museum of Antiquities Library, originally the library of the Society of Antiquaries of Scotland, has been relocated to Chambers Street and amalgamated with the collection there. It is concerned with Scottish history and culture and the archaeology of Europe and an extensive archive of papers, formerly the property of the society, which passed into the library's care in the 19th century.

See also the Scottish United Services Museum (entry 350) and Scottish Life Archive (entry 347).

Acquisitions policy: No active collecting policy. New acquisitions are normally by donation or acquired with an object/specimen.

Archives of organisation: Directors' correspondence 1861– (very incomplete, outgoing correspondence only, 1861–1937).
Edinburgh University Natural History Museum report books: daily, 1822–30, 1845–54; weekly, 1822–31; annual, 1834–6.
Society of Antiquaries of Scotland archives.

Major collections: Natural historians' correspondence, field notes, journals etc, particularly those of J.A. Harvie-Brown (1844–1916), William Jardine (1800–74), William S. Bruce (1867–1921); diary of A. Forbes Mackay. Other, uncatalogued, natural historians' material is in the Natural History Department.
Society of Antiquaries of Scotland: letters of William Smellie (1697–1763); papers of Robert Riddell and miscellaneous antiquarian MSS, 18th and 19th centuries.

Non-manuscript material: Science, Technology and Working Life Department: photography collection, including examples of early photographic techniques and photographs, e.g. Hill and Adamson; technical drawings (*c*300).

Finding aids: Lists of NMS archives for internal use.

Facilities: Photocopying. Photography. Microfilm/fiche readers.

Conservation: Limited in-house paper conservation, otherwise contracted out.

Publications: J. Pitman: *Manuscripts in the Royal Scottish Museum, part 1: William Jardine Papers*, Royal Scottish Museum Information Series: Natural History, 7 (1981).

——— : *Manuscripts in the Royal Scottish Museum , part 2: William S. Bruce Papers and Diary of A. Forbes Mackay*, Royal Scottish Museum Information Series: Natural History 8 (1982).

——— : *Manuscripts in the Royal Scottish Museum, part 3: J.A. Harvie-Brown Papers* , Royal Scottish Museum Information Series: Natural History, 9 (1983).

334 National Trust for Scotland

Address: 28 Charlotte Square, Edinburgh EH2 4ET

Telephone: (0131) 243 9524

Fax: (0131) 243 9599

E-mail: cbain@nts.org.uk

Website: www.nts.org.uk

Enquiries: The Archivist, Carolynn J. Bain

Open: Mon–Fri: 9.30–4.30, by appointment only.

Access: Generally open to anyone with a legitimate interest. Prior contact is required for access to non-manuscript material.

Historical background: The National Trust for Scotland is a conservation charity founded in 1931 to preserve and make accessible to the public, on behalf of the nation, places of cultural and natural significance. The archives project was begun in 1988 to list the administrative and organisational records of the trust. Any archives acquired with properties are usually deposited with the appropriate local record office.

Acquisitions policy: The archives collect the records from head office departments, regional administrative offices and properties.

Archives of organisation: Trust administrative records, especially from the Directorate, the Factorial department and the Law Agent, 1931– .

Non-manuscript material: Photographic libraries and collections of maps, plans and drawings.

Finding aids: General index of files; NRAS 1562.

Facilities: Photocopying.

335 Royal Botanic Garden Library

Parent organisation: Royal Botanic Garden, Edinburgh

Address: 20A Inverleith Row, Edinburgh EH3 5LR

Telephone: (0131) 248 2853 (library enquiries), 552 7171 (switchboard)

Fax: (0131) 248 2901

E-mail: library@rbge.org.uk

Website: www.rbge.org.uk

Enquiries: The Chief Librarian, Mrs Jane Hutcheon

Open: Mon–Thurs: 9.30–4.30; Fri: 9.30–4.00.

Access: Generally open to the public.

Historical background: The garden was founded in 1670. Its large archival collection is the result of its long history and activities, particularly in the field of botany and horticulture.

Acquisitions policy: Attempts to acquire comprehensively material relevant to the research interests of the scientific staff.

Archives of organisation: Archives of the garden and its predecessors: administrative records and scientific papers, including papers of regius keepers and staff.

Major collections: Records of botanical clubs and societies, including the Botanical Society of Edinburgh minute books, 1836– , and the Royal Caledonian Horticultural Society.
Transcribed material and notes made by historians of the garden.
Papers, including J.F. Rock's diaries and photographs; James McNab's journals and scrapbooks; several files of papers and letters, related to expeditions to different parts of the world.
Collection of c30,000 letters, including John Hutton Balfour's worldwide correspondence (c4000) and George Forrest's letters from China (c4000).

Non-manuscript material: Extensive collection of plant drawings, paintings and prints.

Finding aids: MSS indexes.

Facilities: Photocopying. Photography. Microfilm/fiche reader.

Publications: H.R. Fletcher and W.H. Brown: *The Royal Botanic Garden, Edinburgh, 1670–1970* (1970).
I.C. Hedge and J.M. Lamond (eds): *Index of Collectors in the Edinburgh Herbarium* (1970).
M.V. Matthew: *The History of the Royal Botanic Garden Library, Edinburgh* (1987).

336 Royal College of Nursing Archives

Address: 42 South Oswald Road, Edinburgh EH9 2HH

Telephone: (0131) 662 1010

Fax: (0131) 662 1032

E-mail: archives@rcn.org.uk

Website: www.rcnscotland.org

Enquiries: The Archivist, Ms Susan McGann

Open: Mon–Thurs: 10.00–4.45; Fri: 10.00–4.15. An appointment is necessary.

Access: Bona fide researchers. Some administrative records are confidential.

Historical background: The RCN Archives record the growth of the college from its foundation in 1916 to its present position as the largest professional union of nurses, with more than 300,000 members. The records document its role as a professional organisation with international links, as an education body providing the first post-registration courses for nurses, and as a trade union negotiating and campaigning on behalf of nurses. The headquarters are at 20 Cavendish Square, London, a site occupied by the college since 1919. The Scottish Board of the college was also founded in 1916, and in 1991 the RCN Archives were transferred to Edinburgh.

Acquisitions policy: Papers relating to the history of nursing, including those of nursing-related organisations and nurses.

Archives of organisation: RCN archives, 1916– , including council and committee minutes; reports of working parties on professional topics; surveys on nursing policy and practice; records of the professional nursing department, the education department, the labour relations department and the international department; records of fund-raising and public relations; membership records; records of the Scottish Board, the Irish Board, 1917–25, and of various branches.

Major collections: Records of the following nursing organisations: the National Council of Nurses, 1908–62; the Association of Hospital Matrons, 1919–72; the Society of Registered Male Nurses, 1937–67; the National Association of State Enrolled Nurses (NASEN), 1948–70; the Students' Nurses' Association, 1925–68.
Papers and certificates of eminent nurses and others.

Non-manuscript material: Photographs and glass slides (*c*2000).
Oral history collection (*c*200).

Badges (*c*1000).

Finding aids: Catalogues, lists and database.

Facilities: Photocopying. Photography. Microfiche reader.

Publications: G. Bowman: *The Lamp and the Book: the Story of the RCN* (London, 1967).
S. McGann: *The Battle of the Nurses* (London, 1992).
Archives and Oral History Collection leaflet [free].

337 Royal College of Physicians of Edinburgh Library

Address: 9 Queen Street, Edinburgh EH2 1JQ

Telephone: (0131) 225 7324

Fax: (0131) 220 3939

E-mail: library@rcpe.ac.uk

Website: www.rcpe.ac.uk

Enquiries: The Librarian, Iain Milne

Open: Mon–Fri: 9.00–5.00.

Access: Fellows, members of the college and bona fide researchers.

Historical background: The library was founded in 1681 by Sir Robert Sibbald, the principal founder of the college, and has had a continuous existence as a working medical library since then. It also contains good collections of works on botany and natural history down to the mid-19th century.

Acquisitions policy: To fill gaps in historical collections and augment the history of medicine section.

Archives of organisation: College archives relating to the institution, with lists of members, minutes, accounts and records, general correspondence, college buildings, fellows' petitions etc, 1681– .

Major collections: Reports and correspondence concerning lunatic asylums in Scotland, 1814–85.
Records and papers of the Medical Provident Institution of Scotland, 1826–34.
MSS Collection: *c*1000 vols, including 18th-century lecture notes of lectures in Edinburgh Medical School; MSS of William Cullen (1710–90), including consultation letters; MSS of Sir James Young Simpson (1811–70); MSS of the

three Alexander Monros (1697–1767, 1733–1817, 1773–1859).

MSS of Thomas Laycock (1812–76); diaries of Sir Alexander Morison (1779–1866); MSS of Sir R.W. Philip (1857–1939); MSS of Sir Sydney A. Smith (1883–1969).

Non-manuscript material: College portraits.
Albums of engravings of medical men, 18th and 19th centuries.
Other prints, engravings and photographs, including those from the collection of J.D. Comrie.

Finding aids: Inventory of muniments (1914; TS; copy in National Archive of Scotland, see entry 329). Various other indexes. W.J. Robertson: *A Checklist of Manuscripts in the RCPEd* (TS). Detailed and summary listings of larger MSS collections.

Facilities: Photocopying. Photography. Microfilm/fiche reader.

338 Royal College of Surgeons of Edinburgh

Address: Nicolson Street, Edinburgh EH8 9DW

Telephone: (0131) 527 1600

Fax: (0131) 557 6406

E-mail: library@rcsed.ac.uk

Website: www.rcsed.ac.uk

Enquiries: The Secretary, Miss A.S. Campbell
The Hon. Archivist, Dr A.H.B. Masson
The Archivist, Mrs Suzy Cuthbert

Open: Mon–Fri: 9.00–5.00, by prior arrangement.

Access: Enquirers should first write to the Secretary for written permission to use the college's archives, then contact the college's Archivist to arrange a suitable time. There is a fee-based research service.

Historical background: From the beginning the college has been concerned with the training, examination and licensing of prospective surgeons. In 1505, after petitioning the Town Council, the barbers and surgeons of Edinburgh were granted a Seal of Cause, which enabled them to be enrolled among the Incorporated Crafts of the Burgh. The crafts of Barbers and Surgeons were separated by a decree of the Court of Session in 1722, after which records were kept separately for the two crafts. Both the Barbers and Surgeons continued to use the same premises for meetings until 1893, when the Society of Barbers met for the last time. In 1778 a royal charter was granted to the Incorporation of Surgeons, which conferred the present title, and in 1979 a new charter was granted.

Acquisitions policy: The college collects all papers relating to itself and papers belonging to its fellows and licentiates or concerning them.

Archives of organisation: Bound records of the College, 1581– ; college council minutes, 1822– ; charters, 1504–1979; examination records, 1581– ; apprentices' indentures, 1709–1872; building of Old Surgeons' Hall, 1696–1710; records of the Surgeons Widows' Fund, 1820–90; plans for the present college building, 1829–32; list of fellows, 1581– ; lists of licentiates, 1770–1873; triple qualification examination schedules, 1886– ; annual reports of the college, 1937– ; laws of the college, 1793–1977.

Major collections: Papers of the extra-mural medical school of the royal colleges.

Papers of the Society of Barbers.

Papers of the Royal Odonto-Chirurgical Society of Scotland.

Papers of Sir James Young Simpson (1811–70), physician; John Robert Hume (?1781–1857), physician; John Smith (1792–1833), professor of medical jurisprudence; Sir John Struthers (1823–99), anatomist; Joseph Lister (1827–1912), Dr Joseph Bell (1837–1911) and Sir Henry Wade (1877–1955).

Non-manuscript material: Portraits, prints, photographs, audio and video tapes, rare books.

Finding aids: Typescripts for most collections; card indexes; web pages in preparation. Summary of the college's archival holdings freely available on the computer. Sent to the NRAS and the Medical Archives and Manuscripts Survey at the Wellcome Library (entry 844).

Facilities: Photocopying. Photography. Scanning.

Publications: A.H.B. Masson: *Portraits, Paintings and Busts in the Royal College of Surgeons of Edinburgh* (The Royal College of Surgeons of Edinburgh, 1995).

Heritage publication in preparation.

339 Royal Highland and Agricultural Society of Scotland

Parent organisation: Royal Highland Education Trust

Address: The Library, Royal Highland Centre, Ingliston, Edinburgh EH28 8NF

Telephone: (0131) 335 6227

Fax: (0131) 333 5236

E-mail: rhet@rhass.org.uk

Website: www.sfacet.org.uk

Enquiries: The Education Manager, Mrs Carole Snell

Open: Mon–Fri: 9.30–5.00.

Access: Generally open to the public, by appointment.

Historical background: The society was founded in 1784 to promote agricultural interests and education, as well as the study of the Gaelic language and Scottish poetry and music.

Acquisitions policy: To maintain the archives and collections.

Archives of organisation: Minutes, 1784–1967; abstracts of premiums offered, 1874–1925; reports and premium certificates, 1785–1890; accountancy records, 1834–1967; plans of show yards, 1837–47.

Sederunt books, 1842–1945, and journals.

Correspondence, papers and photographs *re* St Kilda Fund, 1851–1931; also J.M. Macleod of St Kilda, letters to J.M. Maxwell *re* conditions on St Kilda, 1859–66.

Major collections: Ingliston papers: MSS relating to Gaelic matters, including essays on Highland music, fisheries and other subjects, 1793–1809; papers *re* publication of Gaelic dictionary, 1809–38; and much other correspondence, mainly 19th century.

Non-manuscript material: Transactions of the Highland Society, 1799– .

Large collection of bound volumes of pamphlets.

Finding aids: NRA 12271.

Facilities: Photocopying.

340 Royal Observatory

Parent organisation: Particle Physics and Astronomy Research Council

Address: Blackford Hill, Edinburgh EH9 3HJ

Telephone: (0131) 668 8397

Fax: (0131) 662 1668

E-mail: library@roe.ac.uk

Website: www.roe.ac.uk/atc/library

Enquiries: The Librarian, Mr A.R. Macdonald

Open: Mon–Fri: 9.00–5.30.

Access: Serious researchers in the history of science, by appointment.

Historical background: The observatory was founded in 1818 as the observatory of the Astronomical Institution of Edinburgh and was designated 'Royal' in 1822. It moved to its present site in the 1890s.

Acquisitions policy: To maintain and consolidate the archives.

Archives of organisation: Correspondence, administrative and scientific papers and notebooks of the Astronomical Institution of Edinburgh and the observatory, 1764– .

Papers and correspondence of Astronomers Royal for Scotland and their staffs, 1834– , including those of Charles Piazzi Smyth (1819–1900).

Considerable collection of material from the (26th) Earl of Crawford's private observatory at Dunecht, Aberdeenshire, 17th-19th centuries.

Major collections: Royal Society of Edinburgh's collections on Charles Piazzi Smyth.

Notes of A.P. Norton, Astronomical Society of Edinburgh.

Non-manuscript material: Photographic collection of glass negatives and prints.

Finding aids: NRAS 2657.

Facilities: Photocopying. Photography.

Publications: H.A. Brück: *The Royal Observatory, Edinburgh, 1822–1972* (Edinburgh, [1972]).

Catalogue of the Archives of the Royal Observatory Edinburgh, 1764–1937 (Edinburgh, 1981).

341 Royal Scots Regimental Museum

Parent organisation: The Royal Scots Regimental Headquarters

Address: The Castle, Edinburgh EH1 2YT

Telephone: (0131) 310 5014

Fax: (0131) 310 5019

E-mail: rhqroyalscots@edinburghcastle.fsnet.co.uk

Enquiries: The Curator, Lt-Col R.P. Mason

Open: April–Oct: Mon–Sun: 9.30–5.30; Oct–March: Mon–Fri: 9.30–4.00.

Access: Bona fide researchers, on written application.

Acquisitions policy: Collection of documents relevant to the regimental history.

Archives of organisation: Regimental war diary, 1914– , and register of services, 1877– .
Regimental record books; minutes of officers' mess.
Account book of distribution of pay and subsistence *re* 1st Battalion, 1776–9.
Official correspondence of officers of the Royals, Ireland, 1786.

Major collections: Diaries, autobiographies and memoirs, mainly World War I.
Miscellaneous documents and letters, some concerning the early history of the regiment, 1650s.

Non-manuscript material: Photographs and albums, drawings and scrapbooks.
Copies of *The Thistle* and regimental magazines; rolls of honours and materials (mainly printed) on casualties and war graves.

Finding aids: Card index. NRAS 2273.

342 Royal Scottish Academy

Address: 3rd Floor, 17 Waterloo Place, Edinburgh EH11 3BG

Telephone: (0131) 225 6671

Fax: (0131) 557 6147

E-mail: info@royalscottishacademy.org

Website: www.royalscottishacademy.org

Enquiries: The Assistant Librarian/Keeper, Mrs Joanna Soden

Open: Mon–Fri: 9.30–5.00.

Access: Generally open to the public, by appointment only. Enquiries may be answered by letter; a donation is requested for this service, except from schoolchildren and matriculated students.

Historical background: The Royal Scottish Academy was founded in 1826 to promote the visual arts in Scotland and to improve conditions of living artists. It is therefore the oldest surviving art organisation in Scotland. One of the founding aims was to establish a library devoted to the visual arts, and this has been maintained since that time. The archives of the RSA date back to its foundation and they form part of the Library collections.

Acquisitions policy: The library of the Royal Scottish Academy aims to collect material relevant to past and present members of the academy and to the visual arts generally in Scotland. Archival material is acquired mainly by gift or bequest.

Archives of organisation: Annual reports, minute books and other records, 1826– .
Annual exhibition catalogues, 1827– , and sales records, 1861– .
Life class registers and associated material, 1843–53; 1866–1901.
Letter collection, 1825–94.

Major collections: William George Gillies RSA (1898–1973) Bequest: letters, cuttings, photographs, notes, catalogues, personal memorabilia and an extensive collection of paintings and drawings.
Files on most 20th-century members and associate members of the RSA, including correspondence, news cuttings and catalogues.

Non-manuscript material: Paintings, drawings, sculptures, photographs, books, catalogues, news cuttings, memorabilia and objects.

Finding aids: Main letter collection listed chronologically with partial name index. Some minute books indexed. Photographs indexed by sitter. NRAS 1464.

Facilities: Photocopying.

Conservation: Limited contracting out.

Publications: E. Gordon: *The Royal Scottish Academy, 1826–1976* (1976).

—— : *The Making of the Royal Scottish Academy* (RSA, 1988).

343 Royal Society for the Relief of Indigent Gentlewomen of Scotland

Address: 14 Rutland Square, Edinburgh EH1 2BD

Telephone: (0131) 558 7097

Fax: (0131) 229 0956

E-mail: admin@igfund.freeserve.co.uk

Enquiries: The Secretary, George F. Goddard

Open: Mon–Fri: 8.45–5.00.

Access: Bona fide researchers; an appointment is necessary.

The society was founded in 1847 to assist spinsters and widows with professional or business backgrounds who exist on low incomes and have limited capital resources. It has enjoyed royal patronage since 1930. Among archives held are loose application books of ladies seeking admission to the roll, records of donations and legacies and annual reports, 1850– . A 150th anniversary history is available.

344 Royal Zoological Society of Scotland

Address: Scottish National Zoological Collection, Murrayfield, Edinburgh EH12 6TS

Telephone: (0131) 334 9171/2/3

Fax: (0131) 316 4050

E-mail: d.waugh@rzss.org.uk

Website: www.edinburghzoo.org.uk

Enquiries: The Director, Dr David R. Waugh

Open: Mon–Fri: 9.00–6.00.

Access: Bona fide researchers, by appointment only.

The Royal Zoological Society was constituted in 1910 and opened its zoological gardens in Edinburgh in 1913. It received its royal charter in 1947. The society has been involved in recent years in the provision of a major zoological collection, for conservation of species, environment education, research and recreation. Although there is no formal archive, correspondence documenting the society's history and animal collection is maintained. There are also collections of plans, drawings and photographs.

Films have been deposited with the Scottish Film and Television Archive (entry 399).

345 School of Scottish Studies

Parent organisation: University of Edinburgh

Address: 27 George Square, Edinburgh EH8 9LD

Telephone: (0131) 650 4159 (Archive Assistant)

Fax: (0131) 650 4163

E-mail: r.w.talbot@ed.ac.uk

Website: www.sss.ed.ac.uk

Enquiries: The Archive Assistant, Ms Rhona Talbot

Open: Mon, Tues, Thurs, Fri: 9.30–12.30, 2.00–5.00.

Access: Bona fide researchers, with advance notice; there are charges for extensive use of tape-recordings.

Historical background: The school was founded as an independent research institute of the University of Edinburgh, and the first fieldworker started accumulating transcripts and sound recordings in 1951. The Sound Archive, backed by photographic, film and videotape archives and a manuscript collection, is the basis for the school's research and its undergraduate teaching, which started in 1971 after the school had become part of the Faculty of Arts in 1965.

Acquisitions policy: Ethnology, including material culture information; folklore, including custom and belief, traditional tales, songs, riddles, rhymes, proverbs etc; ethnomusicology/ folk and national music; oral history, including local and social history, life stories and reminiscences, place names, Scots and Gaelic dialects. Principally sound recordings made by own staff and students in Scotland and Scots communities elsewhere, augmented by donations.

Major collections: Written material in this archive supports sound material which constitutes the main archive.

Manuscript Archive: fieldwork notes, tape transcripts and other relevant typescripts, cuttings, microfilms etc, student projects and dissertations, 1951– .

Lucy Broadwood folksong MSS, mainly Gaelic.

Lady Evelyn Stewart-Murray Gaelic folktales MSS from Atholl.

Royal Celtic Society MSS from storytelling competitions at various Gaelic Mòds, 1920s–1940s.

Maclagan MSS: information on Gaelic folklore (mostly in English) collected by helpers of Dr R.C. Maclagan (9200 sheets; deposited by the Folklore Society, entry 610).

Non-manuscript material: Sound Archive: field recordings, with place-name survey, linguistic survey, lecture tapes, cassettes, direct-recorded discs and commercial discs, 1951– (c10,000).

John Levy Archive: ethnomusicological recordings, mainly Asian, and ancillary material, including photographs and films.

Will Forret Bequest: large collection of sound recordings of Scottish popular and folk music, 1930s– .

Tapes and transcripts from MSC oral history projects in Scotland, e.g. Working People's Oral History in SE Scotland, 1983–5.

There is also a separate photographic archive, including the Atkinson Collection on Scottish islands, for which the Archivist is not responsible.

Finding aids: Card index for all media. Sound recordings, catalogued in detail since the early 1980s, are now accessible only on a database on the website. The accession register from 1951 is fully computerised and will also be available on the website. NRAS informed of oral history recordings.

Facilities: Photocopying. Photography. Sound recording technician available to approved researchers (price-lists available). Printouts from computerised catalogue.

Publications: Material from the archives is published regularly in the school's magazine *Tocher* and the Scottish Tradition series of recordings (now published by Greentax). Information on oral history holdings has been published in the Newsletter of the Scottish Oral History Group, *By Word of Mouth*, 15.

346 Scottish Catholic Archives

Address: Columba House, 16 Drummond Place, Edinburgh EH3 6PL

Telephone: (0131) 556 3661

Enquiries: The Keeper, Dr Christine Johnson

Open: Mon–Fri: 9.30–1.00, 2.00–4.30.

Access: Bona fide researchers, by appointment only.

Historical background: Material was collected by Bishop Kyle from various sources at the seminary of Aquhorties College (Deeside), 1799–1829; Preshome (near Buckie), 1829–69; and Blairs College (near Aberdeen), 1829– . The Blairs material was brought to Edinburgh in 1958, the Preshome material in the 1970s and other collections have been added.

NB There is no genealogical material.

Acquisitions policy: Each diocese or other body preserves its own modern records but they are encouraged to deposit their older records centrally. Material is acquired throughout Scotland, with priority given to older records.

Major collections: Archives of Archdiocese of St Andrews and Edinburgh and of dioceses of Argyll, Dunkeld, Galloway and Motherwell, 1878–1980.

Archives of Blairs College, 1829–1986.

Records of Friendly Societies, 1812–1970s.

Papers relating to the post-Reformation Roman Catholic Church in Scotland: Archbishop James Beaton (*d* 1603); Scottish mission, 16th–19th centuries, including the Blairs and Preshome letters (c50,000 items).

College of the Continent, 16th–19th centuries; in Scotland, 18th–20th centuries; Scots Abbey in Germany, 1177–19th century; Eastern District of Scotland, 19th–20th centuries; Northern and Western Districts of Scotland, 19th century.

Non-manuscript material: Printed books and pamphlets relevant to post-Reformation Scottish Catholicism.

Finding aids: Catalogues. All material prior to 1878 also calendared or (for large collections of letters) at least indexed. A computerised printout of *Summary Handlist of Holdings up to 1878* is available.

Facilities: Photocopying.

Publications: D. McRoberts: 'The Scottish Catholic Archives, 1560–1978', *Innes Review*, xxviii (1977), 59–128.

M. Dilworth: 'The Scottish Catholic Archives', *Catholic Archives*, 1 (1981), 10–19.

See also articles on ongoing work in *Catholic Archives* 4–6, 9–10.

National Inventory of Documentary Sources, Chadwyck-Healey microfiche (1984–).

347 Scottish Life Archive

Parent organisation: National Museums of Scotland

Address: Chambers Street, Edinburgh EH1 1JF

Telephone: (0131) 247 4076/4073 (direct line)

Fax: (0131) 247 4312

E-mail: dik@nms.ac.uk eme@nms.ac.uk

Enquiries: The Curator, Ms D.I. Kidd
The Assistant Curator, Ms E.M. Edwards

Open: Mon–Fri: 9.00–5.00.

Access: Bona fide researchers; a prior appointment is advised and preferred. A charge may be made for any research which is undertaken.

Historical background: The National Museums of Scotland were formed in 1985 from the amalgamation of the Royal Scottish Museum and the National Museum of Antiquities of Scotland (NMAS). The archive, established in 1959 as the Country Life Archive of the NMAS, has since extended its remit to include maritime, urban and industrial collections. It was previously called the Scottish Ethnological Archive.

Acquisitions policy: To acquire, through research, donation or purchase, material illustrating Scotland's social and economic history from the early 18th century onwards.

Major collections: Memoirs, diaries, letters, scrapbooks and recorded MS evidence.

Non-manuscript material: Printed ephemera, cuttings, maps, plans and bibliographical references.
Photographs (c100,000) and slides (c10,000). Small collection of tape-recorded interviews, film and videotape.

Finding aids: Subject catalogue.

Facilities: Photocopying. Photography.

Conservation: In-house paper conservators.

Publications: D.I. Kidd: *To See Ourselves: Rural Scotland in Old Photographs* (NMS/Harper Collins, 1992).
L. Leneman: *Into the Foreground: a Century of Scottish Women in Photographs* (NMS/Alan Sutton, 1993).
I. McGregor: *Bairns: Scottish Children in Photographs* (NMS, 1994).
M.E. Burnett: *Scotland's Magazine Collection: an Index* (NMS, 1997).

Guide and Subject Index to the Scottish Life Archive (NMS, 1998).

348 Scottish National Gallery of Modern Art
Archive and Library

Parent organisation: National Galleries of Scotland

Address: Belford Road, Edinburgh EH4 3DR

Telephone: (0131) 624 6312

Fax: (0131) 343 2802

E-mail: ann.simpson@natgalscot.ac.uk

Enquiries: The Curator, Archive and Library, Mrs Ann Simpson

Open: Mon–Fri: strictly by appointment.

Access: The archive is open to bona fide scholars on completion of a visitor application form. An appointment is essential and at least 10 days' notice is required.

Historical background: The Scottish National Gallery of Modern Art opened in 1960 and is part of the National Galleries of Scotland (see National Gallery of Scotland, entry 330, and Scottish National Portrait Gallery, entry 349). The gallery collection comprises paintings, sculptures, drawings, prints, photographs and video pieces covering the period 1900 to the present day. The archive collection mirrors the range of the artworks collection. The acquisition in 1994 of the Roland Penrose Archive and Library and the bequest of the Gabrielle Keiller Collection in 1996 has given the archive particular strength in the areas of Dada and surrealism.

Acquisitions policy: Material relating to exhibitions organised by the gallery, including papers, sketchbooks, photographs, videos and tape recordings concerning 20th-century art, in particular Dada and surrealism and Scottish Art and Arts.

Archives of organisation: Administrative papers and material relating directly to works in the collection and exhibitions held in the gallery, 1960– .

Major collections: The Roland Penrose Collection: papers, photographs and books belonging to Roland Penrose (1900–84), including important material concerning his involvement with surrealism, and also with

Picasso, Miro, Tapies, and the Institute of Contemporary Art.

The Gabrielle Keiller Collection of Dada and Surrealism: papers and literature including MS letters from Duchamp, Dali, Andre Breton, Georges Hugnet, many livres d'artistes with MS additions and inscriptions.

Papers of the Richard DeMarco Gallery, 1966– .

Other major holdings include artists papers of Joan Eardly (1921–63); Ian Hamilton Finlay (*b* 1925); Sir W.O. Hutchison, (1889–1970), William MacTaggart (1903–81); James Pryde (1866–1941); Scottie Wilson (1889–1972).

Material concerning The 57 and New 57 Gallery, Edinburgh, 1957–88; the Society of Eight, 1920s; the Society of Scottish Artists, 1899– .

Non-manuscript material: Photographs, sketchbooks, recordings, videos, plus large collection of printed material (mainly from the 1920s–1940s) relating to Dada and surrealism.

Finding aids: Handlists; card index.

Facilities: Microfiche reader.

Conservation: In-house conservation; some work contracted out.

Publications: Scottish National Gallery of Modern Art Concise Catalogue (1993).
E. Cowling: *Surrealism and After: the Gabrielle Keiller Collection* (1997)
National Galleries of Scotland Triennial Report 1994–1997 (1998).

349 Scottish National Portrait Gallery
Portrait Archive

Parent organisation: National Galleries of Scotland

Address: 1 Queen Street, Edinburgh EH2 1JD

Telephone: (0131) 556 8921

Fax: (0131) 558 3691

E-mail: natgalscot.ac.uk

Website: www.natgalscot.ac.uk

Enquiries: The Director, James Holloway

Open: Mon–Fri: 10.00–12.30, 2.00–4.30.

Access: Bona fide researchers, by appointment only.

Historical background: Since the establishment of the gallery in the late 19th century, comprehensive records have been kept of Scottish portraits and portrait painters.

Acquisitions policy: Engravings, drawings, early photographs and photographs of portraits are acquired on a historical basis for the importance of the sitter in Scottish history, rather than for artistic merit. The gallery does not collect MS material.

Non-manuscript material: Portrait engravings (14,000).
Portrait drawings (750).
Hill and Adamson calotypes (5000).
Photographs of portraits in other collections (30,000).
Biographical details of Scottish artists.
Analyses of information about costume, furniture and other aspects of social history.

Finding aids: All materials are indexed by sitter, by artist and for all social history features.

Publications: R.K. Marshall: 'The Scottish National Portrait Gallery as a Source for the Local Historian', *Local Historian*, ii (1975), 382.
——: 'Scottish Portraits as a Source for the Costume Historian', *Costume*, xv (1981), 67.
S. Stevenson: *David Octavius Hill and Robert Adamson* (National Galleries of Scotland, 1981) [catalogue of holdings].
H. Smailes: *Concise Catalogue* (Edinburgh, 1990) [illustrated; lists portrait drawings as well as paintings in the collection].

350 Scottish United Services Museum Library

Parent organisation: National Museums of Scotland

Address: The Castle, Edinburgh EH1 2NG

Telephone: (0131) 225 7534 ext. 204

Fax: (0131) 225 3848

E-mail: edith@nms.ac.uk

Enquiries: The Curatorial Assistant, Library/ Archive, Edith Philip

Open: Mon–Fri: 10.00–1.00, 2.00–5.00.

Access: Bona fide researchers, by appointment only.

Historical background: The Scottish United Services Museum was established in 1930. Scots Greys MSS have been returned to the regiment.

Acquisitions policy: To acquire by purchase and donation material on the history of the Scottish soldier, sailor and airman. There is limited purchase of MS material. Most new items are acquired with museum objects.

Archives of organisation: Complete MSS accessions register.

Correspondence of former keepers of the museum.

General records of buildings and administration.

Major collections: 603 (City of Edinburgh) Squadron correspondence, combat reports, benevolent fund etc, 1927–52.

Ronald Ball's notes on the Scots Army (unaccessioned, unindexed, uncatalogued; used only by staff).

Dalrymple-White papers, 1720–1954.

Henry McCance: notes for regimental history of the Royal Scots, 1913.

Regimental order books, 1745– .

Wilson of Bannockburn, clothing contractors: correspondence with regiments, 18th and 19th centuries.

Papers relating to Maj. John McBain, Scots Guards, c1830–c1884.

Correspondence of Gen. Sir David Baird (1759–1829), 1799–1828, with related papers, 1772– c1855.

Papers of Admiral Adam Duncan, 1st Viscount Camperdown, 1731–1804.

Non-manuscript material: Set of World War I trench maps and aerial photographs.

Print and photographs collection (c10,000 items).

World War I service medal roll (microfiche, slightly imperfect).

Cumberland Papers (microfilm; originals in Royal Archives, entry 1204).

Finding aids: Catalogues of all material. Baird: NRA 27982.

Facilities: Photocopying. Photography. Microfilm/fiche readers.

Conservation: Limited paper conservation through National Museums of Scotland Library (entry 333).

351 University of Edinburgh Library

Address: George Square, Edinburgh EH8 9LJ

A Special Collections

Telephone: (0131) 650 8379

Fax: (0131) 650 6863

E-mail: special.collections@ed.ac.uk

Website: www.lib.ed.ac.uk/lib/resources/collections/specdivision

Enquiries: The Special Collections Librarian, Richard Ovenden

Open: Term: Mon–Thurs: 9.00–6.00.
Vacation: Mon–Fri: 9.00–5.00.
Closed 2nd week of August, Scottish spring and autumn holidays.

Access: Bona fide researchers, on written application.

Historical background: The library was founded by the bequest of books from the library of Clement Little in 1580 to the Town and Kirk of Edinburgh; it was transferred to the town's college (later university) in 1584.

Acquisitions policy: To strengthen existing collections in certain fields by purchase and donation.

Major collections: Laing Collection: rich in material relating to Scottish letters and history.
Oriental MSS (c650): include MSS transferred from New College (entry 978) and a small collection of palm-leaf MSS.
Western MSS: medieval items (c330), Scottish Enlightenment, medicine, Africa, Scottish Gaelic; modern Scottish literary collections include Hugh MacDiarmid (1892–1978), George Mackay Brown (1921–96) and Norman Macaig (1910–96); archives of other 20th-century writers: Arthur Koestler (1905–83), John Middleton Murry (1889–1957), Robert Nye (*b* 1939) and John Wain (1925–94); papers of many scientists, geologists and doctors, especially those associated with the university.
Business archives, including Thomas Nelson & Son Ltd, publishers, including John Buchan correspondence, and Christian Salvesen Ltd, Leith, *re* whaling in Antarctica.

Non-manuscript material: Architectural drawings and plans of W.H. Playfair (1789–1857),

Sir Robert Rowand Anderson (1834–1921), Sir Robert Lorimer (1864–1929).

Thomson-Walker collection of engraved portraits of medical men.

University medals.

Kennedy-Fraser wax cylindrical recordings.

Rare book collections in all fields, 15th–20th centuries.

Finding aids: Guide to Manuscript Collections in the Main Library [Library Guide No. 51]. Index to MSS acquired before 1987, accessible on the Internet. Handlists to individual collections. Some manuscripts are catalogued on the library's on-line OPAC.

Facilities: Photocopying. Photography. Microfilm/fiche reader.

Conservation: In-house conservator.

Publications: Rev. J. Anderson (ed.): *Calendar of the Laing Charters, AD 854–1837, Belonging to the University of Edinburgh* (Edinburgh, 1899).

Report on the Laing Manuscripts Preserved in the University of Edinburgh, Historical Manuscripts Commission (London, 1914–25) [2 vols].

C.R. Borland: *A Descriptive Catalogue of the Western Medieval Manuscripts in Edinburgh University Library* (Edinburgh, 1916).

M.A. Hukk, H. Ethé and E. Robertson: *A Descriptive Catalogue of the Arabic and Persian Manuscripts in Edinburgh University Library* (Hereford, 1925).

R.B. Serjeant: *A Handlist of the Arabic, Persian and Hindustani MSS of New College* (London, 1942).

J.R. Walsh: 'The Turkish Manuscripts in New College, Edinburgh', *Oriens*, xii (1959), 171.

Index to Manuscripts (Boston, 1964) [2 vols]; First Supplement (Boston, 1981).

N.R. Ker: *Medieval Manuscripts in British Libraries*, ii (Oxford, 1977), 589.

M.C.T. Simpson: 'The Special Collections', in J.R. Guild and A. Law (eds), *Edinburgh University Library, 1580–1980* (1982).

The Koestler Archive in Edinburgh University Library: a Checklist (Edinburgh, 1987).

B University Archives

Telephone: (0131) 650 6865

Fax: (0131) 650 6863

E-mail: arnott.wilson@ed.ac.uk

Website: www.lib.ed.ac.uk/lib/resources/collections/archived/index.shtml

Enquiries: The University Archivist, Arnott T Wilson

Open: Term: Mon–Thurs: 9.00–6.00; Fri: 9.00–5.00.
Vacation: Mon–Fri: 9.00–5.00.
Closed second week of August, Scottish spring and autumn holidays.
Appointments are necessary.

Access: Bona fide researchers; access to recent official records is subject to the agreement of the appropriate university staff and in accordance with university policies and legislation. Charges are made for certain types of written enquiries.

Historical background: The university has generated records and archives from its inception in 1583. While a few items date from this time, the bulk of the holdings are for much later periods because the university was established and effectively controlled by Edinburgh Town Council until the Universities (Scotland) Act of 1858. Consequently, earlier material relating to the university is to be found among the Edinburgh City Archives (see entry 319). The first University Archivist was appointed in 1994.

Acquisitions policy: To collect archives generated by or relating to the University of Edinburgh and its predecessor institutions, by donation, deposit, departmental transfer or purchase.

Archives of organisation: Archives concerned with the administration, students and teaching of the university 1583– , mainly 19th and 20th centuries, and including the archive of the Moray House Institute of Education, which itself includes Edinburgh Church of Scotland Training College and Normal School, 1845–1907; Edinburgh United Free Church Training College, 1843–1907; Edinburgh Provincial Training College, 1907–59, and Moray House College of Education, 1959–86.

Major collections: Records of student and other clubs and societies including Diagnostic Society, 1816–1966; Dialectic Society, 1787–1960; Celtic Society, 1848– c1960; Philosophical Society, 1871–1946 and the Royal Physical Society of Edinburgh, 1775–1911.

Non-manuscript material: Drawings and plans of the university.

Finding aids: A variety of manual card indexes, sheaf binders and lists. Some material relating to the university archives held as part of the manuscript collections can be searched remotely at http:datalib.ed.ac.uk/projects/scimms/.

Facilities: Photocopying. Microfilming. Photography at the discretion of the University Archivist.

Conservation: In-house.

Publications: A Catalogue of the Graduates in the Faculties of Arts, Divinity and Law of the University of Edinburgh to 1858 (Edinburgh, 1858).
List of the Graduates in Medicine in the University of Edinburgh, 1705–1866 (Edinburgh, 1867).
Alphabetical List of Graduates of the University of Edinburgh, 1859–1888 (Edinburgh, 1889).
A. Logan Turner: *History of the University of Edinburgh 1883–1933* (Edinburgh, 1933).
A. Morgan and R. Kerr Hannay (eds): *Charters Statutes Acts 1583–1858* (Edinburgh, 1937).
D.B. Horn: *A Short History of the University of Edinburgh 1556–1889* (Edinburgh, 1967).
G. Donaldson (ed.): *Four Centuries: Edinburgh University Life 1583–1983* (Edinburgh, 1983).

C Lothian Health Services Archive

Telephone: (0131) 650 3392

Fax: (0131) 650 6863

E-mail: lhsa@ed.ac.uk

Website: www.lhsa.lib.ed.ac.uk

Enquiries: Dr Mike Barfoot

Open: Term: Mon–Thurs: 9.00–6.00; Fri: 9.00–5.00.
Vacation: Mon–Fri: 9.00–5.00.

Access: Generally open to the public, but appointments for new users are preferred. Special permission is required to access personal health records closed for 75 years and administrative records closed for 30 years.

Historical background: The Royal Infirmary of Edinburgh was founded in 1729. It established a professional archive service in 1968. In 1974 the remit of the archivist was widened to cover the entire Lothian Health Board catchment area. Since 1994 the Archive has been directly managed by the university library on behalf of the local NHS funders of the service.

Acquisitions policy: To acquire NHS and other similar records relating principally to the Lothian area. Gifted and deposited material relating to the history of Edinburgh medicine and Scottish medicine generally is also collected.

Archives of organisation: Records of Royal Infirmary, Royal Edinburgh Hospital, Chalmers Hospital, Royal Hospital for Sick Children, Leith Hospital, City Hospital, Royal Maternity (Simpson's), Edinburgh Dental Hospital and School, South Eastern Regional Hospital Board, North and South Lothian District, Lothian Health Board.

Major collections: Personal papers of Alexander Murray Drennan (1884–1984), pathologist; Sir Derrick Melville Dunlop (1902–80), Christison Professor of Therapeutics and Clinical Medicine; Ernst Julius Levin (1887–1975), neurologist; Elsie Stephenson (1916–67), Director of Nursing Studies Unit.
Institutional papers of Medico-Chirurgical Society of Edinburgh, 1821–1959; Royal Infirmary Samaritan Society; and Edinburgh and South-East Scotland Blood Transfusion Service.

Non-manuscript material: Photographic collection (*c*10,000 images); printed book collections relating to midwifery and mental health in Scotland; some artefacts.

Finding aids: TS lists are available for most collections. Card indexes to photographs and some other printed collections. A summary catalogue and fully searchable top-level finding aid is available on the website.

Facilities: Photocopying. Photography. Microfilming.

D New College Library

Address: Mound Place, Edinburgh EH1 2LU

Telephone: (0131) 650 8957

Fax: (0131) 650 6579

E-mail: new.college.library@ed.ac.uk

Website: www.lib.ed.ac.uk/lib/sites/newcoll.shtml

Enquiries: The New College Librarian, Mrs Pamela Gilchrist

Open: Term: Mon–Thurs: 9.00–9.30; Fri: 9.00–5.00; Sat: 9.00–12.30.
Vacation: Mon–Fri: 9.00–5.00.

Access: Bona fide researchers, on written application.

Historical background: The college was founded in 1843 when training for the Free Church ministry began. The library has become one of the chief British research collections in theological, religious, historical and other subjects. After the Church Union of 1900, a large proportion of the library of the United Presbyterian Church College (Synod Hall) was acquired, and in more recent years the General Assembly (Tolbooth) Library of the Church of Scotland was incorporated. In 1935, as a result of the 1929 Reunion, New College formally became also the university's Faculty of Divinity, and in 1963 the library was placed on permanent deposit with the university. It is now administered as a detached section of the university library and includes a recently established Centre for the Study of Christianity in the Non-Western World.

Acquisitions policy: To add to the Thomas Chalmers archive by purchase or gift. To add to existing collections of papers of Scottish church leaders, and, selectively, other material relevant to the religious life of Scotland, and to the ecumenical and hymnology collections.

Archives of organisation: New College archives and historical papers. Papers of principals and professors of New College, 19th and 20th centuries, including John Baillie (1886–1960) and James Stuart Stewart (1896–1990).

Major collections: Archive of Thomas Chalmers (1780–1847).
MSS relating to individuals and events in Scottish church history, including Alexander Thomson (1798–1868) of Banchory; papers of John White (1867–1951) relating to reunion of Church of Scotland and United Free Church of Scotland, 1929; James King Hewison papers on the Covenanters, 17th century; letters, journals and sermons of Robert Baillie, 1637–62; James Kirkwood, provision of the Irish Bible in Scotland, and establishment of Highland libraries, 1676–1709; Thomas Brown archive for Annals of the Disruption, 1843; James Denney (1856–1917) of Glasgow United Free College.
Westminster Assembly of Divines minutes, 1643–52.
Sermons of Covenanters, 17th century; and Secession ministers, 18th century.

Ecumenical Collection, including Church of Scotland Special Committee on Anglican-Presbyterian relations, 1961–6; Christian Unity Association, 1904–56.
Centre for the Study of Christianity in the Non-Western World collections, including archives of Regions Beyond Missionary Union, c1880–1991; and Leprosy Mission International, 1874–1980.
Balfour of Burleigh papers on church reunion, to 1913.
Archibald Campbell Craig (1888–1985).
J.H. Oldham (1874–1969), papers.

Non-manuscript material: James Thin hymnology collection (7000 printed items).
Rare book collections in theological subjects, 15th–20th centuries.

Finding aids: Inventories and indexes.

Facilities: Photocopying. Microfilm/fiche readers. Microfilming and photography in main university library building.

Conservation: In-house conservator at main library.

Publications: H. Watt: *New College, Edinburgh: a Centenary History* (Edinburgh, 1946).
D.F. Wright and G.D. Badcock: *Disruption to Diversity: Edinburgh Divinity, 1846–1996* (Edinburgh, 1996).

E Reid Music Library

Address: Alison House, 12 Nicolson Square, Edinburgh EH8 9DF

Telephone: (0131) 650 2436

Fax: (0131) 650 2425

E-mail: reid.music.library@ed.ac.uk

Website: www.lib.ed.ac.uk/lib/sites/music.shtml

Enquiries: The Music Librarian, Mr J. Upton

Open: Term: Mon–Fri: 9.00–5.30; Sat: 9.30–12.30.
Vacation: Mon–Fri: 9.00–5.00.

Access: Bona fide researchers, on written application

Historical background: The teaching of music began at Edinburgh University in 1839 with the appointment of the first Reid professor of music. The collections were built up through the late 19th century and early 20th century by the Reid professors. The library became the music section of Edinburgh University Library in 1947.

Acquisitions policy: Selectively to add material relevant to the musical life of Edinburgh University.

Major collections: Letters, writings, music library and other papers of Donald Francis Tovey (1875–1940).
Music manuscripts of Kenneth Leighton (1929–88).
Papers of Leonard Friedman, violinist.

Non-manuscript material: Early texts on music theory.
Complete printed music of Luigi Dallapiccola.

Finding aids: Inventories and indexes.

Facilities: Photocopying. Microfilm/fiche readers. Microfilming and photography in main university library building.

Conservation: In-house conservator at main library.

Publications: J.M. Allan: 'The Reid Music Library', *Library World* 51 (1948), 99–101.
H. Gal: *Catalogue of Manuscripts, Printed Music and Books on Music up to 1850 in the Reid Library, Edinburgh* (1941).

352 The Writers' Museum

Parent organisation: City of Edinburgh Museums and Galleries

Address: Lady Stair's House, Lady Stair's Close, Lawnmarket, Edinburgh EH1 2PA

Telephone: (0131) 529 4901

Fax: (0131) 220 5057

E-mail: enquiries@writersmuseum.demon.co.uk

Enquiries: The Curator, Elaine Greig

Open: Mon–Fri: 10.00–5.00, by appointment.

Access: Researchers are requested to apply in writing.

Historical background: The museum was opened in 1907. Since the 1960s it has housed literary collections relating to the lives and works of Robert Burns (1759–96), Sir Walter Scott (1771–1832) and Robert Louis Stevenson (1850–94).

Acquisitions policy: No active policy for acquiring archives.

Major collections: Various papers relating to Robert Burns, Sir Walter Scott, Robert Louis Stevenson and George Meilde Kemp (1795–1844), architect of the Scott Monument.

Non-manuscript material: Plans and drawings of George Meilde Kemp.
Collection of photographs relating to Robert Louis Stevenson and, in particular, to his later life in the South Seas; also personal belongings, paintings and early editions.

Finding aids: General catalogue/card index.

Facilities: Photocopying. Photography.

353 Royal Holloway Archives

Parent organisation: University of London

Address: The Archive Service, Royal Holloway, University of London, Egham, Surrey TW20 0EX

Telephone: (01784) 443814

Fax: (01784) 435841

E-mail: archives@rhul.ac.uk

Website: www.rhul.ac.uk/archives

Enquiries: The College Archivist, Ms Sophie Badham

Open: Mon–Fri: 9.00–5.00; an appointment is necessary.

Access: Bona fide researchers; proof of identity is needed on the first visit. Student and staff records are closed for 100 years after the birth of the individual. College records are closed for 30 years.

Historical background: The Royal Holloway College, built in French Renaissance style to the design of the architect William Henry Crossland, was founded and endowed in 1883 by Thomas Holloway, the Victorian philanthropist who made a fortune from patent medicines. It was officially opened by Queen Victoria in 1886. Originally instituted as a women's college, it began admitting men in 1965. In 1985 the new college was formed by a merger with Bedford College, founded in 1849 as a women's college by Elizabeth Jesser Reid (1789–1866), which moved to Egham from Regent's Park. It has faculties of arts, music and science.

Acquisitions policy: To collect official records of the college in all its aspects and to acquire miscellaneous material relating to the history of the

Royal Holloway College, including its picture gallery, and of Bedford College. Collections are being sought relating to women and higher education as part of the archive's role in the Bedford Centre for the History of Women.

Archives of organisation: Board of Governors' records, 1886–1949, and Council records, 1949– ; records of the academic board, academic departments, library, administrative and residence departments, associations, committees, clubs and societies.
Records of Bedford College governing body, 1849– .

Major collections: Papers of Elizabeth Jesser Reid, 1789–1866; Caroline Spurgeon, 1869–1942; Lillian Penson, 1896–1963.

Non-manuscript material: A variety of miscellaneous material relating to the college and the parent colleges, including photographs of the buildings and of members of the college and their activities; items relating to Thomas Holloway and his family; historical notes, newspaper articles and cuttings; reminiscences and memoirs of members of the college; verses and fiction; prints, drawings and watercolours. Plans of the colleges. College publications, including magazines, prospectuses, annual reports, calendars.

Finding aids: Lists of additions to the catalogues and of personal papers; sent to NRA.

Facilities: Photocopying.

Conservation: Contracted out.

Publications: M. Tuke: *A History of Bedford College for Women, 1849–1937* (1939).
C. Bingham: *The History of Royal Holloway College, 1886–1986* (1987).
J. Elliott: *Palaces, Patronage and Pills. Thomas Holloway: His Sanatorium, College and Pictures Gallery* (1986).
Leaflets on the College Archives and the Bedford Centre for the History of Women.

354 Elgin Museum

Parent organisation: Moray Society

Address: 1 High Street, Elgin, Moray IV30 1EQ

Telephone: (01343) 543675

Fax: (01343) 543675

Website: www.elginmuseum.demon.co.uk

Enquiries: Susan Bennett

Open: April–Oct: Mon–Fri: 10.00–5.00. Winter: by appointment.

Access: Generally open to the public. An appointment is necessary.

Historical background: Elgin and Morayshire Scientific Association (now the Moray Society) was founded in 1836. The museum was opened to the public in 1843.

Acquisitions policy: Modern policy is mostly concerned with collections relating to Moray.

Archives of organisation: Accession books, minutes, letters, newspaper cuttings etc, 1856– .

Major collections: Dr George Gordon of Birnie (1801–93): family history material and scientific correspondence, including with Thomas Huxley (1825–95) and Charles Darwin (1809–92).
Watson Papers: accounts and letters relating to an Elgin sawmill, 1880s.
Moray Farmers' Club archives.

Non-manuscript material: Election posters, 19th century.

Facilities: Photocopying.

Publications: M. Collie and S. Bennett: *George Gordon: An Annotated Catalogue of his Scientific Correspondence* (Scolar Press, 1966).

355 Gordonstoun

Address: Elgin, Moray IV30 2RF

Telephone: (01343) 830445

Fax: (01343) 837838

Website: www.gordonstoun.org.uk

Enquiries: The Hon. Archivist, Mrs Jane Thomas

Open: By arrangement only.

Access: By appointment to researchers.

Historical background: An ancient Scottish estate since the 13th century, Gordonstoun has been a public school since 1934. Gordon Cumming private family papers (owners of Gordonstoun from 17th century to 1934) are deposited in the National Library of Scotland (entry 331).

Acquisitions policy: Any papers on the estate, past and present staff, former pupils, or past governors are most welcome.

Archives of organisation: Minutes of boys', staff and governors' meetings; material relating to the school's varied activities; letters to/from past headmasters, governors and old boys; general administrative papers.

Non-manuscript material: Pamphlets and photographs.
Plans, maps and drawings.

Finding aids: Various lists and indexes.

Facilities: Photocopying.

Publications: H.L. Brereton: *Gordonstoun* (Aberdeen, 1968/R1981).
D.A. Byatt: *Kurt Hahn: an Appreciation of his Life and Work* (Gordonstoun).

356 Local Heritage Centre

Parent organisation: Moray Council

Address: Grant Lodge, Cooper Park, Elgin, Moray IV30 1HS

Telephone: (01343) 544475

Fax: (01343) 549050

E-mail: graeme.wilson@techleis.moray.gov.uk

Enquiries: The Local Heritage Officer, Graeme Wilson

Open: Mon, Wed–Fri: 10.00–5.00; Tues: 10.00–8.00; Sat 10.00–12.00.

Access: Generally open to the public; pre–1975 local government records require 24 hours' notice.

Historical background: The former Moray District Record Office was established in 1975 and was amalgamated with the local studies section of Elgin Public Library in 1998 to form the Local Heritage Centre. Until structural work has been carried out on Grant Lodge, the kirk session, justice of the peace and customs and excise records have been returned to the National Archives of Scotland (entry 329). Records of commissioners of supply, parish councils, parochial boards and school records are presently held by Aberdeen City Archives (see entry 3).

Acquisitions policy: Records relating to Moray.

Archives of organisation: Usual local authority record holdings: archives of pre–1975 authorities in Moray, including three royal and nine police burghs, county councils and district councils, 1268–1975.

Major collections: Records of J. & H.W. Leask, solicitors, Forres, 17th–20th centuries.
Records of Anderson's Institution (free school), Forres, 1823–88, and Elgin, 1834–1958.

Non-manuscript material: Architectural plans of Wittets Ltd, Elgin, 1826–1970, and AJ Morrison & Co., Elgin, 1850–1974, including distillery plans of Charles Chree Doig (1855–1918).
Photographs of Moray, c1855–1998 (c20,000).

Finding aids: Lists, calendars, card and computerised indexes of persons, places and subjects.

Facilities: Photocopying. Microform readers/printer.

357 Pluscarden Abbey Library

Address: Elgin, Moray IV30 3UA

Fax: (01343) 890258

E-mail: monks@pluscardenabbey.org

Website: www.pluscardenabbey.org

Enquiries: The Librarian, Dom Augustine Holmes

Open: By appointment only.

Access: Bona fide researchers, on application to Rt Rev. Fr Abbot.

Historical background: The abbey was founded in 1230 and refounded in 1948. Medieval charters are on deposit at John Rylands Library, Manchester (see entry 875). Other medieval and early modern documents are among Duff House Charters at Aberdeen University Library (see entry 5).

Acquisitions policy: To maintain the archives of the Abbey.

Archives of organisation: Select charters, 1233–1551.
Private community archive, 1948– .

Major collections: Certain papers of P.F. Anson (1889–1975), writer, artist and former member of the community, and of Abbot Aelred Carlyle (1874–1955), founder of the community.

Non-manuscript material: Some books from local Catholic Missions collected by Fr. Antony Ross, mainly 18th century.
Photographs of the abbey.

358   David Owen Archive

Parent organisation: The Waterways Trust

Address: The Boat Museum, South Pier Road, Ellesmere Port, Cheshire CH65 4FW

Telephone: (0151) 355 5017

Fax: (0151) 355 4079

E-mail: boatmuseum@easynet.co.uk

Website: boatmuseum.org.uk

Enquiries: The Archives Officer, Ms Diana Sumner

Open: Mon–Fri: 10.30–4.30; telephone to confirm opening.

Access: Generally open to the public; appointments are preferred.

Historical background: The Boat Museum opened in 1976 with a modest collection of four craft of the inland navigations and then began gathering documents, photographs, artefacts, books and information relating to canals worldwide. The David Owen Archive was officially opened in 1990 and is now an important repository of canal records. The museum is situated in the old transhipment dock of Ellesmere Port which connects the Shropshire Union Canal to the Manchester Ship Canal. It represents an embodiment of the canal age based very largely on the evidence of the archive.

Acquisitions policy: To collect material and informative evidence relating to the history of inland navigations. This includes craft, artefacts, boatbuilding drawings, maps, working records, documents, parliamentary material, photographs, books, audio-visual evidence and other relevant items. The collecting policy extends beyond British canals to world canals where appropriate.

Archives of organisation: Archives of the Boat Museum Trust.

Major collections: David Owen Collection of documents, photographs, slides and artefacts.
Denys Hutchings Collection of papers, books and slides.
Weaver Navigation Files (on loan from British Waterways, NW Division).

Non-manuscript material: Michel Ware Collection of photographs and postcards.
John Heap Collection: Library of the Inland Waterways Association (on long-term loan).

Daphne Roswell Collection of artefacts, books and slides.
Hadfield Collection of books, articles and slides relating to world canals.
Robert Aickman Collection of photographs.
National Waterways Sounds Recording Project Collection.

Finding aids: Card indexes and collection lists. Computerisation in progress.

Facilities: Photocopying. Photography.

Conservation: Paper conservation is carried out by the North West Museums Service.

Publications: The Boat Museum Brochure.
Development of a Dock Area (Archive Pack no. 1).
Canals in Cheshire (Archive Pack no. 2).

359   Fermanagh County Museum

Parent organisation: Fermanagh District Council

Address: Enniskillen Castle, Castle Barracks, Enniskillen, Co. Fermanagh BT74 7HL

Telephone: (02866) 325000

Fax: (02866) 327342

E-mail: castle@fermanagh.gov.uk

Enquiries: Ms H. Lanigan Wood

Open: By appointment only.

Access: Bona fide researchers, by prior arrangement.

Historical background: The County Museum is situated within the precincts of the 15th-century Enniskillen Castle, which houses a separate regimental museum for the Royal Enniskillen Fusiliers.

Acquisitions policy: To maintain and build on the collection relating to Co. Fermanagh only.

Major collections: Co. Fermanagh criminal books, 1861–1969, and proclamations.
Lady Dorothy Lowry-Corry correspondence, 1931–5.
Canon W.H. Dundas (*d* 1941), family papers.

Non-manuscript material: Photographs, maps, posters, sound archives and ephemera.

Facilities: Photocopying.

Conservation: Contracted out.

360 Epsom College Archive

Address: Epsom College, Epsom, Surrey KT17 4JQ

Telephone: (01372) 821022

Fax: (01372) 821023

E-mail: a-scadding@epsomcollege.sch.uk

Enquiries: The Archivist, Mr A.G. Scadding

Open: During school term, by arrangement.

Access: Bona fide researchers, by appointment.

Historical background: Epsom College was founded in 1851 as the Royal Medical Benevolent College in direct response to the inadequacies perceived in the medical profession during the epidemics of the 1830s and 1840s. It opened as a school and asylum for the medical profession in 1855. Development by 1900 resulted in an independent school of international reputation. Strong links with medical colleges were formed in the 1890s, by which time the college was one of the pioneers of science education. The archive was begun in 1980, but inherited material from the foundation in 1851, relating to the money-raising activities of the profession, the public elections to pensioners and scholarships, the growth of the school, royal connections and the development of buildings.

Acquisitions policy: Records from the school and the charity by collection and as a part of record-keeping policies within the institutions. Gifts of interested Old Epsomians and friends. Non-school or charity related items are passed on to the relevant county or national archive.

Archives of organisation: Bound minutes, accounts, photograph albums, headmasters' book, scrapbooks etc, 1851– .
Headmasters' archive: collection of interesting correspondence.
Bursars' archive: documents relating to diet; trenches and evacuation in event of invasion in 1940s; rationing; employment and plans of development.
Trivia boxes: general collections of school-related items for every ten years.
Special collections of sports club, society (natural history) and departmental material.

Non-manuscript material: Photograph boxes, 19th century– .
Maps and plans.
Drainage and works records, including plans by Sir Joseph Bazalgette (1819–91).

Finding aids: Handlists with keys to main sources.

Facilities: Photocopying. Some photographic facilities on request.

Publications: M.A. Salmon, *Epsom College: the First 125 Years.*

361 Lord's Day Observance Society

Address: Unit 3 Epsom Business Park, Kiln Lane, Epsom, Surrey KT17 1JF

Telephone: (01372) 728300

Fax: (01372) 722400

E-mail: johnroberts@lordsday.co.uk

Website: www.lordsday.co.uk

Enquiries: The General Secretary, Mr John Roberts

Open: By arrangement only.

Access: Students and those involved in research regarding the Lord's Day, by appointment with the General Secretary.

Historical background: The society was founded in 1831 by Joseph Wilson and Rev. Daniel Wilson (later Bishop of Calcutta), and it seeks to promote the observance of the Lord's Day for worship. It united with the Working Men's Lord's Day Rest Association in 1920, with the Lord's Day Observance Association of Scotland in 1953 and with the Imperial Alliance for the Defence of Scotland in 1965. Some of the archives were destroyed during World War II.

Acquisitions policy: To maintain the archives.

Archives of organisation: Some records of predecessor society. Minutes, reports and journals, 1830– .
Annual accounts, 1978– .

Non-manuscript material: Magazine *Day One*, 1948– .

Facilities: Photocopying.

362 Evesham Public Library

Parent organisation: Worcestershire County Council

Address: Oat Street, Evesham, Worcestershire WR11 4PJ

Telephone: (01386) 442291

Fax: (01386) 765855

E-mail: eveshamlib@worcestershire.gov.uk

Enquiries: The Librarian, Mrs L. Downes

Open: Mon, Tues, Fri: 9.30–5.30; Thurs: 9.30–8.00; Sat: 9.30–1.00.

Access: Generally open to the public. No appointment is necessary but there are restrictions on the use of the photograph collection.

Principally non-MS material, including the collection of E.A.B. Barnard (*d* 1953), local historian. Complete holding of *Evesham Journal* and its photograph collection. Photocopying and microfilm/fiche reader/printer are available.

363 Courtenay Archives

Address: Powderham Castle, Kenton, Exeter, Devon EX6 8JQ

Telephone: (01626) 890243

Fax: (01626) 890729

E-mail: courtsoc@courtsoc.demon.co.uk

Enquiries: The Archivist

Open: Mon–Fri: 9.30–12.00.

Access: Approved researchers and genealogists, by appointment only. The charge depends on the level of staff involvement.

Powderham Castle has been owned and occupied by the Courtenay family, Earls of Devon, since 1393. The archives consist of family and estate records, plans and maps, mainly from the 18th century onwards, earlier material being deposited in Devon Record Office, Exeter (entry 365). Genealogical records of the Courtenay family worldwide are maintained. There is an index to the MSS and pictures and lists are sent to the NRA. There are facilities for photocopying and photography and the following publications by Dorothy Presswell are available: *The History of Powderham Castle*, *Browsing in the Archives* and *Browsing in the Archives Again*.

364 Devon and Exeter Institution Library

Address: 7 Cathedral Close, Exeter, Devon EX1 1EZ

Telephone: (01392) 251017

Website: www.ex.ac.uk/~ijtilsed/lib/devonex.html

Enquiries: The Librarian-in-Charge, Ms Madeleine Midgley
The Hon. Secretary (archives of institution), Mrs M. Rowe

Open: Mon–Fri: 9.00–5.00.

Access: Members and bona fide day researchers (temporary membership available), by appointment.

Historical background: The Devon and Exeter Institution is an independent subscription library founded in 1813. Since 1972 its library has been administered by the University of Exeter (see entry 368).

Acquisitions policy: Material relating to the south-western counties of England, Devon, Cornwall, Somerset and Dorset.

Archives of organisation: Records of the Devon and Exeter Institution, 1813– , including meteorological registers, 1817–1975.

Major collections: Archive of the Bonus family (Exeter), 19th and 20th centuries.
Correspondence of Henry Whiteway & Co., cider makers of Whimple, Devon, 1897–8.
Business archives of Fox & Co, woollen mill, Wellington, Somerset, 1737–1812.

Non-manuscript material: Devon map and topographical prints collection.
Scrapbooks of the Exeter Diocesan Architectural Society.
Grant-Sturgis family (Cullompton, Devon), photograph album and scrapbook.

Finding aids: Card catalogue and computer. Catalogue records integrated into Exeter University Library on-line public access catalogue.

Facilities: Photocopying. Microfiche reader.

Publications: N. Longridge: *The Devon & Exeter Institution, 1813–1988* (R.N. Longridge, 1988, repr. 1995).

365 Devon Record Office

Address: Castle Street, Exeter, Devon EX4 3PU

Telephone: (01392) 384253

Fax: (01392) 384256

E-mail: devrec@devon.gov.uk

Website: www.devon.gov.uk/dro

Enquiries: The County Archivist, Mr John Draisey

Open: Mon–Thurs: 10.00–5.00; Fri: 10.00–4.30. Closed first two weeks in February.

Access: Generally open to the public, but proof of identity is required. Some documents are kept at an out-store and require 48 hours' notice for production in the Search Rooms. No original documents will be produced between 1.00 pm and 2.00 pm or within 30 minutes of closing time. A paid genealogy research service is available; details may be found on the website. Service points for consultation of microfiches of records are available at a number of locations throughout the county; leaflets giving details are available.

Historical background: The old County Record Office was established in 1952 and the former Exeter City Record Office (originally Exeter MSS Department of the library) was established in 1947. In 1974 the latter became the East Devon Office, and it amalgamated with the old County Office in 1977. The office also acts as the Diocesan Record Office for Exeter and is recognised as a place of deposit for public records. There are branch offices at Barnstaple (entry 52) and Exeter Cathedral (entry 366). The Plymouth and West Devon Record Office (entry 1029) was a branch office from 1974 to 1998

Acquisitions policy: Archival material relevant to the historic county of Devon.

Archives of organisation: Usual local authority record holdings.

Major collections: Deposited collections, including the following which have a wider significance:

Papers of Henry Addington, first Viscount Sidmouth (1757–1844); Gen. John Graves Simcoe, relating to Canada and the campaign in the West Indies, 1776–97.

Non-manuscript material: Microfilms of papers of William Buckland (1784–1856), geologist, and his son Frank Buckland (1809–91), naturalist.

Finding aids: Catalogues and indexes; sent to NRA.

Facilities: Photocopying. Photography and microfilming by arrangement. Microfilm reader/printer.

Conservation: In-house department.

Publications: List available on request.

366 Exeter Cathedral

A Archives

Address: The Cloister Library, Diocesan House, Palace Gate, Exeter, Devon EX1 1HX

Telephone: (01392) 495954

Website: www.ex.ac.uk/library/cathedral.html.

Enquiries: Mrs A.A. Doughty

Open: Mon–Wed: 2.00–5.00, by arrangement.

Access: Serious researchers, by appointment only.

Historical background: A monastery existed here as early as 670 ad. A cathedral church was established in 1050 and consecrated in 1113. The archives are now administered by the Devon Record Office (entry 365) on behalf of the Dean and Chapter of Exeter Cathedral, and the archives of the Archdeaconry of Exeter have been transferred there.

Acquisitions policy: Restricted to records directly relating to the cathedral, its personnel and its present and former properties.

Archives of organisation: Capitular archives: royal diplomas, 10th–11th centuries; charters, deeds, leases; lawsuits etc; chapter acts, late 14th century– ; registers, cartularies etc; rentals, surveys, manorial records, maps, plans etc; accounts, 12th century–; deeds, agreements and manorial records, 18th–19th centuries, redeposited by the Church Commissioners.
Archives of the College of vicars choral, 13th–20th centuries, of a similar nature to the capitular archives.
Papers of Henry Phillpotts, Bishop of Exeter (1778–1869).

Non-manuscript material: Accumulating collection of photographs and coloured photographic slides, mainly of architectural and sculptural details of the cathedral, primarily to record the continuing conservation programme.

Finding aids: MS catalogue of part of the capitular archives (compiled by A. Stuart Moore, 1873); gradually being superseded by numerous lists, card catalogues and indexes in progress. Complete summary class lists in typescript of records of the College of Vicars Choral and of the Archdeaconry of Exeter. Phillpotts: NRA 25909.

Facilities: Photocopying. Photography by arrangement. Microfiche reader.

Conservation: Work undertaken by Devon Record Office, with grants from the Friends of the Cathedral.

Publications: L.J. Lloyd and A.M. Erskine: *The Library of Exeter Cathedral, with a Short Description of the Archives* (Exeter, 1967/R1974).
A.M. Erskine (ed. & trans.): *The Accounts of the Fabric of Exeter Cathedral, 1279–1353*, Devon & Cornwall Record Society, new series, vols 24, 26 (Exeter, 1981, 1983).

B Library

Address: Old Bishop's Palace, Diocesan House, Palace Gate, Exeter, Devon EX1 1HX

Telephone: (01392) 272894

Fax: (01392) 263871 [University Library]

E-mail: p.w.thomas@exeter.ac.uk

Website: www.exeter-cathedral.org.uk/admin/library.html

Enquiries: Mr P.W. Thomas

Open: Mon–Fri: 2.00–5.00.

Access: Generally open to the public; an appointment is appreciated if medieval MSS are required for study.

Historical background: The library was founded by a gift of 66 MSS by Leofric, Bishop of Exeter (*d* 1072), and has had a continuous history since that date. It is now under the administration of the University of Exeter (entry 368).

Acquisitions policy: The collection is virtually static, though gifts would be considered, and an attempt might be made to acquire any MSS of direct relevance to the existing stock.

Archives of organisation: Early catalogues, former librarians' annual reports, unpublished notes on MSS, and other papers, 20th century.

Major collections: Medieval MSS, including the Exeter Book of Poetry, 10th century, and the Exon Domesday, 11th century. Books, pamphlets and a few MSS, post-medieval.

Non-manuscript material: Printed material on MSS and photographs.

Finding aids: MSS catalogued on Exeter University computer catalogue; lists, some on microfilm.

Facilities: Photocopying. Photography. Microfilming (by Exeter University reprographic department). Microfiche reader.

Publications: HMC Report on Manuscripts in Various Collections, IV, 23–95 (1907).
M.P. Crichton: *A Catalogue of the Medical Books and Manuscripts, including a Selection of Scientific Works, in Exeter Cathedral Library* (Exeter, 1934).
N.R. Ker: *Medieval Manuscripts in British Libraries*, ii (Oxford, 1977), 800–46.
L.J. Lloyd and A.M. Erskine: *The Library of Exeter Cathedral, with a Short Description of the Archives* (Exeter, 1967/R1974).

367 Exeter Central Library

Parent organisation: Devon Library and Information Services

Address: Castle Street, Exeter, Devon EX4 3PQ

Telephone: (01392) 384216 (direct line)

Fax: (01392) 384228

E-mail: exelib@dial.devon-cc.gov.uk

Website: www.devon-cc.gov.uk/library/locstudy

Enquiries: The Westcountry Studies Librarian

Open: Mon, Fri: 9.30–6.00; Tues, Thurs: 9.30–8.00; Wed: 10.00–5.00; Sat: 9.30–4.00.

Access: Generally open to the public; a prior enquiry is advisable. Paid research is undertaken by Devon Record Office (see entry 365). Current details with charges are available at www.devon-cc.gov.uk/dro

Historical background: Devon Library Services was formed from a number of separate library authorities on local government reorganisation in 1974; Plymouth and Torbay regained independent status in 1998. Exeter Public Library had been established in 1869 and had considerable MS collections. Its archives are now administered by Devon Record Office. Most MSS in Devon Library Services are now non-archival in nature and relatively few in number; they are to be found mainly in the Westcountry Studies Library in Exeter. Smaller local history collections are at Barnstaple, Exmouth, Newton Abbot, Bideford and some other branch libraries.

Acquisitions policy: To acquire non-archival MSS and other types of documentation which reflect the development of Devon and South-West England.

Major collections: Several hundred MSS and TSS, mainly on local antiquarian or genealogical topics, including the writings of historians such as Tristram Risdon (?1580–1640) and James Davidson (1793–1864), armorials and several surveys of Devon churches.

A few literary MSS by R.D. Blackmore (1825–1900), John Galsworthy (1867–1933), Eden Phillpotts (1862–1960), Sabine Baring-Gould (1834–1924) and Neil Bell.

Devon and Cornwall Record Society collection of transcripts of parish records (1200 vols; available to members only).

J. Brooking Rowe Collection of rubbings of monumental brasses.

Non-manuscript material: Extensive collections of illustrations, newspaper-cutting files, ephemera, maps relating to South-West England. Brooking-Rowe bookplate collection.

Rare book collection, including 2500 pre-1800 imprints.

Small collections of sound and video recordings.

Finding aids: Card indexes and computerised database giving access by author, place and subject. Catalogue of local studies monograph material, including MSS, on Internet.

Facilities: Photocopying. Microfilm/fiche reader/printers.

Conservation: Some work undertaken by Devon Record Office; other work contracted out.

Publications: Some MS material listed in A. Brockett (comp.): *The Devon Union List* (Exeter, 1977).

Some MS items in *Abbots Bickington to Zeal Monachorum: a Handlist of Devon Parish Histories* (Exeter, 1994).

Publications list available.

368 University of Exeter Library

Address: Stocker Road, Exeter, Devon EX4 4PT

Telephone: (01392) 263862

Fax: (01392) 263871

E-mail: library@exeter.ac.uk

Website: www.ex.ac.uk/library/archives

Enquiries: The Assistant Librarian (Special Collections), Madeleine Midgley
The Archivist, Ian Mortimer

Open: Mon–Fri: 2.00–5.00.

Access: Bona fide researchers, on written application to the librarian.

Historical background: The university library dates from 1955, when the university received its charter. The earliest acquisitions were miscellaneous gifts to the library of the University College SW, the predecessor institution. Archives prior to 1955 are held by Devon Record Office (entry 365), post-1955 archives are held by the university, not the library.

Acquisitions policy: Archives and MSS are occasionally purchased but the majority of items are gifts.

Major collections: Literary papers and MSS of R.D. Blackmore (1825–1900), Henry Williamson (1895–1977), Jack Clemo (1916–94), Charles Causley (*b* 1917) and Ted Hughes (1930–98).

Papers of A.L. Rowse (1903–97), historian.

Notebooks and photograph albums of Denton Welch (1915–48).

Autographs: small collection of 19th-century autographs and letters.

Astronomy: archives of Sir Norman Lockyer (1836–1920).

West Indies: collection of papers relating to estates and slavery in Jamaica.

Non-manuscript material: Theatre: large collection of playbills of the Theatre Royal, Exeter, *c*1890–early 1950s.

Local history: local newspapers, prints and MSS.

Early maps, mainly of Devon and Cornwall.

Photographs relating to former British colonies.

American music collection of tapes, records and CDs, especially jazz and blues but also covering

Cajun to North American Indian music (*c*7500).

Finding aids: Lists.

Facilities: Photocopying. Photography.

Publications: Guide in preparation.

369 Ronald Duncan Papers: The New Collection

Parent organisation: The Ronald Duncan Literary Foundation

Address: Faculty of Arts and Education, University of Plymouth, Douglas Avenue, Exmouth, Devon EX8 2AT

Telephone: (01395) 255390

Fax: (01395) 255303

E-mail: a.munton@plymouth.ac.uk

Enquiries: The Archivist, Dr Alan Munton

Open: Mon–Thurs: 9.30–5.30.

Access: Bona fide researchers, after written application, preferably with a letter of introduction.

Historical background: The Ronald Duncan Trust (f. 1973) aims to further the study and assessment of the work of Ronald Frederick Henry Duncan (1914–82) and other artists. It has shared a storage agreement with the University of Plymouth since 1993 to house, collate and catalogue the collection of documentation and memorabilia which illustrates developments in post-1930s literary culture. Other holdings can be found in Kings College Library, Cambridge (entry 185) and at the University of Texas.

Acquisitions policy: Primary source material and correspondence of Duncan, material relevant to the biographical/critical study of his career, ephemera, records, documents, memorabilia, by purchase or as a loan/gift to the collection.

Archives of organisation: Information provided by the Ronald Duncan Literary Foundation, 1973– .
Background material on the University of Plymouth archives project (1993).

Major collections: The personal (and related) papers of the author Ronald Duncan, including original draft manuscripts of poems, plays and novels, diaries, correspondence, journalism, photographs, artwork, scrapbooks, periodicals, cuttings.

Non-manuscript material: Photographs, including family albums and play productions. Audio tapes, interviews, orchestral records, poetry readings, playtext readings.
Programmes, periodicals, playbills, news cuttings, libretti, related published works.

Finding aids: Catalogue (part 1): *The Handlist of the Ronald Duncan Papers: the New Collection* (1995); see NRA 38395.
Searchable database available on request.

Facilities: Photocopying. Microfiche readers.

Conservation: Minor conservation work is undertaken on the premises, with major binding/repair work contracted out.

Publications: The Handlist of the Ronald Duncan Papers: the New Collection (University of Plymouth, 1995).

370 Eyam Hall

Address: Eyam, Hope Valley, Derbyshire S32 5QW

Telephone: (01433) 631976

Fax: (01433) 631603

E-mail: nicwri@eyamhall.co.uk

Website: www.eyamhall.co.uk/

Enquiries: Managing Partner, Nicola Wright

Open: By appointment.

Access: Generally open to scholars, by prior arrangement.

Eyam Hall was built in 1671–2 by a junior branch of the Derbyshire family of Wright of Great Longstone. It has been the home of the Wrights of Eyam ever since and is today the home of R. H. V. Wright Esq. Archives consist of family papers, deeds (mainly for Derbyshire), late 17th century– , papers relating to lead-mining, and photographs. A list of the collection is in preparation. Photocopying, with some restrictions, is available.

371 Falkirk Library

Parent organisation: Falkirk Council

Address: Hope Street, Falkirk FK1 5AU

Telephone: (01324) 503605

Fax: (01324) 503606

E-mail: falkirk-library@falkirk-library.demon.co.uk

Enquiries: The Reference Librarian

Open: Mon–Tues, Thurs: 9.30–8.00; Wed, Fri–Sat: 9.30–5.00.

Access: Generally open to the public, by appointment.

Major collections: Scottish Metalworkers' Union minutes; Falkirk Town Council minutes.

Non-manuscript material: Local newspapers, 1845– .
Census returns.
Press cutting collection.
Small collection of photographs, films and videos of Falkirk social events.

Finding aids: Index to press cuttings; partial index to newspapers.

Facilities: Photocopying. Microfilm reader/printer.

372 Falkirk Museums History Research Centre

Parent organisation: Falkirk Council

Address: Callander House, Callander Park, Falkirk FK1 1YR

Telephone: (01324) 503770

Fax: (01324) 503771

E-mail: callanderhouse@falkirkmuseums.demon.co.uk

Website: www.falkirkmuseums.demon.co.uk

Enquiries: The Archivist, Ms M. Elspeth Reid

Open: Mon–Fri: 10.00–12.30, 1.30–5.00.

Access: Generally open to the public.

Historical background: Falkirk Museum was founded in 1926 from a bequest by Mungo Buchanan, architect and antiquarian, and was based on his collection of MSS and photographic material. The collections were extended to form a local history archive primarily for the town of Falkirk. After local government reorganisation in 1975 the remit was extended to cover the whole of Falkirk district, and records of local businesses and organisations were actively collected. Since 1996, with local government reorganisation, the records of local

authorities have been transferred to Falkirk Museums, which now provides the archives service for Falkirk Council. Most of the records for the predecessor authority of Stirling County are held in Stirling Council Archives (see entry 1133).

Acquisitions policy: To acquire records relating to the area served by Falkirk Council and its predecessors, including records of local authorities, local businesses, industries, organisations, clubs, trade unions, private individuals and families; records relating to museum objects, photographs, ephemera and books.

Archives of organisation: Burgh records of Falkirk, 1803–1975; Grangemouth, 1872–1975; Bo'ness, 1663–1975; Denny and Dunipace, 1833–1975.
District councils records of Stirling County (Eastern Nos. 1, 2, 3, Central No. 2), 1930–75, West Lothian County (Bo'ness, Carriden), 1930–75, Falkirk, 1975–95.
School board records, school log books and admissions registers for schools in the Falkirk area, 1873–1980; valuation rolls and electoral registers for burghs, 1864–1975 (gaps), and Falkirk District, 1975– ; cemetery records.
Falkirk Museums records, 1926– .

Major collections: Records of local businesses and organisations, including Grangemouth Dockyard Co., 1920s–1970s; P. & M. Hurll (Birkhill Clay Mine), 1939–80; J. Baird & Co. (Sawmill), 1934–78; Grahamston Iron Co., 1868–1991; Falkirk Temperance Café Trust, 1919–91; Bo'ness United General Seabox Benificient Society, 1613–20th century.
Records of local estates and families, including Forbes of Callendar Papers, 1530–1932; Burns Family, Falkirk, 1791–1921; James Love Collection *c*1679–1920s (local antiquarian, *d* 1928).
Buchanan Collection: site plans, sketches.

Non-manuscript material: Photograph collection, 1840–1990s, including local life and places, archaeological digs, museum objects and examples of the work of local photographers; incorporates collections of Grangemouth Dockyard Co. and local authority planning department and local authority leisure collection (*c*28,000).
Maps and plans, Falkirk area, 18th and 19th centuries.
Callander Estates maps and plans, 1780s–1950s.
Grangemouth Dockyard Co. ship plans.
Foundry catalogues, 1860s–1980s.
Small oral history collection.

Finding aids: Card and computerised lists and indexes, fonds-level finding aids. Lists sent to NRAS. Bibliographical and trades indexes.

Facilities: Photocopying. Photography. Microfiche reader/printer. Slide hire.

Conservation: Contracted out.

Publications: Various publications based on photographs from the collections.

373 St Michael's Abbey

Address: 280 Farnborough Road, Farnborough, Hampshire GU14 7NQ

Telephone: (01252) 546105

Fax: (01252) 372822

E-mail: prior@farnboroughabbey.org

Website: www.farnboroughabbey.org

Enquiries: The Archivist/Librarian

Open: Strictly by appointment only.

Access: By previous private arrangement.

The church and monastery were built between 1883 and 1888 and stand opposite the former residence of the Empress Eugénie (1826–1920). In 1895 they were occupied by Benedictine monks from the Abbey of Solesmes, France, and 50 years later were handed over to English monks. Monastic archives exist, 1895– , plus plans, drawings etc of the grade I abbey church. There is also an abbey library with special reference to the French Second Empire (1848–70).

374 Falconer Museum

Parent organisation: Moray Council, Department of Technical & Leisure Services, Museums Service

Address: Tolbooth Street, Forres IV36 0PH

Telephone: (01309) 673701

Fax: (01309) 675863

E-mail: alasdair.joyce@techleis.moray.gov.uk

Website: www.moray.org/museums/homepage.htm

Enquiries: The Senior Museums Officer, Alasdair Joyce

Open: Nov–March: Mon–Fri: 11.00–1.00, 2.00–4.00.

April: Mon–Fri: 10.00–5.00.
May–Oct: Mon–Sat: 10.00–5.00.

Access: Bona fide researchers, preferably with a reference and by written appointment.

Historical background: The Falconer Museum is the headquarters of the Museums Division. It was established in 1871 following a bequest by Alexander Falconer in the 1860s and was transferred to the custody of the local authority in 1975.

Acquisitions policy: To collect documentary material relating to Moray when it supplements museum specimens or collections, or is an addition to archival collections already held.

Archives of organisation: Archives of Moray Council are at Moray Council HQ.
Minutes of the Falcolner Trust, 1853–1975, 1991–94 with Museums Service.

Major collections: Archive of Hugh Falconer (1808–65), palaeontologist and botanist, 1836–65.
Diaries and correspondence of Peter Anson (1889–1975), marine painter and recorder of maritime topics, 1919–75.

Finding aids: Simplified catalogue database available on Internet.

Facilities: Photocopying. Photography. Computer scanning.

Publications: Set of information leaflets available.
P.J. Boylan: *The Falconer Papers, Forres* (Leicestershire Museums, Art Galleries and Records Services, 1977).

375 West Highland Museum

Address: Cameron Square, Fort William, Inverness-shire PH33 6AJ

Telephone: (01397) 702169

Fax: (01397) 701927

Enquiries: The Curator, Fiona C. Marwick

Open: Nov–May: Mon–Fri: 10.00–4.00; Jun–Oct: 10.00–5.00.

Access: Anyone may consult the records, but preference will always be given to members; an appointment is essential.

The museum was founded in 1922. It is independent and self-financing and was set up to collect and preserve everything of relevance to the West Highlands. The principal collection is of Jacobite papers, including Cluny family correspondence, 1578–1825 (NRA 13685). The Lochaber Oral Recording Archive begun in 1996 is also housed here.

376 Gateshead Libraries and Arts Service
Local Studies Department

Parent organisation: Gateshead Metropolitan Borough Council

Address: Central Library, Prince Consort Road, Gateshead NE8 4LN

Telephone: (0191) 477 3478

Fax: (0191) 477 7454

E-mail: local@gateslib.demon.co.uk

Website: www.gateshead.mbc.gov.uk/ls

Enquiries: The Local Studies Librarian, Miss E. Carnaffin

Open: Mon, Tues, Thurs, Fri: 9.00–7.00; Wed: 9.00–5.00; Sat: 9.00–1.00.

Access: Generally open to the public.

The local history collection has existed since the opening of the library in 1884. It became a separate local studies and archives department in 1974. Acquisitions are restricted to material relating to the area covered by Gateshead Metropolitan Borough Council. Major collections have been transferred to Tyne and Wear Archives Service (see entry 921), but the general local history collections for the borough include some manuscripts, photographs and maps. See F.W.D. Manders: *Gateshead Archives: a Guide* (1968).

377 British Motor Industry Heritage Trust

Parent organisation: Ford Group

Address: Banbury Road, Gaydon, Warwick CV35 0BJ

Telephone: (01926) 641188

Fax: (01926) 641555

E-mail: gbardsle@landrover.com

Website: www.heritage.org.uk

Enquiries: The Archivist, Gillian Bardsley

Open: Mon–Fri: 10.00–5.00.

Access: Generally open to the public, by prior appointment. There is a 30-year closure on business records and no access to engineering drawings.

Historical background: The trust, formerly Leyland Historic Vehicles and BL Heritage Ltd, was established in 1983. At the same address the trust operates the Heritage Motor Centre (Motor Museum). Material relating to British commercial vehicles may be found in the British Commercial Vehicle Museum, at King Street, Leyland, Lancashire. Some business records of the Rover Group and associated companies are in the trust's deposit at the Modern Records Centre (entry 261).

Acquisitions policy: Material relating to the marques formerly belonging to the Rover Group and to the development of the British motor industry since its inception.

Archives of organisation: Business records, engineering drawings, photographs and films, technical and sales literature for Austin, Morris, Wolseley, Riley, Rover, Standard-Triumph and other British firms.

Major collections: Papers of Herbert Austin, Baron Austin (1866–1941); William Richard Morris, Lord Nuffield (1877–1963), and Sir Alec Issigonis (1906–88).

Non-manuscript material: Substantial photograph and film collections.

Finding aids: Computer database (in progress) Registers of photographic negatives.

Conservation: Provided by Warwickshire Record Office (entry 1189).

378 Gillingham Central Library

Address: High Street, Gillingham, Kent ME7 1BG

Telephone: (01634) 332714

E-mail: lyn.rainbow@medway.gov.uk

Enquiries: The Information Officer

Open: Mon: 9.30–7.00; Tues: 10.00–7.00; Wed–Fri: 9.30–5.30; Sat: 9.30–5.00.

Access: Generally open to the public.

Historical background: The present library was built and opened in 1937, but local collections predate this. Methodist church archives have been transferred to Medway Archives and Local Studies Centre (entry 1062).

Acquisitions policy: To strengthen the existing collection of Gillingham material by purchase and donation.

Major collections: Special collections relating to Louis Brennan (1852–1932); J.B. McCudden, VC (1895–1918); and Will Adams (1564–1620), the first Englishman to settle in Japan (the Adams Collection contains little original archival material).

Non-manuscript material: Photographs and prints (c800); slides (250).
Oil paintings, mostly by Henry Hill.
Microfilms of census returns for Gillingham, Rainham and parts of north-east Kent, 1841–91, and of parish records, c1558–1985.

Finding aids: Indexes and lists.

Facilities: Photocopying. Microfilm/fiche reader/printer.

Publications: Local History Series nos. 1–12 and leaflets 1–6.

379   Angus Folk Museum

Parent organisation: National Trust for Scotland

Address: Kirkwynd Cottages, Glamis, by Forfar DD8 1RT

Telephone: (01307) 840288

Fax: (01307) 840233

Enquiries: The Property Manager, Miss Kathleen Ager

Open: May–Sept: Mon–Sun: 11.00–5.00. July and Aug: 10.00–5.00.

Access: Only serious students; an appointment is preferred.

The museum was founded in 1957. It acquires items relating to rural Angus, domestic and agricultural, until c1920. The museum holds a small quantity of MS items, including school exercise books, 19th century, farm account books, 1834–1961, and town plans, c1832, plus miscellaneous accounts and correspondence relating to the Shaw family, 1759–1916. There are also photographs of the Angus area. See NRA 19893 (NRAS 1262) and *Angus Folk Museum Guide* (1994).

380   Glamis Castle

Parent organisation: Strathmore Estates

Address: Glamis, by Forfar, Angus DD8 1RJ

Telephone: (01307) 840393

Website: www.great-houses-scotland.co.uk/glamis

Enquiries: The Archivist, Jane Anderson

Open: By arrangement.

Access: Bona fide researchers, by appointment. A charge is made.

The castle holds family and estate papers, including farm plans and architectural drawings, of the Lyon and Bowes Lyon family, Earls of Strathmore from the 14th century. See NRAS 885.

381   Archdiocese of Glasgow Archive

Address: 196 Clyde Street, Glasgow G1 4JY

Telephone: (0141) 226 5898

Fax: (0141) 225 2600

E-mail: archives@rcag.org.uk

Website: www.rcag.org.uk

Enquiries: Rt Rev. Mgr Hugh N. Canon Boyle Dr Mary McHugh

Open: By appointment.

Access: Approved readers, usually on written application. There are restrictions on certain categories of records containing personal details of individuals.

Historical background: The modern Archdiocese of Glasgow was established in 1878, although some papers date from the arrival of Archbishop Charles Eyre (1817–1902) in 1869.

Acquisitions policy: To collect material relating to the Archdiocese of Glasgow and its parishes. Deposits from related diocesan organisations and parishes are encouraged.

Archives of organisation: Archives of the Episcopal Chancery and Diocesan Curia, 1878– .
Archdiocesan parish registers, including the cathedral parish, 1795– .
Education papers prior and subsequent to Education (Scotland) Act 1918.

Major collections: Catholic Union records, 1885–1940s.

Non-manuscript material: Plans of some ecclesiastical buildings.
Archbishop J.D. Scanlan, photographs, 20th century.
Canon Michael Condon, photograph albums, 19th century.

Finding aids: Catalogue, which is being computerised.

Facilities: Photocopying.

Publications: M. McHugh: 'Glasgow Archdiocesan Archive', *Catholic Archives*, 5 (1985), 19–33.

382 Brookwood Library, Bearsden

Parent organisation: East Dunbartonshire Libraries

Address: 166 Drymen Road, Bearsden, Glasgow G61 3RJ

Telephone: (0141) 942 6811/776 8090

Fax: (0141) 943 1119

Enquiries: The Reference and Information Librarian, Mr Don Martin

Open: Mon–Thurs: 10.00–8.00; Fri–Sat: 10.00–5.00.

Access: Generally open to the public. An appointment is necessary if advice is required.

Historical background: The service was reorganised in 1996. Brookwood is now a branch office of the East Dunbartonshire service based at the William Patrick Library, Kirkintilloch (see entry 492).

Acquisitions policy: Local authority records which rest in East Dunbartonshire Council; also material deposited by local individuals, firms and organisations.

Archives of organisation: Bearsden and Milngavie town and burgh minutes. Bearsden burgh records of formation, 1957/8.
Records of Bearsden and Milngavie District Council, 1975–96.

Major collections: Local collections, including: Westerton Garden Suburb ledgers, 1912–66, and Co-operative Society minutes, 1915–25.
Bearsden Ladies Club records, 1947–83.

Federation of Bearsden Ratepayers Association records, 1959–76.
Douglas Park Golf Club records, 1897–1977.

Non-manuscript material: Local newspaper, 1901– .
Photographs and maps relating to district.

Finding aids: Computerised catalogue.

Facilities: Photocopying. Microfilm/fiche readers/printers.

Publications: Leaflets available on 'Archives', 'Local History' and 'Family History'.

383 Clydebank District Libraries and Museum

Address: Central Library, Dumbarton Road, Clydebank, Glasgow G81 1XH

Telephone: (0141) 952 8765/1416

Fax: (0141) 951 8275

Enquiries: The District Librarian

Open: Mon–Thurs: 9.30–8.00; Fri: 9.30–5.00; Sat: 10.00–5.00.

Access: Generally open to the public, but prior notification is appreciated.

Acquisitions policy: Generally to acquire all local studies material relating to Clydebank district, but specific interests are local shipbuilding, Singer Sewing Machine production and the Clydebank Blitz. This archive is supplemented by the museum collection, which has shipbuilding memorabilia and a large collection of Singer and non-Singer sewing machines.

Archives of organisation: Minute books and related records of Clydebank Town Council, 1886–1975, and Clydebank District Council, 1975– .

Major collections: Usual local history material, including local shipbuilding companies: J. & G. Thomson Ltd, John Brown & Co. Ltd, Wm Beardmore & Co. Ltd, Napier Miller; Singer Manufacturing Co.; and the Clydebank Blitz, 1941.

Non-manuscript material: *Clydebank & Renfew Post*, 1891–1921, *Clydebank Press*, 1921–83, and *Clydebank Post*, 1983– .
Photographs of Clydebank district (including Old Kilpatrick, Hardgate, Duntocher), late 19th century– .

Near complete set of OS maps of Clydebank district from 1st edition, 6 inch (1:10000) and 25 inch (1:2500)

Facilities: Photocopying. Microfiche reader/ printer.

Publications: J. Hood (ed): *History of Clydebank* (1988).
List of other local history publications available.

384 David Livingstone Centre

Parent organisation: The Scottish National Memorial to David Livingstone Trust

Address: 165 Station Road, Blantyre, Glasgow G72 9BT

Telephone: (01698) 823140

Fax: (01698) 821424

E-mail: kcarruthers@nts.org.uk

Enquiries: The Property Manager, Karen Carruthers

Open: April–Oct: Mon–Sat: 10.00–6.00;
Sun: 12.30–6.00.
Nov–March: Mon–Sat:10.30–4.30;
Sun: 12.30–5.00.

Access: Generally open to the public, by museum entry ticket. An appointment is necessary.

Historical background: The National Memorial to the David Livingstone Trust was established in 1926, with the building opening to the public in 1929. Its main function is the preservation of his birthplace but it is regarded as the main repository for Livingstonia.

Acquisitions policy: Livingstonia; social history relating to Blantyre Mills, where Livingstone worked as a boy; ethnography and natural history relating to areas of southern and East Africa in which he explored.

Archives of organisation: Records relating to the museum.

Major collections: Letters and journals belonging to David Livingstone (1813–73).
Original letters, 1846–76, including notebooks, 1871–4.

Non-manuscript material: Photographs, original hand-drawn maps, books on Livingstone.
Blantyre Mill Works Library.
Paintings and prints by Haswell Millar (30).

Finding aids: Catalogue is available on request.

Facilities: Photocopying. Photography by arrangement.

385 East Renfrewshire Local History Department

Parent organisation: East Renfrewshire Cultural Services

Address: Glen Street, Barrhead, Glasgow G78 1QA

Telephone: (0141) 577 3500

Fax: (0141) 577 3501

E-mail: mcgettiganl@eastrenfrewshire.gov.uk

Website: www.eastrenfrewshire.gov.uk

Enquiries: The Information Services Manager

Open: Mon, Wed, Fri: 2.00–8.00;
Tues, Thurs, Sat: 10.00–5.00.

Access: Generally open to the public.

Historical background: A local history collection is held at East Renfrewshire Local History Department, Giffnock Library, Station Road, Giffnock, East Renfrewshire G46 6JR.

Acquisitions policy: To collect material relevant to the history of East Renfrewshire.

Archives of organisation: Local authority records of East Renfrewshire, mainly 1890– .

Major collections: Glasgow and East Kilbride Railway Development Society records.
Crum Memorial Library papers.

Non-manuscript material: Maps, 1796– , photographs c1880– .

Finding aids: Index to local history holdings.

Facilities: Photocopying. Microfilm/fiche readers.

Publications: A number of publications on the history of the area (list available).

386 Glasgow Caledonian University Library

Address: CLIC, Glasgow Caledonian University, Cowcaddens Road, Glasgow G4 0BA

Telephone: (0141) 331 3920 (John Powles); 3199 (Carole McCallum)

Fax: (0141) 331 3005

E-mail: j.powles@gcal.ac.uk
c.mccallum@gcal.ac.uk

Website: www.lib.gcal.ac.uk/about/speccoll/
index.htm

Enquiries: The Collection Manager, Mr John Powles
The Archivist, Carole McCallum

Open: Mon–Fri: 9.00–5.00; other times may be possible by appointment.

Access: Members of the university and external bona fide researchers, by appointment only.

Historical background: The Glasgow School of Cookery was founded in 1875 and opened the following year. In 1878 the West End School of Cookery also opened in the city. The two schools were amalgamated in 1908 and formed a Scottish Central Institution under the title the Glasgow and West of Scotland College of Domestic Science (Incorporated), affectionately known as the Dough School. In 1975 this College became the Queen's College, Glasgow (the Queen had been patron since 1944). In 1971, under Glasgow Corporation, Glasgow College of Technology opened. It passed to the Strathclyde Regional Council in 1975 and became a Scottish Central Institution in 1985. The name Glasgow College was adopted in 1987 (although Glasgow College of Technology remained its official name), and it became Glasgow Polytechnic in 1991. In 1993 Glasgow Polytechnic and the Queen's College, Glasgow, amalgamated to form Glasgow Caledonian University. The Heatherbank Museum of Social Work moved to the university in 1994. Before it became a university, work on establishing an institutional archive at Glasgow Polytechnic had begun. This was developed at the time of the merger, and material is still being found from the various sites. In 1995 the university was gifted a collection of several thousand books and pamphlets from Janey Buchan (The Norman and Janey Buchan Collection). The first archive collection, however, was that of the RSSPCC (Children 1st), also in 1995. The STUC Archive was acquired in 1998 in conjunction with the Gallacher Memorial Library. The Heatherbank Museum of Social Work (entry 391) moved to Glasgow Caledonian University in 1994.

Acquisitions policy: To consolidate the archives of predecessor institutions, maintain records of the university and acquire materials to support the curricula and research activities of the university.

Archives of organisation: Archives of the university's parent institutions, 1875–1993, including minutes, student records and prospectuses. Archives of Glasgow Caledonian University, 1993– .

Major collections: The RSSPCC (Children 1st) Archive: case records and associated materials covering the activities of the RSSPCC, mainly 1940–76.
Anti-Apartheid Movement in Scotland Archive: committee minutes and papers, correspondence, conference papers, journals, pamphlets and ephemera, 1965–94 (mainly 1976–94).
Scottish Trades Union Congress (STUC) Archive: records include reports of the STUC General Council, Labour Party, TUC, ICTU and, minutes of the STUC General Council, 1897– , correspondence, background papers and campaign material, 1985– .
Social Democratic Party Archive: administrative and committee papers, some conference proceedings, newspapers and pamphlets documenting the activities of the SDP in Scotland.

Non-manuscript material: History Picture Library (part of the Heatherbank Museum of Social Work archives): mainly photographs covering the themes of social work and social history, pictures, slides and negatives (c7,000).

Finding aids: Handlists to all collections. Computer catalogues in preparation for institutional archives and the picture library.

Facilities: Photocopying. Photography by arrangement.

Publications: E. Miller: *Century of Change 1875–1975: One Hundred Years of Training Home Economics' Students in Glasgow* (Glasgow, c1975).
A. Tuckett: *The Scottish Trades Union Congress: the First 80 Years 1897–1977* (1986).
K. Aitken: *The Bairns o'Adam: the Story of the STUC* (Edinburgh, 1997).
W. Thompson and C. McCallum: *Glasgow Caledonian University: its Origins and Evolution* (1998).
Collection leaflets.

387 Glasgow City Archives

Parent organisation: Glasgow City Council

Address: Mitchell Library, North Street, Glasgow G3 7DN

Telephone: (0141) 287 2913

Fax: (0141) 226 8452

E-mail: archives@gcl.glasgow.gov.uk

Website: www.glasgow.gov.uk/gcl/home.htm

Enquiries: The City Archivist, Mr A.M. Jackson

Open: Mon–Thurs: 9.30–4.45; Fri: 9.30–4.00. At other times by arrangement.

Access: Generally open to the public.

Historical background: The Glasgow City Archives Department was established in 1964, and following reorganisation in 1975 became the Strathclyde Regional Archives. As a result of the 1996 reorganisation of Scottish local government the office reverted to its former title, but it still holds many collections relating to the wider area, as well as the archives of the regional council itself.

Acquisitions policy: In view of the history of the office it retains a wider geographical role, but does not acquire collections solely or primarily concerning parts of the former region which now have their own archive services.

Archives of organisation: Usual local authority record holdings.

Major collections: Deposited collections, including the following which have a wider significance:
Extensive shipbuilding and engineering records, including the Fairfield Shipbuilding and Engineering Co. Ltd and its predecessors, 1860– c1970; G.L. Watson & Co., marine architects; and Sir William Arrol & Co. Ltd, bridge builders.
Records of Clydeport Ltd (formerly Clyde Navigation Trust) and the Scottish Co-operative Wholesale Society.
Family collections, including Maxwell of Pollok, Stirling of Keir, Colquhoun of Luss and Cochrane-Baillie of Lamington.

Non-manuscript material: Large collection of architectural and estate plans; photographs, including commercial collections; some audio material.

Finding aids: Lists, indexes and computer files. Lists are sent to NRAS.

Facilities: Photocopying and plan printing. Photography and microfilming by arrangement. Microfilm/fiche readers. Digitisation.

Conservation: In-house conservation. Outside work is undertaken occasionally.

388 Glasgow School of Art
Archives

Address: 167 Renfrew Street, Glasgow G3 6RQ

Telephone: (0141) 353 4592

Fax: (0141) 353 4670

E-mail: c.mcgread@gsa.ac.uk

Website: www.gsa.ac.uk/library/archives

Enquiries: The Archivist, Adele Ashley-Smith

Open: Mon–Fri: 9.30–5.00, by appointment only.

Access: Bona fide scholars, who should write in advance with their enquiry and request for appointment. First-time visitors should provide proof of address. Most records over 30 years old are available for consultation; contact the Archivist for further details. A paid research service is available (hourly rate).

Historical background: Glasgow School of Art is one of the last remaining independent art schools in Britain. Founded as a Government School of Design in 1845 with funding from the Haldane Trust, it was also able to initiate teaching in the fine arts. First situated in Ingram Street, the school later moved to the McLellan Galleries before settling at its present site at Renfrew, Street, in a building designed by Charles Rennie Mackintosh. An archivist has been in post since 1995.

Acquisitions policy: Primarily material relating to GSA, its staff and students, but increasingly material recording art education in Scotland and records of Scottish artists, designers, architects, artistic societies and groups.

Archives of organisation: Minutes and correspondence of the governors, 1852– ; correspondence and working papers of the directors, 1844– ; annual reports and prospectuses, 1845– ; school ephemera, pageants and theatrical events and posters from activities week and student fashion shows; minutes, correspondence and financial papers of the building committee; student records of the school 1882– ; press cuttings and photographic collection, 1864– ; papers, including correspondence, from staff, students and individual departments.

Major collections: Charles Rennie Mackintosh (1868–1928) sketchbooks, and 'Glasgow Style' artists material, including *The Magazine*, 1893–96.
Records of Scottish stands at the Women's Work Exhibition, London, 1900; Glasgow International Exhibition, 1901; Exhibition of Modern Furniture, Budapest, 1902; and Brussels Exhibition, 1910.
Records of Scottish Pavilion at the Turin Exhibition of Decorative arts, 1902; Scottish Society of Art-Workers, 1898–1900; Glasgow School of Art Club, 1897–1950.
Duncan Brown Photographs, *c*1850–1896, of school staff, local dignitaries and areas in and around Glasgow.
Records of Glasgow League of Artists, 1971–82. Scottish Art & Design Collection, incorporating the collections of NSEAD (Scottish Region) and Stuart W. MacDonald.
Sketchbooks and papers from former students relating to study at GSA, *c*1910–1960.
Keppie Collection of ephemera from London and Scottish artists' clubs and 'The Immortals' photograph album.

Non-manuscript material: Architectural plans by Charles Rennie Mackintosh, Eugene Bourdon, Alexander 'Greek' Thomson, James Black Fulton and others. Some sketchbooks of former students and staff, including Maurice Greiffenhagen, RA.

Finding aids: Catalogues of governors' and directors' papers, 1854–1945, and for deposited collections and some other material. Copies of lists at NRAS.

Facilities: Photocopying. Photography. Microfilm reader.

Conservation: Contracted out.

Publications: See website and *Journal of Design History*, 11/2(1998), 173–4.

389 Glasgow University

A Archives & Business Records Centre

Address: 13 Thurso Street, Glasgow G11 6PE

Telephone: (0141) 330 5515

Fax: (0141) 330 4158

E-mail: dutyarch@archives.gla.ac.uk

Website: www.archives.gla.ac.uk

Enquiries: The Duty Archivist

Open: Mon–Wed, Fri: 9.30–5.30; Thurs: 9.30–8.00; appointments are recommended.

Access: Generally open to the public, by appointment. Photographic proof of identity is required. A paid research service is available.

Historical background: The University of Glasgow was founded by Pope Nicholas V in 1451 and the archives date from that time. Since the 1950s the department has built up not only an institutional archive of national significance but also a collection of Scottish business records of international importance. The first archivist was appointed in 1955. From then the collections were housed in a number of locations until 1998, when the archival holdings were merged at Thurso Street to become Glasgow University Archives & Business Records Centre (GUABRC).
The Scottish Brewing Archive (entry 398) is also stored at Thurso Street, and the Greater Glasgow Health Board Archive (entry 390) is adminstered from the GUABRC office although it is stored elsewhere.

Acquisitions policy: To collect unique and original records relating to the university and to Scottish business broadly conceived.

Archives of organisation: Records of the prime functions of the university, 1451– .
Records of affiliated institutions including Anderson's College of Medicine, 1841–1965; Queen Margaret College, 1835–1935; Glasgow Veterinary School, 1866–1990, and the Royal Scottish Academy of Music and Drama, 1870–1985.
Records and papers of staff, students and societies, mainly 19th–20th centuries.

Major collections: Estate and parish collections, including Beith and other Ayrshire parish papers, 1610–1924; Garscube Estate (Sir Archibald Campbell), 1837–1960; Gartshore Estate (Viscount Whitelaw), Glasgow, 1849–1953.
Personal and family papers, including Duncan Black (1908–91), economist; Frederick O. Bower (1885–1928), botanist; Archibald A. Bowman (1883–1936), philosopher; Sir Alec Cairncross (1911–98), economist; Archibald C. Corbett, 1st Baron Rowallan, MP (1856–1933); Sir Maurice Denny (1886–1955), shipbuilder;

John 'Soda' Ferguson (*d* 1915), chemist; Sir Hector Hetherington (1888–1956), university administrator; Sir Robert Horne, MP (1871–1940), Chancellor of the Exchequer; Sir John Graham Kerr (1869–1957), zoologist; Sir James Lithgow (1883–1952), shipbuilder; John Scott Maclay, 1st Viscount Muirshiel, MP (1905–90), Secretary of State for Scotland; Very Rev. Robert Herbert Storey (1835–1907), Principal, Glasgow University; William D. Weir, Viscount Weir of Eastwood (1877–1959), industrialist and public servant.

Business records, including Allied Distillers Ltd, Dumbarton, 1668–1980; Anchor Line, shipowners, Edinburgh and Glasgow, 1790–1980; Babcock & Wilcox Ltd, boilermakers, Renfrew, 1891–1985; Andrew Barclay Sons & Co. Ltd, locomotive builders, Kilmarnock, 1876–1970; Barr & Stroud Ltd, optical instrument makers, Glasgow, 1880s–1980s; William Beardmore & Co., engineers, Glasgow, 1864–1976; Blackie & Son, publishers, Glasgow, 1794–1980s; British Alcan plc, London and Fort William, 1880s–1980s; John Brown & Co. (Clydebank) Ltd, shipbuilders, 1847–1971; City of Glasgow Bank, 1840–82; Clyde Shipping Co. Ltd, Glasgow, 1875–1980s; Coats Paton plc, cotton thread manufacturers, Glasgow and Paisley, 1830–1980s; William Collins, Son & Co. Ltd, publishers, Glasgow, 1822–1986; William Denny & Bros., shipbuilders, Dumbarton, 1844–1952; John Elder & Co., shipbuilders, Glasgow, 1869–1916; Ellerman Lines Ltd (including City Line), shipowners, London, 1839–1970s; James Finlay & Co. plc, textile manufacturers and merchants, Glasgow, 1789–1972; Gourock Ropework Co., Port Glasgow (including New Lanark Mills), 1774–1972; Highland Distilleries Co. plc, whisky distillers, Glasgow, 1882–1984; House of Fraser Group (Army & Navy Stores, Dickens & Jones etc), Glasgow and elsewhere, 1820s–1980s; Ivory & Sime plc, investment trust managers, Edinburgh, 1880–1986; John Lean & Sons, muslin manufacturers, Glasgow, 1850–1925; Lithgows Ltd, shipbuilders, Port Glasgow, 1875–1977; Lumsden of Arden, stationers, Glasgow, 1661–1984; Sir Robert McAlpine & Sons Ltd, Glasgow, 1882–1971; North British Locomotive Co. Ltd, locomotive builders, Glasgow, 1903–48; Robertson & Baxter Ltd, whisky merchants, Glasgow, 1903–82; Scott & Sons, shipbuilders, Bowling, 1857–1979; Scotts Shipbuilding & Engineering Co., Greenock, 1780–1984; A.W. Smith & Co. Ltd, sugar machinery manufacturers, Glasgow, 1841–1966; Alexander Stephen & Sons, shipbuilders, Glasgow, 1848–1968; William Teacher & Sons Ltd, whisky distillers, Glasgow, 1856–1900; TSB Scotland, 1795–1985.

Non-manuscript material: W.J. Jackson collection of photographs relating to Scottish life, 1902–1930s (5000).

Photographs relating to Scottish topography and industry, university life and buildings (100,000).

Plans relating to the university (3000).

Technical drawings of buildings, locomotives, cranes, optical instruments and ships (20,000).

Technical, business and university history library (6000 vols).

Finding aids: Computerised catalogues, handlists and indexes. Lists sent to NRAS.

Facilities: Photography. Photography. Microfilming. Plan copying.

Conservation: Contracted out.

Publications: Munimenta Alme Universitatis Glasguensis: Records of the University of Glasgow from its Foundation till 1727 (Glasgow 1854) [3 vols].

W.I. Addison: *A Roll of the Graduates of the University of Glasgow, 1727–1897* (Glasgow, 1898).

James Coutts: *A History of the University of Glasgow from its Foundation in 1451 to 1909* (Glasgow, 1909).

W.I. Addison: *The Matriculation Albums of the University of Glasgow from 1728–1858* (Glasgow, 1913).

J.D. Mackie: *The University of Glasgow, 1451–1951* (Glasgow, 1954).

A.L. Brown and M. Moss: *The University of Glasgow, 1451–1996* (Edinburgh, 1996).

Glasgow University Archives & Business Records Centre List of Collections (Glasgow, 1998) [also available on the website].

Dunaskin News: the Quarterly Newsletter of GUARBC.

B Library Department of Special Collections

Address: Hillhead Street, Glasgow G12 8QE

Telephone: (0141) 330 6767

Fax: (0141) 330 3793

E-mail: d.weston@lib.gla.ac.uk

Website: http://special.lib.gla.ac.uk

Enquiries: The Keeper of Special Collections, Mr David Weston

Open: Term: Mon–Thurs: 9.00–8.30; Fri: 9.00–5.00; Sat: 9.00–12.30.
Vacation: Mon–Fri: 9.00–5.00; Sat: 9.00–12.30. (not Christmas).
Closed Glasgow Fair (July) and Glasgow Autumn Holiday (September) weekends.

Access: Members of Glasgow University and all other bona fide researchers. Prior written application is desirable.

Historical background: Glasgow University was founded in 1451. A MS catalogue of 1691 shows the library with a stock of 3300 volumes. From 1709 to 1836 the library enjoyed the copyright privilege and by 1791 (the year of its first published catalogue) its holdings had risen to 20,000 volumes. Vast collections were acquired by gift and bequest in the 19th and 20th centuries, and in 1994 the library's stock approached 1,700,000 volumes.

Acquisitions policy: To augment the following archival collections by purchase, gift and deposit: 18th-century medicine, with special emphasis on William Hunter and his work in anatomy and obstetrics.
Scottish theatre history.
History of art in the 19th and 20th centuries, with special emphasis on James McNeill Whistler and his circle.
History of Glasgow and the west of Scotland.
History of the university.
Alchemy and the early history of chemistry.

Major collections: Medieval MSS (*c*240); oriental MSS (*c*200).
Post-medieval MSS and archives, particularly covering the following subjects: 18th-century medicine and anatomy; alchemy and early chemistry; 19th- and 20th-century art history; Gaelic literature (*c*300,000 separate items).
Art and architecture: papers of James McNeill Whistler (1834–1903); art history papers of James Laver (1899–1975), D.S. MacColl (1859–1948), Denys Millar Sutton (1917–91) and Harold Wright (1885–1961); Jessie Marion King (1875–1949); Campbell, Hislop & Welsh, Glasgow architects, 1885–1975.
Music: scores of several late 19th- and early 20th- century Scottish composers, including Frederick Lamond (1868–1948); Hamish MacCunn (1868–1916); Sir John Blackwood McEwen (1868–1948).
Philosophy: MSS collected by Sir William Hamilton (1788–1856).

Politics and economics: papers of William Robert Scott (1868–1940) relating to Adam Smith (1723–90); Alexander MacCallum Scott (1874–1928); Rudolf Schlesinger (1901–69) on communism; Isaac Deutscher (1907–67) on Leon Trotsky (1879–1940).

Religion: letters of Thomas Chalmers (1780–1847), Free Church of Scotland founder; and sermons, 18th–20th centuries.

Science and medicine: alchemical MSS collected by John Ferguson (1837–1916); papers of William Thomson, Lord Kelvin (1824–1907); James Douglas (1675–1742); William Hunter (1718–83); William Cullen (1710–90); R.D. Laing (1927–89).

Sinology: papers of Theophilus Siegfried Bayer (1694–1738).

Large collection of material relating to Glasgow and the West of Scotland, including papers of David Murray (1842–28); Boyd of Trochrig family documents, 1485–*c*1759; Gaelic MS and transcriptions and papers *re* history of Glasgow University.

Scottish Theatre Archive, mainly 19th and 20th century, including archives of Scottish Ballet, Edinburgh Festival Fringe and Glasgow Citizens' Theatre

Non-manuscript material: Robert Dougan collection of early photography, including David Octavius Hill (1802–70) and Robert Adamson (1821–48).
Caricatures of the Franco-Prussian War and the Paris Commune (*c*3000).
Scottish Theatre Collection: Sean Hudson photographic archive of Scottish theatre; programmes, posters, photographs and scripts.

Finding aids: On-line catalogues:
http:special.lib.gla.ac.uk/manuscripts.
It is hoped to bring the Scottish Theatre Archive catalogue on-line.

Facilities: Photocopying. Photography. Microfilming. Microfilm/fiche readers.

Conservation: In-house department.

Publications: J. Young and P. Henderson Aitken: *A Catalogue of the Manuscripts in the Library of the Hunterian Museum in the University of Glasgow* (Glasgow, 1908).
J. Mackechnie: *Catalogue of Gaelic Manuscripts in Selected Libraries in Great Britain and Ireland*, i (Boston, MA, 1973), 365–454.
N.R. Ker: *Medieval Manuscripts in British Libraries*, ii (Oxford, 1977), 871–933 [details of

the non-Hunterian medieval MSS in Glasgow University Library].

J. Baldwin: 'Glasgow University Library's Manuscripts: the non-Hunterian Collections', *The Bibliotheck*, viii (1977), 127.

Kelvin Papers: Index (Glasgow, 1977).

Whistler, MacColl, Wright: Art History Papers, 1850–1950, in Glasgow University Library (Glasgow, 1979).

N. Thorp: *The Glory of the Page: Medieval & Renaissance Illuminated Manuscripts from Glasgow University Library* (London, 1987).

C. Helen Brock: *Dr William Hunter's Papers and Drawings in the Hunterian Collection of Glasgow University Library: a Handlist* (Cambridge, 1990).

——: *Dr James Douglas's Papers and Drawings in the Hunterian Collection of Glasgow University Library: a Handlist* (Cambridge, 1994).

390 Greater Glasgow Health Board Archive

Address: 77–81 Dumbarton Road, Glasgow G11 6PW

Telephone: (0141) 330 4543 (Mon–Wed); 287 2906 (Thurs–Fri)

Fax: (0141) 330 4158

E-mail: gghb@archives.gla.ac.uk

Website: www.archives.gla.ac.uk/gghb

Enquiries: The GGHB Archivist

Open: Thurs 9.30–4.45; Fri: 9.30–4.00; other times by arrangement.
The collections are held in the Mitchell Library (see entry 393) and are made available in the City Archives reading room.

Access: Generally open to the public, subject to usual confidentiality; an appointment is advisable.

Historical background: The Greater Glasgow Health Board was created in 1974 to assume the functions of the former Western Regional Hospital Board and its boards of management in the Greater Glasgow area. The GGHB Archive was established in 1975 to collect and administer the records of the GGHB and its predecessor bodies. The records are now stored at the Mitchell Library.

Acquisitions policy: Records relating to the hospital service and health care, including personal papers of individuals active in the provision of health care, in Glasgow and the west of Scotland.

Archives of organisation: Administrative records of Western Regional Hospital Board and constituent boards of management, 1948–74, and of GGHB, 1974– .

Major collections: Administrative, financial and clinical records of Glasgow hospitals, 1787– ; records of hospitals in the surrounding area, particularly Paisley.
Personal papers of Glasgow medical practitioners, 19th–20th centuries.

Non-manuscript material: Architectural plans. Videotaped interviews.

Finding aids: Fully searchable collection-level descriptions on website. Collection, series and item-level lists in archive; sent to NRAS.

Facilities: Photocopying. Photography.

Publications: A.G. Tough: *Medical Records of Glasgow and Paisley: a guide to the Greater Glasgow Health Board Archive* (Glasgow, 1993) [also available on-line].

391 Heatherbank Museum of Social Work

Address: Glasgow Caledonian University, Cowcaddens Road, Glasgow G3 0BA

Telephone: (0141) 331 3920

Fax: (0141) 331 3005

E-mail: a.ramage@gcal.ac.uk

Website: www.lib.gcal.ac.uk/hbank/index.htm

Enquiries: The Curator, Alastair Ramage

Open: Mon–Fri: 10.00–2.00.

Access: The reference and picture libraries are available for research on application to the Curator.

Historical background: The Heatherbank Press and Museum were founded in 1974 to stimulate public interest in social welfare history by developing the Picture Library, encouraging wider preservation of social welfare archives and publishing occasional papers. It is concerned with buildings, costume, objects, literary evidence and visual evidence.

Acquisitions policy: Actively collects archives *re* social work and welfare history.

Major collections: Association of Poor House Governors of Scotland, register and minute books, 1880–1939.
Lennox Castle, report books, 1930–48.
Glasgow Discharged Prisoners Aid Society, minute books, 1856–1974 (4 items).
Ross and Cromarty County Council records, including asylum patient rolls, 1920–56.
Miscellaneous patients' records.
Association of Directors of Social Work (Scotland), records, 1968–98.

Non-manuscript material: Large collections of photographs, slides, prints and drawings, resource and ephemera material.
Reference library.

Finding aids: NRA 30643.

Facilities: Photocopying.

Publications: C. Harvey: *Social Welfare Archives in Britain and the USA*, Occasional Paper No. 1 (Milngavie, 1980).
*c.*50 titles produced by Heatherbank Press.

392 Lesbian Archive and Information Centre

Address: Glasgow Women's Library, 101 Trongate, Glasgow G1 5HD

Telephone: (0141) 552 8345

E-mail: gwl@globalnet.co.uk

Website: www.womens-library.org.uk/laic.htm

Enquiries: The Lesbian Archive

Open: Tues–Fri: 1.00–6.00; Sat: 2.00–5.00.

Access: Access is for women only; there are restrictions on some materials according to donors' wishes.

The archive was established in 1984 to collect material past and present of specific interest to lesbians and to house it safely and confidentially. After many years as a London-based resource it moved to Glasgow in 1995. It is unfunded and relies on membership and donations. The archive currently holds a wide variety of records, including MSS, diaries and letters, as well as oral histories, press cuttings, artwork, reference and fiction books, magazines, newspapers and newsletters and audiovisual material, which dates mostly from 1950 onwards although it relates to earlier decades. Catalogues, indexes and lists are available.

There is a computerised information database and photocopying is available. See NRA 36162.

393 Mitchell Library, Arts Department

Parent organisation: Glasgow City Libraries and Archives

Address: 201 North Street, Glasgow G3 7DN

Telephone: (0141) 287 2933

Fax: (0141) 287 2815

E-mail: arts@gcl.glasgow.gov.uk

Website: www.gov.uk/gcl/ref.htm

Enquiries: The Departmental Librarian, Arts Department, Hamish Whyte

Open: Mon–Thurs: 9.00–8.00; Fri, Sat: 9.00–5.00.

Access: Generally open to the public; prior notice of particular requirements is helpful.

Historical background: The library was opened in 1877 as Glasgow's first free public reference library, following a bequest by Stephen Mitchell, a tobacco manufacturer in Glasgow, of £70,000 to the town council for that purpose. Baillie's library stock was incorporated in 1982. The Rare Books and Manuscripts Department was incorporated in the Arts Department in 1994. The library's own archives are deposited with Glasgow City Archives (entry 387).

Acquisitions policy: Archives are sought relating to Glasgow, and to the library's major special collections in Scottish poetry, drama, family history and regimental history, and trade unions. Other archives are normally now directed to Glasgow City Archives or the Glasgow University Archives & Business Records Centre (entry 389A) as appropriate.

Major collections: Extensive MSS and archival holdings, including estate and family papers, records of business, societies, schools, and trade unions (*c*100). Examples include Glasgow and West of Scotland Association for Women's Suffrage, 1902–19; Alfred Morton diaries, 1887–1941; Scottish Council for Community Service during Unemployment, 1935–51; Guy Aldred papers, 1905–67; Scottish Women's Hospitals, 1914–22.

Non-manuscript material: North British Locomotive Company Collection includes plate glass negatives (10,000) in addition to order books and weight diagram books.

History and Glasgow Room: material relating to Glasgow, including MSS, maps and illustrations; Scottish local history, topography and genealogy, with extensive map collection.

Architectural drawings by Alexander 'Greek' Thomson (1817–75) (c50).

Finding aids: Interim catalogue of MSS (cards xeroxed in sheets and bound), gradually being superseded by detailed looseleaf catalogue with card index. Aldred: NRAS 1410; John L. Kinloch: NRAS 0465. Literary manuscripts: a checklist.

Facilities: Photocopying. Photography. Microfilm/fiche reader/printers.

Conservation: Full paper conservation facilities available in house; specialist outside contract work undertaken.

Publications: The North British Locomotive Company Collection (1974).
The Mitchell Library, Glasgow, 1877–1977 (Glasgow, 1977).

394 Royal College of Physicians and Surgeons of Glasgow

Address: 234–42 St Vincent Street, Glasgow, Strathclyde G2 5RJ

Telephone: (0141) 221 3204/3234

Fax: (0141) 221 1804

E-mail: james.beaton@rcpsglasg.ac.u
carol.parry@rcpsglas.ac.uk

Enquiries: The Librarian, Mr James Beaton
The Archivist, Mrs Carol Parry

Open: Mon–Fri: 9.15–5.00.

Access: Fellows and members of the college; registered medical practitioners; college examination candidates and postgraduate students. Other approved readers on written application to the Librarian.

Historical background: The college was established in 1599 by the grant of a royal charter from King James VI to Maister Peter Lowe and Professor Robert Hamilton, to regulate the practice of medicine in the west of Scotland. The original title of the college was the Faculty of Physicians and Surgeons of Glasgow. The faculty's privileges were confirmed by Act of Parliament in 1672. It had the exclusive right to examine and license practitioners of surgery in the west of Scotland, and no individual could practise medicine within its boundaries without its express permission. In 1909 the corporation became the Royal Faculty of Physicians and Surgeons of Glasgow, until the change to its present designation as a Royal College in 1962. Many outstanding individuals, such as Lister, Macewen, Livingstone and many names famous in the context of the Glasgow Medical School, have been associated with the college.

Acquisitions policy: Records relating to fellows and members of the college both past and present and to the history of medicine in Glasgow and the west of Scotland.

Archives of organisation: College minutes, 1602–88, 1733– ; examination registers, 1815– ; Widows' Fund records, 1792–1899; vaccination registers records, 1801–96; papers and correspondence, 1635– (mainly 20th century).

Major collections: Papers of Sir William Macewen (1848–1924), 1872–1943; Sir Ronald Ross (1857–1932), 1892–1931; Lord Lister (1827–1912), 1869–1927; Dr William Mackenzie (1791–1868), 1814–1913; Professor Archibald Young (1873–1939), 1891–1939.

Student lecture notes, 18th–19th centuries; casebooks, 1792–1913; MS works on medicine, 17th–19th centuries.

Records of Glasgow Medical Society, 1814–43; Royal Medico-Chirurgical Society of Glasgow, 1844–1987; Glasgow Pathological and Clinical Society, 1873–1909; Glasgow Medico-Chirurgical Society, 1820–9; Glasgow and West of Scotland Medical Association, 1889–1908; Glasgow Northern Medical Society, 1903–41; Partick and District Medical Society, 1908–20; Greenock Medical and Chirurgical Association, 1820–51.

Minute books of the Medical Faculty, St Mungo's College, 1889–1945.

Non-manuscript material: Photographs and illustrations, c1870– .

Extensive collection of medical tracts, 15th–19th centuries, and works by authors such as Boerhaave, Cullen etc.

Medical artefacts, 18th century– .

Finding aids: Lists. Copies sent to NRAS.

Facilities: Photocopying. Photography by arrangement.

Publications: J.J. Beaton, R. Miller and I.T. Boyle (eds): *Treasures of the College* (Glasgow, 1998).

395 Royal Faculty of Procurators Library

Address: 12 Nelson Mandela Place, Glasgow G2 1BT

Telephone: (0141) 332 3593

Fax: (0141) 333 9104

E-mail: rfpg@clara.net

Website: www.rfpg.clara.net

Enquiries: The Librarian, Alan McAdams

Open: Mon–Thurs: 9.00–9.00; Fri: 9.00–5.00; Sat: 9.00–1.00; Sun: 1.00–5.00.
Not Sat and Sun on bank holiday weekends.

Access: Members of the Royal Faculty of Procurators of Glasgow; authorised members of the legal profession (sheriffs, advocates); bona fide research workers, on application to the librarian.

Historical background: Although its existence dates from the latter part of the 18th century, the library was officially founded by the Faculty of Procurators in 1817 and has been housed in the present building since 1857. Its purpose was, and is, to provide practising members of the legal profession in Glasgow with a specialised law library where they can find all the legal information necessary for their daily work and research.

Acquisitions policy: No active policy for acquiring archives.

Archives of organisation: Archives of the Royal Faculty of Procurators, 1668– .

Major collections: Archives of the Hutcheson-Hill family, 16th century– , including some genealogical MSS.
Hill Collection: a record of Glasgow in the 19th century, of sociological interest.

Non-manuscript material: Maps of Glasgow, 18th century– .
Prints.

Finding aids: Catalogue. Card index to Hill Collection, also NRAS 0534.

Facilities: Photocopying.

Conservation: Contracted out.

Publications: Printed catalogue of Hill Collection (1905).

396 Royal Scottish Academy of Music and Drama

Address: 100 Renfrew Street, Glasgow G2 3DB

Telephone: (0141) 332 4101

Fax: (0141) 332 8901

E-mail: i.fowler@rsamd.ac.uk

Website: www.rsamd.ac.uk

Enquiries: The Director of Finance & Administration, Mrs Isobel Fowler

Open: Mon–Fri: 9.00–5.00, by arrangement.

Access: Records are accessible by application to the Company Secretary. A charge is made for copies of the annual accounts.

The Royal Scottish Academy of Music and Drama was incorporated as the Glasgow Athenaeum in 1900. The Glasgow Athenaeum had been established in 1847 to provide further education for adults in the fields of commerce, science and the arts. Archives are held of Glasgow Athenaeum, Scottish National Academy of Music, Royal Scottish Academy of Music, College of Dramatic Art and Royal Scottish Academy of Music and Drama.

397 Royal Scottish Geographical Society

Address: Graham Hills Building, 40 George Street, Glasgow G1 1QE

Telephone: (0141) 552 3330

Fax: (0141) 552 3331

E-mail: r.s.g.s.@strath.ac.uk

Website: ossian.geo.ed.ac.uk/~rsgs/

Enquiries: The Director, Dr David M. Munro

Open: By prior arrangement.

Access: Bona fide researchers, providing a written reference, by appointment. Charges may be made.

Historical background: The idea of forming a Scottish Geographical Society was conceived by the daughter of the missionary-explorer David Livingstone. The society was founded in 1884 to 'advance the science of Geography'.

Acquisitions policy: To maintain its own archive of material relating to the history of the society, the science of geography and Scottish travellers and explorers.

Archives of organisation: Council and committee minutes and papers; correspondence, 1884– .

Major collections: Scottish National Antarctic Expedition, 1902–4.
Isobel Wylie Hutchison (1899–1982), botanist and traveller in Arctic regions.

Non-manuscript material: Photographic slides; a substantial collection of maps of Scotland.

Finding aids: Indexes to maps.

Facilities: Photocopying.

Conservation: Contracted out.

Publications: Early Maps of Scotland [published by the society; 2 vols].
I.H. Adams and others: *The Making of Scottish Geography* (1984).

398   Scottish Brewing Archive

Address: University of Glasgow, Archives & Business Records Centre, 13 Thurso Street, Glasgow G11 6PE

Telephone: (0141) 330 6079

Fax: (0141) 330 4158

E-mail: a.topen@archives.gla.ac.uk

Enquiries: The Archivist, Mrs Alma Topen

Open: Tues, Thurs, Fri: 9.30–5.00.

Access: Generally open to the public, by appointment only.

Historical background: The Scottish Brewing Archive was established in 1981 at Heriot-Watt University, an institution with a long connection with the industry through its degree course in brewing. The archive moved to Glasgow University in 1991.

Acquisitions policy: To collect records of brewing, malting and other related industries (excluding distilling), and the licensed trade in Scotland.

Major collections: Records of more than 120 companies, including James Aitken & Co. (Falkirk) Ltd, 1900–65; T. & J. Bernard Ltd, Edinburgh, 1895–1960; Drybrough & Co. Ltd, Edinburgh, 1778–1983; Belhaven Brewery, Dunbar, 1871–1973; John Fowler & Co. Ltd, Prestonpans, 1926–69; John Jeffrey & Co. Ltd, Edinburgh, 1850–1970; Lorimer & Clark Ltd, Edinburgh, 1871–1973; Wm. McEwan & Co. Ltd, Edinburgh, 1856–1959; J. & R. Tennent Ltd and Tennent Caledonian Breweries Ltd, 1776–1998; Thomas Usher & Son Ltd, Edinburgh, 1834–1980; George Younger & Son Ltd, Alloa, 1875–1969; Wm. Younger & Co. Ltd, Edinburgh, 1805–1960.

Non-manuscript material: Photographs of brewing processes, buildings and workers, 1860s–1980s; plans of buildings, c1900–1970s; anti-prohibition leaflets, 1920s; library of technical and historical books, 1726– ; beer labels, 1850– , and beer mats, 1950s– ; advertising ephemera, 1880s– ; artefacts, including bottles, cans, glasses, trays, coopering and malting tools, hydrometers, c1850s– .

Finding aids: Catalogue of archive collections. Lists sent to NRAS. Computerised database for library and artefacts.

Facilities: Photcopying. Photography. Plan copying. Microfilming. Microfilm/fiche reader.

Conservation: Contracted out.

Publications: Scottish Brewing Archive *Newsletter*, 1982– ; *Journal*, 1998– .

399   Scottish Film and Television Archive

Address: Dowanhill, 74 Victoria Crescent Road, Glasgow G12 9JN

Telephone: (0141) 302 1700

Fax: (0141) 302 1711

E-mail: info@scottishscreen.demon.co.uk

Website: www.scottishscreen.demon.co.uk

Enquiries: The Curator, Ms Janet McBain

Open: Mon–Fri: 9.00–12.30, 2.00–5.00.

Access: Initial enquiries are free; researchers are advised to give prior notice of their intention to visit. Viewings of film are by appointment only, and are free to academic and bona fide students; a fee is charged for commercial and television users. Consultation on the premises is preferred, although arrangements can be made to despatch available viewing copies to an enquirer.

Historical background: The Scottish Film Archive, a division of the Scottish Film Council, was established in 1976 as a job creation project, and permanent status followed in 1978. Active research into the sources of film and cinema history in Scotland has been undertaken since 1977, with a steadily growing collection of material.

Acquisitions policy: Actuality and non-fiction film relating to Scottish culture and history in the 20th century. Emphasis on local material.

Archives of organisation: Archives of the Scottish Film Council and its constituents, 1934–97, including minute books 1934- 74, publications, reports of conferences, papers of the Scottish Educational Film Association, Scottish Central Film Library, Edinburgh Film Festival and Cosmo Cinema (now Glasgow Film Theatre).

Major collections: Principally non-MS material (see below); also Scottish film and cinema industry records.

Non-manuscript material: Locally produced cinema newsreels, comprising calendar customs, visits of celebrities, freedom of city ceremonies etc.
Upper Clyde Shipbuilders Ltd: official films of launches and trials of vessels constructed by component companies, 1926–71.
Educational and documentary films on Scotland, 1935– .
Television news and documentaries, *c*1965– .
Oral recordings: former cinema staff, film renters, exhibitors in Scotland.
Photographs of cinemas. Cinema memorabilia and publicity.

Finding aids: Subject and personality index system. Alphabetical and chronological lists of titles. Cataloguing in progress.

Facilities: 35mm and 16mm film viewing facilities. Beta SP, S/VHS and VHS video.

Publications: Printed catalogue, 3000 titles (1995).
J. Sherrington: *To Speak its Pride: the Work of the Films of Scotland Committee, 1938–1982* (SFC, Glasgow, 1996).
J. McBain and K. Cowle (eds): *With an Eye to the Future: the Films of Donald Alexander and Budge Cooper* (Glasgow, 1997).

400 Scottish Jewish Archives Centre

Parent organisation: Scottish Jewish Archives Committee

Address: Garnethill Synagogue, 127 Hill Street, Glasgow G3 6UB

Telephone: (0141) 332 4151

Fax: (0141) 332 4151

E-mail: harv1998@aol.com

Enquiries: The Director, Mr Harvey Kaplan

Open: Monthly open day; otherwise by arrangement.

Access: Generally open to the public, by appointment only.

The collection was begun in 1984 and the Archives Centre opened in 1987. The centre collects a wide range of material relating to the history of Jews in Scotland from the late 18th century. The holdings include synagogue and communal organisations' minutes and registers; financial records, accounts and annual reports; newspapers and cuttings books; brochures and other publications; and photographs. There is a computerised catalogue and a biannual *Newsletter* issued to Friends of Scottish Jewish Archives. See also K. Collins: *Second City Jewry* (1950).

401 University of Strathclyde

A John Anderson Campus

Address: Archives Department, McCance Building, 16 Richmond Street, Glasgow G1 1XQ

Telephone: (0141) 548 2397/2179

Fax: (0141) 552 0775

E-mail: suarchives@mis.strath.ac.uk

Website: www.strath.ac.uk/departments/archives

Enquiries: The Archivist, Dr James S. McGrath
The Assistant Archivist, Mr Roddy MacKenzie

Open: Mon–Fri: 9.15–4.45.

Access: Bona fide researchers, by appointment. Recent official records by arrangement with the Secretary to the University.

Historical background: Anderson's Institution was established in 1796 according to the instructions contained in the will of John Anderson, Professor of Natural Philosophy at the University of Glasgow, as a 'place of useful learning' for those excluded from the university system. During the 19th century the institution spawned the Glasgow Mechanics' Institution, developed a medical school and changed its name (Anderson's University, then Anderson's College). In 1887 it became the Glasgow and West of Scotland Technical College, at which point the Medical School became independent and was finally absorbed into Glasgow University in 1947. The Technical College was renamed the Royal Technical College in 1912 and then the Royal College of Science and Technology in 1956. In 1964 it merged with the Scottish College of Commerce (which started in 1847 as the Glasgow Athenaeum). Later in 1964 the merged institution became the University of Strathclyde. In 1993 the university merged with the Jordanhill College of Education. Strathclyde University Archives (John Anderson Campus) was established in 1977. Most of the archives previously held by the Department of History have been transferred to Glasgow University Archives & Business Records Centre (see entry 389A).

Acquisitions policy: The university archives collect the records of the university and its antecedents, and the papers of former staff and students. There is no policy of seeking other records, although some non-university collections were inherited.

Archives of organisation: Anderson's Institution and University, including Anderson's Medical School, Allan Glen's Institution, the Atkinson Institution etc, 1796–1887.
Glasgow Mechanics' Institution, 1823–87.
Glasgow and West of Scotland Technical College, later the Royal Technological College, then the Royal College of Science and Technology, 1887–1964.
Glasgow Athenaeum, later the Glasgow and West of Scotland Commercial College, then the Scottish College of Commerce, 1847–1964.
University of Strathclyde, 1964– .

Major collections: Leith-Buchanan family and estate papers (Dunbartonshire and Inverness-shire), c1600–1900.
Glasgow Typographical Society, 1817–1960.
Glasgow Dilettante Society, 1825–43.
Wm. Baird & Co. (steelworks), c1840–1968.
Society of Chemical Industry (Glasgow and West of Scotland branch), 1884–1962.
Scottish Association for the Promotion of Technical and Secondary Education, 1891–1925.
Gem Line (steamship company), c1945–1960.
International Union of Food Science & Technology, c1970– .

Papers of James 'Paraffin' Young, c1811–1883; Sir Patrick Geddes, c1854–1932; Sir George Pepler, c1882–1959.

Non-manuscript material: Photographs and films of campus, staff and students; some sound material; some supporting printed material.

Finding aids: Most collections are catalogued and indexed.

Facilities: Photocopying. Photography. Microfilm reader.

Conservation: Contracted out.

Publications: J.S. McGrath, V. Welter and S. Searle: *Catalogue of the Papers of Sir Patrick Geddes* (Glasgow, 1998) [6 vols incl. index].

B Jordanhill Library

Address: Jordanhill Campus, 76 Southbrae Drive, Glasgow G13 1PP

Telephone: (0141) 950 3300 ext. 3308

Fax: (0141) 950 3150

E-mail: jordanhill.library@strath.ac.uk

Website: www.strath.ac.uk/departments/jhlibrary/archfr.html

Enquiries: The Librarian, Mrs Margaret Harrison

Open: Term: Mon–Thurs: 9.00–9.00; Fri, Sat: 9.00–5.00.
Vacation: Mon–Fri: 9.00–5.00; Sat: 9.00–12.00.

Access: Bona fide researchers. Readers are advised to contact the librarian before visiting the collection.

Historical background: Jordanhill College of Education originated in the pioneering teacher-training work of David Stow (1793–1864) and had become, on the eve of its merger with Strathclyde University, the largest teacher-training institution in the UK. The Jordanhill archive was set up as a special collection within the college library in 1983, and the archives are now managed by the Jordanhill Campus Library on behalf of Strathclyde University Archives.

Acquisitions policy: Records of the college and its antecedents, and the papers of former staff and students. Also material relating to the development of teacher training and education in Scotland. Local history of the Jordanhill area of Glasgow.

Archives of organisation: Glasgow Infant School, 1828–34.

Glasgow Normal Seminary, 1835–45.

Glasgow Church of Scotland Training (or Normal) College, 1845–1907.

Glasgow Free Church Training (or Normal) College, 1845–1907.

University of Glasgow Local Committee for the Training of Teachers (King's students), 1903–6.

Glasgow Provincial Training College, later Jordanhill College of Education, 1907–93.

Hamilton College of Education, 1966–81.

Major collections: Association of Directors of Education in Scotland (ADES) archive, 1920–96.

Non-manuscript material: Photographs of the former college and its staff.

Materials relating to the educational pioneer David Stow, 1793–1864 (chiefly secondary sources).

Collections relating to the development of teacher education, including papers of Robert Rusk and Marjorie Cruickshank (1920–83), to the Jordanhill estate and district of Glasgow, and to Jordanhill College School.

Finding aids: Most collections are catalogued.

Facilities: Photocopying. Photography. Microfilm reader.

Conservation: Contracted out.

Publications: M.M. Harrison and W.B. Marke (eds): Teaching the Teachers: the History of Jordanhill College of Education, 1828–1993 (Edinburgh, 1996).

402 Glossop Library

Parent organisation: Derbyshire County Council

Address: Victoria Hall, Talbot Street, Glossop, Derbyshire SK13 7DG

Telephone: (01457) 852616

Fax: (01457) 856329

Enquiries: The Librarian, Mrs J. Powell

Open: Mon, Wed–Fri: 10.00–7.00; Tues, Thurs: 10.00–5.00; Sat: 9.30–1.00.

Access: Generally open to the public.

Acquisitions policy: To acquire, by donation, deposit or purchase, material relevant to the history and study of Glossop and its immediate surroundings in liaison with Derbyshire Record Office (entry 896).

Major collections: Usual local history collection, including papers and estate records of the Howard family, Dukes of Norfolk; material on local cotton production; parish registers; records of Littlemoor Congregational Church.

Non-manuscript material: Local newspapers, 1859– (on microfilm), and newspaper cuttings. Census returns.

Finding aids: Non-conformist records: NRA 19179. Card index of newspaper cuttings. International Genealogical Index.

Facilities: Photocopying. Microfilm/fiche readers.

403 British Waterways Archive

Parent organisation: Waterways Trust

Address: Llanthony Warehouse, The Docks, Gloucester GL1 2EJ

Telephone: (01452) 318041

Fax: (01452) 318076

E-mail: roy.jamieson@britishwaterways.co.uk

Enquiries: The Head of Archives and Records, Paul Sillitoe
The Archives Assistant, Roy Jamieson.

Open: Mon–Fri: 10.00–5.00.

Access: Generally open to the public; an appointment is essential.

Historical background: Nationalisation of the canals and inland waterways in 1947 was followed by the creation of the British Transport Commission (BTC). The BTC was dissolved in 1963 and the British Waterways Board was created through the Transport Act of 1962. The archive collection began in 1963 at the Canal Museum (Stoke Bruerne), and was moved to its present location in 1989. The collection transferred to the management of the Waterways Trust in 1999 along with National Waterways Museum (Gloucester), the Boat Museum at David Owen Archive (Ellesmere Port, see entry 358), and the Canal Museum (Stoke Bruerne).

Acquisitions policy: Principally internal records of British Waterways, but other material relating to canals is also acquired.

Archives of organisation: Records of canal companies pre-nationalisation, 1690–1947.

British Transport Commission (Docks and Inland Waterways Executive) 1947–63, British Waterways Board, 1963– .

Major collections: Plans by William Jessop (1745–1841), Thomas Telford (1757–1834), John Rennie (1761–1821) and Sir Joseph Whitworth (1803–87).

Non-manuscript material: Photograph collection, 1890– , including work of J.W. Millner, Cyril Arapoff and Arthur Watts (10,000 negatives).

Finding aids: Computer database of archives and photographs.
Retro-cataloguing and Internet project in progress.

Facilities: Photocopying. Microfilm/fiche reader/printer.

Conservation: Contracted out.

404 Gloucester Cathedral Library

Address: 2 College Green, Gloucester GL1 2LR

Telephone: (01452) 528095

Fax: (01452) 300469

Enquiries: The Cathedral Librarian, Mr L. Maddison

Open: By arrangement only.

Access: Bona fide researchers, by appointment only.

Historical background: The long room which contains the present cathedral library dates from the end of the 14th century during the time of Abbot Froucester, who built it to house the monastic library of St Peter's Abbey. When Henry VIII dissolved the abbey early in 1540, he dispersed the books. The present cathedral library dates from the end of the Commonwealth period, when the cathedral received 200 books from the library of John Selden; thanks to the interests of the Dean and Chapter, there were many fine acquisitions during the 18th century.

Acquisitions policy: To maintain the archives.

Archives of organisation: Archives of the Dean and Chapter, 1617–1990.

Major collections: Medieval MSS and registers, including 400 charters, 1072–1539.

Post-medieval MSS, including tithes and offerings of Trinity Parish, Gloucester, 1618–45.
Three Choirs Festival collection of programme books, and documents, 19th century– .

Non-manuscript material: Architectural plans and photographs of the cathedral.
Selden and Wheeler Collection of 17th- and 18th-century books.

Facilities: Photocopying.

Publications: S.M. Eward and others: *Catalogue of Gloucester Cathedral Library* (1972).
A. Boden: *Three Choirs: a History of the Festival* (1992).

405 Gloucester Library
Gloucestershire Collection

Parent organisation: Gloucestershire County Library, Arts and Museums Service

Address: Brunswick Road, Gloucester GL1 1HT

Telephone: (01452) 426979

Fax: (01452) 521468

Enquiries: The Senior Librarian, Local Studies, Graham Baker

Open: Mon, Tues, Thurs: 10.00–7.30; Wed, Fri: 10.00–5.00; Sat: 9.00–1.00.

Access: Generally open to the public; there is restricted access on some collections. An appointment for film/fiche readers is advisable.

Historical background: The nucleus of the Gloucestershire Collection was a bequest by J.J. Powell, QC, who left to the City of Gloucester several volumes of cuttings from Gloucestershire newspapers, with the understanding that should a public library be established they be kept there. On the death of Judge Powell in 1891 the bequest was added to by others, and since the library opened in 1900 other gifts and bequests, coupled with a policy outlined below, has seen the collection become a major one.

Acquisitions policy: All forms of material relating to the county, city, towns and villages of Gloucestershire, and items written by persons connected by birth or residence with the city or county.

Major collections: Hockaday MSS Collection: abstracts of ecclesiastical records relating to the diocese of Worcester and Gloucester, 1187–

(compiled from diocesan records and other sources).

Ivor Gurney MSS Collection: material, comprising music, poems, correspondence.

Smyth of Nibley Papers: papers, documents and letters concerning the business and personal affairs of John Smyth the elder, who was steward of the Hundred of Berkeley (c2000 items).

The Dancey Gift: MSS, books, pamphlets and prints relating to the city and county of Gloucester (225 vols, 321 pamphlets, 282 prints and portraits), includes a series of MSS illustrating the histories of the Saxon churches of Gloucestershire, which have been compiled from city records, parish registers and records and other source, and Dancey's handbooks, which are full of matters relating to local history.

Non-manuscript material: Gloucester Journal, 1722–1992; *Citizen*, 1876– ; *Gloucester Chronicle*, 1833–1928.

Hitchings Collection of Bibles and New Testaments, 1540–1906.

Finding aids: Card catalogue, being replaced by computerised catalogue.

Facilities: Photocopying. Photography. Microfilm/fiche readers.

Conservation: Contracted out .

Publications: Catalogue of the Gloucester Collection (1928).
Your Local History, Your House Has History and *Routes to Roots* [leaflets].

406 Gloucestershire Record Office

Parent organisation: Gloucestershire County Council

Address: Clarence Row, Alvin Street, Gloucester GL1 3DW

Telephone: (01452) 425295

Fax: (01452) 426378

E-mail: records@gloscc.gov.uk

Website: www.archives.gloscc.gov.uk

Enquiries: The County and Diocesan Archivist, Mr N. Kingsley

Open: Mon: 10.00–5.00; Tues, Wed, Fri: 9.00–5.00; Thurs: 9.00–8.00.

Access: By reader's ticket, on application. Proof of identity is required and a fee is charged. Closure for stocktaking usually December (2 weeks).

Historical background: The County Record Office was founded in 1936 and was appointed Diocesan Record Office for Gloucester in 1954. Some archives of the diocese and of the city previously held in the City Library were transferred to the Record Office at local government reorganisation in 1974. The office is recognised as a place of deposit for public records. The county archivist acts as honorary archivist to Berkeley Castle, where muniments are kept, and enquiries for access to these should be sent in the first instance to the county archivist.

Acquisitions policy: Public and private archives relating to Gloucestershire.

Archives of organisation: Records of Gloucestershire County Council, 1889– , and predecessor authorities, including records of Gloucestershire Quarter Sessions with indictment books, 1660– , order books, 1672– , order rolls, depositions and gaol calendars, 1728– ; records relating to the administration of bridges, highways, prisons, police stations and asylums, mainly 19th century; land tax assessments, 1775–1832, and registers of electors, 1832– ; police records, 1839–1980s.

Major collections: Other public and local authority records, including borough, district and parish councils and their predecessor bodies; hospital and health authority records, including Gloucestershire Royal Hospital, 1754–1972, and Barnwood House Private Mental Hospital, 1794–1970s; poor law union records, 1835–1930s; records of individual schools, school boards and managers, mainly 19th–20th centuries; water authorities' records, including waterworks companies, drainage boards and Severn River Board, mainly 19th–20th centuries; coroners' records, 17th–20th centuries; records of the lord lieutenant and militia, 19th–20th centuries.

Registers and records of Anglican parishes, 16th–20th centuries; of the Diocese of Gloucester, 1541– , which includes probate records, 1541–1858, and tithe maps, mid–19th century; of the estates of the Dean and Chapter of Gloucester, 16th–20th centuries; and of many non-conformist churches, 17th–20th centuries.

Records of local societies and voluntary associations, mainly 19th–20th centuries; and of local charities, 16th–20th centuries.

Estate and family archives, often incorporating records relating to property and family elsewhere in Britain and overseas, including:

Bathurst of Cirencester, 14th–20th centuries.

Bathurst of Lydney: correspondence of C.B. Bathurst, MP, 1767–1828.

Beaufort of Badminton, 13th–20th centuries.

Berkeley of Berkeley: correspondence of Capt. H. Berkeley, RN, in Zanzibar, 1843–98, and of F.H.F.Berkeley, MP, 1854–64.

Berkeley of Stoke Gifford, 13th–20th centuries.

Blathwayt of Dyrham: estates in Somerset, 16th–20th centuries; drawings for the building of Dyrham Park by James Wyatt, 1692–1706; political papers of William Blathwayt, Secretary at War, Commissioner of Trade etc, 1662–1716.

Bowly of Cirencester: diplomatic papers of Melchior Guydickens in Russia, 1749–53, and Gustavus Guydickens in Germany, 1760–68.

Codrington of Dodington: Bethell family estates in East Yorkshire, 1795–1846.

Colchester-Wemyss of Westbury-on-Severn: correspondence of M.W. Colchester-Wemyss with the King of Siam, 1903–25.

Commeline of Gloucester: correspondence from a soldier in South Africa, 1879–84.

Ducie of Tortworth: architectural drawings by A.W.N. Pugin and B. Bucknall, c1848–55.

Dutton of Sherborne: Stawell family, c1200–18th century; papers of the Rt. Hon. H.B. Legge, Chancellor of the Exchequer, 1742–64.

Freeman-Mitford of Batsford: 16th–20th centuries; political papers of John Freeman-Mitford, 1st Baron Redesdale, 1748–1830; John Thomas Freeman-Mitford, 2nd Baron and 1st Earl of Redesdale, 1805–86, and Algernon B. Freeman-Mitford, 1st Lord Redesdale of the 2nd creation, 1837–1916.

Hanbury-Tracy of Toddington: estate records, c1300–19th century.

Hicks Beach of Coln St Aldwyn: political papers of Sir Michael Hicks Beach, 1st Earl St Aldwyn, re South Africa and Ireland, 1865–1915.

Hyett and Dickinson of Painswick: political papers of Sebastian Dickinson, MP, 1820–78, and W.H. Dickinson, MP, 1878–1943; correspondence of Gen. Sir Richard Meade in India, 1857–93.

Jenner-Fust of Hill: Indian and Afghanistan records, 1803–82.

Kingscote of Kingscote: Col. R.N.F. Kingscote's Crimean War journal, 1854–6.

Lloyd-Baker of Hardwicke Court: papers relating to Hardwicke Reformatory, 1882–1910; correspondence and other records of Bishop William Lloyd of Worcester, 1627–1717, Archbishop John Sharp of York, 1645–1714, and Granville Sharp, philanthropist, particularly relating to the anti-slavery movement and parliamentary reform, 1735–1813.

Maclaine of the Isle of Mull: estate records, 18th–19th centuries; Gaelic songs, 1689–c1810.

Price of Tibberton: papers of Morgan Philips Price, MP (1855–1973).

Provost of Stinchcombe: correspondence from John and Thomas Keble, 1824–93.

Ridley of Naunton: constituency correspondence files of Nicholas Ridley, MP, 1970–8.

Rooke of St Briavels: naval orders and letters of Admiral Sir George Rooke, 1694–1702.

Sotheron-Estcourt of Shipton Moyne: political papers of Thomas Estcourt, MP (1748–1818), T.G.B. Estcourt, MP (1775–1853) and T.H.S. Sotheron Estcourt, MP (1801–76); also military records of Admiral F. Sotheron (d 1859) and Gen. J.B. Estcourt (1802–55) while serving in Canada, the Middle East and the Crimea.

Whitmore of Lower Slaughter: diaries and other papers re military service of Maj.-Gen. F.L. Whitmore, Gen. Sir A. Whitmore and Maj.-Gen. G.S. Whitmore in France, the Mediterranean and the Crimea, 1789–1882.

Records of local businesses and firms, including many solicitors' practices, comprising family and estate papers, and details of local societies, public undertakings and commercial activities, mainly 17th–20th centuries; canal companies' records, including the Thames and Severn Canal, 1792–20th century.

Businesses, including Winterbotham, Strachan and Playne of Minchinhampton, cloth manufacturers, 1829–1980; Gloucester Railway Carriage and Wagon Company, 1860–1880s; Lister & Co. of Dursley, cycle manufacturers etc, 1867–1971; Sisson & Co. of Gloucester, marine engineers, 1850s–1960s; H.H. Martyn & Co. of Cheltenham, sculptors, woodcarvers and architectural decorators, 1900–65; Bruton Knowles and Co. of Gloucester, estate agents, 19th–20th centuries.

Antiquarian collections, including Sir Thomas Phillipps', relating to Gloucestershire, 13th–19th centuries (mainly title deeds but also including an account roll for Gloucester Castle, 1263–6); Rev. D. Royce's notes and transcripts of the histories of many Cotswold churches and parishes, 19th–20th centuries.

Non-manuscript material: Substantial photographic collection relating to Gloucestershire and elsewhere, 19th–20th centuries.

Large collection of microfilm/fiche copies of material held elsewhere, including Gloucester Cathedral act books, 1617–19th century; the 1851 census enumerators' returns; medieval accounts and title deeds for the Berkeley family's estates in Gloucestershire and elsewhere; part of the West Indian correspondence of the Codrington family of Dodington, 17th–20th centuries.

The library of Sir Francis Hyett, containing a collection of contemporary tracts on the Civil War in Gloucestershire; full series of the *Transactions* of the Bristol and Gloucestershire Archaeological Society and of the Cotteswold Naturalists Field Club.

Printed county maps and sets of the 1st, 2nd and 3rd edition OS maps of Gloucestershire.

Finding aids: Catalogues, lists and indexes. All catalogues sent to NRA.

Facilities: Photocopying. Photography. Microfilming. Microfilm reader.

Conservation: Paper, parchment, seal and map conservation facilities in-house.

Publications: I.M. Kirby: *Catalogue of the Records of the Dean and Chapter* (1967) [Diocese of Gloucester].

——: *Catalogues of the Records of the Bishop and Archdeacons* (1968) [Diocese of Gloucester].

Handlist of the Contents of the Gloucestershire Record Office (1988).

Handlist of Genealogical Records (1992, new edition forthcoming).

Archive teaching books: *Gloucestershire Turnpike Roads* and *Gloucestershire Towns*.

Gloucestershire Family History (1993).

Your House Has History (1993).

Handlist of the Contents of Gloucestershire Record Office (4/1999).

407 Prinknash Abbey Archives

Address: Our Lady & St Peter, Cranham, Gloucester GL4 8EX

Telephone: (01452) 812455

Fax: (01452) 813305

E-mail: peter_prinknash@compuserve.com

Enquiries: The Archivist

Open: By arrangement.

Access: Bona fide researchers, by agreement of the Abbot and Community. An appointment is necessary.

Historical background: The community was founded in 1896 within the Church of England. Initially there were frequent moves before the community settled on Caldey Island in 1906. Conversion to Roman Catholicism took place in 1913 and a further move to Prinknash followed in 1928. The archive represents the accumulation of material since the year of foundation.

Acquisitions policy: To maintain the archive.

Archives of organisation: Monastic archives, 1896– .

Personal correspondence of the community, 1896– .

Anglo-Catholic material, 1890– .

Records of the construction of new Abbey building, 1939– .

Prinknash Pottery material, 1945– .

Major collections: Archives of Dom Aelred Carlyle, the founder, 1896–1955; Peter F. Anson, 1913–72; and Dom Michael Hanbury, 1920–75.

Material of Father Ignatius of Llanthony, late 19th century.

Letters of Eric Gill (1882–1940), mid-1940s.

Non-manuscript material: Plans of new abbey building, 1939– .

Community photographs, 1900– .

Videos of community activities and abbey construction.

Finding aids: Catalogue in process of production.

Facilities: Photocopying.

Conservation: Necessary work in consultation with Gloucestershire Record Office (see entry 406).

Publications: Preliminary guide published in community magazine *PAX*, no. 359, (Autumn, 1984).

408 Charterhouse

Parent organisation: Sutton's Hospital

Address: Godalming, Surrey GU7 2DX

Telephone: (01483) 291508/291516/291671 (answerphone)

Fax: (01483) 291594

Website: www.charterhouse.co.uk

Enquiries: The Archivist, Mrs S F Corke

Open: By arrangement, preferably during term.

Access: Approved researchers, on written application and by appointment. A charge is made for lengthy searches.

Historical background: Sutton's Hospital in the Charterhouse was founded in 1611 by Thomas Sutton to provide a home for 40 deserving men pensioners and to offer board and education to 40 boys, nominated in turn by the governors. They were housed in London until 1872, when the school was moved to newly built premises in Godalming. In London the school also educated day boys, who lodged in private boarding houses, though for many years these were not recorded as part of the establishment.

Acquisitions policy: To add, by purchase or donation, books, photographs, documents etc, by or about Old Carthusians. To house anything of interest to the school, its history and pupils.

Archives of organisation: Governing body minutes and papers; school admission, discipline and attendance books; headmaster's and housemasters' records, records of departments and administration and school activities.
Records of the Charterhouse Mission in Southwark, 1884– .

Major collections: Personal scrapbooks relating to the school, kept by Mrs Haig Brown, wife of the headmaster who moved the school from London, and Mr Girdlestone, an assistant master who founded the house which bears his name and was housemaster of it for many years, 1872– c1902.
Letters and papers of former pupils, including W.M. Thackeray, Robert Baden Powell, Ralph Vaughan Williams, Max Beerbohm, J.C. Bowen (*re* Robert Graves), and Sir Ronald Millar (theatrical and political). Letters and papers of masters, including W.C. Sellar and R.L. Arrowsmith. Diaries and letters of pupils.

Non-manuscript material: School photographs, c1870; school and house magazines, 1872– .
Cartoons and drawings by John Leech, W.M. Thackeray, Max Beerbohm and Osbert Lancaster.

Carthusian Collection: works by and about Old Carthusians, notably John Wesley, W.M. Thackeray, Robert Baden-Powell, Robert Graves.

Finding aids: Handlist to archives; incomplete computerised index by subject.

Facilities: Some photocopying and photography may be possible. Microfilm/microfiche readers.

Conservation: Contracted out.

Publications: A. Quick: *Charterhouse: a History of the School* (London, 1990).

409 Franciscan Missionaries of the Divine Motherhood
General Archives

Address: Ladywell, Godalming, Surrey GU7 1ST

Telephone: (01483) 426371

Fax: (01483) 426244

Enquiries: The Archivist, Sr Victoria Batchelor

Open: By appointment only.

Access: Bona fide researchers, strictly by arrangement.

Historical background: The Missionary Sisters of the Third Order of St Francis started in Hampstead in 1887, and a community of this congregation was founded in Aldershot in 1892. In 1911 many of the Hampstead Sisters joined another congregation and the Aldershot community became independent. In 1947 the Congregation acquired its present name. Having moved from Aldershot to Guildford, the archives transferred to Godalming in 1956.

Acquisitions policy: To acquire selected documents related to the history of the Franciscan Missionaries of the Divine Motherhood and of the Missionary Sisters of the Third Order of St Francis.

Archives of organisation: Records of the sisters' life as a congregation 1887–, religious formation, 1929– ; administration, 1888– ; the congregation, 1882– .

Non-manuscript material: Photographs/prints of sisters and the works of the congregation in various countries. Films and videos showing the work of the congregation. Publications, 1948– .

Finding aids: Descriptive list.

Facilities: Photocopying subject to discretion.

410 Godalming Museum

Parent organisation: Waverley Borough Council

Address: 109A High Street, Godalming, Surrey GU7 1AQ

Telephone: (01483) 426510

Fax: (01483) 869495

E-mail: godalming-museum@ndirect.co.uk

Website: www.meaco.com/godalming.html

Enquiries: The Curator, Alison Pattison

Open: Tues–Fri: 1.30–4.00.

Access: Generally open to the public, by appointment.

Historical background: There has been a museum in Godalming since at least 1908, originally in the old Town Council building (the 'Pepperpot' or 'Pepperbox'). It moved to its present location in 1987 and has had a professional curator since that time, paid by the borough council.

Acquisitions policy: Material relating to Godalming and surrounding area, particuarly archives of local industries and businesses.

Archives of organisation: Copy minutes of the borough council and its committees, 1893–1973, of the Town Council, 1973– , and of Waverley District Council, 1973– .

Major collections: Gertrude Jekyll (1843–1932), notebooks and pictures.
Local history notes and transcripts of Percy Woods (1842–1922) and deeds pertaining to the Godalming area mainly collected by him.
Records of local firms, including RFD (Rescue from Disaster, f. 1920) makers of inflatable dinghies, life-rafts and life-jackets.
Records of local societies.

Non-manuscript material: Museum Library: histories of the area, biographies of local people and *Transactions of the Surrey Archaeological Society* (Surrey Archaeological Collections), 1854– .

Finding aids: In progress

Facilities: Photocopying. Photography.

411 Goole Local Studies Library

Parent organisation: East Riding of Yorkshire Council, Library and Information Services

Address: Carlisle Street, Goole, East Riding of Yorkshire DN14 5DS

Telephone: (01405) 762187 (reference department)

Fax: (01405) 768329

Enquiries: The Reference Librarian, J. Briody

Open: Mon, Wed: 10.00–7.00;
Tues, Thurs, Fri: 10.00–5.00; Sat: 9.00–1.00.

Access: Generally open to the public. A paid research service is available. Appointments are necessary to use microfiche readers.

Historical background: The origins of the collection lie in a donation of material from a local historian, Mr Harold Garside, which has been added to by other interested members of the public. In addition the Goole Borough Library, which developed from the Goole Free Library of 1905, was able to contribute historical books, papers and photographs to create the collection. The holdings of archive material relate mainly to Goole, but also cover the marshland areas of Swinefleet and Adlingfleet, Snaith and Howden.

Acquisitions policy: Purchase, donation and deposit of all types of material in all subject areas relating to Goole and district.

Archives of organisation: Usual local authority holdings, including poor books, drainage books, rate books.

Major collections: Deeds, indentures and local historians' collections, including those of Harold Garside, 1682–c1950.

Non-manuscript material: Photographs, small collections of maps, local newspapers.
Census microfilms, 1841–91, newspaper microfilms, 1870– .

Finding aids: Card catalogues. Indexes.

Facilities: Microfilm/fiche reader/printer.

Publications: Leaflet on the local studies library.

412 Gracehill Moravian Church

Parent organisation: Moravian Church, London (see entry 700)

Address: Moravian Manse, 25 Church Road, Gracehill, Co. Antrim BT42 2NL

Telephone: (028) 25653141

Enquiries: The Minister, Rev. Victor D. Launder

Open: By appointment.

Access: Generally open to the public, by appointment; a donation towards the church is appreciated.

The Moravian Church in Gracehill was started in 1759. Records consist of church diaries (kept by the Moravian ministers), accounts, deeds, registers of members, baptisms, marriages and burials. There are also diaries and records of the former Dublin congregation, 1748–1980, and registers and records of the former congregations. The records and congregations diaries of the Lower Ballinderry Moravian Church, 1755– , were received in 1996. Microfilm and lists are at the Public Record Office of Northern Ireland (see entry 81).

413 Belvoir Castle

Telephone: (01476) 870262

Fax: (01476) 870443

E-mail: info@belvoircastle.com

Website: www.belvoircastle.com

Enquiries: The Archivist, J.R. Webster

The Belvoir Archive contains MSS, estate records, accounts and maps, 14th century– ; and personal papers of the Manners family, 15th century– . This is a private archive; the muniment room is not open, but applications from bona fide researchers may be given consideration. There is a very brief catalogue.

414 Wordsworth Library

Parent organisation: The Wordsworth Trust

Address: Dove Cottage, Townend, Grasmere, Cumbria LA22 9SH

Telephone: (01539) 435003/435544

Fax: (01539) 435748

E-mail: enquiries@wordsworth.org.uk

Enquiries: The Curator, Jeff Cowton

Open: Mon–Sun: 9.30–5.30; weekends by arrangement.

Access: Bona fide researchers, by prior arrangement with the Trustees (please allow 3–4 weeks).

Historical background: This charitable trust was founded in 1890 with the purchase of the house and a mission to preserve the house and its collections 'for lovers of poetry all over the world'. A museum opened in 1935 with provision for a library in 1950. The current specially designed museum opened in 1981 and houses special exhibitions, an education programme, a 'writer-in-residence' scheme, and special events and conferences.

Acquisitions policy: The trust collects manuscripts, books, artefacts and fine art related to Wordsworth and the development and influence of Romanticism; and to the development of the Lake District, art and culture.

Major collections: Verse, prose and correspondence of William Wordsworth (1770–1850), his family and circle, including Dorothy Wordsworth (1771–1855), Samuel Taylor Coleridge (1772–1834) and Thomas De Quincey (1785–1859).

Integral collections of papers associated with Wordsworth and the Lake District and associated family estate papers, including the Shepherd papers, the 'G' papers, the Spedding papers (c1700–1940), and the Moorsom papers of the Calvert and Stanger families of Keswick, 18th century– .

Non-manuscript material: Paintings, drawings, prints, photographic archive.

Lifetime editions, collected works, biographical and critical works of William Wordsworth and his contemporaries.

Books owned by, and associated with, Wordsworth and his circle.

Collection of Lake District books.

Finding aids: Indexes, lists, catalogues, computer records available, to varying degrees of detail; Calvert and Stanger papers: NRA 26173.

Facilities: Photocopying by arrangement. Photography.

Conservation: Preventative conservation in-house. Remedial conservation contracted out.

Publications: Catalogues relating to special exhibitions. Publication list available.

415 Great Yarmouth Central Library

Parent organisation: Norfolk County Council

Address: Tolhouse Street, Great Yarmouth, Norfolk NR30 2SH

Telephone: (01493) 844551/842279

Fax: (01493) 857628

E-mail: peter.ransome@nlis.btinternet.com

Enquiries: The Team Specialist (Information and Norfolk Studies), East Area, Peter Ransome

Open: Mon–Fri: 10.00–5.30; Sat: 9.00–5.00.

Access: Generally open to the public. There is a booking system for microfilm/fiche readers.

Acquisitions policy: Local studies material on Great Yarmouth and East Norfolk, mainly books, pamphlets, newspaper cuttings and illustrations. Most archival material relating to Great Yarmouth is held by Norfolk Record Office (entry 939).

Major collections: Herbert Tinkler Collection: MSS and press cuttings *re* entertainments in Great Yarmouth, c1900–1960s.

Non-manuscript material: Emm's Papers: notes and press cuttings on history of Gorleston, 1970s.
Yallop Collection: glass plate negatives of late Victorian and Edwardian Great Yarmouth (350).
W.A.S. Wynne Collection: material *re* history of south-east and north-east Norfolk, c1900–74.

Finding aids: Local studies catalogue with indexes to newspaper cuttings and local illustrations.

Facilities: Photocopying. Microfilm/fiche readers.

Publications: Guide to the local history collections.

416 Great Yarmouth Museums

Parent organisation: Norfolk Museums Service

Address: Central Library, Tolhouse Street, Great Yarmouth, Norfolk NR30 2SH

Telephone: (01493) 745526

Fax: (01493) 745459

Enquiries: The Collections Officer, Damian Eaton

Open: Mon–Fri: 9.30–5.00, by appointment.

Access: Generally open to the public; however, access is limited as it depends on staff availability, and an appointment is essential.

Great Yarmouth Museums does not actively collect archives except where they relate closely to museums' collections; Norfolk Record Office (see entry 939) is the primary collector of archives for the area. However, it holds records of Great Yarmouth Gaol, 1798–1877, plans from local shipyards, early 20th century, and photographs relating to the maritime history of Great Yarmouth. There is a list of gaol records, and photocopying and photography are available.

417 Inverclyde District Libraries

Address: Watt Library, 9 Union Street, Greenock PA16 8JH

Telephone: (01475) 720186

Enquiries: Mrs I. Couperwhite

Open: Mon, Thurs: 2.00–5.00, 6.00–8.00; Tues, Fri: 10.00–12.30, 2.00–5.00; Wed, Sat: 10.00–1.00.

Access: Generally open to the public.

Historical background: Opened in 1837 as a memorial to James Watt, the Watt Library was originally a subscription library; it was taken over in 1974 by Inverclyde District Council and is used as a centre for the local archive material for the area.

Acquisitions policy: To collect material relating to the Inverclyde area by purchase, donation or deposit.

Major collections: Corporation minutes of Greenock, Gourock and Port Glasgow.
Local cemetery, hospital and institution records.

Non-manuscript material: Pamphlets; photographs; tapes; newspapers; rare books.

Finding aids: Indexes to newspapers, including ship-launches, and births, marriages and deaths. Catalogue of main collections.

Facilities: Photocopying. Microfilm reader/printer.

418 North East Lincolnshire Archives

Parent organisation: North East Lincolnshire Council

Address: Town Hall, Grimsby, Lincolnshire DN31 1HX

Telephone: (01472) 323585

Fax: (01472) 323582

E-mail: john.wilson@nelincs.gov.uk

Website: www.nelincs.gov.uk/ic/index.htm

Enquiries: The Archivist, Mr J.F. Wilson

Open: Mon–Fri: 9.30–12.00, 1.00–4.30.

Access: Generally open to the public. An appointment is advisable and essential for users of microfilms.

Historical background: The office was established in 1976 and covers the administrative areas of North Lincolnshire and North East Lincolnshire, and is a recognised place of deposit for public records. The office is not a diocesan record office and enquiries about parish registers, wills and bishops' transcripts should be directed to the Lincolnshire Archives (see entry 519). Archives formerly in the custody of the North Lincolnshire Museum, Oswald Road, Scunthorpe DN15 7AB, are deposited in this office but can also be returned to the museum by arrangement.

Acquisitions policy: North-East Lincolnshire Council and predecessor authorities since 1201; geographic area of North Lincolnshire and North East Lincolnshire.

Archives of organisation: Usual local authority record holding of archives created by Great Grimsby Borough, 1227– ; and by rural district, urban district and borough councils in North Lincolnshire and North East Lincolnshire, including records of lighting inspectors, local boards of health, sanitary authorities, burial boards, school boards, parish councils, schools, Grimsby Borough Police and Grimsby Education Committee.

Major collections: Deposited local collections, including board of trade records for Grimsby, notably merchant vessel crew lists, 1863–1913; fishing vessel crew lists, 1884–1914; registers of sea-going apprentices, 1880–1937, and registers of Grimsby ships, 1824–1925.

Parkinson family of East Ravendale: family and estate papers, 1699–1937.

Sheffield family of Normanby Hall: family and estate papers, 1720–1927.

Winn family of Nostell Priory (Yorks.) and Appleby Hall: ironstone leases and related papers for North Lincolnshire, 1839–1942, principally of Rowland Winn (1820–93), 1st Lord St Oswald.

Correspondence received by Canon the Hon. Douglas Hamilton Gordon (1824–1901), chiefly from his father George Hamilton Gordon (1784–1860), 4th Earl of Aberdeen and Prime Minister, about school, church preferment and current affairs, 1836–62.

Letters to Arthur Moore, MP, on electoral management of Grimsby borough, 1695–1715.

John Wintringham, solicitor, Grimsby: correspondence concerning railway development, 1845–97.

Business records of British Steel Corporation: records of predecessor iron and steel manufacturers in Scunthorpe area, 1885–1965; Consolidated Fisheries Ltd, trawlers, Grimsby, 1896–1983; Cooper Snowden Ltd, Grimsby, timber merchants, 1874–1947; Peter Dixon and Company Ltd, Grimsby, paper manufacturers, 1909–73; Elswick-Hopper Cycle and Motor Company Ltd, Barton on Humber, 1899–1976; Great Grimsby Ice Company, 1896–1990; Humber Graving Dock and Engineering Company Ltd, Immingham, 1909–47; Marshall Knott and Barker, Grimsby, timber merchants, 1875–1945; Sir Thomas Robinson and Son (Grimsby) Ltd, trawlers, 1891–1976.

Non-manuscript material: Oral history recordings of domestic servants, farm and fishing workers, in Grimsby and North Lincolnshire, 1900–85.

James Jillott (1800–80), drawings of streets and buildings in Grimsby, 1822–77.

Finding aids: Lists sent to NRA.

Facilities: Photocopying. Microfilm readers.

Conservation: Comprehensive in-house facilities.

Publications: Guide to the South Humberside Area Archive Service (1993).

419 Surrey Archaeological Society

Address: Castle Arch, Guildford, Surrey GU1 3SX

Telephone: (01483) 532454

Fax: (01483) 532454

E-mail: surreyarch@compuserve.com

Website: www.ourworld.compuserve.com/homepages/surreyarch/

Enquiries: Mrs S. Ashcroft

Open: By appointment.

Access: Members; non-members by appointment.

Historical background: The library was founded with the society in 1851.

Acquisitions policy: Local history material relating to the history and archaeology of Surrey.

Archives of organisation: Records of the society, 1851– .

Non-manuscript material: Many collections of local material, comprising plans, drawings, photographs, maps, newspaper cuttings, books and paintings.

Finding aids: Card catalogue being computerised.

Facilities: Photocopying.

Conservation: Contracted out.

Publications: Library Guide.

420 University of Surrey

Address: Guildford, Surrey GU2 5XH

A George Edwards Library

Telephone: (01483) 259287

Fax: (01483) 259500

E-mail: library.enquiries@surrey.ac.uk

Website: www.lib.surrey.ac.uk

Enquiries: The Librarian, Mr T.J.A. Crawshaw
The University Archivist, Arthur C. Chandler

Open: Term: Mon: 10.00–10.00; Tues–Fri: 9.00–10.00; Sat:1.00–6.00; Sun: 2.00–6.00.
Vacation: Mon–Fri: 9.00–5.00.
Some additional hours in some vacation periods. Details on application.

Access: Bona fide researchers.

Historical background: Battersea College of Technology, founded in 1894 as the Battersea Polytechnic, was awarded a charter as the University of Surrey in 1966. The library supports the teaching and research of the university. The archives are housed in the library and are under the control of the librarian, supported by part-time archives staff.

Acquisitions policy: The library collects administrative and other documents from departments. There is no other policy, except to preserve items of historical interest about the institution and its courses.

Archives of organisation: Administrative and other records of the university and its predecessors. Calendars, staff and student magazines and newsletters.

Major collections: Ernest H. Shepard (1879–1976), illustrator and cartoonist: material in his possession after selling the rights of *Winnie the Pooh* to the Disney Corporation, including many original illustrations, drawings and manuscripts, with photographs and memorabilia from the two World Wars.
British Guild of Travel Writers' papers.

Non-manuscript material: Some tape-recordings of older staff and others on the institution's history. Some photographs and insignia.

Finding aids: Collection partly indexed, with work still in progess.

Facilities: Photocopying. Photography. Microfilm/fiche reader/printer.

B National Resource Centre for Dance

Telephone: (01483) 259316

Fax: (01483) 259500

E-mail: h.roberts@surrey.ac.uk

Website: www.surrey.ac.uk/nrcd/nrcd.html

Enquiries: The Manager, Helen Roberts

Open: Mon–Fri: 9.30–5.00, by appointment only.

Access: Researchers, students and teachers, by arrangement. A visit fee is charged.

Historical background: The NRCD was established at the University of Surrey in 1982 as a result of the Calouste Gulbenkian Foundation report on dance education and training in the UK (1980) and operates as a self-financing fee-based service. There are numerous collections donated by companies, solo artists, dance organisations and individuals involved in dance.

Acquisitions policy: The focus of the collection is on dance, especially the dance heritage of the UK, mainly from the 20th century. Materials are acquired purely by donation, either as a result of a proactive approach from the NRCD or as a gift from the donor. The NRCD has several regular contributors to the archive, which contains a number of complete collections and others which are added to periodically.

Major collections: Arts Council Dance Panel records, c1950–c1990; Dance and the Child International (daCi), 1978– ; International Council of Kinetography Laban (ICKL), mid-1950s–1995.

Records of companies: Dance Advance; Educational Dance-Drama Theatre: Extemporary Dance Theatre; Green Candle Dance Company; Janet Smith and Dancers; Kickstart Dance Company; EMMA/ Midlands Dance Company; Rosemary Butcher Dance Company; Shobana Jeyasingh Dance Company; V-TOL Dance Company.

Papers of Rudolf Laban, movement theorist and educator (1897–1958); Lisa Ullmann, teacher and associate of Laban (1907–85); Joan Russell, dance educator (1921–89); Betty Meredith Jones, dance educator and movement therapist (1908–96).

Non-manuscript material: Extensive holdings of artwork, audio and video recordings, newspaper clippings, periodicals, photographs, posters, theatre programmes and books.

Finding aids: Paper catalogues to some of the major collections, paper printouts from the NRCD's database of holdings (user interface to be developed), card indexes to journals and publicity.

Facilities: Photocopying. Photography.

Conservation: Contracted out.

Publications: J.A. Chapman (comp.): *Dance Film and Video Catalogue* (NRCD, 1993).

Catalogues covering eleven collections available for purchase. Leaflet guide outlining the archives of the NRCD available on request.

421 Haileybury and Imperial Service College

Address: Haileybury, Hertford SG13 7NU

Telephone: (01992) 447710 (College)

Fax: (01992) 583649 (Archivist); (01992) 467603 (College)

Enquiries: The Hon. Archivist, Mr Andrew Hambling

Open: Weekdays, by arrangement.

Access: Bona fide scholars, by appointment with the Archivist.

Historical background: Haileybury was founded in 1862 on the site of the East India College (EIC), which between 1802 and 1858 trained administrators for the Honourable East India Company. The library and records of the East India College were transferred to the India Office (entry 561E) on its closure, although a small proportion has since been returned to Haileybury.

Acquisitions policy: The acquisition of archive material by purchase is minimal, but gifts of material of interest are welcomed by the archivist.

Archives of organisation: A wide range of historical material originating from the following institutions: The East India College; Haileybury College; United Services College; Imperial Service College; Haileybury & ISC; and the Haileybury Junior School, Windsor; and some items from Haileybury College, Melbourne; and the Haileybury School of Mining, Ontario.

Major collections: Manuscript of Kipling's *Stalky & Co.*.

Non-manuscript material: Complete run of *The Haileybury Observer* and *The Haileyburian* magazines.
Photographs, sound and film archives related to EIC and Haileybury.

Finding aids: Indexing in progress.

Facilities: Photocopying.

Conservation: Contracted out as necessary.

Publications: I. Thomas: *Haileybury 1807–1987.*
W. Blunt: *The Buildings of Haileybury.*
R.L. Ashcroft: *Random Recollections of Haileybury.*

The Haileybury Register [published by the Haileybury Society about every tenth year].

422 West Yorkshire Archive Service: Calderdale District Archives

Parent organisation: West Yorkshire Joint Services

Address: Calderdale Central Library, Northgate House, Northgate, Halifax, West Yorkshire HX1 1UN

Telephone: (01422) 392636

Fax: (01422) 341083

E-mail: calderdale@wyjs.org.uk

Website: www.archives.wyjs.org.uk

Enquiries: The Principal District Archivist, Miss Pat Sewell

Open: Mon, Tues, Thurs, Fri: 10.00–5.30. Open evenings to 7.00 and Sat 10.00–5.00 for microform only. Closed one week in February and one week in November for stock–taking.

Access: Generally open to the public, by appointment. A paid research service is available.

Historical background: The Calderdale Archives Service is very much a development of the Halifax Borough Archives Service, which was established in 1964 and which acquired the accumulations of the Halifax Museums Service and the Halifax Antiquarian Society. In 1974 the archives service took control of the archival records of the nine amalgamating local authorities within Calderdale, and in 1983 it joined the West Yorkshire Archive Service. It moved to its present purpose-built accommodation in 1983. It acts as the Diocesan Record Office for Bradford (Shelf parish records) and is recognised as a place of deposit for public records.

Acquisitions policy: Archives relating to the Calderdale MBC geographical area.

Archives of organisation: Records of Calderdale MBC and nine predecessor authorities, with inherited archives, including records of civil townships, 1665– , and Halifax Town Trustees, 1762–1849.

Major collections: Family and estate archives, including Lister of Shibden Hall, 1329–1937, Armytage of Kirklees Hall, 1200–1800, and Stansfeld of Fieldhouse Sowerby, 1701–1920. Political and labour holdings, including records of local co-operative societies, 1832–1972, friendly societies, 1769–1981, political parties, 1874–1981, and trade unions, 1834–1983. Business archives, especially textile records, 1562–1983, including John Crossley and Sons, carpet manufacturers, 17th–20th centuries.

Finding aids: Lists and detailed indexes available. Link to West Yorkshire Archive Service computerised database. Catalogues sent to NRA.

Facilities: Photocopying. Photography by arrangement. Microfilm/fiche readers/printers.

Conservation: Undertaken by West Yorkshire Archive Service Headquarters, Wakefield (entry 1184).

Publications: *Archives in Calderdale* (1976; annual supplements, 1977–84).
A. Betteridge and P. Sewell (comp.): *Calderdale Archives, 1964–1989: an Illustrated Guide to Calderdale District Archives* (1990); supplement covering 1990–92 accessions (1993).

423 Hamilton Central Library

Parent organisation: South Lanarkshire Libraries

Address: 98 Cadzow Street, Hamilton, Lanarkshire ML3 6HQ

Telephone: (01698) 452403

Fax: (01698) 286334

E-mail: hamilton.reference@south-lanarkshire.co.uk

Enquiries: The Reference Services Manager, Ms Isabel Walker

Open: Mon, Tues, Thurs: 9.15–7.30; Fri: 9.30–7.30; Wed, Sat: 9.15–5.00.

Access: Generally open to the public.

Historical background: South Lanarkshire Libraries was formed in 1996. Hamilton Library was formerly part of Hamilton Burgh to 1975, then Hamilton District Libraries to 1996.

Acquisitions policy: To collect material relating to Hamilton and the surrounding area, within the policy guidelines of South Lanarkshire Libraries.

Major collections: Burgh of Hamilton: council minute books, 1701–1975; abstract of accounts, 1879–1975; register of electors, 1851–1975 (incomplete); Hamilton Police Commissioners minute books, 1857–1901; Hamilton Road Trustees minute books, 1808–65; Hamilton Combination Poor House (later Hamilton Home) minute books, 1864–1975.
Lanark County Council minute books, 1890–1975.
Hamilton District: Council minute books, 1975–96.
Small collection of 18th- and 19th-century estate papers relating to the Duke of Hamilton's estates in Lanarkshire.

Non-manuscript material: Maps of Hamilton and the surrounding area (*c*2000).
Microfilm of old parish registers and census returns for the Hamilton area, 1841–91.
Local newspapers, 1856– .

Finding aids: List of Hamilton estates papers; NRA 36701 (NRAS 3438).

Facilities: Photocopying. Microfilm/fiche reader/printer.

424 Rothamsted Experimental Station Library

Parent organisation: BBSRC Institute of Arable Crops Research

Address: IACR Rothamsted, Harpenden, Hertfordshire AL5 2JQ

Telephone: (01582) 763133

Fax: (01582) 760981

E-mail: liz.allsopp@bbsrc.ac.uk

Enquiries: The Librarian

Open: Mon–Thurs: 9.00–5.30; Fri: 9.00–5.00.

Access: Bona fide enquirers, by prior arrangement only.

Historical background: Rothamsted Experimental Station, now IACR Rothamsted, was founded in 1843 by Sir John Bennet Lawes and his partner Sir Henry Gilbert to study crop nutrition. A number of the experiments they began continue today, and Rothamsted's remit is still to study the processes involved in plant growth.

Acquisitions policy: No active policy for collecting archives; other departments retain their own records.

Major collections: Sir John Lawes and Sir Henry Gilbert: a few personal papers and much correspondence and other documents relating to scientific work, preparation of lectures and printed papers and Rothamsted administration, 1840s–early 20th century.
Sir A.D. Hall and Sir E.J. Russell, 20th-century directors of Rothamsted: personal and working papers.
Lawes Agriculture Trust: correspondence and minutes, 1880s–early 20th century.
Rothamsted Farm, Woburn Experimental Station and Fruit Farm: diaries and working note-books, mid-19th–mid-20th centuries.
Rothamsted staff: working note-books of Robert Warrington (1838–1907) and of a few 20th-century staff members.

Non-manuscript material: British livestock prints and paintings (*c*200).
Early agricultural books, 1480–1840 (*c*3500).

Finding aids: Various catalogues and lists; some sent to NRA.

Facilities: Photocopying. Microfilm/fiche reader.

Conservation: Contracted out.

Publications: M. Harcourt Williams: *Rothamsted Experimental Station: Catalogue of the Records in the Station Library* (1987).
Catalogue of the Correspondence of Lawes and Gilbert (1989).
G.V. Dyke: *John Bennet Lawes: the Record of his Genius* (Research Studies Press, 1991).
——: *John Lawes of Rothamsted* (Hoos Press, 1993).

425 Society of the Divine Saviour (SDS)

Address: Salvatorian Provincial Office, 129 Spencer Road, Harrow Weald, Middlesex HA3 7BJ

Telephone: (020) 8427 4673

Fax: (020) 8427 6924

Enquiries: Fr Edmund Lanning

Open: By appointment.

Access: Bona fide scholars, by appointment only.

The Salvatorians were founded in Rome in 1882 and came to England in 1901. Their archives relate to the administration of the Province, its houses and members, and links with various dioceses and international houses. The society is a registered charity. There is a catalogue and further listing is in progress.

426 Harrow School

Address: 5 High Street, Harrow-on-the-Hill, Middlesex HA1 3HP

Telephone: (020) 8422 2196 ext. 305

Fax: (020) 8423 3112

E-mail: gibbs@archives.freeserve.co.uk

Enquiries: The Archivist, Rita M. Gibbs

Open: By arrangement during school term.

Access: Bona fide students or researchers.

Historical background: The school was founded *de novo* in 1572 in the parish of Harrow by John Lyon of Preston, who, in the absence of children of his own, endowed it with a series of properties. The income from the Lyon estates was also used towards the maintenance of local roads, the provision of apprenticeship money and of dowries and other approved purposes until the Public Schools Act of 1868, when a second school, the John Lyon School, was partially funded from the surplus of the original endowment. Although the school was originally established as a free grammar school for boys from the locality, as early as 1592 the headmaster was permitted to take in fee-paying pupils, who shortly outnumbered the parishioners. It is now an independent fee-paying school controlled by a board of governors.

Acquisitions policy: To consolidate the existing collection of material relating to the school, its governors, staff and pupils, and to John Lyon's other charities.

Archives of organisation: Estate documents, 14th century– .
Governors' minutes and account books, 1615– .
Headmasters' papers, *c*1805– ; masters' papers, *c*1800– .
School lists, 1770– .

Major collections: Literary and other autographs; material relating to Richard Brinsley Sheridan (1751–1816), Lord Byron (1788–1824) and Anthony Trollope (1815–82).

Non-manuscript material: Photographs of individuals, groups, teams and buildings, late 1850s– .

Architectural drawings, particularly by William Burges (1827–81) and Sir John Gardner Wilkinson (1797–1875).

Finding aids: Computerisation of cataloguing in progress.

Facilities: Photocopying.

Conservation: Contracted out.

Publications: E.J.L. Scott: *Records of the Grammar School Founded by John Lyon* (Harrow, 1886).
J.S. Golland: *The Harrow Apprentices* (Harrow, 1981).

427 Hartlepool Central Library

Parent organisation: Hartlepool Borough Libraries

Address: 124 York Road, Hartlepool TS26 9DE

Telephone: (01429) 263778/272905

Fax: (01429) 275685

E-mail: reflib@hartlepool.gov.uk

Website: www.hartlepool.gov.uk

Enquiries: The Reference Librarian, Miss M.E. Hoban

Open: Mon–Thurs: 9.30–7.00; Fri, Sat: 9.30–5.00.

Access: Generally open to the public. Prior notice is needed for access to older and more fragile material; a booking system operates for microfilm readers.

Historical background: There have been a number of local government boundary changes over the years with consequent variations in the local authority's name. The collection is based upon that formed in West Hartlepool, where the Central Library (now replaced) was opened in 1895. The town's boundaries were extended over the years until, in 1967, the neighbouring authorities of Hartlepool and West Hartlepool merged to form the County Borough of Hartlepool. In 1974 Cleveland County was formed and Hartlepool Borough became a district within the county. In 1996 Cleveland County was replaced by four separate unitary authorities formed from the county districts. The Borough of Hartlepool is one of these unitary authorities. Hartlepool Port and Harbour Commission records are now at Teesside Archives (entry 901).

Acquisitions policy: The primary area of interest is the geographical area within the Hartlepool district boundaries; material for neighbouring areas is included in the collection, which is based on a stock covering the old counties of Northumberland, Durham and North Yorkshire. All subjects are included and all formats — books, pamphlets, ephemera, photographs, postcards, maps, periodicals, videos, manuscripts, microfilm, CD-ROM.

Major collections: Usual local history collection, including William Gray & Co., shipbuilder: yardbooks, 1878–1942 (incomplete); L. Blumer and Son, shipbuilder & ship repairer: account books, 1853–68 (4 vols).
J. Proctor, printer, binder and stationer: invoices and accounts, 1865–7.
MSS collection of Sir Cuthbert Sharp, author and antiquary.

Non-manuscript material: Local studies collection covering the north-east, with special emphasis on Hartlepool. Genealogical sources are included in this collection.
Photographs (*c*5000), including the Ferriday Collection.
Substantial collection of 19th-century maps.

Finding aids: Selective index to newspapers, 1865–89; index to photograph collection; catalogue of maps; index to ships listed in Gray's yardbooks; index to vessels listed in Blumer's account books.

Facilities: Photocopying. Photography by arrangement. Microfilm/fiche readers/printers.

Conservation: By arrangement with Teesside Archives.

Publications: List of Directories in the Local Studies Collection.
Selective List of Genealogical Sources in the Local Studies Collection.

428 Haslemere Educational Museum

Address: 78 High Street, Haslemere, Surrey GU27 2LA

Telephone: (01428) 642112

Fax: (01428) 645234

E-mail: haslemeremuseum@compuserve.com

Website: www.ourworld.compuserve.com/homepages/richard_hawkes

Enquiries: The Curator, Diana M. Hawkes

Open: Tues: 10.00–5.00; Sat: 10.00–1.00.

Access: Generally open to the public. An appointment is essential to consult archive material. Administrative archives of the museum are not open to the public.

Historical background: The museum, now a charitable trust, was founded by Jonathan Hutchinson (1828–1913) in Haslemere in 1888 predominantly as a natural history museum.

Acquisitions policy: Suitable documents relating to local history and personalities connected with the district and museum.

Archives of organisation: Annual reports (published), 1914– ; local press reports of museum activities and events, 1897– .

Major collections: Field note-books, sketches and MSS belonging to Sir Archibald Geikie (1834–1924), geologist.
Flora and fauna records of the district, 19th century– .
Local history collection includes MSS, notes of Rev. T.S. Cooper (1850–1918), Chiddingfold antiquarian; J.W. Penfold (1828–1909), architect; W.A. Sillick (*c*1877–1955), local journalist; and E.W. Swanton (1870–1958), museum curator and antiquarian.

Non-manuscript material: Press cuttings, *c*1870– ; parish magazines, maps, photographs and postcards of the district. Small audio-visual archive of local interest.

Finding aids: Computer database, currently for staff use only with long term aim of providing information on the Internet.

Facilities: Photocopying.

Publications: E.W. Swanton: *A Country Museum* (1947).
M. Kane: *A Country Museum Revisited* (1995).
Quarterly *Newsletter* and *Annual Report.*

429 Haslingden Library

Address: Higher Deardengate, Haslingden, Rossendale, Lancashire BB4 5QL

Telephone: (01706) 215690

Fax: (01706) 215690

Enquiries: The Librarian

Open: Mon, Tues: 9.30–12.30, 1.30–7.30; Thurs, Fri: 9.30–12.30, 1.30–5.00; Sat: 9.30–4.00.

Access: Generally open to the public.

Historical background: The local history collection was started before World War II, but some items have been copied and the originals placed in Lancashire Record Office (entry 1044)

Acquisitions policy: Acquires local history material relevant to Haslingden and neighbouring towns in Rossendale.

Major collections: Usual local history collection, including minutes of Haslingden Borough, 1927–74, Rossendale, 1974– .
Halstead Collection: a few transcripts of local church and other records, including Haslingden Parish Church registers, 1650–96, and Haslingden vestry books, 1780–1911, with diaries and scrapbooks.
Collection *re* local cricket club and Lancashire League, 1875– .

Non-manuscript material: Cassette recordings of local dramatic society productions and of the Rossendale Male Voice Choir.
Photographs (1500) and slides.

Finding aids: NRA 1296 and more recent typed list.

Facilities: Photocopying. Microfilm reader. Film projectors.

Publications: J. Dunleavy: *The Fall and Rise of Haslingden Library.*

430 Hastings Museum and Art Gallery

Parent organisation: Hastings Borough Council

Address: Cambridge Road, Hastings, East Sussex TN34 1ET

Telephone: (01424) 781155

Fax: (01424) 781165

E-mail: museum@hastings.gov.uk

Enquiries: The Curator, Miss V.A.G. Williams

Open: Museum: Mon–Sat: 10.00–5.00; Sun: 2.00–5.00.
Access to records is by appointment, Monday to Friday only.

Access: Generally open to the public.

Historical background: The museum was founded in 1890 and moved to its present site in 1928. Originally only a museum and art gallery, it gradually attracted records. In 1973 parish

and other ecclesiastical records were transferred to the East Sussex Record Office (entry 513).

Acquisitions policy: Donations of local MSS are accepted from time to time.

Archives of organisation: Hastings borough records, 1584– .

Major collections: Archives of Hastings and the Cinque Ports, 12th century–20th century.
Archives of local families, including the Milwards.

Non-manuscript material: Large collections of photographs, maps, prints and ephemera with the gallery collections.

Finding aids: Various registers and indexes.

Facilities: Normal archive office facilities cannot be provided. However, help will always be given to genuine researchers. Not suitable for student projects.

Publications: Various historical publications relating to Hastings.

431 Hatfield House Library

Address: Hatfield House, Hatfield, Hertfordshire AL9 5NF

Enquiries: The Librarian and Archivist to the Marquess of Salisbury, Mr R.H. Harcourt Williams

Open: By arrangement with the Librarian.

Access: Approved academic (normally postgraduate) researchers, on written application.

Historical background: Hatfield House was built in 1612 by Robert Cecil, 1st Earl of Salisbury. It has remained in the possession of his direct descendants and is now the home of the 6th Marquess of Salisbury.

Acquisitions policy: To maintain the estate's own records and papers of the Cecil family.

Archives of organisation: Papers of William Cecil, 1st Baron Burghley (1520–98), Secretary of State and afterwards Lord Treasurer to Queen Elizabeth I.
Papers of Robert Cecil, 1st Earl of Salisbury (1563–1612), Secretary of State and Lord Treasurer to King James I (a microfilm copy of these papers may be consulted in the British Library, Special Collections, see entry 561).
Papers of Robert Gascoyne-Cecil, 3rd Marquess of Salisbury (1830–1903), Foreign

Secretary and Prime Minister to Queen Victoria.

Non-manuscript material: Maps and architectural drawings.

Finding aids: Calendar of the Salisbury (Cecil) Manuscripts, vols i–xxiv (1883–1976), covers all papers up to 1668 (i.e. those of Lord Burghley and the 1st and 2nd Earls of Salisbury).
J.F.A. Mason: *Calendar of the Private Foreign Office Correspondence of Robert, 3rd Marquess of Salisbury*, 2 vols (NRA typescript, 1963; available at the NRA).
Card index at Hatfield House for remaining correspondence of the third Marquess.

Facilities: Photocopying (certain collections only).

Conservation: Contracted out.

Publications: Robert, 5th Marquess of Salisbury: 'The library at Hatfield House, Hertfordshire', *The Library*, 5th ser., xviii/2 (1963), 83.
R.A. Skelton and Sir J. Summerson: *A Description of Maps and Architectural Drawings in the Collection made by William Cecil, First Baron Burghley, now at Hatfield House* (Oxford, 1971).
Royal Commission on Historical Manuscripts: 'Estate papers of the Cecil family, Marquesses of Salisbury', HMC *Annual Review, 1989–1990* (HMSO, 1990), 29–31.

432 Haverfordwest Library Local Studies Department

Parent organisation: Pembrokeshire County Council Cultural Services Department

Address: Dew Street, Haverfordwest, Pembrokeshire SA61 1SU

Telephone: (01437) 764551

Fax: (01437) 769218

E-mail: anita.thomas@pembrokeshire.gov.uk

Enquiries: The Assistant Librarian, Reference and Local Studies, Mrs A. Thomas

Open: Mon, Wed, Thurs: 9.30–5.00; Tues, Fri: 9.30–7.00; Sat: 9.30–1.00.

Access: Generally open to the public. Booking is required for microfilm and CD-Rom use. There is a charge for postal enquiries.

Historical background: The Local Studies Collection contains material relating to Pembrokeshire which has been collected over a period of more than 50 years. Much of the archival material was gathered in the absence of a record office before local government reorganisation in 1974.

Acquisitions policy: To collect material directly related to Pembrokeshire. Donations of relevant material are accepted.

Major collections: Francis Green Collection of genealogical material, comprising copies of documents dating from 13th to early 20th centuries (33 vols). There is also a supplementary collection of sheet pedigrees relating to West Wales families.

Non-manuscript material: Photographs and slides, mainly topographical, 19th and 20th centuries (c5500).
Maps, 17th–20th centuries (c1000).
Local newspapers, 1844–1924 (on microfilm), 1960– (bound, incomplete); newspaper cuttings, 1976– .

Finding aids: Card indexes. Bibliographies prepared for certain localities (copies sent to National Library of Wales, Aberystwyth; see entry 9).

Facilities: Photocopying. Microfilm/fiche readers.

Publications: *Genealogical Sources in Haverfordwest Library.*
Newspapers and Periodicals in Haverfordwest Library.

433 Pembrokeshire Record Office

Parent organisation: Pembrokeshire County Council

Address: The Castle, Haverfordwest, Pembrokeshire SA61 2EF

Telephone: (01437) 763707

Fax: (01437) 768539

E-mail: recordsoffice@pembrokeshire.gov.uk

Enquiries: The County Archivist, Miss Claire Orr

Open: Mon–Thurs: 9.00–4.45; Fri: 9.00–4.15; Sat (1st Sat in month except bank holiday weekends): 9.30–12.30.

Access: Generally open to the public.

Historical background: The first county archivist was appointed in 1963 and the office was established as Pembrokeshire Record Office in 1967. It also acts as the Diocesan Record Office for St David's (parish records only) and is recognised as a place of deposit for public records.

Acquisitions policy: Material of significance to and generated by the county of Pembroke.

Archives of organisation: Usual local authority record holdings.

Major collections: Deposited local collections, including business and family records relating to Angle (John Mirehouse); Bush (Meyricks); Carew Court (Carew); Cresselly (Allen); Lawrenny (Lort-Phillips); Pentre (Saunders-Davies); Scotlon (Higgon) and Henllan (Lewis).
Deeds and documents of the Starbuck family of Sherborn, Nantucket Island, Massachusetts, 1660–1780.

Non-manuscript material: Maps; photographs.

Finding aids: Catalogues and indexes. Lists sent to NRA.

Facilities: Photocopying. Microfilm/fiche readers/printer.

Conservation: In-house facilities; minimum outside work undertaken.

434 Flintshire Record Office

Parent organisation: Flintshire County Council

Address: The Old Rectory, Hawarden, Flintshire CH5 3NR

Telephone: (01244) 532364

Fax: (01244) 538344

E-mail: archives@flintshire.gov.uk

Website: www.llgc.org.uk/cac/cacoo32.htm

Enquiries: The County Archivist, Mr Rowland Williams

Open: Mon–Thurs: 9.00–4.45; Fri: 9.00–4.15; an appointment is usually necessary.

Access: Generally open to the public. The office operates the CARN reader's ticket system.

Historical background: Flintshire Record Office was originally established in 1951 but formed part of Clwyd Record Office from 1974 to 1996, when it regained its independence. The office also acts as the Diocesan Record Office

for St Asaph (parish records) and is recognised as a place of deposit for public, manorial and tithe records. The county archivist is honorary archivist to the St Deniol's Library, Hawarden, whose archive collections, the Glynne-Gladstone MSS, including correspondence of W.E. Gladstone (1809–98), Herbert, Viscount Gladstone (1854–1930) and the 5th Duke of Newcastle (1811–64), are made available for research only at the Record Office.

Acquisitions policy: All archives relating to the present county and accruals to existing series (policy available on request).

Archives of organisation: Usual local authority record holdings, including records of quarter sessions, 1720– ; Poor Law Union, 1834– ; county council and district and parish/community councils.

Major collections: Deposited local collections from landed estates, business and industry, Anglican and non-conformist churches and public services; also political papers and antiquarian collections.

Non-manuscript material: Extensive collections of photographs, newspapers, prints, drawings, watercolours and maps.

Finding aids: Most collections catalogued; detailed indexes in electronic and hard copy form. Catalogues sent to NRA.

Facilities: Photocopying (including colour and large format). Photography. Microfilm/fiche reader/printer.

Conservation: In-house facilities; outside work can be undertaken.

Publications: A.G. Veysey: *Guide to the Flintshire Record Office* (1974) [includes St Deniol's Library collections].
D. Pratt and A.G. Veysey: *Handlist of Topographical Prints of Clwyd* (1977).
D. Pratt: *Calendar of the Flintshire Quarter Sessions Rolls, 1747–52* (1983).
A.G. Veysey: *Guide to the Parish Records of Clwyd* (1984).
C.J. Williams: *Handlist of the Grosvenor (Halkyn) MSS* (1988).
——: *Handlist of the Glynne-Gladstone MSS in St Deniol's Library, Hawarden* (List and Index Society, Special Series Vol. 24, 1990).

435 Hawick Museum

Parent organisation: Scottish Borders Council

Address: Wilton Lodge Park, Hawick, Roxburgh TD9 7JL

Telephone: (01450) 373457

Fax: (01450) 378506

E-mail: hawickmuseum@hotmail.com

Enquiries: The Curator, Fiona Colton

Open: April–Oct: Mon–Fri: 10.00–12.00, 1.00–5.00; Sat, Sun: 2.00–5.00.
Oct–April: Mon–Fri: 1.00–4.00; Sun: 1.00–4.00.

Access: Generally open to the public, preferably by appointment.

Historical background: Hawick Museum's collection was founded in 1857 as a result of the collecting activities of the Hawick Archaeological Society. The current museum has been on the site since 1910 and now houses that collection and the library and archive of the society.

Acquisitions policy: Actively seeks to augment existing MS material and contemporary photographs relating to all aspects of Roxburgh district.

Major collections: Hawick Archaeological Society archive and strong local collections, including:
Roxburgh copy of the *National Covenant*, 1638.
Ancrum Papers (Buccleuch), 18th century.
Heritors papers from the original parish church.
Comprehensive monumental inscriptions of Roxburghshire graveyards.
Local estate, church and farming papers, 18th century– .
Local knitwear records, mid-19th century– .
Local archaeological excavations records.
Motor vehicle licensing records (Roxburgh), 1904–27.

Non-manuscript material: Photographic archive (*c*4500 originals) and glass negatives and early slides, late 19th century– .
Extensive maps and plans of Hawick area, 1658– .
Local newspapers, 1877– .

Finding aids: Lists available. Computerised indexes underway. Estate plans and photographs: NRA 17662.

Facilities: Photocopying and photography by arrangement.

Conservation: Contracted out to Scottish Museums Council or Gateshead College.

Publications: Z. Oddy: *A History of Wilton Lodge* (Jedburgh, 1990).

436 Brontë Parsonage Museum Library

Parent organisation: The Brontë Society

Address: Church Street, Haworth, Keighley, West Yorkshire BD22 8DR

Telephone: (01535) 642323

Fax: (01535) 647131

E-mail: bronte@bronte.prestel.co.uk

Website: www.bronte.org.uk

Enquiries: The Curator, Rachel Terry

Open: April–Sept: Mon–Fri: 10.00–5.30.
Oct–Mar: 11.00–5.00.
The Brontë Parsonage Museum itself is also open at weekends.

Access: Bona fide researchers, with written academic references and strictly by prior appointment.

Historical background: The Brontë Society was founded in 1893 and a museum opened in Haworth in 1895. Early Brontë Society representatives obtained material from important sales of MSS. The Brontës' former home was purchased for the society by a local benefactor and it became a museum in 1928. Since then items have been donated, purchased, bequeathed or loaned, thus adding to the collection. The research library is housed within the museum itself.

Acquisitions policy: The acquisition of material related to, or connected with, the Brontë family, their friends and relatives, and the work of the Brontës.

Archives of organisation: Early Brontë Society correspondence.

Major collections: Brontë Society Collection: work of the Brontë family, including MSS, juvenilia, letters, poetry, French exercises, drawings, administration papers and books. Letters and miscellaneous items of the Brontës' friends and relatives.
Indentures, letters, certificates concerning Haworth and district.

Bonnell Collection: MSS, letters, books and drawings, bequeathed by Henry Houston Bonnell.

Seton Gordon Collection: mainly letters from Charlotte Brontë to her publishers, Smith Elder & Co.

Grolier Collection: mainly letters.

Non-manuscript material: Library collections, including transcripts of Brontë MSS; complete set of Brontë Society *Transactions*; editions of the works, biography, literary criticism and drama archive related to the Brontës.
Collection of published material and facsimiles.

Finding aids: Several catalogues. Computer database of books, MSS and museum objects for staff use only, to prepare selective listings for researchers. Facsimiles of primary source material available for study.

Facilities: Photocopying.

Conservation: Contracted out to recommended conservators.

Publications: Brontë Society *Transactions* [published biannually].
C. Alexander: *A Bibliography of the Manuscripts of Charlotte Brontë* (1982).
C. Lemon: *A Centenary History of the Brontë Society, 1893–1993.*

437 EMI Music Archives

Parent organisation: EMI Group plc

Address: Central Research Laboratories, Dawley Road, Hayes, Middlesex UB3 1HH

Telephone: (020) 8848 2000

Fax: (020) 8848 2018/9

E-mail: edger@emigroup.com

Enquiries: The Archivist

Open: Tues–Thurs: 9.30–4.30.

Access: By appointment only; detailed requests in writing are required.

Historical background: The Gramophone Co. was founded in 1897 to exploit Emile Berliner's European patents. Several rival record companies were acquired before 1931, when the Gramophone Co. and the Columbia Graphophone Co. merged to form Electric & Municipal Industries Ltd (EMI). Capital Records was purchased in 1955 and expansion into the leisure industry followed. EMI merged with Thorn in 1979 as Thorn EMI. It demerged in 1996.

Acquisitions policy: To acquire material of significance relating to the group's activities.

Archives of organisation: Records relating to the gramophone, radio and television industry and to household appliance manufacturers, including minutes, contracts, correspondence with performers, recording ledgers, 1890s– .

Non-manuscript material: Discs, CDs, videos, master tapes and video masters, catalogues, photographs.

Finding aids: Card indexes; computer-aided microfilm retrieval.

Facilities: Photocopying. Photography. Microfilm reader by arrangement.

Publications: P. Martland: *Since Records Began: EMI: the First Hundred Years* (1997).
L. Jobey (ed): *The End of Innocence* (1997).
B. Southall, A. Rouse and P. Vince: *Abbey Road* (1997).

438 Boys' Brigade

Address: National Training Centre, Felden Lodge, Hemel Hempstead, Hertfordshire HP3 0BL

Telephone: (01442) 231681

Fax: (01442) 235391

E-mail: felden@boys-brigade.org.uk

Website: www.boys-brigade.org.uk

Enquiries: The Brigade Secretary

Open: Mon–Fri: 9.00–5.00.

Access: Members and bona fide researchers, usually by appointment.

Historical background: The Boys' Brigade was founded by William A. Smith in Glasgow in 1883 as part of the Free Church College Mission. It was the first uniformed youth organisation and now has a membership of about 400,000 in more than 60 countries. The celebration of the centenary in 1983 prompted the development of brigade archives.

Acquisitions policy: To acquire records, publications and other relevant material relating to the brigade and its close links with other similar organisations.

Archives of organisation: Archives of the brigade both at central and local level, 1883– .

The *BB Gazette* (in which the original *Scouting for Boys* by Baden-Powell was published), 1889– (monthly).

Major collections: Records and papers of William A. Smith (1854–1914).

Non-manuscript material: Photographs, programmes, certificates, publicity material, handbooks, badges, medals, uniform regalia and other artefacts; film library.

Finding aids: Cataloguing not complete or comprehensive; personal assistance provided if necessary.

Facilities: Photocopying. Photography by arrangement.

Publications: The Boys' Brigade Gazette [published bi-monthly].
Archives Press [booklet series dealing with a variety of aspects of Boys' Brigade history].

439 Hereford Cathedral Library

Address: The Cathedral, Hereford HR1 2NG

Telephone: (01432) 359880

Fax: (01432) 355929

E-mail: library@herefordcathedral.co.uk

Enquiries: The Cathedral Librarian, Miss Joan Williams
The Archivist, Mrs Rosalind Caird

Open: Tues–Thurs: 10.00–4.00; Sat (1st of month): 10.00–12.30.
Closed for two weeks in January.

Access: Approved readers. Medieval MSS and rare books by appointment only; appointment is preferred for archives.

Historical background: The archives are formed by the natural accretion of records relating to the history and administration of the Cathedral of Hereford and of the affairs of the Dean and Chapter. They are closely associated with the cathedral library, which acts as a repository for the cathedral music and material relating to the cathedral's function as a place of learning.

Acquisitions policy: The archives continue to take in material from the administrative and legal offices of the Dean and Chapter. Gifts and deposits are accepted of material relating to or associated with any aspect of the cathedral's history.

Archives of organisation: Acts of the Dean and Chapter, 1132– .
Archives of the College of Vicars Choral, 1575–1937.

Major collections: Archives of Kington Free School, 1632–1899; St Michael's College, Tenbury Wells, 1852–1985; Hereford Choral Society, 1836– .
Library: 227 MSS works, 8th–15th centuries.

Non-manuscript material: Library: photographic negatives of the cathedral and contents (*c*1000).

Finding aids: Typescript calendars and lists. Card indexes.

Facilities: Photocopying and photography by arrangement. Microfilm reader.

Publications: F.C. and P.E. Morgan: *Hereford Cathedral Libraries and Muniments* (2/1975) [illustrated].
R.A.B. Mynors and R.M. Thomson: *Catalogue of the Manuscripts of Hereford Cathedral Library* (Cambridge, 1993).

440 Hereford City Library

Parent organisation: Herefordshire Libraries and Information Service

Address: Broad Street, Hereford HR4 9AU

Telephone: (01432) 272456

Fax: (01432) 359668

E-mail: herefordlibrary@herefordshire.gov.uk

Website:
www.librariesinfo.herefordshire.gov.uk

Enquiries: The Senior Librarian, Mr Robin Hill

Open: Tues, Wed: 9.30–6.00; Thurs: 9.30–5.00; Fri: 9.30–8.00; Sat: 9.30–1.00.

Access: Generally open to the public, but a prior appointment is appreciated.

Historical background: The city library was independent from 1871 until 1974, when it came under the control of the county of Hereford and Worcester; in 1998 this became Herefordshire Council. It was a record repository until the establishment of Hereford County Record Office in the 1960s, when its collection of parish records and deeds was transferred.

Acquisitions policy: Material relevant to previous donated or purchased collections, otherwise MS items only; most offers of archival material are referred to Herefordshire Record Office (entry 441)

Major collections: Notes on the county of Herefordshire by Thomas Blount (*d* 1679); notes by John Duncumb and others towards a county history (including those for unpublished volumes).

MS collections relating to the history of Herefordshire by James Hill (*d* 1727), Thomas Bird (*d* 1836), and C.J. Bird.

Correspondence of the artist John Scarlett Davies.

MS of John Williams's *History of Radnorshire.* Pilley Collection.

Non-manuscript material: Alfred Watkins and F.C. Morgan photograph collections.

Small collection of cine film, some of local interest.

Local newspapers, 1770– .

Finding aids: Card catalogues and indexes. Local collection records will be available on OPAC.

Facilities: Photocopying. Microfilm reader/printer. Photographs in negative collection by arrangement.

Publications: Brief guide to local collection.

441 Herefordshire Record Office

Parent organisation: Herefordshire Council

Address: The Old Barracks, Harold Street, Hereford HR1 2QX

Telephone: (01432) 260750

Fax: (01432) 260066

E-mail: shubbard@herefordshire.gov.uk

Website: www.herefordshire.gov.uk/records_office/pol_records_intro.htm

Enquiries: The Record Office Manager, Miss D.S. Hubbard

Open: Mon: 10.00–4.45; Tues–Thurs: 9.15–4.45; Fri: 9.15–4.00.
Annual closure for two weeks in autumn; telephone for details.

Access: Generally open to the public. The CARN reader's ticket system is operated. Prior booking for microfilm/fiche readers is essential.

Historical background: Hereford County Record Office was established in 1959, became a dependent repository of Hereford and Worcester Record Office in 1974 and became Herefordshire Record Office following the separation of the counties in 1998. It also acts as the Diocesan Record Office for Hereford and is recognised as a place of deposit for public records. Most Hereford and Worcester County Council records are held at Worcestershire Record Office (see entry 1217).

Acquisitions policy: Records of the County and predecessor authorities. Hereford diocesan records: parish records within the county of Herefordshire. Private records within the Herefordshire county area are accepted as gifts (preferred) or on long term loan.

Archives of organisation: Records of Hereford County Council, 1888–1974 and Herefordshire Council, 1998– .

Major collections: Deposited local collections, some of national standing, including Edward Elgar correspondence with Percy Hull, 1903–33.

Non-manuscript material: Bustin of Hereford, photographers: plate glass negatives, *c*1890–1920 (*c*6000).

Finding aids: Parish, subject and biographical indexes; most lists are indexed. Lists sent to NRA.

Facilities: Photocopying. Photography. Microfilming. Microfilm/fiche readers.

Conservation: Joint conservation unit for both Hereford and Worcester Record Offices based here. Outside work is undertaken to a limited degree.

Publications: General leaflets: *Visiting Herefordshire Record Office*; *Tracing Your House at HRO*; *Tracing Your Family at HRO.* Source Guides: *Census Records available at HRO*; *Parish Registers available at HRO*; *School Records available at HRO*; *Parish Officers' Records available at HRO.*

442 Hertford Museum

Parent organisation: Trustees of Hertford Museum

Address: 18 Bull Plain, Hertford SG14 1DT

Telephone: (01992) 582686

Fax: (01992) 534797

Enquiries: The Senior Curator, Andrea George

Open: Tues–Sat: 10.00–5.00.

Access: Generally open to the public; an appointment is necessary.

Historical background: The museum was founded by Robert and William Andrews during the 19th century and is owned by the trust they set up in 1915.

Acquisitions policy: Material relating to the east Hertfordshire area.

Major collections: Usual local history collections, including amateur dramatic handbills, auction details, and a large collection of election posters, mainly 19th century.
Andrews family collections of topographical and antiquarian notes.
Wigginton Collection: papers of Wigginton family of Hertford.

Non-manuscript material: James Wilcox (1778–1861): collection of his topographical sketches and watercolours.
Rev. R. H. Newell (1778–1852) and C. A. Newell (1818–c1870): sketches of local buildings and holidays.

Facilities: Photocopying.

443 Hertfordshire Archives and Local Studies

Parent organisation: Hertfordshire County Council

Address: County Hall, Hertford SG13 8EJ

Telephone: (01438) 737333

Fax: (01992) 555113

E-mail: hals@hertslib.hertscc.gov.uk

Website: www.hertsdirect.org.uk

Enquiries: The Heritage Services Manager, Mrs Christine Shearman

Open: Mon, Wed, Thurs: 9.30–5.30; Tues: 10.00–8.00; Fri: 9.30–4.30; Sat: 9.00–1.00.
Annual stock-taking closure during first week in February.

Access: Generally open to the public; a charge is made for Family History Centre (records on microfilm and fiche). Prior booking is advisable. Documents must be pre-ordered for Tuesday evenings and Saturday mornings. A paid research service is available.

Historical background: A records committee was established in 1895 and the present premises opened in 1939. The office also acts as the Diocesan Record Office for St Albans and is recognised as a place of deposit for public records. In 1997 the St Albans City archives were transferred to the record office from St Albans Central Library.
The Hertfordshire Film Archive, established in 1978, is housed in the Register Office Block, County Hall, Hertford, tel: (01992) 556624.

Acquisitions policy: A detailed policy is available on request. The geographical coverage is the present administrative county of Hertfordshire and the pre-1974 county, including Barnet and Totteridge.

Archives of organisation: Usual local authority record holdings.

Major collections: Deposited local collections, of which the following have a wider significance:
Family and estate papers of Cowper (Panshanger), 13th–19th centuries; Desborough, 19th and 20th centuries; Lytton (Knebworth), 14th–19th centuries; Delmé-Radcliffe, 13th–20th centuries; Martin Leake, including explorers in the Near and Middle East, 15th–20th centuries; Verulam (Gorhambury), 14th–19th centuries.
Ebenezer Howard (1850–1928), founder of Letchworth and Welwyn Garden Cities, personal letters concerning his publications, 1879–1935.

Non-manuscript material: Local studies library of materials, in a variety of formats, pertaining to Hertfordshire, including photographs, maps, films and printed material.

Finding aids: Manual catalogues and indexes (gradually being converted onto computer). Lists sent to NRA.

Facilities: Photocopying. Photography. Microfilm/fiche readers. Education service.

Conservation: In-house; some outside work undertaken. Book binding and conservation contracted out.

Publications: W. Le Hardy: *Guide to the Hertfordshire Record Office, Part 1: Quarter Sessions and other Records in the Custody of the Officials of the County* (1961).
Catalogue of Manuscript Maps (1969).
Genealogical Sources (1999).

444 Rochdale Libraries
Local Studies Collection

Address: Heywood Library, Church Street, Heywood, Lancashire OL10 1LL

Telephone: (01706) 360947

Enquiries: The Town Librarian or The Local Studies Librarian at Rochdale Library

Open: Mon: 10.00–7.30; Tues, Fri: 10.00–5.30; Wed: 10.00–12.30; Thurs: 10.00–5.30; Sat: 9.30–1.00, 2.00–4.00.

Access: Generally open to the public.

Historical background: The dynamic growth of Rochdale, Middleton and Heywood during the 19th century produced a wealth of material relating to the area. In 1974 it was decided that the local collection pertaining to Heywood only should be retained at Heywood Library, under the general supervision of the Local Studies Librarian at Rochdale Library (entry 902).

Acquisitions policy: The collection of documentary material relating to all aspects of life in the former Borough of Heywood.

Major collections: Administrative material from the former Heywood borough, mainly 20th century, including council minutes and accounts; the Medical Officer of Health's reports; records of the Heywood and Middleton Water Board; electoral registers.

Non-manuscript material: Complete runs of local newspapers (original and microfilm copies).
Books, pamphlets, audio-visual material, photographs, maps, plans, 19th–20th centuries.

Facilities: Photocopying. Microfilm/fiche readers.

445 Gresham's School

Address: Holt, Norfolk NR25 6EA

Telephone: (01263) 711743

Fax: (01263) 712028

E-mail: postmaster@holtsch.demon.co.uk

Website: www.holtsch.demon.co.uk

Enquiries: The Archivist

Open: Term: Mon, Wed, Fri: 9.00–1.00, 2.00–9.00; Sat: 9.00–1.00; Tues, Thurs: 9.00–1.00, 4.00–9.00.

Access: Generally open to the public by appointment.

The School was founded in 1555 by Sir John Gresham (1519?–1579) and governorship was vested in the Worshipful Company of Fishmongers. The archives include registers of pupils 1562– , school lists, 1900– , and school magazines, 1900– . There is also a foundation collection of books begun in 1639 by the bequests of Thomas Tallis, headmaster, 1606–40 and of John Holmes, headmaster, 1729–60.

446 Ulster Folk and Transport Museum

Parent organisation: National Museums and Galleries of Northern Ireland

Address: Cultra, Holywood, Co. Down BT18 0EU

Telephone: (028) 90428428

Fax: (028) 90428728

Enquiries: The Librarian

Open: Mon–Fri: 9.00–5.00.

Access: Bona fide researchers, preferably by appointment.

Historical background: In 1967 two institutions, the Ulster Folk Museum, established by Act of Parliament in 1958, and the Belfast Transport Museum, established by Belfast City Council and opened to the public in 1962, were merged to form the Ulster Folk and Transport Museum. In 1988 the Ulster Folk and Transport Museum was merged with the Ulster Museum and the Ulster American Folk Park to form the National Museums and Galleries of Northern Ireland.

Acquisitions policy: The museum's library acquires material that relates to the museum's collections of artefacts and which relates more generally to its role in illustrating the life past and present of the people of Northern Ireland.

Major collections: Professor K.H. Connell Collection: material covering Irish economic and social history, 18th–20th centuries.
Ulster Dialect Archive.

Non-manuscript material: Extensive collection of photographs (*c*320,000), including W.A. Green Collection, c1900–30, and Harland & Wolff Shipbuilding Collection.

Sound Archive: folklore, oral history, folk music and song (*c*3000 items), and the BBC, Northern Ireland, Sound Archive.

Finding aids: Specialised list and indexes.

Facilities: Photocopying. Photography.

447   Christ's Hospital Archives

Address: Horsham, West Sussex RH13 7LE

Telephone: (01403) 252547

Fax: (01403) 211580

E-mail: archives@christs-hospital.org.uk

Enquiries: The Archivist, Rhona Mitchell

Open: By arrangement only, and usually during school term.

Access: Any responsible person with a serious interest in the history of the school, by appointment only.

Historical background: Christ's Hospital was founded in 1552 for the children of those in need in the City of London. The boys' school moved to Horsham in 1902, and the girls' school moved from Hertford in 1985, thus re-establishing a co-educational school. Most of the administrative records and registers of children prior to the 20th century are deposited at Guildhall Library, London (entry 624).

Acquisitions policy: By donation, deposit and occasionally by purchase, anything relevant to the history of the school.

Archives of organisation: MS material of administrative and educational interest, primarily 20th century.

Major collections: MSS of Edmund Blunden (1896–1974).

Non-manuscript material: Ephemera of educational and antiquarian interest.
Portraits of benefactors and a fine photographic archive collected within the new Christ's Hospital Museum.

Finding aids: Catalogue and inventory in progress.

Facilities: Photocopying. Photography.

Publications: G.A.T. Allan: *Christ's Hospital.*

448   Horsham Museum

Parent organisation: Horsham District Council

Address: 9 The Causeway, Horsham, West Sussex RH12 1HE

Telephone: (01403) 254959

Fax: (01403) 217581

E-mail: museum@horsham.gov.uk

Enquiries: The Curator, J. Knight

Open: Mon–Sat: 10.00–5.00.

Access: Generally open to the public. An appointment needs to be made to consult documents, with the minimum of notice of three (preferably five) days.

Historical background: Horsham Museum was founded by Horsham Museum Society in 1893. From its beginnings the society collected documents, and in 1950 William Albery, saddler, local historian and author, gave his collection to the town and Horsham Museum Society looked after them. In 1989 the collection of documents was handed over to the museum staff to manage. Since 1966 the Museum Society has ceased to collect documents but Horsham Museum continues to collect as a function of the council.

Acquisitions policy: Documents relating to the town, surrounding area and people/businesses connected with Horsham. A close liaison is maintained with West Sussex Record Office (entry 241) over acquisitions.

Archives of organisation: Archives of Horsham Museum Society, 1893– .
Archives of Horsham Museum collections, 1893– .

Major collections: William Albery Collection, consisting of:
Medwin papers: records of elections, Horsham, New Shoreham, Steyning, 1736–1832; Horsham Borough records; Norfolk papers; private and business papers of T. Medwin, P. Medwin (1770–1870).
Albery papers: business and personal records of a saddler, *c*1830–1950s, local history research records, *c*1910–50.
MSS relating to Clough and Butler, Fletcher, Padwick, Rawlinson, Lord and Lady Irwin.
Miscellaneous documents, title deeds, inventories, wills, plus a number of documents relating to the Shelley family, including Percy Bysshe Shelley (1792–1822), poet, and Thomas Medwin, biographer of Byron and Shelley.
Whitehouse papers, covering Sussex & Dorking Brick Company.
Chasemore family papers.

Non-manuscript material: Extensive holdings of ephemera, notably political squibs and sale posters, 1790–1990; civic functions and miscellaneous items.

Maps, postcards and photographs of the town, plus Felici Beato/Samuel Bourne photographs of India, Japan, Borneo, China and USA (320).

Finding aids: Catalogue produced by West Sussex Records Office in preparation.

Facilities: Photocopying. Photography.

Conservation: Contracted out.

Publications: Sussex Archaeological Collections, 69, p.117, describes many of the Albery manuscripts.

449 Royal Society for the Prevention of Cruelty to Animals

Address: The Causeway, Horsham, West Sussex RH12 1HG

Telephone: (01403) 264181

Fax: (01403) 241048

E-mail: enqserv@rspca.org.uk

Website: www.rspca.org.uk

Enquiries: The Information Officer, Chris Reed

Open: Mon–Fri: 9.00–5.00, by arrangement.

Access: Generally open to the public, by appointment only.

Historical background: The society was founded in 1824 as the Society for the Prevention of Cruelty to Animals. Royal patronage was granted in 1840.

Acquisitions policy: To maintain the archives, which include ephemera, publications and artefacts. Other animal welfare related items are acquired.

Archives of organisation: Minutes of council and other committees, 1830–1992.
RSPCA records, including some individual branch records, 1800–76; annual reports, 1932–97, and publications, 1860–1998.

Finding aids: Typed indexes to most material; development of computer catalogue started in 1999.

Facilities: Photocopying. Microfiche reader.

Conservation: Contracted out.

450 Hounslow Local History Collection

Parent organisation: London Borough of Hounslow

Address: Local Studies Department, Hounslow Library, 24 Treaty Centre, Hounslow, Middlesex TW3 1ES

Telephone: (020) 8570 0622 ext. 7892

Fax: (020) 8569 4330/8862 7602

Enquiries: The Senior Officer Heritage Services, Miss Andrea Cameron

Open: Mon, Wed, Fri, Sat: 9.30–5.30; Tues, Thurs: 9.30–8.00.

Access: Generally open to the public.

Historical background: Material is collected pertaining to all aspects of the history of the London Borough of Hounslow and its predecessors. The collections at Chiswick Library, Dukes Avenue, London W4 2AB, and Hounslow Library have been built up since the beginning of this century and contain material on all the original parishes within those two areas. The collection at Feltham Library, 210 The Centre, Feltham TW13 6AW, has been in existence only since 1965 and is much smaller in extent, although containing material relating to the original parishes within the area.

Acquisitions policy: All material pertaining to the history of the London Borough of Hounslow or any of its constituent parts, by purchase, donation or deposit.

Archives of organisation: Local authority archives, including minutes, ratebooks, electoral registers, c1870– .

Major collections: Parish records of All Saints Church, Isleworth, 1564–c1900; St Lawrence's Church, Brentford, 18th century only; St Mary the Virgin, transcript copies only.

Non-manuscript material: Layton Collection: 12,000 books, maps and prints of British topography, 16th–19th centuries.
Several hundred large-scale maps covering most parts of the borough, 1635– .
Prints, paintings and photographs covering all parts of the borough, c1750– .
Local newspapers, c1870– .

Finding aids: Chiswick and Hounslow libraries: subject catalogue and indexes to local newspapers and deeds. Hounslow Borough Records: NRA 13857.

Facilities: Photocopying. Photography. Microfilm/fiche reader/printer.

Conservation: Contracted out.

Publications: A wide range of local publications are available from Chiswick and Hounslow libraries.

451 Hove Reference Library
Wolseley Collection

Parent organisation: Brighton and Hove Council

Address: 182–186 Church Road, Hove, East Sussex BN3 2EG

Telephone: (01273) 296942

Fax: (01273) 296931

Website: www.libraries.brighton-hove.gov.uk

Enquiries: The Reference Library Officer

Open: Tues: 9.30–7.30; Wed–Fri: 9.30–5.30; Sat: 9.30–5.00.

Access: Bona fide scholars, by appointment only. Access through special collections membership only — details on application; research charges apply.

Historical background: There has been a library in Hove since the late 19th century. The present library opened in 1908, and was built with funds provided by Andrew Carnegie. The Wolseley Collection was offered to the library in 1924, and an additional accession via the Royal United Services Institute came in 1965. The collection was officially opened in 1970.

Acquisitions policy: Anything relating to Lord Wolseley and his family, by gift, purchase or deposit.

Major collections: Collection of Field Marshal Lord Wolseley (1833–1913): covers his career and campaigns and includes scrapbooks and autograph letters from leading figures in his day; also correspondence of his wife and with his family, who lived in East Sussex (c8000 items).
Papers of Lord Wolseley's daughter, Lady Frances Garnet Wolseley, who was a pupil of Gertrude Jekyll and had a school of gardening in Glynde, including scrapbooks, notebooks and privately printed catalogue.
Biography of Sir Walter Mieville (1855–1929) and his family.

Non-manuscript material: Small collections of early children's books and private press books.

Finding aids: Name index, rough lists, catalogue of Wolseley Collection.

Facilities: Photocopying. Photography by arrangement. Microfilm/fiche readers.

Conservation: On-going in-house conservation.

Publications: J. Dale: *All Sir Garnet* [catalogue of exhibition on Lord Wolseley, 1981].

452 University of Huddersfield Library

Address: Queensgate, Huddersfield, West Yorkshire HD1 3DH

Telephone: (01484) 422288 ext. 3168/473168 (direct line)

Fax: (01484) 517987

E-mail: e.a.h.haigh@hud.ac.uk

Website: www.hud.ac.uk/schools/library/libarch.htm

Enquiries: The Archivist, Mrs E.A. Hilary Haigh

Open: Mon, Tues, Thurs, Fri: by appointment.

Access: Researchers from within and beyond the university. Appointments should be made with the Archivist.

Historical background: The university has its origins in the Huddersfield Mechanics' Institute, founded in 1841 as the Young Men's Mental Improvement Society. In 1884 the Mechanics' Institute amalgamated with the Female Educational Institute and became the Technical School and Mechanics' Institution. This, successively, was known as the Huddersfield Technical College (1896–1958), Huddersfield College of Technology (1958–70), the Polytechnic of Huddersfield (1970–92) and the University of Huddersfield (1992–). The archive was established in the 1960s by the principal of the College of Technology, Dr W.E. Scott. Much of the institution's historical archive was transferred to the library during the 1970s and 1980s. A professional archivist was first employed in 1991.

Acquisitions policy: Official archives of the university and its predecessors, and collections of archives and other materials deposited by reason of their direct connection with the work of the university and its predecessors. Major collections reflect university research interests in educational and political history.

Archives of organisation: Huddersfield Mechanics' Institute, 1843–84; Huddersfield Female Educational Institute, 1846–83; Huddersfield Technical School and Mechanics' Institution, 1884–96; Huddersfield Technical College, 1896–1958; Huddersfield College of Technology, 1958–70; Huddersfield Foreign Library Society, 1851–70; Huddersfield Literary and Scientific Society, 1857–82; Huddersfield Fine Art and Industrial Exhibition, 1882–4.

Major collections: Records of Colne Valley Labour Party, 1891–1970 (including bound volumes of the *Colne Valley Guardian*, 1896–1976), and Huddersfield Labour Party, 1918–63 (including bound volumes of the *Huddersfield Citizen*, 1926–51); National Adult School Union, 1862–1994.

Non-manuscript material: G.H. Wood Collection: journals, pamphlets and books, c1850–1910 (5000), on economics, politics, and social and industrial history. Wood was a professional statistician and social reformer ultimately employed as the secretary of the Huddersfield Woollen Manufacturers' Association. The collection includes 300 pamphlets on the labour problem; other areas of special significance are trade unions, wage histories, bimetallism, free trade, early socialism, Fabianism, the textile and mining industries, and industrial health, safety and welfare; MS wage notes covering all industries, 1850–1910 (20 vols).
Microfilm copies of manuscripts and indexes held in the PRO and other repositories; significant holdings of newspapers, both local and national; some census material; 18th-century pamphlets.
Yudkin Collection of historical material relating to food and nutrition.
Local History Collection relating to Huddersfield and West Yorkshire.
Research collection of House of Commons and House of Lords journals, rare books and journals relating to many disciplines.

Finding aids: Lists of all the archive collections; some sent to NRA. Detailed catalogue of the G.H. Wood Collection.

Facilities: Photocopying. Photography. Microfilm/fiche readers/printer.

Conservation: Contracted out.

Publications: A note on the G.H. Wood Collection appeared in *Bulletin of the Society for the Study of Labour History*, 4 (spring 1980), 47.
J. O'Connell: 'From Mechanics' Institution to Polytechnic' in E.A. Hilary Haigh (ed.) *Huddersfield: a Most Handsome Town: Aspects of the History and Culture of a West Yorkshire Town* (1992).
Catalogue of the G.H. Wood Collection and *A Guide to the Archives and Special Collections* [in preparation].

453 West Yorkshire Archive Service: Kirklees

Parent organisation: West Yorkshire Joint Services

Address: Central Library, Princess Alexandra Walk, Huddersfield, West Yorkshire HD1 2SU

Telephone: (01484) 221966

Fax: (01484) 518361

E-mail: kirklees@wyjs.org.uk

Website: www.archives.wyjs.org.uk

Enquiries: The Principal Archivist, Miss J. Burhouse
The County Archivist, Mrs S. Thomas

Open: Mon, Thurs: 10.00–5.00; Tues 10.00–8.00; Fri: 10.00–1.00.
Closed one week in February.

Access: Generally open to the public, by appointment. A paid research service is available.

Historical background: The post of archivist was established in 1959. In 1982 Kirklees joined the West Yorkshire Archive Service; close links with the local studies department are still maintained.

Archives of organisation: Local authority records of all predecessor authorities.

Major collections: Estate and family records of the Beaumonts of Whitley, 12th–19th centuries; Ramsdens of Longley and Huddersfield, 16th–20th centuries; Thornhills of Fixby, 18th–20th centuries; Saviles of Thornhill, 17th–18th centuries (held at Dewsbury Library).
Parish and non-conformist church records, 17th–20th centuries.

Education records: school boards' records, education departments' log-books, minutes, 19th–20th centuries.

Societies' records: Co-operative, Chamber of Commerce, Thespians, Glee and Madrigal, Oddfellows, 19th–20th centuries.

Business records of firms of architects, joiners, accountants, engineers, woollen manufacturers.

Poor Law records, 18th–20th centuries.

Finding aids: Lists sent to NRA. Link to West Yorkshire Archive Service computerised database.

Facilities: Photocopying. Photography. Microfilm/fiche readers.

Publications: J. Burhouse and E. Briggs (comps): *Kirklees Archives 1959–1989: an Illustrated Guide to Kirklees District Archives* (1989), and supplement.

454 Hull City Archives

Parent organisation: Hull City Council

Address: 79 Lowgate, Hull HU1 2AA

Telephone: (01482) 615102/615110

Fax: (01482) 613051

E-mail: city.archives@hullcc.gov.uk

Enquiries: The Archivist, Mr Martin Taylor

Open: Tues, Thurs: 9.00–12.15, 1.30–4.45; Wed: 9.00–12.15; Fri: 9.00–12.15, 1.30–4.15.

Access: Generally open to the public, subject to relevant closure periods; appointments are essential. A paid research service is available.

Historical background: The office was established in 1968 and moved to specially converted premises in 1979. It is recognised as a place of deposit for public and manorial records.

Acquisitions policy: Records relating to all subject areas within the City of Hull.

Archives of organisation: Usual local authority record holdings, including minutes, 1445– ; accounts, 1320– ; correspondence, 15th century– ; building and specification contracts, c1780– ; architectural drawings, 1835– .

Major collections: Deposited local collections, including records of Hull Subscription Library, 1682–1900; Hillyer Bros., trawler owners, c1890–1975; Thomas Hamling and Co., trawler owners, c1890–1980; Rosedowns, manufacturers of machinery for oil mills etc, c1790–1960;

Premier Oil, seed crushers, c1900–1970; Hebblethwaite and Son, land agents, c1850–1940; Hull United Charities, 17th–20th centuries.

Non-manuscript material: OS maps for the city and adjacent areas, 1853– .

Local photographic images, c1930– (10,000).

Finding aids: Guide (in progress); lists; indexes of names, places and ships. Lists sent to NRA.

Facilities: Photocopying. Photography. Microfilm/fiche reader.

Conservation: Conservation unit; outside work undertaken.

Publications: L.M. Stanewell: *City and County of Kingston upon Hull: Calendar of the Ancient Deeds, Letters, Miscellaneous Old Documents* (1951).

Guide Part I.

World War II.

Transport by Sea, Rail and Inland Navigation.

455 Hull Local Studies Library

Parent organisation: Hull City Council

Address: Central Library, Albion Street, Hull HU1 3TF

Telephone: (01482) 210077

Fax: (01482) 616858

E-mail: local.studies@hullcc.gov.uk

Website: www.hullcc.gov.uk/libraries

Enquiries: The Specialist Librarian, Local Studies, David Smith

Open: Mon–Thurs: 9.30–8.00; Fri: 9.30–5.30; Sat: 9.00–4.30.

Access: Generally open to the public.

Historical background: The local history collections were originally part of the Central Reference Library, which opened in 1901 and became a separate department in 1962, with collections covering the city of Kingston upon Hull and the old East Riding of Yorkshire. The service became part of Humberside Libraries on local government reorganisation in 1974, and the coverage was extended to include printed material on the new county of Humberside. Following local government reorganisation in 1996 the service became part of Hull City Council. It now collects material on Hull and the East Riding of Yorkshire.

Acquisitions policy: To maintain and strengthen the collections of printed, manuscript and ephemeral material on the areas covered. Archive material is collected by purchase, donation and deposit, in conjunction with the statutory acquisition requirements of the Hull City Archives (entry 454) and the East Riding Archive Office (entry 90).

Major collections: Non-conformity: Congregational records, 1768–1942; Primitive Methodist, district, circuit and church records, 1833–1920.

Forster and Andrews, organ builders of Hull: order books, specifications and miscellaneous material on the company, 1844–1969.

Winifred Holtby (1898–1935), writer: letters, cuttings, literary MSS etc (*c*25,000 items); includes material on the writer's social and political activities, reflecting her work for the League of Nations Union in the cause of world peace, for feminism, and for the cause of South African trade unionism.

Log-books of Hull whaling vessels, 19th century.

Civil War Tracts: of local and national significance, 1641–60.

Non-manuscript material: Illustrations, 18th century– (*c*7000).

Theatre bills for Hull and district, late 18th century– (*c*7000).

Hull and district newspapers, 1787– (most on microfilm).

Extensive collection of maps (*c*1500).

Small collection of audio tapes, slides, records, videotapes.

Hull Health Department Photographs, *c*1890s–1930s (*c*2000).

Census microfilms for Hull and Sculcoates, 1841–91, and East Yorkshire, 1851 (street indexes available for all years and surname indexes available for 1851, 1881, 1891).

Finding aids: Classified card catalogues. Various lists and indexes.

Facilities: Photocopying. Photography by arrangement. Microfilm/fiche reader/printer.

Publications: Select Bibliography of the County of Humberside (1980).

Winifred Holtby (1898–1935): a Catalogue (1985).

Local history study sheets: series of annotated student guides.

456   Hull Maritime Museum

Parent organisation: Hull Museum and Art Galleries

Address: Queen Victoria Square, Hull, East Riding of Yorkshire HU1 3DX

Telephone: (01482) 613902

Fax: (01482) 613710

E-mail: museums@hullcc.gov.uk

Website: www.hullcc.gov.uk/museums

Enquiries: The Keeper, Mr. A.G. Credland

Open: Mon–Sat: 10.00–5.00. An appointment is necessary.

Access: Generally open to the public; application, preferably in writing, is essential.

Historical background: The museum was established in 1912 as the Hull Maritime Museum, and the collections derive from those of the Hull Literary and Philosophical Society, which was founded in 1823. The Wilberforce Collection of personal and family papers of William Wilberforce (1759–1833) and slavery archive is maintained at Wilberforce House; contact the Keeper of Social History, tel. (01482) 613902.

Acquisitions policy: To acquire material relating to whaling, especially arctic, fishing, merchant shipping and Hull docks.

Major collections: Hull whaling: ship log-books and minute books of shipowners, 1754–1869; records of fishing and trawler companies, 19th and 20th centuries.

Merchant shipping: logs, journals and miscellaneous material, 18th–20th centuries.

Hull and Humberside shipyard records; ship plans.

Non-manuscript material: Small collection of rare pamphlets on whaling, 1826–35. Marine paintings, 18th–20th centuries. Photographs of ships, docks etc, *c*1870– .

Finding aids: Handlists, card indexes.

Facilities: Photocopying. Photography.

Publications: Museum publications, exhibition catalogues and Hull shipping books.

457   Reckitt's Heritage

Parent organisation: Reckitt Benekiser Ltd

Address: Dansom Lane, Hull HU8 7DS

Telephone: (01482) 582910

Fax: (01482) 582532

Website: www.reckittbenekiser.com

Enquiries: The Manager, Reckitt's Heritage, Mr G.E. Stephenson

Open: Wed–Thurs (with occasional variation): 8.30–12.45, 1.00–4.45.

Access: Bona fide researchers, by prior appointment only.

Historical background: Isaac Reckitt, a Lincolnshire-born Quaker, established a starch manufacturing business in 1840, subsequently expanding into laundry blue and grate polish. A private company, Reckitt & Sons Ltd, was formed in 1879 and, following its conversion to a public company in 1888, the Hull-based enterprise became a company of international repute producing cleaning products commonly used in the home. In 1905 Brasso metal polish was introduced and many other household-name products soon followed as the business entered a period of major expansion both at home and abroad. Pharmaceutical interests began with the launch of Dettol in 1933 followed by Disprin in 1948. Before World War I, close working relationships had been established with the Chiswick Polish Company of London and J. & J. Colman of Norwich, which eventually led to the amalgamation of all three major businesses in 1954 to form Reckitt & Colman Holdings Ltd, whose head office transferred from Hull to London in 1970.

Acquisitions policy: Deposited materials are actively sought.

Archives of organisation: Records of Reckitt & Colman plc and subsidiaries world-wide, 1840–.

Non-manuscript material: Plans, photographs, films and supporting printed material.

Household toiletries, pharmaceutical packs and advertising materials, including press, TV, cinema, posters, show cards and promotional materials.

Finding aids: Lists and indexes.

Facilities: Photocopying. Microfiche readers.

Publications: B.N. Reckitt: *History of Reckitt & Sons Ltd* (2/1958).

458 University of Hull
Brynmor Jones Library

Address: Cottingham Road, Hull HU6 7RX

Telephone: (01482) 465265

Fax: (01482) 466205

E-mail: archives@acs.hull.ac.uk

Website: www.hull.ac.uk/lib/archives

Enquiries: The University Archivist, Mr B. Dyson

Open: Mon–Fri: 9.00–1.00, 2.00–5.00. Other times by arrangement.

Access: Bona fide researchers, with initial contact in writing and by appointment.

Historical background: Hull University College was opened in 1928 and received its charter as a university in 1954. Archives and manuscripts have been collected since 1928.

Acquisitions policy: To extend and strengthen existing collections, by gift, purchase or deposit, particularly in the fields of labour and political history.

Archives of organisation: Records of principal officers and administrative departments, 1928–.

Major collections: Pressure groups: records of Justice, 1959–; Liberty (formerly the National Council for Civil Liberties), 1934–; Women's Co-operative Guild, 1886–; Union of Democratic Control, 1914–66; Socialist Health (formerly Medical) Association, 1930–; Joint Council for the Welfare of Immigrants, 1967–.

Business records: Ellerman's Wilson Line, 1825–1972; Earle's Shipbuilding and Engineering Company, 1858–1909; Hull Printers, 1897–1978; Hull & East Riding Co-operative Society, 1858–1980; Horsley Smith Ltd, 1864–1968; Kay and Backhouse Ltd, 1891–1970; Needlers Ltd, 1901–86.

Landed families and estates: Barnard of South Cave, 1400–1945; Beaumont (Stapleton) of Carlton, late 11th century–1979; Forbes-Adam (Beilby, Lawley, Thompson, Wenlock) of Escrick, 1387–1988; Gee (Hall, Watt) of Bishop Burton, 1194–1931; Hotham of South Dalton, 1311–1982; Lloyd-Graeme of Sewerby, 12th century–1950; Maxwell-Constable of Everingham, 1125–1959; Pennington of Warter, 1538–1877; St Quintin of Harpham, 1220–1960; Sykes of Sledmere, 1300–1980; Wickham-Boynton of Burton Agnes, 1172–1944.

Trade union and labour: local (Hull and East Yorkshire) trade union and friendly society records, 19th–20th centuries; Frederick W. Dalley (1885–1960); W.E. Jones (1895–1973); Charles George Ammon, 1st Baron Ammon (1873–1960); Julia Varley (1871–1952); Vicky (Victor Weisz) (1913–66).

Political archives: records and papers of Hull Labour Party, 1955– ; Beverley and Haltemprice Social Democratic Party, 1981–8; Campaign for Labour Party Democracy, 1973–91; Revolutionary Communist Party, 1944–9; Sir Patrick Cormack (b 1939); Bernard Floud, MP (1915–67); Anne Kerr, MP (1925–73); Kevin McNamara, MP (b 1934); John Prescott, MP (b 1936); Austin Mitchell, MP (b 1934); Christopher Price, MP (b 1932); David Winnick, MP (b 1933); Eric Lubbock (Lord Avebury) (b 1928); Thomas Perronet Thompson, MP (1783–1869); Sir Mark Sykes, MP (1879–1919); Sir Patrick Wall, MP (b 1916); Henry Grattan (1746–1820); Howard Hill (1913–80); Robin Page Arnot (1890–1980); Jock Haston (1913–86); Harold Laski (1893–1950).

Religious archives: records and papers of Society of Friends, Hull & Pickering Monthly Meeting, 1636–1990; some records of Selby Abbey, 1349–1538, and Marrick Priory, 1154–1539; papers of the Anglican Evangelical Group movement, 1907–72; papers of the Christian Socialists Rev. Conrad Noel (1869–1942) and Canon Stanley Evans (1912–65).

Modern English literary MSS and archives: papers of Douglas Dunn (b 1942), Gavin Ewart (1916-96), Philip Larkin (1922–85), Andrew Motion (b 1952), Alan Plater (b 1935), Howard Sergeant (1914–87), Stevie Smith (1902–71), Henry Treece (1911–66) and Anthony Thwaite (b 1930); records of the magazines *Wave*, 1970–74, *Phoenix*, 1967–75 and *Reality Studio*, 1978–88; and the archives of Hull Literary Club, 1879–1979, and Hull Subscription Library, 1775–1970.

South-East Asian texts and research collections, 19th century– .

Non-manuscript material: Pamphlets, maps, local playbills and broadsides in general collection in main library.

Finding aids: 'HUMAD' on-line guide. Calendars or initial lists of collections also available via website; copies sent to NRA. Indexes of places, personal names and subjects. Subject and other guides issued regularly. Lists of maps, manorial records, enclosure records, wills etc.

Facilities: Photocopying, photography, microfilm/fiche readers.

Conservation: In-house conservation unit.

Publications: Paragon Review (1992) [annual].

P. Larkin: *A Lifted Study-Storehouse: the Brynmor Jones Library, 1929–1979* (Hull, 1979; rev. 1987).

S.K. Mitra, D.A. Reid and G.D. Weston (eds): *Catalogue of Primary and Secondary Material on Indian Studies in the Brynmor Jones Library, University of Hull* (Hull, 1989).

J. Saville: *The Labour Archive at the University of Hull* (Hull, 1989).

B. Dyson: 'Business Records in the Archives of the University of Hull', *Business Archives* (Nov 1990), 14–23.

——: 'Records and Research for Co-operation: Records in Britain', *Journal of Co-operative Studies*, 69 (Sept 1990), 52–6.

——: 'Archives at the University of Hull: a Research Resource', *History of Education Society Bulletin*, 47 (spring 1991), 62–4.

——: 'HUMAD: Hull University's On-Line Guide to Archives and Manuscripts', *Local Studies Librarian*, 10/2 (autumn 1991), 13–15.

B. Dyson and H. Roberts: 'Northern riches: the University of Hull Brynmor Jones Library', *Archives*, XXII, no. 96 (1997), 3–14.

459 Cambridgeshire Archives Service
County Record Office, Huntingdon

Parent organisation: Cambridgeshire County Council

Address: Grammar School Walk, Huntingdon, Cambridgeshire PE29 3LF

Telephone: (01480) 375842

Fax: (01480) 375842

E-mail: county.records.hunts@cambridgeshire.gov.uk

Website: www.cambridgeshire.gov.uk

Enquiries: The Senior Archivist, Alan Akeroyd

Open: Tues–Thurs: 9.00–12.45, 1.45–5.15; Fri: 9.00–12.45, 1.45–4.15; Sat (2nd of every month): 9.00–12.00.

Access: Generally open to the public. The office operates the CARN reader's ticket system. Disabled visitors are asked to contact the office in advance.

Historical background: The office was established in 1947. Between 1969 and 1974 it was administered with the Northamptonshire Record Office. In 1974 it became one of two offices serving the enlarged county of Cambridgeshire responsible for official and unofficial deposited records within the area of the former county of Huntingdonshire, and local government records of the former Soke of Peterborough, which was amalgamated with Huntingdonshire in 1965. Since April 1998 the office has reverted to collecting official and unofficial deposited records for the area of the former county of Huntingdonshire only. Some official and most deposited collections relating to Peterborough currently remain the responsibility of the Northamptonshire Record Office (entry 931). The office contains the records of the Archdeanconry of Huntingdon (until 1837 in Lincoln Diocese, since then in Ely), is a Diocesan Record Office for parish records in the archdeanconry and is recognised as a place of deposit for public records.

Acquisitions policy: Records relating to the area of the former county of Huntingdon (see also Cambridge County Record Office, entry 166).

Archives of organisation: Usual local authority record holdings.

Major collections: Deposited local collections, including the following which have a wider significance:
Records of the Earls and Dukes of Manchester of Kimbolton, 13th–20th centuries.
Bush Collection of Cromwell family records, 1579–1832 (some exhibited in adjacent Cromwell Museum).
Estate records of the Fellowes family, Baron De Ramsey, of Ramsey and Abbots Ripton, 1622–1955.

Non-manuscript material: OS papers and plans for Huntingdon.
Photographs of Maddison and Hinde of Huntingdon, 1867–1925.

Facilities: Photocopying. Photography. Microfilming. Microfilm reader/printer.

Conservation: Undertaken in-house at the Cambridge Office.

Publications: G.H. Findlay: *Guide to the Huntingdonshire Record Office* (1958).
P.G.M. Dickinson: *Maps in the County Record Office, Huntingdon* (1968).

Annual Reports: Northants and Hunts Archives Committee (1969–74), Cambridgeshire County Archivist (1974–93).

460 Knowsley Archives

Parent organisation: Knowsley MBC

Address: Huyton Library, Civic Way, Huyton, Knowsley L36 9GH

Telephone: (0151) 443 3738

Fax: (0151) 443 3739

E-mail: ehume@oakedge.demon.co.uk

Website: www.knowsley.gov.uk/leisure/libraries/local

Enquiries: The Local Studies and Archives Librarian, Mrs Eileen Hume

Open: Mon–Fri: 9.15–7.00; Sat: 10.00–4.00; Sun: 12.00–4.00; an appointment is necessary.

Access: Bona fide researchers.

Historical background: Knowsley Library Service came into being in 1974 following local government reorganisation. The area covers Cronton, Huyton, Kirkby, Knowsley, Prescot, Roby, Simonswood, Tarbock and Whiston. The Local Studies and Archives Collection was assembled during the first years of the library service, before the new Central Library was opened in Huyton in 1998.

Acquisitions policy: To strengthen existing collections regarding the history of areas presently incorporated in the Metropolitan Borough of Knowsley, by purchase, donation or deposit.

Major collections: Council minutes for Huyton-with-Roby, Kirkby and Prescot UDCs; Council minutes and Clerks' working papers for Whiston RDC, c1890–1974.
Prescot Grammar School archives, 15th–19th centuries.
National Union of Mineworkers (Cronton Branch) minute books, 1952–71.
Huyton Cricket Club records, 1860-c1970.
Preston and Whiston Co-operative Society records, c19th–20th centuries.

Non-manuscript material: Photographic collection (c6000).
Large map collection.
Prescot Report, 1858–1975.
Parish registers, census returns, directories, copies of tithe maps and awards, newspaper cuttings and electoral registers.

Finding aids: Most archive collections listed and partly indexed. Indexes to photographic collection. Some census returns indexed by street and name.

User guides and help sheets.

Facilities: Photocopying. Photography by arrangement. Microfilm/fiche readers/printer.

Publications: W.L. French (ed.): *Registers of Kirkby St Chad's Chapelry*, i: *Baptism, 1610–1839* (1977); ii: *Marriages and Burials, 1610–1839* (1979).
J. Knowles (ed.): *Prescot Records: the Court Rolls, 1602–1648* (1980-81).
B. Burgess: *Tracing your Family History in the Knowsley Area at Huyton Library* (1989).

461 Hythe Town Archives

Parent organisation: Hythe Town Council

Address: Town Council Offices, Stade Street, Hythe, Kent CT21 6BG

Telephone: (01303) 266152/3

Enquiries: The Hythe Town Archivist, Mrs M.P. Shaw

Open: Wed: 9.45–1.00; 2.00–4.45; other days may be possible by prior arrangement.

Access: Generally open to the public, by appointment.

Archives of organisation: The town council holds the records of the former Borough of Hythe, c1278–1974; some records, not registers, of the parish of St Leonard, Hythe, c1412–1850; and various private deposits.

Finding aids: Catalogue, in house style of Centre for Kentish Studies, in preparation. NRA 19570.

Facilities: Limited photocopying.

Publications: H.D. Dale and C. Chidell: *Catalogue of Documents Belonging to the Corporation of Hythe, 11th to 20th century*.
M.P. Shaw: *A Revised Catalogue of Documents* (1985).

462 Barnardo's Photographic and Film Archive

Address: Tanners Lane, Barkingside, Ilford, Essex IG6 1QG

Telephone: (020) 8550 8822 ext. 345

Fax: (020) 85516870

Website: www.barnardos.org.uk

Enquiries: The Photographic Resources Officer/Archivist, John Kirkham

Open: Mon–Fri: 9.30–5.00, by appointment.

Access: Bona fide researchers

The photograph and film archive complements the Barnardo Archive held by the University of Liverpool (entry 529). It consists of prints, negatives and plates, 1864– (500,000), and of films (200), illustrating the history of childcare and residential education and includes material donated by the public. A database of the collection is maintained and there is in-house conservation. Photocopying and photography are available; films may be viewed.

463 Redbridge Local Studies & Archives

Parent organisation: London Borough of Redbridge

Address: Redbridge Central Library, Clements Road, Ilford IG1 1EA

Telephone: (020) 8478 3020 ext. 2417/2452

Fax: (020) 8553 3299

E-mail: local studies@redbridge.gov.uk

Enquiries: The Archivist, Tudor Allen

Open: Mon–Fri: 9.30–8.00; Sat: 9.30–4.00; by appointment.

Access: Generally open to the public.

Historical background: Redbridge Borough Council came into existence in 1965. The predecessor authorities for the area were Ilford Borough Council and Wanstead and Woodford Borough Council. Archival material was acquired haphazardly over a number of years from 1909, mainly by donations from local residents. Since 1965 a more definite policy has been pursued. The Local History Library has been designated as the repository for all council archives, and to this end departments are transferring material to the library. In 1999 an Archivist was appointed to set up a full archives service.

Acquisitions policy: To acquire, by donation, loan, purchase or transfer, archives of any organisation or individual currently or formerly based in the London Borough of

Redbridge and any other archives relating to the borough.

Archives of organisation: Material relating to the activities and functions of the various departments of the council of the London Borough of Redbridge.

Major collections: Admission registers, reports, papers etc, relating to the former Infant Orphans Asylum (later the Royal Infant Orphanage, later the Royal Wanstead School), Snaresbrook, Wanstead.
Sales reports, staff and workforce details, reports, maps, minutes of board meetings etc, relating to the former chemical manufacturers Howards of Ilford, Ltd.

Non-manuscript material: Local History Collection: local maps and plans of Ilford, Wanstead and Woodford, mainly 19th and 20th centuries; pamphlets and news cuttings (c45,000); photographs (17,000) and slides (4000).
Local newspapers, 1869– (on microfilm).

Finding aids: The majority of archive material is as yet uncatalogued. Classified index for all illustrative material and pamphlet file material (not complete). Ilford Local History Collection: NRA 3007. 4th Earl of Mornington correspondence: NRA 24051.

Facilities: Photocopying. Photograph copying service. Microfilm reader/printers.

Conservation: Contracted out.

Publications: A Catalogue of Local History Departments (London Borough of Redbridge Libraries Department, 1977).

464 Traquair House

Address: Innerleithen, West Lothian EH44 7PN

Telephone: (01896) 830323

Fax: (01896) 830639

E-mail: enquiries@traquair.co.uk

Website: www.traquair.co.uk

Open: By appointment only.

Access: Bona fide researchers only. A daily charge is made.

Traquair House was originally a royal hunting lodge. It holds domestic and estate papers of the Stuarts of Traquair, 17th–19th centuries, including state papers and royal letters of the 1st Earl of Traquair, who was Lord High Treasurer to Charles I. There are catalogues and photocopying facilities.

465 Highland Council Archive

Parent organisation: Highland Council

Address: The Library, Farraline Park, Inverness, Highland IV1 1NH

Telephone: (01463) 220330

Fax: (01463) 711128

Website: www.highland.gov.uk

Enquiries: The Council Archivist, Mr Robert Steward

Open: Mon–Thurs: 10.00–1.00, 2.00–5.00; by appointment.

Access: Generally open to the public; an appointment is recommended. A genealogical research service is available.

Historical background: The Highland Council Archive was formally established in 1990 as the Highland Regional Archive, although local authority records had been collected from 1975 in Inverness Library. The archive acts as the official repository for the records of the former counties of Inverness, Nairn, Ross and Cromarty, and Sutherland; part of north Argyll, and of the former Burghs of Inverness, Nairns, Dingwall, Dornoch, Fortrose, Fort William, Tain, Cromarty, Invergordon, Grantown and Kingussie, which were in existence prior to local government reorganisation in 1975. Similarly, the archive is responsible for the records of the Highland Regional Council and seven District Councils (excepting Caithness) which operated from 1975 until 1996, when the Highland Council came into being. The Highland Regional Archive became the Highland Council Archive at the time of local government reorganisation. There is an area office in Wick (entry 1196).

Acquisitions policy: The Highland Council Archive covers the geographical boundaries of the administrative area of the Highland Council. It has a particular responsibility for the records of local government, but accepts other records deemed of archival significance, which reflect the social and economic life of the Highlands.

Archives of organisation: Usual Scottish local authority record holdings, pre- and post-1975

reorganisation. Records of Inverness and Fortrose Burghs, 16th century– . The Inverness Burgh archives reflect the town's significance as the administrative and legal centre of the Highlands.

Major collections: Deposited local collections of particular significance include Macdonald and Fraser, solicitors, Portree, Isle of Skye, relating to the factoring of Skye estates and including material on the Skye crofting disturbance, 1855–1952.
Baillie of Dunain papers, including military campaigns in south India and Ireland, 1725–1850.
Alexander and John Fraser, timber merchants, Inverness, including papers on religious, charitable and municipal life in Inverness and the Highlands, 1775–1851.
Northern Meeting records, papers, including the organising of Highland balls, games and piping competitions, 1788–1957.
Harris Tweed Association records, 1851–1963.
A.I. Welders, Inverness, records including international trading in welding equipment, 1875–1990.
Tartan Archive: papers *re* history of tartan, collected by D.C. Stewart and J. Scarlett, *c*1830–1990.

Non-manuscript material: Extensive OS holdings and full set of Roy's military survey of the Highlands, 1747–55 (on 35mm slides).

Finding aids: Catalogues and lists; lists sent to NRA.

Facilities: Photocopying. Microfilm/microfiche reader/printer.

Conservation: Contracted out.

Publications: Guide to the Highland Council Archive (1996).

466   Highland Health Board Archives

Address: University of Stirling, Highland Campus, Old Perth Road, Inverness, Highland IV2 3FG

Telephone: (01463) 705269

Fax: (01463) 713454

E-mail: hhsl1@stir.ac.uk

Website: www.nm.stir.ac.uk/hhsl/hhsllibrary.htm

Enquiries: The Assistant Information Officer, Rob Polson

Open: By appointment only.

Access: Bona fide researchers. Administrative records are closed for 30 years, medical records for 75 years.

Acquisitions policy: Pre- and post-NHS material from the Highlands and inner Islands of Scotland.

Archives of organisation: Records relating to hospitals and health authorities in the area including minutes, financial records, patient and staff registers, case notes, nurse training records and annual reports, *c*1850– .
Administrative records of the Northern Regional Hospital Board and local authority health departments, including MOH annual reports.
Minutes and financial records of the Royal Northern Infirmary, 1798–1950.

Finding aids: Lists.

Facilities: Photocopying. Photography.

467   Inverness Museum and Art Gallery

Parent organisation: Highland Council

Address: Castle Wynd, Inverness, Highland IV2 3EB

Telephone: (01463) 237114

Fax: (01463) 225293

E-mail: catherine.niven@highland.gov.uk

Enquiries: The Museum Curator

Open: Mon–Sat: 9.00–5.00.

Access: Generally open to the public, by appointment.

Historical background: The museum dates from 1825, when the Northern Institution for the Promotion of Science and Literature in Inverness was founded. The collection, badly neglected, was taken over by the Inverness Field Club in 1876 and a permanent building was opened in 1882. In 1907 a new policy of making the museum chiefly a Highland and Jacobite collection was adopted and in the following year management was transferred to the library committee. A new building was erected on the same site in 1966, and in the 1975 local government reorganisation the museum assumed an independent role under the district council's Leisure and Recreation Committee. Following local government reorganisation in 1996 it became part of Cultural and Leisure Services for the Inverness Area, as part of the Highland Council.

Acquisitions policy: Items relating to Inverness and the surrounding area.

Archives of organisation: Inverness Museum guide books, 1909– .

Major collections: Inverness Town Council and District Council committee minutes, 1894– . Small collections of estate papers, accounts and letters of local families, 18th–20th centuries.

Non-manuscript material: M.E.M. Donaldson collection of glass plates of the Highlands, c1900–1920.
Photograph collection: Inverness and district, topography, industry, agriculture, society, architecture, transport, communications etc.
Inverness Courier, 1915– ; *Northern Chronicle*, 1915–49.
Local prints and drawings.

Finding aids: Donaldson catalogue.

Facilities: Photocopying.

468 Queen's Own Regimental Museum

Address: Correspondence: Queen's Own Highlanders Museum, Fort George, Inverness, Highland IV2 7TD

Telephone: (01463) 224380

Fax: (01463) 224380

Enquiries: The Curator

Open: April–Sept: Mon–Sun: 10.00–6.00. Oct–Mar: Mon–Fri: 10.00–4.00.

Access: Anyone with a genuine interest in the history of the regiment, by appointment.

The archives are held at the Regimental Museum at Fort George, Ardersier, Inverness, where the collection was established in 1967. The regiment maintains photograph albums, war diaries, documents, some enlistment books and published records, and actively acquires material relating to its own history, that of antecedent regiments, and the military history of the North Highlands. Archives are included in the museum's database of accessions.

Photocopying and microfilm/fiche readers are available.

469 Hadleigh Guildhall Archives

Parent organisation: Hadleigh Town Council

Address: Market Place, Hadleigh, Ipswich, Suffolk IP7 5DN

Telephone: (01473) 827752

Fax: (01473) 823884

Enquiries: The Town Clerk, Mr R. Stevens

Open: Mon–Fri: 9.30–12.30, by appointment only.

Access: Generally open to the public.

Historical background: The borough's records start in 1619, but it also has responsibility for two charities, Hadleigh Market Feoffment (f. 1438) and the Grand Feoffment and its predecessors formed c.1850, consisting of the Pykenham Charity (f. 1497) and several other charities.

Acquisitions policy: Maintaining the records of Hadleigh parish.

Archives of organisation: Borough records, 1619– .
Records of Hadleigh Market Feoffment, 1438–, and the Grand Feoffment and its predecessors, 1497– .

Non-manuscript material: Large collection of photographs.

Finding aids: Computer catalogue.

Facilities: Photocopying.

Conservation: Contracted out to County Archive Service.

470 Suffolk Record Office
Ipswich Branch

Parent organisation: Suffolk County Council

Address: Gatacre Road, Ipswich, Suffolk IP1 2LQ

Telephone: (01473) 584541

Fax: (01473) 584533

E-mail: ipswich.ro@libher.suffolkcc.gov.uk

Website: www.suffolkcc.gov.uk/libraries.and.heritage/sro

Enquiries: The Public Services Manager, Mrs Bridget Hanley

Open: Mon–Sat: 9.00–5.00.

Access: Generally open to the public. The office operates the CARN reader's ticket system.

Historical background: The Ipswich and East Suffolk Record Office was established in 1950 and became the Ipswich branch of the Suffolk Record Office in 1974. It also acts as the Diocesan Record Office for St Edmundsbury and Ipswich (Archdeanconries of Ipswich and Suffolk) and is recognised as a place of deposit for public records. The Local Studies Library is an integral part of the record office.

Acquisitions policy: Archival and printed material relating to the former administrative county of East Suffolk, excepting the area served by the Lowestoft branch (entry 865).

Major collections: Deposited local collections, including the following which have a wider significance:

Sir Thomas Phillipps Collection of medieval manuscripts and Suffolk antiquaries' notes; Cornwallis papers, including letter-book of 1st Marquis Cornwallis, Governor-General of Bengal; diaries and political papers of Gathorne Hardy, 1st Earl of Cranbrook; correspondence of William Lowther MP and James William Lowther, 1st Viscount Ullswater; military, naval and political papers of 1st–7th Earls of Albemarle, Admiral Viscount Keppel, General Sir William Keppel and Baron Egerton; naval papers of Admiral Sir James Saumarez and Sir Philip Bowes Vere Broke; papers of George Pretyman (Tomline), Bishop of Lincoln and Winchester, including material *re* William Pitt the Younger; papers of Mary C. Greenup (wife of Gen. J.T. English) *re* South America; diaries of Canon J.H. Turner *re* the Canadian Arctic; papers of William Leathes, ambassador, and of Carteret Leathes and Hill Mussenden, MPs.

Collections relating to Jamaican estates of the Long family; Bristol and Gloucestershire estates of the Gonning family; London and Lincolnshire estates of the Boucherett family; Kent estate of the Barne family; various lands of the Hanbury-Bateman families; London estate of the Kerrison family; South Carolina estate of the Middleton family; Lincolnshire estate of the Pretyman-Tomline families; Nevis (West Indies) estate of the Maynard family; Lancashire, Northamptonshire and Irish estates of the Purcell-Fitzgerald family; Hertfordshire and other estates of Lord Rendlesham.

Business archives of Richard Garrett and Sons of Leiston; British Xylonite Co. of Homerton, Hale End and Brantham; Ransomes and Rapier of Ipswich; the Norsk Hydro Fertilisers Group; Paul's Malt Ltd of Ipswich, Associated British Maltsters and subsidiary companies.

Non-manuscript material: Local Studies Library: extensive photographic and illustrative collections, oral history collection.

Finding aids: Catalogues and indexes; catalogues sent to NRA; annual summary of accessions .

Facilities: Photocopying. Photography. Microfilm reader/printers. Microfilming.

Conservation: Available in-house.

Publications: Guide to Genealogical Sources (5:1998).
C. Clark and R. Munting: *Suffolk Enterprise* (2000).

471 Salford City Archives

Parent organisation: Salford Heritage Services

Address: Archives Centre, 658–662 Liverpool Road, Irlam, Manchester M44 5AD

Website: www.gmcro.co.uk/reposit.htm

Enquiries: The Archivist

Open: Mon–Fri: 9.00–4.30

Access: Open to the public by appointment. There are the usual closure periods on local authority and personal records.

Historical background: The Archives Centre was established in 1974 with the reorganisation of local government. Salford Town Hall, Bexley Square, Salford, is recognised as a place of deposit for public records and keeps quarter sessions, coroner's and local health authority records.

NB Since this entry was compiled the Archives Centre has been closed and the collections have been moved to the Museum & Art Gallery, Peel Park, The Crescent, Salford M5 4WU, where access is via the Local Studies Library, entry 1092.

Archives of organisation: Records of the City of Salford and its local authority predecessors, 1687– .

Major collections: Bridgewater Estates plc collection, 1771–1980 (chiefly 19th century).

Ironbridge

Nasmyth, Wilson and Co., records, 1836–1922. James Nasmyth correspondence, 1849–88.

Non-manuscript material: F. Mullineux's photograph collection of glass plates and prints, including photos by Samuel L. Coulthurst, covering local district, Manchester Ship Canal and Holland and Wales, 1880s–1910.

Finding aids: Catalogues, indexes. Copies of catalogues sent to NRA.

Facilities: Photocopying.

Publications: Information leaflets on genealogical sources and the history of houses [available on request]. Handlist leaflet (1998).

472 Ironbridge Gorge Museum Trust

Address: Ironbridge, Telford, Shropshire TF8 7AW

Telephone: (01952) 432141

Fax: (01952) 432237

E-mail: library@ironbridge.org.uk

Website: www.ironbridge.org.uk

Enquiries: The Museum Librarian, Mr John Powell

Open: Mon–Fri: 9.00–5.30.

Access: By prior appointment only, with the Librarian.

Historical background: The Ironbridge Gorge Museum Trust was established in 1968 to conserve for posterity the unique industrial remains of the area's former period of greatness. It consists of the world's first iron bridge (1779), the furnace where coke smelting was first introduced in 1709, the Coalbrookdale Museum of Iron, the Severn Warehouse, Blists Hill Open Air Museum, Coalport China Works Museum and other sites within an area of six square miles. The library and archive collections have been built up since 1968. The Omnibus Society (entry 473) library, including an archive of the bus and coach industry, is now held at the museum.

Acquisitions policy: Material relating to social, industrial and economic history of the East Shropshire coalfield. Technological history in general and industrial archaeology. Special interest in Thomas Telford, oral history and notable industrial historians. The majority of items are received as donations.

Archives of organisation: Internal administrative records of IGMT and Friends of IGMT, 1969– .

Major collections: Archives relating to the following companies: Coalbrookdale Company; Horsehay Company; Lilleshall Company; Maw & Co.; Hathernware Company (of Loughborough, Leics).
Material *re* Dunhill decorative tiles.
Collection pertaining to the life and works of Thomas Telford (1757–1834): official correspondence, reports and accounts of the Gloucester and Berkeley Canal and his involvement in the Exchequer Loans Commission Board; draft versions of Telford's autobiography, with correspondence relating to its publication.
Darby family archives.

Non-manuscript material: Illustrative material in the Telford Collection and xerox and microfilm copies of all known Telford MS material and printed parliamentary reports containing Telford references.
Elton Collection: material relating to the Industrial Revolution.
Maps and plans (c200); postcards and photographs (c15,000).
Film collection on local industries and Ironbridge; oral history recordings (c100).

Finding aids: Lists and indexes. Major lists sent to NRA.

Facilities: Photocopying. Photography. Microfilming.

473 Omnibus Society
John F. Parke Memorial Library & Archive

Address: The Museum of Iron, Coalbrookdale, Ironbridge, Telford, Shropshire

Website: www.omnibussoc.org/library.htm

Enquiries: A.W. Mills, The Hon. Librarian & Archivist, 4 Connaught Close, Walsall WS5 3PR. Tel. (01922) 631867

Open: Weds (1st & 3rd) in the month: 9.00–4.30; other times by arrangement.

Access: Free to Omnibus Society members; a fee is payable by other researchers.

The Omnibus Society was founded in 1929 to study the development and history of all aspects of road passenger transport: buses, trolley buses, trams and light rail. In addition to the society's own records, its library (in association with the Transport Trust) holds Traffic Commissioners' Notices & Proceedings, 1931– ; maps; timetables (some on microfilm); photographs; periodicals, 1920s– ; and books, 1930s– . The Society's official journal is the *Omnibus Magazine*.

474 Scottish Maritime Museum

A Museum Collection

Address: Laird Forge, Gottries Road, Irvine, Ayrshire KA12 8QE

Telephone: (01294) 278283

Fax: (01294) 313211

Enquiries: The Curator, Emily Cook

Open: Mon–Fri: 10.00–5.00.
NB Study times are not identical with those of the museum.

Access: Bona fide researchers, by appointment.

Historical background: The Scottish Maritime Museum Trust was founded in 1983. The museum itself offers harbour quayside exhibits and vessels with visitor access and an exhibition hall. It is housed in a Grade A-listed engine shop rebuilt in 1991 from the Linthouse Shipyard, Govan. The collections are broad and include vessels, machinery, archives and a special library.

Acquisitions policy: All aspects of Scottish maritime history and activity, including inland water, with particular interest in shipbuilding. Archival collections are being developed in co-operation with other major Scottish depositories and include ship/boatbuilding business records.

Archives of organisation: Records relating to the museum and the Scottish Maritime Museum Trust, 1981– .

Major collections: Business records of Wm. Fife & Sons of Fairlie and their successors, the Fairlie Yacht Slip Co., 1915–85. (The main technical material is at Fairlie Restoration Ltd, c/o Hamble Yacht Services, Port Hamble, Batchell Lane, Hants, tel. (01703) 456336).

Non-manuscript material: Samples, manufacturers' catalogues, photographs, postcards, ephemera and cuttings albums.

Finding aids: Business archives cataloguing in progress. Details to be sent to National Archives of Scotland (entry 329).

Facilities: Photocopying. Photography.

Conservation: Contracted out.

B Denny Ship Model Experiment Tank

Address: Castle Street, Dumbarton, G82 1QS

Telephone: (01389) 763444

Fax: (01389) 743093

Enquiries: The Curator, Veronica Hartwich (at address for A above)

Open: Mon–Sat: 10.00–4.00.

Access: Bona fide researchers, by appointment.

Historical background: The Experiment Tank was founded in 1883 by Messrs Wm. Denny & Bros. and was operated by them until 1963, when ownership passed to Vickers Shipbuilding & Engineering Ltd. The establishment was closed down in 1983. The building and its contents were salvaged by a consortium of museums, including the Scottish Maritime Museum, which owns the building and ground and most of the collections.

Acquisitions policy: Existing collections (object and archival) are defined by their direct association with the tank itself. The general objective is to improve and fill gaps in the archive. Expansion to include records of hydrodynamics not ongoing in Dumbarton is under consideration.

Archives of organisation: Hydrodynamic test records of Messrs Wm. Denny & Bros., tank business records, 1883–1963.

Vickers records, mainly lists of models and dates of tests, 1963–83.

Non-manuscript material: Large number of hull lines, plans and drawings for models tested.

Photographic archive of Vickers tests at Dumbarton, 1960s.

Tank original library of books and periodicals appropriate to work.

Finding aids: Master list summarising the content of the collections; detailed catalogue of test records.

Conservation: Contracted out.

475 British and Foreign School Society
Archives Centre

Address: Brunel University, Osterley Campus, Lancaster House, Borough Road, Isleworth, Middlesex TW7 5DU

Telephone: (020) 8891 0121 ext. 2615

Fax: (020) 8891 8211

E-mail: brian.york@brunel.ac.uk

Website: www.brunel.ac.uk

Enquiries: The Archivist, Brian York

Open: Wed, Fri: 10.00–4.00.

Access: Generally open to the public; no prior appointment is necessary but notice of a visit is helpful. Access to some recent records is at the discretion of the Archivist.

Historical background: BFSS was founded in 1808 by supporters of Joseph Lancaster (1778–1838) and his system of undenominational popular education. Its headquarters were at Borough Road, Southwark, where the society's original training institution for elementary teachers was also established. When Borough Road College was moved to Isleworth in 1890, many of the society's records were moved there and so escaped the destruction of the society's London offices in 1940– . The society's recent records were moved to West London Institute (now Brunel University) in 1980. See also entry 1179.

Acquisitions policy: To add to the society's collection of documents, photographs and printed books relevant to the history of its colleges, schools and overseas work, as well as its central administration.

Archives of organisation: Records of the BFSS, including minute books, secretaries' letters and papers, overseas correspondence, annual reports, 1808– .
Records of the society's schools and colleges: Borough Road College, Saffron Walden College, Stockwell College and Darlington College, including minute and logbooks, registers, students' journals and prospectuses, c1814– .

Major collections: Correspondence of Joseph Lancaster and his contemporaries, 1810–12.

Non-manuscript material: The Salmon Collection of books and pamphlets on elementary education, early 19th century.

Photographs and prints of the society's colleges and schools.
Educational Record, 1848–1929.
Collections of children's books, 19th and early 20th centuries.

Finding aids: Typescript bibliography of books, articles, unpublished typescripts, relevant to the history of BFSS and produced since 1965. Card index. Lists sent to NRA.

Facilities: Photocopying. Photography by arrangement.

Publications: BFSS Archives Centre General Prospectus [available on request].
Detailed reports of the Archives Centre are given in the following: *Journal of Educational Administration and History* (July 1980); *History of Education* (Oct 1981); *Local Historian,* xiv/4 (1984).

476 University of Keele Library
Special Collections and Archives

Address: Keele Information Services, Library, Keele University, Keele, Staffordshire ST5 5BG

Telephone: (01782) 583237

Fax: (01782) 711553

E-mail: h.burton@keele.ac.uk

Website: www.keele.ac.uk/depts/li/

Enquiries: The Special Collections and Archives Assistant, Miss Helen Burton

Open: Mon–Fri: 9.00–5.00.

Access: Bona fide researchers, by appointment. A reader's ticket is essential for access to the Wedgwood and Spode MSS; application forms are available from, respectively, the Curator, Wedgwood Museum, Darlaston, Stoke-on-Trent ST12 9ES and the Curator, the Spode Museum, Church Street, Stoke-on-Trent ST4 1BX.

Historical background: In 1957 the University College of North Staffordshire (later the University of Keele) purchased the papers of the Sneyds of Keele, which had by then become part of the collection of the late Raymond Richards, FSA, FRHistS, of Gawsworth, Cheshire. Most of the rest of this collection was purchased at the same time and became the nucleus of the MS holdings. Subsequent deposits and gifts and some further purchases, mainly of archive material, have been added.

Acquisitions policy: Acquisitions should conform with the teaching and research profile of the University, be of strategic local interest, or supplement an existing collection.

Archives of organisation: Keele University Senate minutes, 1951– .

Major collections: Wedgwood MSS: reflecting the history of the family and of the firm; rich in material relating to the fine arts, the history of science and the development of humanitarian movements, as well as the history of the manufacture of ceramic products (*c*75,000 separate items, plus vols).
Spode MSS: business records, correspondence etc, 19th–20th centuries (*c*1000 items).
Raymond Richards Collection: Sneyd family papers and older collections such as the Hatton Wood MSS, a large proportion of which consists of medieval evidence of title, 12th century– .
Tamworth court rolls, items, 13th–16th centuries (*c*300).
Arnold Bennett (1867–1931): literary MSS, letters, pictorial material.
Lord Lindsay of Birker (1879–1952), political philosopher and first principal of the University College of North Staffordshire: family and personal correspondence, journals, photographs, lectures and articles.
Sociological Society (later the Institute of Sociology) records, including the papers of Victor Branford and Alexander Farquharson. Complementary to these are the papers of the eminent sociologist Karl Mannheim.

Non-manuscript material: Photographs, including Warrillow Collection of Potteries material; cartoons; drawings and paintings; music; printed ephemera.

Finding aids: Catalogues, calendars, lists, indexes. Copies of the lists sent to NRA.

Facilities: Photocopying. Photography. Microcard/fiche/film readers.

Conservation: Contracted out.

Publications: M.K. Dale: *Abstracts of Tamworth Court Rolls* (1959).
I.H.C. Fraser: 'Manuscripts in the Library of the University of Keele', *North Staffordshire Journal of Field Studies*, 7 (1967), 58–62.
R. Studd: *The Tamworth Court Rolls: an Introduction* (Ormonde Publishing Ltd, 1987).
C. Fyfe: 'Manuscripts in Keele University Library', *Staffordshire Studies*, i (1988).

477 University of Keele
Air Photo Library

Address: Brian Stokes Building, Keele University, Keele, Staffordshire ST5 5BG

Telephone: (01782) 583395

Fax: (01782) 583395

E-mail: m.c.beech@keele.ac.uk

Enquiries: The Archive Manager, Mrs M.C. Beech

Open: Mon–Fri: 9.00–1.00, 2.00–5.00.

Access: Access is strictly by appointment. Requests for access to photographs covering specific areas should state the name of the site and position to nearest latitude and longitude. There is an administrative search fee.

Historical background: The library is composed of a significant part of the air photo print library of the Allied Central Interpretation Unit from RAF Medmenham, and it holds allied forces reconnaissance air photographs. It is recognised as a place of deposit for public records. The archive is housed in the Environmental Social Sciences Department.

Major collections: Exclusively non-MS material (see below).

Non-manuscript material: Vertical air photographs from World War II (5½ million). There is no cover of any country which was neutral during World War II or of the UK.

Finding aids: The collection is catalogued by latitude and longitude.

Facilities: Copy-print service.

478 Cliffe Castle Museum

Parent organisation: City of Bradford Metropolitan District Council

Address: Spring Gardens Lane, Keighley, West Yorkshire BD20 6LH

Telephone: (01535) 618243

Fax: (01535) 610536

Enquiries: The Curator

Open: Tues–Sat: 10.00–5.00; Sun 12.00–5.00.

Access: Bona fide students and researchers, by appointment only.

The collection of local documentary material was formed by Keighley Museum. It includes papers relating to the Butterfield family of Keighley, builders of Cliffe Castle, and printed ephemera, mainly of local interest. Archives related to the museum's natural sciences collections are also held. Most MS material, including the Eshton Hall Collection of estate papers of the Currer and Wilson families, is now deposited with Bradford District Archives (entry 125).

479 Keighley Reference Library

Parent organisation: Bradford Metropolitan Libraries

Address: Public Library, North Street, Keighley, West Yorkshire BD21 3SX

Telephone: (01274) 758215

Fax: (01274) 758214

Enquiries: The Reference Librarian, Pauline L. Barfield

Open: Mon, Wed: 9.00–7.00; Tues: 9.00–1.00; Thurs: 9.30–7.00; Fri, Sat: 9.00–5.00.

Access: Generally open to the public, but 24 hours' notice is necessary for archives.

Historical background: Although now part of Bradford Metropolitan Libraries, the Reference Library remains largely a relic of the former Keighley Borough (1882–1974), within which its local collection has been steadily accumulating from 1904 onwards. The main emphasis of the archives relates to Keighley and outer communities which were formerly included in Keighley Borough, such as Haworth and Oxenhope, although there is a smaller amount of wider West Yorkshire material.

Acquisitions policy: To collect materials relating primarily to the area of the former Keighley Borough. A major subject area tends to be local government, owing to the demise of the borough in 1974, with consequent movement of its records.

Major collections: Minutes of Keighley Improvement Commissioners, 1824–57; Select Vestry, 1798–1854; Local Board of Health, 1855–82; Borough Council, 1882–1974; Poor Law Union, 1837–1930; North Bierley Poor Law Union, 1848–1930.
Miscellaneous letter files.
Keighley and Worth Valley Methodist archives, 18th–20th centuries; Keighley Independent and Congregationalist archives and Baptist archives (excluding registers), 19th and 20th centuries.

Brigg Collection: mainly documents relating to Yorkshire/Lancashire border properties, 15th–19th centuries.
Records of Keighley Independent Labour Party, c1890s–1920s, and Keighley Cooperative Society, c1860–1950.
Gordon Bottomley (1874–1948), poet and playwright: letters, photographs, inscribed first editions.
Keighley Township papers, 1658–1921.

Non-manuscript material: Philip Snowden Library: personal book collection of former Chancellor of the Exchequer, particularly strong in early socialist pamphlets.
Brontë Collection: scrapbooks and ephemera, 19th century.

Finding aids: Catalogue (but only of broad headings); local index (in permanent process of compilation). Lists of Brigg Collection and Methodist Archives.

Facilities: Photocopying. Microfilm reader.

480 Cumbria Archive Service
Cumbria Record Office, Kendal

Address: County Offices, Kendal, Cumbria LA9 4RQ

Telephone: (01539) 773540

Fax: (01539) 773439

E-mail: kendal.record.office@kendalcc.gov.uk

Enquiries: The County Archivist, Mr Jim Grisenthwaite (service-wide enquiries)
The Assistant County Archivist, Ms Anne Rowe (office enquiries)

Open: Mon–Fri: 9.00–5.00.

Access: Generally open to the public. The office operates the CARN reader's ticket system. A paid research service is provided.

Historical background: The office was established in 1962 under a joint archives committee for the former counties of Cumberland and Westmorland and the City of Carlisle. Few archives other than local authority records had been acquired before that date. The office is recognised as a place of deposit for public records and acts as the Diocesan Record Office for Carlisle (former Westmorland parishes), and holds records of Cumbrian parishes in the Diocese of Bradford. It provides administrative assistance to Levens Hall near Kendal. See also the offices at Carlisle (entry 223) and Barrow-in-Furness (entry 53).

Acquisitions policy: Official and unofficial archives for the former county of Westmorland and the Sedbergh, Garsdale and Dent areas (formerly West Riding of Yorkshire).

Archives of organisation: Usual local authority record holdings.

Major collections: Deposited local collections, of which the following have a wider significance:
Lady Anne Clifford (1590–1676): Appleby Castle estate and personal records.
T.H. Mawson, landscape architect, plans and photographs of gardens and parks, late 19th–20th centuries.

Finding aids: Catalogues and indexes. Some collections are unlisted. Selected catalogues sent to NRA.

Facilities: Photocopying. Photography. Microfilming. Microfilm/fiche readers/printer. Ultra violet light.

Conservation: Cumbria Archive Service Conservation Unit is in Carlisle. Outside work is undertaken.

Publications: B.C. Jones: 'Cumberland, Westmorland and Carlisle Record Office, 1960–65', *Archives*, vii/34 (1965), 80.
——: 'Cumberland and Westmorland Record Offices, 1968', *Northern History*, iii (1968), 162.
E.M. Wilson: *Much Cry of Kendal Wool: an Anthology (1420–1720)*, Curwen Archives Trust, Occasional Publications No. 1 (1980).
E.L. Ashcroft: *Vital Statistics: the Westmorland 'Census' of 1787*, Curwen Archives Texts No. 1 (1992).
Cumbrian Ancestors (3/1998).
Curwen Archives Trust: *Plans of Kendal in 1787, 1833 and 1853 by John Todd, John Wood and Henry Hoggarth* [reproductions].

481 Keswick Museum and Art Gallery

Parent organisation: Allerdale Borough Council

Address: Station Road, Keswick, Cumbria CA12 4NF

Telephone: (01768) 773263

Fax: (01768) 780390

E-mail: keswick.museum@allerdale.gov.uk

Enquiries: The Curator, Hazel Davison

Open: Easter–Oct: Mon–Sun: 10.00–4.00.

Access: Generally open to the public, by appointment only.

Historical background: The museum was founded in 1873 and has been administered by the Fitz Park Trust for much of its history. In 1994 it was taken over by Allerdale Borough Council. The collection of literary MSS of the Romantic poets was initiated by Canon Rawnsley (1851–1920), founder of the National Trust.

Acquisitions policy: MSS of the Romantic poets and local history in North Lakes area.

Major collections: MSS of Robert Southey (1774–1843), Poet Laureate, 1813–43; William Wordsworth (1770–1850); and Sir Hugh Walpole (1884–1941), novelist.
Records of Keswick Gas Company and Crosthwaite Boys School.
Miscellaneous material relating to Keswick.

Non-manuscript material: Maps of Keswick and district.
Photographic collection.
Newspapers: *English Lakes*, *Visitor* and *Keswick Guardian*, 1882–1910.

Conservation: North West Museums Service.

Publications: Southey and Wordsworth MSS listed in *The Wordsworth Circle* (winter 1980).

482 Drayton House

Address: The Drayton Estate Office, Drayton Road, Lowick, Kettering, Northamptonshire NN14 3BG

Telephone: (01832) 732405

Fax: (01832) 732082

Enquiries: The Librarian, Bruce Bailey

Open: Strictly by appointment only.

Access: Approved academic researchers, on written application.

Historical background: Drayton House dates from medieval times. It was owned by the Mordaunt family during the 16th and 17th centuries, passed to the Sackvilles in 1769 and is still with their descendants. Medieval and 16th-century estate records are held at Northamptonshire Record Office (entry 931).

Archives of organisation: Background material to estate and house, mainly c1700–1800.

Major collections: Material on Lord George Germain (Sackville) (1716–85), who inherited Drayton in 1769 (mostly published in HMC Report).

Finding aids: Historical Manuscripts Commission: *Report on the manuscripts of Mrs Stopford-Sackville*, 1904, 1910 [2 vols]. Northamptonshire Record Office *Calendar* lists some material. Other material is still being sorted and catalogued.

Facilities: Limited photocopying.

483 British Geological Survey Library

Address: Kingsley Dunham Centre, Keyworth, Nottinghamshire NG12 5GG

Telephone: (0115) 936 3472

Fax: (0115) 936 3200

E-mail: g.mckenna@bgs.ac.uk

Website: www.bgs.ac.uk

Enquiries: The Archivist, Mr Graham McKenna
The Records Officer, Mr R.C. Bowie

Open: Mon–Thurs: 9.00–5.00; Fri: 9.00–4.30.

Access: Generally open to the public; an appointment is preferred. Charges are made for some services.

Historical background: The collection and organisation of the survey's archives began in 1967 in order to bring together and preserve MS, graphic, photographic and ephemeral printed material of all kinds relating to the history of British geological sciences, and in particular to the history of the British Geological Survey and its forerunners, the Institute of Geological Sciences, the Geological Survey, the Museum of Practical Geology, and Overseas Geological Surveys. The scope of the collection, more than 30,000 items, has been widened to include material about geology on an international basis, the overall aim being to provide a national geological archive available for public reference on site at Keyworth comprising the BGS Library Archives and the materials housed in the National Geosciences Records Centre. BGS Keyworth is recognised as a place of deposit for public records.

Acquisitions policy: To add to the existing collection in pursuance of the survey's role as a repository for national geological archives.

Archives of organisation: The survey's own archives, which include constituent bodies, the Geological Survey, Museum of Practical Geology, Mining Record Office and Royal School of Mines.
Correspondence and papers, paintings, drawings, photographs; registered files; official field records generated by the survey's staff, 1835– .

Major collections: A wide range of other collections includes the records of the Palaeontographical Society, 1847–1950.
Correspondence and notes of celebrated geologists in many varied collections.

Non-manuscript material: Photographs (survey and geology) (75,000).
British Association for the Advancement of Science, geological photographs of Britain, 1861–1940s.
Drawings and ephemera.

Finding aids: TS registers to the whole collection are available in the survey's libraries at Keyworth and Edinburgh (entry 316), BGS London Information Office, and the Public Record Office (entry 1058). The collection is currently being indexed in detail and a card index is maintained in each library. The existing card indexes are being digitised and will be made available on the BGS Library's website.

Facilities: Photocopying. Photography. Microfilm/fiche reader/printers.

484 Brintons Historical & Design Archives

Address: Brintons Ltd, PO Box 16, Exchange Street, Kidderminster, Worcestershire DY10 1AG

Telephone: (01562) 820000

Fax: (01562) 515597 or (01562) 742487 (Design Dept)

Enquiries: The Design Archivist, David L. Thompson

Open: Mon–Fri: 9.00–5.00.

Access: Students and researchers, by appointment only. Personal papers kept by individual members of the Brinton family are not generally available to the public.

Historical background: Brintons was founded in 1783 by William Brinton and remains a family-owned private company. Today it is a worldwide organisation providing high quality designer carpets. The Design Archive includes copies of original tracings, 1842–72, which were publicly registered, see Public Record Office (entry 1058).

Acquisitions policy: To maintain the historical and design archives.

Archives of organisation: Board reports and some correspondence, mid-19th century– .
Price lists, 1905– ; photograph books, 1908– ; brochures, c1930– ; house magazine collection.

Non-manuscript material: Drawings and photographs of manufacturing equipment, 19th century– .

Finding aids: Catalogue of the archives.

Facilities: Photocopying and photography allowed with permission.

Publications: Design Archives and Library brochure (1998).

485 Dick Institute

Parent organisation: East Ayrshire Council, Museums & Arts Section

Address: Elmbank Avenue, Kilmarnock, Ayrshire KA1 3BU

Telephone: (01563) 554343

Fax: (01563) 554343

E-mail: donnachisum@east-ayrshire.co.uk

Enquiries: The Museums and Arts Manager, Mr Charles Woodward

Open: Mon, Tues, Thurs, Fri: 9.00–8.00; Wed, Sat: 9.00–5.00.

Access: Generally open to the public; access to MSS by appointment.

Historical background: The foundation stone of the Dick Institute was laid in 1898 by Mrs Dick, wife of the donor, and the building was formally opened in 1901. The museum owes its origin chiefly to James Thomson, who gifted a rare and valuable collection of corals, fossils and minerals, to which extensive additions were made by Dr Hunter-Selkirk of Braidwood and others.

Acquisitions policy: MSS of local interest or relating to museum subject areas.

Major collections: Various collections, 14th–20th centuries, including poems and letters of Robert Burns (1759–96); papers of Boyds of Kilmarnock, and Rawden-Hastings and Campbell families; records of local town councils, trade guilds and trade unions.

Non-manuscript material: Local maps.
Engineering and architectural plans and drawings.
Penkill Collection: notebooks, watercolours and sketchbooks mostly by William Bell Scott (1811–90), a Pre-Raphaelite artist from Penkill Castle, Ayrshire.
Paintings and prints (c1500).
Photographs and slides (c10,000).
Local newspapers.

Finding aids: Catalogues and indexes to most collections. Rawden-Hastings and Campbell: NRA 18854.

Facilities: Photocopying. Photography. Microfilm reader.

486 Lynn Museum

Parent organisation: Norfolk Museums Service

Address: Old Market Street, King's Lynn, Norfolk PE30 1NL

Telephone: (01553) 775001

Enquiries: The Curator

Open: Tues–Sat: 10.00–5.00.

Access: There is a small admission charge to the museum.

Historical background: The museum was founded as a society museum in 1844 with a collection of natural history specimens and curiosities. It was taken over by King's Lynn Borough Council and the present building was opened in 1904. In 1973 a branch museum of social history was opened, now located at 46 Queen Street, King's Lynn, and in 1974 both museums were included in the newly formed Norfolk Museums Service.

Acquisitions policy: To collect material and information relating to King's Lynn and West Norfolk.

Archives of organisation: Museum records, 1844– .

Natural history: a few records relating to the museum's collections.

Major collections: Archaeological: records of excavations in King's Lynn etc.

Engineering: a vast collection of works' drawings and accompanying ledgers and papers from Dodman's of Lynn (f. *c*1850) relating to boilers, agricultural machinery, traction engines, marine equipment etc; works' drawings, ledgers etc relating to Savages of Lynn, important manufacturers of fairground machinery, traction engines etc.

Topographical: papers, MS letters etc, relating to the history of Lynn, including some deeds and business records.

Miscellaneous MSS relating to Thomas Baines (1822–75) and Captain G.W. Manby (1765–1854).

Non-manuscript material: Pamphlets and broadsheets relating to Lynn.

Poster Collection: local theatres, politics, religion, sales and auctions etc, 18th century–(*c*6000).

Photographic collections relating to the museum collections and to West Norfolk.

Local paintings, prints, sketches etc, including maritime subjects.

Finding aids: Various lists and indexes. A few select catalogues. Automated catalogue of part of the collection.

Facilities: Photocopying of small documents at the discretion of the curator.

487 Kingston Museum and Heritage Service

Parent organisation: Royal Borough of Kingston upon Thames

Address: Local History Room, North Kingston Centre, Richmond Road, Kingston upon Thames, Surrey KT2 5PE

Telephone: (020) 8547 6738

Fax: (020) 8547 6747

E-mail: king.mus@rbk.kingston.gov.uk

Enquiries: The Heritage Officer, Mrs Anne McCormack
The Archivist, Mrs Jill Lamb

Open: Mon, Thurs, Fri: 10.00–1.00, 2.00–5.00; Tues: 10.00–1.00, 2.00–7.00.

Access: Generally open to the public, by appointment (two days' notice required). Council material is restricted for at least 30 years. A paid research service is available.

Historical background: Archives are held under the various provisions of the Municipal Corporations Act 1882, the Local Government (Records) Act 1962, as modified by the London Government Act 1963, and the Public Records Acts 1958 and 1967.

Acquisitions policy: Records of the Royal Borough of Kingston upon Thames, its predecessors, other bodies, businesses and individuals living in, or connected with, places within the royal borough.

Archives of organisation: Records of the Royal Borough of Kingston, including substantial deed groups for corporation property, 1238– .

Major collections: A small number of private papers.

Non-manuscript material: Plans (all other material is held in the local history room).

Finding aids: Lists and name and place index to deeds. Lists sent to NRA.

Facilities: Photocopying and microfilm readers available in the Local History Room.

Conservation: Contracted out.

Publications: Guide to the Borough Archives (1971).
Archive Teaching Units: *Kingston Children*; *Kingston Market Place*; *Kingston in Maps*; *Theatres & Cinemas*; *Road, Rail & River*.

488 Kirkcaldy Central Library

Parent organisation: Kirkcaldy District Libraries

Address: War Memorial Grounds, Kirkcaldy, Fife KY1 1YG

Telephone: (01592) 412878

Fax: (01592) 412750

E-mail: info@kirkcaldy.fife.lib.net

Enquiries: The Reference Librarian, Miss Sheila Campbell

Open: Mon–Thurs: 10.00–7.00; Fri, Sat: 10.00–5.00.
Closed first Monday in May and Monday of third week in July.

Access: Generally open to the public, preferably by prior appointment. A booking system is in operation for the use of microform readers.

Historical background: Kirkcaldy Central Library opened in 1928 and was part of

Kirkcaldy Public Libraries until local government reorganisation in 1975. Kirkcaldy District Libraries took over and continued until 1996, when Fife Council Libraries assumed responsibility for library services in Fife.

Acquisitions policy: To collect material for central area of Fife in particular and Fife in general.

Major collections: Papers of Hutchison family, burgesses of Kirkcaldy, 16th–20th centuries.
MSS of Jessie Patrick Findlay, local author, 20th century.
G. Allen Hutt/Proudfoot papers, 1920s–1940s, posters, pamphlets, correspondence and newspapers, especially concerning General Strike, 1926.

Non-manuscript material: Local study collection: books, maps, press cuttings, slides and photographs.
Fife census returns 1841–91.
Fife old parish registers.
Newspapers.

Finding aids: Press cuttings index. Family history Sources in Kirkcaldy Central Library. Hutt/Proudfoot list: NRAS 1878.

Facilities: Restricted photocopying. Photography by arrangement. Microform print-outs.

Publications: List of local history publications available.

489 Kirkcaldy Museum and Art Gallery

Parent organisation: Fife Council

Address: War Memorial Gardens, Kirkcaldy, Fife KY1 1YG

Telephone: (01592) 412860

Fax: (01592) 412870

Enquiries: The Curator

Open: Mon–Fri: 10.30–5.00.

Access: Generally open to the public, by appointment only.

Historical background: The museum and art gallery was founded in 1925 as a general museum for Kirkcaldy. It is now responsible for central Fife. The archive is only part of the large general museum and art collections. Much earlier local material is deposited with the National Archives of Scotland (entry 329). The bulk of the 19th and 20th century government

material is now held by Fife Council Archive Centre (entry 893).

Acquisitions policy: By donation and deposit, material relevant to the museum collections and to the history of central Fife.

Major collections: Records of the linoleum industry, including plans, buildings and machinery, 1840s–1990s; trade guilds, 1700–1850; trade unions, local branches, 20th century; local government, 19th–20th centuries; friendly societies, 19th century.

Non-manuscript material: Photographic collections of the district. Most non-MS material is held by Kirkcaldy Central Library (entry 488).

Finding aids: Some indexing. NRAS lists, including Kirkcaldy Burgh Museum and Art Gallery: NRAS 744.

Facilities: Photocopying by arrangement.

490 Hornel Library

Parent organisation: National Trust for Scotland

Address: Broughton House, 12 High Street, Kirkcudbright, Dumfries and Galloway DG6 4JX

Telephone: (01557) 330437

Fax: (01557) 330437

Enquiries: The Librarian, Mr James Allan

Open: April–June, Sept–Oct: Mon–Sun: 1.00–5.30; at other times by arrangement only.
July–Aug: Mon–Sun: 11.00–5.30.

Access: Generally open to the public; an appointment is necessary.

Historical background: The property and its contents, including the library, were left to the community by the artist E.A. Hornel, under a trust deed which became operative in 1950. In 1994 the property was transferred to the National Trust for Scotland by the E.A. Hornel Trust.

Acquisitions policy: Acquisition by donation, deposit or purchase within the fields covered by the collection.

Major collections: The Dumfries and Galloway Collection, covering the old counties of Dumfries, Kirkcudbright and Wigtown: diaries, accounts, military documents, genealogies, ecclesiastical papers, writs, covenanting papers, 17th–19th centuries.

Literary MSS, including correspondence of Sir Walter Scott, 1802–31, and Thomas Carlyle, 1819–78.

Large collection of MSS of local authors and correspondence *re* ballads and local traditions, including the William McMath Collection, relating mainly to English and Scottish popular ballads.

Correspondence of E.A. Hornel (1864–1933).

Non-manuscript material: Robert Burns Collection, including many early editions, and information about Burns clubs throughout the world.

Finding aids: Catalogues. NRAS 0118 (NRA 10178).

Facilities: Photocopying and photography by arrangement.

491 The Stewartry Museum

Parent organisation: Dumfries and Galloway Council

Address: St Mary Street, Kirkcudbright DG6 4JG

Telephone: (01557) 331643

Fax: (01557) 331643

E-mail: davidd@dumgal.gov.uk

Enquiries: The Curator, Dr D. Devereux

Open: Mon–Fri: 9.00–5.00, subject to the availability of the Curator. NB These opening times are not identical with those of the museum.

Access: Open to all responsible researchers; an appointment with the Curator is desirable. A postal enquiry service is offered on a fee-paying basis.

Historical background: The archive collection was begun in 1881 with the foundation of the Stewartry Museum. The operation of the museum was taken over by Stewartry District Council in 1990, and at this time responsibility for the district council's collection was transferred to the Museum Service, which from 1996 became part of Dumfries and Galloway Museums Service.

Acquisitions policy: In collaboration with Dumfries and Galloway Council's Libraries, Archives and Information Service. Material of all types relating to the human and natural history of the collecting area, which is the area currently under the local government

administration of Stewartry District Council, together with those areas formerly administered by the County Council of the Stewartry of Kirkcudbright and now outwith the bounds of Stewartry District.

Archives of organisation: Records relating to the foundation and subsequent management of the Stewartry Museum, 1881–1990; these include minute books, financial accounts, correspondence and the collections register of the Stewartry Museum Association.

Major collections: Kirkcudbright Town Council records, later 16th century–1975, including minute books, 1576–1975.

Burgh court records and annual accounts, c1700– .

Stewartry Burgh records for New Galloway, Castle Douglas and Gatehouse of Fleet (various dates).

Stewartry District Council minute books, 1975–96.

Kirkcudbrightshire Yeomanry Cavalry records, 1804–36.

Local estate records: Auchendolly, Redcastle, Queenshill, Gelston, Orchardton, Livingstone.

Non-manuscript material: Small collections of plans and drawings of local bridges.

Maps, especially Kirkcudbright, late 18th century– .

Photographic collection for the Stewartry area. Small collection of films.

Supporting printed material includes graveyard surveys and newspaper indexes.

Finding aids: A computer-based inventory is in preparation. Survey of Stewartry Museum Collection: NRA 9002.

Facilities: Photocopying. Photography by arrangement.

Conservation: Active conservation programme, contracted out.

492 William Patrick Library

Parent organisation: East Dunbartonshire Libraries

Address: 2 West High Street, Kirkintilloch, East Dunbartonshire G66 1AD

Telephone: (0141) 776 8090

Fax: (0141) 776 0408

Enquiries: The Reference and Information Librarian, Mr Don Martin

Open: Mon–Thur: 10.00–8.00; Fri–Sat: 10.00–5.00.

Access: Generally open to the public.

Historical background: The service was set up in 1996 as a result of the reorganisation of local government in Scotland. There is a branch office at Brookwood Library, Bearsden (entry 382).

Acquisitions policy: To provide accommodation for local authority records which vest in East Dunbartonshire Council; also material belonging to local individuals, firms and organisations who wish to deposit locally.

Archives of organisation: Records of the former burghs of Kirkintilloch and Bishopbriggs; also a small quantity of records of former county district councils which now vest in East Dunbartonshire Council. Records of the former Strathkelvin District Council.

Major collections: Archives of local organisations, families and individuals, including minute books, accounts books, scrapbooks etc, of Kirkintilloch YMCA, Kirkintilloch Funeral & Mortcloth Society, Lenzie Public Hall Trustees and Kirkintilloch Town Mission.
J.F. McEwan Collection of Scottish railway history.
Documents of local interest collected by individuals and families.

Non-manuscript material: Catalogues, drawings and photographs of the former Lion Foundry Co.
Extensive holdings of local material, including books, pamphlets, maps, photographs, photographic slides, local newspapers, news cuttings, leaflets and posters.

Finding aids: Catalogues.

Facilities: Photocopying. Photography. Microfilm/fiche reader/printer.

Publications: Leaflets on 'Archives', 'Local History' and 'Family History'.

493 Orkney Archives

Parent organisation: Orkney Islands Council

Address: The Orkney Library, Laing Street, Kirkwall, Orkney KW15 1NW

Telephone: (01856) 873166

Fax: (01856) 875260

E-mail: alisonf@oic4.orkney.gov.uk

Enquiries: The Archivist, Miss Alison Fraser

Open: Mon–Fri: 9.00–1.00, 2.00–4.45.
Closed for three weeks in mid-February.

Access: Generally open to the public, by appointment.

Historical background: The office was formally established in 1973 by Orkney Education Authority; it is now administered by the Department of Education and Recreation Services of Orkney Islands Council.

Acquisitions policy: MS and printed material; film, video, photographs, sound recordings, maps, plans etc relating to Orkney.

Archives of organisation: Usual local authority holdings, 1669– .

Major collections: Balfour of Balfour and Trenabie, c1570–1886; Watt of Breckness & Skaill, c1720–1850; Sutherland Graeme of Graemeshall, c1600–1938; Ernest W. Marwick, c1770–1977; Earldom of Orkney, 1536–1880.
Business records of Highland Park Distillery and Orkney Islands Shipping Company.
Church records and records of Orkney sheriff court, customs and excise.

Non-manuscript material: Plans and maps.
Photographs (20,000).
Sound archive (1600 tapes).
Microfilm copies of local newspapers, census and old parish registers.

Finding aids: Descriptive lists available for main series of records and many of the deposited collections; lists sent to NRAS.

Facilities: Photocopying. Photography. Microfilm/fiche readers/printer.

494 University of Wales, Lampeter

Address: Lampeter, Ceredigion SA48 7ED

Telephone: (01570) 424708

Fax: (01570) 423641

Website: www.lamp.ac.uk

Enquiries: The Archivist, Rev. Dr John R. Guy

Open: By appointment.

Access: Generally open to the public.

Historical background: The college opened in 1827, and for many years most of the graduates entered the ministry of the Anglican Church, although the college was never simply a theological college. In 1971 the college became a constituent institution of the University of Wales.

Acquisitions policy: To retrieve and preserve all material concerned with the history of the college.

Archives of organisation: Archives of the college, including tutors' registers, which provide biographical material on all students of the college.

Major collections: Papers of Archbishops Edwin Morris and G.O.Williams, and of Rev. Professor Thomas Wood.

Non-manuscript material: College magazines; many photographs.

Finding aids: Various lists and indexes.

Facilities: Photocopying. Microfilm readers.

495   Lanark Library

Parent organisation: South Lanarkshire Libraries

Address: Lindsay Institute, Hope Street, Lanark ML11 7LZ

Telephone: (01555) 661144

Fax: (01555) 665884

Enquiries: The Reference and Local Studies Section

Open: Mon, Tues, Thurs: 9.15–7.30; Fri: 9.30–7.30; Wed, Sat: 9.30–5.00.

Access: Generally open to the public. An appointment is advisable if a microfilm reader is required.

Historical background: South Lanarkshire Libraries were formed in 1996. Material in this repository was formerly held by the Royal Burgh of Lanark, the Burgh of Biggar and Lanark County Council, and from 1975 to 1996 by Lanark/Clydesdale District Council.

Acquisitions policy: To collect material relating to Lanark and the Clydesdale area, within the policy guidelines of South Lanarkshire Libraries.

Archives of organisation: Records of the Royal Burgh of Lanark, 1150–1975.
Records of Biggar Town Council, 1863–1963 (incomplete).

Lanark/Clydesdale District: council minute books, 1975–96.

Non-manuscript material: Maps of Lanark and the Clydesdale area (c3200).
Microfilms of old parish registers, 1645–1854, census returns, 1841–91.
Local newspapers, 19th century– .
Photographs and illustrations (c2500).

Finding aids: Lists sent to NRAS. Royal Burgh of Lanark: NRA 26114.

Facilities: Photocopying. Microfilm/fiche readers/printer.

Conservation: Minor work and protective measures carried out in-house; otherwise contracted out.

496   Lancaster District Library
Local Studies Department

Address: Market Square, Lancaster, Lancashire LA1 1HY

Telephone: (01524) 580708

Fax: (01524) 580709

E-mail: lancaster.reference@lcl.lancscc.gov.uk

Enquiries: The District Librarian, Mr S.J. Eccles
The Reference Librarian, Jennifer Lovridge

Open: Mon, Tues, Wed, Fri: 9.30–5.00; Tues, Thurs: 9.30–7.00; Sat: 9.30–4.00.

Access: Generally open to the public; a prior appointment will save time.

Historical background: Formerly Lancaster City Library, the library became part of the Lancashire Library in 1974. The City Library was formed in 1893, inheriting volumes from the Mechanics' Institute, Amicable Society etc, which date from the late 18th century. Between World Wars I and II the library was designated an official repository of archives by the Master of the Rolls before the creation of Lancashire Record Office (entry 1044). Most archive material has been acquired since 1900. The Yorkshire Collection is now housed at Morecambe Library.

Acquisitions policy: Material is bought on a regular basis and acquired by donation.

Major collections: Local history collection (c9000 MSS), for the area within 15 miles radius of Lancaster, including apprentice registers and Port Commissioners' archives.

Cumbria and Lancashire Collection: general interest material.

Non-manuscript material: Cumbria, Lancashire and Yorkshire map collections.
Local newspapers, 1801– .

Finding aids: Indexes to all local collections are sheaf catalogues with general subject lists as guides to their use. Newspapers are partly indexed, but the quality of the indexing varies.

Facilities: Photocopying (excluding bound newspapers). Photography (subject to conditions). Microfilm reader/printer.

Publications: Local Studies Classification Scheme Indexes [booklet].
Guide to Parish Registers on Microfiche.

497 Lancaster University Library

Address: Bailrigg, Lancaster, Lancashire LA1 4YH

A Rare Books and Archives

Telephone: (01524) 592544/65201 (Library

Fax: (01524) 63806

E-mail: l.newman@lancs.ac.uk

Website: www.lancs.ac.uk

Enquiries: The Curator of Rare Books and Archives, Dr L.M. Newman
The Centre for NW Regional Studies, Dr Elizabeth Roberts

Open: Mon, Wed, Fri: 2.00–4.00.

Access: Members of the university library and other accredited research workers; prior written application is desirable.

Major collections: MSS from the library of Burnley Grammar School, 13th–17th centuries (9 items).
Miscellaneous correspondence of John Ruskin.
Wordsworth MSS, including a variant of a late sonnet.
Wolfenden Report: papers and oral evidence submitted to the Wolfenden Committee on the future of voluntary organisations, 1974–6.
Barclay Report: papers and oral evidence submitted to the Barclay Committee on the role and task of social workers, 1981.
Robert Fitzgibbon Young (*d* 1960): some papers and press cuttings.

Non-manuscript material: Map collection, census, slides, extensive microfilm archives.
Centre for North West Regional Studies: tapes, with transcripts, of interviews on social and family life in Barrow, Lancaster and Preston, 1890–1970 (500).

Finding aids: Some indexes, including full index to CNWRS transcripts.

Facilities: Photocopying. Photography. Microfilm/fiche reader/printers.

Conservation: Contracted out.

B Ruskin Library

Telephone: (01524) 593587

Fax: (01524) 593580

E-mail: ruskin.library@lancaster.ac.uk

Website: www.lancs.ac.uk/users/ruskinlib

Enquiries: The Deputy Curator, Rebecca Finnerty

Open: Mon–Fri: 10.00–4.00, by appointment.

Access: Bona fide researchers who can supply a reference, by prior appointment.

Historical background: The collection was begun by J. Howard Whitehouse (1873–1955) in the 1890s and taken to Bembridge with him in 1919, when he founded Bembridge School, Isle of Wight. It became part of the Education Trust property when the trust was established in 1921. The galleries at Bembridge were built by Whitehouse to house the collection in 1929. In 1932 he bought Brantwood at Coniston and opened it to the public as an international memorial to John Ruskin (1819–1900). The collection moved to Lancaster University in 1997.

Acquisitions policy: To collect items by or relating to John Ruskin and his associates.

Major collections: John Ruskin: correspondence with his parents and friends (*c*1000 items); letters to his cousin, 1864–95 (2500 items); diaries, 1835–89 (26 vols); literary manuscripts and notebooks.

Non-manuscript material: Sketches and drawings by Ruskin (*c*1000) and by artists associated with him (*c*600). His collection of daguerreotypes (125); also large collection of photographs relating to him and of his works.
Ruskin's library (500 vols) and an extensive collection of books by and about him.

Finding aids: Handlist of manuscript and letters (available on request). See also NRA 11475. On-line catalogue of photographs, pictures and books available on the website.

Facilities: Photocopying. Photography. Microfilm reader.

Publications: J.S. Dearden: *Ruskin, Bembridge and Brantwood* (1994).

498 Lancing College Archives

Address: Lancing College, Lancing, West Sussex BN15 0RW

Telephone: (01273) 452213 ext. 267

Fax: (01273) 464720

E-mail: jp@lancing.org.uk

Website: www.lancing.org.uk

Enquiries: The College Archivist, Mrs J. Pennington

Open: Term: by arrangement only.

Access: Approved readers, on written application. An appointment is necessary and a small search fee is made for lengthy postal requests.

Historical background: The college was founded by Nathaniel Woodard (1811–91), canon of Manchester, in 1848. A collection of Woodard schools papers, made by Henry M. Gibbs during the 19th century, has been gradually added to since. See also Woodard Corporation Archives (entry 856).

Acquisitions policy: To acquire further material relating to the past of Lancing College and to preserve present material, including tape-recordings and video recordings.

Archives of organisation: Correspondence and papers of Nathaniel Woodard, 1846–90 (*c*15,000).

Major collections: Papers of Edmund Field, chaplain of Lancing College, 1854–92, and Basil Handford (1900–91), pupil and master. Memoirs and other papers.

Non-manuscript material: Photographs and architectural drawings, in particular of the construction of the chapel, 1868–1979.

Finding aids: Catalogue. Report on the records compiled by the Royal Commission on Historical Manuscripts.

Facilities: Photocopying.

Conservation: Contracted out.

Publications: K.E. Kirk: *The Story of the Woodard Schools* (Abbey Press, *R*1952). B. Heeney: *Mission to the Middle Classes: the Woodard Schools, 1848–1891* (SPCK, 1969). B. Handford: *Lancing College: History and Memoirs* (Phillimore, 1986). R.J. Tomlinson: *Lancing College: a Portrait* (Lancing College, 1998).

499 Henry Moore Institute

Parent organisation: Henry Moore Foundation

Address: 74 The Headrow, Leeds, West Yorkshire LS1 3AA

Telephone: (0113) 246 9469

Fax: (0113) 246 1481

E-mail: archive@henry-moore.ac.uk

Website: www.henry-moore-fdn.co.uk

Enquiries: The Archivist, Adeline van Roon

Open: Mon–Sun: 10.00–5.30; Wed: 10.00–9.00; an appointment is advisable.

Access: Open to everyone with a serious interest. There is public access to the Institute's general files only in exceptional cases; some artist files are accessible on request.

Historical background: The Centre for the Study of Sculpture was established by the Henry Moore Foundation and Leeds City Council in 1982. In 1993 it moved from Leeds City Art Gallery to the new Henry Moore Institute next door. The institute promotes the study of sculpture. Most material relating to Henry Moore (1898–1986) is kept at the foundation's premises in Much Hadham, Hertfordshire (entry 911).

Acquisitions policy: To maintain and develop a library and archive devoted to the history and practice of sculpture. The centre aims to preserve documents relating to the preparation, production and reception of sculpture, and holds a significant collection of sculptors' drawings in addition to other kinds of documentation.

Archives of organisation: Henry Moore Institute archive, 1980s– .

Major collections: Papers of Laurence Henderson Bradshaw (1899–1978); Jacob Epstein (1880–1959); John Hoskin (1921–90);

David Nash (*b* 1945) and Sir Hamo Thorneycroft (1850–1925).

Letters of Joseph Herbert Cribb (1892–1967); Alfred Gilbert (1854–1934); Clare Consuelo Sheridan (1885–1970).

Jacob Epstein, complete studio photographs and sketchbooks.

Henry Moore, early note-book and juvenilia from his time at Leeds; photographs of his works.

Gilbert Ledward (1888–1960), preparation drawings for 'Westminster Guards Memorial' (1922); typescript of his unpublished autobiography; all studio photographs.

Eric Gill (1882–1940), correspondence with the sculptor Joseph Cribb.

Stephen Cox (*b* 1946), two sketchbooks.

Wood's Monumental Masonry Album of 222 designs for church monuments by various artists working in Britain, used by the workshop of the Wood family of Bath and Bristol, late 18th and early 19th centuries.

John Galizia Foundry, London, casting ledgers, 1930–65 (4 vols), and photographic archive (500).

Non-manuscript material: Material, mainly photographic, with some drawings relating to the works of Henry Hugh Armstead, Count Gleichen (1828–1905); Stephen Joseph Cox (*b* 1946); George Frampton (1860–1928); Eric Gill; Peter (Laszlo) Peri (1899–1967); Ellen Mary Rope (1855–1934); and Austin Wright (1911–97).

Slide library, especially of exhibitions, outdoor sculpture and ecclesiastical sculpture (10,000 images).

Finding aids: Thornycroft papers indexed and catalogued. Smaller holdings are listed on the Artists' Papers Register database on www.hmc.gov.uk.

Facilities: Photography by arrangement. Slide sets for loan.

500 Leeds Central Library
Local Studies Department

Parent organisation: Leeds Libraries and Information Service

Address: Municipal Buildings, Calverley Street, Leeds, West Yorkshire LS1 3AB

Telephone: (0113) 247 8290

Fax: (0113) 247 8290

Enquiries: The Departmental Manager, Local Studies Library, Michele Lefevre

Open: Mon, Wed: 9.00–8.00; Tues, Fri: 9.00–5.30; Thurs: 9.30–5.30; Sat: 10.00–5.00.

Access: Generally open to the public.

Historical background: The reference library has always maintained a collection of material relating to Leeds and the rest of Yorkshire. In 1991 the Local History Department was expanded to include material and research facilities for the study of family history and became the Local and Family History Library. The Leeds Archives Department (now West Yorkshire Archive Service: Leeds; entry 506), originally housed in the library building, moved to separate premises in the 1960s and is administered independently.

Acquisitions policy: Maps, periodicals, newspapers etc relating to Leeds or by Leeds authors, and some relating to the rest of Yorkshire, are purchased.

Major collections: Usual local history collection, including a minor collection of such items as minutes of local societies and original MSS of works by local authors.

Non-manuscript material: Maps of Leeds and Yorkshire.

Illustrations of Yorkshire, mostly of the Leeds area (*c*32,000).

Leeds playbills (6000).

Wide range of printed transcripts and microfilm copies of parish registers.

Microfilm of Yorkshire census returns and Leeds newspapers.

Books and pamphlets on Leeds and Yorkshire or by local authors (*c*90,000).

Finding aids: Index to Leeds and Yorkshire items in newspapers and periodicals (incomplete). Index to illustrations. Index to census returns: Yorkshire by town and village, Leeds Metropolitan District by street names.

Facilities: Photocopying. Photography. Microfilm printer.

Publications: Leeds City Libraries: *Guide to Local and Family History* and *Guide to Census Enumerator's Returns, Yorkshire.*

501 Leeds Diocesan Archives

Address: Leeds Diocesan Pastoral Centre, 62 Headingley Lane, Leeds, West Yorkshire LS6 2BU

Telephone: (0113) 244 2406

Fax: (0113) 244 2406

Enquiries: The Diocesan Archivist, Very Rev. Mgr G.T. Bradley
The Assistant Archivist, Mr Robert Finnigan

Open: Mon–Fri: 10.00–4.00, by appointment.

Access: Bona fide students, by written application to the Archivist.

Historical background: The collection is part of the archives of the Vicars Apostolic of the Northern District (1688–1840) and the papers of the Vicar Apostolic of the Yorkshire District (1840–50), the Bishop of Beverley (1850–78) and the Bishops of Leeds (1878-).

Acquisitions policy: The records of the Diocese of Leeds are all eventually passed to the Diocesan Archives; also deposited are any records of importance from parishes in the diocese. The registers of certain parishes established before 1900 have been microfilmed.

Major collections: Papers of the Roman Catholic Church in Yorkshire, 1688– ; some papers for other parts of the North of England before 1840.

Hogarth MSS: 19th-century transcripts of the papers of the secular clergy in Yorkshire, 1660– .

Non-manuscript material: Printed pastorals of bishops and miscellaneous diocesan publications.

Small collection of theological pamphlets for the period of the archives.

Finding aids: Some lists and indexes (1821–61); other parts are in the process of being catalogued.

Facilities: Photocopying by arrangement. Microfiche reader.

Conservation: Contracted out.

Publications: G.T. Bradley: 'Leeds Diocesan Archives: a Provisional Summary', *Newsletter for Students of Recusant History*, 4 (Nijmegen, 1962), 26.

——: 'The Leeds Diocesan Archives', *Catholic Archives*, 2 (1982), 46–51.

502 Leeds University Library
Brotherton Library

Address: Woodhouse Lane, Leeds, West Yorkshire LS2 9JT

A Special Collections

Telephone: (0113) 233 5518

Fax: (0113) 233 5561

E-mail: special-collections@library.leeds.ac.uk

Website: www.leeds.ac.uk/library/spcoll

Enquiries: The University Librarian and Keeper of the Brotherton Collection
The Head of Special Collections, Mr C.D.W. Sheppard

Open: Mon–Thurs: 9.00–7.00; Fri: 9.30–7.00 (no document delivery after 5.00); Sat: 10.00–1.00.

Access: Open to all at the discretion of the Librarian. Non-members of the university should apply in advance to the Librarian and should provide a letter of introduction from a person of recognised status if so required.

Historical background: The university library, of which the Brotherton Library forms part, began as the library of the Yorkshire College in 1874.

Acquisitions policy: General, with a bias towards the research interests of the university.

Major collections: Archives of West Riding wool textile manufacturers, mainly 18th century– ; Dean and Chapter of Ripon, medieval; various Yorkshire Quaker meetings, 17th century– ; Leeds Chamber of Commerce, 19th century– ; Leeds Philosophical and Literary Society, 19th and 20th centuries; Association of Education Committees, 20th century.
Woolley Hall estate papers, medieval.
Roth MSS on Jewish history and culture, medieval.
Papers and diaries of Herbert Thompson, music critic, 19th and 20th centuries.
Correspondence of Jethro Bithell, mainly with mid-20th-century German writers.
Papers of John Wilson of Broomhead, near Sheffield, antiquarian, 18th century.
Leeds Russian Archive, 20th century.
Miscellaneous cookery and recipe books, 16th century– ; medical treatises and papers, 18th century– .

Diaries, letters and papers of various professors and other members of the university staff, 19th and 20th centuries.

Papers of Lord Boyle, and other political papers, 20th century.

Leeds Queen's Square and Park Square art gallery archives, 20th century.

Finding aids: Various handlists.

Facilities: Photocopying. Photography. Microfilming. Microfilm/fiche reader.

Conservation: In-house

Publications: C. Roth: 'Catalogue of Manuscripts in the Roth Collection', *Alexander Marx Jubilee Volume: English Section* (1950), 503–35.

P. Hudson: *The West Riding Wool Textile Industry: a Catalogue of Business Records* (1975).

B The Brotherton Collection

Historical background: The basis of the collection is the private library of Lord Brotherton of Wakefield (1856–1930), presented to the university 'for the Nation' shortly after his death. It is now greatly increased in size through subsequent purchases from endowed funds and through further gifts. Since 1993 the Brotherton Collection has been amalgamated with the other special collections of the university library, but for historical and funding reasons it retains a degree of autonomy.

Acquisitions policy: Major current collecting fields are: English drama and poetry, 1600–1750, and material from this period relating to travel, science, language, translation, and political and economic thought; 19th- and 20th-century literary MSS and printed books; Romany subjects.

Major collections: Literary MSS, especially verse miscellanies, 17th and 18th centuries.

MSS of 19th century writers, including the Arnolds, the Brontës, A.C. Swinburne (1837–1909) and George Borrow (1803–81).

Marrick Priory deeds and charters, 12th century– .

Archives of the Loder-Symonds family and Henry Marten (1602–80), regicide.

Papers of Thomas Townshend, 1st Viscount Sydney (1733–1800); the Novello and Cowden-Clarke families, 19th century.

MSS and correspondence of Sir Edmund Gosse (1849–1928), P.H. Gosse (1810–88) and Dr Philip Gosse, 1867–1928; Edward Clodd (1840–1930); W.W. Gibson; Lascelles Abercrombie (1881–1938); John Drinkwater (1882–1937); W.R.M. Childe; Bonamy Dobrée; Francis Berry and G. Wilson Knight and many contemporary British poets.

Correspondence of Bram Stoker (1847–1912) and Sir Henry Irving (1838–1905); Henry Arthur Jones (1851–1929); G.A. Sala (1828–96); Clement Shorter (1857–1926).

Papers of Arthur Ransome (1884–1967).

Letters and MSS of Mendelssohn.

Correspondence files of the *New Statesman*, 1914–19.

Archives of the *London Magazine*, 1972– , and *Strand*, 1952– .

Documents relating to the Chevalier D'Eon.

Papers of T.W. Thompson, gypsy scholar.

Non-manuscript material: Some paintings and other artefacts, particularly in Romany and Novello & Cowden-Clarke collections.

Finding aids: Many lists and indexes.

Facilities: Photocopying. Photography. Microfilming. Microfilm/fiche reader.

Conservation: In-house.

Publications: J.S. Symington: *The Brotherton Library: a Catalogue of Ancient Manuscripts and Early Printed Works Collected by Edward Allen, Baron Brotherton of Wakefield* (Leeds, 1931).

Annual Report of the Brotherton Collection Committee (1936–).

A Catalogue of the Gosse Correspondence in the Brotherton Collection 1867 to 1928 (Leeds, 1950).

The Novello Cowden-Clarke Collection (Leeds, 1955).

Catalogue of the Romany Collection formed by D.U. McGrigor Phillips LL.D and Presented to the University of Leeds (Edinburgh, 1962).

D.I. Masson: 'The Brotherton Collection of Rare Books and Manuscripts', *University of Leeds Review*, xxi (1978), 135.

The Brotherton Collection, University of Leeds: its Collections Described with Illustrations of Fifty Books and Manuscripts (Leeds, 1986).

The Brotherton Collection Review (1989–) [triennial account of selected new acquisitions].

C The Liddle Collection

Telephone: (0133) 335566

Fax: (0133) 335561

Enquiries: The University Librarian
The Head of Special Collections

Open: Generally open to the public, by appointment.

Access: Open to all at the discretion of the Librarian. Non-members of the university should apply in advance to the Librarian and should provide a letter of introduction from a person of recognised status if so required.

Historical background: The collection, which dates from 1964, was conceived by Dr Peter Liddle as a source of original material for research on World War I, with a particular emphasis on the personal experience of individuals involved in the conflict. In 1988 the collection was acquired by the university library.

Acquisitions policy: Any original documentary material in the form of letters, diaries, artwork, scrapbooks and official papers, and also maps, books, artefacts, souvenirs, weapons and uniforms relating to 1914–18 and the period immediately before and after World War I. Also MS, typescript and tape-recorded recollections of personal experience in any aspect of the war. The domestic front and conscientious objection are areas considered as significant as the fighting fronts.

Major collections: The 1914–18 papers and/or recollections of over 6000 veterans (many men and women of outstanding eminence).

Non-manuscript material: Large newspaper collection of national, local, army and navy, and foreign issues, with many unusual specialist items, including trench news sheets.

Map collection for all the fighting fronts.

Museum collection of uniforms, weapons, souvenirs and various artefacts.

Tape-recorded recollections of all areas of personal experience in the war.

Finding aids: Lists and leaflets. Developing database of holdings. Card index to tape-recordings; transcripts in progress. Lists for the newspapers, maps and museum collections.

Facilities: Photocopying. Photography.

Conservation: Contracted out.

Publications: The Poppy and the Owl (1990–), [Journal for the Friends of the Liddle Collection].

D University Archives

Address: Baines Wing, University of Leeds, Leeds, West Yorkshire LS2 9JT

Telephone: (0113) 233 5061

E-mail: m.a.s.shipway@leeds.ac.uk

Website: www.leeds.ac.uk/library/spcoll/archive/index.htm

Enquiries: Assistant Archivist, Mark Shipway

Open: Mon–Thurs: 9.00–5.00; Fri: 9.30–5.00, preferably by appointment.

Access: Bona fide researchers, preferably by appointment. Some university records are subject to a 30-year closure and certain other records are restricted at the request of donors.

Historical background: The Yorkshire College of Science, precursor of the University of Leeds, was founded in 1874 and merged with the Leeds School of Medicine (f. 1831) in 1884 to become one of the constituent colleges of the Victoria University in 1887. The University of Leeds was created an independent institution in 1904 and the university archives were established in 1977.

Acquisitions policy: Administrative and teaching records and papers of the University of Leeds and such personal papers as may be appropriate.

Archives of organisation: Records of Leeds School of Medicine, 1831–84; Yorkshire College (of Science), 1874–1903; University of Leeds, 1904– , including administrative, committee, academic, staff and student records.

Major collections: Personal papers of former members of staff, including Rt. Hon. Lord Boyle of Handsworth, Vice-Chancellor, 1970–81; Archibald Durwald, Professor of Anatomy, 1936–64; Albert Hemingway, Professor of Physiology, 1936–67; Frank Maudsley Parsons, Urological Surgery/Renal Medicine, 1951–83; Leslie Norman Pyrah, Professor of Urological Surgery, 1956–64; Frank Smith, Professor of Education, 1933–47; Frederick William Spiers, Professor of Medical Physics, 1950–72.

Non-manuscript material: Photographs; building plans, printed material.

Finding aids: Various lists and indexes in process of compilation.

Facilities: Photocopying. Photography.

Conservation: Undertaken by the Conservation Unit of the University Library, or contracted out.

Publications: P.H.J.H. Gosden and A.J.Taylor (eds): *Studies in the History of a University 1874–1974: to Commemorate the Centenary of the University of Leeds* (Leeds, 1975).

503 Museum of the History of Education

Parent organisation: University of Leeds

Address: Parkinson Court, University of Leeds, Leeds, West Yorkshire LS2 9JT

Telephone: (0113) 233 4665

Fax: (0113) 233 4541

E-mail: museum@education.leeds.ac.uk

Website: http://education.leeds.ac.uk/edu/inted/museum.htm

Enquiries: The Curator, Dr E.J. Foster

Open: Mon–Fri: 2.00–4.30; Wed: 2.00–4.30; Thurs: 9.30–12.30, 1.30–4.30.

Access: Generally open to the public, by arrangement.

Historical background: The University of Leeds was founded as the Yorkshire College in 1874. The museum was established in the 1950s, aimed at the documentation of the history of education and the promotion of research and publication.

Acquisitions policy: Acquires children's work, equipment, artefacts and books to illustrate the history of education.

Major collections: Children's exercise books, 17th century– .
Trainee teachers' work and records of their progress.
Records of education societies and material concerning education in the former West Riding of Yorkshire, 1902–74.

Non-manuscript material: Children's practical work, including needlework.
School textbooks, 17th century– .
Examples of science teaching apparatus and school furniture.

Finding aids: Computerised catalogue in progress.

Facilities: Photocopying. Photography. Microfilm/fiche readers.

504 Royal Armouries Library

Parent organisation: Trustees of the Royal Armouries/Department of Culture, Media and Sport

Address: Royal Armouries, Armouries Drive, Leeds, West Yorkshire LS10 1LT

Telephone: (0113) 220 1832

Fax: (0113) 220 1934

E-mail: library@armouries.org.uk

Website: www.armouries.org.uk

Enquiries: The Librarian, Philip Abbott

Open: Mon–Fri: 10.30–4.30.

Access: Generally open to the public. Some records are restricted.

Historical background: The Royal Armouries is the national collection of arms and armour. The collections grew steadily from the 18th century. Until its abolition in 1855 the Board of Ordnance, with its headquarters in the Tower of London, designed and tested prototypes and organised the production of huge quantities of regulation weapons of many sorts. Examples of most types survive in the Royal Armouries today. It moved to Leeds from the Tower of London and opened in a newly designed building in 1996.

Acquisitions policy: Records relating to the Royal Armouries and its collections, and to the history and use of arms and armour.

Archives of organisation: Archives of the Royal Armouries Museum, Leeds.

Archives of the Royal Armouries (active files only; inactive files at the Tower of London).

Major collections: Papers of collectors and scholars of arms and armour, 19th and 20th centuries, including Seymour Wilkinson, Rolf Muller, Richard Williams, Noel Corry, John Hayward.

Non-manuscript material: Photographic library: black and white prints (c40000); colour transparencies (c3000); slides (c15,000); films and videos (c100).

Facilities: Photocopying. Microfilm/fiche reader. In-house photographic department.

Conservation: Contracted out.

505 Thoresby Society

Address: Claremont, 23 Clarendon Road, Leeds, West Yorkshire LS2 9NZ

Enquiries: The Hon. Librarian

Open: Tues, Thurs: 10.00–12.00 (except Tues following a bank holiday).

Access: Members of the society; others on written application.

The Thoresby Society was founded in 1889 to foster interest in the history of Leeds and district; it collects relevant MSS, pictures, maps and plans and printed material. A catalogue, lists and indexes are available. The society publishes monographs, editions of records and articles relating to the history of Leeds and district: *Publications of the Thoresby Society's* vols I–LXIII (1889–1990); Second Series, vol. I–(1991–).

506 West Yorkshire Archive Service: Leeds

Parent organisation: West Yorkshire Joint Services

Address: Chapeltown Road, Sheepscar, Leeds, West Yorkshire LS7 3AP

Telephone: (0113) 214 5814

Fax: (0113) 214 5815

E-mail: leeds@wyjs.org.uk

Website: www.archives.wyjs.org.uk

Enquiries: The Principal District Archivist, Mr W.J. Connor

Open: Tues–Fri: 9.30–5.00 (limited service 12.00–2.00).
Annual stock–taking closure usually early February and early November; generally closed on the day following public holidays. An appointment is essential.

Access: Bona fide researchers, subject to any restrictions laid down by depositors. A paid research service is available.

Historical background: The office was established in 1938 in Leeds City Reference Library, where manuscripts had been collected since the late 19th century. It moved to its present premises in 1965 and became part of the West Yorkshire Archive Service in 1982. It does not incorporate a printed local history collection. As one of the few offices established in the West Riding before 1974, its collections derive from a much wider geographical area than might be expected, including Craven, Ripon and Harrogate as well as the heartland of the present West Yorkshire. It is a Diocesan Record Office for the dioceses of Bradford and Ripon and is recognised as a place of deposit for public records.

Acquisitions policy: Archives of all kinds arising within the local authority area or associated with existing holdings.

Archives of organisation: Leeds City Council and absorbed authorities, 1662– , including the boroughs and districts of Aireborough, Garforth, Horsforth, Morley, Otley, Pudsey, Rothwell, Wetherby and Wharfedale.

Major collections: Family and estate archives, including Baines family of Leeds, 1784–1890, notably Edward Baines (1774–1848), Matthew Talbot Baines (1799–1860) and Sir Edward Baines (1800–90); Gascoigne family of Parlington; Gossip and Hatfield families of Thorp Arch, 1558–1970; Earls of Harewood, notably papers of George Canning, 1780–1827, Earl Canning, 1833–62, and Marquises of Clanricarde, 1816–1910; Ingilby family of Ripley Castle; Lane Fox family of Bramham Park; Earls of Mexborough, notably correspondence of Sir John Reresby, 1639–88; Newby Hall Estate, notably London Port Books, 1717–20, and correspondence of 1st and 2nd Lords Grantham, 1736–1801; Nostell Priory; Ramsden family of Byram, notably Rockingham and Fitzwilliam correspondence, 1765–1801, and Sir J.W. Ramsden (1831–1914); Samuel Smiles (1812–1904), papers; Studley Royal Estate, notably Fountains Abbey monastic records, 12th century–1540, and correspondence of 1st and 2nd Lords Grantham, 1725–71; Temple Newsam (Ingram family and estate), notably English and Irish customs accounts, 1604–45, the Commissary of Minorca, 1735–55, and records of the Council of the North, 1585–1636.

Antiquarian collections include Bacon Frank, J.E.F. Chambers (including Plumpton family) and papers of William Farrer.

Business records include T. and M. Bairstow of Sutton in Craven, worsted manufacturers, 1801–1964; British Coal, pre-vesting date records for North Yorkshire Area; Burton group of Leeds, clothing manufacturers, notably papers of Sir Montague Burton, 1896–1952; Fairbairn Lawson of Leeds, engineers, 1843–1980; Ford Ayrton of Bentham, silk spinners,

1871–1971; Grand Theatre and Opera House, Leeds, 1876– ; Greenwood and Batley of Leeds, engineers, 1856–1969; Hathorn Davey of Leeds, pump manufacturers, 1852–1939; Kirkstall Forge of Leeds, engineers, 1752– ; Leeds Industrial Co-operative Society, 1847– ; Middleton Colliery of Leeds, 1760–1907; Joshua Tetley of Leeds, brewers, 1786– ; John Waddington of Leeds, printers and games manufacturers, 1907– ; John Wilson of Leeds, linen manufacturers, 1754–1836; Yorkshire Patent Steam Waggon Co. of Leeds, 1903–53; and solicitors' and estate agents' papers.

Ecclesiastical records of Anglican and non-conformist churches, including Diocese of Ripon and Archdeaconry of Richmond, 1474– , deposited parish records and Yorkshire Congregational Union, 1812– .

Records of charities and societies include Arthington Trust, Conchological Society of Great Britain and Northern Ireland, Leeds Institute, Yorkshire Ladies' Council of Education, Yorkshire Naturalists' Union.

Non-manuscript material: Many photographs, usually associated with archives, such as surveys of slum clearance area, civil engineering projects, industrial processes and products.

Finding aids: Card indexes of names, places and probate records. Links to West Yorkshire Archive Service and NRA computerised databases. Catalogues sent to NRA.

Facilities: Photocopying. Photography. Microfilm/fiche readers. Ultra-violet lamp.

Conservation: In-house department which undertakes outside work.

Publications: A Brief Guide to Yorkshire Record Offices (1968).

P. Hudson: *The West Riding Wool Textile Industry: a Catalogue of Business Records* (1975).

J.M. Collinson: *Sources of Business and Industrial History in the Leeds Archives Department* (Leeds, 1977).

——: 'The Leeds Archives Department', *Northern History,* xv (1979), 210.

Leeds Archives, 1938–1988: an Illustrated Guide to Leeds District Archives (Wakefield, 1988).

West Yorkshire Archive Service: *Guide for Family Historians* (1992).

507 West Yorkshire Archive Service: Yorkshire Archaeological Society

Address: Claremont, 23 Clarendon Road, Leeds, West Yorkshire LS2 9NZ

Telephone: (0113) 245 6362

Fax: (0113) 244 1979

Website: www.wyjs.org.uk

Enquiries: Senior Librarian and Archivist, Mr R.L. Frost
The Principal District Archivist, Mr W.J. Connor

Open: Tues, Wed: 2.00–8.30; Thurs –Sat: 10.00–5.00.

Access: Generally open to the public; an appointment is necessary. A limited paid research service is available, subject to availability of staff time.

Historical background: The society was formed in 1863 and has built up extensive collections of books and documents relating to the whole of Yorkshire. From 1976 to 1982 the society's archives were administered by West Yorkshire County Council, and since 1982 they have formed part of the West Yorkshire Archive Service, which seconds staff from its headquarters in Wakefield (entry 1184). The Thoresby Society (entry 505) operates from the same address.

Acquisitions policy: To acquire items additional to collections already held, material relating to Yorkshire as a whole, antiquarian MSS and the results of research and fieldwork carried out by society members.

Archives of organisation: The society's own records, 1863– .

Major collections: Estate and family archives, including Osborne, Duke of Leeds; Clifford of Skipton; Slingsby of Scriven; Fawkes of Farnley; Lister, Lord Ribblesdale of Gisburn; Middleton of Stockeld; Beaumont, Viscount Allendale of Bretton; Clarke-Thornhill of Fixby.
Manorial, most notably Wakefield court rolls, 1274–1940s.
Leeds Freemasons' records, 18th–20th centuries.
Antiquarian collections, including those of the Horsley family, herald painters, 16th–17th centuries; Roger Dodsworth, 17th century; Ralph

Thoresby (1658–1725), historian of Leeds, and Joseph Hunter, historian of South Yorkshire.

Non-manuscript material: The society maintains an extensive library of Yorkshire books, prints, maps and photographs.

Finding aids: Lists and indexes. Link to West Yorkshire Archive Service computer database. Lists sent to NRA.

Facilities: Photocopying. Microfilm/fiche readers.

Conservation: Undertaken at West Yorkshire Archive Service HQ.

Publications: E.W. Crossley: *Catalogue of Manuscripts and Deeds in the Library of the Yorkshire Archaeological Society, 1867–1931* (2/1931; R1986).
S. Thomas: 'The Archives of the Yorkshire Archaeological Society', *Yorkshire Archaeological Journal*, lvi (1984).
——: *Guide to the Archive Collections of the Yorkshire Archaeological Society, 1931–1983, and to Collections Deposited with the Society* (Wakefield, 1985).

508 Record Office for Leicestershire, Leicester and Rutland

Parent organisation: Leicestershire County Council, Leicester City Council and Rutland County Council

Address: Long Street, Wigston Magna, Leicester LE18 2AH

Telephone: (0116) 257 1080

Fax: (0116) 257 1120

E-mail: recordoffice@leics.gov.uk

Website: www.leics.gov.uk

Enquiries: The County Archivist, Mr Carl Harrison

Open: Mon, Tues, Thurs: 9.15–5.00; Wed: 9.15–7.30; Fri: 9.15–4.45; Sat: 9.15–12.15.

Access: Generally open to the public. The office operates the CARN reader's ticket system. A paid research service is available.

Historical background: Archives were collected by Leicester Museum from 1849 and the City Museums Archives Department was set up in 1930. The County Record Office was established in 1947. With reorganisation in 1974 the Museums Archives Department was amalgamated with the County Record Office. In 1997 Leicester City Council and Rutland County Council became archive and library authorities (for their administrative areas, but continue to support the record office as a joint service). In 1992 the Leicestershire Collection, the county's local studies library, was amalgamated with the record office. The office also acts as the Diocesan Record Office for Leicester (parish records) and Peterborough (Rutland parish records) and is recognised as a place of deposit for public records.

Acquisitions policy: All appropriate archives and local studies resources for Leicestershire, Leicester and Rutland.

Archives of organisation: Usual local authority record holdings.

Major collections: Deposited local archive collections. Local studies library.

Non-manuscript material: Photographs, maps, film and sound collections, local studies library.

Finding aids: Archive lists/indexes. Lists sent to NRA. Local studies library catalogue.

Facilities: Photocopying. Photography. Microfilming. Microfilm/fiche readers/printers.

Conservation: In-house.

Publications: M. Bateson, H. Stocks and G.A. Chinnery: *Records of the Borough of Leicester, 1103–1835*, vols I–VII (1899–1974).

Brief Guide to the Muniment Room, City of Leicester Museum and Art Gallery (1949).

Handlist of the Records of the Leicester Archdeaconry (1954).

A.M. Woodcock: *Records of the Corporation of Leicester* (1956).

H. Broughton: *Village History in Records* (1982).

G. Jones: *Quarter Sessions Records in the Leicestershire Record Office* (1985).

J. Farrel: *A Guide to Tracing your Family Tree in the Leicestershire Record Office* (1987).

G. Jones: *The Descent to Dissent: a Guide to the Nonconformist Records at the Leicestershire Record Office* (1989).

H.E. Broughton: *Family and Estate Records in the Leicestershire Record Office* (2/1991).

509 University of Leicester Library

Parent organisation: University of Leicester

Address: PO Box 248, University Road, Leicester LE1 9QD

Telephone: (0116) 252 2046

Fax: (0116) 252 2066

E-mail: library@leicester.ac.uk

Website: www.le.ac.uk/li/

Enquiries: The Stack Librarian

Open: Mon–Fri: 9.00– 5.00.

Access: Any registered readers. External readers should give prior notification of their visit.

Historical background: The university was founded in 1921. University archives are kept separately; contact Ms M.G. Clark.

Acquisitions policy: It is not a primary goal of the library to build up extensive archival collections. Acquisitions are occasionally made by purchase or donation, where these complement existing strengths, or where there are strong local connections.

Archives of organisation: Archives of Leicester University Library.

Major collections: Papers of Sir B.C. Brodie (1817–80), Waynflete Professor of Chemistry at Oxford.
Capital Guarantee Society: minutes, correspondence, registers of borrowers, share certificates, 1874–1914.
Robert Benson Dockray, resident engineer of the London & Birmingham Railway and L&NWR: journal, 1850–60 (3 vols), and commonplace book, 1852–69.
Papers of Joe Orton (1933–67), playwright.
Correspondence between Laura (Riding) Jackson and George Fraser, 1971–80.

Finding aids: Brief catalogue. Brodie papers: NRA 9991. Lists sent to NRA. Catalogue of the Joe Orton Collection.

Facilities: Photocopying. Photography by arrangement. Microfilm/fiche/card readers.

Conservation: Small in-house conservation unit; other work contracted out.

Publications: B. Burch and J. Clark: *A Handlist of the Manuscript Collection* (Leicester University Library, 1998).

B. Burch: *The University of Leicester: a History, 1921–1996* (University of Leicester, 1996).

510 Wigan Archives Service

Parent organisation: Wigan Council

Address: Town Hall, Leigh, Lancashire WN7 2DY

Telephone: (01942) 404430

Fax: (01942) 404425

E-mail: heritage@wigannbc.gov.uk

Website: www.wigannbc.gov.uk

Enquiries: The Archivist, Mr N.P. Webb

Open: Mon, Tues, Thurs, Fri: 10.00–1.00, 2.00–4.30, by appointment.

Access: Generally open to the public. NB Church registers are normally shown on microfilm only, and these are now accessible at the History Shop, Library Street, Wigan WN1 1DG, not at the Archives Service.

Historical background: Wigan Record Office was established in 1968 to serve the former Wigan County Borough. In 1974, when the present Wigan Metropolitan Borough was created, the office moved to larger premises in Leigh. In 1989 the office became part of the new Wigan Heritage Service, which also includes local history libraries and museums, and the title Archives Service was adopted. The service acts as Diocesan Record Office for Liverpool (parish records), and is approved as a place of deposit for public, manorial and tithe records.

Acquisitions policy: Records relating to the locality, by deposit or gift.

Archives of organisation: Records of the old borough, including charters, court leet, 1626–1834, borough sessions, 1733–1971, burgess lists and accounts.
Records of Wigan Municipal and County Borough, 1835–1974; the other pre-1974 constituent authorities, including Leigh Municipal Borough and civil townships, 17th–19th centuries.

Major collections: Family and estate archives, including Anderton, Dicconson, Earls of Crawford, Holt Leigh, Scarisbrick, Standish.
Wigan Grammar School.
Wigan and Leigh Boards of Guardians.
Hospital records, pre-1948.

Records of solicitors, businesses and societies. Motor vehicle licensing files and indexes. Edward Hall Collection of diaries.

Non-manuscript material: Local photographic collection of regional significance.
Comprehensive OS map collection for the locality.
Census microforms, 1841–91, for the present Metropolitan Borough area.

Finding aids: Most collections have been listed and indexed.

Facilities: Photocopying. Photography. Microfilming. Microform readers.

Conservation: Mostly contracted out.

Publications: Guide to the Archives (1996).
Guide to Genealogical Sources (1994).
Past Forward Heritage Service free magazine [thrice yearly].
Information leaflets (free); local history publications programme (list available).

511 Shetland Archives

Parent organisation: Shetland Islands Council

Address: 44 King Harald Street, Lerwick, Shetland ZE1 0EQ

Telephone: (01595) 696247

Fax: (01595) 696533

E-mail: shetland.archives@zetnet.co.uk

Enquiries: The Archivist, Mr Brian Smith

Open: Mon–Thurs: 9.00–5.00; Fri: 9.00–4.00. Closed on local public holidays.

Access: Generally open to the public. An appointment is preferable but not essential.

Historical background: The archives department was founded in 1976 and is now part of the leisure and recreation department of Shetlands Islands Council.

Acquisitions policy: Records and oral material relating to Shetland.

Archives of organisation: Usual local authority record holdings, 1750– .

Major collections: Deposited collections, 16th century– ; Crown records, including sheriff court, customs and excise and procurator fiscal, 15th century– .

Non-manuscript material: Oral history collections, with transcripts.

Finding aids: Lists, many available on computer with text-search facilities.

Facilities: Photocopying. Photography. Microfilm reader/printer.

Publications: H. Ballantyre and B. Smith (eds.): *Shetland Documents 1195–1579* (Lerwick, 1994).
——: *Shetland Documents 1580–1611,* (Lerwick, 1994).

512 United Distillers & Vintners Archive

Parent organisation: Diageo plc

Address: Balfour Building, Banbeath, Leven, Fife KY8 5HD

Telephone: (01333) 433040

Fax: (01333) 423915

E-mail: c.jones@guinness.com

Enquiries: The Archivist, Christine Jones

Open: Mon–Fri: 9.00–5.00.

Access: At the discretion of the company: to approved researchers, on written application; to interested members of the public, by postal or telephone enquiry only.

Historical background: In 1987 Distillers Company Ltd (formed 1877) was acquired by Guinness plc (entry 625) and United Distillers plc emerged as the spirits division of Guinness plc. In 1997 Guinness plc and GrandMet merged to form Diageo plc, and International Distillers & Vintners (of GrandMet) merged with United Distillers to become United Distillers & Vintners.

Acquisitions policy: To strengthen the existing collection as evidence of the activities and achievements of the company and its brands worldwide.

Archives of organisation: Archives of Distillers Company Ltd, 1877– ; United Distillers plc, 1987– ; United Distillers & Vintners 1997– , including minutes, letter books, sales records, awards, plans and production records.
Archives of constituent distilling, blending, bottling & trading companies including John Walker & Sons (f.1820), John Dewar & Sons (f.1846), James Buchanan & Co. (f. 1885) & Tanqueray Gordon & Co. (f. 1898).

Non-manuscript material: Advertising and art-work; labels; bottles; artefacts; photographs; films and videos.

Finding aids: Database. Photo-CD. CD-Rom.

Facilities: Photocopying. Photography.

Conservation: Contracted out.

513 East Sussex Record Office

Address: The Maltings, Castle Precincts, Lewes, East Sussex BN7 1YT

Telephone: (01273) 482349

Fax: (01273) 482341

E-mail: archives@eastsussexcc.gov.uk

Website: www.eastsussexcc.gov.uk/archives/mainstop.htm

Enquiries: The County Archivist, Mrs Elizabeth Hughes

Open: Mon, Tues, Thurs: 8.45–4.45; Wed: 9.30–4.45; Fri: 8.45–4.15.
Second Sat of each month, please enquire.

Access: Generally open to the public. The office operates the CARN reader's ticket system. A paid research service is available.

Historical background: The office was established in 1949. It also acts as a Diocesan Record Office for Chichester (East Sussex parish records), houses Sussex Archaeological Society records, and is recognised as a place of deposit for public records

Acquisitions policy: All appropriate material for the East Sussex area.

Archives of organisation: Usual local authority record holdings.

Major collections: Deposited collections, including the following which have a wider significance:
Sheffield Park archives concerning John Baker Holroyd, 1st Earl of Sheffield, politician and authority on commercial and agricultural topics, late 18th century.
Sussex Archaeological Society records, including papers of the Gage family (American material) and the Fuller family of Rosehill (West Indian material).

Non-manuscript material: Usual local history collection.

Finding aids: Catalogues. Lists. Indexes.

Facilities: Photocopying. Microfiching by arrangement. Microform reader/printer.

Conservation: In-house.

Publications: *Descriptive Report on the Quarter Sessions, other Official, and Ecclesiastical Records in the Custody of the County Councils of West and East Sussex* (1954).
F.W. Steer: *The Records of the Corporation of Seaford* (1959).
——: *Catalogue of the Shiffner Archives* (1959).
R.F. Dell: *Winchelsea Corporation Records* (1963).
——: *The Glynde Place Archives* (1964).
J.A. Woodbridge: *The Danny Archives* (1966).
H.M. Warne: *Catalogue of the Frewen Archives* (1972).
J.A. Brett: *Catalogue of the Battle Abbey Estate Archives* (1973).
——: *The Hickstead Place Archives* (1975)
——: *East Sussex Record Office: a Short Guide* (1988).
F.W. Steer: *The Ashburnham Archives* [out of print].
R.F. Dell: *The Records of Rye Corporation: a Catalogue* [out of print].

514 Festival Opera Archive

Address: Glyndebourne, Lewes, East Sussex BN8 5UU

Telephone: (01273) 812321 ext. 2214

Fax: (01273) 812783

E-mail: switchboard@glyndebourne.com

Website: www.glyndebourne.com

Enquiries: The Archivist, Julia Aries

Open: Mon–Fri: 9.30–5.30.

Access: Researchers, by prior appointment. A research fee is charged.

Historical background: Glyndebourne Festival Opera was founded in 1934 by John Christie (1882–1962) and his wife Audrey, and has become renowned for its annual festival. Glyndebourne Touring Opera was established in 1968, with Arts Council support, to encourage young singers and to take the festival's productions to a wider audience. The archive was set up in 1987.

Acquisitions policy: To acquire, by gift or purchase, all material relevant to the history of

Glyndebourne and the personnel connected with it.

Archives of organisation: Large collection of correspondence relating to the festival and touring opera companies, 1930s– .

Major collections: Material relating to James Atkins (1912–91), singer.

Non-manuscript material: Plans, posters, programmes, leaflets, press cuttings, recordings, videos, costume and set designs. Oral history interviews, in association with the National Sound Archive (entry 561D), with singers, conductors, former members of the administrative staff etc (*c*40). Black and white contact sheets (*c*170) and colour slides (2000) recording the demolition of the old theatre and building of the new Opera House, 1991–4.

Finding aids: Computer database for all Glyndebourne Festival productions and performers, 1934– . Many lists.

Facilities: Photocopying.

Publications: W. Blunt: *John Christie of Glyndebourne* (London, 1968).
S. Hughes: *Glyndebourne: a History of the Festival Opera* (London, 1981).
J. Julius Norwich: *Fifty Years of Glyndebourne: an Illustrated History* (London, 1985).
M. Binney and R. Runciman: *Glyndebourne: Building a Vision* (London, 1994).
P. Campion and R. Runciman: *Glyndebourne Recorded* (London, 1994).

515 Museum of the Staffordshire Regiment

Address: Whittington Barracks, Lichfield, Staffordshire WS14 9PY

Telephone: (0121) 311 3229

Fax: (0121) 311 3205

E-mail: museum@rhq.fsnet.co.uk

Enquiries: The Curator

Open: Tues–Fri: 10.00–4.00, by arrangement.

Access: Archive open to the public, by appointment only. A donation to the Museum Trust is requested.

The Staffordshire Regiment (the Prince of Wales's) incorporates the former South and North Staffordshire regiments, which were amalgamated in 1959. Its origins go back to four numbered regiments of foot, formed in 1705

(38th), 1756 (64th), 1793 (80th) and 1824 (98th). In 1782 the 38th was given the subsidiary title '(1st Staffordshire)' and the 64th '(2nd Staffordshire)'. The 80th adopted 'Staffordshire Volunteers' on formation. The 98th was designated 'Prince of Wales's' in 1876. Under the Cardwell Army Reforms of 1881 the 38th and 80th amalgamated to form the South Staffordshire Regiment and the 64th and 98th became the North. The archive does not hold personal records of soldiers (except for the 80th, from 1817 to mid-1914) and has very few original documents dating from before 1815. Histories and copies of documents refer back to 1705. There is a photograph collection. Lists and indexes are available and there are photocopying and photography facilities.

516 Samuel Johnson Birthplace Museum

Parent organisation: Lichfield City Council

Address: Breadmarket Street, Lichfield, Staffordshire WS13 6LG

Telephone: (01543) 264972

Fax: (01543) 258441

E-mail: sjmuseum@lichfield.gov.uk

Website: www.lichfield.gov.uk

Enquiries: The Museums and Heritage Officer, Annette French

Open: Mon–Fri: 10.30–5.00.

Access: Generally open to the public, by appointment.

Historical background: The museum was opened in 1901. A large number of papers relating to Samuel Johnson (1709–84) was acquired in the first decade of the 20th century; these have subsequently been added to by donation and purchase.

Acquisitions policy: MS material relating to Samuel Johnson, especially his family, and other eminent citizens, including Anna Seward (1747–1809) and David Garrick (1717–79), actor.

Major collections: A.C. Reade Collection: documents and papers relating to Johnson's family.
Lichfield and Johnson papers collected by Thomas George Lomax.
Papers relating to Johnson and Jacob Tonson.
Anna Seward papers.
Gregory King (1648–1712), statistical papers.

Non-manuscript material: Large library relating to Johnson and the 18th century, including association copies.

Conservation: Contracted out.

Publications: K.K. Yung: *Handlist of Manuscripts and Documents in the Johnson Birthplace Museum* (1972).

517 Staffordshire and Stoke-on-Trent Archive Service
Lichfield Record Office

Parent organisation: Staffordshire County Council and Stoke-on-Trent City Council

Address: Lichfield Library, The Friary, Lichfield, Staffordshire WS13 6QG

Telephone: (01543) 510720

Fax: (01543) 510715

E-mail: lichfield.record.office@staffordshire.gov.uk

Website: www.staffordshire.gov.uk/archives/lich.htm

Enquiries: The Archivist-in-charge, Mr Martin Sanders

Open: Mon Fri: 9.30–5.00, by arrangement.

Access: Generally open to the public, by appointment only.

Historical background: The office was established in 1959 as a branch of the Staffordshire Record Office to house the Lichfield probate and, on completion of purpose-built accommodation in 1968, diocesan records, since when it has been jointly financed by the Lichfield City (now District) and Staffordshire County councils. It is now run as part of the Staffordshire & Stoke-on-Trent Archive Service. It also acts as the Diocesan Record Office for Lichfield, and is recognised as a place of deposit for public records.

Acquisitions policy: Archives from the City of Lichfield and Lichfield diocesan records.

Archives of organisation: Usual local authority record holdings.

Major collections: Lichfied diocesan archives. Deposited local collections relating to Lichfield and including Lichfield Cathedral archives.

Finding aids: Catalogues of diocesan and non-diocesan records; surname index to original wills; general subject index to non-diocesan records. Lists sent to NRA.

Facilities: Photocopying. Microfilming by arrangement. Microfilm/fiche readers.

Conservation: In-house at Staffordshire & Stoke-on-Trent Archive Services, Stoke (see entry 1139).

Publications: Staffordshire Record Office *Cumulative Hand List*, part 1: *Lichfield Joint Record Office, Diocesan, Probate and Church Commissioners Records* (2/1978).

518 Bishop Grosseteste College

Address: Newport, Lincoln, Lincolnshire LN1 3DY

Telephone: (01522) 527347 ext. 227

Fax: (01522) 530243

E-mail: registry@bgc.ac.uk

Website: www.wisdom.bgc.ac.uk

Enquiries: The Archivist, Mrs G. Moyes

Open: By arrangement. Seven days' notice by telephone is required.

Access: Bona fide students and researchers. There is no access to unlisted material and restricted access to some other material. Charges may be made for some services.

Historical background: Bishop Grosseteste College, a college of higher education specialising in primary education, was founded in 1862 as the Lincoln Diocesan Training College. Until 1998 it held the National Primary Education Archives including the papers of Robin Tanner, HMI (see Institute of Education, entry 653).

Acquisitions policy: To maintain the college archive and accept material of local interest.

Archives of organisation: College archives, 1862– ; including Governors' minutes, students records, photographs, artefacts and the College *Chronicle*, 1896– .

Major collections: Tom Baker Lincolnshire Collection: a local history collection of books and papers.

Finding aids: Internal indexes. Lists will be sent to NRA.

Facilities: Photocopying.

Conservation: Contracted out.

Publications: Papers of Robin Tanner, HMI, 1904–1989: a Summary List (Bishop Grosseteste College, 1993).

519 Lincolnshire Archives

Parent organisation: Lincolnshire County Council

Address: St Rumbold Street, Lincoln LN1 2EZ

Telephone: (01522) 526204

Fax: (01522) 530047

E-mail: archives@lincsdoc.demon.co.uk

Website: www.lincs-archives.com

Enquiries: The Principal Keeper, Mrs Susan Payne

Open: Mon: 1.00–7.00 (1.00–5.00 Nov–Feb); Tues–Fri: 9.00–5.00; Sat: 9.00–4.00.

Access: By reader's ticket only.

Historical background: A Diocesan Record Office was established in 1936 and Lincolnshire Archives Office was formally established in 1948. It also acts as the Diocesan Record Office for Lincoln, and is recognised as a place of deposit for public records.

Acquisitions policy: Documents, in any category, which are of lasting historical significance and relate to the county of Lincolnshire, are accepted either by gift or on indefinite loan.

Archives of organisation: Usual local authority record holdings.

Major collections: Deposited local and family collections, 11th century– .

Finding aids: Lists and indexes. Longer lists sent to NRA. CD-ROM titles.

Facilities: Photocopying. Digital photography. Microfilming. Microfilm/fiche reader.

Conservation: Full conservation service available; outside contracts accepted.

Publications: Archivist's Reports (1948–77; with indexes, 1948–68) [available from the office].
K. Major: *Handlist of the Records of the Bishop of Lincoln and of the Archdeacons of Lincoln and Stow* (1953).
D.M. Williamson: *Muniments of the Dean and Chapter of Lincoln* (1956).
Lincolnshire Archives: *Poor Law Union Records.*
Lincolnshire Archives: *Deposited Parish Registers and Bishops' Transcripts.*
Indexes, Genealogical Resources and Foster Library Catalogue (1998) [CD-ROM].
Indexes of Wills 1700–1900 [CD-ROM].
Guide to Collections, Archivists' Reports and Accessions 1948–1997 [CD-ROM].
Publications leaflet available.

520 Lincolnshire County Library

Parent organisation: Lincolnshire County Council

Address: Local Studies Section, Lincoln Central Library, Free School Lane, Lincoln LN1 2EZ

Telephone: (01522) 510800

Fax: (01522) 575011 (marked FAO: Local Studies)

E-mail: lincoln.library@lincolnshire.gov.uk

Website: www.lincolnshire.gov.uk

Enquiries: The Local Studies Librarian

Open: Mon–Fri: 9.30–7.00; Sat: 9.30–4.00. Tennyson Research Centre: by appointment only.

Access: Generally open to the public. A letter of authority is usually required for the Tennyson Research Centre.

Historical background: The Tennyson Research Centre was founded in 1964 following the deposit by the Tennyson Trustees. Since 1983 the collection has been owned by Lincolnshire County Council.

Acquisitions policy: Any material relating to Sir Joseph Banks (1743–1820), botanist, or Alfred, Lord Tennyson (1809–92).

Major collections: Joseph Banks Collection: MS material covering a range of subjects relating to Lincolnshire, the militia etc, including many letters to and from Banks (*c*700 items).
Tennyson Centre: correspondence between Tennyson and members of his family, and letters from Browning, Gladstone, Lear, Sullivan, FitzGerald etc (*c*8000 items); most complete MS of *In Memoriam*, plus MSS of Tennyson's plays, poems, extracts from poems etc; miscellaneous material, including day-books, diaries, journals, household account books, 19th century (mainly 1850–92).

Non-manuscript material: Joseph Banks Collection: topographical drawings of Lincolnshire by C. Nattes and others, late 18th century, commissioned by Banks (4 folio vols, *c*770 sketches); biographies of Banks together with copies of his works.

Tennyson Centre: proofs and trial-books of Tennyson's poems (*c*220 items); illustrations, including photographs by Julia Margaret Cameron (*c*100); sound recordings and tapes of Tennyson's works; music based on Tennyson's poetry; biographical and critical material, mainly monographs and pamphlets (*c*1200 items); Tennyson family library and collection of his works.

Finding aids: Banks: NRA 5342.

Facilities: Photocopying. Photography. Microfilm/fiche reader/printer.

Publications: The letters in the Banks Collection are included in W.R. Dawson (ed.): *The Banks Letters* (1958).

N. Campbell (comp.): *Tennyson in Lincoln: a Catalogue of the Collections in the Research Centre,* vol. 1: *The Family Libraries*; vol. 2: *Tennyson's Works, Biographies and Criticism, Parodies, Music, Illustrations* (Tennyson Society, 1971, 1973).

C.Y. Langand and E.F. Shannon (eds): *The Letters of Alfred, Lord Tennyson, 1821–1870* (1981, 1987).

521   Littlehampton Museum

Parent organisation: Littlehampton Town Council

Address: Manor House, Church Street, Littlehampton, West Sussex BN17 5EP

Telephone: (01903) 738100

Fax: (01903) 731690

E-mail: ian.friel@arun.gov.uk

Enquiries: The Curator, Dr I. Friel

Open: Tues–Sat: 10.30–4.30.

Access: Generally open to the public, on application one week in advance.

Historical background: The museum was founded in 1926 by the local Natural History and Archaeology Society and the Town Council. It was taken over in 1974 by Arun District Council and is now administered by Littlehampton Town Council. The museum's own archive was established in 1928 and a town photo archive in the 1930s.

Acquisitions policy: To add to collections on the town's and the district's history, with emphasis on seafaring and shipbuilding. Non-local material collected for maritime history and photography.

Archives of organisation: Documentation, including photographic prints and negatives, supporting the museum's collections, 1928– .

Major collections: Local history collection, including:
Records of the Romano-British villa excavation in Gosden Road and Angmering.
Transcripts of Capt. Robinson's history of the Robinson shipping family.
Company records of John Eede Bull & Sons.

Non-manuscript material: Maps of the harbour development, mid-18th century– .
Extensive ephemera collection.
Prints of railway charts and maps, mid-19th century– .
Photographs, prints and paintings concerning the history of the town.

Finding aids: Card index. Computerisation started in 1994.

Facilities: Photocopying. Photography by arrangement.

Publications: A *Littlehampton Chronology, 1945–1970* (1970).
Littlehampton. Archive photographs series (1998).

522   Athenaeum, Liverpool

Address: Church Alley, Liverpool L1 3DD

Telephone: (0151) 709 7770

Fax: (0151) 709 0418

E-mail: library@athena.force9.net

Website: www.athena.force9.co.uk

Enquiries: The Librarian

Open: Mon–Fri: 10.00–4.00.

Access: This is a private library for use by the proprietors. Facilities are made available to researchers on application in writing.

Historical background: Founded in 1797 as a literary and scientific institution, the Athenaeum contains a historic general library strong in local history.

Acquisitions policy: Acquisitions are now limited to works of local interest.

Major collections: Roscoe Collection: Renaissance Italian and English MSS collected by William Roscoe (1753–1831), historian.
Gladstone Collection: papers, documents and MSS relating to local history collected by Robert Gladstone (1866–1940).

Non-manuscript material: Liverpool playbills, 1773–1830 (22 vols).
Comprehensive collection of maps of Liverpool and district included in local collection.
Extensive pamphlet collection: J. Hampden Jackson economic pamphlets.
Bound single plays, mainly 18th century (100 vols).

Finding aids: Card and shelf catalogues; indexes to pamphlets and plays; handlist of maps.

Facilities: Limited photocopying. Microfiche reader.

Publications: Catalogue (1864; supplements, 1892, 1905).
R.W. MacKenna: *The Athenaeum* (Liverpool, 1928).
N. Carrick and E. L. Ashton: *The Athenaeum, Liverpool, 1797–1997* (Liverpool, 1998).

523 Crosby Library
Local History Unit

Parent organisation: Sefton Metropolitan Borough Council

Address: Crosby Library, Crosby Road North, Waterloo, Liverpool L22 0LQ

Telephone: (0151) 257 6401/6408

Fax: (0151) 330 5770

Enquiries: The Local History Librarian

Open: Mon, Tues, Fri: 10.00–5.00; Wed: 10.00–8.00; Thurs, Sat: 10.00–1.00.

Access: The local history unit is generally open to the public, but an appointment is recommended for detailed research, and for use of microfilm/fiche machines. All archives are available on application. There is a fee for postal enquiries for non-residents.

Historical background: Sefton Metropolitan Borough was formed after local government reorganisation in 1974. It combined the areas of Bootle, Crosby, and Southport with parts of

the West Lancashire District. Material relating to Southport is held at Southport Library (entry 1124).

Acquisitions policy: There is no active collecting policy, but archives are taken in on request.

Archives of organisation: Local government records of Bootle County Borough, Crosby Municipal Borough, Litherland Urban District and predecessor authorities.

Non-manuscript material: Newspapers, photographs, maps, film/audio, microfilm/fiche.

Finding aids: Handlists; index to newspapers. NRA 2553.

Facilities: Photocopying. Microfilm/fiche readers/printer.

Conservation: Contracted out.

Publications: Assorted local history titles; details on request.

524 Institute of Popular Music

Parent organisation: The University of Liverpool

Address: Roxby Building, Liverpool L69 3BX

Telephone: (0151) 794 3101

Fax: (0151) 794 2566

E-mail: ipm@liverpool.ac.uk

Website: www.liv.ac.uk/ipm

Enquiries: The Institute Secretary, Ms Natasha Gay

Open: By arrangement.

Access: University members of staff and approved external readers, on written application and by appointment.

Historical background: The Institute of Popular Music was set up in 1988 with a particular interest in broadening the academic study of popular music.

Acquisitions policy: Actively develops undergraduate and research collections (books, journals, sound recordings) in the area of popular music, through donations from private collections, record stations and libraries.

Non-manuscript material: Robert Pring-Mill Collection: selection of printed material, cassettes and vinyl discs on Spanish American political song.

Robert Shelton Collection: personal library of writings, books, records and research material of the late author and journalist, including the entire collection of Shelton's American writing, 1958–68.

Large sound archive including rock and pop albums (c5000), jazz albums (5000), soul and dance albums (1000) and a large collection of country, folk and blues records, as well as soundtracks, comedy and pre-1950s popular music.

Finding aids: Database of the Robert-Pring Mill Collection.

Facilities: Photocopying.

Publications: Album Covers from the Vinyl Junkyard (Booth-Clibborn Editions, 1997).

525 Liverpool Medical Institution

Address: 114 Mount Pleasant, Liverpool L3 5SR

Telephone: (0151) 709 9125

Fax: (0151) 707 2810

E-mail: library@lmi.org.uk

Website: www.lmi.org.uk

Enquiries: The Resident Librarian, Mrs M. Pierce Moulton

Open: Mon–Fri: 9.30–6.00; Sat: 9.30–12.30.

Access: Approved readers, by appointment.

Founded in 1779 as the Liverpool Medical Library, the institution adopted its present name in 1840 and was granted a royal charter of incorporation in 1964. The archives comprise minutes of council meetings, 1779– , ordinary meetings (scientific), 1839– , and the Library Committee, 1840– . There are also deposited MSS, which are included in W.A. Lee: *Catalogue of the Books in the Liverpool Medical Institution Library* (Liverpool, 1968). See also J.A. Shepherd: *A History of the Liverpool Medical Institution* (1979).

526 Liverpool Record Office and Local Studies Service

Parent organisation: Liverpool City Council

Address: Central Library, William Brown Street, Liverpool L3 8EW

Telephone: (0151) 233 5817

Fax: (0151) 233 5824

E-mail: recoffice.central.library@liverpool.gov.uk

Website: www.liverpool.gov.uk

Enquiries: The Record Office and Local Studies Manager, Mr David Stoker

Open: Mon–Thurs: 9.00–7.30; Fri: 9.00–5.00; Sat: 10.00–4.00.
Closed 3rd and 4th weeks in June.

Access: Generally open to the public, on application. There is a 30-year closure on some collections, while the permission of the depositor is needed for others. An authorised reader's ticket is required for archives, rare books, maps, photographs and watercolours. Appointments are necessary to use microfilm/fiche and there is an advance booking fee.

Historical background: The 'Local Collection' was begun in the Liverpool Public Library in 1852 and local material has been acquired continuously since then. The Liverpool Record Office was formally opened in 1953 as a repository for Liverpool archives. It is recognised as a place of deposit for public records and since 1977 has acted as the Diocesan Record Office for Liverpool.

Acquisitions policy: Official and non-official archives of and relating to Liverpool. Books and other non-manuscript material covering Liverpool and Merseyside in detail and the surrounding areas of Lancashire and Cheshire in general.

Archives of organisation: Usual local authority records of Liverpool City Council and Corporation, including city charters, 1207– , minutes of the council and committees, 1550– , freeman's registers, 1692– . Department records, including cemeteries: interment registers; education: school managers' minutes, logbooks, registers; housing: photographs of corporation estate and clearance areas.

Major collections: Liverpool Diocesan Registry, parish records: Church of England, 1586– , and Roman Catholic, 1741– ; non-conformist and Jewish records.
Liverpool Borough Sessions, 1836– .
Statutory authorities, 19th–20th centuries: Liverpool School Board, Board of Guardians, including workhouse registers; records of out-townships subsequently incorporated.

Business organisations, including Liverpool Chamber of Commerce, 1860– , Liverpool Cotton Association, 1842– , Liverpool Stock Exchange, 1836– .

Local general and specialist hospitals, 18th–20th centuries.

Records relating to public health, including MOH letter books and report books, 1849–89, and extensive correspondence of Florence Nightingale (1820–1910) and William Rathbone VI (1819–1902).

Papers of prominent Liverpool figures and local families, including letters of Dr James Currie (1756–1805), physician and slave-trade abolitionist; non-estate papers of the Earls of Derby, statesmen, 19th–20th centuries; Holt and Durning-Holt families, 19th–20th centuries; papers of Joseph Mayer (1803–86), antiquarian and collector; correspondence of George Melly (1830–94), merchant and MP; Moore deeds and papers, 13th–18th centuries; papers of James Muspratt (1798–1886), founder of alkali industry in Lancashire; Nicholson family, merchants and Unitarians, 17th–20th centuries; deeds and papers of the Norris family of Speke, 15th–18th centuries; papers of the Parker family, with interests in America and the West Indies, 18th–19th centuries; Plumbe Tempest, deeds of property in and around Liverpool, 16th–19th centuries; letters of William Roscoe (1753–1831), banker, MP, poet and philanthropist who corresponded with many eminent figures, early 19th century; the Liverpool estate and manorial records of the Marquess of Salisbury, 15th–20th centuries; Molyneux, Earls of Sefton, diaries and papers, 1815–1953; papers of the Tarleton family of Liverpool, landowners and West India merchants, 17th –19th centuries.

Records of many Liverpool societies, charities and trade unions, including Literary and Philosophical Society, 1812–1937, Liverpool Society for the Prevention of Cruelty to Children, 1883–1957, Liverpool Trades Council, 1852– .

Records of the Liverpool Playhouse (Repertory) Theatre, 1911– .

Non-manuscript material: Maps.

Newspapers, 1756– .

Photographs and prints, topographical watercolours, films, tape and video recordings.

Microfilm of Liverpool directories, 1766–1904, Liverpool newspapers, Town Books, 1550–1835, obituary notices, 1879–1920s, census returns.

Finding aids: Archive lists; copies of significant lists sent to NRA. Calendars of older collections and index to unlisted archives accessions. Handlist of maps. Indexes to photographs and watercolours.

Facilities: Photocopying. Photography by arrangement. Microfilm/fiche readers/printer.

Conservation: Paper and bookbinding conservation department on premises.

Publications: Brief information sheets available.
A Handlist of Church of England Parish Records.
Map of Church of England Parishes in Liverpool and District c1900.
A Handlist of Roman Catholic Parish Records.
A Handlist of Cemetery and Burial Records.

527   Merseyside Record Office

Parent organisation: Liverpool City Council

Address: Central Library, William Brown Street, Liverpool L3 8EW

Telephone: (0151) 233 5817

Fax: (0151) 233 5824

E-mail: recoffice.central.library@liverpool.gov.uk

Website: www.liverpool.gov.uk

Enquiries: The Manager, Mr David Stoker

Open: Mon–Thurs: 9.00–7.30; Fri: 9.00–5.00; Sat: 10.00–4.00.
Closed 3rd and 4th weeks in June.

Access: Generally open to the public. An appointment is essential for Rainhall Hospital and coroners' records. A reader's ticket is required, which is issued upon proof of name and address.

Historical background: The Merseyside County Archives were established in 1974 as part of the new county's museum service. At the abolition of the county council (MCC) in 1986 the records passed to the Merseyside Residuary Body (MRB), with the exception of maritime archives, records relating to the museums' artefact collections and archives acquired by the museums before 1974, which were transferred to the National Museums and Galleries on Merseyside (successor to the County Museums). In 1989 the records, now including the records of the MCC (and later of the MRB), passed to Liverpool City Council, which administers the service on behalf of the five Merseyside district councils by means of an endowment from the funds of the MRB. The office is recognised as a place of deposit for public records.

Acquisitions policy: Seeks to acquire official and non-official records and documents relating to the whole of the county of Merseyside or to more than one of the metropolitan districts.

Archives of organisation: Usual local authority record holdings of Merseyside County Council and Merseyside Residuary Body.

Major collections: Deposited local collections of coroners, hospitals, Methodist and United Reformed Churches, social welfare organisations, businesses, societies and some family and estate papers, including records of Merseyside Passenger Transport Executive and Merseyside Fire Service and their predecessor bodies, 1845–1970s; Rainhall Hospital, 1851–1981; Peter Walker, brewers, 1850s–1970s; Crawfords Biscuits, family and business papers, 20th century; Woodall, architects, 1864–1980; Child Welfare Association, 1870–1970; League of Welldoers, 1856–1986; Personal Service Society, 1858–1983; Weld-Blundell family, c1667–1974; Merseyside Communist Party, 1940s–1992.

Non-manuscript material: Merseyside Development Corporation photographic archive, 1981–98.

Finding aids: Lists and indexes. Handlists of holdings and of genealogical sources. Significant lists sent to NRA.

Facilities: Photocopying. Photography by arrangement.

Conservation: In-house.

Publications: Public Health on Merseyside: a Guide to Local Sources (1991).

Archives on Merseyside (1997).

Education on Merseyside: a Guide to the Sources (1992).

The Irish Community in North-West England: a Guide to Local Archive Sources (1993).

Transport on Merseyside: a Guide to Local Sources (1994).

528 National Museums and Galleries on Merseyside
Archives Department

Address: c/o Maritime Archives and Library, Merseyside Maritime Museum, Albert Dock, Liverpool L3 4AQ

Telephone: (0151) 207 0001 (switchboard); 478 4424 (enquiries)

Fax: (0151) 478 4590

E-mail: maritime@nmgmrhl.demon.co.uk

Website: www.nmgm.org.uk

Enquiries: The Curator of Archives

Open: Tues–Thurs: 10.30–4.30. Closed first three weeks of January.

Access: Bona fide researchers, preferably by prior appointment. Several collections require at least two weeks' notice. Modern business and charity records may include confidential material.

Historical background: An archivist was appointed after the county of Merseyside came into existence in 1974, and the museum archives collections (which had themselves developed from Liverpool City functions) were incorporated; the latter included valuable maritime archives, particularly in connection with the Maritime Museum, finally established in 1980. The abolition of the county council led to the transfer of charity, hospital and non-conformist archives to the Merseyside Residuary Body and subsequently to Merseyside Record Office (see entry 527). The department is recognised as a place of deposit for public records. For horological material previously held, contact Prescot Museum, 34 Church Street, Prescot, tel. (0151) 430 7787.

Acquisitions policy: To extend the holdings of the following: archives of the National Museums and Galleries on Merseyside; maritime and business archives; archives associated with museum specialisms, especially shipping and trade, natural history, the King's Regimental Museum and the Museum of Labour History.

Archives of organisation: Records of the Museums and Art Galleries, 1849– .

Major collections: Maritime archives: Mersey Docks and Harbour Board and its antecedents; Dockland Survey Archive (South Docks); Register of Shipping, 1739–1942.

Business records: including shipping company records and correspondence about American Civil War and trade abroad, slave trade, marine insurance and associations for shipping; BICC plc (cables); Meccano Ltd; engineering records, including Vulcan Locomotive Works.

Natural history records, including 13th Earl of Derby's correspondence, 1799–1850.

Business and family papers: Danson family of Barnston and Birkenhead in Wirral (shipping insurance), 19th–20th centuries; Bryson Collection, 17th–20th centuries.

Non-manuscript material: Stewart Bale photographic archive: glass negatives covering all aspects of business activity in the North-West and elsewhere, c1910–1975.

Maritime history research library, photographic and sound archives.

Reference library of printed books, pamphlets and periodicals, including Lloyd's Registers, 1764– , Lloyd's Lists, 1741– , Customs Bills of Entry, c1820–1939 (incomplete), and museum catalogues.

Finding aids: Some 100 lists and indexes.

Facilities: Photocopying. Photography. Microfilm/fiche reader.

Publications: G. Read and M.K. Stammers (eds): *Guide to the Records of Merseyside Maritime Museum*, Vol. 1 (1994).
D. Littler (ed): *Guide to the Records of Merseyside Maritime Museum*, Vol. 2 (2000).

529 University of Liverpool
Special Collections and Archives

Address: Sydney Jones Library, PO Box 123, Liverpool L69 3DA

Telephone: (0151) 794 2696

Fax: (0151) 794 2681

Website: sca.lib.liv.ac.uk

Enquiries: The Head of Special Collections and Archives

Open: Mon–Fri: 9.00–1.00, 2.00–4.45. An appointment is preferred.

Access: Generally open to bona fide researchers. There are access restrictions on certain deposited archives, including archives of organisations devoted to child welfare.

Historical background: The University of Liverpool was founded initially as University College in 1881, when it was joined by the Medical School (f. 1834). The University received its charter in 1903. The Tate Library, established in 1892, was superseded in 1938 by the Harold Cohen Library. In 1976 the Sydney Jones Library was established. From that date the holdings of the Harold Cohen Library were concentrated in science and medicine while those of the Sydney Jones Library focused on the arts and social sciences. Special Collections and the University Archives were established in 1938 and 1968 respectively.

Acquisitions policy: To enhance and extend resources by purchases, donation or deposit, particularly in the following areas: gypsy studies; science fiction; papers of University staff and students; social work with children.

Archives of organisation: Medical School archives, 1834– .
University College archives, 1881–1903.
University archives, 1903– .

Major collections: Manuscripts: Oxyrhynchus papyri; Medieval, Renaissance and Oriental manuscripts in three collections: the University Collection, the Mayer Collection on deposit from the National Museums and Galleries on Merseyside, and the Radcliffe Collection on deposit from Liverpool Cathedral Library.

Deeds, autograph letters, and modern papers, including those of Ted Hughes, Seamus Heaney, and D.H. Lawrence.

Archives: Papers of former staff and students of the university, including Sir Cyril Burt; Lord Holford; Sir Charles Reilly; Sir Oliver Lodge and Professor R. Allison Peers.

Records of the Cunard Steamship Co., 1840–1970.

Archives of national sporting bodies: British Universities' Sport Association, 1919–97; English Table Tennis Association, 1919–98; Leeds Swedish Gymnastic Association, 1918–67; and Lord Aberdare's collection of papers, c1932–85, on the history of tennis and rackets.

Child Welfare Archives: Barnardo's, 1867–1998; National Children's Home, now NCH Action for Children, 1869–1996; the Fairbridge Society, 1908–98; Family Service Units, 1940–96; and the Simon Community, 1964–90.

Archives of the Liverpool Royal Institution, 1813–1942; the Liverpool Philomatic Society, 1825–1929; the Royal Society for the Prevention of Accidents, 1917–94; the Liverpool School of Tropical Medicine, 1898–1995.

Papers of the Rathbone Family of Liverpool, 1721–1991; John and Katharine Bruce Glasier, 1879–1975; Josephine Butler, 1853–1906; Jose Blanco White, 1805–44; Rt. Hon. Lord Owen, principally relating to the Social Democratic Party (SDP), 1981–92.

Archives of the Gypsy Lore Society, 1896–1974, and the R.A. Scott Macfie Gypsy Collection.

Science Fiction Archives: Olaf Stapledon, 1900–50; Eric Frank Russell, c1950–78; John Wyndham, c1935–69; Ramsey Campbell, c1970; Brian Aldis, c1990.

Papers of the Flat Earth Society, c1950–69.

Deeds of the Norrish family of Speke Hall, c1220–1637, and of the Aston family of Cheshire, 16th–19th centuries; Widnes Halmote rolls, 1748, 1799–1863.

Non-manuscript material: Printed book collections in all fields, 15th–20th centuries; Science Fiction Foundation Collection (c25,000 vols).

Collections of early children's books (c10,000 vols); Scott Macfie Gypsy Collection, includes photographs (3500) and vols (c5000).

Audio-visual material, mainly in the University Archives, Science Fiction Collections, and Gypsy Collections.

Finding aids: On-line and paper-based finding aids for Gypsy Collections, Rathbone Papers, Glasier Papers, Manuscripts Collections. Paper-based finding aids and information sheets for the University Archives, papers of staff and students, organisations devoted to child welfare and deposited collections. Lists sent to NRA. Website includes on-line access to finding aids for several collections.

Facilities: Photocopying (availability dependent upon age and condition). Photography. Microfilming. Microfilm/fiche reader/printer. Audio equipment.

Conservation: Contracted out.

Publications: Guide to the Manuscript Collections in Liverpool University Library (Liverpool, 1962).
T. Kelly: *For the Advancement of Learning: the University of Liverpool, 1881–1981* (Liverpool, 1981).
A.R. Allan and J.A. Carpenter (comps): *Redbrick University: a Portrait of University College Liverpool and the University of Liverpool, 1881–1981* (Liverpool, 1981).
N.R. Kerr: *Medieval Manuscripts in British Libraries,* iii (Oxford, 1983).

M. Proctor (ed): *Education on Merseyside: a Guide to the Sources* (Merseyside Archives Liaison Group, 1992).
Medieval Manuscripts on Merseyside: Catalogue of an Exhibition (Liverpool, 1993).
S. Harrop: *Decade of Change: the University of Liverpool, 1981–1991* (Liverpool, 1994).

530 West Lothian Council Archives

Parent organisation: West Lothian Council

Address: 7 Rutherford Square, Brucefield Industrial Estate, Livingston, West Lothian EH54 9BU

Telephone: (01506) 460 020

Fax: (01506) 416 167

Website: www.westlothian.gov.uk/libraries

Enquiries: The Archivist/Records Manager, Miss Alice Stewart

Open: Mon–Thurs: 9.00–5.00; Fri: 9.00–4.00.

Access: Generally open to the public, by appointment.

Historical background: West Lothian Council was formed in 1996 from West Lothian district and Lothian regional councils. Livingston New Town Development Corporation was included in 1997. The Archives/Records Management Service was established in 1995; before this material was acquired by the Local History Library.

Acquisitions policy: All types of material relevant to, created in or having some connection with West Lothian, including Linlithgow, Bathgate, Livingston, Broxburn.

Archives of organisation: Records of local authority committees including education, transport, social work, 1890s–1998.
Archives of West Lothian District Council, 1974–96; West Lothian Council, 1996– ; Livingston New Town Development Corporation, 1962–97; Lothian Regional Council, 1974–96.

Major collections: Records of Bathgate Forge Ltd/Chieftain Forge Ltd, 1908–1980s.

Non-manuscript material: Livingston New Town Development Corporation: photographic, plan and drawing archives, including films and supporting material.

Landscape Development Unit: site rehabilitation drawings.

Finding aids: Computerised catalogue.

Facilities: Photocopying. Microfilm/fiche readers.

Conservation: Contracted out.

531 Powys County Archives Office

Parent organisation: Powys County Council

Address: County Hall, Llandrindod Wells, Powys LD1 5LG

Telephone: (01597) 826088

Fax: (01597) 826872

E-mail: archives@powys.gov.uk

Website: powys.gov.uk/english/education/archives

Enquiries: The County Archivist, Gordon Reid

Open: Tues–Thurs: 10.00–12.30, 1.30–5.00; Fri: 9.00–12.30, 1.30–4.00.

Access: Generally open to the public. An appointment is recommended to avoid disappointment.

Historical background: An archivist was first appointed in Powys in 1985, based in the County Library Headquarters in Llandrindod. In 1991 the new County Archives Office was established on the County Hall site and the collections were relocated there. In addition, virtually all collections of official and public records relating to the old counties of Brecon, Montgomery and Radnor have been transferred from the National Library of Wales (see entry 9). Many private deposits relating to these counties and all ecclesiastical parish records remain at the National Library. However, the County Archives Office has purchased copies of all tithe maps and registers of baptisms, marriages and burials for Powys.

Acquisitions policy: To collect archival material relating to the old counties of Brecon, Montgomery and Radnor and the modern county of Powys, as laid down in a policy document agreed with the county's libraries and museums.

Archives of organisation: Virtually all records of local government for the three counties, including quarter sessions, county councils, urban and rural district councils, and parish and community councils. Also some Brecon Beacons National Park records.

Major collections: Deposited local collections, of which the following have a wider significance:

The Abercamlais Estate: deeds, correspondence and related papers, 16th–19th centuries, including correspondence and other papers of Archdeacon Richard Davies of Brecon, late 18th–early 19th centuries.

Brecknock Museum Transfer: large collection of assorted material relating to Breconshire, including papers of the Brecon and Abergavenny Canal and miscellaneous great and quarter sessions records.

Bonner-Maurice of Llanfechain, 17th–early 20th centuries.

Sandbach Family of Bryngwyn: diaries, correspondence and papers, 1813–1929.

Lewis of Y Neuadd: Lewis Lloyd and Lewis families of Nantgwyllt, 1548–1973.

Welsh Water Authority: records and plans of Elan Valley waterworks, 1890s–1930s.

Non-manuscript material: OS and other maps; topographical prints and engravings. Some photographs and postcards.

Finding aids: TS catalogues; sent to NRA and National Library of Wales. Detailed card index to places only. Accessions catalogued since 1992 on computer with free-text search facility.

Facilities: Photocopying. Photography. Microfilm/fiche readers/printer.

Conservation: Contracted out.

Publications: Guide to the Powys County Archives Office (1993).
G. Reid: 'The County Archives', *Transactions of the Radnorshire Society*, LXIII (1993).
Regular reports, including new accessions relating to Breconshire, are published in *Brycheiniog*, the journal of the Brecknock Society.

532 Llanelli Public Library

Address: Vaughan Street, Llanelli, Carmarthenshire SA15 3AS

Telephone: (01554) 773538

Fax: (01554) 750125

E-mail: richdavies@sirgar.gov.uk

Enquiries: The Borough Librarian

Open: Mon, Thurs, Fri: 9.30–7.00; Tues: 9.30–6.00; Wed: 9.30–6.00; Sat: 9.30–5.00.

Access: Generally open to the public.

Historical background: The Public Library was established in 1892; it incorporated the Mechanics' Institute, which was established in 1847.

Acquisitions policy: The library is a general library which also has collections on all aspects of local matters, with special emphasis on the coal industry, tinplate making, ships and shipbuilding and local government. Material in any form in these specialised areas is collected.

Major collections: Llanelli Harbour Trust records.
Local government records for Llanelli area.

Non-manuscript material: Coal-mining plans for Carmarthenshire.
Photographic prints (*c*15,000), transparencies (*c*2000) and 16 mm cine-films, all devoted to local subjects, e.g. industry, town development, special events.
Tape interviews of local people.

Finding aids: Indexes, including local newspapers, 1863– .

Facilities: Photocopying. Microfilm/fiche readers. Cine-film and slide projectors.

Publications: Llanelli Public Library Local History Research Group Series [details on application].

533 Anglesey County Record Office

Archifdy Ynys Môn

Parent organisation: Isle of Anglesey County Council

Address: Glanhwfa Road, Llangefni, Anglesey LL77 7TW

Telephone: (01248) 752080

Website: www.ynysmon.gov.uk

Enquiries: The County Archivist, Anne Venables

Open: Mon–Fri: 9.00–1.00; 2.00–5.00.
Annual closure 1st week of November.

Access: Generally open to the public. The office operates the CARN reader's ticket system. A paid research service is offered.

Historical background: The office was set up in 1974 following local government reorganisation, and before that Anglesey County Library did some collecting. It is recognised as place of deposit for public records.

Acquisitions policy: Material relating to Anglesey.

Archives of organisation: Usual local authority record holdings.

Major collections: Deposited local collections.

Non-manuscript material: Plans, photographs, tape interviews.

Finding aids: Indexes, catalogues. Lists sent to NRA and National Library of Wales (entry 9).

Facilities: Photocopying. Photography. Microfilm/fiche readers.

Conservation: Undertaken at Caernarfon Area Record Office (entry 160).

Publications: D.O. Jones (ed.): 'Guide' in *Anglesey Bibliography* (1976).
Recent accessions published twice yearly in the *Newsletter* of the Anglesey Antiquarian Society and on the office's website.

534 Midlothian Council Archives and Local Studies Centre

Address: Library Headquarters, 2 Clerk Street, Loanhead, Midlothian EH20 9DR

Telephone: (0131) 271 3976

Fax: (0131) 440 4635

E-mail: local.studies@midlothian.gov.uk

Website: www.earl.org.uk/partners/midlothian/index.html

Enquiries: The Archivist, Ms Ruth Calvert

Open: Mon: 9.00–5.00, 6.00–8.00; Tues, Thurs: 9.00–5.00; Fri: 9.00–3.45.

Access: Generally open to the public.

Historical background: The library was established as Midlothian County Library in 1921 under the Education (Scotland) Act of 1919. Following local government reoganisation parts of the area were transferred to East Lothian, West Lothian and Edinburgh district and to the Borders region. Material previously deposited with Edinburgh District Archives has now been returned to the library.

Acquisitions policy: The library attempts to acquire, by purchase, gift or otherwise, items relating to the area.

Major collections: Local collection covering Midlothian district.

Records of the former burghs of Dalkeith, 1760–1975; Bonnyrigg and Lasswade, 1865–1975; Loanhead, 1909–75; and Penicuik, 1867–1975.

School Board letter-books and cash books; school log-books, *c*1870–1970.

County council and district council minutes.

Family papers.

Non-manuscript material: Maps and plans, prints and photographs.

Finding aids: Bibliographies, catalogues and shelf-lists. Local newspaper index in preparation.

Facilities: Photocopying. Microfilm/fiche reader/printers.

Publications: New Statistical Account of Midlothian, pt 1 (1987); pts 2 & 3 (1988) [reprint of the 1845 2nd Statistical Account with additional notes and illustrations].

J. Wilson: *The Annals of Penicuik, being a History of the Parish and of the Village* (1985) [reprint of the 1891 history of Penicuik].

Leaflet *Local Studies in Midlothian* outlining the main archive holdings and local history collections.

535 Argyll and Bute District Council

Address: Manse Brae, Lochgilphead, Argyll PA31 8QU

Telephone: (01546) 604120

Fax: (01546) 606897

E-mail: murdo.macdonald@argyll-bute.gov.uk

Enquiries: The Archivist, Mr Murdo MacDonald

Open: Tues–Fri: 10.00–1.00, 2.00–4.30

Access: Generally open to the public. An appointment is advised.

Historical background: A part-time archivist's post was established by Argyll County Council three years before local government re-organisation in 1975. The post was expanded by the successor authority, Argyll and Bute District

Council, and again in 1996 by Argyll and Bute Council within an expanded geographical area.

Acquisitions policy: To encourage the deposit and donation of records relating to the Argyll and Bute Council area.

Archives of organisation: Records of the present council's predecessors i.e. the small burghs, the county councils, and the former district council, 17th century– .

Major collections: Diocese of Argyll and the Isles (Episcopal) records, 19th–20th centuries.

Papers of Malcolm of Poltalloch, 18th–20th centuries; Campbell of Kilberry, 18th–20th centuries; MacTavish of Dunardry, 18th–20th centuries; Sporat & Cameron, solicitors, Tobermory, 19th century.

Non-manuscript material: Architectural drawings in the Dean of Guild Court records of the former burghs, *c*1880–1975.

Finding aids: Lists sent to NRAS.

Facilities: Photocopying.

Conservation: Contracted out.

536 ActionAid Central Archive

Address: Resource Centre, Hamlyn House, Macdonald Road, Archway, London N19 5PG

Telephone: (020) 7561 7561

E-mail: cgale@actionaid.org.uk

Website: www.actionaid.org.uk

Enquiries: The Archives Assistant

Open: Tues, Thurs: 10.00–4.30, by appointment only.

Access: Generally open to the public upon advance application in writing (though some record classes are restricted).

Historical background: In 1971, under the leadership of Cecil Jackson-Cole, the Voluntary and Christian Services Trust set up a standing Christian Youth Appeal sub-committee to raise funds for the sponsorship of orphans and the provision of medical assistance in the UK. The name of the appeal was changed in 1972 to Action in Distress, and again in 1980 to ActionAid, reflecting a sharpening focus upon overseas development (rather than relief) work. Regional and national offices have been set up in areas in which the agency works, and several European affiliates have been established. ActionAid is the UK's third largest development agency, and works in more than 30 countries in Africa, Asia, Latin America and the Caribbean. The public and private papers of Cecil Jackson-Cole (1901–79) are held at West Sussex Record Office (entry 241).

Archives of organisation: Minute books, 1971– ; other institutional records, including archives of UK departments, country programme plans and budgets, and reports.

Non-manuscript material: Printed annual reports; supporter and staff newsletters, magazines etc; small photograph collection.

Finding aids: Location database.

Facilities: Photocopying.

537 Alfred Dunhill Archive

Address: 27   Knightsbridge,   London SW1X 7YB

Telephone: (020) 7838 8233

Fax: (020) 7838 8556

E-mail: peter.tilley@alfreddunhill.co.uk

Website: www.dunhill.com

Enquiries: The Curator, Mr Peter Tilley

Open: Mon–Fri: 9.00–5.00, by appointment only.

Access: At the discretion of the company, by telephone or written application.

Historical background: Alfred Dunhill Ltd was established in 1893, but Dunhill traders can be traced back to the 18th century. Much material was destroyed by bombing in 1941; nonetheless some 12,000 documents are held. However, the museum was reinstated and is at 48 Jermyn Street, London SW1Y 6LX with c2500 antique products.

Acquisitions policy: Maintains archives of the company. Other accessions relate mainly to museum objects.

Archives of organisation: Records of the business, 1899– .

Non-manuscript material: Catalogues, press-cuttings, photographs and video materials. Library on tobacco, pipes and smoking-related topics (c400 books).

Finding aids: Old catalogues are available.

Facilities: Photocopying. Photography.

Publications: M. Balfour: *Alfred Dunhill: One Hundred Years and More* (1992).
M. Dunhill: *Our Family Business* (1979).

538 Alpine Club

Address: 55   Charlotte   Road,   London EC2A 3QF

Telephone: (020) 7613 0755

Fax: (020) 7613 0755

E-mail: library@alpine.club.org.uk

Website: www.alpine-club.org.uk/library.htm

Enquiries: The Hon. Archivist, Peter Berg

Open: Mon–Fri: 10.00–5.00, by appointment. The archivist is available on Tuesdays.

Access: Members of the Alpine Club and bona fide researchers. It is necessary to make an appointment with the Hon. Archivist by contacting the Assistant Secretary or the Librarian. A modest donation is appreciated.

Historical background: The Alpine Club was founded in 1857 and its archives include mountaineering records dating back to the 18th century. The material comprises a unique collection of MSS, letters and photographs of mountain exploration, in which the Alpine Club has always played a leading role, from the earliest days up to the present time.

Acquisitions policy: To encourage the deposit and donation of records relating to the Alpine Club and its members and mountaineering in general.

Archives of organisation: Alpine Club records: minutes and correspondence, 1857– .
Ladies' Alpine Club records, 1907–75.

Major collections: Collections of personal papers, including diaries of J.P. Farrar (1857–1929); W.N. Ling (1873–1953); C. Schuster (1869–1956); and T.G. Longstaff (1875–1964). Papers of S. Spencer (1862–1950); E. Strutt (1874–1948); and H. Montagnier (1877–1933). Correspondence of E. Whymper (1840–1911); G. Winthrop Young (1876–1958); D. Freshfield (1854–1934); W. Coolidge (1850–1926); M. Bourrit (1739–1819); and Eric Shipton (1907–77).

Non-manuscript material: Newspaper cuttings, 1891– (36 vols).
Photographs are held in the club library.

Finding aids: Indexes.

Facilities: Photocopying.

539 Anthroposophical Society in Great Britain

Address: Rudolf Steiner House, 35 Park Road, London NW1 6XT

Telephone: (020) 7224 8398

Fax: (020) 7724 4364

E-mail: rsh@cix.compulink.co.uk

Enquiries: The Librarian/Archivist, Mrs M. Jonas

Open: Tues–Thurs: 11.00–1.00, 2.00–5.00; Tues late opening to 7.30 in term time; Fri: 1.00–6.00; Sat (except Aug.): 12.00–5.00.

Access: Generally open to the public, by prior appointment only.

Historical background: The society was founded in 1923 to further the work of Rudolf Steiner (1861–1925). The library dates from the early 1920s, and the collection refers to the early days, from 1912 onwards, before and during the founding of the society. Most material relates to the 1920s and 1930s but has been added to for the 1980s and 1990s.

Acquisitions policy: Any relevant material is welcomed.

Archives of organisation: Records relating to the founding of the society in Great Britain and worldwide.
Council minutes, reports, correspondence, and records of daughter movements, including Waldorf Education, 1920s– .
Records of the Anthroposophical Medical Movement and of branches of the Anthroposophical Society, 1920s– , including public and members' lectures, events, conferences and performances.

Non-manuscript material: Photographs of Rudolf Steiner, his colleagues, major centres and members' conferences.
Plans and development of Rudolf Steiner House.

Finding aids: Box lists.

Facilities: Photocopying. Photography by arrangement.

540 Architectural Association Library

Address: 36 Bedford Square, London WC1B 3ES

Telephone: (020) 7636 0974 ext. 236

Fax: (020) 7414 0782

E-mail: hsklar@aaschool.ac.uk

Website: www.aaschool.ac.uk/library

Enquiries: The Librarian, Hinda F. Sklar

Open: Term: Mon–Fri: 10.00–8.00; Sat: 11.00–3.00.
Vacation (except summer): Mon–Fri: 10.00–6.00.

Access: Bona fide scholars and members of the Architectural Association. An appointment is necessary and a research fee is charged to non-members.

Historical background: The Architectural Association was founded as an evening school for architectural students in 1847. A day school was started in 1901. The library began in 1862 and is principally a resource for staff, students and members.

Acquisitions policy: Material relating to subject areas of teaching units in general: architecture, art, landscape planning, town planning, philosophy.

Archives of organisation: Archives of the AA, including membership index, 1847– .

Major collections: Small MS collection, including a Repton 'Red Book'.

Non-manuscript material: Slide library and print studio.
Theses and essays.

Facilities: Photocopying.

Publications: Guide to the Library.
Annual Reports.

541 Art Workers' Guild

Address: 6 Queen Square, London WC1N 3AR

Telephone: (020) 7713 0966

Fax: (020) 7713 0967

Enquiries: The Secretary, Gerald Southgate

Open: Mon–Wed.

The guild is an association of architects and artists founded in 1884 by members of the arts and crafts movement. It maintains its own archives, including minute books, and accepts deposits relating to members. There is a card catalogue and the archive is open to bona fide researchers, by appointment with the Honorary Librarian. See H.J.L.J. Masse: *The Art Workers' Guild, 1884–1934* (London, 1935).

542 Association of Anaesthetists of Great Britain and Ireland

Address: 9 Bedford Square, London WC1B 3RA

Telephone: (020) 7631 8806

Fax: (020) 7631 4350

E-mail: info@aagbi.org

Website: www.aagbi.org

Enquiries: The Archivist, Ms Trish Willis

Open: Mon–Fri: 9.30–5.00, by prior arrangement with the Archivist.

Access: Members of the AAGBI and bona fide researchers.

The AAGBI was founded in 1932 by Dr Henry W. Featherstone (1874–1967). There are extensive archives relating to the association as well as much relating to anaesthesia as a whole, a large photographic and video collection and a museum display that changes on a yearly basis. In addition there is a library of anaesthesia books and technical literature. Items relating to resuscitation, anaesthesia, intensive care and pain management are collected.

543 Athenaeum

Address: 107 Pall Mall, London SW1Y 5ER

Telephone: (020) 7930 4843

Fax: (020) 7839 4114

Website: www.athenaeum.co.uk

Enquiries: The Librarian, Miss S.J. Dodgson

Open: Private club. Visiting by arrangement only.

Access: Bona fide researchers, on written application to the Librarian.

The Athenaeum was founded in 1824 by John Wilson Croker (1780–1857) and others, and is one of the most celebrated London clubs. Its archives consist solely of internal administrative records. The librarian will answer reasonable requests about them submitted in writing. The club has no papers of past members; the letters of Herbert Spencer (1820–1903) have been transferred to the University of London (entry 833). An automated catalogue of former members is in progress, and a handlist of archives has been compiled which may be consulted only in the club. Photocopying is available. The Victorian periodical *The Athenaeum* is not connected with the club or library in any way. See H. Ward: *The Athenaeum* (1924); Anon: *The Athenaeum 1824–1974* (1974); and Tait and Walker: *The Athenaeum Collection* (1999).

544 BT Group Archives

Parent organisation:
British Telecommunications plc

Address: Third Floor, Holborn Telephone Exchange, 268–270 High Holborn, London WC1V 7EE

Telephone: (020) 7492 8792

Fax: (020) 7242 1967

E-mail: archives@bt.com

Website: www.bt.com/archives/

Enquiries: The Group Archivist, David Hay

Open: Mon–Fri: 10.00–4.00.

Access: Generally open to the public, including many records less than 30 years old. Prior appointments are necessary.

Historical background: The telegraph service, begun by private companies from the 1830s, was taken over by the Post Office (PO) in 1870. The telephone service, also initiated by private companies from 1878, was taken over in 1912. As a central government department (the Postmaster General sat in Cabinet) the PO was the virtual monopoly supplier of telecommunications services in the UK from this date. In 1969 the PO was established as a public corporation under the Post Office Act of that year and was split into two divisions, Posts and Telecommunications. The British Telecommunications Act 1981 established British Telecom as a distinct corporation, although the telecommunications division of the PO had been known as British Telecom since the previous year. British Telecom was incorporated as a public limited company in 1984 as British Telecommunications plc under the Telecommunications Act of that year. The 1984 Act also abolished British Telecom's exclusive privilege of running telecommunications services. It now requires a licence to operate such services and is subject to scrutiny and review by the Office of Telecommunications. BT, the company's trading name since 1991, remains legally obliged under the Public Records Acts to safeguard its historical records created up to the date of privatisation, including those of its predecessors. BT Archives, created in embryonic form during 1984, rapidly expanded from 1986 to consolidate in one repository the various telecommunications collections held throughout BT and elsewhere. It moved to its purpose-adapted accommodation in 1997 and in 2001 the document collections of BT Museum were transferred. It is recognised as a place of deposit for public records.

Acquisitions policy: To collect all multi-media material reflecting the development of services provided in the UK and overseas by BT and its predecessors.

Archives of organisation: Private telegraph companies, 1846–70; private telephone companies, 1878–1912; PO telegraph service, 1866–1969; PO telephone service, 1878–1969; PO telecommunications, 1969–80; British Telecommunications (public corporation), 1981–4; British Telecommunications plc, 1984–.

Major collections: Records of telegraph companies taken over by the PO, including: English Telegraph Co., 1852–69; Electric (and International) Telegraph Co., 1846–70; London and Provincial Telegraph Co., 1859–68; United Kingdom Telegraph Co., 1851–70; Universal Private Telegraph Co., 1861–70.
Records of telephone companies taken over by the PO, including: the Telephone Co. Ltd, 1878–80; Edison Telephone Co., 1879–80; United Telephone Co., 1880–8; National Telephone Co., 1892–1913.

Non-manuscript material: Historical phone book collection, 1880–.
Historical telecommunications photograph and film library, 19th century–.
Phonecard collection, 1985–.
Publicity artwork, 1930s–1960s.
Telecommunications library, 1769–.

Finding aids: Catalogues (mostly computerised).
CD-ROM, video and 16mm film viewers.

Facilities: Photocopying. Photography. Microfilm/fiche readers.

Conservation: Contracted out.

Publications: F.G.C. Baldwin: *History of the Telephone in the United Kingdom* (1938).
H. Robinson: *Britain's Post Office* (1953).
D.C. Pitt: *The Telecommunications Function in the British Post Office* (1980).
BT Archives: *Guide to Events in Telecommunications* (Issue 3, 1999).
BT Archives: *Events in Telecommunications History* (2000) [web publication].

545 Bank of England

Address: Threadneedle Street, London EC2R 8AH

Telephone: (020) 7601 4889/5096

Fax: (020) 7601 4356

E-mail: archive@bankofengland.co.uk

Enquiries: The Archivist, Henry Gillett

Open: By appointment only.

Access: Records over 30 years old are normally available for inspection, although records relating to customers may need to be withheld.

Historical background: The Bank of England was incorporated by Act of Parliament and charter in 1694, and in return its proprietors subscribed funds to help finance the war being fought by William III against Louis XIV of France. The subscribers were granted a royal charter on 27 July 1694, under the title 'The Governor and Company of the Bank of England'. Of the original charter, the only clauses now remaining unrevoked are those relating to the incorporation of the bank, the common seal, legal suit and the holding of property. The Bank of England Act of 1946 brought the bank into public ownership, but provided for the continued existence of 'the Governor and Company of the Bank of England' under royal charter.

Acquisitions policy: No external acquisitions.

Archives of organisation: Records covering the principal activities of the bank: advice to government; market operations; management of government, bank and private accounts;

management of government and other stock issues; economic intelligence; relations with financial institutions abroad; industrial liaison; banknote printing; supervision of UK financial institutions; exchange control.

Finding aids: Descriptive lists and computer database. Lists sent to NRA.

Facilities: Limited photocopying.

Conservation: Contracted out.

Publications: Free guide (64pp) available.

546 Bankside Gallery

Address: 48 Hopton Street, London SE1 9JH

Telephone: (020) 8928 7521

Fax: (020) 8928 2820

E-mail: re&rws@bankside-gallery.demon.co.uk

Enquiries: The Archivist, Simon Fenwick

Open: Mon: by appointment only.

Access: Bona fide researchers, on application; a charge is made.

Historical background: Bankside Gallery has been home to the Royal Watercolour Society (RWS; f. 1804 as the Royal Society of Painters in Water Colours) and the Royal Society of Painter-Printmakers (RE; formerly the Royal Society of Painter-Etchers and Engravers) since 1980. An archive facility has been maintained since 1994.

Acquisitions policy: Archives are acquired relevant to the RWS and the RE and their members.

Archives of organisation: Bankside Gallery records.

Major collections: RWS (also known as the Old Watercolour Society) Archives: minute books; catalogues and records of sale, 1804– ; and records of the RWS Art Club. Also papers collected by Joseph John Jenkins, secretary to the society, 1954–64, including files on 19th-century artists with significant material relating to Samuel Palmer, William Henry Hunt and David Cox; and papers of Elizabeth Scott-Moore (1904–1993).

RE Archives: correspondence of Seymour Haden, 1877, *re* foundation of the society; minute books, sale catalogues and exhibition sales, 1880– . Also records of the Print Collectors Club, 1921–88, and scientific papers of Sir Frank Short (1857–1945), including

account book of W.B. Cooke, engraver for J.M.W. Turner (1775–1851).

Non-manuscript material: Photographs of members of the RWS, *c*1860– .
Photographs of pictures in the RWS Diploma Collection.
Slides and photographs of work by current members of both societies; files of ephemeral material on various members.

Finding aids: Lists sent to NRA.

Facilities: Photocopying.

Conservation: Contracted out.

Publications: S. Fenwick and G. Smith: *The Business of Watercolour: a Guide to the Archives of the Royal Watercolour Society* (Ashgate, 1997).

547 Barbers' Company

Address: Barber-Surgeons' Hall, Monkwell Square, Wood Street, London EC2Y 5BL

Telephone: (020) 7606 0741

Fax: (020) 7606 3857

E-mail: clerk@barberscompany.org

Website: www.barberscompany.org

Enquiries: The Archivist, Mr I.G. Murray

Open: Mon–Wed: 10.30–4.30, by appointment.

Access: To approved researchers, on written application. Users are referred in the first instance to the microfilmed copies of company records at Guildhall (entry 624).

Historical background: The company, which practised both barbery and surgery, is first mentioned in 1308, when Richard le Barbour was presented as Master before the Court of Aldermen. It had a hall in Monkwell Street by 1443 and received its Charter of Incorporation in 1462. In 1540 by Act of Parliament it was united with the Fellowship of Surgeons to form the Worshipful Company of Barbers and Surgeons of London, with a monopoly of the two trades throughout London and the suburbs, and later the right to examine surgeons for the Navy and East India Company. In 1745 the surgeons left to form what was to become the Royal College of Surgeons (see entry 758), leaving the hall and its contents to the Barbers. The present hall dates from 1969, the previous ones having been destroyed in 1666 and 1940.

Acquisitions policy: Modern records are added to the archives from time to time in the usual way. The company also maintains a library, on barbery, and anatomy and surgery before 1745, to which material is added by gift or purchase.

Archives of organisation: Charters, ordinances, Grant of Arms etc, 1462–1685; court minutes, 1551– ; court and livery lists, 1711– ; freedom admission registers, 1522–1801; apprentice bindings and turnover books, 1657–1829; quarterage books, 1717–1860; company accounts, 1603–1881; dinner accounts, 1676–1790; tradesmens' receipt books, 1722–1818; records of examination of naval surgeons, 1709–45; charity fund accounts, 1764–1917; pension accounts, 1716–1894; property inventory, 1711–45; title deeds to company property, 1555– .

Non-manuscript material: Biographical material on members.
Photographs, portraits and illustrative material.

Finding aids: List of archive holdings; sent to NRA. Indexes to court minutes.

Publications: S. Young: *Annals of the Barber-Surgeons* (London, 1890).
J. Dobson and R. Milnes-Walker: *Barbers and Barber-Surgeons of London* (London, 1979).
The Worshipful Company of Barbers [free pamphlet].

548 Barnet Archives and Local Studies Centre

Parent organisation: London Borough of Barnet

Address: Hendon Catholic Social Centre, Egerton Gardens, Hendon, London NW4 4EH
Correspondence to be addressed c/o Hendon Library, The Burroughs, Hendon, London NW4 4BQ

Telephone: (020) 8359 2876

Fax: (020) 8359 2869

E-mail: hendon.library@barnet.gov.uk

Website: www.earl.org.uk/earl/members/barnet/history

Enquiries: The Information Adviser, Mr David Bicknell

Open: By arrangement only.

Access: Generally open to the public, by appointment only.

Historical background: Archives have been collected by the library since 1932. Barnet Borough was created in 1965 out of the boroughs of Finchley and Hendon and the urban districts of Barnet, East Barnet and Friern Barnet.

Acquisitions policy: To collect material of relevance to present and former administrative authorities and deposited archives within the limits of the area of the present borough.

Archives of organisation: Usual local authority record holdings.

Major collections: Deposited local records.

Non-manuscript material: Maps, photographs, prints, local newspapers, iconographic material.

Finding aids: Card index to places, persons, and subjects. Catalogues of all listed deposits; lists sent to NRA.

Facilities: Photocopying. Photography. Microfilm/fiche reader/printers.

Conservation: Contracted out.

Publications: S. Gillies and P. Taylor: *Finchley and Friern Barnet* (Phillimore, 1992).
——: *Hendon, Childs Hill, Golders Green and Mill Hill* (Phillimore, 1993).
P. Taylor & J. Corden: *Barnet, Edgware, Hadley and Totteridge* (Phillimore, 1994).
P. Taylor (ed): *A Place in Time* (Barnet, 1991) [a history of the borough to c1500].
Full list of publications available.

549 Birkbeck College

Parent organisation: University of London

Address: Malet Street, London WC1E 7HX

Telephone: (020) 7631 6257

Fax: (020) 7631 6224

Website: www.bbk.ac.uk

Enquiries: The College Secretary

Open: By prior arrangement only.

Access: Bona fide researchers.

Historical background: The college was founded in 1823 as the London Mechanics' Institution and was modelled on the Glasgow Mechanics' Institution. Dr George Birkbeck (1776–1841) became its first president. Its original building was in Chancery Lane. In 1891 it was called the Birkbeck Institute and combined with two other bodies to form the City

Polytechnic; however, in 1907 it reverted to being a separate institution called Birkbeck College. Although it had teachers recognised by the University of London from the 1890s, it became part of the university only in 1920. The college maintains a commitment to provide education to working people and mature students.

Acquisitions policy: To maintain the archive.

Archives of organisation: Early registers and papers, 1823–1910 (incomplete); governors' minutes and records, 1910–50; financial records, including appeals, 1897–1925; staff records; building records, 1914–45; departmental papers.
Papers re London County Council, 1906–35; University of London, including records of first application, 1908–50; and University Grants Committee, 1921–48.
War papers, 1938–46.

Major collections: Letters of George Birkbeck. Papers of Sir John Lockwood (1903–65), principally concerning development of university education in East Africa; Dr R. Fürth, physicist, and Prof. David Bohm (1917–92), physicist.

Non-manuscript material: Photographs and college calendars.

Finding aids: Outline list.

Facilities: Photocopying by arrangement.

Publications: C. Delisle Burns: *A Short History of Birkbeck College* (London, 1924).
E.H. Warmington: *A History of Birkbeck College, University of London, during the Second World War, 1939–1945* (London, 1955).

550 Bishopsgate Institute Reference Library

Address: 230 Bishopsgate, London EC2M 4QH

Telephone: (020) 7247 6198

Fax: (020) 7247 6318

Enquiries: The Reference Librarian, Alice Mackay

Open: Mon–Fri: 9.30–5.30; Thurs: 11.00–5.30.

Access: Generally open to the public.

Historical background: The institute began as a cultural centre in 1894, funded by the Bishopsgate Foundation, a federation of St Botolph parish charities. The reference library

opened in 1895 and is still supported entirely by the foundation.

Acquisitions policy: The library acquires the archives of associations and individuals connected with radical politics, especially the co-operative movement, and secularism.

Major collections: Howell Collection: papers and library of George Howell (1833–1910), trade unionist and MP, including the archives of the Reform League; the diaries of Ernest Jones (1819–69), chartist; and the minutes of the First International, 1864–76.
Holyoake Collection: diaries and MSS of George Jacob Holyoake (1817–1906), socialist and founder of the co-operative movement.
National Secular Society Archives (f. 1866), including correspondence and papers of its founder, Charles Bradlaugh (1833–91), and archives of the Rationalist Peace Association, 1910–21.
London Co-operative Society Archives, including those of constituent societies, and their predecessors, c1850– .
Women's Co-operative Guild.
Derrick Collection: International Co-operative Alliance.
Raphael Samuel Archive.

Non-manuscript material: London History Collection: includes plans, photos and maps.

Finding aids: Typescript lists. NRA 10203, 10204.

Publications: George Howell Collection: Index to the Correspondence (R1975).
E. Royle: *The Bradlaugh Papers: a Descriptive Index* (East Ardsley, 1975).
D.R. Webb: *Bishopsgate Foundation Centenary History* (1991).

551 Black Cultural Archives

Parent organisation: The African People's Historical Monument Foundation

Address: 378 Coldharbour Lane, Brixton, London SW9 8RP

Telephone: (020) 7738 4591

Fax: (020) 7738 7168

E-mail: 106464.3650@compuserve.com

Enquiries: The Director, Mr S.H. Walker

Open: Mon–Fri: 10.00–4.00.

Access: Researchers and interested members of the public; an appointment is essential.

Historical background: The African People's Historical Monument Foundation (UK) exists to promote the collection, documentation and dissemination of the culture and history of African peoples in the diaspora. The Black Cultural Archives project was begun in 1982 as a centre for collection and preservation of all primary source materials relating to black experience and community events, both past and present. Display and exhibition of materials are top priorities.

Acquisitions policy: To acquire, by donation or purchase, historical and contemporary material by, or pertinent to, people of African origin.

Archives of organisation: Official records, working papers and photographic evidence of the growth of the archives project, 1982– .

Major collections: Jamaican slave papers, 18th century– .
Documentation of the lives and achievements of eminent black persons in Britain, 18th–20th centuries.

Non-manuscript material: Rare books documenting European imperialism in Africa.
Handbills, posters and photographs of community events, both current and historical.
Rare maps.
Paintings by local and international artists; African sculpture and carvings.
Oral evidence of black experience.

Finding aids: General index to all collections.

Facilities: Photocopying. Photography by arrangement. Computers.

Publications: Mary Seacole Teacher's Resource Pack.

552 Brent Community History Library and Archive

Parent organisation: London Borough of Brent

Address: Cricklewood Library, 152 Olive Road, London NW2 6UY

Telephone: (020) 8937 3541

Fax: (020) 8450 5211

E-mail: archive@brent.gov.uk

Website: www.brent.gov.uk

Enquiries: Ian Johnston

Open: Mon: 1.00–5.00; Tues, Sat: 10.00–5.00; Thurs: 1.00–8.00.

Access: Generally open to the public; an appointment is preferred. A paid research service is available.

Historical background: A local history library was opened in 1977 in the Grange Museum. The collections were moved to Cricklewood Library (f. 1929) in 1993.

Acquisitions policy: Material illustrating the life of the people of the Borough of Brent and its predecessors, Wembley, Willesden and Kingsbury.

Archives of organisation: Minutes of the present borough and its predecessors, with Medical Officer of Health reports.
Vestry minutes, overseers' and churchwardens' records for Willesden, 17th century– .

Non-manuscript material: British Empire Exhibition, Wembley, 1924–5, including guides, maps, photographs, music and souvenirs.
Wembley History Society Collection, including hundreds of mounted photographs.
Photographs and postcards, prints and drawings of the area.
Large map collection, especially strong on Willesden, including tithe and enclosure maps.
Collections of work by local authors, including Harrison Ainsworth, W.H.G. Kingston, Louis Wain, Gunby Hadath.

Finding aids: Index to the collection and partial index to the local newspapers *Willesden Chronicle*, 1880–1985, and *Wembley Observer*, 1965–85. Some lists sent to NRA.

Facilities: Photocopying. Photographic reprint service. Microfilm/fiche reader/printer.

Conservation: Contracted out.

Publications: Series of local history publications, 1975– .

553 British Academy

Address: 10 Carlton House Drive, London SW1Y 5AH

Telephone: (020) 7969 5200

Fax: (020) 7969 5300

Enquiries: The Secretary

Open: Mon–Fri: 9.30–5.30.

The British Academy is the premier national learned society for the humanities and the social sciences. It was founded in 1902 by royal charter, and the official records and working papers from that time are maintained and made available to bona fide researchers, by appointment. No other material is acquired but there is a collection of photographs of fellows.

554   British Deaf Association

Address: BDA Head Office, 1–3 Worship Street, London EC2A 2AB

Telephone: (020) 7588 3520 (Text); (020) 7588 3520 (Voice)

Fax: (020) 7588 3527

E-mail: info@bda.org.uk

Website: www.bda.org.uk

Enquiries: The Information Department

Open: Normal office hours throughout the year.

Access: Generally open to the public, by appointment only.

The association is the oldest national charity in the United Kingdom for deaf people. It was founded as the British Deaf and Dumb Association in 1890, in response to the report by the Royal Commission on the Education of the Blind and the Deaf and Dumb which endorsed the ousting of sign language from teaching. The present name was adopted in 1971. Its aim is 'to advance and protect the interests of all deaf people' and 'to ensure that deaf people using sign language have the same rights and entitlement as any other citizens'. The association maintains its own archives and acquires any material relevant to the history of the deaf and to the association.

555   British Dental Association Library

Address: 64 Wimpole Street, London W1M 8AL

Telephone: (020) 7935 0875 ext. 205

Fax: (020) 7487 5232

E-mail: enquiries@bda-dentistry.org.uk

Enquiries: The Librarian

Open: Mon–Fri: 9.00–5.30.

Access: Bona fide researchers. An appointment is essential.

Historical background: The BDA was founded in 1880, and in 1923 it was linked with the Incorporated Dental Society through the Public Dental Service Association, which provided a forum for both professional negotiating bodies. Following the establishment of the NHS in 1948, all three associations amalgamated as the BDA.

Acquisitions policy: To maintain BDA records, and other collections or material of historical dental interest.

Archives of organisation: Records of BDA, including minutes of central committees, e.g. Council and Representation Board, and of branches and sections, 1880– .
Records of Incorporated Dental Society, 1934–49, and Public Dental Service Association, 1923–49.

Finding aids: Holdings list.

Facilities: Photocopying.

556   British Film Institute

Address: 21 Stephen Street, London W1P 1PL

Telephone: (020) 7255 1444

Fax: (020) 7436 2338

A   Special Collections

E-mail: janet.moat@bfi.org.uk

Website: www.bfi.org.uk

Enquiries: The Special Collections Manager, Ms Janet Moat

Open: Mon, Tues, Thurs, Fri: 10.30–5.30; Wed: 2.00–5.30.

Access: Bona fide researchers, by appointment only. Preference given to BFI library members and postgraduates.

Historical background: The BFI was founded in 1933 'to encourage the development of the art of the film, to promote its use as a record of contemporary life and manners, and to foster public appreciation and study of it'. In 1961 the BFI's Memorandum of Association was amended to include television. The Special Collections incorporate the holdings of unpublished scripts, press-books and special collections which have been acquired gradually since 1933.

Acquisitions policy: All types of material relating to film and television, including ephemera, are acquired by purchase, donation and exchange, but priority is given to British cinema and TV.

Major collections: These currently number more than 100, and include papers of Carol Reed (1906–76), director/producer; Michael Balcon (1896–1977), producer; Joseph Losey (1909–84), director; Derek Jarman (1942–94), director/scriptwriter/designer; David Puttnam (*b* 1941), producer; Ivor Montagu (1904–84), director/producer /scriptwriter.
Unpublished scripts (*c*20,000) and press-books (25,000).

Non-manuscript material: Audio cassettes (*c*100), plus listening copies of the BECTV Oral History Project cassettes; see also below.

Finding aids: Script card catalogue. Lists of special collections; sent to NRA. Computerisation in progress.

Facilities: Photocopying. Photography. Microfilm/fiche readers.

Conservation: Contracted out.

Publications: 'Preserving British Cinema History', *Contemporary Record*, 8/2 (1994).
'The Aileen and Michael Balcon Special Collection', *Historical Journal of Film, Radio and Television*, 16/4 (1996).
'The Business of Film', *Business Archives*, no. 72 (Nov 1996).

B National Film and Television Archive

Fax: (020) 7580 7503

E-mail: olwen.terris@bfi.org.uk

Enquiries: The Chief Cataloguer, Ms Olwen Terris

Open: Mon–Fri: 10.00–5.30.

Access: The catalogue of the film and TV collection is generally open to the public for consultation. Research viewings can also be arranged by appointment. Details of charges are available on request. The film and TV collection is not available for loan or hire.

Historical background: The NFTVA, part of the Collections Department of the British Film Institute, was founded in 1935 'to maintain a national repository of films of permanent value'. Its brief was extended to include television in the 1950s. A large complementary collection of stills, posters and designs is also held by the Stills, Posters and Designs Department. The NFTVA is a founder-member of the International Federation of Film Archives.

Acquisitions policy: To select, acquire, preserve, document and make permanently available for research and study a national collection of films and television programmes of all kinds exhibited or transmitted in the UK, from any source and of any nationality, which have lasting value as works of art, or are examples of cinema and television history, historical or scientific records, portraiture, or records of contemporary life and behaviour.

Non-manuscript material: Film and television collection comprising feature and short films, documentaries, newsreels animation and amateur films, 1895– (*c*300,000 titles).

Finding aids: Computerised database to holdings with search criteria such as title, country or director. Comprehensive subject and personality indexes, plus shot-lists for *c*10 per cent of the collection.

Facilities: 35 mm and 16 mm flatbed table viewers for film study. Video players and monitors for videocassette viewings. Microfilm readers.

Conservation: Conservation centre for core collections, i.e. film and video materials, and an active preservation policy. Paper conservation is normally contracted out.

Publications: British Films, 1927–39, 1971–81.
Catalogue of Stills, Posters and Designs.
Film and Television Periodical Holdings (1982).
Film/Video Production and Funding (1984).
TV Documentation: a Guide to BFI Library Services Resources (1985).
British Cinema Resource Book (1994).
Some special subject bibliographies.
BFI annual listing of publications.

557 British Humanist Association

Address: 47 Theobald's Road, London WC1X 8SP

Telephone: (020) 7430 0908

Fax: (020) 7430 1271

E-mail: robert@humanism.org.uk

Website: www.humanism.org.uk

Enquiries: The Executive Director, Robert Ashby

Open: Mon–Fri: 9.30–5.00.

Access: Generally open to the public, by prior arrangement.

Originally founded as the Union of Ethical Societies (later known as the Ethical Union) in 1896, the British Humanist Association is the UK's largest association of humanists. It has its own archives, including minutes and published documents, from the foundation onwards.

558 British Institute of Radiology
Bernard Sunley Library

Address: 36 Portland Place, London W1N 4AT

Telephone: (020) 7307 1405/7580 4085

Fax: (020) 7255 3209

E-mail: admin@bir.org.uk

Website: www.bir.org.uk

Enquiries: The Library and Information Services Manager, Mrs Kate Sanders

Open: Mon, Wed, Fri: 9.00–5.00; Tues, Thurs: 10.00–6.00 , by prior arrangement only.

Access: Bona fide scholars may apply for research tickets. Special permission is required to consult the archives and historic books. Charges are made for certain services.

Historical background: The present British Institute of Radiology, incorporated by royal charter in 1958, has its origin in the Röntgen Society, founded in March 1897, 16 months after the discovery of X-rays. The basic constitution of the institute dates from 1927. Application for membership may be made by any person, medically qualified or not, with interests in radiology. The archives derive from the initial collection of minutes and associated correspondence; artefacts derive from the initial gifts of X-ray tubes (currently on loan to the Science Museum) and historic books. Journals gained considerably from the Mackenzie Davidson Collection donated in 1923.

Acquisitions policy: To maintain and extend records of the evolution of the institute and of activities stimulated by its members.

Archives of organisation: Minute books of the Röntgen Society and successive bodies, including records of property transactions, membership lists and handbooks, 1897– .

Major collections: Minutes of the British X-Ray and Radium Protection Committee, 1921–48. Proceedings of the Radium Commission, 1929–48.
Book of Radiation Martyrs, with source material collected by F.G. Spear (1895–1980).
Notebooks of J. Read (1908–93), pioneer in radiation biology and the effects of oxygen on radiosensitivity.

Non-manuscript material: Group photographs of institute and international meetings and individual portraits.
Recordings of lectures.
Manufacturers' catalogues.
Newspaper cuttings on radiology, 1921–3.
Collections of X-ray prints in albums.
K.C. Clark Slide Library on Positioning in Radiography, based on lectures, 1935–80.

Finding aids: Outline list of archives (full details in preparation). Full catalogue of historic books.

Facilities: Photocopying.

Publications: P.J. Bishop: 'The Evolution of the British Journal of Radiology', *British Journal of Radiology*, x/6 (1973), 833–6.
——: 'The Library's Historical Collection', *British Institute of Radiology Bulletin*, i/3 (1975), 5.
Annual Reports of the British Institute of Radiology include summaries of work on archives and books.

559 British Library Newspaper Library

Address: Colindale Avenue, London NW9 5HE

Telephone: (020) 7412 7353

Fax: (020) 7412 7379

E-mail: newspaper@bl.uk

Website: www.bl.uk

Enquiries: The Information Officer

Open: Mon–Sat: 10.00–5.00. Applications must be made before 4.15.

Access: Holders of a Newspaper Library pass or British Library pass (for the purposes of research and reference not readily available in other libraries). There is no access for those under 18.

Historical background: The library was opened in 1905 as the British Museum Newspaper Repository to house English provincial, Welsh, Scottish and Irish newspapers. In 1932 it became the Newspaper Library and all the British Museum's newspapers were transferred to Colindale, with the exception of the pre-1801 London newspapers and newspapers in oriental languages. In 1973 it became part of the British Library.

Acquisitions policy: All UK and Irish newspapers received through legal deposit, also weekly and fortnightly popular magazines, comics and specialist titles (trade etc). Foreign newspapers are acquired in Western and Slavonic languages.

Major collections: Newspapers and magazines (600,000 vols; 270,000 reels of microfilm). Includes full sets of the main London editions of all national daily and Sunday papers from start of publication to the present day. Local newspapers are held from all over England, Wales, Scotland and Ireland. Foreign newspapers in Western and Slavonic languages are acquired from almost every country in the world.

Finding aids: On-line catalogues available at Colindale and Bloomsbury.

Facilities: Full range of copying services, including self-service microfilm reader/printers.

Conservation: In-house conservation workshop and bindery.

Publications: Catalogue of the Newspaper Library, Colindale (1975).
J. Westmancoat: *Newspapers* (1985).
Newsplan reports (in progress).
Bibliography of British Newspapers (vols in progress).

560 British Library of Political and Economic Science

London School of Economics

Parent organisation: University of London

Address: 10 Portugal Street, London WC2A 2HD

Telephone: (020) 7955 7223

Fax: (020) 7955 7454

E-mail: document@lse.ac.uk

Website: www.lse.ac.uk/blpes/archives/

Enquiries: The Archivist, Ms S. Donnelly

Open: Mon–Thurs: 10.00–7.30; Fri: 10.00–5.30 (5.00 during vacation); Sat: 11.00–5.30 (term and Easter vacation).
Closed for one week at Easter.

Access: Approved readers undertaking original research; students must produce evidence of their status and degree course. Some categories of reader will be charged a fee. An appointment is not necessary but readers are strongly advised to contact the Archivist before their first visit.

Historical background: The library of the London School of Economics was founded in 1896.

Acquisitions policy: Modern British political, economic and social history, social anthropology (mainly post-1890); history of the London School of Economics.

Archives of organisation: LSE archives, 1894–1968.

Major collections: Papers of Beatrice Webb (1858–1943) and Sidney Webb (1859–1947); John Stuart Mill (1806–73); Hugh Dalton (1887–1962); Bronislaw Malinowski (1884–1942); George Lansbury (1859–1940); Walter Citrine (1887–1983); Anthony Crosland (1918–77), James Meade (1907–95).
Archives of National Institute of Industrial Psychology, 1919–74; Political and Economic Planning, c1931–73; Independent Labour Party National Administrative Council, minutes and other papers, c1893–1950; Liberal Party, c1924–1982; Nationalised Industries Chairmen's Group, 1973–89; Royal Economic Society, 1890–1990; Fabian Society, 1881–1980s; International African Institute, 1920s–1980s.
Charles Booth Survey of London, 1885–1905 (426 vols).
New Survey of London Life and Labour, 1928–33.
Hall-Carpenter Archives of Lesbian and Gay History, c1957–1994.

Non-manuscript material: Webb Collection on Trade Unions.
G.B. Shaw (1856–1950), photographic collection.
Extensive collections of rare books on political, economic and social questions, and on socialism, 1485–1951.

UK election leaflets and other ephemera for most general and some other elections, 1945– .

Finding aids: Catalogues/handlists for most collections; an on-line catalogue is available in the Archives Division providing collection-level descriptions for all holdings and complete descriptions of all major collections. Searches can be undertaken on behalf of readers.

Facilities: Photocopying, microforms and photography by arrangement. Readers may use personal computers (but not scanners) and power points are provided. Microfilm/fiche readers/printers.

Publications: A Guide to Archives and Manuscripts in the University of London, 1 (1984), 1–35.

561 British Library Special Collections

Address: 96 Euston Road, London NW1 2DB

Telephone: (020) 7412 7501

Fax: (020) 7412 7400

Website: www.bl.uk

Enquiries: The Director of Special Collections.

Open: Mon: 10.00–5.00; Tues–Sat: 9.30–5.00.

Access: By reader's pass, valid for all reading rooms, available on application to the Reader Admissions Office (Mon: 10.00–6.00; Tues-Thurs: 9.30–6.00; Fri, Sat: 9.30–4.30).

Historical background: The foundation collections (Sloane, Cotton, Harley) date back to the establishment of the British Museum in 1753. MSS of all kinds, including music, maps and oriental material, were represented in these early collections and have been added to constantly ever since. The Philatelic Collections were founded in 1891 with the Tapling Collection bequest. The British Library was founded from the library departments of the British Museum in 1973. In 1982 the administration of the India Office Library and Records was transferred from the Foreign and Commonwealth Office to the British Library Board and has since been amalgamated with the Oriental Collections. In 1983 the British Institute of Recorded Sound joined the British Library as the National Sound Archive. All the Special Collections departments contain material of potential interest to archive and manuscript researchers. Since 1999 they have all been housed in the St. Pancras building. The British Library is recognised as a place of deposit for public records. The British Library Newspaper Library is administered separately (entry 559).

Acquisitions policy: There is an active policy of acquisition by purchase and gift in the field of historical papers and in many others, literary, artistic, cartographic, musical etc, of national interest.

Archives of organisation: Archives of the British Library since its foundation in 1973.

Facilities: Photocopying. Photography. Microfilm/fiche readers/printers.

Conservation: Full in-house facilities.

A Manuscripts Collections

Telephone: (020) 7412 7513

Fax: (020) 7412 7745

E-mail: mss@bl.uk

Enquiries: The Manuscripts Librarian

Major collections: Historical collections include important MSS from the 8th century onwards; letters and documents of virtually all of the British sovereigns; manorial rolls, charters, seals, cartularies, chronicles and estate maps. The collections are particularly strong in the papers of statesmen, prime ministers, diplomats, and military officers.

Literary MSS include the Anglo-Saxon Beowulf and the medieval Thomas Malory's Le Morte D'Arthur. Most of the major figures in English literary history are well represented, and there are significant collections of the MSS and letters of modern British authors, such as Evelyn Waugh and Virginia Woolf.

Larger archives include those of the publishers Macmillan & Co., the Society of Authors, and the Royal Literary Fund.

Significant holdings of medieval romances, Greek and Latin classical texts, and the works of later continental authors.

Theatre collections include plays submitted to the Lord Chamberlain's Office for examination and licensing, 1824–1968, and plays submitted under the terms of the Theatres Act, 1968– . Related collections include the archives of playwrights, and other theatrical figures.

Illuminated, biblical and liturgical manuscripts: important English and Continental illuminated MSS from the 7th-century 'Lindisfarne

Gospels' onwards; also two of the earliest surviving manuscript Bibles.

Papers of scientists, medical researchers and explorers. Also collections of antiquarians, particularly useful for the study of local history.

Non-manuscript material: Large collection of seals.

Original photographs.

Portraits, paintings, prints, drawings, plans.

Finding aids: Published catalogues of additions and catalogues of named collections. Supplementary unpublished finding aids available in Manuscripts Reading Room.

Amalgamated Index of Manuscripts.

NRA holds published catalogues and annual printouts. See NRA 13548 [*Guide to MSS*].

Card catalogues, lists and indexes, and many contemporary finding aids are available.

Catalogue of Additions to the MSS (including retro-converted records going back to mid-18th century) available on website.

Publications: M.A.E. Nickson: *Guide to the Catalogues and Indexes of the Department of Manuscripts.*

B Map Library

Telephone: (020) 7412 7702

Fax: (020) 7412 7780

E-mail: maps@bl.uk

Enquiries: The Map Librarian

Major collections: The national map library of Great Britain, with a collection of more than four million atlases, maps, globes and books on cartography, dating from the fifteenth century to the present day. The modern collections include Ordnance Survey, important deposits from the Ministry of Defence, worldwide topographical collections, a good collection of geological maps for the UK and worldwide and a comprehensive collection of fire insurance and shopping centre plans (most significant are those produced by the London-based firm Charles E. Goad Ltd).

Finding aids: Catalogue of MS maps, charts and plans.

Publications: British Library Map Catalogue (Primary Source Media, Reading, 1998), [CD-ROM].

C Music Collections

Telephone: (020) 7412 7527/7752

Fax: (020) 7412 7751

E-mail: music-collections@bl.uk

Enquiries: The Head of Music Collections

Major collections: Western Music Manuscripts: music manuscripts and papers relating to music and musicians, 1500– .
The Royal Music Library: contains some 5000 items, of which *c*1000 are manuscripts, including a unique collection of Handel autographs (97 vols).
The Zweig Collection: autograph manuscripts of many classical composers.

Non-manuscript material: Printed Music: music published in all European countries, late 15th century– , including English and Italian madrigalists; instrumental collections, such as those published by members of the Playford family; first editions of music by the major European composers; numerous collections of dance music, 17th and 18th centuries; and popular music, 1937– .

Publications: A. Hughes-Hughes: *Catalogue of Manuscript Music in the British Museum* (London, 1906–9; reprint 1964–6).
P. Willetts: *Handlist of Music Manuscripts acquired 1908–1968* (London, 1970).
CPM Plus: Catalogue of Printed Music (Bowker-Saur, London, rev. 1997), [CD-ROM].

D National Sound Archive

Telephone: (020) 7412 7440

Fax: (020) 7412 7741

E-mail: nsa.bl.uk

Non-manuscript material: Curatorial sections covering Western music; drama, poetry and documentary recordings; folk, traditional and world music; jazz; popular music; wildlife sounds; oral history.
UK commercially published recordings (through a system equivalent to legal deposit of books at the British Library).
Overseas commercially published recordings.

Recordings of BBC, ITV and Channel 4 broadcasts off transmission.

Duplicate pressings and tapes of BBC Sound Archive recordings.

NSA's own recordings.

National Life Story Collection recordings and Millennium Oral History Project.

Deposited collections of commercial and non-commercial recordings.

Major collection of historic recording machines.

Published discographies and record company catalogues.

Finding aids: CADENSA: on-line catalogue of sound recordings.

E Oriental & India Office Collection

Telephone: (020) 7412 7873

Fax: (020) 7412 7641

E-mail: oioc-enquiries@bl.uk

Website: www.bl.uk/collections/oriental/

Open: Mon–Fri: 10.00–5.00; Tues–Fri: 9.30–5.00.

Major collections: Oriental collections:
More than 45,000 oriental MSS, the largest collections being in Hebrew, Arabic, Persian, Turkish, Chinese and the languages of South and South-East Asia; especially rich in illuminated and illustrated Islamic MSS and Hebrew and Arabic religious and literary texts.

Stein Collection of Chinese Tibetan and Sanskrit, Khotanese, Vighur MSS from Chinese Turkestan (*c*25,000).

India Office Collections:
Archives of the East India Company, 1600–1858; the Board of Control, 1784–1858; the India Office, 1858–1947; and the Burma Office, 1937–48; while concentrating upon South Asia, the archive also covers the general history of the British penetration of Asia, ranging at different periods from St Helena, via South and East Africa, the Middle East, Malaysia, Indonesia and China, to Japan; includes maps (*c*20,000 items).

Oriental MSS (*c*27,800): major collections in Persian and Arabic, many illuminated and illustrated.

European MSS (*c*50,000): private papers of such individuals as Robert, 1st Baron Clive, and his son, Edward Clive (1751–1803); Sir Stamford Raffles (1781–1826). Papers of Viceroys including 1st Viscount Chelmsford, 1916–21;

Marquess Curzon, 1899–1905; India, Marquess of Dufferin and Ava, 1884–8; 8th Earl of Elgin, 1862–3; 9th Earl of Elgin, 1894–8; 1st Earl of Halifax, 1926–31; 5th Marquess of Lansdowne, 1888–94; 1st Baron Lawrence, 1864–9; 2nd Marquess of Linlithgow, 1936–43; 1st Earl of Lytton, 1876–80; 1st Earl of Northbrook, 1872–6; 1st Marquess of Reading, 1921–6; 1st Earl Wavell, 1943–7.

Non-manuscript material: Oriental Collections:
Early block-printed books from the Far East. More than 630,000 printed books, serials and newspapers, representing all the literary languages and cultures of Asia and of North and North-East Africa.

Growing collections of microforms.

Large intake of official publications from Asian countries.

India Office Collections:
India Office Records: official publications: (*c*70,000 vols).

India Office Library: European printed books (*c*58,000).

Oriental printed books (*c*270,000).

Prints, drawings and paintings (*c*30,000).

Photographs (*c*250,000).

Finding aids: A large number of lists and indexes are available, including many contemporary finding aids. The catalogues of European Manuscripts and of Prints, Drawings and Photographs have now been computerised.

Publications: Guide to the Department of Oriental Manuscripts and Printed Books (1977) [published catalogues (covering more than 100 languages) are listed and described].

A. Farrington: *The Records of the East India College, Haileybury, and other Institutions* (London, 1976).

I.A. Baxter: *A Brief Guide to Biographical Sources* (London, 1979).

A. Griffin: *A Brief Guide to Sources for the Study of Burma in the India Office Records* (London, 1979).

P. Tuson: *The Records of the British Residency and Agencies in the Persian Gulf* (London, 1979).

A.K. Jasbir Singh: *Gandhi and Civil Disobedience: Documents in the India Office Records, 1922–1946* (London, 1980).

L.A. Hall: *A Brief Guide to Sources for the Study of Afghanistan in the India Office Records* (London, 1981).

J. Sims: *A List and Index of Parliamentary Papers relating to India, 1908–1947* (London, 1981).

A. Farrington: *A Guide to the Records of the India Office Military Department* (London, 1982).

A Select List of Private Collections in the European Manuscripts (London, 1985).

R. Seton: *The Indian 'Mutiny', 1857–58. A Guide to Source Material in the India Office Library and Records* (London, 1986).

M.I. Moir: *A General Guide to the India Office Records* (London, 1988).

D.M. Blake: *Catalogue of the European MSS in the Oriental and India Office Collections of the British Library* (London, 1998).

F Philatelic Collections

Telephone: (020) 7412 7635/7636

Fax: (020) 7412 7780

Enquiries: The Head of Philatelic Collections

Major collections: Collections were established in 1891 with the bequest of the Tapling Collection and consist of more than eight million items, including postage and revenue stamps, postal stationery, artwork, essays, proofs, covers and entries, 'Cinderella' material, specimen issues, airmails, some postal history materials, official and private posts etc, for almost all countries and periods.

562 British Medical Association

Address: BMA House, Tavistock Square, London WC1H 9JP

Telephone: (020) 7383 6588

Fax: (020) 7383 6717

E-mail: rbirch@bma.org

Website: www.bma.org.uk

Enquiries: The Archivist

Open: Mon–Fri: 9.00–5.00.

Access: BMA members and other bona fide researchers, by appointment only. A letter of introduction is required from non-BMA members. Official records of the association are subject to a closure period.

Historical background: The BMA was founded in 1832 by Sir Charles Hastings to promote the medical and allied sciences and to maintain the honour and interests of the medical profession. Originally called the Provincial Medical and Surgical Association, it adopted its present name in 1856. The BMA is also a registered company and trade union. The archive was set up in 1993.

Acquisitions policy: The records of the association at both central and local level and other material relating to the history of the BMA, including personal papers of BMA members and officers, and records of related organisations.

Archives of organisation: Minutes of committees and annual meetings, 1834– .

Correspondence and subject files, *c*1900s– .

Deposited collections of minutes and other records of BMA divisions and branches, 1830s– .

Major collections: Records of the World Medical Association, 1946– ; Commonwealth Medical Association, 1962– , and its predecessor the British Commonwealth Medical Council, 1947– ; Panel Committee for the County of London, 1914– , and its successor, the London Medical Committee, 1948– .

Various small collections including those of Sir Charles Hastings (1794–1866) and Sir Henry Brackenbury (1866–1942).

Non-manuscript material: Photographs of BMA events, members and other medical personalities, 19th and 20th centuries.

Plans of BMA House, including some by Sir Edwin Lutyens.

The 'Hastings Collection of rare medical and related books.

Finding aids: Lists and indexes.

Facilities: Photocopying and photography by arrangement.

Conservation: Contracted out.

Publications: E. Muirhead Little: *History of the British Medical Association 1832–1932* (BMA, 1932).

E. Grey-Turner and F.M. Sutherland: *History of the British Medical Association Vol II: 1932–1981* (BMA, 1982).

P. Bartrip: *Themselves Writ Large: The British Medical Association 1832–1966* (BMJ, 1996).

E. Naish: *Promoting the Medical and Allied Sciences ... a Short History of Science at the BMA* (1995).

563 British Museum
Central Archives

Address: Great Russell Street, London WC1B 3DG

Telephone: (020) 7323 8224

Fax: (020) 7323 8118

E-mail: archives@thebritishmuseum.ac.uk

Website: www.thebritishmuseum.ac.uk

Enquiries: The Head of Archives, Mr Christopher Date

Open: Tues, Thurs: 10.00–1.00, 2.00–4.30.

Access: Generally open to the public, by appointment. Records less than 30 years old are closed under the terms of the Public Records Act 1958, and a small number of other records are closed for a longer period by order of the Lord Chancellor.

Historical background: The British Museum was founded in 1753 and has been governed throughout its history by a board of trustees. Its present-day curatorial departments have evolved from one original department of antiquities. It also included, until the 1880s, the departments which now form the Natural History Museum and, until 1973, the departments which now form part of the British Library. The museum's archives are public records and an archivist was first appointed in 1974.
Detailed documentation of the museum's collections of antiquities is held by the various departments.

Acquisitions policy: Material relating to the history of the museum is accepted by gift and may be acquired by purchase when appropriate.

Archives of organisation: Archives of the British Museum Trustees, Director and Museum Secretary, 1675– , including records of buildings and staff; purchases and donations of museum objects; finance; reading room of the former British Museum Library; excavations; deeds of title; administrative correspondence and papers.
Printed staff lists, 1847–1967.

Major collections: Papers of Charles Townley (1737–1805).

Non-manuscript material: Printed copies of statutes and proceedings of parliamentary commissions relating to the museum, 18th and 19th centuries; photographs of British Museum buildings, galleries and staff, 1840s– ; plans and drawings of the museum buildings and galleries, 1725– ; sound and visual recordings of museum staff and events.
Microfilm of the main classes of archives.

Finding aids: Class lists and indexes to the main classes; databases of photographs and plans.

Facilities: Photocopying (unbound MSS only). Photography. Microfilm reader-printers.

Publications: Introductory guide to Central Archives.
J. Wallace: 'The Central Archives of the British Museum', *Archives*, xix/84 (1990), 213–23.
M.L. Caygill and C. Date: *Building the British Museum* (British Museum Press, 1999).

564 British Orthodox Church

Parent organisation: Coptic Orthodox Patriarchate of Alexandria

Address: Church Secretariat, 10 Heathwood Gardens, Charlton, London SE7 8EP

Telephone: (020) 8854 3090

Fax: (020) 8244 7888

E-mail: boc@cwcom.net

Enquiries: The Librarian, James Kirby Tomblin
The Archivist, Dr Gregory Tillet

Open: By appointment only.

Access: Bona fide enquirers, on written application.

Historical background: The British Orthodox Church dates its foundation to 1866, when Jules Ferrette (1828–1904) was consecrated Bishop of Iona in the apostolic succession of the Syrian Orthodox Church. Having remained outside the structures of canonical orthodoxy for most of its history, in 1994 it entered into union with the Coptic Orthodox Patriarchate of Antioch under Pope Shenouda III.

Acquisitions policy: To maintain all records of the church.

Archives of organisation: Church records, registers and correspondence, 1866– .

Major collections: Private papers of Metropolitan Mar Georgius (1905–79), Bishop W.B. Crow (1895–1976) and Bishop U.V. Herford (1866–1938).

Papers of the now defunct Archdiocese of Antwerp, 1947–85, and the Apostolic Vicariate for France, 1952–70.

Collection relating to the history of the Orthodox Church in Great Britain; Old Catholicism and various small autocephalous churches.

Non-manuscript material: The Newman Collection of books, pamphlets and photographs relating to the Catholic Apostolic Church (commonly known as Irvingites).

Photographic collection, press cuttings and pamphlets.

Library of books on liturgy and Eastern Christendom, especially the Coptic and other oriental Orthodox Churches.

Finding aids: Card index. Catalogues of books and MSS (in progress).

Facilities: Very limited photocopying and photography.

565 British Province of the Society of Jesus Archives

Address: 114 Mount Street, London W1Y 6AH

Telephone: (020) 7493 7811

Fax: (020) 7495 6685/7499 0549

E-mail: tmmccoog@compuserve.com

Enquiries: The Archivist, Rev. Thomas M. McCoog
The Archivist Emeritus, Rev. T.G. Holt
Please address all correspondence for the attention of the Archivist.

Open: Mon–Fri: 10.00–1.00, by appointment only. Arrangements may be made for longer daily periods where researchers come from a distance.

Access: Bona fide students, on written application. Official policy forbids access to any Jesuit's papers until forty years after his death.

Historical background: The province archives supplement and continue the collection of MSS held at Stonyhurst, which virtually began with the Jesuit mission to England, Scotland and Wales from 1580. Original papers at Farm Street begin c1623 and cover England and Wales, and Scotland from 1857.

Acquisitions policy: All kinds of archival material concerning the history of the Society of Jesus, especially in England, Scotland and Wales, is received. The main accessions come from Jesuit houses, especially those which close, and from the papers of deceased Jesuits.

Archives of organisation: Official and private correspondence, registers and accounts of missions, c1623– .

Major collections: Correspondence of John Morris (1826–93); John Hungerford Pollen (1820–1902); Joseph Stevenson (1806–95); Herbert Thurston (1856–1939); and other members of the British Province.

Non-manuscript material: Large collections of transcripts, photocopies and microfilms of material from many British and continental archives concerning the British Jesuits in particular and British Catholics in general.

Extensive collection of printed books and pamphlets on Jesuit and British Catholic topics, 1525– , with special emphasis on the 16th and 17th centuries and the Victorian period.

Complete set of the English Recusant Literature reprint series. The archives holds copies of most of the works written by members of the British Province and is currently seeking to fill in the gaps.

Finding aids: Card index (not in general available, but cards of subjects of interest to researchers are shown them by an archivist or assistant).

Facilities: Limited photocopying. Microfilm reader.

Publications: F. Edwards: 'The Archives of the English Province of the Society of Jesus', *Journal of the Society of Archivists*, iii (1966), 107.

566 British Psycho-Analytical Society

Address: Institute of Psycho-Analysis, 112A–114, Shirland Road, London W9 2EQ

Telephone: (020) 7286 3028

Fax: (020) 7289 2264

E-mail: 106027.3376@compuserve.com

Enquiries: The Hon. Archivist, Dr Riccardo Steiner

Open: Mon–Fri: 10.00–6.00.
Closed in August.

Access: Researchers are allowed access by previous permission of the Honorary Archivist.

Historical background: The BPAS was founded in 1919 and the institute's library started in 1926. Ernest Jones (1879–1958) was president of the society and his correspondence forms the basis of the collections. A working party now exists to deal with the archives and MS collections.

Acquisitions policy: Donations of papers of people associated with the society.

Archives of organisation: British Psycho-Analytical Society archives, including minutes, correspondence and memoranda, 1919– .

Major collections: Personal and professional papers of Ernest Jones, c1900–1958.
Papers of James Strachey (1887–1967), translator of Freud; John Rickman (c1890–1951); Sylvia Payne (1880–1971); and Susan Isaacs (1885–1948), colleague of Melanie Klein.

Non-manuscript material: Newspaper cuttings.

Finding aids: Computer database.

Facilities: Photocopying.

567 British Railways Board Records Centre

Parent organisation: Strategic Rail Authority

Address: 66 Porchester Road, London W2 6ET

Telephone: (020) 7922 6627

Fax: (020) 7922 6557

Enquiries: The Records Officer, Mr Allan R. Leach

The Records Centre at Royal Oak is the custodian of the records of the British Railways Board (since 2000 the Strategic Rail Authority) and acts as a conduit between the board, the Public Record Office (entry 1058), the National Railway Museum (entry 1224) and the county/local record offices for papers no longer required by the board. The board holds documents, maps and plans dating from 1837 and is in the process of rationalising and cataloguing the holdings, some of which will be transferred to the PRO and other appropriate repositories. Material is not generally available for consultation, although bona fide researchers may contact the centre by writing.

568 British Red Cross Museum and Archives

Parent organisation: British Red Cross Society

Address: 9 Grosvenor Crescent, London SW1X 7EJ

Telephone: (020) 7201 5153

Fax: (020) 7235 0876

E-mail: enquiry@redcross.org.uk

Enquiries: The Archivist

Open: By arrangement only.

Access: Generally open to the public, by appointment only.

Historical background: The Red Cross movement was started in 1863 to help the sick and wounded of both sides in war. The British society was founded in 1870, when it was known as the British National Society for Aid to the Sick and Wounded in War. In 1905 it became the British Red Cross Society.

Acquisitions policy: To acquire records and artefacts relating to the history of the British Red Cross.

Archives of organisation: Minute books, 1905– ; other records of the society, including official reports on British Red Cross activities in a number of wars, c1870– ; Voluntary Aid Detachment personnel record cards, World Wars I and II.
Records of British Red Cross county branches, 1909– .
Limited information on overseas branches in pre-independence colonial territories.

Major collections: Records of Royal Star and Garter Home for Disabled Sailors, Soldiers and Airmen, Richmond, Surrey, 1915–87.
Voluntary Blood Donors Association, minute books, 1932–64.
Records of the Joint Committee of the British Red Cross Society and Order of St John, including records of its predecessor bodies the Joint War Committee, the Joint Council and the Joint War Organisation, 1914– . These bodies co-ordinated voluntary aid to the armed services during both World Wars, and their records include information about services to prisoners of war, medical work, fund-raising and personnel.
Papers of Col. Robert Loyd-Lindsay, later Lord Wantage (1832–1901), founder and first chairman of BRCS. These contain important

material on the Franco-Prussian War, 1870–1, and the South African War, 1899–1902.

Non-manuscript material: Museum Collection, including medical and nursing equipment, medals and badges and decorative textiles.
Large amount of printed and published posters, leaflets, first-aid handbooks, reports, etc, c1870– .
Large photograph collection.
Small collection of oral history tapes.
Training films and films showing International Red Cross work.

Finding aids: Lists. Accessions register. Subject names and geographical card indexes. Survey lists for items acquired before May 1985. Computerised finding aids currently being implemented. Some lists sent to NRA.

Facilities: Photocopying. Photography by arrangement.

Conservation: Contracted out.

Publications: B. Oliver: *The Red Cross in Action* (London, 1966).
M. Poulter: 'The Archives of the British Red Cross', *Social History of Medicine*, vi/1(1993), 143–7.
E. Wood: *The Red Cross Story* (1995).

569 British Veterinary Association

Address: 7 Mansfield Street, London W1M 0AT

Telephone: (020) 7636 6541

Fax: (020) 7436 2970

E-mail: bvahq@bva.co.uk

Enquiries: The Head of Veterinary Services, Ms Chrissie Nicholls

Open: Mon–Fri: 9.30–5.00

Access: Members and bona fide researchers only. An information service is provided for the media, parliamentarians and occasional researchers.

The association was founded in 1881 and retains its own archives. Collections of veterinary interest are normally referred to the Royal College of Veterinary Surgeons (entry 759).

570 Brompton Oratory

Address: Brompton Road, London SW7 2RP

Telephone: (020) 7589 4811

Fax: (020) 7584 1095

Enquiries: The Fr Librarian

Open: By arrangement only.

Access: Bona fide researchers, by appointment.

Historical background: The oratory was opened in 1854, although a library had existed from 1847.

Acquisitions policy: The oratory maintains its own archives and collections.

Archives of organisation: Internal records, 1854– . Recorded notes of general congregations.

Major collections: Letters of or about F.W. Faber (1814–63), superior of the oratory, and MSS of his works; Ralph Francis Kerr (1874–1932); and John Henry Newman (1801–90); as well as other London oratorians.
MSS of Thomas Francis Knox (1822–82).

Finding aids: NRA 16631.

Publications: The London Oratory, 1884–1984 (London, 1984).

571 Camden Local Studies and Archives Centre

Parent organisation: London Borough of Camden

Address: Holborn Library, 32–38 Theobalds Road, London WC1X 8PA

Telephone: (020) 7974 6342

Fax: (020) 7974 6284

E-mail: localstudies@camden.gov.uk

Website: www.camden.gov.uk

Enquiries: The Principal Officer, Local Studies and Archives, Mr R.G. Knight

Open: Mon, Thurs: 10.00–7.00; Tues: 10.00–6.00; Fri: 10.00–1.00; Sat: 10.00–1.00, 2.00–5.00.

Access: Generally open to the public. Appointments are needed for some archives and there is restricted access to items less than 30 years old. The Kate Greenaway Collection is available by special application only.

Historical background: In 1965 the London Borough of Camden was formed by the amalgamation of the former metropolitan boroughs of Hampstead, Holborn and St Pancras. Each borough had collected archives and local history material since the first library service was established in 1896. The Local Studies and Archives Centre holds many archives of the London Borough of Camden and its predecessors, and many local organisations have deposited their records.

Acquisitions policy: The centre aims to record life and events in Camden: its people, buildings and institutions.

Archives of organisation: London Borough of Camden and its predecessor bodies. Parish records, 1617–1900, including vestry and committee minutes, churchwardens' accounts, poor law records, paving records, ratebooks and other items (but excluding parish registers). District boards of works records, 1856–1900. Local commissioners' and boards' records, 1850–1906. Metropolitan Boroughs of Hampstead, Holborn and St Pancras records, 1900–65, including council and committee minutes, ratebooks and valuation lists. London Borough of Camden records, 1965–80, including council and committee minutes, ratebooks and valuation lists.

Major collections: Hampstead Manor: copy of minute books, 1742–1843, and papers concerning disputes and court cases, particularly concerning Hampstead Heath.

Highgate Cemetery: burial registers and other records, 1839–1984.

Transcriptions of monumental inscriptions, 1860s–80s, including ones by F.T. Cansick for Holborn and St Pancras and R. Milward for Hampstead.

Other collections include records from local societies and bodies, some local business records, personal papers, title deeds and other documents.

Non-manuscript material: Local newspapers; cuttings from local and national newspapers; ephemeral items, including theatre programmes and posters.

Illustrations, including photographs, slides, prints, watercolours, drawings and other works of art (c40,000).

Ordnance Survey, parish and other London and local maps (c3000).

Oral history tapes, films, videos etc.

Census returns for area of present London Borough of Camden, 1841–91 (microfilm).

Bellmoor Collection: compiled by Hampstead historian Thomas J. Barratt (21 vols).

Dalziel Collection: proof engravings by the Dalziel brothers, who lived and worked in Hampstead and Camden Town (c250).

Ambrose Heal Collection: ephemera, illustrations, maps, playbills and manuscripts about St Pancras up to 1913.

G.B. Shaw Collection: books (including first editions), pamphlets, photographs, letters and other items.

Kate Greenaway Collection: printed items, illustrations, including original drawings, etc (c1400 items).

St John, Hampstead, parish registers, 1560–c1842 (microfilm).

Finding aids: Card catalogues. Various lists and indexes. Lists sent to NRA.

Facilities: Photocopying. Photography by arrangement. Microfilm/fiche readers/printers.

Conservation: In-house conservation unit.

Publications: Camden Now and Then: a Student's Guide to the Local Studies Library (1989).
Camden Local Studies and Archives Centre: a Brief Guide to the Collections (1994).
New guide in preparation.
Various other publications; list available.

572 Carlton Club

Address: 69 St James's Street, London SW1A 1PJ

Telephone: (020) 7399 0901

Fax: (020) 7495 4090

E-mail: secretary@carltonclub.co.uk

Enquiries: The Secretary, Mr A.E. Telfer

Open: Mon–Fri: by arrangement.
Closed August.

Access: Bona fide researchers, by appointment.

The Carlton Club, a club for Conservative Party supporters, was founded in 1832. Most of the records and the library were destroyed by enemy action in 1940, but some archives of the club survive, including members' records from 1832. The club owns a number of portraits of 19th- and 20th-century Conservative leaders. Photocopying facilities are available. See Sir Charles Petrie: *The Carlton Club*; Barry Phelps: *Power and the Party* [includes 1st and 2nd Carlton Lectures].

573 Carpenters' Company

Address: Carpenters' Hall, 1 Throgmorton Avenue, London EC2N 2JJ

Telephone: (020) 7588 7001

Fax: (020) 7638 6286

Website: www.thecarpenterscompany.co.uk

Enquiries: The Archivist

Open: Mon–Fri: 9.30–4.30.

Access: Bona fide researchers, by appointment only. Prospective researchers should write in the first instance, outlining their area of interest.

Historical background: The records of the Carpenters' Company (an ancient City of London guild) survive from 1438, although the company is much older. The company received its grant-of-arms in 1466 and its first charter in 1477. Originally established to control the carpentry trade, the company's main concerns are the administration of its charities and estates. Its earliest archives (principally court and membership records) are on long-term deposit at Guildhall Library (entry 624). The records retained at the Hall are principally records relating to property or charities, 19th and 20th centuries.

Acquisitions policy: To acquire archival items relating to the Carpenters' Company and its activities, primarily through the retention of historically important modern records.

Archives of organisation: Foundational records; court and committees papers; membership records; charity and estate records; and administrative files.

Non-manuscript material: The combined technical libraries of the company and the Institute of Carpenters.

Finding aids: Biographical card index of members, 16th century– .
Catalogue currently in progress.

Conservation: Contracted out.

Publications: J. Ridley: *A History of the Carpenters' Company* (1995).

574 Central St Martins College of Art and Design

Parent organisation: The London Institute

Address: Southampton Row, London WC1B 4AP

Telephone: (020) 7514 7146

Fax: (020) 7514 7024

E-mail: museumcollection@csm.linst.ac.uk

Enquiries: The Head of Museum and Study Collections, Sylvia Backemeyer

Open: Term: Mon–Fri, by appointment only.

Access: Staff and students of London Institute and bona fide researchers.

Acquisitions policy: History of the founding colleges; work by alumni of the Central School, St Martins and Central St Martins.

Archives of organisation: Collection of documents relating to the history of the founding colleges.

Non-manuscript material: German and UFA film posters; prints and drawings; Joyce Clissold Textile Archive; the Lethaby Archive of Teaching Examples; the School of Book Production Collection and the Central Lettering Record.
Study collection of books similarly acquired and used as teaching examples.

Finding aids: On-line database with digitised images for part of the collection; complete database available in-house.

Publications: S. Backemeyer: *Object Lessons: Central St Martins Art and Design Archive* (Lethaby Press/Lund Humphries, 1996).

575 Central School of Speech and Drama
Learning & Information Services

Address: Embassy Theatre, 64 Eton Avenue, London NW3 3HY

Telephone: (020) 7559 3942

Fax: (020) 7586 1665

E-mail: library@cssd.ac.uk

Website: www.cssd.ac.uk

Enquiries: The Library Services Manager, Peter Collis

Open: Term: Mon–Thurs: 9.30–7.45; Fri: 9.30–4.45; Sat: 1.00–4.45.
Vacation: Mon–Fri: 11.00–4.45.

Access: Generally open to the public; an appointment is necessary and fees are charged.

The Central School of Speech and Drama was founded in 1906 by Elsie Fogerty, to offer an entirely new form of training in speech and drama for young actors and other students. In 1956 the school moved to its current location at the Embassy Theatre in Swiss Cottage. There is a very small archive concerned with the history and development of the school. Donations of material concerned with the history of CSSD are accepted, although space constraints mean that it is not current policy to expand the archive significantly.

576 Chartered Institute of Bankers

Address: 90 Bishopsgate, London EC2N 4DQ

Telephone: (020) 7444 7111

Website: www.eubfn.com/index.html

Enquiries: The Librarian

Open: Mon–Fri: 9.00–5.00.

Access: Anyone wishing to consult the institute's archives should apply to the Librarian in writing.

The Institute of Bankers was founded in 1879 to provide the educational background for bankers at all stages of their careers. The organisation maintains a library, formed in 1879, and owns a historical collection of paper money which is now housed in the British Museum. The archives include council minutes and there is a small collection of documents relating to the work of the institute in the field of banking education. The CIB is now branded as the Institute of Financial Services. See E. Green: *Debtors to their Profession: a History of the Institute of Bankers, 1879–1979* (Institute of Bankers, 1979).

577 Chartered Institute of Public Finance and Accountancy

Address: Information Centre, CIPFA, 3 Robert Street, London WC2N 6BH

Telephone: (020) 7543 5600

Fax: (020) 7543 5700

Website: www.cipfa.org.uk

Enquiries: The Information Manager, Margaret Conlon

Open: Mon–Fri: 9.00–5.00.

The institute was founded in 1885 as the Corporate Treasurers' and Accountants' Institute. It was incorporated under the Companies Acts in 1901 as the Institute of Municipal Treasurers and Accountants (IMTA), and was granted a royal charter under that name in 1959. In 1973 the present name was adopted. A library was formally established in 1985 and this incorporated the institute's archives, including the institute journal, annual report and publications, 1885– ; archives of associated bodies are also held, notably the Association of Health Service Treasurers and IMTA students' societies. The Information Service was established in 1998 following the closure of the library, and the archive is now stored off site. It conducts research enquiries but does not give access to the archives.

578 Chartered Insurance Institute

Address: The Library, 20 Aldermanbury, London EC2V 7HY

Telephone: (020) 7417 4415/6

Fax: (020) 7972 0110

E-mail: info@cii.co.uk

Open: Mon, Tues, Thurs: 9.00–5.00; Wed: 10.00–5.00; Fri: 9.00–4.45.

Access: Members and bona fide researchers. An admission charge is made for non-members.

The Federation of Insurance Institutes of Great Britain and Ireland was established in 1897. Ten years later it was replaced by the Chartered Insurance Institute of Great Britain and Ireland, which in 1912 became the Chartered Insurance Institute. The institute holds its own archives, which are primarily for internal use only, and it does not actively acquire records. There are also substantial catalogued collections of insurance policies and other insurance ephemera, 17th–20th centuries, as well as a rare book collection. See *Sources of Insurance History: a Guide to Historical Material in the CII Library* (London, 1990). The institute's Insurance History Committee actively promotes interest in insurance archives.

579 Chelsea College of Art and Design

Parent organisation: The London Institute

Address: Manresa Road, London SW3 6LS

Telephone: (020) 7514 7773

Fax: (020) 7514 7785

E-mail: mr-lib@linst.ac.uk

Website: www.linst.ac.uk/library/

Enquiries: Dr Stephen Bury

Open: Mon–Fri: 10.00–1.00, 2.00–5.00, by appointment only.

Access: Bona fide researchers, by prior arrangement.

Historical background: The college was formerly Chelsea School of Art, which was part of the South Western Polytechnic from 1895 to 1922, then Chelsea Polytechnic from 1922 to 1956, Chelsea College of Science and Technology from 1957 to 1966, and autonomous from 1963 to 1986. It subsumed Regent Street Polytechnic Art School in 1963 and Hammersmith School of Arts in 1976. It has been part of the London Institute since 1986. Staff and student records are held by Kings College London (entry 669).

Acquisitions policy: The college acquires material relating to its mission of supporting teaching, learning and research in contemporary art.

Major collections: Correspondence of S.J. Bury, Germano Celant and others.
Archive of Kurt Schwitters (1887–1948), including Lords Gallery files.
Women's International Art Club (from papers of Gwen Barnard), 1950–76.

Non-manuscript material: Prospectuses, playscripts, programmes, 1895–1963.
Slides of works, prospectuses, exhibition catalogues, photographs, 1964– .
Ian Hamilton Finlay (*b* 1925): plans, prints etc.

Facilities: Photocopying.

Conservation: Contracted out.

Publications: S. Bury: *Artists' Books* (Aldershot, 1995).

580 Chelsea Physic Garden

Parent organisation: Chelsea Physic Garden Company

Address: 66 Royal Hospital Road, London SW3 4HS

Telephone: (020) 7352 5646

Fax: (020) 7376 3910

Website: www.cpgarden.demon.co.uk

Enquiries: The Curator

Open: Apr–Oct: Mon–Wed: 12.00–5.00; Sun: 2.00–6.00.

Access: Bona fide scholars, by appointment only.

Historical background: The Chelsea Physic Garden Company is a registered charity set up in 1983 to continue to administer the Chelsea Physic Garden, founded in 1673 by the Society of Apothecaries. In 1899 control of the Society of Apothecaries passed to the City Parochial Fund. Most of Chelsea Physic Garden's archives are housed at the Guildhall Library (entry 624).

Acquisitions policy: To maintain its archives.

Archives of organisation: A few fragmentary records, including catalogues of seeds sown and accounts, 1785–1842.
Committee of management minutes, 1899– ; attendance records, 1912–76.

Major collections: Alicia Amherst, Lady Rockley (1865–1941): MSS, including material on gardening history.

Non-manuscript material: Photographs of the garden, including collection of William Hales, curator, 1899–1937.
Publications, including guide books, seed lists etc, 1900– .
Herbarium collection.

Facilities: Photography by prior arrangement.

Publications: Catalogue of the Library of the Chelsea Physic Garden (1956) [includes MSS].

581 Children's Society Archive

Parent organisation: The Children's Society

Address: Block A, Floor 2, Tower Bridge Business Complex, 100 Clement's Road, Bermondsey, London SE16 4DG

Telephone: (020) 7252 2966

Fax: (020) 7837 3902

E-mail: archives@the-childrens-society.org.uk

Website: www.the-childrens-society.org.uk

Enquiries: The Records Manager and Archivist, Ian Wakeling

Open: Mon–Fri: 9.30–5.00.

Access: Generally open to the public, by appointment. There is restricted access to case records.

Historical background: The society was founded in 1881 by Prebendary Edward de Mountjoie Rudolf (1852–1933) as the child-care organisation of the Church of England. Known originally as the Church of England Society for Providing Homes for Waifs and Strays, it was renamed the Church of England Children's Society in 1946. The society adopted its present title in 1982. Until the 1970s it ran a large number of residential children's homes and specialised in the field of adoption, fostering and boarding-out. The 1970s saw a shift in practice that led to the development of community-based social work projects and preventative work with children, young people and their families. The earlier records are incomplete, some having been lost through bombing during the war.

Acquisitions policy: Records relating to the development of the society's child-care and fundraising practices and policies.

Archives of organisation: Annual reports, branch minute books, diet books, admission and discharge registers, correspondence *re* the administration of children's homes and projects, and general promotional material, including leaflets and posters.
Society journals: *Our Waifs and Strays* (1882–1953), *Gateway* (1953–1993) and *Brothers and Sisters* (1891–1971).

Major collections: Children's case files, 1882–1926 (30,000).
Papers of the Churches Association for Family Welfare, 1924–90.

Non-manuscript material: Photograph collection of prints and negatives, 19th century–(10,000).

Finding aids: A provisional catalogue for the records of the society's homes is available. The majority of the earlier photographs have catalogue lists and an index. Index entries to homes and projects in the publications *Our Waifs and Strays* and *Gateway*.

Facilities: Photocopying. Photography.

Publications: J. Stroud: *Thirteen Penny Stamps* (London, 1971).

582 Church of England Record Centre

Parent organisation: Archbishops' Council of the Church of England

Address: 15 Galleywall Road, Bermondsey, London SE16 3PB

Telephone: (020) 7898 1030

Fax: (020) 7898 1031

E-mail: archivist@c-of-e.org.uk

Website: www.cofe.anglican.org

Enquiries: The National Society Archivist, Ms S. Duffield

Open: Mon, Weds: 10.00–4.30; Tues: 11.00–4.30.

Access: Bona fide researchers, by appointment. Records are open to the public, except for 100-year closure on personal files and 30-year closure on certain administrative files. Access to the archives of the ecumenical bodies is at the discretion of the organisation concerned.

Historical background: The record centre came into operation in 1989, and incorporates the former archives of the Church Commissioners, the General Synod, and the National Society for Promoting Religious Education with a few smaller collections, including the records of the former British Council of Churches. The centre also assists the voluntary organisations of the Church of England on request, and acts as a clearing-house for information on all Anglican records.

Acquisitions policy: Generally restricted to the records of the parent organisations, but the papers of voluntary bodies are occasionally housed as an emergency measure, and there are papers of leading churchmen (normally having connections with one or more of the parent bodies). Only central Anglican records are accepted; parish and diocesan records are cared for by the relevant diocesan record office (normally the county record office).

Major collections: Church Commissioners: archives, including those of predecessor bodies, Queen Anne's Bounty, 1704–1948, the Church Building Commissioners, 1818–56, and the Ecclesiastical Commissioners, 1836–1948; the bulk relates to the estates which were inherited from the bishops and deans and chapters in the 19th century, and the involvement of the Church Commissioners and their predecessors in a great variety of specific church matters as a result of various Acts and Measures.

General Synod: departmental material, mainly 20th century, but inherited papers include those of the Church of England Purity Society, 1887– ; the Church Defence Institution, 1859– ; the Church Reform League, 1895– , and the Colonial/Overseas Bishoprics Fund (f. 1841).

Personal papers include those of Dr Francis Eeles (1876–1954), former secretary of the Central Council for the Care of Churches, a leading liturgical scholar and an authority on women's ministry; and certain correspondence of Lord Hugh Cecil, Lord Quickswood (1869–1956), primarily on church affairs of the 1920s and 1930s.

National Society: minute books and annual reports, 1811– ; School and Teaching Training College, correspondence, c1816– .

Records of Church of England Sunday School Institute, 1843–1936, and St Christopher's College, Blackheath, 1908–1960s.

Records of Church of England schools in the diocese of London and Southwark.

Non-manuscript material: The reference library includes sets of published Church Assembly/General Synod debates and papers; *Church of England Yearbook*, 1883– ; *Crockford/Clergy List*; and *Chronicles of the Convocation of Canterbury*.

Small photographic archive.

The National Society has an important library relating to the history of education.

Finding aids: Chiefly contemporary finding aids, some being computerised. Some lists of General Synod material. Some lists sent to NRA.

Facilities: Photocopying and photography.

Conservation: Very limited in-house facilities.

Publications: A. Savidge: *The Foundation and Early Days of Queen Anne's Bounty* (1955).

M.H. Port: *Six Hundred New Churches* (1961) [history of the Church Building Commissioners].

G.F.A. Best: *Temporal Pillars* (1964) [history of Queen Anne's Bounty and the Ecclesiastical Commissioners].

A. Savidge: *The Parsonages in England* (1964).

C.J. Kitching: *The Central Records of the Church of England: a Report and Survey presented to the Pilgrim and Radcliffe Trustees* (London, 1976).

Series of leaflets on main classes of records.

583   City of London Club

Address: 19 Old Broad Street, London EC2N 1DS

Telephone: (020) 7588 7991

Fax: (020) 7374 2020

Website: www.cityclub.uk.com

Enquiries: The Club Secretary

Open: Mon–Fri: 8.00–5.00.

Access: Non-members of the club must write to the general committee via the Club Secretary for access.

Historical background: The City of London Club was founded in 1832 by a group of prominent bankers, merchants and shipowners, who formed a committee under the chairmanship of Mr John Masterman, MP.

Archives of organisation: Minutes of committee meetings (c30 vols); membership lists; menus; album of photographs of original members of the club; miscellaneous documents, 1832– .

Original plans drawn by Philip Hardwick, the architect of the club (52).

Facilities: Photocopying.

584   City University Library

Address: Northampton Square, London EC1V 0HB

Telephone: (020) 7477 8193

Fax: (020) 7477 8194

E-mail: library@city.ac.uk

Enquiries: The Deputy Librarian
The Hon. Archivist

Open: Term: Mon–Thurs: 9.00–9.00; Fri: 9.00–8.00.
Vacation: Mon–Fri: 9.00–5.00.

Access: Bona fide researchers.

Founded in 1894 as the Northampton Institute and renamed the City University in 1966, the university does not have an active policy relating to its archives. Surviving material, including governing body and council minutes, is held. In addition the library has marked files with contributors' names of *The Athenaeum*, a forerunner of the *New Statesman*, late 19th–early 20th centuries, and papers of Sir Robert Birley (1903–82), educationist and Professor of Social Sciences and Education in the university. There is a published history by J. Teague: *The City University History* (London, 1980).

585 Clothworkers' Company

Address: Clothworkers' Hall, Dunster Court, Mincing Lane, London EC3R 7AH

Telephone: (020) 7623 7041

Fax: (020) 7283 1289

E-mail: enquiries@clothworkers.co.uk

Website: www.clothworkers.co.uk

Enquiries: The Archivist, Mr D.E. Wickham

Open: Mon–Fri: 9.30–4.30.

Access: After acceptance of details of purpose and requirements of study, and by appointment only; suitable written reference is required in advance. Problems of supervision and accommodation mean that random enquiries are not encouraged.

Historical background: The company was incorporated by royal charter in 1528 and its records are practically complete to date. The company's involvement with clothworking (i.e. cloth finishing) was always limited to London, and the records are not normally of use for any aspect of the cloth trade of Kent, East Anglia or the Cotswolds.

Acquisitions policy: Restricted to records relating directly to the company, its prominent members, its history, and its post-industrial revolution status as a charitable organisation. To a large extent these items are self-generating.

Archives of organisation: All aspects of the history and modern work of this City of London livery company and its associated charitable foundation, 1528– .

Finding aids: Some lists and indexes.

Conservation: On-going contracted-out programme.

Publications: T. Girtin: *The Golden Ram: a Narrative History of the Clothworkers' Company, 1528–1958* (1958).
D.E. Wickham: *Clothworker's Hall in the City of London* (1989).

586 College of Arms

Address: Queen Victoria Street, London EC4V 4BT

Telephone: (020) 7248 2762

Fax: (020) 7248 6448

E-mail: enquiries@college-of-arms.gov.uk

Website: www.college-of-arms.gov.uk

Enquiries: The Officer in Waiting (heraldic and genealogical matters)
The Archivist, Mr R.C. Yorke (academic matters)

Open: Mon–Fri: 10.00–4.00.

Access: Through an officer of arms or the Archivist; prior contact by academic enquirers recommended. A fee may be charged.

Historical background: The English heralds were made a body corporate in 1484. The College of Arms has been on its present site since 1555, being rebuilt after the Great Fire of 1666. The archives comprise both the official records of the college and the collections of many individual heralds, who have included well-known antiquaries. There is medieval material dating from well before 1484.

Acquisitions policy: The archives are augmented by the generation of records within the college, and by the acquisition of collections from heralds. Relevant material may be purchased from, or given by, outside sources.

Archives of organisation: Official records: these include visitations; grants of arms; enrolments of royal warrants, pedigrees etc; royal and other ceremonials; records of Garter King of Arms; records of the Court of Chivalry; and the administrative records of the college.
Semi-official and unofficial records include rolls of arms, armorials, pedigrees, painters' work-books, and papers relating to orders of chivalry.

Major collections: Arundel MSS; Combwell Priory and other charters; miscellaneous family and estate papers.
Some 50 collections of individual heralds and others.

Non-manuscript material: Bookplate and seal collections.

Finding aids: Various lists and indexes. L.M. Midgley: Report on *Miscellaneous Deeds, including Charters relating to Combwell Priory in the Collections of the College Arms* (1980) [typescript].

Facilities: Photocopying. Photography and microfilming by arrangement. All reproduction is subject to permission; official records may not be copied.

Conservation: In-house facility.

Publications: W.H. Black: *Catalogue of the Arundel Manuscripts in the College of Arms* (1829).

A.R. Wagner: *The Records and Collections of the College of Arms* (1952).

F. Jones: *Catalogue of Welsh Manuscripts in the College of Arms* (1988).

L. Campbell and F. Steer (comps): *A Catalogue of Manuscripts in the College of Arms: Collections,* i (1988).

587 Commonwealth Institute
Commonwealth Resource Centre

Address: Kensington High Street, London W8 6NQ

Telephone: (020) 7603 4535 ext. 210

Fax: (020) 7602 7374

E-mail: info@commonwealth.org.uk

Website: www.commonwealth.org.uk

Enquiries: The Head of Library and Information Services

Open: Mon–Sat: 10.00–4.00, by appointment.

Access: Serious users over the age of 18.

Historical background: The present centre dates from 1962, when the new institute building was opened in Kensington High Street. Before that, as the Imperial Institute at a site in South Kensington, there had existed a library, most of which was dispersed at the time of removal. It is believed that some archival materials, dealing with life in the colonial possessions, and particularly a large collection of photographic slides, were destroyed before removal to the new premises. The library in the new building was originally intended for use by teachers and collected materials mainly concerning contemporary life in Commonwealth countries. The library was opened to the general public from *c*1972. In 1977 most of the archives of the Imperial Institute, up to 1958, were deposited at the Public Record Office (entry 1058).

Acquisitions policy: There is no positive acquisitions policy, and no funding is available to acquire archival material relating to the Commonwealth from external sources.

Major collections: Garfield Todd (Zimbabwe) Archive: letters from Mrs G. Todd and her husband, ex-Prime Minister of Rhodesia, explaining conditions under detention, confinement and imprisonment during the period of Unilateral Declaration of Independence, *c*1965– .

Harold Ingrams Archive: miscellaneous papers, articles and MS books covering his career as colonial administrator, journalist and writer, *c*1900–1970s.

Non-manuscript material: Special collection of Commonwealth literature (in English), consisting of published creative writing and critical responses from most Commonwealth countries.

Newscuttings and articles on writers; recordings of readings, dramatic productions and interviews.

Finding aids: Lists of some collections, including literature, recordings and audio-visual materials [list available on application].

Facilities: Photocopying. Range of audio-visual hardware.

588 Corporation of London Records Office

Address: PO Box 270, Guildhall,, London EC2P 2EJ

Telephone: (020) 7332 1251

Fax: (020) 7710 8682

E-mail: clro@ms.corpoflondon.gov.uk

Website: www.cityoflondon.gov.uk

Enquiries: The City Archivist, Mr J.R. Sewell

Open: Mon–Fri: 9.30–4.45; an appointment is necessary to see rate books.

Access: Generally open to the public.

Historical background: The office is the official record office for the archives of the Corporation of the City of London. It is recognised as a place of deposit for public records.

Acquisitions policy: To accept any official record of the corporation that is intended for permanent preservation and which is, in the opinion of the professional staff, worthy of inclusion among the archives.

Archives of organisation: Official archives of the corporation, 11th–20th centuries, including records of admissions to the freedom of the city, 1681–1940; at many periods the principal classes include much of national interest.

Other classes of records reflect special responsibilities or associations of the corporation and jurisdiction and property interests outside the city boundaries; these records include:

Bridge House Estates, deeds, rentals, accounts, minute books etc, relating to maintenance of London Bridge and, later, other bridges within the city, 11th century– .

Royal Contract Estates, records of estates in many counties granted by the Crown in 1628 for sale to settle crown debts, 17th century.

Brokers' admission records, 1691–1886.

Southwark: coroners' records, 1788–1932; sessions of the peace records, 1667–1870; manorial records, 1539–1959.

Finsbury: manorial records, 1550–1867; property records, 1567–1867.

City of London Lunatic Asylum (later known as City of London Mental Hospital and Stone House Hospital) records, 1859–1948.

Guildhall School of Music and Drama records, 1878–1989.

Emanuel Hospital, Westminster, and Brandesburton Estate, Yorkshire, records, early 17th–20th centuries.

Thames Conservancy records, 17th–19th centuries.

Lieutenancy of the City of London, commissions, lists and minutes, 17th–19th centuries.

Irish Society records of the plantation of Ulster and management of estates there, 17th–20th centuries.

Non-manuscript material: Large collection of plans of civic estates and buildings, 15th century– .

Finding aids: Subject indexes; various personal name indexes; lists and schedules.

Facilities: Photocopying. Photography by arrangement. Microfilm/fiche readers.

Conservation: In-house.

Publications: P.E. Jones and R. Smith: *Guide to the Records at Guildhall London*, pt I: *The Corporation of London Records Office* (1951).
H. Deadman and E. Scudder: *An Introductory Guide to the Corporation of London Records Office* (1994).
Many calendars of medieval and later records [list available].
Research guides and information sheets [list available].

589 Council for the Care of Churches

Parent organisation: Archbishops Council of the Church of England

Address: Church House, Great Smith Street, London SW1P 3NZ

Telephone: (020) 7898 1884

Fax: (020) 7898 1881

E-mail: enquiries@ccc.c-of-e.org.uk

Enquiries: The Librarian, Miss Janet Seeley

Open: Mon–Fri: 9.30–4.30.

Access: Generally open to the public, by appointment only.

Historical background: The council was established in 1921 as the central co-ordinating body for the Diocesan Advisory Committees for the Care of Churches. The library and National Survey of Churches were developed from the outset. The council supplies photographic and documentary information on the work of contemporary artists and craftsmen who are interested in ecclesiastical commissions.

Acquisitions policy: To strengthen the National Survey of Churches, by donation and purchase; to acquire special collections through bequests and gifts; to augment records of contemporary craftsmanship and conservation, by donation from practitioners.

Archives of organisation: National Survey of Churches files, many including photographs and guide books, on most of the 17,000 churches and chapels of the Church of England; the collection is particularly rich in postcards and photographs, c1900–50.

Major collections: Canon B.F.L. Clarke Collection of MS notes, covering c11,000 Anglican churches, with details of 18th- and 19th-century restorations; also photographs.
Canon P.B.G. Binnall's card index and MS notes on 19th-century stained glass.
Gordon Barnes Collection of MS notes and photographs, with emphasis on Victorian church architecture, especially in London and Worcestershire.

Non-manuscript material: Canon B.F.L. Clarke Collection of postcards (c20,000).
Printed items on ecclesiastical art and architecture, with special reference to Anglican churches and their furnishings (c12,000).

Finding aids: Card catalogue.

Facilities: Photocopying.

Publications: Information sheet [available from the librarian].

590 Courtauld Institute of Art

Parent organisation: University of London

Address: Somerset House, The Strand, London WC2R 0RN

Telephone: (020) 7848 2706

Fax: (020) 7873 2887

E-mail: susan.scott@courtauld.ac.uk

Website: www.courtauld.ac.uk

Enquiries: The Librarian, Book Library

Open: Term: Mon–Fri: 9.30–7.00.
Vacation: Mon–Fri: 10.30–5.00. (Closed one month during the summer vacation.)
Appointments are always necessary.

Access: Bona fide researchers; enquiries should be made well in advance of a visit.

Historical background: The Institute opened in 1931 in Home House, Portman Square. It moved to its present location, Somerset House, in 1989. The library (called the Book Library) was started in 1933.

Acquisitions policy: No proactive acquisitions policy, but material offered may be accepted if considered appropriate.

Archives of organisation: Records of the Institute, 1931– .

Major collections: Academic papers of Professor Anthony Blunt (1907–83).
Papers of Lord Lee of Fareham (1868–1947).
Correspondence of Philip Webb (1831–1915), architect.

Finding aids: Catalogues or checklists for all collections.

Facilities: Photocopying. Photography. Microfilm/fiche reader/printer.

Publications: Guide to the archives available on website.

591 Coutts & Co (Archive Department)

Parent organisation: Royal Bank of Scotland Group

Address: 440 Strand, London WC2R 0QS

Telephone: (020) 7753 1000

Fax: (020) 753 1051

Enquiries: The Archivist, Ms Tracey Earl

Open: By appointment only.

Access: Bona fide researchers; the bank reserves the right to refuse access. The permission of the current head of the family must be obtained before accounts may be viewed. There is no access to material post–1900.

Historical background: Coutts was established in 1692. It absorbed Davison, Noel, Temple, Middleton and Wedgwood in 1816 and Hammersley, Greenwood and Brooksbank in 1840. In 1914 Robarts Lubbock & Co. was absorbed and National Provincial Bank was affiliated in 1920.

Acquisitions policy: Maintains its own archives.

Archives of organisation: Archives of Coutts & Co., 1699– , and Robarts Lubbock & Co., 1772–1914 (incomplete).

Major collections: Limited material on banks absorbed.

Non-manuscript material: Paintings, photographs, furniture, banking paraphernalia.

Finding aids: Card index; computer database of customers.

Facilities: Photocopying at the discretion of the Archivist.

Publications: R. Richardson: *Coutts & Co., Bankers, Edinburgh and London* (1900).
E.H. Coleridge: *The Life of Thomas Coutts, Banker* [2 vols] (1920).
R.M. Robinson: *Coutts: the History of a Banking House* (1929).
E. Healey: *Coutts & Co. 1692–1992: the Portrait of a Private Bank* (1992).

592 Dickens' House Museum

Address: 48 Doughty Street, London WC1N 2LF

Telephone: (020) 7405 2127

Fax: (020) 7831 5175

E-mail: dhmuseum@rmplc.ac.uk

Website: www.dickensmuseum.com

Enquiries: Curator, Andrew Xavier

Open: Mon–Fri: 10.00–5.00.
NB Opening times are not identical to those of the museum.

Access: Generally open to the public; appointments are necessary.

Historical background: The Dickens' House Museum was founded by the Dickens Fellowship in 1925. The fellowship acquired the house, where Dickens had lived, put together the basis of a collection, and set up an independent trust to run the museum. Working in close co-operation with the fellowship since that date, the house has gradually built up a major collection of memorabilia, pictures, books, ephemera and MSS (not Dickens' papers as such, since in 1858 Dickens himself burnt all the letters he had received).

Acquisitions policy: Written material relating to the life, works, circle and times of Charles Dickens (1812–70), and relevant objects.

Archives of organisation: Records relating to the museum and the Dickens Fellowship.

Major collections: Collections assembled by Dickens scholars and admirers, including the following: B.W. Matz (1865–1925); F.G. Kitton (1856–1903); Thomas Wright (1859–1936); Comte Alain de Suzannet (1882–1950), these include letters and scrapbooks; Sir Felix Aylmer (1889–1979), concerning his acting studies of Dickens; W.J. Carlton (1886–1973); Leslie Staples (1896–1980); Gladys Storey (1892–1978); Noel O. Peyrouten (1924–68); and the National Dickens Library. In addition there are various collections built up piecemeal by the museum.

Non-manuscript material: Memorabilia, pictures, photographs, books (including Dickens first editions in volume form and parts), scrapbooks.
Copies of The Dickensian, 1902– [journal published by the Dickens Fellowship].

Facilities: Photocopying. Photography by arrangement.

Conservation: Contracted out.

Publications: Useful articles in The Dickensian.

593 Dr Williams's Library

Address: 14 Gordon Square, London WC1H 0AG

Telephone: (020) 7387 3727

Fax: (020) 7388 1142

E-mail: 101340.2541@compuserve.com

Enquiries: The Director, Dr David Wykes

Open: Mon, Wed, Fri: 10.00–5.00; Tues, Thurs: 10.00–6.30.

Access: Open to persons duly introduced and guaranteed in accordance with the regulations made by the trustees. Regulations, membership forms etc may be had on personal application or by post from the Librarian.

Historical background: The library forms part of the charitable trust established under the will of Daniel Williams, DD (d 1716), a Presbyterian minister; its nucleus was the founder's personal library, principally of divinity. To this collection of printed books, MSS, for the most part relating to English non-conformity, began to be added by purchase, gift or deposit very soon after the library opened in 1729/30. The library also administers the Congregational Library (f. 1831).

Acquisitions policy: Occasional purchases are made. Such MSS as are acquired are given or, in some cases, deposited. Very little is added that is not related to English non-conformity or to material already held.

Major collections: Minutes of the Westminster Assembly, 1643–52, and the Fourth London Classis, 1646–59; John Evans List of Dissenting Congregations, 1715–29, and similar lists of c1770 by Josiah Thompson; correspondence of Joseph Priestley, Theophilus Lindsey and others associated with them; correspondence and other papers of Richard Baxter (1615–91); collections made by Roger Morrice, including the late 16th-century Second Parte of a Register and Morrice's political diary covering the years 1677–91; the collections for the history of dissenting churches made by Walter Wilson (1781–1847); the miscellaneous and largely personal collections of John Jones (1700–70), which include a MS of George Herbert's poems, English and Latin; the diary, reminiscences and letters of Henry Crabb Robinson (1775–1867); items by William Law and others in the collection of books and MSS deposited by Christopher Walton (1809–77); the MSS from New College, London, including much correspondence and papers of Philip Doddridge (1702–51).

The Congregational Library collection includes correspondence of Isaac Watts (1674–1748), as well as letters and sermons of prominent non-conformists.

Non-manuscript material: The MSS are really an adjunct to the printed books (133,000 vols), which are pre-eminent for the study of English Protestant non-conformity.

Finding aids: Handlists of MSS and partial name index.

Facilities: Microfilm reader. Some items suitable for photocopying on premises.

Publications: The Baxter Treatises: a Catalogue of the Richard Baxter Papers (other than the Letters) in Dr Williams's Library (1959).
I. Elliott: *Supplement* to index in Edith Morley: *Henry Crabb Robinson on Books and their Writers* (1960).
J. Creasey: *Index to the John Evans List of Dissenting Congregations and Ministers, 1715–1729, in Dr Williams's Library* (1964).
K. Twinn: *Guide to the Manuscripts in Dr Williams's Library* (1969).
Nonconformist Congregations in Great Britain: a List of Histories and other Material in Dr Williams's Library (1974).
Thomas Jollie's Papers: a List of the Papers in Dr Williams's Library, Manuscript no. 12.78.

594 Drapers' Company

Address: Drapers' Hall, Throgmorton Avenue, London EC2N 2DQ

Telephone: (020) 7588 5001

Fax: (020) 7628 1988

E-mail: mal@thedrapers.co.uk

Website: www.thedrapers.co.uk

Enquiries: The Archivist, Miss P.A. Fussell

Open: Mon–Fri: 9.30–6.00.

Access: Generally open to the public, by prior appointment only.

Historical background: The company evolved from a religious fraternity and trading association of cloth merchants in the City of London, and was granted a royal charter in 1364. The hall has occupied its present site since 1543, although it has since been damaged by fire; the facade and interior of the present hall date mainly from 1860. The company is principally concerned with supporting charities, especially in education, medicine and the arts, and the relief of need.

Irish estate archives, c1585–1900, are mostly held at the Public Record Office of Northern Ireland (entry 81).

Acquisitions policy: To maintain its archives.

Archives of organisation: Land and other documents, 1180– ; accounts, 1415– ; meetings, 1515– ; grants of arms, including earliest surviving English grant, 1439– ; charters, 1364– ; charity trust deeds and documents, 1408– .

Major collections: Papers of Lambarde family, c1540–1980; Thomas Howell Trust, 1519– ; rectory of St Michael Cornhill, 1502– ; Francis Bancroft Trust, late 18th century– .

Non-manuscript material: Published works of William Lambarde, late 16th century.
Sir Thomas Phillips Survey of the Plantations of the City of London and the Livery Companies in Ireland, illuminated, 1622.

Finding aids: Catalogues and lists; sent to NRA.

Facilities: Photocopying and photography only by express permission of the Master and Wardens.

Publications: A.H. Johnson: *History of the Worshipful Company of Drapers of London* (1914) [5 vols].
T. Girtin: *The Triple Crowns: a Narrative History of the Drapers' Company, 1364–1964* (1964).
P. Hunting: *A History of the Drapers' Company* (1989).

595 Drivers Jonas Archive

Address: Drivers Jonas, 6 Grosvenor Street, London W1X 0DJ

Telephone: (020) 7896 8069

Fax: (020) 7896 8330

E-mail: jamesgriggs@djonas.co.uk

Enquiries: The Information Officer, James Griggs

Open: Mon–Fri: 9.30–4.30, by appointment.

Access: Bona fide researchers, at the discretion of the Information Officer.

Historical background: This firm of chartered surveyors was founded *c*1725 by Charles Driver, master baker and market gardener, who became an estate improver, land valuer and surveyor. The nursery business was retained until 1802. As valuers and auctioneers, the business was particularly involved in land acquisition for railways and then the break-up of great landed estates. The Drivers and Jonas families were dominant until the 1970s; there have been no family members in the partnership since 1995.

Acquisitions policy: To maintain the archive.

Archives of organisation: The business archive of the firm, including auction particulars, cash books and rent books, 1725– .

Non-manuscript material: Architectural plans and ordnance survey maps.

Finding aids: Computerised catalogue.

Facilities: Photocopying by arrangement.

Publications: H. Barty-King: *Scratch a Surveyor* (1975).

596 Duchy of Cornwall Office

Address: 10 Buckingham Gate, London SW1E 6LA

Telephone: (020) 7931 9541

Fax: (020) 7931 9541

Enquiries: The Archivist and Records Manager, Miss E. A. Stuart

Open: Wed: 2.00–5.00, by prior arrangement.

Access: On written application. The archive is private and part of the working estate. While limited public access can be allowed, the priority is the long-term maintenance of the archive as an internal resource.

Historical background: The Duchy of Cornwall was created by Edward III in 1337 to provide an income for his eldest son, Edward (often called the Black Prince). As such, it is a major landed estate whose holdings are concentrated largely, though not exclusively, in the West Country. Apart from the period of the Interregnum, the Duchy has existed continuously since the fourteenth century and continues to maintain the heir to the throne.

Acquisitions policy: Material relating to the Duchy, mainly from within the organisation.

Archives of organisation: Mainly the usual records of a landed estate, with some significant additions:
Extensive series of medieval account rolls of the receivers, ministers and court officials of the Duchy.
Household receipts and vouchers for Frederick and subsequently Augusta, Prince and Princess of Wales respectively, 1728–72.
Estate correspondence, 19th–early 20th centuries.

Non-manuscript material: Duchy photograph collection. Prints and engravings, including 18th-century Vauxhall Gardens prints.

Finding aids: Cataloguing is in progress.

Facilities: Limited photocopying and photography at the discretion of the Archivist.

Conservation: Extensive programme in progress.

Publications: R.L. Clowes: 'On the Historical Documents in the Duchy of Cornwall Office', *Royal Cornwall Polytechnic Society Annual Report* (1930).

597 Dulwich College
The Wodehouse Library

Parent organisation: Alleyn's College of God's Gift

Address: College Road, London SE21 7LD

Telephone: (020) 8299 9201

Fax: (020) 8299 9245

E-mail: archives@dulwich.org.uk

Website: www.dulwich.org.uk/history/archives.htm

Enquiries: Dr J.R. Piggott or Mr P. Fletcher

Open: Term only, by prior arrangement.

Access: Bona fide researchers, by appointment.

Historical background: Founded in 1619 by Edward Alleyn (1566–1626), the college is administered by a board of governors. In the mid-19th century it was refounded as a public school. The archives of the original library were rehoused in air-conditioned units in 1981.

Acquisitions policy: Materials relating to Dulwich College.

Archives of organisation: Alleyn's personal papers and those of Philip Henslowe (c1555-1616), his wife's step-father.

Records of the college, 1619– .

Deeds of the Manor of Dulwich, 14th century– .

Major collections: P.G Wodehouse (1881–1975) collections, including assorted MSS and his voluminous correspondence with William Townend.

Music MSS collection, early 18th century.

Medical records of College Mission, 1909–37.

Non-manuscript material: Architectural drawings for college buildings by Charles Barry (1823–1900).

Sir Ernest Shackleton: original photographs of *The Endurance* expedition.

Alleyn's library and subsequent gifts.

Finding aids: Computerised catalogues in preparation.

Facilities: Photocopying. Photography and microfiche by arrangement.

Conservation: Contracted out.

Publications: G. Warner: *Catalogues of the Manuscripts and Muniments* (1881; 2nd series, 1903).

J.R. Piggott: *Dulwich College: a Brief History and Guide to the Buildings* (1990).

598 Ealing Local History Centre

Parent organisation: London Borough of Ealing

Address: Central Library, 103 Ealing Broadway Centre, London W5 5JY

Telephone: (020) 8567 3656 ext. 37

Fax: (020) 8840 2351

E-mail: localhistory@hotmail.com

Enquiries: The Archivist, Mr Jonathan Oates

Open: Tues, Thurs: 9.30–7.45; Wed, Fri, Sat: 9.30–5.00.

Access: Generally open to the public; appointments are advisable.

Historical background: The Local History Library is formed from the collections of the former boroughs of Acton, Ealing and Southall and contains material on the area of the London Borough of Ealing. Many of the archives are stored off-site, principally those of the predecessor bodies of the London Borough of Ealing, and cannot be viewed without a prior appointment.

Acquisitions policy: Donations and deposits of material covering the London Borough of Ealing are accepted.

Archives of organisation: Archives of the London Borough of Ealing and its predecessor bodies, including the boroughs of Acton, Ealing and Southall and the civil parishes of Ealing, Hanwell, Greenford and Norwood.

Major collections: Minutes of the Acton School Board, 1875–1903; Acton Education Committee, 1903–44; Ealing Works Committee, 1883–1956; Ealing Education Committee, 1903–65; Southall Council School Managers, 1903–31; Ealing Sanitary Inspectors' Journal, 1899–1940.

Large collection of school log-books.

Hanwell Wesleyan Methodist Church, minutes and miscellaneous documents, 1882–1969.

Ealing Swimming Club, 1882–1934.

League of Nations Union (Ealing Branch), including minute books, 1931–6.

Martin Brothers & Martinware: papers of Sydney K. Greenslade, 1880–1933.

E.K. Venables (1893–1970), diaries, photographs and papers; H.A.F. St John (1911–79) diaries, 1922–68; General Sir F.A. Wetherall (1754–1842), papers, 1800–79; Ealing Tenants Ltd, 1901–74; Ealing and Brentford Volunteer Corps, 1798–1965; the Order of the Sons of Temperance, 1887–1917.

Non-manuscript material: Photographic survey of Borough of Ealing, c1902, and other photographs and postcards (c18,500).

Finding aids: Accession lists: copies sent to London Metropolitan Archives (entry688). Index to local newspaper, 1866– .

Facilities: Photocopying strictly at the discretion of the Archivist; in general no archival material may be copied. Microfilm reader/printer.

Conservation: Contracted out.

Publications: Full list of reproduction maps, postcards and monographs available.

Guide to Sources for Family History.

599 Egypt Exploration Society

Address: 3 Doughty Mews, London WC1N 2PG

Telephone: (020) 7242 1880

Fax: (020) 7404 6118

E-mail: eeslondon@compuserve.com

Website: www.ees.ac.uk

Enquiries: The Secretary, Dr Patricia Spencer

Open: Mon–Fri: 10.30–4.30, by appointment only.

Access: Bona fide researchers approved by the society's committee.

Historical background: The Egypt Exploration Society was founded as the Egypt Exploration Fund in 1882 by Amelia Edwards, Sir Erasmus Wilson and scholars from the British Museum to study the culture of ancient Egypt and promote excavation and survey work in the Nile Valley. The society's excavation costs are mostly covered by an annual grant from the British Academy, with donations from museums and individuals; it also maintains an Egyptological library for the use of members. The Graeco-Roman branch of the society was established in 1897 for the discovery and publication of Greek or Latin documents from Egypt.

Archives of organisation: The society's archive, consisting mainly of the records of excavations, as well as note-books, correspondence, photographs and negatives, 1882– .

Finding aids: Handlist of early correspondence. Lists for most of the photographic record.

Facilities: Photocopying. Photography by arrangement.

Publications: Journal of Egyptian Archaeology. Results of fieldwork are incorporated in more than 170 publications.

600 Electoral Reform Society of Great Britain and Ireland

Parent organisation: The McDougall Trust

Address: Lakeman Library for Electoral Studies, 6 Chancel Street, London SE1 0UU

Telephone: (020) 7620 1080

Fax: (020) 7928 1528

E-mail: admin@mcdougall.org.uk

Enquiries: The Executive Secretary, Paul Wilder

Open: Mon–Fri: 9.30–5.30, by arrangement.

Access: Bona fide researchers, by appointment.

Historical background: Founded in 1884 as the Proportional Representation Society, it changed its name in 1959 but holds the same aims. The archives are now the responsibility of the society's associated charity, the McDougall Trust, which was established by the society in 1948 from a bequest by a member of the flour-milling family. Its charitable objectives include the study of economic and political science and methods of election and government.

Acquisitions policy: Maintains own archives and accepts material relating to elections and electoral methods. An active policy of acquiring papers, books, journals and reports on all aspects relating to democracy and elections in newly emerging democracies.

Archives of organisation: Records of the society, including minute books and early publications.

Major collections: Papers of individuals associated with reform and parliamentary change, including Lord Courtenay of Penwith, Sir John Lubbock (Lord Avebury), A.R. Droop and Dr J.F.S. Ross.

Non-manuscript material: Pamphlets on proportional representation in Britain, Europe, America and Australia, 1844–1918.

Publications from various electoral reform groups in the UK, Ireland and abroad, c1880s– .

Large collection of dated and sourced newspaper cuttings about electoral politics, 1905– (also on microfilm).

Parliamentary papers about reform from Commonwealth and European countries.

Finding aids: Database catalogue.

Facilities: Photocopying.

Publications: The Best System (London, 1984) [centenary history].

E. Lakeman: *Twelve Democracies: Electoral Systems in the European Community* (1991).

Representation: Journal of Representative Democracy [published quarterly by the McDougall Trust].

601 Enfield Local History Unit

Parent organisation: London Borough of Enfield

Address: Southgate Town Hall, Broomfield Lane, London N13 4EY

Telephone: (020) 8379 2774

Fax: (020) 8379 2761

Website: www.enfield.gov.uk/lochist.htm

Enquiries: The Local History Officer, Mr G.C. Dalling

Open: Mon, Tues, Thurs, Fri: 10.00–5.00.

Access: Generally open to the public; an appointment is essential.

Historical background: The former boroughs of Enfield and Edmonton each had a local collection, and there was also a collection of books, pamphlets, photographs and drawings at Broomfield Museum in Southgate. All archive material was removed from the museum to Southgate Town Hall in 1975 and escaped the fire in 1984.

Acquisitions policy: To obtain, by donation, purchase or photocopy, material on the area of the London Borough of Enfield. To acquire non-current documents by transfer from other local authority departments.

Archives of organisation: Usual local authority record holdings.

Major collections: Local history and topography collections relating to Edmonton, Enfield and Southgate, including Edmonton Friendly Benefit Society records, 1820–1912; Stamford Hill and Green Lanes Turnpike Trust records, 1764–1805.
Edmonton rate books, 1764–1850, and valuation lists, 1878, 1884, 1892 and 1905; Edmonton and Enfield Enclosure Awards.

Non-manuscript material: Paintings, drawings and prints (500). Photographs (15,000) and transparencies (1500). Newspaper cuttings (14,000).
Local newspapers and microfilms of census returns.
All non-current maps of the area.

Finding aids: General index on cards. Detailed classified catalogue: books, pamphlets and printed ephemera. Name indexes to census records, World War II civilian casualties etc. See NRA 25942, 25947.

Facilities: Photocopying. Microfilm reader/printer.

Publications: Brief guide.

602 English Heritage

Address: 23 Savile Row, London W1X 1AB

Telephone: Main switchboard: (020) 7973 3000 Record Office: 7973 3104 Historic Properties Group: 7973 3731 (London Sites and Monuments Record)

Fax: (020) 7973 3001

Website: www.english-heritage.org.uk

Enquiries: The National Programmes Service Manager, Alphena Gordon

Open: By arrangement.

Access: By prior appointment only.

Historical background: The Historic Buildings and Monuments Commission, the predecessor of English Heritage, was set up in 1984 to be responsible for securing the preservation of England's architectural and archaeological heritage and for the management of more than 350 monuments and buildings formerly under the Secretary of State for the Environment (DoE). In 1986 it took over the conservation work carried out by the GLC Historical Buildings Division. The public repository for records of historic monuments is the National Monuments Record (entry 1158) and enquiries should normally be directed to them in the first instance. English Heritage's record holdings relate to its own statutory and management responsibilities and are working papers rather than archives.

Acquisitions policy: To maintain the archives of the commission.

Archives of organisation: Record Office: records related to scheduled ancient monuments, listed buildings, registered parks and gardens.
Historic Properties Group: the Historic Plans Room is the official repository for English Heritage and the DoE/Property Services Agency permanent record drawings, survey notes, photographs of work in progress, glass negatives, deeds and deed plans.
London Division: London Sites and Monuments Record, London blue plaques files, survey drawings associated with the Survey of London volumes, some research reports

prepared in connection with public enquiries and proposals to change the character of listed buildings. Survey drawings were sent to the archives division of the Royal Commission of Historical Monuments of England in 1995, but English Heritage has kept copies.

Files on buildings recommended for listing.

The Photographic Unit, Fortress House, provides new photography for internal use for works and presentation purposes

Publications: Annual reports; Conservation Bulletin; list of publications available.

603 English National Ballet Archives

Address: Markova House, 39 Jay Mews, London SW7 2ES

Telephone: (020) 7581 1245

Fax: (020) 7225 0827

E-mail: info@ballet.org.uk

Enquiries: The Archivist, Ms Jane Pritchard

Open: By appointment only.

Access: Bona fide research students, on written application.

Historical background: The archive was established in 1975 to maintain the records of English National Ballet, formerly known as London Festival Ballet, which was founded by Julian Braunsweg, Anton Dolin and Alicia Markova in 1950.

Acquisitions policy: Primary and secondary material relating to the history of London Festival Ballet. Also material relating to the history of ballets in the company's repertoire and to the careers of artists who have worked with the company. The emphasis is on 20th-century ballet. Material is acquired by donation, purchase and deposit.

Archives of organisation: Principally records of the English National Ballet Company.

Non-manuscript material: Photographic collection.
Video library, including tapes of productions and classes; some films.
Audio recordings.
Designs for Festival Ballet productions.

Finding aids: Cataloguing in process.

604 English National Opera Archive

Address: The ENO Works, 40 Pitfield Street, London N1 6EU

Telephone: (020) 7729 9610

Fax: (020) 7729 9610

E-mail: ccolvin@eno.org

Enquiries: The Archivist, Ms C. Colvin

Open: By arrangement.

Access: Bona fide researchers, by appointment only.

Historical background: Sadler's Wells Opera moved to the London Coliseum in 1968 and changed its name to English National Opera (ENO) in 1974. ENO purchased the London Coliseum in 1992.

Acquisitions policy: To acquire material relevant to ENO, Sadler's Wells Opera and the Coliseum.

Archives of organisation: Administrative records of Sadler's Wells Opera and ENO, 1931– .

Major collections: Material on the Coliseum, 1904– .

Non-manuscript material: Photographs of productions; press cuttings; posters, audio and video tapes.

Finding aids: Lists, indexes and database.

Facilities: Photocopying. Photography. Tape copying.

605 Ethical Society Library

Parent organisation: South Place Ethical Society

Address: Conway Hall, 25 Red Lion Square, London WC1R 4RL

Telephone: (020) 7242 8037/8034

Fax: (020) 7242 8036

E-mail: library@ethicalsoc.org.uk

Website: www.ethicalsoc.org.uk

Enquiries: The Librarian, Jennifer Jeynes

Open: Mon–Fri: 2.00–5.00.

Access: Bona fide researchers, by appointment.

Historical background: The society evolved in 1793 from a group of Christian non-conformists who rejected the doctrine of eternal hell. It has developed to be a forum for discussion on humanist issues. In 1823 it became the South Place Religious Society on moving to a new chapel in South Place, and in 1988 it adopted its present name, SPES. It moved to the Conway Hall in 1929. The library has grown gradually with additions from free-thought societies, most recently from the Rationalist Press Association.

Acquisitions policy: Papers of persons significant in the history of the society.

Archives of organisation: Archives, including minutes and annual reports, 19th century– .

Major collections: Papers of Moncure Conway (1832–1907), Staunton Coit, William Janus Fox (1786–1864) and William Lovett (1800–77).

606 Evangelical Library

Address: 78A Chiltern Street, London W1V 5HB

Telephone: (020) 7935 6997

E-mail: stlibrary@aol.com

Website: evangelical-library.org.uk

Enquiries: The Librarian

Open: Mon–Sat: 10.00–5.00

Access: Bona fide scholars, by arrangement. The archives are also open to members who pay an annual donation. A paid research service is available.

Historical background: The library was begun in about 1924 as the personal collection of Geoffrey Williams (1886–1975), whose aim was to build up a worldwide evangelical library. Towards the end of World War II the library was moved from Surrey into central London, largely due to the influence of the preacher Dr D. Martyn Lloyd-Jones (1899–1981).

Major collections: MSS and letters of eminent non-conformists, including sermon notes of Matthew Henry (1662–1714), commentator and non-conformist minister; letters received by George Whitefield (1714–70), leader of Calvinistic Methodists.

Non-manuscript material: Large collection of small portraits of evangelicals.

Wilberforce and McGhee collections of pamphlets of the National Club, 19th century. Puritan and Robinson collections of works by Evangelicals of the 17th and 18th centuries.

Facilities: Photocopying.

Publications: Bulletin [biannual]. Numerous printed catalogues for sale.

607 Faber and Faber Archives

Address: 3 Queen Street, London WC1N 3AU

Telephone: (020) 7465 7575

Fax: (020) 7465 0034

E-mail: colimp@faber.co.uk

Website: www.faber.co.uk

Enquiries: The Archivist, Mr Colin Penman

Open: By appointment only.

Access: Access to some records may be refused, in accordance with the access policy. A fee will be charged for substantial research carried out by the Archivist.

Historical background: Faber and Gwyer was founded in 1925, and reconstituted as Faber and Faber Ltd in 1929. From the beginning, with the appointment of T.S. Eliot (1888–1965) as a director, the company has enjoyed a high reputation as a general literary publisher, and six Faber writers have been awarded the Nobel Prize for Literature. It remains one of the few independent publishers in the UK. A strong music list led to the formation of a separate company, Faber Music, in 1965.

Acquisitions policy: Main acquisitions from the records of the company. Other material may be acquired which is of direct relevance to Faber and Faber and its history.

Archives of organisation: Records of Faber and Faber, 1929– , and of its predecessor, Faber and Gwyer, 1925–9.

Non-manuscript material: One copy of every book and dust jacket published by the company is retained in the archives. Other material includes paintings and sculpture, works on paper related to book production, and company memorabilia.

Finding aids: Card index.

Conservation: Contracted out.

Publications: Faber Books 1925–75: Impressions of a Publishing House (1975).

Faber Music: Notes of a Decade, National Book League exhibition (1975).
A Sampler of Sixty Years of Faber & Faber Book Jackets and Covers (1986).

608 Family Records Centre

Address: 1 Myddelton Street, London EC1R 1UQ

Telephone: (01704) 569824/(020) 8392 5200

E-mail: enquiry@pro.gov.uk
certificate.services@statistics.gov.uk

Website: www.familyrecords.gov.uk
www.statistics.gov.uk

Enquiries: Family history enquiries: Family Records Centre
Certificate enquiries: General Register Office, PO Box 2, Southport, Merseyside PR8 2JD

Open: Mon, Wed, Fri: 9.00–5.00; Tues, Thurs: 10.00–7.00; Sat: 9.00–5.00.

Access: The centre is open to the public; appointments are only necessary for large groups. Access to the records is on a self-service basis. Staff are on hand for advice.

Historical background: The Family Records Centre (FRC), formerly Office of Population Censuses and Surveys, St Catherine's House, and Public Record Office Census Reading Rooms, is a joint service run by the Office for National Statistics' General Register Office and the Public Record Office (entry 1058). The centre houses the General Register Office's Public Search Room and the Public Record Office's Census and Wills Reading Rooms. The General Register Office (GRO) was founded in 1837 when a service was created for the state registration of births and deaths and the solemnization and registration of marriages in England and Wales. The GRO exists as a statutory body under the direction of the Registrar General, who is also the Director of the Office for National Statistics.

Acquisitions policy: The register records accumulate as registration of events proceeds. Census records are made available after the statutory closure period of 100 years.

Archives of organisation: Indexes of births, marriages and deaths, 1837– .
Indexes of births, marriages and deaths of some British citizens abroad, late 18th century– .
Indexes of legal adoptions, 1927– .
Microfilms of census returns 1841–91.

Microfilms of Estate Duty Office death duty registers, 1796–1858.
Non-parochial registers, 1567–1858.
Registered copies of wills from Prerogative Court of Canterbury, pre–1858.

Finding aids: Indexes to birth, death and marriage registers. Street and some surname indexes to the censuses. Family search on CD-ROM.

Publications: Contact Public Record Office for full lists of publications and Office for National Statistics for leaflets and details of publications: (0151) 471 4357, website: www.ons.gov.uk/services.

609 Federation of British Artists

Address: 17 Carlton House Terrace, London SW1Y 5AH

Telephone: (020) 7930 6844

Fax: (020) 7839 7830

Website: www.mallgalleries.org

Enquiries: The Archivist/Librarian

Open: Mon–Sun: 10.00–5.00.

The federation was established in 1962 and links the following organisations: the Hesketh Hubbard Society; the New English Art Club; the Pastel Society; the Royal Institute of Painters in Water Colours (f. 1831); the Royal Society of British Artists (f. 1823); the Royal Society of Marine Artists; the Royal Society of Portrait Painters (f. 1891); and the Society of Wildlife Artists. In spite of the age of some of these bodies, it appears that archives have not been systematically preserved and details are not available. A fire in 1985 destroyed some material, although this was mainly catalogues. Some records are held by presidents of the societies and, although access is not encouraged, enquiries can be addressed to the federation.

610 Folklore Society

Address: University College London, Gower Street, London WC1E 6BT

Telephone: (020) 7387 5894

Enquiries: The Hon. Archivist

Open: Strictly by arrangement only.

Access: Members of the society and bona fide researchers, by appointment.

Historical background: The Folklore Society was formed in 1878 and was the first organisation in the world to be devoted to the study of traditional culture. Today the society continues to stimulate folklore studies throughout the world, and it provides a valuable point of contact for isolated collectors and scholars.

Acquisitions policy: Most acquisitions are by donation from society members, mainly in the form of TS and MS materials, but also a limited number of photographic materials.

Major collections: Collections, large and small, deposited by past society members, including Sir George and Lady Alice Gomme, T.F. Ordish and Andrew Lang, 1890s– .
Daily Mirror 'Live Letters' collection.

Finding aids: Cataloguing and indexing in progress.

Facilities: Photocopying and photography by arrangement.

Publications: Folklore and *FLS News*, in which reports of past donations to the archive and a current annual report are included.

611 Football Association

Address: 25 Soho Square, London W1D 4FA

Telephone: (020) 7262 4542

Fax: (0207) 7454546

E-mail: info@the-fa.org

Website: www.the-fa.org

Enquiries: Mr David Barber

Open: By arrangement.

The association was founded in 1863 and retains its minutes from that time, as well as a collection of historical books and programmes. The library holds *c*2000 volumes, including early *Annuals*, 1870– . A short article by D. Barber, 'FA Records', appeared in the *FA Year Book*, 1980–81.

612 Franciscan Archives English Province

Address: Franciscan Friary, 56 St Antony's Road, Forest Gate, London E7 9QB

Telephone: (020) 8472 6012

Fax: (020) 8503 5797

E-mail: friarsminor@btinternet.com

Enquiries: The Archivist

Open: By arrangement.

Access: Bona fide scholars, by appointment only.

Historical background: The archive collection was begun in 1629.

Acquisitions policy: To acquire any material dealing with the English Franciscan Province.

Archives of organisation: Chapter registers, 1629–1838.
Correspondence dealing with the business of the province.
Deeds and wills connected with benefactors and relatives of Franciscans.
Provincial registers; procurators' account books; note-books of Franciscan provincials; notifications from Major Superiors in Rome and the Low Countries.

Non-manuscript material: Photographs.

Facilities: Photocopying.

613 French Protestant Church of London

Address: 8–9 Soho Square, London W1V 5DD

Telephone: (020) 7437 5311

Fax: (020) 7434 4579

E-mail: eglisoho@globalnet.co.uk

Enquiries: Pasteur Leila Hamrat

Open: Mon–Fri: 9.00–5.00, by appointment.

Access: Generally open to the public; charges are made.

Historical background: The French Protestant Church was founded in 1550, when Edward VI gave a charter to Protestant refugees. French Huguenots occupied a church in Threadneedle Street from 1550 to 1841, then in St Martins le Grand until 1887. Links were maintained with other Huguenot churches in England, notably at Canterbury, Norwich and Southampton. The church moved to its present site in 1893.

Acquisitions policy: To complement the archives of the past and document the church's ongoing activities.

Archives of organisation: Records, including *actes du consistoire* (vestry minutes), 1560– ; account books; lists of members' pews and poor relief; indentures of apprentices; *livres des témoignages*; royal approbations.

Non-manuscript material: Library of specialist literature, including incunabula, particularly 18th century– (*c*1400 vols).

Facilities: Photocopying/microfilm/fiche readers.

Publications: R. Smith (comp.): *The Archives of the French Protestant Church of London* (London, 1972).
Y. Jaulmes: *The French Protestant Church of London and the Huguenots* (London, 1993).

614 Freud Museum

Address: 20 Maresfield Gardens, London NW3 4SX

Telephone: (020) 7435 2002

Fax: (020) 7431 5452

E-mail: freud@gn.apc.org

Website: www.freud.org.uk/fmrese.htm

Enquiries: The Research Director, Michael Molnar

Open: Mon–Fri: 10.00–5.00.

Access: Generally open to the public; an appointment is necessary.

Historical background: The Freud Museum was opened in 1986 in the house inhabited by Sigmund Freud (1856–1939) during 1938–9 and by his daughter Anna (1895–1982) until her death. Some of the original papers have been transferred to the Sigmund Freud collection at the Library of Congress, Washington, and replaced by photocopies.

Acquisitions policy: Papers relating to Sigmund Freud and psychoanalysis.

Archives of organisation: Records of the Vienna Psychoanalytic Society, 1913–14, and the training committee and ambulatorium, 1925–38.

Major collections: Papers of Sigmund Freud and Anna Freud.

Non-manuscript material: Freud family photograph collection.
Newspaper cuttings, 1930s.

Finding aids: Computer catalogue.

Facilities: Photocopying.

Conservation: Contracted out.

Publications: M. Molnar (ed.): *The Diary of Sigmund Freud, 1929–1939* (1992).

615 Froebel Archive for Childhood Studies

Parent organisation: Incorporated Froebel Educational Institute

Address: Grove House, Roehampton Lane, London SW15 5PJ

Telephone: (020) 8392 3000 (switchboard); 8392 3323 (answerphone for out of hours enquiries)

Fax: (020) 8392 3331

E-mail: j.read@roehampton.ac.uk

Website: roehampton.ac.uk/about/colleges/froebel/facs

Enquiries: The Archivist, Ms Jane Read

Open: Tues, Wed, Fri: 10.00–3.00: visits outside these hours may be possible; an appointment is required.

Access: Bona fide researchers and other interested persons.

Historical background: The Froebel Society was founded in 1874 to promote Friedrich Froebel's educational ideology, particularly his concept of the Kindergarten. The Froebel Educational Institute opened in 1892, moved to Roehampton in 1921 and since 1978 has been a constituent college of Roehampton Institute London, now University of Surrey Roehampton. The Froebel Archive for Childhood Studies, formerly known as the Early Childhood Collection, was established to preserve a unique set of source material tracing the development of the Froebel movement in this country, and to provide information and research facilities for the college community and for researchers from this country and abroad.

Acquisitions policy: To acquire any further relevant material to strengthen the existing collection.

Archives of organisation: Archives of the institute, 1892–.
Minute books of the Froebel Society and the National Froebel Foundation, 1874–.

Non-manuscript material: The Froebel 'Gifts and Occupations'.
Publications relating to the work of Froebel (1782–1852) in English and German.

Publications relating to key figures in early childhood education including Margaret McMillan, Montessori, Steiner, Susan Isaacs and others.
Teaching apparatus and games by Montessori, Decroly and others.
Examples of students' work, 1890s– .
Photographs of college, staff, students, kindergartens, demonstration schools, nursery schools.

Finding aids: Card catalogue of holdings; database version in preparation. Card indexes of Froebelian subjects.

Facilities: Photocopying by arrangement.

Conservation: Contracted out.

Publications: The Froebel Educational Institute: a Centenary Review (London, 1992).
Froebel: Drawings and Photographs of the Froebel Institute College (London, 1992).
P. Weston: *Friedrich Froebel: his Life, Times and Significance* (1998).
——: *From Roehampton Great House to Grove House to Froebel College: an Illustrated History* (1998).
Introductory leaflet (1998).

616 GFS Platform for Young Women

Address: Townsend House, 126 Queens Gate, London SW7 5LQ

Telephone: (020) 7589 9628

Fax: (020) 7225 1458

E-mail: platform@gfs.u-net.com

Website: www.tabor.co.uk/gfs/

Enquiries: Mrs Anne Monk

Open: Mon–Fri: 10.00–5.00, by appointment.

Access: Generally open to the public, by prior arrangement. A donation to the society would be appreciated.

Historical background: The society was founded as the Girls Friends Society in 1875 to work with women and girls, particularly those moving to the towns and cities to work.

Acquisitions policy: To maintain the archives.

Archives of organisation: Archives, 1875– , including minutes, correspondence and papers, annual reports, registers, diocesan and branch records.

Non-manuscript material: Photographs, drawings, artwork and memorabilia.

Finding aids: Printed list/index.

Facilities: Photocopying.

617 Garrick Club

Address: 15 Garrick Street, London WC2E 9AY

Telephone: (020) 7836 1737

Fax: (0207) 3795966

Enquiries: The Librarian

Open: Wed: 10.00–5.00, by arrangement.
Closed last two weeks of August and first week of September.

Access: Bona fide researchers, who should write stating the subject of their research. An appointment is necessary and a fee may be charged.

Historical background: The Garrick Club was founded in 1831 by the art collector Francis Mills. The formation of a library was in the first constitution. It now contains *c*7500 volumes connected with the theatre.

Acquisitions policy: Material relating to British drama and the theatre, especially 18th and 19th centuries.

Major collections: Garrick Collection: correspondence, cuttings and illustrations relating to David Garrick (1717–79).
Northcote Collection: archives of Drury Lane Theatre.

Non-manuscript material: Irving Collection: 20 scrapbooks relating to Henry Irving (1838–1905).
Playbills and programmes, 18th century– .
Press cuttings.

Finding aids: Card index.

Facilities: Photography by arrangement only.

Publications: G. Boas: *The Garrick Club, 1831–1947* (1948).
R. Hough: *The Ace of Clubs* (1986).
G. Ashton, K.A. Burning and A. Wilton (eds), G. Ashton (comp.): *Pictures in the Garrick Club* (1997).

618 Geological Society

Address: Burlington House, Piccadilly, London W1V 0JU

Telephone: (020) 7434 8975

Fax: (020) 7439 9875

E-mail: enquiries@geolsoc.org.uk

Website: www.geolsoc.org.uk

Enquiries: The Hon. Archivist

Open: Mon–Fri: 9.30–5.30.

Access: Bona fide researchers, by appointment

Historical background: The Geological Society of London was founded in 1807.

Acquisitions policy: Any donations of MSS relating to the society and its fellows are gratefully received.

Archives of organisation: Administrative records: a full series of official records, including minutes, 1807– ; fellowship and financial records; MSS relating to society publications, including the *Journal.*

Major collections: Collections from fellows and others, in particular Roderick I. Murchison (1792–1871).
Collection of note-books, diaries and letters.

Non-manuscript material: Maps. Illustrations.

Finding aids: MSS catalogue.

Facilities: Photocopying.

Publications: J.C. Thackray: 'The Archives of the Geological Society', *Journal of the Geological Society* (1986), repr. with additions, from *Earth Sciences History,* 3/1 (1984), 3–8.
Various 19th-century catalogues of the library.

619 Girls' Day School Trust

Address: 100 Rochester Row, London SW1P 1JP

Telephone: (020) 7393 6666

Fax: (020) 7393 6789

Website: www.gdt.net

Enquiries: The Hon. Archivist, Miss Margaret Walker, GDST, c/o the School Office, Croydon High School, Old Farleigh Road, Selsdon, Croydon, Surrey CR2 8YB; tel. (020) 8651 5020.

Open: By appointment, usually Mon–Fri: 9.30–5.00.

Access: Bona fide researchers.

Historical background: The Girls' Day School Trust was founded in 1872 as the Girls' Public Day School Company to provide junior day schools. The first school was established in the following year in Chelsea, and the trust currently runs 24 schools in England plus one (in association) in Wales. Teacher-training departments were often attached to the schools, and the trust also had responsibility for Clapham Teacher Training College from 1900 to 1949. Charitable status was acquired in 1950. The bulk of the archives is now held at Croydon High School; duplicate minutes are also held at the GDST Office. 'Public' was dropped from the name in 1998.

Acquisitions policy: To maintain the archives of the trust and its schools.

Archives of organisation: Records of the trust, including minutes of council and committees, 1874– ; financial and legal papers, 1872– ; correspondence, 1879– ; estate and building records, including architects' plans, 18th–20th centuries; pupil admission registers, 1873– ; inspectors' and headmistresses' reports, 1880s– ; prospectuses and press cuttings, 1860s– .

Facilities: Photocopying. Microfilm/fiche reader.

Publications: L. Magnus: *The Jubilee Book of the Girls' Public Day School Trust, 1873–1923* (1924).
J. Sondheimer and P. Bodington (eds): *A Centenary Review* (1972).
L. Richmond and B. Stockford: *Company Archives* (1986), 118–23 [gives a detailed survey of the trust's records].

620 Gray's Inn Library

Parent organisation: Honourable Society of Gray's Inn

Address: South Square, Gray's Inn, London WC1R 5EU

Telephone: (020) 7458 7800

Fax: (020) 7458 7850

Website: www.graysinn.org.uk

Enquiries: The Librarian, Mrs T.L. Thom

Open: Legal term: Mon–Fri: 9.00–8.00. Shorter hours during vacations, please enquire.

Access: Members only, though others may be admitted by arrangement at the Librarian's discretion and after written application.

Historical background: The library has been in existence since the mid-16th century, although bombing destroyed a large part of the collections in 1941.

Archives of organisation: Records of Gray's Inn, mainly 18th and 19th centuries, but including orders in pension, 1569– , MS books, 12th–16th centuries.
Records of Barnard's Inn, 17th–19th centuries.

Major collections: Papers of James Richard Atkin, Baron Atkin (1867–1944), judge.

Non-manuscript material: Portraits, prints and photographs.
Roman law books collected by Robert Warden Lee (1868–1958), lawyer.

Finding aids: Typescript guide, 1971; NRA 17004.

Facilities: Photocopying. Microfilm reader.

Publications: A.J. Horwood: *Catalogue* (1869). N.R. Ker: *Medieval Manuscripts in British Libraries*.

621 Greenwich Local History and Archives Library

Parent organisation: London Borough of Greenwich

Address: 'Woodlands', 90 Mycenae Road, Blackheath, London SE3 7SE

Telephone: (020) 8858 4631

Fax: (020) 8293 4721

E-mail: local.history@greenwich.gov.uk

Website: www.greenwich.gov.uk/council/publicservices/lhistory.htm

Enquiries: The Senior Library Manager, Mr Julian Watson

Open: Mon, Tues: 9.00–5.30; Thurs: 9.00–8.00; Sat: 9.00–5.00.

Access: Generally open to the public. Appointments are desirable for the use of microfilm/fiche readers.

Historical background: The department opened as a local library and art gallery in 1970,

enabling the separate collections of the former metropolitan boroughs to be amalgamated. There is as yet no systematic records programme. The department also acts as the Diocesan Record Office for Southwark (Greenwich parish records), and is recognised as a place of deposit for public records.

Acquisitions policy: Printed documents, MSS, illustrations, and other visual media for the London Borough of Greenwich (Greenwich, Deptford, Charlton, Woolwich, Plumstead, Shooters Hill, Eltham, Kidbrook and Blackheath). Relevant archives of local organisations except those within the collections policy of London Metropolitan Archives (entry 688), i.e. ecclesiastical registers, schools, hospitals, magistrates courts etc.

Archives of organisation: Usual local authority record holdings, including archives of London Borough of Greenwich, 1965– , and its predecessors: the metropolitan boroughs of Woolwich and Greenwich, and former civil parishes of Greenwich, St Nicholas Deptford, Charlton, Plumstead, and Kidbrooke, and Woolwich Board of Health, 1848–99.

Major collections: Deeds, 16th–20th centuries.
Family and estate papers relating to Martin, Newton and Fuller families.
Records of Christchurch School, East Greenwich, 1870–1950.
Business records, including Woolwich Ferry Company, 1811–15; Furlongs Estate Agency; and Sykes Pumps.
Records of Greenwich and Lewisham Antiquarian Society, 1905– ; Greenwich Historical Society; and West Kent Natural History Society, 1871– .
The collection of Alan Roger Martin (1901–74).

Non-manuscript material: MS plans and surveys.
Extensive picture and photographic collections.
Spurgeon Collections of photographs of street life in Greenwich, 1884.
Watercolours and drawings, early 18th–20th centuries (c900).

Finding aids: Catalogues, lists and indexes. Some lists sent to NRA, see NRA 7826, 26583.

Facilities: Photocopying. Photography. Microfilm/fiche reader.

Conservation: Contracted out.

Publications: Greenwich Local History Library: *A Guide to Sources*.

L. Reilly: *Family History in Greenwich: a Guide to Sources* (1992).

622 Grenadier Guards Regimental Archives

Address: Regimental Headquarters, Wellington Barracks, Birdcage Walk, London SW1E 6HQ

Telephone: (020) 7414 3221

Fax: (020) 7414 3443

Enquiries: The Curator/Archivist

Open: Tues, Thurs: by appointment.

Access: Open to ex-Grenadiers and their relations, and also to bona fide researchers on application.

Historical background: The regiment was founded in 1656 by Charles II.

Acquisitions policy: Maintains the regimental archive and accepts personal papers.

Archives of organisation: Records of the regiment, including activities of each Battalion, 1656– .
Records of promotions, awards, births, deaths and marriages.
Attestation papers of all members of the regiment (3000 box files).

Major collections: Diaries, letters and biographical material.

Non-manuscript material: Photographs, 1850– .
Grave locations.

Finding aids: Catalogue in preparation. Personal files of all officers in alphabetical order and other ranks by regimental number.

Facilities: Photocopying.

623 Guide Association

Address: 17–19 Buckingham Palace Road, London SW1W 0PT

Telephone: (020) 7834 6242 ext. 255

Fax: (020) 7828 8317

E-mail: chq.guides.org.uk

Website: www.guides.org.uk

Enquiries: The Archivist, Mrs M.S. Courtney

Open: Mon–Fri: 10.00–4.00.

Access: Bona fide scholars, who should supply references and make an appointment. There are restrictions on certain records.

Historical background: The Guide Association was founded as the Girl Guides Association in 1910 by Lord Baden-Powell (1857–1941) as a counterpart to the Boy Scouts (see National Scout Archive, entry 713).

Acquisitions policy: Accepts donations of guiding material and papers relating to guiding personnel. Local records are held by regional and county offices.

Archives of organisation: Records and publications of the association, 1910– , including minutes of council and committees; annual and conference reports and correspondence; training material.

Major collections: Small collection of Baden-Powell family letters.

Non-manuscript material: Photographic collection, 1908– .
Film collection (transferred to video).
Badges, awards and exhibits.
Audio collection (being transferred to CD).

Finding aids: Catalogues. Indexes. Photographic catalogue in preparation.

Facilities: Photocopying. Microfilm/fiche reader.

Conservation: Contracted out.

624 Guildhall Library
Manuscripts Section

Parent organisation: Corporation of London

Address: Guildhall Library, Aldermanbury, London EC2P 2EJ

Telephone: (020) 7332 1863

Fax: (020) 7600 3384

E-mail: manuscripts.guildhall@ms.corpoflondon.gov.uk

Website: ihr.sas.ac.uk/ihr/ghmnu.html

Enquiries: The Keeper of Manuscripts

Open: Mon–Fri: 9.30–4.45; Sat: 9.30–4.45 (but no delivery from strongrooms, 12.00–2.00).
The library closes on all bank holiday Saturdays and any Saturdays which immediately precede or follow the Christmas and New Year holidays.

Access: Generally open to the public; an appointment is not normally necessary. Access to some modern (mostly business) records is dependent on the depositor's permission and requires 24 hours' notice of a visit.

Historical background: Guildhall Library was founded in 1824 and is primarily a library of London history, holding not only printed books but also prints, maps, drawings and paintings and MSS. The Manuscripts Section is, in effect, the local record office for the City of London (excepting the archives of the Corporation of London, entry 588). The office also acts as Diocesan Record Office for London and is recognised as a place of deposit for public records.

Acquisitions policy: Records relating to or emanating from the City of London (excepting the archives of the Corporation of London).

Major collections: Records of Diocese of London, 14th–20th centuries; Archdeaconry of London, 14th–20th centuries; parish records for the City of London, 15th–20th centuries; and Dean and Chapter of St Paul's Cathedral, 11th–20th centuries.

Records of 79 of the City of London's ancient livery companies and related organisations, 12th–20th centuries.

Businesses and business organisations, 16th–20th centuries, including merchant banks: Brown Shipley, Hambros, Kleinwort Benson, Morgan Grenfell; insurance companies: Commercial Union, Hand-in-Hand, Royal Exchange, Sun Insurance Office; London Chamber of Commerce; Association of British Commerce; London Stock Exchange; Lloyd's of London; Institute of Chartered Accountants.

Records of Christ's Hospital School, 16th–20th centuries and Corporation of Trinity House, 16th–20th centuries.

Finding aids: General catalogue. General subject, name and place indexes. Several specialised indexes, lists and guides.

An updated guide is available on website.

Facilities: Photocopying. Microfilm/fiche readers.

Conservation: Parchment, paper and photograph conservation and binding are undertaken in-house. Some work is contracted out.

Publications: Vestry Minutes of Parishes within the City of London (2/1964).

London Rate Assessments and Inhabitants Lists in Guildhall Library and the Corporation of London Records Office (2/1968).
Churchwardens' Accounts of Parishes within the City of London (2/1969).
Guide to the Archives of City Livery Companies and Related Organisations in Guildhall Library (3/1989).
Handlist of Parish Registers, pt 1: Parishes within the City of London (6/1990); pt 2: *Parishes in Greater London outside the City* (7/1994).
A Handlist of Business Archives at Guildhall Library (2/1991).
Handlist of the Non-Conformist, Roman Catholic, Jewish and Burial Ground Registers (2/1993).
D.T. Barriskill: *A Guide to the Lloyd's Marine Collection at Guildhall Library* (2/1994).
The British Overseas: a Guide to Records of their Births, Baptisms, Marriages, Deaths and Burials available in the United Kingdom (3/1994).
R. Harvey: *A Guide to Genealogical Sources in Guildhall Library* (4/1997).
A Guide to Archives and Manuscripts at Guildhall Library (7/1999).
Greater London History Sources, Vol. 1: *City of London* (2000).

625 Guinness Archives

Parent organisation: Guinness Ltd (part of Diageo plc)

Address: Park Royal Brewery, London NW10 7RR

Telephone: (020) 8963 5278

Fax: (020) 8963 5173

E-mail: garlands@guinness.com

Enquiries: The Archivist, Sue Garland

Open: Mon–Fri: 9.00–5.00, by appointment.

Access: Bona fide researchers, at the discretion of the company.

Historical background: The Guinness brewery in Dublin was founded in 1759 and became a limited company on the British Stock Exchange in 1886. Park Royal Brewery opened in 1936 and is now the headquarters for Guinness's international operations which have developed since the 1960s.

Acquisitions policy: Material related to Guinness companies and branches in Britain and overseas, although Irish material is held mainly in Dublin.

Archives of organisation: Statutory records, 1886– ; operational records relating to Park Royal Brewery, mid–1930s– .
Advertising (British) material, 1929– .

Non-manuscript material: Advertising posters, TV and radio commercials, and artefacts. Photographs of breweries and some site plans. Packaging, including bottles, cans and labels.
S. Dennison and O. MacDonagh: 'Guinness, 1886–1939, from Incorporation to Second World War' (TS).

Finding aids: Manuscript and typed lists. Computer database.

Conservation: Contracted out (mainly for advertising artwork).

Publications: B. Sibley: *The Book of Guinness Advertising* (1985).
J. Davies: *The Book of Guinness Advertising* (1998).

626 HM Land Registry

Address: 32 Lincoln's Inn Fields, London WC2A 3PH

Telephone: (020) 7917 8888

Fax: (020) 7955 0110

Website: www.landreg.gov.uk

Open: Mon–Fri: 9.00–5.00.

Access: Generally open to the public.

Under the Land Registration (Open Register) Rules 1991, anyone may inspect and obtain copies of the register and filed plans and any documents (other than a charge or a lease) referred to in the register that the Land Registry holds. A fee is payable for this service. The Land Registry was established in 1862, but only a handful of properties were registered in the 19th century. Compulsory registration on a sale or a grant of a long lease was first introduced in inner London between 1899 and 1902, and by 1990 extended to the whole of England and Wales. Compulsory registration now applies to sales, gifts, assents and first mortgages of unregistered land. It is estimated that about 70 per cent of properties in England and Wales are registered. The Land Registry is an executive agency under the Lord Chancellor's Department.

The Land Registry does not, as a rule, retain the deeds of title which are submitted for registration. The records kept by the registry are retained only for the periods required by the Public Records Act 1958, except in the case of permanently retained documents still under the provisions of the Land Registration Acts, 1925 & 1988, and Rules.

627 HSBC Holdings plc
Group Archives

Address: 10 Lower Thames Street, London EC3R 6AE

Telephone: (020) 7260 0108/7609

Fax: (020) 7260 7977

E-mail: group.archives@hsbcgroup.com

Enquiries: The Deputy Archivist, Sara Kinsey
The Assistant Archivist, Rachel Huskinson

Open: Mon–Fri: 9.00–5.00, by appointment only.

Historical background: The Shanghai Banking Corporation (HSBC) was established in Hong Kong in 1865 to finance trade between the Far East, India and Europe. In 1959 it took over the Mercantile Bank of India and the British Bank of the Middle East. A UK-based holding company, HSBC Holdings plc, was established in 1991, and the following year Midland Bank became a wholly-owned subsidiary of HSBC Holdings plc. Both Midland Bank and HSBC had established archive units in the 1970s, and these were merged in 1993 when the HSBC archive was transferred from Hong Kong to London.

Acquisitions policy: Collects records covering all aspects of the activities of the HSBC Group.

Archives of organisation: Archives of Midland Bank and its constituent banks, late 18th century– ; Hong Kong and Shanghai Banking Corporation, 1865– ; the British Bank of the Middle East, formerly the Imperial Bank of Persia, 1889– ; the Mercantile Bank of India, formerly the Chartered Mercantile Bank of India, London & China, 1853–1983.

Non-manuscript material: Plans of bank buildings. Photographs of branches, bank buildings and staff.
Oral history collections.
Film and video collections.

Finding aids: Descriptive lists and computer databases.

Facilities: Photocopying. Photography.

Conservation: Contracted out.

Publications: E. Green: *Midland: 150 Years of Banking Business* (1986).
G. Jones: *The History of the British Bank of the Middle East* (1986–7).
H.H. King: *The History of the Hong Kong and Shanghai Banking Corporation* (1987–91).
E. Green and S. Kinsey: 'The Archives of the HSBC Group', *Financial History Review*, 3 (1996).

628 Hackney Archives Department

Parent organisation: London Borough of Hackney

Address: 43 De Beauvoir Road, London N1 5SQ

Telephone: (020) 7241 2886

Fax: (020) 7241 6688

E-mail: archives@hackney.gov.uk

Website: www.hackney.gov.uk

Enquiries: The Archivist, Mr D.L. Mander

Open: Mon, Tues, Thurs: 9.30–1.00, 2.00–5.00; Sat (1st and 3rd of each month): 9.30–1.00, 2.00–5.00.

Access: Generally open to the public; an appointment is necessary. Certain classes of records are closed for specified periods (details from the department). A paid research service is available.

Historical background: The department was established in 1965 and administers the official and inherited records of the former metropolitan boroughs of Hackney, Shoreditch and Stoke Newington and their predecessors, as well as the local history collections of the former authorities. Deposited records are also held.

Acquisitions policy: Formal policy approved by Hackney Council. Collects records about or associated with the area of the London Borough of Hackney and its immediate environs. In certain cases records relating to areas outside the geographical boundaries may be acquired, either because they form part of a record group with a Hackney association or for other reasons.

Archives of organisation: Usual local authority record holdings, including those transferred from the former Greater London Council.

Major collections: Deposited records with substantial business collections, including records of Abney Park Cemetery Company, 1840–1980; Berger, Jensen & Nicholson, paint manufacturers, 1773–1980; Bryant & May Ltd, match manufacturers, and subsidiaries, c1850–c1965, J. & W. Nicholson of Clerkenwell and Bow, gin distillers, 1763–1969; British Xylonite Co. Ltd, plastic manufacturers, corporate and some manufacturing records, 1877–1969; Carless, Capel & Leonard, distillers and oil refiners of Hackney Wick, 1860–1988.

Non-manuscript material: Local history library, which includes local directories; local newspapers (available on microfilm); theatre material, including posters and programmes for four Shoreditch theatres, c1831–1910, and for the Hackney Empire, c1910– ; and OS and other printed and copy maps of the Hackney area.

Visual collection of photographs; oil, watercolour and other paintings; film (mostly available on VHS video).

John Dawson Collection: books printed before 1767 (600), believed to be the only surviving parochial library in London, with MS notebooks and Dawson's diary.

Finding aids: Lists of archive collections sent to NRA. Lists of deposited records have been microfilmed by Chadwyck-Healey. Indexes. General information and guide available via website.

Hackney on Disk digitized map image database.

Facilities: Photocopying. Digital photographic service. Microprinter reader and microfilm/fiche readers. Video monitor. Cassette listening facility.

Conservation: In-house service; available to external institutions.

Publications: Hackney section of *Guide to London Local History Resources*.

Leaflets on using sources.

Various publications on the history of Hackney stocked for sale; publications list available (send SAE).

629 Hahnemann House Trust

Address: 2 Powis Place, Great Ormond Street, London WC1 3HT

Telephone: (020) 7286 9892

E-mail: jbrock4884@aol.com

Enquiries: J.T. Brock, 15 Cheadle Court, Henderson Drive, London NW8 8UD

Open: Strictly by appointment.

Access: Bona fide scholars by prior arrangement.

The trust was established in 1910 to exhibit artefacts of Samuel Hahnemann, and others of homoeopathic interest. It holds records of the British Homoeopathic Society and the Faculty of Homoeopathy, mainly 19th and early 20th centuries, as well as the papers of Frederic Quin (1798–1878) and Sir John Weir (1879–1941).

630 Hammersmith and Fulham Archives and Local History Collection

Parent organisation: London Borough of Hammersmith and Fulham

Address: The Lilla Huset, 191 Talgarth Road, London W6 8BJ

Telephone: (020) 8741 5159

Fax: (020) 8741 4882

Website: www.lbhf.gov.uk

Enquiries: The Borough Archivist, Ms Jane Kimber

Open: Mon: 9.30–8.00; Tues: 9.30–1.00; Thurs: 9.30–4.30;
Sat (1st of each month): 9.30–1.00.

Access: Generally open to the public, by appointment only.

Historical background: Hammersmith and Fulham libraries accumulated material from the late 19th century. In 1955 the Metropolitan Borough of Hammersmith appointed an archivist, and on the amalgamation of the borough with Fulham in 1965 appropriate material was also transferred to the archives, then based at Shepherds Bush. In 1992 the entire archives plus the two separate local history collections moved into a new purpose-built Archives and Local History Centre next to the Ark building in Hammersmith. The centre is recognised as a place of deposit for public, manorial and tithe records.

Acquisitions policy: In addition to preserving and making available the records of the London Borough of Hammersmith and Fulham and its predecessors, deposits are accepted, and in some cases purchases are made, of material relevant to the history of the area.

Archives of organisation: Usual local authority record holdings, including vestry minutes, rate books etc, 1620s– .

Major collections: Deposited local collections, including records of some local churches, businesses and schools, plus the following of particular note: Hammersmith Bridge Company records, 1824–80; Fulham Bridge Company records, 1729–1865; Dorville and Scott families, estate papers, 1607–1853; Bult family of Brook Green, correspondence, 1796–1846; Fulham manorial records, 1810–1929; West London Hospital records, 1866–1979; Fulham Pottery records, 1865–1968; Sir William Bull's collection of antiquarian papers, 1882–1930; Hammersmith Convent's records (IBVM, later Benedictine, now Sacred Heart), 1672–1866; William Morris (1834–96) and Edward Burne-Jones (1833–98), miscellaneous papers.

Non-manuscript material: Extensive collection of photographs, drawings and prints (c60,000); maps, printed ephemera, theatre programmes; local newspapers, including *West London Observer*, 1855–1984, and *Fulham Chronicle*, 1888– ; newspaper cuttings; electoral registers; local directories.

Collections of local pottery and paintings, such as the Cecil French Bequest, which includes 25 works by Burne-Jones.

Census returns, 1841–91 (microform).

Finding aids: Name and place index. Lists of deposited collections: copies sent to NRA. Brief guide to holdings on website.

Facilities: Photocopying and photography by arrangement. Microform reader/printer.

Conservation: Conservation section with one in-house full-time conservator. Outside work is not undertaken.

631 Haringey Museum and Archive Service

Parent organisation: London Borough of Haringey

Address: Bruce Castle, Lordship Lane, London N17 8NU

Telephone: (020) 8808 8772

Fax: (020) 8808 4118

E-mail: museum.services@harringey.gov.uk

Website: www.brucecastlemuseum.org.uk

Enquiries: The Local History Officer, Ms Rita Read

Open: By arrangement only.

Access: Generally open to the public, by appointment.

Historical background: Bruce Castle was opened as a world history museum in 1926 and subsequently acquired an important collection of material on the history of the British Post Office. It is now a museum of local and postal history. The collection of archival material relating to Tottenham commenced early; since the formation of the London Borough of Haringey in 1964, Hornsey and Wood Green material has been added. The material comprising the museum of the Middlesex Regimental Association has been transferred to the National Army Museum (entry 706).

Acquisitions policy: Limited to public and private records relating to the Haringey area.

Archives of organisation: Usual local authority record holdings, 1850– .

Major collections: Court rolls of the Manor of Tottenham, 1318–1732.
Records of the parishes of Tottenham and Hornsey, 15th century– .
Administrative records of the Alexandra Park and Palace, 1866–1966.

Non-manuscript material: Collection of local history material, consisting of printed books and pamphlets, maps and plans (c1000); newspapers; photographs (c10,000); prints and paintings; census returns.

Finding aids: Lists of parochial and manorial holdings and indexes by person and place to the archive collections in general. Translations of manorial court rolls fully indexed. Census material and newspapers in process of indexing.

Facilities: Photocopying. Photography by arrangement. Microfilm reader.

Publications: Guide to London Local Studies Resources [includes details of archive holdings and local history material in the Haringey return].
Handlist no. 1: Deposited Parish Records [Tottenham and Hornsey].
Court Rolls of the Manor of Tottenham [translations appearing so far (6 vols): 1318–99 and 1510–82].
Illustrated exhibition catalogues covering education, leisure activities, housing and transport.

632 Harrods Ltd
Company Archives
Address: Knightsbridge, London SW1X 7XL

Telephone: (020) 7730 1234 ext. 8027

Fax: (020) 7581 0470

E-mail: archives@harrods.com

Website: www.harrods.com

Enquiries: The Company Archivist

Open: Mon–Fri: 10.00–7.00.

Access: At the discretion of the company. Appointments should be made with the Company Archivist.

Historical background: The business was founded as a small grocery retail store in 1849 by Charles Henry Harrod (1799–1885). It grew into a large homewares and food retail business under his son Charles Digby Harrod (1841–1905), who retired in 1889, when the business was floated as a limited company. Rapid development of the business occurred during the next 20 years under the Managing Director Richard Burbridge, who was succeeded by his son in 1917, and his grandson in 1935. Harrods Ltd was taken over by the House of Fraser in 1959. The Fayed family acquired the House of Fraser Group in 1985.

Acquisitions policy: Company records.

Archives of organisation: Archives of the company, 1889– , including financial, personnel, administrative and advertising records.

Non-manuscript material: The advertising records comprise cuttings books, 1917– , catalogues, photographs and account mailers, 1890s– .

Finding aids: Manually compiled lists. Computer cataloguing programme being developed.

Facilities: Photocopying. Microfiche reader/printer. Photography can be arranged if permission is granted to reproduce material from the collection.

Publications: A. Turton and M. Moss: *A Legend in Retailing: the House of Fraser* (1989).
S. Callery: *Harrods Knightsbridge: the Story of Society's Favourite Store* (1991).
T. Dale: *Harrods: the Store and the Legend* (1991).
——: *Harrods: a Palace in Knightsbridge* (1995).

633 Highgate Literary and Scientific Institution

Address: 11 South Grove, London N6 6BS

Telephone: (020) 8340 3343

Fax: (020) 8340 5632

E-mail: admin@hlsi.demon.co.uk

Enquiries: The Secretary, Archives Committee

Open: Tues–Fri, by arrangement.

Access: Members and bona fide scholars, by appointment only.

Historical background: The institution was founded in 1839 by Harry Chester (1806–68), educationalist, and others. It has been at the present address since 1840. The scientific book collection was completely dispersed after World War II and the institution now concentrates on literature and local history.

Acquisitions policy: Material of local interest accepted by donation.

Archives of organisation: Records of the institution, including minute books, annual reports, printed programmes, lectures, correspondence, scrapbooks and newspaper cuttings, 1838– .

Major collections: Deeds of Pauncefort Almshouses, c1700–c1900.
Book Society minute books, 1822–1922.
Highgate Dispensary books, 1787–1840.
Mothercraft Training Society archives, 1918–1950s.
Highgate Horticultural Society minute books, 1903– .
Robert Whipple Trust minute books.
Papers of Samuel Taylor Coleridge (1772–1834) and Sir John Betjeman (1906–84).

Non-manuscript material: Local history collection, including photographs, prints, glass plate slides and negatives.

Finding aids: Outline lists and card indexes for some collections.

Publications: A.E. Barker: 'Improving the Records of Highgate: the Story of the Literary and Scientific Institution', *Camden History Review*, no.8 (1980), 13–16.
Heart of a London Village (Archives Committee, 1989).

634 Highgate School

Address: North Road, London N6 6AY

Telephone: (020) 8340 1524

Fax: (020) 8340 7674

Website: www.highgate.org.uk

Enquiries: The Record Keeper, Mr T.G. Mallinson

Open: By prior arrangement only.

Access: Bona fide researchers, by appointment.

Historical background: Highgate School is an independent institution, founded in 1565 by Sir Richard Cholmeley. The archives have been developed systematically only since the 1980s following the return of the governors' records, formerly housed separately, into school curatorship.

Acquisitions policy: All items in any way connected with Highgate School and its present and former staff and pupils.

Archives of organisation: Documents relating to the foundation, history, administration, finance, staff and pupils of the school, mid-16th century– .

Major collections: Some documentary material relevant to the history of Highgate village.

Non-manuscript material: Plans, drawings, photographs and uniforms, as an integral part of the archive.
Tape-recorded interviews, with transcripts, of former staff and pupils, mainly covering early 20th century.

Finding aids: Manual card index catalogue and users' guide.

Publications: T. Hinde: *Highgate School: a History* (London, 1992).

635 Honourable Artillery Company

Address: Armoury House, City Road, London EC1Y 2BQ

Telephone: (020) 7382 1541

Fax: (020) 7382 1538

Website: www.hac.org.uk

Enquiries: The Archivist, James Armstrong

Open: By written appointment.

Access: Bona fide researchers. Enquiries are answered by post and a donation may be requested.

Historical background: The Honourable Artillery Company was incorporated by Royal Charter in 1537 and is the oldest volunteer regiment in the world. The company is governed by an annually elected Court of Assistants. The archives, which date from 1656 onwards, are of particular interest for 17th– and 18th–century militia and City matters.

Acquisitions policy: Records of the Honourable Artillery Company and personal papers of members of the Company.

Archives of organisation: Minutes of the Court of Assistants, 1656– ; financial and membership records; minutes of other HAC committees.

Major collections: Personal papers of Maj. George Goold Walker (*d* 1955), Lt. Col. John Bamford Smith (1885–1987), and Capt. John Beaven (1906–87).

Non-manuscript material: Artworks by Adrian Hill (1895–1977), official war artist.
Photographs. Prints and drawings. Maps and plans, including World War I trench maps.
Printed histories, leaflets and ephemera of the HAC and related literature.

Finding aids: Lists in progress.

Facilities: Photocopying. Photography.

Conservation: Contracted out.

Publications: G.A. Raikes: *The History of the Honourable Artillery Company*, 2 vols (London, 1878–9).
B. Williams and E. Childers (eds): *The H.A.C. in South Africa* (London, 1903).
HAC Journal (1923–).
G. Goold Walker (ed.): *The Honourable Artillery Company in the Great War, 1914–1919* (London, 1930).

R.F. Johnson: *Regimental Fire!: the Honourable Artillery Company in World War II, 1939–1945* (London, 1958).
G. Goold Walker: *The Honourable Artillery Company, 1537–1987* (London, 3/1986).

636 House of Lords Record Office
The Parliamentary Archives

Address: Westminster, London SW1A 0PW

Telephone: (020) 7219 3074

Fax: (020) 7219 2570

E-mail: hlro@parliament.uk

Website: www.parliament.uk

Enquiries: The Clerk of the Records

Open: Mon–Fri: 9.30–5.00.
Closed last two weeks of November.

Access: Open to the public, preferably by appointment. There is a 30-year closure period on administrative records and longer closure periods on a few classes, e.g. certain committee records.

Historical background: The records of the House of Lords have been kept at Westminster since 1497 (earlier records are to be found among the Chancery and Exchequer records in the Public Record Office entry 1058). The House of Lords records escaped the fire of 1834 which gutted most of the medieval Palace of Westminster, but the House of Commons records were destroyed, with the exception of the original *Journals* dating from 1547. In 1864 the Lords records were moved into the Victoria Tower of the new Palace of Westminster, where they are still housed. The record office was established in 1946 and now has custody of both the House of Lords records and of the *House of Commons Journals* and post-1834 records, as well as some deposited private papers.

Acquisitions policy: To acquire records relating to proceedings in either House of Parliament; the history, architecture and decoration of the Palace of Westminster; peers, MPs and officials particularly concerned with the running of Parliament.

Archives of organisation: Acts of Parliament, 1497– (*c*60,000).
Papers laid before the House of Lords, 1531– .
House of Lords Journals, 1510– .

House of Commons Journals, 1547– .
Committee proceedings, 1610– .
Plans of canals, railways, roads and other works, 1794– .
Peerage claims, 1604– .
Historical collections: parliamentary diaries, clerks' papers etc, 1545– .

Major collections: Private political papers, 1712– , including those of Lord Beaverbrook (1879–1964), David Lloyd George (1863–1945) and Andrew Bonar Law (1858–1923).

Non-manuscript material: Plans and drawings of the Palace of Westminster, including drawings by Barry and Pugin, c1840–60.
Photographs of the Palace of Westminster and of peers and MPs, 1852– .

Finding aids: Automated finding aids available.

Facilities: Photocopying. Photography. Microfilm/fiche reader.

Conservation: In-house bindery; outside work undertaken.

Publications: M.F. Bond: *Guide to the Records of Parliament* (1971).
A Guide to Historical Collections of the Nineteenth and Twentieth Centuries Preserved in the House of Lords Record Office, House of Lords Record Office *Memorandum*, no.60 (1978).
Historical Manuscripts Commission Reports 1–14 [include lists of House of Lords MSS, 1498–1693].
The Manuscripts of the House of Lords, 1693–1718 [12 vols].
Witness before Parliament: a Guide to the Database of Witnesses in Committees on Opposed Private Bills 1771–1917, House of Lords Record Office *Memorandum*, no.85 (1997).

637 Howard de Walden Estate

Address: 23 Queen Anne Street, London W1G 9DL

Telephone: (020) 7580 3163

Fax: (020) 7436 8152

Website: www.howard-de-walden.co.uk

Enquiries: The Archivist, Richard Bowden

Open: Tues–Wed: 10.00–5.00, by prior appointment only.

Access: Bona fide researchers only. A 30-year closure rule applies.

Historical background: The Howard de Walden Estate comprises approximately 90 acres in Marylebone, north of Oxford Street. The area began to be developed c1715 by Edward Harley, 2nd Earl of Oxford. His only daughter and heir married William Bentinck, 2nd Duke of Portland, and so, until 1879, it was known as the Portland Estate. Ten years after the death of the 5th Duke of Portland in 1879 the estate passed to his sole surviving sister, Lucy, Lady Howard de Walden, and the Howard de Walden Estate came into existence. Although sizeable portions of the estate were sold at the beginning of the 20th century, Harley Street and the streets on either side of it, including Portland Place and most of Marylebone High Street, still remain part of it. Additional archives relating to the estate are at Westminster City Archives (entry 846) and Nottingham University Library (entry 946). There are no family papers in this collection, and because of war damage almost no records from the 18th century.

Archives of organisation: Estate records, 19th–20th centuries, including ground plans and lease contract details for individual properties, 1812–c1960, with indexes for the current estate. Correspondence files for individual properties, c1900– .

Non-manuscript material: Architectural drawings of estate properties, c1890– (13,000).

Finding aids: Database of architectural drawings.
Lists of estate records, 19th and 20th centuries.

Facilities: Photocopying and photography by arrangement.

Publications: R. Bowden: 'Oxford Street Two Hundred Years Ago: the Portland Estate Block Plans, c1805–1870', *London Topographical Record*, xxviii (2001).

638 Huguenot Library

Parent organisation: The Huguenot Society of Great Britain and Ireland

Address: University College London, Gower Street, London WC1E 6BT

Telephone: (020) 7380 7094

E-mail: s.massil@ucl.ac.uk

Website: www.ucl.ac.uk/ucl-info/divisions/library/huguenot.htm

Enquiries: The Librarian

Open: Mon–Wed: 10.00–4.00, strictly by appointment with the Librarian.

Access: Fellows of the society and bona fide researchers. Genealogical enquiries from non-members are dealt with by the society's research assistant (details on application).

Historical background: The Huguenot Library is the joint library of the French Protestant Hospital, founded by royal charter in 1718 (now at Rochester), and of the Huguenot Society of London, founded in 1885. It was housed at the hospital until its transfer on deposit to University College in 1957, but it is not administered by the college archivists.

Acquisitions policy: Books and archives relating to the Huguenots, in particular those who came to Britain, and their descendants.

Major collections: French Protestant Hospital archives, with some associated Huguenot philanthropic bodies.
Huguenot Society records, plus collection of Huguenot pedigrees and other genealogical material made by the late Henry Wagner.
'Royal Bounty' MSS.

Conservation: Contracted out.

Publications: Huguenot Society: *Quarto Series* (1885–) [59 vols], including all surviving registers of the Huguenot churches in England and Ireland; lists of denizations and naturalisations; the 'Royal Bounty' papers by Raymond Smith (vol.51); and all remaining archives by Irvine Gray (vol.56). Vols 1–47 available in microfiche.
Annual Proceedings (1885-).
General Index to the Proceedings and Quarto Series, 1885–1985 (1986).
Huguenot Society New Series (monographs) 1–3.
Master (name) Index to Proceedings I–XXVI (1998).

639 Hulton Getty Picture Collection

Address: Unique House, 21–31 Woodfield Road, London W9 2BA

Telephone: (020) 7579 5700

Fax: (020) 7266 2662

E-mail: info@getty-images.com

Website: www.hulton.getty.com

Enquiries: The Picture Research Manager

Open: Mon–Fri: 9.00–6.00.

Access: Generally open to the public, by appointment. Researchers can also telephone with a description and then fax the information. A search fee is charged. Those wishing to purchase a photograph for their personal use should contact the Hulton Getty Picture Gallery, 3 Jubilee Place, London SW3 3TP, tel: (020) 7376 4525, fax: (020) 7376 4524. A price guide is available.

Historical background: The collection is the direct descendant of the library originally created by Edward Hulton, the publisher of *Picture Post.* The collection was part of the BBC until 1988, when it was acquired by Brian Deutsch. Since 1997 it has been part of the Getty Group.

Acquisitions policy: Hulton Getty represents Reuter News Pictures and manages Mirror Syndication International, ensuring contemporary images are being added to the collection.

Non-manuscript material: Many photographic collections, including:
Picture Post Collection, 1938–58.
Topical Press Agency, 1902–57.
Sasha, 1920s and 1930s (theatre portraits and literary figures).
Baron, 1935–56 (personalities, society and performing arts).
Studio Lisa, 1936–54 (royal family).
Charles Downey, 1860–1920 (portraits).
London Stereoscopic Company, 1854–1914 (topographical).
Keystone, Fox, Central Press and Three Lions, 20th century.
Large collection of historical engravings.
Images from *Evening Standard*, Ernst Haas, Slim Aaron, Weegee.

Finding aids: Basic and advance search tools on web-site. Search facilities on internal production database.

Facilities: Photocopying. CD-ROM research facilities.

Conservation: In-house conservation department.

Publications: Quarterly newsletter *HDC*, 1994– .

CD guides: *The Decades*, 1920s–1950/60s, with 2500 images each.
7 Ages of Man [catalogue].
All Human Life [booklet].

640 ING Baring Holdings Ltd

Address: 60 London Wall, London EC2M 5TQ

Telephone: (020) 7767 1401

Fax: (020) 7767 7131

E-mail: john.orbell@ing-barings.com
jane.waller@ing-barings.com

Enquiries: The Archivist and Records Manager, Dr M.J. Orbell
The Assistant Archivist, Jane Waller

Open: Mon–Fri: 10.00–5.00, by appointment.

Access: Bona fide researchers. A letter of introduction is required, and ING Baring wish to see research prior to publication.

Historical background: The bank was established in 1762 as John & Francis Baring & Co. and for many years was known as Baring Brothers & Co. Ltd. Its original function was merchanting, but the business was soon diversified into finance of international trade and into security issuance. Barings vied with Rothschilds for leadership of the London international capital market between 1800 and 1914. The company was closely involved with finance in Argentina, Russia, the USA and Canada, and financed railway construction in the 19th century.

Acquisitions policy: Papers and three-dimensional material relating to Barings, the Baring family and individuals who worked or were otherwise connected with the bank.

Archives of organisation: General ledgers, customer ledgers and other accounting records, 1762–20th century.
Correspondence of partners and senior managers, *c*1820–20th century.
Department records, including personnel, premises, credit and securities, 20th century.

Major collections: Northbrook papers, of Sir Francis and Sir Thomas Baring, 1st and 2nd Lords Northbrook, 1760s–1910.
Ashburton family papers, 1808–98.
Papers of William Windham and of the Windham family of Felbrigg, 1769–1870; Labouchere family, 1621–1822; the 3rd Earl of Cromer, 1926–82.

Archives of H.S. Lefevre & Co., merchant bankers, 1880–1949.

Non-manuscript material: Security certificates, early 19th century– .
Plans and drawings *re* premises, mid–19th century– .
Plans and maps of projects financed, 1796– .
Portraits of Baring family and staff, 18th century– .
Photographs of premises and staff, late 19th century– .

Finding aids: Manual catalogue of 18th- and 19th-century archives; card index (people and institutions) to 18th-century and 19th-century catalogue; sent to NRA.
Computer-based catalogue of 20th-century archives.

Facilities: Photocopying restricted to documents from which it is difficult to make notes, e.g. tables of statistics.

Conservation: Contracted out.

Publications: J. Orbell: *A History of Baring Brothers to 1939* (1985).
P. Ziegler: *The Sixth Street Power: Baring, 1762–1929* (1988).
J. Orbell: *Guide to the Baring Archive at ING Barings* (2/1997).

641 ITC Archive and Records

Parent organisation: Independent Television Commission

Address: 33 Foley Street, London W1P 7LB

Telephone: (020) 7306 7781

E-mail: troake.p@itc.org.uk

Enquiries: The Records and Archive Administrator, Mr Paul Troake

Open: Mon–Fri: 8.30–5.30.

Access: Members of the public and staff. The 30-year rule applies, but special requests to view less sensitive recent information may be made.

Historical background: ITC was founded in 1991 to regulate and licence commercial television (i.e. non-licence fee funded) services provided in and from the UK.
The Independent Broadcasting Authority (IBA) archive was established as a collection during 1991 and subsequent records belong to the ITC; an official ITC Archive is currently being established.

Acquisitions policy: Relevant donations are accepted.

Archives of organisation: IBA Archive, 1954–90, including Radio Division Archive.
Cable Authority Archive, 1984–90.
Special collection held by Library of Associated Rediffusion Archive: Programme Sales Collection, 1955–68.
ITC Archive, 1990– .

Non-manuscript material: Some film footage of IBA promotions; memorabilia; trade test transmission slides and photographs.

Finding aids: Lists, indexes. Database using keyword searches.

Facilities: Photocopying. Microfiche printer.

Conservation: Paper conservation undertaken in-house.

Publications: B. Sendall: *Independent Television in Britain*, vols 1 & 2 (1982, 1983).
J. Potter: *Independent Television in Britain*, vols 3 & 4 (1989, 1990).
P. Bonner and L. Aston: *Independent Television in Britain*, vol. 5 (1998).

642 ITV Network Ltd

Address: 200 Grays Inn Road, London WC1X 8HF

Telephone: (020) 7843 8000

Fax: (020) 7843 8158

Website: www.itv.co.uk

Enquiries: The Archivist/Records Manager

Open: By appointment.

Access: Bona fide researchers, by written application to the Archivist. The company reserves the right to refuse access.

Historical background: Between 1954 and 1958 an alliance of ITV contractors was established known as the Television Programme Contractors Association. This was followed by a more formalised arrangement with the incorporation of the Independent Television Companies Association (ITCA). In 1987 the ITCA changed its name to the Independent Television Association (ITVA) and, in response to the 1990 Broadcasting Act and a change in function, the ITVA was restructured and known from 1993 as the ITV Network Centre. In 1998 the ITVA officially changed its name to ITV Network Ltd.

Acquisitions policy: Acquisitions arise as part of a records management programme, and they will reflect the work of the organisation and its predecessors.

Archives of organisation: Records of the ITCA and its successor bodies, 1958– , relating to corporate policy, European affairs, marketing, agency recognition, copy clearance of commercials, research and development (including engineering), network scheduling, film acquisitions, industrial relations, rights, training and the commissioning of networked programmes. Records relating to the British Regional Television Association and the British Bureau of Television Advertising.

Non-manuscript material: Promotional and programme presentation material on a variety of tape formats.

Finding aids: In-house records management database.

Facilities: Photocopying.

Conservation: Contracted out.

Publications: Independent Television in Britain, Vol. 1: (1982–).
B. Sendall: Vol. 1: *Origin and Foundations, 1946–62* (London, 1982).
——: Vol. 2: *Expansion and Change, 1958–68* (London, 1983).
J. Potter: Vol. 3: *Politics and Control, 1968–80* (London, 1989).
——: Vol. 4: *Companies and Programmes, 1968–80* (London, 1990).
P. Bonner with L. Aston: Vol. 5: *ITV and IBA, 1981–82: the Old Relationship Changes* (London, 1998).

643 Imperial College

Parent organisation: University of London

Address: Room 455, Sherfield Building, Imperial College, London SW7 2AZ

Telephone: (020) 7594 8850

Fax: (020) 7584 9353

E-mail: a.barrett@ic.ac.uk

Website: www.ic.ac.uk

Enquiries: The College Archivist, Mrs Anne Barrett

Open: Mon–Fri: 10.00–12.30, 2.00–5.00, by appointment.

Access: Open to bona fide scholars who produce evidence of their identity. There is a 25-year closure on administrative records. There is a longer period for some records and some material is not available for consultation.

Historical background: Imperial College was established by royal charter in 1907 and was a federation of the Royal School of Mines, the Royal College of Science and the City and Guilds College. In 1988 St Mary's Hospital Medical School (f. 1854; see also entry 792) was merged with the college.
The National Heart and Lung Institute (NHLI) merged with the college in 1995 and became part of Imperial College School of Medicine in 1997. It emerged from the Brompton Hospital Medical School (f. 1843), which joined the British Postgraduate Medical Federation in 1946 and became the Institute for Diseases of the Chest in 1947; a further merger with the Institute of Cardiology in 1972 formed the Cardiothoracic Institute, which became NHLI in 1988.
Westminster Medical School became part of Imperial College School of Medicine in 1997; founded in 1834, it merged with Charing Cross Medical School (f. 1822) in 1984. Westminster Hospital records are at London Metropolitan Archives (see entry 688); West London Hospital records are in the Hammersmith and Fulham Archives and Local History Centre (see entry 630)
The British Postgraduate Medical School (f. 1935) became part of the British Postgraduate Medical Foundation in 1947 as the Postgraduate Medical School of London. In 1974 it regained independence and the title Royal Postgraduate Medical School (RPMS). It merged with the Institute of Obstetrics and Gynaecology in 1986 and further merged with Imperial College School of Medicine in 1997.
See entry 760 for the archives of the Royal Commission for the Exhibition of 1851.

Acquisitions policy: Material collected is directly related to the college, including constituent colleges, or any of its past or present staff and students.

A College Archives & Collections

Archives of organisation: Records of the Royal College of Chemistry, 1845–53; the Royal School of Mines, 1851– ; the Royal College of Science, 1881– ; the City and Guilds College, 1884– ; Imperial College, 1907– .

Records of Westminster Medical School, including minute-books and journals, 1830s– . Student registers, 1890–1932, with some other material, are held in the library of the Chelsea and Westminster Hospital, London SW10.

Records of NHLI and predecessor bodies, including minutes.

Records of RPMS, including minute books and annual reports, 1935–, (housed at Hammersmith Hospital campus, London W12).

Major collections: Collections of papers of scientists associated with the college including: Sir Andrew Ramsay (1814–91), geologist; Lyon Playfair (1818–98), chemist and politician; T.H. Huxley (1825–95), member of staff, 1854–95; William Cawthorne Unwin (1838–1933), civil engineer; Henry Edward Armstrong (1848–1937), chemist; Silvanus P. Thompson (1851–1916), electrical engineer; H.A. Humphrey (1868–1951), engineer; Edward Frankland Armstrong (1878–1945), chemist; James Watson Munro (1888–1968), entomologist; Herbert Dingle (1890–1978), historian of science; Dennis Gabor (1900–79), electrical engineer, inventor of holography and television engineering pioneer; Willis Jackson (1904–70), electrical engineer; Sir Patrick Linstead (1902–66), chemist and rector of the college; Colin Cherry (1914–79), electrical and telecommunications engineer.

Non-manuscript material: Photographs, maps, plans and models of college buildings; photographs of staff and students; records and videotape interviews; microfilms of financial records; scientific drawings and teaching apparatus; medals etc.

Finding aids: Handlists for most collections. Listing in progress for Westminster Medical College and NHLI. Lists sent to NRA.

Facilities: Photocopying and photography at Archivist's discretion. Microfilm/fiche readers in college library.

Conservation: Contracted out.

Publications: A. Barrett and R.G. Williams: *Imperial College: a Pictorial History* (London, 1988).

A. Barrett (ed.): *A History of the Future: Imperial College School of Medicine* (London, 1998).

B Charing Cross Campus

Address: Medical Library, Reynolds Building, St Dunstan's Road, London W6 8RP

Telephone: (020) 8846 7152

Fax: (020) 8846 7565

E-mail: librarycx@ic.ac.uk

Website: www.lib.ic.ac.uk/cx/main.html

Enquiries: The Assistant Librarian, Howard Hague

Open: Mon–Thurs: 9.00–9.00; Fri: 9.00–8.00; Sat (term): 9.00–12.00.

Historical background: See A above.

Acquisitions policy: Material relating to the history of Charing Cross Hospital and its medical school is accepted.

Archives of organisation: Charing Cross Hospital records, including management minutes, 1818–1976.
CCH Medical School records, 1823–1984, including student registers, 1882–1934.

Major collections: Biographical files for prominent Charing Cross and Westminster Hospitals personalities.

Non-manuscript material: Photographs, albums, newspaper cuttings. Collection of books by Charing Cross doctors, 19th–20th centuries.

Finding aids: Interim lists.

Facilities: Photocopying. Photography.

Conservation: Contracted out.

644 Imperial War Museum
Department of Documents

Address: Lambeth Road, London SE1 6HZ

Telephone: (020) 7416 5220/1/2/3

Fax: (020) 7416 5374

E-mail: docs@iwm.org.uk

Website: www.iwm.org.uk

Enquiries: The Keeper of the Department of Documents, Mr R.W.A. Suddaby

Open: Mon–Sat: 10.00–5.00, preferably by appointment (essential for Sats).
Closed last two full weeks of November.
NB Other reference departments in the museum have different opening hours.

Access: Bona fide researchers over the age of 15. Some collections are governed by special access conditions.

Historical background: Although the museum has been collecting MSS relating to 20th century warfare since its formation in 1917, the Department of Documents has its origins in the Foreign Documents Centre, which was set up in the museum and supported by a grant from the Leverhulme Trust from 1964 to 1969. On the expiry of the grant the centre was incorporated into the museum as the Department of Documents and assumed responsibility for the acquisition and administration of collections of British private papers, while continuing in its role of custodian of major series of foreign records for the period 1933 to 1945. The department is recognised as a place of deposit for public records.

Acquisitions policy: To expand the museum's holdings of unpublished records written by officers and other ranks of all three services and by civilians where they relate to their experiences in 20th century conflict, particularly World Wars I and II.

Major collections: Foreign documents: copies of papers relating to the following areas: the German military high command and the conduct of land campaigns of World War II; Luftwaffe planning and supply, 1939–45; German aerial, armaments, industrial and technical research during the period of the Third Reich; the Nuremberg and Tokyo War Crimes Trials.

British private papers: notable collections include the papers of Field Marshals Sir John French (1852–1925), Sir Henry Wilson (1864–1922) and Viscount Montgomery of Alamein (1887–1976); Sir Henry Tizard (1885–1959), scientist; Isaac Rosenberg (1890–1918), war poet.

Several thousand collections of unpublished diaries, letters and memoirs written by officers and other ranks, many of them civilians in uniform (i.e. not regulars), during, between and since World Wars I and II.

Series of biographical files on persons who have been decorated with the Victoria or George Crosses.

Department of Art: unique collection of correspondence with artists who were commissioned under the war-artist schemes in World Wars I and II.

Non-manuscript material: Film and Video Archive: including record footage from service film units; officially sponsored information and propaganda films and newsreels; equivalent material from Allied and enemy sources; television 'histories' and amateur records (c45 million feet).

Photograph Archive: including those taken by official war photographers and others acquired from private sources (c5 million).

Department of Printed Books: reference library comprising books (c100,000) as well as extensive collections of pamphlets, propaganda leaflets, periodicals, maps and technical drawings.

Sound Archive: recorded material, including interviews conducted by museum staff covering the period from the Boer War to Bosnia; also broadcast recordings and sound effects (c20,000 hours/45 million feet).

Finding aids: In-house lists and indexes.

Facilities: Photocopying. Microfilming. Special area for readers wishing to use typewriters or dictaphones. Copy prints can be made to order from the Photograph Archive's collections.

Conservation: Contracted out.

Publications: Leaflet outlining the holdings of the department.
A Catalogue of the Records of the Reichsministerium für Rüstung und Kriegsproduktion, pt 1 (1969).
For further information about individual collections of British private papers in the museum, see C. Cook: *Sources in British Political History, 1900–1951* (especially vols ii and vi), and S.L. Mayer and W.J. Koenig: *The Two World Wars: a Guide to Manuscript Collections in the United Kingdom.*

645 Inner Temple Archives

Parent organisation: The Honourable Society of the Inner Temple

Address: c/o Treasurer's Office, Inner Temple, London EC4Y 7HL

Telephone: (020) 7797 8251 (Archives); 7797 8219 (Library)

Fax: (020) 7797 8178 (Archives); 7797 8224 (Library)

E-mail: library@innertemple.org.uk

Website: www.innertemple.org.uk

Enquiries: The Archivist, Dr C.M. Rider

Open: Thurs–Fri: by arrangement.

Access: Approved researchers, strictly by appointment.

Historical background: The Temple acquired its name from the Knights Templars, who held the site from about 1150 until 1320, when the order was dissolved. It was then granted to the Order of St John of Jerusalem but, after 1339, when the courts were permanently established at Westminster, it became increasingly the home of lawyers, who very soon formed themselves into two legal societies, the Inner and Middle Temples. These were two of the four Inns of Court with powers to train barristers and call them to the Bar, and their authority was confirmed by letters patent of 1608, when the Temple was conveyed to the two societies for this purpose 'for all time to come'. The division of the site between them was confirmed by a formal Deed of Partition in 1732. The library is recognised as a place of deposit for public records.

Acquisitions policy: Modern records from the society are added to the archives periodically.

Archives of organisation: Records of the society relating to admission and call, domestic administration, the management of the Temple Church, and the building and maintenance of chambers, including admission registers, 1547– ; admission papers, 1805–1927; students' address books, 1871–1962; bar bonds, 1642–1873; records of call to the Bar, 1590– ; Bench Table orders, 1668– ; committee minutes, 1876– ; Acts of the Parliament of the Inn, 1505– ; admissions to chambers, 1615–67; chamber reference books, 1693–1962; chamber rent accounts, 1821–1962; Commons records, 1672– ; Christmas account book, 1614–82; financial records, 1606– .

Major collections: Library: MS collections of historical, legal and literary interest, principally the Petyt Collection (386 vols); the Barrington Collection (57 vols); the Mitford Collection of legal MSS (79 vols); miscellaneous MSS (211 vols).

Series of bound volumes of administrative records, 16th–18th centuries, separate from the archives.

Non-manuscript material: Building plans, c1820– ; photographs, engravings etc. of the Inn.

Library: printed books on the Inn and the Inns of Court in general.

Finding aids: Handlist of the archives; sent to NRA. Index to admissions, 1505–1929.

Facilities: Photocopying.

Conservation: Contracted out.

Publications: F.A. Inderwick, R.A. Roberts and B. Given (eds): *A Calendar of the Inner Temple Records* (1896–1992) [8 vols, covering the period 1505–1835].
J.C. Davies (ed.): *Catalogue of Manuscripts in the Library* (1972) [3 vols; sets available for sale on application to the librarian].
J.H. Baker: *The Inner Temple: a Brief Historical Description* (1991).

646 Institute and Guild of Brewing

Address: 33 Clarges Street, London W1Y 8EE

Telephone: (020) 7499 8144

Fax: (020) 7499 1156

E-mail: enquiries@igb.org.uk

Website: www.igb.org.uk

Enquiries: The Principal Technical Support Officer, M. Butterworth

Open: Mon–Fri: 9.00–5.00.

Access: Members of the Institute of Brewing, and bona fide scholars, by appointment only.

Historical background: The institute's origins date back to 1886, with the foundation of a Laboratory Club by a group of brewing chemists. In 1940 Brewers Hall was bombed and most of the archives were destroyed.

Acquisitions policy: Books and occasionally MSS on historical technical machinery and brewing.

Archives of organisation: Charters and lists of members, 1886–1935.
Minutes and records, 1940– .

Non-manuscript material: Institute's publications and journals, 1895– .
Technical brewing journals and brewing trade magazines, 1941– .

Facilities: Photocopying.

Publications: *A History of the Institute of Brewing, 1886–1951* (1955).
The Institute of Brewing Centenary, 1886–1986 (1987) [pictorial history].

647 Institute of Actuaries

Address: Staple Inn Hall, High Holborn, London WC1V 7QJ

Telephone: (020) 7632 2100

Fax: (020) 7632 2111

E-mail: libraries@actuaries.org.uk

Website: www.actuaries.org.uk

Enquiries: The Assistant Librarian
The Librarian, Miss Sally Grover

Open: Mon–Thurs: 9.15–5.00; Fri: by appointment only.

Access: Actuaries and bona fide researchers, by appointment only.

Historical background: The institute was formed in 1848 and received the Royal Charter of Incorporation in 1884. It has been housed in Staple Inn since 1887, apart from 11 years following the destruction of the hall in 1944. In 1990 the education service and the main library moved to Oxford, leaving the rest of the secretariat, archives and historical texts in Staple Inn. The formation of a library was one of the original objects of the institute, and many early members were also FRS or FSS.

Acquisitions policy: Maintaining the institute archives and acquiring collections on actuarial and related material, including MSS and associative copies of historical texts.

Archives of organisation: Minutes of council and miscellaneous committees; formal business of council; lists of members, 1848– .
Year Book and *Members' Handbook*, 1851– .

Major collections: Correspondence and MSS of Frank Mitchell Redington (1906–84), president, 1958–60.
Records relating to the Students' Society/Staple Inn Actuarial Society.
Biographical research papers on John Finlaison (1783–1860), 1st president (1848–60).

Non-manuscript material: Photographs of presidents and other prominent members.
Newmarch Collection of 19th-century pamphlets.
Books, journals and papers on actuarial and related matters, including historical texts (mainly British).
A few early 20th-century calculating machines.

Finding aids: Database, document/book catalogue includes details of major MS collections. Lists available; sent to NRA.

Council and committee minutes indexed in each volume.
Index to photographs.

Facilities: Photocopying subject to conservation appraisal.

Conservation: Some in-house facilities. Binding of archival and historical texts contracted out.

Publications: Printed catalogue (1935); later additions listed in *Journal of the Institute* (now *British Actuarial Journal*) or *The Actuary*.
Reading lists available covering historical texts.
Occasional articles and reviews in *Journal* and *The Actuary* on historical texts and MSS.
Landmarks of Actuarial Science (1985) [exhibition catalogue].
Proceedings of the Institute of Actuaries Centenary Assembly, vol. 1(1952) [catalogue of the exhibition].
Modelling of the Future: a celebration of the UK Actuarial Profession: (1998) [150th anniversary exhibition catalogue].

648 Institute of Advanced Legal Studies

Parent organisation: School of Advanced Study, University of London

Address: 17 Russell Square, London WC1B 5DR

Telephone: (020) 7637 1731

Fax: (020) 7580 9613

E-mail: ials.lib@sas.ac.uk

Website: http://ials.sas.ac.uk

Enquiries: The Archivist, Clare Cowling

Open: Mon–Fri: 9.30–8.00; Sat: 10.00–5.30.

Access: Bona fide researchers, by application to the Archivist or the Librarian.

Historical background: The institute was founded in 1946 as a national institution to support and promote legal research. The institute library is the foremost national legal research library. The Records of Legal Education Archive (RLEA) was established under a Leverhulme Trust grant in 1995.

Acquisitions policy: Maintains archives of the Institute and acquires records from organisations whose archives are already held and from organisations connected with legal education with no institutional home if under threat.

Archives of organisation: Archives of the institute, 1946– .

Major collections: Archives of Council of Legal Education, 1845–1996; Society of Public Teachers of Law, 1908–96; United Kingdom National Committee of Comparative Law, 1960–89; Association of Law Teachers, 1965–96; Committee of Heads of University Law Schools, 1974–97; Commonwealth Legal Education, 1972–95; Commonwealth Legal Records Project, 1987–93; Socio-Legal Studies Association, 1989–96; Legal Skills Research Group, IALS, 1989–96.
Minutes of the Standing Conference on Legal Education, 1991–4.
Papers of Professor William L. Twining, law teacher, 1965–94; Dr S Marsh, law teacher, 1968–95; and Professor James S. Read, law teacher, 1972–83.

Finding aids: RLEA detailed list available on website.

Facilities: Photocopying.

Conservation: Contracted out.

Publications: Guide to the Records of Legal Education (1999).

649 Institute of Chartered Accountants in England and Wales

Address: Chartered Accountants' Hall, Moorgate Place, London EC2P 2BJ

Telephone: (020) 7920 8620

Fax: (020) 7920 8621

E-mail: library@icaew.co.uk

Website: www.icaew.co.uk

Enquiries: The Librarian, Ms S.P. Moore

Open: Mon–Thurs: 9.00–5.30; Fri: 10.00–5.30.
Closed for three weeks in August.

Access: On written application.

Historical background: The institute was founded in 1880 by the amalgamation of the five smaller societies of accountants. It absorbed the Society of Incorporated Accountants and Auditors (f. 1886) in 1956. The institute is the major professional body for accountants in England, with 113,000 members. The library was founded on the basis of the small collection made by the Institute of

Accountants (f. 1870) and is now the major accounting library in Britain. It began collecting early books on book-keeping in 1882, and continues to do so.

Records of the ICAEW and of Incorporated Accountants are now housed at the Guildhall Library (entry 624).

Acquisitions policy: Occasionally acquires interesting MS account books and other material relevant to the history of accounting.

Major collections: Files of comments by interested persons, companies, firms etc on exposure drafts of accounting standards issued by the Accounting Standards Board and on exposure drafts of auditing standards and guidelines issued by the Auditing Practices Board (committee of the Consultative Committee of Accountancy Bodies (f. 1971)).

Account books illustrating the development of book-keeping practice, including the journal of Francesco Doni, 1534–42; Linzer Marckt-Strazza journal, 1659; and a West Country draper's waste book, 1654–67 (10 vols).

Miscellaneous collection of letters, documents and MSS relating to the history of accounting, including the notebook of R.P.A. Coffy (*d* 1867); the patent granted on his book-keeping system to E.T. Jones (1767–1833); a number of MSS of 19th- and early 20th-century books on accounting; copies of indentures, articles and partnership agreements of some 19th-century accountants; letters and the MS library catalogue of C.P. Kheil (1843–1908).

Leaf of a piyyut for Yom Kippur, 15th century, used as a binding for Pacioli's *Summa de arithmetica*, 1494.

Non-manuscript material: Books on book-keeping and accounts in English, French, German, Dutch, Russian, Spanish, Japanese and ten other languages, 1494–1914 (*c*3000 vols).

Finding aids: Handlist of MSS. Computer database of 20th-century collection. NRA 36719. Card catalogue of Rare Book Collection.

Facilities: Photocopying allowed only of comments on ASB and APB exposure drafts.

Publications: G.A. Lee, 'The Melekh Manuscript: a Discovery in the English Institute Library', *The Accountant* (16 Nov 1972), 622–4.

Library of the ICA: *Historical Accounting Literature: a Catalogue of the Collection of Early Works on Book-Keeping and Accounting* (London, 1975).

M.F. Bywater and B.S. Yamey: *Historical Accounting Literature: a Companion Guide* (London, 1982).

650 Institute of Classical Studies and Library of the Hellenic and Roman Societies

Parent organisation: School of Advanced Study, University of London

Address: Senate House, Malet Street, London WC1E 7HU

Telephone: (020) 7862 8709

Fax: (020) 7862 8724

E-mail: ch.annis@sas.ac.uk

Website: www.sas.ac.uk/icls/

Enquiries: The Librarian, Mr C.H. Annis

Open: Mon–Fri: 10.00–6.00; Sat: 10.00–4.30; Term: Tues, Thurs: 10.00–8.00.
Closed for two weeks to include the late summer bank holiday.

Access: Open to members of the Hellenic Society and the Roman Society (subscription and sponsor required) and the Institute of Classical Studies (university teachers, museum staff and registered postgraduate students are eligible for membership if working on subjects within the scope of the institute). Postal and telephone enquiries are accepted from the general public. An appointment is preferable for the consultation of MSS.

Historical background: The Hellenic Society was founded in 1879 and the library was begun in 1880; the Roman Society was formed in 1910 and the library became a joint library. The Institute of Classical Studies (University of London) was founded in 1953. The societies then handed over primary published material to the institute, which took responsibility for the primary (reference) library; they kept responsibility for the secondary (lending) library and slides collection. The two libraries are housed and run as one unit, but separate ownership is maintained. Black and white slides are now housed at King's College London (entry 669).

Acquisitions policy: MSS: to accept donations where appropriate. Printed material and slides: to maintain and improve the coverage of all aspects of classical antiquity, in close co-operation with other libraries whose interests overlap.

Major collections: Wood donation (property of the Hellenic Society), including diaries and sketchbooks relating to Robert 'Palmyra' Wood (?1717–71) and his travels.

Bent diaries and notebooks (property of Hellenic Society), mainly diaries of Mabel Bent (*d* 1929) with note-books of Theodore Bent, covering travels, 1883–98.

Non-manuscript material: Unpublished University of London theses on classical subjects, mainly 1954– (350 vols).

Library covering all aspects of classical antiquity: *c*97,000 books, pamphlets and bound periodicals; *c*1100 sheets of maps (3125 items on microfilm or microfiche); coloured slides (6800).

Photographic collections on microfiche: the index of ancient art and architecture of the German Archaeological Institute in Rome; Ancient Roman architecture.

Finding aids: Handlist to Wood Collection. List of the Bent papers. Card catalogue of unpublished theses, which are listed in University of London and Aslib lists. Catalogues, including catalogue of colour slides.

Facilities: Photocopying. Photography by request. Microfilm/fiche reader.

Publications: Annual Report of the Hellenic Society, xxii (1926) [on the Wood donation].

C.A. Hutton: 'The travels of "Palmyra" Wood in 1750–51', *Journal of Hellenic Studies,* xlvii (1927), 102.

University of London Bulletin, xiv (1974), 5.

P.T. Stevens: *The Society for the Promotion of Hellenic Studies, 1879–1979: a Historical Sketch* (London, 1979).

J.A. Butterworth: 'Robert Wood and Troy', *Bulletin of the Institute of Classical Studies,* xxxii (1985), 147.

——: 'The Wood Collection', *Journal of Hellenic Studies,* cvi (1986), 197.

Guide to Classic Libraries and Collections, LRCC Classics Sub-Committee (London, 1993).

Hellenic and Roman Societies, Slide Collections: Greek Catalogue (1993); *Roman Catalogue* (1994).

Guide to the Library of the Institute of Classical Studies and the Library of the Hellenic and Roman Societies (London, 2/1994).

651 Institute of Commonwealth Studies

Parent organisation: School of Advanced Study, University of London

Address: 28 Russell Square, London WC1B 5DS

Telephone: (020) 7862 8842

Fax: (020) 7862 8820

E-mail: icommlib@sas.ac.uk

Website: www.sas.ac.uk/ commonwealthstudies/archives/archives.html

Enquiries: The Archivist, Mr David Ward

Open: Term: Mon–Fri: 9.30–6.30. Vacation: Mon–Fri: 9.30–5.30.

Access: Any member of the Institute of Commonwealth Studies, or anyone entitled to use the ICS Library. Membership of ICS is free to academic staff and postgraduate students from the UK or abroad, on production of identification. Undergraduates can use the library as non-paying occasional readers. Non-academic researchers can use the library by becoming members, or as occasional readers, for which a small charge is made.

Historical background: Founded in 1949, the Institute of Commonwealth Studies is now the only postgraduate academic institution in the UK devoted to the study of the Commonwealth. Its purpose is to promote inter-disciplinary and inter-regional research on the Commonwealth, and all of its member nations, in the fields of history, politics, economics, and other social sciences. Archives have been collected since the 1950s.

Acquisitions policy: Focused on the Caribbean, Sri Lanka and Southern Africa, but there is material relevant to most regions in the Commonwealth. ICS is also collecting the records of Commonwealth non-government organisations.

Archives of organisation: A complete set of unpublished papers presented to seminars and conferences held at the institute, 1949– .

Major collections: Strengths lie in material relating to the Caribbean (18th–20th centuries) and 20th century Southern Africa, including papers of Ellis Ashmead-Bartlett (1881–1931), war correspondent; Ruth First (1925–92), South African anti-apartheid activist, journalist and writer; Sir Keith Hancock (1898–1988),

Australian historian, ICS's first director; C.L.R. James (1910–89), Trinidadian activist and writer; Richard Jebb (1874–1953), influential Empire theorist; Sir Ivor Jennings (1903–65), constitutional advisor to newly independent nations, first head of Ceylon University; Simon Taylor (1740–1813), Jamaica sugar planter and merchant.

Records of West India Committee, 1769–1988; Commonwealth Telecommunications Organisation, 1926–95; Commonwealth Press Union, 1909–86.

Non-manuscript material: Collection of Commonwealth political party, trade union and pressure group materials including manifestos, conference proceedings, pamphlets, constitutions and campaign material from more than 1000 organisations throughout the Commonwealth, late 1950s– .

Foreign and Colonial Office Confidential Print.

Finding aids: Lists and collection-level descriptions. Lists sent to NRA.

Facilities: Photocopying. Microfilm/fiche readers.

Conservation: Contracted out.

Publications: Series of short guides to resources for Commonwealth regions and countries: Africa, Asia, Australia, Caribbean, Pacific, Mediterranean.

V.J. Bloomfield: 'African Ephemera', in J.D. Pearson (ed.) *Proceedings of the International Conference on African Bibliography, Nairobi, 1967*, (London, 1969) [in Commonwealth Political Party Collection].

B. Willan: *The Southern African Materials Project, University of London, 1973–76* (London, 1980).

D. Blake: 'Indian Political Ephemera at the Institute of Commonwealth Studies', *South Asia Library Group Newsletter*, no.29 (Jan 1987), 1–7.

652 Institute of Contemporary History and Wiener Library

Address: 4 Devonshire Street, London W1N 2BH

Telephone: (020) 7636 7247

Fax: (020) 7436 6428

E-mail: lib@wl.u-net.com

Website: www.wienerlibrary.co.uk/

Enquiries: The Librarian, Colin Clarke

Open: Mon–Fri: 10.00–5.30.

Access: Bona fide researchers and students who may become members, on payment of a moderate fee.

Historical background: The Wiener Library collection was founded by Dr Alfred Wiener in Amsterdam in 1933 and brought to London in 1939. After giving help to the war effort, the library assisted the prosecution at the Nuremberg trials, assembled the world's first collection of eyewitness accounts of the Holocaust and, through its *Wiener Library Bulletin*, encouraged the academic study of Nazi Germany and the Holocaust.

Acquisitions policy: To build its existing collections in the areas of racism and fascism; modern Jewish history; anti-semitism; the Weimar Republic; the Nazi party; the Third Reich; the Holocaust and World War II; and modern German history.

Major collections: Eye-witness and fate of survivors reports; unpublished memoirs.

Collection on the Nazi Party in Spain.

Gestapo files and Himmler papers.

International War Crimes Tribunal prosecution documents (*c*40,000).

Much material is held on microfilm.

Non-manuscript material: Press archives: more than a million cuttings drawn from an international range of newspapers and covering a wide range of subjects relating to events in Europe and other countries before, during and after World War II; also includes a special collection of files covering biographical information on several thousand individuals considered relevant to the library's holdings.

Ephemeral pamphlets, leaflets and brochures.

Finding aids: Guides and indexes, computerised catalogue.

Facilities: Photocopying. Microfilm reader/printer.

Publications: Various reference works, including:

I. Wolff and H. Kehr (eds): *Wiener Library Catalogue Series* (1949–78) [7 vols].

The Wiener Library Newsletter (3 per annum).

653 Institute of Education

Parent organisation: University of London

Address: 20 Bedford Way, London WC1H 0AL

Telephone: (020) 7612 6063/76080

Fax: (020) 7612 6093

E-mail: lib.enquiries@ioe.ac.uk

Website: www.ioe.ac.uk/library

Enquiries: The Archivist

Open: Mon–Thurs: 9.30–12.30, 1.30–5.00; Fri: 10.30–12.30, 1.30–5.00, by prior appointment.

Access: Bona fide researchers, who must produce evidence of their identity, by arrangement only. Material from some collections may be closed and the permission of the owner may be required.

Historical background: The Institute of Education, University of London, was founded in 1902 as the London Day Training College. Financed and controlled by the London County Council and with the academic support of the University of London, it was initially a college for training elementary-school teachers to work in the capital. In 1909 it became a School of the University of London. It lost this status when, in 1932, it was transferred wholly to the control of the university, at which time it changed its name to the Institute of Education. During these years it had gradually expanded its role, starting to train secondary-school teachers and to offer higher degrees and research. Particularly important were its work in training teachers for colonial service and the establishment of the Child Development Department. In 1949 its role was extended under the Area Training Organisation for London, which brought it into close relationship with the other constituent teacher-training colleges. This arrangement was dissolved in 1975 and in 1987 the institute once again became a school of the University of London, incorporated by royal charter.

Acquisitions policy: Records of organisations and personal papers relating to education and allied areas. Archival acquisitions are intended to reflect the broadest possible range of issues and concerns surrounding teaching and lifelong learning. This includes all levels of education, from pre-school onwards, in all settings, and it covers research, practice, policy and thought in education and related areas.

Archives of organisation: Records of the Institute of Education, 1902– , including student records, committee minutes and papers, administrative, subject and correspondence files, photographs and some audio-visual material.

Major collections: Records of a wide range of educational organisations, including the Assistant Masters Association, 1891–1978; the College of Preceptors (f. 1846); the Board of Education Inspectors' Association, 1919–92; The Moot (f. 1939); German Educational Reconstruction, 1943–58; the National Commission on Education, 1991–5; the Programme for Reform in Secondary Education; the Schools Curriculum Award; the Schools Council for Curriculum and Examinations, 1964–84; the Society for Teachers Opposed to Physical Punishment, 1968–89; the National Union of Women Teachers, 1904–61; the World Education Fellowship (f. 1921), and the Universities Council for the Education of Teachers (f. 1966).

Personal papers of educationists and others, including Fred Clarke (1880–1952), Isabel Fry (1869–1958), Nicholas Hans (1888–1969), Susan Isaacs (1885–1948), Joseph Lauwerys (1902–81), Harry Rée (1889–1991), R.H. Tawney (1880–1962), Christian Schiller (1895–1976), Margaret Read (1889–1991) and Robin Tanner (1904–89).

Non-manuscript material: Photographic archive of the Architects and Building Branch, Ministry of Education, and successors, 1940s–1980s.

Brenda Francis collection of photographs of home economics teaching, *c*1930s–1980s.

David Medd (*b* 1917), educational architect, photographs, slides, plans and drawings.

Eileen Molony (1914–1982), films about primary education.

Examples of children's art work, photographs and audio-visual material.

Finding aids: Summary guide to the major deposited collections on website.

Handlists available for some collections; a searchable database is under construction.

Facilities: Limited photocopying. Microfilm reader/printer.

Publications: University of London Institute of Education Jubilee Lectures (London, 1952).

University of London Institute of Education Studies and Impressions (London, 1952).

C. Willis Dixon: *The Institute: a Personal Account of the History of the University of London Institute of Education, 1932–1972* (London, 1986).

L. Elvin: *Encounters with Education* (London, 1987).

A centenary history of the Institute of Education, to be published in 2002, is currently being researched and written.

654 Institute of Germanic Studies

Parent organisation: University of London

Address: 29 Russell Square, London WC1B 5DP

Telephone: (020) 7580 3480

Fax: (020) 7436 3497

E-mail: igslib@sas.ac.uk wabbey@sas.ac.uk

Website: www.sas.ac.uk/igs

Enquiries: The Librarian, Mr W. Abbey

Open: Mon–Fri: 9.45–6.00; strictly by appointment.

Access: Bona fide researchers in relevant fields of study.

Historical background: The institute was founded in 1950 as an independent centre within the University of London. It has since been recognised as playing a national role in its field and in 1994 became a constituent member of the University's School of Advanced Study. Its objects are to promote the advanced study of German language, literature and related subjects, and to provide facilities for research and opportunities for contacts between scholars, the former through its extensive library, the latter through regular symposia, seminars and lectures.

Acquisitions policy: To strengthen existing archive collections, very occasionally by purchase, principally by encouraging donations or deposits of material relating to the language, literature, theatre, history etc. of the German-speaking countries or of German-speaking communities elsewhere.

Major collections: Papers of Berthold Auerbach (1874–1960), Germany's leading theatrical agent before World War II, now incorporated into a newly established archive for German theatre history.

Papers of German scholars, including Dr Mary Beare (1897–1985); Jethro Bithell (1878–1962); Professor Karl Breul (1860–1932); Professor E.M. Butler (1885–1959); Professor August Closs (1898–1990); Professor William Rose (1894–1961); and Professor Gilbert Waterhouse (1888–1977).

Exile collection covering all aspects of German and Austrian exile, 1933– .

Friedrich Gundolf (1880–1931) archive: Professor Gundolf of Heidelberg was associated with the poet Stegan and his circle.

Records of Conference of University Teachers of German in Great Britain and Ireland and material collected by it relating to the history of German studies in Great Britain.

English Goethe Society: records and papers.

Non-manuscript material: Pamphlets and broadsheets of the 1848 revolution in Berlin; maps and other illustrative documents; offprints; newspaper cuttings; theatre programmes; and visiting cards.

Postcards and photographs.

Finding aids: Detailed on-line catalogue (for staff use only) for several collections; all others have handlists and/or box-lists with varying degrees of detail.

Facilities: Photocopying. Microfilm/fiche reader.

Publications: C.V. Bock: 'First Report on the Gundolf Papers at the Institute of Germanic Languages and Literature in the University of London', *German Life and Letters* (new series), 15 (1961–2), 16–20.

C. Neutjens: *Friedrich Gundolf: ein bibliographischer Apparat* (Bonn, 1969) [includes almost complete list of the Gundolf Archive].

J.L. Flood: 'Die mittelalterlichen Handschriften der Bibliothek des Institute of Germanic Studies, London', *Zeitschrift für deutsches Altertum und deutsche Literatur*, 129 (1991), 325–30.

W. Abbey: 'Closs Papers in the Institute of Germanic Studies', *German Studies Library Group Newsletter*, no.18 (1995), 14–16.

J. Hogarth: 'A Treasure Trove: Exploring the Institute's Archives', *Institute of Germanic Studies Friends Newsletter* (1996–7), 12–14.

——: '1848 and All That: More from the Institute's Archives', *Institute of Germanic Studies Friends Newsletter* (1998), 4–7.

W. Abbey: 'Theatre Directors at the Institute', *Institute of Germanic Studies Friends Newsletter* (1998), 7–8.

655 Institute of Materials Library

Address: 1 Carlton House Terrace, London SW1Y 5DB

Telephone: (020) 7451 7300 (switchboard); (020) 7451 7360 (enquiries – direct line)

Fax: (020) 7451 7349

E-mail: admin@materials.org.uk
hilda_kuane@materials.org.uk

Website: www.materials.org.uk

Enquiries: The Information Officer, Hilda Kuane

Open: Mon–Fri: 9.30–12.30, 2.30–5.30; by prior appointment.

Access: Generally open to members of the institute and the public.

Historical background: The institute was founded in 1869 as the Iron and Steel Institute. It is a learned society incorporated by royal charter and a professional body for materials scientists and engineers. Members of the institute work in fields involving the use and application of engineering materials such as ceramics, metals, polymers and composites. In 1993 it amalgamated with the Institute of Metals (1985), the Institute of Ceramics (1986), the Plastics and Rubber Institute (1975) and the British Composite Society (1987).

Acquisitions policy: To acquire relevant material mainly by donation.

Archives of organisation: Annual reports, presidential addresses, records of council and committee meetings of the institute and most of its predecessors.

Major collections: Sir Henry Bessemer Collection (1813–98): artefacts, photographs, portrait, letters, drawings and books, 1850–. Papers of John Parry (1817–89), metallurgist.

Non-manuscript material: Photographs, biographies and obituaries of past presidents, authors and key individuals, 1870– (2500 items).
Paintings and portraits of individuals of great importance and interest in the field and institute, 1869–.

Technical drawings.
Antiquarian books relating to metallurgy (*c*150).

Finding aids: Lists.

Facilities: Photocopying. Photography.

656 Institute of Physics

Address: 76 Portland Place, London W1N 3DH

Telephone: (020) 7470 4800

Fax: (020) 7470 4848

E-mail: physics@iop.org

Website: www.iop.org

Enquiries: The Librarian, Mrs Sue Lowell

Open: Mon–Fri: 9.30–5.00.

Access: Bona fide researchers, by appointment.

The present institute is the result of the amalgamation of the Physical Society (f. 1874), the Optical Society (f. 1907) and the Institute of Physics (f. 1918). It was granted a royal charter in 1970. It holds its own archives, 1874–, which include minute books of council and some committees, and all publications of constituent bodies.

657 Institution of Civil Engineers

Address: 1–7 Great George Street,, London SW1P 3AA

Telephone: (020) 7222 7722 ext. 2043

Fax: (020) 7976 7610

E-mail: arrowsmith_c@ice.org.uk

Website: www.ice.org.uk/

Enquiries: The Archivist, Carol Arrowsmith

Open: Mon–Fri: 9.15–5.30.

Access: Items may be consulted in the library by members of the institution, and by approved readers by prior arrangement.

Historical background: The institution was founded in 1818 and the first royal charter was received in 1828; it is the learned society and qualifying body for the civil engineering profession. The library has as its nucleus the gifts of Thomas Telford (1757–1834), who became the institution's first president in 1820. The archive collections consist of records relating to the institution and to the civil engineering profession.

Acquisitions policy: All important ICE records. Select civil engineering archives, usually acquired by gift, very occasionally by purchase.

Archives of organisation: ICE archives: records of meetings, membership, accounts; council and committees' minutes; MSS of early papers; minute books of the Society of Civil Engineers, 1771–92, and the Society of Smeatonian Civil Engineers, 1793– .
Archives of the Institution of Municipal Engineers (absorbed in 1984); Society of Civil Engineering Technicians; Société des Ingénieurs Civils de France (British section); Council of Engineering Institutions.

Major collections: MS records relating to the work of Thomas Telford; the Rennie family: John Rennie (1761–1821), George Rennie (1791–1866) and Sir John Rennie (1794–1874); John Smeaton (1724–92); William Mackenzie (1794–1851), contractor, and his family (non-engineering material in Buckinghamshire Records and Local Studies Service, see entry 37); Sir Joseph Bazalgette (1819–91); Robert Stephenson (1803–59); Sir Marc Isambard Brunel (1769–1849); and the Thames Tunnel.
J.G. James Collection relating to the history of iron bridges.

Non-manuscript material: Engineering drawings and plans; prints; paintings; portraits; slides; photographs.
J.G. James Collection of architectural and civil engineering slides.
Medals; various artefacts, e.g. drawings and instruments belonging to Telford.

Finding aids: Various indexes and lists, including Archives of the ICE provisional list (1979) and Collections of Prints and Drawings (1978) [duplicated TS].
All recent additions notified to NRA.
On-line computer catalogue.

Facilities: Photocopying. Microform reader/printer.

Conservation: Contracted out.

Publications: Save Engineering Records (1979) [pamphlet].
M.M. Chrimes: 'The Institution of Civil Engineers Library and Archives: a Brief Introduction', *Construction History*, 5 (1989), 59–65.

658 Institution of Electrical Engineers
Archives Department

Address: Savoy Place, London WC2R 0BL

Telephone: (020) 7344 5395

Fax: (020) 7240 7735

E-mail: lsymons@iee.org.uk

Website: www.iee.org.uk/archives

Enquiries: The Archivist, Mrs E.D.P. Symons

Open: Mon–Fri: 9.45–5.00.

Access: Bona fide researchers, by appointment.

Historical background: The institution was founded in 1871 as the Society of Telegraph Engineers and took its present name in 1888. A royal charter granted in 1921 recognised it as the representative body of electrical engineers in the United Kingdom. The institution houses a library (formed in 1880) and an archives department (formed in 1975), which holds MS material relating to the history and development of magnetism and electricity from medieval times to the present, and modern papers relating to the development of telegraphy, the submarine cable, electrical engineering and physics.

Acquisitions policy: To acquire, by donation, deposit or purchase, material relevant to the history and development of electrical engineering and electronics, and allied fields, including modern industrial records.

Archives of organisation: Archives of the institution including official records and working papers, 1871– .
Archives of the Institution of Electronic and Radio Engineers (amalgamated 1988) and the Institution of Production/Manufacturing Engineers (merged 1991).

Major collections: Special Collection MSS: including medieval MSS; the scientific papers of Michael Faraday (1791–1867); Sir Francis Ronalds (1788–1873); Oliver Heaviside (1850–1925); Sir William Fothergill Cooke (1806–79), including letters from Sir Charles Wheatstone (1802–75); several 19th- and 20th-century engineers and academics.
National Archive for Electrical Science and Technology: modern technical and manufacturing records and engineering drawings.

Archives of the Women's Engineering Society, 1919–85, and of the Electrical Association for Women, 1924–86.

Non-manuscript material: Portraits (mainly photographs and engravings) of eminent scientists and electrical engineers, presidents of the institution, 18th–20th centuries.
Photographs of electrical equipment and institution events.
Silvanus Phillips Thompson Collection of rare books relating to magnetism and electricity, 15th–19th centuries (1000).
Sir Francis Ronalds Collection of rare books (2000) and pamphlets (3000) relating to magnetism and electricity and the development of the telegraph, 17th–19th centuries.

Finding aids: General index to all collections. Handlists for most collections. Index to photograph collections. Lists sent to NRA.

Facilities: Photocopying. Photography by arrangement.

Conservation: Contracted out.

Publications: F. Ronalds: *Catalogue of Books and Papers relating to Electricity, Magnetism, the Electric Telegraph* (1880).
S.P. Thompson: *Handlist of Magnetic and Electrical Books* (1914).

659 Institution of Gas Engineers

Address: 21 Portland Place, London W1N 3AF

Telephone: (020) 7636 6603

Fax: (020) 7636 6602

E-mail: anita@igaseng.demon.co.uk

Website: www.igaseng.com

Enquiries: The Librarian

The institution was founded in 1863 and retains some archives, including printed bound transactions, as well as a small number of MS items donated by individuals. Access is limited and requests to consult material should be made by arrangement with the Librarian. Various indexes are available and a database is under construction. A charged research service and photocopying are also available. See W.T.K. Braunholtz: *The First Hundred Years, 1863–1963* (London, 1963).

660 Institution of Incorporated Engineers

Address: Savoy Hill House, Savoy Hill, London WC2R 0BS

Telephone: (020) 7836 3357

Fax: (020) 7497 9006

E-mail: iie@dial.pipex.com

Website: www.iie.org.uk/iie

Enquiries: Kevin Foley

Open: Mon–Fri: 9.00–5.00.

Access: By arrangement.

Historical background: The institution was created in 1998 on the amalgamation of the Institute of Engineers and Technicians, the Institution of Electronics and Electrical Incorporated Engineers and the Institution of Mechanical Incorporated Engineers. Of these, the Institution of Mechanical Incorporated Engineers was itself the result of merger between the Institution of Technical Engineers in Mechanical Engineering and the Institution of Mechanical and General Technician Engineers (f. 1864). The latter was started as the Vulcanic Society by apprentices at Maudslay, Son & Field Ltd of Lambeth and underwent several name changes, most notably functioning as the Institution of Junior Engineers.

Acquisitions policy: To maintain membership records and associated memorabilia.

Archives of organisation: Institution of Junior Engineers council minute books, 1894–8, 1903– .
Minutes of committees, including finance and general purposes, 1898–1912; benevolent fund, 1947–88.
Minutes of members' ordinary meetings, 1912–61; membership registers, 1914–38; subscription book, 1919–68, and other financial records.
Papers on awards of medals, 1953–78.
Papers of the Institution of Electronics and Electrical Incorporated Engineers and the Institute of Engineers and Technicians from inception to 1998.

Non-manuscript material: Architectural plans relating to former HQ at 33 Ovington Square, London.
Small collections of photographs and memorabilia.

Finding aids: Brief listing.

Facilities: Photocopying. Photography.

Publications: Institution of Mechanical and General Technical Engineers Centenary, 1884-1984 (IMGTechE, 1984).

661 Institution of Mechanical Engineers

Address: 1 Birdcage Walk, London SW1H 9JJ

Telephone: (020) 7222 7899

Fax: (020) 7222 8762

E-mail: k.moore@imeche.org.uk

Enquiries: The Senior Librarian/Archivist, Mr Keith Moore

Open: Mon–Fri: 9.15–5.30.

Access: Bona fide researchers, by appointment only.

Historical background: The institution was founded in Birmingham in 1847 and moved into its current premises in 1899. The library contains some 150,000 publications covering all aspects of engineering and associated subjects.

Acquisitions policy: To maintain the collection on mechanical engineering, by purchase, donation or presentation.

Archives of organisation: Council and committee minutes; biographical records of members (proposal forms) and signature books, 1847– . Archives of organisations later merged with IMechE, including the Institution of Automobile Engineers (f. 1905) and the Institution of Locomotive Engineers (f. 1911).

Major collections: Correspondence and papers of George Stephenson (1781–1848), first president, and Robert Stephenson (1803–59).
Note-books and engineering drawings of James Nasmyth (1808–90); Charles Algernon Parsons (1854–1931); Frederick William Lanchester (1868–1946); David Joy (1825–1903); and Joseph Whitworth (1803–87).
Personal papers of Christopher Hinton (1901–83), Baron Hinton of Bankside, nuclear engineer.
Company records, including papers of the Livesey-Henderson Company (f. 1865), overseas railway consulting engineers.

Non-manuscript material: Portraits of eminent engineers, 19th century.
Photographs of engineering works, notably Robert Howlett's series on Isambard Kingdom Brunel and the construction of the *Great Eastern*.
Engineering medals and artefacts.

Finding aids: Catalogue on a CAIRS-IMS database. Handlists to particular collections available; sent to NRA. Summary of collections on website.

Facilities: Photocopying. Microfilm reader/printer.

Conservation: Contracted out.

Publications: R.H. Parsons: *A History of the Institution of Mechanical Engineers, 1847–1947* (1947).
J. Pullin: *Progress through Mechanical Engineering: the First 150 Years of the Institution of Mechanical Engineers* (1997).
K. Moore: *1 Birdcage Walk: the Home of Mechanical Engineering* (1998).

662 Irish in Britain Archive

Parent organisation: University of North London

Address: Tower Building, Holloway Road, London N7 8DB

Telephone: (020) 7753 5018

Fax: (020) 7753 7069

E-mail: isc@unl.ac.uk

Enquiries: The Administrator, Tony Murray

Open: By arrangement.

Access: Generally open to the public, by appointment.

Historical background: The Irish Studies Resource Centre was established by the University of North London in 1986 and the archive is housed in the university library. Much material is on permanent loan from the Irish in Britain History Group and the video collection was recently donated by the Activision Irish Project. It focuses on a wide range of topics, including the Irish in London, migration, racism, homelessness and Irish culture, and is particularly rich in materials covering the experience of the 1940s/50s migrants. For University of North London see entry 834.

Acquisitions policy: Actively welcomes donations of material covering Irish culture of contemporary or historical interest.

Major collections: Subject files of personal reminiscences, memorabilia, photographs and pamphlets, including also British media and Ireland.

Non-manuscript material: Activision Irish Project: large video collection.
Irish Post, 1970– .
Books and articles of Irish literary and historical interest (*c*400).
Cassette recordings.

Facilities: Photocopying.

Publications: Guide to Resource Centre (1994). Information packs.

663 Islington Archives

Parent organisation: London Borough of Islington

A Islington Central Library

Address: 2 Fieldway Crescent, London N5 1PF

Telephone: (020) 7527 6931/2

Fax: (020) 7527 6939

E-mail: is.loc.his@dial.pipex.com

Website: www.islington.gov.uk

Enquiries: The Local History Manager, Ms Vada Hart

Open: Mon, Wed, Thurs: 9.30–8.00; Tues, Fri, Sat: 9.30–5.00.

Access: Generally open to the public; an appointment is necessary. Appointment times are more restricted than general library opening hours.

Historical background: The London Borough of Islington was formed in 1965 by the amalgamation of the metropolitan boroughs of Finsbury and Islington. Both library services had collections of local history material and held records of the borough councils and their predecessors. The two local history collections are housed separately and their scope reflects the pre-1965 borough boundaries. Some post-1965 records have been transferred to the Islington collection. The metropolitan borough of Islington (1900–65) was formed from only one civil parish, St Mary's, Islington.

Acquisitions policy: To acquire all possible material relating to the local area by purchase, donation or deposit.

Archives of organisation: Local government records: some post–1965 council records; records of the metropolitan borough of Islington, including council minutes and rate books; records of the civil parish of St Mary's, Islington, including vestry minutes, rate books, churchwardens' and overseers' accounts.
Records of Islington Turnpike Trust (later Hampstead and Highgate Turnpike Trust), 1717–1826.

Major collections: Records of Islington Literary and Scientific Society, 1832–76.
Records of the Royal Agricultural Hall, Islington, 1862–1981.
Records of Dove Brothers, builders, 1855–1970.

Non-manuscript material: Very large collections of graphic material and news cuttings.
Registers of electors for Islington, 1860– (incomplete).
Many local newspapers, 1865– (mainly on microfilm).
Islington local directories, 1852–1916.
Census returns, 1841–81 (microfilm).
Special collections relating to Walter Sickert (1860–1942) and Joe Orton (1933–67).

Finding aids: Various catalogues, card indexes and lists. Where possible lists sent to NRA.

Facilities: Photocopying. Photography by arrangement. Microfilm/fiche reader/printer.

Conservation: Contracted out.

B Finsbury Library

Address: 245 St John Street, London EC1V 4NB

Telephone: (020) 7527 7994

Fax: (020) 7527 7998

E-mail: is.loc.his@dial.pipex.com

Website: www.islington.gov.uk

Enquiries: The Local History Manager, Ms Vada Hart

Open: Mon, Thurs: 9.30–8.00; Tues, Sat: 9.30–5.00; Fri: 9.30–1.00.

Access: Generally open to the public; an appointment is necessary. Appointment times are more restricted than general library opening hours.

Historical background: The metropolitan borough of Finsbury (1900–65) was formed from the civil parishes of St James and St John, Clerkenwell, St Luke, the Liberty of Glasshouse Yard, St Sepulchre (part) and Charterhouse (part). In 1965 it became part of the London Borough of Islington. The collection covers the area within the former borough boundaries, i.e. the Pentonville district, north of the Angel and Islington south of the Angel.

Acquisitions policy: To acquire all possible material relating to Finsbury, by purchase, donation or deposit.

Archives of organisation: Inherited Finsbury records contain the following:
Records of the constituent parishes of Finsbury, including vestry minutes and rate books; Clerkenwell and St Luke's Guardians' records.
Records of the metropolitan borough of Finsbury, including council minutes and rate books.
Records of Old Street Turnpike, 1752–1826, and City Road Turnpike Trust, 1786–1827.
Records of the Clerkenwell Explosion Relief Fund (set up after the Fenian bomb incident), 1867–81.

Major collections: Sadler's Wells Theatre Archives (includes much printed material), 18th century– .
Penton estate records, 1695–1938.
Records of Finsbury Dispensary, 1795–1920.

Non-manuscript material: Very large collections of graphic material and news cuttings.
Islington Gazette, 1856–1904, 1955–60 (on microfilm).
Registers of electors: Clerkenwell, 1842; combined parishes of Islington and Finsbury etc, 1873–85 (arranged in alphabetical order of electors).
Census returns, 1841–81 (microfilm).

Finding aids: Various catalogues and card indexes. Where possible lists sent to NRA.

Facilities: Photocopying. Photography by arrangement. Microfilm/fiche readers.

Conservation: Contracted out.

664 J. Henry Schroder & Co. Ltd

Parent organisation: Schroders plc

Address: 31 Gresham Street, London EC2V 7QA

Telephone: (020) 7658 6000

Fax: (020) 7658 3950

Website: www.schroders.com

Enquiries: The Company Secretary, Mr Bainbridge

Open: Mon–Fri: 9.00–5.00, by appointment.

Access: Generally open to the public, by prior arrangement.

Historical background: Established in 1818 as a banking entity, Schroders evolved into a merchant bank and in 1962 merged with Herbert Wagg & Co. Ltd. In 1995 the firm resumed the original name of J. Henry Schroder & Co. Ltd and now operates in more than 30 countries.

Acquisitions policy: Maintains own archive supplemented by occasional material from third parties.

Archives of organisation: Records of J. Henry Schroder & Co, 1829–1962; Herbert Wagg & Co., 1848–1902.
Files on securities issued, 1853– .

Non-manuscript material: Photograph collection, 19th century– .

Finding aids: Computerised index.

Facilities: Photocopying.

Publications: R. Roberts: *Schroders: Merchants and Bankers* (1992).

665 Japan Society Library

Address: Suite 6/9, Morley House, 314–22 Regent Street, London W1R 5AH

Telephone: (020) 7636 3029

Fax: (020) 7636 3089

E-mail: info@japansociety.org.uk

Website: www.japansociety.org.uk

Enquiries: The Library Manager, Mr Patrick Knill via Secretariat of the Japan Society

Open: Thurs: 2.30–5.00.
Closed when national holidays (British and Japanese) fall on a Thursday.

Access: Members of the Japan Society. Others by appointment, please contact the Library Manager.

Historical background: The society was founded as the Japan Society of London in 1891. The library and the archives, where they survive, also date from that time. The name changed to the Japan Society in 1986.

Acquisitions policy: To maintain the archives and MSS.

Archives of organisation: Some archive material, including minutes of the council, is held by the secretariat and the library.

Non-manuscript material: Some early printed books, 17th–18th centuries.

Finding aids: Card catalogues under author, subject and title.

Publications: Records of the society are incorporated in *Transactions and Proceedings of the Japan Society of London* (1891–World War II), continued by *Bulletin of the Japan Society of London* (1950–85) and *Proceedings* (of the Japan Society, 1986–).

666 The Jewish Museum

A Camden

Address: 129/131 Albert Street, London NW1 7NB

Telephone: (020) 7284 1997

Fax: (020) 7267 9008

E-mail: admin@jmus.org.uk

Website: www.jewmusm.ort.org/camden.htm

Enquiries: The Curator

Open: Sun–Thurs: 10.00–4.00.
Closed Jewish and public holidays.

Access: MSS can only be inspected by prior appointment, by qualified researchers.

Historical background: Founded in 1932 and relocated in 1995, the museum has amalgamated with the former London Museum of Jewish Life and is on two sites. The museum's collections of secondary genealogical material have been transferred to the Anglo-Jewish Archives, now at the University of Southampton (entry 1122) and the Mocatta Library, now incorporated into University College London (entry 832).

Acquisitions policy: Relevant material is acquired relating to individuals or organizations.

Major collections: Records of Canterbury Jewish congregation, 1783–1870; Exeter Hebrew Congregation, 1827–1932; Great Synagogue, London, 1696–19th century; London Jewish community circumcision register, 1775–1913.
Papers of Aaron Levy Green (1821–83), Jewish Minister and scholar; Numa Edward Hartog (1846–71), mathematician; Sir Moses Haim Montefiore (1784–1885), letters to Lewis Emmanuel, 1869–85.

Finding aids: Lists. See also NRA 30955.

Publications: E. Samuel: *The Portuguese Jewish Community in London, 1656–1830* (London, 1992).
A.J. Kershen (ed.): *150 Years of Progressive Judaism in Britain 1840–1900* (1988).

B Finchley

Address: The Sternberg Centre, 80 East End Road, London N3 2SY

Telephone: (020) 8349 1143

Fax: (020) 8343 2162

E-mail: jml.finchley@lineone.net

Website: www.jewmusm.ort.org/finchley.htm

Enquiries: The Curator, Carol Seigal

Open: Mon–Thurs: 10.30–5.00.

Access: Generally open to the public, by appointment.

Historical background: The museum was initially established in 1984 as the Museum of the Jewish East End.

Acquisitions policy: Documents, photographs, artefacts and memorabilia relating to the social and cultural history of London's Jewish community.

Major collections: Personal papers and records of organisations relating to the Jewish East End, including immigrant trades, Yiddish theatre, East East synagogues and refugees from Nazism.
Records of Jewish Friendly Society, late 19th and 20th centuries.
Collection of unpublished memoirs and research papers.
Personal papers of Israel Zangwill (1854–1926).

Non-manuscript material: Boris the Studio Photographer Collection: photographs of Jewish weddings, 1920s and 1930s.

Photograph archive (c15,000) and oral history library (c400 tapes); collection of gramophone records.

Facilities: Photocopying. Photography by arrangement.

Publications: Boris, the Studio Photographer (1986).
D. Mazower: *Yiddish Theatre in London, 1880–1987* (2/1996).

667 Keats House

Parent organisation: London Metropolitan Archives (LMA)

Address: Wentworth Place, Keats Grove, Hampstead, London NW3 2RR

Telephone: (020) 7435 2062

Fax: (020) 7431 9293

E-mail: keatshouse@corpoflondon.gov.uk

Website: www.corpoflondon.gov.uk

Enquiries: The Access and Enquiries Section, LMA (entry 688).

Open: By written appointment only.

Access: By prior appointment. During the major repair project (2000–2004) access to Keats House MS and printed book collections will be at the LMA Reading Room. A paid research service is available.

Historical background: The Keats Collection was begun in 1897 by Hampstead Public Library and transferred in 1921 to Keats House, where John Keats lived from 1818 to 1820. It was opened to the public in 1925. The Corporation of London has run Keats House since 1997, with LMA becoming responsible for the management in 1999. It is currently undergoing a five-year repair project.

Acquisitions policy: To add to the collections on Keats, Shelley, Byron, Leigh Hunt and their circles and to maintain the collection on general Romantic literature. To add, where possible, to the relics of the poets.

Major collections: Dilke Collection: MSS, books, paintings, relics of Keats.
Leigh-Browne Lockyer Collection: commonplace books relating to friends of Keats (20).

Non-manuscript material: Kate Greenaway Collection: original drawings, proofs, Christmas cards and books.

Charles Lamb Collection: books on Lamb (c1000).
Maurice Buxton Forman Collection: books on Keats and his circle (c2500).
Smaller collections from the families of Fanny Brawne, Charles Brown, Joseph Severn and Fanny Keats.

Finding aids: Catalogue of MSS and relics (1966). Card catalogue of pamphlets and ephemera. Recataloguing in progress.

Facilities: Photocopying. Scanning. Microfilming.

Conservation: Full service at LMA.

668 Kensington and Chelsea Local Studies Centre

Parent organisation: Royal Borough of Kensington and Chelsea

Address: Kensington Central Library, Phillimore Walk, London W8 7RX
Chelsea Reference Library, Old Town Hall, King's Road, London W8 7RX

Telephone: (020) 7937 2542 (Kensington); (020) 77352 6056 (Chelsea)

Fax: (020) 7361 2976 (Kensington)

E-mail: information.services@rbkc.gov.uk

Website: www.rbkc.gov.uk/libraries/general/

Enquiries: The Local Studies Librarian

Open: (Kensington): Tues, Thurs: 10.00–8.00; Fri: 9.30–5.00; Sat: 10.00–1.00.
Chelsea: Mon, Tues, Thurs: 10.00–8.00; Fri: 9.30–5.00; Sat: 10.00–1.00.

Access: It is necessary to telephone to make an appointment. There are restrictions on certain deposits and council records. Charges are made for postal and e-mail enquiries involving more than 15 minutes' work.

Historical background: The Royal Borough of Kensington and Chelsea was formed in 1965 by the amalgamation of the boroughs of Kensington and Chelsea. Both library services had collections, founded in 1887, of local history materials and held records of the councils and their predecessors. The two collections reflect the pre-1965 borough boundaries. However, all post-1965 civic records are held at Kensington, where a borough records management scheme is in operation.

Acquisitions policy: To acquire by donation, deposit or purchase all material irrespective of format, relating to the royal borough.

Archives of organisation: Usual local authority record holdings, *c*1700– .
Archives of Alexander Estate, (South Kensington) *c* 1800–*c*1950; Alexander Family (Aubrey House), 1870–1950; Kensington Housing Trust and others, 1930–60.

Major collections: Kensington: Correspondence of Frederic, Lord Leighton (1830–96). Sambourne family diaries and papers, 1880s–1960s.
Local deeds (50,000 items).
Manor rolls for Earls Court, 1554–1865, and Abbotts, Kensington, 1554–1856.
Chelsea: Records of Chelsea Arts Club, 1890– .

Non-manuscript material: Original sketches and design material relating to the work of Walter Crane (1845–1915).
Extensive collections of illustrations, topographical prints, photographs, newspaper cuttings and maps.
John Bignel photographic work, 1950–1990s.

Finding aids: Some card catalogues and indexes. Transcript of Leighton collection. Lists sent to NRA.

Facilities: Photocopying. Photography.

Publications: A number of publications, including *Historic Kensington in Maps, 1741–1894* and *Historical Chelsea in Maps, 1700–1894* [list of publications available at the Central Library].

669 King's College London

Parent organisation: University of London

Address: Strand, London, London WC2R 2LS

Telephone: (020) 7873 2015/2187

Fax: (020) 7873 2760

E-mail: archives.web@kcl.ac.uk

Enquiries: The Director of Archive Services, Miss Patricia Methven

Open: Term: Mon–Fri: 9.30–5.30.
Vacation: Mon–Fri: 9.30–4.30.
Closed last fortnight of August.

Access: Open to bona fide scholars and members of the public able to demonstrate a serious interest in the records, by appointment. Records relating to college business are closed for 30 years. Student and personnel files are closed for 80 years. A limited number of the collections in the Liddell Hart Centre for Military Archives are closed. Readers seeking to use the Centre for Military Archives and the Modern Greek Archives are required to agree to submit texts for publication to the trustees and/or another designated authority.

A College Archives and Library Manuscripts

Website: www.kcl.ac.uk/kis/archives/newhome.htm

Historical background: KCL was founded in 1828. Both King's College (the senior department) and King's College School (the junior department) opened to students in 1831. In 1839 the first King's College Hospital was established in Portugal Street; it moved to Denmark Hill in 1913, where the Medical School followed in 1915. From 1849 the college provided evening and occasional education for Londoners. Academic education co-existed with training for would-be entrants to the Civil Service, telegraphists and surveyors of taxes, and workshop classes were set up with, among others, the Clothworkers' Company (entry 585). An offshoot of the Civil Services classes was a commercial school, the Strand School, which moved into the basement of the college when the boys' school moved to Wimbledon in 1897. With reconstitution of the University of London in 1900, the college shed its non-academic commitments. In 1909 responsibility was transferred to independent governing bodies for the hospital and KCS and to the LCC for the Strand School. The abolition of the Test Act in 1903 led to the partial separation of the college into University of London King's College for the majority of subjects and KCL for the Theological Department. In 1915 King's College for Women (f. 1871) transferred from Kensington, except for the Household and Social Science Department, which became recognised as a school in its own right and was renamed Queen Elizabeth College in 1953. In the 1980s the divisions of the college went into partial reverse. The Theological College was reunited with the rest of the college in 1980, the whole to be known again as KCL. In 1983 King's College Hospital Medical and Dental School was also reunited, followed in 1985 by Queen Elizabeth College. In 1985 the college was merged with Chelsea College, founded in 1891 as the South Western Polytechnic, later

Chelsea Polytechnic, a college of advanced technology, and eventually a school of the university in 1966. In 1998 the college merged with the United Medical and Dental Schools and the Institute of Psychiatry.

Acquisitions policy: Internal records, private papers of members of the college, and papers supporting research in the specialist fields of literature in translation and modern Greece.

Archives of organisation: All major records relating to KCL, 1828–, including its constituent colleges, except UMDS and the Institute of Psychiatry.

Records relating to KCS, and the Strand School, mainly during the periods when they formed part of the college, but 19th-century pupil admission forms are held by KCS.

King's College Hospital records, 1839–1976, including minutes, policy files, title deeds and the records of the merged Nursing School; case files, 1840–1939; Belgrave Hospital for Children case papers, 1904–39.

Major collections: Papers of former members of the college, including Prof. T.J. Brown (1923–87); Dr R.M. Burrows (1867–1920); Prof. J.F. Daniell (1790–1845); Maureen Duffy (*b* 1933); Prof. R.R. Gates (1882–1962); Prof. E.J. Hanson (1919–73); Prof. F.J.C. Hearnshaw (1869–1946); Prof. Donald Hey (1904–87); Dr C.W.F. McClare (1937–77); Rev. W.R. Matthews (1881–1974); Rev. F.D. Maurice (1805–72); Prof. J.C. Maxwell (1831–79); Prof. E. N. W. Mottram (1924–98); Evelyn Underhill (1875–1941); Prof. Sir Charles Wheatstone (1802–75).

Other collections: P.H. Leathes (*d* 1838), especially 18th-century antiquarian and topographical literature, *c*1650–1844; William Marsden (1754–1836), especially oriental MSS and records *re* Portuguese missionaries, 1580–1780; Frida Mond Collection, including Goethe and Schiller papers, 1794–1831; King George III Museum Collection, especially Richmond Observatory records, 1769–83.

Archives of Modern Poetry in Translation, 1965–83; *Adam International Review*, 1920–86; the Greek Relief Fund, 1948–84; League for Democratic Freedom in Greece, 1940–83. Nuffield Foundation Science Education Projects, 1960–76.

Non-manuscript material: Photographs and engravings of college life and history.

Sir Charles Wheatstone Collection of photographs *re* his work on stereoscopes.

Finding aids: Handlists.

Facilities: Restricted photocopying and photography.

Publications: F.J.C. Hearnshaw: *The Centenary History of King's College London* (London, 1929).

H. Willoughby Lyle: *King's and Some King's Men: being a Record of the Medical Department of King's College London from 1830–1909 and of King's College Hospital Medical School from 1909–1934* (London, 1935; addendum to 1948, 1950).

H. Silver and S.J. Teague (eds): *Chelsea College: a History* (London, 1977).

G. Huelin: *King's College London, 1828–1978* (London, 1978).

F. Miles and G. Cranch: *King's College School: the First 150 Years* (London, 1979).

W.O. Skeat: *King's College London Engineering Society, 1847–1947* (London, 1979).

N. Marsh: *The History of Queen Elizabeth College* (London, 1986).

D.J. Britten (ed.): *The Story of King's College Hospital and its Medical School* (London, 1991).

C.E. Handler: *Guy's Hospital, 250 Years* (London, 1976).

F.G. Parsons: *The History of St Thomas's Hospital* (London, 1932–6) [3 vols].

British Postgraduate Medical Federation Institute of Psychiatry, 1924–1974 (1974).

B Liddell Hart Centre for Military Archives

Website: www.kcl.ac.uk/lhcma/top.htm

Historical background: Founded in 1964, the centre was in the vanguard of repositories and museums which actively sought out private papers bearing on the military affairs of the 20th century. It was named after Captain Sir Basil Liddell Hart (1895–1970) to mark the acquisition of his papers and library in 1973.

Acquisitions policy: Private papers of higher commanders of the armed services and defence personnel holding senior office during the 20th century. Archives of related documentary television programmes made by independent production companies.

Major collections: Collections of private papers (*c*550), including those of FM Viscount Alanbrooke (1883–1963); FM Viscount Allenby (1861–1936); ACM Sir Robert

Brooke-Popham (1878–1953); Sir Arthur Bryant (1899–1985); Brig. John Charteris (1877–1946); Sir Frank Cooper (*b* 1922); Sir Maurice Dean (1906–78), Maj.-Gen. C.H. Foulkes (1875–1969); Maj.-Gen. J.F.C. Fuller (1878–1966); Gen. Sir Ian Hamilton (1853–1947); Gen. Lord Ismay (1887–1965); Sir Charles Johnson (1912–86); Gen. Sir Richard O'Connor (1889–1981); ACM S.W.B. Menaul (1915–87); FM Sir Archibald Montgomery-Massingberd (1871–1947); FM Sir William Robertson (1860–1933); Gen. Sir Hugh Stockwell (1903–86).

Television documentary archives, including *The Nuclear Age, The Death of Yugoslavia, The Washington Version* (Gulf War), and *The Fall of the Wall.*

Non-manuscript material: Numerous photographs illustrating the life and work of the armed services from the Boer War onwards; especially important are those relating to the development of photographic reconnaissance at the turn of the century.

Microfilm (800 reels) and microfiche (5000) copies of original material, mainly American, relating to defence studies.

Finding aids: Handlists. Collection-level descriptions available on website. Detailed cataloguing in progress.

Facilities: Restricted photocopying, photography and microfilming.

670 Laban Centre for Movement and Dance

Address: Laurie Grove, New Cross, London SE14 6NW

Telephone: (020) 8692 4070 ext. 120

Fax: (020) 8694 8749

E-mail: r.cox@laban.co.uk

Website: www.laban.co.uk

Enquiries: The Librarian, Ralph Cox

Open: Term: Mon, Wed, Thurs: 9.00–7.30; Tues: 9.00–5.00; Fri: 9.00–1.00. Vacation: Mon–Fri: 9.00–5.00.

Access: Generally available to the public. An appointment is necessary and a charge is made. Paid research facilities are available.

Historical background: The Laban Centre for Movement and Dance is an institution for higher education in dance offering graduate, postgraduate and research degree courses. The centre developed from the Art of Movement Studio opened by Lisa Ullmann, an associate of Rudolph Laban, in Manchester in 1946. The library and archives developed considerably during the early 1980s into a major dance resource, although the archives of the Art of Movement Studio and the Laban Centre are not at present available for public use.

Acquisitions policy: All forms of dance and movement are covered, including dance therapy and dance in the community. Equally all forms of printed and audio-visual materials on dance are acquired.

Major collections: Peter Williams Collection: the working collection of Peter Williams, editor of the journal *Dance and Dancers*, 1950–77, consisting principally of photographs, theatre programmes, publicity material.

Laban Collection: documents, books and photographs of the work of Rudolph Laban (*d* 1958) in pre-war Europe.

Peter Brinson Collection covering sociology, education, ballet for all.

Shirim Lynne Collection on notation.

Non-manuscript material: Records of notation, photographs, theatre programmes, video, sound tapes and ephemera.

Finding aids: Computer catalogues are in preparation.

Facilities: Photocopying. Microfilm/fiche reader. Video viewing facilities.

671 Lambeth Archives Department

Parent organisation: London Borough of Lambeth

Address: Minet Library, 52 Knatchbull Road, London SE5 9QY

Telephone: (020) 7926 6076

Fax: (020) 7926 6080

E-mail: lambetharchives@hotmail.com

Website: www.lambeth.gov.uk

Enquiries: The Archives Managers, Mr Jon Newman/Ms Sue McKenzie

Open: Mon: 1.00–8.00; Tues, Thurs: 10.00–6.00; Fri: 10.00–1.00; Sat: 9.00–5.00.

Access: Generally open to the public; it is advisable to make an appointment. There are restrictions on certain records. A paid research service is available.

Historical background: William Minet donated the library to the vestries of Lambeth and Camberwell in 1890, together with his local history collection, which related to the whole of Surrey before 1888. The collection of MSS, illustrations, maps and printed material was built up, and in 1956 the library became part of the Borough of Lambeth public library service and took on its archive function. It is recognised as a place of deposit for public and manorial records.

Acquisitions policy: The records of the London Borough of Lambeth and predecessor authorities and of business organisations and individuals situated within or connected with the borough.

Archives of organisation: Usual local authority record holdings: Lambeth, Clapham and Streatham civil parish records up to 1855; Vestry of St Mary Lambeth, 1855–1900; Metropolitan Borough of Lambeth, 1900–65; London Borough of Lambeth, 1965– .

Major collections: Manorial, parochial, charity, Poor Law and non-conformist records.
Deeds (*c*13,000).
Special collections, including Magdalen Hospital Trust, 1757–1975.
Theobald Papers, papers of an 18th-century steward of the Dukes of Bedford at Streatham.
Minet Estate records, Camberwell, 1767–1975.
Papers of the Graham and Polhill families of Clapham, including letters and diaries, 1803–55; and of the Thorntons of Clapham, mainly 19th century.
Correspondence of Henry Beaufoy, relating mostly to the setting up of Ragged Schools, 1847–51.
Artagen records (Artisans, Labourers and General Dwellings Company), 1867–1975.

Non-manuscript material: 10,000 illustrations, including 'extra-illustrated' vols (e.g. Manning and Bray's Surrey); 4 vols of Phillips watercolours; Petrie watercolours.
Playbills and theatre programmes.
Vauxhall Gardens song books, playbills, news cuttings etc.
Printed books, guides, pamphlets and news cuttings relating to the Crystal Palace.
Cuttings collection (includes ephemera), mainly post-1956.

Maps and plans (printed and MS), 17th-century– .
Periodicals, newspapers, directories, pamphlets, including all standard printed material as well as rarer items.

Finding aids: Catalogue of, and person, place and subject indexes to, deeds and special collections. Street index to census returns (on microfilm) and trade index to 1841 census. Vauxhall Gardens songs index. Rate books name index, 1729–73. Lambeth Vestry minutes subject index, 1652–1858. Norwood Cemetery index to tomb inscriptions. South London Press index, 1909–14. GRO index to births in UK. Lists sent to NRA.

Facilities: Photocopying. Photography. Microfilm/fiche reader/printer. Map copying service.

Conservation: Contracted out.

Publications: House History at Lambeth Archives (1996).
Family History at Lambeth Archives (1996).
Guide to Lambeth Archives (1999).
Series of Information Guides on particular topics.

672 Lambeth Palace Library

Address: Lambeth Palace Road, London SE1 7JU

Telephone: (020) 7898 1400

Fax: (020) 7928 7932

Website: www.lambethpalacelibrary.org

Enquiries: The Librarian and Archivist, Dr Richard Palmer

Open: Mon–Fri: 10.00–5.00.
Closed for ten days from Good Friday.

Access: Bona fide students, at the discretion of the Librarian; new readers are required to provide a letter of introduction from a person or institution of recognised standing, two passport photographs, and evidence of permanent address. The library operates a system of readers' tickets. Special permission is needed for access to some categories of MSS (e.g. illuminated MSS).

Historical background: Lambeth Palace Library is the historic library of the archbishops of Canterbury. It was founded as a public library by Archbishop Bancroft in 1610. Its original endowment included a celebrated collection of medieval MSS and a large quantity of English and foreign printed books, to which considerable additions have been made. The Church Commissioners are now responsible for the maintenance of the library, and it is recognised as a place of deposit for public records. Manuscript collections, pamphlets and pre-1850 books have been transferred from Sion College Library.

Acquisitions policy: Records of the archbishops of Canterbury. Historical records of the central institutions of the Church of England, with the exception of records of the Church Commissioners and the General Synod and its associated bodies (see Church of England Record Centre, entry 582). Papers of ecclesiastics of national distinction and of statesmen where these fall within the library's general area of interest.

Archives of organisation: Registers of the archbishops of Canterbury, 13th–20th centuries.
Correspondence and papers of the archbishops of Canterbury, 16th century– .
Records of the estates of the See of Canterbury, 13th–19th centuries.
Archives of the Province of Canterbury, including those of the Court of Arches, the Faculty Office, the Vicar General's Office, and Convocation, mainly 17th century– .
Records of the Archbishop's Peculiars of Arches, Croydon and Shoreham, particularly testamentary, 17th–mid-19th centuries.
Records of the Lambeth Conferences, 1860– .

Major collections: Medieval MSS.
Collections of 16th-century MSS, including Bacon, Carew, Shrewsbury and Talbot papers.
Records of societies within the Church of England, including the Church of England Men's Society, Church of England Temperance Society, Church Society, Church Union, Clergy Orphan Corporation. Confraternity of the Blessed Sacrament, Incorporated Church Building Society (ICBS).
Papers of the bishops of London, including extensive collections concerning colonial America and the West Indies, 17th century– .
Papers of distinguished bishops, churchmen and statesmen, such as G.K.A. Bell (1883–1958), Bishop of Chichester; A.C. Headlam (1862–1947), Bishop of Gloucester; E.J. Palmer (1869–1954), Bishop of Bombay; Christopher Wordsworth (1807–85), Bishop of Lincoln; Baroness Burdett-Coutts (1814–1906); John Keble (1792–1866); Athelstan Riley (1858–1945); Isaac William (1802–65); 1st Earl of

Selborn (1812–95); William Gladstone (1809–98); William Scott (1813–72).
Ecclesiastical records of the Commonwealth, 1643–60.
Records of the Commission for Building Fifty New Churches in London and Westminster, 18th century.
Records of Doctors Commons.
Registers of foreign churches, e.g. Basra, Khartoum, Shanghai and Shangtung.

Non-manuscript material: Books (c200,000), particularly strong in English and foreign books published from the invention of printing to 1800. Includes pre-1850 books from Sion College Library.
Large collection of pamphlets.
ICBS includes extensive collection of plans of churches, 1818–1982.

Finding aids: Catalogues, indexes, database for ICBS records. *Handlist of Catalogues and Indexes of the Archives and Manuscripts in Lambeth Palace Library* (1998).

Facilities: Photocopying. Photography and microfilming by arrangement. Colour transparencies available for loan.

Publications: Apart from catalogues noted in Robert Collison: *Published Library Catalogues* (1973), 137–8, see:
C.R. Batho: *A Calendar of the Shrewsbury and Talbot Papers in Lambeth Palace Library and the College of Arms, ii: Talbot Papers in the College of Arms* (1971) [collection purchased by Lambeth Palace in 1983].
E.G.W. Bill: *A Catalogue of Manuscripts in Lambeth Palace Library, MSS 1222–1860* (1972); *MSS 2341–3119* (1983).
J. Houston: *Index of Cases in the Records of the Court and Arches at Lambeth Palace Library, 1660–1913* (1972).
J.E. Sayers and E.G.W. Bill: *Calendar of the Papers of Charles Thomas Longley, Archbishop of Canterbury, 1862–1868, in Lambeth Palace Library* (1972).
Index to the Papers of Anthony Bacon (1558–1601) in Lambeth Palace Library (MSS 647–662) (1974).
W.W. Manross: *S.P.G. Papers in the Lambeth Palace Library: Calendar and Indexes* (1974).
M. Barber: *Index to the Letters and Papers of Frederick Temple, Archbishop of Canterbury, 1896–1902, in Lambeth Palace Library* (1975).
E.G.W. Bill: *The Queen Anne Churches: a Catalogue of the Papers in Lambeth Palace Library of the Commission for Building Fifty*

New Churches in London and Westminster, 1711–1759 (1979).
Index to the Letters and Papers of Edward White Benson, Archbishop of Canterbury, 1883–1896, in Lambeth Palace Library (1980). For recent accessions, see Library's *Annual Review*.

673 Law Society Library

Address: 113 Chancery Lane, London WC2A 1PL

Telephone: 0870 606 2511

Fax: (020) 7831 1687

E-mail: lib-enq@lawsociety.org.uk

Enquiries: The Librarian

Open: Mon–Fri: 9.00–5.00.

Access: Members and academic researchers, by written appointment. Charges for enquiries passed to records department on individual solicitors and firms.

Historical background: The Law Society was formerly known as the Society of Attorneys, Solicitors and Proctors and others not being Barristers, practising in the Courts of Law and Equity of the United Kingdom; the Law Institution; and the Incorporated Law Society. It was founded in 1825 and remains on the same site. The archives are limited and do not include the papers of individual solicitors, their firms or their clients.

Acquisitions policy: To maintain the society's archives. Private papers and MSS are not acquired.

Archives of organisation: Incomplete archives, including minutes of council and committees; AGM and SGM annual reports; committee reports; charters and bye-laws.

Major collections: Records of the Society of Gentlemen Practisers, 1739–1819. Certain records of Staple Inn.

Non-manuscript material: Architectural plans of 113 Chancery Lane by Vulliamy, Hardwick and others.
Some photographs of solicitors, mainly presidents of the society.
Publications of the Metropolitan Provincial Law Association.

Finding aids: Computer catalogue (limited detail).

Facilities: Archival material is not normally copied, but photocopying and microform reader/printers are available.

Conservation: Contracted out.

Publications: Handbook of the Law Society (London, 1938) [gives brief description].
D. Sugarman: *History of the Law Society* (1995).

674 Leathersellers' Company

Address: 15 St Helen's Place, London EC3A 6DQ

Telephone: (020) 7330 1444

Fax: (020) 7330 1445

E-mail: enquiries@leathersellers.co.uk

Website: www.leathersellers.co.uk

Enquiries: The Clerk

Open: Strictly by appointment only.

Access: On a restricted basis following discussion with the Clerk.

Historical background: The Leathersellers' Company appears to have been the successor of two earlier and minor fraternities that existed in the early 13th century. Reference to a Fraternity of Leathersellers appears in 1372. Articles for the regulation of the craft were applied for in 1398, and in 1444 the Leathersellers obtained a Charter of Incorporation. The company has possessed six halls and has provided technical education since 1909, with the establishment of the Leathersellers' Technical College, re-established as the National Leathersellers' College in 1951, and now known as the British School of Leather Technology, Nene College, Northampton.

Acquisitions policy: To maintain the company's archives; the company also relies on the goodwill of members of the profession and families who present items of historical interest.

Archives of organisation: Minutes, 1608– ; warden's accounts, 1471– ; books of wills, 1470–1799; apprenticeship books, 1629– ; registers for freedom, 1630– ; livery books, 1706– ; charters and ordinances.

Publications: W.H. Black: *History of the Antiquities of the Worshipful Company of Leathersellers of the City of London* (London, 1871) [includes facsimiles and lists archives].

P. Hunting: *The Leathersellers' Company: a History* (London, 1994).

675 Leighton House Museum and Art Gallery

Parent organisation: Royal Borough of Kensington and Chelsea

Address: 12 Holland Park Road, London W14 8LZ

Telephone: (0207) 602 3316

Fax: (0207) 371 2467

E-mail: danielrobbins@rbkc.gov.uk

Website: www.rbkc.gov.uk/leightonhousemuseum

Enquiries: The Curator, Daniel Robbins

Open: Mon, Wed–Sun: 11.00–5.30.

Access: Bona fide researchers, by appointment.

Leighton House acquired the papers of Frederic, Lord Leighton (1830–96), which consist of *c*600 items of juvenilia and correspondence with family and friends, 1840–96. Some of the letters have been transferred from the G.F. Watts Gallery, Compton, and those are listed in B. Curle: *Catalogue of Leighton Letters* (Royal Borough of Kensington and Chelsea, 1983). A computerised catalogue is in progress.

676 Lewisham Local Studies Centre

Parent organisation: London Borough of Lewisham

Address: Lewisham Library, 199–201 Lewisham High Street, London SE13 6LG

Telephone: (020) 8297 0682

Fax: (020) 8297 1169

E-mail: local.studies@lewisham.gov.uk

Website: www.lewisham.gov.uk

Enquiries: The Archivist, Ms Jean Wait

Open: Mon: 10.00–5.00; Tues, Thurs: 9.00–8.00; Fri, Sat: 9.00–5.00.
Closed for two weeks in December.

Access: Generally open to the public; appointments are advisable. There are restrictions on some official and deposited collections.

Historical background: An archives and local history department (later called the Local History Centre) was established by the Metropolitan Borough of Lewisham in 1960 at the Manor House, Lee. Since 1965 it has acted as the archive repository and local history library for the London Borough of Lewisham, including the former Metropolitan Borough of Deptford. In October 1994 it changed its name to Lewisham Local Studies Centre and moved to the new Lewisham Library. The centre is recognised as a place of deposit for local public, manorial and tithe and parish records (parishes in East and West Lewisham).

Acquisitions policy: To collect, preserve and make available all types of archive and local history materials relating to the London Borough of Lewisham, within the terms of the relevant Local Government Acts and the centre's formal appointments.

Archives of organisation: Local government records: metropolitan boroughs of Lewisham and Deptford, Lewisham Board of Works, Lee and Plumstead Board of Works, Greenwich Board of Works, St Paul's Deptford Committee, parishes of Lewisham, Lee and St Paul's Deptford, 18th–20th centuries.

Major collections: Anglican parish records: parishes within the deaneries of East and West Lewisham, 16th–20th centuries.
Non-conformist records: Lewisham and Peckham Methodist Circuit and constituent churches, 19th–20th centuries; Deptford Wesleyan Mission, 19th–20th centuries; Deptford and Brockley Congregational churches, 18th–20th centuries; Lewisham Unitarian Church, 20th century.
Family and estate records: Baring Estate, Lee, including manorial records, 16th–19th centuries; Mayow Estate, Sydenham, 17th–20th centuries; Evelyn Estate, Deptford, 19th–20th centuries; other lesser estates and miscellaneous deeds, 16th–20th centuries; Forster estate, southern Lewisham, 18th–20th centuries.
Charity records: Deptford Fund (Albany Institute), 19th–20th centuries; parochial and other charities and voluntary bodies, 17th–20th centuries.
Business records: Chiltonian Ltd, biscuit manufacturers, 20th century; Cobbs of Sydenham, department store, 19th–20th centuries; Stone's foundry, Deptford, 19th–20th centuries (restricted access).
Education records: Blackheath Proprietary School, 19th–20th centuries; St Dunstan's

College, Catford, 19th–20th centuries; Prendergast Grammar School, Lewisham, 19th–20th centuries; Lee Church of England Schools, 19th–20th centuries.

Clubs and societies records: Bellingham Bowling Club, 20th century; Catford Cycling Club, 19th–20th centuries; Old Brocklejan Society, 20th century.

Political: records of local Labour and Liberal parties, 20th century.

Non-manuscript material: Prints of Lewisham, London and Kent, 18th–20th centuries (1400 items).

Art collection: mainly Lewisham topography and local artists, 19th–20th centuries (500 items).

Photographic prints, postcards, negatives and transparencies, c1857– (c30,000 items).

Printed maps and plans: Lewisham, London, Kent, OS etc, 16th–20th centuries.

Local newspapers, 1834- (originals and microfilm).

Local census returns, 1841–91 (microfilm).

Audio-visual materials: miscellaneous local films (mainly home movies); tape-recordings of local events and oral history reminiscences.

Printed books and pamphlets: Lewisham, London and Kent, local history topics, works by local authors (e.g. John Evelyn, Edgar Wallace, Henry Williamson), 16th–20th centuries.

Various indexes of inhabitants of the area.

Finding aids: Lists and card indexes. Some lists are word-processed and can be searched by keyword. Lists sent to NRA.

Facilities: Photocopying. Photography. Microfilm/fiche readers/printer.

Conservation: Contracted out.

Publications: Lewisham Section of the *Guide to London Local History Resources.*
Sources for Family History.
Various local history publications.

677 Library and Museum of Freemansonry

Parent organisation: United Grand Lodge of Free and Accepted Masons of England

Address: Freemasons' Hall, Great Queen Street, London WC2B 5AZ

Telephone: (020) 7395 9251

Fax: (020) 7404 7418

Enquiries: The Director, Mrs Diane Clements

Open: Mon–Fri: 10.00–5.00.

Access: The library and museum are open to the public. Access to the records is free to members and, after discussion with the Director, to non-members by appointment. There is a charge for genealogical enquiries.

Historical background: The Grand Lodge of England was formed in 1717. The library and museum were established in 1837 to manage the archives of the Grand Lodge and its sister organisation the Grand Chapter of the Royal Arch, and to develop a comprehensive library on freemasonry, together with a reference collection of regalia, medals and orders, and artefacts with either a masonic use or incorporating masonic decoration in their design. While concentrating on the development of English freemasonry, the collections include material on freemasonry wherever it is or has been practised throughout the world.

Acquisitions policy: Active policy of collecting printed, MS, documentary and ephemeral material on English freemasonry.

Archives of organisation: MS and printed minutes of Grand Lodge, 1723– , and Grand Chapter, 1766– .
Membership registers of Grand Lodge, 1751– , and Grand Chapter, 1766– .
Letter-books, c1770.

Major collections: Historical correspondence: correspondence from lodges and individual freemasons (worldwide), c1770–c1890 (c150,000 items).
Masonic warrants, charters, patents of appointment, certificates etc (c200,000 items).

Non-manuscript material: Large collection of printed ephemera concerning lodges, personalities and masonic events.
Portraits, prints, drawings, photographs, engravings of persons, masonic scenes, artefacts (c100,000 items).
Printed books and pamphlets (c44,000).

Finding aids: Documents indexed by recipient and issuing body. Correspondence indexed by writer, recipient and subjects.

Facilities: Photocopying and photography by arrangement.

Publications: J. Stubbs and T.O. Haunch: *Freemasons' Hall: Home and Heritage of the Craft* (London, 1983).

J.M. Hamill: *The History of Freemasonry: Souvenir of an Exhibition* (London, 1986).

678 Library Association

Address: 7 Ridgmount Street, London WC1E 7AE

Telephone: (020) 7255 0500

Fax: (020) 7255 0501

E-mail: info@la-hq.org.uk

Website: www.la-hq.org.uk

Enquiries: The Archivist, Maris Mathias

Open: Mon, Tues, Thurs: by arrangement.

Access: Open to members and bona fide researchers. An appointment is essential.

Historical background: The Library Association was established in 1877 to promote libraries and professional librarianship and received its royal charter in 1898.

Acquisitions policy: Restricted to Library Association records.

Archives of organisation: Library Association archives, 1877– , including council minutes and proceedings, committee papers and files, conference reports, the *Record* and predecessor journals; and records of some predecessor/absorbed bodies, including Birmingham Library Association.

Major collections: Records of the Association of Assistant Librarians, 1890s– ; the Association of Chief Metropolitan Librarians; and the Cataloguing and Indexing Group.

Non-manuscript material: Newspaper cuttings, late 1800s–mid-1960s.
Glass plate negatives of library buildings, 1930s.

Finding aids: Computerised listing in progress.

Publications: W. A. Munford: *The History of The Library Association, 1877–1977* (Library Association Publishing, 1976).

679 Lincoln's Inn Library

Parent organisation: Honourable Society of Lincoln's Inn

Address: Holborn, London WC2A 3TN

Telephone: (020) 7242 4371

Fax: (020) 7404 1864

E-mail: mail@lincolnsinn.org.uk

Website: www.lincolnsinn.org.uk

Enquiries: The Librarian

Open: Mon–Fri: 9.00–8.00;
Aug–mid-Sept: Mon–Fri: 9.30–5.30.

Access: Members of Lincoln's Inn, and bona fide enquirers by appointment with a letter of recommendation.

Historical background: One of the four Inns of Court, with uncertain origins in the 14th century or earlier. The library was established by c1475.

Archives of organisation: Principal archives of Lincoln's Inn, including Black Books: minutes of the governing body, 1422– ; Red Books: finance and building, 1614–1877 [7 vols]; Account Books Vacation Commons, 1629–35, 1649–58, 1660–80; treasurers' accounts, 1672–81, 1713–22; Works Department accounts, 1779–84; cook's accounts, 1806–32; admission registers, 1573– ; Bar Books, 1757– ; deeds and property records, 1228– ; chapel registers, 1695– .

Non-manuscript material: Some drawings, plans and photographs of Lincoln's Inn.

Finding aids: Catalogue. NRA 17005.

Publications: R. Megarry: *An introduction to Lincoln's Inn* (1997).
Printed editions of the Black Books (1422–1914) and Admission Registers (1422–1893).

680 Linnean Society of London

Address: The Library, Burlington House, Piccadilly, London W1V 0LQ

Telephone: (020) 7434 4479

Fax: (020) 7287 9364

E-mail: gina@linnean.demon.co.uk

Website: www.linnean.org.uk

Enquiries: The Librarian and Archivist, Miss Gina Douglas

Open: Mon–Fri: 10.00–5.00.
Closed the day after a bank holiday.

Access: Bona fide scholars; non-fellows by written appointment only.

Historical background: The society was founded in 1788. Linnaeus's MSS were acquired in 1828 from the founder, J.E. Smith, who purchased them in 1784. Other MSS have been acquired by bequest or gift.

Archives of organisation: Charters, minute books, accounts, records relating to collections of specimens, correspondence, ephemera etc, 1788– .

Papers read at society meetings, most published in society *Transactions*.

Zoological Club of the Linnean Society, minutes and papers, 1822–9.

Major collections: Carolus Linnaeus (1707–78), MSS, including correspondence, MS copies of his work and other MSS from contemporary naturalists.

James Edward Smith (1759–1828), MSS, including correspondence (*c*3000 letters).

William Swainson (1789–1855), correspondence.

MSS, including correspondence of Alexander and William Sharpe MacLeay; Richard Pulteney (1730–1801) and John Ellis (?1705–1776).

Archives of the Society for Promoting Natural History, 1783–1801; Selborne Society, including minute books and Gilbert White MSS; and the Council for Nature.

Non-manuscript material: Prints, watercolours and sketches included in collections.

Collection of portraits of naturalists.

Finding aids: Card catalogue; slip index of correspondents; individual handlists. Lists sent to NRA.

Facilities: Photocopying. Photography by arrangement. Microfiche reader.

Conservation: Limited in-house facilities. Specific projects contracted out.

Publications: Linnean Society of London: *Catalogue of the Manuscripts in the Library of the Linnean Society of London*, pt I: *The Smith Papers* (by Warren Dawson, 1934); pt II: *Caroli Linnaei Determinationes in Hortum Siccum Joachimi Burseri* (by Spencer Savage, 1937); pt III: *Synopsis of the Annotations by Linnaeus and Contemporaries in his Library of Printed Books* (by Spencer Savage, 1940); pt IV: *Calendar of the Ellis Manuscripts* (by Spencer Savage, 1948).

W.T. Stearn and G. Bridson: *Commemorative Catalogue* (1978).

G. Bridson, W. Phillips and A.R. Harvey: *Natural History Manuscript Resources in the British Isles* (Mansell, 1981) [lists collections and holdings].

National Inventory of Documentary Sources, Chadwyck-Healey microfiche (1984–).

W.T. Stearn: *History of the Linnean Society London* (1988).

681 Little Sisters of the Assumption
Anglo-Scottish Province Archives

Address: Provincial House, 52 Kenneth Crescent, Willesden Green, London NW2 4PN

Telephone: (020) 8452 1687

Fax: (020) 82083625

E-mail: margarch@lsacon.ssnet

Enquiries: The Provincial Archivist, Sr Margaret Lonergan

Open: By arrangement.

Access: The archives are private, and access is normally limited to members. However, bona fide researchers who can authenticate their request by a letter of referral are assured that enquiries are welcome. There is a 50-year closure on personal records.

Historical background: The religious order known as the Little Sisters of the Assumption was founded in 1865 in Paris for the care of needy families by means of nursing and social work. The first convent in England opened in Bow, London, in 1880 and the first Scottish community opened in 1946. It is now present in 30 countries. The Welsh communities are linked to the Irish Province.

Acquisitions policy: To maintain, preserve and acquire archival material relating to the order and its associate works and organisations.

Archives of organisation: Archives relating to the early history of the province, 1865–83, as well as sisters, communities and convents in England, 1880– , and in Scotland, 1946– .

Administrative records of the history of each convent, nursing and social work.

Medical registers detailing patients nursed, 1880– (closed).

Major collections: Pernet MSS: correspondence and transcripts relating to the Founder, Venerable Stephen Pernet, 1824–99.

Fage papers: correspondence of Antoinette Fage, foundress with Fr Pernet, and first sister, 1824–83.

Non-manuscript material: Albums and photographs depicting the sisters, convents and associates.

Films and transparencies.

Finding aids: Some lists and indexes.

Facilities: Photocopying.

Publications: Sr M. Lonergan: 'The Archives of the Anglo-Scottish Province of the Little Sisters of the Assumption', *Catholic Archives*, 11 (1991), 17–24.

682 Lloyd's Register of Shipping
Information Centre

Address: 71 Fenchurch Street, London EC3M 4BS

Telephone: (020) 7423 2475 (Information Officer and Archivist); (020) 7423 2348 (Records Centre Manager)

Fax: (020) 7488 4796

Website: www.lr.org

Enquiries: The Information Officer and Archivist, Mrs Barbara Jones
The Records Centre Manager, Mr Iain Mayoh

Open: Information Office: Mon–Fri: 9.30–12.00, 1.00–4.30.
Records Centre: by appointment only.

Access: Information Office: generally open to the public.
Records Centre: bona fide researchers, by appointment; prior application is necessary to view records of ships (existing or wreck); the owner's permission must be obtained by the enquirer.

Historical background: Lloyd's Register was founded in 1760 and is now the oldest and largest ship classification society. It has diversified into many other technical areas, notably offshore gas and oil and land-based industrial work of all kinds. The Information Centre holds a complete collection of all the published works of Lloyd's Register, including the Register of Ships, 1764– . The Records Centre holds plans and survey reports of current classed ships and an index to those of Lloyd's Register's plans and reports retained by the National Maritime Museum (entry 710).

Acquisitions policy: Lloyd's Register's own publications and additions to maritime reference library.

Archives of organisation: Register of ships, 1764– .
Merchant shipbuilding returns, 1888– .
Statistical returns, 1878– .
Casualty returns, 1890– .
Liverpool Underwriters Register for Iron Ships, 1862–84.
British Corporation Registers, 1893–1947.
Plans and reports of ships classed by Lloyd's Register, 1834– (incomplete).
Register of yachts, 1878–1980.

Non-manuscript material: Reference library concerning maritime history (*c*3000 vols).

Facilities: Photocopying.

Conservation: On-going conservation programme contracted out.

683 Lloyds TSB Group Archives

Parent organisation: Lloyds TSB Group plc

Address: Secretary's Department, 71 Lombard Street, London EC3P 3BS

Telephone: (020) 7356 1032

Fax: (020) 7929 2901

Enquiries: The Group Archivist

Open: Mon–Fri: 9.30–4.30, by appointment.

Access: At the discretion of the company, by application in writing to the Group Archivist.

Historical background: Lloyds Bank was established in Birmingham in 1765 as Taylors and Lloyds. In 1865 it became a joint-stock company, and by 1923 it had acquired more than 50 smaller banks. Lloyds Bank International, formed in 1971 following the takeover of the Bank of London and South America (BOLSA) and its union with Lloyds Bank Europe, was merged with the clearing bank in 1986. Cheltenham and Gloucester Building Society joined Lloyds in 1994. The TSB's origins lie in the local savings banks established in the early 19th century. In 1986 TSB Group plc was floated as an independent bank, and the following year the merchant bank Hill Samuel Group plc was acquired. In 1995 TSB Group merged with Lloyds Bank to form Lloyds TSB Group plc. Scottish Widows joined Lloyds TSB Group in 2000.

Acquisitions policy: Records of parent company and its constituents.

Archives of organisation: Records of Lloyds Bank, 1765– , and its constituents, including Liverpool Union Bank, 1835–1900, Bucks and Oxon Union Bank, 1853–1914, Devon and Cornwall Bank, 1831–1906, Wilts and Dorset Bank, 1835–1914, Capital and Counties Bank, 1877–1918, Fox Bros., Fowler and Co., 1787–1921, Cox and Co., army agents, 1758–1923, London and River Plate Bank, 1862–1924, Bank of London and South America, 1924–70; TSB Group plc and its constituent savings banks, 1816– ; TSB Association (f. 1887); Hill Samuel Group plc and its constituents, including M. Samuel and Co., (f. 1832); constituents of Cheltenham and Gloucester Building Society, 1853–1993.

Non-manuscript material: Photographs of branch premises; banking artefacts; banknotes; banking periodicals; numerous histories of savings bank movement in general, and individual savings banks.

Finding aids: Computer database and manual catalogues. Some lists sent to NRA.

Facilities: Photocopying. Photography.

Conservation: Contracted out.

Publications: H.O. Horne: *A History of Savings Banks* (1947).
R.S. Sayers: *Lloyds Bank in the History of English Banking* (1957).
D. Joslin: *A Century of Banking in Latin America* (1963) [BOLSA centenary].
J.R. Winton: *Lloyds Bank, 1918–1969* (1982).
M. Moss and I. Russell: *An Invaluable Treasure: a History of the TSB* (1994).

684   London College of Fashion

Parent organisation: London Institute

Address: 20 John Princes Street, London W1M 0BU

Telephone: (020) 7514 7410

Fax: (020) 7514 7580

E-mail: k.baird@linst.ac.uk

Website: www.linst.ac.uk

Enquiries: The Head of Learning Resources, Katherine Baird

Open: By arrangement.

Access: By appointment.

Historical background: The college was founded in 1820 and specializes in courses in fashion, style and beauty.

Acquisitions policy: Maintains archives of the college and acquires special collections relating mainly to tailoring.

Archives of organisation: Archives of the college, c1820s– .

Major collections: Special collections, 19th century– , relating to clothing and tailoring techniques, and including the Clothing and Footwear Institute archive.

Non-manuscript material: Photographs and slides (c1000).

Finding aids: Special collection catalogue.
College archive in process of digitisation with creation of metadata.

Facilities: Photocopying.

Publications: H. Reynolds: *Costume or Trade; an Early Pictorial Record of the London College of Fashion* (Phillimore, 1997).

685   London College of Printing

Parent organisation: The London Institute

Address: Elephant and Castle, London SE1 6SB

Telephone: (020) 7514 6500 ext. 6527

Fax: (020) 7514 6597

E-mail: info@lcp.linst.ac.uk

Website: www.lcp.linst.ac.uk

Enquiries: The Head of Learning Resources, Elizabeth Davison

Open: Term: Mon–Thurs: 9.30–8.15; Fri: 10.00–5.00.
Vacation: Mon–Fri: 10.00–4.30 (opening times subject to change).

Access: External researchers should apply in writing to the Head of Learning Resources.

Historical background: The London College of Printing was an ILEA specialist college until the formation of its new parent body, when it became a federated member of the London Institute. It subsequently merged with the College for the Distributive Trades and is now the largest college within the London Institute.

Acquisitions policy: To maintain the college archives and acquire materials to support the teaching, learning and research needs of the staff and students of the college. Principal areas of work are printing, graphic design, media, business and management, retail studies and professional studies.

Archives of organisation: College archives, including those of its predecessor, the London School of Printing, 1894–1922.

Non-manuscript material: Printing Historical Collection: specimens of printing, 1485– ; private press and artists books; substantial ephemera collection, including posters and calendars. Collection of film scripts (located at Back Hill site); Distribution Industrial Training Board Collection (located at Davies Street site).

Finding aids: Catalogue on BLCMP library system. Manual index to special collections' catalogues held at each site.

Facilities: Photocopying. Photography. Microfilming.

Conservation: In-house facilities.

Publications: Series of guides to collections.

686 London Guildhall University

Address: 41–71 Commercial Road, London E1 1LA

Telephone: (020) 7320 1867

Fax: (020) 7320 2831

Website: www.lgu.ac.uk

Enquiries: The Subject Librarian, Richard Farr

Open: Term: Mon: 10.15–8.00; Tues–Thur: 9.00–8.00; Fri: 9.00–5.00.
Vacations: Mon–Fri: 1.00–5.00.

Access: Bona fide enquirers, by appointment.

In 1848 Rev. Charles Mackenzie established the Metropolitan Evening Classes for Young Men in Bishopsgate. These were reconstituted as the City of London College in 1861 and came under the supervision of the London County Council in 1907. The college buildings were bombed in 1940 and many of the archives were lost. In 1970 the City of London Polytechnic was formed through the amalgamation of the college with Sir John Cass College, founded in 1899 as the Sir John Cass Technical Institute. In 1977 the polytechnic took responsibility for the

Fawcett Library, now the Women's Library (see entry 855). In 1980 the London College of Furniture, formerly Shoreditch Technical Institute (f. 1902), joined the polytechnic, which became London Guildhall University in 1992.

The Learning Resources Centre is responsible for the surviving archives of the university and its predecessors. The library of the Commercial Road site houses the Atcraft Archive Collection, which was deposited after the closure of Atcraft of Wembley, manufacturers of furniture, formerly active in East London. The collection consists primarily of ledgers, accounts books and product catalogues.

687 London Library

Address: 14 St James's Square, London SW1Y 4LG

Telephone: (020) 7930 7705

Fax: (020) 7766 4766

E-mail: inquiries@londonlibrary.co.uk

Website: www.londonlibrary.co.uk

Enquiries: The Librarian

Open: Mon–Wed, Fri, Sat: 9.30–5.30; Thurs: 9.30–7.30.

Access: Members and accredited students. A prior appointment is essential.

Historical background: The London Library was established in 1841 as a subscription library with an extensive collection of printed books (now c1 million vols) for reference and loan to members.

Acquisitions policy: Collecting is now concentrated on the library's own history from the founder, Thomas Carlyle (1795–1881), onwards.

Archives of organisation: Minute books, 1845– ; some early issue registers; membership lists, annual reports etc.

Major collections: Thomas Carlyle, various letters.
J.F. Baddeley Collection on Caucasian studies, 1882–1914.
C.W. Shirley Brooks (1816–74), editor of *Punch*, diaries.
Sir Samuel Egerton Brydges (1762–1857), miscellaneous papers.
James Mill (1773–1836), commonplace books (5 vols).

John Addington Symonds (1840–93), MS memoirs.

James Maurice Wilson (1836–1931), canon of Worcester, memoirs, books and family papers.

Non-manuscript material: Charles Reade (1814–84), scrapbooks.

Finding aids: NRA 20043 (summary only).

Facilities: Photocopying. Microfilm/fiche readers.

Conservation: Contracted out.

Publications: J. Wells: *Rude Words: a Discursive History of the London Library* (London, 1991).

688 London Metropolitan Archives

Parent organisation: Corporation of London

Address: 40 Northampton Road, London EC1R 0HB

Telephone: (020) 7332 3820

Fax: (020) 7833 9136

E-mail: lma@ms.corpoflondon.gov.uk

Website: www.cityoflondon.gov.uk/ organisation/index.htm

Enquiries: The Head Archivist, Dr Deborah Jenkins

Open: Mon, Wed, Fri: 9.30–4.45; Tues, Thurs: 9.30–7.30.
Closed first two weeks in November.

Access: Generally open to the public. Access is granted wherever possible, but a few special collections require written permission and/or 48 hours notice of a visit. A Family History Research Service is available and an Adoption and Care Counselling Service is provided.

Historical background: London Metropolitan Archives (LMA) was established in 1997 as a successor to the Greater London Record Office formed in 1965. It traces its roots to the former counties of Middlesex and London which each had a county record office until 1965. The Greater London Record Office and the Members Library moved from County Hall to Clerkenwell in 1982. Following abolition of the Greater London Council in 1986, the Modern Records Section likewise moved to Clerkenwell in 1994 with the official archives of the GLC, ILEA and LRB. LMA is the Diocesan Record Office for London, Southwark and Guildford

and is recognised as a place of deposit for public records. It is responsible for Keats House (see entry 667).

Acquisitions policy: Archives relating to the area of Greater London (especially pan-London or cross-borough collections). Regional records for London and the South-East. Archives of national organisations based in London.

Archives of organisation: Records of London Residuary Body, 1986–96; Greater London Council, 1965–86; Inner London Education Authority, 1965–90 and their predecessors including records of the Middlesex Sessions, 1549–1971, Metropolitan Board of Works, 1855–89, London Commissions of sewers, 1557–1855, the School Board for London, 1870–1904, and the Middlesex Deeds Registry, 1709–1938.

Major collections: Hospital records of more than 50 hospitals, including St Thomas' Hospital Group, Guy's Hospital, Westminster Hospital Group, 1556–1974, and London Regional Health Authorities, 1948–90, the Foundling Hospital (Thomas Coram Foundation for Children), 1739–1995.

Charities' records, 19th and 20th centuries, including Charity Organisation Society, National Council of Voluntary Organisations, National Council of Women.

Business records, 17th–20th centuries, including brewing companies such as Truman, Hanbury and Buxton; Barclay Perkins; Fuller Smith and Turner; Courage; builders such as Higgs and Hill; Mowlem; Trollope and Colls; retailers such as J. Lyons and Co.; Curry's; British Tyre and Rubber Company.

Utilities' records, 17th–20th centuries, including Thames Water and British Gas predecessors.

Anglo-Jewish records, 18th–20th centuries, including Board of Deputies; United Synagogue; Office of Chief Rabbi; Jews' College; Jews' Free School.

Manorial, family and estate records, 13th–20th centuries, including family papers of Earls of Jersey, Marquesses of Anglesey, Dukes of St Albans, Canon Barnett, 1844–1913; estate papers of Duke of Bedford (Covent Garden and Southwark), Marquess of Northampton (Canonbury and Clerkenwell), Maryon-Wilson (Hampstead and Charlton) and Charterhouse.

Political papers, 19th–20th centuries, including London Labour Party, London Liberal Party,

Hartley Booth MP (*b* 1946), 1st Baron Latham (1888–1970) and Ken Livingstone, MP (*b* 1945).

Housing records, 19th–20th centuries, including Peabody Trust, Society for Improving the Conditions of the Labouring Classes, William Sutton Trust, the Metropolitan Association, Improved Industrial Dwellings Company, Hampstead Garden Suburb.

Non-conformist records of more than 500 chapels, 17th–20th centuries, including Wesley's Chapel, City Road, and London Congregational Union.

Court records, 18th–20th centuries, including magistrates and coroners courts.

Regional archives, 20th century, including South East Regional Planning Committee (SERPLAN), and London Regional Passengers Committee (LRPC).

Non-manuscript material: Library of 100,000 books, including many primary sources to support official records, with important local government holdings; printed maps (15,000); prints and drawings (40,000); plans (1,000,000).

GLC photographic collection: 500,000 images (1.2 million negatives).

Finding aids: Computer-generated catalogues. Lists and indexes. Annual return of accessions and lists sent to NRA.

Facilities: Comprehensive reprographics service, including photocopying, microfilming, scanning, photography. Microfilm and microfiche reader, self-service reader/printers.

Conservation: Full in-house provision.

Publications: We Think You Ought to Go: the Evacuation of London's Children (1993).
Parish Registers: County of Middlesex, Diocese of London (1998) [microfiche].
Electoral Registers (1998) [microfiche].
Surrey Marriage Bonds and Allegations (1998) [microfiche].
Middlesex Sessions Records, 1549–1688; Old series vols 1–4, New series vols 1–4.
Greater London Record Office: a General Guide to Holdings (1994) [2 vols].

689 London School of Hygiene and Tropical Medicine

Parent organisation: University of London

Address: Keppel Street, London WC1E 7HT

Telephone: (020) 7927 2283

E-mail: library@lshtm.ac.uk

Website: www.lshtm.ac.uk/library/libintro.htm

Enquiries: The Librarian and Director of Information Services, Mr Brian Furner

Open: Term: Mon–Fri: 8.30–8.25; Sat: 9.00–12.30.
Vacation: Mon–Fri: 9.30–7.30; Sat: 9.00–12.30.

Access: Bona fide researchers. Records containing personal information are generally closed for 100 years.

Historical background: The school was opened in 1899 and the library has existed since that date. There is a broad coverage of all aspects of exotic diseases and public health as well as the history of both subjects. The school's administrative archives are kept by the Secretary and Registrar's office and are not available.

Acquisitions policy: To maintain the existing archival collections.

Archives of organisation: Papers, architects' drawings and correspondence *re* competition for the design of LSHTM, 1924, and its construction in Keppel Street, 1926–9.
Papers of Sir Andrew Balfour (1873–1930), first director of LSHTM.
Student registers, 1899– c1970.
Examination records of candidates for service in the 'Colonies and Protectorates', 1898–1919.

Major collections: Sir Ronald Ross (1857–1932) Archives: MSS, correspondence and reprints relating to his life and work (c20,000 items).
Sir Patrick Manson (1844–1922) Collection: diaries covering his work in China and including many case histories, also artefacts.
Robert Thomson Leiper (1881–1969), Professor of Helminthology: material relating to his work and family.
Sir (William) Allen Daley (1887–1969): papers relevant to his life and work.
Sir Leonard Rogers: MSS and original medical illustrations concerning leprosy.
Timothy Lewis note-books, including case histories, 1870s.
Records of the Mott Malaria Clinic, Horton Hospital, Epsom: clinical records of patients treated for neurosyphilis by induced malaria, 1925–60.

Non-manuscript material: Photographs of personalities connected with the history of the school and Ross Institute.

Finding aids: Catalogue of the Ross Archives. Some MSS in library card catalogue.

Facilities: Photocopying. Microfilm/fiche reader.

Publications: G.K Hall: *Dictionary Catalogue of the London School of Hygiene and Tropical Medicine* (Boston, 1965; suppl. 1970) [7 vols]. M.E. Gibson: *Catalogue of the Ross Archives* (London, 1983) [microfiche].

690 London School of Jewish Studies Library

Address: Schaller House, Albert Road, London NW4 2SJ

Telephone: (020) 8203 6427/8/9

Fax: (020) 8203 6420

E-mail: enquiries@lsjs.ac.uk

Website: www.lsjs.ac.uk

Enquiries: The Head Librarian, Mr Esra Kahn
The Librarians, Miss Kayla Robery, Mrs Erla Zimmels

Open: Mon, Tues, Thurs: 9.00–6.00; Wed: 9.00–9.00; Fri: 9.00–1.00; Sun: 9.30–12.30.
Closed all Jewish holy days and public holidays.

Access: Open to those who are interested in Hebrew and Jewish studies. Students, scholars and other enquirers who need guidance should telephone prior to a visit and produce a letter of introduction.

Historical background: The library was founded in 1860. The archives of Jews' College have been transferred to London Metropolitan Archives (see entry 688), where a catalogue is available.

Acquisitions policy: Acquisition is dependent on the amount of donations received. Financial assistance is welcomed as well as donations, from individual books to entire collections.

Major collections: Jews' College Collection of MSS (*c*150 vols).
Montefiore Collection of MSS (*c*600 vols).

Non-manuscript material: Collection of printed books and pamphlets (*c*100,000 vols).
Montefiore Collection of printed books (*c*3000 vols).
Hebrew and Jewish periodicals collection.

Facilities: Photocopying.

Conservation: Contracted out.

Publications: H. Hirschfield: *Descriptive Catalogue of the Hebrew MSS of the Montefiore Library* (London, 1904, 1969).

691 Madame Tussaud's Archives

Address: Marylebone Road, London NW1 5LR

Telephone: (020) 7487 0227

Fax: (020) 7465 0862

Website: www.madame-tussauds.com

Enquiries: The Archivist, Ms Rosy Canter

Open: By appointment.

Access: Preferably by letter in the first instance, thereafter by appointment only, if appropriate. There are restrictions on certain material.

Historical background: Madame Marie Tussaud (1760–1850) inherited a small wax exhibition from her uncle in Paris. She brought it to England in 1802 and travelled with it for many years, settling in London permanently in 1835. Other members of the Tussaud's group include Rock Circus, London; the London Planetarium; Chessington World of Adventures; Alton Towers; and Scenerama, Amsterdam.

Acquisitions policy: To enlarge the collection of material relating to or produced by Madame Tussaud's; and, to a much lesser extent, to collect material relating to 19th-century wax exhibitions.

Archives of organisation: Archives of Madame Tussaud's group; Tussaud family documents.

Non-manuscript material: Collection of embossed scrap reliefs and scrap albums, 18th and 19th centuries.
Exhibition catalogues, posters, publications written by members of staff.

Finding aids: List in course of preparation.

Facilities: Photocopying. Photography of certain items.

Publications: P. Chapman: *Madame Tussaud in England* (1992).

692 Marks & Spencer Company Archive

Parent organisation: Marks & Spencer plc

Address: B169 Michael House , Baker Street, London WC1U 8EP

Storage and Research Facility: Marks & Spencer, Wood Green Store, 46 High Road, London N22 6BX

Telephone: (020) 7268 3115

Fax: (020) 7268 2643

E-mail: rebecca.walker@marks-and-spencer.com

Website: www.marks-and-spencer.co.uk

Enquiries: The Company Archivist, Rebecca Walker

Open: Mon–Fri: 9.30–5.00.

Access: Any genuine researcher may consult the records, subject to company's access policy restrictions, by appointment only and on completion of a reader's application form. Certain records are closed and the company reserves the right to refuse access. Advance notice is required as the records are out stored.

Historical background: The business derives from a stall, with the goods priced at one penny, established in Leeds in 1884 by Michael Marks (*d.* 1907), a Russian Jewish refugee. He formed a partnership in 1894 with Tom Spencer (*d.* 1905), the cashier of a supportive local wholesaler. By 1900 the partnership had 36 outlets and in 1903 the business became Marks & Spencer Ltd. Simon Marks, son of Michael, became a director in 1911 and was chairman from 1916 until his death in 1964. In 1917 he was joined by his school friend, Israel Sieff. A period of growth began and in the 1920s and 1930s the company's quality control and staff welfare policies developed. The company's property suffered extensively during the 1939–45 war, but expansion and modernisation were resumed post-war and advantage taken of food technology developments to expand the product range. The company archive was established as part of the centenary celebrations in 1984 and the first professional archivist was appointed in 1997.

Acquisitions policy: Material relating to the activities of Marks & Spencer and its subsidiaries. Records, including sample merchandise, generated by the business in the course of its activities. Also family/personal papers of Marks and Sieff.

Archives of organisation: Archives of Marks & Spencer plc and its preceding organisations, c1890– , including limited records of its subsidiaries.

Major collections: Personal papers of notable individuals relating to the company: Simon Marks (1888–1964); Israel Sieff (1890–1972); Rebecca Sieff (née Marks) (1890–1966); Harry Sacher (1881–1971); and Flora Solomon (1895–1984).

Non-manuscript material: Samples of merchandise and clothing, 1890s– .

Large collection of photographs of stores, store interiors, window displays, staff, customers, directors, Marks and Sieff families, 1900– .

Collection of films, video, audio material including staff training, advertising and informational material, 1950s– .

Finding aids: Outline lists only.

Facilities: Photocopying. Photography.

Conservation: Contracted out

Publications: A. Briggs: *Marks & Spencer: a Centenary History* (1984).

K.K. Tse: *Marks & Spencer: Anatomy of Britain's Most Efficently Managed Company* (Pergamon Press, 1985).

P. Bookbinder: *Marks and Spencer: the War Years* (1989).

——: *Simon Marks: Retail Revolutionary* (1993).

A. Burns and B. Hyman: *100 Years of Partnership* (Marks & Spencer, 1994).

693 Marx Memorial Library

Address: Marx House, 37a Clerkenwell Green, London EC1R 0DU

Telephone: (020) 7253 1485

Fax: (020) 7251 6039

E-mail: marxlibrary@britishlibrary.net

Website: www.marxmemoriallibrary.sageweb.co.uk

Enquiries: The Librarian, Tish Collins

Open: Mon: 1.00–6.00; Tues–Thurs: 1.00–8.00; Sat: 10.00–1.00.

Access: Library members. An annual subscription is charged. Enquiries are welcomed.

Historical background: The library was started in 1933 as a response to Hitler's Fascism and the burning of Marxist and progressive books, and to commemorate the fiftieth anniversary of Karl Marx's death.

Acquisitions policy: To build and maintain a library relating to all aspects of Marxism, the history of socialism and the working-class movement.

Major collections: Spanish International Brigade Archives, including letters, cuttings, pamphlets and books.

Non-manuscript material: Books, pamphlets and periodicals on all aspects of Marxism and the Labour movements, including John Williamson Collection of the American Communist and Labour Movement; James Klugmann Collection of Chartist and radical literature, 1640s–1900; J.D. Bernal Peace Collection.

Finding aids: Author, subject and title catalogues. NRA 11083.

Publications: A. Rothstein: *The House on Clerkenwell Green.*
Marx Memorial Library Bulletin.

694 Marylebone Cricket Club Library

Address: Lord's Cricket Ground, St John's Wood, London NW8 8QN

Telephone: (020) 7289 1611

Fax: (020) 7432 1062

Enquiries: The Curator, Mr Stephen E.A. Green

Open: Mon–Fri: 9.30–5.30, by appointment; most Saturdays and some Sundays in the cricket season.

Access: Approved readers, on written application.

Historical background: Lord's was founded in 1787 and has had a historical collection of paintings since 1864. All the early records of the club were destroyed by a fire in 1825. The MCC library dates from 1893.

Acquisitions policy: To build up a representative body of material on the history of cricket.

Archives of organisation: Domestic archives of the MCC, 1787– .

Major collections: Middlesex County Cricket Club archives.

MS collections concerning other cricket clubs and famous players.

Non-manuscript material: Books, photographs, films and oral history collections concerning cricket.

Finding aids: Catalogues to much of the collection. NRA informed of accessions.

Facilities: Photocopying. Photography.

Conservation: Contracted out.

Publications: S. Green: 'Some Cricket Records', *Archives,* 80 (Oct 1988), 187–98.
Many publications relating to Lord's.

695 Medical Mission Sisters Central Archives

Address: 41 Chatsworth Gardens, Acton, London W3 9LP

Telephone: (020) 8992 6444

Fax: (020) 8896 2397

Website: archives@gn.apc.org

Enquiries: The Archivist

Open: Mon–Fri: 8.30–4.30.

Access: Not open to the public, but the Archivist will deal with enquiries.

Historical background: The Society of Catholic Medical Missionaries, also known as Medical Mission Sisters, is an international religious congregation founded in 1925 in Washington, DC. In 1939 the mother house moved to Philadelphia, and in 1958 the Society's Generale was established in Rome. It moved to its present location in 1983. District archives are held at individual houses but are mainly duplicated in the central archives.

Acquisitions policy: Society archives.

Archives of organisation: The history of the society.
Papers of the foundress, Dr Anna Dengel.
Papers of the society.

Non-manuscript material: Collection of photographs and slides of the foundress, the sisters and the work of the society in various countries.
Books and other printed works relating to medical missions.

Finding aids: Some preliminary inventories are available.

Facilities: Photocopying.

Conservation: Facilities for paper conservation.

696 Mercers' Company

Address: Mercers' Hall, Ironmonger Lane, London EC2V 8HE

Telephone: (020) 7776 7244 (direct line)

Fax: (020) 7600 1158

E-mail: ursulac@mercers.co.uk

Website: www.mercers.co.uk

Enquiries: The Archivist, Ursula Carlyle

Open: Mon–Fri: 9.30–5.00.

Access: Approved readers, by prior appointment only.

Historical background: The Worshipful Company of Mercers is the premier city livery company and one of the ancient merchant guilds of London. The word 'mercer' derives originally from the French word for merchant, but later became associated particularly with the trade in luxury goods, especially cloth. The records start in 1348 but the company is certainly older. From an early date the mercers administered estates in land and money left to them by wealthy members and non-members, such as Richard Whittington; Dean Colet, the founder of St Paul's School; Sir Thomas Gresham, the founder of the Royal Exchange and Gresham College; and the Earl of Northampton. These charities were and are for the poor and for educational purposes.

Acquisitions policy: To acquire material closely related to the history of the company and its members, by purchase, permanent loan or donation.

Archives of organisation: Records of the Mercers' Company and of the charitable estates in its care.

Non-manuscript material: A small collection of books printed at the Mercers' Chapel, London.

Finding aids: Extensive lists and catalogues.

Facilities: Limited photocopying.

Publications: J. Watney: *Some Account of the Hospital of St Thomas of Acon and of the Plate of the Mercers' Company* (London, 1892; 2/1906).

——: *An Account of the Mistery of Mercers of the City of London* (London, 1914).

L. Lyell and F. Watney (eds): *The Acts of Court of the Mercers' Company, 1453–1527* (Cambridge, 1936).

J. Imray: *The Charity of Richard Whittington, 1424–1966* (London, 1968).

——: *The Mercers' Hall,* London Topographical Society Publication, 143 (1991).

A.F. Sutton: *The Mercers' Company's First Charter, 1394* (Mercers' Company, 1994).

I. Doolittle: *The Mercers' Company 1579–1959* (Mercers' Company, 1994).

G. Huelin: *Think and Thank God: the Mercers' Company and its Contribution to the Church and Religious Life since the Reformation* (Mercers' Company, 1994).

697 Middle Temple Archive

Parent organisation: The Honourable Society of the Middle Temple

Address: Middle Temple Library, Middle Temple Lane, London EC4Y 9BT

Telephone: (0207) 427 4830

Fax: (0207) 427 4831

E-mail: library@middletemple.org.uk

Website: www.middletemple.org/library.htm

Enquiries: The Archivist, Mrs Lesley Whitelaw
The Keeper of the Library, Miss Vanessa Hayword

Open: Mon–Fri: 10.00–5.00.
Closed for the first fortnight in August.

Access: Access to non-members is strictly by appointment and at the Librarian's discretion.

Historical background: The Middle Temple is one of the four Inns of Court, which alone have the right of calling members to the Bar, i.e. of admitting them as barristers who, after completing 12 months pupillage, will enjoy rights of audience in all the superior courts of England and Wales. Apprentices in law first settled in the Temple in the mid-14th century. The earliest records of the Middle Temple date from 1501, by which time it was already providing education for students, accommodation for practitioners and a professional and social framework for barristers, functions which it continues to discharge. The governing body of Parliament is composed of senior judges and practitioners who are elected Masters of the Bench. The Under Treasurer is responsible to Parliament for the running of the Inn.

Acquisitions policy: There is no active acquisitions policy. The Inn maintains its own archive and this involves the transmission of non-current administrative and financial records to the archive. Occasional gifts and deposits of papers of members or societies associated with the Inn are accepted.

Archives of organisation: Records relating to administration, 1501–1988; finance, 1608–1991; membership, 1501–1987; deeds and legal papers, 1608–1994; rents, chambers and property, 1621–1969; building works, 1670–1976; commons, kitchens, entertainment, 1612–1971; staff, 1601–1991; library, 1641–1992; scholarships, prizes, charities, 1877–1985; pictures and plate, 1717–1967; New Inn, 1605–1904; legal education, 1846–1993; liaison with legal institutions, 1894–1992; Temple Church, 1591–1990; House of Commons Bills affecting Middle Temple, 1855–1958; Inns of Court Regiment, 1896–1959.

Major collections: A small number of deposited records, mainly letters patent, registrations of arms and collections of papers pertaining to prominent lawyers, including Sir Alexander Cockburn, QC, mid-19th century; A.M. Sullivan, KC, 1919; John Dunning, Lord Ashburton, 1768; Lord Diplock, 1948–56; Helena Normanton, KC, 1948.

Correspondence of Samuel Annesley, East India Company, Surat, 1695–97.

The library holds MSS (mostly law case notes and judgements) by Sir George Treby (?1644–1700), Charles Butler (1750–1832), Sir Soulden Laurence (1751–1814), Sir Vicary Gibbs (1751–1820), John Scott, Earl of Eldon (1751–1838), and Sir Henry Dampier (1758–1816).

Non-manuscript material: Plans and architectural drawings including those by Sir Christopher Wren, 1680; H.J. Wadling, 1903; Sir Aston Webb, 1924; Clyde Young, 1946–7; Sir Edward Maufe, RA, 1950–58.

Large illustration collection relating to the Inn and its members and to Temple Church.

Video (taken from nitrate film), with soundtrack, of the Inns of Court during the blitz.

Finding aids: Most of the archive is catalogued; catalogues will be sent to NRA when listing is completed.

Facilities: Photocopying by approval of the Archivist. Photography on payment of a disturbance fee.

Conservation: Conservation programme being undertaken by a part-time paper conservator. Specific repairs also contracted out.

698 Middlesex Hospital Archives Department

Parent organisation: University College London Hospitals

Address: Mortimer Street, London W1T 3AA

Telephone: (020) 7636 8333 ext. 4498

Fax: (020) 7380 9264

Enquiries: Mr Martin Sturridge

Open: Mon–Fri: 9.00–5.00.

Access: By written application only; an appointment is essential. There is closure on some records depending on the date.

Historical background: The Middlesex Hospital was founded in 1745. The Hospital for Women, Soho Square, was founded in 1842. St Luke's Woodside, Psychiatric Hospital, was founded in 1751 and houses its own records. The other collections were brought together in 1971.

Acquisitions policy: To strengthen the existing collection of written, printed and photographic records relating to the Middlesex Hospital and illustrating its work and organisation since its foundation in 1745.

Archives of organisation: Middlesex Hospital: Board of Governors' minutes, 1748–1975; Medical Committee minutes, 1851– ; admissions registers, 1747– ; lying-in registers, 1747–1829; case notes, 1855– ; register of surgeons' pupils and house surgeons, 1763– ; physicians' pupils, 1766– ; register of refugee French clergy, 1789–1814; hospital reports, 1820–1940 (incomplete); register of nurses, 1867– .

Hospital for Women: reports, 1843–1940; Committee of Management minutes, 1843–1939.

Non-manuscript material: Numerous photographs, etchings, portraits, maps and some film. Pamphlets.

Finding aids: List and indexes in course of revision.

699 Ministry of Defence

A Admiralty Library

Address: Mezzanine 3, 3–5 Great Scotland Yard, London SW1A 2HW

Telephone: (020) 7218 5445

Enquiries: The Admiralty Librarian, Miss J.M. Wraight

Open: By appointment only.

Access: Generally open to the public. As there are only two staff, and visitors from outside MoD must be escorted at all times, the number of visitors and hours of opening may be restricted.

Historical background: The library served the information needs of the Admiralty from c1809–1964, but following the creation of the Ministry of Defence in that year it became the Library of the Navy Board, administered by the Naval Historical Branch. Upon moving to Great Scotland Yard, the library was temporarily absorbed within the MoD Whitehall Library, but was returned to the Naval Historical Branch in 1996, and reverted to its original title of Admiralty Library. Because of pressure on space in London, the collections have now been divided into three. The Admiralty Library retains works on operations, policy, doctrine, strategy, tactics, administration, gunnery, naval aviation, and prize law. Atlases, maps, charts, and works on hydrography, geography, voyages, navigation, seamanship, astronomy, and allied subjects, are currently in the care of the UK Hydrographic Office in Taunton (entry 1162). Works on personnel, social history, military history, courts martial, the mercantile marine, naval architecture, engineering, fuel, sciences, medicine and law are housed with the library of the Royal Naval Museum in Portsmouth (entry 1041).

Major collections: An important collection of signal books is retained in London. Most other manuscripts have been placed either in Taunton or Portsmouth, according to their subject matter. The Royal Naval Museum holds the papers of Admiral John Arbuthnot Fisher, covering the period 1898–1918; Alfred C. Dewar papers relating to his work with the Naval Intelligence Division, 1917–18, and Historical Section, 1919–48; and Admiral Sir Henry Bradwardine Jackson, private papers whilst First Sea Lord, 1915–16.

Non-manuscript material: Monographs, atlases, maps and pamphlets.

Finding aids: Various lists and indexes. A union catalogue is in process of preparation, and corrections and additions will be sent to the NRA.

Facilities: Photocopying. Photography. Microfilm/fiche readers.

Conservation: The UK Hydrographic Office has its own conservator. Other work contracted out.

B Information and Library Service

Address: Whitehall, London SW1A 2HW

Telephone: (020) 7218 5446 (enquiries)

Fax: (020) 7218 8210

Enquiries: The Chief Librarian, MoD, Mr Richard Searle

Historical background: The MoD Whitehall opened in its newly refurbished building in 1989. The emphasis on the historical work of the library has declined in recent years and it is now essentially a working collection geared to current information needs. Almost all archival material formerly held in the Library has now been transferred to the Public Record Office (see entry 1058) or other public collections.

700 Moravian Church Archive and Library

Parent organisation: Moravian Church in Great Britain and Ireland

Address: Moravian Church House, 5–7 Muswell Hill, London N10 3TJ

Telephone: (020) 8883 3409/1912

Fax: (020) 8365 3371

E-mail: archive@moravianchurch.freeserve.co.uk

Website: www.moravian.org.uk

Enquiries: The Archivist, Paul Blewitt

Open: Mon, Tues: 10.00–4.30; by appointment only. Where possible, records needed for consultation should be ordered in advance.

Access: Access is free to anyone with an interest in the church and its history, by appointment with, and the consent of, the Archivist.

Historical background: The Moravian Church is the oldest established Protestant church in the world and the first English congregation settled in London in 1742. The church started its missionary work in 1732 and the library and archive contain records relating to both the church in Britain and missionary activities in the UK and overseas.

Acquisitions policy: To maintain the archives and library of the church.

Archives of organisation: Records of the Moravian Church in the British Province (UK), 1742–, including General Synod, congregational material and records of the churches' missionary activities overseas.

Major collections: Collection of diaries and MSS, including correspondence of John Wesley (1703–91) and Charles Wesley (1707–88) with James Hutton (1715–95).

Non-manuscript material: Plans and maps, including those of Moravian settlements built in the UK; illustrations and photographs. Copies of Periodical Accounts, communications from missionaries working abroad, 1790– . Collection of books on the history of the church and Moravian theology; collection of hymn books, 18th century– .

Finding aids: Catalogue in progress.

Facilities: Photocopying. Photography and microfilming by arrangement.

Conservation: Contracted out.

701 Morden College Archives

Address: 19 St Germans Place, London SE3 0PW

Telephone: (020) 8858 3365 ext. 228

Fax: (020) 8293 4887

Enquiries: The Archivist and Librarian, Mrs Elizabeth Wiggans

Open: By arrangement only.

Access: Researchers, by appointment arranged on application to the Clerk to the Trustees.

Historical background: The archives department holds administrative records from the foundation of the charity in 1695 and other documents relating to its endowment, the Manor of Old Court.

Acquisitions policy: To maintain the archives.

Archives of organisation: Minute books, 1708– . Early account books, 1705– . Maps, plans and expired leases relating to the college estates. Deeds relating to the appointment of trustees. Documents relating to the admission of members.

Major collections: Charles Kelsall (1782–1857): sketch books, architectural drawings, literary works.

Non-manuscript material: Plans, prints, drawings, photographs, maps.

Finding aids: Database in course of compilation.

Facilities: Photocopying.

Conservation: Contracted out.

Publications: H. Lansdell: *Princess Aelfrida's Charity* (1911–15) [7 parts plus index]; history of the college.
P. Joyce: *Patronage and Poverty in Merchant Society: the History of Morden College , Blackheath* (1982).
Morden College: a Brief Guide and Handbook (6/1995).

702 Mothers' Union

Address: The Mary Sumner House, 24 Tufton Street, London SW1P 3RB

Telephone: (020) 7222 5533

Fax: (020) 7222 1591

E-mail: mu@themothersunion.org

Website: www.themothersunion.org

Enquiries: The Consultant Archivist, Dr Cordelia Moyse

Open: By arrangement.

Access: Members of the Mothers' Union and bona fide researchers. There is a general 30-year closure rule, although this may vary in certain cases.

Historical background: The Mothers' Union (MU) was started in England in 1876 by Mary Sumner, wife of an Anglican clergyman. She wished to enable mothers to fulfil their responsibility for the material and spiritual well-being of their children. The union quickly grew outside the British Isles, taking root throughout the British Empire. Today it has 750,000 members world-wide, committed to supporting the family through prayer and practical action both locally and globally. The MU has played an important role in the political and religious life of many countries.

Acquisitions policy: To maintain the archives of the union: there is an active records management programme.

Archives of organisation: Minutes and correspondence of committees and departments, 1893– .

Non-manuscript material: Mothers' Union photographs and publications including its journals: *Mothers' Union Journal, Mothers in Council, Workers' Papers, Mothers' Union News* and *Home and Family*

Finding aids: Catalogue. Card index to executive committee and central council minutes.

Facilities: Photocopying by arrangement.

703 Museum in Docklands

Parent organisation: Museum of London

Address: Unit C14, Poplar Business Park, 10 Prestons Road, London E14 9RL

Telephone: (020) 7515 1162

Fax: (020) 7538 0209

E-mail: docklands@museum-london.org.uk

Website: www.museumoflondon.org.uk

Enquiries: The Librarian, Mr R. Aspinall

Open: Mon, Tues, Thurs: 2.00–6.00; Wed, Fri: 9.00–5.00, strictly by prior telephone appointment.

Access: Generally open to the public, students and researchers, strictly by appointment with the Librarian.

Historical background: The Museum of London began collecting material relating to London's docklands, with the assistance of the Port of London Authority (PLA), in the 1970s. In 1985 discussions between the two institutions resulted in the PLA's library and archives being deposited with the museum for curatorial purposes. Until then, this was the largest collection of business records in the UK outside a museum or record office.

Acquisitions policy: To maintain and consolidate the collections relating to the Port of London and London's docklands.

Major collections: Port of London Authority archives, 1770– , including minute books of London dock companies and Thames navigation authorities, and departmental records of PLA administration, 1909– .
British Ports Association archives, 1911–70.
Registers of vessels licensed to operate on the tidal River Thames, 1890–1950.

Non-manuscript material: Newspaper cuttings *re* all events in the docks, including strikes, 1889–1960s.
Photographs, including dock activities, riverside and aerial views, 1865–1970 (c20,000).
Films and videos, 1924–70.
Engineering and architectural drawings of docks, 1805–1970s (20,000).
Expanding collection on the regeneration of Docklands, 1981– , drawn from a wide variety of sources.

Finding aids: Catalogues and indexes for PLA and BPA archives and newspaper cuttings collection. Computer list of dock company employees, 1800–1909. See also NRA 25615.

Facilities: Photocopying. Photography by arrangement.

Conservation: Contracted out.

Publications: M. Chrimes: 'Drawing on the Past', *New Civil Engineer* (19 May 1988), 26 [gives details of engineering drawings].
R. Aspinall: 'Liquid History: the Archives of the Port of London Authority', in M.V. Roberts (ed.) *Archives and the Metropolis* (1998), 185–8 [describes the collections].

704 Museum of London

Address: 150 London Wall, London EC2Y 5HN

Telephone: (020) 7600 3699 ext. 221

Fax: (020) 7600 1058

E-mail: sbrooks@museumoflondon.org.uk

Website: www.museumoflondon.org.uk

Enquiries: The Library Officer, Ms Sally Brooks

Open: By appointment.

Access: Bona fide researchers.

Historical background: The Museum of London was opened in 1976, created by the amalgamation of two major collections, the Guildhall Museum of the City of London (1826–1975) and the London Museum (1911–75). The archaeological archive and printed ephemera store are managed separately from the library.

Acquisitions policy: The museum collects, conserves and records evidence relating to the development of London and to life in London from earliest times. Documentary evidence is excluded unless it falls within one of the following categories: records created by the museum or by others (individuals or societies) in the course of research on London; material relating to or illuminating aspects of the existing object-collections. Archives which form an integral part of an object-collection are acquired.

Archives of organisation: Archives of the Guildhall and London museums, c1908–75.

Major collections: The Young MSS: commonplace books, household accounts and letters of the Young family of Limehouse (family of G.F. Young, shipbuilder), 1736–1862.
Whitefriars Glass Company archives, 1680–1980.
Suffragette Collection, 1800– , including, Women's Social and Political Union Archive and the research papers of David Mitchell, author of *The Fighting Pankhursts.*
Miscellaneous deeds, letters etc, 15th century– .
Archaeological Archive: site records of archaeological excavations in the City, 1930s– ; miscellaneous other site records from other parts of Greater London.

Non-manuscript material: Tangye Collection, contemporary printed works and some MSS of Civil War/Commonwealth period.
W.G. Bell Collection, similar collection of material concerning the Plague and Fire of London.
London guide books, 18th century– .
Maps and plans of London, 1553–1994.
Printed Ephemera Collection: includes trade cards, 16th century– ; valentines, 19th century; material from London pleasure gardens and theatres, 18th–20th centuries.
Historic photograph collection, 1840s– .
Prints, drawings and paintings of London.

Finding aids: Indexes and catalogues to the collections.

Facilities: Photocopying. Photography. Microfilm/fiche reader/printer.

Conservation: Limited in-house facilities; some work contracted out.

Publications: F. Sheppard: *The Treasury of London's Past: an Historical Account of the Museum of London and its Predecessors, the Guildhall Museum and the London Museum* (London, 1991).

705 Musicians' Union

Address: Union Headquarters, 60–62 Clapham Road, London SW9 0JJ

Telephone: (020) 7582 5566

Fax: (020) 7582 9805

E-mail: info@musiciansunion.org.uk

Website: www.musiciansunion.org.uk

Enquiries: The General Secretary, Derek Kay

Open: By arrangement.

Access: Bona fide scholars, by appointment.

Historical background: The Manchester Musical Artistes' Protective Association, 1874–6 (a branch of a similar organisation in London), and the Birmingham Orchestral Association, 1874–8, were forerunners of the Amalgamated Musicians' Union established in Manchester in 1893. In 1921 this merged with the National Union of Professional Orchestral Musicians and adopted its present name.

Acquisitions policy: To maintain its archives.

Archives of organisation: Manchester Musical Artistes' Protection Association minutes, 1874–6. Musicians' Union Executive Committee minutes, 1894– , and Glasgow Branch minutes, 1902– .
Rules, 1894– (incomplete), and membership records, c1930– .
Reports and Journals, 1895– .

Finding aids: NRA 9877.

Publications: E.S. Teale: 'The Story of the Amalgamated Musicians' Union', *Musicians' Journal* (1929–30) [4 articles].

706 National Army Museum

Address: Royal Hospital Road, London SW3 4HT

Telephone: (020) 7730 0717 ext. 2222

Fax: (020) 7823 6573

E-mail: info@national-army-museum.ac.uk

Website: www.national-army-museum.ac.uk

Enquiries: The Head of Archives, Photographs, Film and Sound, Dr P.B. Boyden

Open: Tues–Sat: 10.00–4.30.
Closed last two weeks in October.

Access: By reader's ticket, which must be obtained in advance.

Historical background: The museum developed from the collections of the Royal Military Academy, Sandhurst (entry 162), which provided museum facilities for relics of the pre-partition Indian Army and the Irish regiments disbanded in 1922. In 1960 the National Army Museum was established by royal charter. The museum moved to purpose-built premises in Chelsea in 1971, an extension to which was opened in 1980.

Acquisitions policy: The acquisition by gift and purchase of collections of private, regimental and business archives relating to the history of the British Army, the Indian Army to 1947, and British colonial land forces to relevant independence dates.

Major collections: Papers of Gen. Lord Rawlinson of Trent (1864–1925); Gen. Sir James Outram (1803–63); Gen. Sir Aylmer Hunter-Weston (1864–1940); Lt.-Gen. Sir William Inglis (1763–1837); Maj.-Gen. Sir Clement Milward (1877–1951); FM Lord Birdwood (1865–1951); FM Sir George Nugent (1757–1849); Lt.- Gen. Robert Ballard Long (1771–1825); Gen. Lord Chelmsford (1827–1905); Gen. Lord Raglan (1788–1855) and Gen. Sir William Codrington (1804–84) *re* Crimean war; 1st Marquis of Anglesey (1768–1854), as Colonel of 7th Hussars; FM Lord Roberts (1832–1914); FM Viscount Gough (1779–1869); Gen. Sir Frederick Haines (1812–1909); Gen. Sir Henry Warre (1819–98); Lt.-Gen. Reginald Savory (1894–1980); Gen. Sir Roy Bucher (1895–1980); FM Lord Harding of Petherton (1896–1989); Maj.-Gen. Sir Edmund Hakewill Smith (1896–1986); Brig. Peter Young (1915–88); Sir A.F. Andrew N. Thorne (1885–1970); Lt.-Gen. Sir Gerald Ellison (1861–1947); Prof. H. Spenser Wilkinson (1853–1937); Brig. Gen. J.E. Gough (1871–1915); F.M. Lord Combermere (1773–1865) and others.

Regimental records of Middlesex Regiment, Womens' Royal Army Corps (and predecessors), Surrey Yeomanry, 4th Battalion London Regiment, and various Indian Army units.
Business archives of some military tailors.
Tidworth Tattoo records, 1920–39; United Service Club records, 1815–1970.

Non-manuscript material: Prints and drawings, including the Crookshank Collection of British military campaigns and the Cambridge Collection of British military costumes (*c*25,000).
Albums (*c*1000) and photographs (*c*400,000).
Printed books (*c*40,000).
Oral history interviews (*c*400) and sound discs of military music (*c*2000).
Small collection of privately shot cine film.

Finding aids: Card catalogue for pre-1984 accessions; more recent additions on microfiche catalogue and computer database. Lists and calendars of large collections. Lists sent to NRA.

Facilities: Photography. Photocopying. Microfiche/film reader.

Conservation: Facilities available in-house.

Publications: Articles on the collections in the archives appear in the *Annual Report* and *Yearbook*.
P.B. Boyden: 'The National Army Museum Archive Collection, 1960–1985', *Journal of the Society of Archivists*, viii/1 (1986), 23–9.

707 National Council of Women of Great Britain

Address: 36 Danbury Street, London N1 8JU

Telephone: (020) 7354 2395

Fax: (020) 7354 9214

E-mail: ncwgb@danburystreet.freeserve.co.uk

Website: www.ncwgb.org

Enquiries: The Office Manager

Open: Mon–Fri: 9.00–5.00, by appointment only.

Access: Bona fide researchers, with a letter of introduction and a prior appointment.

The National Council of Women, a leading women's organisation, was founded in 1895 to bring together women working to improve the quality of life. It soon developed into an organization promoting views and the exchange of information and ideas of women. It has attracted many prominent women, and speakers at its first conference included Beatrice Webb (1858–1913) and Millicent Fawcett (1849–1927). Archives, including branch records, 1895–1980, are held by London Metropolitan Archives (see entry 688) and a catalogue is available. The NCW still holds conference reports, yearbooks and house magazines.

708 National Gallery Archive

Address: Trafalgar Square, London WC2N 5DN

Telephone: (020) 7747 2831

Fax: (020) 7747 2892

E-mail: lad@ng-london.org.uk

Website: www.nationalgallery.org.uk

Enquiries: The Archivist, Isobel Hunter

Open: Mon–Fri: 9.30–5.30.

Access: Bona fide researchers.

Historical background: The National Gallery, founded in 1824, houses the national collection of European painting dating from the mid-13th to the early 20th century. The archive is recognised as a place of deposit for public records.

Acquisitions policy: To collect, by purchase, gift or deposit, material related to the National Gallery and the people associated with it.

Archives of organisation: Records of the activities of the National Gallery, 1824– , including minutes, correspondence, photographs, plans, publications and press cuttings.

Major collections: Correspondence of Sir Abraham Hume and Giovanni Maria Sasso, 1787–1805.
Note-books of Sir Charles Eastlake (1793–1865), 1852–64, and his correspondence with Jeremiah Harman, 1821–5.
Diaries of Otto Mündler, 1855–8.
Correspondence of Sir William Boxall, 1848–78; and of Ellis Waterhouse, 1925–56.
Papers of Ralph Nicholson Wornum, 1812–77.

Finding aids: Basic lists of most of the collection; some detailed lists and indexes.

Facilities: Limited photocopying. Photography of some material permitted. Microfilm reader/printer.

709 National Institute for Social Work
Dame Eileen Younghusband Collection

Address: 5–7 Tavistock Place, London WC1H 9SN

Telephone: (020) 7387 9681

Fax: (020) 7387 7968

E-mail: info@nisw.org.uk

Website: www.nisw.org.uk

Enquiries: The Librarian

Open: Mon–Fri: 9.30–5.30.

Access: Bona fide research students; a letter of application and an appointment are essential; certain materials are restricted.

The institute was started in 1961 by Eileen Louise Younghusband (1902–81), a pioneer in social work, and on her death it accepted her extensive collection of papers (NRA 24768). Information about the institute's own archives is not available.

710 National Maritime Museum

Address: Romney Road, Greenwich, London SE10 9NF

Telephone: (020) 8858 4422

Fax: (020) 8312 6632

Website: ww.nmm.ac.uk

Enquiries: The Curator of Manuscripts, Mr Duncan Harting

Open: Mon–Fri: 10.00–5.00; Sat: 10.00–1.00, 2.00–5.00; prior arrangement is necessary. Closed 3rd week in February.

Access: By reader's ticket, issued to prospective readers who can prove their identity. Access to certain items, including the museum's archives, is restricted.

Historical background: The museum was formally established by Act of Parliament in 1934 for the instruction and study of the maritime history of Great Britain and opened in 1937. The MS collections began to be assembled before this date. The museum is recognised as a place of deposit for public records. The Information Access Section of the museum's

Maritime Information Centre is responsible for MSS.

Acquisitions policy: To collect, by purchase, gift or deposit, MSS relating to British maritime affairs.

Archives of organisation: Records of acquisitions, policy and management, early 1930s– , including papers of first director, Sir Geoffrey Callender.

Major collections: Admiralty, Navy Board and dockyard records, 17th–19th centuries.

Business records, including P&O and subsidiary companies; Lloyd's Register Surveys, c1833– c1964; Shipbuilders and Repairers National Association, c1889–1977; Marine Society, 1756–1977.

Personal papers: c300 collections, including Edward Hawke (1705–81); Lord Hood (1724–1816); Viscount Nelson (1758–1805); Matthew Flinders (1774–1814); Lord Beatty (*d* 1936); Baron Chatfield (1873–1967); John Montagu, 4th Earl of Sandwich (1718–92).

Artificial collections, including the maritime papers collected by Sir Thomas Phillipps.

Items acquired singly by the museum, e.g. atlases, logs, signal books, letter- and order-books; tapes relating to seamen and shipboard life.

Non-manuscript material: Maritime Information Centre: books and pamphlets (c50,000).

Ships' Draught Collection, including the Admiralty Draught Collection.

Chart collection.

Photographic collection.

Finding aids: Lists are available for most of the collections. Index of people, places, ships and subjects. Lists sent to NRA.

Facilities: Photocopying. Photography. Microfilming. Microfilm/fiche reader.

Conservation: In-house service; outside work undertaken occasionally. Some binding contracted out.

Publications: R.J.B. Knight (ed.): *Guide to the Manuscripts in the National Maritime Museum,* i: *The Personal Collections* (1977); ii: *Public Records, Business Records and Artificial Collections* (1980).

Guide to British Naval Papers in North America.

711 National Monuments Record
London Branch

Address: NMR Public Services, 55 Blandford Street, London W1H 3AF

Telephone: (020) 7208 8200

Fax: (020) 7224 5333

E-mail: info@rchme.gov.uk

Website: www.rchme.gov.uk

Open: Tues–Fri: 10.00–5.00; an appointment is strongly advised.

Access: Generally open to the public.

The main office is at Swindon, where further information about NMR may be found (see entry 1158). Material relating to the Greater London area is held at the London Branch.

712 National Portrait Gallery
Heinz Archive and Library

Address: St Martin's Place (entrance in Orange Street), London WC2H 0HE

Telephone: (020) 7306 0055 ext. 257

Fax: (020) 7306 0056

Website: www.npg.org.uk

Enquiries: The Head of Archive and Library, Robin Francis

Open: Mon–Fri: 10.00–5.00, by appointment.

Access: Researchers in the field of portraiture who cannot find their material elsewhere.

Historical background: The National Portrait Gallery was founded in 1856. The archive and library were originally built up to aid staff in the acquisition of portraits, in the compiling of catalogues of the collection, and to help answer general enquiries. The gallery is recognised as a place of deposit for public records.

Acquisitions policy: Photographs, engravings, drawings and MSS that extend the collection of information on British portraiture are acquired by purchase and donation.

Major collections: Sketchbooks and diaries of Sir George Scharf (1820–95), first director.

Artists' sitters' books, notably Joseph Wright of Derby (1734–97), account books, and letters, including many by George Frederic Watts (1817–1904).

Collection of MSS on the history of the National Portrait Gallery and the building.

Non-manuscript material: Extensive collection of reference photographs and other reference material on portraits in collections other than the gallery's.
Portrait engravings.
Original portrait photographs and negatives (*c*150,000 items), including large collections of the work of Camille Silvy, Madame Yevonde, Howard Coster, the Bassano Studio and Cecil Beaton (1904–80).

Finding aids: Card catalogue to library and MSS. Card index of portraits. Listing of special collections.
Database of reserve collection of engravings. Handlist to Collery muniments.

Facilities: Limited photocopying. Photography.

Publications: A. Davies and E. Kilmurray: *Dictionary of British Portraiture* (1979–81) [4 vols; based on information in the archive].
K.K. Yung (comp.): *Complete Illustrated Catalogue* (1981).

713 National Scout Archive

Parent organisation: The Scout Association

Address: Baden-Powell House, Queen's Gate, London SW7 5JS

Telephone: (020) 7584 7030

Fax: (020) 7581 9953

E-mail: archives@scout.org.uk

Website: www.scoutbase.org.uk

Enquiries: The Archivist, Mr Paul Moynihan

Open: Mon–Fri:10.00–4.00, by appointment.

Access: Members of the scout movement, and other approved readers by application in writing to the Archivist.

Historical background: The Scout Association's national archive was established in 1976 to provide the movement with a reference facility covering the history of scouting and the life of its founder, Lord Baden-Powell (1857–1941).

Acquisitions policy: To receive, by gift or purchase, any relevant material.

Archives of organisation: Minute books, letters, documents and official documents of the movement, 1907– .

Some material relating to the Boer War and the Siege of Mafeking.

Major collections: Diaries, papers and original MSS of Lord Baden-Powell.
Papers and letters of Sir Percy W. Everett (1870–1952), Deputy Chief Scout, and Percy B. Nevill (1887–1975).

Non-manuscript material: Large collection of photographic items, including prints, negatives and slides relating to world scout jamborees, rover moots and scouting activities generally. Also cine and video films and sound recordings. Large collection of uniforms, badges, postcards, cigarette cards, artefacts and memorabilia.
Collection of pamphlets, secondary works and general reference works on the history of scouting.

Finding aids: General card index.

Facilities: Photocopying. Photography. Microfilm/fiche reader.

Conservation: Contracted out.

Publications: Subject fact sheets.

714 National Society for the Prevention of Cruelty to Children (NSPCC)

Address: The Library, NSPCC National Centre, 42 Curtain Road, London EC2A 3NH

Telephone: (020) 7825 2706

Fax: (020) 7825 2706

E-mail: nmalton@nspcc.org.uk

Website: www.nspcc.org.uk

Enquiries: The Archivist, Nicholas Malton

Open: Mon–Fri: 9.30–4.30.

Access: Bona fide readers. There is a 100-year closure period for any records from which children can be identified, and a 30-year closure for most unpublished administrative records. Children's legal case files are not included in the archive.

Historical background: The NSPCC was founded by Rev. Benjamin Waugh (1839–1908) in 1884, following the example of local societies in New York and Liverpool.

Acquisitions policy: Records of or directly relating to the NSPCC and of local societies that have merged into it.

Archives of organisation: National and local administrative records and annual reports.
The Society's official journals and other NSPCC publications.

Major collections: Collection of material relating to Rev. Benjamin Waugh, founder and first director.

Non-manuscript material: Photographs and films.
Collecting boxes, badges, uniforms, portraits, plaques and posters.

Finding aids: Catalogues: due to confidentiality, these are not open to public use, but it may be possible to supply researchers with lists tailored to their specific enquiry.

Facilities: Limited photocopying by permission.

715 National Trust Archives

Address: 36 Queen Anne's Gate, London SW1H 9AS

Telephone: (020) 7447 6648

Fax: (020) 7222 5097

E-mail: lddlct@smtp.ntrust.org.uk

Website: www.lddlct@smtp.ntrust.org.uk

Enquiries: The Corporate Information and Records Manager, Jonathan Whiting

Open: By appointment only.

Access: Bona fide researchers. Material will generally be available after 30 years but restrictions may be applied.

Historical background: The trust was established in 1895 and holds its own internal archives.

Acquisitions policy: Papers acquired with properties are generally family and estate papers, and are normally deposited in an appropriate local repository.

Major collections: The trust also owns papers of Rudyard Kipling (1865–1936), housed at University of Sussex library (entry 136A); family and political papers of Benjamin Disraeli (1804–81), at the Bodleian Library (entry 958); and papers of Thomas Carlyle (1795–1881), at the National Library of Scotland (entry 331).

Finding aids: Lists only.

Facilities: Photocopying.

Publications: R. Fedden: *The National Trust, Past and Present* (1974).
J. Gaze: *Figures in a Landscape: a History of the National Trust* (1988).
M. Waterson: *The National Trust: the First 100 Years* (1994).

716 Natural History Museum

Address: Cromwell Road, London SW7 5BD

Telephone: (020) 7942 5507

Fax: (020) 7942 5559

E-mail: s.snell@nhm.ac.uk

Website: www.nnm.ac.uk/info/library/index.html

Enquiries: The Archivist and Records Officer, Susan Snell

Open: Mon–Fri: 10.00–4.30.

Access: Tickets are issued (no museum admission charge applies); prior notice is required.

Historical background: The British Museum (Natural History) was established at South Kensington in 1881, having separated from the British Museum, Bloomsbury, in that year. The natural history collections date from the time of Sir Hans Sloane (1660–1753), who bequeathed his vast private collection to the nation. This formed the nucleus of the British Museum. A few important MS collections were transferred to South Kensington in 1881, but the bulk of the museum's holdings have been acquired since that date. The museum changed its name to the Natural History Museum in 1989. It is recognised as a place of deposit for public records.

Acquisitions policy: To obtain, by purchase, gift or exchange, all published and unpublished materials relevant to the work of the museum.

Archives of organisation: The museum archives comprise mostly post-1881 documents, although some departmental records go back to 1800 and a few are pre-1800. They contain reports, correspondence etc relating to the collections and the development of the museum.

Major collections: Large collections of MSS associated with the following scientists: Sir Joseph Banks (1743–1820) and his associates; Robert Brown (1773–1858); Albert C.L.G.

Günther (1830–1914); Sir John Murray (1841–1914); Sir Richard Owen (1804–92); Lionel Walter, 2nd Baron Rothschild (1868–1937); Daniel Solander (1736–82); James Sowerby (1757–1822) and later generations of the Sowerby family; Richard Meinertzhagen (1878–1967); Miles J. Berkeley (1803–89); William Jardine (1800–74); David A. Bannermann (1886–1979); John Gould (1804–81); Philipp C. Zeller (1808–83); Arthur Russell (1878–1964); William Roxburgh (1759–1815); Henry T. Stainton (1822–92); Alfred Russel Wallace (1823–1913); Edward A. Wilson (1872–1912).

Documents relating to Captain James Cook's three expeditions, 1768–71, 1772–5, 1776–80.

Non-manuscript material: Large collections of watercolour paintings, pencil sketches etc, of natural history subjects, including works by, or commissioned by, the following: Ferdinand Bauer (1760–1826); Franz Bauer (1758–1840); Thomas Baines (1822–75); Georg D. Ehret (1708–70); Thomas Hardwicke (1755–1835); Bryan H. Hodgson (1800–94); Sydney Parkinson (1745–71); John Reeves (1774–1856); John Latham (1740–1837); Alfred Waterhouse (1830–1905); Richard Owen (1804–92); George E. Lodge (1860–1954); John Abbot (1751–c1842); Eugel Terzi (d c 1944); Arthur Smith (1916–91); Thomas Watling (1762?).

Challenger voyage photographs; Indian botanical drawings; portraits of naturalists collection.

Finding aids: The automated catalogue of the museum libraries contains catalogue entries for MSS and drawings; various more detailed lists are available. Lists and indexes of the museum archives are available. An index of letters is in the course of compilation. Lists sent to NRA.

Facilities: Photocopying. Photography. Microform viewing.

Publications: W.T. Stearn: *The Natural History Museum at South Kensington* (London, 1998).

R.E.R. Banks: 'Resources for the History of Science in the Libraries of the British Museum (Natural History)', *British Journal for the History of Science*, xxi (1988), 91–7.

J.M.V. Harvey, P. Gilbert and S. Martin: *A Catalogue of Manuscripts in the Entomology Library of the Natural History Museum, London* (London, 1996).

J.C. Thackray: *A Catalogue of Manuscripts and Drawings in the General Library of the Natural History Museum, London* (London, 1995).

——: *A Catalogue of Portraits, Paintings and Sculpture at the National History Museum, London* (London, 1995).

——: *A Guide to the Official Archives of the Natural History Museum, London* (London, 1998).

717 New Church Conference Library

Parent organisation: The General Conference of the New Church

Address: Swedenborg House, 20 Bloomsbury Way, London WC1A 2TH

Telephone: (020) 7229 9340

Enquiries: The Library Secretary, Mrs Frances Fisher

Open: By arrangement.

Access: The collections may be consulted by anyone, but an appointment is necessary.

Historical background: The General Conference of the New Church is an organisation of followers of the Christian theological teaching of Emanuel Swedenborg (1688–1772), the Swedish scientist, philosopher and theologian. They first met for separate worship in 1787 and a national organisation began in 1789. The General Conference was incorporated in 1872. It is a registered charity under the Companies Act. The library was established in 1913 and is under the supervision of a library and documents committee.

Acquisitions policy: To collect as fully as possible records of New Church organisations in this country.

Archives of organisation: Minute books and similar records, with some correspondence, of the General Conference, its various committees and some related bodies, early 19th century– . Baptismal, marriage and funeral registers and minute books of individual New Church societies (congregations) in the UK. Also overseas missions records.

Non-manuscript material: Photographs of New Church buildings, meetings and individuals. Early Latin editions and English translations of the works of Emanuel Swedenborg. Many miscellaneous New Church printed pamphlets.

Finding aids: Loose-leaf catalogue of principal archives.

718 Newham Archives and Local Studies

Parent organisation: London Borough of Newham

Address: 3 The Grove, Stratford, London E15 1EL

Telephone: (020) 8430 6881

Fax: (020) 8430 6867

E-mail: r.durack@newham.gov.uk

Website: www.newham.gov.uk/leisure/libraries/local.htm

Enquiries: The Archives and Local Records Advisor, Richard Durack

Open: Mon: 1.00–5.30; Tues, Fri, Sat: 9.30–5.30; Thurs: 9.30–8.00.

Access: Generally open to the public. An appointment is necessary.

Historical background: Newham Archives and Local Studies was opened in 1978 and forms part of the Stratford Library. It moved to its current premises in 2000. The collection contains material on Essex, London and the former county boroughs of East and West Ham. A large amount of pre–20th-century material, especially official records, is in Essex Record Office (entry 228). The library is recognised as a place of deposit for public records.

Acquisitions policy: To collect materials directly related to the London Borough of Newham, the former county boroughs of East and West Ham, and Essex and London materials where relevant.

Archives of organisation: Archives of Newham Borough and its former constituent authorities. West Ham Quarter Sessions rolls, 1894–1965; manorial rolls and books, 1603–24, 1736–1922.

Major collections: Parochial and religious records: East Ham, 1809–1965; Little Ilford, 1887–1900; West Ham, 1646–1965; Newham, 1964– .
Minute and rate books of Stratford Abbey Landowners, 1715–1874.
Records of local charities, 17th–19th centuries.
Deeds and family papers: Rawstorne of Plaistow, 17th–19th centuries; Henniker of Stratford and East Ham, 17th–19th centuries.
Non-conformist records, 19th and 20th centuries.
Air Raid Precaution files relating to East and West Ham, 1939–45.

Records relating to HMS *Albion* disaster, 1898, and Silvertown Explosion, 1917, relief funds.
Jack Cornwell, VC (1900–16), papers.
James Keir Hardie, first Labour MP (South West Ham, 1892–5), letters, photographs etc.

Non-manuscript material: Newspapers and journals; newspaper cuttings, 18th–20th centuries.
Maps and surveys of East and West Ham, 1741– .
Photographs (c25,000), paintings, drawings, films, videos, sound recordings.
Microfilms of directories, electoral registers, newspapers and parish registers.
Theatre Royal, Stratford, posters, programmes.
Wanstead House scrapbooks, 19th and 20th centuries.

Finding aids: Catalogue. Various indexes.

Facilities: Photocopying. Microfilm reader/printer.

Conservation: Contracted out.

*Publications: Family History Notes.
Local Studies Notes.*

719 Newham Museum Service

Parent organisation: London Borough of Newham

Address: c/o Leisure Service Department, 292 Barking Road, London E6 3BA

Telephone: (020) 8430 2457

Fax: (020) 8430 1075

E-mail: sean.sherman@newham.gov.uk

Website: www.newham.gov.uk/leisure/museums

Enquiries: The Museum Services Manager, Sean Sherman

Open: By appointment only.

Access: Generally open to the public.

Historical background: The Newham Museum Service, formerly the Passmore Edwards Museum, was reviewed in 1994 and the collections rationalised to retain principally material relating to the London Borough of Newham: non-Newham archives have been transferred to the Essex Record Office (entry 228).

Acquisitions policy: Acquisition, by donation or purchase, of material relating to the London

Borough of Newham and any material relating to the Great Eastern Railway.

Archives of organisation: Some East and West Ham and London Borough of Newham archives.

Major collections: Great Eastern Railway records, 19th and 20th centuries.
Local manorial and industrial records, 16th century– .
Correspondence and papers of Raphael Meldola (1849–1915), chemist, 1864–1908.

Non-manuscript material: Essex Pictorial Survey (photographs and engravings).

Finding aids: Lists. Meldola: NRA 12102.

Facilities: Photocopying. Photography by arrangement.

720 News International Record Office

Parent organisation: News Corporation

Address: Archive Department, News International plc, 1 Virginia Street, London E98 1ES

Telephone: (020) 7782 6890

Fax: (020) 7782 3967

E-mail: nick.mays@newsint.co.uk

Enquiries: The Deputy Archivist, Nicholas Mays

Open: Mon–Fri: 10.00–1.00, 2.00–5.00.

Access: By prior appointment at the discretion of the Archivist. Strictly by application only, with two references taken up beforehand. Written enquiries are welcome. A 30-year closure rule is in operation. The back files of newspapers and the cuttings collections are the responsibility of the company's reference library, which is not a public library.

Historical background: News of the World Organisation Ltd was founded in 1960. The company was purchased by Rupert Murdoch in 1969 and News International Ltd was formed in 1971 under a change of name. News International plc was formed in 1982, following the purchase of Times Newspapers Limited (f. 1966) from the Thomson Organisation. It owns four titles, *The Times, The Sunday Times, News of the World* and *The Sun*; and owned *Today*, 1987–95, plus Times Supplements Ltd and HarperCollins. The company also has a holding of 40 per cent in BSkyB. *The Times* was first published as *The Daily Universal Register* in 1785 and renamed three years later. *The Sunday Times* was first published in 1821 as *The New Observer* and renamed the following year, though it has always been a separate editorial concern. *News of the World* was first published in 1843 by John Browne Bell. *The Sun* was first published in its modern form in 1969.

The archive of *The Times* was brought together in the early 1930s for the publication of the official history of the paper, though the earliest reference to the 'office archives' is in a letter written in 1899. Times Newspapers Ltd established a records management operation in 1981, which was amalgamated with the archives in 1982 to form the TNL Record Office. In 1985 the responsibilities of this department expanded to embrace the whole company, creating the News International Record Office. The records of the *Daily Herald* are not known to have survived, but its photograph archive is held by the National Museum of Photography, Film & Television (entry 123).

Acquisitions policy: The collection and preservation of all material, except press-cuttings, relevant to the company's current and past newspaper titles and the companies which have owned them.

Archives of organisation: The Times: papers of proprietors, 1785– ; editors, managers, editorial staff and correspondents, departments, subject files etc, 1840s– ; managers' letter-books (indexed), 1847–1915; marked copies of *The Times*, 1890–1966; editors' leader diaries, 1857– ; *The Times House Journal*, 1920– ; business and corporate records, 1780s– ; staff records, c1845– ; the Times Book Club, 1905–82; the Times Book Company, 1909–82.

Times Supplements: marked copies of *The Times Literary Supplement*, 1902–77; with stock books, 1909–74; editorial correspondence, 1902– (the bulk, 1958–). Marked copies of *The Times Educational Supplement*, 1910–77, and other supplements.

News of the World: corporate records, 1891–1979; property, 1920–69; staff and pension fund, 1937–80; publishers' statements and report books, 1936–84; editorial correspondence relating to features, 1930–72; plus records relating to production, advertising and promotion, circulation and distribution, publications and industrial relations.

Sunday Times: staff records, 1890– ; editorial papers, production records and advertising material, 1960– .

Today: pre-launch dummy copies and advertising material, 1986–7.

Major collections: The Times: Walter family papers, 1785–1968; Lord Northcliffe (1865–1922), papers, 1908–22; John Thadeus Delane (1817–79), correspondence, 1841–77; William Stebbing (1831–1926), papers, 1868–1926; George Earle Buckle (1854–1935), papers, 1884–1935, Geoffrey Dawson (1874–1944), papers, 1912–41; Henry Wickham Steed (1871–1956), papers, 1896–1922; Charles Moberly Bell (1847–1911), papers, 1889–1911; Sir William Howard Russell (1820–1907), diaries, 1854–1904, and correspondence, 1844–1903; Sir James Richard Thursfield (1840–1923), papers, 1878–22; Ralph Deakin (1888–1952), papers, 1921–52; letters from Winston Churchill (1874–1965), 1898–1954 (43).

Sunday Times: Denis Hamilton (1918–88), papers, 1940s–1966; Harold Evans (*b* 1928), papers, 1967–81.

News of the World: Derek Jameson (*b* 1929), papers, 1981–4.

The Sun: Politicians' Complaints Commission papers.

Non-manuscript material: Books and pamphlets by or about all titles, or written by staff correspondents, the majority relating to *The Times* (c2500 items). More than 1000 reels of microfilm, mainly marked copies of *The Times*, its supplements and its press-cuttings books. Significant collections of artefacts, paintings, posters, drawings, cartoons, photographs, videos, films, audio tapes and CD-ROMS are also held.

The Jack Hill newspaper collection and library: c2000 newspapers, 1640s–1990s (150 books).

Finding aids: Computer indexes and catalogues; card indexes; lists sent to NRA.

Facilities: Photocopying. Microfilm reader.

Conservation: Contracted out.

Publications: History of the Times, 1785–1981, 6 vols (1935–93).

H. Hobson: *The Pearl of Days: an Intimate Memoir of The Sunday Times, 1822–1972* (1972).

G. Phillips: 'The Archives of *The Times*' *Business Archives,* 41 (1976).

C. Bainbridge and R. Stockdill: *The News of the World Story, 1843–1993* (1993).

News International: *From the Archives* (web publication, 2000).

721 Order of St John Library and Museum

Address: St John's Gate, Clerkenwell, London EC1M 4DA

Telephone: (020) 7253 6644

Fax: (020) 7490 8835

Enquiries: The Curator

Open: Mon–Fri: 10.00–5.00, by arrangement.

Access: Generally open to the public, by appointment.

Historical background: The collection was started after the establishment of the Venerable Order of St John in 1831 and more particularly after the acquisition in 1874 of St John's Gate, where the collection is housed. St John's Gate and Priory Church are the remains of the priory of the medieval Order of St John, dissolved in 1540. The museum was opened to the public on a regular basis in 1978. The British Royal Order of Chivalry runs two major charitable foundations, St John Ambulance and St John Ophthalmic Hospital.

Acquisitions policy: Material relevant to the history of the Knights of St John, the Most Venerable Order and the charitable foundations, by purchase and donation.

Archives of organisation: MS records of the Order of St John, including documents relating to British properties, and estates in France, Malta and Rhodes, 1140– (c5000).

Records relating to the foundation of St John Ambulance and its activities in various wars, including Zulu, Boer and World Wars I and II, 1860s– .

Records of the St John Ophthalmic Hospital, Jerusalem.

Non-manuscript material: Prints and drawings collection. Photographs and glass negatives.

Pamphlets and books relating to the Order of St John, 15th–20th centuries.

Coins: Crusader and Order of St John (including the King, Wilkinson and Sprawson collections).

St John Ambulance collections.

Finding aids: Catalogue and handlists. Indexes. Lists sent to NRA.

Facilities: Photocopying. Photography.

Publications: The Early Statutes of the Knights Hospitallers (1932).
The Thirteenth-Century Statutes of the Knights Hospitallers (1933).
Six Documents relating to Queen Mary's Restoration of the Grand Priories of England and Ireland (1935).
Notes on the History of the Library and Museum (1945).
J. Toffoto: *Image of a Knight* (1988).
P. Willis: *Brief History of the Order of St John.*
Mason and Willis: *Maps of Malta* (1989).
Knights of St John in Essex (1992).

722 Palestine Exploration Fund

Address: 2 Hinde Mews, Marylebone Lane, London W1M 5RR

Telephone: (020) 7935 5379

Fax: (020) 7486 7438

E-mail: pefund@compuserve.com

Enquiries: The Executive Secretary, Dr R. Chapman

Open: Mon–Fri: 10.00–5.00, by appointment.

Access: Subscribers and bona fide researchers, by prior arrangement.

Historical background: The fund was established in 1865 as a non-political, non-sectarian learned society, and supports research in all areas of the study of the geographical area now occupied by Israel, Jordan and neighbouring countries.

Acquisitions policy: To maintain the archives and acquire the papers of individuals associated with the fund.

Archives of organisation: Records of the fund, including reports of Jewish excavations, 1865–6, 1867–70; and other excavations, 1860s–1930s; Survey of Western Palestine, 1871–7; and Survey of Eastern Palestine.

Major collections: Papers, including those of Edward Henry Palmer (1840–82); Sir Walter Besant, secretary of PEF, 1868–86; Prof. T. Hayter Lewis, 1870s–1890s; William Flinders Petrie (1853–1942); and documents by and relating to Gen. Sir Charles Warren (1840–1928), Maj.-Gen. Sir Charles Wilson (1836–1905), FM Lord Kitchener of Khartoum (1850–1916) and T.E. Lawrence 'of Arabia' (1888–1935).

Field and study records of excavations of Dr Duncan Mackenzie (1861–1934); Prof. J. Garstang (1876–1936), Olga Tufnell (1904–85) and others.

Non-manuscript material: Photographs, 19th and early 20th century, Palestine, Lebanon, Syria, and Trans-Jordan, places, landscapes, people, antiquities, etc.
MSS maps of Palestine, including the fund's Survey of Western Palestine MSS and the surviving MSS of the map of Lt. C.W.M. Van de Velde, RE.
Archaeological and ethnographic artefacts.
Paintings and drawings, including a selection of the 'Simpson Watercolours' focusing on the exploration of underground Jerusalem by Gen. Sir Charles Warren (1867–70).
Collection of rare and antiquarian books relating in particular to early travel and exploration in the Levant.

Finding aids: Detailed list: NRA 16370.

Facilities: Photocopying.

Conservation: Contracted out.

Publications: Occasional monograph series covering various specialist topics of study falling within the region of interest (available for purchase).
Palestine Exploration Quarterly [biannual journal].

723 Performing Right Society Archives

Parent organisation: MCPS-PRS Alliance

Address: 29/33 Berners Street, London W1P 4AA

Telephone: (020) 7306 4660 (direct line)

Fax: (020) 7306 4050

E-mail: jhodgetts@prs.co.uk

Enquiries: The Information Security Manager, Jonathan Hodgetts

Open: Private business archive, access by appointment only.

Access: Academic researchers and historians by prior appointment. Access will usually be restricted to public and non-confidential documents. Prior permission may have to be obtained for access to members' personal files.

Historical background: The PRS was formed in 1914 to represent composers and publishers of music in the collection of royalties from public performances of their music. Most British composers in the 20th century were members of PRS. Through reciprocal agreements with overseas affiliated societies, PRS collects royalties for music from around the world performed in UK territories. In 1998 the MCPS (Mechanical Copyright Protection Society) and PRS formed an alliance to jointly administer their rights. The PRS established a Records Management Department in 1992 to manage the society's extensive records. Since then an archive has been established, consisting mostly of material held by the Secretarial and Membership Departments.

Acquisitions policy: To maintain the archives of the PRS.

Archives of organisation: Formation papers; board minutes; contracts; directors' reports and accounts; correspondence files, 1914– , including all composer and publisher members, associated organisations, broadcasters, overseas agents and affiliated societies; internal reports and memoranda; in-house publications.

Non-manuscript material: Performing Right News, 1922– .

Facilities: Photocopying.

Publications: C. Ehrlich: *Harmonious Alliance* (OUP, 1989).

724 Polish Institute and Sikorski Museum
Archives Department

Address: 20 Princes Gate, London SW7 1PT

Telephone: (020) 7589 9249

Enquiries: The Keeper of Archives, Andrzej Suchcitz

Open: Tues–Fri: 9.30–4.00.

Access: All bona fide researchers; there are restrictions on certain deposited collections.

Historical background: The institute was founded in 1945 as the General Sikorski Historical Institute, and took its present name in 1966 after amalgamating with the Polish Research Centre. The institute's archives contain the largest collection outside Poland of primary sources concerning that country, with special emphasis on World War II. The documents in the institute's archives do not concern only Polish history and related subjects, nor are

they exclusively in Polish. Researchers will also find sources relating to international politics in general, and to Central and East European affairs in particular.

Acquisitions policy: To acquire, by donation or deposit, material relevant to the history of Poland and her citizens.

Major collections: Records of Polish Civil Service, including the Chancellery of the President of Poland, the Polish National Council, the Council of Ministers, ministries, embassies, legations and consulates, 1939–49; Polish armed forces, including army, navy and air force, 1939–47.

Papers of the Polish government in exile, 1945–90.

Private and subject collections(c575), including those of Gen. Władysław Sikorski (1881–1943), soldier and statesman; Gen. Władysław Anders (1892–1970); Count Edward Raczynski (1891–1993), diplomat; Tadeusz Romer (1894–1978), diplomat; Joseph Heironym Retinger (1888–1960), political adviser; Adam Ciołkosz (1901–78), politician and writer; Jan Ciechanowski (1887–1973), diplomat; Count Jan Szembek (1881–1945), diplomat; Stanisław Kot (1888–1975), professor of literature and politician.

Non-manuscript material: Film, photographs, maps, paintings and engravings, 15th–19th centuries.
Military memorabilia.

Finding aids: General index to all collections. Register of subject files to most collections.

Facilities: Photocopying. Microfilm reader.

Publications: Guide to the Archives of the Polish and Sikorski Museum, i (London, 1985).

725 Polish Library

Parent organisation: Polish Social and Cultural Association

Address: 238–246 King Street, London W6 0RF

Telephone: (020) 8741 0474

Fax: (020) 8746 3798

E-mail: polish.library@mailbox.ulcc.ac.uk

Website: ourworld.compuserve.com/homepages/posk_polish_cent

Enquiries: The Librarian, Dr Z. Jagodzinski

Open: Mon, Wed: 10.00–8.00; Fri: 10.00–5.00; Sat: 10.00–1.00.

Access: Generally open to readers, students, scholars and researchers, subject to the rules and regulations of the library.

Historical background: The Polish Library was established in 1942 by the Ministry of Education of the Polish government in exile. Between 1948 and 1953 the library became part of the Polish University College in London. It was subsidised by the Committee for the Education of Poles until 1977. In 1967 the newly formed Polish Social and Cultural Association took over the responsibility for the upkeep of the library as a legal owner on behalf of the Polish community in the UK. Funds were raised to build a centre at 238–246 King Street, Hammersmith, where eventually the Polish Library was transferred in 1977.

Acquisitions policy: To collect and preserve records of literary, cultural, social and political activities of Poles abroad. To propagate the use of the unique archival resources which the library amassed during the first period of its development and provide an infrastructure to match the international research importance of its collections.

Major collections: Genealogical archives of Poles in the UK, 1830– .

Private diaries, biographical materials, literary works, diploma works of Polish writers, scholars, politicians and artists in the UK and abroad, including papers of Joseph Heironym Retinger (1888–1960), politician; Joseph Conrad (1858–1924); Kazimierz Wierzyński, poet (1894–1969); Sergiusz Piasecki (1899–1964), writer; Bolesław Boyom Szcześniak, publicist, researcher.

Archives of the Joseph Conrad Society; Polish Solidarity Campaign; Union of Polish Artists in the UK; Federation of Polish Medical Organizations abroad.

Non-manuscript material: Large collection of Anglo-Polonica, pamphlets, photographs, maps, engravings and books.

Press archives of the Polish Socialist Party in the UK and *Fighting Poland.*

More than 3800 titles of periodicals and extensive collection of Solidarnosc and underground materials, 1976–90.

Finding aids: Inventory books. Joseph Conrad: NRA 15220. OPAC database.

Facilities: Photocopying.

Conservation: Minimal amount contracted out.

Publications: Polish Library, 1942–1992 [for 50th anniversary].

726 Post Office Heritage Services

Parent organisation: Consignia plc

Address: Freeling House, Phoenix Place, Mount Pleasant Complex, London EC1X 0DL (entrance in Phoenix Place)

Telephone: (020) 7239 2570

Fax: (020) 7239 2576

E-mail: mmartin.rush@postoffice.co.uk

Website: www.consignia.com/heritage

Enquiries: The Archives Manager, Mr Martin Rush

Open: Mon–Fri: 9.00–4.15.

Access: Generally open to the public; proof of identity is required.

Historical background: The General Post Office (GPO) was founded by royal proclamation in 1635, and at first operated on a farming basis. Its public records date from 1677, and these were being administered as a public archive by 1890. The Heritage Services holds all the archives of the GPO, including those on broadcasting, the Post Office Savings Bank, and some on telecommunications, up to 1969 when the Post Office was established as a public corporation.

The National Postal Museum was established on the initiative of R. M. Phillips, who donated his stamp collection to the Post Office in 1965. It was administratively amalgamated with P.O. archives in 1996 to form a business unit, P.O. Heritage Services, now part of the renamed Consignia plc.

Heritage Services is recognised as a place of deposit for the organisation's public records.

Alliance and Leicester Girobank (entry 117) and British Telecom (entry 544) are now separate organisations, with their own archives units.

Acquisitions policy: Through the operations of its records centre, to maintain the archive and ensure its completeness from 1969. All aspects of the development of Post Office operations and services are covered, wherever these occur.

Archives of organisation: Administrative records reflecting all aspects of Post Office operations and services, at home and overseas, and employee records, late 17th century– .

Major collections: Papers of Sir Roger Whitley, Deputy Postmaster-General, 1672–77; John Palmer (1742–1818), Surveyor and Comptroller of Mails, 1788–1813; Sir Rowland Hill (1795–1879), Secretary to the Post Office, 1836–79; and Sir William Preece (1834–1913), Engineer-in-Chief, 1854–1913.

Correspondence of the De La Rue Company, stamp printers, 1855–1955 (available on microfilm).

The R.M. Phillips Collection of British stamps and related material, 1837–1901 (available on microfilm).

The Frank Staff postal history collection.

Non-manuscript material: Portraits and other pictures, c1800– .

Maps showing the circulation of mail in local areas as well as over major routes, 1760– .

Photographs reflecting the work of the Post Office, late 19th century– .

Library covering the history of the Post Office, c1850– .

Artefacts relating to Post Office operations: prints, paintings, vehicles, uniforms; supporting printed material.

The Post Office's collection of artists' designs for postage stamps, essays, die proofs and registration sheets, mid–19th century– .

Stamps of the world collection.

Finding aids: Catalogues; copies held at PRO (entry 1058).

Facilities: Photocopying (NB photocopying of philatelic material is limited for reasons of conservation). Photography. Microfilm reader. Use of laptop computers.

Conservation: Contracted out.

Publications: J. Farrugia: *Guide to Post Office Archives* (1986).

Information leaflets and a list of other publications available.

727 Principal Registry of the Family Division

Address: First Avenue House, 42–49 High Holborn, London WC1 6NP

Telephone: (020) 7947 6000

Enquiries: Probate Enquiries Room or Divorce Enquiries Room.

Open: Mon–Fri: 10.00–4.30.

Access: Generally open to the public, to view and purchase copies of grants of representation and wills of deceased persons' estate issued in England and Wales since 1858. There is a restriction on most divorce records, but copies of some documents are available to the public. The office is recognised as a place of deposit for public records.

Major collections: Probate: copies of all grants of representation and all wills proved in England and Wales, 1858– .

Divorce: petitions issued in PRFD, 1858– ; index of all decree absolutes issued throughout England and Wales, 1858– .

Finding aids: Probate: index available for public inspection.

Divorce: index for staff inspection only.

Facilities: Photocopying. Microfiche readers.

728 Prudential plc Archives

Address: 142 Holborn Bars, London EC1N 2NH

Telephone: (020) 7548 3582

Fax: (020) 7548 3583

E-mail: jennie.campbell@prudential.co.uk

Enquiries: The Group Archivist, Jennie Campbell

Open: By appointment only.

Access: Bona fide researchers, on application in writing to the Group Archivist. The company reserves the right to refuse access.

Historical background: The Prudential Mutual Assurance Investment and Loan Association was founded in 1848 and entered into industrial assurance in 1854. Following amalgamation with the British Industry Life Assurance Co. (f. 1852) in 1860 the name British Prudential Assurance was adopted. During the following decade a number of other companies were acquired and the name was changed to the Prudential Assurance Co. General insurance business started in 1919 and overseas business began shortly afterwards, with branches being established in most British colonies during the 1930s. In 1936 British Widows Assurance Co. Ltd (f.1902) was absorbed. Prudential Corporation Ltd was established as a holding company in 1978 and the shorter name of Prudential plc was taken in 1999. The Scottish

Amicable was taken over in 1997, but its archives remain located in its headquarters in Stirling.

Acquisitions policy: Records relating to the corporation and its subsidiaries.

Archives of organisation: Archives of Prudential Assurance Company, 1848– . Some records of organisations acquired in the 19th century, and of British Widows Assurance Co. Ltd, 1902– .

Non-manuscript material: Architectural drawings by Alfred Waterhouse.
Photographs, video and film.

Finding aids: Computerised catalogue in progress.

Facilities: Photocopying. Photography.

Conservation: Contracted out.

Publications: A Century of Service: the Story of Prudential, 1848–1948 (1948).
L. Dennett: *A Sense of Security: 150 Years of Prudential* (Cambridge, 1998).

729 Punch Library and Archives

Parent organisation: Punch Ltd

Address: Trevor House, 100 Brompton Road, London SW3 1ER

Telephone: (020) 7225 6710/6711

Fax: (020) 7225 6712

E-mail: library@punch.co.uk

Enquiries: The Library Manager, Miranda Taylor

Open: Mon–Fri: 10.00–1.00, 2.30–5.30.

Access: Bona fide researchers, by appointment only. A paid research service is available.

Historical background: Punch magazine first appeared in 1841 and published without a break until 1992. It began republishing in 1996. The present library and archive date from around the 1940s; they moved to their current premises in 1996.

Acquisitions policy: Maintains its own records; no active policy for acquiring archives.

Archives of organisation: Correspondence by writers and artists connected with *Punch*, 19th and 20th centuries.

Bradbury & Evans printing and publishing records, including various paper and prints ledgers, 1830– ; account books and contributors' ledgers, authors' ledgers, 1843–1946; letter-books, 1893–1953.

Major collections: Henry Silver (1828–1910), staff writer: bequest of original sketches and proofs of *Punch* cartoons and the *Silver Diary of Punch Table Talk* (1858–70).
R.G.G. Price (1910–89), staff writer and author of *A History of Punch* (1959): bequest of *Punch*-related papers, notebooks, original typescripts and books.

Non-manuscript material: Complete run of *Punch* with covers, advertisements and supplements.
Substantial collection of *Punch* publications, including *Punch's Pocket Book* (1843–81).
British and foreign imitations of *Punch*.
Books about *Punch*, and by and about *Punch* contributors/artists.
Biographical information on contributors/artists.
Punch ephemera and cuttings.
Original *Punch* cartoons, 19th and 20th centuries (c1000).

Finding aids: MS subject index, compiled before 1900, of *Punch* cartoons and articles, 1841–91. Author index for each volume, 1902–92, descriptive index, 1841–1901. Computerised subject/artists index to cartoons published 1893–1963. Card subject indexes, 1969–92. Lists of cartoonists. Computerised catalogue of original cartoon collection.

Facilities: Photocopying. Photography service by order.

Conservation: Contracted out.

730 Queen Mary

Parent organisation: University of London

Address: Mile End Road, London E1 4NS

Telephone: (020) 7882 3305

Fax: (020) 8981 0028

E-mail: a.c.nye@qmw.ac.uk

Website: www.qmw.ac.uk

Enquiries: The Archivist, Mr Anselm Nye

Open: Mon–Fri: 9.00–5.00, by arrangement.

Access: Approved readers, on written application.

Historical background: Westfield College, Hampstead, was founded in 1882 as a residential college for women preparing for University of London degrees. The MS collection was built up from donations and occasional purchases. Queen Mary College traces its foundation from the opening of the People's Palace in the East End in 1884 and the start of its Technical Schools in 1887. The latter expanded from part-time evening classes to the status of a full school of the University of London, shown in its changes of name first to the East London Technical College, in 1892, then to East London Technical College and finally to Queen Mary College, in 1934. The two colleges merged in 1990 as Queen Mary & Westfield College, the present name was adopted in 2000.

The Geology Department holds records of the Geologists' Association.

Acquisitions policy: To maintain archives of relevance to both colleges.

Archives of organisation: Westfield College archives, 1882–1990.

Archives of the People's Palace: minutes, correspondence and press cuttings, 1884–1920.

Archives of East London College and Queen Mary College, 1892–1990.

Major collections: Letters of the Lyttelton family, especially Gen. Sir Neville Lyttelton (1845–1931), with relevance to British and South African history, late 19th and early 20th centuries (*c*10,000).

Archive of Constance Louisa Maynard (1848–1935), first mistress of the college, including personal papers and diaries, 1860–1930s.

Papers of Peter Shore local MP (1923-2001), 1963–97; Donald Chesworth (1923–91), social activist, former warden of Toynbee Hall and founder of the Spitalfields Trust; Professor Clive Schmithoff, connected with the college's Centre for Commercial Law Studies, covers family records as well as legal and academic matters.

Small collections on 19th-century British art, especially Benjamin Robert Haydon (1786–1846), John Martin (1789–1854) and James Smetham (1821–89).

Finding aids: Draft catalogue for Westfield College archives. Lyttelton Collection catalogue almost complete.

Facilities: Photocopying. Photography. Microfilm reader.

Publications: J. Sondheimer: *A Castle Adamant in Hampstead* (London, 1983).

G.P. Moss and N.V. Saville: *From Palace to College* (London, 1985).

C.M. Maynard: *The Diaries of Constance Maynard* (Brighton, 1987) [14 reels of microfilm, including the diaries, Effie note-books and unpublished autobiography].

731 Queen's College

Address: 43–49 Harley Street, London W1N 2BT

Telephone: (020) 7291 7000

Fax: (020) 7291 7070

E-mail: queens@qcl.org.uk

Website: www.qcl.org.uk

Enquiries: The Archivist

Open: Term: Mon–Fri: 10.00–3.30.

Access: Bona fide researchers, at the discretion of the Principal and by appointment only. There are restrictions on certain MSS and a charge is made.

Historical background: Queen's College, the first institution to provide a sound academic education and proper qualifications for women, was founded in 1848 by F.D. Maurice. The college had strong links with King's College in the University of London (see entry 669), many of whose professors also lectured at Queen's, and with the Governesses' Benevolent Association. In 1853 Queen Victoria, the first patron, granted a royal charter to the college and a school for younger girls was started. The college continues to flourish in its present site, now considerably expanded, in Harley Street.

Acquisitions policy: Anything of major interest concerning former students or members of staff and the history of Queen's College.

Archives of organisation: Records and registers of students, 1848– . Committee of Education and Council minutes, accounts, annual reports, prospectuses, 1848– .

Major collections: Early correspondence of founders and original professors, including F.D. Maurice, David Laing, W. Sterndale Bennett (1816–75), R. Chenevix Trench (1807–86).

Articles and note-books of early students, including Katherine Mansfield (1888–1923), writer, and Louisa Twining (1820–1911), social reformer.

Non-manuscript material: Early photographs of the college and former students.
Queen's College Calendar, 1879–1931; *Queen's College Magazine,* 1881– .

Finding aids: Automated lists; copies to be sent to NRA.

Facilities: Photocopying.

Conservation: Simple conservation undertaken in house; other work sent to outside conservator.

Publications: The First College for Women: Memories and Records of Work Done, 1848–1898.
R.G. Grylls: *Queen's College, 1848–1948* (1948).
E. Kaye: *A History of Queen's College, London* (1972).
M. Billings: *A History of Queen's College* (1999).

732 Rambert Dance Company Archives

Address: 94 Chiswick High Road, London W4 1SH

Telephone: (020) 8995 4246

Fax: (020) 8747 8323

E-mail: rdc@rambert.org.uk

Enquiries: Jane Pritchard

Open: By appointment only.

Access: Company members and bona fide researchers.

Historical background: The archive was established in 1982 to document the history of Ballet Rambert/Rambert Dance Company and related organisations. The archive documents the life and career of the company's founder, Marie Rambert (1888–1982), choreographers, composers, designers and dancers who worked with the company and the productions they created.

Acquisitions policy: The collection and preservation of a wide range of documentation on the history and activities of the company. This is primarily British, but includes records of overseas tours.

Archives of organisation: Administrative and artistic records, 1926– .

Major collections: Collections of Marie Rambert, 1888–1982; Walter Gore-Paula Hinton, 1910–97; Andrée Howard, 1910–68. Papers from numerous former company members.

Non-manuscript material: Production designs, set models, video and sound tapes.

Finding aids: Cataloguing in progress.

Facilities: Photocopying.

Conservation: Occasionally contracted out.

Publications: J. Adshead Lansdale and J. Layson, 'Rambert Dance Company Archive', *Dance History* (Routledge, 1994).

733 Reform Club

Address: 104 Pall Mall, London SW1Y 5EW

Telephone: (020) 7747 4608

Fax: (020) 7930 1857

E-mail: libreform@aol.com

Enquiries: The Librarian

Open: Strictly by arrangement only.

Access: Members only; other bona fide researchers, by member's introduction or special arrangement with the Librarian.

Historical background: The Reform Club was founded in 1836 by Edward Ellice (1781–1863), MP and promoter of the 1832 Reform Bill, for the benefit of Liberal politicians.

Acquisitions policy: To maintain its own archives.

Archives of organisation: Extensive archives of the club, including committee and AGM minutes, annual reports and membership records, 1836– .

Major collections: Papers of W.M. Eager (1884–1966), secretary of the Liberal Land Committee, 1920s.

Finding aids: Catalogue.

Facilities: Photocopying.

Conservation: Contracted out.

Publications: L. Fagan: *The Reform Club: its Founders and Architect, 1836–1886* (1887).
G. Woodbridge: *The Reform Club, 1836–1978* (1978).

734 Reuters Archive

Address: 85 Fleet Street, London EC4P 4AJ

Telephone: (020) 7542 7132

Fax: (020) 7542 4066

E-mail: john.entwisle@reuters.com

Website: www.reuters.com

Enquiries: The Manager, Mr John Entwisle

Open: By appointment.

Access: Bona fide researchers, at the discretion of the company and on written application.

Historical background: After attempts in Paris in 1849, and in Aachen in 1850, Paul Julius Reuter (1816–99) established his new agency in London in 1851. The business was incorporated in 1865, and in 1916 Reuters Ltd was created as a private company. By 1941 Reuters was jointly owned by the Press Association Ltd and the Newspaper Proprietors Association Ltd and a trust was formed, guaranteeing the independence and integrity of Reuters news services. In 1984 Reuters became a public company.

Acquisitions policy: Maintains archives relating to the company's activities.

Archives of organisation: Records of Reuters Ltd and associated activities, 1849– , including information on many well-known figures who worked for Reuters.

Non-manuscript material: Some video, film and microform material.

Finding aids: Computer database and card index.

Facilities: Photography. Photocopying. Microfilm/fiche reader/printer.

Conservation: Contracted out.

Publications: G. Storey: *Reuters' Century: 1851–1951* (1951).
J. Laurence and L. Barber: *The Price of Truth* (1952).
D. Read: *The Power of News* (1992).

735 Rio Tinto plc

Address: 6 St James's Square, London SW1Y 4LD

Telephone: (020) 7753 2123 (direct line)

Fax: (020) 7753 2211

E-mail: fiona.maccoll@riotinto.com

Website: www.riotinto.com

Enquiries: The Records Manager, Ms Fiona Maccoll

Open: Mon–Fri: 10.00–4.00, by appointment only.

Access: Anyone with a legitimate interest; an appointment is always necessary. There is restricted access to some of the archives.

Historical background: Rio Tinto plc was formed in 1997 with the merger of the RTZ Corporation plc and its associate company CRA Ltd (of Australia). The RTZ Corporation Ltd itself was formed in 1962 on the merger of the RTC Ltd (f. 1873) and the Consolidated Zinc Corporation Ltd (f. 1949). The Rio Tinto Company Ltd had been formed in 1873 by a consortium of banks to acquire the Spanish copper mine of the same name. The majority interest was sold to a consortium of Spanish banks in 1954; the remaining interest was divested in 1990. The proceeds of the sale in 1954 were invested in projects in Africa and Australasia. The Consolidated Zinc Corporation Ltd had been incorporated to acquire the interests of the Zinc Corporation Ltd (f. 1911), the Sulphide Corporation (reg. 1898), the Broken Hill Corporation Ltd (reg. 1947) and the Imperial Smelting Corporation Ltd (inc. 1929). The Zinc Corporation Ltd was formed to treat the tailing dumps from the Broken Hill mine in New South Wales, Australia. The Broken Hill Corporation Ltd held a substantial interest in the New Broken Hill Consolidated Ltd mine. The Sulphide Corporation Ltd was a producer of sulphuric acid, superphosphate and cement. The Imperial Smelting Corporation, based in the UK, was the sole zinc producer in the country, mainly using raw material from the Broken Hill mines. It also produced sulphuric acids, chemicals, fertilisers and fluorine and fluorine compounds in plants in Avonmouth and Swansea.

Archives relating to the Australian operations are held at the University of Melbourne Archive, Victoria, Australia. Records of some former UK subsidiaries have been deposited with local and specialist repositories in the UK.

Acquisitions policy: Only material relating to the group's activities is collected.

Archives of organisation: The Rio Tinto Company Ltd: headquarters records of the Rio Tinto mine in Spain and records on the African,

Canadian and Australian operations, 1873–1962.

Rio Tinto plc: headquarters records of the corporation's activities around the world, 1962– .

Non-manuscript material: Photographs of main group operations, 1890s– .
Film/video archive of selected operations, 1949– .

Finding aids: Lists.

Facilities: Photography by arrangement.

Conservation: Occasional contracting out.

Publications: D. Avery: *Not on Queen Victoria's Birthday: the Story of the Rio Tinto Mines* (London, 1974).
C.E. Harvey: *The Rio Tinto Company: an Economic History of a Leading International Mining Concern* (Penzance, 1982).

736 Rothschild Archive

Parent organisation: The Rothschild Archive Trust

Address: New Court, St Swithin's Lane, London EC4P 4DU

Telephone: (020) 7280 5874

Fax: (020) 7280 5657

E-mail: info@rothschildarchive.org

Website: www.rothschildarchive.org

Enquiries: The Archivist

Open: Mon–Fri: 10.00–4.15.

Access: Written requests only, supported by two references. Access is by appointment only. Material is generally available up to 1930.

Historical background: The Rothschild Archive was established in 1978 in order to arrange and make available the records of N.M. Rothschild & Sons, and to provide a repository for the records of the Rothschild family generally. In 1999 the board of directors of N.M. Rothschild & Sons Ltd formally transferred the ownership of the archives to the Rothschild Archive Trust.

Major collections: The archives of N.M. Rothschild & Sons, merchant bankers, 1809–1930, including correspondence with sister houses in Frankfurt, Paris, Vienna and Naples; correspondence with agents and ledgers.
Papers relating to the activities of the Rothschild family in France, c1880–1939; correspondence of the Rothschild family once resident at Gunnersbury, West London, c1835–1884.

Non-manuscript material: Photographs of the Rothschild family and their houses; a collection of several hundred autochrome plates of English gardens and European cities, c1912–1920s.
Books written by members of the Rothschild family.

Finding aids: Guide to the collection, available in database form; computerised name and place index to various series; transcripts of major family correspondence.

Facilities: Photocopying. Microfilm reader.

Conservation: Contracted out.

Publications: M. Aspey (ed.): *The Rothschild Archive: a Guide to the Collection.*
N. Fergusson: *The World's Banker: the History of the House of Rothschild* (1998).
I. Roldán de Montaud: 'Nathan Mayer Rothschild & Sons de Londres y su archivo en la city de Londres', *Hispania* (1999).

737 Royal Academy of Arts

Address: Burlington House, Piccadilly, London W1V 0DS

Telephone: (020) 7300 5768

Fax: (020) 7300 5765

E-mail: mark.pomeroy@royalacademy.org.uk

Website: www.raa.org.uk

Enquiries: The Archivist, Mark Pomeroy

Open: Tues–Thurs: 10.00–1.00, 2.00–5.00.

Access: Bona fide students and scholars.

Historical background: The Royal Academy was established by George III in 1768 for 'promoting the arts of design'. Records of the proceedings of the academy, and its finances, were specifically preserved from the foundation for reasons of accountability. The institutional records have never left the custody of the academy. Responsibility for the archives passed from the Secretary to the Librarian of the academy and is now vested in the Archivist.

Acquisitions policy: To maintain the archives of the academy and to accept donations of members' papers.

Archives of organisation: Archives of the Royal Academy, including Summer and Loan

Exhibition catalogues, General Assembly and Council minutes, annual reports and students' register.

Major collections: Summer Exhibition catalogues, 1769–1850, annotated by J.H. Anderdon (26 vols).
Graphic Society laws, minutes and letters, 1833–90.
Society of Artists records, 1759–1807.
Papers of Sir George Clausen (1852–1944); John Gibson (1790–1866); Ozias Humphrey (1742–1810) (8 vols); Sir Thomas Lawrence (1769–1830) (5 vols); Sir Joshua Reynolds (1723–92), including 27 sitters' books.

Non-manuscript material: Collection of works of art and photographs, mostly connected with members of the Royal Academy.
Rare books relating to architecture and bound volumes of engravings by artists.

Finding aids: General and separate indexes to most MS material. See NRA 14837.

Facilities: Photocopying. Photography by arrangement.

Publications: S.C. Hutchinson: *History of the Royal Academy of Arts, 1768–1986* (London, 2/ 1986).
'The Royal Academy Schools, 1768–1830', *Walpole Society,* xxxvii [includes transcript of first schools' register].

738 Royal Academy of Dramatic Art

Address: 18–22 Chenies Street, London WC1E 7EX

Telephone: (020) 7636 7076

Fax: (020) 7323 3868

Website: www.rada.org.uk

Enquiries: The Librarian, Jayne Mann

Open: Term: Mon–Fri: 9.30–7.00.

Access: Generally open to the public, by appointment.

Historical background: The academy was founded in 1904 by Sir Herbert Beerbohm-Tree (1852–1917) and has been in its present home since 1905. It received its royal charter in 1920. Members of council have included, George Bernard Shaw, a major benefactor of RADA library, and Irene Vanbrugh. Many distinguished members of the theatrical profession have attended RADA.

Acquisitions policy: To maintain the archives. The library expands to support productions.

Archives of organisation: Archives include records of council meetings, 1906– ; student records and cast lists.

Non-manuscript material: Albums of press cuttings on George Bernard Shaw (40).

Facilities: Photocopying.

739 Royal Academy of Music Library

Parent organisation: Royal Academy of Music

Address: Marylebone Road, London NW1 5HT

Telephone: (020) 7873 7323

Fax: (020) 7873 7322

E-mail: library@ram.ac.uk

Website: www.ram.ac.uk

Enquiries: The Acting Librarian, Ms Kathryn Adamson

Open: Term: Mon–Fri: 9.00–6.00; Sat: 9.00–12.00.
Vacation: enquire before visit.

Access: Bona fide researchers, by appointment only.

Historical background: The academy was founded in 1822 to provide training facilities for those seeking careers in all branches of music. The library incorporates a room to house early printed music and MSS.

Acquisitions policy: Material relating to music and performance.

Archives of organisation: Academy archives, including student registers, papers and prospectuses (incomplete).

Major collections: Papers and scores of Sir Henry Wood (1869–1944), conductor, a former student and teacher at RAM. Papers of other eminent performers, including Harriet Cohen (1896–1967), pianist.
Savage-Stevens Collection of 18th-century music scores.
David Munrow and Robert Spencer Collections.

Non-manuscript material: Collection of early sound recordings.

Large collection of printed music, pre-1850, and supporting collection of early literature.

Finding aids: Computerised catalogues, lists and indexes.

Facilities: Photocopying. Microfilm/fiche reader. Sound recording listening facilities.

Publications: Catalogue of Microfilms of RAM Holdings.

740 Royal Aeronautical Society Library

Address: 4 Hamilton Place, London W1V 0BQ

Telephone: (020) 7670 4361/4362

Fax: (020) 7670 4359

E-mail: library@raes.org.uk

Enquiries: The Librarian and Information Officer, A.W.L. Nayler

Open: Mon–Fri: 10.00–5.00.

Access: Any member of an Engineering Council institution may have access to the society's library. Non-members are charged a small daily access fee.

Historical background: The society was founded in 1866 and is the oldest aeronautical society in the world; it incorporated the Institute of Aeronautical Engineers in 1927, the Helicopter Association of Great Britain in 1960 and the Society of Licensed Aircraft Engineers and Technologists in 1987. A royal charter, granted in 1949, recognised it as the representative body for those concerned with the general advancement of aeronautical art, science and engineering, and that it facilitated the exchange of information and ideas. The library, formed in 1866, holds an extensive collection of books, technical reports, papers and archival material.

Acquisitions policy: To acquire, by donation, deposit or purchase, material relevant to the history and development of aeronautical engineering, aviation and aerospace, and allied fields.

Archives of organisation: Official records and working papers of the society, 1866– .

Major collections: Collections built up by John Cuthbert (*fl.* 1820s), John Hodgson (1875–1952) and Frederick Poynton (1869–1944), including MSS, prints and ephemera relating to early flight and ballooning, mainly 19th century.

Papers of Sir George Cayley, 1800–50; John Stringfellow (1799–1883); Wilbur Wright (1867–1912); Orville Wright (1871–1948); Katherine Wright (1874–1929); Lawrence Hargrave (1850–1915); Maj. B.F.S. Baden-Powell (1860–1937); G.G. Grey (1875–1953).

Air Commodore E.M. Maitland (1880–1921) airship collection.

Aircraft design notebooks of Captain F.S. Barnwell (1880–1938).

Non-manuscript material: Portraits of eminent aeronautical engineers and aviators, presidents of the society, 1866– .

Photographic Collection of aviation images from the early days of ballooning to modern technology, including aircraft, equipment, society events and members (*c*100,000).

Finding aids: General catalogue to all collections. Index to the photographic collections. Cayley: NRA 1055.

Facilities: Photocopying. Photography by arrangement.

Publications: J.E. Hodgson: *History of Aeronautics in Great Britain* (Oxford, 1924) [includes details of collections].

F. MacCabee: *Publications Index, 1897–1977* [index to the *Aeronautical Journal*, Aerospace Conferences etc].

741 Royal Air Force Museum
Department of Research and Information Services

Address: Grahame Park Way, Hendon, London NW9 5LL

Telephone: (020) 8358 4850 (Senior Keeper); (020) 8358 4873 (archive and library enquiries); (020) 8358 4808 (photographic, film and fine art enquiries)

Fax: (02) 8358 4991 (office hours only); (020) 8200 1751 (24 hours)

Website: www.rafmuseum.org.uk

Enquiries: The Keeper of Research and Information Services, Mr P.J.V. Elliott

Open: Mon–Sun: 10.00–6.00, by appointment.

Access: Bona fide researchers.

Historical background: The museum was founded in 1964 and opened at Hendon in 1972.

The Department of Research and Information Services comprises the former departments of Aviation Records (archives and library) and Visual Arts (film, photographs and fine art). The museum is recognised as a place of deposit for public records.

Acquisitions policy: To collect material, by donation and purchase, which relates to the history of the RAF and its antecedents, associated air forces and aviation generally, where a link with the RAF is established. The subject emphasis is on British military aviation, but includes records of British aircraft companies.

Archives of organisation: Museum files, 1964– ; minutes of trustees' meetings, 1965– .

Major collections: Papers of a number of senior officers of the period up to 1945, including Marshal of the RAF Lord Trenchard (1873–1956), ACM Sir Arthur Harris (1892–1984), and Lt.-Gen. Sir David Henderson (1862–1921); also leading figures in British aviation, including Lord Brabazon of Tara (1884–1964) and Sir Frederick Handley Page (1885–1962), and aircraft companies, including Supermarine, Fairey and Handley Page.
Material relating to ordinary airmen and women, notably aircrew log-books, World War I casualty records and record cards for RAF aircraft, vehicles and marine craft.

Non-manuscript material: Extensive collections of manufacturers' drawings of aircraft and engines, with site plans for RAF airfields and non-flying stations.
Photographs, films and works of art, including the Air Ministry element of the collection assembled by the War Artists Advisory Committee.

Finding aids: Catalogues and accession lists for most collections. Lists sent to NRA.

Facilities: Photocopying. Microform (fiche, film and aperture card). Photography. Researchers may use their own tape-recorders and other aids in the reading room.

Conservation: Contracted out.

Publications: Series of leaflets explaining how to trace unit and personnel records, the history of RAF stations and the service histories of individual aircraft.

742 Royal Albert Hall

Address: Kensington Gore, London SW7 2AP

Telephone: (020) 7589 3203 ext. 2207

Fax: (020) 7823 7725

E-mail: jackyc@royalalberthall.com

Enquiries: The Archivist, Ms Jacky Cowdrey

Open: Tues–Thurs: 10.00–6.00, strictly by appointment only.

Access: Bona fide researchers. Charges are applicable for any commercial use applied for and approved by the hall. Please note seating is very limited.

Historical background: The Royal Albert Hall was opened in 1871, part of the arts and science development of the surrounding area following the 1851 Great Exhibition. Since 1941 it has been the home of the annual Promenade Concerts founded by Sir Henry Wood in 1895.

Acquisitions policy: The collection, acquisition and preservation of all material relating to events staged at the Royal Albert Hall and to the building itself.

Archives of organisation: Royal Albert Hall Council minutes, 1869– .
Programmes of events, 1913– .

Non-manuscript material: Drawings of the hall, 1871– .
Original sepia photographs of the building; Heraton's photographs, 1940s–1960s.
Transparencies and colour negatives of events, 1982–94.

Finding aids: Various lists. Programmes arranged chronologically.

Facilities: Photocopying. Photography.

Publications: R.W. Clark: *The Royal Albert Hall* (London, 1958).
J.R. Thackrah: *The Royal Albert Hall* (1983).

743 Royal Anthropological Institute of Great Britain and Ireland

Address: 50 Fitzroy Street, London W1P 5HS

Telephone: (020) 7387 0455

Fax: (020) 7383 4235

E-mail: admin@therai.org.uk

Website: www.therai.org.uk

A Manuscript and Archive Collection

Enquiries: The RAI Representative, c/o Museum of Mankind, 6 Burlington Gardens, London W1X 2EX

Open: By arrangement.

Access: Accredited scholars, after written application. Fragile collections are closed.

Historical background: The institute was founded in 1871, incorporating the Ethnological Society and the Anthropological Society of London. It is recognised internationally as the representative body in the UK for the whole field of the study of man. In 1976 the library was donated to the British Museum and merged with the departmental library of the Museum of Mankind, where the Manuscript and Archive Collection is now also stored.

Acquisitions policy: Donations are accepted.

Archives of organisation: Domestic archives of the institute, consisting of minute books, committee reports and other documents relating to its administrative history, mid–19th century– .

Major collections: MSS of fieldwork and papers of the following: E.H. Man, 1875–1920; Sir Everard im Thurn, 1887–1923; H.B.T. Somerville, 1889–1900; M.E. Durham, 1900–36; M.W. Hilton-Simpson, 1906–9; R.S. Rattray, 1919–27; J.D. Unwin, 1919–34; Marian W. Smith, 1945.

Non-manuscript material: See entry B below. Film library of c150 films is managed by the Scottish Film and Television Archive, Glasgow (entry 399).

Finding aids: Typescript catalogues, entry by author with author/subject index (compiled by B.J. Kirkpatrick).

B Photographic Collection

E-mail: photo@therai.org.uk

Website: rai.anthropology.org.uk/photo/photo.html

Enquiries: The Photo-Librarian

Open: Usually Mon–Tues: 9:30–5:30, by appointment.

Access: Consultation of the illustrated catalogue is open to all. Access to the original photographs is restricted and by written application only.

Historical background: The photographic collection predates the institute (f. 1871), some of the photographs having come from one or other of the parent societies, the Ethnological Society and the Anthropological Society of London. Few photographs in the collection can be dated earlier than the 1860s. The taking of photographs was actively encouraged by the institute in *Notes and Queries on Anthropology* (first published in 1874). The photographs taken by these early 'travellers and anthropological observers', as well as those by some of the pioneers of modern anthropological fieldwork, were lodged with the institute. Attempts to classify the photographs began in 1899, at first independently, and then in conjunction with the British Association. This scheme was abandoned by 1911. After a period of inactivity work began again on the collection in 1974 and this has led to more recent acquisitions. In 1995 the RAI initiated an on-going computer cataloguing project for the collection.

Acquisitions policy: To encourage the deposit or donation of photographs relating to the study of anthropology, including early photographs with anthropological content, and recent or present-day fieldwork photographs with associated documentation. The institute has very limited resources for purchase.

Non-manuscript material: Two sets of photographs of 'The Natives of Greater Russia', organised by Professor A. Bogdanov for the Moscow Ethnographic Exhibition in 1867.
Prince Roland Bonaparte's portraits of the Lapps, 1884.
Album of photographs (c700) selected from the collection of portraits of North American Indians made by the US Geological Survey in the 1870s, and presented by F.V. Hayden, geologist in charge of the survey.
Other collections: E.H. Man (Andaman and Nicobar Islands), Sir Everard im Thurn (Indians of Guyana), P.A. Johnston and T. Hoffman (Sikkim, Nepal and Tibet), Vice-Admiral H.B.T. Somerville (Solomon Islands and New Hebrides), all 19th century; R.W. Williamson (Melanesia), C.G. Seligman (Vedda of Sri Lanka, Sudan, New Guinea), Emil Torday (Congo), Mary Edith Durham (Bosnia, Serbia and Albania), Prof. I. Schapera (Southern Africa), M.W. Hilton-Simpson (Algeria), all early 20th century; E.E. Evans-Pritchard (Africa), Sir Max Gluckman (Southern Africa),

1930s and 1940s; Dr Audrey Richards (East Africa).

Finding aids: Illustrated catalogue cards for three-quarters of the prints and some of the negatives. Various lists.

Facilities: Photocopying. Photography. Copy prints may be supplied on loan to general users (publishers etc), as well as to specialists and students. Loan and reproduction fees charged are available on application.

Publications: R. Poignant: *Observers of Man: a Catalogue of an Exhibition of a Selection of Photographs from the Collection of the Royal Anthropological Institute* (1980).
E. Edwards (ed): *Anthropology and Photography, 1860–1920* (Yale UP and RAI, 1992).

744 Royal Artillery Historical Branch

Parent organisation: Royal Artillery Institution

Address: Old Laboratory Office, Royal Arsenal (West), Warren Lane, Woolwich, London SE18 6ST

Telephone: (020) 8316 7393

E-mail: raht@btinternet.com

Enquiries: The Historical Secretary, Royal Artillery Instittution, Brigadier K.A. Timbers The Archivist

Open: Mon–Fri:10.00–12.30, 2.00–4.30.

Access: Bona fide researchers, by appointment only and subject to the approval of the Royal Artillery Historical Affairs Committee, on application to the Historical Secretary. A contribution towards costs is requested from most enquirers and users of library facilities who are not members of the Royal Artillery Institution or the Royal Regiment of Artillery. Most material relating to the administration of the Royal Artillery Institution is not currently available to outside researchers.

Historical background: The Royal Artillery Library is a private reference library, which can trace its origins to the Royal Military Repository established at the Royal Arsenal in 1778 to assist in the training of members of the Royal Regiment of Artillery. The Royal Artillery Institution was formally established in 1838 in order to further the study of technical and scientific matters by officers of the RA. The library and historical collections are administered by a charitable trust, and comprise material relating to the history, tactical use, technology and manufacture of British and foreign artillery, and to all aspects of the history and development of the RA. Its historical collections were relocated on a single site in purpose-built premises at the old Royal Arsenal in 2001.

Acquisitions policy: Collection of archival material in whatever format relating to the history, tactics and technology of artillery and the history of the Royal Regiment of Artillery from 1716. Most material is donated to the library, though purchases are occasionally made.

Major collections: Papers, technical manuals and official material relating to British ordnance and artillery matters, 17th century– , mainly 19th century.

Papers of c80 military personnel, notably Maj.-Gen. Sir Alexander Dickson (1777–1840), including his collection of historical MSS, and printed maps and plans, c1695–1838; Gen. Sir R.W. Gardiner (1781–1864), including material relating to the Peninsular War; Lt.-Gen. Sir J.H. Lefroy (1817–90); Gen. Sir Robert Biddulph (1835–1918), including material relating to his period as High Commissioner for Cyprus, 1879–86; Maj. A.F. Becke (1871–1947), mainly comprising research material relating to the First World War; Brig. O.F.G. Hogg (1887–1979), including material relating to his history of the Royal Arsenal, Woolwich.

Collection of Lt-Col. Samuel Cleaveland relating to the early history of the Royal Artillery, 1698–1813.

Regimental archives, 18th century– .

Non-manuscript material: Illustrative and photographic collections, 1850s– .
Military sketches and caricatures by Col. L.G. Fawkes, RA, 19th century (2 portfolios).
Royal Carriage Dept, Woolwich, lithographed general assembly plates of artillery equipment, 19th century.
Rare books.

Finding aids: Lists of deposited material, with a manual index. This is at present being computerised. Lists sent to NRA.

Facilities: Photocopying. Microfilm/fiche reader.

Publications: H.W.L. Hime: *History of the Royal Regiment of Artillery, 1815–1853* (London, 1908).

J.R.J. Jocelyn: *History of the Royal and Indian Artillery in the Mutiny of 1857 (Crimean War Period* (London, 1911).

———: *History of the Royal and Indian Artillery in the Mutiny of 1857* (London, 1915).

C. Callwell and J. Headlam: *The History of the Royal Artillery from the Indian Mutiny to the Great War* (3 vols, 1931–1940).

M.E.S. Laws: *Battery Records of the Royal Artillery, 1716–1877* (London, 1952) [2 vols].

M. Farndale: *History of the RA*, vol. I: *Western Front, 1914–1918* (c1986); vol. II: *Forgotten Fronts and the Home Base* (c1988); vol V: *The Years of Defeat, 1939–1941* (London, 1996).

B.P. Hughes: *History of the RA*, vol. III: *Between the Wars* (1992).

N.W. Routledge: *History of the RA*, vol. IV: *Anti-Aircraft Artillery, 1914–1955* (c1994).

P.R.F. Bonnett: *A Short History of the Royal Regiment of Artillery* (1994).

745 Royal Asiatic Society Library

Address: 60 Queen's Gardens, London W2 3AF

Telephone: (020) 7724 4741

Fax: (020) 7706 4008

E-mail: mjp@royalasiaticsociety.org

Website: www.royalasiaticsociety.co.uk

Enquiries: The Librarian, M.J. Pollock

Open: Tues: 11.00–8.00; Wed, Thurs: 11.00–5.00.
Closed August.

Access: Fellows, and other visitors on written or telephone application.

Historical background: The society was founded by Henry Thomas Colebrooke in 1823 and received its first royal charter that year for 'the investigation of subjects connected with and for the encouragement of science, literature and the arts in relation to Asia'. Many distinguished scholars have been associated with the society and their work has been presented at its meetings.

Acquisitions policy: Material in the field of oriental studies, mainly by donation, but some limited purchases.

Archives of organisation: Minutes of the council and general meetings; and printed lists of members, 1823– .

Major collections: Collections of European language MS material including the Rawlinson Collection *re* Sir Henry Creswicke, 1810–98. Eckstein Collection, includes letters from and about Sir Richard Burton (1821–90). Oriental MSS (c1500).

Non-manuscript material: Prints (c2000), drawings, paintings and busts.
Books, including Storey Collection of Arabic and Persian literature, and Burton Collection.

Finding aids: Catalogues and handlists for all book, MSS and prints and drawings collections.

Facilities: Photocopying. Photography. Microfilm/fiche readers.

Conservation: Some in-house service for prints and drawings collection.

Publications: S. Simmonds and S. Digby: *The Royal Asiatic Society: its History and Treasures* (London, 1979).

746 Royal Astronomical Society

Address: The Library, Burlington House, Piccadilly, London W1V 0NL

Telephone: (020) 7734 3307/4582

Fax: (020) 7494 0166

E-mail: info@ras.org.uk

Website: www.ras.org.uk

Enquiries: The Librarian, Mr P.H. Hingley

Open: By arrangement.

Access: Private library, but access may be granted to bona fide researchers, on application in writing to the Librarian or by recommendations of a fellow.

Historical background: The astronomical library has been accumulated by the Royal Astronomical Society since its foundation in 1820. The founder president was William Herschel, and through the benefactions of his family and others associated with it the society has become the owner and guardian of many MSS and archives of value. The archives were temporarily stored at Churchill College, Cambridge, and the collection was catalogued by a temporary archivist, appointed by the Council of the Society between 1974 and 1976.

Acquisitions policy: Gifts of astronomically significant archives and books are considered on their merits.

Archives of organisation: The society's general correspondence, 1820– .

Papers generated by the society: minutes, register books, papers relating to expeditions etc.

Major collections: MSS, mainly 35 named collections.

Herschel Archive: papers of Sir William Herschel (1738–1822), Sir John Herschel (1792–1871) and Caroline Herschel (1750–1848) (housed at Churchill College, Cambridge (entry 171) and not available for study, but microfilm copy at Burlington House).

Non-manuscript material: Astronomical drawings.

Astronomical portrait and telescope photographs.

Extensive library of astronomical and some other scientific works (of which *c*2500 are pre–1850).

Finding aids: Guide to library.

Facilities: Photocopying. Microfilm/fiche reader. Microfilming.

Publications: J.A. Bennett: 'Catalogue of the Archives of the Royal Astronomical Society', *Memoirs of the RAS*, lxxxv (1978).

747   Royal Automobile Club

Address: 89–91 Pall Mall, London SW1Y 5HS

Telephone: (020) 7747 3398/3350

Fax: (020) 7451 9980

E-mail: library@royalautomobileclub.co.uk

Website: www.royalautomobileclub.co.uk

Enquiries: The Librarian, Trevor Dunmore

Open: Mon–Fri: 9.00–5.00.

Access: Members and bona fide scholars, by appointment only.

Historical background: The club was founded in 1897 as the Automobile Club of Great Britain, the society for the protection, encouragement and development of automobilism. It was granted a royal charter and renamed the Royal Automobile Club in 1907. Since 1911 it has been housed at its present address, previous locations being in Whitehall Court and

Piccadilly. The archives are still in the process of being sorted.

Acquisitions policy: To maintain the club's archive and to acquire documentation and memorabilia relating to the history of motoring, by purchase or donation.

Archives of organisation: Archives of RAC, including minute books, 1897– , annual reports, letters, journals, posters and programmes.

Major collections: Early correspondence of F.R. Simms (1863–1944), founder of the club.

Non-manuscript material: Photographs (*c*4000).

Small collection of films and videos.

Memorabilia, including badges and models.

Finding aids: Lists and computerised catalogue.

Facilities: Photocopying. Microfilm reader/printer.

Conservation: Contracted out.

Publications: D. Noble (ed.): *The Jubilee Book of the Royal Automobile Club, 1897–1947* (London, 1947).

P. Brendon: *The Motoring Century, 1897–1997* (London, 1997).

Guide to Library and Archives.

748   The Royal Bank of Scotland Archives

Address: Archive Department, The Royal Bank of Scotland Group, PO Box 348, Regent's House, 42 Islington High Street, London N1 8XL

Telephone: (020) 7615 6127

Fax: (020) 7837 7560

E-mail: archives@rbs.co.uk

Website: www.rbs.co.uk

Enquiries: The Head of Archives, Ms A. Turton

Open: Mon–Fri: 9.30–5.00

Access: By appointment only. There is no access to customers' records less than 100 years old or to others less than 30 years old without special permission. The bank reserves the right to refuse access.

Historical background: Founded as a corporation by royal charter in 1727, the Royal Bank opened for business in Edinburgh and was quickly involved in a bank-note circulation war with the older Bank of Scotland. It pioneered 'cash-credit', the forerunner of the overdraft, in 1728. In 1783 the bank opened a branch in Glasgow, and it acquired a considerable number of other branches in the aftermath of the collapse of the Western Bank of Scotland in 1857 and of the City of Glasgow Bank in 1878. In 1874 it opened a branch office in London. The Royal Bank acquired Drummonds Bank (f. 1717) in 1924; Williams Deacon's Bank (f. 1771) in 1930; and Glyn, Mills & Co. (f. 1753), which owned Holt & Co. (f. 1809) and Child & Co. (f. 1580s), in 1939. William Deacon's and Glyn, Mills continued to operate as separate entities and the business became known as the Three Banks Group. In 1969 the Royal Bank of Scotland merged with National Commercial Bank of Scotland, formed in 1959 by the merger of National Bank of Scotland (f. 1825) and the Commercial Bank of Scotland (f. 1810) and supplemented in 1966 by the acquisition of the English and Welsh branches of the National Bank (f. 1835). In 1970 the three London clearing-bank subsidiaries combined as Williams & Glyn's Bank Ltd. In 1985 the business of the Royal Bank of Scotland Ltd and Williams & Glyn's Bank Ltd was merged and the group became the Royal Bank of Scotland plc. Thereafter the bank restructured, refocusing on its core activity of retail banking, and in 1993 it acquired the private bank of Adam & Company (f. 1983). In 2000 the Royal Bank of Scotland acquired the National Westminster Bank plc, integrating the two business as The Royal Bank of Scotland Group but retaining the Royal Bank and NatWest brands on the high street.

National Westminster Bank commenced trading in 1970 following the merger of National Provincial Bank, its subsidiary District Bank and Westminster Bank. The bank's origins can, however, be traced back over three centuries, through the amalgamation of nearly two hundred banks. Westminster Bank was created from the union in 1909 of London & Westminster Bank (f. 1834) and London & County Bank (f. 1836). The merged bank acquired Ulster Bank (f. 1836) in 1917 and amalgamated with Parr's Bank (f. 1780s). National Provincial Bank was formed in 1833 as National Provincial Bank of England. In 1918 it merged with Union of London & Smiths Bank (f. 1839) to form National Provincial & Union Bank of England. National Provincial acquired the subsidiaries Coutts & Co. (f.1692) in 1920, North Central Finance (f.

1861) in 1958 and District Bank (f. 1829) in 1962.

Acquisitions policy: Maintains the records of The Royal Bank of Scotland Group and its constituents in Great Britain.

Archives of organisation: Records of The Royal Bank of Scotland, 1727– ; National Westminster Bank, 1968–2000; Commercial Bank of Scotland, 1810–1959; National Bank of Scotland, 1824–1959; National Provincial Bank, 1833–1969; Westminster Bank, 1833–1969; District Bank, 1829–1969; Glyn, Mills & Co. 1754–1970; Williams Deacon's Bank, 1836–1970; the National Bank, 1835–1970; London & County Banking Co., 1836–1909; Parr's Bank, 1788–1918; Prescott's Bank, 1766–1903; Smith family banks, 1762–1902; Union of London & Smiths Bank, 1839–1917; County Bank, 1862–1935; Williams, Deacon & Co., 1808–90; Child & Co., 1663– ; Messrs Drummonds, 1697– ; Sheffield & Rotherham Bank, 1792–1907; International Westminster Bank, 1913–82; Beckett & Co., 1776–1921; Bank of Whitehaven, 1838–1916; Jones, Loyd & Co., 1803–64; and many other private and joint stock constituent banks in London and the provinces. Also records of the Company of Scotland Trading to Africa and the Indies, 1695–1907; and the Equivalent Company, 1724–1850.

Non-manuscript material: Coins, banknotes, public relations and training films, and branch photographs.

Finding aids: Computer-based catalogues and indexes. Collections guide.

Facilities: Photocopying. Photography. Microfilm reader.

Conservation: Contracted out.

Publications: J.L. Anderson: *The Story of the Commercial Bank of Scotland, 1810–1910* (1910).
N. Munro: *History of the Royal Bank of Scotland, 1727–1927* (1928).
H. Withers: *National Provincial Bank 1833–1933* (1933).
T.E. Gregory: *The Westminster Bank through a Century* (1936).
H. Bolitho and D. Peel: *The Drummonds of Charing Cross* (1966).
Williams Deacon's, 1771–1970 (1971).
M. Slattery: *The National Bank, 1835–1970* (1972).

P. Clarke: *The First House in the City* (1973) [Child & Co.].

S.G. Checkland: *Scottish Banking: a History, 1695–1973* (1975).

The Royal Bank of Scotland: a History (1997).

National Westminster Bank: a Short History (1989).

A Guide to the Historical Records of The Royal Bank of Scotland (2000).

749 Royal British Nurses' Association

Address: Duke of York's Headquarters, 424 Left Wing, Turks Row, London SW3 4RY

Telephone: (020) 7730 0624

Enquiries: The Vice President, Miss H.M. Campbell, SRN, SCM

Open: Thurs: 10.00–4.00, by prior arrangement.

Access: Bona fide researchers, strictly by appointment. Space is limited. Donations are welcomed.

Historical background: The Royal British Nurses' Association (RBNA) was founded in 1887, the first professional organisation for nurses in the world. One of the main aims of its founders, Dr and Mrs Bedford Fenwick, was the registration of nurses, which was achieved in 1919. The RBNA opposed the opening of the (Royal) British College of Nursing in 1916. For many years it maintained a club for nurses at 194 Queen's Gate in London and today it operates a charity for sick and disabled nurses. The link with Mrs Bedford Fenwick (1857–1947) remained up to her death, and the RBNA's archives, which were fully opened to the public in 1998, reflect this.

Archives of organisation: Minutes, 1887–1982; membership registers, 1888–1966; letters from Princess Christian, the RBNA's first President, 1893–1921; annual reports and accounts, 1902– ; annual reports and accounts of the Trained Nurses Annuity Fund, 1887–1921; and accounts of the Ethel Mary Fletcher Fund, 1963– . RBNA letters and papers, 1886–1994, including material from the many pre-1919 organisations with which Mrs Bedford Fenwick was connected.

Major collections: Records of the British College of Nurses, 1926–56, including material from its special collections on the history of nursing, 1870–1956, and on Florence Nightingale, 1852–1939.

Papers relating to Mrs Bedford Fenwick, 1896–1938, and to the International Council of Nurses, 1900–37.

Non-manuscript material: Large collection of illustrations and photographs.

Periodicals, including *Nursing Journal*, 1902– ; *British Journal of Nursing*, 1888–1955; *Nursing Journal*, 1891–1918; *International Nursing Review*, 1929–39; *Journal of the RBNA*, 1947–63.

Finding aids: The archive has recently been fully catalogued. Copy at NRA.

Facilities: Photocopying. Photography.

Publications: 1999 Handbook includes details of the archives.

750 Royal College of Art

Address: College Library, Kensington Gore, London SW7 2EU

Telephone: (020) 7590 4230

Fax: (020) 7590 4500

E-mail: e.rae@rca.ac.uk

Enquiries: The Archives Assistant

Open: Mon, Fri: 10.00–12.15; Tues: 10.00–12.15, 2.15–4.15; Wed, Thurs: 2.15–4.15.

Access: Generally open to all researchers, by appointment only.

Historical background: The college was founded in 1837 and obtained a royal charter in 1967.

Acquisitions policy: Maintains own archives and acquires material relating to students or staff of the RCA before 1950, with a particular interest in 19th-century material. Student lists most desirable.

Archives of organisation: Archives, including annual reports and prospectuses, student magazines, and degree show catalogues.

Student and staff records are housed in the College Registry.

Major collections: Henry Wilson (1864–1934), architect and designer, notebooks and copious correspondence and writings, late 19th–early 20th century.

Collection of manufacturers' pattern books, 19th–20th centuries.

Non-manuscript material: Black and white photographs of student work, 1950s–1970s.

Finding aids: Catalogue.

Facilities: Photocopying.

751 Royal College of General Practitioners

Address: 14 Princes Gate, Hyde Park, London SW7 1PU

Telephone: (020) 7581 3232 ext. 275

Fax: (020) 7584 1992

E-mail: cjackson@rcgp.org.uk

Website: www.rcgp.org.uk

Enquiries: The Archivist, Claire Jackson

Open: Mon–Fri: 9.00–5.00, an appointment is necessary.

Access: Members of the college and bona fide researchers. Restrictions on access to college archives less than 30 years old.

Historical background: The Royal College of General Practitioners was founded in 1952 to provide an 'academic headquarters for general practice [and] to raise the standards and status of general practice'. The college purchased its present headquarters in 1962. The archives document the college's role in the development of general practice as a specialist branch of medicine, by establishing academic standards and promoting training and research.

Acquisitions policy: To maintain administrative archives of the college and to consolidate holdings through acquisition of papers relating to the activities of the college and its members.

Archives of organisation: Minutes and papers of council, committees and working groups, 1952– .
Administrative records of central departments and other sections, including research units and regional organisations (faculties), 1952– .

Major collections: Papers of Lord Hunt of Fawley (1905–87), William Pickles (1885–1969), Patrick Byrne (1913–80) and John Fry (1922–94).
Transactions and reports of the National Association of General Practitioners, 1844–6.

Non-manuscript material: Photographs and audio-visual collections, including video interviews with eminent members.

Small collection on the history of the headquarters building.

Finding aids: Database catalogue of institutional records, 1952–c1970.
Brief hand-lists for most collections.

Facilities: Photocopying. Photography and consultation of audio-visual material by arrangement.

Conservation: Contracted out.

Publications: J. Fry, Lord Hunt of Fawley and R.J.F.H. Pinsent (eds): *A History of the Royal College of General Practitioners: the First 25 Years* (1983).
Prof D.J. Pereira Gray (consultant ed.): *Forty Years On: the Story of the First Forty Years of the Royal College of General Practitioners* (1992).

752 Royal College of Midwives

Address: 15 Mansfield Street, London W1M 0BE

Telephone: (020) 7872 5100

Fax: (020) 7872 5101

Enquiries: The Hon. Archivist, Ms Cathy Thornton

Open: By arrangement only.

Access: Bona fide researchers, by appointment.

Historical background: The RCM was founded in 1881 as the Matrons' Aid or Trained Midwives' Registration Society (later the Midwives' Institute) to campaign for the registration and training of midwives. The former aim was realised with the Midwives Act of 1902. By 1905 there were over 22,000 registered midwives; other midwives' associations were encouraged to affiliate with the institute, which became the leading representative of the profession. Its importance as a training institution was recognised by the change of title to College of Midwives in 1941, and the prefix Royal was granted six years later.

Acquisitions policy: To maintain and consolidate the college's archives and collections.

Archives of organisation: Records of the college, including incorporation documents; minutes of Council and other committees, including advisory and teachers; financial records, including benevolent funds, 1881–c1960; reports and correspondence *re* maternal mortality, 1934–8, and Rushcliffe Committee on salaries, 1941–7.

Major collections: Some midwives' case books and lecture notebooks, 1917–59.

Non-manuscript material: Memorabilia, including certificates and photographs.

Finding aids: Preliminary inventory, 1981. NRA 19150.

Publications: B. Cowell and D. Wainwright: *Behind the Blue Door: a History of the Royal College of Midwives, 1881–1981* (London, 1981).

753 Royal College of Music

Address: Prince Consort Road, London SW7 2BS

Telephone: (020) 7589 3643

Fax: (020) 7589 7740

E-mail: phorton@rcm.ac.uk

Website: www.rcm.ac.uk

Enquiries: The Reference Librarian, Dr Peter Horton
The Keeper of Portraits, Mr Oliver Davies
The Museum Curator, Mrs Elizabeth Wells

Open: Library: Mon–Thurs: 9.30–6.15; Fri: 9.30–5.30.
Portraits: Mon–Fri: 10.00–5.30.

Access: Generally open to the public, but space is extremely limited during term. Specialised enquiries and parties by appointment only.

Historical background: The Royal College of Music was founded by the Prince of Wales, later King Edward VII, in 1883. The important library of the Sacred Harmonic Society was bought for it by public subscription in that year, and very large collections of MSS and early printed music, musical instruments and portraits have accumulated since, mainly by donation. The Museum of Instruments opened in 1970 and the Department of Portraits opened in 1971.

Acquisitions policy: Library: to extend all classes of material held, by purchase as well as donation.

Archives of organisation: Official records (including student registers), 1883– .
Archives of National Training School for Music, 1876–82.

Major collections: Library: MSS, much of English origin, 16th century– .
MSS of people connected with the college, e.g. Hubert Parry (1848–1918) and Herbert Howells (1892–1983).
Full scores of British choral music, mainly autograph, from Novello's publishing house, 19th century.
Autograph MSS of Walford Davies (1869–1941), Havergal Brian (1876–1972) and Malcolm Arnold (*b* 1921); Frank Bridge (1879–1941) Trust MSS.

Non-manuscript material: Portraits Department: the most comprehensive British collection of likenesses of musicians, comprising 320 original portraits and many thousands of prints and photographs.
Extensive collections of opera illustration, instrumental and concert hall design, title pages.
Concert programmes, 1780– (600,000).
Reference library on musical iconography and performance history; documentation on musical portraiture.
Museum: Keyboard, stringed and wind instruments, *c*1480– (*c*600), including the Tagore, Donaldson, Hipkins, and Ridley and Hartley collections.
Reference library on musical instruments.

Finding aids: Author-title index to MSS and printed books. Handlist of original portraits. Indexes of sitters, opera representation, illustration in music periodicals.
Programme index by artists and first performances.

Facilities: Photocopying of approved material. Photography. Microfilm readers/printer.

Publications: *Guide to the Collection* (1984).
H. Howells: *The Music Manuscripts in the Royal College of Music* (1992).
J. Doane: *A Musical Directory for the Year 1793* (1993).

754 Royal College of Obstetricians and Gynaecologists

Address: 27 Sussex Place, London NW1 4RG

Telephone: (020) 7772 6277

Fax: (020) 7723 0575

E-mail: archives@rcog.org.uk

Website: www.rcog.org.uk

Enquiries: The College Archivist, Clare Cowling

Open: Three days per week, by arrangement with the College Archivist.

Access: Bona fide researchers may apply for access; letters sent to the archivist will be vetted by the college secretary. A 20-year closure rule is applied. A written undertaking must be given, and an appointment is necessary.

Historical background: The college was founded in 1929 from a group within the Gynaecological Visiting Society in the north of England. It moved from Queen Anne Street to a new building on its present site, that of the former Sussex Lodge, in 1960. A royal charter was granted in 1947.

Acquisitions policy: To acquire papers of former presidents and fellows of the college.

Archives of organisation: Records of the founding of the college, 1926–9; council and committee minutes and papers, with records of honorary officers, 1929– ; fellowship selection records, 1930–76.

Special reports, surveys and projects conducted or supported by RCOG, including abortion, contraception, artificial insemination by donor, childbirth, maternity services in general and rare tumour registry, 1950s–1990s.

Major collections: Papers of William Blair-Bell (1871–1936), founder and first president; and of William Fletcher Shaw (1878–1961), first honorary secretary and later president.
NB The library also holds a number of MS collections (unlisted).

Non-manuscript material: Aquarelles (cystoscopic drawings), 1930–45.
X-rays, photographs, plans and drawings, and press cuttings.
Obituary notices (in college library).

Finding aids: Class lists. Indexes. Updated lists will be sent to NRA.

Facilities: Photocopying. Microfilm reader.

Publications: W. Fletcher Shaw: *Twenty Five Years: the Story of the Royal College, 1929–54* (London, 1954).
J. Peel: *The Royal College of Obstetricians and Gynaecologists, 1929–1979* (London, 1979).
C. Cowling and R. Byrne: *Subject Guide 1: A Guide to Personal and Professional Papers of Fellows and Members of the RCOG in the College Archives* (RCOG, 1997).
——: *Subject Guide 2: A Guide to Wartime Papers in the Archives of the RCOG* (RCOG, 1997).
—— : *Subject Guide 3: A Guide to Papers relating to Midwifery in the Archives of the RCOG* (RCOG, 1998).
——: *College Archives: Notes for Fellows, Members and other Researchers* (RCOG, 1998).

755 Royal College of Pathologists

Address: 2 Carlton House Terrace, London SW1Y 5AF

Telephone: (020) 7930 5861

Fax: (020) 7321 0523

E-mail: registrar@rcpath.org

Enquiries: The College Secretary

Open: Mon–Fri: 9.30–5.00, by arrangement.

Access: Bona fide researchers, by appointment.

Historical background: The college was founded in 1962 having developed from the Pathological Society of Great Britain and Ireland, which was established at the beginning of the 20th century when academic pathology became recognised as a distinct subject. Papers of Herbert Maitland Turnball (1875–1955), have been transferred to the Royal London Hospital Archives (see entry 772) and of Sir Roy Cameron to University College London [see entry 832).

Acquisitions policy: To maintain the college archives.

Archives of organisation: Minutes of the Pathological Society of Great Britain and Ireland, 1906–62.
Archives of the college, including annual reports, 1962– .

Non-manuscript material: Photographs and memorabilia of members and fellows.

Facilities: Photocopying.

756 Royal College of Physicians of London

Address: 11 St Andrews Place, Regent's Park, London NW1 4LE

Telephone: (020) 7935 1174 ext. 312/3

Fax: (020) 7486 3729

E-mail: info@rcplondon.ac.uk

Enquiries: The Archivist

Open: Mon–Fri: 9.00–5.00.

Access: Most materials are open to bona fide researchers. There is restricted access to college archives less than 20 years old. Documents containing medical details of patients are not normally available until they are 100 years old.

Historical background: The college was granted its first charter in 1518. It has maintained a library since the 16th century. In 1950 the college decided that its library should concentrate on medical history, and in recent years the library has assumed responsibility for college archives in addition to its MS collections. It is recognised as a place of deposit for public records.

Acquisitions policy: To collect material relating to medical history and biography, with special reference to the college and its fellows.

Archives of organisation: Annals, i.e. records of proceedings of the college, 1518– ; deeds and charters, 1510–1865; other records, 1607– .

Major collections: Western MSS: 13th–20th centuries (several thousand), including collections of papers of individual physicians, mainly 19th and 20th centuries.

Oriental MSS: mostly Arabic, 12th–20th centuries (*c*66 vols).

Non-manuscript material: Paintings, prints and photographs (chiefly medical portraits).

Books, pamphlets and journals.

Sound and video tapes from the college's oral history programme.

Finding aids: Card index. Electronic catalogue in preparation. Catalogues of legal documents (1924) and oriental MSS (1951).

Facilities: Photocopying. Photography and microfilming by arrangement (advance notice required).

Conservation: Contracted out.

Publications: National Inventory of Documentary Sources, Chadwyck-Healey microfiche (1984–).

757 Royal College of Psychiatrists Library

Address: 17 Belgrave Square, London SW1X 8PG

Telephone: (020) 7235 2351

Fax: (020) 7245 1231

E-mail: rcpsych@rcpsych.ac.uk

Website: www.rcpsych.ac.uk

Enquiries: The Archivist (part-time)
The Librarian

Open: Mon–Fri: 8.00–6.00.

Access: Bona fide researchers, strictly by appointment. A letter of introduction is required. There is a day charge.

Historical background: The Association of Medical Officers of Asylums and Hospitals for the Insane was founded in 1841 and changed its name to the Medico-Psychological Association in 1865. It was granted a royal charter in 1926 and in 1971 became the Royal College of Psychiatrists.

Acquisitions policy: To maintain the college's archives. The college does not have a policy of collecting archives from external sources.

Archives of organisation: Minutes of annual meetings, 1841– ; quarterly, council, education and parliamentary committee meetings, mid/late 19th century–1971.

Examination question papers and lists of successful candidates in mental nursing examinations (examinees' names and hospitals only), 1890s–1950s.

Non-manuscript material: Small collection of prints, photographs and newspaper cuttings.

Finding aids: Minutes of annual, quarterly, council, education and parliamentary committee meetings have been abstracted onto an in-house database. Card index to prints, photographs and news cuttings collection.

Facilities: Photocopying.

Conservation: Contracted out.

Publications: The Journal of Mental Science, 1850s– [includes minutes and membership lists].

758 Royal College of Surgeons of England

Address: 35–43 Lincoln's Inn Fields, London WC2A 3PN

Telephone: (020) 7405 3474

Fax: (020) 7405 4438

E-mail: archives@rcseng.ac.uk

Website: www.rcseng.ac.uk/facility/lib&1sc.htm

Enquiries: The Archivist

Open: Mon–Fri: 9.00–6.00.
Closed August.

Access: Approved readers, on written application. New readers should enclose a letter of introduction.

Historical background: The college was founded in 1800 as the successor to the Surgeons' Company, which broke away from the Barber-Surgeons' Company in 1745. It is recognised as a place of deposit for public records

Acquisitions policy: To acquire, by gift, deposit or purchase, material relating to the college and its fellows and the history of surgery and its specialities.

Archives of organisation: Records of the Royal College of Surgeons and its predecessor, the Corporation of Surgeons Company, 1745– .

Major collections: Papers and letters of John Abernethy (1764–1831); Sir Charles Bell (1774–1842); Matthew Baillie (1761–1823); Sir Anthony Bowlby (1855–1929); Sir John Bland-Sutton (1866–1936); Sir Buckston Browne (1850–1945); Edward Browne (1644–1708); George Busk (1807–86); William Clift (1775–1849); Sir Astley Paston Cooper (1768–1814); William Cruikshank (1745–1800); George Dance (1741–1825); Sir Humphry Davy (1778–1829); Thomas Denman (1733–1815); Michael Faraday (1791–1867); Sir Everard Home (1756–1832): John Hunter (1728–93); William Hunter (1718–83); Edward Jenner (1749–1823); Frederic Wood Jones (1879–1954); Robert Keate (1777–1857); Sir Arthur Keith (1866–1955); Rudyard Kipling (1865–1936); Sir William Lawrence (1783–1867); Lord Lister (1827–1912); Wolfgang Amadeus Mozart (1756–91); Sir Richard Owen (1804–92); Sir James Paget (1814–99); Louis Pasteur (1822–95); Sir John Simon (1816–1904); Benjamin

Travers (1783–1858); Sir Frederick Treves (1853–1923); Dorothy Wordsworth (1771–1855); William Wordsworth (1770–1850).
Records of the London Lock Hospital, 1746–1948.
Autograph letters, mainly 19th and 20th centuries.
Surgical papers, casebooks and lecture notes, 18th–20th centuries.

Non-manuscript material: Extensive collection of medical drawings and illustrations, 18th–19th centuries.
Engraved portraits and photographs (c3000); plans, medals, busts.

Finding aids: Various lists and indexes.

Facilities: Photocopying. Photography. Microfiche reader.

Conservation: Contracted out.

Publications: V.G. Plarr: *Catalogue of Manuscripts in the Library of the Royal College of Surgeons of England* (London, 1928).
Z. Cope: *The Royal College of Surgeons of England: a History* (London, 1959).

759 Royal College of Veterinary Surgeons
Wellcome Library

Address: 62–64 Horseferry Road, London SW1P 2AS

Telephone: (020) 7222 2001

Fax: (020) 7222 2004

E-mail: library@rcvs.org.uk

Website: www.rcvs.org.uk

Enquiries: The Librarian, Tom Roper

Open: Mon–Fri: 10.00–5.00.

Access: All those on the statutory register of the college. Others on introduction by a member of the college or a librarian.

Historical background: The college was incorporated by royal charter in 1844, and members immediately offered to present books to form the nucleus of a library. Several important collections have been acquired by bequest.

Acquisitions policy: To strengthen existing collections, by purchase, exchange and donation.

Archives of organisation: Minute books and other records of the college, 1844– .

Major collections: Papers of Sir Frederick Smith (1857–1929) concerning veterinary history, veterinary physiology and army history, particularly South African Wars.

Non-manuscript material: Portraits of presidents of the college.
A few drawings and prints; small collection of photographs.

Finding aids: Individual MSS indexed in main library catalogue. Contemporary indexes to some minute books.

Facilities: Photocopying.

Conservation: Contracted out.

760 Royal Commission for the Exhibition of 1851 Archive

Address: Room 456A, Sherfield Building, Imperial College, Exhibition Road, London SW7 2AZ

Telephone: (020) 7589 5111 ext. 58850

Fax: (020) 7594 8794

Website: www.ic.ac.uk

Enquiries: The Archivist, Mrs Valerie Phillips

Open: Mon–Thurs: 10.00–12.30, 2.00–5.00.

Access: Bona fide scholars, with evidence of identity, by appointment only. There is a 30-year closure on most material and 50 years on personal files.

Historical background: The commissioners were appointed by royal charter in 1850 to plan and promote the Exhibition of the Works of Industry of All Nations (held in London in 1851). When the affairs of the exhibition were wound up, the commissioners remained a permanent body to administer the surplus funds to 'increase the means of industrial education and extend the influence of science and art upon productive industry'. On their estate in South Kensington they have established an educational centre as well as schemes of fellowships and scholarships for advanced study and research in science, engineering and art.

Acquisitions policy: Maintaining the records of the 1851 commission and acquiring some material from other organisations relating to the commissioners' activities.

Archives of organisation: 1851 exhibition correspondence.

Correspondence on the South Kensington estate, including institutions, e.g. Royal Albert Hall, Royal College of Music, Royal College of Art, Science Museum, Natural History Museum, Victoria and Albert Museum, Royal College of Organists, Imperial Institute, Imperial College.
Files of science research scholars, industrial bursars and naval architecture scholars.
Windsor archives on the 1851 exhibition (on permanent loan).

Non-manuscript material: Maps, plans, drawings, photographs.
Publications of the commissioners.

Finding aids: Detailed list in preparation.

Facilities: Photocopying. Photography.

Conservation: Contracted out.

Publications: Records of Science Research Scholars [1891 to date] in preparation.

761 Royal Entomological Society

Address: 41 Queen's Gate, London SW7 5HR

Telephone: (020) 7584 8361

Fax: (020) 7581 8505

E-mail: reg@royensoc.demon.co.uk

Website: www.royensoc.demon.co.uk

Enquiries: The Librarian, Berit Pedersen

Open: Mon–Fri: 9.30–5.00; an appointment is necessary.

Access: Bona fide researchers, on application; a charge may be made to non-members.

Historical background: The society was founded as the Entomological Society of London in 1833, and became 'Royal' in 1933. Its archives consist of the society's administrative records as well as other collections and individual items given over the years; the records are housed in the society library; an archivist is employed on contract.

Acquisitions policy: Records relating to entomology, to the society and its membership.

Archives of organisation: Council and committee minutes, 1833– ; files on individual members, late 19th century– ; society 'obligations book' illustrated by J.O. Westwood (1805–93), 1883.

Major collections: Collections of journals, correspondence and papers, including records of Alexander Henry Haliday (1807–70), who lived in Italy and corresponded in Italian, French and German; Herbert Druce (1846–1913); Roland Trimen (1840–1916), Curator of the South African Museum in Cape Town and friend of Charles Darwin; Hugh Warner Bedford (1893–1975), relating to locust control in the Sudan; Colbran Joseph Wainwright (1867–1949); George Charles Champion (1851–1927), who worked in Central America.

Numerous journals of collecting trips made both in the UK and overseas.

Records of other entomological societies.

Non-manuscript material: Photographs of members.

Various collections of drawings, including two by Alfred Russel Wallace (1823–1913).

Insect cartoons by F.N. Pierce and Harry Eltringham (1873–1941).

Finding aids: Records are currently being catalogued and indexed.

Facilities: Photocopying.

Conservation: Contracted out.

Publications: S.A. Neave: *The History of the Entomological Society of London, 1833–1933* (London, 1933).
A History of the Society and Guide to its Archives (RES, 1999).

762 Royal Free Hospital Archives Centre

Parent organisation: Royal Free Hampstead NHS Trust

Address: The Hoo, 17 Lyndhurst Gardens, Hampstead, London NW3 5NU

Telephone: (020) 7794 0692

E-mail: enquiries@royalfreearchives.org.uk

Website: www.royalfreearchives.org.uk

Enquiries: The Archivist

Open: Mon–Thurs: 9.30–5.00.

Access: Generally open to the public, strictly by appointment. There is a 30-year closure on administrative records and 100-year closure on clinical records.

Historical background: The Free Hospital was founded in Hatton Garden by William Marsden in 1828, became the Royal Free in 1837 and in 1842 moved to Gray's Inn Road, where it remained until transferring to the new building in Hampstead in 1974. This brought together on one site Hampstead General, the London Fever Hospital and Lawn Road Hospital, which had formed the Royal Free Group following the establishment of the National Health Service in 1948. New End and Coppett's Wood Hospitals joined the group in 1966. In 1974 the group became North Camden District (later Hampstead Health Authority). The Royal Free Hampstead NHS Trust was set up in 1991. From 1878 the Royal Free provided clinical teaching facilities for the London School of Medicine for Women, which was founded in 1874 and became the Royal Free School of Medicine when it became co-educational in 1947. Following a merger with University College School in 1998, the school became the Royal Free University College School of Medicine. The archive was first established in 1974 and the Archives Centre opened in 1992, a recognised place of deposit for public records. It houses records of the constituent hospitals of the group and the Medical School, a particularly valuable source for the study of early women's medical education.

Acquisitions policy: Records produced by or directly relating to any of the hospitals or staff associated with the Royal Free Hospital and Hampstead Health Authority and its predecessors. Records produced by or directly relating to the Royal Free Hospital Medical School, its staff and students.

Archives of organisation: Royal Free Hospital administrative records, 1828-, and case books, 1891–1920; staff records, 1968–78; London Fever Hospital administrative records, 1802–1948, and patient records, 1837–1948; Hampstead General Hospital, including North West London Hospital, administrative records, 1882–1948; patient notes and social work records, 1930s–1970s (very incomplete); Children's Hospital, Hampstead, administrative records, 1876–1948; New End Hospital patient records, including birth and death registers, 1914–86 (pre-1948 administrative records in London Metropolitan Archives (see entry 688)); North Western Fever Hospital nursing and domestic staff records, 1887–1950 (patient registers, 1900–48, in London Metropolitan Archives); Coppett's Wood Isolation Hospital, case notes, 1936–1970s.

Records of North Camden and Hampstead health authorities, 1974–89.

Major collections: Royal Free Hospital Medical School records, 1874–1998, including annual reports, council and committee minutes, application forms, student magazines and some student records.

Non-manuscript material: Medical school press cuttings, 1874–1984; hospital press cuttings, 1939–45, c1985– ; extensive photographic collection for both hospital and medical school; microfilmed patient records, 1920–48; various works of art and artefacts, including old medical apparatus; small audio-visual collection, including taped memoirs of some hospital staff.

Finding aids: Most main collections listed and partly indexed: finding aids are constantly updated and enquiries on particular collections should therefore be made directly to the Archivist.

Facilities: Photocopying. Photography. Microfilm reader.

Conservation: Contracted out.

Publications: The Illustrated History of the Royal Free Hospital (1996).

763 Royal Fusiliers (City of London Regiment) Museum and Archives

Parent organisation: The Royal Regiment of Fusiliers

Address: HM Tower of London, London EC3N 4AB

Telephone: (020) 7488 5611

Fax: (020) 7481 1093

Enquiries: The Chief Clerk and Archivist, Mr J.P. Kelleher

Open: Mon–Fri: 9.30–5.00, by arrangement.

Access: Generally open to the public, by appointment and with 48 hours' notice. Postal enquiries are welcome; an SAE is required.

The regiment was raised in the Tower of London in 1685 and amalgamated in 1968 into the Royal Regiment of Fusiliers. There have always been close links with the City of London. The archive includes documents about the raising of the regiment but the bulk of the material dates from World War I. There is a substantial number of deposited collections relating to members of the regiment as well as photographic and sound archives. Indexing is in

progress and additions to the collections are actively acquired.

764 Royal Geographical Society

Address: 1 Kensington Gore, London SW7 2AR

Telephone: (020) 7591 3000

Fax: (020) 7591 3001

E-mail: archives@rgs.org

Website: www.rgs.org

Enquiries: The Archives Assistant, Huw Thomas
The Keeper, Dr Andrew Tatham

Open: Usually Fri: 11.00–5.00.

Access: Fellows of the society and bona fide researchers (by prior application to the Keeper). An appointment is necessary.

Historical background: The society was founded in 1830 to encourage exploration and geographical research. From the time of its foundation the society collected books, maps, pictures, MSS and museum artefacts relevant to its interests. The Institute of British Geologists is now part of the society.

Acquisitions policy: To accept gifts of MSS relevant to the history of geography, cartography, exploration and travel or relevant to notable fellows of the society.

Archives of organisation: Minute books, administrative records, correspondence and working papers of the society, and of the Institute of British Geographers (1930–95).

Major collections: Special collections of the papers of Dixon Denham (1786–1828); Ney Elias (1844–97); David Livingstone (1813–73); Sir Clements Markham (1830–1916); F.W.H. Migeod; Sir Henry C. Rawlinson (1810–95); Henry M. Stanley (1841–1904); Captain R.F. Scott's *Discovery* expedition, 1901–04.
Files of worldwide astronomical observations (to fix positions) and meteorological and topographical observations.

Non-manuscript material: Large collections of maps and pictorial material (Map Room and Picture Library respectively; enquiries should be directed to the Map Curator or Picture Library Manager, as appropriate).

Archives: illustrated MSS diaries, photographs and press cuttings, mostly 19th century.

Finding aids: Author card index. Catalogues available on microfiche.

Facilities: Photocopying. Photography and microfilming by arrangement.

Conservation: Contracted out.

Publications: C. Kelly (comp.): The RGS Archives: a Handlist [reprinted fromGeographical Journal, 141, 142 and 143, plus supplement, vol. 154, part 2; lists accessions up to Dec 1987].

765 Royal Historical Society

Address: c/o University College London, Gower Street, London WC1E 6BT

Telephone: (020) 7387 7532

Fax: (020) 7387 7532

E-mail: royal histsoc@ucl.ac.uk

Enquiries: The Hon. Librarian, Mr D.A.L. Morgan

Open: Mon–Fri: 10.00–5.00, by prior arrangement with the Executive Secretary.

Access: Bona fide researchers, on written application to and at the discretion of the Hon. Librarian.

Historical background: The Historical Society was founded in 1868 and became the Royal Historical Society in 1887. In 1897 the Camden Society was amalgamated with the Royal Historical Society.

Acquisitions policy: No intention of acquiring MSS.

Archives of organisation: Archives of the society and the Camden Society, including minute books, accounts and correspondence, 1867– .

Major collections: Papers of Sir George Prothero (1848–1922), including diaries, letters, notebooks, newspaper cuttings, printed pamphlets and proofs.
Solly Flood MS (a history of the writ of Habeas Corpus by Solly Flood, HM Attorney-General in Gibraltar).

Non-manuscript material: The library consists mainly of printed primary sources for British history.

Finding aids: Duplicated list and supplementary handwritten list of the Prothero papers.

Publications: Report on the Archives of the Camden Society and the Royal Historical Society, 1867–97, Royal Commission on Historical Manuscripts (1977).
Transactions; Camden Series; Guides and Handbooks series and supplementary series.

766 Royal Horticultural Society
Lindley Library

Address: Vincent Square, London SW1P 2PE

Telephone: (020) 7821 3050

Fax: (020) 7828 3022

E-mail: library-enquiries@rhs.org.uk

Website: www.rhs.org.uk

Enquiries: The Librarian, Dr Brent Elliott

Open: Mon–Fri: 9.30–5.30.

Access: Members of the RHS; members of the public with bona fide horticultural enquiries, preferably by appointment.

Historical background: The Horticultural Society of London was founded in 1804 and became the Royal Horticultural Society in 1861. The original library was sold in 1859 and the Lindley Library established in 1868.

Acquisitions policy: Material relating to horticulture worldwide, with subordinate emphasis on botany, garden history, garden design, flower arrangement and botanical art.

Archives of organisation: Archives of Horticultural Society of London, later Royal Horticultural Society: minutes of council and committees.
Architectural drawings for RHS garden at Kensington (1861–88), exhibition halls in Westminster (1904 and 1928), and sundry other buildings.
Flower show records.

Major collections: Personal papers of Edward Augustus Bowles (1865–1954); Ernest Tetley Ellis (1893–1953); Vera Higgins (1892–1968); Lanning Roper (1912–83).

Non-manuscript material: Botanical drawings (c18,000).
UK's largest collection of horticultural trade catalogues.
Photographic collections.

Finding aids: Archives in course of cataloguing.

Facilities: Photocopying and photography may be arranged.

Conservation: Contracted out.

Publications: G. Bridson and others: *Natural History Manuscripts Resources in the British Isles* (1981), 273.
W.L. Tjaden: 'The Loss of a Library', *Garden* [Journal of RHS], 112 (1987), 386–8.
—— : 'The Lindley Library of the Royal Horticultural Society, 1866–1928', *Archives of Natural History*, 20 (1993), 93–128.
B. Elliott: 'Pictures at an Exhibition', *Garden*, 118 (1993), 108–112.
—— : *Treasures of the Royal Horticultural Society* (Herbert Press, 1994).

767 Royal Humane Society

Address: Brettenham House, Lancaster Place, London WC2E 7EP

Telephone: (020) 7836 8155

Fax: (020) 7836 8155

Website: rhs@supanet.com

Enquiries: The Secretary, Maj. Gen. C. Tyler

Open: Mon–Thurs: 10.00–4.00.

Access: Bona fide researchers, by appointment.

Historical background: The society is a national charity founded in 1774 as 'an Institution for the Recovery of Persons apparently dead by Drowning etc.' The founders, mainly medical men, wanted to encourage and disseminate a wider knowledge of the proper methods of restoring the apparently drowned, and the society was instrumental in saving so many lives in the first 20 years that it became an established national institution enjoying royal patronage. Originally based in a receiving house by the Serpentine in Hyde Park, the society gradually extended its activities along all the waterways of London and the surrounding area. Nowadays the society is concerned with granting awards to rescuers.

Acquisitions policy: To maintain the society's archives.

Archives of organisation: Annual reports, minute books, accounts, 1774– ; anniversary sermons, 1775– , and proceedings of anniversary festivals, 1845, 1849–52; case books, 1823– .
Receiving house bathing books and correspondence, 1860–1952.

Non-manuscript material: Plans, drawings and engravings.

Facilities: Photocopying.

Conservation: Contracted out.

Publications: P.J. Bishop: *A Short History of the Royal Humane Society* (London, 1974) [available from the society].

768 Royal Institute of British Architects
British Architectural Library

Address: Manuscripts and Archives Collection 66 Portland Place, London W1N 4AD
British Architectural Library Drawings Collection, 21 Portman Square, London, W1H 9HF

Telephone: (020) 7307 3615

Fax: (020) 7631 1802

E-mail: jane.collings@inst.riba.org

Website: ww.riba.org

Enquiries: The Archivist, Ms Jane Collings

Open: Mon: 1.30–5.00; Tues: 10.00–8.00; Wed– Fri: 10.00–5.00; Sat: 10.00–1.30. Closed August.

Access: Generally open to the public. A charge is made. The Drawings Collection and the Photograph Collection are by appointment only. A paid research service is available.

Historical background: The RIBA was founded in 1834 for the general advancement of civil architecture and for promoting and facilitating knowledge of the various related arts and sciences. From the beginning the British Architectural Library (BAL) has formed an important part of the institute's activities and has always included special collections of drawings, MSS, photographs, pamphlets, and early printed works, in addition to its reference and loan libraries. There is a long tradition of members and well-wishers presenting material to the library, which is funded by members of the RIBA and by a trust fund of donated money. In 2002 the majority of the Drawings Collection will be moved to the Victoria and Albert Museum (entry 838).

Acquisitions policy: To strengthen existing collections relating to the work of architecture, and in particular British architecture, by encouraging donations or deposits, and by purchase.

Archives of organisation: RIBA Archives: administrative records of the institute, documenting the affairs of the RIBA and the preoccupations of the architectural profession, and containing biographical information on its members, 1834– ; includes the archives of the Society of Architects, 1884–1926, and the Architectural Union Company, 1857–1916.

Major collections: BAL MSS Collection: the largest collection in Britain of the papers of architects, architectural organisations and related groups (including MSS, TSS and printed ephemera), 17th century– , but mainly British 19th- and 20th-century material (600 metres). Included are papers of the Scott family; Sir William Chambers (1723–96); the Cockerell family; Godfrey H. Samuel (1904–82); Sir Edwin Lutyens (1869–1944); Oliver Hill (1887–1968); Erno Goldfinger (1902–87); Sir Herbert Baker (1862–1946); Sir Edward Maufe (1883–1974); Sir John Ninian Comper (1864–1960); and Sir John Summerson (1904–92).

Non-manuscript material: BAL Drawings Collection (*c*500,000): the largest collection in Britain of architectural drawings, mainly British, but including important groups of foreign drawings, 16th century– (particularly rich in 19th-century material).
BAL Photographic Collection (*c*400,000 prints): several collections covering British and foreign architecture and topography of all periods; collection of photographic portraits of architects.

Finding aids: Various lists, card indexes and computer databases for use in the library.

Facilities: Photocopies or photographs may sometimes be provided. Microfilm/fiche readers.

Conservation: Limited in-house facilities for drawings, otherwise contracted out.

Publications: Catalogues of the Drawings Collection of the Royal Institute of British Architects (Amersham, 1969–) [8 alphabetical vols; 11 special vols (on Colen Campbell, Gentilhatre, Inigo Jones and John Webb, Lutyens, J.B. Papworth, the Pugin family, the Scott family, Alfred Stevens, Visentini, Voysey, the Wyatt family)].
National Inventory of Documentary Sources, Chadwyck-Healey microfiche (1984–).

A. Mace: *The RIBA: a Guide to its Archive and History* (London, 1986).
——: *Architecture in Manuscript, 1601–1886* (London, 1998).
Architecture and Design Illustrated (London, 1998) [CD-Rom; over 2000 images from the collections].

769 Royal Institute of International Affairs

Address: Chatham House, 10 St James's Square, London SW1Y 4LE

Telephone: (020) 7957 5723

Fax: (020) 7957 5710

E-mail: chume@riia.org

Website: www.riia.org

Enquiries: The Librarian, Mrs Catherine Hume

Open: Mon–Fri: 10.00–5.30 (Enquiry Desk staffed from 11.00).
Closed part of August each year and for occasional extra days around some public holidays.

Access: Bona fide researchers, with suitable references and on written application. A fee is charged. There is a 30-year closure on all archives; archives dealing with purely internal Chatham House affairs are closed indefinitely.

Historical background: The institute was established in 1920 as a result of discussions between British and US delegates to the Paris Peace Conference of 1919. Its royal charter, granted in 1926, precludes it from expressing opinions of its own, so opinions expressed in its publications or at meetings are the responsibility of the authors and speakers. Its aim is to advance the objective study and understanding of all aspects of international affairs and to encourage informed policy-oriented debate on these issues.

Acquisitions policy: To maintain the institute's archives.

Archives of organisation: Records of Chatham House from its foundation, including correspondence and texts of off-the-record meetings held at the institute (speakers include many of international repute); unpublished material from the research and meetings departments of the institute.

Non-manuscript material: An important press-cuttings collection on most aspects of international affairs, 1924–97 (1924–39 is on film at Chatham House but 1972–97 is hard copy; 1940–71 is at the British Library Newspaper Library, see entry 559).

Finding aids: Handlists.

Facilities: Photocopying (self-service copying facilities for the press cuttings). Microfilm/fiche readers.

770 Royal Institution of Great Britain

Address: 21 Albemarle Street, London W1X 4BS

Telephone: (020) 7409 2992

Fax: (020) 7629 3569

E-mail: ril@ri.ac.uk

Website: www.ri.ac.uk

Enquiries: The Director of Collections, Dr Frank James

Open: Mon–Fri: 10.00–5.30.

Access: Bona fide readers, by appointment.

Historical background: Founded in 1799 by, among others, Benjamin Thompson, Count Rumford, to promote the study and advancement of science, the institution has since that time occupied the same premises, where many major scientific discoveries have been made. Apart from specific research project grants, the Royal Institution receives no financial support from government and activities are funded by income from property endowments, donations and subscriptions from members.

Acquisitions policy: Donations and deposits of material relevant to the Royal Institution and those who have worked in it.

Archives of organisation: Royal Institution archives.

Major collections: MSS, administrative records, correspondence and research notes of eminent scientists of the 19th and 20th centuries associated with the Royal Institution, notably Sir Humphry Davy (1778–1829); Michael Faraday (1791–1867); Sir William Grove (1811–96); John Tyndall (1820–93); James Dewar (1842–1923); Sir William H. Bragg (1862–1942); William Lawrence Bragg (1890–1971); Sir Eric K. Rideal.
Journals of Thomas Archer Hirst (1830–92).

Non-manuscript material: Pictures and busts. Large photographic archive.
Prospectuses and lecture lists.

Finding aids: Lists and indexes. Rideal: NRA 22229.

Facilities: Photocopying. Photography. Microfilm/fiche reader.

Conservation: Contracted out.

Publications: T. Martin (ed.): *Faraday's Diary, 1820–1862* (London, 1932).
Proceedings of the Royal Institution: Managers' Minutes, 1799–1903 (1971).
J.R. Friday, R.M. MacLeod and P. Shepherd: *John Tyndall: Natural Philosopher, 1820 1893: Catalogue of Correspondence, Journals and Collected Papers* (1974) [microfiche].
W.H. Brock and R.M. MacLeod: *The Journals of Thomas Archer Hirst, FRS* (1980) [microfiche].
I.M. McCabe and F.A.J.L. James: 'History of Science and Technology Resources at the Royal Institution of Great Britain', *British Journal for the History of Science*, xvii (1984), 205–9.
F.A.J.L. James: *The Correspondence of Michael Faraday* (1991–).

771 Royal Institution of Naval Architects

Address: 10 Upper Belgrave Street, London SW1X 8BQ

Telephone: (020) 7235 4622

Fax: (020) 7259 5912

E-mail: hq@rina.org.uk

Website: www.rina.org.uk

Enquiries: The Technical Officer, Mr D. Culnane

Open: Mon–Fri: 9.30–5.00.

Access: Bona fide researchers, by appointment.

The institution was founded in 1860 and incorporated by royal charters in 1910 and 1960. It has established an international reputation as a qualifying body and learned society in the field of marine technology. It maintains its own archives, which include membership records; institution transactions and written papers; and shipping registers, 1860– . Photocopying is available.

772 Royal London Hospital Archives

Parent organisation: Barts & the London NHS Trust

Address: The Royal London Hospital Archives and Museum, Royal London Hospital, Whitechapel, London E1 1BB

Telephone: (020) 7377 7608

Fax: (020) 7377 7413

E-mail: rjevans@mds.qmw.ac.uk

Enquiries: The Archivist, Mr R.J. Evans

Open: Mon–Fri: 10.00–4.30 (Term: Reading Room open to 7.00).

Access: Generally open to the public, by appointment. Usual restrictions on public (hospital) records: bona fide researchers can be granted access on completion of relevant documentation.

Historical background: The London Hospital (now Royal London) was founded in 1740 and was granted a royal charter in 1758. It was controlled by a Court (later Board) of Governors, which continued after the hospital joined the NHS in 1948 until it became part of Tower Hamlets Health District in 1974. After the first archivist was appointed in 1984, the archives assumed responsibility for the records of all hospitals within the district, and this was subsequently extended to include records of hospitals and health authorities in Newham. From 1994 the hospital was joined by St Bartholomew's Hospital (entry 788) and the London Chest Hospital as part of the Royal Hospitals NHS Trust since renamed; the Queen Elizabeth Hospital for Children joined the trust in 1996, when the archives became responsible for its records. In 1995 the medical college became part of a combined medical school at Queen Mary and Westfield (now Queen Mary, see entry 730). The archive is a recognised repository for public records.

Acquisitions policy: Records produced by or relating to the Royal London Hospital, its alumni and staff; records of health care in Tower Hamlets. The archives also collect records of the London Hospital Medical College and training schools, past and present, associated with health care in the district.

Archives of organisation: Records of the London (now Royal London) Hospital, 1740– ; London Hospital Medical College, 1785–1995; London Hospital School of Nursing, 1873–1967; Princess Alexandra and Newham College of Nursing and Midwifery, 1967–92; the Royal London NHS Trust, 1991–4; Albert Dock Hospital, 1890–1979; Bethnal Green Hospital, 1906–90; City and East London Area Health Authority (Teaching), 1973–82; East London Hospital for Children, 1868–1948; Eastern Dispensary, 1808–1957; East End Maternity Hospital, 1884–1991; East Ham Memorial Hospital, 1926–48; Forest Gate Hospital, 1914–66; London Chest Hospital, 1848– ; London Jewish Hospital, 1926–80; Mildmay Mission Hospital, 1878–1982; Mile End Hospital, 1898–1988; Newham District Health Authority, 1982–93; Plaistow Maternity Hospital, 1890–1978; Poplar Hospital, 1858–1964; Queen Elizabeth Hospital for Children, Hackney, 1868–1998; Queen Mary's Hospital for the East End, Stratford, 1948– ; Queen Mary's Maternity Home, Hampstead, 1919–72; St Andrew's Hospital, Bromley-by-Bow, 1873–1977; St Clement's Hospital, Bow, 1891–1974; Tower Hamlets District Health Authority, 1982–93; Whitechapel Clinic, 1927–57.

Major collections: Records of the London Hospital Medical Club, 1792–1985; Marie Celeste Samaritan Society (f. 1791), 1837–1983; Royal London Hospital League of Nurses (f. 1931); British Society for the Study of Orthodontics, 1907–90; United Hospitals Rugby Football Club, 1872–1910.

Papers and illustrations of Henry Hamilton Bailey, medical teacher, 1928–61; Francis Camps, forensic pathology, including material collected by Sir Bernard Spilsbury and Sir William Bentley Purchase, c1910–1973.

Papers of Kenneth Cross, physiologist, 1946–82; Eva Luckes, matron and writer, including correspondence with Florence Nightingale and Edith Cavell, 1880–1919; Douglas Northfield, neurosurgeon, c1926–1976; Sydney Holland, 2nd Viscount Knutsford, 1897–1931; Dorothy Stuart Russell, pathologist, c1945–1960; Hubert Maitland Turnball, pathologist, 1906–46.

Non-manuscript material: Photographs of wards, medical and nursing staff, 19th and 20th centuries.

Films of hospital subjects, surgery, nursing etc, 1930s– .

Library of books about and by 'Old Londoners', 18th–20th centuries.

Journals: *The Hospital*, 'marked file' series with editor's manuscript annotations, 1890–1921; *London Hospital Gazette*, 1896– .

Reference library of historical medical texts, 16th–20th centuries (2000 items).

A registered museum containing paintings, silverware, instruments and uniforms, trophies etc relating to the Royal London Hospital and health care in East London.

Finding aids: All main archives of organisations and many of the major collections catalogued. Lists sent to NRA.

Facilities: Photocopying. Photography. Microfilm/fiche readers.

Conservation: Contracted out.

Publications: J. Pepler: 'The Archives of Tower Hamlets Health Authority', *Society for the Social History of Medicine Bulletin*, xxxix (Dec. 1986), 80–2.

S. Francis Fish: *The Dental School of the London Hospital Medical College, 1911–1991* (1991).

J. Evans: 'The Royal London Hospital Archive Centre & Museum', *London Hospital Gazette*, new series, xvii (1992).

S.M. Collins: *The Royal London Hospital: a Brief History* (1995).

E.R. Parker and S.M. Collins: *Learning to Care: a History of Nursing and Midwifery Education at the Royal London Hospital, 1740–1993* (1998).

773 Royal National Mission to Deep Sea Fishermen

Address: 43 Nottingham Place, London W1M 4BX

Telephone: (020) 7487 5101

Fax: (020) 7224 5240

E-mail: rnmdsf@msa.com

Enquiries: The Secretary

Open: Mon–Fri: 8.30–4.30.

Access: Generally open to the public, by appointment.

Historical background: The mission was founded in 1881 by Ebenezer Mather, and granted a royal charter in 1896, to offer a spiritual and welfare ministry to fishermen and their families. In early years it visited and ministered to fleets of fishing-boat crews from its own mission ships, known as 'Bethel' ships. Present operations concentrate on mission centres located in fishing ports.

Acquisitions policy: To acquire, nearly always by donation, material relevant to early days of fishing and obscure records of the mission's service.

Archives of organisation: Archives of the mission, 1881– , including council and other minutes (mainly on microfiche).

Major collections: Papers of Sir Wilfred Grenfell (1865–1940), medical missionary in Labrador.

Non-manuscript material: Photo album relating to early history, including photographs of mission ships and a few hospital ships.
Mission magazines (many on fiche).

Facilities: Photocopying. Microfiche readers.

774 Royal National Theatre Archive

Address: Rear of Salisbury House, 1–3 Brixton Road SW9 6DE Address for correspondence Royal National Theatre, South Bank, London SE1 9PX

Telephone: (020) 7820 3512

Fax: (020) 7820 3512

E-mail: archive@nationaltheatre.org.uk

Website: www.nationaltheatre.org.uk/archive

Enquiries: The Archivist, Louise Ray

Open: Mon, Wed, Fri: by appointment only. Telephone enquiries: Mon–Fri: 10.00–4.30.

Access: Accredited researchers, by appointment only. There is restricted access to certain categories of administrative records.

Historical background: The first detailed scheme for a national theatre was drawn up in 1907 by the critic William Archer and the actor/playwright Harley Granville Barker. In 1908 supporters of the scheme joined forces with a group interested in establishing a national memorial to Shakespeare to campaign for a Shakespeare Memorial National Theatre. The committee of the SMNT purchased a site in Cromwell Road in 1937, but the outbreak of World War II delayed the building of a theatre. In 1949 the National Theatre Bill was passed, authorising the use of public funds to establish a National Theatre on a South Bank site. The first NT performance took place on 22 October 1963 at the Old Vic, which housed the NT for the next 13 years. Building on the present site began in 1969 and in 1976 the first production was staged in the Lyttelton Theatre. The archive was established in 1993 with the assistance of the Foundation for Sport and the Arts.

Acquisitions policy: Records and memorabilia of the Royal National Theatre Company's work since 1963. Material relating to the Shakespeare Memorial National Theatre Committee and the early initiatives for a National Theatre.

Archives of organisation: Company archives of the Royal National Theatre, including programmes, posters, press cuttings, production and administrative files, prompt scripts, board minutes, 1963– .

Non-manuscript material: Production photographs/drawings and stage plans; video recordings of the theatre's mainhouse productions, 1995– .

Finding aids: Index in preparation.

Facilities: Photocopying. Photography.

Conservation: Contracted out.

775 Royal Opera House

Address: The Archives, Royal Opera House, Covent Garden, London WC2E 9DD

Telephone: (020) 7212 9353

Fax: (020) 7212 9489

E-mail: francesca.franchi@roh.org.uk jane.jackson@roh.org.uk

Website: www.roh.org.uk/house

Enquiries: The Archivist, Miss Francesca Franchi

Open: Mon, Tues, Thurs, Fri: 10.30–1.00, 2.30–5.30

Access: Approved readers, by appointment. Some administrative records are confidential, some available only following written application. A research fee is charged.

Historical background: The Royal Opera House is the third theatre to have been built on the Covent Garden site and was opened in 1858. The first two theatres opened in 1732 and 1809. On account of the fires that destroyed these two buildings in 1808 and 1856, relatively little material remains relating to their history. There have been various museums and archives at Covent Garden over the years, and when the Royal Opera House reopened after World War II the archives were re-established in the 1950s.

The collection concentrates on performances that have been given at Covent Garden and by the Royal Opera House companies, the Birmingham Royal Ballet, the Royal Ballet and the Royal Opera, with biographical information on the people involved and related general information where possible (e.g. prints/photos of world premières of operas/ballets not at Covent Garden). There has been a full-time archivist since 1969, when the present cataloguing system was introduced.

Acquisitions policy: Material mainly from within the Opera House and from donations. Acquisitions are restricted to items necessary to consolidate the collection and provide general reference material.

Archives of organisation: Correspondence and administrative papers.

Non-manuscript material: Playbills, 1750s–1840s (c5000).

Programmes, 1850s– (complete from 1946).

Prints and photographs of singers, dancers, composers, choreographers, designers, producers, productions, Royal Opera House personnel.

Prints, plans and photographs of the three theatres.

Costume designs by Attilio Comelli (c1000); some other costume and set designs, stage plans etc.

Small reference library of books and periodicals.

Press-cutting library.

Finding aids: Various lists and statistics available. Opera and theatre collection almost completely catalogued; ballet catalogue in the process of being fully completed.

Facilities: Photocopying. Photography.

Conservation: Contracted out.

776 Royal Pharmaceutical Society of Great Britain

Address: 1 Lambeth High Street, London SE1 7JN

Telephone: (020) 7735 9141 ext. 354

Fax: (020) 7793 0232

E-mail: museum@rpsgb.org.uk

Website: www.rpsgb.org.uk/infocentre/ mus_index.htm

Enquiries: The Museum Curator, Caroline M. Reed

Open: By appointment.

Access: Bona fide researchers by appointment only; there are limited research facilities available. Special permission is required for access to the society's council and committee minutes and other internal records.

Historical background: The Pharmaceutical Society of Great Britain was founded in 1841, incorporated by royal charter in 1843 and granted the title 'Royal' in 1988. Historically it has acted as the professional and regulating body for the profession of pharmacy in Great Britain. The Scottish Department, located in Edinburgh, maintains its own library and archive (see NRAS 6743).

Acquisitions policy: Limited to material generated by the society, its staff and members in an official capacity; containing information directly relevant to the society; relating closely to museum collections.

Archives of organisation: Minute books, administrative records, correspondence and working papers of the society, 1841– (incomplete).

Major collections: Limited MSS collection, 15th–20th centuries, mostly recipe books, retail pharmacists' prescription records, some fragmentary business records, minor collections of teaching and research materials relating to pharmacy and pharmacology.
Personal correspondence of Jonathan Pereira (1804–53), Jacob Bell (1810–59) and Daniel Hanbury (1825–75).

Non-manuscript material: Extensive object collection.
Early printed works, including herbals, pharmacopoeias and prints.
Photographs and ephemera.
Audio taped interviews.

Finding aids: Computerised inventory of society archive and deposited MSS collections; see also NRA 26284.
Entry in 'Survey of the Historical Records of the Pharmaceutical Industry' (BAC/Wellcome Trust) database available at Wellcome Library (see entry 844).

Facilities: Photography by arrangement.

Publications: S.W.F. Holloway: *Royal Pharmaceutical Society of Great Britain, 1841–1991: A Political and Social History* (Pharmaceutical Press, 1991).

777 Royal Society

Address: 6 Carlton House Terrace, London SW1Y 5AG

Telephone: (020) 7451 2606

Fax: (020) 7930 2170

E-mail: library@royalsoc.ac.uk

Website: www.royalsoc.ac.uk

Enquiries: The Head of Library and Information Services.
The Archivist, Mrs Joanna Corden

Open: Mon–Fri: 10.00–5.00.

Access: Fellows of the Royal Society and bona fide researchers, who should contact the library in advance of their first visit.

Historical background: The Royal Society was founded in 1660 and has been in continuous existence since that date. One of its earliest activities was to collect scientific books and MSS to form a library.

Acquisitions policy: To collect administrative records of the Royal Society, as well as original papers and correspondence of past presidents and officers and some Fellows.

Archives of organisation: Royal Society Archives: journal books (of meetings), 1660– ; register books, 1661–1738 (21 vols); letterbooks, 1661–1740 (31 vols); classified papers, 1660–1740 (39 vols); early letters, 1660–1740 (38 vols); letters and papers, 1741–1806 (70 vols); referees' reports, 1832– .

Major collections: MSS collections, including Robert Boyle (1627–91), letters and papers (53 vols); Charles Blagden (1748–1820), letters and papers, diary (25 vols); Sir John Herschel (1792–1871), scientific correspondence (35 vols); Sir John William Lubbock (1803–65), correspondence (42 vols); John Smeaton (1724–92), engineering drawings (11 vols).
Papers of Sir Frederick Bawden (1908–72); Lord Blackett (1897–1974); Sir George Lindor Brown (1903–71); Sir Henry Dale (1875–1968); Sir Alfred Egerton (1886–1959); Lord Florey (1898–1968); Sir John Henry Gaddum (1900–65); Sir Cyril Hinshelwood (1897–1967); Sir James Jeans (1877–1946); Otto Loewi (1873–1961); Sir Robert Robinson (1886–1975); Sir Francis Simon (1893–1956); Sir Arthur Tansley (1871–1955); Sir Harold Thompson (1908–83); Lawrence Wager (1904–65).

Non-manuscript material: Tape-recordings of some fellows, also the society's named lectures, 1974– .
Some collections of early photographic material.
A limited number of artefacts from the society's history.

Finding aids: General card catalogue in the library.

Facilities: Microfilming. Microfilm/fiche reader/printer.

Publications: M. Boas Hall: *The Library and Archives of the Royal Society, 1660–1990* (London, 1992).
K. Moore and M. Sampson: *A Guide to the Archive and Manuscripts of the Royal Society* (London, 1995).

778 Royal Society for the Encouragement of Arts, Manufactures and Commerce

Address: 8 John Adam Street, London WC2N 6EZ

Telephone: (020) 7930 5115 ext. 276

Fax: (020) 7839 5805

E-mail: nicola.gray@rsa.org.uk

Website: www.rsa.org.uk

Enquiries: The Archivist, Nicola Gray

Open: Mon, Tues, Thurs: 10.00–1.00; Wed: 10.00–1.00, 2.00–5.00; by appointment.

Access: Fellows of RSA and bona fide researchers.

Historical background: The society was founded in 1754 to encourage arts, manufactures and commerce through the award of premiums and prizes. Its present headquarters was built for it by the Adam brothers in 1774. It was incorporated by royal charter in 1847 and granted the title 'Royal' in 1908. It is a charity which uses its independence and the resources of its international fellowship to stimulate discussion, develop ideas and encourage action.

Acquisitions policy: To maintain the society's archive and acquire fugitive items and other material relevant to the society's history.

Archives of organisation: The society's records: minutes, 1754– ; correspondence, c1755–1851 (c10,000 items).

Major collections: John Scott Russell Collection on the Great Exhibition of 1851 (5 vols).
Transactions and *Journal* of the society, 1754– .
Catalogues of exhibitions held by the Free Society of Artists, 1760–90.
Collection of material relating to international exhibitions in UK and overseas, 1848–1951.

Non-manuscript material: Pamphlets and tracts forming part of the society's library, all pre-1830 (c400).
Collection of mechanical and architectural drawings and paintings relevant to its early 'premium' offers, 1754–c1840.

Finding aids: Card catalogue for MS correspondence.

Facilities: Photocopying of unbound MS items only.

Conservation: Contracted out.

Publications: Series of studies in the society's history and archives, published in *Journal of the Royal Society of Arts* (1958-).
D.G.C. Allan: *William Shipley, Founder of the Society of Arts* (1968).
D.G.C. Allan and J.L. Abbott (eds): *The Virtuoso Tribe of Arts and Sciences* (1992).

779 Royal Society of Chemistry
Library and Information Centre

Address: Burlington House, Piccadilly, London W1V 0BN

Telephone: (020) 7437 8656

Fax: (020) 7287 9798

E-mail: library@rsc.org

Website: www.rsc.org/library

Enquiries: The Librarian, Peter Hoey

Open: Mon–Fri: 9.30–5.30.

Access: Bona fide researchers; an appointment is necessary. Charges are made for extensive research work.

Historical background: The Royal Society of Chemistry was founded in 1980 as a result of the unification of the Chemical Society (f. 1841) and the Royal Institute of Chemistry (f. 1877).

Acquisitions policy: To maintain the archives and accept donations of other relevant material.

Archives of organisation: Minutes of council meetings, 1841– .

Major collections: Note-books, lecture drafts and correspondence of Sir Henry Enfield Roscoe (1833–1918) (*c*700 items).

Non-manuscript material: Nathan Collection of monographs on explosives and firearms, 1598–1990 (978).
Cribb Collection of portraits and cartoons of chemists, 1538–1890 (433).

Finding aids: Searchable catalogue of library images and archives available on the website.

Facilities: Photocopying. Microfilm/fiche readers.

Conservation: Contracted out.

Publications: History of Chemistry Sources of Information [short annotated guide; free on request].

780 Royal Society of Literature

Address: 1 Hyde Park Gardens, London W2 2LT

Telephone: (020) 7723 5104

Fax: (020) 7402 0199

E-mail: rslit@aol.com

Enquiries: The Secretary, Maggie Fergusson

Open: By arrangement.

Access: Bona fide researchers, by appointment.

The society was founded in 1820 by George IV, but many moves of premises have resulted in the loss of much of its archival material. What remains is concerned largely with the administration of the society and consists principally of council minutes and correspondence, with full sets of reports of its proceedings and lectures, 'transactions' and 'essays by divers hands'. Photocopying is available. See E. W. Brabrook, *The Royal Society of Literature of the United Kingdom: a Brief Account of its Origins and Progress.*

781 Royal Society of Medicine

Address: 1 Wimpole Street, London W1M 8AE

Telephone: (020) 7290 2900 ext. 4960

Fax: (020) 7290 2939

E-mail: claire.jackson@roysocmed.ac.uk

Website: www.roysocmed.ac.uk

Enquiries: The Archivist, Claire Jackson

Open: Mon–Fri: 9.00–8.30; Sat: 10.00–5.00; an appointment is necessary.

Access: By arrangement with the Archivist. Access is free to fellows, and temporary library membership is available to non-fellows for a nominal charge.

Historical background: The Medical and Chirurgical Society, a breakaway body from the Medical Society of London, was formed in 1805. A royal charter was granted to the society in 1834 and a new charter in 1907 when a number of other societies amalgamated with it to form the Royal Society of Medicine. The old societies then became specialist sections of the Royal Society of Medicine.

Acquisitions policy: Papers relating to the Royal Society of Medicine, its predecessor organisations and people who have played a prominent role in the society.

Archives of organisation: Records of Royal Society of Medicine, 1907– , and of predecessor societies, including the Royal Medical and Chirurgical Society, 1805–1907; Society of Anaesthetists, 1893–1908; British Balneological and Climatology Society, 1895–1909; Society for the Study of Diseases in Children, 1900–08; Dermatological Society of London, 1882–1907; Clinical Society of London, 1868–1907; British Electrotherapy Society, 1901–07; Epidemiology Society, 1850–1907; British Gynaecological Society, 1884–1907; British Laryngological, Rhinological and Otological Association, 1888–1907; Neurological Society, 1886–1907; Obstetrical Society of London, 1858–1907; Odontological Society of Great Britain, 1856–1907; Pathological Society of London, 1846- 1907; Therapeutical Society, 1902–07.

Major collections: Considerable collection of lecture notes, correspondence and case notes, including Robert Bayfield (*c*1629–70); John Abernethy (1764–1831); Matthew Baillie (1761–1823); Joseph Black (1728–1799); Sir Astley Cooper (1768–1841); William Cullen (1710–90); John Hunter (1728–93); William Hunter (1755–1812); Sir William Jenner (1815–98); Percival Pott (1714–88); Herman Boerhaave (1668–1738); Thomas Young (1773–1860); William Withering (1741–99); Percivall Willughby (1596–1685); Alexander Monro (1692–1762); Alexander Monro II (1753–1817);

Marshall Hall (1790–1857); William Hawes (1736–1808).

Non-manuscript material: Portraits of medical men, photographs, plans, medals, microscopes. Diamond photographic collection on 19th-century lunacy.

Finding aids: NRA 19231.

Facilities: Photocopying. Photography. Microfilm reader.

Conservation: Contracted out.

Publications: Report on the Records of the Royal Society of Medicine, 1805–1968, Royal Commission on Historical Manuscripts no. 75/42 (London, 1975).

782 Royal Society of Musicians of Great Britain

Address: 10 Stratford Place, London W1N 9AE

Telephone: (020) 7629 6137

Enquiries: The Secretary

Open: Mon, Wed, Fri: 10.15–3.45.

Access: Approved readers, on written application.

Historical background: Founded in 1738 as a benevolent fund for musicians and their families, the society took its present name in 1785 and was granted a royal charter five years later. The Royal Society of Female Musicians was subsequently absorbed in 1866. The society is still administered by governors and a court of assistants.

Acquisitions policy: Donations of relevant material are accepted.

Archives of organisation: Minute books of governors, 1785– ; minutes of annual general meetings, 1792– ; files on members, c1776– ; other minute books and cash books; annual lists of subscribers, 1742– .
Many letters from distressed musicians and correspondence relating to public functions.

Major collections: MS scores of Joseph Haydn (1732–1809), Carl Maria von Weber (1786–1826), Philip Cipriani Potter (1792–1871) and Sir Henry Rowley Bishop (1786–1855).

Non-manuscript material: Portraits and photographs of members, 19th and 20th centuries.

783 Royal Society of Tropical Medicine and Hygiene

Address: Manson House, 26 Portland Place, London W1N 4EY

Telephone: (020) 7580 2127

Fax: (020) 7436 1389

E-mail: mail@rstmh.org

Website: www.rsthm.org

Enquiries: The Hon. Secretaries

Open: By arrangement.

Access: Fellows only; other bona fide scholars strictly by arrangement with the Hon. Secretaries.

The society was founded in 1907 by James (later Sir James) Cantlie and George Carmichael Low. Patrick Manson (1844–1922) was the first president, and it became the Royal Society in 1920. It retains its council minutes and membership applications from that date. All other material has been transferred to the Wellcome Library (entry 844). *Transactions* have been published since 1907.

784 Royal Statistical Society

Address: 12 Errol Street, London EC1Y 8LX

Telephone: (020) 7638 8998

Fax: (020) 7638 0946

E-mail: j.foster@rss.org.uk

Website: www.rss.org.uk

Enquiries: The Archives Consultant, Janet Foster

Open: By arrangement.

Access: Generally open to the public by arrangement. An appointment is essential.

Historical background: The Statistical Society of London was founded in 1834 and renamed the Royal Statistical Society in 1887. The founders included Charles Babbage and T.R. Malthus and members of the society were, and are, known as fellows. The principle activities of the society were the publication of its *Journal* and the holding of monthly meetings. The society's activities began to expand in the 20th century with the establishment of the Industrial and Agricultural Research Section. In 1993 the Institute of Statisticians, founded in 1948 as a professional and examining body for statisticians, was merged with the society. The society has changed premises nine times causing significant gaps in the archives, especially in the later 19th century.

Acquisitions policy: The society maintains its own archives and accepts donations of material having a direct relevance to its activities and fellows.

Archives of organisation: Archives of the Royal Statistical Society, 1834– , comprising reports of Council, lists of Fellows and byelaws, 1834–; minutes of Council and committees, Anniversary, Annual and Ordinary meetings, 1834–1995; Fellowship records, 1834– ; administration records, 1834–1980s; finance records, 1834–1980s; minutes and papers of research and study Sections; and Library registers, catalogues and papers, 1851– .

Major collections: Papers of William Newmarch (1820–1882), banker, 1753–1880, principally concerning prices and the movement of money. William Stanley Jevons (1835–82) charts.

Non-manuscript material: Photographs of presidents and eminent statisticians.

Finding aids: Catalogue. Detailed listing in progress. NRA 14718.

Facilities: Photocopying. Photography.

Conservation: Contracted out.

785 Royal Television Society

Address: Tavistock House East, Tavistock Square, London WC1H 9HR

Telephone: (020) 7430 1000

Fax: (020) 7430 0924

E-mail: royaltvsociety@btinternet.com

Website: www.rts.org.uk

Enquiries: The Consultant Archivist, Ms C. Colvin

Open: By arrangement with the Archivist.

Access: Members of the society and bona fide researchers, by appointment only.

Historical background: The Television Society was founded in 1927 and granted the royal title in 1966. The society's activities include the organisation of lectures and a major annual symposium, the publication of *Television* and the society's *Bulletin*, annual awards to the industry, and, more recently, courses of training for television. In these activities it is supported by 14 regional centres. The library and archives suffered considerable damage during the war and were not maintained until the appointment of an archivist in 1986. The records chart the history and development of television and include material on electrical engineering.

Acquisitions policy: To acquire material relevant to the society about the history and development of television.

Archives of organisation: Archives of the society: official and working papers, 1927– .

Major collections: Lecture notes of Sir Ambrose Fleming (1849–1945).
MSS, photographs and printed ephemera on John Logie Baird (1888–1946), W.C. Fox, and other pioneers of television.

Non-manuscript material: Photographs of television equipment, personalities and society events.
Small collection of books on the history of television.

Finding aids: A catalogue of the collection is in preparation.

Facilities: Photocopying. Photography and the copying of tapes by arrangement.

786 Royal Veterinary College
Historical Collections and Veterinary Museum

Parent organisation: University of London

Address: Royal College Street, London NW1 0TU

Telephone: (020) 7468 5162

Fax: (020) 7468 5162

E-mail: d.walker@rvc.ac.uk

Website: www.rvc.ac.uk/general/library/historic.htm

Enquiries: The Archivist

Open: Mon–Fri: 9.00–4.45, by appointment.

Access: Generally open to the public; a donation to assist in the preservation of the collections would be appreciated. A charge is made for research by staff.

Historical background: The Royal Veterinary College was established in 1791. The college was the first of its kind in the English-speaking world, and was granted its royal charter in 1875. The RVC became a school of the University of London in 1949. The historical collections have been formally gathered together since 1990 and the Veterinary Museum was created in 1992.

Acquisitions policy: Primarily material relating to the history of the college, but gifts of material relating to the development of veterinary science in general are very welcome.

Archives of organisation: Archives of the college, including minutes, 1790–1905; register of pupils, 1794–1907; student entry books, 1839–1930; illuminated scrapbook *re* fundraising 'The Book of the Nosebag' appeal, 1934–5.
Letter-books of Richard Atherton Norman Powys, first college secretary (1876–1913), 1879–1909 (7 vols).

Major collections: James Beart Simonds (1810–1904), first Chief Inspector and Veterinary Advisor to the Privy Council (1865), and RVC Principal (1872–81), papers on veterinary matters, especially cattle plague, pleuro-pneumonia, variolar ovina, 19th century (9 scrapbooks and 70 'tract volumes').
A.M. Johnston Collection: papers relating to cattle plague in Scotland, 19th century.
Frederick Smith (1857–1929) MS notes for a biography of Napoleon Bonaparte (unpublished).
Day books of the Beaumont Animals Hospital, 1933–64.
Papers and letters of the London Veterinary Medical Society, 1813–36, and of the Veterinary Medicine Association, including minutes, 1836–84.

Non-manuscript material: Books, pamphlets and periodicals, pre-1901 (*c*4000), reputedly one of the finest historical veterinary collections in the world.
Veterinary instruments.
Photographs of college staff, students and buildings, *c*1860– .

Finding aids: NRA 35652.

Facilities: Photocopying. Photography by arrangement. Microfilm reader/printer.

Publications: Catalogue of the Books, Pamphlets and Periodicals up to 1850 (1965).
'Historical Manuscripts at the Royal Veterinary College, University of London', *Librarians World*, 1/2 (1992), 2–4.

'The Scrapbooks of the Simonds Collection at the Royal Veterinary College', *Veterinary History*, 7/2(1992), 39–45.
Royal Commission on Historical MSS: *Annual Review, 1992–1993* [gives a summary of the archives].
Guide to Historical Collections and *A Brief History of the RVC* [leaflets; available free].

787 Saddlers' Company

Address: Saddlers' Hall, 40 Gutter Lane, London EC2V 6BR

Telephone: (020) 7726 8661/6

Fax: (020) 7600 0386

E-mail: archivist@saddlersco.co.uk

Enquiries: The Clerk to the Company, Group Captain W.S. Brereton Martin
The Company Archivist, Mrs E.A. Seymour

Open: By appointment only.

Access: By written application, and at the discretion of the company.

Historical background: The Worshipful Company of Saddlers is one of the oldest established livery companies in the City of London; its first recorded charter was granted in 1363, and its incorporation charter in 1365. The company maintained close control over the saddlery trade in the City of London until the 19th century. Today it is closely involved in saddlery education and supports the work of the Society of Master Saddlers. Its charitable activities are funded through a series of trusts, the oldest of which was founded in 1557. The company lost many of its records in 1940 when the hall was destroyed during the blitz.

Acquisitions policy: To acquire material closely related to the history of the company, its members and the saddlery trade.

Archives of organisation: Records of the Worshipful Company of Saddlers, mainly 1946– , but including 'Testament' or record book, and 'Freedom Roll', which is signed by all new members, 17th century– ; Court Minute Book, 1605–66.

Non-manuscript material: Audio and visual material recording the history of the company and the saddlers' craft.
Information on the company through research at other archives.
Small collection of books on saddlery.

Finding aids: Handlists and indexes of company members.

Facilities: Photocopying.

Publications: J.W. Sherwell: *The History of the Guild of Saddlers of the City of London* (1889; rev. 1937, 1956).

K.M. Oliver: *The History of the Worshipful Company of Saddlers of the City of London* (1995).

—— : *The Treasures and Plate of the Worshipful Company of Saddlers* (1995).

788 St Bartholomew's Hospital

Parent organisation: Barts and the London NHS Trust

Address: West Smithfield, London EC1A 7BE

Telephone: (020) 7601 8152

E-mail: marion.rea@bartsandthelondon.nhs.uk

Enquiries: The Archivist, Ms Marion Rea

Open: Mon–Fri: 9.00–5.00, by appointment.

Access: Generally open to the public. There is a 30-year closure on administrative records and a 100-year closure on medical records.

Historical background: St Bartholomew's Hospital was founded, with a monastic priory, in 1123. It was re-established by Henry VIII in 1546 and thereafter controlled by a board of governors, which continued after the hospital joined the National Health Service in 1948 but became defunct following the reorganisation of the NHS in 1974. The archives department at St Bartholomew's was set up after the appointment of the hospital's first achivist in 1934. In 1974 St Bartholomew's became part of the City and Hackney Health District, and the archives department assumed responsibility for the records of all hospitals within the district. In 1994 the hospital joined the Royal London and London Chest Hospitals to form the Royal Hospitals NHS Trust, now Barts and the London NHS Trust. The archives department is recognised as a place of deposit for public records. A museum was opened in 1997.

Acquisitions policy: Restricted to records produced by St Bartholomew's and associated hospitals, or directly relating to any of them or to prominent members of staff.

Archives of organisation: Records of St Bartholomew's Hospital, 12th century– ; Medical College, 1832– ; School of Nursing, 1877–1970s; Alexandra Hospital for Children with Hip Disease, 1866–1958; Eastern Hospital, 1874–1972; German Hospital, Dalston, 1843–1970; Hackney Hospital, 1876–1983; Metropolitan Hospital, 1836–1977; Mothers' Hospital, 1913–84; St Leonard's Hospital, 1885–1969; and St Mark's Hospital, City Road, 1857–1988.

Records of the Central Group Hospital Management Committee, 1948–66; Hackney Group Hospital Management Committee, 1948–74.

Major collections: Parish records of St Bartholomew the Less, 1547– , and St Nicholas Shambles, 1452–1546.

Records of the Royal General Dispensary, Bartholomew Close, 1894– .

Non-manuscript material: Maps and plans of St Bartholomew's Hospital and its estates, 17th–20th centuries (c500 items).

Photographs, mainly of hospital buildings, staff and patients, c1880– .

Portraits and sculptures of eminent physicians, surgeons and benefactors of St Bartholomew's Hospital, and prints and drawings, mainly 17th–20th centuries.

Museum of silverware, instruments and other hospital-related objects.

Hospital publications.

Finding aids: Index and calendar of medieval deeds of St Bartholomew's. Card catalogues of all holdings (computerised catalogue in preparation). St Bartholomew the Less: index of baptisms, 1547–1894, marriages, 1547–1847, burials, 1547–1848.

Facilities: Photocopying. Photography. Microfilm reader.

Conservation: Contracted out.

Publications: N.J. Kerling: *Cartulary of St Bartholomew's: a Calendar* (London, 1973).

—— : 'Archives', in *The Royal Hospital of St Bartholomew, 1123–1973*, ed. V. Medvei and J.H. Thornton (London, 1974), 299.

—— : *Descriptive Catalogue of Archives of the Hospitals in the City and Hackney Health District from the beginning of each Hospital to 1974* (Historical Manuscripts Commission, 1977) [includes records held by other repositories].

Minute Books, Accounts and other Records, 1547–1801 (World Microfilms Publications, 1988).

G. Yeo: *Resources in the Archives Department: a Guide for Users* (London, 1990).

789 St Bride Printing Library

Parent organisation: Corporation of London

Address: St Bride Institute, Bride Lane, London EC4Y 8EE

Telephone: (020) 7353 4660

Fax: (020) 7583 7073

E-mail: stbride@corpoflondon.gov.uk

Enquiries: The Librarian, Nigel Roche

Open: Mon–Fri: 9.30–5.30.

Access: Generally open to the public; an appointment is recommended for special collections.

Historical background: The parish of St Bride has long been a centre of printing and allied trades. In 1894 the St Bride Foundation Printing School opened, its library financed by J. Passmore Edwards. The school moved in 1922 to Southwark, to form the London College of Printing (see entry 685), but the library remained and has been administered by the City Corporation since 1966.

Major collections: Records of several firms and printing organisations, including Association Typographique Internationale; British Printing Industries Federation; Double Crown Club; Electrotypers and Stereotypers Managers' and Overseers' Association; Printing Historical Society; Wynkyn de Worde Society.
London Society of Compositors and other unions, archival material and publications.
Collections of trade documents on labour relations in trade, 1785–1913.
Richard Taylor (1781–1858), personal and family papers *re* printing and publishing of scientific journals, records of his business.
Specimens of printing: a small group of Western and oriental MSS.

Non-manuscript material: Newspapers, broadsides, book jackets, chapbooks etc, with a large collection of ephemera, mostly 18th–19th centuries (*c*6000 entries).

Finding aids: Lists and indexes.

Facilities: Photocopying.

790 St George's Hospital NHS Trust and Medical School

Address: The Library, Hunter Wing, St George's Hospital Medical School, Cranmer Terrace, London SW17 0RE

Telephone: (020) 8725 5466/3255

Fax: (020) 8767 4696

E-mail: nthevaka@sghms.ac.uk

Website: www.sghms.ac.uk/depts/library/hist.htm

Enquiries: The History Librarian, Nallini Thevakarrunai

Open: Mon–Fri: 9.00–6.00, by appointment.

Access: Accredited researchers and interested persons.

A Archives

Historical background: St George's Hospital was founded in 1733. It was controlled by a board of governors, which continued after the hospital joined the National Health Service in 1948. The Atkinson Morley Hospital at Wimbledon was built (1867–9) originally for convalescents, but is now the neurological and neurosurgical department; in addition it provides some psychiatric in-patient facilities. The governors were given the management responsibility for the Victoria Hospital for Children and the Royal Dental Hospital, Leicester Square, which closed in 1964 and 1985 respectively. In 1954 St George's began to refurbish derelict wards at the Grove Fever Hospital, Tooting, and in 1968 the building of the new St George's began on the sites of the Grove and Fountain Hospitals. In 1974 the board of governors was replaced by Merton, Sutton and Wandsworth Health Authority, which was itself replaced by the Wandsworth District Health Authority in 1981. In these reorganisations St George's and the Atkinson Morley hospitals were grouped with St James', South London for Women, St Benedict's, Weir, Springfield and Bolingbroke hospitals. Closures of the Weir, St Benedict's, South London for Women and St James' took place in 1979, 1980, 1984 and 1988 respectively. St George's at Hyde Park Corner was closed in 1980 and the new hospital at Tooting was formally opened in 1980. St George's NHS Healthcare Trust was formed in 1993 and includes St George's, Atkinson Morley and Bolingbroke hospitals.

Acquisitions policy: Restricted to records relating to St George's, Atkinson Morley and Tite Street hospitals, St James', South London for Women and Bolingbroke hospitals.

Archives of organisation: Records of weekly boards of St George's Hospital, 1733–1948. Records of Tite Street, Atkinson Morley, Bolingbroke, St James', South London for Women and Springfield hospitals.

Non-manuscript material: Photographs, pictures, plans.

Finding aids: List of main material. NRA 9767.

Facilities: Photocopying.

B Medical School Library

Historical background: The medical school at St George's was built in 1834, but the hospital has been associated with the teaching of medicine since its foundation in 1733. Physicians and surgeons of the hospital were permitted to have a limited number of pupils and the register of these past students is still preserved in the medical school. A number of celebrated men have been associated with the school, including John Hunter (1728–93), Edward Jenner (1749–1823), Sir Benjamin Collins Brodie (1783–1862) and Henry Gray (1872–1912). In 1901 the school was incorporated as a clinical school within the University of London and in 1976 pre-clinical teaching began at Tooting. All clinical teaching ended at Hyde Park Corner in 1980, when the medical school was transferred to the Tooting site.

Acquisitions policy: Donations of material directly related to the existing collection.

Archives of organisation: Records of the library, 1836–1946 (incomplete).

Major collections: MSS of or relating to Sir Benjamin Collins Brodie.
Student notes of lectures delivered at St George's Hospital, late 18th and 19th centuries.
MSS of Hyde Park Corner Whist Club, 1891–1925.
MSS of St George's Hospital Medical and Surgical Society (later Hunterian Society), 1833–1956.

Non-manuscript material: Photographs, pictures, plans, late 19th and 20th centuries.

Finding aids: List of principal items of interest.

Facilities: Photocopying.

Publications: National Inventory of Documentary Sources, Chadwyck-Healey microfiche (1984–).

791 St Joseph's Missionary Society
Archives of the Mill Hill Missionaries

Address: St Joseph's College, Lawrence Street, Mill Hill, London NW7 4JX

Telephone: (020) 8959 8254

Enquiries: The Archivist, Fr Tom O'Brien

Open: Mon–Fri: 9.00–12.30.

Access: Bona fide researchers. There is a 50-year closure on all personal correspondence.

Historical background: St Joseph's Missionary Society is a Roman Catholic society for primary evangelisation outside Europe. It was founded in 1866 by Herbert Vaughan (1832–1903), later Cardinal-Archbishop of Westminster.

Acquisitions policy: Maintaining of the archives and minor acquisition of printed matter and photographs.

Archives of organisation: Correspondence between headquarters and mission territories in Africa, Asia, Latin America and Australasia; society's publications.

Major collections: Papers and memorabilia of Cardinal Vaughan; diaries of other missionaries.

Non-manuscript material: Photographs from missionary countries.
Publications of similar societies.

Facilities: Photocopying.

Publications: D. Henige: 'The Archives of the Mill Hill Fathers', *African Research and Documentation*, xxii (1980), 18–20.
W. Mol: 'Our Archives', *Millhilliana*, 1 (1981), 31–6.
——: 'The Archives of the Mill Hill Missionaries', *Catholic Archives* (1982), 19–27.

792 St Mary's Hospital Archives

Parent organisation: St Mary's NHS Trust

Address: St Mary's Hospital, Paddington, Praed Street, London W2 1NY

Telephone: (020) 7886 6528

Fax: (020) 7886 6739

E-mail: kevin.brown@st-marys.nhs.uk

Enquiries: The Trust Archivist and Curator, Mr Kevin Brown

Open: Mon–Fri: 9.00–5.00, by appointment only.

Access: Generally open to the public. The 30-year closure rule applies. Appointments are essential.

Historical background: St Mary's Hospital was founded as a voluntary hospital in 1845 and opened in 1851; St Mary's Hospital Medical School was founded in 1854. In 1948 the hospital become part of the National Health Service, and its medical school became an independent institution within the University of London. The St Mary's Teaching Group of Hospitals was extended to include the Samaritan Free Hospital for Women; Western Ophthalmic Hospital; Paddington Green Children's Hospital; Princess Louise Hospital Kensington; and St Luke's Hospital for Advanced Cases. The group was joined by Paddington General Hospital in 1968 and by St Charles' Hospital in 1991. St Mary's had its own board of governors until 1974 when it passed to health authority control. Since 1992 it has been governed by St Mary's NHS Trust. The Medical School merged with Imperial College (see entry 643) in 1988 and became part of ICSM in 1997. An archivist was appointed in 1989 as a joint appointment between the hospital and medical school. The archives department administers the Alexander Fleming Laboratory Museum (f. 1993).

Acquisitions policy: To acquire material relating to St Mary's Hospital, St Mary's Hospital Medical School, the constituent hospitals, their staff and students, and Sir Alexander Fleming (as part of the Alexander Fleming Laboratory Museum).

Archives of organisation: Archives of St Mary's Hospital, 1845– ; St Mary's NHS Trust, 1991– ; St Mary's Hospital Medical School, 1854–1988; Imperial College School of Medicine at St Mary's, 1988– , Inoculation Department, St Mary's Hospital, 1907–48; Wright Fleming Institute, 1948–67; Paddington Green Children's Hospital, 1883–1987; Samaritan Free Hospital for Women (formerly Gynaepathic Institute), 1847–1997; Princess Louise Hospital, Kensington, 1900–74; St Luke's Hospital for the Dying Poor, 1893–1974; Ophthalmic Hospital, 1856– ; Paddington General Hospital deeds, 1800–1935; St Charles' Hospital, Ladbroke Grove, 1881–1991.

Records of student societies; Ladies' Association, 1906– .

Major collections: Paddington and North Kensington Health Authority records, 1986–88.

Parkside District Health Authority archives, 1988–91.

St Columba's Hospital archives (formerly Friedenheim Hospital), 1901–52.

British Hospital records (Forbes Winslow Memorial Hospital), 1894–1946.

West End Hospital for Nervous Diseases, records, 1908–34.

Child psychiatry papers of Dr Donald Winnicott (1896–1971).

St Marylebone General Dispensary, records, 1835–1936.

Non-manuscript material: Plans, drawings and photographs.

St Mary's Hospital Gazette, 1895–1998.

Small collection of oral history tapes.

Fundraising posters and other printed ephemera.

Museum collections of artefacts.

Finding aids: Catalogues and lists; sent to NRA.

Facilities: Photocopying and photography by arrangement.

Publications: K. Brown: *St Mary's Hospital: an Illustrated History* (1991).

A. Barrett and K. Brown (eds.): *St Mary's Hospital Medical School: an Historical Anthology* (1990).

St Mary's Hospital Gazette was edited and published from St Mary's Hospital Archives, 1996–8, and contains information on the archives and collections.

K. Brown and T. Allen (eds.) *Hospitals and Nursing, 1845–1948* and *Alexander Fleming and Penicillin* (1998) [Education packs available from the Archivist].

793 St Paul's Girls' School

Address: Brook Green, Hammersmith, London W6 7BS

Telephone: (020) 7603 2288

Fax: (020) 7602 9932

E-mail: howard.bailes@spgs.org

Website: www.spgs.org

Enquiries: The Archivist, Dr Howard Bailes

Open: Term: Mon–Fri: 8.40–5.00.

Access: Generally open to the public, by appointment.

Historical background: The school was founded in 1904 by the Mercer's Company, and is a sister school of St Paul's School (entry 794).

Acquisitions policy: To maintain the archives.

Archives of organisation: Archives of the school, 1904– , including MSS of Gustav Holst (1874–1934), Director of Music at the School, 1905–34; Imogen Holst (1907–84); and Ralph Vaughan Williams (1872–1958).
School magazine, *Paulina*, 1904– .

Major collections: Significant material on successive high mistresses.

Non-manuscript material: The personal library of Sir Siegmund Warburg (1902–82).

Facilities: Photocopying. Photography.

Publications: Catalogue of the Warburg Library.

794 St Paul's School Archives

Address: Lonsdale Road, London SW13 9JT

Telephone: (020) 8748 9162

Fax: (020) 87489 557

E-mail: sent@stpauls.richmond.sch.uk

Website: www.stpaulschool.org.uk

Enquiries: The Archivist, Mr David May

Open: Mon–Fri: 9.30–4.30, during term, by appointment.

Access: Bona fide researchers, on written application; there is very limited accommodation.

Historical background: St Paul's School was founded by Dean Colet, probably in 1509. The school and most of its records were destroyed in the Great Fire of London (1666); any surviving early records are held by the Mercers' Company (entry 696). The library and archives both have items connected with the history of the school and its pupils.

Acquisitions policy: The library purchases books and MSS by Old Paulines. The archives have no funds but actively encourage donations and deposits by the school, old boys and masters.

Archives of organisation: School Archives: apposition lists, 1749– ; governors' minutes, 1876–1973.
School magazines, 1831– ; calendars, 1881– ; club lists of masters and boys, 1918– ; examination papers; team photographs. School reports; records of school societies; memoirs by old boys.

Major collections: Correspondence of Duke of Marlborough (1650–1722); William Camden (1551–1623); Judge Jeffreys (1648–89); Benjamin Jowett (1817–93); Thomas Clarkson (1760–1846); Ernest Raymond (1888–1974); Viscount Montgomery (1887–1976).
Literary MSS of Rev. R.H. Barham (1788–1845); Laurence Binyon (1869–1943); G.K. Chesterton (1874–1936); E.C. Bentley (1875–1956).

Non-manuscript material: Engravings of the school.
Naimaster Collection of engravings of Old Paulines and high masters.
Books by and about Edward Thomas (1878–1917).
Books relating to the early history of the school, including grammars, 1575– , preces, 1644– , and sermons, 1674– .
School copy books, 17th and 18th centuries.

Finding aids: Card indexes of authors, subjects, masters and boys.

Facilities: Photocopying.

795 Salters' Company

Address: The Salters' Hall, 4 Fore Street, London EC2Y 5DE

Telephone: (020) 7588 5216

Fax: (020) 7638 3679

E-mail: company@salters.co.uk

Enquiries: The Archivist, Mrs Katie George

Open: By appointment only.

Access: Bona fide researchers, by arrangement. Access is restricted.

Historical background: The company had its origins in a religious fraternity founded in 1394

and received charters of incorporation as a livery company in 1559 and 1607.

Acquisitions policy: Continuous policy of incorporating current material in the company archives and of acquiring relevant material for the company and other (e.g. almshouses) archives as they become available.

Archives of organisation: Charters and other constitutional documents.
Court minutes, 1627– .
Reports of other committees.
Documents on charitable matters (e.g. almshouses and Salters' Institute of Industrial Chemistry).
Documents relating to the company's English estates.
Records relating to admission to the freedom, 1716– ; apprenticeship, 1678– ; and livery, 1714– .

Non-manuscript material: Photographs, drawings and plans.

Finding aids: Checklist; calendar.

Publications: J. Steven Watson: *History of the Salters' Company* (1963).
H. Barty-King: *The Salters' Company, 1394–1994* (1994).

796 Salvation Army International Heritage Centre

Address: William Booth College, House 14, Denmark Hill, London SE5 8BQ
Correspondence: 101 Queen Victoria Street, London EC4P 4EP

Telephone: (020) 7332 0101 ext. 8704

Fax: (020) 7332 8099

E-mail: heritage@salvationarmy.org

Website: www.salvationarmy.org/history

Enquiries: The Director, Maj. James Bryden
The Archivist, Gordon Taylor

Open: Mon–Fri: 9.00–3.30.

Access: Generally open to the public, by appointment; access may be restricted on some documents. Limited research can be undertaken by staff in response to enquiries.

Historical background: The East London Christian Mission was founded by William Booth in 1865 and changed its name to the Salvation Army in 1878. As well as being a denomination of the Christian Church, the army is active in all areas of social welfare. The archives were first officially organised in 1978, although much material was lost in World War II.

Acquisitions policy: To maintain the archives and accept donations of material relevant to the army and Salvationists.

Archives of organisation: Minute books, conference minutes, files and correspondence, 1866– . Some records of army establishments, e.g. Mother's Hospital, Clapton (f. 1884).

Major collections: Papers of William Booth (1829–1912), his daughter Catherine Booth-Clibborn (1858–1955), his grand-daughter Catherine Bramwell-Booth (1883–1987) and James Allister Smith (1866–1960).
Diaries, letters and papers of Salvationists in Britain and abroad, 19th–20th centuries.

Non-manuscript material: Books, pamphlets, photographs, artefacts, videos, sound recordings.

Finding aids: Computer databases, card catalogue, lists and indexes.

Facilities: Photocopying. Photography. Microfilm reader/printers.

797 Save the Children Fund Archives

Address: Mary Datchelor House, 17 Grove Lane, Camberwell, London SE5 8RD

Telephone: (020) 703 5400 ext. 2269

Fax: (020) 7703 2278

E-mail: s.sneddon@scfuk.org.uk

Website: www.savethechildren.org.uk

Enquiries: The Archivist, Susan Sneddon

Open: Mon–Fri: 9.30–4.30, by arrangement.

Access: Bona fide researchers. There is a general 30-year closure rule, although this may vary in certain cases.

Historical background: The Save the Children Fund was founded in 1919 by Eglantyne Jebb (1876–1928) to distribute money for the relief of children and their families in postwar Europe. Since then the fund has given grants or run projects in more than 130 countries. It has also campaigned on behalf of children's rights in the UK and internationally. It was a pioneer of development aid and started the playgroup movement in the UK. The archives have been organised since 1991.

Acquisitions policy: Archives of the fund, through an active records management programme. Outside material relating to the fund's work, especially in the early years.

Archives of organisation: Minutes of committees, 1920–85; administrative papers, 1920–7; Director-General's papers, 1965–86; finance papers, 1963–86; Overseas department, 1946–80; UK department, 1926–80.

Major collections: Various papers relating to Eglantyne Jebb; Edward Fuller (1889–1958), editor of *The World's Children*; Mosa Anderson (*c*1895–1978) and Bridget Stevenson (1909–85), relief workers; and Dorothy Buxton (*née* Jebb, 1881–1962).
Material relating to the International Save the Children Union, 1926–46.

Non-manuscript material: *The World's Children*, 1920– , and advertising material, 1919–85; films and photographs, 1919–90; artefacts relating to Eglantyne Jebb.

Finding aids: General guide to the collections, continuously updated.

Facilities: Photocopying.

798 Savoy Group Archives

Parent organisation: The Savoy Hotel Ltd

Address: 1 Savoy Hill, London WC2R 0BP

Telephone: (020) 7420 2344

Fax: (020) 7836 9736

E-mail: info@savoy-group.co.uk

Website: www.savoy-group.co.uk

Enquiries: The Archivist, Susan Scott

Open: Mon, Tues, Fri: 10.00–4.00.

Access: Bona fide researchers, by appointment only. Access to some documents may be restricted.

Historical background: The success of the Gilbert and Sullivan operas led the impresario Richard D'Oyly Carte (1844–1901) to build the Savoy Theatre (1881), and then the Savoy Hotel (1889). With the acquisition of Claridge's (1894) and the Berkeley (1900), the Savoy Group was born. After D'Oyly Carte's death,

expansion continued, and Simpson's-in-the-Strand (1903), the Connaught Hotel (1956) and the Lygon Arms (1986) are today the other major properties in the group, which was purchased by the Blackstone Group in 1998. The Savoy Group Archives were founded in the mid-1970s, in the run-up to the Savoy's 90th birthday in 1979.

Acquisitions policy: Material relating to the running and promotion of the enterprises, past and present, of the Savoy Group.

Archives of organisation: Archives of the Savoy Hotel, 1889– , and all other Savoy enterprises, except the Savoy Theatre. In addition to the hotels and restaurants, this includes material relating to the Savoy's bands, the Savoy Orpheans, the Savoy Hotel Orpheans, and the Savoy Havana Band.

Non-manuscript material: Photographs, advertising and other printed promotional ephemera, press cuttings.

Finding aids: Catalogues, lists and indexes.

Facilities: Photocopying. Photography.

Conservation: Contracted out.

Publications: S. Jackson: *The Savoy: a Century of Taste* (1989).

799 School of Oriental and African Studies
SOAS, Centre for Africa and Asia

Parent organisation: University of London

Address: Thornhaugh Street, Russell Square, London WC1H 0XG

Telephone: (020) 7898 4180

Fax: (020) 7436 2388

E-mail: docenquiry@soas.ac.uk

Website: www.soas.ac.uk/archives/home.html

Enquiries: The Archivist, Mrs R.E. Seton

Open: Term, Christmas and Easter vacations: Mon–Thurs: 9.00–7.00; Fri: 9.00–5.00; occasional Saturday mornings.
Summer vacation: Mon–Fri: 9.00–5.00.
Closed for one week in June.

Access: An archives ticket permits free access to the archives and manuscripts for up to twenty days in any one year. For a longer period a reference ticket should be requested, for which there is, in certain circumstances, a charge. A letter of recommendation should be submitted with the completed application form. The Archivist is most willing to help with guidance and advice, but it is first advisable to make an appointment.

Historical background: SOAS, founded in 1916, provides courses in the study of the art, archaeology, languages, literature, history, geography, law, religion and social sciences of Africa, Asia and the Pacific area. It also acts as a centre of research in those areas. The library holds some 800,000 volumes, receives 5000 periodicals currently, and has many thousands of microforms, 45,000 sheet maps, 45,000 photographs and sound recordings on disc and tape. The archives and MSS division of the library has grown rapidly since the library moved into its new accommodation in 1973.

Acquisitions policy: Primary source materials of research value relating to Asian and African studies in the following categories: (i) missionaries, missionary organisations and religious groups; (ii) business organisations and individuals involved in business; (iii) humanitarian organisations and political non-governmental groups; (iv) individuals whose life or work has been of special relevance to the study of Asia and Africa.

Major collections: Missionary Archives: archives of missionary and related organisations, including the China Inland Mission (now the Overseas Missionary Fellowship), c1872–1951; the Conference of British Missionary Societies, 1910–12; the London Missionary Society (now the Council for World Mission), 1795–1970; the Melanesian Mission, c1872–1970; the Presbyterian Church of England's Foreign Missions Committee, c1900– , and the Religious Tract Society (now the United Society for Christian Literature), 1799–1976. Individual missionaries represented in the collections include Gladys Aylward, James Legge, David Livingstone, Robert Morrison, Mabel Shaw and James Hudson Taylor.

Overseas Aid Agencies: records of Christian Aid, 1946–70.

Business and Trade: collections include the archives of John Swire & Sons, 1869–1967; the China Association, 1889–1969; the Guthrie Corporation, c1900–1960; the Imperial British East Africa Company, c1874–1892, and the British India Steam Navigation Company (in the papers of Sir William Mackinnon); papers of members of the Chinese Maritime Customs.

Private Paper Collections: papers of overseas administrators, diplomats, scholars and businessmen, including Sir Charles Addis (1861–1945), Sir John Addis (1914–83), Sir T.W. Arnold (1864–1930), Dr R.W. Cole (1907–95), Prof. C. von Fürer Haimendorf (1909–95), J.S. Furnivall (1878–1960), Andrew Hake (*b* 1925), Sir Robert Hart (1835–1911), Sir Alwyne Ogden (1899–1981), Sir E. Denison Ross (1871–1940) and A.N. Stencl (1897–1983).

Non-manuscript material: Cassettes (with transcripts) of reminiscences of men and women who experienced the partition of India and the end of British rule (*c*360).
Photographs, many relating to missionary work (22,000).

Finding aids: Various lists and inventories. Card index to MSS, arranged by language. Automated database to archives and manuscripts.

Facilities: Photocopying. Photography and microfilming (small orders only). Microfilm/fiche readers.

Publications: Guide to Archive and Manuscript Collections (1994).
Published guides to the archives of the London Missionary Society, the Methodist Missionary Society, John Swire & Sons, the papers of Sir William Mackinnon and Sir Charles Addis, and the collection of Arabic MSS in the school's library.

800 School of Slavonic and East European Studies

Parent organisation: University College London

Address: Senate House, Malet Street, London, London WC1E 7HU

Telephone: (020) 7862 8523

Fax: (020) 7642 8644

E-mail: l.pitman@ssees.ac.uk

Website: www.ssees.ac.uk/archives/newarchi.htm

Enquiries: The Librarian and Director of Information Services, Lesley Pitman

Open: Term: Mon–Fri: 9.00–7.00.
Christmas and Easter vacations: Mon–Fri: 10.00–7.00.
Summer vacation: Mon–Fri: 10.00–6.00.

Access: Approved readers, following written application.

Historical background: The school was founded at King's College London in 1915 and became an institute of the University of London in 1932. In 1999 the school merged with University College London (see entry 832).

Acquisitions policy: The library accepts donations and deposits from individuals or organisations with a connection to the areas studied by the school: Russia, the countries of Eastern and South-Eastern Europe (excluding Greece) and Finland.

Major collections: The library holds more than 190 archive collections. Most of them are fairly small collections and many contain material in a Slavonic language. The more significant include: papers of Manó Kónyi (1842–1917) and Count Menyhért Lónyay relating to Hungarian politics and the constitutional settlement of 1867; correspondence, notes and papers of Sir Bernard Pares (1867–1949) relating to Russia and Russian history; papers of Robert William Seton-Watson (1879–1951), historian, publicist and politician; and Karel Lisicky, Czech diplomat.

Non-manuscript material: Photograph albums depicting the life of Countess Natalia Sergeevna Brasova (1880–1952) with the Grand Duke Mikhail Aleksandrovich, 1909–13.

Finding aids: On-line guide and catalogues. NRA 24277.

Facilities: Photocopying. Photography and microfilming by arrangement. Microfilm/fiche readers.

801 Science Museum Library

Parent organisation: National Museum of Science and Industry

Address: Imperial College Road, South Kensington, London SW7 5NH

Telephone: (020) 7938 8218/8234

Fax: (020) 7938 9714

E-mail: smlinfo@nmsi.ac.uk

Website: www.nmsi.ac.uk/library

Enquiries: The Archivist, Robert Sharp

Open: Mon–Sat: 9.30–5.15, by appointment.

Access: Bona fide researchers. Proof of identity is required. For collections in other departments apply to the relevant Senior Curator.

Historical background: The Science Museum evolved from the science-based collections of the South Kensington Museum (f. 1857) and from the Patent Office Museum (merged 1883–7), and became administratively separate from the Victoria and Albert Museum in 1909. Both the museum and its library (which is housed in a separate building as Imperial College and Science Museum Libraries) have acquired MS material, including large archival collections, throughout their history. An archives collection was set up within the library in 1979 to coordinate future acquisitions and to centralize and catalogue existing collections. It is a recognised place of deposit for public records. Some material has been transferred to the National Museum of Photography, Film and Television (see entry 123) and to the National Railway Museum (see entry 1224).

Acquisitions policy: Records relating principally to the museum's collecting areas in the history of science, technology and medicine; records in the general field of physical science and technology for which there is no suitable local or specialist repository.

Archives of organisation: Administrative records of the Science Museum, 1851–, are held by the Archives Collection in the library and the Documentation Centre (tel. (020) 7938 8036) in the museum, both of which form part of the Collections Division. Broadly, early and non-current material is held by the former, current material by the latter. Either can advise on the location of particular records.

Major collections: Major collections of individuals including Charles Babbage (1791-1871), mathematician, notes and drawings relating to calculating engines, 1832–71; George P. Bidder (1806–78), 'calculating boy' and engineer; R.E.B. Crompton, electrical pioneer, papers, 1853–1950s; Joshua Field, engineer, c1805–65; Stanley Gill, computer scientist, papers, 1947–75; Simon Goodrich, mechanician to the Navy Board, papers and drawings, c1797–1840s; H. Kavelaars, extensive Schneider Trophy-related material, 1913–31; George Neumann, railway engineer, 1828–58; Sir Charles A. Parsons, engineer and scientist, papers, 1881–1951; Oswald Silberrard and the Silberrard Laboratory, 1881–1948; H.E.S. Simmons, papers *re* British windmills and watermills; Charles Urban, papers *re* early motion pictures, 1905–24; Barnes Wallis, papers, 1905–73.

Major collections of industrial and company records including Bramah & Robinson, engineering drawings, c1804–1852; Gibb engineering companies, drawings, c1801–1914; Thomas Hawksley/T. & C. Hawksley & Co., water engineers, drawings, 1830–1918; Hooper (Coachbuilders) & Co. Ltd, motor car construction records, c1910–50; Humphreys & Glasgow, negatives of gas plant designs, 1892–1952; Maudslay, Sons & Field, engineers, 1800–92, Negretti & Zambra, scientific instrument makers, c1900–80; S. Pearson & Son, civil engineering contractors with major subsidiary oil interests, 1876–1955; Robert Stephenson & Co. Ltd, locomotive manufacturers, 1825–59; Price & Reeves, civil engineering contractors, 1890–1927; John Taylor/Taylor & Sons, water engineers, drawings c1846–1957.

Non-manuscript material: Map Collection, including early railway maps.
Pictorial Collection (tel. (020) 7938 8212): extensive collections of portraits, prints, oil paintings.
Science & Society Picture Library (tel. (020) 7938 9748): vast collection of photographs.
Trade literature, transport ephemera, ships' plans etc are divided between the library and museum curatorial departments.

Finding aids: Catalogue of most of the material in the archives collection accessible via the joint database of Imperial College and Science Museum Libraries on the website.
Various lists and indexes to major collections are kept at the point of administration of the collection, the STS (Science & Technology Studies) desk on Level 3 of the library. Lists sent to NRA.

Facilities: Photocopying. Photography by arrangement through S & SPL. Microfilming. Video player.

Conservation: Contracted out.

802 Scots Guards Regimental Headquarters

Address: Wellington Barracks, London SW1E 6HQ

Telephone: (020) 7414 3419

Fax: (020) 7414 3445

Website: www.army.mod.uk/infantry/scotsgrd/

Enquiries: The Archives Clerk

Open: Mon–Fri: 8.30–4.30, by appointment.

Access: Generally open to the public, by prior written arrangement only. A charge may be made in some cases.

Historical background: The Scots Guards were formed in 1642 and established into the British Army in 1661. The regiment now comprises one regular Foot Guards Battalion, one incremental Foot Guards Company and a Regimental Headquarters.

Acquisitions policy: Any Scots Guards material accepted by donation; also selected items, mainly medals, swords, silverware, purchased at auction.

Archives of organisation: Personal records of soldiers (non-effective), c1806– .
Biographical list of officers, 1642– .
Regimental orders books, 18th–20th centuries.
Soldiers' enlistment and discharge record books, c1800–1960s.

Non-manuscript material: Photograph album collection, c1850– .
Medals, banners and flags.

Finding aids: Catalogues, indexes and lists.

Facilities: Photocopying and photography by arrangement.

Conservation: In-house.

Publications: F. Maurice: *History of the Scots Guards from the Creation of the Regiment to the Great War*, 2 vols (London, 1934).
D. Erskine: *History of the Scots Guards, 1919–1955* (London, 1995).
M. Naylor: *Among Friends: the Scots Guards, 1956–1993* (1995).

803 Shaftesbury Homes and Arethusa

Address: The Chapel, Royal Victoria Patriotic Building, Trinity Road, London SW18 3SX

Telephone: (020) 8875 1555

Fax: (020) 8875 1954

E-mail: shaftesburyhomes@hotmail.com
shaftesbury.homes@virgin.net

Enquiries: The External Relations Director, Edward Hardman

Open: Mon–Fri: 9.00–5.30, by appointment only.

Access: Bona fide researchers, plus all Friends and Old Boys and Girls. Access to personnel files may be restricted. No charge will be made but donations will be most welcome.

Historical background: The organisation was founded by William Williams in 1843 and staunchly supported by the 7th Earl of Shaftesbury, from whom the society takes its name. The aim of the society is to help, educate and care for children and young people who are suffering from the lack of a stable family upbringing or other social or educational disadvantage, and to enable them to take their place in society as happy and responsible citizens. Throughout its history the society has maintained a number of residential schools, at Bisley, Twickenham, Esher, Sudbury and Ealing, and supported over 250 boys at any one time in the training ship *Arethusa*. The collection has grown considerably since the late 19th century and has only recently been consolidated.

Acquisitions policy: To maintain and accrue archives.

Archives of organisation: The material relates solely to the work and records of the Shaftesbury Homes and *Arethusa*, and includes: minutes of the General Committee of the National Refuges, 1904– , and of the Shaftesbury Homes and *Arethusa*, c1850– ; admission/discharge registers for the Homes c1870– ; annual reports, 1843– ; deeds of properties and trust funds.

Non-manuscript material: Photographs, c1900– .
The Fo'c's'le, 1920–1940s; *Our Log Book,* c1900– .

Finding aids: Catalogue of holdings and alphabetical index to admission registers (in preparation).

Facilities: Photocopying, restricted at the discretion of the Director.

Publications: History of the Shaftesbury Homes (in preparation).

804 Shaftesbury Society

Address: 16 Kingston Road, London SW19 1JZ

Telephone: (020) 8239 5555

Fax: (020) 8239 5580

Website: www.shaftesburysoc.org.uk

Enquiries: The Public Relations Manager

Open: By arrangement only.

Access: Bona fide scholars, by appointment.

The society was founded as the Ragged School Union in 1844, added Shaftesbury Society to its name in 1914, and has been known by that title only since 1944. Its early concern with the education and welfare of poor children has led the society to develop a number of socio-medical functions. The society has moved frequently, with resultant loss of records; however, some archives have survived and are maintained. These include minutes, 1841– ; and correspondence with reports relating to individual homes, schools and centres, mainly post-1945. Bound copies of the society's magazine exist from 1849. Photocopying is available.

805 Sir John Soane's Museum

Address: 13 Lincolns Inn Fields, London WC2A 3BP

Telephone: (020) 7440 4251

Fax: (020) 7831 3957

E-mail: library.soane1@ukgateway.net

Website: www.soane.org

Enquiries: The Archivist, Susan Palmer

Open: Tues–Fri: 10.00–1.00, 2.00–5.00; Sat: 10.00–1.00.

Access: Generally open to the public; an appointment is necessary for the library and archives.

Historical background: The museum was founded by Sir John Soane, RA (1753–1837), architect, who obtained an Act of Parliament in 1833 that vested the property in trustees. On his death in 1837 the trustees were placed under obligation to maintain the house and collections as they then stood (from funds left by Soane). The Act remained in force until 1969, when a scheme was made under the Charities Act, but the character of the museum remains unchanged. No.12 Lincolns Inn Fields was added to the museum in 1970.

Acquisitions policy: The collection being personal and static, there is no provision for acquisitions. Gifts and objects having a close association with Soane are sometimes accepted.

Archives of organisation: The personal and professional papers of Sir John Soane.
Administrative records of the museum, 1837– .

Non-manuscript material: Architectural drawings by Sir John Soane and others, including the Adam brothers (*c*30,000; microfilmed).
Sir John Soane's library.

Finding aids: Archive catalogue in progress. Catalogues of books and drawings.

Facilities: Photocopying. Photography. Microfilm/fiche readers/printers.

Conservation: Paper conservation in-house.

Publications: A New Description of Sir John Soane's Museum (1955; 10/2000).

806 Skinners' Company

Address: Skinners' Hall, 8 Dowgate Hill, London EC4R 2SP

Telephone: (020) 7236 5629

Fax: (020) 7236 6590

Enquiries: The Clerk

Open: By appointment only.

Access: Bona fide researchers.

The Skinners, the guild of furriers, had their first hall during Henry III's reign. The first charter was granted in 1327 and the final charter by James I. The company funds four schools, Tonbridge School, (f. 1553); Judd School, Tonbridge (f. 1888); School for Boys, Tonbridge (f. 1886); School for Girls, North London (f. 1889), and has almshouses at Palmers Green, which were established in 1894, and Hounslow, established in 1986. Its archives include title deeds 1249– , accounts 1491– , records of apprentices and freemen admitted 1496– and court books 1551– . All archives dating from before World War II are held by Guildhall Library (see entry 624).

807 Society for the Protection of Ancient Buildings

Address: 37 Spital Square, London E1 6DY

Telephone: (020) 7377 1644

Fax: (020) 7247 5296

E-mail: info@spab.org.uk

Website: www.spab.org.uk/

Enquiries: The Archivist, Miss C.Y. Greenhill

Open: Mon–Fri: 9.30–5.00; possibly closed on days following bank holidays.

Access: Members and bona fide researchers, by prior appointment only.

The society was founded in 1877 by William Morris (1834–98) and maintains its own archives, which include some thousands of case histories as well as minute books (although these are held elsewhere). There is a list available, see NRA 24467.

808 Society of Antiquaries of London

Address: Burlington House, Piccadilly, London W1V 0HS

Telephone: (020) 7479 7084/7085

Fax: (020) 7287 6967

E-mail: library@sal.org.uk

Enquiries: The Librarian, Mr E.B. Nurse

Open: Mon–Fri: 10.00–5.00. Closed in August.

Access: Fellows and approved readers; others by appointment.

Historical background: The present society was founded in 1707 by Humphrey Wanley and has had a continuous existence from 1717. There was no connection with the Elizabethan Society of Antiquaries. A royal charter was granted in 1751, commanding the society to devote itself 'to the study of antiquity and history of former times'. The society moved to the present premises in 1875, having previously occupied premises in Chancery Lane (1753–80) and Somerset House (1780–1875).

Acquisitions policy: To acquire material, by purchase, donation, deposit, etc.

Archives of organisation: Minutes, accounts, lists of fellows, election books and certificates, papers and correspondence, 1717– .

Major collections: MSS reflecting the varied interests of past and present fellows, 10th–20th centuries (950).
Many MSS of heraldic interest, especially from the collections of Sir A.W. Franks (1821–97), Oswald Barron (1868–1939) and Charles James Russell (*fl.* 1860–1907); some are described in A.R. Wagner (see *'Publications'*).
Rubbings are deposited of almost all brasses listed in Mill Stephenson (see *'Publications'*).

Important local collections include Habington, Lyttelton and Prattinton collections on Worcestershire; Canon J.E. Jackson (1805–91) on Wiltshire; Edward James Willson (1787–1854) on Lincolnshire; John Thorpe (1682–1750) on Kent (Rochester Diocese); and Thomas Wakeman on Monmouthshire.

Archives of the Roxburghe Club, the Society of Dilettanti and the Royal Archaeological Institute are deposited in the library; permission from the respective secretaries must be given before access is granted.

Non-manuscript material: Prints and drawings of a topographical nature (*c*20,000).
Broadsides, 1400– (3000).
Lowther Collection: Printed books (200) and tracts (1500) relating largely to the Civil War period.
Casts of seals (10,000).

Finding aids: Topographical and subject catalogue. Catalogues of MSS and of broadsides. Lists sent to NRA.

Facilities: Photocopying. Photography. Microfilm reader.

Conservation: Contracted out.

Publications: H. Ellis: *A Catalogue of Manuscripts in the Library of the Society of Antiquaries of London* (London, 1816).
Mill Stephenson: *A List of Monumental Brasses in the British Isles* (London, 1926); *Appendix* (Ashford, 1938).
E.A.B. Barnard: *The Prattinton Collections of Worcestershire History* (Evesham, 1931).
A.R. Wagner: *Catalogue of English Medieval Rolls of Arms* (London, 1950).
J. Evans: *A History of the Society of Antiquaries* (1956).
N.R. Ker: *Medieval Manuscripts in British Libraries* (Oxford, 1969).
I. Gray: *Report on the Manuscript Collections of the Society of Antiquaries of London, 12th–20th Century* (1985).

809 Society of Apothecaries Archives

Parent organisation: The Worshipful Society of Apothecaries of London

Address: Apothecaries' Hall, Black Friars Lane, London EC4V 6EJ

Telephone: (020) 7248 6648

Fax: (020) 7329 3177

E-mail: archivist@apothecaries.org

Website: www.apothecaries.org

Enquiries: The Archivist, Mrs Dee Cook

Open: By prior arrangement.

Access: Bona fide scholars and researchers. An appointment is necessary. In the first instance, application should be made in writing to the Archivist, giving details of research interest.

Historical background: Apothecaries were originally members of the Grocers' Company. They obtained their own charter in 1617, incorporating them as the Worshipful Society of Apothecaries of London, and acquired a hall in 1632. Formerly the guesthouse of the Dominican Priory of the Black Friars, it was destroyed in the Great Fire of 1666 but was rebuilt by 1672 on the same site, where it still stands. In 1704 the apothecaries won the right to prescribe medicines, formerly the sole right of physicians, in addition to dispensing them, and thus became general practitioners. Their status was further ratified by the Apothecaries' Act (1815) by which the society was given the legal authority to conduct examinations and to grant licences to practise and regulate medicine throughout England and Wales. In 1671 the society decided to establish a laboratory in its hall and, until 1922 when the businesses were sold, manufactured and retailed medicines and drugs. In 1673 the society founded Chelsea Physic Garden where raw drugs and medicinal plants were grown. The garden is now managed by a trust. The society is the largest livery company in the City of London.

A large number of the Society's early records have been deposited in Guildhall Library (see entry 624), however a substantial quantity of previously unknown and inaccessible historical material has recently been uncovered at Apothecaries' Hall. A major records survey in 1997 led to an archive being established at the hall.

Archives of organisation: Charters, 1617, 1685; grant of arms, 1617; rules and ordinances, 1618– ; court minutes, 1926– ; membership lists and yearbooks, 1702– ; financial records, 17th–20th centuries; court of examiners records, 1815– ; records of the stock companies and retail pharmacy, 1703–1922; Chelsea Physic Garden minute books, accounts, botany prizes and correspondence, 18th–19th centuries, faculty papers, 1959– ; administrative records including the clerks' letter books, 1876–1953, cases for counsel's opinion, hospitality and ceremonial records, papers concerning royal commissions of enquiry, etc, 18th–20th centuries; records of gifts and charities, 18th–20th centuries; hall, contents and property records, 1617– .

Non-manuscript material: Plans, prints, engravings, photographs, glass slides, copperplates, rare books and artefacts, including medicine chests, drug jars, pill chests, surgical instruments, pharmacy equipment, early 19th-century laboratory glassware.

Finding aids: Listing in progress.

Facilities: Photocopying. Microfilm/fiche reader.

Conservation: Some is carried out by Guildhall Library.

Publications: C.R.B. Barrett: *The History of the Society of Apothecaries* (1905).
E.A. Underwood, H.C. Cameron and Cecil Wall: *A History of the Worshipful Society of Apothecaries of London,* Vol. 1: *1617–1815* (1963).
W.S.C. Copeman: *The Worshipful Society of Apothecaries of London: a History, 1617–1967* (1967).
City Livery Companies. A Guide to their archives in Guildhall Library (Guildhall Library Research Guides (3rd edn, 1989), 8–11 [summary list].
I. Field: *The Worshipful Society of Apothecaries: a Guide to the Society and Apothecaries' Hall* (1992).
P. Hunting: *A History of the Society of Apothecaries* (1998).

810 Society of Chiropodists and Podiatrists

Address: 1 Fellmonger's Path, Tower Bridge Road, London SE1 3LY

Telephone: (020) 7234 8620

Fax: (020) 7234 8621

E-mail: enq@scpod.org.uk

Enquiries: The Editorial Officer, Dr Georgina Stevens

Open: Mon–Fri: 9.30–4.45.

Access: Bona fide researchers, by appointment.

The Society of Chiropodists was formed in 1945 by the amalgamation of the following organisations: the Incorporated Society of Chiropodists (f. 1912), the first in Europe; the Northern Chiropodists' Association (f. 1925); the Chelsea Chiropodists' Association (f. 1926); the British Association of Chiropodists (f. 1931); and the Chiropody Practitioners (f. 1942). The society maintains its own archives which include some records of its constituent bodies, 1912– . There is material relating to the formation of the London Foot Hospital (f. 1913) and to the schools of chiropody.

811 Society of Friends

Address: Library of the Religious Society of Friends, Friends House, Euston Road, London NW1 2BJ

Telephone: (020) 7663 1135

Fax: (020) 7663 1101

E-mail: library@quaker.org.uk

Website: www.quaker.org.uk

Enquiries: The Librarian

Open: Mon, Tues, Thur, Fri: 1.00–5.00; Wed: 10.00–5.00 (and approx. 8 Sats per year).
Two annual closed weeks (variable year to year); telephone or write for details.

Access: Open to members of the Society of Friends, and to bona fide researchers, who are asked to provide advance introductions or letters of recommendation on arrival. There is an hourly fee for genealogical research. Documents less than 50 years old are not normally available.

Historical background: The library was founded in 1673 and serves as the main reference library and central archive repository of the Religious Society of Friends (Quakers) in Great Britain. It moved from Devonshire House, Bishopsgate, London EC2, in 1926 to the present location. Most Irish Quaker records are held at Friends Historical Library, Dublin, and the Public Record Office of Northern Ireland (entry 81).

Acquisitions policy: Society archives; to strengthen MS collections of Quaker private and family papers and archives of bodies with Quaker associations, by donation, deposit and (occasionally) purchase.

Archives of organisation: The central archives of Britain (until 1995 London). Yearly Meeting including records of its committees; digest register of births, marriages and burials, c1650– (now on microfilm).

Archives of London and Middlesex area meetings.

Most other local Quaker records are deposited in the appropriate local authority record offices or university libraries.

Major collections: Swarthmore MSS: c1400 letters and transcripts relating to the early history of Quakerism, 17th century.

A.R. Barclay MSS: letters of early Friends, 1654–88 (250).

Gurney MSS: letters, written mainly by or to members of the Gurney family of Norfolk (including Joseph John Gurney and Elizabeth Fry), c1750–1850 (c1900).

Wilkinson MSS: letters, written mainly to Thomas Wilkinson (1751–1836) of Yanwath, Westmorland (c500).

Lloyd MSS: letters and papers relating to the Lloyd family of Dolobran, Montgomeryshire, and Birmingham, c1680–1850 (c800).

Barclay (Bury Hill) MSS: letters and papers relating to the Barclay family of Urie, Aberdeenshire; London; and Bury Hill, Surrey, c1650–1850.

Non-manuscript material: Picture collections, including some oil paintings and watercolours; engravings, etchings and lithographs; a sizeable collection of photographs of Friends, meeting houses and Quaker work.

Most British printed Quaker works since 1650, listed in J. Smith: *Descriptive Catalogue of Friends' Books* (2 vols, London, 1867; suppl., 1893); a substantial proportion of other Quaker printed works to date.

Printed works relating to peace, slavery, conscientious objection and relief work.

Quaker periodicals, early 19th century– .

Finding aids: Card catalogues, lists and indexes. Lists sent to NRA.

A typescript dictionary of Quaker biography is in progess (currently 20,000 entries), in collaboration with Haverford College, Pennsylvania.

Facilities: Photocopying. Photography. Microfilm reader.

Publications: Journal of Friends Historical Society (1903–) [indexed; includes numerous references to material in the library; now published annually c/o the library].

O. Goodbody: *Guide to Irish Quaker Records, 1654–1860* (1968).

812 Society of Genealogists

Address: 14 Charterhouse Buildings, Goswell Road, London EC1M 7BA

Telephone: (020) 7250 0291 (Library); 7250 799 (main switchboard)

Fax: (020) 7250 1800

E-mail: library@sog.org.uk

Website: www.sog.org.uk

Enquiries: The Librarian, Sue Gibbons
The Archivist, Sarah Henning

Open: Tues, Fri, Sat: 10.00–6.00; Wed, Thurs: 10.00–8.00; an appointment is necessary for certain material on Sat.
Closed first full week in February.

Access: Open to members paying an annual subscription; to non-members on payment of hourly, half-daily or daily fees.

Historical background: Founded in 1911, the society is a registered charity and limited company. Its objects are to transcribe and index original material to make it readily available to genealogical researchers and to be a pressure group for promoting easier access to records of all kinds. The library of the society provides one of the finest resources for the study of genealogy, family and community history, biography and demography.

Acquisitions policy: To provide a safe depository for archives and MSS, not wanted by other repositories, relevant to genealogical, family history or biographical research.

Archives of organisation: Minutes of the executive and other committees; correspondence files; card index of former members, 1911– ; annual reports.
Genealogists Magazine, 1925– , *Computers in Genealogy*, 1978– .

Major collections: Document collections, 1538– including family history collection with diaries, notebooks and marriage settlements.

Collection of original apprenticeship indentures, 1641–1888; mortgage bonds; Civil Service evidences of age, 1855–1939; Trinity House petitions, 1780–1854 (128 vols); Bank of England will extracts, 1717–1845 (176 vols); Great Western Railway stock transfer registers, 1835–1932.

Special MS collections relating to inhabitants of Berkshire (Snell Collection), Cornwall (Rogers bequest), Norfolk and Suffolk (Campling and

Whitehead Collections), Scotland (Macleod Papers) and the West Indies (Smith Collection).
Jewish collections: Collyer-Fergusson; D'Arcy Hart; Hyamson and Mordy.

Transcripts of church registers, monumental inscriptions, wills etc, mainly relating to the British Isles but including some former colonies and other countries; Boyd's Marriage Index (for England), 1538–1837, and London Burials, 1538–c1853.

General card index of names, c1538–c1900; other specialised indexes, including Bernau Index to Chancery and other Proceedings, pre-1900; Culleton index to British Museum and other sources.

Non-manuscript material: Topographical material arranged by county or country; Army and Navy lists; directories and poll-books; family histories; peerages; school, university professional registers; heralds' visitations; will calendars and indexes, including indexes to lost Irish wills; marriage allegations; genealogical periodicals.

Book-plate collection (60,000).

Finding aids: Computerised catalogue, available on website, where weekly accessions are posted.

Facilities: Photocopying. Microfilm/fiche readers/printers. Microfilming by arrangement. Computer downloading.

Publications: Library Sources Guides including:

List of Parishes in Boyd's Marriage Index (1994).

Directories and Poll Books in the Library of the Society of Genealogists (London, 6/1995).

School, University and College Registers and Histories in the Library of the Society of Genealogists (London, 1996).

Will Indexes and other Probate Material in the Library of the Society of Genealogists (London, 1996).

Maritime Sources in the Library of the Society of Genealogists (London, 1997).

Census Copies and Indexes in the Library of the Society of Genealogists (London, 3/1998).

Sources for Irish Genealogy in the Library of the Society of Genealogists (London, 2/1998).

Using the Library of the Society of Genealogists (1999).

Genealogists' Magazine [quarterly; contains accessions lists].

813 Society of St John the Evangelist

Address: 22 Great College Street, London SW1P 3QA

Telephone: (020) 7222 9234

Fax: (020) 7799 2641

E-mail: frpeterssjeuk@talk2.com

Enquiries: The Secretary and Treasurer, Fr. Peter Huckle

Open: By arrangement only.

Access: Bona fide researchers, by consultation with the Secretary.

Historical background: The society was founded in 1866 when Revs Richard Meux Benson, Charles Grafton and Simeon Wilberforce O'Neill took vows of celibacy, poverty and obedience as Mission Priests of St John the Evangelist in Oxford. It later had houses in India, Canada, the USA and South Africa, but work in those countries ended some years ago.

Acquisitions policy: Maintains the society's archives.

Archives of organisation: Archives of the society, consisting of minutes, writings, sermons and retreat addresses, 1888– .
Records of Cowley, Wantage and All Saints Missionary Association mission work in India.

Non-manuscript material: Photograph albums, c1880– .
Cowley parish magazine, 1867–1904; *The Cowley Evangelist*, 1900–68; *Star in the East*, 1893–1962.

Publications: Fr. Martin Smith SSJE (ed): *Benson of Cowley* (OUP, 1980).

814 Society of the Sacred Heart
Provincial Archives

Parent organisation: Generalate of the Society of the Sacred Heart, Rome

Address: Convent of the Sacred Heart, Digby Stuart College, Roehampton Lane, London SW15 5PH

Telephone: (020) 8876 9880

Fax: (020) 8876 9880

Enquiries: The Archivist, Sr M. Coke

Open: Mon–Fri: 9.30–5.00, by previous arrangement.

Access: Anyone interested in archival matters and bona fide researchers, with a recommendation; an appointment is necessary.

Historical background: The Society of the Sacred Heart, a Roman Catholic order of nuns, was founded in 1800 in France. It is an international religious institute and houses in the British Isles were first founded in 1842. The work of the society is chiefly education at all levels. The archives of individual houses were centralised in each province in 1972, those of England and Wales at Roehampton, London.

Acquisitions policy: Material relevant to the work of the order and its members, particularly in England and Wales, including publications by members.

Archives of organisation: Records of the order and its work, including St Mary's College, Newcastle, 1906–85; Digby Stuart College, Roehampton, 1874– ; Sacred Heart High School, Hammersmith, 1893– , and other boarding and day schools.

Major collections: Plans and legal documents concerning the Goldsmid and Ellenborough families and others, and their tenure of the site of Digby Stuart College, 1724–1850.

Plans and legal documents relating to the previous occupants of the site of the Sacred Heart High School, Hammersmith: the Institute of the Blessed Virgin Mary, 1672–1792, and the Benedictines, 1799–1865.

Letters and writings of Mabel Digby (1835–1911) and Janet Stuart (1857–1914), who promoted education in the late 19th and 20th centuries.

Archives of the Association for Religions in Education (ARE), 1928–97.

Non-manuscript material: Photographs of pictures of 17th- and 18th-century mansions of the manors of Wimbledon and Mortlake and of many of the personalities involved, e.g. the Ellenborough family.

Photographs and memorabilia supporting printed and MS records of the work of the order, c1820– .

Finding aids: Checklist of holdings. Catalogue in preparation.

Facilities: Photocopying.

815 South Bank University
Perry Library

Address: 250 Southwark Bridge Road, London SE1 6NJ

Telephone: (020) 7815 6699

Fax: (020) 7815 6699

E-mail: cousina@sbu.ac.uk

Website: www.sbu.ac.uk

Enquiries: The Senior Information Adviser, Mrs Alison Cousins

Open: Mon–Fri: 9.00–5.00.

Access: Bona fide researchers; an appointment is essential.

Historical background: The institution was originally the Borough Polytechnic (f. 1892), was renamed the South Bank Polytechnic in 1971 and became the South Bank University in 1992.

Acquisitions policy: Any material relating to the history of the university.

Archives of organisation: Collections held include minutes of Brixton School of Building (part); Battersea College of Education; National College of Heating, Ventilation and Fan Engineering; National Bakery School; Westminster College (part).
Articles of foundation, internal committee papers, student magazines, publications, prospectuses, 1892– .

Non-manuscript material: Photographs and a few working drawings on building extensions.

Facilities: Photocopying.

816 Southlands College

Parent organisation: University of Surrey, Roehampton

Address: 80 Roehampton Lane, London SW15 5SL

Telephone: (020) 8392 3401 ext. 4242

Fax: (020) 8392 3431

Website: www.roehampton.ac.uk/abt

Enquiries: The College Archivist, Stuart Brenner

Open: By arrangement.

Access: Bona fide researchers, an appointment is necessary.

Southlands College was founded in 1872 in Battersea. It moved to Wimbledon in the 1930s and, in 1997, to a new, purpose-built college in Roehampton Lane. The college holds its own archives, 1872– , as well as building plans, photographs and artefacts. Donations of material relating to the college are welcomed. Cataloguing is in progress.

817 Southwark Archdiocesan Archives (Roman Catholic)

Address: 150 St Georges Road, Southwark, London SE1 6HX

Telephone: (020) 7928 5592

Fax: (020) 7928 7833

Enquiries: The Diocesan Archivist

Open: By arrangement.

Access: Approved persons, on written or phone application and by appointment only. There are restrictions on certain deposited papers.

Historical background: The Diocese of Southwark (Roman Catholic) was formed in 1850 on the restoration of the hierarchy in that year.

Acquisitions policy: The archive will acquire any historical papers relevant to the development of the Catholic Church in South-East England.

Archives of organisation: Collection of papers, documents and letters on all matters of church administration relevant to the Diocese of Southwark, 1850– ; includes collections of letters from chaplains in the Crimean War and the Indian Mutiny.

Major collections: Tierney/Rock Collection: MSS collected by Dr Daniel Rock, antiquarian and historian, and Dr Mark Tierney, historian, including naval diaries of Admiral Sir William Monson (1569–1643), Dr Stonor's Roman Agency diaries, and correspondence of Cardinal Barberini and his secretary George Conn (*d* 1640), Papal Agent to Queen Henrietta Maria.
Papers of Dr William Brown (*d* 1950) relevant to the visitation of Scottish dioceses in 1919 and the Scots Education Act of 1917.
Research papers of Dr Percival Styche on Marian priests and martyrs, 1535–1688.

Non-manuscript material: Many rare works and first editions of religious books, 16th–19th centuries.

Finding aids: TS list. The Tierney/Rock Archives have a separate MSS catalogue: NRA 27760.

Facilities: Photocopying. Microfiche reader.

Publications: Rev. M. Clifton: 'Southwark Diocesan Archives', *Catholic Archives*, 4 (1984), 15–24.

818 Southwark Local Studies Library

Parent organisation: London Borough of Southwark

Address: 211 Borough High Street, London SE1 1JA

Telephone: (020) 7403 3507

Fax: (020) 7403 8633

E-mail: local.studies.library@southwark.gov.uk

Website: www.southwark.gov.uk

Enquiries: The Local Studies Librarian, Mr Leonard Reilly

Open: Mon, Thurs: 9.30–8.00; Tues, Fri: 9.30–5.00; Sat: 9.30–1.00.

Access: Generally open to the public, except in the case of some categories of modern council records to which restrictions of varying duration apply.

Historical background: The London Borough of Southwark was formed in 1965 by the merger of the metropolitan boroughs of Southwark, Bermondsey and Camberwell. These metropolitan boroughs in their turn were formed in 1900 from ten vestries which had governed their parishes from Tudor times.

Acquisitions policy: Acquisitions comprise records which are transferred from the custody of departments of the London Borough of Southwark, and various private deposits which relate to institutions and individuals within the borough or its predecessors.

Archives of organisation: Records of the civil parishes up to 1900: vestry minutes, rate books, Poor Law records, churchwardens' accounts, highway records and other series of the parishes of St Saviour, St Olave, St Mary Magdalen

(Bermondsey), St Mary (Rotherhithe), St Mary (Newington), St Giles (Camberwell), St John Horselydown, St Thomas, St George and Christ Church, 1546– ; notably Poor Law records, late 18th and early 19th centuries, and vestry records, 1856–1900.

Records of the boroughs, 1900– .

Major collections: Deposited private collections, including local deeds, 1747– (30,000), and a large collection of local Methodist records.

Non-manuscript material: Printed books, pamphlets, press cuttings and other ephemera; microfilms of local newspapers, parish registers, census returns and directories; photographs and prints; maps; gramophone records and tape-recordings of older residents' memories; videos and films.

Finding aids: Calendar of 10,000 deeds, with indexes by name, place and trade.
Detailed lists of many deposits of unofficial records, with index in progress.
Summary catalogue of official records, indexed by subject, with some more detailed lists. A few thematic lists are available. Author and subject card-catalogue of the non-MS items, plus a computer catalogue of most of them.

Facilities: Photocopying. Microfilm/fiche reader/printer.

Conservation: Contracted out.

Publications: A Guide to the Archives in Southwark Local Studies Library (1992).
Family History in Southwark: a Guide to Tracing your Southwark Ancestors (1996).

819 Spanish and Portuguese Jews' Congregation of London
Congregational Archives

Address: 2 Ashworth Road, London W9 1JY

Telephone: (020) 7289 2573

Fax: (020) 7289 2709

E-mail: howard@sandpsyn.demon.co.uk

Enquiries: The Hon. Archivist, Miss M. Rodrigues-Pereira

Open: Strictly by arrangement.

Access: Private archive, not generally open to the public. Queries and requests submitted in writing by bona fide researchers will be considered.

Historical background: The Congregation of Spanish and Portuguese Jews was formed in 1656 under the protection of Oliver Cromwell by Jews escaping from the persecution of the Spanish and Portuguese Inquisitions. The first synagogue was opened in the City of London in 1657. This was replaced in 1701 by a new building, which is still in use. The archives were formally established in 1915 and since then have been maintained by a small number of volunteers.

Acquisitions policy: To acquire, mainly by deposit and donation, material relating to the history of the congregation and its institutions and to the lives of its members.

Archives of organisation: Archives of the congregation and of its charitable and educational institutions, 1663– .
Registers of marriages and burials, 17th century– ; registers of births and circumcisions, 17th–early 20th centuries (incomplete).
NB Records were kept in Portuguese (some in Spanish) until 1819.

Non-manuscript material: Printed orders of service for special occasions, 19th and 20th centuries.
Tape recordings of London Sephardi liturgical music.

Finding aids: Catalogue of MS books and papers in preparation.

Conservation: Contracted out.

Publications: L.D. Barnett: *El libro de los acuerdos: Translation of the Records and Accounts, 1663–1681* (Oxford, 1931).
——: *Bevis Marks Records*, pt I: *The Early History of the Congregation, 1656–1800*, pt II: *Abstracts of Marriage Contracts, 1686–1837* (Oxford, 1940, 1949).
R.D. Barnett: *The Burial Register of the Spanish and Portuguese Jews, London, 1657–1735* (Jewish Historical Society of England, 1962).
G.H. Whitehill (ed.): *Bevis Marks Records*, pt III: *Marriage Registers, 1837–1901* (with Jewish Historical Society of England, 1973).
R.D. Barnett and M. Rodrigues-Pereira (eds): *Bevis Marks Records*, pt IV: *The Circumcision Register of Isaac and Abraham de Paiba, 1715–1775*; *Record of Circumcisions, 1679–99, Marriages, 1679–89, and some Female Births, 1679–99* (with Jewish Historical Society of England, 1991).

M. Rodrigues-Pereira and C. Loewe (eds): *Bevis Marks Records*, pt V: *The Birth Register, 1767–1881, of the Congregation, together with Four Related Circumcision Registers, and the Jewish Births, 1707–63, in the Registers of the College of Arms* (1993).
M. Rodriguez-Pereira and C. Loewe (eds): *Bevis Marks Records*, pt VI: *The Burial Register, 1733–1918, of the Novo (New) Cemetery of the Congregation* (1997).
A.M. Hyamson: *The Sephardim of England* (Methuen, 1951; repr. 1991).

820 Spurgeon's College

Address: 189 South Norwood Hill, London SE25 6DJ

Telephone: (020) 8653 0850

Fax: (020) 8771 0959

E-mail: enquiries@spurgeons.ac.uk

Website: www.spurgeons.ac.uk

Enquiries: The Librarian

Open: Mon–Fri: 9.30–5.00.

Access: Approved readers, on written application and by prior appointment only.

Historical background: The college was founded in 1856 by the Victorian preacher Charles Haddon Spurgeon (1834–92) for the purpose of preparing students for the Christian ministry within the Baptist denomination at home and overseas. In 1923 the college, which was originally sited at the rear of the Metropolitan Tabernacle in Newington Butts, became residential and moved to the house and estate of Falkland Park, South Norwood. The Heritage Room above the college chapel was opened in 1957.

Acquisitions policy: To acquire, by donation or purchase, all material relating to the life and writings of Charles Haddon Spurgeon.

Archives of organisation: Archives of the college, including reports as published in the *Sword and Trowel*, 1866– .

Major collections: Extensive collection of material by and about Spurgeon, including his sermon notes, letters, and photocopies of published writings.

Non-manuscript material: Most of the publications of Spurgeon (including translations),

biographies, volumes of newspaper cuttings and portraits.

Facilities: Photocopying.

821 Stationers' and Newspaper Makers' Company

Address: Stationers' Hall, London EC4M 7DD

Telephone: (020) 7248 2934

Fax: (020) 7489 1975

E-mail: archivist@stationers.org

Enquiries: The Hon. Archivist, Robin Myers

Open: Mon, Tues: 10.00–4.00, by appointment. Other days by special arrangement.

Access: Approved researchers, on written application. Members of the Bibliographical Society of London.

Historical background: A gild of London stationers (or text-writers), illuminators, parchminers, paper-makers and bookbinders, was established in 1403, incorporated by royal charter in 1557 and liveried in 1560. Until 1695 membership was confined to those working in the book trades within the City of London. A trade qualification is still required, now including librarians, archivists and journalists. Women have been admitted since 1977. Censorship, controlled by entering permitted publications in the company's registers, was replaced in 1710 by copyright registration which continued until 1911. In 1924 a voluntary registry was set up, mainly for unpublished material. The *English Stock*, established by letters patent in 1603 and in operation until 1963, was a semi-charitable, joint-stock publishing venture, whose shareholders were members of the company; it held a monopoly, disallowed in 1774, in certain popular works, the most lucrative being almanacks in English. The company maintained a school from 1858 to 1984. In 1933 the Stationers were joined by the Newspaper Makers' Company and the present name was assumed. The present hall, dating from 1674, replaces one burnt down in the Great Fire of 1666.

Acquisitions policy: The main purpose of the archive is to maintain and make available, through microfilm and publication, the records of the company; however, occasional purchases or gifts of relevant material are received.

Archives of organisation: The company's records comprise royal charters, letters patent, decrees and ordinances, orders of court, 1603– ; membership records, 1556– ; entry books and copyright registers, 1556–1842 (thereafter to 1924 at the Public Record Office, entry 1058); wardens' accounts and other financial records, 1554– ; pension lists, 1608– ; wills and documents relating to charities, 1593– ; records relating to property, including surveys and plans, 1674– .

Records of the *English Stock*, 1644–1961, including dividend registers, share transfers, wills and stock holdings.

Records of the company's school, 1858–1984.

Major collections: Papers and deeds of the Baskett and Tottel families, 18th–20th centuries.

Papers of the Rivington family.

Correspondence of Sidney Hodgson (1879–1973), Hon. Archivist.

Records and ledgers of Kellie and Sons, bookbinders, 1767–1962.

Non-manuscript material: Runs of almanacs, 1675–1920s, housed in the company's library of books relating to the company and other livery companies.

Finding aids: M. Turner (comp): Database of members of the company, 1801–50.
W.P. Williams: Index to the Stationers' Register, 1640–1708.
A. Shell and A. Emblow: Index to Court Books, 1779–1817.
Indexes to published editions of the court books (see below).

Conservation: Ongoing programme by private conservators and by Camberwell College students.

Publications: An extensive published literature includes:
E. Arber: *Transcript of the Registers of the Stationers' Company, 1554–1640* (5 vols, 1875–94).
G.E.B. Eyre and C.R. Rivington: *Transcript of the Registers 1640–1708* (3 vols, 1913).
W.W. Greg and E. Boswell: *Records of the Court 1576–1602* (1930).
W.A. Jackson: *Records of the Court, 1602–40* (1957).
D.F. McKenzie: *Stationers' Company Apprentices, 1603–1800* (3 vols, 1958–78).
C. Blagden: *The Stationers' Company: a History, 1554–1959* (1960).

R. Myers (ed.): *Microfilm Records of the Worshipful Company of Stationers, 1554–1929* (115 reels, Chadwyck-Healey, 1987) [includes abstracts and indexes].
——: *The Archive of the Stationers' Company, 1554–1984, a Companion to the Records* (1990).
——: *The Stationers' Company: a History of the Later Years, 1800–200/2001.*

822 Tate Gallery Archive

Address: Tate Gallery, Millbank, London SW1 3RG

Telephone: (020) 7887 8831

Fax: (020) 7887 8637

E-mail: yvonneoliver@tate.org.uk

Website: www.tate.org.uk

Enquiries: The Head of Archive and Gallery Records, Mrs Jennifer Booth

Open: Tues, Thurs, Fri: 10.00–1.00, 2.00–5.30, by appointment only.

Access: Postgraduates and approved readers, by written application with two letters of reference.

Historical background: The archive was established in 1970. It is the national archive of 20th-century British art and a recognised place of deposit for public records.

Acquisitions policy: Personal and institutional papers relating to 20th-century British art.

Archives of organisation: Archives of the Tate Gallery, 1897– .

Major collections: Papers of David Bomberg (1890–1957); Kenneth Clark (1903–83); Cecil Collins (1908–89); Alan Durst (1883–1970); Naum Gabo (1890–1977); Cedric Morris (1889–1982); John Nash (1893–1977); Paul Nash (1889–1946); Ben Nicholson (1894–1982); Sir John Rothenstein (1901–92); Stanley Spencer (1891–1959); Julian Trevelyan (1910–88); George Frederick Watts (1817–1904).
Artists International Association, official records and correspondence, 1933–71.
Charleston Trust: correspondence of Vanessa Bell, Clive Bell, Roger Fry, Duncan Grant and others, 1902–60.
Records of Contemporary Art Society; National Art Collection Fund; Institute of Contemporary Art, 1947–87.

Non-manuscript material: Sales records of MSS relevant to the archive's own collections.
Interviews with artists and personalities in the art world (*c*1800).
Drawings and prints, usually part of the MSS collections.
Microform: more than 80 collections of loan material.
Photographs of British and 20th-century art and artists, including installation photographs of exhibitions, photographs of artists, their work and their studios.
Artist-designed posters (*c*1600).
A large collection of press cuttings.
Private view cards of exhibitions, mainly 1970– .

Finding aids: Lists and indexes.

Facilities: Photocopying. Photography. Microfilm/fiche reader.

Conservation: Some in-house facilities; work is also contracted out.

Publications: A. Causey: *Paul Nash's Photographs: Document and Image* (1973).
S. Fox Pitt: 'The Tate Gallery Archive of 20th Century British Art and Artists', *AICARA: Journale pour la documentation de l'art moderne* (March 1983).
——: 'The Tate Gallery Archive of 20th Century British Art, its Formation and Development', *Archives*, xvii/74 (1985), 94–106.
C. Colvin: 'Forms of Documentation and Storage in the Tate Gallery Archive', *Archives*, xvii (April 1986), 144–52.
Index to the Tate Gallery Archive on Microfiche (1986).
D. Fraser Jenkins: *John Piper: a Painter's Camera* (1987).

823 Theatre Museum

Parent organisation: Victoria and Albert Museum

Address: 1E Tavistock Street, Covent Garden, London WC2E 7PA

Telephone: (020) 79434 700

Fax: (020) 7443 4777

Website: www.theatremuseum.org

Enquiries: The Head of Library and Information Services, Claire Hudson

Open: Wed–Fri: 10.30–1.00, 2.00–4.30.

Access: Readers should write or telephone in advance with specific enquiries. Access is by appointment only.

Historical background: The Gabrielle Enthoven Theatre Collection, which was given to the Victoria and Albert Museum in 1924, formed the basis of the museum, with later additions from the British Theatre Museum Association and the Friends of the Museum of Performing Arts. The Theatre Museum was finally established in 1974, and opened to the public in its new premises in Covent Garden in 1987.

Acquisitions policy: To collect material on all aspects of the performing arts, while strengthening the existing collections.

Major collections: Gabrielle Enthoven Theatre Collection: comprehensive archive of playbills, programmes, letters and prompt scripts relating to the history of the theatre, opera, ballet, pantomime, circus etc in Britain, *c*1718– .
British Theatre Museum Association Collection: extensive collection on the London theatre, 18th–20th centuries.
London Archives of the Dance and Cyril Beaumont Collection relating to the history of dance, 19th and 20th centuries.
William Archer Collection *re* British Theatre Association and English Stage Company Archive.

Non-manuscript material: Harry R. Beard Collection of prints and other material, with particular strength in the history of opera and Italian festival theatre.
Gift of Dame Bridget D'Oyly Carte: designs for Gilbert and Sullivan operas.
Antony Hippisley Coxe Circus Collection.
Friends of the Museum of Performing Arts Collection: costumes, backcloths, designs and other material relating to Diaghilev and the Ballets Russes.
Arts Council Collection: modern theatre designs.
British Council Collection: post-war theatre design.
Guy Little Collection of historic photographs, *c*1857–90.
Houston Rogers Collection of theatre photographs, 1930s–1950s.
Baron Nicholas de Rakoczy circus photographs.
British Theatre Association play library.

Finding aids: Various lists and indexes, but no comprehensive catalogue for the entire collection. Catalogues of finite collections are in the course of preparation.

Conservation: V&A Museum Conservation Department.

Publications: Spotlight (1981) [exhibition catalogue].
Victorian Illustrated Music Sheets (1981).
Images of Show Business (1982).
Oliver Messel (1983) [exhibition catalogue].
Theatre Posters (1983).
Stage by Stage (1985).
The Theatre Museum (1987).

824 Theosophical Society in England

Address: The Library, 50 Gloucester Place, London W1U 8EA

Telephone: (020) 7935 9261

Fax: (020) 7935 9543

E-mail: theosophical@freenetname.co.uk

Website: theosophical-society.org.uk

Enquiries: The Librarian, Janet Grayson

Open: By arrangement.

Access: Members of the Theosophical Society, or non-members upon previous appointment with the Librarian.

The society was formed in New York in 1875 by Madame Blavatsky (1831–91). The international headquarters are now in Madras, India, with branches in more than 60 countries worldwide. The library specialises in theosophy, comparative religion, mysticism and occultism. It holds a collection of the works and pamphlets of Annie Besant (1847–1933), MSS, photographs and a press cuttings book of other members of the society, plus a growing collection of audio cassettes (c400) and videos (24). There is a catalogue and photocopying is available.

825 Tower Hamlets Local History Library and Archives

Parent organisation: London Borough of Tower Hamlets

Address: Bancroft Library, 277 Bancroft Road, London E1 4DQ

Telephone: (020) 8980 4366 ext. 129

Fax: (020) 8983 4510

Enquiries: The Archivist, Mr Malcolm Barr-Hamilton

Open: Tues, Thurs: 9.00–8.00; Fri: 9.00–6.00; Sat: 9.00–5.00.

Access: Generally open to the public. An appointment is advisable for microform use.

Historical background: Following the creation of the London Borough of Tower Hamlets in 1965, the local collections of archives and local history material from the former metropolitan boroughs of Bethnal Green, Poplar and Stepney were amalgamated to form Tower Hamlets Local History Library. Some local records are held by the London Metropolitan Archives (entry 688) and Guildhall Library (entry 624), and others were destroyed during World War II. In 1986 an archivist was appointed, and in 1988 an air-conditioned strongroom was opened to house the archives.

Acquisitions policy: To collect, preserve and make available material in all formats relevant to the history of the London Borough of Tower Hamlets and its people.

Archives of organisation: Committee minutes and other records of the London Borough of Tower Hamlets, 1965– , and the metropolitan boroughs of Bethnal Green, Poplar and Stepney, 1900–65.
Records of the predecessor authorities, including rate books, land tax assessments, vestry records, Poor Law records etc, 16th century– .

Major collections: Deposited records of some local organisations, including non-conformist churches and schools, 18th–20th centuries; some East India Company records, 1709–1871.
Census returns for Poplar and Blackwall, 1821, 1831, and (on microfilm) for the whole borough, 1841–91.
Title deeds, 16th century– (c15,000).
Daniel Bolt Shipping Collection: books, pamphlets, illustrations, MS ship indexes, mostly 1850–1920, and MS ships' log-books, 1797–1914 (c10).

Non-manuscript material: Photographs and prints (c20,000), transparencies (c5000); books, pamphlets and theses (c18,000); newspaper cuttings (c500 boxes); maps (c2000).
Small collections of sound recordings, films and videos.

Microfilms of local newspapers, 1857– , and some parish registers.

Finding aids: Several catalogues and indexes to the local history collections. Handlists; sent to NRA.

Facilities: Photocopying. Photography by arrangement. Microfilm/fiche readers/printer.

Conservation: Contracted out.

Publications: H. Finch: *The Tower Hamlets Connection: a Biographical Guide.*
T. Ridge: *Central Stepney History Walk.*
Leaflets on family history and other resources in the collection are available.

826 Town and Country Planning Association

Address: 17 Carlton House Terrace, London SW1Y 5AS

Telephone: (020) 7930 8903/4/5

Fax: (020) 7930 3280

Website: www.tcpa.org.uk

Enquiries: The Director

Open: Mon–Fri: 9.30–5.30.

Access: Town planners and bona fide academic researchers; an appointment is necessary.

Historical background: The association was founded in 1899 as the Garden Cities Association by 13 men, influenced by Ebenezer Howard. It was renamed the Town and Country Planning Association in 1941. Subsequently Frederick J. Osborn, Honorary Secretary of TCPA, 1955–70, campaigned against the construction of tower blocks and deck-access flats. In recent years the TCPA has set up demonstration projects to encourage community initiatives and has urged government to decentralise decision-making on environment issues. It is a voluntary body and a registered educational charity. The archive has been substantially depleted by changes of offices and war-time destruction.

Acquisitions policy: To maintain and consolidate the archive.

Archives of organisation: Council and executive committee minutes, 1913–20, 1938–76; minutes of AGMs, 1901–67.
Other administrative records, including papers and proceedings of conferences; evidence submitted by the association; correspondence files

of F.J. Osborn; complete set of annual reports, 1941– .

Major collections: Administrative material on Letchworth and Welwyn Garden Cities (2 box files).

Non-manuscript material: Pamphlets and leaflets commissioned or sponsored by TCPA. Press cuttings and scrapbooks, 1937–70. Photograph albums, glass slides, posters and ephemera.

Finding aids: NRA 24472.

Facilities: Photocopying.

827 Transport for London Archives and Records Management Service

Address: 55 Broadway, London SW1H 0BD

Telephone: (020) 7918 4142

Fax: (020) 7918 3727

E-mail: kathrynthomas@tfl.gov.uk

Enquiries: The Archivist, Kathryn Thomas

Open: Normal office hours, by appointment only.

Access: Bona fide researchers by prior arrangement. There is no access to staff records or those containing personal information less than 75 years old, or to other records less than 30 years old.

Historical background: Transport for London (TfL) was established in July 2000, and is an executive arm of the Greater London Authority, reporting to the Mayor of London. TfL is responsible for the delivery of the mayor's integrated transport strategy. As well as buses, the organisation is responsible for river services, Victoria Coach Station, light rail and trams, street management and taxi and private hire licensing. TfL will assume responsibility for London Underground on completion of the proposed Public Private Partnership. Before July 2000, the Archives and Records Management Service was part of London Transport (LT). The London Passenger Transport Board was established by Act of Parliament in 1933 with powers to take over and operate all bus, tram, trolleybus and underground railway services in London and adjacent counties. Predecessor companies included London General Omnibus Company Ltd (originally registered in Paris in 1855); the Metropolitan Railway, the world's first underground railway (1863); the City and South London Railway, the world's first deep-level tube railway (1890); Underground Electric Railways of London Ltd, initially comprising the District railway, and the projected Bakerloo, Piccadilly and Hampstead tubes; and the London United Tramways (1902). Since 1933, LT has been constituted variously as an executive of the British Transport Commission (1947), and an executive of the Greater London Council (1969). In 1984 the London Regional Transport Act transferred control back to central government. London Underground Ltd and London Buses Ltd were established as operating subsidiaries.

Photographs and library materials relating to the history of LT are held at the London Transport Museum, Covent Garden, access to these is by appointment (tele. (020) 7379 6344). London Transport has deposited 3,500 items in London Metropolitan Archives (see entry 688).

Acquisitions policy: To select records which best illustrate the development, history and business processes of Transport for London and its predecessors. Main acquisitions come through the records management programme and document management framework project. Related material is also acquired, e.g. of staff associations.

Archives of organisation: Archives of London Transport and its predecessor companies, c1820– .

Finding aids: The service is in the process of cataloguing archives created by London Transport and recataloguing earlier deposits with London Metropolitan Archives. Completed catalogues are available.

Facilities: Photocopying and photography by arrangement, and in accordance with the service's preservation policy.

Conservation: Contracted out.

Publications: T.C. Barker and R.M. Robbins: *A History of London Transport* (1963, 1974).

C. Barman: *The Man who Built London Transport: a Biography of Frank Pick* (1979).

S. Taylor: *A Journey through Time: London Transport Photographs, 1880–1965* (1992).

D.F. Croome and A.A. Jackson: *Rails Through the Clay, a History of London's Tube Railways* (1993).

O. Green and J. Rause-Davies: *Designed for London: 150 Years of Transport Design* (1995).

828 UK National Digital Archive of Datasets (NDAD)

Parent organisation: University of London/ Public Record Office

Address: UL Computer Centre, 20 Guilford Street, London WC1N 1DZ

Telephone: (020) 7692 1212

Fax: (020) 7692 1234

E-mail: support@ndad.ulcc.ac.uk

Website: ndad.ulcc.ac.uk

Enquiries: The Senior Archivist

Open: The NDAD website is the means of access to the archive's catalogues and its holdings of data and documentation. The website may be consulted at any time except scheduled down-times due to maintenance, which will be announced on the website in advance. A service providing access to the website via a dedicated terminal at the University of London Library (see entry 833) is available for users who lack their own connection to the Internet. This service is available Mon–Fri: 9.00–5.00, by appointment only.

Access: Access to data and related documentation is via links in NDAD's on-line catalogues. There is no charge for access. Access is restricted to registered users and anyone may register by completing a registration form; details are available on the website or by contacting NDAD.

Historical background: NDAD is operated by the University of London (UL) as an agent of the Public Record Office (PRO; entry 1058). Following a period of testing and development in late 1997/early 1998, NDAD has offered a public service since March 1998.

Acquisitions policy: Electronic datasets and related documentation are selected by the PRO for transfer to NDAD. The archive's contents are therefore drawn primarily from those bodies covered by the Public Records Acts. The archive is actively acquiring material.

Archives of organisation: Records of the acquisition of datasets and the administration of the service, 1997– . Archives of the central services of the University of London are held at the University of London Library.

Major collections: Court Service: Judicial Statistics database, 1986–96; Education Departments: Schools' Census (Form 7) datasets, 1976, 1993; Home Office: British Crime Survey, 1996; Metropolitan Police: Crime Statistics System (ME), 1990–6; Agricultural Departments: Agricultural Census — Parish Summaries, 1989–90, and County Summaries, 1994–6, Internal Drainage Board Database, 1994–5; Coast Protection Survey of England, 1993–6; Forestry Commission: National Inventory of Woodlands and Trees Grampian Region dataset, 1994–7; Statistical Departments: Historic Mortality data files 1901–92, and Primary Births, 1963–4; Transport Departments: Survey of Heavy Goods Vehicles, 1976–97; HM Customs and Excise: Beer Duty dataset, 1993–8; Health Departments: Anatomy dataset, 1992–8; Museums and Galleries Commission: Digest of Museum Statistics (DOMUS), 1991–8; Welsh Office: Contaminated Land Survey, 1987–98, and Coastal Survey of Wales, 1992–6; Coal Authority: Mining Report System, 1800s–1998; Nature Conservation Departments: Welsh Bats database, *c*1982–*c*1996, and British Bats database, *c*1982–*c*1996.

Non-manuscript material: Documentation relating to datasets, including a series of maps produced by the Welsh Office to accompany the Coastal Survey — Wales dataset. Paper documentation is normally scanned and made available electronically.

Finding aids: The following finding aids are available on the NDAD website: series, datasets and documentation catalogues; administrative histories of transferring departments. Facilities are available for free-text and thesaurus-assisted keyword searching of the finding aids. Paper and electronic copies of datasets and documentation can be ordered by registered users via the NDAD website.

Conservation: Minor repairs to paper documentation are made in-house; more extensive repairs are contracted out as necessary. Conservation advice and guidance is provided by the University of London Library's Preservation and Conservation Department.

Publications: Information leaflet.

829 Unilever Historical Archives

Parent organisation: Unilever plc

Address: Correspondence: Unilever House, Blackfriars, London EC4P 4BQ Repository: The Lyceum, Bridge Street, Port Sunlight, Wirral L62 3VJ, London

Fax: (020) 7822 5464

E-mail: jeannette.strickland@unilever.com

Enquiries: The Corporate Archivist, Ms J. Strickland

Open: Mon–Fri: 10.00–4.00, by appointment.

Access: At the discretion of the company, strictly by appointment. Applications should be made in writing to the Corporate Archivist in London, although it should be noted that most archives are housed in Port Sunlight.

Historical background: Lever & Co. began soap production in 1885 and became Lever Bros. Ltd in 1890, following its move to Port Sunlight. Unilever was formed in 1929 from the merger of Lever Bros. Ltd and the Margarine Union, a European partnership of Van den Berghs, Jurgens and Schichts. The company now specialises in packaged consumer goods. An archive service has been provided since 1983. Records deposited elsewhere include Colman title deeds, in Norfolk Record Office (entry 939); Niger Co. Ltd, in Rhodes House Library (entry 994) Price's Patent Candle Co. Ltd, in Wirral Archives (entry 97); and United Africa Co. Ltd, in the PRO (entry 1058).

Acquisitions policy: To maintain the archives of all Unilever companies, past and present, in the UK. Accepts papers of individuals connected with the company.

Archives of organisation: Records of head office departments and subsidiary companies including A.F. Pears, 1781– ; D. & W. Gibbs, 1820s– ; Joseph Crosfield, 1820s– ; J. & J. Colman, 1820s– ; also records relating to numerous dormant and struck-off companies.

Major collections: William Hesketh Lever, 1st Viscount Leverhulme (1851–1925), business correspondence, 1894–1925.

Non-manuscript material: Films, videos, microfilms, photographs, packaging and ephemera, paintings.
Histories of individual companies.

Finding aids: Computer database and descriptive lists.

Facilities: Photocopying and photography by arrangement. Microfilm readers.

Conservation: Contracted out.

Publications: C. Wilson: *The History of Unilever*, 3 vols. (1954, 1968; 4th vol. in preparation).

D.K. Fieldhowe: *Unilever Overseas: the Anatomy of a Multinational* (1978).

——: *Merchant Capital and Economic Decolonization: the United Africa Company, 1929–1989* (1994).

830 United Kingdom Temperance Alliance

Address: Alliance House, 12 Caxton Street, London SW1H 0QS

Telephone: (020) 7222 4001/5880

Fax: (020) 7799 2510

E-mail: info@ias.org.uk

Enquiries: The Librarian, Mrs T. Levonen

Open: Mon–Fri: 10.00 4.30, by appointment only.

Access: Generally open to the public.

Historical background: The United Kingdom Alliance was founded in 1853 'to suppress the drink traffic by legislative means'. The United Kingdom Temperance Alliance Ltd was formed in 1942 as an educational charity, taking over all the work of the UKA except for its political activities. The temperance library and research centre was developed in 1975 by the Christian Economic and Social Research Foundation under the umbrella of the UKTA, which (since the removal of the CESRF to another headquarters) now runs the library.

Archives of organisation: Records of UKA, including minute books, 1871–1923; minute book of UKA Agency Committee, 1902–25; *Alliance Reports*, 1953– ; *Year Book*, 1910–52.

National Commercial Temperance League: general minute books, 1894–1924; minutes of various committees, 1899–1939.

Scottish Temperance League register, 1916, and tracts.

Non-manuscript material: Alliance News; *Outlook* (NCTL; incomplete run).

Pamphlets, duplicated material and memorabilia of the temperance movement.

Original prints by Cruikshank of 'The Bottle' and 'The Drunkard's Daughter'.

Finding aids: Card index. List of temperance movement material by B. Harrison.

Facilities: Photocopying.

831 United Society for the Propagation of the Gospel (USPG)

Address: Partnership House, 157 Waterloo Road, London SE1 8XA

Telephone: (020) 7928 8681

Fax: (020) 7928 2371

E-mail: archive@uspg.org.uk

Enquiries: The Archivist, Mrs C. Wakeling

Open: Mon–Thurs: by appointment only.

Access: Open to bona fide researchers, upon production of a letter of introduction. Some records are closed for 30 years and personal records are closed for 50 years from the date of death.

Historical background: The USPG was formed in 1965 by the merging of two missionary organisations: the Society for the Propagation of the Gospel in Foreign Parts (SPG), founded in 1701, and the Universities Mission to Central Africa (UMCA), founded in 1857. The majority of the archives of SPG (1701–1965), UMCA (1857–1965) and the Cambridge Mission to Delhi (1857–1968) are at Rhodes House Library (entry 994).

Acquisitions policy: Gifts of appropriate missionary papers are accepted.

Archives of organisation: USPG archives, 1965– .

SPG and UMCA missionaries personal files, 19th century–1965.

Small proportion of SPG and UMCA archives, pre-1965.

Non-manuscript material: Photographs.

The society's films are deposited at the National Film and Television Archive (entry 556B).

Finding aids: Calendars of the earliest correspondence and lists of archives at Rhodes House Library.

Card index to missionary files. Card index/catalogue to USPG archives.

Facilities: Photocopying.

Publications: C.F. Pascoe: *Two Hundred Years of the SPG: an Historical Account of the Society for the Propagation of the Gospel in Foreign Parts, 1701–1900* (London, 1901).
H.P. Thompson: *Into all Lands: the History of the Society for the Propagation of the Gospel in Foreign Parts, 1701–1950* (London, 1951).
A.E.M. Anderson-Morshead and A.G. Blood: *The History of the Universities Mission to Central Africa* (3 vols, London, 1955, 1957).
M. Dewey: *The Messengers* (Oxford, 1975).

832 University College London
Special Collections

Parent organisation: University of London

Address: Gower Street, London WC1E 6BT

Telephone: (020) 7380 7796 (direct line); 7387 7050 ext. 7793 (general enquiries only)

Fax: (020) 7380 7727

E-mail: mssrb@ucl.ac.uk

Website: www.ucl.ac.uk/library/special-coll
www.cadb.ucl.ac.uk/

Enquiries: The Head of Special Collections, Ms Gillian Furlong

Open: Mon–Fri: 10.00–5.00.

Access: Open to bona fide scholars, on application to the Director of Library Services or to the Head of Special Collections, preferably giving prior notice.

Historical background: The college was founded in 1827 by a group led by Henry Brougham (1778–1868) and Thomas Campbell (1777–1844), supported by whig, radical and non-conformist interests. In 1836 the government established the University of London as a purely examining and degree-granting body and the Gower Street College was granted a royal charter as London University College. The library was opened in 1829, a year after the University of London first admitted students. The first acquisitions of MS material were donations or bequests, the most notable being the Bentham MSS (1849), the Society for the Diffusion of Useful Knowledge (SDUK) papers (1848), the Chadwick papers (1898) and the Graves Library (1870). Major purchases included the Brougham papers and a collection of very interesting MSS that came with the Ogden Library (1953) and a succession of purchases of early MSS in 1911, 1921 and 1927. The large collection of Latin American business archives was transferred to the library, from firms going into liquidation in the 1960s, as a result of a survey undertaken on behalf of the *Guide to MS Sources for the History of Latin America and the Caribbean in the British Isles* (ed. P. Walne, 1973). Following reorganisation in the late 1980s, MSS and archives of Jewish interest, in particular those formerly part of the Library of the Jewish Historical Society of England (or Mocatta Library), were incorporated in 1993. The Gaster papers were transferred in 1994. Records of the Geological Sciences Department are now held by the Zoology Museum, Biology Department. College archives, other than those detailed below, are held by the college records office (contact Mrs Rosamund Cummings).
NB The Special Collections department will be rehoused in 2002.

Acquisitions policy: To strengthen existing collections, by gift, loan, deposit or purchase, and to encourage the deposit of archival material relating to college history, including professorial papers.

Archives of organisation: College archives, including correspondence, 1825–1905; professorship applications, 1827–1920; professors' fee books, 1833–80; and committee papers, 1836–1918.
Archives of UCH Medical School.
Archives of Slade School of Art (f. 1871), including student signing-in books, 1878– , but mainly 1949– , with photographs of student works, 1950s– (incomplete).
Archives of Institute of Archaeology (f. 1937), including excavation records, photographs, and working note-books of Prof. Gordon Childe, former director.

Major collections: Correspondence and papers of eminent political, literary and scientific figures, including Lord Brougham (1778–1868) (c60,000 MSS); Jeremy Bentham (1748–1832), (c75,000 MSS); Sir Edwin Chadwick (1800–90); Dr Moses Gaster (1856–1939); George B. Greenough (1778–1855); Karl Pearson (1857–1936); Sir Francis Galton (1822–1911); Lionel Penrose (1878–1972); George Orwell (1903–50).
Diaries and letters of Sir Moses Montefiore (1827–72).

Publishing archives of Routledge & Kegan Paul Ltd, 1853–1973; and the Society for the Diffusion of Useful Knowledge, 1824–48.

Papers of former UCL professors, including Sir William Ramsay (1852–1916); A.F. Murison (1847–1934); W.P. Ker (1855–1923); Sir J. Ambrose Fleming (1849–1945); R.W. Chambers (1874–1942); J.Z. Young, FRS (1907–97).

Latin American business archives: the largest collection outside South America, covering, in particular, banking, trade, railways and shipping, mainly 19th century.

Smaller collections include 99 medieval MSS in nine different languages; 40 Phillips MSS relating to Swiss towns; 40 Graves MSS relating to the history of mathematics and science; 102 Ogden MSS covering a wide range of subjects.

Non-manuscript material: Photograph collection covering UCL history, members of staff, buildings etc.
Several MS collections contain photographs.

Finding aids: Handlists and/or card indexes to most collections. Lists sent to NRA.
Summary guides comprising collection-level descriptions available on webpage; also MAARS on-line catalogue.

Facilities: Photocopying. Photography. Microfilming. Microfilm/fiche reader.

Conservation: Contracted out.

Publications: D.K. Coveney: *Descriptive Catalogue of Manuscripts in the Library of University College* (London, 1935).
A. Taylor Milne: *Catalogue of the Manuscripts of Jeremy Bentham in the Library of UCL* (1937).
N.R. Ker: *Medieval Manuscripts in British Libraries,* I:*London* (1969).
J. Percival: *Manuscript Collections in the Library of University College London,* Occasional Publications of UCL Library no. 1 (London, 2/1978).
Occasional Publications of UCL Library nos. 3–8 [handlists to the Chadwick, Chambers, Sharpe and SDUK papers and to the archives of Routledge & Kegan Paul and of the Peruvian Corporation].
M. Merrington and others: *A List of the Papers and Correspondence of Lionel Sharples Penrose (1898–1972)* (London, 1979).
J. Golden: *A List of the Papers and Correspondence of George Bellas Greenough (1778–1855)* (London, 1981).

M. Merrington, J. Golden and others: *A List of the Papers and Correspondence of Karl Pearson (1857–1936)* (London, 1983).
J. Percival (ed.): *A Guide to the Archives and Manuscripts in the University of London,* i (London, 1984).
J. Golden: *A List of the Papers and Correspondence of Henry Clark Barlow MD (1806–1976)* (London, 1985).
N. Harte and J. North: *The World of UCL, 1828–1990* (London, 1991).

833 University of London Library

Parent organisation: University of London

Address: Senate House, Malet Street, London WC1E 7HU

Telephone: (020) 7862 8470

Fax: (020) 7862 8480

E-mail: jetherton@ull.ac.uk

Website: www.ull.co.uk

Enquiries: The Archivist, Ms Judith Etherton

Open: Term: Mon: 9.30–8.45; Tues–Fri: 9.30–6.00; Sat: 9.30–1.00, 2.00–5.15.
Vacation: Mon–Fri: 9.00–6.00; Sat: 9.30–1.00, 2.00–5.15.

Access: By appointment. There are restrictions on certain collections and some of the university archives.

Historical background: The University of London Library has, historically, been the central library of the university. Its origins go back to 1838, though its real expansion dates from the gift of the De Morgan Collection in 1877. The library was based first in Burlington Gardens and then, from 1906, in South Kensington, before it moved to its present accommodation in Senate House in 1937. The Palaeography Room contains a library of printed material on MS studies and archives, and its staff are responsible for administering the library's holdings of MSS and archives. In 1901 Herbert S. Foxwell (1849–1936) sold his collection of books, pamphlets and MSS relating to economic history to the Worshipful Company of Goldsmiths and in 1903 the company gave this collection to the university. This subject interest partly influenced the subsequent acquisitions policy for MS material, especially for the period covering the 15th to the

19th centuries. The Institute of Historical Research has transferred its MS holdings to the library.

Acquisitions policy: At present the library only accepts MS material which adds to or complements existing collections or which falls within the collecting policy, defined as follows: material relating to the history of the university, especially personal papers of prominent figures, and to the history of higher education; papers of historians and of literary figures, especially 1850– ; material which complements the University of London Library's Special Collections, including Goldsmiths' Library: social and economic history, 15th–19th centuries; Sterling Library: literary MSS and correspondence, mainly 19th century; Harry Price Library: psychical research.

Archives of organisation: The archives of the central administration of the university, 1836– , comprising records created by statutory bodies, administrative departments, federal activities, student facilities and other functions associated with the Federal University.

Major collections: Individual historical and literary MSS and autograph letters, 12th–20th centuries; includes the foundation collection of MSS acquired with the Goldsmiths' Library of Economic Literature.

Collections of papers of individuals and institutions, including the following: Charles Booth (1840–1916); (Henry) Austin Dobson (1840–1921); Duckworth Publishers, c1936–56; Professor Augustus De Morgan (1806–71); Thomas Sturge Moore (1870–1944); Anne Isabella Ritchie (1837–1919); Herbert Spencer (1820–1903).

Captain A.W. Fuller's collection of documents and seals, 13th–20th centuries.

MSS transferred from the Institute of Historical Research.

Papers of Harry Price (1881–1948), including correspondence of Sir A. Conan Doyle (1859–1930).

Literary MSS collected by Sir Louis Sterling (*d* 1958).

Non-manuscript material: Considerable quantity of microfilm copies of MS material held elsewhere.

Detached seals, proofs and casts.

University of London Collection: relating to the history of the university.

Finding aids: Card index to holdings. TS catalogue to post–1930 MS acquisitions. Handlists

to many collections. TSS lists. NRA notified of new acquisitions and lists sent.

Facilities: Photocopying. Photography. Microfilm/fiche reader/printer.

Conservation: Full in-house service.

Publications: R.A. Rye: *Catalogue of Manuscripts and Autograph Letters in the University Library* (London, 1921; suppl. 1921–30, 1930).
P. Kelly: *Modern Historical Manuscripts in the University of London Library: a Subject Guide* (London, 1972).
J. Gibbs and P. Kelly: 'Manuscripts and Archives in the University of London Library', *Archives*, xi/51 (1974), 161.
H. Young: *Guide to Literary Manuscripts.*
Catalogue of the Goldsmiths' Library of Economic Literature, iii (1982) [including MSS].
J. Percival: *A Guide to Archives and Manuscripts in the University of London*, 1 (London, 1984).

834 University of North London
TUC Library

Address: Learning Centre, 263 Holloway Road, London N7 6PP

Telephone: (020) 7753 3184

Fax: (020) 7753 3191

E-mail: c.coates@unl.ac.uk

Enquiries: The Librarian, TUC Collections, Chris Coates

Open: Mon–Fri: 9.15–4.45, by appointment only.

Access: Bona fide scholars.

Historical background: The University of North London was formerly the Polytechnic of North London which was the amalgamation of the Northern Polytechnic (f. 1896) and North Western Polytechnic (f. 1929). The TUC Library Collections were deposited in 1996 although the TUC Archive is held by the Modern Records Centre (see entry 261). Archives of the University, 1890s– , are held separately and are not currently available.

Acquisitions policy: Material relevant to existing holdings will be considered.

Major collections: TUC Library Collections, c1868– , including Gertrude Tuckwell (1861–

1951) Collection, c1890–1921; Workers Education Association National Archive and Library, 1903– ; Marjorie Nicholson (1914–97) papers, c1918–97.

Non-manuscript material: TUC Library of pamphlets and periodicals.
Oral history collection (in progress).

Finding aids: Nicholson: NRA 41904.

Facilities: Photocopying. Microfilm/fiche readers.

Conservation: Occasionally contracted out.

Publications: A. Mason: *WEA National Archive Catalogue* (1999).

835 University of Westminster Archives

Address: ISLS, 4–12 Little Titchfield Street, London W1P 7FW

Telephone: (020) 7911 5000 ext. 2524

Fax: (020) 7911 5894

E-mail: archive@westminster.ac.uk

Enquiries: The University Archivist, Brenda Weeden

Open: By appointment.

Access: Generally open to the public; proof of identity is required and an appointment is necessary. Some institutional records are generally closed for 30 years; student and staff files are closed for 80 years.

Historical background: In 1838 the Polytechnic Institution (from 1841 the Royal Polytechnic Institution) opened at 309 Regent Street. It was founded to promote science and technology through exhibition, teaching and research and became associated particularly with the development of photography and with magic lantern shows. The Polytechnic Institution failed in 1881, and the building was bought by Quintin Hogg. Hogg's philanthropic and education work began with the establishment of a ragged school in Covent Garden in 1864. In 1871 he founded the Young Men's Christian Institute, and the Young Women's Institute was opened in 1888. Following the move to Regent Street, the YMCI became known as the Polytechnic and became the model for similar institutions across London. From 1893 the Polytechnic was increasingly funded by the London County Council.

The Polytechnic of Central London (PCL) was formed in 1970 by the merger of Regent Street Polytechnic and Holborn College of Law, Languages and Commerce. Sidney Webb College of Education, opened in 1961, merged with PCL in 1975 and closed in 1980. In 1900 Harrow College for Further Education also merged with PCL, which became the University of Westminster in 1992.

Acquisitions policy: To acquire and preserve the records of the university and of its antecedents.

Archives of organisation: Royal Polytechnic Institution, records, 1838–81, including some material *re* foundation, and printed programmes, 1873–78 (c100 items).
The Polytechnic, Regent Street, minutes of governing body, 1891–1970 (incomplete), *Polytechnic Magazine*, 1879–1971; prospectuses, 1901–65; administrative records and records of some sports and social clubs.
The Quintin School, some records of pupils, school magazines and memorabilia.
PCL, Sidney Webb College of Education and Harrow College of Further Education, administrative records (incomplete).

Non-manuscript material: Engravings and photographs.

Finding aids: Partial descriptive list. Database in preparation.

Facilities: Restricted photocopying. Photography.

Conservation: Contracted out.

Publications: E.M. Wood: *A History of the Polytechnic* (London, 1965).
L.C.B. Seaman: *The Quintin School, 1886–1956* (London, 1956).
160 Years of Innovation: from Polytechnic Institution to University of Westminster, 1838–1998 (London, 1998) [short pictorial history].

836 Upper Norwood Joint Library

Address: Westow Hill, Upper Norwood, London SE19 1TJ

Telephone: (020) 8670 2551

Fax: (020) 8670 5468

Enquiries: The Reference and Local History Librarian, Mr J.G. Savage

Open: Mon: 10.00–7.00; Tues, Thurs, Fri: 9.00–7.00; Sat: 9.00–5.00; an appointment is advisable.

Access: Generally open to the public.

Historical background: The library is situated close to the borough boundary between Lambeth and Croydon. It opened in 1900 and has been run since then as an independent public library financed jointly by Croydon and Lambeth.

Acquisitions policy: To supplement the local history collection with any materials of interest concerning the Upper Norwood area.

Major collections: Principally non-MS material (see below).

Non-manuscript material: Local history collection, including pamphlets, programmes and handbills, newspapers, press cuttings, maps, videos and books, covering the Upper Norwood area and to a lesser extent the surrounding localities of Croydon, Dulwich, Camberwell, Sydenham, Southwark, Anerley and Penge. There is a considerable amount on the Crystal Palace, which stood nearby until 1936, including photographs of interior and exterior views.
J.B. Wilson (*d* 1949) Collection: personal collection of a local historian, covering Upper and especially West Norwood.
Gerald Massey Collection: books, newspaper and magazine articles, photographs, on the life and interests of Gerald Massey (1828–1907), poet, chartist, spiritualist and Egyptologist.

Finding aids: Card indexes of subjects, individuals and buildings for the local history and Crystal Palace collections.

Facilities: Photocopying.

Publications: Fact-sheets on early history of Norwood and on the Crystal Palace.

837 Vaughan Williams Memorial Library

Parent organisation: English Folk Dance and Song Society

Address: Cecil Sharp House, 2 Regent's Park Road, London NW1 7AY

Telephone: (020) 7485 2206

Fax: (020) 7284 0534

E-mail: library@efdss.org

Website: www.efdss.org

Enquiries: The Librarian, Malcolm Taylor

Open: Mon–Fri: 9.30–5.30
Sound library closed 12.00–2.00 daily.

Access: Generally open to the public, but non-members of the society are charged a daily fee. Access to the sound collection is restricted; contact the Librarian for details.

Historical background: Cecil Sharp (1859–1924) was an assiduous collector of English folk music and dance traditions and founded the English Folk Dance Society (EFDS) in 1911 to encourage and promote these traditions. Cecil Sharp House was opened in 1930 and in 1932 the society amalgamated with the Folk Song Society (f. 1898). The library was renamed in 1958 in honour of Ralph Vaughan Williams (1872–1958), president of EFDSS.

Acquisitions policy: To acquire materials of any media relevant to British folk culture and elements of it found in other communities, particularly North America and Ireland.

Archives of organisation: Archives of the Folk Song Society, 1898–1932, the EFDS, 1911–32, and the EFDSS, 1932– .

Major collections: MS collections of most early 20th-century folk song and dance collectors, including Cecil Sharp, Lucy Broadwood, Janet Blunt, Anne Gilchrist, George Gardiner, George Butterworth, Hammond brothers, Maud Karpeles and James Madison Carpenter (some on microfilm).

Non-manuscript material: Sound collection, 1906– , including field recordings of major collectors such as Percy Grainger and Mike Yates. BBC film/video collections.

Finding aids: Indexes to photographs, Cecil Sharp's informants, films and videos, and BBC archive of folk music and folklore.
Sound collection catalogue and various indexes.
Blunt: NRA 35006; Broadwood: NRA 35004; Butterworth: NRA 35007; Gardiner: NRA 35005; Sharp: NRA 34987.

Facilities: Photocopying. Microfilm/fiche reader/printer. Audio-visual playback equipment.

Conservation: Contracted out.

Publications: Catalogue (1973).
Study guides to Morris dancing, sword dancing, English folk song, clog and step dancing, and May Day in England.

838 Victoria & Albert Museum National Art Library
Special Collections

Address: Cromwell Road, London SW7 2RL

Telephone: (020) 7938 8315

Fax: (020) 7938 8461

E-mail: enquiries@nal.vam.ac.uk

Website: www.nal.vam.ac.uk

Enquiries: Public Services

Open: Tues–Sat: 10.00–5.00.
Closed for three weeks after late August bank holiday for stock-taking.

Access: Bona fide researchers and holders of V&A Library reader's tickets.

Historical background: MSS have entered the library from the inception of the School of Design after 1836. Documentary and illuminated MSS were collected from the 19th century and consolidated into a collection in the 1950s.

Acquisitions policy: To collect MSS that document the history and practice of all branches of art and design; to collect illuminated and calligraphic MSS that document the development of book production and book design from the Middle Ages, with special emphasis on the post-medieval survival of medieval bookmaking crafts, the 19th-century revival and subsequent development in the 20th century of calligraphy, lettering and illumination. The MSS Collection usually acquires material that lacks an archival context; archive groups are passed to the Archive of Art and Design (see entry 839A).

Archives of organisation: The MSS Collection holds material relating to the history of the V & A, most notably the papers of Henry Cole (1808–82).

Major collections: Edwin Landseer (1803–73), correspondence.
Records of Carrington & Co., silversmiths and jewellers, 1870–1930; J. Smith & successors, picture dealers, 1812–1908.
Pugin family records, 19th century.
The Library of John Forster (1812–76) includes MSS of Charles Dickens's novels; correspondence of David Garrick (1717–79); papers of James Butler, Duke of Ormonde, and his successor, relating to Ireland, c1642–c1700; miscellaneous papers of Jonathan Swift (1667–1745).

Finding aids: Pre–1987 card catalogue on microfiche. Post–1987 acquisitions on automated library catalogue available on website. NAL Heritage Project will extend automated catalogue.
Handlists to some self-contained collections.
Annual returns to NRA.

Facilities: Photography. Microfilm/fiche readers/printers.

Conservation: In-house museum department; some work contracted out.

Publications: J.I. Whalley: *Catalogue of English Non-Illuminated Manuscripts in the National Art Library up to December 1973* (1975) [reproduced typescript; with annual supplements up to 1978].
Forster Collection: a Catalogue of the Paintings, Manuscripts, Autograph Letters, Pamphlets, etc. with Indexes (HMSO, 1893).
The Forster and Dyce Collections from the National Art Library at the V&A Museum, London: an inventory to Parts 1 and 2 of the Harvester Microform Collection (1987).

839 Victoria and Albert Museum National Art Library
Museum Archives

Address: Blythe House, 23 Blythe Road, London W14 0QF

E-mail: archive@vam.ac.uk

Website: www.nal.vam.ac.uk/archives.html

A Archive of Art and Design

Telephone: (020) 7603 1514

Fax: (020) 7602 0980

Website: www.nal.vam.ac.uk/nalaad.html

Enquiries: The Archivist

Open: Tues–Thurs: 10.00–4.30, by appointment.
Closed for three weeks after late August bank holiday for stock-taking.

Access: An appointment, by telephone or in writing, is required. Identification with signature and proof of address is also required and references may be necessary for access to certain materials.

Historical background: The Archive of Art and Design was set up in 1978 to conserve, catalogue and make available archive groups formerly held by and offered to the curatorial departments of the Victoria and Albert Museum, with particular emphasis on the 20th century.

Acquisitions policy: To collect archive groups with special reference to the fields covered by the collections of the Victoria and Albert Museum. Major strengths are in the fields of textiles, fashion, graphic design and book illustrations, stained glass, exhibition design, interior design, metalwork and ceramics.

Major collections: Archives of Heal & Son Ltd, bedding and furniture manufacturers, 1810–1995; John French, fashion photographer, c1948–85; Misha Black, industrial and exhibition designer and architect, 1922–78; the Rt. Hon. Baron Reilly of Brompton, former director of the Design Council, c1920–c1990; Gaby Schreiber, consultant designer for industry, c1940–89; Francis Marshall, fashion and social illustrator, 1868–1986; Japan Festival 1991 Ltd, c1986-92; the Crafts Council, c1960–1994; Royal College of Art, Department of Design Research, c1960–1986; Bernhard Baer, 1947–85; *The Ambassador,* the British export magazine for textiles and fashion, 1933–87.
Records of James Powell & Sons (Whitefriars) Ltd, stained-glass making company, 1845–1973; William Comyns & Sons Ltd, manufacturing silversmiths, 1896–1987; Arts and Crafts Exhibition Society (later Society of Designer-Craftsmen), papers, 1886–1984.
E.W. Godwin, architect, furniture and theatre designer, papers, 1844–88.
Eileen Gray, architect, furniture and interior designer, papers, designs and photographs, 1913–74.
Archive of Robin and Lucienne Day, furniture and textile designers respectively, c1950–c1990.

Non-manuscript material: A large number of the archive groups contain a wide variety of media, from glass negatives to film and other audio-visual material.
The Krazy Kat Arkive of 20th-century popular culture includes toys, robots, games, books, journals and tear sheets.
Ephemera collection.

Finding aids: Each archive group is described on the computer catalogue of the National Art Library; list of titles of all archive groups and lists for larger collections also available.

Facilities: Photography. Microfiche readers. Video and tape recorders. Slide projector. Light table.

Conservation: In-house museum department.

Publications: E. Lomas: *Guide to the Archive of Art and Design, Victoria & Albert Museum* (2001).

B Beatrix Potter Collections

Telephone: (020) 7602 0281 ext. 212

Fax: (020) 7602 6907

Enquiries: The Frederick Warne Curator of Children's Literature

Open: Tues–Thurs: 10.00–4.30, by appointment only.
Closed for three weeks after late August bank holiday for stock-taking.

Access: Identification with signature and proof of address required.

Historical background: The basis for the collections was the bequest by Leslie Linder (1904–73) of his substantial collection of Beatrix Potter material.

Acquisitions policy: Individual items and groups of material relating to Beatrix Potter.

Major collections: The Linder Bequest: correspondence, drawings and watercolours, photographs, literary MSS and other memorabilia of Beatrix Potter (1866–1943) relating to her farming interests as well as her books; includes a group of letters from W.E. Gladstone.
The Linder Archive: letters and other working papers of Leslie Linder.

Non-manuscript material: The Linder Collection: drawings (280) and early editions of Potter books.
Exhibition catalogues.
Photocopies of Potter letters.

Finding aids: List of the Linder Archive.

Facilities: Photography.

Conservation: In-house museum department.

Publications: A. Stevenson Hobbs and J.I. Whalley: *Beatrix Potter: the V&A Collection. The Leslie Linder Bequest* (London, 1985).

C V & A Archive

Telephone: (020) 7602 8832

Fax: (020) 7602 0980

E-mail: archive@vam.ac.uk

Website: www.nal.vam.ac.uk/archives.html

Enquiries: The Assistant Archivist, Victoria and Albert Museum

Open: Tues–Thurs: 10.00–4.30, strictly by appointment.
Closed for three weeks after late August bank holiday for stock-taking.

Access: Identification with signature and proof of address required. Records less than 30 years old are closed under the terms of the Public Records Act 1958; some confidential material is closed for longer.

Historical background: The museum was established on its present site in South Kensington in 1857. Papers in the archive go back to the 1840s but are not rich for the 19th century. The V & A Archive was formally set up when an archivist was appointed in 1992 to take charge of records management procedures and to look after the museum's historical archives. It is recognised as a place of deposit for public records

Acquisitions policy: To collect material relating to the V & A Museum and the people associated with it.

Archives of organisation: Archives of the V & A Museum, formerly the South Kensington Museum, 1852– ; and of its predecessor, the Government School of Design, 1837–48.
Archives of the separate branches and departments of the V & A, including the Bethnal Green Museum of Childhood, the National Art Library, the Theatre Museum (see entry 823) and the Wellington Museum.

Finding aids: Some lists available.

Facilities: Photography. Microfiche readers.

Conservation: In-house museum department.

840 Wallace Collection Library

Address: Hertford House, Manchester Square, London W1M 6BM

Telephone: (020) 7935 0687 ext. 15

Fax: (020) 7224 2155

E-mail: admin@wallcoll.demon.co.uk

Website: www.demon.co.uk/heritage/wallace

Enquiries: The Museum Assistant, Grania Lyster

Open: Mon–Fri: 9.00–1.00, 2.00–5.00.

Access: Bona fide researchers; an appointment by phone or in writing is required.

Historical background: The collection was acquired during the 19th century by the 3rd and 4th Marquesses of Hertford and the latter's illegitimate son, Sir Richard Wallace. It includes old master paintings, 18th-century French works of art, and arms and armour. The collection was bequeathed to the nation by Lady Wallace in 1897 and opened as a national museum in 1900. The library is recognised as a place of deposit for public records.

Acquisitions policy: Any material relating to the founders, their properties and their collections. Also material relating to the history of the museum since 1900.

Archives of organisation: Extensive archives on the founders, their ancestors and descendants; their property and collections, including receipts, inventories, letters and wills.
Archives relating to the Sèvres porcelain factory (mainly microfilm).

Major collections: Hertford-Mawson letters, 1848–61.

Non-manuscript material: Photographs of the founders, their properties and collections, and of the museum, 1900– .
Numerous French and British sale catalogues, 18th and 19th centuries.
Books and sale catalogues from Richard Wallace's Library.

Finding aids: Index.

Facilities: Photocopying. Microfilm/fiche reader.

Conservation: Contracted out.

Publications: J. Ingamells (ed.): The Hertford-Mawson Letters (London, 1981).
P. Hughes: The Founders of the Wallace Collection (London, 1992).
The Wallace Collection: a Guide (London, 1992).

841 Waltham Forest Archives and Local History Library

Parent organisation: London Borough of Waltham Forest

Address: Vestry House Museum, Vestry Road, Walthamstow, London E17 9NH

Telephone: (020) 8509 1917

E-mail: vestry.house@al.lbwf.gov.uk

Website: www.lbwf.gov.uk

Enquiries: The Archivist, Josephine Parker

Open: Tues, Wed, Fri: 10.00–1.00, 2.00–5.15; Sat: 10.00–1.00, 2.00–4.45.
Annual stock-taking closure for two weeks (usually February–March).

Access: Generally open to the public, strictly by appointment.

Historical background: Vestry House Museum was opened as the Walthamstow Borough Museum in 1931, with recognition as an approved repository for local manorial records. Following the formation of the London Borough of Waltham Forest in 1965, the manuscript and printed local history collections of the former boroughs of Chingford, Leyton and Walthamstow were amalgamated at the museum, forming the basis of Waltham Forest Archives and Local History Library. Records of parishes in Waltham Forest Deanery have been held since 1982, when diocesan approval was granted.

Acquisitions policy: To hold the records of the former boroughs of Chingford, Leyton and Walthamstow; to hold and continue to receive official and private records relevant to the Waltham Forest area.

Archives of organisation: Usual local authority records.

Major collections: Deposited local collections, including research notes and transcripts of state papers relating to the Leyton area by John Brant, c1919–1929.
MS works of John Drinkwater (1882–1937), poet and dramatist, c1912–1934.
Records of Chingford Mount Cemetery, 1884–1970.

Non-manuscript material: Prints, drawings and some ephemera.
Waltham Forest Photographic Archive (c60,000 images).
Tape-recordings, with transcripts, generated by the Waltham Forest Oral History Workshop.
The Local History Library holds books, directories, pamphlets, local newspapers, ephemera, printed maps and plans (enquiries to the Local History Librarian).

Finding aids: Archive catalogues; lists sent to NRA. Name index to Chingford, Leyton and

Walthamstow parish registers and rate books, pre-1880, and to local census returns up to 1881. Indexed calendars of certain deeds series for Leyton and Walthamstow.

Facilities: Photocopying. Microfilm/fiche reader/printer.

842 Wandsworth Local History Collection

Parent organisation: London Borough of Wandsworth

Address: Battersea Library, 265 Lavender Hill, London SW11 1JB

Telephone: (020) 8871 7753

Fax: (020) 7978 4316

E-mail: wandsworthmuseum@wandsworth.gov.uk

Website: www.wandsworth.gov.uk

Enquiries: The Archivist, Julie Gregson

Open: Tues, Wed: 10.00–8.00; Fri: 10.00–5.00; Sat: 9.00–1.00; other times by appointment.

Access: Generally open to the public; an appointment is advised. A paid research service is available.

Historical background: The London Borough of Wandsworth is an amalgamation of the two old metropolitan boroughs of Battersea and Wandsworth. The collection covers the old parishes of Battersea, Putney, Streatham, Tooting Graveney, Wandsworth and, to a small extent, Clapham. Original paintings and drawings previously in the library are now held at the Wandsworth Museum.

Acquisitions policy: Any material relating to the above, by purchase, donation and deposit.

Major collections: Records of parishes listed above, including rate books; vestry minutes; Poor Law records; minutes of metropolitan and local Boards of Works; metropolitan boroughs of Battersea and Wandsworth and the London Borough of Wandsworth.
Correspondence of Edward P. Thomas (1878–1917) of Battersea, poet and critic.

Non-manuscript material: Illustrations, mainly photographs, c1870– (14,000).

Finding aids: Card and loose-leaf indexes only. Very few MSS catalogued.

Facilities: Limited photocopying. Photography by arrangement. Microfilm/fiche readers.

843 Warburg Institute

Parent organisation: University of London: School of Advanced Study

Address: Woburn Square, London WC1H 0AB

Telephone: (020) 7862 8912

Fax: (020) 7862 8939

E-mail: dmcewan@sas.ac.uk

Website: www.sas.ac.uk/warburg

Enquiries: The Archivist, Dr. Dorothea McEwan

Open: Mon–Fri: 10.00–6.00; Sat: 10.00–1.00 (except Aug and Sept), strictly by appointment with the Archivist.

Access: Bona fide researchers on written application, with academic reference, to the Director, at least 14 days prior to visit.

Historical background: The institute is named after its founder, Aby Warburg (1866–1929), historian of Renaissance art and civilisation. In 1913 Warburg was joined by Fritz Saxl (1890–1948), who in 1921 turned the library in Hamburg into a research institute. After the rise of the Nazi regime it was transferred to London, where, in 1934, it was housed at Thames House, then moved in 1937 to the Imperial Institute, South Kensington. In 1944 it was incorporated into the University of London, and in 1958 moved to its permanent home in Woburn Square. The institute is concerned with the study of the Classical tradition, i.e. those elements of European thought, literature, art and institutions which derive from the ancient world.

Acquisitions policy: Archive material is not actively sought.

Archives of organisation: Records of the Warburg Institute, 1896– , including working materials and correspondence of Aby Warburg, Fritz Saxl, Gertrud Bing and Frances A. Yates (1899–1991).

Major collections: Working papers of Henri Frankfort (1897–1954); Robert Eisler (1882–1949); Roberto Weiss (1906–69); Evelyn Jamison (1877–1972); A.A. Barb (1901–79).

Yorke Collection: papers of and concerning Aleister Crowley and the Order of the Golden Dawn.

Non-manuscript material: Photographic collection, designed primarily for the study of iconography relating to the areas of scholarship represented in the library.

Menil Foundation Photographic Archive (contact the Photographic Curator, Dr E. McGrath)

Finding aids: Catalogue of Aby Warburg's working papers. Computerised catalogue of correspondence of Aby Warburg and of the Kulturwissenschaftliche Bibliothek Warburg. Photographic collection arranged by subject; card index supplies cross-references.

Conservation: In-house service; some contracting out.

Publications: Summary Guide to the Photographic Collection of the Warburg Institute, University of London (London 1988).
Catalogue of the Yorke Collection (London, 1999).
Annual Report.
Newsletter (twice yearly) [also available on the website].

844 Wellcome Library for the History and Understanding of Medicine

Parent organisation: The Wellcome Trust

Address: 183 Euston Road, London NW1 2BE

Telephone: (020) 7611 8888

Fax: (020) 7611 8703

E-mail: archives+mss@wellcome.ac.uk
library@wellcome.ac.uk

Website: www.wellcome.ac.uk/library

Enquiries: The Head of Special Collections, Miss J.G.A. Sheppard
The Archivist, Archives and Manuscripts, Dr R. Aspin
The Curator of Oriental MSS and Printed Books, Dr N. Allan
The Curator of Iconographic Collections, Mr W.M. Schupbach

Open: Mon, Wed, Fri: 9.45–5.15; Tues, Thurs: 9.45–7.00; Sat: 9.45–1.00.
Archives are available after 5.15 and on Saturday by prior appointment only.

Access: Generally open to the public. An appointment is advised for access to archives and manuscripts and readers will be expected to sign a reader's undertaking. Permission of the owner may be required and some collections are closed.

Historical background: The library is owned and maintained by the Wellcome Trust, a charity established under the will of Sir Henry Wellcome (1853–1936). Wellcome amassed a vast amount of material covering the whole history of man, with medicine as a central core. Although a great deal of the Wellcome Collection was dispersed by gift or sale after his death, the remaining collections have a wide scope. He built up a historical medical museum and library, the latter being opened to the public in 1949. The museum was transferred on indefinite loan to the Science Museum (entry 801) in 1976, and the Wellcome Institute (so called 1968–1999) housed the library and academic research centre. The library was renamed in 1999 when the administration of the Academic Unit was transferred to University College London. The Contemporary Medical Archives Centre (1979–2000) inherited the collections of the Wellcome Tropical Institute on its closure in 1989, and became responsible for the Wellcome Archives collection. The CMAC and Western Manuscripts Departments merged in 2000. Apart from papers and records of 20th-century medical scientists and practitioners, there is a Hospital Records Project with the Public Record Office (entry 1058) and the Medical Archives and Manuscripts Survey (MAMS), 1660–1945; both these databases are available on the Wellcome website.

Records of the Wellcome Foundation pharmaceutical company, 1880–c1960, were transferred to the Wellcome Trust by Glaxo Wellcome (now Glaxo Smith Kline) in 2001.

Acquisitions policy: To strengthen existing primary and secondary collections in the history of medicine and allied subjects by purchase, donation or deposit.

Archives of organisation: Wellcome Trust archives, 1936– , are maintained by the Records Manager, R. Maclean.

Major collections: Archives and MSS: including correspondence, diaries, accounts, minutes, medical treatises, lecture notes, recipe books, case notes, prescription books, laboratory notes, 11th–20th centuries.

MS collections of the Medical Society of London, and the Hunterian Society of London, 1819–1989.

Papers of individuals, including Sir Ernst Chain (1906–79), Thomas Hodgkin (1798–1866), Edward Jenner (1749–1823), Melanie Klein (1882–1960), Sir Thomas Lewis (1881–1945), Joseph Lister (1827–1912), Sir Peter Medawar (1915–87), Florence Nightingale (1820–1910), E.A. Sharpey-Schafer (1850–1935), Dr Marie Stopes (1880–1958) and Dr Cicely Williams (1894–1992).

Records of charities, professional bodies and other organisations, including the Abortion Law Reform Association, 1935–83; British Pharmacological Society, 1921–79; Chartered Society of Physiotherapists (f. 1894); Health Visitors' Association (f. 1896); Eugenics Society, 1908–79; Lister Institute, 1889–1960; Medical Women's Federation, 1916– ; Pioneer Health Centre (Peckham experiment), 1920s– ; Queen's Nursing Institute (f. 1887).

Records of Ticehurst House, Sussex, lunatic asylum, 1787–1980.

Records and papers of general practitioners.

Collections of tropical interest, including administrative records of the Royal Society of Tropical Medicine and Hygiene.

Wellcome Archives Collection: personal papers of Sir Henry Wellcome and records of his research institutions, including the Wellcome Museum of Medical History, 1880s–1960s.

Royal Army Medical Corps Muniment Collection: papers of individuals serving in the RAMC, c1850– , including Sir John Hall (1794–1866) and Sir Thomas Longmore (1816–1895) (c2000 accessions).

American Collection of MSS, especially Mexico.

Oriental MSS: representing 43 languages (c11,000 MSS; one of the major collections in the UK), especially Indian material, including Sanskrit and Hindi; Singalese palm leaf MSS (c470); Batak MSS (24). Extensive MS collections of Arabic and Chinese block-printed works, earliest from Egypt, c1100 BC.

Non-manuscript material: Iconographic collections: paintings, drawings, prints, photographs, films, eastern and western, 14th–20th centuries, including portraits, posters, topography, medical and surgical scenes, Boer War and World War I material, saints and martyrs, caricatures etc.

Tape-recordings (c300).

The trust also maintains a separate film collection and medical photographic library: contact Medical Film and Video Library (020) 7611 8596.

Finding aids: Various guides, handlists, indexes and sources leaflets; databases of some of the archival collections; on-line catalogue; videodisc. See also website.

Facilities: Photocopying. Photography. Microfilm/fiche reader/printer.

Conservation: In-house conservation department.

Publications: Series of descriptive booklets on South Asian, Oriental, American, Iconographic collections, Western Manuscripts and Contemporary Medical Archives Centre (1984–95).
Catalogues include:
Warren R. Dawson: *Manuscripta medica: a Descriptive Catalogue of the Manuscripts of the Medical Society of London* (1932).
R. Burgess: *Portraits of Doctors and Scientists* (1973).
S.A.J. Moorat: *Catalogue of Western Manuscripts on Medicine and Science* (1962, 1973) [3 vols].
A.Z. Iskandar: *A Catalogue of Arabic Manuscripts on Medicine and Science* (1967).
R.M. Price: *An Annotated Catalogue of Medical Americana* (1983).
J. Symons: *Wellcome Institute for the History of Medicine: a Short History* (1994).
R.J. Palmer: *Catalogue of Western Manuscripts in the Wellcome Library for the History and Understanding of Medicine: Western Manuscripts, 5120–6244* (2000).
Guide to Contemporary Medical Archives Centre (2000).
Articles on collections in the library regularly included in series 'Illustrations from the Wellcome Institute Library', in *Medical History* and *Friends of the Wellcome Newsletter*.
Many published catalogues of Oriental MSS. Full publication list available on website.

845 Westminster Abbey Muniments and Library

Address: London SW1P 3PA

Telephone: (020) 7222 5152 ext. 228

Fax: (020) 7654 4827

E-mail: library@westminster-abbey.org

Website: www.westminster-abbey.org

Enquiries: The Keeper of the Muniments, Dr Richard Mortimer
The Librarian, Dr Tony Trowles

Open: Mon–Fri: 10.00–1.00, 2.00–4.45.

Access: Consultation by telephone or written appointment; there are restrictions on certain classes of modern records.

Historical background: The Benedictine monastery founded in the 10th century was replaced in 1540 by a collegiate institution; after a brief restoration of the Benedictines under Queen Mary, the present collegiate chapter was founded in 1560.

Acquisitions policy: Anything relevant to the abbey or its special collections.

Archives of organisation: Estate and administrative archives of the medieval monastery and of the post-medieval collegiate foundation; coronation and funeral records; Jewish starrs (shetaroths); coroners' inquests for the City of Westminster, 1760–1880; various papers from St Margaret's Westminster, including the parish registers.

Major collections: Collections of personal papers include those of Lady Margaret Beaufort (1443–1509) and Sir Reginald Bray (*d* 1503), John Nedham (c1670–1710), and Sir Thomas Modyford (?1620–1679), Governor of Jamaica.
NB The Chapter Library holds a substantial collection of MSS; access is by arrangement with the Assistant Librarian.

Non-manuscript material: Plans, engravings and photographs relating to the abbey.

Finding aids: Extensive index and calendar to the muniments available in the Muniment Room. Much later material is awaiting cataloguing.

Facilities: Photocopying. Photography by arrangement.

Conservation: Contracted out; some in-house book conservation

Publications: J. Armitage Robinson and M.R. James: *The Manuscripts of Westminster Abbey* (Cambridge, 1909).
L.E. Tanner: 'The Nature and Use of the Westminster Abbey Muniments', *Transactions of the Royal Historical Society*, xix (1936).

Westminster Abbey Record Series (1997–).

846 Westminster City Archives

Address: City of Westminster Archives Centre, 10 St Ann's Street, London SW1P 2XR

Telephone: (020) 7641 5180

Fax: (020) 7641 5179

Enquiries: The City Archivist

Open: Mon, Fri, Sat: 9.30–5.00; Tues–Thurs: 9.30–7.00.

Access: Generally open to the public; permission is needed to consult the Grosvenor Estate archives. A paid research service is available.

Historical background: Westminster became a city on the foundation of the episcopal see in 1540. From the 16th century local government was by parishes and by the Court of Burgesses, the court gradually losing most of its powers to the parishes and being abolished in 1900. The ten Westminster parishes were united in 1900 to form the City of Westminster. In 1965 the boroughs of Paddington and St Marylebone, which had each been a single civil parish before 1900, and the City of Westminster formed the present city. The Archives Centre also acts as the Diocesan Record Office for London (South Westminster parish records) and is recognised as a place of deposit for public records. The two separate collections formerly held at Victoria and Marylebone libraries have been amalgamated and are now held at the purpose-built Archives Centre, which opened in 1995.

Acquisitions policy: Records relating to Westminster are acquired.

Archives of organisation: Usual local authority record holdings.

Major collections: Records of the parishes which constitute Westminster.
Archives of Grosvenor Estates, c1700–1960; Howard de Walden, formerly Portland, Estate, 18th–20th centuries; Royal Botanic Society, 1838–1931; St Marylebone Charity School for Girls, 1750–1932; Jaeger, 1883–1987; Gillow, 1731–1932; Liberty, 1883–1988; Westminster Fire Office, 1717–1943; Royal Institute of Chartered Surveyors, 1868–1956; Grey Coat Hospital, 1698–1950.

Non-manuscript material: Prints and photographs (56,600); theatre programmes (30,200); newspaper cuttings (64,000); slides (5600); maps (4400); books (18,200); microfilms (local studies) (1200); microfilms (archives (3500).

Finding aids: Lists and indexes. Lists sent to NRA. Guide to holdings.

Facilities: Photocopying. Photography by arrangement. Microfilm/fiche readers/printers.

Conservation: In-house conservation facilities.

Publications: *Westminster Review* [annual journal].
E. Cory: *Guide to Sources for Family History held by Westminster City Archives.*
A. Kenney: *Tracing the History of your House.*

847 Westminster Diocesan Archives (Roman Catholic)

Address: 16a Abingdon Road, London W8 6AF

Telephone: (020) 7938 3580

Enquiries: The Archivist, Rev. Ian Dickie

Open: Tues–Thurs: 10.00–5.00 (with lunch break). Closed in August.

Access: Generally open to the public, by appointment only. A 30-year closure rule applies as far as possible.

Historical background: After the Elizabethan Reformation settlement in 1559, Roman Catholic life was organised initially from centres abroad such as the seminary college at Douai. From 1623, however, a rudimentary national network, known as the Old Chapter, was created for secular priests, though it lacked papal recognition and ecclesiastical authority, especially in relation to the religious orders. In 1688 England and Wales were divided into four districts under bishops, known as Vicars Apostolic, who enjoyed ecclesiastical jurisdiction of a limited nature (albeit under penal laws and some persecution) until 1850; the number of districts was doubled in 1840. In 1850 a normal diocesan jurisdiction was restored, though with the reservation of certain powers to Rome, since Britain was predominantly a non-Catholic country. These reservations were gradually abolished only in the 20th century. A small amount of St Edmund's College archives remains with the college at Old Hall Green, Ware, Hertfordshire.

Acquisitions policy: At present restricted to central diocesan archives, but no relevant deposits are refused.

Archives of organisation: Records of organisation of Catholics in the London district (Home Counties) and correspondence with other areas, 16th–19th centuries; papers of some agents abroad (especially Roman), recovered *c*1815; administrative records and correspondence of Westminster diocese, 1850– (except 1865–92); records of bishops' meetings, 1865–1945.

Major collections: Records of St Edmund's College, school and seminary, mainly 1794–*c*1950.

Non-manuscript material: Small pamphlet collection; a few plans and elevations; photographs and scrapbooks concerning most cardinals of Westminster.

Finding aids: Various lists and indexes. Archives of St Edmund's College: NRA 16303.

Facilities: Photocopying, generally of 19th- and 20th-century material. Microfilming of earlier material may sometimes be arranged.

Conservation: In-house facilities.

Publications: P. Hughes: 'The Westminster Archives', *Dublin Review*, cci (1937) [gives an account of papers earlier than mid-19th century, but further material of this period has been discovered].

848 Westminster School Archive and Library

Address: 17 Dean's Yard, London SW1 3PB

Telephone: (020) 7963 1018

Fax: (020) 7963 1006

E-mail: eddie.smith@westminster.org.uk

Website: www.westminster.org.uk

Enquiries: The Archivist

Open: During school terms, by appointment only.

Access: On application, to researchers with specific enquiries or interests.

Historical background: Westminster School has been established on a site adjacent to Westminster Abbey since at least 1361 and its history is closely bound up with the ecclesiastical and political history of Westminster.

Acquisitions policy: To extend the collection of books, relics and records connected with the history of the school.

Archives of organisation: The school archive: an extensive collection of records and documents concerning the history of the school from its foundation.

Non-manuscript material: Prints and photographs of school history.
The Busby Library: a private 17th-century academic library left to the school by Richard Busby, headmaster, in 1695.
The Greene Library: a collection of first editions of works by Westminster authors.

Finding aids: Computerised catalogue and data retrieval system.

849 Whitechapel Art Gallery

Address: Whitechapel High Street, London E1 7QX

Telephone: (020) 7522 7888 (general information); 7522 7879 (archives)

Fax: (020) 7377 1685

E-mail: archive@whitechapel.org

Website: www.whitechapel.org

Enquiries: The Archivist, Janeen Haythornthwaite

Open: By appointment.

Access: Access to publicity materials is unrestricted. Permission is required to consult any administrative records. Charges are made for research done on behalf of enquirers.

Whitechapel Art Gallery, which opened in 1901, is an unendowed charitable trust administered by an independent board of trustees representing national and local interests. It has an internationally recognised tradition of presenting major exhibitions of British and international art. It also aims to encourage young artists, to facilitate the exchange of exhibitions with other galleries and to promote contemporary visual arts. Since 1901 the gallery has held more than 600 exhibitions, which are documented with catalogues, press cuttings, other publicity materials and administrative records. There are also photographs of exhibited works of art and of exhibition installations as well as audio tapes of interviews with artists and others associated with the gallery. Photocopying is available and a catalogue is being planned.

850 Whitelands College

Parent organisation: University of Surrey, Roehampton

Address: West Hill, Putney, London SW15 3SN

Telephone: (020) 8392 3000

Fax: (020) 8392 3531

Website: www.roehampton.ac.uk

Enquiries: The Principal's Office

Open: By appointment.

Access: Generally open to all enquirers; there is a 30-year closure on personal records.

Historical background: The college was founded in 1841 by the National Society (Church of England) to be a training institution for women teachers and soon became important in the professional qualification and academic advancement of women generally. It had connections with Baroness Burdett-Coutts (1814–1906) and especially with John Ruskin (1814–1900), who gave substantial donations of books, illustrations etc and who inspired the institution of the May Queen Festival in 1881. Ruskin also interested Edward Burne-Jones and William Morris in the decoration of its chapel. The college was in Chelsea from 1841 to 1930. In the 1920s and early 1930s its interests were greatly promoted by Winifred Mercier, OBE, who moved the college to a building in Putney specially designed by Giles Gilbert Scott. Since 1978 it has been a constituent college of Roehampton Institute, offering degrees awarded by the University of Surrey.

Acquisitions policy: To enlarge the existing collection by donations from former staff and students of examples of work, mementos, letters etc.

Archives of organisation: Student records, 1842– (c3000).
College annual reports, 1849– ; minute books and account books of governing body.
Chapel files: complete correspondence, 1881–1907, including Burne-Jones and William Morris.
Guild of Old Students: annuals and complete records, 1881– .
Documents covering all aspects of college development, including administrative, financial, curricular and social, especially 1870– .

Non-manuscript material: Extensive photographic collection; films and videos.

May Queen collection: dresses, jewellery, books, photographs, some MSS, 1887– .
Gifts from Ruskin of books, illustrations, pictures etc; and other donations from former staff and students to the college and its chapel.
Some educational equipment of historical interest.
Specimens of students' work, e.g. in needlework.

Finding aids: Computer catalogue in progress. Card index.

Facilities: Photocopying. Photography.

Publications: M. Cole: *The History* (1932).
——: *The Chapel* (1935).
H. Henstridge: *Whitelands College Archive Catalogue* (London, 1979).
M. Cole: *The May Queen Festival* (1981).

851 William Morris Gallery Library

Parent organisation: London Borough of Waltham Forest

Address: Water House, Lloyd Park, Forest Road, Walthamstow, London E17 4PP

Telephone: (020) 8527 3782

Fax: (020) 8527 7070

Website: www.lbwf.gov.uk/wmg

Enquiries: The Keeper, Norah C. Gillow

Open: Tues–Sat: 10.00–1.00, 2.00–5.00; Sun (1st of each month): 10.00–1.00, 2.00–5.00.

Access: The archive/reserve collection may be viewed by prior appointment only, and access is restricted to bona fide students/academics.

Historical background: Water House was the boyhood home of the designer, craftsman, writer and socialist William Morris (1834–96) from 1848 to 1856. Since 1950 it has housed the gallery, a permanent collection illustrating the achievements and influence of Morris as a designer and writer.

Acquisitions policy: By purchase and gift, within the period relevant to the gallery's collections, i.e. Morris and his associates, the Arts and Crafts Movement, early 20th-century design.

Major collections: Correspondence and MS writings of William Morris and his associates; Arthur H. Mackmurdo (1851–1942) and Frank Brangwyn (1867–1956), artist.

Non-manuscript material: In addition to the main gallery collections there are the following: photographs, articles and catalogues of relevant exhibitions; contemporary periodicals, e.g. *The Studio, The Yellow Book, The Century Guild Hobby Horse.*
Kelmscott Press books and printed ephemera.

Finding aids: All items catalogued on cards/files. NRA 11835, 11836.

Facilities: Limited photocopying. Photography.

Conservation: Contracted out via Southern Museums Service.

Publications: K.L. Goodwin: *A Preliminary Handlist of Manuscripts and Documents of William Morris* (1983).
N. Kelvin: *The Collected Letters of William Morris* (Princeton, 1984).

852 Wimbledon College Archives

Address: Wimbledon College, Edge Hill, London SW19 4NS

Telephone: (020) 8946 2533

Fax: (020) 8947 6513

E-mail: enquiries@wimbledoncollege.org.uk

Website: www.wimbledoncollege.org.uk

Enquiries: The Archivist, Mr McDonald

Open: Term: Mon–Thurs: 9.00–3.30; Fri: 9.00–1.40.

Access: Bona fide researchers, on written application and by prior appointment. There are restrictions on certain collections.

Historical background: Wimbledon College was founded by the Jesuit Fathers in 1892 as the first of two secondary day-schools for boys in the London area. In 1893 the school moved to its present buildings, formerly occupied by Wimbledon School, founded by the Rev. John Matthew Brackenbury, an Anglican clergyman, in 1860. Initially a fee-paying school, Wimbledon College became a voluntary-aided grammar school in 1944 and adopted comprehensive status in 1969. From 1898 to 1919 an independent Army Department, also conducted by the Jesuits, flourished on the same site.

Acquisitions policy: To acquire, by donation or deposit, material relevant to the history and development of Wimbledon School,

Wimbledon College and Wimbledon College Army Department and their respective pupils.

Archives of organisation: Archives of Wimbledon College, including admissions registers and financial records, 1892– .
Archives of Wimbledon College Army Department, 1898–1919.
A very small number of records relating to Wimbledon School, 1860–92.

Non-manuscript material: Photographic collection: staff and pupils, sports clubs etc, 1892– .
Architect's plans, 1938– .
Wimbledon College Magazine, 1923– .

Finding aids: General index to all collections.

Facilities: Photocopying.

Publications: M. Whitehead: *Archives at Wimbledon College* (1980).
A. Poole: *A History of Wimbledon College* (1992).

853 Wimbledon Lawn Tennis Museum
Kenneth Ritchie Wimbledon Library

Parent organisation: The All England Lawn Tennis Club

Address: Church Road, Wimbledon, London SW19 5AE

Telephone: (020) 8946 6131

Fax: (020) 8944 6497

Website: www.wimbledon.org

Enquiries: The Hon. Librarian, Mr Little

Open: Tues–Fri: 10.30–1.00, 2.00–5.00.
Closed during the championships.

Access: Approved researchers, on written application and strictly by appointment only.

The Wimbledon Lawn Tennis Museum was opened in 1977 to mark the centenary of the championships. The library forms an integral part of the museum, although the archives are administered for the club via the Librarian. It houses a collection of British and foreign lawn tennis books, annuals, periodicals, programmes, photographs and postcards, covering the game from its origin in 1874. Photocopying and photography is by arrangement. See J.A. Little: *The Kenneth Ritchie Wimbledon Library* (1998) [catalogue].

854 Women's Art Library

Address: Fulham Palace, Bishop's Avenue, London SW6 6EA

Telephone: (020) 7731 7618

Fax: (020) 7384 1110

E-mail: womensart.lib@ukonline.co.uk

Website: www.womensart.org.uk

Enquiries: The Director, Ceri Hand
The Librarian, Althea Greenan

Open: Tue– Fri: 10.00–5.00.

Access: Generally open to the public. An appointment is advisable for complex searches. A postal research service is available.

Historical background: The library was established in 1984 in Battersea Arts Centre as the Women Artists' Slide Library and renamed in 1993. The archives of the Society of Women Artists (f. *c*1855), previously held by the library, have been returned to the Society.

Acquisitions policy: Accepts donations of documentation, photographs, slides, cuttings, films and videos, by or about women artists; also artists' books.

Major collections: Women's International Art Club records, 1900–78.
Historical Documentation Collection, including material *re* Elena Gaputyte (1927–91), Elisabeth Frink (1930–93), Jo Spence (1934–92) and Pauline Boty (1938–66).
Archival files, including *Guerrilla Girls, Fanny Adams.*
Work of Danish and European artists (*c*5000 files).
Women of colour index, 1985–95.

Non-manuscript material: Photographs, including large collection on life and works of Dame Laura Knight (1877–1970).
Historical unpublished papers and theses.

Finding aids: Indexed and listed on database.

Facilities: Photocopying. Photography.

855 The Women's Library
(formerly Fawcett Library)

Parent organisation: London Guildhall University

Address: Calcutta House, Old Castle Street, London E1 7NT

Telephone: (020) 7320 1189

Fax: (020) 7320 1188

E-mail: fawcett@lgu.ac.uk

Website: www.lgu.ac.uk/fawcett

Enquiries: The Head of Special Collections, Ms Jennifer Haynes

Open: Term: Mon: 10.15–8.30; Wed: 9.00–8.30; Thurs–Fri: 9.00–5.00.
Vacation: Mon, Wed–Fri: 9.00–5.00, preferably by appointment.

Access: By subscription. Charges are payable for a day visit, or at different rates per annum for individuals, full-time students and the unwaged.

Historical background: The library began as the Women's Service Library, which was the library of the London and National Society for Women's Service (now the Fawcett Society), the direct descendant of the London Society for Women's Suffrage, founded in 1867. The society was at the centre of the non-militant campaign for women's suffrage under the leadership of Millicent Garrett Fawcett, and accumulated a certain amount of material from the campaign and related issues. In the 1920s the society decided to organise this material for the use of members and in 1926 the first librarian was appointed. Over the years the library acquired a number of other smaller collections, including the Cavendish-Bentinck and Edward Wright libraries (originally suffrage collections with a high proportion of old and rare books), the Crosby Hall Collection, the Sadd Brown Library (on women in the Commonwealth) and the library of the Josephine Butler Society (formerly the Association for Moral and Social Hygiene). Gradually the Fawcett Library became a major national research resource. In 1977, as the society could no longer support the library, it was transferred to the City of London Polytechnic, which became the London Guildhall University in 1993. The library was renamed in 2000 and moved into new purpose-built premises in 2001.

Acquisitions policy: Papers relating to women's organisations and individual women are actively collected, mainly by gift.

Major collections: Archive material, mainly 19th and 20th centuries, including records of societies concerned with suffrage, especially the archive of the Fawcett Society; equal status; emigration; business and professional bodies, including trade unions; repeal of the Contagious Diseases Acts and other moral issues, including papers of feminists involved in the controversy of 1863–6; and records of the Association for Moral and Social Hygiene and the National Vigilance Association.

Papers of individuals, including Millicent Garrett Fawcett (1847–1929) and Dr Elizabeth Garrett Anderson (1836–1917), correspondence of Josephine Butler (1828–1906) and miscellaneous letters.

20th-century archives include papers of women-centred cultural and campaigning groups, notably the Movement for the Ordination of Women; papers of organisations and individual women connected with the Women's Liberation Movement and feminist scholarship.

Non-manuscript material: Photographs, many of individual women involved in suffrage movements; posters relating to suffrage campaign; newspaper cuttings on all aspects of women.

Special collections include: Josephine Butler Library (previously library of the Association for Moral and Social Hygiene); Cavendish-Bentinck Collection (mainly rare and antiquarian works); Sadd Brown Collection, devoted to the role of women in the Commonwealth.

Finding aids: Typed list to major collections. NRA 8556, 10648, 20625, 21465. On-line *Outline Guide to the Fawcett Library Archives* (1997) available on library website (to be superseded by web-based access to archival finding aids).

Facilities: Photocopying. Microfiche reader.

Publications: M. Barrow: *Women, 1870–1918: a Select Guide to Printed and Archival Sources in the United Kingdom* (1981), 192–215.

J. Uglow: 'The Fawcett Library', *Times Literary Supplement* (7 Sept 1984), 994–5.

Women's Studies International Forum, x/3 (1987) [special issue on the Fawcett Library].

H.L. Smith: 'Archival Report: British Women's History: the Fawcett Library Archival Collections', *Twentieth Century British History*, 2/2 (1991), 215–23.

856 Woodard Corporation Archives

Address: c/o Lee, Bolton and Lee, 1 The Sanctuary, Westminster, London SW1P 3JT

Telephone: (020) 7222 5381

Fax: (020) 7222 7502

Enquiries: The Registrar, P.F.B. Beesley
The Registrar can direct enquirers to the relevant school or office (see below).

Open: Office hours, by arrangement.

Access: Approved readers, on written application.

Historical background: The Rev. Nathaniel Woodard (1811–91) established the corporation in 1848 to provide schools for the middle classes, in which education should be in accordance with Anglican principles. From his first schools at Lancing and Hurstpierpoint, the corporation has developed five geographical divisions which now control 23 schools, the largest single grouping of independent schools in England. South, Midland, West, North and East divisions each have a company office from which their schools are controlled. Records are kept in the offices and the schools and also in the registrar's central office. The corporation's archive provides a unique source for educational development in the independent sector in all parts of England. A consultant has identified records throughout the corporation, listing them and advising schools, officers and the corporation on future archive policy.

Acquisitions policy: Each school and office maintains records.

Archives of organisation: The most important single collection is at Lancing College (see entry 498), where the letters of the founder, Nathaniel Woodard, are stored.

Finding aids: Every school and office has its own archive list. Each division holds the lists of all its schools. The office of the registrar holds all archive lists for the corporation. Copies of all lists at NRA.

Facilities: These vary from school to school.

Publications: There is a number of published works on the history of the corporation and of some of its schools; these are noted in the archive lists.

857 Working Men's College

Address: 44 Crowndale Road, London NW1 1TR

Telephone: (020) 7387 2037

Fax: (020) 7383 5561

E-mail: info@wmcollege.ac.uk

Website: www.wmcollege.ac.uk

Enquiries: The Director of Resources, Mr Chris Firmin

Open: By arrangement.

Access: Researchers and students, by appointment.

Historical background: The college was founded in 1854 by F.D. Maurice and a group of Christian Socialists.

Acquisitions policy: To maintain the archive.

Archives of organisation: College records, including committee papers, accounts, records of early students, attendance registers, 1854– .

Major collections: Papers of the founders, lecturers and students, including correspondence of F.D. Maurice (1805–72), Malcolm Forbes Ludlow (1821–1911), F.J. Furnivall (1825–1920), John Ruskin (1819–1900) and Dante Gabriel Rossetti (1828–62).
General correspondence from individuals such as William Morris (1834–96) and E.M. Forster (1879–1970).

Non-manuscript material: Newspaper cuttings and scrapbooks, 1880– , including collected newpaper articles of A.V. Dicey (1835–1922), English jurist.

Finding aids: NRA 16341. Another catalogue in preparation.

Facilities: Photocopying.

Publications: J. Harrison: *History of the Working Men's College, 1854–1954.*

858 Worshipful Company of Goldsmiths

Address: The Library, Goldsmiths' Hall, Foster Lane, London EC2V 6BN

Telephone: (020) 7606 7010

Fax: (020) 7606 1511

E-mail: the.clerk@thegoldsmiths.co.uk

Website: www.thegoldsmiths.co.uk

Enquiries: The Librarian, David Beasley

Open: Mon–Fri: 10.00–5.00.

Access: Generally open to bona fide researchers, by appointment.

Historical background: The library was established after World War II to provide access to company records.

Acquisitions policy: All relevant material on hallmarking, assaying, and the precious metals as functional or decorative works of art.

Archives of organisation: Company records, including wardens' accounts and court minutes, 1334– (lacking 1579–92), books of ordinances, estate documents.
Trial of Pyx records.
London Assay Office records.

Non-manuscript material: Philip Hardwick (1792–1870), drawings of the hall.
Edward Spencer metalwork designs.
Omar Ramsden workbooks.
Twining Collection of material on regalia throughout the world.
Trade papers, 1950s– .
Photographs; slides; films.
Specialist collections of books on precious metals.

Finding aids: Catalogues, index of members.

Facilities: Limited photocopying.

Publications: *The Early History of the Goldsmiths' Company.*
History of the Assay Office.
Exhibition catalogues [list available from the Librarian].

859 Young Men's Christian Association

Parent organisation: National Council of YMCA (Inc.)

Address: 640 Forest Road, Walthamstow, London E17 3DZ

Telephone: (020) 8520 5599

Fax: (020) 8509 3190

E-mail: info@ymca.org.uk

Website: www.ymca.org.uk

Enquiries: Sue Ralph

Open: Mon–Fri: 10.00–4.00.

Access: Generally open to the public, on written application and by appointment.

The National Council was founded in 1882 but YMCAs were founded from 1844 onwards. Records, including photographs, reports and handbooks, relate mainly to the national body but some local YMCA material is available. Papers on certain founder members and material relating to the movement's activities in World War I are also held.

860 Young's Brewery Archive

Parent organisation: Young & Co.'s Brewery plc

Address: Ram Brewery, Wandsworth High Street, London SW18 4JD

Telephone: (020) 8875 7000

Fax: (020) 8875 7100

Enquiries: The Archivist and Records Manager

Open: Tues–Wed: 9.30–5.00, by appointment only.

Access: At the discretion of the Archivist and by prior arrangement only.

Historical background: The business was founded in 1831 when the partnership of Charles A. Young and Anthony F. Bainbridge purchased, from the Tritton family, the Ram Brewery (est. prior to 1675) in High Street, Wandsworth, London. Later Charles F. Young (son of C.A. Young) and Herbert Bainbridge (son of A.F. Bainbridge) entered the partnership, which was dissolved in 1883. The business was carried on by C.F. Young, trading as Young & Co., and on his death in 1890 was registered as a limited liability company, Young & Co.'s Brewery Ltd. Debenture stock was first issued in 1898, but the company did not become fully public until 1955. The company took over William Wells & Co. Ltd (est. 1834), Britannia Brewery, Kensington, London, in 1924; Foster-Probyn Ltd (est. 1791), beer and mineral water bottlers, Islington, London, in 1962; Cockburn & Campbell Ltd (est. 1796), wine merchants and shippers, in 1973; and H.H. Finch Ltd (est. 1865), Bishopsgate, London, public management company, in 1991.

Acquisitions policy: Material, in whatever media, that is directly relevant to Young's and its subsidiary companies, i.e. that has been produced by the parent organization or its subsidiaries, as well as the families connected with those companies, arising mainly from the records management programme.

Archives of organisation: Archives of Young & Co.'s Brewery plc, 1831– ; William Wells & Co., 1834–1903; Cockburn & Campbell, 1834–1973; A.F. Probyn Ltd, 1894–1958; M.B. Fosters Ltd, 1877–1962; H.H. Finch Ltd, 1865–1991; also subsidiary companies of Probyn, Fosters and Finch.

Non-manuscript material: Photographs relating to brewing, publications, shire horses (*c*4000). Museum artefacts relating to the history of drink and of Young's.

Finding aids: Lists for most of the archives, but not complete for Young's Brewery, A.F. Probyn and M. B. Fosters. Computer catalogue to the photograph collection.

Facilities: Photocopying. Photography.

Conservation: Contracted out.

Publications: H. Osborn: *Inn & Around London: a History of Young's Pubs* (1991).

861 Zoological Society of London

Address: Regent's Park, London NW1 4RY

Telephone: (020) 7449 6293

Fax: (020) 7586 5743

E-mail: library@zsl.org

Enquiries: The Archivist, Mr Michael Palmer

Open: Mon–Fri: 9.30–5.30; an appointment is essential.

Access: Generally open to the public, by purchase of a library membership ticket either for a day or a year, or by becoming a fellow of ZSL. Proof of address is required.

Historical background: The society was founded in 1826. It is an educational charity comprising the learned society itself; London Zoo; Whipsnade Wild Animals Park; and the Institute of Zoology. Much of the correspondence was destroyed during World War II.

Acquisitions policy: Important back files from various departments are added to the archives. Donations of material relevant to the society's history are welcomed.

Archives of organisation: Administrative records, 1826– , including council minutes; committee minutes, including Scientific; Publications; Finance; Animal Welfare; and Husbandry Committees; Daily Occurrences books for London Zoo and Whipsnade; post-mortem and veterinary books; list of fellows; staff records; account books; records of the Zoological Club; 19th-century letter collection.

Major collections: Papers of Samuel Richard Tickell, naturalist (*d* 1875); Brian Houghton Hodgson, naturalist (1800–94).
Field journals of Maj. Eustace Poles, Chief Ranger of the Game & Tsetse Control Dept. Northern Rhodesia, 1947–50.
Archives of the Fauna Preservation Society.

Non-manuscript material: Paintings, drawings, photographs, press cuttings, lists of fellows, zoo guides, annual reports.

Finding aids: In preparation.

Facilities: Photocopying. Photography. Microfiche reader/printer.

Publications: S. Zuckerman (ed): *Symposia of the ZSL No. 40: the Zoological Society of London, 1826–1976 and Beyond* (London, 1976).
J. Edwards: *London Zoo from Old Photographs, 1852–1914* (London, 1996).

862 St Columb's Cathedral Chapter House Library

Address: c/o the Dean, The Deanery, 30 Bishop Street, Londonderry, Co. Londonderry BT48 6PP

Telephone: (02871) 262746 (Dean);   267313 (Cathedral)

Enquiries: The Dean, Very Rev. Dr W.M. Morton

Open: Mon–Fri:10.00–4.00, by arrangement.

Access: Bona fide scholars; an appointment is essential and a charge will be made.

Historical background: The collection was begun in 1922 by Dean R.G.S. King (*d* 1958), supported by the Cathedral Select Vestry.

Acquisitions policy: To maintain and consolidate the collections relating to the history of Londonderry and Derry Diocese.

Archives of organisation: Parish records, 1642– .

Major collections: Collections of transcripts relating to the City and County of Londonderry, by A.M. Munn (*d* 1937) and Tenison Groves (*d* 1938).

Non-manuscript material: Sir Frederick Heygate (*d* 1940) Collection of pamphlets on Irish affairs, 17th century.
Prints relating to the cathedral and its history.

Facilities: Reprography by permission of the Dean.

Conservation: Contracted out.

863 Loughborough University Archives

Address: Pilkington Library, Loughborough University of Technology, Loughborough, Leicestershire LE11 3TU

Telephone: (01509) 222359/222357

Fax: (01509) 223993

E-mail: jgclark@lboro.ac.uk

Enquiries: The University Archivist, Mrs J.G. Clark

Open: Thurs, Fri: 9.00–12.30, 2.00–4.30.

Access: Bona fide researchers, by appointment. There are restrictions on some records.

Historical background: Loughborough Technical Institute (renamed Loughborough College in 1920) was established by the Leicestershire County Council in 1909 and was an 'Instructional Factory' for the Ministry of Munitions during World War I. In 1952 Loughborough College was divided into four separate institutions: Loughborough College of Technology; Loughborough Training College (later renamed Loughborough College of Education); Loughborough College of Further Education (later renamed Loughborough Technical College and now known as Loughborough College); and Loughborough College of Art. Loughborough College of Technology received its charter as a university in 1966; in 1977 the university and the College of Education were amalgamated; and in 1998 the College of Art was also merged with the university. The University Archives were established in 1980.

Acquisitions policy: Administrative and other records of the university and its predecessors; papers of former staff and students as appropriate.

Archives of organisation: Administrative and other records relating to Loughborough College, 1909–52; Loughborough College of Technology, 1952–66; Loughborough College of Education, 1952–77; Loughborough University of Technology, 1966– .

Records of Loughborough Students' Union, 1918–, and the Past Students' Association, 1948– .

Major collections: Personal and business papers of Norman Swindin (1880–1976), chemical engineer and Hon. Reader in Chemical Technology, c1890–1970.

Papers and memorabilia of Dan Maskell (1908–92), tennis player and commentator, c1920–90.

Papers of Commander F.W. Collins (1905–89) relating to athletics and 1948 Olympic Torch Relay, c1933–64.

John Lucas Literary Collection: correspondence received by Professor John Lucas from poets and writers, c1930–80.

Non-manuscript material: Photographs of the 'Instructional Factory', 1914–18.

University publications, calendars, prospectuses, journals, newspapers etc, and student publications; photographs; slides; film and tape-recordings of university events; technical drawings and plans.

Finding aids: Catalogues, lists and indexes; list sent to NRA.

Facilities: Photocopying.

864 National Co-operative Archive

Address: Co-operative College, Stanford Hall, Loughborough, Leicestershire LE12 5QR

E-mail: archive@co-op.ac.uk

Website: www.co-op.ac.uk

Enquiries: The Archivist, Mrs G. Lonergan

Open: Mon–Fri: by appointment.

Access: Bona fide scholars, students and research workers, by appointment only.

Historical background: The Co-operative Union was founded in 1869 to link the scattered co-operative societies of that time into a movement, to arrange annual national co-operative congresses for the exchange of information and ideas on co-operation, and to advise in the formation of co-operative societies. Today the union is still the national co-ordinating, advisory and information body of the co-operative consumer movement. The library was properly established in 1911. Following the movement of the Co-operative College to Loughborough, the College Archive and the Co-operative Union Archive developed separately. The

opportunity has been taken to merge the two archives as the basis for a National Co-operative Archive, bringing together collections from other sources and making them available to researchers in many cases for the first time.

NB As this book was going to press the Archive was relocated to Holyoake House, Hanover Street, Manchester M60 0AS, tel: (0161) 246 2925, fax: (0161) 246 2946.

Acquisitions policy: Records of all branches of the co-operative movement, all aspects of modern co-operation and the history of the Labour movement.

Major collections: Letters and documents of Robert Owen (1771–1858), social reformer, philanthropist and co-operator, 1821–58 (c3000), George Jacob Holyoake (1817–1906), co-operative leader, secularist and social reformer, 1835–1903 (3500), and Edward Owen Greening (1836–1923), pioneer of co-operative co-partnership societies and founder of the International Co-operative Alliance, 1861–1923 (c11,000).

Records of co-operative societies in the Midlands and south Midlands area.

Non-manuscript material: Complete run of the co-operative movement's official newspaper, the *Co-operative News*, 1871– , *The Co-operator*, 1860–71, *New Moral World*, 1840–42, and *Brighton Co-operator*, 1828–30.

Pamphlets on co-operation, 19th century.

Co-operative Party Collection: comprehensive collection of jubilee and centenary histories of individual co-operative retail and productive societies.

Finding aids: Catalogues of Owen, Holyoake and Greening MS collections. Checklist on historical periodicals, Co-operative Women's Guild, Co-operative Party, Rochdale Pioneers, Co-operative Youth Movements, Co-operative Education, Dividend, Co-operative Plays and Sketches.

Facilities: Photocopying. Photography by arrangement.

865 Suffolk Record Office
Lowestoft Branch

Parent organisation: Suffolk County Council

Address: Central Library, Clapham Road, Lowestoft, Suffolk NR32 1DR

Telephone: (01502) 405357

Fax: (01502) 405350

E-mail: lowestoft.ro@libher.suffolkcc.gov.uk

Website: www.suffolkcc.gov.uk/
libraries_and_heritage/sro

Enquiries: The Public Service Manager, Mrs Louise Clarke

Open: Mon, Wed–Fri: 9.15–5.30; Tues: 9.15–6.00; Sat: 9.15–5.00.

Access: Generally open to the public; the office operates the CARN reader's ticket system. Appointments are accepted for microform readers.

Historical background: The branch was established in 1985 to serve the north-eastern part of Suffolk. Its area for the purpose of collecting archives and printed local studies material is that of the Waveney District. It is recognised as a place of deposit for public records and is a Diocesan Record Office for parish records.

Acquisitions policy: Archival and printed material relating to the north-east part of Suffolk.

Archives of organisation: Usual local authority record holdings.

Major collections: Deposited local collections, including shipping records, c1750–1980s; Adair of Flixton Hall, family and estate records, 13th–20th centuries; Somerleyton Hall estate, 1645–1958.

Non-manuscript material: Local studies library as integral part of record office.

Finding aids: Catalogues and lists; some sent to NRA. Indexes to persons, subjects, places and particular types of record, e.g. photographs, maps and plans, building plans, architects/surveyors.

Facilities: Photocopying. Photography. Microfilming by arrangement. Microfilm/fiche readers/printers (some self-service).

Conservation: In-house service.

Publications: Guide to Genealogical Sources (5/1998).
Annual summary of accessions.

866 Luton Museum

Parent organisation: Borough of Luton

Address: Wardown Park, Luton, Bedfordshire LU2 7HA

Telephone: (01582) 546723

Fax: (01582) 746763

E-mail: adeye@luton.gov.uk

Enquiries: The Keeper of Local History, Dr Elizabeth Adey

Open: Mon–Fri:10.00–4.00 by appointment.

Access: Generally open to the public; an appointment is necessary, and because of the limited space in the study room the number of researchers must be restricted to a maximum of eight.

Historical background: Luton Museum commenced collecting local history material as soon as it was established in 1927. The collection consists of a library, documents and photographs.

Acquisitions policy: Acquisition is limited to items which have a local relevance or which relate to a specific area of the collection, e.g. lace or rural crafts.

Major collections: Documents relating to all aspects of Luton life: industry (particularly hats), education, social life etc.
Maps, plans and other documents produced by local firm of architects, 1890s–1960s (20,000).
MS vols, including the Guild Book of the Fraternity of the Holy Trinity, a guild based in Luton, 1474–1547; the register of the Fraternity of St John the Baptist, based in Dunstable.
Vols of sketches and notes produced by W.G. Smith (1835–1917), a Dunstable antiquarian.

Non-manuscript material: Photographic negatives from *Luton News* (c1,250,000).
Photographs by Frederick Thurston of Luton, 1870s–1930.

Facilities: Photocopying. Photography.

Conservation: Contracted out.

Publications: S. Bunker: *North Chilterns Camera, 1863–1954, from the Thurston Collection in Luton Museum* (Dunstable, 1989).

867 The Silk Museum

Parent organisation: Macclesfield Museums

Address: The Heritage Centre, Roe Street, Macclesfield, Cheshire SK11 6UT

Telephone: (01625) 613210

Fax: (01625) 617880

E-mail: postmaster@silk-macc-u-net.com

Website: www.silk-macclesfield.org

Enquiries: Ms Louanne Collins

Open: Mon–Fri: 9.00–5.00, by appointment only.

Access: Generally open to the public.

Historical background: The Museum and Heritage Centre was established in 1981 by Trustees of the Macclesfield Sunday School, Macclesfield Borough Council and Friends of Macclesfield Silk Heritage. The building was originally a Sunday school which closed in the 1970s.

Acquisitions policy: Acquires records relating to the silk industry, including relevant and local Macclesfield company archives.

Archives of organisation: Sunday School records, 1796–1970s.
Annual reports and accounts, Sunday School Heritage Trust, 1982-, and Macclesfield Museums Trust, 1987- .

Major collections: Cartwright & Sheldon Company records, 1912–81 (incomplete).
Silk manufacturers' pattern books, 1800- .

Non-manuscript material: Large collection of oral history transcripts.
Photograph collection.
Maps.

Finding aids: Catalogues. Lists. Indexes.

Facilities: Photocopying. Photography.

Conservation: Contracted out to Cheshire and Chester Archives (see entry 236).

Publications: J. Norris: *The Last Handloom Weavers, Paradise Hill* (1984).
L. Collins and M. Stevenson: *Silk-sarsenets, Steels, & Stripes: 150 Years of Macclesfield Textile Design.*
——: (comps) *Macclesfield Silk Industry* [photo archive] (1995).
L. Collins: *Silk Museums in Macclesfield* (1989).
——: *Macclesfield Sunday School* (1996)

868 Centre for Kentish Studies

Parent organisation: Kent County Council Arts and Libraries

Address: Sessions House, County Hall, Maidstone, Kent ME14 1XQ

Telephone: (01622) 694363

Fax: (01622) 694379

E-mail: archives@kent.gov.uk

Website: www.kent.gov.uk/e&l/artslib/archives/archiveshome.htm

Enquiries: The County Archivist, Miss Patricia Rowsby

Open: Tues, Wed, Fri: 9.00–5.00; Thurs 10.00–5.00; Sat (2nd & 4th in month): 9.00–1.00. Closed 2 weeks in January.

Access: Generally open to the public. The office operates the CARN reader's ticket system.

Historical background: The office (previously Kent Archives Office) was established in 1933. It merged with the former County Local Studies Library to form the Centre for Kentish Studies in 1990. It also acts as the Diocesan Record Office for Rochester (Archdeaconry of Tonbridge) and Canterbury (Archdeaconry of Maidstone). It is recognised as a place of deposit for public records. The local studies collections at Tonbridge Library are now administered by the Centre for Kentish Studies but are still made available at Tonbridge. See also Canterbury Cathedral Archives (see entry 209) and East Kent Archives Centre (see entry 289).

Archives of organisation: Usual local authority record holdings.

Major collections: Deposited collections, including the following which have a wider significance:
Correspondence of Frederick North, 5th Earl of Guildford, principally concerning activities as Governor of Ceylon, 1798–1805.
Wykeman Martin MSS, including correspondence relating to American affairs, 18th century.
Cornwallis (Mann) MSS, including correspondence of Charles, Marquis Cornwallis, as Governor General of India, later Lord Lieutenant of Ireland, 1786–1804.
Sackville of Knole MSS, including correspondence about the Young Pretender, 1746; military papers of Lt.-Col. Sir Francis Whitworth concerning Gibraltar and West Indies, 1777–1807.
Mackeson MSS: correspondence from John Mackeson while in the army in India, 1801–3, and in West Indies, 1807–14.
Papers of Sir Jeffrey, 1st Lord Amherst, covering his military career in Europe, America and, after 1764, England.
Talbot MSS, including diaries of Lady Caroline Stuart Wortley, 1814–18; travel diaries of J.G. Talbot and others, 19th–20th centuries.

Garnett MSS, including military correspondence of General Robert Garnett, 1841–64.

Papers of Charles, Baron Hardinge of Penshurst (1858–1944).

Papers of George Harris, 1st Baron Harris, covering his life in India and the Seringapatam Campaign, 1789–1800.

Romney MSS, including correspondence of Sir John, 1st Baronet, 1656–83.

Papers of Thomas Papillon (1623–1702), London merchant and politician, and his Huguenot family.

Business and personal correspondence of Sir Mark Wilks Collett, Bart, especially about the American cotton market, 1816–1905.

Pratt MSS, including political correspondence of Sir Charles Pratt, 1st Earl Camden (1714–94), Lord Chancellor; and John Jeffreys Pratt, 2nd Earl and 1st Marquess, 1795–1829.

United and Cecil Club records, 1882–1961.

Sir John Rodgers, Bart, MP for Sevenoaks, 1950–79, official and family papers.

Society of Holy Cross records, 1855–1978.

Extensive correspondence with many eminent figures is included in the following collections:

Faunce Delaune MSS.

Knatchbull and Banks MSS, including correspondence relating to the families of Jane Austen and Sir Joseph Banks.

Sir William Knollys, treasurer and controller of household of Prince of Wales, 1863–77.

Lady Rose Weigal (d 1921) and family.

Rt Hon. J.H. Thomas, MP (1874–1949).

De L'Isle MSS: Sydney family of Penshurst, 14th century– (available only with the permission of Lord De L'Isle of Penshurst Place).

Stanhope of Chevening MSS: official, literary and scientific papers of the seven Earls Stanhope, with family and estate papers, including most of the letters from the 4th Earl of Chesterfield to his son, 1738–68.

Non-manuscript material: The County Local Studies Collection: books and pamphlets relating to the historic county of Kent; printed maps, illustrations; microfilms and microfiche, including census returns, 1841–91; small collection of audio-visual material.

Finding aids: Catalogues, lists and indexes.

Facilities: Photocopying. Photography. Microfilming. Microfilm reader.

Conservation: In-house service. Outside work undertaken; contact Canterbury Cathedral Archives (see entry 209).

Publications: Guide to Kent Archives Office (1958);*First Supplement, 1957–68* (1971); *Second Supplement, 1969–80* (1982).

Handlist of County Council Records, 1889–1945 (1972).

Handlist of Parish Registers and Transcripts (1997).

869 Kent Biological Archives and Records Centre

Address: Natural History Section, Maidstone Museums & Art Gallery, St Faith's Street, Maidstone, Kent ME14 1LH

Telephone: (01622) 754497

The archive was started in 1971 to maintain records of all natural history in the present administrative county of Kent. Photographs of habitats and species (c1000) are kept and a collection of local naturalists' note-books and other MS material has also been started. Records before 1971 are treated as historical records and are recorded under species headings. All records for 1971 onwards are treated as recent records and are filed under species and locality headings.

870 Thomas Plume's Library

Address: Market Hill, Maldon, Essex CM9 7PZ

Telephone: 01621 854051

Enquiries: The Librarian, William Petchey, 22 London Road, Maldon, Essex CM9 6HD

Open: Tues–Thurs: 2.00–4.00; Sat: 10.00–12.00. Open at other times by arrangement.

Access: Generally open to the public, by appointment.

The library was the private collection of Archdeacon Thomas Plume (1630–1704) and was bequeathed to the people of Maldon on his death. Minute books of the Plume Trustees survive from 1704. There are early MS catalogues of the library, which holds pamphlets, bills and miscellaneous documents (c1500) on a wide range of subjects, including theology, mathematics, science, astronomy and travel, 16th–19th centuries.

871 Malvern College Archives

Address: College Road, Malvern, Worcestershire WR14 3DF

Telephone: (01684) 892333

Fax: (01684) 572398

E-mail: inquiry@malcol.org.uk

Website: www.malcol.org.uk

Enquiries: The Archivist, Norman Rosser

Open: Term: Mon–Fri: 9.30–4.30, by appointment

Access: Bona fide researchers, on written application.

The college was founded for boys in 1865. In 1992 it incorporated Ellerslie girls' school and Hillstone preparatory school. It holds governors' minutes, 1863– ; registers of teachers, pupils and old Malvernians, 1865– ; calendars, 1902– ; rolls of honour from two world wars; photographs; school magazines and newspaper cuttings. See G.H. Chesterton: *Malvern College: 125 Years* (1990).

872 Barclays Group Archives

Parent organisation: Barclays plc

Address: Dallimore Road, Wythenshawe, Manchester M23 9JA

Telephone: (0161) 946 3035

Fax: (0161) 946 0226

E-mail: jessie.campbell@barclays.co.uk

Website: www.barclays.co.uk

Enquiries: Group Archivist, Jessie Campbell

Open: Mon–Fri: 10.00–4.00, by appointment

Access: Bona fide researchers only, at the discretion of the company after receipt of an acceptable letter of introduction. Researchers are required to deposit a copy of their work. Company records are closed for 30 years and customer records for 100 years.

Historical background: Barclays was formed as a limited company in 1896 by a group of private banks, one of which was called Barclay, Bevan and Company, founded in Lombard Street in 1690. Many banks were subsequently taken over, in particular Martins Bank in 1969. Three overseas banks were acquired in 1925 and renamed Barclays Bank Dominion, Colonial and Overseas. The archives were moved out of

Head Office in London in 1989 and records were collected from departments, regional offices and branches in a programme of centralising the historic records of the group. In 2000 Barclays took over the Woolwich Building Society. The Woolwich was founded in 1847 as the Woolwich Equitable Benefit Building and Investment Association and incorporated in 1875. Between 1941 and 1992 the Woolwich acquired 12 building societies, themselves the results of previous amalgamations.

Acquisitions policy: To act as the corporate memory of Barclays plc by preserving records containing evidence of policy decisions and background papers relating thereto, evidence of rights and obligations and significant records of banks and companies taken over by the group. New accessions result from the records management programme.

Archives of organisation: Business records of Barclays Bank, 1896– ; of Barclays Bank (Dominion, Colonial and Overseas), 1925–85; of constituent banks, 18th century–1969. Records of the Woolwich Building Society and its constituents, 1847– .

Finding aids: Database catalogue and lists.

Facilities: Photocopying and photography by arrangement.

Conservation: Contracted out.

Publications: P.W. Matthews and A.W. Tuke: *History of Barclays Bank* (1926).
G. Chandler: *Four Centuries of Banking...the Constituent Banks of Martins Bank Ltd* (1964) [2 vols].
A.W. Tuke and R.H. Gillman: *Barclays Bank Limited 1926–1969* (1972).
J. Crossley and J. Blandford: *The DCO Story, a History of Banking in Many Countries, 1925–71* (1975).

873 Chetham's Library

Address: Long Millgate, Manchester M3 1SB

Telephone: (0161) 834 7961

Fax: (0161) 839 5797

E-mail: chetlib@dial.pipex.com

Enquiries: The Librarian, Michael Powell
The Archivist, Jane Foster

Open: Mon–Fri: 9.00–12.30, 1.30–4.30, by appointment.

Access: Material is available on 24 hours' notice. Readers are asked to provide references. The building may be visited by the public during opening hours.

Historical background: Founded in 1653 by Humphrey Chetham, a Manchester merchant, as a free public library for 'the use of scholars', it was recognised by royal charter in 1665; it was founded with Chetham's School (now the School of Music).

Acquisitions policy: The library concentrates on the history and topography of north-western England.

Archives of organisation: Chetham family papers, hospital and library minute books, 1653–.

Major collections: A varied collection, including *c*40 medieval MSS.
The majority of MSS and archives are concerned with the history of Manchester and its region, including:
Papers of the Manchester Sunday Schools, 19th century.
Bishop Fraser, 2nd Bishop of Manchester, Collection, 1818–85.
Hulme Trust deeds, mainly on Manchester, 13th–17th centuries, including papers of John Huntingdon, 1st warden of the Collegiate Church, 1422–58.
Records of Belle Vue Zoological Gardens, 19th–20th centuries.
Poor House and constable's accounts for Sutton, nr Macclesfield, and Over Knutsford, Cheshire, 17th–19th centuries.
Estate papers of Agecroft, nr Manchester, 15th–18th centuries.
Booth Charities Archive, 17th–20th centuries.

Non-manuscript material: Broadsides and tracts (*c*3100); Chetham Popery tracts.
Shorthand collections of John Byrom (1692–1763) and John Harland (1806–38) (*c*49 MSS and 360 printed books).
Photographic slides and engravings (*c*2000).
Scrapbooks (various) relating to the 18th- and 19th-century history of Manchester.
Local newspapers, 18th–19th centuries.
Incunabula (*c*90).

Finding aids: Catalogues, indexes and lists available; the collection is continuously researched and indexed. Lists sent to NRA.

Facilities: Restricted photocopying. Photography by arrangement.

Conservation: In-house service.

Publications: M. Powell: 'Chetham's Library', *Manchester Region History Review,* 2 (1988).
M. Powell: 'Chetham's Library, Manchester', *The Local Historian,* 20 (1990).
Chetham's Library: Three Centuries of the Written Word (Manchester, 1994).
N. Barker: 'Chetham's Library: an appeal', *The Book Collector,* 44 (1995).
J. Foster: *The Archive of the Booth Charities of Salford* (Manchester, 1999).

874 Greater Manchester County Record Office

Parent organisation: Association of Greater Manchester Authorities (AGMA)

Address: 56 Marshall Street, New Cross, Manchester M4 5FU

Telephone: (0161) 832 5284

Fax: (0161) 839 3808

E-mail: archives@gmcro.u-net.com

Website: www.gmcro.co.uk

Enquiries: The County Archivist

Open: Mon, Tues, Thurs, Fri: 9.00–5.00; Wed 9.00–1.00; Sat (2nd and 4th of month): 9.00–12.00, 1.00–4.00.

Access: Generally open to the public. The office operates the CARN reader's ticket system. An appointment is necessary to use microfilm readers.

Historical background: The office was established in 1976 as the county record office for Greater Manchester, with a collecting policy designed to supplement rather than duplicate those of the district record offices. It is recognised as a place of deposit for public records. The Documentary Photography Archive has existed since the early 1970s with Audrey Linkman as its curator.

Acquisitions policy: Archives of the county with a regional significance, i.e. of two or more districts.

Archives of organisation: Usual local authority record holdings, of Greater Manchester Council and some predecessor bodies, plus Greater Manchester Residuary Body records.

Major collections: Deposited local collections, of which the following have a wider significance:

Family papers, including Lord Wilton's family and estate papers relating to Heaton Park, Manchester, and estates in Wrinehill, Cheshire/Staffordshire, and Battesley, West Yorkshire, 1304–1970s; archives of the Assheton family of Middleton, c1300–1830s, Legh of Lyme Hall, Stockport.

Entwisle family of Foxholes, nr Rochdale, 1565–1957.

Canal records, including archives of the Manchester Ship Canal, 1883–1970s; archives of Rochdale Canal Company, 1793–1880s.

Archive of the Paul Graney Memorial Folk Trust.

Architectural records, 19th and 20th centuries.

Business archives, including records of National Vulcan Insurance Company, Manchester, c1860s–1950s; records of Robinsons of Ramsbottom, Bury, bleachers and dyers, 1900–1970s.

Manchester Stock Exchange lists.

Records of Prestorial Hospital, former County Lunatic Asylum.

Non-manuscript material: Documentary Photography Archive, 1840s– .

Engineering drawings (c100,000).

Paul Graney archive of oral histories, legends, music and remembrance.

GMC and Manchester Ship Canal photographic archives.

Finding aids: Catalogues being updated. Lists will be sent to NRA.

Details of collections available on website.

Facilities: Photocopying. Microfilm/fiche readers. Photography by arrangement.

Conservation: Full in-house service except some specialist bookbinding; outside work undertaken.

Publications: Guide to Greater Manchester County Record Office (1998).

A. Linkman: *The Victorians: Photographic Portraits* (London, 1993).

875 John Rylands University Library

Parent organisation: University of Manchester

Address: Deansgate, Manchester M3 3EH

A Library

Telephone: (0161) 834 5343/6765

Fax: (0161) 834 5574

E-mail: p.mcniven@man.ac.uk, j.r.hodgson@man.ac.uk

Website: www.rylibweb.man.ac.uk

Enquiries: The Head of Special Collections, Dr Peter McNiven

The Co-ordinating Archivist, John Hodgson

Open: Mon–Fri: 10.00–5.15; Sat: 10.00–1.00, preferably by appointment.

Access: Manchester University reader's ticket holders; approved researchers on production of a letter of reference.

Historical background: The library was formed by the merger in 1972 of the library of the University of Manchester (f. 1851) and the John Rylands Library (f. 1900). Most MS collections are housed in the former John Rylands Library on Deansgate, notable exceptions being the university's own archive, the *Manchester Guardian* archive and the Manchester Medical Society archives, which are at the University Library, Oxford Road, Manchester M13 9PP (special access arrangements apply).

Acquisitions policy: To strengthen existing collections, by purchase, donation or deposit, particularly in the fields of non-conformity, contemporary literature and the papers of Manchester University, its staff and alumni.

Archives of organisation: University archive, with papers of a number of academics, including W.S. Jevons (1835–82) and Professor T.F. Tout (1855–1929).

Major collections: Oriental collections, including codices, papyri, ostraca, clay tablets and palm leaves, in over 30 languages.

Western MSS: medieval MSS in all major European languages, many from libraries of famous collectors such as Lord Crawford; particularly rich in illuminated Latin MSS of early Germanic and Italian provenance.

Charter Rooms: extensive deeds, genealogical and family papers and other material, relating mainly to Cheshire, Lancashire, Derbyshire, Yorkshire, Warwickshire, Lincolnshire and Suffolk, 12th–20th centuries. Collections for the following families: Bagshawe of Ford Hall and the Oaks, Bromley-Davenport of Capesthorne, Brooke of Mere, Coke of Longford and Holkham; Cornwall-Legh of High Legh; Grey of Dunham Massey (Earls of Stamford); Legh of Lyme, Leycester of Toft; Tatton of Wythenshawe, the Manchester portion of the muniments of the Earl of Ducie; and miscellaneous charter collections.

Other collections, including the following:

Papers of Gen. Sir Henry Clinton (1771–1829) and his brother Gen. Sir William Henry Clinton (1769–1846), with ancillary collections, relating to the Peninsular War and Napoleonic period.

Correspondence and papers of Henry Dundas (1742–1811), 1st Viscount Melville and his son Robert Saunders Dundas (1771–1851), 2nd Viscount Melville, East India Company papers and much other material concerning British rule in India.

World War II papers of FM Sir Claude Auchinleck (1884–1981) and Maj.-Gen. Eric Edward Dorman O'Gowan (1895–1966).

Manchester Guardian newspaper archive, 1821–1970s.

Papers of Mrs Hester Lynch Piozzi (1741–1821) relating to the circle of Samuel Johnson (1709–84) (3000 items).

Correspondence of John Ruskin (1819–1900) and his circle (2000 items).

Collections and 19th-century art, especially William Holman Hunt (1827–1910) the Pre-Raphaelites.

Papers of 20th-century novelists, poets, dramatists, actors and producers including Robert Donat (1905–58), actor; Basil Dean (1888–1978), director; L.P. Hartley (1895–1972), novelist; dom silvester houédard (1924–92), concrete poet; Norman Nicholson (1914–87), poet; and Alison Uttley (1884–1976), children's writer; also the archive of Carcanet Press.

Papers of John Dalton (1766–1844) and other Manchester scientists; archive of Jodrell Bank Radio Telescope.

Industrial archives, especially of the early textile industry, including Samuel Oldknow, McConnel & Kennedy and Rylands & Sons; also archives of trade unions and employers' organizations.

Non-conformist theological collections, particularly significant for the Baptist, Congregationalist, Methodist and Unitarian denominations, as well as archives of the ecumenical movement and feminist theology.

Women's suffrage movement archives, 1892–1920.

Manchester Medical Society manuscripts, 18th–19th centuries.

Extensive 19th-century autograph letter collections.

Non-manuscript material: Maps, plans, photographs and a small quantity of audio-visual archives.

Finding aids: Comprehensive *Guide to Special Collections* available on-line and in printed form. Handlists or calendars for most collections. Some lists sent to NRA, including university archives: NRA 16039, 18558.

Facilities: Photocopying. Comprehensive photographic and microfilming service. Microfilm/fiche readers.

Conservation: Large in-house conservation unit; outside work is not normally undertaken.

Publications: Comprehensive *Guide to Special Collections* (see above); shorter guides and histories; many published handlists and catalogues, some of which have appeared in the *Bulletin of the JRULM*, published thrice-yearly. Many publications available for purchase, together with free items. Publications list available.

B Methodist Archives and Research Centre

Telephone: (0161) 834 5343

Fax: (0161) 834 5574

E-mail: pnockles@fs1.li.man.ac.uk

Website: rylibweb.man.ac.uk/data1/dg/text/method.html

Enquiries: The Librarian in charge of the Methodist Church Archives, Dr Peter Nockles

Open: Mon–Fri: 10.00–5.15; Sat: 10.00–1.00, by appointment.

Access: Those using the manuscript material for the first time will require a letter of recommendation or identification. There is an embargo placed on certain material, and written permission for access to these items must first be obtained from the Secretary of the Methodist Church.

Historical background: Established in 1961 by the Methodist Church, the centre was formerly housed in Epworth House, City Road, London. In 1977 the collection was transferred to Manchester, but Wesley's Chapel (49–51 City Road, London EC1, tel. (020) 7253 2262), retains a small amount of material and has transferred some film and sound archives relating to Methodism to the National Film and Television Archive (entry 556B). The collection remains the property of the Methodist Church and consists of books and MSS devoted to the religious history of the denomination and the doctrinal theological controversies relating to it. Material concerning circuits and churches, and also more recent district material, is normally deposited in local authority record offices or agreed repositories.

Acquisitions policy: To strengthen existing primary and secondary collections in the history of Methodism, Evangelicalism and allied subjects, by purchase and donation.

Archives of organisation: Material of a connexional nature, 1739– , including agendas, conference papers and minutes and district synod minutes. Other material, 1700– .

Major collections: J.J. Colman Collection: surviving diaries and sermon notebooks of John Wesley (1703–91).
Papers, including those of Charles Wesley (1707–88) and Wesley family, George Whitfield (1714–70), the Countess of Huntingdon (1707–91), Thomas Coke (1747–1814), John Ernest Rattenbury (1870–1963), Rupert Davies (1909–94), and Donald Soper (1903–98).
MSS relating to John Fletcher (1729–84) of Madeley and his wife, Mary Bosanquet (1739–1815).
E.S. Lamplough Collection: letters of John Wesley and other members of the family.
Preachers' Letters and Portraits Section: letters of Methodist ministers, mainly 18th and 19th centuries (c50,000), and their diaries and journals (c100).
J.T. Wilkinson Collection: letters of Professor A.S. Peak (1865–1929) (c 4000) and other documents relating to the history of Hartley Victoria College and to Primitive Methodism (11,500 items).
National and district, but not circuit, records.
Much material from the various divisions of the Methodist Church, including home missions, finance, social responsibility, ministries, education and youth and property; also from the forces board and conference office, Hunmanby Methodist Girls' School, Filey (now closed), and the diaconal order.
No genealogical, baptismal or burial records.

Non-manuscript material: 18th-century editions of Wesley's works (2000 vols); Charles Wesley's library (500 vols); John Fletcher's library (130 vols).
Pamphlets and tracts (20,000).
Periodicals (c6200); hymn books (3000); circuit plans (10,000).

Books by Methodist authors; local histories, engravings, portraits and photographs.

Finding aids: Detailed catalogues and finding aids are available for consultation in the Deansgate building of the library; see also the website. Calendar and handlists for major collections. Lists sent to NRA.

Facilities: Photocopying. Photography. Microfilms. Colour slides and all other kinds of work may be supplied.

Conservation: In-house.

Publications: D.W. Riley: 'The Methodist Archives and Research Centre', *Bulletin of the John Rylands University Library of Manchester*, lx, 269; lxii, 3.
H.L. Calking (comp): *Catalogue of Methodist Archival and MSS Collections* (Part 6) (1982).
G. Lloyd and P. Nockles: *A Guide to Manuscript Accessions 1985–1994* (1994).
P.B. Nockles: 'The Work of the Methodist Archives & Research Centre...', in R. Seton (ed.), *Proceedings of a Conference...* (Religious Archives Group, 1993), 1–8.
See also *Proceedings of the Wesley Historical Society and Methodist Magazine*.
Catalogues and handlists for sale; available from centre.

876   Labour History Archive & Study Centre

Parent organisation: John Rylands University Library of Manchester

Address: 103 Princess Street, Manchester M1 6DD

Telephone: (0161) 228 7212

Fax: (0161) 228 5965

E-mail: archives@nmlhweb.org

Website: www.nmlhweb.org/archive.htm

Enquiries: The Archivists, Stephen Bird and Janette Martin

Open: Mon–Fri: 10.00–5.00.

Access: Generally open to the public; an appointment is preferred.

Historical background: The Labour History Archive and Study Centre was established under the auspices of the National Museum of Labour History when it moved from London to Manchester in 1988. In 1990 the Labour

Party Archives were deposited and since then an archive centre has been developed based primarily upon the political wing of the labour movement. In 2000 the management of the centre came under the John Rylands Library (see entry 875) for a period of five years. The museum maintains its own archives, including minutes and correspondence.

Acquisitions policy: To collect records of the political wing of the British labour movement; consequently trade union collections previously held have been de-accessioned.

Major collections: Labour Party Archives, 1900– , including minutes of the National Executive Committee and correspondence.
Parliamentary Labour Party minutes, 1906– .
Communist Party of Great Britain archives including Executive and Policy Committee minutes, 1921–92.
Miniken/Vincent papers, Chartist collection, 1837–41.
Labour and Socialist International papers 1917–57.
Socialist Sunday School collection 1904–73.
Papers of Michael Foot (*b* 1913), 1926–90; Judith Hart, MP (1924–91), 1955–91; Eric Heffer, MP (1922–91), 1946–91; Jo Richardson, MP (1923–93), 1948–50.

Non-manuscript material: Large photographic collection, including Labour Party and Communist Party photograph libraries.
Large pamphlet collection.
Journals relating to Labour history, including *Tribune, Commonweal, New Leader, Labour Weekly* and *Marxism Today.*

Finding aids: Most material has been sorted and listed. Lists sent to NRA.

Facilities: Photocopying. Microfilm/fiche reader.

Publications: Guide to the Labour Party Archives.

877 Manchester Archives and Local Studies

Parent organisation: Manchester City Council

Address: St Peter's Square, Manchester M2 5PD

Telephone: (0161) 234 1980 (archives); 234 1979 (non-manuscript material)

Fax: (0161) 234 1927

E-mail: lsu@libraries.manchester.gov.uk

Website: www.manchester.gov.uk/libraries/arls

Enquiries: The Principal Archivist, Ms Ann Heath
The Local Studies Officer, Richard Bond

Open: Archives: Mon–Thurs: 10.00–4.30.
Local studies material: Mon–Thurs: 10.00–8.00; Fri–Sat: 10.00–5.00.

Access: Generally available, unless restricted by the terms of the deposit. Some archive material must be booked at least 24 hours in advance. There are no restrictions on access to non-MS material.

Historical background: Manchester Public Libraries have collected local studies material (MS and printed) since the establishment of the service in 1852. A separate Local History Library was established in 1957, and an Archives Department in 1966. The two services were merged in 1991 to provide a combined archives and local studies service. The unit is recognised as a place of deposit for public records and as the Diocesan Record Office for Manchester (diocesan and parish records). The unit retains records acquired before the mid-1950s for a wide area around Manchester.

Acquisitions policy: Records of the local authority, organisations, communities and individuals within the City of Manchester.

Archives of organisation: Manchester Public Library archive.

Major collections: Manchester branch of the National Union of Women's Suffrage Societies, 1867–1919; papers of Mrs Millicent Garrett Fawcett, LLD, on women's suffrage etc, 1871–1919.
Manchester Chamber of Commerce minutes, 1794–1964.
Records of the Strutt Mills at Derby, Milford and Cromford, Derbyshire, 1780–1936, and Samuel Greg's Quarry Bank Mill, Styal, Cheshire, 1788–1937.
Papers of Dr William Farrer, editor of *Victoria County History of Lancashire*, 16th–20th centuries.
Letters, mostly from politicians, to George Wilson, chairman of the Anti-Corn Law League, 1827–85; letters to John Benjamin Smith, MP, 1832–74.
Records of the Lancashire, later the National, Public School Association, 1848–62.

Parish records for the Diocese of Manchester, 16th–20th centuries; Methodist records of circuit and chapels in the Manchester and Stockport district, 18th–20th centuries; records of the Society of Friends, Hardshaw East, monthly and preparative meetings, 17th–20th centuries.

Records of many Manchester Jewish organisations.

Records of the Calico Printers' Association, 1774–1969; Boys' and Girls' Welfare Society, 19th–20th centuries; Peter Stubs Ltd, watch and tool makers, and subsidiary interests of the Stubs family, 1775–1933; Renold Chains Ltd, chain manufacturers, and predecessor and subsidiary companies, 1618–1964 (mainly 1860s onwards); Royal Manchester Institution, 1823–1958; J. & N. Philips and Co. Ltd, manufacturers of textiles, tapes and smallwares, including predecessor and subsidiary companies, 1748–1968 (mainly 19th–20th centuries).

Papers of Lord Ernest Darwin Simon of Wythenshawe (1879–1960) and Lady Sheena Dorothy Simon of Wythenshawe (1883–1972), mainly relating to 20th-century politics and education, 1894–1974.

Non-manuscript material: Prints and photographs (*c*143,000), maps (*c*13,000), broadsides (*c*6600), and several hundred press cutting volumes. Microforms (*c*14,000) include local census returns, newspapers, parish registers (including many for Lancashire and Cheshire), directories, electoral registers; also the *International Genealogical Index* for the British Isles and the *National Probate Index*, 1858–1930.

Finding aids: Lists and calendars, sent to NRA. Name, place and subject indexes to the calendars.

Facilities: Limited photocopying and photography. Microfilming.

Conservation: Contracted out to Greater Manchester County Record Office

Publications: Manchester and Lancashire Family History Society (Comp.): *Parish and Non-conformist Registers in Manchester Local History Library ("The Pink Book")* (5/1997) [correct up to the end of 1995].

878 Manchester Cathedral Muniment Room

Address: Manchester Cathedral, Manchester M3 1SX

Telephone: (0161) 833 2220

Fax: (0161) 839 6226

E-mail: manchester.cathedral@btinternet.com

Enquiries: The Archivist, Mrs Rose Gore

Open: By arrangement.

Access: Bona fide scholars, students and family history researchers. A small charge is made.

Historical background: The cathedral is the ancient parish church of Manchester, formerly known as the Collegiate Church, founded in 1421. It became a cathedral in 1847.

Acquisitions policy: To maintain the parochial and capitular records: anything appertaining to Collegiate and Cathedral Church, fabric, choir, chapter and personnel.

Archives of organisation: Principally, registers, 1543– , including baptisms, marriages, burials, charters, 1421– . The records of the collegiate foundation, including wardens' and fellows' Act books, 1635–20th century; surveys and valuations relating to lands in the Manchester area, 1422– , and financial archives, 1861– . Records of the parish, including parish registers, 1573– (*c*450 vols).

Non-manuscript material: Drawings and plans of ancient holdings of Collegiate Church; service sheets, 1950– .
The Bishop Wickham Library.

Finding aids: Typewritten catalogue.

Facilities: Photocopying.

Publications: A.E.J. Hollander: 'The Muniment Room of Manchester Cathedral', *Archives*, i/5 (1951), 3–10.

879 Manchester Jewish Museum

Address: 190 Cheetham Hill Road, Manchester M8 8LW

Telephone: (0161) 834 9879

Fax: (0161) 834 9801

E-mail: info@manchesterjewishmuseum.com

Website: www.manchesterjewishmuseum.com

Enquiries: The Director, Jim Garretts

Open: Mon–Thurs: 10.30–4.00; Sun: 10.30–5.00, by appointment.

Access: Generally open to the public on presentation of a form of bona fides if not previously known to the institution. Researchers wishing to consult archives must book in advance.

Historical background: The museum's archives developed from those collected under the auspices of a project based at Manchester Polytechnic in the 1970s and transferred to the museum when it opened in 1984. Major archives of Jewish-owned companies are acquired by Manchester Archives and Local Studies Division (see entry 877). A Jewish Heritage Committee exists, which acts as a discussion forum for the deposition of archives; the museum and the city library are represented on this committee.

Acquisitions policy: Archival material that relates to the Jewish community in the Manchester region from its inception to the present. If the museum has the opportunity to secure significant material that falls outside the normal geographical boundaries, then consultation with other interested parties will take place before a decision is made.

Major collections: Papers and records mostly relating to local Jewish families and businesses, 19th century– .

Non-manuscript material: Photography and oral history holdings.

Finding aids: Most of the manuscript archives can be accessed via a simple database. Photographs can be accessed by name of depositor or by subject; oral history archives can be accessed by name of interviewee.

Facilities: Photocopying. Photography. Cassette tape/copying.

Conservation: All relevant conservation work is done by the North West Museums Service, or by specific agencies recommended by them.

880 Manchester Literary & Philosophical Society

Address: Churchgate House, 56 Oxford Street, Manchester M60 7HJ

Telephone: (0161) 228 3638

Fax: (0161) 228 3571

E-mail: man.litphil@virgin.net

Website: www.manlitphil.org

Enquiries: The Hon. Curator and Librarian, Miss S.J. Lowe

Open: Mon–Fri: 10.30–4.00.

Access: Restricted use by the public; an appointment is necessary.

The society was instituted in 1781. Its archives were largely destroyed in 1940 although minutes survive after this date. The Dalton MSS are now in the possession of the John Rylands University Library (entry 875). Some deeds are deposited in the Manchester Archives and Local Studies Unit (entry 877), and other papers are held by the Manchester Museum of Science and Industry (entry 882). The society houses the *Manchester Memoirs* (formerly *Memoirs and Proceedings*), 1781– . Material is collected on the history of the society and on selected members. Photocopying is available.

881 Manchester Metropolitan University Library

Address: All Saints, Oxford Road, Manchester M15 6BH

Telephone: (0161) 247 6108/6644

Fax: (0161) 247 6349

E-mail: artdesign-lib-enq@mmu.ac.uk

Website: www.mmu.ac.uk/services/library

Enquiries: The Special Collections Library/ Conservator

Open: Mon–Fri: 10.00–4.00.

Access: Bona fide researchers, by appointment.

Historical background: Manchester Polytechnic was created in 1970, when the Regional College of Art, the John Dalton College of Technology and the Manchester College of Commerce merged. Didsbury College of Education and Hollings College were also brought into the polytechnic in 1977. Further mergers took place in 1983 with the City of Manchester College of Higher Education and in 1992 with Crewe and Alsager College of Higher Education. University status was granted in 1992. The Jimmy Deane Archive has been transferred to the Modern Records Centre, University of Warwick (entry 261).

Acquisitions policy: To strengthen existing undergraduate research collections in subject areas taught in the university and to acquire specialised materials where necessary.

Archives of organisation: A collection of ephemeral material relating to the college of art, the polytechnic and the university. Official records are housed elsewhere within the university, and archives relating to other founding colleges are commonly held at the appropriate site library.

Major collections: Artists' Archive: primary source material, including correspondence, original design work, wood blocks, artist's and printer's proofs. Artists represented include Barnett Freedman (1901–58), John Farleigh (1900–65), Rigby Graham (*b*1931) and Peter Reddick (*b*1924).

Design Process Collection: a small collection resulting from an exhibition, which refers mainly to the development of Hygena kitchens, 1950s–mid-1970s.

Fleece Press Archive: correspondence and proofs relating to book production at Simon Lawrence's Fleece Press, 1979–98.

Lancashire Cotton Trade: *re* the development of trade unions, newspapers and parliamentary representations, early 20th century– .

The Pratt Collection: design archive of H. Pratt (Jacquard Designers) Ltd, comprising design inspiration albums, fabric samples and original design work.

Non-manuscript material: The Seddon Collection: Victorian and Edwardian seasonal greetings cards (32,000) and Victorian valentines (2000).

Book Design Collection: books demonstrating physical aspects of book production, 18th-century, including examples of most of the major British private presses.

Children's Book Collections: 19th- and 20th-century children's books and periodicals.

Manchester Society of Architects Library: historical books on 18th- and 19th-century architecture.

Home Studies Collections: books on cooking and household management, 17th–mid-20th-century.

Finding aids: Handlists for most collections.

Facilities: Microfilm/fiche printers. No photocopying permitted from Special Collections. Researchers are allowed to photograph items.

Conservation: In-house conservation facilities; no external work undertaken.

Publications: W.H. Shercliff: *Morality to Adventure: Manchester Polytechnic's Collection of Children's Books, 1840–1939* (1988).

G. Smith: *Sentimental Souvenirs: Victorian Scrap Albums from the Sir Harry Page Collection* (1989).

I. Rogerson: *Barnett Freedman: Painter, Draughtsman, Lithographer* (1990).

G. Smith: *Trade Catalogues: a Hundred Years 1850–1949* (1992).

L. Seddon: *A Gallery of Greetings: a Guide to the Seddon Collection* (1992).

I. Rogerson: *The John Farleigh Collection* (1993).

L. Seddon: *Victorian Valentines: a Guide to the Laura Seddon Collection of Valentine Cards in Manchester Metropolitan University Library* (1996).

882 Museum of Science and Industry in Manchester
Library and Record Centre

Address: Liverpool Road, Castlefield, Manchester M3 4FP

Telephone: (0161) 606 0503

Fax: (0161) 834 5135

E-mail: archive@msim.org.uk

Website: www.msim.org.uk

Enquiries: The Senior Archivist, Penny Feltham

Open: Mon–Fri: 10.00–4.30.

Access: Generally open to the public. Some records are subject to a 30-year closure period. Access to the museum's archive collections will be via the new Collection Centre. There is no charge for access to the museum, but charges for reproductions will apply.

Historical background: The Museum of Science and Industry opened in the world's oldest surviving passenger railway station in 1983 and its collections incorporate those developed by the North Western Museum of Science and Technology (f .1969). The Library and Record Centre is the searchroom and study centre for the museum. The redeveloped Centre opened in 2001, when the Lancashire Mining Museum collections, previously held in Salford, were transferred.

Acquisitions policy: Archives and records relating to the development of Manchester as an industrial city, as the centre of the industrial conurbation of Greater Manchester and as a centre of scientific activity.

Archives of organisation: Corporate, departmental and project records relating to the museum's development.

Major collections: Archives of the Electricity Council, 1957–90, and predecessor agencies, including Central Electricity Board, 1927–48, British Electricity Authority, 1947–54, Central Electricity Authority, 1955–57, and British Electrical Development Association, 1919–90. Business records, including Beyer Peacock & Co. 1854–1966; Joseph Cockshoot & Co. Ltd, 1867–1965; Craven Brothers Ltd, 1860–1967; Ferranti International, 1790–1990; GEC Alsthom — Trafford Park, and predecessor agencies, 1902–90; Linotype and Machinery Ltd, 1890–1990; Coats Viyella, records relating to the discovery of Terylene, 1929–68; Gainwest Ltd, papers relating to the Hacienda and Factory Communications, c1977–96; A.V. Roe & Co., aircraft manufacturers; papers of Roy Chadwick (1893–1947), chief designer, and Jimmy Orrell (1903–88), chief test pilot; Mather and Platt, Manchester, engineers; Crossley Brothers, Manchester, engine manufacturers, c1890–c1960; W.T. Glover & Co. Ltd, Trafford Park, electric cable makers, 1868–c1968.

John Alcock and Arthur Whitten-Brown: papers relating to transatlantic flight, 1919.

William Perkin, research papers relating to the discovery of aniline dyestuffs, c1840–1960.

Non-manuscript material: Calico Printers Association and Birch Vale collections of fabric samples, 1795–1946; Dimoldenberg design samples, c1920–1965.

National Paper Museum collections, including Clayton-Beadle, Clapperton, Schieland watermark collections; J.B. Green and Wakeman collections of paper samples; library of publications relating to papermaking history.

Prints, photographs, engineering drawings, trade literature.

Finding aids: Handlists. Card index. Computer database of images in Beyer Peacock Archive. Lists sent to NRA.

Facilities: Photocopying. Photography. Microfilm/fiche reader.

Publications: P. Webb and E. Sprenger: 'Persuading the Housewife to Use Electricity? An Interpretation of Material in the Electricity Council Archive', *British Journal for the History of Science*, 26 (1993).

Electricity Council Archive Handlist and Guide (1994).

Catalogue of Photographic Images in the Beyer Peacock Archive (1995).

883 National Archive for the History of Computing

Parent organisation: University of Manchester

Address: Centre for the History of Science, Technology and Medicine, Mathematics Tower, The University, Manchester M13 9PL

Telephone: (0161) 275 5850

Fax: (0161) 275 5699

E-mail: nahc@fs4.ma.man.ac.uk

Website: www.man.ac.uk/science_engineering/chstm/nahc.htm

Enquiries: The Director

Open: Mon–Fri: 10.00–5.00, by appointment.

Access: Generally open to the public, by arrangement.

Historical background: The NAHC was founded in 1987 within the Centre for the History of Science, Technology and Medicine at Manchester University in collaboration with the Department of Computer Sciences and the John Rylands University Library (entry 875).

Acquisitions policy: Materials relating to the development of computing in Britain, including company records, personal papers, advertising literature and ephemera.

Major collections: International Computers Ltd (ICL) historical collection, c1900– .

Computer records of the National Research Development Corporation, 1949–65.

Records of the Department of Computer Science, University of Manchester, 1946– .

Open System Interconnection (OSI), records, British Standards Institution, 1978– .

Non-manuscript material: Photographic collection of 20th-century punched-card and computing machinery. Computer industry film and slide collections.

Oral history collection.

Finding aids: Catalogue available on website. Lists sent to NRA.

Facilities: Photocopying.

884 National Gas Archive

Parent organisation: Transco plc

Address: Common Lane, Partington, Manchester M31 4BR

Telephone: (0161) 777 7193/7121

Fax: (0161) 777 7055

E-mail: enquiries@gasarchive.org

Website: www.lattice-com/ community_environment/gas-archive/index

Enquiries: The Archive Manager, Helen Ford

Open: Mon–Fri: 9.00–5.00, by appointment only.

Access: Generally open to the public; there are restrictions on some material.

Historical background: On nationalisation in 1949, twelve area gas boards were established and absorbed over 1,000 local gas undertakings. The Gas Council acted as a liaison body. The 1972 Gas Act abolished the Gas Council and established the British Gas Corporation. In 1986 the gas industry was privatised and British Gas plc was formed. The geographical structure of the company was replaced by functional business units such as Transco. In 1997, British Gas demerged to form two separate companies, BG plc (responsible for Transco, the transmission and storage of gas) and Centrica (responsible for domestic supply/retail). Centrica trades as British Gas in the UK. Records of many pre-1949 local undertakings are deposited in local record offices. In 2000, following the demerger of the BG Group, the archive became part of Transco plc.

Acquisitions policy: Regular transfer of material from corporate centre to the National Gas Archive (NGA). Records from the other business units within the company are transferred intermittently. A small amount of external material has been deposited. The collections cover the UK, although holdings for some regions are poor.

Archives of organisation: Corporate records of Gas Council and area gas boards, 1949–72; British Gas Corporation and regions, 1972–86; British Gas plc (1986–97) and BG plc, 1997– . Records of many subsidiary companies, both UK and overseas, 1970s– .

Records of area gas boards and regions, 1949–92, (incomplete).

Major collections: Archives of the pre-nationalisation gas undertakings, 1812–1949, arranged on a regional basis and including collections transferred from the John Doran Gas Museum. Laboratory books from London Research Station/Watson House, 1930s–1960s.

Non-manuscript material: Large collection of technical drawings, gas works site plans and maps for most of the country, mid-19th century–1980s.

Extensive photographic collection of prints, slides and glass negatives of gas works, plant, personnel, showrooms and appliances (c500,000).

A large collection of retail and domestic appliance catalogues, advertising and retail material, early 20th century– .

Collection of co-partnership and company journals/magazines.

Large collection of films and videos.

Library of technical material, journals including *Gas Journal*, 1849– , papers of the Institute of Gas Engineers and other associations.

Finding aids: Most regional material and pre-nationalisation records listed, with catalogues in production.

Facilities: Photocopying, including map/plan copying up to A0 size. Microfiche/film reader/ printers.

Conservation: Contracted out.

Publications: S. Everard: *History of the Gas Light and Coke Company* (1949).
T. Williams: *A History of the British Gas Industry* (Oxford, 1981).
H. Barty-King: *New Flame: How Gas Changed the Commercial, Dramatic and Industrial Life of Britain, 1813–1984* (Tavistock, 1984).

885 Nazarene Theological College

Parent organisation: Church of the Nazarene

Address: Dene Road, Didsbury, Manchester M20 8GU

Telephone: (0161) 445 3063 ext. 212

Fax: (0161) 448 0275

E-mail: library@nazarene.ac.uk

Enquiries: The Librarian, Mrs Heather Bell

Open: Mon–Fri: 9.00–5.00, by appointment only.

Access: To any person with a relevant enquiry, by arrangement only.

The Church of the Nazarene was founded in 1906 and the Theological College in 1944. Any material relating to the Church in the British Isles is acquired, and personal papers of the Rev. Dr Jack Ford, 1908–80, are held. A card catalogue and subject lists are available. There are photocopying facilities and microfilm/fiche readers are available.

886 North West Film Archive

Parent organisation: Manchester Metropolitan University

Address: Minshull House, 47–49 Chorlton Street, Manchester M1 3EU

Telephone: (0161) 247 3097

Fax: (0161) 247 3098

E-mail: n.w.filmarchive@mmu.ac.uk

Website: www.mmu.ac.uk/services/library/west.htm

Enquiries: The Access Assistants, Liza Warren and Anoush Simai

Open: Mon–Fri: 9.00–5.00; viewings are by prior appointment only.

Access: Bona fide researchers, on an appointment basis and with staff assistance. A comprehensive search service is provided and a charge is made to commercial production companies.

Historical background: The North West Film Archive (NWFA) grew out of a research project into the history of the local film and cinema industry. It was established in 1977 by Manchester Polytechnic (now Manchester Metropolitan University) and the North West Arts Association (now North West Arts Board). The project concentrated on the location and acquisition of film that was made in or about the North-West of England. The success of this search, together with the demand for a documentary collection within the region and the urgent need for specialist preservation work, led to the establishment of a regional film archive.

Acquisitions policy: Documentary material about life in Lancashire, Cheshire and Greater Manchester. All film gauges are included and the archive also acquires master videotapes. The collection includes cinema newsreels, documentaries, promotional material, television programmes, home movies and other amateur footage.

Non-manuscript material: Films, 1896– , of local events and traditions such as Whit Walks; life at work, e.g. textile industry; leisure activities such as sport; holidaying throughout the region, particularly Blackpool; street scenes; life on the home front in the two world wars; local personalities, such as Gracie Fields.

Corporate collections include Co-operative Wholesale Society films and the Manchester Ship Canal Company Collection.

Extensive collections of television programmes from BBC North and Channel 4, with restrictions on access.

Copy photographs, taped interviews, posters, advertising material and ephemera on the north-west cinema industry.

Finding aids: Computerised database of *c*4000 titles within the film and video collection, by title, date, subject, place and producer. Also detailed shot lists for many.

Facilities: A range of specialised equipment for film, video and sound. Facility to transfer all film gauges to video tape to broadcast standard.

Conservation: All conservation work is undertaken in-house. Film copying is undertaken by external professional laboratories.

Publications: Moving Memories [Video series: compilation videos showcasing the archive's collections (4)].
M. Gomes: *The Picture House* (1988) [a photographic album of north-west film and cinema].

887 Portico Library and Gallery

Address: 57 Mosley Street, Manchester M2 3HY

Telephone: (0161) 236 6785

E-mail: emma.marigliano@theportico.org.uk

Website: theportico.org.uk

Enquiries: The Librarian, Emma Marigliano

Open: Mon–Fri: 9.30–4.30.

The Portico is a private subscription library dating from 1806. The archives are a comprehensive record of the library from its foundation, including minute books, annual reports, library acquisition and issue books, members' subscription books, letter-books and press cuttings. Any interested person may consult the archives and there is a detailed list available. See NRA 35387.

888 Royal Northern College of Music

Address: The Library, 124 Oxford Road, Manchester M13 9RD

Telephone: (0161) 907 5241

Fax: (0161) 273 7611

E-mail: rosemary.williamson@rncm.ac.uk

Website: www.library.rncm.ac.uk/libare.htm

Enquiries: The Librarian, Dr Rosemary Williamson

Open: Term: Mon–Thurs: 9.00–7.00; Fri: 9.00–5.00; Sat: 9.00–1.00.
Vacation: Mon–Fri: 10.00–1.00, 2.00–4.30.
Closed August.

Access: Generally open to the public, by appointment only.

Historical background: The RNCM was founded in 1972 from an amalgamation of the Royal Manchester College of Music (f. 1893) and the Northern School of Music (f. 1920).

Acquisitions policy: To maintain and consolidate the collections.

Archives of organisation: Royal Manchester College of Music archive, 1893–1973, including student registers, professors' attendance books, council minutes and correspondence.

Major collections: Correspondence of Sir Charles Hallé (1819–95), founder of RNCM (149 items).
Adolph Brodsky (1851–1929) Collection: autograph letters from contemporary musicians, including Tchaikovsky, Brahms, Grieg, Elgar, Busoni and Richter, as well as photographs (many signed), concert programmes and press cuttings relating to performances by Brodsky and the Brodsky Quartet.
Philip Newman (1904–66) Collection of letters, photographs, press cuttings and artefacts.
MS compositions of Alan Rawsthorne (1905–71).

John Ogdon (1937–89), manuscripts of compositions, mainly unpublished, by the pianist and former RNCM student.

Non-manuscript material: First editions of Handel, Gluck and other 18th-century music.
Hansen Collection of 20th-century Scandinavian music.
Henry Watson Collection of historical music instruments.
Halifax Collection of scores and piano music; Gordon Green collection of piano music.
Dame Eva Turner (1892–1990) Collection of songs with MS annotations.

Finding aids: Card catalogue. Computer catalogue. Collection-level descriptions and some catalogues available on website.

Facilities: Photocopying. Microfilm/fiche readers.

889 University of Manchester Institute of Science and Technology

Address: PO Box 88, Manchester M60 1QD

Telephone: (0161) 200 4946

Fax: (0161) 200 4941

E-mail: jbart@fs3.li.umist.ac.uk

Website: www.umist.ac.uk/umist_library

Enquiries: Ms Janet Barratt

Open: By arrangement.

Access: Bona fide researchers.

Historical background: Founded as the Manchester Mechanics' Institution in 1824, it was renamed Manchester Technical School in 1883 and Manchester Municipal School of Technology in 1902. It was incorporated as the Faculty of Technology in the University of Manchester in 1905, and renamed Manchester Municipal College of Technology in 1918 and Manchester College of Science and Technology in 1955. It was awarded a royal charter as an independent university in 1956 and became known as University of Manchester Institute of Science and Technology in 1966.

Acquisitions policy: Material to support the teaching and research of the institute.

Archives of organisation: Records of UMIST and its predecessors, 1824– ; some departments retain their own archives as well.

Major collections: Records of the National Federation of Building Trade Operatives, 1918–76.
Note-books and some correspondence of J.P. Joule (1818–89), scientist.

Non-manuscript material: Joule Collection: library of J.P. Joule.
UMIST theses.

Finding aids: Joule: NRA 9527.

Facilities: Photocopying. Microfilm/fiche reader/printers.

890 Mansfield Library

Parent organisation: Nottinghamshire County Council

Address: Four Seasons Centre, Westgate, Mansfield, Nottinghamshire NG18 1NH

Telephone: (01623) 627591

Fax: (01623) 629276

Enquiries: The Local Studies Librarian, Mr D. Crute

Open: Mon, Tues, Thurs: 9.00–6.30; Wed, Sat: 9.00–1.00; Fri: 9.00–5.30.

Access: Generally open to the public.

Acquisitions policy: Donations and deposits are accepted if donors are unwilling to let material out of the town; the Nottinghamshire Archives (entry 945) is the designated repository.

Major collections: Mansfield Borough and successor district diaries, 1892– , and council minutes, 1928– .
Note-books of Albert Sorby Buxton (1867–1932).
Correspondence of Joseph Whitaker (1850–1932).

Non-manuscript material: Photographs, slides, prints and picture postcards of Mansfield and environs, 1870– .
Parish registers up to 1900; census returns of Mansfield and nearby towns and villages in Nottinghamshire; local newspapers, 1846– ; wills made within the area of the Peculiar Court of the Manor of Mansfield, 1640–1857 (microform).
Oral history recordings with transcripts.

Finding aids: Archive material is catalogued, classified and indexed by subject. Nottinghamshire Archives have a list of major items. Place and subject index to photographs,

slides, prints and picture postcards on cards. Subject and place index to *Mansfield and North Nottinghamshire Advertiser*, 1871–1950. Card index to wills.

Facilities: Photocopying. Microfilm/fiche readers/printer.

Conservation: Work undertaken by Nottinghamshire Archive Office conservation unit.

Publications: The census returns have published surname indexes, compiled by the Nottinghamshire Family History Society.

891 Mining Records Office

Parent organisation: The Coal Authority

Address: 200 Lichfield Lane, Berry Hill, Mansfield, Nottinghamshire NG18 4RG

Telephone: (01623) 427162

Fax: (01623) 622072

Website: www.coal.gov.uk

Enquiries: The Manager, Mr D. Clarke

Open: Mon–Thurs: 9.00–4.30; Fri: 9.00–4.00, by appointment only.

Access: Generally open to the public. A room hire charge is levied for the inspection of geological and Coal Commission records. No charge is made for the inspection of abandonment plans.

Historical background: The statutory depositing of abandonment plans began with the Coal Mines Regulation Act 1872. The plans were kept in London until 1939, when, due to the war, they were transferred to Buxton. In the early 1950s the coal plans were split from the plans of minerals other than coal and placed in the custodianship of the National Coal Board under the terms of a memorandum of agreement. The Coal Authority took over custodianship on its formation in 1994, after which post-nationalisation records from all departments of the industry for England and Wales were transferred to the Public Record Office (see entry 1058) and certain pre-nationalisation records (up to 1947) were distributed to relevant county record offices. The office was previously known as the Central Coal Benefits Archive Centre.

Acquisitions policy: Plans are added to the collection on the completion of opencast sites or colliery closures. Active pursuit of information/plans to supplement existing collection is also ongoing.

Archives of organisation: Coal Commission records *re* transfer in ownership of coal prior to nationalisation (*c*26,500).
Ex-British Coal prospecting data of open cast holes (*c*1 million) and deep mine bores (*c*20,000).

Non-manuscript material: Coal abandonment plans 1872– (*c*100,000).
Microfilms of all plans.

Finding aids: All plans are catalogued by graticule square onto the old county reference system. Coal Commission and prospecting data researched by geographic area.

Facilities: Microfilm reader/printers.

Conservation: In-house conservation.

892 Margate Library
Local History Collection

Parent organisation: Kent County Council

Address: Cecil Square, Margate, Kent CT9 1RE

Telephone: (01843) 223626

Fax: (01843) 293015

Website: www.kent.gov.uk

Enquiries: The Local Studies Librarian, Beth Thomson

Open: Tues, Fri: 2.00–6.00; 1st Sat in month: 9.30–1.00, 2.00–5.00.

Access: Generally open to the public.

Historical background: The basis of the Margate Local History Collection was the bequest of a local antiquary, Dr Arthur Rowe, in 1926. It consisted of every kind of material relevant to the development of Margate, which he was researching in order to write and illustrate a parish history. The collection has continued to be augmented by purchases and donations.

Acquisitions policy: To acquire material relating to Margate, by purchase, donation and loan.

Major collections: Rowe MSS: part of Rowe Collection, documenting streets, buildings, local families, sea bathing, archaeology, 1900–20.
Pridden MSS: a description of the Isle of Thanet in Kent, by Rev. John Pridden, 1780–90,

including 100 original drawings; *c*100 letters of John Anderson relating to the founders of the Sea Bathing Hospital; pedigrees of Thanet families (copy on microfilm).
Edward White's MS extracts from Kent newspapers, archives, state and domestic papers, parish registers, gravestones; W.J. Mercer's scrapbooks and indexes, 1850–1900.

Non-manuscript material: Rowe Collection: more than 2000 items relating to Margate, including books, pamphlets, programmes, maps, illustrations, plans, photographs, bills, posters.
Parker Collection: more than 10,000 items relating to Kent, including books, pamphlets, maps, 7000 prints and 1000 illustrations.
Other items include press cuttings, illustrations and ephemera, scrapbooks covering Margate and Kent, photographs, postcards and many guide books and directories.

Finding aids: Catalogue. Some original indexes. The collection is being exhaustively recatalogued, with a computer index to the illustrations.

Facilities: Photocopying. Photography by arrangement. Microfilm readers/printer.

893 Fife Council Archive Centre

Address: Carleton House, Balgonie Road, Markinch, Fife KY6 7AH

Telephone: (01592) 416504/413256

Fax: (01592) 417477

E-mail: andrew.dowsey@fife.gov.uk

Enquiries: Archivist, Andrew Dowsey

Open: Mon–Fri: 9.00–5.00, by appointment.

Access: Generally open to the public

Historical background: Fife Council (formed in 1995 following the reorganisation of local government in Scotland) has inherited records from predecessor authorities including Fife Regional Council, North East Fife District Council, Dunfermline District Council, Kirkcaldy District Council, Glenrothes Development Corporation, Fife County Council and pre-1975 Fife Burgh Councils.

Acquisitions policy: Maintains local government records and seeks to acquire archives relating to the Fife area.

Archives of organisation: Mainly local authority records including: Commissioners of Supply records, 1709– ; records of Glenrothes Development Corporation, 1948–95; and burgh records for Culross, Dysart, Kinghorn, Kirkcaldy, Leslie.

Major collections: Papers of Rothes family of Leslie, c1645–1966.

Records of trade bodies, families and miscellaneous organisations.

Finding aids: Indexes.

Facilities: Photocopying.

Publications: A. Campbell: *The Archives of Fife*, Fife Family History Society.

894 Marlborough College

Address: Archives   Room,   Marlborough College, Marlborough, Wiltshire SN8 1PA

Telephone: (01672) 892401

Fax: (01672) 892207

Website: www.marlborough.org

Enquiries: The Honorary Archivist, T.E. Rogers

Open: By arrangement.

Access: Bona fide researchers, on written application. There is restricted access to personal files.

The college was founded in 1843 as an independent boarding school with a few day pupils. Girls were admitted to the sixth form in 1968 and the college has been co-educational since 1989. The archival collections were first organised in the 1950s and documents and memorabilia appertaining to the college and its former pupils are actively collected. There is extensive documentation of the foundation and earlier years of the college, including architectural drawings, and a large collection of pupils' reminiscences. A partial computerised index exists and photocopying is available. See T. Hinde: *Paths of Progress: a History of Marlborough College* (James and James, 1992); A.G. Bradley and J. Murray: *History of Marlborough College* (1893, 1923).

895 Derbyshire Libraries and Heritage Department
Local Studies Library

Parent   organisation: Derbyshire   County Council

Address: County Hall, Matlock, Derbyshire DE4 3AG

Telephone: (01629) 585579

Fax: (01629) 585049

E-mail: derbyshire.libraries@derbyshire.gov.uk

Website: www.derbyshire.gov.uk

Enquiries: The Librarian, Mrs Ruth Gordon

Open: Mon–Fri: 9.00–5.00; occasional Sats: 9.30–1.00. Appointments are essential for the use of microfilmed material.

Access: Generally open to the public. A paid research service is available.

Historical background: The Local Studies Department was originally housed in the Central Lending Library, St Mary's Gate, Derby. The collections were moved to Matlock in 1966 and housed in the branch library, and transferred to the county offices in 1969.

Acquisitions policy: To strengthen and enlarge existing primary and secondary collections on the county of Derbyshire.

Major collections: Peach Collection: MS and printed play, film and radio scripts of L. du Garde Peach (1890–1975), Derbyshire dramatist.

Barmasters Library: includes, in addition to printed material, MSS, account books and ledgers relating to lead-mining industry in Derbyshire, 1730–1915.

Non-manuscript material: Wolley MSS (British Museum Add. MSS 6666–6718), on microfilm, covering Derbyshire; MSS 6676–6686 relate to the Derbyshire lead-mining industry.

Census returns for Derbyshire and some small portion of surrounding counties, 1841–91 (on microfilm).

Derby Mercury, 1735–1800; *Derbyshire Times*, 1854– ; *Derbyshire Courier*, 1831–53; *High Peak News*, 1890–1959; *Matlock Mercury*, 1937– (on microfilm).

Illustrations covering all aspects of Derbyshire life (c2500).

Maps, historical and modern, of the county (various scales).

A wide range of genealogical research materials, including St Catherine's House indexes, 1837–1965; International Genealogical Index: Quaker registers, Roman Catholic registers (microfilm).

Finding aids: Various lists and indexes. Card index to Wolley MSS.

Facilities: Photocopying. Microfilm/fiche reader/printer.

Publications: Catalogue and Indexes of the British Museum Additional MSS 6676–6686 (Derbyshire County Library, 1977).
Derbyshire Local Studies Collections: a Guide to Resources (Derbyshire Library Service, rev. 1988).
Family History in Derbyshire (1994).
List of library publications available on request.

896 Derbyshire Record Office

Parent organisation: Derbyshire County Council

Address: New Street, Matlock, Derbyshire DE4 3AG
Correspondence address: County Hall, Matlock DE4 3AG

Telephone: (01629) 580000 ext. 35201; 585347 (searchroom)

Fax: (01629) 585144

Enquiries: The County Archivist, Dr Margaret O'Sullivan

Open: Mon–Fri: 9.30–4.45

Access: User registration is required, with proof of identity and address; an appointment is advisable. There is a charge for research services.

Historical background: Derbyshire Record Office was established in 1962, although archive collections had been acquired earlier. It is the Diocesan Record Office for the Diocese of Derby and is recognised as a place of deposit for public records and for manorial and tithe records.

Acquisitions policy: Archival material, of all types, of Derbyshire origin: official, ecclesiastical, industrial, business, family and estate.

Archives of organisation: Archives of Derbyshire County Council and its predecessors; ecclesiastical parishes in the diocese of Derby; superseded local authorities and institutions throughout Derbyshire.

Major collections: National Coal Board, Derbyshire colliery records of pre-vesting date.
Lead-mining and related records, 17th–19th centuries.
Engineering company records, late 18th–20th centuries.
Private deposits, including:
Estate papers of Harpur-Crewe of Calke, 12th–20th centuries.
Fitzherbert of Tissington papers, including Treby papers concerning the Titus Oates plot and papers of Lord St Helens (1753–1839), diplomat.
Gell of Hopton and Trustees papers, including civil war papers, 17th century.
Longsdon of Little Longstone papers, including textile manufacturing interest, 18th century.
Catton Hall archive, including political papers of Sir Robert Wilmot *re* Ireland, mid–18th century, and Sir Robert John Wilmot Horton *re* population, emigration and slavery, 1820s–1830s.

Non-manuscript material: Strutt Collection of printed Derbyshire topographical material, late 19th century.

Finding aids: Catalogues, card indexes, handlists. Lists sent to NRA.

Facilities: Photocopying. Photography. Microfilming. Microfilm/fiche readers/printers.

Conservation: In-house.

Publications: Handlist of Tithe Maps (1992).
Derbyshire Record Office Guide (2/1994).
List of Derbyshire Parish Registers (1998).
List of Derbyshire Non-Conformist Registers (1998).
Archives First (1994–) [series of introductions to Derbyshire Archives].
Annual Supplement to Record Office Guide (1995–).

897 National Tramway Museum
John Price Memorial Library

Parent organisation: Tramway Museum Society

Address: Crich, Matlock, Derbyshire DE4 5DP

Telephone: (01773) 852565

Fax: (01773) 852326

E-mail: ntm_library@online.rednet.co.uk

Website: www.tramway.co.uk

Enquiries: The Librarian, Mrs R. Thacker

Open: Mon–Fri: 9.00–5.00.

Access: Generally open to the public, by appointment.

Historical background: The Tramway Museum Society was formed in 1955 to preserve tramcars and associated material. The museum premises were acquired in 1959. The depots accommodate more than 70 horse, steam and electric tramcars. The library is housed in its own air-conditioned building.

Acquisitions policy: Material relevant to tramways, urban transport and LRT systems worldwide is acquired, by donation or bequest.

Archives of organisation: Records of the Tramway Museum Society, 1964– , including annual reports.

Major collections: Production records and official photographs of Edgard Allen Ltd, Sheffield, tramway equipment manufacturers.

Minutes of the Municipal Tramways and Transport Association and the Municipal Passenger Transport Association.

Records of transport operators, including those previously lodged with the Bus and Coach Council.

Archive of British Electric Traction (BET).

Non-manuscript material: Manufacturers and transport department drawings, including Maley & Taunton, Glasgow.

Large photographic collection, including R.B. Parr, N. Forbe, H.B. Priestley, M.J. O'Connor and H. Nicol.

Film archive (*c*400).

Postcard collection (*c*50,000).

Finding aids: Computer catalogue (not photographs). List sent to NRA.

Facilities: Photography. Photocopying. Microfilm reader.

Conservation: Digitising of photographs done in-house. Service available to other departments.

898 Society of the Holy Child Jesus
Provincial Archives

Parent organisation: Society of the Holy Child Jesus

Address: Convent of the Holy Child, Mayfield, East Sussex TN20 6PH

Telephone: (01435) 873575

Fax: (01435) 873575

E-mail: hforshaw1@yahoo.co.uk

Website: www.shcj.org

Enquiries: The Archivist, Sr Helen Forshaw

Open: By arrangement.

Access: Anyone with a genuine interest or connection.

Historical background: The Society of the Holy Child was established in 1846 by the Venerable Cornelia Connelly mainly as a teaching order. There are convents in the three provinces of Europe, Africa and the USA. The archive will probably be moved to a London location within the next few years.

Acquisitions policy: Records of the society's government and communities. When a convent closes all material relating to it is transferred.

Archives of organisation: General and provincial chapter minutes and communications.
Annals, compiled from the house diaries of each community.
Brief obituaries of sisters from all three provinces.

Non-manuscript material: Province newsletters.
Books and articles by or about members of the order.
Audio tapes; slides; photographs; films.
Books on women's orders.

Finding aids: Loose-leaf inventory.

Facilities: Limited photocopying.

899 Merthyr Tydfil Central Library

Address: High Street, Merthyr Tydfil, Mid Glamorgan CF47 8AF

Telephone: (01685) 723057

Fax: (01685) 370690

E-mail: library-service@merthyr.gov.uk

Enquiries: The Assistant Chief Officer (Libraries), Leisure and Amenities Department, Mr G.H. James

Open: Mon, Fri: 9.00–6.00; Tues: 9.00–7.30; Wed, Thurs: 9.00–5.30; Sat: 9.00–12.00.

Access: Generally open to the public. Material held at Dowlais Library is made available through staff at Merthyr Tydfil Central Library.

Historical background: The Central Library opened in 1935.

Acquisitions policy: Primary and secondary material relating to the Merthyr Tydfil area.

Archives of organisation: Borough Council minutes and County Borough Council and education minutes, 19th–20th centuries.

Major collections: Aberfan Disaster Archive, 1966– , original material from Merthyr Tydfil Borough Council and the Aberfan Disaster Fund (held at Dowlais Library) and a collection of material from local sources, including tribunal reports, newspaper articles, personal memories, photographs and monographs.
Rate books and rate account books of the iron masters, 19th century.
Dowlais Iron Company letters (held at Dowlais Library).
Archive of local author Horace Charles Jones.

Non-manuscript material: Photographic collection.
Maps, including OS maps of the Merthyr Tydfil area, 1832– , and later surveys.
Extensive collection of pamphlets and photocopied material.
Oral history collection; small collection of cine and video material.
Merthyr Express, 1864– ; *Merthyr Guardian,* 1833–74; *Western Mail,* 1960– ; *Merthyr Telegraph*; *Merthyr & Dowlais Times* (microfilm).
Census returns, 1841–91.
Bishops transcripts, 1717– , and chapel records, 1786–1837 (microfilm).
Register of electors, 1890– (incomplete).

Finding aids: Catalogue of Aberfan Disaster Archive (1997) available on www.nuff.ox.ac.uk/politics/aberfan/home.htm.
Material is filed by subject with a separate author/title index.

Facilities: Photocopying. Microfilm/fiche reader.

Publications: Guide to the Local History Collection (1976).
Bibliography (1982); *Supplement* (1984).

900 Claydon House

Parent organisation: Claydon House Trust

Address: Claydon House, Middle Claydon, Buckinghamshire MK18 2EY

Enquiries: The Archivist, Mrs Susan Ranson

Open: By arrangement.

Access: Bona fide researchers, by written application: a daily charge is made.

Historical background: Claydon House has been the home of the Verney family since the 17th century. It is now administered by the National Trust. A member of the Verney family lives in the house, and the archives are managed by a special trust set up for that purpose.

Acquisitions policy: To maintain the archives.

Archives of organisation: Verney family archives, including deeds, 12th century– , estate papers, and letters.
Correspondence of Sir Ralph Verney (1613–98) (microfilm copies at Buckinghamshire Records and Local Studies Service (see entry 37), the British Library (entry 561) and Yale University).

Major collections: Nightingale Papers: letters of the Nightingale family, 1796–1874; correspondence of Florence Nightingale (1820–1910) with Frances Parthenope Nightingale (later Verney) and other members of the Verney family, 1827–1910 (photocopies at the Wellcome Library, see entry 844).

Non-manuscript material: Maps and plans.

Finding aids: Catalogue available at Buckinghamshire Record Office and NRA.

Facilities: Photocopying.

Publications: F.P. Verney and M.M. Verney (eds): *Memoirs of the Verney Family,* 4 vols (1892–9; 1970) [relates to the 17th century].
M.M. Verney and P. Abercrombie: 'Letters of an Eighteenth Century Architect, Sir Thomas Robinson Bart., to Ralph, 2nd Earl of Verney', *Architectural Review,* lix (1926), 258–63; lx (1926), 1–3, 50–3, 92–3.

M.M. Verney (ed): *The Verney Letters of the Eighteenth Century, 1717 to 1799*, 2 vols (1930).
S. Goldie (comp.): *A Calendar of the Letters of Florence Nightingale* (Oxford, c1977; microfiche) [includes the Claydon House letters].

901 Teesside Archives

Address: Exchange House, 6 Marton Road, Middlesbrough TS1 1DB

Telephone: (01642) 248321

Fax: (01642) 248391

Enquiries: The Archivist, Mr D.H. Tyrell

Open: Mon, Wed, Thurs: 9.00–5.00; Tues: 9.00–9.00; Fri: 9.00–4.30.

Access: Generally open to the public. The office operates the CARN reader's ticket system. A paid search service is provided.

Historical background: The office was established in 1974 following the creation of Cleveland County, comprising the former county boroughs of Teesside and Hartlepool and parts of the former counties of Durham and the North Riding of Yorkshire. Since the abolition of Cleveland County Council in 1996, the service has been jointly run by the borough councils of Hartlepool, Middlesbrough, Stockton on Tees and Redcar, and Cleveland. The department acts as the Diocesan Record Office for York (Cleveland parish records), and is recognised as a place of deposit for public records.

Archives of organisation: Usual local authority record holdings.

Major collections: Deposited collections, all of purely local interest.

Non-manuscript material: Sound archives of Radio Cleveland, 1971– .

Facilities: Photocopying. Photography. Microfilm/fiche reader/printers, by arrangement.

Conservation: In-house facilities.

902 Rochdale Libraries
Local Studies Collection

Parent organisation: Rochdale Metropolitan Borough Council

Address: Middleton Area Central Library, Long Street, Middleton M24 6DU

Telephone: (0161) 643 5228

Fax: (0161) 654 0745

Enquiries: The Assistant Librarians, Mrs P.M. Elliott and Mrs M. Payne

Open: Mon: 10.00–7.30; Tues, Thurs, Fri: 10.00–5.30; Wed: 10.00–12.30; Sat: 9.30–1.00, 2.00–4.00.

Access: Open to the public.

Historical background: The dynamic growth of Rochdale, Middleton and Heywood during the 19th century produced a wealth of material relating to the area. Before 1974 the substantial local collections of Heywood, Middleton and Rochdale were located at the central libraries in those areas, and on local government reorganisation it was decided that each should retain a separate collection under the general supervision of a local studies librarian based at Rochdale.

Acquisitions policy: The collection of documentary material relating to all aspects of life in the Middleton area.

Major collections: Local administrative records: early administrative records, including highway rates, Poor Law administration and administrative material from the constituent authorities of the metropolitan borough, 19th century; includes Middleton Poor Book, 1838, and Suffield Rental, 1784.
Church records: church rates, leys, tithe commutation maps, plans, deeds etc.

Non-manuscript material: Complete runs of local newspapers, 1877– (originals and microfilm copies).
Books, pamphlets, audio-visual material, photographs, maps, plans, broadsheets, political handbills, theatre programmes.

Finding aids: Newspaper index.

Facilities: Photocopying. Microfilm/fiche readers/printer.

903 Open University Library

Address: Walton Hall, Milton Keynes, Buckinghamshire MK7 6AA

Telephone: (01908) 653138 ext. 53795

Fax: (01908) 653571

E-mail: m.barnes@open.ac.uk

Website: www.open.ac.uk/library

Enquiries: The Archivist, Michelle Barnes

Open: By arrangement with the Archivist.

Access: Bona fide researchers, by appointment only.

The Open University was founded in 1969. A professional archivist has been employed since 1999, and full searchroom facilities were established in 2001. Records of the Open University and working collections, personal papers and records of OU staff or other persons connected with the OU are acquired. At present the major collection consists of the personal papers of Jennie Lee, Baroness Lee of Asheridge (1904–88), including correspondence, articles and some political material. Photocopying is available.

904 Society of the Sacred Mission Archives

Parent organisation: St Antony's Priory, Durham

Address: SSM Priory, 1 Linfield Lane, Willen, Milton Keynes, Buckinghamshire MK15 9DL

Telephone: (01908) 234546

Fax: (01908) 234546

Enquiries: The Archivist

Open: By arrangement.

Access: On written application to the Archivist.

Historical background: The society, an Anglican religious community, was founded in 1893 by Fr Herbert Kelly (1860–1950). The archives were moved to Willen from Kelham, near Newark, in 1973.

Acquisitions policy: To maintain the archives of the society and the collections of papers of members of the society.

Archives of organisation: Administrative records of the society, 1890– , including student and other records of Kelham Theological College, 1891–1971.

Major collections: Personal and academic papers of Herbert Kelly (1860–1950), director, 1893–1910; David Jenks (1866–1935), director, 1910–20; Gabriel Hebert (1884–1963), 1884–1963; and Alfred Kelly (1872–1950).

Finding aids: Major revision in progress. Society of the Sacred Mission: NRA 26270.

905 Flintshire Library and Information Service

Parent organisation: Flintshire County Council

Address: Library HQ, County Civic Centre, Mold, Flintshire CH7 6NW

Telephone: (01352) 704400

Fax: (01352) 753662

E-mail: lawrence_rawsthorne@flintshire.gov.uk

Enquiries: The Head of Libraries and Archives, Mr L. Rawsthorne

Open: Mon–Fri: 9.00–5.00; Sat: 9.00–12.30.

Access: Generally open to the public; an appointment is recommended for viewing special collections.

The library comes under the unitary authority established in 1996. It holds a local history collection of books, pamphlets, journals, newspapers, maps, prints, a selection of photographs, oral history tapes, in Welsh and English, and ephemeral material relevant to Flintshire. In addition there is a substantial collection of printed material on the Arthurian legends (c2000 vols) and collections of works by and about Daniel Owen (1836–95), local novelist, and William Gladstone (1809–98).

906 Clogher RC Diocesan Archives

Address: Bishops House, Monaghan, Co. Tyrone

Enquiries: The Archivist

Open: Mon–Wed: 11.00–1.00.

Access: Bona fide researchers.

The archives house the papers of James Donnelly, Bishop of Clogher, 1864–93, and the parish baptismal and marriage records to 1880. Photocopying is available and microfilm copies and a catalogue are in the Public Record Office of Northern Ireland (entry 81).

907 Montrose Library Archive

Parent organisation: Angus Council

Address: 214 High Street, Montrose, Angus DD10 8HE

Telephone: (01674) 671415

Fax: (01674) 671810

E-mail: culmonarc@angus.gov.uk

Website: www.angus.gov.uk/history/
history.htm

Enquiries: The Local Studies Librarian/Archivist, Mrs Fiona Scharlau

Open: Mon–Fri: 9.30–5.00.

Access: An appointment is recommended.

Historical background: Angus District Council was established following local government reorganisation in 1975, taking over the functions of six former burghs and the former county council. In 1989 all archival material held by these burgh libraries was transferred to the Montrose Library and in 1996 all records were transferred to Angus Council. In addition Angus County Council records previously held by Dundee City Council were also transferred.

Acquisitions policy: Administrative, social, personal and economic records relating to the geographic boundaries of Angus District Council by transfer and donation.

Archives of organisation: Records of Angus County Council, 1718–1975; Angus District Council, 1975–96; Angus Council, 1996– .
Records of former burghs: Arbroath, 1530–1975; Brechin, 1672–1975; Carnoustie, 1884–1975; Forfar, 1666–1975; Kirriemuir, 1834–1975; Montrose, 1458–1975; Monifieth, 1890–1975.

Major collections: Council minutes, burgh correspondence and charters, 1232–1975.
Trades records for Arbroath, Brechin and Forfar, 16th–19th centuries.
Subscription library and trades library records for Arbroath, Brechin, Forfar and Montrose, 1810–1904.
Business records including R. & D. Duke, Brechin; J. & G. Paton, Montrose; Francis Webster, Arbroath; Carnoustie Co-operative Association, 1921–59; Arbroath Harbour Board, 1889–1975.
Local societies' records: Montrose Society, 1852– ; Montrose Female Society, 1817–24; Brechin Total Abstinence Society 1853–1963; St James Lodge of Gardeners, Brechin, 1784–1836; National Union of Boot and Shoe Operatives, Arbroath, 1886–1918; Forfar Young Women's Christian Association, 1838–66.
Personal papers, including William Baillie, Writer to the Signet, Montrose, 1777–95; J.M.

Barrie, 1860–1937; David Dakers Black, Town Clerk, Brechin, 1838–66; Frederick A. Ferguson, Town Clerk, Brechin, 1925–59; Andrew Jervaise, historian, Brechin, 1869–78; Margaret F. Mills, Montrose, 1910–45; David Waterson, artist, Brechin, 1930s.
Estate papers, including Speid of Ardovie, 17th century–1865; Scott of Commieston, 1703–1820; Wedderburn of Pearsie, 1833–56; Fowlis Easter Estate, 1839–91.
Genealogical collection: families of Binny, Forfar; Burns, Scotland; Duke, Brechin; Inglis, Lochlee & Edzwell; Seivwright, Arbroath.
Church records: Forfar Baptist Church, 1872–1926; Associate Congregation of Brechin, 1764–1868.
Records of schools throughout Angus, 1873–1975.

Non-manuscript material: Dean of Guild plans for Montrose, Forfar and Kirriemuir, Monifieth and Brechin.
Gravestone and other photographs and maps.

Finding aids: Lists for burgh collections, business records and miscellaneous collections. Name and subject index for miscellaneous collection, burgh and county council records.

Facilities: Photocopying. Microfilm/microfiche readers.

Conservation: Contracted out.

Publications: Angus Archives guide [leaflet].
Scottish Record Association datasheet no. 6 [leaflet].
House History [leaflet]
Burn the Witch! The Story of the Forfar Witches, 1660–1663.

908 Montrose Museum

Address: Panmure Place, Montrose, Angus DD10 8HE

Telephone: (01674) 673232

E-mail: montrose.museum@angus.gov.uk

Enquiries: The Curator, Mrs Rachel Benvie

Open: Mon–Sat: 10.00–5.00.

Access: Generally open to the public, on written application.

Historical background: The museum was built and opened by Montrose Natural History and

Antiquarian Society in 1842. Since 1975 it has been part of Angus District Libraries and Museums.

Acquisitions policy: Any local material for Montrose and Angus.

Major collections: Montrose Natural History and Antiquarian Society minutes, 1836–1951.
Payroll of Forfar & Kincardine Militia, 1803. Rifle Volunteer papers.
Miscellaneous local voluntary and friendly society records, 18th and 19th centuries.
Log of whaling ship *Snowdrop*, 1907.
Autograph collection includes Sir Walter Scott (1771–1832); Alfred, Lord Tennyson (1809–92); Richard Chenevix Trench (1807–86); William Harrison Ainsworth (1805–82); Alex Burness ('Bokhara Burness') (1805–41); Joseph Bonaparte; Admiral Sir Charles Napier (1786–1860).

Non-manuscript material: Local maps and plans, 17th–19th centuries.
Local photographs.

Finding aids: Index of Montrose Natural History and Antiquarian Society members, 1836–1931.

Facilities: Photocopying by arrangement.

909 Northumberland Archive Service

Morpeth Records Centre

Parent organisation: Northumberland County Council, Amenities Division

Address: The Kylins, Loansdean, Morpeth, Northumberland NE61 2EQ

Telephone: (01670) 504084

Fax: (01670) 534521

Website: www.swinhope.demon.co.uk/genuki/nbl

Enquiries: The Senior Archivist, Mrs S. Wood, Northumberland Archive Service, Newcastle upon Tyne (see entry 920)

Open: Mon, Wed, Fri: 9.30–1.00, 2.00–5.00; Tues: 9.30–1.00, 2.00–8.00.

Access: Generally open to the public. Records in microform are available only in this form; advance booking of a microfilm reader is essential.

Historical background: Opened in 1989 as a modern records centre, part of the building was converted to an archive strongroom and small public searchroom in 1991 to house certain classes of archives formerly held at Newcastle upon Tyne. The searchroom was further extended in 1994 to allow sources on microfilm to be transferred. The office is recognised as a place of deposit for public records and as a Diocesan Record Office for Newcastle, which is mostly coterminous with the boundaries of Northumberland before 1974 but includes a small part of Cumbria. Principal classes of archives are now divided between the two offices, while there is a branch office at Berwick upon Tweed (entry 87) which provides a comprehensive service for North Northumberland.

Archives of organisation: Usual local authority holdings, comprising records of the county council and other past and present local authorities, ecclesiastical records and public records.

Major collections: Deposited local collections.

Finding aids: Catalogues and lists.

Facilities: Photocopying. Photography and microfilming by arrangement.

Publications: List of genealogical publications available.

910 Motherwell Heritage Centre

Parent organisation: North Lanarkshire Council

Address: 1 High Road, Motherwell ML1 3HU

Telephone: (01698) 251000

Fax: (01698) 253433

E-mail: motherwellheritagecentre@compuserve.com

Enquiries: The Local Studies Librarian, Margaret McGarry

Open: Mon–Wed, Fri, Sat: 10.00–5.00; Thurs: 10.00–7.00.

Access: Generally open to the public.

Historical background: The local history collection has been growing and developing since the opening of Motherwell Public Library in 1906. All relevant materials were transferred to the newly built Motherwell Heritage Centre in 1996. Focusing on the historical, social and political life of the community since the beginnings of industrialisation in the mid-nineteenth century, the collection also reflects the changes in the administration of the area. The Burgh of Motherwell amalgamated with the Burgh of Wishaw in 1920, leading in turn to the formation of Motherwell District Council in 1975 and the establishment of North Lanarkshire Council in 1997.

Acquisitions policy: Historical material relating to the area within the boundaries of North Lanarkshire Council.

Archives of organisation: Minutes of police commissioners of the burgh of Motherwell, 1864–1900; commissioners of the burghs of Motherwell and Wishaw, 1931–60; Motherwell District Council 1975–96; North Lanarkshire Council, 1997– .

Major collections: Lord Hamilton of Dalzell Collection of books and MSS, including several relating to the Owenite Orbiston community experiment.

Non-manuscript material: Hurst Nelson Collection of photographs of rolling stock. Microfilms of old parish records and census returns and complete runs of local newspapers. Large collection of photographs, historical and OS maps relating to the local area. Motherwell Football Club database. Videos and oral history tapes.

Finding aids: Indexes to *Motherwell Times*, 1883–1983, *Wishaw Press*, 1873–1984, Hurst-Nelson collection of photographs, 1851 census (various parishes in Lanarkshire).

Facilities: Photocopying. Microform reader/printer.

Publications: List available.

911 Henry Moore Foundation

Address: Dane Tree House, Perry Green, Much Hadham, Hertfordshire SG10 6EE

Telephone: (01279) 843333

Fax: (01279) 843647

E-mail: archive@henry-moore-fdn.co.uk

Website: www.henry-moore-fdn.co.uk/hmf/research.htm

Enquiries: Alice Beckley

Open: Mon–Fri: 10.00–1.00, 2.00–5.00, by appointment only.

Access: Bona fide researchers, who should complete an appointment application form.

Historical background: The object of the Henry Moore Foundation, set up in 1977, and generously endowed by Mr Moore, is 'to advance the education of the public by the promotion of their appreciation of the fine arts and in particular the works of Henry Moore'. The foundation established the Henry Moore Institute in 1982 (see entry 499).

Acquisitions policy: To maintain the collection.

Major collections: Letters to and from Henry Moore, 1917–86.

Finding aids: Cataloguing and indexing in progress.

Facilities: Photocopying or photography may be permissable by special request.

912 Much Wenlock Town Council

Address: The Corn Exchange, Much Wenlock, Shropshire TF13 6AE

Telephone: (01952) 727509

Enquiries: The Town Clerk

Open: No regular opening. Any time can be arranged after reasonable notice.

Access: Bona fide researchers.

Historical background: The Borough of Wenlock was founded by charter in 1468. The Corn Exchange is recognised as a place of deposit for public records. Early borough records as well as court and parish records are now at the Shropshire Records and Research Centre (see entry 113).

Archives of organisation: Borough and town council records, including minutes, 1892– .

Major collections: Records of Agricultural Reading Society and Olympian Society, which led to modern Olympic Games, 1840– .

Non-manuscript material: Penny Brookes Herbarium.

Finding aids: Card index.

Facilities: Photocopying.

913 Nelson Library

Parent organisation: Lancashire County Council Education and Cultural Services Directorate

Address: Market Square, Nelson, Lancashire BB9 7PU

Telephone: (01282) 692511

Fax: (01282) 603166

Enquiries: The Reference Librarian

Open: Mon, Tues, Thurs, Fri: 9.30–5.00; Wed: 9.30–7.00; Sat: 9.30–4.00.

Access: Generally open to the public.

Historical background: The collection relates specifically to the present area of Pendle district, with emphasis on the western half of the area. See also Colne Library (see entry 254) and Barnoldswick Library (see entry 49).

Major collections: Council minutes, 1864– . Rate books; census enumerators' returns, 1841–91.

Non-manuscript material: Usual local history collection, including local newspaper files, 1863– ; maps, 1848– ; directories, 1814– . Microfilm of parish registers, 1599– .

Facilities: Photocopying. Microfilm/fiche readers.

Publications: Guide to Lancashire Local Studies Collections (1998), 124–9.

914 British Horological Institute

Address: Upton Hall, Upton, Newark, Nottinghamshire NG23 5TE

Telephone: (01636) 813795/6

Fax: (01636) 812258

E-mail: clocks@bhi.co.uk

Website: www.bhi.co.uk

Enquiries: The Institute Secretary, Mrs H. Bartlett

Open: Mon–Fri: 9.00–1.00, 2.00–5.00.

Access: Members. Others by special concession only.

The British Horological Institute is a founder horological society of the world, established in 1858. It moved to Upton in 1972. It retains the archives of the institute as well as a substantial number of MSS, including the Louis Baume Archives and a collection on the history of clock and watch manufacture.

915 Newark Museum

Parent organisation: Newark and Sherwood District Council

Address: Appletongate, Newark, Nottinghamshire NG24 1JY

Telephone: (01636) 655740

Fax: (01636) 655745

E-mail: museums@newark-sherwooddc.gov.uk

Website: www.newark-sherwooddc.gov.uk

Enquiries: The Museums and Heritage Manager, Ms Melissa Hall

Open: (April–Sept) Mon–Wed, Fri–Sat: 10.00–1.00, 2.00–5.00; Sun: 2.00–5.00.

Access: Generally open to the public; an appointment is always necessary to consult the archives.

Historical background: Established in 1912 as the museum of the borough of Newark, the collection passed, under local government reorganisation in 1974, to the Newark and Sherwood District Council. Newark Borough records have been transferred to Nottinghamshire Archives (entry 945).

Acquisitions policy: Acquisitions consist of ephemera circulated in the district, items relating to local government and local material.

Major collections: Usual local history collection, principally of non-MS material.

Non-manuscript material: W.N. Nicholson & Sons Ltd, agricultural engineers, Newark: printed catalogues, photographs and negatives, c1860–1967.
Negatives and photographs of the locality.
Negatives of illustrations from the *Newark Advertiser*, 1949– .
Pamphlets of local interest.

Finding aids: Place-name, subject, biographical and author indexes.

Facilities: Photocopying. Photography. Microfilm/fiche reader.

916 Borough Museum and Art Gallery

Parent organisation: Newcastle under Lyme Borough Council

Address: Brampton Park, Newcastle under Lyme, Staffordshire ST5 0QP

Telephone: (01782) 619705

Fax: (01782) 626857

E-mail: nulmuseum@newcastle-staffs.gov.uk

Enquiries: The Museum and Arts Officer, Delyth Copp

Open: Mon–Sat: 10.00–5.30; Sun: 2.00–5.30.

Access: Bona fide researchers, by appointment.

Historical background: The museum was founded in 1943, and the borough archives were deposited at that time.

Acquisitions policy: Continues to acquire borough records and related material, mostly directly from the council.

Archives of organisation: Borough council records, including minute books of council meetings, lists of burgesses (electors), electoral registers, rate books, reports of medical officers of health, minute books of court cases, 14th century– .
Archives of the borough museum, including accession registers, correspondence, committee resolutions, policies, 1943– .

Major collections: Miscellaneous documents relating to local history, 17th century– .

Non-manuscript material: Staffordshire and Newcastle maps, 18th–19th centuries.
Some plans of buildings erected or acquired by the council.
Large photographic collection (duplicated at Newcastle Library).
Town directories.

Finding aids: Subject and author indexes.

Facilities: Photocopying.

Conservation: Contracted out.

917 Hancock Museum

Natural History Society of Northumbria

Parent organisation: University of Newcastle upon Tyne

Address: Barras Bridge, Newcastle upon Tyne NE2 4PT

Telephone: (0191) 222 7418

Fax: (0191) 222 6753

E-mail: hancock.museum@newcastle.ac.uk

Enquiries: The Curator, S.G. McLean

Open: Mon–Fri: 10.00–5.00.

Access: Any bona fide enquirer.

Historical background: The Natural History Society of Northumberland, Durham and Newcastle upon Tyne was founded in 1829 as an offshoot of the Literary and Philosophical Society of Newcastle upon Tyne (entry 918). The society's museum included donations made to the parent society, but was founded on the private collections of Marmaduke Tunstall (1743–90) of Wycliffe and George Allan (1736–1800) of Darlington. The museum was administered solely by the society until the later 1950s, when the University of Newcastle began to provide financial support. The university took overall control in 1974, and since 1992 the Hancock Museum has been administered by Tyne and Wear Museums under an agreement.

Acquisitions policy: Archives relating to natural history and natural history collections in northern England.

Archives of organisation: Archives relate principally to the Natural History Society and the scientific achievements of its members; also letters and documents about the Hancock Museum and the Tyneside Naturalists Field Club.

Major collections: Many collections of papers, including those of Joshua Alder (1792–1867); Thomas Belt (1832–78); Thomas Bewick (1753–1828); R.B. Bowman (1808–82); G.S. Brady (1832–1921); H.B. Brady (1835–91); Abel Chapman (1851–1929); Albany Hancock (1806–73); W.C. Hewitson (1806–78); P.J. Selby (1788–1867); N.J. Winch (1768–1838).

Finding aids: Partly catalogued: lists available on site.

Facilities: Photocopying. Photography.

Publications: Natural history collections listed in P. Davis and C. Brewer: *A Catalogue of Natural Science Collections in North-East England*, North of England Museums Service (Durham, 1986).

918 Literary and Philosophical Society of Newcastle upon Tyne

Address: 23 Westgate Road, Newcastle upon Tyne NE1 1SE

Telephone: (0191) 232 0192

Fax: (0191) 261 2885

E-mail: litphil.library@btinternet.com

Enquiries: The Librarian, Pat Southern

Open: Mon, Wed–Fri: 9.30–7.00; Tues: 9.30–8.00; Sat: 9.30–1.00.

Access: Generally open to the public; an appointment is desirable.

Historical background: The society was founded in 1793, since when it has had a major role in all scientific, industrial, literary, antiquarian and literary movements in the North-East.

Archives of organisation: Minutes, reports etc, 1793– .

Major collections: Northern Arts MS Collections: works by most of the region's living writers, especially poets and dramatists, including Thomas Bewick, Edward Bond, Basil Bunting, Tony Harrison, Tony Jackson and Alan Plater.
The Douglas W. Dickenson Collection: material relating to the history of the Northern Architectural Association.

Non-manuscript material: Early scientific and technological material.
Local collection, including a large number of pamphlets, local maps and plans.
Mordern Tower Poetry Reading posters.
Newcastle University theatre programmes.

Facilities: Photocopying subject to the librarian's consent.

Publications: R.S. Watson: *The History of the Literary and Philosophical Society of Newcastle upon Tyne, 1793–1896* (1897).
C. Parish: *The History of the Literary and Philosophical Society of Newcastle upon Tyne,* vol. 2, 1896–1989 (1990).
J. Phillipson (ed.): *Literary and Philosophical Bicentenary Lectures* (1994).
S. Harbottle: *The Reverend William Turner: Dissent and Reform in Georgian Newcastle upon Tyne* (1997).

919 Newcastle upon Tyne Local Studies Library

Address: City Library, Princess Square, Newcastle upon Tyne NE99 1DX

Telephone: (0191) 277 4100

Fax: (0191) 261 1435

Enquiries: The Local Studies Librarian

Open: Mon, Thurs: 9.30–8.00; Tues, Wed, Fri: 9.30–5.00; Sat: 9.00–5.00.
Closed Saturdays preceding bank holiday Mondays.

Access: Generally open to the public. An appointment is necessary to consult the Pease (Bewick) Collection in its entirety.

Historical background: The Mechanics' Institute formed the basis of the central library. The collection was founded in 1884 to include all local material (books, photographs, archives etc). In recent years most of the archives have been transferred to the appropriate record offices.

Acquisitions policy: Any printed works, photographs, maps, audio and video recordings on Northumberland, Durham and Tyne and Wear, with special emphasis on Newcastle upon Tyne.

Major collections: Mechanics' Institute minute books, 1834– .

T. and G. Allan Collection: Tyneside song MSS, 1860s.

Seymour Bell Collection, part of a collection compiled by the Bell family of Newcastle and Gateshead during their work as booksellers and land surveyors. It includes plans, inventories of properties, valuations, correspondence, surveys and auctioneers' notices relating to estates in Newcastle and Northumberland, late 18th–early 20th centuries (25 portfolios).

T. Bell material about the River Tyne, 1844–50; papers relating to printing, 19th century.

Literary and other correspondence of Wilfred Gibson, poet, 1930–44.

Gowland MSS relating to estates and collieries in Durham, early 18th century (4 vols).

MSS of Joe Wilson, songwriter, c1850s.

Letters relating to Durham collieries, 1838–57 (c100).

Early letters and papers relating to the Stockton and Darlington Railway.

Patent library, including UK patent abridgements, 1617– , and specifications 1924– ; USA abridgements, 1954– .

The C.P. Taylor Collection: includes scripts etc written by the local playwright C.P. Taylor (1929–81) (146 folders).

Non-manuscript material: Pease (Bewick) Collection: books, engravings, wooden blocks, toolbox of Thomas Bewick (1753–1828) and his pupils, 1753–1882.
Illustrations and photographs (*c*70,000).
Street plans and early maps.
OS maps from 1st edn to current.

Finding aids: Card catalogue.

Facilities: Photocopying. Microfilm/fiche reader/printers.

Conservation: Contracted out.

Publications: Bewick Collection Catalogue.
List of Parish Register Transcripts.
Fact sheets and user guides.

920 Northumberland Archive Service

Parent organisation: Northumberland County Council, Education Directorate, Amenities Division

Address: Northumberland Record Office, Melton Park, North Gosforth, Newcastle upon Tyne NE3 5QX

Telephone: (0191) 236 2680

Fax: (0191) 217 0905

Website: www.swinhope.demon.co.uk/genuki/ nbl

Enquiries: The Senior Archivist, Mrs S. Wood

Open: Wed: 9.30–1.00, 2.00–8.00; Thur–Fri: 9.30–1.00, 2.00–5.00.

Access: Generally open to the public. Records that have been microfilmed are normally available only in this form. A paid research service is available.

Historical background: In 1957 a county records committee was appointed, which established a record office in the Moothall, Newcastle, in 1958. The record office moved to a former anti-aircraft operations centre in North Gosforth in 1962. It is recognised as a place of deposit for certain classes of public records and as a Diocesan Record Office for Newcastle, which is mostly coterminous with the boundaries of Northumberland before 1974. Since the opening of other repositories for Northumberland, the principal classes of archives are split between the offices at Melton Park and Morpeth (see entry 909), while there is a branch record office at Berwick upon Tweed (see entry 87) which offers a comprehensive service for North Northumberland. Melton Park remains the administrative centre for Northumberland Archives Service.

Archives of organisation: Usual local authority record holdings.

Major collections: Deposited local collections, principally family, estate and business archives, including the following of special significance:
Records of the North of England Institute of Mechanical and Mining Engineers, including records of the London Lead Company (f. 1692), with interests in the North Pennines and North Wales, 17th–20th centuries.
Butler (Ewart) MSS, 17th–20th centuries; includes papers relating to the social reformer Josephine Butler.
Ridley (Viscount Ridley) MSS, 16th–20th centuries: includes correspondence relating to national policies, late 19th century.
Culley (agricultural improvers) MSS: includes correspondence with leading agriculturalists in the UK, 18th–19th centuries.
Records of the Society of Antiquaries of Newcastle upon Tyne: includes part of the Bell Collection of plans and valuations relating to Northumberland, 18th–20th centuries.

Non-manuscript material: Extensive photographic collections include those of J.P. Gibson of Hexham (1838–1912) and the Blankenburgs Collection: landscape and forestry in the area of Kielder forest and reservoir, *c*1947–71.

Finding aids: Detailed catalogues and place, personal name and subject index cards. Lists sent to NRA.

Facilities: Photocopying. Photography. Microfilming.

Conservation: Contracted out.

Publications: List of genealogical publications available.

921 Tyne and Wear Archives Service

Address: Blandford House, West Blandford Square, Newcastle upon Tyne NE1 4JA

Telephone: (0191) 232 6789

Fax: (0191) 230 2614

E-mail: twas@dial.pipex.com

Website: www.thenortheast.com/archives/index.html

Enquiries: The Chief Archivist, Ms E.A. Rees
The Project Director, Northern Region Film &
TV Archive, Chris Galloway

Open: Mon, Wed–Fri: 9.00–5.15; Tues: 9.00–8.30.
Documents required for Tuesday evening must
be ordered before lunchtime that day.

Access: Generally open to the public. A paid
research service is available. Booking is
required for microfilm readers.

Historical background: The service is jointly
run by the five metropolitan districts which
formerly made up Tyne and Wear County:
Gateshead (lead authority), Newcastle upon
Tyne, North Tyneside, South Tyneside and
Sunderland. It is recognised as a place of deposit
for public records.

Acquisitions policy: To secure the preservation
of significant archives relating to the Tyne and
Wear area, even when the records may not
relate primarily to activities in the area.
Film and videotape material produced in, or
relating to, the social, economic, industrial and
political history of the North-East, both amateur and professional productions.

Archives of organisation: Usual local authority
record holdings.

Major collections: Deposited collections, some
of which have a wider significance, including:
Papers of Sir W.G. Armstrong & Co. (later
Armstrong Whitworth, then Vickers), Elswick,
Newcastle upon Tyne, relating to engineering
and armaments, 1847–1981.
Papers of Sir Joseph Wilson Swan about the
invention of incandescent electric light bulbs,
the improvement of photographic processes
etc, 1863–1959.
Joseph Cowen, politician and newspaper pro-
prietor, correspondence, 1833–1937.
Messrs Merz & McLellan, Newcastle, consulting engineers; reports, minutes, specifications,
photographs, 1900–47.
Sir Charles Parsons' plans of the *Turbinia*,
1893–1904.
A.J. Fenwick Collection of circus material,
1773–1974.

Messrs Ralph Beilby and Thomas Bewick,
Newcastle engravers, financial records, 1752–
1881.
Associated Lead Manufacturers Ltd, papers,
1780–1980.
Records of most of the former shipbuilding
firms of the Tyne and the Wear, 19th–20th centuries.

Non-manuscript material: North East Region
Film and Television Archive incorporating the
collections of Trade Films Ltd (formerly
Northern Film & Television Archive), including National Coal Board films, 1947–83, with
photocopies of material from the NCB production files; North-East Development Council
films, 1966–74; Trade Film productions, 1981–;
home movies; collection of film material produced during the Miners' Strike, 1984–5.
Photographic archive, including the nationally
significant collection of Turner Film and
Photographic, Newcastle upon Tyne.

Finding aids: User guides on various topics
available on website, or by mail free of charge.
Lists sent to NRA.

Facilities: Photocopying. Photography.
Microfilming. Microfilm/fiche reader/printer.

Conservation: In-house service for all types of
archive conservation.

*Publications: Guide to Sources for Family
Historians at Tyne & Wear Archives Service.*

922 University of Newcastle upon Tyne
The Robinson Library

Address: Newcastle upon Tyne NE2 4HQ

Telephone: (0191) 222 7671

Fax: (0191) 222 6235

E-mail: lib-specenq@ncl.ac.uk

Website: www.ncl.ac.uk/library/speccoll/
spechome.html

Enquiries: The Special Collections Librarian,
Dr Lesley Gordon

Open: Mon–Fri: 9.15–4.45 (Special Collections
Reading Room).

Access: By appointment and written application
to the Special Collections Librarian.

Historical background: The university has a
complicated history, involving the College of

Medicine (f. 1834) and the College of Physical Science (f. 1871). At first part of the University of Durham, the Newcastle colleges, after several changes of name, became in 1963 the independent University of Newcastle upon Tyne. The Gertrude Bell photographic archive is housed in the university. The originals are kept by the library, but copies are available for viewing in the Department of Archaeology (University of Newcastle upon Tyne, Newcastle upon Tyne NE1 7RU), where all enquiries should be addressed.

Acquisitions policy: Selective strengthening of MS and printed materials.

Major collections: Papers of four Trevelyans: Sir Walter Calverley (1797–1879), Sir Charles Edward (1807–86), Sir George Otto (1838–1928), Sir Charles Philips (1870–1958).
Papers of Robert Spence Watson (1837–1911), political and educational reformer; Walter Runciman, 1st Viscount Runciman of Doxford (1870–1949), politician; Bernard Bosanquet (1848–1923), philosopher; Helen Bosanquet (1860–1925), social reformer; Gertrude Bell (1868–1926), traveller; Frederick Whyte (1867–1941), publisher, translator and biographer of W.T. Stead and William Heinemann; Jack Common (1903–68), novelist and journalist; Mary Moorman (1905–94), biographer of Wordsworth, including letters from her father, G.M. Trevelyan (1876–1962), historian; Sid Chaplin (1916–86), writer.
Travel diaries and book MSS of Thomas Hodgkin (1831–1913), historian.
Musical MSS of Charles Villiers Stanford (1852–1924).

Non-manuscript material: Robert White Collection, notably English and Scottish literature, border history and ballads.
Election ephemera, chapbooks and broadsides, 19th century.
Newcastle Cathedral books.
Burman Collection of Alnwick printed books.
Joseph Cowen tracts on political, social and economic topics.
Hindson-Reid Collection of 19th-century Newcastle woodblocks.
Thomas and John Bell's material on the northeast book trade.
Pybus History of Medicine Collection.

Finding aids: Series of catalogues of Trevelyan papers. Catalogue of Chaplin papers in preparation. Handlists or indexes of the Bosanquet,

Whyte, Common and Hodgkin material. Lists sent to NRA.
Gertrude Bell website: www.gerty.ncl.ac.uk/home/index.htm.

Facilities: Photocopying. Photography. Microfilm equipment.

Conservation: In-house service. Outside work undertaken by arrangement with the Conservation Unit (see: www.ncl.ac.uk/bindery/bindhome.html).

Publications: B.C. Raw: *Lives of the Saints: a Description of MS.1 in the University Library* (Newcastle upon Tyne, 1961).
S. Hill, L. Ritchie and B. Hathaway (comps): *Catalogue of the Gertrude Bell Photographic Archive* (Newcastle upon Tyne, 2/1965).
W. C. Donkin: *The Letters and Papers of Gertrude Bell: a List* (1966).
J.S. Emmerson (comp.): *Catalogue of the Pybus Collection of Medical Books, Letters and Engravings, 15th–20th Centuries, Held in the University Library, Newcastle upon Tyne* (Manchester, 1981).
C.J. Hunt: 'Scottish Ballads and Music in the Robert White Collection', *Bibliothek*, v (1983), 138–41.
Special Collections Guide (1994) [also available on the library webpage].

923 University of Northumbria

Address: Library Building, Sandyford Road, Newcastle upon Tyne NE1 8ST

Telephone: (0191) 227 4125 (direct line)

Fax: (0191) 227 4563

E-mail: kate.duggan@unn.ac.uk

Website: www.unn.ac.uk/central/isd

Enquiries: The Assistant Director, Information Services

Open: Term: Mon–Thurs: 9.00–9.00; Fri: 9.00–7.00; Sat: 9.30–5.00; Sun: 11.00–5.00.
Vacation: Mon, Wed–Fri: 9.00–5.00; Tues: 9.00–9.00.

Access: Generally open to the public by prior application.

Newcastle Polytechnic was founded in 1969 incorporating three predecessor colleges: the Rutherford College of Technology, the Regional College of Art and Design and the College of Commerce. It became a university in 1992. The library holds the Thomson

Newspaper Archive, comprising cuttings, 1900–81, with particular emphasis on the 1970s; and the Visual Arts (UK) Archive, including minutes and correspondence of the various organisation which set up the Year of the Visual Arts in the north of England in 1996.

924 National Horseracing Museum

Address: 99 High Street, Newmarket, Suffolk CB8 8JL

Telephone: (01638) 667333

Fax: (01638) 665600

Website: www.nhrm.co.uk

Enquiries: The Curator, Mr Graham Snelling

Open: Tues–Sat: 10.00–5.00; Sun: 12.00–4.00. Closed December to March.

Access: Generally open to the public, on written application. An appointment is necessary.

Historical background: The national horseracing museum is an independent museum which was opened in 1983. Its regency building is an integral part of racing history, being adjacent to the Jockey Club. The archives were established at the time of opening.

Acquisitions policy: Material relating to racing, including racing calendars, paintings, memorabilia and books.

Major collections: Archives of the Jockey Club, early 19th century– .
Small collections of memorabilia of famous jockeys, including Sir Gordon Richards (*b* 1904), Stephen Donoghue (1884–1945), Fred Archer (1857–86).

Non-manuscript material: Heber's Turf Calendar, 1763– , and Stud Books (2nd edn) c1750– .
Large collection of photographs of jockeys and horses, 1880s– .
Watercolours, prints and films.

Finding aids: Handwritten index and register. Jockey Club archives to be computerised.

Facilities: Photocopying. Photography by arrangement.

925 Newport Libraries

Address: Central Library, John Frost Square, Newport, Gwent NP20 1PA

Telephone: (01633) 211376

Fax: (01633) 222615

E-mail: central.library@newport.gov.uk

Enquiries: The Information Librarian, Ian Evans

Open: Mon–Wed: 9.30–6.00; Thurs: 9.30–5.00; Fri: 9.00–6.00; Sat: 9.30–5.00.

Access: Generally open to the public.

Historical background: Newport Public Library opened in 1870. An extensive general reference library and local collection was built up over 100 years. In 1974 much archival material was transferred to Gwent County Record Office (entry 272).

Acquisitions policy: MSS are occasionally acquired, by donation only.

Major collections: Chartist riots, verbatim reports of trials affecting Newport and district (30 vols).
Mary Delany (1700–88), correspondence with well-known figures of the day, including Fanny Burney (1752–1840).
Correspondence of Sir Charles Hanbury Williams (1708–59), satirist and diplomat, 1750s.

Non-manuscript material: Maps.

Finding aids: Card catalogues.

Facilities: Photocopying. Microfilm reader.

926 Isle of Wight County Record Office

Address: 26 Hillside, Newport, Isle of Wight PO30 2EB

Telephone: (01983) 823820/1

Fax: (01983) 823820

E-mail: record.office@iow.gov.uk

Website: www.dina.clara.net/iowfhs/recoffic.htm

Enquiries: The County Archivist, Mr Richard Smout

Open: Mon: 9.30–5.00; Tues–Fri: 9.00–5.00; Wed (1st in each month) 5.00–7.30, by appointment.

Access: Generally open to the public. Booking is required for microform readers.

Historical background: The record office was founded in 1958. It acts as the Diocesan Record Office for Portsmouth (Isle of Wight parish records), and is recognised as a place of deposit for public records.

Acquisitions policy: Archival material relating to the Isle of Wight and its inhabitants.

Archives of organisation: Usual local authority record holdings.

Major collections: Deposited local collections, including estate papers of Oglander family of Nunwell, *c*1200–20th century, and the Barrington/Simeon families of Swainston, 14th–20th centuries.

Non-manuscript material: Photographs/postcards relating to the Isle of Wight, *c*1860– .

Finding aids: Extensive personal names index to parish register entries pre-1900. Catalogues and indexes. Lists sent to NRA.

Facilities: Photocopying. Microfilm/fiche reader/printer.

Conservation: Contracted out.

Publications: Hampshire Archivists Group: *Poor Law* (1970); *Transport* (1973); *Education* (1977).
P.D.D. Russell (ed.): *The Hearth Tax Returns for the Isle of Wight, 1664–1674*, Isle of Wight Record Series, vol. 1.
S.F. Hockey (ed.): *The Cartulary of Carisbrooke Priory*, Isle of Wight Record Series, vol. 2.
——: *The Charters of Quarr Abbey*, Isle of Wight Record Series, vol. 3.

927 Scottish Mining Museum Archives

Parent organisation: The Scottish Mining Museum Trust

Address: Lady Victoria Colliery, Newtongrange EH22 4QN

Telephone: (0131) 663 7519

Fax: (0131) 654 1618

E-mail: enquiries@scottishminingmuseum.org

Website: www.scottishminingmuseum.com

Enquiries: The Curator

Open: Mon–Sun: 10.00–5.00.

Access: Generally open to the public, by appointment only. Study times are not identical to those of the museum.

Historical background: The Scottish Mining Museum Trust was formed in 1984 to co-ordinate previous efforts which had started in the early 1970s. The museum is based at a 90-year-old colliery which closed in 1981. The main source of the collection has arisen from the relatively rapid decline of the industry in recent years. The library's core holdings are from the now-closed Hood School of Mining, Heriot Watt University.

Acquisitions policy: To collect both artefacts and archival material recording the history of Scottish coal-mining, its life and times from the discovery of coal to the present day.

Major collections: National Coal Board/British Coal Corporation, annual reports and accounts, technical specifications, 1947– .
National Union of Mineworkers (Scottish Area) McDonald Memorial Collection, including Miners Federation of GB/NUM annual reports and minutes, 1900– ; Scottish executive committee minutes, 1945– , closure consultation minutes, 1950–70.
Royal commissions on the coal industry, 1842–1940.
Annual reports of the Mines Inspectors (national and divisional), 1900– ; Inspectors' incident reports, 1920– .
Lothian Coal Company archives, including ledgers, 1889–1947.

Non-manuscript material: Technical drawings, pictures, photographs, maps.
Tape-recordings.
Official government and union publications, including annual reports of NUM and MFGB.
Trade catalogues.

Finding aids: Catalogues are in preparation.

Facilities: Photocopying. Limited photography.

Conservation: Contracted out.

Publications: *A Short History of Mining in Scotland.*

928 Robert Owen Memorial Museum

Address: The Cross, Broad Street, Newtown, Powys SY16 2BB

Telephone: (01686) 626345

Fax: (01686) 626345

E-mail: johnd@robert-owen.midwales.com

Website: www.robert-owen.midwales.com

Enquiries: The Hon Curator, Mr John Hatton Davidson

Open: By arrangement.

Access: Students by prior appointment.

Historical background: The museum was founded in 1929 in memory of Robert Owen (1771–1858), industrialist and social reformer.

Acquisitions policy: Material relating to the life and work of Robert Owen and his associates.

Archives of organisation: Records of the Robert Owen Museum and its precursor committee, 1920-, and of the Robert Owen Statue Committee.

Major collections: Some letters and papers of Robert Owen, including collected letters on spiritualism; and of George Jacob Holyoake (1817–1906).

Non-manuscript material: Portraits of Owen and his associates; prints and photographs of places associated with Owen; books by and about Owen and his associates.

Finding aids: Ordered schedule of collection and indexes.

Facilities: Photography by arrangement.

Conservation: Contracted out.

929 North Yorkshire County Record Office

Address: Malpas Road, Northallerton, North Yorkshire DL7 8TB
Correspondence: County Hall, Northallerton, North Yorkshire DL7 8AF

Telephone: (01609) 777585

Fax: (01609) 777078

Website: www.northyorks.gov.uk/education/archives.shtm

Enquiries: The County Archivist, Mr M.Y. Ashcroft

Open: Mon, Tues, Thurs: 9.00–4.45; Wed: 9.00–8.45; Fri: 9.00–4.15.

Access: Generally open to the public, by appointment. The majority of records are made

available on microfilm. Research services are available.

Historical background: The present office was established in 1974 with local government reorganisation; previously the office had covered the old North Riding area. The first archivist was appointed in 1949, although records had been collected from 1938. The office acts as a Diocesan Record Office for Bradford, Ripon and York (parish records), and is recognised as a place of deposit for public records.

Acquisitions policy: Records relating to North Yorkshire.

Archives of organisation: Usual local authority record holdings.

Major collections: Deposited local collections.

Non-manuscript material: Includes some photographs; printed maps (e.g. Ordnance Survey maps).

Finding aids: General and detailed guides (available for purchase); lists in Search Room; major lists in NRA; indexes to parish registers.

Facilities: Photocopying. Photography. Microfilming. Microfilm reader/printer.

Conservation: In-house.

Publications: A list of publications is available.

930 Northampton Museum

Parent organisation: Northampton Borough Council

Address: Guildhall Road, Northampton NN1 1DP

Telephone: (01604) 238548 ext. 5104

Fax: (01604) 238720

E-mail: museums@northampton.gov.uk

Website: www.northampton.gov.uk/museums

Enquiries: The Keeper of the Boot and Shoe Collection, Sue Constable

Open: Mon–Sat: 10.00–5.00; Sun: 2.00–5.00.

Access: Generally open to the public, on application and by appointment.

Historical background: The County Museum was established in 1865. Since 1873 it has collected objects related to shoes and shoemaking worldwide, though the greater part of the collection still relates to shoes as worn in the UK and the history of shoemaking in Northamptonshire.

Acquisitions policy: Objects related to the history of Northampton, and in the shoe department to continue to acquire material related to the history of shoes and shoemaking worldwide.

Major collections: Accounts and account books; apprenticeship indentures; documents relating to shoe unions, and education; shoe designs, mostly 19th century.

Non-manuscript material: Pictures, prints and photographs of shoemakers, factory exteriors, shoe shops and transport.
Shoe price lists and catalogues; shoe tool and machinery catalogues, handbooks, c1870–c1930.
Advertisements.

Finding aids: Card indexes of the above. Card indexes of shoemakers, bucklemakers, lastmakers, machinery makers. History of shoemaking by Northamptonshire parishes. NRA 22281.

Facilities: Photocopying. Photography.

Publications: J.M. Swann: *Catalogue of Shoemaker Pictures and Works of Art* (1975).

931 Northamptonshire Record Office

Address: Wootton Hall Park, Northampton NN4 8BQ

Telephone: (01604) 762129

Fax: (01604) 767562

E-mail: archivist@nro.northamptonshire.gov.uk

Website: www.nro.northampshire.gov.uk

Enquiries: The County Archivist

Open: Mon–Wed: 9.00–4.45; Thurs: 9.00–7.45; Fri: 9.00–4.15; Sat (2nd in month): 9.00–12.15.
Office may close 1.00–2.00 without prior notice; documents required for Thursday evenings, Saturday mornings and weekdays, 12.00–2.00, should be ordered in advance.

Access: Generally open to the public.

Historical background: The Northamptonshire Record Society founded and ran the record office from 1920 to 1951, when it was taken over by a joint archives committee. In 1972, it came under the administration of Northamptonshire County Council. The office also acts as the Diocesan Record Office for Peterborough and is recognised as a place of deposit for public records.

Acquisitions policy: Official and private archives relating to Northampshire and the former Soke of Peterborough, pre-1974.

Archives of organisation: Usual local authority record holdings, including Quarter Sessions, c1520– .

Major collections: A wide range of important family archives of which the following have more than local significance:
Annaly (Holdenby): Diaries of the 1st Lord Dover, 1814–33.
Cartwright (Aynhoe): Diplomatic papers of Sir Thomas Cartwright, 1833–50, and Sir Fairfax Cartwright, 1900–12; correspondence and diaries of William Cornwallis Cartwright, 1860–1915.
Ellesmere (Brackley): Bridgewater estate and canal accounts, 1759–1806.
Elwes (Great Billing): Records of Admiral Rye, 1791–1815, despatch books of Charles Fitzgerald, Governor of Gambia, 1844–51.
Finch Hatton: Genealogical, historical and literary collections of Sir Christopher Hatton, letter books of the 2nd Earl of Nottingham, 1702–04, papers of the 1st Lord Hatton and 1st Viscount Hatton as governors of Guernsey, 1662–72, papers relating to the gardens at Kirby, 1685–86, poems of Anne Finch, Countess of Winchelsea.
Fitzwilliam (Milton): Correspondence, 1514–1864, including letters of Sir William Paget to the Duke of Somerset, 1547–49, and letters of Edmund Burke, 1764–97. Papers of Sir William Fitzwilliam as Governor in Ireland, 1558–99; architectural plans of Milton.
Isham (Lamport): Correspondence and diaries, 1563–1824, including correspondence of Sir Justinian Isham and Bishop Brian Duppa, 1650–60.
Knightley (Fawsley): Charters, 12th century– , diaries of Louisa, Lady Knightley, 1856–1913.
Montagu (Broughton): Letter books, 1537–1758, including those of the Duke of Shrewsbury, 1694–1700. Papers of the 2nd Duke of Montagu as Master General of the Ordnance, 1742–9.
Scott (Broughton): Naval records and photograph albums of Admiral Lord Charles Scott, 1853–86.

Spencer of Althorp Collection, including charters, deeds and court rolls, mainly for Bedfordshire, Northamptonshire, Surrey and Warwickshire, mid-12th–20th centuries.

Westmoreland (Apethorpe): Account book for the household of Edward, Duke of York, 1409–10; Fotheringhay College accounts, 1469–1535; papers of Sir Walter Mildmay as Under Treasurer of England, 1567–89; household account books, 1593–6, 17th century.

Letters of Warren Hastings to J.P. Auriol, 1802–18.

Diaries of John Clifton, carpenter, of Oundle, 1763–84.

Finding aids: Catalogues, sent to NRA.

Facilities: Photocopying. Photography and microfilming (subject to delays). Microfilm/fiche readers/printers.

Conservation: In-house.

Publications: C.R. Chapman: *Tracing Ancestors in Northamptonshire: Local, Social and Family History* (1994).

932 Northamptonshire Studies Collection

Parent organisation: Northamptonshire Libraries and Information Service

Address: Central Library, Abington Street, Northampton NN1 2BA

Telephone: (01604) 462040

Fax: (01604) 462055

Website: www.northamptonshire.gov.uk

Enquiries: The Subject Specialist: Local Studies, Mr T. Bracher

Open: Mon: 9.30–8.00; Tues–Fri: 9.30–7.00; Sat: 9.30–4.00.

Access: Generally open to the public; an appointment is necessary to see the John Clare Collection.

Historical background: The amalgamation of local collections at Northampton and Northamptonshire County Libraries led to the establishment of the collection in its present form in 1974.

Acquisitions policy: To collect and preserve all printed and photographic material on Northamptonshire, its footwear and leather industry, and on John Clare.

Major collections: John Clare (1793–1864): collection of MSS, with his library; books and cuttings.

Beeby Thompson Geological Collection: files and volumes of published papers on geology and water supply of Northamptonshire.

Sir Henry Dryden (1818–99) Collection: drawings and plans of churches and buildings in UK and Europe (several thousand).

Non-manuscript material: Charles Bradlaugh (1833–91) Collection: works by and about him, portraits, illustrations, posters and news cuttings.

Northamptonshire Studies Collection: illustrations; photographs, including glass and celluloid negatives; engravings and printed maps (14,000).

Newspaper files, including *Northampton Mercury*, 1720– .

Large collection of books, theses and journals on leather and footwear.

Finding aids: Indexes. Catalogues of Dryden and Clare Collections: NRA 14253 and 10984.

Facilities: Photocopying. Photography. Microfilm reader/printer.

Publications: Catalogue of the John Clare Collection in the Northampton Public Library (Northampton, 1965); Supplement (1971).

933 Northwich Library

Parent organisation: Cheshire Libraries and Archives

Address: Witton Street, Northwich, Cheshire CW9 5DR

Telephone: (01606) 44221

Fax: (01606) 48396

E-mail: northwich.infopoint@cheshire.gov.uk

Website: www.cheshire.gov.uk/library/northwch.htm

Enquiries: The Group Librarian, Sheila Scragg

Open: Mon, Tues: 9.30–5.00; Wed, Sat: 9.30–1.00; Thurs, Fri: 9.30–7.00.

Access: Generally open to the public. Booking is necessary for the microform readers and Internet.

Historical background: The public library dates from 1885, and there has always been a small local history collection for reference use.

Acquisitions policy: Donation and purchase of material relating to the history of Northwich and district, and selected material more broadly on Cheshire.

Major collections: Usual local history collection, comprising MS material (1.5 metres), microfilm (390 rolls), printed maps (*c*555), photographs, printed vols (*c*1200).

Non-manuscript material: Northwich Guardian, 1861– ; *Northwich Chronicle,* 1885– (incomplete); census returns (Northwich area), 1841–91, and parish registers, 1558–1903 (microfilm).

Finding aids: County-wide local studies computer database.

Facilities: Photocopying. Photography by arrangement. Microfilm/fiche readers.

Conservation: Contracted out to Cheshire and Chester Archives and Local Studies Service (see entry 236).

934   London Bible College

Address: Green Lane, Northwood, Middlesex HA6 2UW

Telephone: (01923) 826061

Fax: (01923) 836530

E-mail: library@londonbiblecollege.ac.uk

Enquiries: The College Librarian, Alan Linfield

Open: Mon–Fri: 9.00–5.00, by appointment only.

Access: Bona fide scholars and researchers engaged in academic study. Due to limited space, access is usually restricted to vacations for those outside the college.

The London Bible College is the largest international theological college in Western Europe, founded in 1943. The library has been built up steadily over the years and now boasts a collection of *c*40,000 books, making it one of the best collections of academic theology in the UK, being particularly strong in biblical theology. It holds mainly publications, but also some tape-recordings and videos relating to academic theology and contemporary Christianity, and the personal papers of Dr Donald Guthrie (1916–92).

935   Bridewell Museum

Parent organisation: Norfolk Museums Service

Address: Bridewell Alley, Norwich, Norfolk NR2 1AQ

Telephone: (01603) 667228

Fax: (01603) 614018

Enquiries: The Assistant Keeper of Social History, Mr John Renton

Open: Mon–Sat: 10.00–5.00.

Access: Bona fide researchers by appointment.

Historical background: Bridewell Museum opened as a museum of local trades and industries in 1925.

Acquisitions policy: Acquires material relating to trades and industries of the city of Norwich and immediate suburbs.

Major collections: Costing, design and order books relating to Norwich textile industry, *c*1790–1950s.
Boston pawnbrokers, Norwich, pledge registers, *c*1930s–1960s.
Prescription books, registers, correspondence relating to named East Anglian pharmacies.

Non-manuscript material: Photographic prints (3800) and glass negatives (1700) of local topography, trades and industries, commerce and retailing.
Small number of oral history tapes.
Printed trade catalogues and ephemera.

Finding aids: Manual catalogue and computerised records.

Facilities: Photocopying.

Conservation: Contracted out to Conservation Department, Norwich Castle Museum (see entry 940).

936   CGNU plc Group Archive

Parent organisation: CGNU plc

Address: 8 Surrey Street, Norwich, Norfolk NR1 3NG

Telephone: (01603) 840498/687280

Fax: (01603) 840499

E-mail: anna_stone@cgnu.net

Enquiries: The Group Archivist, Anna Stone

Open: Archive: Mon–Fri: 10.00–5.30.
Museum: by appointment.

Access: Bona fide researchers, on written application and at the discretion of the Archivist and/or Company Secretary.

Historical background: The Norwich Union Fire Insurance Society was established in 1797 and the Life Insurance Society in 1808, both by Thomas Bignold. The Life Insurance Society acquired the Amicable Society (f. 1706) in 1866 and the share capital of the Fire Office in 1925. Other major UK acquisitions include Scottish Union and National (f. 1824) and Norwich and London Accident Insurance (f. 1856). The Norwich Union was demutualised in 1997.

Commercial Union was established in 1861 following a meeting of merchants opposed to increases in fire insurance premiums after the Tooley Street fire in June 1861. A life department was established in 1862 and a marine department in 1863. By the 1890s business was being conducted in over 20 countries. Several American companies were taken over following the San Francisco earthquake of 1906. Major UK acquisitions include Hand-in-Hand (f. 1696), West of England (f. 1807), North British and Mercantile Insurance Co. (f. 1809) and Northern Assurance (f. 1836). European acquisitions include Delta Lloyd in 1973, L'Epargne de France in 1984 and Groupe Victoire in 1994. Commercial Union was incorporated as a plc in 1990. CGNU plc group was formed in 2000 with the merger of Norwich Union and CGU, a company itself formed following the merger in 1998 of Commercial Union and General Accident. Major archival collections of some subsidiaries are held at Guildhall Library (see entry 624), the Mitchell Library Glasgow (entry 393), and Aberdeen University (entry 5). West of England records are held at Devon Record Office (entry 365).

Acquisitions policy: Material relating to the group and its associated companies, and to the Bignold family.

Archives of organisation: Archives, including board minute books, policy records and claims registers, of Norwich Union Life and Fire Insurance societies, 1821– ; Commercial Union, 1861– ; General Accident, 1885– ; Amicable Society, 1706- – ; Hand-in-Hand, 1696– ; Yorkshire Insurance, 1924– ; Provident Mutual, 1871– ; and other acquired companies.

Non-manuscript material: House magazine photographs, 1886– ; advertising ephemera and other memorabilia; firemen's uniforms and equipment.

Finding aids: Database.

Facilities: Photocopying.

Conservation: Contracted out.

Publications: R. Bignold: *Five Generations of the Bignold Family* (1948).
R.J. Ryan: *A History of Norwich Union Fire and Life Insurance Society, 1797–1914* (1982).
J. Mantle: *Norwich Union – The First 200 Years* (1997).
E. Living: *Century of Insurance: the CU Group 1861–1961* (1961).
B. Henham: *Hand-in-Hand: the Story...1696–1996* (1996).
P. Young: *A Premium Business: a History of General Accident* (1999).
F.H. Sherriff: *Provident Mutual Life Assurance Association: from Then... ... Till Now* (1940).
A. Champness: *A Century of Progress: the General Life Assurance Company* (1937).

937 History of Advertising Trust

Address: Hat House, 12 Raveningham Centre, Raveningham, Norwich, Norfolk NR14 6NU

Telephone: (01508) 548623

Fax: (01508) 548478

E-mail: archive@hatads.org.uk

Website: www.hatads.org.uk

Enquiries: The Secretary, Michael Cudlipp
The Archive Manager, Margaret Garrod

Open: Mon Fri: 9.00–5.00, by arrangement.

Access: Bona fide researchers, by appointment only.

Historical background: The trust, a registered charity, was set up in 1978 as an educational foundation to encourage and sponsor the serious study of all aspects of the growth and development of advertising. It is recognised internationally as a prime source of historical research on British print advertising, and its rapidly growing collection of more than one million unique images and artefacts dates from the 1800s. Its extensive library dates from the 19th century. There are research facilities and an information service, as well as exhibitions and publications. The trust has a membership scheme which is open to the public.

Acquisitions policy: Records of organisations connected with advertising; advertising material in general, including advertising proofs, research background to campaigns, competitive press and magazine advertising, artwork, television commercials, point of sale material, early commercial television records and rate cards, posters and historic company records.

Major collections: Collections from the Advertising Association, Association of Independent Radio Contractors, Institute of Practitioners in Advertising, Institute of Public Relations, and other national bodies; also from major advertising agencies, e.g. Charles Barker Group, Ogilvy & Mather and J. Walter Thompson Co.
Advertising material from major companies, including H.J. Heinz, Hovis and Selfridges.

Non-manuscript material: Pearl and Dean cinema commercials.
Selective record of advertisements in various two-dimensional pictorial forms: posters, cards, slides, transparencies, filmstrips, video cassettes etc.
Specialised library on the history of advertising.

Finding aids: Lists and indexes. Computer catalogue. Select bibliography of the history of advertising (available on request).

Facilities: Photocopying. Photography and colour scanning by arrangement.

Publications: T.R. Nevett: *Advertising in Britain: a History* (Heinemann, 1982).
B. Henry (ed.): *British Television Advertising: the First 30 Years* (Century Benham, 1986).
Journal of Advertising History.
Monthly newsletters and *Hatnews Extra* (twice yearly).

938 John Innes Centre

Parent organisation: John Innes Foundation and Biotechnology and Biological Sciences Research Council (BBSRC)

Address: Norwich Research Park, Colney, Norwich, Norfolk NR4 7UH

Telephone: (01603) 452571 ext. 2674/2676

Fax: (01603) 456844

E-mail: elizabeth.stratton@bbsrc.ac.uk

Website: www.jic.bbsrc.uk/history/archives/index.htm

Enquiries: The Archivist, Miss E.A. Stratton

Open: Mon–Fri: 9.00–5.00.

Access: Any interested person, by appointment only.

Historical background: The centre was previously known as the John Innes Institute, which merged with the Cambridge Laboratory and the Nitrogen Fixation Unit to form the present organisation. From 1910 to 1981, when the archives section was established, the archives were in the care of the librarian.

Acquisitions policy: All material pertaining to the history and work of the John Innes Centre. Also material concerning the Innes family, the history of the Plant Breeding Institute, Cambridge, and the history of genetics.

Archives of organisation: Administrative, scientific and historical records of the institute, 1910– .

Major collections: Note-books, original and copy letters of William Bateson (1861–926), pioneer geneticist and first director, 1910–26.

Letters and papers of the Innes family.

Papers relating to the work of the Plant Breeding Institute, Cambridge.

Haarland and Hutchinson collections on the genetics of cotton.

Genetical Society archives.

Non-manuscript material: John Innes Rare Botanical Books: early botanical books and herbals, 1536– .

History of genetics library (c6000 vols).

Finding aids: Card and computer catalogues of John Innes archive collections.

Computer catalogues of Bateson letters (see also NRA 2554) and history of genetics library.

Catalogue of John Innes Rare Books.

Facilities: Photocopying. Photography. Microfilm/fiche readers/printer.

Publications: R.D. Harvey: 'The William Bateson Letters at the John Innes Institute', *Mendel Newsletter*, no. 25 (Nov 1985).

R.D. Harvey: 'Pioneers of Genetics: a Comparison of the Attitudes of William Bateson and Erwin Baur to Eugenics', *Notes and Records Royal Society of London*, 49/1 (1995), 105–17.

JIC Annual Reports, 1910– .

939 Norfolk Record Office

Address: Gildengate House, Anglia Square, Upper Green Lane, Norwich, Norfolk NR3 1AX

Telephone: (01603) 761349

Fax: (01603) 761885

E-mail: norfrec.nro@norfolk.gov.uk

Website: http://archives.norfolk.gov.uk

Enquiries: The County Archivist, Dr John Alban

Open: Mon–Fri: 9.00–5.00; Sat: 9.00–12.00.

Access: Generally open to the public. The office operates the CARN reader's ticket system. There is a limited paid research service, and also transcription and translation services.

Historical background: The office was founded in 1963, taking over from the archives department of Norwich Public Libraries. It acts as the Diocesan Record Office for Norwich and Ely (deaneries of Feltwell and Fincham) and is recognised as a place of deposit for public records. The previous building was severely damaged by fire in 1994 but no records were lost. The record office will move to new purpose-built premises adjacent to County Hall during 2003.
The Borough of King's Lynn archives are stored at the Regalia Rooms, Saturday Market Place, King's Lynn PE30 5DQ, but arrangements to see them there should be made in advance with the record office.

Acquisitions policy: Records of historical significance relating to the county of Norfolk, excluding mainly photographic and audiovisual material.

Archives of organisation: Usual local authority record holdings, including records of the City of Norwich and Norwich diocesan records.

Major collections: Deposited local collections, including:
Norwich Cathedral archives to 1900.
Estate and family records, including Hobart of Blickling; Meade of Earsham; Ketton-Cremer of Felbrigg; Bulwer of Heydon; le Strange of Hunstanton; Wodehouse of Kimberley; de Grey of Merton; Hare of Stow Bardolph.
Literary MSS of Sir Henry Rider Haggard (1856–1925) and Ralph Hale Mottram (1883–1971).

Music and other MSS of Dr William Crotch (1775–1847) and musicological notes of Dr Arthur Henry Mann (1850–1929).
Antiquarian collections of Harry Bradfer-Lawrence (*d* 1965), Walter Rye (*d* 1929) and the Colman family.

Finding aids: Lists and card indexes of archives received or catalogued since 1963; lists and card catalogue of MSS held by Norwich Public Libraries pre-1963. Lists sent to NRA.

Facilities: Photocopying. Photography. Microfilming. Microfilm/fiche readers/printer.

Conservation: In-house service; some work contracted out.

Publications: P. Rutledge: *Guide to the Great Yarmouth Borough Records* (1973).
Norfolk Record Office Guide to Genealogical Sources (3/1993).
F. Meeres: *A Guide to the Records of Norwich Cathedral* (1998).

940 Norwich Castle Museum

Parent organisation: Norfolk Museums Service

Address: Castle Museum, Norwich, Norfolk NR1 3JU

Telephone: (01603) 493624

Fax: (01603) 765651

Website: www.norfolk.gov.uk/tourism/museums

Open: By appointment.

Access: Bona fide researchers, by prior arrangement.

Historical background: The original museum was opened in 1825. After Norwich Castle ceased to be the county prison in 1887 it was converted to a museum and opened in 1894. Since 1974 the museum has been part of the Norfolk Museums Services.

A Archaeology

Telephone: (01603) 493630

Enquiries: The Keeper of Archaeology, Dr John Davies

Acquisitions policy: To collect material relating to the archaeology of Norfolk.

Archives of organisation: County excavation archives.

Major collections: Collection of historical manuscripts.

Helmington Breviary, a medieval English liturgical manuscript.

Archives relating to Norwich Castle as a jail, including minute books, jailers' and surgeons' journals, visitors books, death warrants and chapel books, 19th century– .

Woodward papers and correspondence.

Non-manuscript material: Collection of county maps, historical photographs.

Finding aids: Indexes; some material on computer database.

Facilities: Photocopying. Microfiche reader.

B Art

Telephone: (01603) 493633

Fax: (01603) 493661

Enquiries: The Curator & Keeper of Art, A.W. Moore
The Assistant Keeper of Art, Norma Watt

Acquisitions policy: To acquire material relating to art in Norfolk, i.e. on artists, works of art, collections, with particular emphasis on the Norwich School of Artists.

Major collections: Correspondence, account books, treatises, notes by artists, mainly of Norwich School.

Minute books of Norfolk Contemporary Art Society and Norwich Art Circle.

Papers of R.J. Colman (1861–1946) including James Reeve manuscript catalogues relating to Norwich School artists; Col. E.A.E. Bulwer (1834–1934) relating to teapot collection.

Non-manuscript material: Small number of photographs and printed ephemera relating to Norwich School artists and Decorative Art collections.

Facilities: Photocopying. Photography by arrangement.

C Natural History

Telephone: (01603) 493647

Enquiries: The Keeper of Natural History, Dr A.G. Irwin

Acquisitions policy: To acquire items and documents relating to the natural history and geology of Norfolk and build up a supporting library for reference.

Archives of organisation: Annual reports, accessions registers.

Major collections: Papers of E.A. Ellis (1909–86); S.A. Manning (*d*1993); R. Gurney (1879–1950), including Sutton Freshwater Laboratory work.

Collections of letters, journals, etc, mostly from naturalists working or resident in the county of Norfolk, including M.E. Fountaine (1862–1940) and H. Stevenson (1833–88).

Non-manuscript material: Large collection of reprints, long runs of local natural history society publications, E.A. Ellis collections of 35 mm colour transparencies.

Finding aids: Catalogue in progress.

Facilities: Photocopying. Photography by arrangement. Microfiche reader.

941 University of East Anglia

A Archive Collections

Address: The Library, University of East Anglia, Norwich, Norfolk NR4 7TJ

Telephone: (01603) 593492

Fax: (01603) 259490

E-mail: d.n.sharpe@uea.ac.uk

Website: www.lib.uea.ac.uk/libinfo/archives/ archives.htm

Enquiries: The Curator, Archive Collections

Open: Mon–Fri: 9.30–4.30.

Access: Generally available to scholars. Prior written application is advised. A paid research service is available.

Historical background: The archive collections are housed in the university library, which opened to readers in 1963. Collection of MSS and related material began in 1981 with the transfer from the English Faculty Library, Cambridge University, of the Library of Contemporary Cultural Records, subsequently renamed the Holloway Collection of Modern Cultural Records in honour of its founders, John Holloway, Professor of Modern English at Cambridge, and his wife Joan, formerly librarian of the English Faculty. In recent years papers of former UEA staff and alumni have also been accepted.

Acquisitions policy: Continuing development of the Holloway Collection; collection of material relating to the history and work of the university. Acceptance of other donations or deposits can be considered only where there is a close relationship with existing collections or with the university's teaching and research programmes. Copies of the full policy statement can be supplied.

Archives of organisation: The bulk of the university records are not yet open to researchers.

Major collections: Holloway Collection: ephemera representative of the arts and media in their institutional aspects, 1965– , with emphasis on regional and local activity.

Papers of Lord Zuckerman (1904–93), anatomist and government scientific adviser, including material on medical/biological research, civil defence research and air operations planning in World War II, and post-war science policy.

Papers of John Pritchard (1899–1992), engineer and furniture-maker, including records of the Isokon Company and correspondence relating to architecture and design, with special reference to the work of ex-Bauhaus designers in Britain.

Papers of Anne and Jessie Kenney, suffragettes, including correspondence and MSS writings, suffragette newspapers, photographs, cuttings and memorabilia.

Personal papers of former staff and alumni.

Non-manuscript material: Local theatre memorabilia collection.

Pamphlets, posters, photographs, film, video, news cuttings and microscope slides.

Some maps, plans and microforms.

Finding aids: On-line catalogues of Zuckerman and Pritchard papers; printed guide to Pritchard papers.

Descriptive brochures and handlists. Lists sent to NRA.

Facilities: Photocopying. Scanning. Microfilm/fiche readers/printer. Video facility.

Conservation: Contracted out.

Publications: B. Gillies, M. St John, and D. Sharp: *The Pritchard Papers: a Guide* (UEA, 1998).

B East Anglian Film Archive

Address: University of East Anglia, Norwich, Norfolk NR4 7TJ

Telephone: (01603) 592664

Fax: (01603) 458553

E-mail: eafa@uea.ac.uk

Website: www.uea.ac.uk/eafa

Enquiries: The Director, David Cleveland
The Deputy Director, Jane Alvey

Open: By arrangement.

Access: Historians, programme makers, students and the general public.

Historical background: Established in 1976, the East Anglian Film Archive (EAFA) was the first regional film archive in the UK. It aims to collect and preserve moving images relating to East Anglia and to provide a service of access and presentation where copyright allows. EAFA is a non-profit making organisation supported by money raised through the services it provides and applications for funding. It receives an annual grant from Eastern Arts.

Acquisitions policy: Film and video of all types representing life in the wider East Anglian region of Bedfordshire, Cambridgeshire, Essex, Hertfordshire, Norfolk and Suffolk.

Non-manuscript material: Non-fiction film, on all film gauges and video formats, 1896– , including documentaries, local and national newsreel and news magazines, promotional and publicity films, educational productions, and home movies. Particularly well represented are images of people at work, town and village life, farming and fishing, transport, holidays and family life.

Finding aids: Catalogue, with full descriptions of all the films for which viewing copies exist, currently being updated for Internet publication.

Facilities: Film printing. Film to video transfers.

Conservation: EAFA specialises in printing small gauge films onto 16mm for preservation and access and carries out printing for archives and other customers around the world.

942 Boots Company Archives

Parent organisation: The Boots Company plc

Address: D31 Building, The Boots Company plc, Nottingham NG2 3AA

Telephone: (0115) 9594228

Fax: (0115) 9593500

E-mail: katey.logan@boots-plc.com

Enquiries: The Company Archivist, Katey Logan

Open: Mon–Fri: 9.00–4.00, by appointment only.

Access: Bona fide researchers, at the discretion of the company archivist.

Historical background: Boots has been in retailing since 1849. Its main subsidiary, Boots the Chemist, is the UK's leading retailer of health and beauty products, with stores ranging from small community pharmacies to city-centre department stores. Timothy Whites & Taylors Ltd was acquired in 1968. Boots' pharmaceutical business was sold to BASF (Germany) in 1995. The Company Archives have been professionally managed since 1995.

Acquisitions policy: Main acquisitions are through internal records management; some records are also deposited by members of the public.

Archives of organisation: Business records of the parent company, 1888–1982, and of Timothy Whites, 1930–81.

Non-manuscript material: Company magazines, 1919– ; merchandise; bulletins, 1924– ; store plans and photographs.

Finding aids: Catalogues, lists, indexes and database.

Facilities: Photocopying.

Publications: S.D. Chapman: *Jesse Boot of Boots the Chemists* (1974).
C. Weir: *Jesse Boots of Nottingham* (1994).

943 Media Archive for Central England

Address: Institute of Film Studies, School of American and Canadian Studies, University of Nottingham, University Park, Nottingham NG7 2RD

Telephone: (0115) 846 6448

Fax: (0115) 951 4270

E-mail: james.patterson@nottingham.ac.uk

Enquiries: The Director, James Patterson
The Archivist, James Taylor

The Media Archive for Central England (MACE) is the emerging public-sector moving-image archive serving the East and West Midlands. MACE will be moving to a permanent location in due course. It continues to seek funding to collect, preserve and make accessible the film culture and heritage of the regions. Its core collection will be the regional news and local programming of the independent television companies ATV, Central and Carlton. MACE will be seeking out other material to develop collections once the facilities are in place. MACE welcomes enquiries from researchers and from the public and will endeavour to find material either from its own or other specialist collections relating to the regions.

944 Nottingham Diocesan Archives

Parent organisation: Roman Catholic Diocese of Nottingham

Address: Willson House, Derby Street, Nottingham NG1 5AW

Telephone: (0115) 953 9803

Enquiries: The Diocesan Archivist

Open: By arrangement only. Please write in the first instance, enclosing an s.a.e.

Access: Any bona fide enquirer, at the Archivist's discretion. A charge is made for work done on behalf of enquirers. No records later than 1944 may be consulted at present.

Historical background: The Diocese of Nottingham was created in 1850 when the Catholic hierarchy was restored in England and Wales. The diocese at present covers Nottinghamshire (except Bassetlaw), Derbyshire (except parts of the High Peak and Chesterfield areas), Leicestershire, Lincolnshire and Rutland. The diocesan archives have been built up over many decades by various individuals. They were moved to their present site in 1990. Many pre-1850 records are held by Birmingham Archdiocesan Archives (see entry 99).

Acquisitions policy: To acquire material relevant to the history of the Catholic Church, with particular reference to the Diocese of Nottingham and the institutions and individuals which form part of it.

Archives of organisation: Correspondence and other papers of the Bishops of Nottingham.
Files for most of the older parishes of the diocese.
Registers (baptisms, confirmations, marriages, deaths) of many of the parishes (also on microfiche). County record offices for the territory covered by the diocese hold microfiche copies of these registers, which finish before 1910. Much of the information is also available from local or national register offices.

Major collections: Croft papers: material on the history of the diocese collected with a view to publication by Monsignor W. Croft (*d* 1926).
Sweeney Collection: typescript history of the diocese and obituary notices for priests compiled by Canon G.D. Sweeney (*d* 1979).

Non-manuscript material: Catholic Directory, c1840– (incomplete).
Diocesan Year Book, 1921– .

Finding aids: Many of the documents are listed on index cards or on typed sheets. Separate list of parish registers. Arrangements are in hand to computerise records.

Facilities: Photocopying by arrangement. Microfiche reader.

Publications: 'A Short Account of Nottingham Diocesan Archives', *Catholic Archives,* iii (1983), 9–19.
'Building for the Future: Reflections of a Diocesan Archivist', *Catholic Archives,* ix (1989), 41–7.

945 Nottinghamshire Archives

Parent organisation: Nottinghamshire County Council/Nottingham City Council

Address: Castle Meadow Road, Nottingham NG2 1AG

Telephone: (0115) 958 1634/950 4524 (archival enquiries); 924 2749 (Conservation Unit)

Fax: (0115) 941 3997

E-mail: archives@nottscc.gov.uk

Website: www.nottscc.gov.uk

Enquiries: The Principal Archivist, Mr Adrian Henstock

Open: Mon, Wed–Fri: 9.00–4.45; Tues: 9.00–7.15; Sat: 9.00–12.45.

Access: Generally open to the public. A *CARN* reader's ticket is required to consult the original archives (not microfilms).

Historical background: The county office was formally established in 1949, although some archives were collected from an earlier date. In 1975 it amalgamated with the Archives Department of Nottingham Public Library. The office acts also as the Diocesan Record Office for Southwell and is recognised as a place of deposit for public records.

Acquisitions policy: Archival material relating to the geographical county of Nottinghamshire.

Archives of organisation: Usual local authority record holdings.

Major collections: Deposited local collections, of which the following have a wider significance:
Portland papers: medieval charters; disintegration of forests, 16th–17th centuries.
Foljambe papers: medieval charters; correspondence of Sir George Savile MP, late 18th century.
Savile papers: medieval charters; correspondence of Sir John Savile (Lumley), European diplomat, late 19th century. Papers of Dame Laura Knight (1877–1970), artist.
Raleigh Cycle Co. archive.

Non-manuscript material: Nottingham Playhouse photographic archive, 1948–93.

Finding aids: Lists sent to NRA.

Facilities: Photocopying. Photography. Microfilming. Microfilm/fiche readers.

Conservation: Full in-house service.

Publications: P.A. Kennedy: *Guide to the Nottinghamshire County Records Office* (1960).
The Victorian School in Nottinghamshire, Archive Resource Pack no. 1 (1988).
The Great War and Nottinghamshire, Archive Resource Pack no. 2 (1989).
Women's History in Nottinghashire Archives Office, c1550–1950 (1989).
Rufford: From Abbey to Country House, Archive Resource Pack no. 3 (1990).
Watson Fothergill: a Victorian Architect of Nottingham, Archive Resource Pack no. 4 (1993).
The Home Front: Nottinghamshire, 1939–1945, Archive Resource Pack no. 5 (1995).

Nottinghamshire Parish and Denominational Registers: a Finding List for Family Histories (1997).

946 University of Nottingham Library
Department of Manuscripts and Special Collections

Address: University Park, Nottingham NG7 2RD

Telephone: (0115) 951 4565

Fax: (0115) 951 4558

E-mail: mss-library@nottingham.ac.uk

Website: www.mss.library.nottingham.ac.uk

Enquiries: The Keeper of Manuscripts, Dr D.B. Johnston

Open: Mon–Fri: 9.00–5.00, by appointment. Closed for one week in September.

Access: Open to the public on application. There are restrictions on modern records varying from between 30 and 100 years, depending on the type of material.

Historical background: Nottingham University College began collecting MSS in the 1930s after the appointment of the first professional librarian in 1931. The first archivist was appointed in 1947, which led to the development of a separate MSS department within the university library. Nottingham gained full university status in 1948. It is recognised as a place of deposit for public records.

Acquisitions policy: To increase the strength of existing collections, by deposit, donation or occasionally purchase, with particular focus upon local archives, material relating to the research and teaching interests of the university and private papers of former members of the university.

Archives of organisation: Historical records of Nottingham University College (1881–1948); some non-current records of the University of Nottingham.

Major collections: Family collections: title deeds and settlements, manorial and estate records, including court rolls, compoti, accounts, rentals, surveys, maps and plans; estate, political and personal correspondence, with papers covering banking business and other interests, including Chamier, Clifton, Denison, Drury-Lowe, Galway, Manvers, Mellish, Middleton, Newcastle, Portland, Wrench and Kirke families.

Ecclesiastical records: Church of England (Archdeaconry of Nottingham), Unitarian, Baptist, United Reformed Church (Congregational/Presbyterian).

Literary collections: Restoration and 18th-century verse (Cavendish and Harley material in Portland Collection); Henry Kirke White; Coventry Patmore; D.H. Lawrence.

Hospital records of those hospitals in the Nottinghamshire Area Health Authority (Teaching) Nottingham District.

Water authority: records of the former Trent River Authority and its predecessors and other bodies amalgamated with it, including Hatfield Chase Drainage Authority and Brigg Court of Sewers.

Business records, mainly of firms connected with the lace industry.

Trade union records, including those of the Amalgamated Society of Lacemakers.

Specialised collections, including that of Francis Willoughby (1635–72), naturalist and patron of John Ray (1627–1705), a 17th-century natural history collection within the Middleton (Willoughby family) Collection; meteorological records; and Russian and British posters of World War II.

In total there are more than 2,000,000 MSS, 12th–20th centuries.

Non-manuscript material: Included in the MSS collections are photographic material, printed pamphlets, posters, printed sermons, hymn books and related material.

The library's printed book special collections form part of the department's holdings and complement strengths in the MSS in several areas, especially local history.

Finding aids: Handlists, available for purchase; also sent to NRA, copyright libraries and the local record offices (Nottinghamshire, Derbyshire and Lincolnshire). Detailed calendars for a small number of collections, or sections of collections. Some indexes of personal and place names. Some catalogues on website.

Facilities: Photocopying. Photography. Microfilming. Microfilm reader/printer.

Conservation: In-house work undertaken.

Publications: *The University of Nottingham, Manuscripts Department of the University Library*, Information leaflet no. 13.

The University of Nottingham, Report of the Keeper of the Manuscripts [occasional publication].

National Inventory of Documentary Sources, Chadwyck-Healey microfiche (1984–).

947 Nuneaton Library

Parent organisation: Warwickshire County Library

Address: Church Street, Nuneaton, Warwickshire CV11 4DR

Telephone: (024) 7638 4027/7634 7006

Fax: (024) 7635 0125

E-mail: nuneatonlibrary@dial.pipex.com

Enquiries: The Divisional Manager, Mr C.W. Foster

Open: Mon, Wed: 9.00–7.00; Tues, Fri: 9.00–6.00; Thurs: 9.00–5.00; Sat: 9.00–4.00; Sun: 10.00–2.00.

Access: Open to the public.

Historical background: Ephemeral material relating to Nuneaton and the surrounding area has been collected on a non-systematic basis. Other libraries at Warwick, Stratford upon Avon and Leamington hold local history collections. Most genuinely archival material, including the Jodrell MSS and Cross Collection, is held by the Warwickshire County Record Office (see entry 1189).

Acquisitions policy: Donations of archival material relevant to the Nuneaton area are accepted, but may be passed to the county record office. Archival material is not normally purchased.

Major collections: Collection of letters of George Eliot, G.H. Lewes, J.W. Cross and Herbert Arthur Lewes.

Non-manuscript material: George Eliot Collection.
Collection of local illustrations.

Finding aids: Index to George Eliot Collection and to illustrations.

Facilities: Photocopying. Microfilm/fiche reader/printer.

948 Oldham Local Studies and Archives

Parent organisation: Oldham Metropolitan Borough

Address: 84 Union Street, Oldham OL1 1DN

Telephone: (0161) 911 4654

Fax: (0161) 911 4654

E-mail: archives@oldham.gov.uk

Website: www.oldham.gov.uk/local studies

Enquiries: Mrs Maria Sienkiewicz

Open: Mon, Thurs: 10.00–7.00; Tues: 10.00–2.00; Wed, Fri, Sat: 10.00–5.00.

Access: Open to the public. Proof of name and address is required. Advance booking is recommended for microform readers.

Historical background: Oldham Metropolitan Borough was established in 1974 within Greater Manchester County. Oldham's Local Studies Library then became responsible for the records of the predecessor local authorities, adding to substantial local history MSS collected over 100 years. It moved to the present premises in 1982 and the first Archives Officer was appointed in 1991.

Acquisitions policy: In co-operation with the Greater Manchester County Record Office (see entry 874) and other GM district archives services, to collect, permanently preserve and make available for research, public, official, ecclesiastical and private records relating to the area of Oldham Metropolitan Borough.

Archives of organisation: Records of predecessor authorities: Oldham County Borough and urban districts of Chadderton, Crompton, Failsworth, Lees, Royton, Saddleworth, Springhead and Uppermill.

Major collections: Extensive records of local co-operative society and textile trades unions.
Butterworth MSS: including press reports, 1829–43, and research notes for Baines's History of Lancashire (1836).
Rowbottom diaries: daily events in Oldham, 1787–1829.
Personal papers of Dame Sarah and Marjory Lees of Werneth Park, including suffrage material.
Higson antiquarian collection.

Non-manuscript material: Local census and parish registers (microfilm).

Local newspapers and oral history resources. Local studies collections include photographs (20,000), plans (2000), books (16,000) and pamphlets on the history of Oldham.

Finding aids: Lists and indexes (under revision); lists sent to NRA. Local studies classification scheme and indexes.

Facilities: Photocopying. Photography. Microfilm/fiche readers/printer.

Conservation: Contracted out.

Publications: Archive Guide in preparation.

949 Saddleworth Museum Archives Room

Parent organisation: Saddleworth Museum and Art Gallery

Address: High Street, Uppermill, Oldham OL3 6HS

Telephone: (01457) 874093

Fax: (01457) 870336

Enquiries: The Curator, Matthew Richardson
The Hon Archivist, Maurice Dennett

Open: By arrangement.

Access: Generally open to the public, by appointment.

Historical background: Saddleworth Museum was opened in 1962, with the aim of displaying local life, and expanded in 1979. Partly due to a policy of displaying travelling exhibitions, attendance increased steadily, resulting in a flow of gifts of documents and artefacts from local people. As well as the museum's collections, those of the Saddleworth Historical Society are housed and made available for general use.

Acquisitions policy: To accept anything which will help bring alive an awareness and understanding of the district and its history.

Major collections: Howcroft/Shaw papers, architectural and antiquarian, 19th and 20th centuries.
Saddleworth deeds and wills, including documents and maps re Enclosure Act and Award of 1810 and 1834.
Local mill financial, business and processing records, with sample books and correspondence re exports of cloth to the Americas, 1800– .

Weavers' Union books and papers, 1820s–1960s.
Papers of Ammon Wrigley (1861–1946), writer, painter and folklorist, and E.L. Edwards (c1885–1978), local historian.

Non-manuscript material: Photographic archive of local architecture and textile machinery.
Recorded interviews with local people on the history of the area, and the sound of textile looms in operation.
Taped memoirs of Lord Rhodes of Saddleworth.
Microfilms of census returns and parish registers.

Finding aids: Holdings fully listed in typed calendars and card catalogues.

Facilities: Photocopying. Microfilm/fiche readers.

Publications: Saddleworth Archives: *Archives for Research and Education* (1982) [descriptive booklet].

950 Aberdeenshire Library and Information Service

Parent organisation: Aberdeenshire Council

Address: Meadows Industrial Estate, Meldrum Meg Way, Oldmeldrum, Aberdeenshire AB51 0GN

Telephone: (01651) 871220/871219

Fax: (01651) 872142

E-mail: david.catto@aberdeenshire.gov.uk

Enquiries: The Local Studies Librarian, Mr David Catto

Open: Mon Fri: 9.00–5.00; Sat: 9.00–4.30.

Access: Generally open to the public. Some prior notice would be appreciated and an appointment is recommended for use of microfilm/fiche reader/printer. Disabled access is available. Charges for copying. Enquiries from non-Aberdeenshire residents by telephone; letter will incur charges.

Historical background: Formerly the North East of Scotland Library Service, Aberdeenshire Library and Information Service came into being in 1996 with the reorganisation of local government in Scotland. ALIS serves the library and information needs of the residents and council of Aberdeenshire.

Acquisitions policy: To strengthen existing primary and secondary collections of materials relating to Aberdeenshire, by purchase or donation.

Major collections: Strichen Collection: Strichen estate records and plans; records of local societies, Auchmedden estate papers and a small collection of late 19th-century and early 20th-century photographs (microfilm copies are also held at Strichen Branch Library).
George Macdonald Collection: MSS, letters, books and photographs relating to Macdonald (1824–1905), novelist.

Non-manuscript material: The Local Studies collection includes maps and photographs; council minutes, valuation rolls and voters' rolls, mostly 1975– , and community council newsletters and minutes of meetings, 1975– .
School board minutes.
Old Parish registers and census records (on microfilm).

Finding aids: The collection is catalogued and classified accessible through OPAC. Some of the maps are indexed. Periodical and newspaper index. Index to major reference sources.

Facilities: Photocopying (including colour). Microfilm/fiche reader/printer.

951 Cowper Memorial Library

Parent organisation: Cowper and Newton Museum

Address: Orchard Side, Market Place, Olney, Buckinghamshire MK46 4AB

Telephone: (01234) 711516

E-mail: museum@olney.co.uk

Website: www.olio.demon.co.uk/cnmhome.html

Enquiries: The Custodian, Mrs Joan McKillop

Open: March–Dec: Tues–Sat: 10.00–1.00, 2.00–5.00, by arrangement.

Access: Bona fide students, by appointment.

Historical background: The museum was founded in 1900 and is an independent museum run by a board of trustees. The founder was Thomas Wright, author and local historian, who continued to add to his personal collection. Over the past 20 years the lace collection has been expanded, lacemaking being the local cottage industry in Cowper's day and now enjoying a craft revival. Collections include local archaeology, geology, palaeontology, local history and, more recently, family history.

Acquisitions policy: The main object of the Cowper and Newton Museum is to obtain objects and memorabilia of the poet William Cowper (1731–1800) and the Rev. John Newton (1725–1807), and to preserve and maintain and display such objects for the benefit of students as well as the general public. The museum also acquires items which have a close association with Olney and the immediate surrounding villages.

Major collections: The Avenell Collection, the Drinkwater Collection and the Harvey Collection.
Collection of materials towards a life of Cowper.
John Sparrow Collection.
Brian Spiller working papers.

Non-manuscript material: Photographs.

Finding aids: Catalogue of manuscripts. Card index of pamphlets and photographs. NRA 10540.

Conservation: Contracted out.

Publications: 'Handlist', *Cambridge Bibliographical Society Journal*, 4/2 (1965) [letters and MSS relating to Cowper and Newton].

952 Edge Hill College

Address: St Helens Road, Ormskirk, Lancashire L39 4QP

Telephone: (01695) 575171

Fax: (01695) 584298

E-mail: jenkins@mail.ehche.ac.uk

Enquiries: The Head of Library and Information Services

Open: By arrangement only.

Access: Bona fide researchers, by appointment.

Historical background: The college was opened as a teachers' training college for women in 1885. It is now co-educational and offers a wide variety of courses in higher education.

Acquisitions policy: To maintain its archives.

Archives of organisation: College archive: minute books, 1882–1925; staff meeting minutes, 1937–64 (incomplete); governors' minutes, 1933–84 (incomplete); register of students,

1885–1925 and 1930–51; college roll, 1885–1947; letter books, register of students work, 1885–1925; correspondence with the Board of Education, 1888–1907.

Non-manuscript material: College magazine, 1892–1906 (various and incomplete), 1907– . College newsletters, 1943– .

Facilities: Photocopying.

Publications: F.A. Montgomery: *Edge Hill University College: a History, 1885–1997* (1997).

953 Oswestry Town Council

Address: Guildhall, Oswestry, Shropshire SY11 1PZ

Telephone: (01691) 652776

Fax: (01691) 671080

E-mail: dpreston@oswestry.enterprise-plc.com

Website: www.arik.co.uk/oswestry

Enquiries: The Town Clerk, Mr D.J. Preston

Open: Mon, Tues, Thurs, Fri: 9.45–12.45, 2.15–4.30, by appointment.

Access: Bona fide researchers, by application; a registration form must be completed and submitted before a first appointment. Access to records less than 50 years old may be restricted.

Historical background: Oswestry was a chartered borough and, following local government reorganisation, became in 1967 a rural borough functioning as a traditional parish council. In the 1974 reorganisation the rural borough became Oswestry Town Council. In 1986 a strongroom was equipped in the Guildhall, which is a recognised place of deposit for public records. Searchroom accommodation was provided in Powis Hall in 1987. An additional strongroom and improved searchroom facilities were provided in 1999, when the Guildhall was renovated with the aid of a grant from the Heritage Lottery Fund.

Acquisitions policy: To maintain the archives of the Town Council.

Archives of organisation: Charters, 1324–1674; minutes and accounts, 1674– ; burgess books, 1674–1899; court records of civil actions, 1661–2, 1714–1843; deeds and papers *re* markets, waterworks and buildings, 17th century– ; quarter sessions records, 1737–1951; petty sessions records, 1818–97; letter-books and correspondence files, 1890– ; charity records, 1836– ; housing trust records, 1928–68.

Finding aids: Lists, sent to NRA.

Facilities: Photocopying.

Conservation: Contracted out.

Publications: S. Leighton (ed.): 'The Records of the Corporation of Oswestry', reprinted from *Transactions of the Shropshire Archaeological Society* (1879–83).

954 All Souls College

Parent organisation: University of Oxford

Address: Oxford OX1 4AL

Telephone: (01865) 279379

Fax: (01865) 279299

E-mail: codrington.library@all-souls.ox.ac.uk

Enquiries: The Librarian in Charge, Dr N. Aubertin-Potter

Open: Term: Mon–Fri: 9.30–6.30; Sat: 9.30–12.30.
Vacation: Mon–Fri: 9.30–4.30; Sat: 9.30–12.30.

Access: Bona fide researchers, on written application only and strictly by appointment.

Historical background: All Souls College was founded by Henry Chichele, Archbishop of Canterbury, 1414–43, and is a college for postgraduates only. The library was established in 1716 and takes its name from Christopher Codrington (1668–1710). The archives were transferred to the Bodleian Library (see entry 958) in 1966, the college retaining a few groups of documents.

Acquisitions policy: To maintain collections, by accepting relevant gifts and bequests.

Archives of organisation: Items retained by the college include deeds, charters, college registers, stewards' books, plans, miscellaneous papers.

Major collections: Luttrell Wynne MSS, including volumes of parliamentary journals and state papers; East India Company documents, 1619–85; papers concerning maritime law; notebooks of Humphrey Dyson (*d* 1632), lawyer and bibliographer.
Correspondence of Sir George Downing (*c*1623–1684) with Sir William Temple, 1664–7.

Notes of lectures given by Sir William Blackstone (1723–80), judge.

Papers of Sir Charles Vaughan, 1774–1849, traveller and diplomat.

Correspondence of Lord Cranley (5th Earl of Onslow) with Sir Dougal Malcolm (1877–1955) on foreign and domestic politics, 1903–13 (2 vols).

Oriental MSS (50).

Non-manuscript material: Drawings and plans by Sir Christopher Wren (1632–1733) (c 400 items).

Finding aids: Handlist for History of University Project. Calendar of Vaughan Papers: NRA 10564.

Publications: C. Trice Martin: *Catalogue of the Archives in the Muniment Room of All Souls College* (1877) [2 vols + index; annotated copy in Bodleian].

'Catalogue of Sir Christopher Wren's Drawings at All Souls', *Wren Society*, xx (1943), 1–33.

E.F. Jacob: 'All Souls College Archives', *Oxoniensia*, xxxiii (1969), 89–91.

N.R. Ker: *Records of All Souls College Library, 1437–1600* (Oxford, 1971).

955 Ashmolean Library

Parent organisation: University of Oxford

Address: Sackler Library, 1 St John Street, Oxford OX1 2LG

Telephone: (01865) 278088

Fax: (01865) 278098

E-mail: james.legg@saclib.ox.ac.uk

Website: www.saclib.ox.ac.uk

Enquiries: The Librarian, Mr J. Legg

Open: Term: Mon–Fri: 9.00–10.00; Sat: 10.00–5.00.
Vacation: Mon–Fri: 9.00–5.00; Sat: 9.00–1.00.

Access: Members of Oxford University and bona fide researchers on application to the Librarian.

Historical background: The library has developed since the 1880s to support the work of the departments of the Ashmolean Museum and the teaching of archaeology and art history at Oxford University.

Acquisitions policy: To maintain the collections.

Major collections: Papers of Prof. F.J. Haverfield (1860–1919), Roman historian and archaeologist, and Sir Ian Richmond (1902–65), archaeologist.

Material compiled by R.G. Collingwood (1889–1943) and others for the publication of *Roman Inscriptions of Britain*, 1965–95.

Other minor collections of papers of archaeologists and scholars of ancient history.

Non-manuscript material: Includes large-scale plans of archaeological sites, photographs and notebooks, including sketch drawings and text.

Finding aids: Haverfield archive: topographical arrangement by county.
Richmond archive: systematic index of sites.

Facilities: Photocopying.

956 Ashmolean Museum

Parent organisation: University of Oxford

Address: Beaumont Street, Oxford OX1 2PH

Website: www.ashmol.ox.ac.uk

Historical background: The Ashmolean Museum, founded in 1683, comprises a range of collections of art and archaeology. It is not primarily a repository for archives, but some have been deposited in connection with collections acquired by the museum. The collection of old master prints and drawings dates largely from the 19th century and has been enlarged over the years by gifts and purchases. The most important holdings in the Department of Antiquities are the Knossos records of Sir Arthur Evans.

Acquisitions policy: No active policy for acquiring archives, but they are accepted where appropriate.

A Department of Antiquities

Telephone: (01865) 278020

Fax: (01865) 278032

E-mail: antiquities@ashmus.ox.ac.uk

Enquiries: The Curator

Open: Tues–Fri: 10.00–5.00.

Access: Bona fide researchers, by appointment.

Archives of organisation: Archival material relating to the history of the Ashmolean Museum since its foundation.

Major collections: Papers of Sir Arthur Evans (1851–1941) and excavation archives of Knossors.

Air photographs of Major George Allen, c1930s.

Facilities: Restricted photocopying and photography.

Conservation: Contracted out.

B Department of Western Art

Telephone: (01865) 278049

Fax: (01865) 278056

Enquiries: The Keeper of Western Art, Mr Timothy Wilson

Open: Tues–Sat: 10.00–1.00, 2.00–4.00.
Closed Mon and Tues following 1st Sat in Sept.

Access: Generally open to the public

Archives of organisation: Department of Western Art archives, 19th century– .

Major collections: The Pissarro Archives: prints, drawings, books, letters and other documents of Camille Pissarro (1830–1903), Lucien Pissarro (1863–1944), Orovida Pissarro (1893–1968) and other members of the family.
Papers of C.D.E. Fortnum (1820–99).

Finding aids: Card indexes.

Facilities: Photography.

Conservation: In-house paper conservation studio.

Publications: Brief guide to the print room available.

957 Balliol College

Parent organisation: University of Oxford

Address: Oxford OX1 3BJ

Telephone: (01865) 277777 (for appointments; written enquiries only)

Fax: (01865) 277803

E-mail: john.jones@balliol.ox.ac.uk
library@balliol.ox.ac.uk

Enquiries: The Archivist, Dr J.H. Jones
The Librarian, Dr P. Bulloch

Open: Mon–Fri: 9.00–5.00.

Access: Archives: Bona fide researchers, on application in writing; there is a 30-year closure rule.

Library: Bona fide researchers, by appointment.

Historical background: The college was founded about 1263 and given its first statutes in 1282. Few records survive for college activities in the medieval period, except title deeds. Recording of membership and internal matters began in c1520 and was established by 1550. The Archives Room was instituted in 1986 to bring together scattered items. There is little information about the library before 1400, but there have been continuous gifts since that time.

Acquisitions policy: Archives: material is transferred from college departments, offices and undergraduate societies, and occasionally donated by members.

Library: papers of those connected with the college are accepted.

Archives of organisation: Statutes and foundation deeds, decrees of and correspondence with visitors, correspondence, papers and registers *re* benefactors, 13th–20th centuries; membership records, 16th–20th centuries; estate records, 12th–20th centuries; building records, including architectural drawings and plans, mostly 18th–20th centuries; administration and finance records, including bursars' accounts and buttery books, 1568–20th centuries; records of the Balliol-Trinity Laboratories, 1853–1939; records of undergraduate societies, 19th–20th centuries; litigation papers, 17th–20th centuries; estates and ecclesiastical patronage deeds and papers, 13th–20th centuries.

Major collections: Extensive papers of masters, fellows and others connected with the college, including Conroy family papers; Jenkyns family papers, notably Richard Jenkyns (master, 1819–54); substantial material relating to Benjamin Jowett (master, 1870–93); and papers of David Urquhart (1805–77), Sir Robert Morier (1826–93) and the Morier family, T.H. Green (fellow, 1861–82) and A.L. Smith (master, 1916–24), including papers relating to the Workers' Educational Association. Also some papers of Nicholas Crouch (fellow, 1640–8), Frederick Oakeley (fellow, 1827–45), Arthur Hugh Clough (1819–61), Robert Browning (1812–89), Matthew Arnold (1822–88) and his family, A.C. Swinburne (1887–1909), Arnold Toynbee (1852–83), Sir Harold

Nicolson (1886–1968) and Adam von Trott zu Solz (1909–44).

Non-manuscript material: Photographs, portraits, seals, Balliol College stamps (numerous specimens of the unique stamp).

Finding aids: All pre-1939 records are identified, listed and selectively indexed. Lists sent to NRA.

Facilities: Microfilm/fiche reader.

Publications: H.E. Salter: *Oxford Balliol Deeds* (1913).
R.A.B. Mynors: *Catalogue of the Manuscripts of Balliol College, Oxford* (1963).
J. Jones: *The Archives of Balliol College, Oxford: a Guide* (Chichester, 1984).
K. Hudson and J. Jones: *The Conroy Papers: a Guide* (1987).
J. Jones: *The Jenkyns Papers: a Guide* (1988).
—— : *Balliol College: a History* (2/1997).
—— : *The Portraits of Balliol College: a Catalogue* (1990).
R. Darwall-Smith: *The Jowett Papers* (1993).

958 Bodleian Library
Special Collections and Western Manuscripts

Parent organisation: University of Oxford

Address: Broad Street, Oxford OX1 3BG

Telephone: (01865) 277158

Fax: (01865) 277187

E-mail: western.manuscripts@bodley.ox.ac.uk

Enquiries: The Keeper of Special Collections and Western Manuscripts, Mrs M. Clapinson

Open: Term: Mon–Fri: 9.00–10.00 (Modern Papers Reading Room 9.00–7.00); Sat: 9.00–1.00.
Vacation: Mon–Fri:9.00–7.00; Sat: 9.00–1.00.
Closed: Encaenia Day and the week beginning with the late summer bank holiday.

Access: By reader's ticket. Applicants should contact the department in the first instance. They must present themselves in person, and must have either a letter of introduction from, or an application form filled in by, a responsible person familiar with their work. There is a charge for readers not from a UK institution of higher education.

Historical background: Founded in 1488, the Bodleian has a continuous history since the refoundation by Sir Thomas Bodley in 1602. Since that date it has collected MSS and printed books and remains a library of legal deposit. The Indian Institute Library and Rhodes House Library (see entry 994) are dependent libraries but still have a separate identity.

Acquisitions policy: Building the collections in existing areas of strength. The chief growth area is modern personal papers of public figures.

Archives of organisation: Bodleian Library administrative records, 1600– . See entry 982 for University Archives.

Major collections: Large collections of MSS of all periods, including papyri; Byzantine MSS; medieval text and illuminated MSS, especially Italian and English; English historical collections, especially 17th century; local history collections of antiquarian, topographical and estate records; deeds and rolls; music; archives of societies, including the Church's Ministry among the Jews, the Society for the Protection of Science and Learning and the Conservative Party; papers of politicians and other public figures, writers, scientists, scholars and churchmen.

Non-manuscript material: Oxford University theses.
Maps, drawings and photographs.
The John Johnson Collection of printed ephemera.

Finding aids: Variety of lists, catalogues and indexes. Lists sent to NRA.

Facilities: Restricted photocopying. Photography. Microfilm/fiche readers.

Conservation: Full in-house service.

Publications: Quarto catalogues of older named collections (1845–1900): I: *Greek Manuscripts*; II: *Laud*; III: and XI: *Canonici*; IV: *Tanner*; V: *Rawlinson*; IX: *Digby*; X: *Ashmole*.
F. Madan and others: *Summary Catalogue of Western MSS in the Bodleian Library at Oxford* (8 vols, 1895–1953; repr., 1980).
M. Clapinson and T.D. Rogers: *Summary Catalogue of Post-medieval Western MSS. Acquisitions, 1916–1975* (3 vols, 1991).
Lists of notable accessions in *Annual Report of the Curators* (1888–) and *Bodleian Library Record* (1914–).

959 Brasenose College

Parent organisation: University of Oxford

Address: Oxford OX1 4AJ

Telephone: (01865) 277826/7

Fax: (01865) 277822

E-mail: archives@bne.ox.ac.uk

Website: www.bne.ox.ac.uk/history/index.html

Enquiries: The Archivist, Mrs Elizabeth Boardman

Open: Tues, Wed: 9.00–4.45.

Access: Bona fide scholars, by appointment only.

Historical background: The college was founded in 1509, and by the 18th century was considered one of the best endowed colleges in the university. Medieval and other MSS are deposited in the Bodleian Library (see entry 958).

Acquisitions policy: Archives of the college; papers of members of the college.

Archives of organisation: Extensive archive collections include college minutes, 1539– ; accounts, 1516– ; buttery books, 1639–1931; deeds, 12th century– ; other estate records, 1509– ; site and buildings records, 1509– ; benefactions, 1509– ; undergraduate clubs, 1782– ; room books, 1747– ; records of college library, 1550– .

Major collections: Personal papers of Sir Noel Hall (1902–83), principal.
J.H.A. Sparrow Collection of letters, MSS and memorabilia of Walter Horatio Pater (1839–94), writer, critic and fellow.

Non-manuscript material: Plans and drawings for college buildings by Nicholas Hawksmoor, Sir John Soane, Philip Hardwick and Sir Thomas Jackson, 18th–20th centuries.
Estate maps, (c1500), 1607–1869.
Photographs of college site and members.
Photograph negatives and albums of W.T.S. Stallybrass (1883–1948), principal.

Finding aids: Calendar of deeds and some administrative papers to mid–19th century (NRA). Handlist of major administrative records, 1509–1960 (NRA). Card index of most remaining material. Comprehensive catalogue in progress.

Facilities: Photocopying.

Publications: Brasenose College Register (1909).

Articles about the archive collections appear in *The Brazen Nose* (1909–), including R.W. Jeffrey: 'The Brasenose College Muniment Room', *The Brazen Nose*, v (1933), 290–3.

960 Campion Hall

Parent organisation: University of Oxford

Address: Brewer Street, Oxford OX1 1QS

Telephone: (01865) 286104 (Librarian); 286100 (enquiries)

Fax: (01865) 286148

E-mail: norman.tanner@campion.ox.ac.uk

Website: www.campion.ox.ac.uk

Enquiries: The Librarian/Archivist, Rev. Norman Tanner

Open: By arrangement only.

Access: Approved readers, by appointment only.

Campion Hall is a private hall of the University of Oxford, founded in 1896 for members of the Society of Jesus. It holds papers of Gerard Manley Hopkins (1844–89), which are catalogued in H. House and G. Storey (eds): *The Journals and Papers of Gerard Manley Hopkins* (1959), Appendix IV. There are also some drawings by Sir Edwin Lutyens (1869–1944), architect. Photocopying is available.

961 Centre for Oxfordshire Studies

Parent organisation: Oxfordshire County Council

Address: Central Library, Westgate, Oxford OX1 1DJ

Telephone: (01865) 815749

Fax: (01865) 810187

E-mail: cos.occdla@dial.pipex.com

Enquiries: The Head of Oxfordshire Studies, Dr M. Graham

Open: Mon, Fri, Sat: 9.15–5.00; Tues, Thurs: 9.15–7.00.

Access: Generally open to the public. An appointment is required for the county Sites and Monuments Record. A charge is made for advance booking of microform equipment.

Historical background: Oxford City Library was started by Oxford City Council in 1854 and transferred to the county council in 1974. A local history collection was established in 1890 and this was merged with other library and museum resources in 1991 to form the Centre for Oxfordshire Studies.

Acquisitions policy: To maintain and develop the local studies collections, which cover Oxford and Oxfordshire, including the area formerly in north Berkshire.

Non-manuscript material: H.W. Taunt (1842–1922) and others: collections of topographical photographs, c1860– (250,000).
Other extensive collections of illustrative material, including prints and posters.
Local newspapers, 1753- (virtually complete).
Oxfordshire census returns (microfiche).
County Sites and Monuments Record.
Oral History Archive (c3000 tapes), including BBC Radio Oxford Collection.
General Register Office, index 1837–1992 (fiche); Somerset House wills index, 1858–1957 (film); 1881 census index (fiche).
Copies of some local manuscript material.
Local printed ephemera.

Finding aids: Catalogues, lists and indexes.

Facilities: Photocopying. Photography. Microfilm/fiche readers/printers.

Conservation: Contracted out.

Publications: In-house leaflets available.

962 Christ Church

Parent organisation: University of Oxford

Address: Oxford OX1 1DP

Telephone: (01865) 276169

E-mail: archives@christ-church.ox.ac.uk
library@christ-church.ox.ac.uk

Website: www.chch.ox.ac.uk/library

Enquiries: The Archivist
The Librarian

Open: By arrangement.

Access: Bona fide researchers, by appointment.

Historical background: The original college was founded by Cardinal Wolsey in 1525 and refounded by Henry VIII in 1546, although a library was not begun until the 1560s. The medieval records of monasteries suppressed by

Wolsey to endow his college have been deposited in the Bodleian Library (see entry 958). Custody of the archives is divided between the library and muniment room. Papers of John Evelyn have now been transferred to the British Library (entry 561) and to Surrey History Centre (entry 1208).

Acquisitions policy: To maintain the college archives and consolidate the MS collections.

Archives of organisation: Statutes and charters, 1525– ; admission books, 1546– c1960; records of college administration, 1547– ; estate records, including maps, accounts, correspondence and leases, 16th–19th centuries; records of the Dean and Chapter, 1547–c1900. Diocesan records are kept at the Oxfordshire Record Office (see entry 986).

Major collections: Papers of William Wake (1657–1737), Archbishop of Canterbury, C.L. Dodgson (Lewis Carroll) (1832–98), Viscount Portal of Hungerford (1893–1971), Marshal of the RAF, and Thomas Driberg (1905–76), politician.

Finding aids: Typescript catalogues of manorial records; maps and plans; leases; treasury books; other college administrative records; photographs.

Publications: N. Denholm Young: *Cartulary of the Medieval Archives of Christ Church*, Oxford Historical Society, xcii (1931).
W.G. Hiscock: *A Christ Church Miscellany* (1947).
E.G.W. Bill and J.F.A. Mason: *Christ Church and Reform, 1850–1867* (1970).
J. Cook and J.F.A. Mason (eds): *The Building accounts of Christ Church Library, 1716–1779* (1988).
E.G.W. Bill: *Education at Christ Church, Oxford, 1600–1800* (1988).
D. Fletcher: *The Emergence of Estate Maps, Christ Church, Oxford, 1600–1840* (1995).

963 Corpus Christi College

Parent organisation: University of Oxford

Address: Merton Street, Oxford OX1 4JF

Telephone: (01865) 276717

Fax: (01865) 276767

E-mail: michael.stansfield@ccc.ox.ac.uk

Website: ww.ccc.ox.ac.uk/library.htm

Enquiries: The Archivist, Michael Stansfield

Open: Mon, Tues: 9.30–4.45.

Access: Bona fide researchers; an appointment is always necessary.

Historical background: The college was founded in 1517 by Richard Fox (?1448–1528), who made strict regulations for preserving the muniments.

Acquisitions policy: Internal records as they devolve from office holders. Deeds and documents concerning property and estates.

Archives of organisation: Administrative and estate records of the college, including admission registers, 1517– ; bursarial accounts, 1521– ; buttery records, 1648– ; correspondence of Richard Fox and John Claimond, first president; papers of Robert Newlin, steward, c1660–1700; records of undergraduate societies, 19th century.

Major collections: Library Collections: Medieval MSS concerning theology, liturgy, science, medicine and mathematics.
Collection of Christopher Wase (?1625–1690) *re* grammar schools.
Papers of Thomas Hornsby (1733–1810), astronomer, 1768–74.
Correspondence, papers and diaries of Sir Robert C.K. Ensor (1877–1958) *re* foreign policy, socialism and ornithology.
Letters and papers of A.F. Hemming (1893–1964) *re* Irish troubles and the treaty, 1920–22, and the International Committee for Non-Intervention in Spain, 1936–9.
Papers of E.D.M. Fraenkel (1888–1970).

Non-manuscript material: Estate maps, 17th century– .
Photographs of members of College.

Finding aids: Catalogue.

Facilities: Photography.

Conservation: In-house service as part of Oxford Colleges Conservation Consortium.

Publications: J.G. Milne: 'The Muniments of Corpus Christi College', *Oxoniensia*, ii (1937).
——— : 'Berkshire Muniments of Corpus Christi College', *Berkshire Archaeological Journal* (1942), 35–44.
——— : *The Early History of Corpus Christi College* (Oxford, 1946) [Chap. 5 covers the archives].
C. Woolgar: 'Two Oxford Archives in the Early Seventeenth Century', *Archives*, xvi/71 (1984), 258–72.

964   English Faculty Library

Parent organisation: University of Oxford

Address: St Cross Building, Manor Road, Oxford OX1 3UQ

Telephone: (01865) 271050

Fax: (01865) 271054

E-mail: susan.usher@efl.ox.ac.uk

Website: www.users.ox.ac.uk

Enquiries: The Librarian

Open: Term: Mon–Fri: 9.30–7.00; Sat: 9.30–12.30 .
Vacation: Mon–Fri: 9.30–5.00.
Closed during August.

Access: Primarily for members of the university. Other people may be admitted at the discretion of the library committee. Application should be made to the Librarian, giving credentials and special reasons for wishing to use the library.

Historical background: Founded in 1914 to serve the English School, it is essentially a working collection and has been enriched by gifts and bequests.

Acquisitions policy: It is not library policy to buy MS material; working papers of scholars are occasionally deposited.

Major collections: E.H.W. Meyerstein (1889–1952): papers, including unpublished works, copies of letters, collections of family photographs, portraits (40 boxes).
Wilfred Owen (1893–1918) Collection: includes his personal library, some of his MSS (poems etc), family relics, press cuttings, correspondence about his works, and other papers preserved by his brother Harold Owen (1897–1971), an author in his own right; correspondence by or to Wilfred Owen, and later letters from members of his circle or editors, including Siegfried Sassoon (1886–1967) and Edmund Blunden (1896–1974) to Susan and Harold Owen.
Notes and correspondence of Dr Percy Simpson (1865–1962) relevant to the history of the library; Dr K.D. Büllbring (1863–1917); S. Roscoe (1900–77), bibliographer of the Newbery family of booksellers; and Professor H.J. Davis (1893–1967), editor of Swift.

Non-manuscript material: Pamphlet collection of Prof. A.S. Napier (1853–1916), including scarce academic dissertations on Old and

Middle English philology, late 19th–early 20th centuries.

Finding aids: Special handlists for MSS collections. NRA 11902.

Facilities: Photocopying. Microfilm readers.

Conservation: Bodleian Library Conservation Department.

Publications: P. Morgan: *Brief Calendar* (1965) [available in Bodleian Library].
——: *Oxford Libraries outside the Bodleian: a Guide* (Oxford, 2/1980), 169.
J. Harker: *The Historical Development of the English Faculty Library, Oxford* (London, 1980).

965 Exeter College
The Library

Parent organisation: University of Oxford

Address: Oxford OX1 3DP

Telephone: (01865) 279621/279600

Fax: (01865) 279630

E-mail: librarian@exeter.ox.ac.uk

Website: www.exeter.ox.ac.uk

Enquiries: The Librarian and Archivist, Dr J.R. Madicott

Open: Mon–Fri: 9.00–5.00.
Closed for two to three weeks in August and September.

Access: Bona fide scholars, by appointment with the Librarian and Archivist.

Historical background: The college was founded in 1314.

Acquisitions policy: Gifts and bequests are occasionally received from old members, and very occasionally items relating to the college are purchased.

Archives of organisation: College registers, 1539–1915; lists of fellows; statutes; rectors' and bursars' accounts; financial records, 1592– ; buttery books, 1592–1762; SCR papers, 1787–1967; library records; records of clubs and societies; deeds and papers *re* properties in Oxfordshire and elsewhere.

Major collections: Shortridge papers, 1693– .
Secondary material and collections relating to college history.

Non-manuscript material: A large number of photographs, prints and original drawings; scrapbooks; rolled maps and plans of estates, 18th and 19th centuries.

Finding aids: Full typescript handlist (1977, rev. 1993; copy in the Bodleian Library).

Facilities: Photocopying.

Publications: C.W. Boase: *Registration Collegii Exoniensis* (Oxford, 2/1894).
A.B. How: *Exeter College Register, 1891–1921* (Oxford, 1928).
HMC Second Report, XIV App. 127–30 (1).
A.G. Watson: *A Descriptive Catalogue of the Medieval Manuscripts of Exeter College, Oxford* (Oxford, 2000).

966 Harris Manchester College

Parent organisation: University of Oxford

Address: Mansfield Road, Oxford OX1 3TD

Telephone: (01865) 271015/6

Fax: (01865) 271012

Enquiries: The Librarian, Mrs M.A. Sarosi

Open: Mon–Fri 9.30–1.00, 2.00–5.00, by appointment.
Closed in August.

Access: Approved readers, on written application. Letters of recommendation/identification may be required.

Historical background: Manchester College was established in 1786 in Manchester under the name of Manchester Academy. It was one of the last of a long line of dissenting academies founded to provide non-conformists with higher education, and was the direct successor to Warrington Academy. It moved successively to York (1803–40), back to Manchester (1840–53), to London (1853–99) and finally to Oxford (1899-). From the first the college was closely linked to the Unitarian denomination. The name changed to Harris Manchester College in 1996, when the college acquired full collegiate status in the university.

Acquisitions policy: To collect Unitariana and items relating to the history of the college.

Archives of organisation: Minute books of Warrington Academy and Manchester College, 1757–1820, 1885– ; library catalogues from Warrington, Exeter and Manchester academies; lecture notes by students; student magazines.

Major collections: Letters and papers of teachers at Warrington Academy and Manchester College, including John Seddon (1725–70), Joseph Priestley (1733–1804), Charles Wellbeloved (1769–1858), John Kenrick (1788–1877), James Martineau (1805–1900).
Letters and papers of Unitarians, including William Shepherd (1768–1847), Lant Carpenter (1780–1840), Joseph Blanco White (1775–1841), Mary Carpenter (1807–77), Harriet Martineau (1802–76), Robert B. Aspland (1782–1845).

Non-manuscript material: Portraits and prints of teachers and others.
College photographs etc.
Printed material relating to the college and Unitarian history.
Joseph Priestley's globes.

Facilities: Photocopying. Photographs may be arranged.

Conservation: Contracted out when grants obtained.

Publications: Joseph Priestley 1733–1804: Scientist, Teacher and Theologian: a 250th Anniversary Exhibition (Oxford, 1983).
Manchester College, 1786–1986: a Bicentenary Exhibition Organised by Manchester College Oxford at the Bodleian Library (Oxford, 1986).
B. Smith, (ed.): *Truth, Liberty, Religion: Essays Celebrating Two Hundred Years of Manchester College* (Oxford, 1986).
D.S. Porter: *A Catalogue of Manuscripts in Harris Manchester College* (Oxford, 1998).

967 Hertford College

Parent organisation: University of Oxford

Address: Catte Street, Oxford OX1 3BW

Telephone: (01865) 279400

Fax: (01865) 279437

Website: www.hertford.ox.ac.uk

Enquiries: The Archivist, Dr T. Barnard
The Librarian, Dr S. West

Open: By arrangement.

Access: Access to the archives is by courtesy of the principal and fellows, who reserve the right to refuse permission without giving the reasons for their decision. Post–1920 material is not normally available.

Historical background: The origins of the college lie with the foundation of Hart Hall, a medieval establishment connected with Exeter College, which became the first Hertford College in 1740, and Magdalen Hall. The latter was allied to Magdalen College until 1602, moved to the site of the first Hertford College in 1813 and became the second Hertford College in 1874. MSS were deposited in the Bodleian Library (see entry 958) in 1890.

Archives of organisation: Few records survive: they include Magdalen Hall buttery books, 1661, 1663, 1670–1862; Hertford College buttery books, 1879– .
NB A few Magdalen Hall records are among Magdalen College archives (see entry 973).

Non-manuscript material: Broadsides and proclamations, c1660–18th century.

Finding aids: Typescript catalogue of archives (1985): NRA 27928.

Conservation: Contracted out.

Publications: See preface to S.G. Hamilton: *Hertford College* (College Histories, 1903).

968 House of St Gregory and St Macrina Library

Address: 1 Canterbury Road, Oxford OX2 6LU

Telephone: (01865) 552991

Fax: (01865) 316700

E-mail: gensec@sobornost.org

Enquiries: The Librarian
For Webb Collection: Dr S.P. Brock, Oriental Institute, Pusey Lane, Oxford OX1 2LE

Open: By arrangement.

Access: Bona fide researchers, by appointment.

Historical background: The core of the collection comes from the library of the late Rev. Derwas Chitty.

Acquisitions policy: Funds available are minimal: acquisitions are mainly Greek patristic texts of monastic interest.

Major collections: Chitty Collection of papers left by Rev. D. Chitty.
Webb Collection: transcripts of Syriac liturgical MSS made by Rev. Douglas Webb.

Non-manuscript material: Greek patristic texts.

Publications: K. Ware and S.P. Brock: 'The Library of the House of St Gregory and St

Macrina, Oxford: the D.J. Chitty Papers', *Sobornost/Eastern Chronicles Review*, iv/1 (1982), 56–8.

969 Jesus College

Parent organisation: University of Oxford

Address: Oxford OX1 3DW

Telephone: (01865) 279761

Fax: (01865) 279687

E-mail: brigid.allen@jesus.ox.ac.uk

Website: www.lib.ox.ac.uk/guides/jes.htm

Enquiries: The Archivist, Brigid Allen

Open: By arrangement only.

Access: Bona fide researchers, by appointment after written application.

Historical background: The college was founded by Elizabeth I in 1571 and has had strong connections with Wales throughout its history. In 1886 the medieval MSS, including some important Welsh-language ones, were deposited in the Bodleian Library (see entry 958).

Acquisitions policy: Papers of former members may be accepted.

Archives of organisation: Registers and papers relating to the college's internal administration, estates and livings, including bursars' accounts, 1631– ; benefactors' registers, 1625– ; buttery books, 1637– ; admission registers, 1882–1932; college registers, 1660– ; minutes of governing body, 1883– ; records of undergraduate societies, 1858– .

Major collections: Private papers of principals Francis Mansell (1579–1665) and Thomas Pardo (1688–1763), and of Edmund Meyricke (1636–1713), fellow and benefactor.
Papers of John Richard Green (1837–83), historian, and T.E. Lawrence (1888–1935).

Non-manuscript material: Plans, maps and photographs.

Finding aids: Lists available. Guide in preparation.

Facilities: Photocopying where appropriate. Photography via the Bodleian Library.

Conservation: Member of the Oxford Colleges Conservation Consortium.

Publications: J.N.L. Baker: *Jesus College, Oxford, 1571–1971* (Oxford, 1971).
B. Allen: 'The Early History of Jesus College of Oxford, 1571–1603', *Oxoniensia*, (1998 [1999]), 105–24.
W.P. Griffith: 'Jesus College, Oxford and Wales, the first Half-Century', *Transactions of the Honorable Society of Cymmrodorion*, new series 3 (1997), 20–44.

970 Keble College

Parent organisation: University of Oxford

Address: Parks Road, Oxford OX1 3PG

Telephone: (01865) 272727

Fax: (01865) 272705

E-mail: marjory.szurko@keb.ox.ac.uk

Website: www.lib.ox.ac.uk/guides/colleges/keb.htm

Enquiries: The Librarian

Open: By arrangement.

Access: Bona fide scholars, by appointment.

Historical background: The college was founded in 1870 as a memorial to John Keble (1792–1866), poet and divine.

Acquisitions policy: To maintain the archives and accept papers relevant to the theological concerns of the college.

Archives of organisation: Papers of the Keble Memorial Fund, 1866– ; council minutes, accounts, admissions, 1870– ; academic reports on undergraduates, 1873– ; records of student societies, 1870– .

Major collections: Correspondence and papers of John Keble and H.P. Liddon (1829–90) *re* Tractarian Movement.
Collections of medieval and oriental MSS.

Finding aids: TS lists of Keble and Liddon papers, with index of correspondents.

Publications: B. St G. Drennan (ed.): *The Keble College Centenary Register, 1870–1970* (Oxford 1971).
M.B. Parkes: *The Medieval Manuscripts of Keble College, Oxford* (1979).
P. Morgan: *Oxford Libraries outside the Bodleian* (2/1980), 54–5.

971 Lady Margaret Hall

Parent organisation: University of Oxford

Address: Norham Gardens, Oxford OX2 6QA

Telephone: (01865) 274361

Fax: (01865) 511069

E-mail: roberta.staples@lmh.ox.ac.uk

Website: www.lib.ox.ac.uk/guides/colleges/lmh.htm

Enquiries: The College Archivist, c/o the College Librarian

Open: Strictly by arrangement.

Access: Bona fide researchers. There is restricted access to personal records of members of the college.

Historical background: Lady Margaret Hall was founded in 1878 as one of the first two halls for women in Oxford. It has been co-educational since 1979. Papers of Louisa Kathleen Haldane (1863–1961) have been transferred to the Bodleian Library (see entry 958).

Acquisitions policy: Strictly limited to records relating to the college, its fellows, other staff and students.

Archives of organisation: Official records of the college, 1878– , including minute books of the History Club, a society for Oxford women history dons, 1899–1939.

Major collections: MS and TS poems of Ethel Street (LMH, 1918–21), who worked at the Tavistock Clinic and London School of Economics.

Non-manuscript material: Architectural drawings of college buildings and plans of the grounds.
Photographs of buildings and students.

Finding aids: Summary lists. Lists sent to NRA. Haldane: NRA 11605.

Facilities: Photocopying by arrangement.

Conservation: Contracted out.

Publications: J. Agate (ed.): *Lady Margaret Hall Register, 1879–1966* (Cambridge, 1970).
C. Avent and H. Pipe (eds): *Lady Margaret Hall Register, 1879–1990* (Oxford, 1990).

972 Lincoln College

Parent organisation: University of Oxford

Address: Turl Street, Oxford OX1 3DR

Telephone: (01865) 279831

Fax: (01865) 279802

E-mail: archives@lincoln.ox.ac.uk

Website: www.lincoln.ox.ac.uk

Enquiries: The Archivist

Open: By arrangement only.

Access: Genuine historical researchers; an appointment must be made well in advance.

Historical background: Lincoln College was founded in 1429 by Richard Fleming, Bishop of Lincoln, under whom the earliest college buildings were erected. In 1479 Bishop Thomas Rotherham, who is regarded as the second founder, further endowed the college and had the statutes drawn up. The college was given estates in Oxfordshire and elsewhere which, with various benefactions, provided the income of fellows and scholars. The college administration has continued unbroken to the present day, although several series of records survive only from the 17th century. In 1892 the MS collections were deposited in the Bodleian Library (see entry 958).

Acquisitions policy: The college is pleased to accept papers of old members relating to the life of the college.

Archives of organisation: College statutes, charters, registers, 1427– .
Annual accounts, 15th century– (complete, 1600–).
Estate deeds, leases and manorial records, correspondence, 13th–20th centuries.
Records of college clubs and societies.

Major collections: Some letters of John Wesley (1703–17), fellow, and Mark Pattison (1813–84), rector.
Papers of William Ward Fowler (1847–1921), fellow.
Some MSS of Edward Thomas (1878–1917).
Papers of Sir Osbert Lancaster (1908–86).

Finding aids: MS catalogue of medieval deeds and charters.
Catalogue of later material. Handlist and shelf list of archives. Transcripts with subject indexes available in Bodleian Library.

Facilities: Photocopying.

Publications: V.H. Green: *The Commonwealth of Lincoln College, 1427–1977* (Oxford, 1979).

973 Magdalen College

Parent organisation: University of Oxford

Address: Oxford OX1 4AU

Telephone: (01865) 276088

E-mail: robin.darwall-smith@magd.ox.ac.uk

Website: www.magd.ox.ac.uk

Enquiries: The Archivist, Dr R.H. Darwall-Smith

Open: Thurs, Fri: 10.00–1.00, 2.00–4.30, by appointment.

Access: On written application. There is a 30-year restriction on many items; no access is available to records of living persons.

Historical background: The college was founded in 1458 by William Waynflete, Bishop of Winchester.

Acquisitions policy: The integration into the college archive of any material relevant to its history, donated or deposited by former members or by the general public.

Archives of organisation: Administrative and financial records of the college, 15th century– .
Deeds and documents relating to the acquisition and control of college estates, distributed over a wide area of southern and eastern England, 12th century– .
Documents relating to Magdalen College Schools at Oxford, Brackley (Northants) and Wainfleet (Lincs), mainly 19th century.

Major collections: Literary and personal papers relating to members of the college and their associates.
Papers of Sir Douglas Dodds-Parker (*b* 1909), relating to the Sudan, the Second World War, and late 20th-century British politics.

Non-manuscript material: Maps, plans and architectural drawings of college buildings and estates.
Prints and photographs of college members.
Printed material relating to the college and the university.
A small number of microfilms and tape-recordings.

Finding aids: Summary Guide to the Archives of Magdalen College and detailed catalogues of the estate papers of the college (10 vols) and the Dodds-Parker papers (available at the NRA). Other catalogues and lists, including a calendar of medieval deeds (49 vols) and an MS list and card index to documents MSS 222–1119, at the college.

Facilities: Photocopying at the discretion of the Archivist. Photography and microfilm by arrangement.

Conservation: Member of the Oxford Colleges Conservation Consortium.

Publications: J.R. Bloxam: *Register of the Members of St Mary Magdalen College* (Oxford and London, 1853–81) [7 vols].
W.D. Macray: *Notes from the Muniments of St Mary Magdalen College, Oxford, from the Twelfth to the Seventeenth Century* (Oxford and London, 1882).
—— : *Register of Magdalen College*, new series (London, 1894–1915) [8 vols].
C. Woolgar: 'Two Oxford Archives in the Early Seventeenth Century', *Archives*, xvi/71 (1984), 258–72.

974 Mansfield College Library

Parent organisation: University of Oxford

Address: Mansfield College, Mansfield Road, Oxford OX1 3TF

Telephone: (01865) 270975

Fax: (01865) 270970

E-mail: alma.jenner@mansfield.ox.ac.uk

Enquiries: The Librarian, Alma Jenner

Open: Mon–Fri: 9.00–4.00.

Access: By written application to the Librarian.

Historical background: Mansfield College had its origins in Spring Hill College, Birmingham, founded in 1838 for the training of Congregational ministers. The college was transferred to Oxford in 1886, and, being the first non-conformist college to come to Oxford after the abolition of the Religious Tests Act, it trained ministers from any dissenting denomination and provided a free church faculty in theology. In 1955 it was recognised by the university and began to receive undergraduates. It was granted full college status in 1995.

Acquisitions policy: General encouragement from librarian to departments and older members of the college to deposit material.

Archives of organisation: Archives of Spring Hill College, Birmingham, and Mansfield College, Oxford: annual reports; minutes of the

governing body and Board of Education; cash books; bursary records, 1838– .
College magazine.
Responses from other dissenting colleges to questions sent by Spring Hill College on the anti-slavery movement, 1841.
Minutes of college societies, including Discussion Society, 1847–66; Debating Society, 1860–77; Oxford University Congregational Society, 1950–57; Oxford University Nonconformists Union; Rural Mission Society; Rural Churches Committee.

Major collections: Samuel Birch (1813–85), Book of Prayers.
Records of chapels and missioners associated with former students of Spring Hill.
A.L. Thomas, note-books of lectures by Selbie and others, 1919–22 (47).
E. Wilton Rix, letters to his family, 1914–18.
A.G. Matthews (1881–1962), papers concerning non-conformist history.
Records of the Frilford and Longworth Home Mission, 1854–1939.
MS sermons.

Non-manuscript material: Photograph albums of college buildings, interiors and college members; news cuttings.
Tapes of reminiscences of older members of the college.

Finding aids: Computerised catalogue; hard copy available. Handlist. NRA 10965.

Facilities: Photocopying.

Publications: E. Kaye: *Mansfield College Oxford: its Origin, History and Significance* (Oxford, 1996).
'Library Guide', *Mansfield College Magazine* (1988, 1989, 1998) [3 articles by librarian on history of the library].

975 Merton College Library

Parent organisation: University of Oxford

Address: Oxford OX1 4JD

Telephone: (01865) 286477

Fax: (01865) 276361

E-mail: michael.stansfield@merton.ox.ac.uk

Website: www.merton.ox.ac.uk/college/library.html

Enquiries: The Archivist, Michael Stansfield

Open: Wed–Fri: 9.30–4.45.

Access: Bona fide researchers only; an appointment is necessary.

Historical background: The college was founded in 1264 and the library building, begun in 1373, is one of the oldest to survive in England.

Archives of organisation: Records of the college, administration and estates, including wardens' accounts, bursars' and subwardens' rolls, c1300–1660; minutes of the governing body, 1483– ; admission records, 1758– ; parish register of St John the Baptist parish.

Major collections: Two diaries of Griffin Higgs (1589–1659), 1637–8.
Papers of James Harris, 1st Earl of Malmesbury (1746–1820); G.C. Brodrick (1831–1903), warden of the college, and F.H. Bradley (1846–1924), philosopher.
Autobiography of Edward Nares (1762–1841), theological and historical writer.
Papers, drawings and first editions of Sir Max Beerbohm (1872–1956).

Non-manuscript material: First editions of T.S. Eliot.

Finding aids: Supplementary catalogue, 1920. Indexes of deeds, surveys and maps, with handlists. Summary handlist, 1970. Calendar of Oxfordshire Records at Merton (typescript list). List of correspondence of 1st Earl of Malmesbury: NRA 9473.

Facilities: Limited photocopying facilities. Photographs and microfilms may be ordered.

Conservation: Member of the Oxford Colleges Conservation Consortium.

Publications: F.M. Powicke: *The Medieval Books of Merton College* (Oxford, 1931) [includes MSS].
Merton College Register, 1900–1964; 1964–84 (Oxford, 1891–1989) [these registers contain summaries of the biographies of members of the college].
G.H. Martin and J.R.L. Hughfield: *A History of Merton College, Oxford* (Oxford, 1997).

976 Middle East Centre
St Antony's College

Parent organisation: University of Oxford

Address: Oxford OX2 6JF

Telephone: (01865) 284706

Fax: (01865) 311475

E-mail: clare.brown@sant.ox.ac.uk

Website: www.sant.ox.ac.uk/mec/mec.html

Enquiries: The Archivist, Mrs Clare Brown

Open: Mon–Fri: 9.30–12.45, 1.45–5.15.
Closed for four weeks in the summer.

Access: Members of Oxford University; others at the discretion of the Archivist and strictly by appointment. There is a daily charge for non-academics. A letter of introduction is required.

Historical background: The collection was begun in 1961 by Elizabeth Monroe and Albert Hourani with the aim of gathering together the papers, both personal and official, of individuals who served in the Middle East as senior government representatives, members of the armed forces etc,or whose main area of concern (as bankers, businessmen, missionaries or travellers) was the Middle East. The collection has expanded rapidly and now contains the papers of more than 200 individuals, covering the period from 1800 to the present day.

Acquisitions policy: To acquire, by donation or deposit, further collections of private papers of individuals who were involved in the Middle East.

Major collections: H.R.P. Dickson (1881–1959) papers: reports, diaries and correspondence concerning his career as political agent in Bahrain, 1919–21; political resident in the Gulf, 1928; and political agent in Kuwait, 1929–36.
Papers of C.J. Edmonds concerning his service in Iraq, 1915–45, and his study of Kurdistan (topography, language and people), 1915–1960s.
H. St John Philby: correspondence, memos, travel diaries, published and unpublished MSS, relating to Transjordan, Iraq, Palestine and Arabia, 1915–57.
Maj.-Gen. Sir E.L. Spears: papers relating to the Spears Mission to Syria and the Lebanon, 1941–4.
Jerusalem and East Mission: records covering the mission's work in Palestine, Syria, Iraq, Jordan, Iran, Gulf, Egypt, Sudan, Cyprus and North Africa, 1841–1970s.

Non-manuscript material: Photographic Archive: covering all areas of the Middle East, c1860–1960 (c70,000 items).

Finding aids: Handlists are available for approximately one-third of the collections and there is an extensive author and subject index. Lists sent to NRA.

Facilities: Photocopying. Photography by arrangement. Microfiche reader.

Conservation: Contracted out.

Publications: D. Grimwood Jones (ed.): *Sources for the History of the British in the Middle East, 1800–1978: a Catalogue of the Private Papers Collection in the Middle East Centre, St Antony's College, Oxford* (London, 1979).
G.M. Grant (ed.): *Historical Photographs of the Middle East from the Middle East Centre, St Anthony's College, Oxford* (1984) [17,000 photographs on microfiche with a catalogue].

977 Museum of the History of Science

Parent organisation: University of Oxford

Address: Old Ashmolean Building, Broad Street, Oxford OX1 3AZ

Telephone: (01865) 277280/4

Fax: (01865) 277288

E-mail: tony.simcock@mhs.ox.ac.uk

Website: www.mhs.ox.ac.uk

Enquiries: The Archivist, Mr A.V. Simcock

Open: Mon–Fri: 10.00–5.00, by arrangement.

Access: Scholarly readers, by arrangement with the Librarian; prior notice of visits is helpful.

Historical background: Accompanying the collection of scientific instruments of Lewis Evans (1853–1930), with which the museum was founded in 1924, were the founder's library of c1000 books and 120 volumes of MSS on the subjects of his collection — early scientific instruments and associated techniques. The first curator of the museum, R.T. Gunther (1869–1940), built up a museum library around this core, and it has continued to develop by purchase, gift and deposit. The MS collections and iconographic collection (prints, photographs and printed ephemera) have developed in the same way.

Acquisitions policy: MSS are occasionally purchased, but more usually deposited or given, on the subject of scientific instruments, history of science, and other themes relating to the displays, activities and interests of the museum.

Archives of organisation: R.T. Gunther (curator, 1924–40) Archive, relating both to Gunther himself and to the early history and activities of the museum.

Museum Archive, 1924– .

Major collections: Buxton MSS containing important material relating to Charles Babbage (1792–1871).

Radcliffe Observatory MSS, 1750s-c1900.

Papers and antiquarian collections of several historians of science, in particular G.H. Gabb (1868–1948), R.T. Gunther, H.E. Stapleton (1878–1962) and F. Sherwood Taylor (1897–1956).

Small groups of papers of many Oxford scientists, and from various university departments, laboratories and societies, especially strong in the fields of astronomy and chemistry.

Lewis Evans's important collection of MS treatises and other papers on sundials, surveying, and other mathematical instruments and techniques, mostly 17th and 18th centuries.

Archives and collected MSS of the Royal Microscopical Society.

Non-manuscript material: Associated with the general collection of books is a large collection of off-prints and pamphlets.

The iconographic and printed ephemera collection includes portraits of scientists, illustrations of scientific instruments and other scientific subjects, lecture notices and syllabuses and trade literature.

Photographic material – not confined to scientific subjects – ranges from an archive of Sir John Herschel's experimental work from the time of the invention of photography (1839) to pioneering colour photographs (1900s), and to lantern slides used in science lectures (often associated with MS collections).

Finding aids: Catalogue and index of the MSS collections. NRA lists.

Facilities: Photocopying. Photography can be arranged. Microfilm/fiche reader.

Publications: A.V. Simcock: 'An Ark for History of Science', *Iatul Quarterly*, i/3 (1987), 196–215.

P. Morgan: *Select Index of Manuscript Collections in Oxford Libraries outside the Bodleian* (Oxford, 1991) [references for the museum's holdings].

978 New College

Parent organisation: University of Oxford

Address: The Library, New College, Oxford OX1 3BN

Telephone: (01865) 279581

Fax: (01865) 279590

E-mail: caroline.dalton@new.ox.ac.uk

Website: www.new.ox.ac.uk/nc/archives/

Enquiries: The Archivist, Mrs C. Dalton

Open: Mon–Fri: 10.00–1.00, 2.00–5.15; Sat: a.m. at Bodleian Library, by prior arrangement only.

Access: Bona fide scholars and researchers, by appointment.

Historical background: New College was founded by William of Wykeham in 1379 as the senior part of two linked educational institutions, New College and Winchester College. It became co-educational in 1979. The archives have taken their present form partly as a result of provisions made in the founder's statutes for the admission and conduct of members, and partly out of the need to keep track of an income derived from manors and benefices scattered over ten different counties in southern England. Of particular interest is the fact that the endowments of the college already had a written history when they were acquired, together with their documents. This means that the oldest material in the collections antedates the foundation of the college by some 250 years.

Acquisitions policy: The archives absorb as a matter of course non-current administrative papers generated within the college. Any informal record of college life offered by old members or their descendants is accepted with gratitude. The college does not actively seek out archives which might have strayed into private hands in the past, or memorabilia, but if anything is offered for purchase, it is considered on its merits.

Archives of organisation: Records of internal discipline and administration, including bursars' rolls, 1379– , hall books, 1386– , acts of warden and fellows, 17th century– , registers of admission, 1450–1841.

Records of dealings with Winchester College, 16th century– .

Records of the administration of the college estates and admission to college livings, 12th

563

century– , including court rolls, late 13th century– , lease books, 1480–20th century, manorial account rolls, 15th century– .

Records of trusteeships, including foundation and administration of Lord Williams' School, Thame, Oxfordshire, 1559–1900.

Major collections: Woodforde family papers, early 17th– late 19th centuries.

Letters of Rev. Sydney Smith (1771–1845) (*c*500).

The residue of the papers of Alfred Milner, 1st Viscount Milner (1854–1925) not transferred to the Bodleian Library, especially press cuttings, 1893–1905, visitors' books, 1897–1905, and addresses presented to Lord Milner, 1897–1906.

Letters and papers of Warden A.H. Smith (1883–1958).

Cox Archives: letters and papers covering roughly the first half of the life of Sir Christopher Cox (1899–1982).

Cooke Archive: a collection of papers of A. H. Cooke (1912–87), mainly from his period as warden, 1976–85.

Personal archives of H.W.B. Joseph (1867–1943), Professor H.H. Joachim (1868–1938) and A. Robinson (1841–1895).

Manuscript compositions of R.O. Morris (1886–1948).

Letters of Rev. H. Rashdall (1858–1924) to his mother Emily Rashdall (*c*480).

Non-manuscript material: A series of photograph albums depicting rowing crews and some other sporting teams, 1883– .
Estate maps.

Finding aids: Databases of recent archives of administration, early deeds and photographs of individuals or groups. Calendar of the White book (archive 9654). Handlists of the personal archives. Guide to using printed sources and New College archives for biographical research.

Facilities: Photocopying. Photography by arrangement. Microfilm reader. Researchers may bring laptop computers.

Conservation: Contracted out.

Publications: H. Rashdall and R.S. Rait: *New College* (London 1901) [part of the college histories series].

H.F. Westlake: *Hornchurch Priory: a Kalendar of Documents* (1923).

T.F. Hobson: *Manorial Documents at New College, Oxford*, Manorial Society no. 16 (1929).

A.H. Smith: *New College and its Buildings* (Oxford, 1952).

F. Steer: *The Archives of New College, Oxford* (London, 1974).

J. Buxton and P. Williams (eds): *New College, 1379–1979* (1979).

P. Morgan: *Oxford Libraries outside the Bodleian: a Guide* (Oxford, 2/1980), 92.

979 Nuffield College Library

Parent organisation: University of Oxford

Address: Nuffield College, Oxford OX1 1NF

Telephone: (01865) 278550

Fax: (01865) 278621

E-mail: james.legg@nuf.ox.ac.uk

Website: www.nuff.ox.ac.uk/library

Enquiries: The Librarian, Mr James Legg

Open: Oct–Jun: Mon–Fri: 9.30–5.30; Sat: 9.30–12.30, by prior arrangement only

Access: Bona fide researchers, by appointment (letter or e-mail).

Historical background: The college was founded in 1937 as a graduate college in the social sciences. The librarian is responsible for custody of archives and deposited collections. Fabian Society archives have been transferred to the London School of Economics (see entry 560).

Acquisitions policy: To serve the research needs of members of the college.

Archives of organisation: College records, including papers of the founder, Viscount Nuffield (1877–1963), and of Nuffield College Social Reconstruction Survey.

Major collections: Nuffield Trust for the Special Areas.
Papers on Guild Socialism.
Papers of individuals, including Lord Cherwell (1886–1957), William Cobbett (1762–1835), G.D.H. Cole (1889–1957), Lord Gainford (1860–1943), Sir Hubert Henderson (1890–1952).

Non-manuscript material: Books, pamphlets, journals, government publications *re* social sciences.

Finding aids: Detailed lists of some collections and catalogues of most others.

Facilities: Photocopying. Microfilm/fiche readers.

980   Oriel College

Parent organisation: University of Oxford

Address: Oriel Square, Oxford OX1 4EW

Telephone: (01865) 286545

Fax: (01865) 286549

E-mail: archives@oriel.ox.ac.uk

Website: www.oriel.ox.ac.uk/library/archive.htm

Enquiries: The Archivist, Mrs E. Boardman

Open: Mon: 9.00–4.45, by arrangement.

Access: Bona fide scholars, by prior appointment only.

Historical background: The college was founded in 1326, and until the Elizabethan period it was primarily a body of graduate fellows; the number of undergraduates remained small until the nineteenth century. The neighbouring St Mary Hall was absorbed in 1902. The library benefited from a large bequest by Baron Leigh in 1786, as well as the college's connections with the Tractarian movement in the 1830s and 1840s; leaders of the movement were fellows of the college. Medieval MSS (not college archives) are deposited in the Bodleian Library (see entry 958).

Acquisitions policy: Archives of the college (internal deposits). Papers of members of the college. Letters and documents connected with the Tractarian movement.

Archives of organisation: College minutes, 1479– ; accounts, 1409– (incomplete); buttery books, 1643–1952; caution books, 1627– ; estate records, 1326– (deeds from 12th century); site and building records, 1326– ; tutorial registers, 1834–1936; records of undergraduate clubs, 1842– .

Major collections: Archives of St Mary Hall, including Journal, 1764–1899; buttery books, 1715–1874; battels account, 1773– .
Extensive collections of letters and papers of those in the Tractarian movement, including John Keble (1792–1866) and John Henry Newman (1801–90).
Correspondence and papers of Edward Hawkins (1789–1882), provost.

Correspondence of Lancelot Ridley Phelps (1853/4–1936), provost.
Papers concerning R.D. Hampden (1793–1868) controversy.

Non-manuscript material: James Wyatt's plans for the college library, 1787.
Estate maps, 1684– , and plans of college site, 20th century.
Photographs of college members and site, late 19th and 20th centuries.

Finding aids: Calendar of papers relating to the college's foundation and to medieval estates. Card index of college archives (cataloguing in progress). Index of Tractarian and other correspondence.

Facilities: Photocopying.

Publications: C.L. Shadwell: *Catalogue of Muniments*, i–x (1893–1905) [privately printed].
—— : *Registrum Orielense*, i–ii (Oxford 1893, 1902).
G.C. Richards and C.L. Shadwell: *The Provosts and Fellows of Oriel College Oxford* (Oxford, 1922).
G.C. Richards and H.E. Salter: *The Dean's Register of Oriel, 1446–1661* (Oxford, 1926).
C.L. Shadwell and H.E. Salter: *Oriel College Records* (Oxford Historical Society, 1926).
Articles about the archive collections appear in *The Oriel Record* (1909–).

981   Oxfam Archives

Address: 274 Banbury Road, Oxford OX2 7DX

Telephone: (01865) 313764 (Tue, Thurs, Fri); (01869) 355129 (Mon, Wed)

Fax: (01865) 313770

E-mail: cwebb@oxfam.org.uk

Enquiries: The Archivist, Chrissie Webb

Open: Mon–Fri: by arrangement.

Access: Generally open to the public, by appointment only. Access to certain items may be restricted.

Historical background: The Oxford Committee for Famine Relief was formed in 1942 in response to the Allied blockade of Greece and the suffering of its population. In 1943 the committee was registered as a charity. Today, Oxfam's main concerns as a development agency are long-term sustainable development (although it continues to provide emergency relief in times of crisis) and international advocacy. The organisation of the overseas project files began in 1980 and the central archives were established in 1994.

Acquisitions policy: To maintain the archives.

Archives of organisation: Main committee minutes of Oxford committee for Famine Relief, later Oxfam, 1942– .
Minutes of executives and other committees; annual reports and accounts; records of grants, 1943– .
Overseas project files, c1955– .

Non-manuscript material: Publicity and advertising material; appeals and campaign literature. Photographs, film and videos.
Oxfam publications, including development education material, periodicals, etc. Gilbert Murray Memorial Lectures.

Finding aids: Computerised databases.

Facilities: Photocopying.

Publications: M. Black: *A Cause for our Times — Oxfam: the First 50 Years* (1992).

982 Oxford University Archives

Parent organisation: University of Oxford

Address: Bodleian Library, Broad Street, Oxford OX1 3BG

Telephone: (01865) 277145

Fax: (01865) 277145 (office hours); 277182 (other times)

E-mail: enquiries@oua.ox.ac.uk

Website: www.users.ox.ac.uk/~ouainfo

Enquiries: The Archivist, Mr Simon Bailey

Open: Term: Mon–Fri: 9.00–10.00; Sat: 9.00–1.00. Vacation: Mon–Fri: 9.00–7.00.
Sat: 9.00–1.00.
Closed week of August bank holiday.
Opening hours are those of the Bodleian Library (see entry 958); intending visitors should always contact the Archivist in advance.

Access: By prior arrangement with the Archivist. Material from the University Archives is read in the Duke Humfrey reading room in the old Bodleian Library. Access requires a Bodleian reader's ticket, for which a charge is made. All records are closed for 30 years and access to certain classes of material is restricted for up to 80 years.

Historical background: The date of the first extant university charter is 1214. Since then the university has preserved records such as charters, deeds, financial documents and records of students. The first keeper of the archives was elected in 1634, and he and his successor transferred the records from the old Congregation House adjoining St Mary's Church to the lower of the two top rooms in the tower in the old Bodleian Library quadrangle. Expansion led to the acquisition of the upper room in the tower for the archives in 1854 and accommodation in other university buildings more recently. The Bodleian Library and the university Press maintain their own records, as do the individual colleges of the university.

Acquisitions policy: Acquisitions are restricted to the administrative records of the university and its departments.

Archives of organisation: University charters, statutes and title deeds.
Records of Congregation, Convocation and Hebdomadal Council (legislative and executive bodies).
University Chest and Registry (finance and central administration); students (chiefly matriculations and degrees); chancellor's jurisdiction; university delegacies and committees.
Departmental and faculty records.

Non-manuscript material: Plans of the University Museum and the Taylor Institution, 19th and 20th centuries.
Drawings and photographs of the restoration of the Sheldonian Theatre, 1935–7, 1958–63.

Finding aids: Handlist and index to contents of lower archive room; lists of most other records; detailed index to Chancellor's Court records, 1578–1968 (in preparation).

Facilities: (shared with Bodleian Library) Photocopying. Photography. Microfilm/fiche reader/printer.

Conservation: Contracted out.

Publications: *Corpus Statutorum Universitatis Oxoniensis* (Oxford, 1768) [with additions].
J. Griffiths: *Index to Wills and other Testamentary Records of the Chancellor's Court* (Oxford, 1862).
J. Foster: *Alumni Oxonienses/Oxford Men*, 3 vols (1887–93).

The History of the University of Oxford: Vols I–VIII (Oxford, 1984–2000).
J. Griffiths: Statutes of the University of Oxford codified in 1636 (Oxford, 1888).
R.L. Poole: Lecture on the History of the University Archives (Oxford, 1912).
S. Gibson: Statuta Antiqua Oxoniensis (Oxford, 1931).
A.B. Emden: A Biographical Register of the University of Oxford to A.D. 1500/A.D. 1501–1540 (Oxford, 1957/1974).
T.H. Aston and D.G. Vaisey: 'University Archives', in P. Morgan: Oxford Libraries outside the Bodleian (Oxford, 2/1980).
All the pre-1500 university records and some 16th- and 17th-century material have been published, chiefly by the Oxford Historical Society.

983 Oxford University Museum of Natural History

Parent organisation: University of Oxford

Address: Parks Road, Oxford OX1 3PW

Telephone: (01865) 272982

Fax: (01865) 272970

E-mail: stella.brecknell@oum.ox.ac.uk

Website: www.oum.ox.ac.uk/library.html

Enquiries: The Librarian, Ms Stella Brecknell

Open: Mon–Fri: 9.00–1.00, 2.00–5.00.

Access: Members of Oxford University, and staff and students of other universities upon proof of identity. Other bona fide researchers on written application to the Director. All new users (including members of the university) who wish to consult manuscripts must make prior (normally written) application to the Director and, permission having been given, make an appointment with the Librarian.

Historical background: The library is based upon two major benefactions, that of the Rev. F.W. Hope (1849) and that of W.J. Arkell (1956), which created outstanding resources for the study of entomology and Jurassic geology and palaeontology. It also reflects the university's historic decision of 1855 to create a central teaching facility for natural science in a new museum where its scattered natural history collections could be brought together. The library concentrates today on providing curatorial and research resources for the four modern collections of entomology, geology, mineralogy and zoology. The archives of the museum are deposited in Oxford University Archives (see entry 982), but there is a small archive on the history of the building and of the museum.

Acquisitions policy: There is no policy of adding to the archive by purchase.

Major collections: Each collection holds catalogues and correspondence in various degrees of completeness relating to accessioned specimens. In addition there is the following material:
Entomology: W.J. Burchell (1782–1863), MS notes, paintings, correspondence; J.C. and C.W. Dale (1792–1872; 1851–1906), diaries, catalogues, correspondence; F.W. Hope (1797–1862), note-books and correspondence; W. Jones (d 1818), note-books and paintings; O. Pickard-Cambridge (1828–1917) and J.O. Westwood (1805–93), MS notes.
Geology: W.J. Arkell (1904–56) and W. Smith (1769–1839), papers; W. Buckland (1784–1856) and J. Phillips (1800–74), note-books, letters and papers; J.M. Edmonds (1909–82), research notes.
Mineralogy: T.V. Barker (1881–1931), research notes, correspondence; A.H. Church (1834–1915), laboratory note-books, correspondence; H. Muller (1833–1915), correspondence; H.L. Bowman (1874–1942), M.W. Porter (1886–1981), R.S. Spiller (1887–1954) and E.J.W. Whittaker (b 1921), research notes; L.R. Wager (1904–65), research notes, field notes, field notebooks, photographs.
Zoology: W.J. Burchell, MS notes etc.

Non-manuscript material: Plans, drawings and photographs of the early museum.
Paintings and drawings of geological phenomena used as teaching aids by Buckland, Phillips and others, 19th century.
Teaching slide collections, early 20th century.

Finding aids: Catalogues and handlists. Arkell: NRA 24520.

Facilities: Photocopying. Photography.

Publications: K.C. Davies and J. Hull: The Zoological Collections of the Oxford University Museum (Oxford, 1976).
A.Z. Smith: A History of the Hope Entomological Collections in the University Museum, Oxford (Oxford, 1986).

J. Alton: *Catalogue of the Papers and Correspondence of James Marmaduke Edmonds (1909–1982)* (Bath, NCUACS, 1998).

984 Oxford University Press

Parent organisation: University of Oxford

Address: Great Clarendon Street, Oxford OX2 6DP

Telephone: (01865) 267527

Fax: (01865) 267908

E-mail: mawma@oup.co.uk
mcmorrij@oup.co.uk

Enquiries: The Archivist, Dr Martin Maw
The Assistant Archivist, Jenny McMorris

Open: Mon–Fri: 9.00–5.00.

Access: Open to all researchers, by appointment. There are closure periods of 80 years on personal records, 40 years on finance committee minutes and 30 years on delegates' minutes, financial and printing records.

Historical background: The university commissioned its first book in 1478, and obtained a royal charter to print 'all manner of books' in 1636. In the 19th century the press opened a London office (since closed) and now has branches around the world. OUP is governed by a group of university academics and officials — the Delegates of the Press. There is a small museum open by arrangement with the Archivist.

Acquisitions policy: Through its records management programme, the archive collects the administrative, editorial and legal documents governing OUP's activities, generated at its main offices in Oxford. OUP branches outside Britain are responsible for keeping their own current records.

Archives of organisation: Delegates' minute books and accounts, 1668– .
Clarendon Press records, 1867–1976.
Records of OUP London, 1874–1976, very fragmentary, but detailed Music Department records.
Printing business records, 1768– c1960.
Wolvercote paper mill records, c1860–1977 (very fragmentary).
Editorial and administrative files from modern publishing divisions: arts and reference, science, English language teaching, medical and journals, and education.

Major collections: Working files and research material for the *Oxford English Dictionary, Dictionary of National Biography* and *Oxford History of English Literature.*

Non-manuscript material: Substantial Bible library, c1580–1990.
The 'Out of Print' Library includes reference copies of most OUP publications, 19th century– .
Large collection of metal types, including the 'Fell types' bought for the press by Bishop John Fell in the 17th century.

Finding aids: Database catalogue (available only to archives staff).

Facilities: Photocopying.

Conservation: Contracted out.

Publications: H. Carter: *A History of the Oxford University Press,* vol. I (1690–1780) (1975).
N. Barker: *The Oxford University Press and the Spread of Learning* (1978).
P. Sutcliffe: *The Oxford University Press: an Informal History* (1978).
Pamphlet guide.

985 Oxfordshire Health Archives

Address: The Warneford Hospital, Warneford Lane, Headington, Oxford OX3 7JX

Telephone: (01865) 226308

Fax: (01865) 226507

Enquiries: The Archivist, Mrs Elizabeth Boardman

Open: Fri: 9.00–4.45, and one other variable day, by arrangement.

Access: By prior appointment only. There is a 30-year closure on administrative records and 100-year closure on medical material.

Historical background: A part-time archivist was employed by the United Oxford Hospitals in 1969, and this was continued by Oxfordshire Health Authority from 1974 to 1994. The archivist is now employed by the Oxfordshire Mental Healthcare NHS Trust, which contracts the service out to the other Oxfordshire NHS trusts and authorities.

Acquisitions policy: Material relating to NHS hospitals in Oxfordshire and their staff, acquired by internal transfer and by gift or deposit from external sources.

Archives of organisation: Significant archives of the following hospitals and administrative bodies:
Radcliffe Infirmary, 1764–1979; Warneford Hospital (formerly Radcliffe Asylum), 1567–1971; Littlemore Hospital (formerly Oxfordshire County Lunatic Asylum), 1846–1985; Horton Hospital, 1869–1989; Nuffield Orthopaedic Centre (formerly Winfield-Morris Hospital), 1872–1974; Brackley Cottage Hospital, 1876–1968; Oxford Eye Hospital, 1885–1947; Victoria Cottage Hospital, Thame, 1891–1969; Chipping Norton War Memorial Hospital, 1919–86; Bicester Cottage Hospital, 1928–68; hospital management committees, 1948–74.
Records of 15 other hospitals and bodies.

Major collections: Radcliffe Guild of Nurses, 1897–1991; Wingfield League, 1926–94; Radcliffe Infirmary League of Friends, 1967–90; League of Friends of the Littlemore, Warneford and Park hospitals, 1961–89.
Miscellanea relating to J.M. Charcot (1825–93), French neurologist.

Non-manuscript material: Paintings, prints and photographs of staff and hospitals; site plans.

Finding aids: Handlists of all material and catalogues of most collections.

Facilities: Photocopying.

Publications: A.G. Gibson: *The Radcliffe Infirmary* (1926).
M. Bone: *Relief of the Sick and Lame* (1970).
A.H.T. Robb Smith: *A Short History of the Radcliffe Infirmary* (1970).
M. Cheney: *The Horton General Hospital, Banbury, 1872–1972* (1972).
J. Trueta: *Gathorne Robert Girdlestone* (1971).
B. Parry Jones: *The Warneford Hospital, 1826–1976* (1976).
E.J.R. Burrough: *Unity in Diversity: the Short Life of the United Oxford Hospitals* (1978).
B. Parry Jones: 'Peter Hollins at the Warneford Hospital', *Leeds Arts Calendar*, no. 88 (1981).
J. Selby-Green: *History of the Radcliffe Infirmary* (1990).
M. Railton: *Early Medical Services: Berkshire and South Oxfordshire* (1994).
D. Smith: *Brackley Cottage Hospitals, 1876–1996* (1996).

986 Oxfordshire Record Office

Parent organisation: Oxfordshire County Council

Address: St Lukes Church, Temple Road, Cowley, Oxford OX4 2EX

Telephone: (01865) 398200

Fax: (01865) 398201

E-mail: archives@oxfordshire.gov.uk

Website: www.oxfordshire.gov.uk/cshaindex.htm

Enquiries: The County Archivist, Mr Carl Boardman

Open: Mon–Thurs: 9.00–5.00, by appointment only.
Closed for last week of January and first week of February for stock-taking.

Access: Prior booking is advisable. The office operates the CARN reader's ticket system; tickets issued require two passport-size photos. A charge is made for postal enquiries. A 30-year closure may apply to some county council records.

Historical background: Oxfordshire County Record Office was established in 1935 as a sub-section of the legal department of Oxfordshire County Council. In 1987 it was transferred to the newly created Department of Leisure and Arts, and shortly afterwards changed its name to Oxfordshire Archives. In 1984 it took over from the Bodleian Library as Diocesan Record Office for Oxford, and in 1989 it began its policy of providing access to major archive collections held by other organisations in the county through its central searchroom. The office moved from County Hall in 2000 and its name reverted to Oxfordshire Record Office. The archive arranges access to the archives of Oxford City, 1199– , Woodstock Borough, 15th century– , and St Edward's School, Oxford, 1863– .

Acquisitions policy: Material of local significance, which may have relevance for the study of both local and national history, from within the old county boundaries of Oxfordshire (excluding the Vale of White Horse) before 1974, and the present county of Oxfordshire since that date. The office is a recognised place of deposit for public records, tithe and manorial documents. As Diocesan Record Office, it accepts the diocesan archives for Oxford (i.e. the Archdeaconries of Oxford, Berkshire and

Buckingham), but the archdeaconry and parish records for the Archdeaconry of Oxford only.

Archives of organisation: Records of Oxfordshire Quarter Sessions, 1687–1974, and of Oxfordshire County Council (legal and committee service units), 1888– .

Major collections: Local administration: borough records of Banbury, 1554–1974, Chipping Norton, 1600–1966, and Henley-on-Thames, 12th–20th century; urban and rural district council records for pre-1974 Oxfordshire; parish council records; Oxfordshire coroner's records, mainly 20th century; Poor Law union and highway board records for pre-1974 Oxfordshire.

Ecclesiastical: records of Oxford Diocese, 1516–20th century; Oxford Archdeaconry, 1516–20th century; records of parishes in Oxford Archdeaconry, 1244– .

Private deposits: Papers of landed families, including Valentia, early 16th century–20th century; Dillon, 1267–1929; Dashwood, 1316–1954; Fane, 1498–1884; and Saye and Sele, 1339–1932.

Business records, including the Early Blanket Company of Witney, 1648–1988; Frank Cooper (Oxford Marmalade), 1881–1992, and the breweries of Halls, 1537–1947; Courage, 1709–1967; and Brakspear, 1782–1940.

Personal papers of individuals, including Hubert Kestell Cornish, 1803–73, containing extensive correspondence from John Keble; and Madeau Stewart, 20th century, notably with many individuals, including the Mitford family, Stevie Smith, Elizabeth Poston and Elizabeth Goudge.

Records of organisations, including the Oxford Playhouse, 20th century.

Manorial records; deeds; maps.

Non-manuscript material: Library of John Marriott Davenport, clerk of the peace and antiquary.

Finding aids: Computer catalogue. Lists sent to NRA. Calendar of quarter sessions rolls, 1687–1830. Diocesan and parish records catalogued by Bodleian Library prior to transfer; numerous but incomplete indexes to parts of records. Card index of private deposits; comprehensive personal name and place indexes, less comprehensive subject index.

Facilities: Photocopying. Photography can be arranged with a commercial firm. Small number of microforms for use.

Conservation: In-house conservation.

Publications: Oxfordshire County Record Office and its Records (1938).
A Summary Catalogue of the Privately Deposited Records in the Oxfordshire County Record Office (1966).
J. Howard-Drake: *Oxford Church Courts Depositions, 1542–1550* (1991), *1570–1574* (1993), *1581–1586* (1994).
C. Boardman: *Oxfordshire Sinners and Villains* (1994).

987 Pembroke College
McGowin Library

Parent organisation: Oxford University

Address: Oxford OX1 1DW

Telephone: (01865) 276409

Fax: (01865) 276418

E-mail: naomi.vanloo@ox.ac.uk

Enquiries: The Deputy Librarian

Open: Mon–Fri: 10.00–5.00.
Closed in August.

Access: Bona fide researchers, by appointment only. Post-1920 material will not normally be available.

Historical background: Pembroke College, founded by royal charter in 1624, inherited the site and buildings of its direct predecessor, Broadgates Hall. The McGowin Library was opened in 1974.

Acquisitions policy: To maintain and consolidate the college archives and collections.

Archives of organisation: Archives of the college, including statutes, 1624– ; acts of the governing body, 1712– ; accounts, 1651– ; admission records, 1678– ; student societies records, including the Boat Club and the Debating Society, 1842– .

Major collections: Samuel Johnson (1709–84), lexicographer: private devotions and papers (14 bundles).
Log-book of T. Atkinson, Master of *The Victory*, 1804–5.
Correspondence of G.W. Hall, Master, 1809–43, and Sir Peter Le Page Renouf (1822–97).

Finding aids: General index to collection; copy held by NRA.

Facilities: Photocopying. Photography by arrangement. Microfilm/fiche readers.

Publications: J.D. Fleeman: *A Preliminary Handlist of Documents and Manuscripts of Samuel Johnson*, Oxford Bibliographical Society Occasional publications, no.2 (1967).

988   Pitt Rivers Museum

Parent organisation: University of Oxford

Address: Photograph & Manuscripts Collections, Pitt Rivers Museum Research Centre, 64 Banbury Road, Oxford OX2 6RR

Telephone: (01865) 270927

Fax: (01865) 284657

E-mail: prm@prm.ox.ac.uk

Website: www.prm.ox.ac.uk

Enquiries: The Assistant Curator (Archives), Ms E. Edwards

Open: Thurs, Fri: 9.00–5.00, by appointment. Closed for ten days at Easter and Christmas.

Access: Bona fide researchers of postgraduate (or equivalent) status; others at the discretion of the Assistant Curator. There is no access for persons under the age of 18.

Historical background: The museum has been collecting archival material, especially photography, since its foundation in 1884. Its focus has been to collect material which relates to the intellectual frameworks in which the museum functioned rather than the administrative records of the institution itself. Until 1985 the archives were attached to the museum's Balfour Library, but at that date were restructured as a separate curatorial department of the museum.

Acquisitions policy: To strengthen existing collections to meet the teaching and research needs of the museum and department, and to document the development and history of anthropology. Material is added by purchase, exchange, donation and bequest.

Archives of organisation: Very few, mainly from 1884 to 1900.

Major collections: Henry Balfour (1863–1939): diaries and annotated writings.
Miss B. Blackwood (1889–1975): field notes and correspondence.
Sir Baldwin Spencer (1860–1929): correspondence, notes and other papers.

Prof. Sir Edward B. Tylor (1832–1917): correspondence and notes.
Col. R.G. Woodthorpe (1845–98): diaries and sketches.
Various other smaller collections of MSS of anthropological interest.

Non-manuscript material: Photographic collections, which are more significant historically than the MS collections.
A collection of about 125,000 items of anthropological interest, 1860s– . The whole world is represented, but coverage is especially strong on Oceania, Central Asia, Assam and North America.
Collections include: E. Evans-Pritchard (Southern Sudan), B. Blackwood (Melanesia), J.H. Hutton and J. Mills (Assam), Charles Bell and F. Spencer Chapman (Tibet), R. Rattray (Ghana) and Wilfred Thesiger (Middle East and Africa).

Finding aids: Computer listing, manual handlists and indexes for different parts of the collection. MS list sent to NRA.

Facilities: Photocopying (restricted). Photography.

Conservation: Preventative rather than active. Specialist work is contracted out.

Publications: E. Edwards: 'Collecting with a Camera: Pitt Rivers Museum Photographic Collections', *The General's Gift*, ed. B.A.L. Cranstone and S. Seidenburg (Oxford, 1984).
——: (ed.) *Wilfred Thesiger's Photographs: a Most Cherished Possession* (Oxford, 1993) [exhibition publication].
——: 'Photography in Ethnographic Museums: a Reflection', *Journal of Museum Ethnography*, 7 (1995), 131–9.
J. Coole and E. Edwards: 'Images of Benin at Pitt Rivers Museum', *African Arts*, 30/4 (1997), 26–35.

989   Plunkett Co-operative Library

Parent organisation: Plunkett Foundation

Address: 23 Hanborough Business Park, Long Hanborough, Oxford OX8 8LH

Telephone: (01865) 883636

Fax: (01993) 883576

E-mail: library@plunkett.co.uk

Website: www.plunkett.co.uk

Enquiries: The Information Services Manager, Kate Targett

Open: Mon–Fri: 9.00–5.00.

Access: Generally open to the public, by appointment.

Historical background: The foundation was established in 1919 by Sir Horace Curzon Plunkett (1854–1932), Anglo-Irish statesman and father of the Irish agricultural co-operative movement. Based on his private collection, the library was set up to promote the study of co-operative principles and practices throughout the English-speaking world.

Acquisitions policy: Selective acquisition of materials relating to all sectors of co-operatives and other user-controlled enterprises around the world, with emphasis on farmer-controlled business. Supporting section on rural development.

Archives of organisation: Publications of Plunkett Foundation for Co-operative Studies, 1919– .

Major collections: Sir Horace Curzon Plunkett, diaries, 1881–1932; correspondence, 1883–1932; core collection Co-operative Reference Library founded 1914; *Irish Homestead*, 1895–1923.

Non-manuscript material: Records of 1917–18 Irish Convention, of which Plunkett was chairman; documents of Independent Commission into Consumer Co-operation (Gaitskell Commission), 1958.

Finding aids: Index of Plunkett correspondence, NRA 16228; catalogue (undergoing conversion to database); cross-referenced index to correspondence and diaries.

Facilities: Photocopying.

990 Pusey House Library

Address: Pusey House, 61 St Giles, Oxford OX1 3LZ

Telephone: (01865) 278415

Fax: (01865) 278415

E-mail: pusey.house@rc24.net

Enquiries: The Custodian of the Library, Rev. W.E.P. Davage

Open: Mon–Fri: 9.15–12.45, 2.00–4.45. Times are subject to alteration out of the university term.

Access: On written application to the Custodian.

Historical background: The library was founded as a memorial library after the death of E.B. Pusey (1800–82) by his friends, who bought Pusey's own library for the purpose. The library concentrates on patristics, church history, Victorian church sources and liturgy. Since 1989 the library of the St Augustine's Foundation has been at Pusey House, and is available on the same terms as the Pusey House collection.

Acquisitions policy: To strengthen the areas noted above, as well as to augment the extensive 19th-century pamphlet collection.

Archives of organisation: Records of Pusey House, 1884– .

Major collections: Papers and correspondence of various important figures and organisations involved in the High Church movement: the nucleus is the collection of Pusey papers, formed by H.P. Liddon for his *Life of Pusey,* which includes papers of Edward Churton (1800–74); W.K. Hamilton (1808–69); C. Marriott (1811–58); R. Scott (1811–87); H.A. Woodgate; the English Church Union; the Association for the Promotion of the Unity of Christendom.

Collection by and relating to John Henry Newman (1801–90).

Papers of 20th-century Anglican figures, including C.H. Turner (1860–1930), Darwell Stone (1859–1941), Sidney Lesley Ollard (1875–1949), Eric Mascall (*b* 1905).

Non-manuscript material: Pamphlets centring on the Tractarian movement, 19th century (21,500).

H.E. Hall Collection of photographs of 19th-century clergymen.

Finding aids: Catalogues and provisional author list for much of the MS material. Handlist and indexes to pamphlet collection.

Facilities: Photocopying.

991 Queen's College

Parent organisation: University of Oxford

Address: High Street, Oxford OX1 4AW

Telephone: (01865) 279130

Fax: (01865) 790819

E-mail: library@queens.ox.ac.uk

Website: www.queens.ox.ac.uk

Enquiries: The Keeper of the Archives or The Librarian

Open: By arrangement.

Access: Bona fide scholars, by appointment. Access to the medieval archives and MSS deposited in the Bodleian Library is via the Keeper of the Archives at Queen's only.

Historical background: The college was founded in 1340. Many of the medieval deeds and MSS books have been deposited in the Bodleian Library (see entry 958).

Acquisitions policy: To maintain and consolidate the archives and MSS.

A Archives

Archives of organisation: Statutes, letters patent and foundation documents, 1341–19th century; financial records, including annual accounts, 1348–1900; records of college government, 1565–1827; entrance book, 1635–1890; butler's college diary, 1844–1900; records of benefactors and schools, 16th–19th centuries; estate records, principally deeds, c1150–1868, especially re Sherborne Priory, Dorset, and God's House, Southampton, c1190–16th century.

Finding aids: NRA 1097. Handlist, History of the University Project.

Conservation: Contracted out.

Publications: HMC 2nd report (1871), 137–42, and 4th Report (1874), 451–8.
N. Denholm-Young: *Archives of the Queen's College, Oxford* (1931) [4 vols; calendar of deeds and documents].

B Library

Archives of organisation: Library records, 1663–1805.
Student note-books, 17th and 18th centuries, including Jeremy Bentham's notes on Sir W. Blackstone's lectures, c1760– ; records of undergraduate societies, including Halcyon Club, 1869–96, and Addison Society, 1876–1931.
Minutes of meetings and accounts of the proprietors of *Grub Street Journal*, 1730–38.

Major collections: Collections of Thomas Barlow (1607–91), mainly theological MSS, and of Sir Joseph Williamson (1633–1701), including political correspondence and heraldic and genealogical MSS.
MSS and collections of former students and provosts.
Rev. John Barnabas Maude, diary kept during his detention at Verdun, 1802–14.

Finding aids: Manuscript catalogue.

Conservation: Contracted out.

992 Refugee Studies Centre

Parent organisation: University of Oxford

Address: 1st Floor, Dartington House, Little Clarendon Street, Oxford
Postal: Queen Elizabeth House, 21 St Giles, Oxford OX1 3LA

Telephone: (01865) 270298

Fax: (01865) 270721

E-mail: sarah.rhodes@qeh.ox.ac.uk

Website: www.bodley.ox.ac.uk/rsc

Enquiries: The Documentalist, Sarah Rhodes

Open: Mon–Fri: 9.00–5.00.

Access: Generally open to the public, by prior appointment. There may be access restrictions on recent or sensitive archive material.

Historical background: The Refugee Studies Programme was set up in 1982 and is concerned with the causes, consequences and experiences of forced migration. It promotes inter-disciplinary research, teaching and information provision. The Documentation Centre now holds more than 30,000 items, comprising books and unpublished material.

Acquisitions policy: To complement the interests and ongoing projects of the programme.

Major collections: Papers of Paul Weis (1907–92), international refugee lawyer, 1930s–1980s.
Papers of Tristram Betts (1908–83), famine relief and resettlement worker, 1950–1980s.
Derek Cooper (*b* 1912) Archive, work in Middle East, especially Palestinian refugees, 1956–98.
Refugee Health Collection (transferred from London School of Hygiene and Tropical Medicine), 1960–1990s.

Non-manuscript material: Video collection.
Conference proceedings, project reports and UN documentation.

Finding aids: On-line computer catalogue, including dedicated archive database. Lists of videos and periodicals. Weis list will be sent to NRA.

Facilities: Photocopying. Printouts from catalogue. Microfiche readers.

Publications: Documentation Centre: a Guide [free].
Refugee Studies Programme Annual Reports.
Forced Migration Review [newsletter].

993 Regent's Park College
Angus Library

Parent organisation: University of Oxford.

Address: Pusey Street, Oxford OX1 2LB

Telephone: (01865) 288142

Fax: (01865) 288121

E-mail: sue.mills@regents-park.oxford.ac.uk

Website: www.rpc.ox.ac.uk/rpc

Enquiries: The Librarian/Archivist, Mrs Susan J. Mills

Open: Mon–Fri: 9.30–4.00, by appointment only.
Closed for about two weeks at Easter and Christmas and usually most of August

Access: Bona fide researchers, by written application accompanied by a reference, to the Librarian/Archivist. The E.A. Payne papers are closed until 2010. There is a daily charge to private genealogical searchers. Extended use by visiting scholars may incur a fee.

Historical background: The college was founded in Stepney in 1810 as a training centre for Baptist ministers, and moved to Regent's Park in 1856. It transferred to Oxford between 1927 and 1940 and became a permanent private hall of the university in 1957. In 1985 the Baptist Union Library became part of the Angus Library, and in 1989 the archives of the Baptist Missionary Society were deposited with it.

Acquisitions policy: To maintain the archives and build on existing collections of Baptist records, by purchase or gift.

Archives of organisation: College archives, 1810– .

Major collections: Baptist Union of Great Britain (and Ireland) archives, 1812– , including minute books, plus records of the Particular Baptist Fund and other Baptist organisations and associations, 18th century– .
Baptist Missionary Society (BMS) archives, 1792– ; and missionary correspondence, including William Carey (1761–1834) and George Grenfell (1849–1906).
Records of some local Baptist churches, 1643– .
Papers of prominent Baptists, including Andrew Fuller (1754–1815), William Newman (1773–1835), Joseph Kinghorn (1766–1832), William Steele (1689–1769), Anne Steele (1717–78), J.H. Rushbrooke (1870–1947), M.E. Aubrey (1885–1957), E.A. Payne (1902–80).

Non-manuscript material: BMS archives: maps, photographs, glass slides and negatives.
Major collection of oriental and African translations of the Scriptures and linguistic material.

Finding aids: Card catalogues. Lists sent to NRA. Computer database of BMS missionaries and their records.

Facilities: Photocopying at the librarian's discretion. Microfilm/fiche readers.

Conservation: Contracted out.

Publications: 'Baptist Archives', *Religious Archives Group Conference Proceedings* (Sept 1990).
'Angus Library', *Bulletin ABTAPL*, 2/7 (1990), 15.
'Sources for the Study of Baptist History', *Baptist Quarterly*, xxxiv, 6 (1992) [offprints available].

994 Rhodes House Library

Parent organisation: University of Oxford

Address: South Parks Road, Oxford OX1 3RG

Telephone: (01865) 270909

Fax: (01865) 270912

E-mail: rhodes.house.library@bodley.ox.ac.uk

Website: www.bodley.ox.ac.uk/boris/guides/rhl/rhl01

Enquiries: The Librarian, Mr J.R. Pinfold
The Archivist, Mrs A.J. Hill

Open: Term: Mon–Fri: 9.00–7.00; Sat: 9.00–1.00.
Vacation: Mon–Fri: 9.00–5.00; Sat: 9.00–1.00.
Follows Bodleian Library timetable for closure at Christmas and Easter and in early September.

Intending vacation readers are advised to write for information.

Access: Approved readers holding a Bodleian reader's ticket or a short-term ticket available at Rhodes House Library. Suitable credentials are required and written application in advance is preferred.

Historical background: A dependent library of the Bodleian Library (see entry 958), founded by the Rhodes trustees in 1929, it houses the post-1760 Bodleian book and MSS collections relating to the political, economic and social history of the British colonies and Commonwealth (excluding the Indian subcontinent), the USA and sub-Saharan Africa.

Acquisitions policy: Development of existing holdings of archives relating to Britain's imperial and colonial history, through gifts, deposits and some purchases.

Major collections: MS collections relating to areas mentioned above, notably the personal papers of former British colonial officials and development administrators, have been gathered through the Oxford Colonial (and Development) Records Projects, and the library houses the papers of organisations such as the Anti-Slavery Society, the Fabian Colonial Bureau and the Africa Bureau.
Archives of the United Society for the Propagation of the Gospel, 1701– .
Substantial holdings relating to Cecil John Rhodes (1853–1902) and his family; Sir Thomas Fowell Buxton (1786–1845) and Charles Roden Buxton (1875–1942); papers of Arthur Creech Jones (1891–1964), Dame Margery Perham (1895–1982), Lord Lugard (1858–1945), Sir Roy Welensky (1907–91) and Elspeth Huxley (1907–97).
Sarawak materials include papers of the Brooke family and their associates.

Finding aids: Card index; handlists of larger individual collections sent to NRA.

Facilities: Photocopying in library; other photographic services at the Bodleian. Microfilm/fiche readers/printers. Audio-equipment for oral history collections.

Publications: Manuscript Collections of Africana in Rhodes House Library (1968; suppls, 1971, 1978).
Manuscript Collections (1970, suppl., 1978) [excluding Africana].
P.M. Hugh: 'The Oxford Colonial Records Project and Oxford Development Records Project', *Journal of the Society of Archivists*, vi/2 (1978), 76.
Manuscript Collections in Rhodes House Library, 1978–1994 (1996).
A.G. Tough: *African Medical History: a Guide to Personal Papers in Rhodes House Library* (1998).

995 Ruskin College

Address: Walton Street, Oxford OX1 2HE

Telephone: (01865) 554331

Fax: 01865) 554372

E-mail: d.horsfield@ruskin.ac.uk

Website: www.ruskin.ac.uk

Enquiries: The Librarian, David Horsfield

Open: Term: 9.00–5.00.
Vacation: by arrangement.

Access: Approved readers, by prior application in writing.

Historical background: Ruskin College was founded as a residential college for adult education in 1899. The archives collection was commenced in 1969.

Acquisitions policy: Working-class and labour movement history, mainly 20th century.

Archives of organisation: Archives of Ruskin College, 1899– .

Major collections: Papers of James Smith Middleton (1878–1962), secretary of the Labour Party, and Lucy Annie Middleton, MP.
Abe Lazarus Memorial Archives: Oxford labour history, 1930s and 1940s.
Working-class autobiographies.

Non-manuscript material: Books, periodicals, pamphlets relating to the labour movement.

Finding aids: Items listed in typescript. Middleton: NRA 27385.

Facilities: Photocopying. Microfilm/fiche reader. Video player.

Publications: P. Yorke: *Education and the Working Class: Ruskin College, 1899–1909* (Oxford, 1977).
H. Pollins: *The History of Ruskin College* (Oxford, 1984).

996 St Anne's College

Parent organisation: University of Oxford

Address: Oxford OX2 6HS

Telephone: (01865) 274800

Fax: (01865) 274899

E-mail: david.smith@st-annes.oxford.ac.uk

Enquiries: The Librarian and Archivist, Dr David Smith

Open: By arrangement.

Access: Bona fide scholars, strictly by appointment.

The college was originally founded as the Society of Oxford Home Students in 1879 and was given collegiate status in 1952. The college archives, as yet unsorted, are held by the library, which also houses correspondence concerning the fight for women's rights to take degrees. See R.F. Butler and M.H. Pritchard (eds): *St Anne's College: a History* (1957) [2 vols].

997 St Edmund Hall

Parent organisation: University of Oxford

Address: Oxford OX1 4AR

Telephone: (01865) 279000 (College); 279015 (Archivist)

Fax: (01865) 279090

Website: www.seh.ox.ac.uk

Enquiries: The Archivist, Professor R.J. Crampton

Open: By arrangement.

Access: Anyone with a specific reason. An appointment is necessary.

Historical background: St Edmund Hall was, from the 13th century, an academic hall of Oxford University; it has been a college since 1957. MSS and papers of principals and vice-principals, 17th–19th centuries, have been deposited in the Bodleian Library (see entry 958).

Acquisitions policy: Material relevant to the history of the hall and its members.

Archives of organisation: Archives of the hall, including buttery books, 1695–1920; principal's ledger, 1684– ; library borrowers' registers, 1666–74, 1838–81; minutes and accounts of the Boat Club and Debating Society, 1869– .

Major collections: Extensive transcripts of documents relating to the hall and its members made by Dr A.B. Emden, principal, 1929–51.

Finding aids: Handlist for History of the University Project.

998 St Edward's School Archives

Address: Woodstock Road, Oxford OX2 7NN

Telephone: (01865) 319214

Website: www.stedward.oxon.sch.uk

Enquiries: The Archivist, Ms K.A. Garvey

Open: Fri: by arrangement.

Access: Bona fide researchers, by appointment only.

Historical background: St Edward's was established in 1863 by the Rev. Thomas Chamberlain, MA, a follower of the Oxford Movement. In 1873 the school moved from premises in New Inn Hall Street to its current location in Summertown. Originally founded for boys, girls were first admitted to the sixth form in 1983. Since 1998 it has been fully co-educational.

Acquisitions policy: Official and informal material about the school and its members. Mainly written and photographic records, such as diaries and correspondence; memorabilia; and reminiscences.

Archives of organisation: Administrative material dating from the school's foundation, including records of the governing body, warden, bursary, individual houses, teaching departments, student activities and societies and chapel.

Major collections: Early photographic material and wardens' papers. Some photographic and written material relating to famous alumni including Kenneth Grahame (1859–1932), Laurence Olivier (1907–89), Douglas Bader (1910–82) and Guy Gibson (1918–44).

Non-manuscript material: Photographs of pupils, staff and buildings; audio-visual material, memorabilia.

Facilities: Photocopying

Publications: R.D. Hill: *A History of St Edward's School.*

999 St Hilda's College

Parent organisation: University of Oxford

Address: Oxford OX4 1DY

Telephone: (01865) 276882 (Thursdays only; answerphone on other days)

Fax: (01865) 276816

E-mail: archives@sthildas.ox.ac.uk

Website: www.sthildas.ox.ac-uk/information/history

Enquiries: The Archivist, Mrs Elizabeth Boardman

Open: Thurs: 9.30–4.45, by prior appointment only.

Access: Bona fide researchers only.

Historical background: The college was founded in 1893 by Dorothea Beale (1831–1906) and maintains associations with Cheltenham Ladies College, also established by her. The archives are in the custody of the Librarian. It was recognised by the Association of Promoting the Higher Education of Women in Oxford (AEW) in 1896 and by the university as a society for women in 1910. St. Hilda's College was incorporated by royal charter in 1926 and became a full college of the university in 1960. It is the only surviving women's college in Oxford.
Originally established in the early 1980s as a collection of memorabilia, the archive was extended in 1993 to cover all departments of the college. A professional archivist was first appointed in 1995.

Acquisitions policy: Official records of the college and its members. Material relating to the college and its members.

Archives of organisation: Minutes and papers of governing body, committees and principals, 1896–1996; student and staff records, 1896–1990; statutes and rules, 1898–1995; departmental records, 1919–98; records *re* social life, 1905–97.

Major collections: Biographical information and reminiscences of College members including MSS of Dame Elizabeth Maconchy (1907–94) and papers of Baroness Lucy Faithfull (1910–96).
Burrows Collection: papers of the first two principals, Esther Elizabeth Burrows (1847–1935) and Christine Mary Elizabeth Burrows (1872–1959).

Records of old Students Association/Association of Senior Members, 1907–89 and Barbara Pym Society, 1993–5.

Non-manuscript material: Photographs of college buildings, events, groups and individuals, 1894–1998.
Sound Archive: interviews with former students and recordings of College events, 1971–98.

Finding aids: Catalogues, personal name indexes and subject indexes of Burrows Collection and most college records. Card index, with some name and subject indexing, of photographs, memorabilia and biographical collections.

Facilities: Photocopying.

Publications: G. Hampshire: *Memorabilia* (Oxford, 1977).
St Hilda's College Register, 1893–1993 (Oxford, 1994).
M.E. Rayner: *The Centenary History of St Hilda's College* (Oxford, 1994).
Report and *Chronicle,* 1900– [College magazines].

1000 St Hugh's College
Howard Piper Library

Parent organisation: University of Oxford

Address: St Margaret's Road, Oxford OX2 6LE

Telephone: (01865) 274938

E-mail: library@st-hughs.ox.ac.uk

Website: www.st-hughs.ox.ac.uk/library

Enquiries: The Librarian and Archivist, Miss D.C. Quare

Open: Mon–Fri: 9.00–5.00.
Closed mid-August to mid-September.

Access: Bona fide researchers. Written application must be made.

The college was founded in 1886 and maintains its archive from that date, as well as acquiring material from past members, including personal papers, letters and reminiscences, especially relating to the education and awarding of degrees to women. A computerised database is in progress and photocopying is available.

1001   St John's College

Parent organisation: University of Oxford

Address: Oxford OX1 3JP

Telephone: (01865) 277300

Fax: (01865) 277435

Enquiries: The Keeper of the Archives, Dr M.G.A. Vale
The Librarian

Open: By arrangement.

Access: Approved readers, by appointment.

Historical background: St John's College was founded in 1555 by Sir Thomas White, and has a continuous history since that date as an academic corporation with its own endowments, including estates. The college archives were brought together in a single muniment room in 1957 and a summary guide was prepared.

Acquisitions policy: To maintain the college archives.

Archives of organisation: The college archives are essentially those of the governing body and its committees and of its agents in the management of its property: these include annual accounts, 1568– ; bursars' records, 1562– ; estate papers; MS maps and plans, minute books of undergraduate societies, 1880– ; photographic collection, c1860– .

Major collections: Library: A large number of MSS, many by or concerning those associated with the college, including lectures, essays, miscellaneous documents.
Correspondence received by Thomas Hare (1806–91), political reformer.
Account books of Henry Handley Norris (1771–1850), leader of High Church party.
Lectures of Rev. John Rose (1754–1821), fellow and rector of St Martin, Outwith London, describing London society and places, 1800–20.
Letters and papers of Josiah Tucker (1717–99), economist, later Dean of Gloucester.
'Ludicra' collection of limericks and nonsense verses made by Herbert Armitage James, president of college, 1909–31.

Non-manuscript material: Estate maps and plans; house plans (North Oxford Estate); photographs including building record, c1860– .

Finding aids: General guide to the college archives: NRA 9363, revised 1983, and a detailed card index. MS 213–357 described in NRA 7453.

Facilities: Photocopying and photography by arrangement.

Publications: H.M. Colvin: 'Manuscript Maps belonging to St John's College', *Oxoniensia*, xv (1950).
A. and V. Sillery: *St John's College Biographical Register, 1919–1975* (1978).
V. Sillery: *St John's College Biographical Register, 1875–1919; 1775–1875; 1660–1775* (1981; 1987; 1990).
HMC: 4th Report, xvii App. 465–8.

1002   St Peter's College

Parent organisation: University of Oxford

Address: New Inn Hall Street, Oxford OX1 2DL

Telephone: (01865) 278900

Fax: (01865) 278855

E-mail: alistair.ricketts@spc.ox.ac.uk

Website: www.spc.ox.ac.uk

Enquiries: The Librarian, Alistair Ricketts

Open: By arrangement.

Access: Bona fide researchers, at the discretion of the governing body of the college.

St Peter's Hall was founded in 1929 and achieved full college status in 1961. It maintains only its own archives, primarily the records of the governing body, 1929– . Other records are now deposited elsewhere: the parish records of St Peter-le-Bailey in Oxfordshire Record Office (see entry 986) and a small collection of St Helena letters in the Bodleian Library (entry 958). See Eric H.F. Smith: *St Peter's: the Founding of an Oxford College* (Gerrards Cross, 1978).

1003   School of Geography

Parent organisation: University of Oxford

Address: Library, Mansfield Road, Oxford OX1 3TB

Telephone: (01865) 271911/2

Fax: (01865) 271929

E-mail: linda.atkinson@geography.ox.ac.uk

Website: www.geog.ox.ac.uk

Enquiries: The Librarian and Map Curator, Mrs L.S. Atkinson

Open: Term: Mon–Fri: 9.00–6.00; Sat: 9.30–12.30.
Vacation: Mon–Fri: 9.00–1.00, 2.00–5.00.

Access: Bona fide researchers, by appointment.

Historical background: The present school was established in 1899 and the library is one of the largest and best in the subject in Great Britain. The archives have mainly been deposited in the University Archives (see entry 982). Radcliffe Meteorological Station Collection of weather reports, 1815– , is kept in the school, but not in the Library.

Acquisitions policy: Papers and lecture notes of academics, by donation or bequest.

Major collections: Papers and lectures notes of Sir Halford Mackinder (1861–1947), geographer and politician; Prof. A.J. Herbertson (*d* 1914); J.N.L. Baker (1893–1971); Prof. Kenneth Mason (1887–1976); and Prof. E.W. Gilbert (1900–73).

Non-manuscript material: Extensive collection of maps covering the whole world (*c*52,000). Collection of air photographs (*c*4000).

Finding aids: Lists. Mackinder Papers: NRA 18709. Card catalogue of map collection.

Facilities: Photocopying. Photography. Microfilm/fiche readers.

1004 Sherrington Library for the History of Neuroscience

Parent organisation: University of Oxford

Address: University Laboratory of Physiology, Parks Road, Oxford OX1 3PT

Telephone: (01865) 272524

Fax: (01865) 272488

E-mail: library@physiol.ox.ac.uk

Website: www.physiol.ox.ac.uk/library

Enquiries: The Librarian, Mrs Sophie Wilcox

Open: Mon–Fri: 8.00–4.00, except during university closures.

Access: Any interested scholar. There are restrictions on some correspondence and rarer books. An appointment is always necessary.

The Sherrington Library was opened in 1984 as a memorial to Sir Charles Sherrington (1857-1952), Waynflete Professor in the University Laboratory of Physiology, 1913–35, who won the Nobel Prize for medicine in 1932. The collection comprises correspondence (mostly photocopies) of Sir Charles and is being computerised. The actual records of the Laboratory of Physiology are held by the University Archives (see entry 982). Photocopying, photography and a microfiche reader are available.

1005 Somerville College

Parent organisation: University of Oxford

Address: The Library, Somerville College, Oxford OX2 6HD

Telephone: (01865) 270694

Fax: (01865) 270620

E-mail: pauline.adams@somerville.ox.ac.uk

Website: www.lib.ox.ac.uk/guides/colleges/som.htm

Enquiries: The Archivist, Miss P.A. Adams

Open: By appointment only.

Access: Scholars, by appointment. There are restrictions on certain college archives.

Historical background: The college was first so designated in 1894, although it had been founded as a hall for women students in 1879. The papers of Mary Somerville (1780–1872), after whom the college was named, are now deposited in the Bodleian Library (see entry 958), but the college library holds the archives and important collections of 19th- and 20th-century literary MSS.

Acquisitions policy: To maintain the college archives and collections, by donation.

Archives of organisation: Archives of the college, 1879– .

Major collections: Papers and correspondence of Amelia B. Edwards (1831–92), novelist and Egyptologist; and Percy Withers (1867–1945), literary figure.
MSS and correspondence of Violet Paget (1856–1936), author.
Working papers of Muriel St Clare Byrne (1895–1983), historian, and of Gladys Scott Thomson (*d* 1966), archivist and author.
Papers of Margaret Kennedy (1896–1967), novelist; Margaret Mann Phillips (1906- 87), Erasmus scholar.

Non-manuscript material: Collection of pamphlets, press cuttings and correspondence on women's suffrage.
The libraries of John Stuart Mill (1806–73) and Amelia B. Edwards.

Finding aids: Summary lists at NRA.

Facilities: Microfilm/fiche reader.

Publications: M. St Clare Byrne and C. Hope Mansfield: *Somerville College, 1879–1921* (1922).
Somerville College Register, 1879–1971.
P. Adams: *Somerville for Women: an Oxford College, 1879–1993* (1996).

1006 Taylor Institution Library

Parent organisation: University of Oxford

Address: St Giles', Oxford OX1 3NA

Telephone: (01865) 278158

Fax: (01865) 278165

E-mail: enquiries@taylib.ox.ac.uk

Website: www.taylib.ox.ac.uk

Enquiries: The Librarian, Ms E.A. Chapman

Open: Oct–June: Mon–Fri: 9.00–7.00; Sat: 9.00–1.00.
July–Sept: Mon–Fri: 10.00–1.00, 2.00–5.00; Sat: 10.00–1.00.
Closed for the late August bank holiday and the first few days in September (see website for further details).

Access: Graduates and other established researchers.

Historical background: The institution is a centre for the teaching of modern European languages excluding English. It was provided for in the will of Sir Robert Taylor (1714–88), but the establishment was delayed until 1839 and the library was started in 1848. Records of the institution are deposited in Oxford University Archives (see entry 982).

Acquisitions policy: Material relating to continental European languages and literatures, including Slavonic and modern Greek and modern Latin American.

Major collections: Autograph material: an extensive collection of MSS and letters of continental European political, musical, literary and artistic writers, 1700– .

Archives of the International Association of Hispanists.
Papers of academics associated with the institution, including Dr T.D.N. Besterman (1904–76), Voltaire scholar; H.G. Fiedler (1862–1945), professor of German; F. Max Müller (1823–1900), orientalist and philologist.

Finding aids: On-line catalogue of the European writers' letters and MSS (funded by HEFCE). Card index to MSS. Handlist of autograph materials acquired, 1950–70. NRA 11664.

Facilities: Photocopying. Photography by arrangement. Microfilm reader/printer.

Publications: G.G. Barber: 'The Taylor Institution', *The History of the University of Oxford*, vol.6, *Nineteenth-Century Oxford, Part 1*, ed. M.G. Brock and M.C. Curthoys (1997).
D.M. Sutherland: 'The Taylor Institution Library at Oxford', *Stechert-Hafrier Book News*, 8 (March 1954), 77–9.
P. Morgan: *Oxford Libraries outside the Bodleian: a Guide* (1973).

1007 Trinity College

Parent organisation: University of Oxford

Address: Broad Street, Oxford OX1 3BH

Telephone: (01865) 279861

Fax: (01865) 279911

E-mail: archive@unix1.trinity.ox.ac.uk

Enquiries: The Archivist, Mrs Clare Hopkins

Open: By arrangement only.

Access: Bona fide researchers. An appointment is always necessary. Some access is restricted.

Historical background: Trinity College was founded by Sir Thomas Pope in 1555. It stands on the site of the Benedictine Durham College (of which no records remain in Trinity). The archive was rehoused in 1987–8. All early library MSS and the collections of Warton, Ingram and Collins have been deposited in the Bodleian Library (see entry 958).

Acquisitions policy: The college is pleased to accept material of or relating to its own former and present members, especially reflecting the life of the college.

Archives of organisation: Statutes and charters, financial records and college government,

1556– ; property documents, including court rolls, 1556– ; admissions registers, 1648– ; other records of benefactions, college library and buildings.

Major collections: Literary papers of Sir Arthur Quiller-Couch (1863–1944).

Non-manuscript material: Prints of college buildings, 1675– ; photographs of buildings, 1860– , and of members, 1889– ; building plans; some estate maps.
Major collection of 20th-century undergraduate ephemera.

Finding aids: Detailed catalogue under preparation (to be sent to NRA). Brief handlist for History of the University Project.

Facilities: Photocopying. Photography may be permitted.

Conservation: Contracted out.

Publications: Herbert E.D. Blakiston: *Trinity College* (London, 1898).

1008 University College

Parent organisation: University of Oxford

Address: High Street, Oxford OX1 4BH

Telephone: (01865) 276952

E-mail: robin.darwall-smith@univ.ox.ac.uk

Website: www.univ.ox.ac.uk/index.html

Enquiries: The Archivist, Dr Robin Darwall-Smith

Open: Mon–Tues: 10.00–4.30 (1 hour lunch closure), by appointment.

Access: Bona fide scholars, on written application. There is a 30-year restriction on many items and no access to records of living persons.

Historical background: Money for a college was bequeathed to Oxford University by William of Durham, Archdeacon of Rouen (*d* 1249), but the exact date of the founding of the college is disputed. It has, however, definitely been in continuous existence since 1280. In 1882 its MS collections were deposited with the Bodleian Library (see entry 958). Some later private papers have also been deposited there, including the Robert Ross Collection concerning Oscar Wilde, and the papers of Clement Attlee (1883–1967).

Acquisitions policy: The Archivist is willing to consider donations or deposits of any material relevant to the history of the college.

Archives of organisation: Administrative and financial records of the college, 13th–20th centuries, including accounts, 1381– , and admissions register, 1674– .

Major collections: Papers of Obadiah Walker, master, 1676–89; some papers of Anthony Wood, historian (*d* 1695); other personal papers relating to members of the college, mainly 19th–20th centuries.

Non-manuscript material: Maps, plans and architectural drawings of college buildings, with related papers, 17th–20th centuries (including a 17th-century card model).
Maps and plans of college estates, 18th–20th centuries.
Photographs of college members, 1850s– .

Finding aids: A new catalogue of the archives is in progress. Copies of completed sections are with the NRA, as is a guide to the uncatalogued material; all these are regularly updated.

Facilities: Some documents may be photocopied at the discretion of the Archivist. Arrangements can be made for documents to be photographed or microfilmed.

Publications: W. Carr: *University College* (London, 1902).
University College Record (1952–3), 11–12 [summary of the archives].

1009 Wadham College

Parent organisation: University of Oxford

Address: Oxford OX1 3PN

Telephone: (01865) 277900

Fax: (01865) 277937

E-mail: library@wadham.ox.ac.uk

Website: www.wadham.ox.ac.uk

Enquiries: The Keeper of the Archives, C.S.L. Davies (postal only)
The Librarian

Open: By arrangement.

Access: Bona fide researchers, by prior appointment. Enquiries by post only.

Historical background: The college was founded in 1613, and until 1877 the library was housed in its original room dating from that time.

Acquisitions policy: To maintain and consolidate the archives and collections.

Archives of organisation: Records concerned with the foundation and building of the college; admissions registers, 1613– ; bursars' accounts, 1649– ; estate records and maps (16 counties).
Series of minute books and papers of undergraduate societies, including various literary and theological societies, 1934– .

Major collections: Various Spanish MSS of Sir William Godolphin (?1634–96), ambassador in Madrid, and Benjamin Barron Wiffen (1794–1867) relating to Church reform in Spain.
Individual MSS of former members of the college, including Mediterranean diary of John Swinton (1703–77), naval chaplain, 1730–31, and some papers of John Swinton (1703–77), warden.

Finding aids: Catalogue of the Muniments of Wadham College: NRA 8127. Deposited collections: NRA 10095. Handlist for History of the University Project.

Facilities: Photocopying.

Publications: R.B. Gardiner: *The Registers of Wadham College, 1613–1871* (London, 1887–90) [effectively presents everything available in the archives on members of the college].
HMC: 5th Report, pp. 479–81.

1010 Wesley & Methodist Studies Centre

Parent organisation: Westminster Institute of Education

Address: Oxford Brookes University, Harcourt Hill, Oxford OX2 9AT

Telephone: (01865) 488319

Fax: (01865) 488317

E-mail: wmsc.archive@brookes.ac.uk

Website: www.brookes.ac.uk/wmsc/

Enquiries: The Director of the Centre, Rev. Dr. Tim Macquiban
The Methodist Heritage Co-ordinator (Archives & Art), Peter Forsaith

Open: Mon–Fri: 9.00–5.00, by prior arrangement.

Access: Generally open to the public, by appointment.

Historical background: Westminster College was founded in London in 1851 for the training of teachers in the Methodist Church. In 2000 Westminster Institute of Education was formed from the college and Oxford Brookes University School of Education. The centre houses the library of the Wesley Historical Society (WHS), which was founded in 1893 and maintained a library from 1959. The official archives of the Methodist Church have been deposited in the John Rylands Library, Manchester (see entry 875B) and the Methodist missionary archives at the School of Oriental and African Studies, London (entry 799).

Acquisitions policy: Maintaining the college archives and acquiring other records relating to Methodism and education.

Archives of organisation: Archives of constituent colleges of the Westminster Institute: Westminster College, 1851–2000; Bletchley Park College, 1947–65; Lady Spencer Churchill College, 1965–76; Oxford Polytechnic/Oxford Brookes University School of Education, 1976–2000.

Major collections: Wesley Historical Society archives, including minutes and correspondence, 1893– .
Papers, with associated material, of the Avec Resource and Church & Community Development Trust, 1966– .
Small collection of letters of John (1703–91) and Charles Wesley (1707–88).
Journals, sketched 'squarings' and other manuscripts of James Smetham (1821–89), painter and essayist.

Non-manuscript material: Photographs of the college, staff and students.
WHS Library, including extensive collection of periodicals and a cuttings collection, 1791– .
Portraits, photographs and prints of British Methodists.
Art collections, including Methodist Church Modern Christian Art and Smetham Collection.

Finding aids: Lists and indexes of college archives and WHS Library.

Facilities: Photocopying. Microfilm/fiche readers.

Conservation: Contracted out.

Publications: Westminster Wesley Series.

1011 Worcester College

Parent organisation: University of Oxford

Address: Oxford OX1 2HB

Telephone: (01865) 278354

Fax: (01865) 278387

Enquiries: The Librarian, Dr J.H. Parker

Open: Mon–Fri: 9.00–1.00, 2.00–5.00.
Closed for a fortnight at Christmas, a week at Easter and a fortnight in the summer.

Access: Any bona fide scholar, on written application and by prior appointment.

Historical background: Worcester College is an 18th-century foundation in the University of Oxford. Its chief benefactor was George Clarke (1661–1736), virtuoso and politician, who not only built the library block with the help of Hawksmoor, but also left money for further building, plus his own great collection of books.

Acquisitions policy: To add, if possible, to areas where the collection is already strong.

Archives of organisation: In custody of the college archivist: records of the college, including register, bursars' journals, provosts' accounts and annual lists of members, 1714– .
Student note-books on philosophy, theology and the classics, 17th and 18th centuries.
Records of undergraduate societies, 19th and 20th centuries.

Major collections: A large collection of records accumulated by Sir William Clarke (?1623–66), secretary to Cromwell's army, relating to the activities of the army at the height of its political importance; and some papers of his son, George Clarke (1661–1736).
Papers of C.H.O. Daniel (1836–1919), Provost of Worcester, especially relating to the Daniel Press.

Non-manuscript material: Architectural drawings of Inigo Jones (1573–1652) and John Webb (1611–72), and some of the working library of Inigo Jones, copiously annotated in his hand (30 vols).

Finding aids: MS catalogue of all the holdings. NRA 10396. Catalogues of the Clarke papers and the C.H.O. Daniel papers sent to NRA.

Facilities: Photocopying and photography by arrangement. Microfilm reader.

Conservation: Paper conservation is contracted out.

Publications: C.H. Firth (ed.): *The Clarke Papers* (Camden Society, 2nd Series, 1891).
C. Henry Daniel and W.R. Barker: *Worcester College* (London, 1906).
J. Harris and A.A. Tait: *Catalogue of the Drawings by Inigo Jones, John Webb and Isaac de Caus at Worcester College, Oxford.*
H.M. Colvin: *A Catalogue of the Architectural Drawings of the 18th and 19th Centuries in Worcester College* (1964).
G. Aylmer: *Clarke Papers* [Harvester Press microfilm edition].

1012 Zoology Department

Parent organisation: University of Oxford

Address: Library, Department of Zoology, South Parks Road, Oxford OX1 3PS

Telephone: (01865) 271141/2/3

Fax: (01865) 310447

E-mail: zoolib@zoo.ox.ac.uk

Website: http://users.ox.ac.uk/~zoolib/

Enquiries: The Librarian, Dr M.L. Birch

Open: Mon–Fri: 9.00–5.00.

Access: Oxford University members; bona fide researchers, on application to the librarian.

Historical background: The Department of Anatomy and Physiology originated in 1860. It became known as the Department of Zoology in 1961, after several name changes in the intervening years. In 1967 the Department of Zoological Field Studies, itself an amalgamation of the Edward Grey Institute of Ornithological Field Studies and the Bureau of Animal Populations, became part of the Zoology Department bringing together three libraries and their constituent archives. The Edward Grey Institute received its formal university statute in 1938, with W.B. Alexander (1885–1965) as the director and it was he who built up the collections. In 1947 the university assumed full financial responsibility for the institute, which retains its strong links with other ornithological organisations that provide members of its advisory council.

Acquisitions policy: No active policy, but the department accepts material pertaining to zoological research in Wytham Wood and ornithological note-books and manuscripts of eminent ornithologists.

Major collections: The zoology archives include notes, note-books and lectures by several of the department's eminent zoologists, such as P.H. Carpenter, Sir G. De Beer and E.S. Goodrich.
Notes of lectures given by T.H. Huxley at the School of Mines, 1869–71.
H.N. Moseley's notes and photograph album of the *Challenger* expedition, 1871–76, is of special note.
The Alexander Library of the Edward Grey Institute houses manuscripts, mainly orthnithological field notes, by many distinguished people working in Britain and abroad, such as W.B. & H.G. Alexander; T.A. Coward, 1883–1933; C. Oldham, 1883–1939; and E. Selous.
Data and notes on animal populations (particularly small mammals), mostly from Wytham Wood (Oxfordshire), are kept in the Elton Library, with a complete record of all research published from the wood.

Non-manuscript material: Photographs and glass slides with note-books of some ornithologists.

Finding aids: Card catalogues; database lists in Alexander Library and at NRA.

Facilities: Photocopying. Microfilm/fiche reader.

1013 Paisley Museum

Parent organisation: Renfrewshire Council

Address: High Street, Paisley PA1 2BA

Telephone: (0141) 889 3151

Fax: (0141) 889 9240

Enquiries: Susan Geoffrey

Open: Tues–Sat: 10.00–5.00; Sun: 2.00–5.00.

Access: Researchers, by prior appointment.

The museum holds records of J. and P. Coats Ltd, thread manufacturers, Paisley, 1808– ; including employee records, 1833– , minutes 1890– , and plans etc. NRA 20914 (NRAS 3151).

1014 Renfrewshire Archives

Parent organisation: Renfrewshire Council

Address: Local Studies Department, Central Library, 6–8 High Street, Paisley PA1 2BB

Telephone: (0141) 889 2360

Fax: (0141) 887 6468

E-mail: local_studies@renfrewshire.gov.uk

Enquiries: The Local Studies Librarian

Open: Mon–Fri: 9.00–8.00; Sat: 9.00–5.00.

Access: Generally open to the public. Some material is out-stored, so prior contact is advised.

Historical background: The Local Studies Department of Paisley's central library had amassed over the years a quantity of MS and other archival material. In 1975, as a result of the reorganisation of Scottish local government, the records of several burghs and of the former Renfrew county relevant to Renfrew district were deposited with the department.

Acquisitions policy: To acquire, by deposit, donation or purchase, material relating to places, persons and companies within Renfrewshire.

Major collections: Burgh records of Renfrew, 1655– ; Paisley, 1594– ; Johnstone, 1857– ; and Barrhead, 1894– .
Paisley Poor Law volumes.
Strathclyde Regional Council minutes, annual financial statements, 1975–95; Renfrew District Council minutes, statements of reports, annual financial statements, 1975–95; community councils, minutes for all councils within the district, 1975–95; Renfrewshire Council, 1995– .
Records of the co-operative movement in Paisley, late 19th and 20th centuries.
Antiquarian MSS (45 vols).

Non-manuscript material: Plans from Dean of Guild courts in Paisley and Johnstone, late 19th and 20th centuries (c4000).
Newspapers (various titles), 1824– .

Finding aids: List of local authority records to 1975. Indexes to plans.

Facilities: Photocopying. Microfilm/fiche reader/printer.

1015 University of Paisley Library

Address: High Street, Paisley PA1 2BE

Telephone: (0141) 848 3758

Fax: (0141) 887 0812

E-mail: library@paisley.ac.uk

Website: www.paisley.ac.uk/welcome/lp-index.htm

Enquiries: The Chief Librarian, Mr S. James

Open: Term: Mon–Fri: 8.30–9.00; Sat: 9.00–5.00.
Vacation: Mon–Fri: 9.00–5.00.

Access: Upon satisfactory identification and approval of need.

Historical background: The university, previously Paisley College of Technology, was founded in 1897 as Paisley Technical College, with the Paisley Government School of Art and Design (f. 1842) as a constituent. It was granted the status of a central institution in 1950, when the art courses were dropped and development concentrated on science and technology. The library was established in 1963.

Archives of organisation: Materials relating to the history of the college/university.

Major collections: Notes of lectures of Lewis Fry Richardson (1881–1953), principal, 1929–40, and his library, with many volumes annotated by him.
A collection of estimates and contracts relating to the construction of c25 Scottish railway companies, donated to the college in 1967, at the time of closure of St Enoch's Station, Glasgow. Parliamentary papers of Norman Buchan, MP (1922–90).

Non-manuscript material: Maps and plans relating to above material.

Finding aids: Fry Richardson: NRA 26463.

Facilities: Photocopying. Microfilm/fiche readers. Photography by arrangement.

Publications: Calendar of Scottish Railway Documents (1978).
Calendars of the Papers of L.F. Richardson (1983).

1016 Sir Henry Royce Memorial Foundation

Address: The Hunt House, Paulerspury, Northamptonshire NN12 7NA

Telephone: (01327) 811048

Fax: (01327) 811797

E-mail: shrmf@rrec.co.uk

Website: www.henry-royce.org

Enquiries: The Curator, Philip Hall

Open: Mon–Fri: 9.00–5.00; strictly by appointment.

Access: Bona fide researchers; there are hourly and daily charges.

Historical background: The origin of Rolls-Royce Ltd was the agreement of 1904 between C.S. Rolls & Co., London motor traders, and Royce Ltd, engineers of Manchester, for Rolls to sell cars produced by Royce under the name Rolls-Royce. Rolls-Royce Ltd was established in 1906. Aero engines were produced from the First World War onwards. The bankrupt Bentley Motors was acquired in 1931. The foundation is a charitable trust, established in 1977. Modern engineering records are maintained by the Rolls-Royce Company at the Technical Archives Centre, Rolls-Royce Motor Cars Ltd, Pym's Lane, Crewe, Cheshire CW1 3PL.

Acquisitions policy: Any material or artefacts relating to C.S. Rolls (1877–1910), F.H. Royce (1863–1933), Rolls-Royce and Bentley motor cars and aero engines.

Archives of organisation: Rolls-Royce archives, including individual records of every Rolls-Royce and post-1931 Bentley car; extensive technical correspondence.

Major collections: Papers of Hon. C.S. Rolls, Sir Henry Royce and Lord Hives.
Post-war records of James Young Ltd, coachbuilders, Bromley.

Non-manuscript material: Technical records, drawings and blueprints, advertisements, photographs.

Facilities: Photocopying. Photography.

1017 Morrab Library

Address: Morrab Gardens, Penzance, Cornwall TR18 4DA

Telephone: (01736) 364474

Fax: (01736) 364474

Enquiries: The Librarian

Open: Tues–Fri: 10.00–4.00; Sat: 10.00–1.00, by appointment.

Access: By prior arrangement. There is a daily fee for non-members of the library.

Historical background: The Penzance Library was founded by private subscription in 1818. It is especially strong in Cornish material. Thomas Dawson's Napoleonic collection was presented between 1869 and 1877. Much rare material, including all the incunabula, was sold in 1964 and is now at Edinburgh University Library (entry 351)

Major collections: Thomas Dawson scrapbooks relating to Napoleon, including ephemera, engravings and prints, and *re* late 18th- and 19th-century notable figures.
William Borlase collection of his correspondence and other MSS.
Tremenheere papers.

Non-manuscript material: Photographic archives (*c*10,000 negatives) including glass plates.
Sketches and maps, 1770–1840.

Facilities: Limited photocopying facilities.

Conservation: Contracted out.

Publications: The Penzance Library: Celebration Essays...,1818–1988 (1988)

1018 Black Watch Museum Archive

Parent organisation: Trustees of the Black Watch

Address: Balhousie Castle, Hay Street, Perth PH1 5HR

Telephone: (0131) 310 8530

Fax: (01738) 643245

E-mail: bw.rhq@btclick.com

Enquiries: Mr T.B. Smyth

Open: Mon–Fri: 10.00–4.00.

Access: The museum is open to the public. Research in the archives is by appointment only.

Historical background: The Black Watch (Royal Highland Regiment), 42nd and 73rd, traces its origin to six independent companies dating from 1725. These were regimented in 1739, the first muster parade being held in 1740. Since then the regiment has served in many parts of the world. The archive reflects the history of these activities and is part of a registered charitable trust administered by the regimental trustees. Collection of material was begun in a systematic way in 1925.

Acquisitions policy: Material directly relating to the history of the regiment, its militia and territorial battalions and allied regiments.

Archives of organisation: Regimental records of service and diaries; casualty rolls; description book; order books; depot roll books etc, 18th century– .

Major collections: Diaries and memoirs of various regimental personalities, early 19th century– .

Non-manuscript material: Press cuttings/scrapbooks compiled by members of the regiment, illustrating personal and campaign histories.
Large collection of photographs, 1860s– .
Small collection of oral history tapes, and recordings of regimental bands, in particular illustrating pipe music.
Film collection, 1930s- (transferred to videotape).

Finding aids: Regimental documents survey (NRAS).

Facilities: Photocopying. Microfiche reader.

Publications: Bernard Fergusson: *The Black Watch: a Short History.*

1019 Perth and Kinross Council Archive

Parent organisation: Perth and Kinross Council

Address: A.K. Bell Library, 2–8 York Place, Perth PH2 8EP

Telephone: (01738) 477012/477022 (direct lines)

Fax: (01738) 477010

E-mail: archives@pkc.gov.uk

Website: www.scan.org.uk/directory/perth/perthframeset.html

Enquiries: The Archivist, Mr Stephen Connelly

Open: Mon–Fri: 9.30–5.00.

Access: Generally open to the public; an appointment is preferable. A paid research service is provided (5 hours maximum).

Historical background: The Council Archive is the successor of Perth and Kinross District Archive, which it replaced on local government reorganisation in 1996. The service dates back to 1975 and the first full-time archivist was appointed in 1978. It moved to purpose-built premises in 1994.

Acquisitions policy: To locate local authority records for preservation in the council archive and to act as a place of deposit for the records of various local businesses, institutions, families and individuals.

Archives of organisation: Records of the City and Royal Burgh of Perth, 1210–1975.
Records of the burghs of Aberfeldy, Abernethy, Alyth, Auchterarder, Blairgowrie and Rattray, Coupar Angus, Crieff, Kinross and Pitlochry, 1708–1975.
Records of County of Perth, 1650–1975; County of Kinross, 1738–1975; Joint County of Perth and Kinross, 1930–75.
Records of Perth & Kinross District Council, 1975–96.

Major collections: Many deposited collections, including Stewart-Meiklejohn family of Edradynate, 1484–1892, Fergusson family of Baledmund, 1328–1900, Perth Theatre, 1900–98.
Barons Kinnaird of Inchture, c1172–1930; Richardson family of Pitfour, 1740–1890; Murray Threipland family of Fingask, 17th–20th centuries; Stuart of Annat family papers, 1805–1900.

Non-manuscript material: Reports, posters, photographs, maps and plans.

Finding aids: Descriptive lists are available for the main series of records and many of the private deposits. Lists are sent to NRAS.

Facilities: Photocopying. Microfilm/fiche readers.

Conservation: Contracted out.

1020 Perth Museum and Art Gallery

Parent organisation: Perth and Kinross Council

Address: George Street, Perth PH1 5LB

Telephone: (01738) 632488

Fax: (01738) 443505

E-mail: museum@pkc.gov.uk

Enquiries: The Principal Officer, Human History, Ms S. Payne

Open: Mon–Sat: 10.00–1.00, 2.00–5.00.

Access: Generally open to the public, by appointment only.

Historical background: The nucleus was the Literary and Antiquarian Society Collection, built up from 1784. In 1822 part of the present museum was erected; it opened in 1824. In 1902 a separate collection built up by the Perthshire Society for Natural Sciences was transferred to local authority ownership, as was the Literary and Antiquarian Society Collection in 1914. All of the collections were amalgamated in the 1824 building, which was extended and reopened in 1935. The museum has three curatorial sections: Human History, Fine and Applied Art, and Natural Sciences.

Acquisitions policy: The archives are no longer being actively added to, but the museum collects ephemera associated with Perth and Kinross district and the history of Perth Museum and its collections.

Archives of organisation: Records of the museum, 19th century– .

Major collections: Small MSS collections from Kinross Museum and Alyth Folk Museum.
Local history material, including trade archives, 17th century– .
Records of members of the Perthshire Society of Natural Sciences.

Non-manuscript material: Literary and Antiquarian Society Collection, mainly antiquarian tracts and papers, 18th and 19th centuries.
A few plans, mostly of Perth and Perthshire.
Photographic collection (c200,000 items, mostly glass negatives).
Scottish paintings and prints.

Finding aids: NRAS has made lists of the collection. Kinross: NRA 22369. Photographic collection reasonably well indexed.

Facilities: Photocopying. Photography. Laser copying.

Conservation: Work contracted out.

1021 English Nature

Address: Northminster House, Peterborough, Cambridgeshire PE1 1UA

Telephone: (01733) 455000

Fax: (01733) 568834

E-mail: enquiries@english-nature.org.uk

Website: www.english-nature.org.uk

Enquiries: The Archivist, Miss H.J. Taylor

Open: By appointment only.

Access: Bona fide researchers; records are designated public records and held pending transfer to the Public Record Office; the 30-year closure period operates.

Historical background: The Nature Conservancy was founded by royal charter in 1949 and for the period 1965–73 formed part of the Natural Environment Research Council. In 1973 the Nature Conservancy Council was established by Act of Parliament, to be succeeded in 1991 by three country conservation agencies: English Nature, Scottish Natural Heritage and the Countryside Council for Wales. English Nature has inherited and administers the Great Britain headquarters records of the former Nature Conservancy Council. Some records have been transferred to the PRO (entry 1058).

Acquisitions policy: Internal acquisitions only.

Archives of organisation: Council and committee minutes, papers, annual reports, 1949– .
Records of National Nature Reserve and Sites of Special Scientific Interest, 1952– .
Conservation policy files, scientific research policy and data records, 1973– .

Non-manuscript material: Photographs, maps, slides.
Extensive library material.

Facilities: Photocopying. Microfilm/fiche readers.

1022 Peterborough Cathedral

Address: Canonry House, The Precincts, Peterborough, Cambridgeshire PE1 1XX

Telephone: (01733) 562125

Fax: (01733) 552465

Enquiries: Canon J. Higham

Open: By prior arrangement.

Access: Bona fide scholars

Virtually all MSS and early printed books are on loan to Cambridge University Library (entry 165), but the cathedral holds Act books, early registers and a collection of photographs of the cathedral and precincts, as well as a collection of printed books, post–1800. Architects' drawings, 1860–1920, have been transferred to Northamptonshire Record Office (entry 931).

1023 Peterborough Central Library
Local Studies Collection

Parent organisation: Peterborough City Council (Community Services Dept)

Address: Broadway, Peterborough, Cambridgeshire PE1 1RX

Telephone: (01733) 348343

Fax: (01733) 555277

E-mail: aaa413@peterborough.gov.uk

Enquiries: The Local Studies Librarian

Open: Mon, Fri, Sat: 9.30–5.00; Tues–Thurs: 9.30–7.00.

Access: Generally open to the public; an appointment is preferred for certain items, especially those which require supervision. Booking is required for microfilm/fiche readers.

Historical background: The Local Studies Collection was established by Peterborough City Council in 1892 with a collecting area of 35 miles radius of the city. In 1900 the Peterborough Gentlemen's Society Library was absorbed, though little now remains. With local government reorganisation in 1974 the collecting area was reduced.

Acquisitions policy: To collect local history printed material relating primarily to Peterborough and its former Soke, and secondarily to the area within a 10- to 15-mile radius.

Archives of organisation: Minutes of Peterborough City Library Committee, 1892–1974, with various correspondence files and statistics.

Major collections: Peterborough Gentlemen's Society, minute books, 1730–1900, with the society's surviving library, which includes a copy of the life of Edward the Confessor by Ailred of Rievaulx, 15th century.

Non-manuscript material: Usual local history collection, including Kitchin Photograph Collection, 1953–73 (*c*2000; copies available).
Printed maps and plans, 17th century– ; engravings; negatives and photographs, 19th century– .

Facilities: Photocopying. Photography. Microfilm/fiche readers.

Conservation: Conservation contracted out.

Publications: Guide (1998).

1024 Peterborough Museum and Art Gallery

Address: Priestgate, Peterborough, Cambridgeshire PE1 1LF

Telephone: (01733) 343329

Fax: (01733) 341928

E-mail: museum@peterborough.gov.uk

Enquiries: The Museum Services Curator

Open: Mon–Fri: 8.45–5.00, by prior appointment only.

Access: Bona fide researchers. In the case of Clare MSS, proof of bona fides will be requested.

Historical background: The museum was founded by the Peterborough Museum Society in 1879 and taken over by the city council in 1968.

Acquisitions policy: The museum now collects material of local interest (i.e. within the Greater Peterborough area), although collections held in the museum cover a wider area.

Major collections: Archaeological records of excavations, mostly 20th century.
Papers and MSS of John Clare (1793–1864).
Norman Cross Collection: Napoleonic prisoner of war work records, including order of day books, accounts of courts martial, land tenure agreements, inventories, 1797–1816.

Non-manuscript material: Photographs; playbills; maps, 1820– ; topographical collection.

Finding aids: Card indexes.

Facilities: Photocopying and photography by arrangement only.

Publications: M. Grainger: Catalogue of Clare MSS in the Peterborough Museum.

1025 Thomas Cook Archive

Parent organisation: Westdeutsche Landesbank Girozentrale

Address: PO Box 36, Peterborough PE3 6SB

Telephone: (01733) 502024/5

Fax: (01733) 502022

E-mail: paul.smith-archives@thomascook.com

Enquiries: The Company Archivist, Paul Smith

Open: Mon–Fri: 10.00–4.00, strictly by appointment.

Access: At the discretion of the company and by prior arrangement.

Historical background: The Thomas Cook Group was founded in 1841. Initially based in Leicester, Cook opened an office in London in 1865 and persuaded his son, John Mason Cook, to join him. The firm became known as Thomas Cook & Son in 1871 and the travel business was incorporated as Thos Cook & Son Ltd in 1924. A subsidiary, Thos Cook & Son (Bankers) Ltd, was formed at the same time to manage the banking and foreign exchange side of the business. In 1928 the entire share capital of Thos Cook & Son Ltd was sold to the Compagnie Internationale des Wagons-Lits et des Grands Express Européens of Brussels. After the occupation of Belgium in 1940, the Wagon-Lits shareholding in the company was brought under the control of the Official Custodian of Enemy Property for England. In 1942 the government authorised the transfer of the share capital of Thos Cook & Son Ltd to a company controlled by the four mainline railway companies and in 1948, the company became part of the nationalised British Railways under the British transport holding company. In 1972 the company returned to private ownership, bought by a consortium of Midland Bank, Trust House Forte and the Automobile Association. It was rebranded Cook International Ltd in 1973, but this name was dropped the following year and the Thomas Cook Group Ltd was born. Thomas Cook became a wholly-owned subsidiary of the Midland Bank Group in 1977, but was sold in 1992 to Westdeutsche Landesbank, one of the largest banks in Germany.

Acquisitions policy: The Thomas Cook Archive seeks to acquire material, regardless of format, from the UK and overseas, which is directly relevant to the company's history. Material is acquired by internal transfer, donation or purchase.

Archives of organisation: Archives of the Thomas Cook Group Ltd, 1841– , including agreement books, 1870s–1920s; partners' correspondence, 1870s–1920s; travellers' diaries and journals, 1855–1980s.

Non-manuscript material: Travel newspapers and magazines, 1851–1939; photographs, 1860s– ; railway timetables, 1873– ; guidebooks,

1874– ; holiday brochures, 1889– ; staff magazines, 1911– .

Finding aids: Lists and card indexes to certain collections; computer database in preparation.

Facilities: Photocopying.

Conservation: Contracted out.

Publications: P. Brendon: *Thomas Cook: 150 Years of Popular Tourism* (1991).
A. Williamson: *The Golden Age of Travel* (1998).

1026 Arbuthnot Museum

Parent organisation: Aberdeenshire Heritage

Address: St Peter Street, Peterhead, Aberdeenshire AB42 6QD

Telephone: (01771) 477778; (01771) 622906 (Museum Service HQ)

Fax: (01771) 622884

E-mail: general@abheritage.demon.co.uk

Website: www.aberdeenshire.gov.uk/ahc.htm

Enquiries: The Curator of Local History, Dr David M. Bertie

Open: Mon, Tues, Thurs–Sat: 10.30–1.30, 2.30–5.00; Wed: 10.30–1.00.

Access: Generally open to the public, by appointment.

Historical background: The present museum service was formed in 1996 by the amalgamation of North East of Scotland Museums Service and the Agricultural Heritage Centre, and is part of Aberdeenshire Council's Education and Recreation Service. Aberdeenshire Heritage incorporates the following museums: Aberdeenshire Farming Museum, Mintlaw (f. 1980), Arbuthnot Museum, Peterhead (f. 1850), Banchory Museum (f. 1977), Banff Museum (f. 1828), Brander Museum, Huntly (f. 1883), Carnegie Museum, Inverurie (f. 1884), Fordyce Joiner's Workshop Visitor Centre (f. 1993), Garlogie Mill Power House Museum (f. 1995), Maud Railway Museum (f. 1995), Sandhaven Meal Mill, Fraserburgh (f. 1993), and Tolbooth Museum, Stonehaven (f. 1963).

Acquisitions policy: Relevant material relating to Aberdeenshire; although most archive material is referred to Aberdeen City Archives (entry 3).

Archives of organisation: Small collection of museum service's archival material, 1828– .

Major collections: Peterhead Harbours: records of arrivals and sailings, 1865–97; day-books, 1857–1935.
Whaling voyage journals, mid-19th century.
Music MSS of J. Scott Skinner (1843–1927).
Arbuthnot family records, 18th–19th centuries.
Family papers of George Macdonald (1824–1905).

Non-manuscript material: Maps of Peterhead, Stonehaven and Banff.
Astronomical charts of James Ferguson (1710–76).
Large photograph collection covering northeast Scotland.

Finding aids: Catalogue to photograph collection.

Facilities: Photocopying. Photography. Microfiche reader.

Conservation: Referred to Scottish Museums Council.

1027 Blair Castle

Parent organisation: Atholl Estates

Address: Blair Atholl, Pitlochry, Perthshire PH18 5TL

Telephone: (01796) 481207

Fax: (01796) 481487

E-mail: office@blair-castle.co.uk

Website: www.blair-castle.co.uk

Enquiries: The Archivist, Mrs Jane Anderson

Open: Mon–Fri, by appointment only.

Access: Bona fide researchers; an appointment is necessary and a charge is made.

Historical background: Blair Castle has been the seat of the Earls, Marquis and Dukes of Atholl from the 13th century to the present day; the present Duke is the 11th.

Acquisitions policy: Material concerning the Atholl family and their estates (located mainly in Perthshire).

Archives of organisation: Land charters and deeds, 13th–18th centuries.
Correspondence, 17th–20th centuries.
Estate rentals and accounts, 17th–20th centuries.

Major collections: Political papers of Katharine, Duchess of Atholl, MP (1874–1960).

Non-manuscript material: Estate plans and maps.
Architectural drawings.

Finding aids: NRAS 234: covers majority of collection (1600–1900). 19th-century MS catalogue of earlier material (1290–1600). MS bundle list of 20th-century materials.

Conservation: Limited paper conservation carried out in-house; more complex work contracted to Dundee University (entry 302). No outside work is undertaken.

Publications: *Atholl and Tullibardine Chronicles* (private publication, 1908, 1919).

1028 Marine Biological Association of the United Kingdom

Address: Citadel Hill, Plymouth, Devon PL1 2PB

Telephone: (01752) 633266

Fax: (01752) 633102

E-mail: nmbl@pml.ac.uk

Enquiries: The Head of Library and Information Services, Linda Noble

Open: Mon–Fri: 9.00–5.15.

Access: By appointment only.

Historical background: The Marine Biological Association was founded in 1884 and the Plymouth laboratory opened in 1888. The aims are to promote scientific research into all aspects of life in the sea, and the MBA has gained an international reputation for excellence in research, both by resident staff and the many British and overseas visiting workers. The library is one of the most comprehensive in the world in its coverage of the marine literature and maintains an archive collection.

Acquisitions policy: Material related to the history of the MBA and of British marine science.

Archives of organisation: Material relating to the history of the association, laboratory, research programmes, staff, visiting workers, ships, and governing council. Including personal and scientific papers, letters, note-books and MSS, 1870– .

Non-manuscript material: Photographs and illustrations of people, ships, equipment and buildings.

Finding aids: Catalogue. Computer database.

Facilities: Photocopying.

Publications: J. Southward and E.K. Roberts: 'One Hundred Years of Marine Research at Plymouth', *Journal of the Marine Biological Association of the United Kingdom*, 67 (1987), 465–506.
A. Varley: *Catalogue of the Archives of the Marine Biological Association*, Occasional Publication of the MBA no.5 (1997).

1029 Plymouth and West Devon Record Office

Parent organisation: Plymouth City Council

Address: 3 Clare Place, Plymouth, Devon PL4 0JW

Telephone: (01752) 305940

Fax: (01752) 223939

E-mail: pwdro@plymouth.gov.uk.

Enquiries: The City Archivist, Mr Paul Brough

Open: Tues–Thurs: 9.30–5.00, Fri: 9.30–4.00.

Access: Generally open to the public; proof of identity is required. There are some restrictions on access and some charges.

Historical background: The office was set up in 1952 as a section of the Plymouth Central Library, which was administered by the city council. From 1974 to 1998 it was a branch of Devon Record Office (entry 365) under the aegis of Devon County Council. It also acts as the Diocesan Record Office for parishes within the West Devon area and for parts of the South Hams.

Acquisitions policy: Material relating to Plymouth City (unitary authority) and southwest Devon, in collaboration with Devon Record Office (entry 365).

Archives of organisation: Borough archives, 1439– .

Major collections: Parker family of Saltram, Earls of Morley, correspondence, legal and estate papers, 18th–20th centuries.
Bastard family of Kitley and Buckland, family and estate papers, 18th–20th centuries.

Lopes family of Maristow, Barons Roborough of Maristow, family and legal papers, 13th–19th centuries; includes letterbook of George Gilles, agent to Sir Massey Lopes, 1825–32.

Bayly family of Torr, Plymouth, family and estate papers, 17th–20th centuries.

Business records of Millbay Laundry, Cleaning and Dyeing Co., 1896–1972.

Farley Infant Foods of Plymouth.

St Aubyn of Devonport, family and estate papers, 1803–1944.

Non-manuscript material: Western Morning News photographic collection.
Plans; photographs; maps.

Finding aids: Catalogues and indexes; computerised accession database searchings. Lists sent to NRA.

Facilities: Photocopying. Self-service microfiche printing. Microfilm/fiche readers.

Conservation: Conservator on staff.

1030 Plymouth Local and Naval Studies Library

Parent organisation: Plymouth City Council

Address: Plymouth Central Library, Drake Circus, Plymouth, Devon PL4 8AL

Telephone: (01752) 305909

Fax: (01752) 305905

E-mail: localstudies@plymouth.gov.uk

Website: www.plymouth.gov.uk/star/library.htm

Enquiries: The Local and Naval Studies Librarian, Joyce Brown

Open: Mon–Fri: 9.00–7.00; Sat: 9.00–4.00.

Access: Freely open to any member of the public, but prior enquiry as to the availability of items is advisable.

Historical background: The former Borough of Plymouth opened its first free public library in 1876, and has operated from the same central library building since 1910. The library was seriously damaged during the Blitz in 1941, when virtually the entire Devon and Cornwall Library was destroyed. Although some items were irreplaceable, the collection has been rebuilt since World War II by purchase and donation. It is now a valuable resource for the study of Plymouth and the surrounding region. Administered by Devon County Council from 1974, it reverted to Plymouth City Council in 1998, when the council became a unitary authority.

Acquisitions policy: A formal written policy is in preparation; currently the aim is to acquire non-archival MSS and publications in all formats which reflect the development of Plymouth and South-West England.

Archives of organisation: These are held by the Plymouth and West Devon Record Office (entry 1029).

Major collections: A small number of MSS, including antiquarian notes; also the folksong and parish history collections of Sabine Baring-Gould (1834–1924).

Non-manuscript material: Extensive collections of illustrations, newspaper cuttings, ephemera, theatre programmes, maps, films.
Collection of theses on Plymouth area.
Major collection of material on the history of the Royal Navy and contemporary naval studies.

Finding aids: Items are catalogued on either an on-line database or a card catalogue. Biography index. Newspaper cuttings index.

Facilities: Photocopying. Photography and scanning by arrangement. Microfilm/fiche reader/printers.

Conservation: The City Council has its own bindery, and the Plymouth and West Devon Record Office has its own conservator.
Local newspapers are microfilmed as part of the Newsplan project.

Publications: Some material included in A. Brockett: *The Devon Union List* (Exeter, 1977).

1031 South West Film & Television Archive

Address: Melville Building, Royal William Yard, Stonehouse, Plymouth, Devon PL1 2RP

E-mail: enquiries@tswfta.co.uk

Website: www.tswfta.co.uk

Enquiries: The Director, Elayne Hoskin

Open: Mon–Fri: 9.00–5.00.

Access: Generally open to the public, by appointment. Viewings are free for non-profit distributing purposes (including academic and educational viewings). Commercial users will normally be charged a research/viewing fee at the point that they order material, provided that the research or viewing does not take more than one hour.

Historical background: TSW, Television South West Limited, established a registered charity to become the film archive for the South West in 1993, and then gifted both its back catalogue and that of Westward Television to the archive. BBC South West also stores its film library at the archive, with access allowed for the archive's charitable aims and objectives. Active research into the sources of moving image in the South West has been undertaken since the archive's inception, leading to a steadily growing collection of material.

Acquisitions policy: Moving images of and about the South West of England.

Major collections: Principally non-manuscript material.

Non-manuscript material: Westward Television collection (ITV provider), 1961–81.
TSW (ITV provider), 1981–92.
Non-broadcast collections from various organisations, including South West Gas, South West Electricity Board and Dartington Hall.
Many private collections, 1900– .

Finding aids: Database (incomplete); subject index system (incomplete); file notes (incomplete).
Cataloguing in progress.

Facilities: Viewing copies. All gauges film and video viewing facilities. Telecine.

1032 University College of St Mark and St John

Address: Derriford Road, Plymouth, Devon PL6 8BH

Telephone: (01752) 777188 ext. 4200

Fax: (01752) 636820

E-mail: bidgoa@marjon.ac.uk

Website: www.marjon.ac.uk

Enquiries: The Deputy Head of Learning Resources, Alison Bidgood

Open: Mon–Fri: 8.30–8.00; Sat: 10.00–4.45.

Access: Generally open to the public, by appointment.

Formerly Battersea College (later St John's College, Battersea), 1840–1923, and St Mark's College, Chelsea, 1841–1923, the colleges were merged by the National Society in 1923 on the Chelsea site, and moved to Plymouth in 1973. The founding principals were Sir James Kay-Shuttleworth (1840–77) at Battersea and Derwent Coleridge (1800–83) at St Marks. Until 1977 the college was solely for teacher training. An archive exists for the early colleges and the combined college on both sites. Records include registers, council minutes, photographs, plans, books, journals, papers, artefacts and, more recently, video and audio recordings. There is a card catalogue of the collection and computerisation is being considered.

1033 Ackworth School

Address: Ackworth, Pontefract, West Yorkshire WF7 7LT

Telephone: (01977) 611401

Fax: (01977) 616225

E-mail: ackworth@aol.com

Enquiries: The Hon. Archivist, Mr Frederick A. Davis

Open: Postal enquiries only, to the Archivist at the above address.

Historical background: Ackworth School was founded in 1779 by Dr John Fothergill, a celebrated 18th-century Quaker physician, botanist and philanthropist. It is run by the Society of Friends. The original buildings, constructed between 1757 and 1763, were, until 1773, the Yorkshire branch of the London Foundling Hospital, whose archives were transferred from Ackworth to London Metropolitan Archives (entry 688) in 1995.
The extensive administrative records, 18th–early 19th century, covering staff, housekeeping, finance, farm management, estates and buildings are held for conservation and re-cataloguing by West Yorkshire Archive Service, Wakefield (entry 1184).

Acquisitions policy: Deposits by the school, old scholars and members of the Society of Friends (Quakers).

Archives of organisation: Admission details of all scholars, 1779– .
Governors' minutes, 1779– .
Annual reports of the Ackworth Old Scholars' Association, 1881– .

Major collections: Memorabilia of Dr John Fothergill, the school's founder.
Genealogies of some Quaker families.

Non-manuscript material: School copy books, early 19th century– .
A photographic record of teachers, pupils and school servants, mid–19th century– .
Engravings and books on the history of the school.
Quakers samplers, 1780–1860 (*c*100).

Finding aids: Various lists of pupils, staff and officers, 1779– .

Conservation: Some undertaken by West Yorkshire Archive Service, Wakefield.

Publications: E. Vipont, *Ackworth School* (1959; repr. 1991) [copies available from the school].

1034 History of Technology Research Unit

Parent organisation: Bournemouth University

Address: Talbot Campus, Fern Barrow, Poole, Dorset BN12 5BB

Telephone: (01202) 595451

Fax: (01202) 595475

E-mail: fcambroo@bournemouth.ac.uk

Website: http://histech.centre.org.uk http://chide.bournemouth.ac.uk

Enquiries: The Manager, Frances Cambrook

Open: By appointment.

Access: Researchers and educators, on written application. Commercial companies may be charged.

Historical background: Bournemouth University was created in 1992. Formerly it was Bournemouth Polytechnic (1990–92) and Dorset Institute of Higher Education (1976–1990) which had been formed by the amalgamation of Bournemouth College of Technology and Weymouth College of Education in 1976. The unit comprises the Centre for the History of Defence Electronics, founded in 1995, and the Centre for Understanding Technology through Oral Sources, founded in 1998.

Acquisitions policy: Both centres collect oral histories of technology and electronics as well as supporting documents and images.

Major collections: Penley Archive of Telecommunications Research Establishment.

Non-manuscript material: Photographs relating to the early development of radar.
Oral history tapes.

Finding aids: Internet-based catalogue in preparation.

1035 Poole Borough Council

Address: Poole Museum Service, 4 High Street, Poole, Dorset BH15 1BW

Telephone: (01202) 262600

Fax: (01202) 262622

E-mail: mldavidw@poole.gov.uk

Enquiries: The Local History Manager, David Watkins

Open: Mon–Fri: by arrangement.

Access: Generally open to the public. An appointment is needed to view fragile material.

Historical background: Poole Borough Council maintains access to archive material through the Museum and Library sections of Cultural Services. The Poole Borough archive is now lodged at the Dorset Record Office, Dorchester (entry 285).

Acquisitions policy: Material evidence of Poole, its history and its people, including family records, business and association records, title deeds, photographs and supporting material.

Archives of organisation: Corporate records, minute books and deeds, 16th–20th centuries; courts of record, petty sessions and quarter sessions, mid-17th century– .

Major collections: Records of merchant families involved in Newfoundland trade.

Non-manuscript material: Local studies collection, including maps, photographs (*c*20,000), biographical material, trade and commerce data, extensive collection of local publications (mostly microfilmed), books and tapes.

Finding aids: Family name, ship name, occupation and information indexes. Photographic collection partially catalogued.

Facilities: Photocopying. Microfilm printer.

Conservation: Contracted out.

Publications: Census, 1574.
1803 Levée en Masse.

Book of the Staple, 1589–1727.

1036 Royal National Lifeboat Institution

Address: West Quay Road, Poole, Dorset BH15 1HZ

Telephone: (01202) 663000

Fax: (01202) 663167

E-mail: info@rnli.org.uk

Website: www.rnli.org.uk

Enquiries: The Honorary Librarian, Mr Barry Cox

Open: Mon–Fri: 9.30–4.30, by appointment only.

Access: Bona fide researchers into RNLI history. There is no charge but donations are welcome.

Historical background: The RNLI was founded in 1824 by Sir William Hillary to co-ordinate the individual lifeboat services around the coast of Britain. The service has always been provided by volunteer crews.

Acquisitions policy: Items and books relevant to RNLI history. Gifts and donations are appreciated.

Archives of organisation: Minute books, 1824– ; annual reports, 1824– ; Lifeboat Journal, 1852– .

Non-manuscript material: Photographic library: RNLI boats, stations and personnel. Lifeboat station histories.

Finding aids: Library catalogue.

Facilities: Photocopying.

Conservation: Contracted out.

Publications: A. Beilby: Heroes All (Patrick Stephen, 1992).
O. Warner: The Lifeboat Service (Cassell, 1974).

1037 Cable & Wireless Archive

Parent organisation: Cable & Wireless Porthcurno & Collections Trust

Address: Eastern House, Porthcurno, Cornwall TR19 6JX

Telephone: (01736) 810811/810478

Fax: (01736) 810640

E-mail: archive@tunnels.demon.co.uk

Website: www.porthcurno.org.uk

Enquiries: The Curator/Archivist, Ms Mary Godwin

Open: Mon–Fri: by appointment only.

Access: At the discretion of the company, by application in writing to the Curator.

Historical background: Cable & Wireless Ltd was incorporated in 1929 to acquire the shares in Eastern & Associated Telegraph (f.1872), and Marconi (f.1897), while Imperial & International Communications Ltd was established to acquire the communication assets. In 1932 I&IC Ltd acquired the West India & Panama Telegraph Co. Ltd and in the following year it acquired Direct Spanish Telegraph Co. Ltd. I&IC Ltd became Cable & Wireless Ltd in 1934 and was nationalised in 1947. In 1950 the company's UK telecom assets passed to the Post Office and in 1981 it was privatised. The archive, part of which was previously housed in the Modern Records Centre (entry 261), is now managed by a trust based in Porthcurno.

Acquisitions policy: To maintain the archives of Cable & Wireless and its constituent companies.

Archives of organisation: Archives of Cable & Wireless plc, 1870s– , including staff records, c1870– , and staff magazine, 1906–
Records of c90 subsidiary companies, 1860s– .

Major collections: Collection relating to Brunel's Great Eastern and the laying of the first Atlantic cable, 1857–66.

Non-manuscript material: Large photograph collection.
Nautical charts and large collection of technical artefacts and ephemera.

Finding aids: Descriptive lists; subject index. NRA 21652.

Facilities: Photocopying.

Publications: H. Barty-King: Girdle Round the Earth (1979).
M. Godwin: A Short History of Cable & Wireless (1995).
D. Souden: Voices over the Horizon, (1998).
——: Voices of Change (2001.)

1038 Portsmouth Central Library
Historical Collections

Parent organisation: Portsmouth City Council Library Service

Address: Guildhall Square, Portsmouth, Hampshire PO1 2DX

Telephone: (023) 92819311 ext. 234

Fax: (023) 92839855

E-mail: reference.library@portsmouthcc.gov.uk

Enquiries: The City Librarian, J. Thorn (postal) The Historical Collections Librarian, A. King (telephone)

Open: Mon–Fri: 9.30–7.00; Sat: 9.30–4.00.

Access: Anyone may use the local, naval and genealogical collections on production of proof of name and address. Readers requiring detailed help are encouraged to make an appointment. Dickens researchers should write to the City Librarian with the name of a referee.

Historical background: Portsmouth Public Libraries began in 1883, when a local collection was started. The Naval Collection was first brought together in the 1950s and includes the McCarthy Collection of naval history books donated in 1984. The Dickens Collection was transferred from the Charles Dickens Birthplace Museum in Portsmouth in 1967. Portsmouth libraries were part of Hampshire County Library (1974–97) and then reverted to Portsmouth City Council.

Acquisitions policy: Material, including illustrations, maps, pamphlets, periodicals and ephemera, is acquired by purchase and occasionally by donation. Archives are mostly deposited in Portsmouth City Records Office (entry 1039).

Archives of organisation: Annual reports, catalogues, bye-laws relating to Portsmouth libraries; cuttings and photographs illustrating Portsmouth library history.

Major collections: Dickens Collection: letters, speeches, scrapbooks, first editions etc of Charles Dickens (1812–70).
Minutes and reports of the Portsmouth Literary and Philosophical Society.

Non-manuscript material: Collection of Sir F. Madden's Portsmouth theatre playbills.
Navy lists, 1778– ; army lists, 1766– .

Lily Lambert McCarthy Collection of books on naval history, especially Nelson.
Local newspapers, including *Hampshire Telegraph*, 1799–1976.

Finding aids: Items are on the Portsmouth City Libraries catalogue.

Facilities: Photocopying. Photography by arrangement. Microfilm/fiche readers (must be booked in advance).

Conservation: Contracted out.

Publications: Booklet and leaflet guides to collections.

1039 Portsmouth Museums and Records Service

Parent organisation: Portsmouth City Council

Address: Museum Road, Portsmouth, Hampshire PO1 2LJ

Telephone: (023) 92827261

Fax: (023) 92875276

E-mail: info@recordsoffice.co.uk

Website: www.portsmouthmuseums.co.uk

Enquiries: The Collections Manager, Michael Gunton

Open: April–Oct: Mon–Fri: 10.00–5.00. Nov–March: Mon–Fri: 10.00–4.00.

Access: Generally open to the public. Closure periods apply to certain classes of records.

Historical background: The Records Office was established in 1960. It also acts as the Diocesan Record Office for Portsmouth, and is recognised as a place of deposit for public records. Since 1994 it has been part of Portsmouth Museums and Record Service.

Acquisitions policy: Written and printed documents, photographs, maps etc from organisations, families and individuals relating to Portsmouth and south-east Hampshire.

Archives of organisation: Records of Portsmouth City Council and predecessor bodies.

Major collections: Portsmouth Floating Bridge Co., 1838–1961; Portsmouth Water Co., 1741–1967; Portsmouth United Breweries, 1834–1960; Hulbert Jackson, 1650–1985; W. Treadgold & Co. Ltd, iron merchants, 1704–1988; Hoad & Son, wheelwrights, 1777–1984;

Portsea Island Gas Co., 1821–1957; Anglican parish records of the Portsmouth, Havant and Alverstoke deaneries of Portsmouth Diocese; records of the Anglican Diocese of Portsmouth; records of Roman Catholic and non-conformist churches on Portsea Island.

Non-manuscript material: Extensive photographic holdings; film and sound archives transferred to the Wessex Film and Sound Archive at Hampshire Record Office (entry 1199).

Finding aids: Card indexes (name, place, subject); catalogues of collections; ongoing computerisation of indexes and catalogues. Copies of catalogues sent to NRA.

Facilities: Photocopying. Photography by arrangement. Microfilm/fiche readers.

Conservation: In-house.

Publications: Leaflets on various topics are available.

1040　Portsmouth Roman Catholic Diocesan Archives

Address: St Edmund House, Edinburgh Road, Portsmouth PO1 3QA

Telephone: (023) 92822166

Enquiries: The Diocesan Archivist, Rev. Francis P. Isherwood

Open: Mon–Fri: 9.30–5.00, by appointment.

Access: Bona fide researchers, at the discretion of the Archivist.

Historical background: The RC Diocese of Portsmouth was created in 1882 and covers the old counties of Berkshire, Hampshire, the Isle of Wight and Channel Islands. Its premises suffered a direct hit during World War II and few diocesan archives survive.

Acquisitions policy: To assemble and maintain records concerning both the spiritual and temporal affairs of the diocese.

Archives of organisation: Diocesan and parish papers; some parish registers, 1733– , and parish histories.
Letters to Bishop of Southwark from Portsmouth, 1850s– .

Finding aids: Index to diocesan holdings.

Facilities: Photocopying.

1041　Royal Naval Museum Archive

Address: HM Naval Base, Portsmouth, Hampshire PO1 3NH

Telephone: (023) 92727563 (central number); 9727577 (Curator of Manuscripts); 92723795 (Library)

Fax: (023) 92727575

E-mail: rn-museum@compulink.co.uk

Enquiries: The Curator of Manuscripts, Mr Matthew Sheldon.
More general historical enquiries which do not relate to the museum's collections will be answered as a paid research service by the Information Service, at the museum address.

Open: Mon–Fri: 10.00–4.00, by appointment by 3p.m. the preceding day.

Access: Free to all genuine researchers. All manuscripts are consulted in the library and advance application for a library reader's ticket is advised.

Historical background: The museum was founded in 1911 as the Dockyard Museum, and the bulk of its collections were transferred to the new Victory Museum in 1938. In 1972 it was renamed the Royal Naval Museum and major expansion began, as a result of which the museum now presents the history of the Royal Navy from Tudor times until the present day. It is the only museum in the country devoted exclusively to the overall history of the Royal Navy.

Acquisitions policy: The museum aims to collect material for display and research relating to the history of the Royal Navy and its people. Particular emphasis is placed on the navy's social history and the experience of individuals as shown in personal papers and oral history interviews.

Archives of organisation: Correspondence relating to the establishment of the Royal Naval Museum and the formation of the former Victory Museum; correspondence and research notes on museum acquisitions.

Major collections: Records of active service of *HMS Victory*, 1792–1810, and of restoration, 1890–1948.
Records of the Royal Naval Benevolent Society, 1791–1968.
Papers of Admiral Sir Arthur Auckland Cochrane (1824–1905).

Records of the Medical Department of HM Dockyard Portsmouth, 1850–1955.

WRNS Historic Collection.

Many small collections of ships logs, diaries, memoirs and personal papers, 1757–1982.

The Royal Naval Museum also administers most of the important manuscripts of the Admiralty Library (entry 699A) as a separate, discrete collection. Major elements administered by the RNM are: manuscripts of Thomas Corbett (d 1751); papers of Admiral Sir John Jervis, Earl St Vincent (1735–1823); Admiral of the Fleet, John Fisher, 1st Baron Fisher (1841–1920), 1889–1918; Edward Majoribanks, Baron Tweedmouth (1849–1909), as First Lord of the Admiralty, 1905–08; Admiral Sir Henry Jackson (1855–1929), as First Sea Lord, 1915–16; Alfred C. Dewar (d 1969), 1917–48.

Logs, personal diaries, letter- and order-books, ship and establishment plans.

Plans prepared by Robert Seppings (1767–1840) as Surveyor of the Navy, 1813–32.

Non-manuscript material: Photographic archive of ships, men, actions and routines of the Royal Navy, c1860– .

Oral History Collection, c 1900– .

Royal Naval Museum Library and large part of the printed collections of the Admiralty Library, particularly strong on reference works, journals and biography.

Finding aids: Handlist of additions, 1997-, and for parts of the Admiralty Library Manuscript Collection. Annual return to NRA.

Facilities: Photocopying. Photography. Microfiche reader.

Publications: V. Billing: *Catalogue of the Oral History Collection at the Royal Naval Museum* (1997).

M. Sheldon: *Guide to the Manuscript Collections of the Royal Naval Museum* (1997).

1042 University of Portsmouth
Frewen Library

Address: Cambridge Road, Portsmouth PO1 2ST

Telephone: (023) 92843222

Fax: (023) 92843233

E-mail: library@port.ac.uk

Website: www.libr.port.ac.uk

Enquiries: The University Librarian
The Humanities Librarian

Open: Term: Sun–Sat: 8.00–12.00 midnight
Vacation: Sun–Sat: 9.00–6.00, but confirm in advance.

Access: Approved external readers, on written application.

Historical background: The university had its origins in the Portsmouth and Gosport School of Sciences and Art founded in 1869. This subsequently became the Portsmouth Municipal Technical Institute, Portsmouth Municipal College, Portsmouth College of Technology and finally Portsmouth Polytechnic in 1969. Merger with the City of Portsmouth College of Education took place in 1976, and with Portsmouth College of Art, Design and Further Education in 1994.

Acquisitions policy: Archives are not normally acquired.

Archives of organisation: Some MS material, and a large collection of printed ephemera relating to the history of the university, 1869– .

Major collections: Records of the British Federation of Women Graduates (BFWG), c 1907–95, including minutes, correspondence, AGM reports, reports of refugee cases, and members' reports on women's issues.

Non-manuscript material: The BFWG archive includes annual reports of the Association of University Women in India, 1914–22 and the Women Graduates Union, Bombay, 1916–23; also conference reports of the International Federation of University Women.

Finding aids: British Federation of University Women: NRA 39086.

1043 Harris Library
Local Studies Collection

Parent organisation: Lancashire Library

Address: Market Place, Preston, Lancashire PR1 2PP

Telephone: (01772) 404010

Fax: (01772) 555527

E-mail: harris@airtime.co.uk

Enquiries: The Divisional Librarian, Mrs L.M. Farnworth

Open: Mon, Wed, Fri: 10.00–7.30; Tues, Thurs, Sat: 10.00–5.00.

Access: Generally open to the public, preferably by appointment.

Historical background: There has been an organised Local Studies Collection since 1967, although material was acquired previously. The library forms part of Preston District Reference Library and collects material relating to Preston and the immediate area around. The bulk of the collection comprises printed material, and previously held records of Preston police, schools, trades council and businesses have been transferred to the Lancashire Record Office (entry 1044).

Acquisitions policy: MS material is acquired by donation; printed material is purchased as required.

Major collections: Papers of Francis Thompson (1859–1907), poetry and prose.

Non-manuscript material: Harkness Collection of Broadsides.
Lancashire maps.
Transactions of the major historical and record societies of the North-West.
Local newspapers, 1807– .

Finding aids: Computer catalogue of Local Studies Collection.

Facilities: Photocopying. Microfilm/fiche reader/printer.

Publications: Catalogue of the Francis Thompson Collection (Preston, 1959).
Family History: A guide to Sources in the Harris Library (Preston, 1998).

1044   Lancashire Record Office

Address: Bow Lane, Preston, Lancashire PR1 2RE

Telephone: (01772) 263039

Fax: (01772) 263050

E-mail: record.office@ed.lancscc.gov.uk

Website: www.lancashire.gov.uk/education/lifelong/recordindex.shtml

Enquiries: The County Archivist, Mr B. Jackson

Open: Mon, Wed, Thurs: 9.00–5.00; Tues: 9.00–8.30; Fri: 9.00–4.00.
Closed first week in each month.

Access: Generally open to the public. The office operates the CARN reader's ticket system.

Historical background: The record office was established in 1940. Before the reorganisation of local government in 1974 it covered the former County Palatine of Lancashire, including Furness, now in Cumbria, and those areas which formed the metropolitan counties of Greater Manchester and Merseyside. At this time also it lost Warrington and gained a small part of Yorkshire. Since 1998 it has provided archive services, under joint agreements, to the new unitary authorities of Blackburn with Darwen and Blackpool. It acts as a Diocesan Record Office for the Anglican Diocese of Blackburn for the northern deaneries of Liverpool and for the former Yorkshire parishes in Bradford Diocese, as well as for the Roman Catholic Dioceses of Lancaster, Liverpool and Salford. It is recognised as a place of deposit for public records. Lancashire Library moved its headquarters local studies collection to the office in 1999. The office is a listening post for material from the North West Sound Archive (entry 245).

Acquisitions policy: Archives relating to the geographical area covered by Lancashire County Council and the boroughs of Blackburn with Darwen and Blackpool, in addition to diocesan records outside the area.

Archives of organisation: Usual local authority record holdings.

Major collections: Deposited local collections, including many large family and estate collections; several solicitors' collections; business records, including stained glass, engineering and textile manufacturing companies; and the records of trade unions and employers' organisations, particularly relating to the Lancashire textile industry.
Feilden Collection, formerly in Blackburn Museum.

Non-manuscript material: Lancashire Local Studies Library central collection.

Finding aids: Catalogues and lists; index to quarter sessions petitions; catalogues sent to NRA.

Facilities: Photocopying. Photography. Microfilming. Microfilm/fiche readers/printers.

Conservation: In-house. Outside work is not undertaken.

Publications: R. Sharpe France: *Guide to Lancashire Record Office* (1986).

Janet D. Martin: *Guide to Lancashire Record Office: a Supplement* (1992).

Finding Folk: a Handlist of Basic Sources for Family History in the Lancashire Record Office (1999) [also available on CD-ROM].

1045 Myerscough College Library

Address: Myerscough Hall, Bilsborrow, Preston, Lancashire PR3 0RY

Telephone: (01995) 642222 ext. 2551

Fax: (01995) 642333

E-mail: mailbox@myerscough.ac.uk

Website: www.myerscough.ac.uk

Enquiries: The College Librarian, Mr J.R. Humfrey

Open: Mon–Thurs: 9.00–8.00; Fri: 9.00–5.00; Sat: 10.00–3.00.

Access: Generally open to the public.

Historical background: The college was founded in 1893, and called Lancashire College of Agriculture and Horticulture until 1993. It is particularly concerned with agriculture, arbori-culture, the environment, horticulture, land-based industries, leisure and tourism, equine studies and veterinary nursing.

Acquisitions policy: To maintain the college archives.

Archives of organisation: Archives relating to the college, 1919– , including milking records and farm reports, 1948– ; plans and maps of col-lege sites and farms; photographs and glass plates of college and local agriculture, c1900– ; slides of conservation/land-based industries/ farming (3000) and videos (550).

Finding aids: Lists and indexes.

Facilities: Photocopying. Microfilm/fiche read-ers. Video players.

1046 University of Central Lancashire

Address: Library and Learning Resource Services, Preston, Lancashire PR1 2HE

Telephone: (01772) 892285

Fax: (01772) 892937

E-mail: a.turner-bishop@uclan.ac.uk

Website: www.uclan.ac.uk

Enquiries: The Special Collections Librarian, Aidan Turner-Bishop

Open: Term: Mon–Thurs: 8.45–10.00; Fri: 8.45–8.00; Sat: 10.00–6.00; Sun: 10.00–2.00.
Vacation: Mon–Thurs: 8.45–5.30 Fri: 8.45–5.00.

Access: Written application is preferred and an appointment is necessary.

Historical background: Preston Institution for the Diffusion of Knowledge was founded in 1828 by Joseph Livesey (1794–1884), who was a pioneer of temperance. It was later known as the Avenham Institution until it was re-formed in 1882 as the Harris Institute. This became Harris College in 1956 and Preston Polytechnic in 1973. The Preston Municipal Observatory (f. 1881) was incorporated into the polytechnic in 1974. In 1984 it was renamed Lancashire Polytechnic and in 1992 it became the University of Central Lancashire.

Acquisitions policy: To collect all material likely to be relevant to the understanding of the his-tory and development of the university and its predecessors.

Archives of organisation: Astronomical and meteorological records for Preston, 1881–1960s.

Index registers of all Harris Institute/College students, 1882–1965.

Committee minutes, 1828–1920s.

Major collections: Archives of British National Temperance League and its two former constit-uents, including minutes, agents' reports, account books, annual reports, 1845– (incom-plete).

Sheffield Temperance Association records, including minutes, correspondence, subscrip-tion book, 1856–1919.

Band of Hope Shepherd Street Mission minutes and other records.

Non-manuscript material: All prospectuses and reports, 1928– .

Photographs and ephemera, including Charnley Collection *re* Guatemala banana plantations; and collection of design catalogues. Oral history video tapes.

BNTL artefacts, e.g. Joseph Livesey's rattle, memorabilia, lantern slides; films and videos.

Finding aids: Catalogue available on website.

Facilities: Photocopying. Photography. Microfilm readers.

Publications: G. Timmins and others: *Preston Polytechnic: the Emergence of an Institution, 1828–1978* (1979).
R. Pope and K. Philipps: *University of Central Lancashire: a History of the Development of the Institutions since 1828* (1995).
I. Levitt (ed): *Joseph Livesey of Preston: Business, Temperance and Moral Reform* (1996).

1047 Rawtenstall District Central Library
Rossendale Collection

Parent organisation: Lancashire County Library

Address: Haslingden Road, Rawtenstall, Rossendale, Lancashire BB4 6QU

Telephone: (01706) 227911

Fax: (01706) 217014

E-mail: rawtenstall.reference@lcl.lancscc.gov.uk

Enquiries: The Reference Librarian, Laura Waterhouse

Open: Mon, Tues: 10.00–7.30; Wed: 10.00–1.00; Thur, Fri: 10.00–5.00; Sat: 10.00–4.00.

Access: Generally open to the public.

Historical background: Before 1974 Rawtenstall was administered by a borough council, and the Local Studies Collection was quite extensively developed to cover Rawtenstall and the surrounding areas. After the 1974 local government reorganisation Rawtenstall became the district headquarters of Rossendale, one of the 14 districts of Lancashire County Library. (See also Haslingden Library, entry 429). In 1998 a merger with the Hyndburn district formed the South-East Lancashire Division.

Acquisitions policy: To collect materials directly relevant to the Rossendale area, i.e. Bacup, Haslingden, Rawtenstall and Whitworth, as well as Lancashire and the North-West.

Major collections: Rawtenstall and Rossendale Borough Council minutes and electoral registers, 1891– ; Rawtenstall Burial Board records, 1874–9; Rawtenstall Corporation Housing Scheme records, 1922–74.

Sunday school records, 1844–1953; co-operative societies' records, 1876–1956.
Loveclough Printerworkers' Library and Club records, 1892–1944.
Haslingden Gospel Mission minute books, 1890–1983.

Non-manuscript material: Copies of music scores written and used by Deighn Layrocks (Larks of Dean), group of 18th-century musicians. Originals on permanent loan to Lancashire Record Office (entry 1044).
John Willie Johnson Collection: mainly articles and information on Bacup area.
News cuttings and photographs.
Rossendale Free Press, 1883– (on microfilm).
Dissertations on the development of industry within Rossendale.
Maps, 1844– .

Facilities: Photocopying. Microfilm/fiche readers/printer.

Conservation: Conservation work undertaken by Lancashire Record Office.

Publications: J. Harrison: *Tracing your Ancestors in Rossendale* (1982).
Directory of Local Studies Resources in Lancashire (1986).
S. Halstead: *Around Rossendale* (1994).

1048 BBC Written Archives Centre

Address: Caversham Park, Reading, Berkshire RG4 8TZ

Telephone: (0118) 946 9281/2

Fax: (0118) 946 1145

E-mail: wac.enquiries@bbc.co.uk

Enquiries: The Written Archivist, Mrs J.M. Kavanagh

Open: Wed–Fri: 9.45–1.00, 2.00–5.00, by appointment.
Telephone calls taken Mon–Fri: 9.30–5.30.

Access: By written appointment, giving full details of the nature of the enquiry. Correspondence files, 1922–74, are open for research. There is unrestricted access to programme records, programme logs, news bulletins, scripts and publications. Charges are made for some services.

Historical background: The centre was established at Caversham in 1970, when it was decided to move the Historical Records Office (set up in London in 1957 mainly to assist Asa Briggs in his work on *The History of Broadcasting in the UK*) to more spacious accommodation and allow greater access for research. BBC sound and visual archives are held in London. Requests for access to recorded material should be made to the National Sound Archive (entry 561D) and the National Film and Television Archive (entry 556B) respectively.

Acquisitions policy: To maintain the records of the corporation, including BBC publications, and to acquire papers of prominent BBC figures and material closely related to the BBC.

Archives of organisation: Non-current records of the corporation for permanent preservation, including papers from the regional centres and the BBC's commercial activities.
Correspondence, minutes and reports covering all areas of the BBC's activities, 1922– : programmes (including correspondence with contributors), policy, scripts, news bulletins, daily programme logs, audience research, technical developments.

Major collections: Papers of people closely connected with the BBC in some way, including Lord Reith.

Non-manuscript material: Plans and illustrations; microfilm; BBC publications, including *Radio Times* (with regional volumes), *The Listener, World Radio, London Calling*; BBC schools publications; BBC Symphony and Promenade Concert programmes; the *Summary of World Broadcasts* (produced by the BBC Monitoring Service); broadcasting press cuttings; small collection of books on broadcasting.

Finding aids: Title and summary indexes.

Facilities: Photocopying. Microfilm readers.

Publications: For a general introduction to the range and nature of the material available, see A. Briggs: *The History of Broadcasting in the United Kingdom* (Oxford, 1961–95) [5 vols].

1049 Berkshire Record Office

Parent organisation: Reading Borough Council

Address: 9 Coley Avenue, Reading, Berkshire RG1 6AF

Telephone: (0118) 901 5132

Fax: (0118) 901 5131

E-mail: arch@reading.gov.uk

Enquiries: The County Archivist, Dr Peter Durrant

Open: Tues, Wed: 9.00–5.00; Thurs: 9.00–9.00; Fri: 9.00–4.30.
Closed for stocktaking for two weeks in October/November.

Access: Generally open to the public. The office operates the CARN reader's ticket system. An appointment is essential as space is limited.

Historical background: The office was established in 1948. It also acts as the Diocesan Record Office for Oxford (Archdeaconry of Berkshire), and is recognised as a place of deposit for public records.

Archives of organisation: Usual local authority record holdings, including Corporation of Reading records.

Major collections: Deposited local collections.

Finding aids: Catalogues and indexes; catalogues sent to NRA.

Facilities: Photocopying. Photography. Microfilming. Microfilm /fiche reader/printers.

Conservation: In-house service; outside work occasionally undertaken.

Publications: F. Hull: *Guide to the Berkshire Record Office* (1952).

1050 Douai Abbey

Address: Upper Woolhampton, Reading, Berkshire RG7 5TQ

Telephone: (0118) 971 5340

Fax: (0118) 971 5203

E-mail: gscott2006@aol.com

Enquiries: The Archivist, Dom Geoffrey Scott

Open: By arrangement.

Access: Bona fide researchers, by appointment.

Historical background: The English Benedictine community was founded in Paris in 1615, and settled at Douai in northern France after the French Revolution. In 1903 it transferred to Woolhampton. The collections divide into two: material relating to the English Benedictine Congregation, of which the abbey is a member, and archives belonging to Douai

Abbey, its parishes, school and other apostolates.

Acquisitions policy: The abbey serves as a repository for archives of the parishes it administers. It specialises in 18th-century Benedictine and Jacobite material. Microfilms are made of dispersed records.

Archives of organisation: English Benedictine Congregation, 1619– .
Records of community, school and missions attached to the community, including apostolates in Mauritius and Australia.

Major collections: Collections of Dom Benet Weldon (1674–1713), Benedictine annalist.

Non-manuscript material: English Benedictine Congregation photographs.

Finding aids: Subject and chronological catalogues.

Facilities: Photocopying. Microfilm/fiche reader.

Publications: G. Scott: '"The Collector": a Look at Benedictine Archives through the Eyes of Brother Benet Weldon', *Catholic Archives*, 6 (1986), 25–42.

1051 Reading Local Studies Library

Parent organisation: Reading Borough Libraries

Address: Central Library, Abbey Square, Reading, Berkshire RG1 3BQ

Telephone: (0118) 901 5965

Fax: (0118) 901 5954

E-mail: reading.ref@dial.pipex.com

Enquiries: The Local Studies Librarian

Open: Mon, Wed: 9.30–5.00; Tues, Thurs, Fri: 9.30–7.00; Sat: 9.30–4.00.

Access: Generally open to the public, although an appointment is required to consult some material. There is a fee-based research service.

Historical background: Reading is the main local studies library for the historic county of Berkshire. It has been collecting material on Reading and the historic county since a public library was first opened in the town in the 1880s. Maidenhead Library also holds a small amount of MS material on Cookham and Maidenhead.

Acquisitions policy: To collect material relating to the whole of historic Berkshire and neighbouring areas of bordering counties.

Major collections: Literary MSS, diaries, letters and local history note-books and scrapbooks, including Mary Russell Mitford (1787–1855), correspondence and diary; Thomas Noon Talfourd (1795–1855), judge and author, correspondence and legal note-books; Treacher family note-books of River Thames surveyors and their accounts, c1800–c1860.

Non-manuscript material: Illustrations, photographs, prints, slides, maps and plans, books and directories, newspaper files and cuttings. Printed ephemera.

Finding aids: Catalogues.

Facilities: Photocopying. Photography. Microfilm/fiche reader. Self-service microfiche printer.

Conservation: In-house service.

Publications: Local Collection Catalogue (1958; suppl., 1967).
Bibliography of Mary Russell Mitford (1787–1855).

1052 Rural History Centre

Parent organisation: University of Reading

Address: Whiteknights, Reading, Berkshire RG6 6AG

Telephone: (0118) 931 8666 (Archivist); 931 8660

Fax: (0118) 975 1264

E-mail: j.h.brown@reading.ac.uk

Website: www.rdg.ac.uk/instit/im/home.html

Enquiries: The Archivist, Dr J.H. Brown

Open: Mon–Thurs: 9.30–1.00, 2.00–5.00; Fri: 9.30–1.00, 2.00–4.30.

Access: Generally open to the public. A user's card may be issued for study of research collections over a long period. One week's notice is required for consultation of the records of the Agricultural Co-operative Society and certain deposits of national agricultural organisations. There are restrictions on some deposited collections.

Historical background: The Institute of Agricultural History was established in 1968 to co-ordinate and extend teaching and research in agricultural history; to collect, preserve and publish records, documents and other relevant material; and to maintain the Museum of English Rural Life, founded within the University of Reading in 1951 and opened to the public in 1955. The institute became the Rural History Centre in 1993.

Acquisitions policy: To collect material concerned with rural and agricultural history, with special reference to national organisations concerned with agriculture, the countryside, rural and agricultural industry, and food. Geographical coverage: Britain, mainly England.

Major collections: Trade records: business records of over 30 agricultural engineering, servicing and processing firms; technical and advertising literature issued by *c*3000 UK and foreign firms, 19th century– .

National agricultural organisation records: records of Royal Agricultural Society of England (f. 1838), including archives of the Board of Agriculture and Internal Improvement, 1793–1822; National Union of Agriculture and Allied Workers, 1906–1970s; National Farmers' Union, 1909–43; Country Landowners' Association, 1907–58; Royal Agricultural Benevolent Institution, 1880s–1960s; Council for the Protection of Rural England, 1930s–1970s; Council for National Parks; Agricultural Apprenticeship Council, 1949–74. Shorthorn Society and Jersey Cattle Society records and publications.

Agricultural Co-operative Society records, mostly 20th century.

General collections, including personal papers of agricultural writers and scientists.

Farm records, 18th–20th centuries, are housed at Reading University Library (entry 1053): enquiries should be made in the first instance to the University Archivist.

Non-manuscript material: Engineering drawings, trade catalogues and printed ephemera; film and audio tapes.

Photograph library, including reference collections of agricultural organisations and the farming press, mid-19th century– (*c*500,000 prints and negatives).

Finding aids: Lists and catalogues for all principal deposits. Specialised indexes for certain collections. Lists of principal deposits sent to NRA.

Facilities: Photocopying. Photography. Microfilming. Microfilm reader. Copying of engineering drawings.

Publications: Historical Farm Records: a Summary Guide (Reading, 1973).
Ransomes: a History of the Firm and Guide to its Records (Reading, 1975).

1053 University of Reading
Archives and Manuscripts

Parent organisation: The University of Reading

Address: PO Box 223, Whiteknights, Reading, Berkshire RG6 6AE

Telephone: (0118) 9931 8776

Fax: (0118) 9931 6636 (library)

E-mail: g.m.c.bott@reading.ac.uk

Website: www.rdg.ac.uk/serdepts/home.html

Enquiries: The Keeper of Archives and Manuscripts, Mr Michael Bott

Open: Mon–Fri: 9.00–5.00, by appointment.

Access: Generally open to the public. Certain records are restricted.

Historical background: Archives and Manuscripts was established as a department of the library in 1966 on the appointment of Dr J.A. Edwards. Until recently it was the base for work on a location register of 20th-century English literary MSS and letters (published 1988) and its extension to the 18th and 19th centuries (published 1995). The Typography Department holds the Centre for Ephemera Studies, with the Maurice Rickards Collection of Ephemera. Access is via Michael Twyman, Hon. Director.

Acquisitions policy: To acquire literary and historical MSS related to teaching and research in the University of Reading. To preserve university archives through the operation of a records management system.

Archives of organisation: University archives: records of university departments and their antecedents and of members of staff, 1860– .

Major collections: Records of British publishing and printing: collections include George Allen & Unwin; George Bell & Sons; the Bodley Head; Jonathan Cape; Chatto & Windus; Heinemann Educational Books; the Hogarth Press; Isotype Institute; Longman Group;

Macmillan & Co.; Routledge & Kegan Paul; Secker & Warburg.

Historical farm records: mainly of individual working farmers from every English county, 16th–20th centuries.

Records of contemporary writing: letters and MSS of some 200 authors, 1880– , including the largest collection of Samuel Beckett MSS in Europe.

Modern political papers: six collections of 20th-century papers, of which most important are those of Waldorf, 2nd Viscount Astor, and Nancy, Lady Astor.

John Lewis (co-founder with Maurice Rickards of the Ephemera Society) Printing Collection.

Non-manuscript material: Maps. Photographs. Audio-visual material.

Finding aids: Various indexes, catalogues and inventories.

Facilities: Access to all the resources of the university library, including photocopying and photographic services.

Publications: Accessions of General Manuscripts up to June 1970 (1970).
Historical Farm Records: a Summary Guide to Manuscripts and other Material in the University Library Collected by the Institute of Agricultural History (1973).
University of Reading Records Handbook (1977).
M. Bott and J.A. Edwards: *Records Management in British Universities: a Survey with some Suggestions* (1978).
J.A. Edwards: *The Samuel Beckett Collection: a Catalogue* (1978).
The Kingsley Read Alphabet Collection: a Catalogue (1982).
One Hundred Years of University Education in Reading: a Pictorial History, 1892–1992 (1992).
Beckett at Reading: Catalogue of the Beckett Manuscript Collection at the University of Reading (1998).

1054 Sisters of St Joseph of Peace Archive

Address: Sacred Heart Provincial House, 61 Station Road, Rearsby, Leicestershire LE7 8YY

Telephone: (01644) 424251

Enquiries: The Archivist, Sr Bridgetta Rooney

Open: By arrangement.

Access: Students and bona fide researchers only. An appointment is necessary.

Founded in 1884 in Nottingham, the Religious Sisters are concerned with social work, education, the care of sick children, work with people with AIDS, and justice and peace issues. The archive consists mainly of personal papers, including correspondence and photographs of the founder, Mother Francis Clare Cusack (1829–91), and early members of the order. There are catalogues and indexes.

1055 Redcar Reference Library

Parent organisation: Redcar & Cleveland Borough Council

Address: Central Library, Coatham Road, Redcar TS10 1RP

Telephone: (01642) 489292

Fax: (01642) 492253

Enquiries: The Reference Librarian, Mrs Brenda Robinson

Open: Mon, Tues, Wed, Fri: 9.30–7.00; Thurs: 9.30–5.00; Sat: 9.30–12.30.

Access: Generally open to the public.

Redcar was a borough library from 1937 to 1967. From 1967 it was part of Teesside Libraries and later of Cleveland, and in 1996 it came under Redcar & Cleveland Borough Council. It maintains the usual local history collection, which includes the Graham Collection of social history photographs, 1890s–1940s (*c*3000). Photocopying and microfilm/fiche readers are available.

1056 Cornish Studies Library

Parent organisation: Cornwall County Council

Address: 2–4 Clinton Road, Redruth, Cornwall TR15 2QE

Telephone: (01209) 216760

Fax: (01209) 210283

E-mail: cornishstudies.libraries@cornwall.gov.uk

Website: www.cornwall.gov.uk

Enquiries: The Principal Library Officer, Cornish Studies, Mr G.T. Knight

Open: Mon–Fri: 10.00–6.00; Sat: 10.00–4.00.

Access: Generally open to the public. An appointment is strongly advised for the use of microfilm. Some material is in store, so prior enquiry is suggested.

The Cornish Studies Library was established in 1974, based on an earlier large collection at Redruth, but adding collections from Truro and items from elsewhere. A local history collection is maintained, incorporating the A.K. Hamilton Jenkin Collection relating to metal-mining in Cornwall and the Hambly and Rowe and Ashley Rowe general Cornish collections. This is actively developed to complement the archival holdings of the Cornwall County Record Office (entry 1173). There are also 30 newspaper files, Cornish census returns, and a large photograph collection, including the George Ellis Photographic Collection (*c*10,000). A full computer catalogue is available and there is the usual range of reprographic services.

1057 British Mycological Society Library

Address: c/o The Herbarium, Royal Botanic Gardens, Kew, Richmond-upon-Thames, Surrey TW9 3AE

Telephone: (01784) 259198 (Librarian's home)

E-mail: v.barkham@rbgkew.org.uk

Enquiries: The Librarian and Archivist, Mrs Valerie Barkham

Open: By prior arrangement with the Librarian.

Access: Members and associates of BMS.

The BMS was founded in 1896 and its library was founded *c*1949. Originally housed at the Commonwealth Mycological Institute, it moved to the Herbarium in 1990. It holds 1890s drawings by Worthington G. Smith and photographs of early mycologists and some archival material. There is a catalogue and photocopying is available. The society publishes various works, including G.C. Ainsworth and J. Webster (comp.): *Brief Biographies of British Mycologists* ed. D. Moore (1996).

1058 Public Record Office

Address: Ruskin Avenue, Kew, Richmond-upon-Thames, Surrey TW9 4DU

Telephone: (020) 8876 3444; 8392 5200 (enquiries)

Fax: (020) 8878 8905

E-mail: enquiries@pro.gov.uk

Website: www.pro.gov.uk

Enquiries: The Keeper of Public Records, Mrs Sarah Tyacke

Open: Mon, Wed, Fri: 9.30–5.00; Tues: 10.00–7.00; Thurs: 9.30–7.00; Sat: 9.30–5.00 (except Sat prior to bank holidays).
Closed public and privilege holidays and usually the first week of December (for stock-taking).

Access: Generally open to the public, by reader's ticket issued on production of formal documentary proof of identity. No reader's ticket is required for the Family Record Centre.

Historical background: The PRO's original building in Chancery Lane was constructed, following the Public Records Act 1838, between 1851 and 1899. By the 1960s overcrowding led to the building of a new repository at Kew, which was opened in 1977. Records of medieval and early modern government, the Prerogative Court of Canterbury and the census of England and Wales (1841–91), with all legal records, were then held at Chancery Lane, while records of modern government departments were housed at Kew. Following new building at Kew all Chancery Lane records were moved there and the collections were reunited in 1997. Census records remain in central London at the Family Records Centre (entry 608). In 1995 the PRO decided to contract out provision for structured datasets used and produced by government. This service is now provided by the UK National Digital Archive of Datasets (NDAD) at the University of London (see entry 828).

Acquisitions policy: All government archives selected for permanent preservation are transferred to the PRO for the use of the public 30 years after their creation, unless retained for a longer period by the department concerned under statute or on application to the Lord Chancellor. The acquisitions policy directs that records selected should document the nation's social and economic conditions and contact between citizens and governments.

Archives of organisation: Public records of government, 1066– .

Major collections: Many private and semi-official collections of public figures, including the Chatham, Russell, Ramsay MacDonald, Kitchener and Milner papers, and archives of some national non-governmental organisations, including the Imperial Institute, the Association of Municipal Corporations and the Queen's Institute of District Nursing.

Non-manuscript material: One of the most significant collections of maps and plans in the world.
Extensive photograph holdings (mostly scattered among administrative archives).
Some film, sound and machine-readable material (no facilities for use).
Official printed material.
Large library, very strong on English topography, administrative, legal and archival history, and a large collection of periodicals.

Finding aids: Lists, card indexes, indexes, databases, calendars, handbooks etc. Lists sent to NRA. All PRO finding aids are available on the website.

Facilities: Photocopying. Photography. Microfilming. Microfilm/fiche reader/printer.

Conservation: Full in-house facilities.

Publications: Guide to Contents of the Public Record Office (1963–8) [3 vols].
Tracing your Ancestors in the Public Record Office (3/1995).
The Public Record Office Current Guide [regularly updated microfiche edition to 1998].
Calendars, handbooks, pamphlets, readers' guides.
A variety of catalogues of publications including academic titles, popular history, family history and military titles, available on the website and from the PRO's marketing department.

1059 Richmond-upon-Thames Local Studies

Parent organisation: London Borough of Richmond-upon-Thames

Address: Old Town Hall, Whittaker Avenue, Richmond-upon-Thames TW9 1TP

Telephone: (020) 8332 6820

Fax: (020) 8940 6899

E-mail: locstudies@richmond.gov.uk

Website: www.richmond.gov.uk/leisure/libraries/library.html

Enquiries: The Local History Librarian, Miss V. Jane Baxter

Open: Tues: 1.00–5.00; Wed: 1.00–8.00; Thurs, Fri: 1.00–6.00; Sat (2nd, 4th and 5th): 10.00–12.30, 1.30–5.00.

Access: Generally open to the public. A telephone call in advance is advisable to establish the exact location of any given material.

Historical background: The London Borough of Richmond-upon-Thames was formed in 1965 by the amalgamation of the boroughs of Richmond, Twickenham and Barnes. The local material relating to Richmond and East Sheen, Ham, Kew, Mortlake and Petersham is located at Richmond. There is no borough archivist or archives department and the library is not an official archive depository. Local material relating to Twickenham, the Hamptons, Teddington and Whitton is located at Twickenham District Reference Library. The majority of council records are in the custody of the Chief Executive and Town Clerk's Department, Municipal Offices, Twickenham TW1 3AA, tel. (020) 8891 1411.

Acquisitions policy: Local history material by donation, transfer and, occasionally, purchase.

Major collections: Usual local history collections, including:
Local government records, in particular rate books, Richmond vestry minutes and workhouse records, 19th and 20th centuries.
School records, 19th and 20th centuries.
Records of various local clubs and societies, mostly 20th century.
Vancouver Collection: pamphlets, cuttings and books relating to Captain George Vancouver, especially concerning his connections with Richmond and Petersham.
Sladen Collection: scrapbooks of his correspondence, bills, reviews etc (*c*70), compiled by Douglas Sladen, editor of *Who's Who*, who knew many of the literary and society figures of his day.
Long Collection: local material, especially books and playbills.
Collections of the works of local authors, e.g. James Thomson and Mrs Braddon.
Playbill collection.

Non-manuscript material: Maps, 1635– ; photographs; prints; postcards; slides; news cuttings and microfilms of local newspapers; copies and microfilms of census returns, 1841–91.

Collection of playbills relating mainly to the Theatre Royal, Richmond, 1765–1884 (c1000).

Ionides Collection: topographical paintings, drawings and engravings of Richmond, Twickenham and the Lower Thames area (housed at Orleans Gallery, Twickenham).

Finding aids: Index to Sladen letters: NRA 14252. Card catalogues of prints. Index to playbills, artists and local authors.

Facilities: Photocopying. Microfilm/fiche reader/printer.

Publications: The library produces a series of about 60 brief notes on local history which are currently being revised; a complete list of local publications is available.

1060   Royal Botanic Gardens, Kew
Library and Archives

Address: Kew, Richmond-upon-Thames, Surrey TW9 3AE

Telephone: (020) 8332 5417

Fax: (020) 8332 5278

E-mail: librarian@rbgkew.org.uk

Website: www.rbgkew.org.uk

Enquiries: The Archivist, Ms Lesley Price

Open: Tues–Thurs: 10.00–5.00.

Access: On written application.

Historical background: A botanic garden at Kew was begun in 1759 by Princess Augusta. The gardens of the royal estates at Kew became a department of the Crown in 1840. They have been successively managed by the Commissioners of Woods and Forests (1841–51), the Board of Works (1851–1903), the Board of Agriculture (later Ministry of Agriculture, Fisheries and Food) (1903–84), and (since 1984) a board of trustees appointed under the National Heritage Act 1983. The library was set up in 1852; it is recognised as a place of deposit for public records.

Acquisitions policy: Official papers are selected according to Public Record Office rules. Other papers are accepted if relevant to Kew's plant collections and research on plant and fungal systematics, conservation, anatomy, biochemistry, horticulture and economic botany.

Archives of organisation: Extensive archives containing more than 4600 collections from all over the world, including modern registered files, field note-books, diaries etc, mostly 1840– .

Notable are the papers of Sir William Jackson Hooker (1785–1865), his son Sir Joseph Dalton Hooker (1817–1911) and George Bentham (1800–84); correspondence with overseas botanic gardens and departments of agriculture and forestry, especially in colonial territories.

Fewer papers relating to the gardens before 1840 survive: most of the papers of the superintendents William Aiton (1731–93) and his son William Townsend Aiton (1766–1849) were burnt in 1849; some were rescued, including inwards and outwards books and records books, 1793-, and correspondence with Kew collectors, e.g. Francis Masson and others; there are some papers of Sir Joseph Banks (1743–1820).

Archives of the Kew Guild and the Phytochemical Society of Europe, 1956–84.

Major collections: Papers of E.K. Balls (1892–1984), 1932–79; G. Bentham (1800–84), 1807–97; Paul Furse (1904–78), 1938–77; R.E. Holttum (1895–1990), 1922–50; A.F.G. Kerr (1877–1942), 1906–34; J. Lindley (1799–1865), 1831–54; G.W.E. Loder, 1st Baron Wakehurst (1861–1936), 1884–1942; Messrs Lovell Reeve Ltd, publishers (1847–1965); Margaret Mee (1909–88), 1950–88; R.E. Melville (1903–85), 1940–85; R. Roxburgh (1751–1815), 1790–1812; R. Spruce (1817–93), 1842–90.

Non-manuscript material: Periodicals (4000); printed books (130,000); pamphlets (140,000); microforms (10,000); illustrations (175,000); maps (11,000); portraits (500).

Kewensia ; nurserymen's catalogues.

Sound archive.

Large collection of plant illustrations, including many originals, e.g. the Church, Roxburgh, Tankerville and *Curtis's Botanical Magazine* Collections.

Finding aids: General author and subject catalogues. Inventory and Public Record Office lists being computerised. Name index of correspondents. Artists' name index. NRA 25004, 25005.

Facilities: Photocopying. Photography. Microfilm/fiche readers.

Conservation: In-house service.

Publications: G.D.R. Bridson and others: *Natural History Manuscript Resources in the British Isles* (London, 1980) [RBG, Kew entries, nos. 269.1- 387].

R. Desmond: *Kew: the History of the Royal Botanic Gardens* (London: Harvill Press with the Royal Botanic Gardens, Kew, 1995).

1061 Rochdale Local Studies Library

Parent organisation: Rochdale Metropolitan Borough Council

Address: 3rd Floor, Champness Hall, Drake Street, Rochdale, Lancashire OL16 1PB

Telephone: (01706) 864915

Website: www.gmcro.co.uk/reposit.htm

Enquiries: The Local Studies Officer, Mrs P.A. Godman

Open: Wed, Fri: 10.00–1.00, 2.00–5.30; Thurs: 10.00–1.00, 2.00–7.30; Sat: 9.30–1.00, 2.00–4.00.

Access: Generally open to the public. The storage of some records on a separate site necessitates prior notice for access. Appointments are advised for the use of microfilm readers.

Historical background: The dynamic growth of Rochdale, Middleton and Heywood during the 19th century produced a wealth of material relating to the area. The town of Rochdale in particular was fortunate in that the early pioneers of the library service were keenly interested in the development of the area and helped to acquire a large amount of material which formed the basis of the Local Collection. Before 1974 the substantial local collections of Heywood, Middleton and Rochdale were located at the central libraries in those areas, and on local government reorganisation it was decided that each should retain a separate collection under the general supervision of a local studies librarian based at Rochdale. See also Rochdale Libraries, Heywood (entry 444), and Rochdale Libraries, Middleton (entry 902).

Acquisitions policy: The collection of documentary material relating to all aspects of life in the area of the Metropolitan Borough of Rochdale and its previously independent constituent authorities.

Major collections: Local administrative records: early administrative records, including highway rates, Poor Law administration and administrative material from the constituent authorities of the metropolitan borough, mid-18th–early-19th centuries.

Church records: church rates, leys, tithe commutation maps (Middleton only), plans, deeds, etc; Methodist archives, 18th century– .

Family records: material relating to local families, including manorial records, deeds, indentures etc, mainly 19th century.

Trade union records: records of the Rochdale Operative Cotton Spinners Association; the Rochdale Weavers, Winders and Beamers Association, 19th and 20th centuries.

Non-manuscript material: Complete runs of local newspapers (original and microfilm copies).

Books, pamphlets, audio-visual material, photographs, maps, plans, broadsheets, political handbills, theatre posters.

Finding aids: Archive lists.

Facilities: Photocopying. Microfilm/fiche readers.

Conservation: Contracted out.

Publications: Introduction to Local Studies Collections (1981).

1062 Medway Archives and Local Studies Centre

Parent organisation: Medway Council

Address: Civic Centre, Strood, Rochester, Kent ME2 4AU

Telephone: (01634) 332714

Fax: (01634) 297060

E-mail: archives@medway.gov.uk
local.studies@medway.gov.uk

Website: cityark.medway.gov.uk

Enquiries: The Borough Archivist, Stephen Dixon
The Local Studies and Information Officer, Lyn Rainbow

Open: Mon, Thurs, Fri: 9.00–5.00; Tues: 9.00–6.00; Sat (1st and 3rd): 9.00–1.00.
Closed for stock-taking first two full weeks of November.

Access: Generally open the public. Archives are available by appointment only and the centre operates the CARN reader's ticket system.

Bookings are required for microfilm and microfiche holdings.

Historical background: Medway City Archives (Medway Area Archives Office) opened to the public in 1990, the result of an arrangement between Kent County Council, as then archives authority, and the local authority. The local studies collections of Chatham, Rochester and Strood libraries were merged and relocated to join the Archives at the Civic Centre to form the Rochester upon Medway Studies Centre (1993–8). The present service name stems from the inauguration of the new Medway Council unitary authority in 1998. The core collections were originally the local government archives of Rochester upon Medway City Council and its predecessors, to which have been added Medway-related collections previously held by Kent Archives Office, Maidstone (now the Centre for Kentish Studies, entry 868), unofficial collections received directly since 1990 and the Gillingham Borough archives in 1998.

Acquisitions policy: Historical and modern records of the parent local authority.

Archives of organisation: Records of Medway Council, 1998– ; Rochester upon Medway City Council, 1974–98; Gillingham Borough Council, 1903–98; Rochester City Council, 1227–1974; Chatham Borough Council, 1890–1974; Strood RDC, 1897–1974; Hoo RDC, 1897–1935; Strood Intra Parish Meeting, 1894–1935; Gillingham UDC, 1893–1903; Milton next Sittingbourne RDC (Rainham only), pre-1929; Rainham Parish Council, pre-1929; Rochester Highway Board, 1862–96; various courts leet, local boards of health and burial boards; Medway, Strood (North Aylesford) and Hoo Poor Law Unions, 1835–1930; school and education records, 1870– .

Major collections: Records of parish councils and Church of England parishes, Rochester Archdeaconry area, 14th–20th centuries; Rochester Cathedral, 1541–1994; St Andrew's Priory Rochester, Newark Priory, Strood, Leeds Priory, 1080–1541; Methodist Church, Medway Towns Circuit, 1768–1996; Chatham Memorial Synagogue, Rochester, 1834–1972.

Family and estate papers of Earls of Darnley of Cobham Hall, 1537–1974; Best family of Chatham and Boxley, family, estate and brewery business, 1596–1970.

Business papers of Winget of Strood, engineers, 20th century; Blaw Knox of Rochester, engineers, 20th century; Winch and Winch of Chatham, solicitors, clients' papers, 19th–20th centuries; Arnold Tuff & Grimwade of Rochester (Martin Tolhurst Partnership), solicitors, clients' papers, 18th–20th centuries.

Records of charities: Richard Watts' Charity, Rochester, 1579–1979; Hospital of Sir John Hawkins Kt in Chatham [1500], 1594–1984; St Bartholomew's Hospital, Rochester, 1418–1948; Foord Almshouses, Rochester, 1922–87; St Catherine's Hospital, 1697–1958.

Rochester Book Society, 1797–1965.

Medway Ports Authority and Conservancy Board, 1627–20th century; North Aylesford and Medway Petty Sessional Divisions, 1754–1985.

Non-manuscript material: Medway area census microfilms (with index to former Rochester upon Medway area), 1841–91; Kent census index microfiche, 1881; Kent and London *IGI*. Topographical printed histories, directories, maps, photographs and prints; Charles Dickens Collection (formerly housed at Chatham Library); Short Brothers Aeronautical Engineers Collection; HMS *Wildfire* RNR RTC (Chatham) Collection, 1964–94; biographical material on, and works of, Vera Conway Gordon (1874–1955), suffragist; Anne Pratt (1806–93), naturalist; and William J. Saunders (1873–1928), author of *Kalomera*.

Finding aids: Archives: manual descriptive lists and card indexes; CityArk Intranet database available on website.

Local Studies: card indexes, automated library service catalogue.

Facilities: Photocopying. Photography by arrangement. Microfilm/fiche readers.

Conservation: Contracted out.

Publications: A Genealogist's Guide to Sources for Tracing Members of the Armed Forces in the Medway Area, 1550–1950 (rev. 1997).

1063   Rochester Bridge Trust

Address: The Bridge Chamber, 5 Esplanade, Rochester, Kent ME1 1QE

Telephone: (01634) 846706/843457

Fax: (01634) 840125

E-mail: lewis@rochester-bridge-trust.freeserve.co.uk

Enquiries: The Bridge Clerk, Mr Michael Lewis
The Archivist, Dr James M. Gibson

Open: By arrangement.

Access: Archives are not normally available to the public, but may be consulted by bona fide scholars, with the approval of the Rochester Bridge Trust.

Historical background: In 1399 Sir Robert Knolles and Sir John de Cobham, prominent local men, gave and collected endowments in money and lands and obtained a patent of incorporation to ensure a responsible administration of the Rochester Bridge. A new bridge was built and two wardens appointed, who, with the help of a Court of Assistants added in 1576, administered the bridge. This arrangement still pertains. The bridge was specifically excluded from the provisions of the Trunk Roads Act of 1946. The wardens were appointed ex officio presidents of the New College of Cobham when it was refounded under the will of William Brooke, Lord Cobham, a descendant of the original founder, and college records are therefore lodged with those of the bridge, forming a distinct series.

Acquisitions policy: Working papers of the trust.

Archives of organisation: Rochester Bridge: Administrative records, including election registers, 1576– , and minute books, 1663– .
Wardens' accounts, 14th–20th centuries.
Records about the maintenance and construction of the bridge, including sounding charts, engineers' reports, contracts, specifications, and plans, 16th–20th centuries.
Estate records, including title deeds, leases, surveyor's reports, and estate maps, 14th–20th centuries.
Manorial records.
New College of Cobham: administrative records, including payment to pensioners, 1599– ; accounts, 1599– ; bonds, 1599–1877; nominations, certificates and material concerning elections, 1632–1890; estate deeds and surveys.

Non-manuscript material: Maps, plans, photographs and drawings.

Finding aids: Cobham College: NRA 10439, 20714.

Facilities: Photocopying.

Publications: E.S. Scroggs: *Rochester Bridge Trust and the New College of Cobham, Kent: Guide to Classification and Indexing of Records at the Bridge Chamber, Rochester* (1954).

—— : 'The Records of Rochester Bridge and the New College of Cobham', *Archives,* ii/12 (1954), 183.
N. Yates and J.M. Gibson (eds): *Traffic and Politics: the Construction and Management of Rochester Bridge, AD 43–1993* (Boydell and Brewer, 1994).
J.M. Gibson: *Catalogue of the Archives of the Rochester Bridge Trust: 1336–1996.*

1064   Havering Local Studies

Parent organisation: London Borough of Havering

Address: Central Library, St Edward's Way, Romford RM1 3AR

Telephone: (01708) 772393/772394

Fax: (01708) 772391

E-mail: romfordlib2@rmplc.co.uk

Enquiries: The Senior Librarian, Reference and Information Library

Open: Mon–Wed, Fri: 9.30–8.00; Sat: 9.30–4.00.

Access: Generally open to the public; an appointment is preferred. Booking is required for use of the microform readers.

Historical background: Until 1965 Havering was part of the county of Essex, and much archive material relating to the area is therefore to be found at the Essex Record Office (entry 228). However, a small collection of items is held at Romford.

Acquisitions policy: To obtain further archives relevant to the area where possible and also to acquire copies of those deposited in other collections such as the Essex Record Office (mainly in microfilm form).

Major collections: Usual local history collections, including parish rate books for selected areas (especially Romford), 19th century– .
Council minute books for Hornchurch UDC; Romford UDC; Romford Borough; Romford Local Board of Health, 1851–89.
Liberty of Havering treasurer's book, 1835–43.

Non-manuscript material: Microfilm copies of items held at the Essex Record Office, including Romford Workhouse Guardians' minutes; and South Divisional Parliamentary Committee for Essex minute book, 1643–56.
Microfilm and transcript of some of the local parish registers, to mid–19th century.

Pamphlets, posters, postcards and other illustrations (*c*2200).
Census, 1841–91, for London Borough of Havering area (1891 census covers parts of London and Essex).
Local newspapers (microfilm, 1866– ; bound vols, 1930s–).
Maps and plans.

Finding aids: Some lists and indexes available for census and parish material.

Facilities: Photocopying. Microfilm/fiche reader/printers.

1065 Church Lads' and Church Girls' Brigade

Address: 2 Barnsley Road, Wath upon Dearne, Rotherham, South Yorkshire S63 6PY

Telephone: (01709) 878089

Fax: (01709) 876535

E-mail: generalsecretary@church-brigade.syol.com

Website: www.clcgb.org.uk

Enquiries: The General Secretary, Col. (retd) Tony Reed Screen

Open: By appointment only, and currently restricted pending cataloguing/conservation.

Access: Bona fide researchers only.

Historical background: The Church Lads' Brigade was founded in 1891 and amalgamated with London Diocesan Church Lads' Brigade in 1919. The Church Girls' Brigade was founded in 1923, and the two bodies merged to become the Church Lads' and Church Girls' Brigade in 1978.

Acquisitions policy: Any material relating to the brigade's national and regional activities.

Archives of organisation: Minutes of CLB, 1891–1978; CGB, 1923–78; Church Lads' and Church Girls' Brigade, 1978– .
Minutes of the Incorporated Church Scout Patrols, 1909–35.

Non-manuscript material: Printed chronicles and promotional literature.
Photographs and brigade artefacts.

Finding aids: Box lists. Detailed lists in progress.

1066 Rotherham Archives and Local Studies Section

Parent organisation: Rotherham Metropolitan Borough Council

Address: Central Library and Arts Centre, Walker Place, Rotherham, South Yorkshire S65 1JH

Telephone: (01709) 382121 ext. 3616; 823616 (direct line)

Fax: (01709) 823650

E-mail: archives@rotherham.gov.uk

Website: www.rotherham.gov.uk

Enquiries: The Manager, A.P. Munford

Open: Tues, Wed, Fri: 10.00–5.00; Thurs: 1.00–7.00; Sat: 9.30–1.00, 2.00–4.00.

Access: Generally open to the public.

Historical background: The library was administered by Rotherham County Borough until 1974 and then, after local government reorganisation, began collecting material relating to the new metropolitan borough. It is recognised as a place of deposit for public records.

Acquisitions policy: To collect material connected with the area of Rotherham Metropolitan Borough.

Major collections: Local government archives of Rotherham Metropolitan Borough Council and the former constituent authorities of Rotherham County Borough, Kiveton Park and Rotherham rural district councils, and the urban district councils of Maltby, Swinton Rawmarsh and Wath-upon-Dearne.
Non-conformist and quarter sessions records.
Hospital, business and workhouse records.

Non-manuscript material: Photographs and other illustrations of the area. Oral history tapes. Pamphlets, press cuttings, newspapers, maps.

Finding aids: Lists sent to NRA.

Facilities: Photocopying. Microfilm/fiche readers.

Conservation: Work undertaken by Sheffield Archives Conservation Unit (entry 1107).

1067 Bute Museum Library

Parent organisation: Bute Museum Trustees

Address: The Museum, Stuart Street, Rothesay, Isle of Bute PA20 0BR

Telephone: (01700) 502540

Enquiries: The Hon. Librarian/Archivist, Mrs Kathleen Clegg

Open: Wed: 2.30–4.30; other times by appointment only.

Access: Generally open to the public. No charge is made but donations are welcomed.

Historical background: The Archaeological and Physical Society of Bute was founded in 1872 and started a library and museum. Interest in the society waned at the end of the century but was resuscitated in 1905 when the Buteshire Natural History Society was founded. The library and museum had various locations before the present building was erected in 1926. The society continued the administration until 1992, when a trust was formed and the museum became a registered charity.

Acquisitions policy: Archival material and books which are concerned with the history, natural history, geology and archaeology of the Isle of Bute are actively acquired.

Archives of organisation: Records of Archaeological and Physical Society, 1872– ; Buteshire Natural History Society, 1905– ; Bute Museum Trust, 1992– .

Major collections: Examination rolls, marriage and baptismal records for Rothesay parish, 1775–1835 (incomplete).
Deeds and papers *re* parish of Kingarth, 1504–1745, and Ascog Estate, 1507–1752.
Rothesay Town Council records, 1653–1766, and parish session records, 1658–1750; Kingarth parish session records, 1641–1703.
MS sermons, 1765–1824.

Non-manuscript material: Pictures, books, memorabilia, photographs (*c*1500) and glass negatives (200), including several minor collections of photographs of Clyde steamers, buildings on the island now demolished and general landscapes.

Facilities: Photocopying. Photography by arrangement.

Publications: Transactions of Buteshire Natural History Society [23 vols].
D. N. Marshall: *History of Bute* (rev., 1992).

1068   Rugby Library

Parent organisation: Warwickshire County Library

Address: Little Elborow Street, Rugby, Warwickshire CV21 3BZ

Telephone: (01788) 542687/571813/535348

Fax: (01788) 573289

E-mail: rugbylibrary@dial.pipex.com

Enquiries: The Senior Information Librarian, Mrs Joanna M. Grindle

Open: Mon, Thurs: 9.30–8.00; Tues, Wed, Fri: 9.30–5.00; Sat: 9.30–4.00.

Access: Generally open to the public.

The library was founded in 1890. It holds the usual local history collection relating to the borough of Rugby and parts of east Warwickshire. This includes school registers; a large photographic collection; *Rugby Advertiser*, 1946- (microfilm); and a significant collection of almanacs, 1854–1960. A card-catalogue and on-line public access catalogue as well as photocopying and microfilm/fiche readers are available. Conservation work is carried out in-house by staff at Warwickshire County Record Office (entry 1189).

1069   Rugby School

Address: Temple Reading Room, Rugby School, Barby Road, Rugby, Warwickshire CV22 5DW

Telephone: (01788) 556227

Fax: (01788) 556228

E-mail: dsrm@rugby-school.warwks.sch.uk

Enquiries: The Librarian, Mr D.S.R. MacLean

Open: Term: Mon–Fri: 9.00–4.00, by appointment.

Access: Approved readers on written application. All research undertaken by the school will be charged for. Applications may also be made to the Sub-Librarian (Special Collections), University of Birmingham Library (entry 107A).

Historical background: Rugby School was founded by Lawrence Sheriff in 1567. Originally a free grammar school for local boys, it began to attract pupils from further afield during the late 17th century, and 100

years later was an established public school. Dr Thomas Arnold (1795–1842) and Dr Frederick Temple (1821–1902), later Archbishop of Canterbury, were among the 19th-century headmasters. The game of rugby football originated at the school. Old Rugbeians include W.S. Landor (1775–1867), Matthew Arnold (1822–88), A.H. Clough (1819–61), Thomas Hughes (1822–96), Rupert Brooke (1887–1915), Lewis Carroll (1832–98), Arthur Ransome (1834–1922) and William Temple (1881–1944).

Acquisitions policy: Items connected with the school, its pupils and staff.

Archives of organisation: School records: registers, governing body papers, collections of boys' letters etc; the earliest date from the 1670s, most from 1750– .

Major collections: Arnold MSS: letters, diaries and note-books of Dr Thomas Arnold.
Rupert Brooke Collection: MS poems and scrapbook given by Mrs Brooke.
Various items associated with Brooke's schooldays.
Rugby football: MSS and drawings concerning the early history of the game.

Non-manuscript material: Photographs, 1861– .
Portraits of headmasters and distinguished Rugbeians.
Natural History Society: published reports, 1867– , and supporting collections.

Finding aids: Various lists available. NRA 5282.

Facilities: Photocopying and photography, by arrangement.

1070 Denbighshire Record Office

Parent organisation: Denbighshire County Council

Address: 46 Clwyd Street, Ruthin, Denbighshire LL15 1HP

Telephone: (01824) 708250 (enquiries); 708251 (County Archivist)

Fax: (01824) 708258

E-mail: archives@denbighshire.gov.uk

Website: www.denbighshire.gov.uk

Enquiries: The County Archivist, R.K. Matthias

Open: Mon–Thurs: 9.00–4.45; Fri: 9.00–4.15. Closed for one week annually Jan/Feb.

Access: Generally open to the public. Prior reservation of microfilm and microfiche readers is necessary. A paid research service is provided.

Historical background: Denbighshire Record Office was set up in 1972 and was incorporated into the Clwyd Record Office upon local government reoganisation in 1974. It is recognised as a place of deposit for public records. It became the repository for the new county of Denbighshire following the local government reorganisation of 1996.

Acquisitions policy: Archives and manuscript material relating to the present county of Denbighshire; additions to previously deposited series relating to historic county of Denbighshire.

Archives of organisation: Usual local authority holdings.

Major collections: Deposited local collections.
Archives of North Wales (Mental) Hospital, Denbigh, 1848–1980s.

Non-manuscript material: Denbighshire photographic collection; newspapers; index to births, marriages and deaths, 1837–66; index to registers of probate, England and Wales, 1858–1928; database of information on more than 800 nonconformist chapels in the county, with photographic records, 1988. Digitised image database of old photographs of present county (2000).

Finding aids: Lists sent to NRA. Indexed catalogues and handlists. Leaflet aids for searchers. Finding aids also to Flintshire Record Office (entry 434). Access to computerised index for appropriate enquiries. Internet access for appropriate searches.

Facilities: Photocopying. Photography. Microfilming by arrangement. Microfilm/fiche reader/printer. Refreshment room.

Publications: Handlist of Denbigh Borough Records (1975).
Handlist of Denbighshire Quarter Sessions Records (1991).
Handlist of Topographical Prints of Clwyd (1977).
Guide to Parish Records of Clwyd (1984).
Sir Ddinbych/Denbighshire (1996) [Archive Photographs].

1071 Saffron Walden Town Council

Address: 11 Emson Close, Saffron Walden, Essex CB10 1HL

Telephone: (01799) 516501

Fax: (01799) 516503

E-mail: townclerk@swtc.freeserve.co.uk

Website: www.swtc-gov.uk

Enquiries: Mr M.D. White

Open: Mon–Fri: 9.00–5.00, by appointment.

Access: Approved readers, on written application.

Historical background: The Borough of Saffron Walden was granted its first charter in c1300. Saffron Walden Town Council was formed in 1974. It is recognised as a place of deposit for public records.

Acquisitions policy: Anything relating to Saffron Walden Town Council and of general interest concerning Saffron Walden.

Archives of organisation: Borough council and court records, c1300–1974.
Town council records, 1974– .

Major collections: Charity minutes and papers.

Non-manuscript material: Drawings, paintings and prints of Saffron Walden, mainly late 19th and early 20th centuries.

Finding aids: Index available from the Town Clerk.

Facilities: Photocopying available on request.

1072 Victorian Studies Centre

Address: Saffron Walden Library, 2 King Street, Saffron Walden, Essex CB10 1ES

Telephone: (01799) 523178

Fax: (01799) 513642

E-mail: saffronwalden.library@essexcc.gov.uk

Website: www.essexcc.gov.uk/libraries

Enquiries: The Librarian, Martin Everett

Open: Mon, Tues, Thurs: 9.00–7.00; Fri: 10.00–7.00; Sat: 9.00–5.00, Sun: 1.00–4.00.

Access: Generally open to the public. An appointment is necessary.

The Victorian Studies Centre houses the archives of the Saffron Walden Literary and Scientific Institute, which flourished between 1832 and 1967. The records include minute books, reports of various committees, and documents relating to the activities and the winding-up of the organisation. A full catalogue is available. There is also the Dawson-Turner Collection of correspondence relating to London booksellers and publishers, 18th and 19th centuries.

1073 Museum of St Albans

Address: Hatfield Road, St Albans, Hertfordshire AL1 3RR

Telephone: (01727) 819340

Fax: (01727) 837472

E-mail: a.wheeler@stalbans.gov.uk

Enquiries: The Keeper of Social History, Anne Wheeler

Open: Mon–Sat: 10.00–5.00.

Access: Generally open to the public, strictly by appointment only.

Historical background: The museum was founded as Hertfordshire County Museum in 1898; it was taken over by the district council in the 1950s.

Acquisitions policy: Social and local history material relating to the city and district of St Albans.

Archives of organisation: Material relating to the history of the museum, 1898– .

Major collections: Local History Collection, including local MSS, antiquarian notes and children's writing books.
Natural History Collection, including field note-books of collections of ecological and geological field data for South Hertfordshire.

Non-manuscript material: Photographs, drawings, maps, sound archive.
Posters, bills, and other relevant printed ephemera.
Photographs.
Slide collection of ecologically important sites and of geological sections, exposures, etc (7000).

Finding aids: Catalogues.

Facilities: Photocopying and photography by arrangement.

Conservation: Basic paper conservation in-house. Major work sent out.

1074 St Albans Abbey
Muniment Room

Parent organisation: Cathedral and Abbey Church of St Alban

Address: c/o The Deanery, Sumpter Yard, St Albans, Hertfordshire AL1 1BY

Telephone: (01727) 860780

Fax: (01727) 850944

E-mail: mail@stalbanscathedral.org.uk

Website: www.stalbanscathedral.org.uk

Enquiries: The Archivist, Dr D.J. Kelsall

Open: Monday p.m.; otherwise by arrangement.

Access: Any bona fide student, by previous appointment.

Historical background: The abbey church has a long and varied history dating back to Norman times. The diocese was founded in 1877 and the collection, which has only recently been organised, dates mainly from 1800. There is, however, some earlier material in the Hertfordshire Archives and Local Studies (entry 443).

Acquisitions policy: To maintain the records of the cathedral and abbey church.

Archives of organisation: Records relating to the building, its precincts and other property, the parish and its administration, including material relating to the establishment of the See of St Albans and the controversial restoration of the abbey church by Lord Grimthorpe and others, 1870– .

Non-manuscript material: A number of drawings, plans etc, especially those by J.S. Neale, 19th century.

A small collection of pictures and a large collection of photographs and slides, 19th and 20th centuries.

Finding aids: Catalogue. Card index.

Publications: R.M. Thomson: *Manuscripts from St Alban's Abbey, 1066–1235* (1902) [2 vols].

1075 Youth Hostels Association

Address: Trevelyan House, 8 Stephen's Hill, St Albans, Hertfordshire AL1 2DY

Telephone: (01727) 855215

Fax: (01727) 844126

E-mail: customerservices@yha.org.uk

Website: www.yha.org.uk

Enquiries: The National Secretary

Open: By arrangement.

Access: Researchers should apply in writing.

Historical background: A growing interest in the enjoyment of the countryside from the late 19th century led to the setting up of a number of regional bodies and, in 1930, the establishment of a national association to promote youth hostels in Britain. The YHA is governed by a national council and by regional groups, and is now one of the largest youth organisations in the country. Records of Herbert Gatliff, much of which relates to YHA, are at the Bodleian Library (entry 958).

Acquisitions policy: To maintain the archive.

Archives of organisation: General minute books, 1930– (including minutes of a number of committees).
Complete set of annual reports.
Files of memoranda (which were presented to committees, regional groups and secretaries etc), 1933– .
Hostel files (administrative, legal etc), 1936– (incomplete).
Financial records, 1930s– (incomplete).
Copies of all official magazines and some regional booklets, leaflets etc.
Correspondence and administrative files *re* activities and facilities offered by YHA.

Non-manuscript material: Film strips, 1950s. Slides.
Press cuttings, 1970s– .
Maps and plans.

Finding aids: NRA 24465.

Publications: O. Coburn: *Youth Hostel Story* (1950).

1076 British Golf Museum

Address: Bruce Embankment, St Andrews, Fife KY16 9AB

Telephone: (01334) 478880

Fax: (01334) 473306

E-mail: bgm@purplenet.co.uk

Enquiries: The Curator, Elinor Clark
The Assistant Curator, Kathryn Baker

Open: Mon–Fri, by arrangement.

Access: Bona fide researchers, by appointment only.

Historical background: The British Golf Museum opened in 1990 and took responsibility for the administration of the archives of the Royal and Ancient Golf Club in addition to its own resources. The Royal and Ancient Golf Club was founded in 1754 and became the governing authority for the rules of golf in 1897. Among other events it runs the Open and Amateur Championships each year.

Acquisitions policy: Material relating to the development and history of golf in Britain and to British influences on the game abroad.

Major collections: Royal and Ancient Golf Club archives, including minutes, 1754– ; secretary's correspondence, 1890s, and administrative records of the Open championship, 1860– .

Non-manuscript material: Comprehensive museum collections.

Finding aids: Computerised catalogues, accessed by staff.

Facilities: Photocopying.

Publications: P.N. Lewis, R. Clark and F.C. Grieve: *A Round of History at the British Golf Museum* (St Andrews, 1998).
J. Behrend and P.N. Lewis: *Challenges & Champions: the Royal & Ancient Golf Club 1754–1883*, Vol.1 (1998).

1077 Hay Fleming Reference Library

Parent organisation: Fife Council

Address: St Andrews Branch Library, Church Square, St Andrews, Fife KY16 9NN

Telephone: (01334) 412685

Fax: (01334) 413029

E-mail: standrews@fife.gov.uk

Enquiries: The Branch Librarian
The District Librarian, East Fife District Library, County Buildings, Cupar, Fife KY15 4TA, tel. (01334) 412736

Open: Mon–Wed, Fri: 10.00–7.00;
Thurs, Sat: 10.00–5.00.

Access: Generally open to the public.

Historical background: David Hay Fleming (1849–1931), a native of St Andrews and an eminent historian and critic, built up a substantial personal library for his own research and studies. On his death the collection was bequeathed to the town of St Andrews to form the nucleus of a public reference library and further the study of Scottish history. The main scope for the collection is Scottish history, literature, theology and the local history of St Andrews. The library is administered on a day-to-day basis by the staff of North East Fife District Library Service and is managed by a management committee of trustees.

Acquisitions policy: The terms of David Hay Fleming's will stipulated that 'the proceeds of the endowment spent in increasing the said library shall be mainly devoted to the purchase of works bearing directly or indirectly on the civil, political, ecclesiastical and social history of Scotland and on the antiquities of Scotland'. A few important works were purchased each year. Archival material is occasionally acquired by donation.

Major collections: David Hay Fleming Collection: research note-books, correspondence, press cuttings, proofs of publications, local historical records and broadsheets.
Collections of Church of Scotland sermons.
Title and legal documents, 1467–1595.
Ecclesiastical documents, 1613–58.
Papers relating to the financial effects of the town of St Andrews, 1614–1702.
Titles to lands in the town, 1622–1724.
Papers of local trades, including wrights, tailors, weavers.
Congregational rolls of churches.

Non-manuscript material: Printed books and pamphlets (*c*13,000), early photographs and postcard views of St Andrews.
Prints, maps and plans of historical buildings.
Press cuttings.
Broadsides and antiquarian material.

Finding aids: NRAS 1882. MS index to correspondence.

Facilities: Photocopying.

Publications: H.M. Paton: *David Hay Fleming, Historian and Antiquary* (1934).
A. Rodden: 'The Hay Fleming Reference Library, St Andrews', *SLA News*, cxxii (1974), 109 [precis of a paper given to the Dundee Branch of the Library Association, 3 April 1974].

1078 St Andrews Preservation Trust Museum

Parent organisation: The St Andrews Preservation Trust

Address: 12 North Street, St Andrews, Fife KY16 9PW

Telephone: (01334) 477629

Website: www.standrewspreservationtrust.co.uk

Enquiries: The Curator, Matthew Jarron

Open: By arrangement.

Access: Generally open to the public; an appointment is desirable.

Historical background: The St Andrews Preservation Trust was founded in 1937 to preserve the character and history of St Andrews. Its early work concerned chiefly the restoration of old buildings, but in 1962 it purchased the house at 12 North Street and began to hold exhibitions there. It became a permanent museum in the early 1980s.

Acquisitions policy: The museum is interested in any material relating to the social, architectural and industrial history of St Andrews.

Archives of organisation: St Andrews Preservation Trust's minute books, publications, yearbooks etc, 1937– .

Major collections: Collection of scrapbooks of local news-cuttings, 1830s– .
Gillespie & Scott Collection of architectural documents, mainly 1940s–1980s.

Non-manuscript material: Photographs (c5000).
Small oral history collection.
Drawings, engravings, paintings, maps and other objects.

Finding aids: Card index and (partially complete) computer index.

Facilities: Photocopying, lasercopying and photography, all off-site.

Conservation: Contracted out.

Publications: Year Book.

1079 St Andrews University

Address: North Street, St Andrews, Fife KY16 9TR

Telephone: (01334) 462324

Fax: (01334) 462282

E-mail: norman.reid@st-and.ac.uk

Website: www.library.st-and.ac.uk

Enquiries: The Keeper of Muniments and Manuscripts, Dr Norman H. Reid

Open: Mon–Fri: 9.00–5.00.
Term: additional hours Thurs: 5.00–9.00;
Sat: 9.00–12.15.
Open public holidays except Christmas and New Year.

Access: Generally open to the public. An appointment is not necessary, but it is advised for those who require staff assistance.

A Muniments

Historical background: The university was founded in 1411; St Salvator's College in 1450; St Leonard's College in 1512; St Mary's College in 1538; United College in 1747; and University College was conjoined in 1897 (becoming the University of Dundee in 1967). Although there has been continuous provision for custody of records since the foundation, the Muniments Department dates only from 1982.

Acquisitions policy: Official records of the university and its constituent parts. Other relevant material is held in the Manuscripts Department (see below).

Archives of organisation: The university's own records, administrative and academic, 15th–20th centuries, including some earlier title deeds.

Major collections: Dundee Royal Infirmary minutes, 1793–1902.

Non-manuscript material: Photographs, pictures, medals, and a wide miscellany of objects relating to the university's history.
Architectural plans of university buildings, 18th–20th centuries.

Finding aids: Typescript guide (incomplete); separate name indexes to several major series.

Database guide in preparation accessible (with manuscripts database) via website.

Facilities: Photocopying. Photography. Electronic print service. Microfilm/fiche reader/printer.

Conservation: Contracted out.

Publications: No general published guide, but see *Historical Manuscripts Commission 2nd Report* (1871), 206.

R.G. Cant: *The University of St Andrews: a Short History* (Edinburgh, 1992).

J.M. Anderson: *Matriculation Roll of the University of St Andrews, 1747–1897* (Edinburgh, 1905).

———: *Early Records of the University of St Andrews, 1413–1579* (Edinburgh, 1926).

A.I. Dunlop: *Acta Facultatis Artium Universitatis Sancti Andree, 1413–1588* (Edinburgh, 1964).

B Manuscripts Department

Historical background: A few MSS from the medieval religious house and college libraries of St Andrews survive, but the greater portion of the collection has been acquired by the university library in the 19th and 20th centuries.

Acquisitions policy: To acquire scholarly material of or relating to members of the university, and MSS with a local connection or which relate to existing collection strengths, or which otherwise support the teaching and research activities of the university.

Major collections: Western MSS: a miscellaneous collection of more than 100,000 codex MSS, letters and documents, early Middle Ages– . It is particularly strong in scientific correspondence of the 19th and 20th centuries, papers relating to the Roman Catholic Modernist Movement, and material of local and university interest. Includes papers of Sir James Donaldson (1831–1915), James David Forbes (1809–68), Baron Friedrich von Hügel (1852–1925), Sir D'Arcy Wentworth Thompson (1860–1948), and Wilfrid Ward (1856–1916).

Oriental MSS: a small collection (*c*100 volumes), mostly in Arabic, Persian or Turkish. Contains some especially fine copies of the Qur'an.

Records of the former burghs of North East Fife District, as well as the records of the parishes of the former presbyteries of St Andrews and Cupar, are held on deposit from the Keeper of the Records of Scotland.

Non-manuscript material: Photographs: Valentine Ltd, mainly British Isles, 1878–1967 (*c*120,000 images); G.M. Cowie, press photography, Fife, 1930–81 (*c*60,000 images); R.M. Adam, Scottish landscape and botany (especially Scottish highlands) (*c*15,000 images; other smaller collections: zoology, Turkey, Italian architecture, Canada, Fife, continental scenery, farm animals, art photography, highland scenery, 1839– (*c*100,000 images). Includes a fine collection of very early photographs, notably work by Dr John Adamson and D.O. Hill and Robert Adamson.

Architectural Drawings: Gillespie and Scott, Architects, St Andrews, plans, 1870s–1960s, (*c*15,000), with supporting contract documentation; St Andrews Dean of Guild plans, 1890s–1975 (*c*4000).

Finding aids: Unpublished inventories and descriptive lists for particular parts of the collection. Name indexes available for both MSS and photographs. Database guide to MSS in preparation, available from website. Selected images from photographic collections also available via web browser. Full database in preparation.

Facilities: Photocopying. Photography. Electronic print service. Microfilm/fiche reader/printer.

Conservation: Contracted out.

Publications: HMC 2nd Report (1871), 206–9.
St Andrews University Library: an Illustrated Guide (St Andrews, 1948).

R.N. Smart: *An Index to the Correspondence and Papers of James David Forbes (1809–1868) and also to some Papers of his son George Forbes* (St Andrews, 1968).

J.D. Pearson: *Oriental Manuscripts in Europe and North America* (Zug, 1971).

R.N. Smart: *Index to the Correspondence and Papers of Sir D'Arcy Wentworth Thompson* (St Andrews, 1987).

C.M. Gascoigne: *Cedric Thorpe Davie, 1913–1983: Catalogue of Works and Index to Correspondence* (St Andrews, 1988).

Various leaflets on different aspects of the collection.

1080 Wheal Martyn Museum

Address: Carthew, St Austell, Cornwall PL26 8XG

Telephone: (01726) 850362

Fax: (01726) 850362

E-mail: whmartyn@aol.com

Enquiries: The Collections Manager, Fiona M. Spiers

Open: By arrangement

Access: Generally open to the public

Historical background: The Museum is sponsored by English China Clays International (ECCI Ltd).

Acquisitions policy: Archives relating to the china clay industry and supporting industries, as well as to the industrial and social history of the mid-Cornwall area.

Major collections: Records of the china clay industry in Cornall, 19th–20th century.
Archives of ECCI Ltd.

Non-manuscript material: Photographic collection (*c*2000); trade journals and newsletters, maps, plans, books, 18th–20th century.

Finding aids: Indexes.

Conservation: Contracted out.

1081 St Helens Local History and Archives Library

Parent organisation: St Helens MBC

Address: Central Library, Gamble Institute, Victoria Square, St Helens, Merseyside WA10 1DY

Telephone: (01744) 456952

Fax: (01744) 20836

Enquiries: The Local History Librarian and Archivist, Ms L. Hainsworth

Open: Mon, Wed: 9.30–8.00; Tues, Thurs: 9.30–5.00; Sat: 9.30–4.00; appointments are advisable.

Access: Generally open to the public.

Historical background: The borough library service was established in 1872. A separate local history and archives library was established in 1974 to expand existing collections in the reference library and to implement an active archive policy to deal with local government records on reorganisation.

Acquisitions policy: Records of the St Helens Borough Council are stored where appropriate. Donations of other records are accepted. Other records are acquired when known to be at risk.

Major collections: Records of the borough council and historic constituents, 1845– . Poor Law papers for the township of Parr, 1688–1828.
Sherdley estate papers, 1477–1900 (*c*1500 items).
Records of Grundy's Ironmongers, 1913–70; Beechams Pills Co. Ltd, St Helens and abroad; Forsters Glass Co. Ltd, St Helens; Greenall Whitley, Co., St Helens (Brewers) and John Roby Ltd, brass founders, Rainhill.

Non-manuscript material: Gentry Collection: South Lancashire newspapers, including *St Helens Report.*
Maps, local newspapers, 1859– .
Photographs and pamphlets relating to St Helens, Lancashire and local history in general. Large collection of genealogical microforms and CD-ROM.

Finding aids: Index to most archive collections. Newspaper index.

Facilities: Photocopying. Microfilm/fiche readers/printer.

Conservation: Contracted out.

Publications: Numerous leaflet guides to types of material (e.g. genealogical sources).

1082 Jersey Archive

Parent organisation: Jersey Heritage Trust

Address: Clarence Road, St Helier, Jersey, Channel Islands JE2 4JY

Telephone: (01534) 833300/833333 (reader enquiries)

Fax: (01534) 833301

E-mail: archives@jerseyheritagetrust.org

Website: www.jersey.gov.uk/jerseyarchives

Enquiries: The Head of Archives Service

Open: Tues–Sat: 9.00–5.00.

Access: Generally open to the public.

Historical background: The Jersey Archives Services was established in 1993 and is administered by the Jersey Heritage Trust. In 2000 it moved to new purpose-built premises.

Acquisitions policy: The archives service seeks to acquire records of Jersey organisations and individuals.

Archives of organisation: Official records, including States of Jersey departmental records, 17th century– (early records very incomplete). Records from the period of the occupation by German forces, 1940–45; these include the war files from the Bailiff's Chambers and the registration cards and photographs of the population at the time.

Finding aids: Catalogues: the majority of the collections are catalogued and indexed on a database. Lists sent to NRA.

Facilities: Photocopying.

Conservation: In-house.

Publications: C.N. Aubin: *A Glossary for the Historian of Jersey* (1997).

1083   Judicial Greffe

Address: Morier House, Halkett Place, St Helier, Jersey JE1 1DD

Telephone: (01534) 502300

Fax: (01534) 502399

E-mail: jgreffe@super.net.uk

Website: www.jersey.gov.uk

Enquiries: The Registrar of Deeds, Mrs J. Hume

Open: Mon–Fri: 9.00–1.00, 2.00–5.15.

Access: Public Registry: members of the public, 8.30–5.00, as and when working space permits. Facilities are limited and research is not generally possible during office hours, when the records are in use for business purposes.
Royal Court records: members of the public, by prior arrangement with the Judicial Greffier only. Permission is not automatically granted. Some records (e.g. criminal matters) are not available for consultation.
Probate Registry: not open to unsupervised inspection by members of the public.

Historical background: The Judicial Greffe is a civil service department which, among other responsibilities, has custody of records, although this is not a primary function.

Acquisitions policy: The department houses only the documents of the court.

Archives of organisation: Three major categories of documents, as follows:
Public Registry, containing deeds of sale and conveyance, mortgage etc, of real property, 1602– ; wills of real estate, 1851– ; powers of attorney.
Records of the Royal Court, comprising all acts etc of the Royal Court and other related documents.
Probate Registry, containing wills of personal estate, c1660– ; letters of administration, 1848– .

Finding aids: Indexes to relevant court books.

Facilities: Photocopying of some court records and extracts from the Public Registry. The department does not provide a research service by post.

1084   Société Jersiaise

Address: 7 Pier Road, St Helier, Jersey JE2 4XW

Telephone: (01534) 730538

Fax: (01534) 888262

E-mail: library@societe-jersiaise.org

Website: www.societe-jersiaise.org

Enquiries: The Librarian, Miss Mary Billot
The Assistant Librarian, Miss Sally Knight

Open: Mon, Wed, Fri: 9.30–4.30; Thurs: 9.30–7.00; Sat: 9.30–12.30.

Access: Members of the Société Jersiaise and members of the public.

Historical background: The Société Jersiaise was founded in 1873, and includes among its aims the promotion and encouragement of the study of the history, archaeology, natural history, language and many other subjects of interest in the Island of Jersey. The société has a very comprehensive local history library with local genealogical research facilities.

Archives of organisation: Archives of the Société Jersiaise, 1873– .

Major collections: Family papers and correspondence, including La Hague Manor, Pipon, Le Vavasseur dit Durell, Le Couteur and Trinity Manor.
Authors' MSS and notes, including Philip Ahier, E.T. Nicolle, Joan Stevens and Marguerite Syvret.
Ancient MSS, including Chevalier's diary, 1643–51, with translation.
Parish church records, 1540–1842.
Jersey Merchant Seamen's Benefit Society registers, c1830s–1880s (some on microfilm).

Non-manuscript material: Mullins' albums of identified photographic portraits, 1848–73.

German Occupation Ephemera Collection, including ration books, identity cards and *Evening Post*, 1940–45, in English.

Almanacs, 1800– (lists of residents by and/or trade, officers of the militia, shipping, clubs etc, diaries of local events).

Indexes to the parish registers of baptisms, burials and marriages (but not all years or parishes are held).

Index of civil registers (births, deaths and marriages), 1842–1900 on microfiche.

Maps of Jersey and St Helier.

States of Jersey publications, including *Ordres du Conseil*, 1536–1812; *Recueil des Lois*, 1771–, and *States' Minutes*.

Finding aids: Brief list of main archives collections.

Facilities: Photocopying. Microfilm/fiche readers.

Publications: Brief library guide.
Introduction to family history research.

1085 Norris Library and Museum

Address: The Broadway, St Ives, Cambridgeshire PE17 4BX

Telephone: (01480) 497314

E-mail: norris.stives-tc@co-net.com

Enquiries: The Curator, Mr R.I. Burn-Murdoch

Open: May–Sept: Tues–Fri: 10.00–1.00, 2.00–5.00;
Sat: 10.00–12.00.
Oct–April: Tues–Fri: 10.00–1.00, 2.00–4.00;
Sat: 10.00–12.00.

Access: Bona fide researchers.

Historical background: The library and museum opened in 1933, according to the terms of the will of Herbert Ellis Norris (1859–1931). Norris assembled a large collection of antiquities, both historical and archaeological, which he left, together with a substantial trust fund to pay for a building to house them and to allow for future maintenance, to St Ives Borough Council. The present town council continues to administer the library and museum as trustees. Norris collected material from the former county of Huntingdonshire (technically

abolished in 1974). Since 1933 other collections of a similar scope have been added to his foundation, notably those of the Huntingdonshire Literary and Scientific Institution (1840–1959). The present Norris Library and Museum houses material from every part of Huntingdonshire and every period of history.

Acquisitions policy: Material relating to all parts of Huntingdonshire and all periods of history and pre-history. There is a small accessions fund for the library. The museum is dependent on gifts.

Major collections: MS material, including various legal documents, wills etc, 16th–18th centuries.
Field survey of St Ives, 18th century.
MSS by John Clare (1793–1864).
Many minute books etc relating to local government and local charities, 19th century.
Notes by local historians and antiquarians, notably S. Inskip Ladds, Ely Diocesan architect and editor of the *Victoria County History of Huntingdonshire*.

Non-manuscript material: Pamphlets etc relating to the Civil War period, and to Cromwell, in Huntingdonshire.
Runs of local newspapers, including 19th-century editions.
Maps, including Saxton, Speed, Blaeu, 16th–19th centuries.
Photographs, postcards, prints, paintings and drawings of local scenes, various periods.
General collection of books relating to all aspects of the history of Huntingdonshire.

Finding aids: Comprehensive card index in preparation.

Facilities: Limited photocopying by arrangement. Photography by arrangement.

1086 Isles of Scilly Museum

Parent organisation: Isles of Scilly Museum Association

Address: Church Street, St Mary's, Isles of Scilly TR21 0JT

Telephone: (01720) 422337

Fax: (01720) 422337

Website: www.btinternet.com/~severecci/ios/museum/

Enquiries: The Librarian, Miss D. Barnes
The Honorary Secretary, Mr Steve Ottery

Open: Summer season: 10.00–12.00, 1.30–4.30.

Access: Generally to the public, by appointment. Only three seats are available at any one time.

The museum commenced in 1967 and collects anything relevant to the history of the Isles of Scilly. Its local history collection includes custom house books, court record books, ships' logs and lifeboat records, wills and scrapbooks, 17th century– . NRA 33099. A limited photocopying facility is available. This museum has issued a series of publications.

1087 The Greffe

Address: The Royal Court House, St Peter Port, Guernsey GY1 2PB

Telephone: (01481) 725277

Fax: (01481) 715097

E-mail: ken.tough@gov.gg

Enquiries: Her Majesty's Greffier, Mr K.H. Tough.
Assistance is by arrangement with the Archiviste de la Cour Royale (Island Archivist; see entry 1088). Genealogical enquiries should first be addressed to the Priaulx Library (entry 1089).

Open: Mon–Fri: : 9.00–1.00, 2.00–4.00.

Access: Written application should be made to Her Majesty's Greffier. A letter of introduction is recommended.

Historical background: As the record office of the Royal Court of Guernsey, the Greffe has existed in various forms throughout the history of the Royal Court, which is first referred to in a document of 1179. Virtually all records prior to 1948 are in French, and a command of that language is essential for all serious students researching at the Greffe.

Acquisitions policy: All island judicial and legislative records. Deposits of private collections and documents relating to Guernsey are welcomed.

Archives of organisation: Contemporary copies of charters granted to the Bailiwick, 1394– .
Judicial records of the Royal Court of Guernsey, 1526– .
Legislative records, 1553– .
Royal Court letter-books, 1737– .
Documents issued by the Royal Court, c1350– .
Records of land conveyance etc, 1576– .

Records of the Assembly of the States of Guernsey, 1605– .
Registers of births, marriages and deaths, 1840– .
Wills of Real Property from 1841, when it first became possible to make Wills of Realty (Wills of Personalty are held by the Ecclesiastical Court, tel. (01481) 721732).

Major collections: Feudal Court registers, especially Cour St Michel, 1537– .
Private collections deposited by local families, notably the de Sausmarez papers.
Transcripts of documents elsewhere, especially of the Mont St Michel collection (originals destroyed in 1944) and of minute books etc of the Calvinist regime in Guernsey, c1558–1660.
Identity card files, comprising personal forms and photographs, 1940–45 (c20,000).

Finding aids: Typescript calendar of all single documents. Summary of Family History Sources at the Greffe (copies available on request).

Facilities: Photocopying (limited to certain records only). Microfilm reader/printer.

Publications: Lists of records in the Greffe published by the List and Index Society (Special Series, continuing): (i) *Registers and Records in Volume Form* (1969); (ii) *Single Documents under the Bailiwick Seal* (1969); (iii) *Other Documents under Sign Manual, Signature or Seal* (1983).
Recueil d'Ordonnances de la Cour Royale de l'Île de Guernesey, 1533 [24 vols to date].
Actes des Etats de l'Île de Guernesey, 1605–1843 [8 vols; thereafter published as *Billets d'Etat,* in annual vols to date].
Recueil d'Ordres en Conseil d'un Intérêt Général enregistrés sur les Records de l'Île de Guernesey, 1800– [30 vols to date].
For a general introduction, see J.C. Davies: 'The Records of the Royal Court', *La Société Guernesiaise, Report and Transactions,* xvi (1956–60), 404.

1088 Island Archives Service

Parent organisation: States of Guernsey

Address: 29 Victoria Road, St Peter Port, Guernsey GY1 1HU

Telephone: (01481) 724512

Fax: (01481) 715814

Website: http://user.itl.net/~glen/archgsy.html

Enquiries: The Island Archivist, Dr D.M. Ogier

Open: Mon–Fri: 8.30–12.30, 1.30–4.30.

Access: Generally open to the public. An appointment is advisable. States of Guernsey material post–1948 is subject to restriction.

Historical background: The Island Archives Service was established in 1986 by the States of Guernsey for the cataloguing and retention of committee and departmental records and the provision of deposit and research facilities to the wider public.

Acquisitions policy: All island records of an official or unofficial character, public and private.

Archives of organisation: Records of States' committees and departments, 1804–1948; Occupation records, 1940–45.

Major collections: St Peter Port Hospital records, 1742–1950.
Guernsey Chamber of Commerce, 19th centuries– .
Guernsey Methodist Church, 1796– .
Records of several civil parishes, mid–18th century– .
Stevens Guille Collection, 1350–1850.
Manorial records of Fief le Comte, 1479–1971.
Dobrée Collection of commercial and family papers, late 18th–19th centuries.

Non-manuscript material: States' architectural drawings, 1800– .
Film/sound archive, 1917– .

Finding aids: Office lists and indexes.

Facilities: Photocopying (limited to certain records).

Conservation: Contracted out in the UK.

Publications: Brochure.

1089   Priaulx Library

Address: Candie Road, St Peter Port, Guernsey GY1 1UG

Telephone: (01481) 721998

Fax: (01481) 713804

E-mail: priaulx.library@gov.gg

Website: www.gov.gg/priaulx

Enquiries: The Chief Librarian, Mrs M.E.R. Harris

Open: Mon–Sat: 9.30–5.00.

Access: Generally open to the public. An appointment is necessary for the use of microfilm readers.

Historical background: The Priaulx Collection, along with Candie House where it is contained, was donated to the people of Guernsey in 1891, for use as a free library, by Osmond De Beauvoir Priaulx (1805–91). The library is designated as a local studies centre.

Acquisitions policy: Purchasing is now restricted to works produced in the islands or relating to them, plus relevant back-up material.

Major collections: Correspondence relating to shipping and privateering from the firm of Carteret Priaulx, 19th century.
Records of the Royal Guernsey Militia, 18th–19th centuries (incomplete).
Records of the Onesimus Dorey Shipping Co., 19th and 20th centuries.
Genealogical files and pedigree rolls relating to many local families.

Non-manuscript material: Parish registers, cemetery records, civil records of births and deaths and census of Guernsey and Jersey, 1841–91 (microfilm).
Photographs and prints of various locations and personalities of local interest.
Newspapers published in Guernsey, 1791– (microfilm).
Army lists, 1661–1714, 1756–1920.
Regimental histories.
Works of fiction produced by local or locally resident authors, Guernsey imprints, 19th and 20th centuries.

Finding aids: Card index and computer.

Facilities: Photocopying. Some photography. Microfilm/fiche readers/printer.

Conservation: Contracted out.

1090   Trafford Local Studies Centre

Parent organisation: Trafford MBC

Address: Sale Library, Tatton Road, Sale M33 1YH

Telephone: (0161) 912 3013

Fax: (0161) 912 3019

E-mail: trafford.local.studies@free4all.co.uk

Website: www.gmcro.co.uk/reposit.htm

Enquiries: The Local Studies Librarian, Ms Pat Southam

Open: Mon, Thurs: 10.00–7.30; Tues, Fri: 10.00–5.00; Sat: 10.00–4.00.

Access: Generally open to the public. Booking is required 24 hours in advance for some archive material, microfiche and microfilm records.

Historical background: Trafford Metropolitan Borough was formed in 1974 and unites the former Cheshire boroughs of Altrincham and Sale, the former Lancashire borough of Stretford, the Lancashire urban district of Urmston and the three parishes of Carrington, Dunham Massey and Warburton and the township of Parkington, the latter four all being part of the Cheshire rural district of Bucklow. The Local Studies Centre was created in 1990 by combining collections from the area's four main reference libraries.

Acquisitions policy: Material relating to Trafford Metropolitan Borough in all forms, with an emphasis on family history material.

Archives of organisation: Sale Borough Council minutes, 1805– , rate books, 1836– .
Altrincham Borough Council minutes, 1890– .
Stretford minutes, 1884– (incomplete), ratebooks, 1876– .
Urmston UDC minutes, 1931– and rate books, 1895– .
Camington Parish Council minutes, 1894– .
Bowdon Council minutes, 1874– .

Major collections: Extensive family history collections.

Non-manuscript material: Photographs, slides and negatives of the Trafford area (20,000). Map and plan collection, audio-visual collection, including some oral history recordings.

Finding aids: Lists sent to NRA. Archival material is not extensively catalogued. Some newspaper indexes and biographical indexes. Sources leaflets.

Facilities: Photography. Laser printouts from pilot database of 2000 prints/photos. Microform/film readers/printer.

Conservation: Contracted out.

1091   Salford Art Gallery
L.S. Lowry Archive
Parent organisation: City of Salford

Address: The Lowry Centre, Development Co. Ltd, West Pavilion, Harbour City, Salford Quays, Salford M5 2BH

Telephone: (0161) 955 2020

Fax: (0161) 955 2021

E-mail: info@thelowry.org.uk

Website: www.thelowry.com

Enquiries: The Museums Officer, Fine Art, Judith Sandling

Open: Mon–Fri: 10.00–4.45; Sun: 2.00–5.00.

Access: Bona fide researchers, by appointment only. There is restricted access to some parts of the archive.

Salford Museum and Art Gallery was established in 1850. The gallery's association with L.S. Lowry (1887–1976) began in the 1930s and continued until his death. The collection and archive were transferred in 2000 to Salford Quays, which houses the collection of paintings and drawings along with other documents, and the library and archive. Details about The Lowry are available on the website. See M. Leber and J. Sandling: *L.S. Lowry* (Phaidon Press, 1987).

1092   Salford Local History Library
Address: Peel Park, Salford M5 4WU

Telephone: (0161) 736 2649

Fax: (0161) 745 9490

E-mail: salford.museum@salford.gov.uk

Enquiries: The Local History Librarian, Mr Tim Ashworth

Open: Tues, Thurs, Fri: 10.00–5.00 Wed: 10.00–8.00

Access: Generally open to the public.

The library holds local history collections, including the following: James Nasmyth (1808–90), locomotive engineer and inventor of steam hammer: collection of correspondence, engineering drawings and photographs; and Harold Brighouse, author of *Hobson's Choice*: collection of letters and some MSS of his works. NB Salford City Archives (see entry 471) have been transferred here.

1093 University of Salford Library

Parent organisation: University of Salford, Academic Information Services

Address: The Crescent, Salford M5 4WT

Telephone: (0161) 295 5846

Fax: (0161) 295 5888

E-mail: m.p.carrier@ais.salford.ac.uk

Website: www.salford.ac.uk/ais/homepage

Enquiries: Michael Carrier (0161) 296 3508
The Director of Academic Information Services

Open: Term: Mon–Fri: 9.00–9.00; Sat: 9.00–12.00.
Vacation: Mon–Fri: 9.00–5.00.

Access: Bona fide scholars. An appointment is necessary for consultation of archive material.

Historical background: The university is descended from the Salford Royal Technical Institute, founded in 1896. The institute became the Salford Royal College of Advanced Technology before receiving its university charter in 1967. The library was founded in 1957.

Acquisitions policy: To support the teaching and research interests of the university.

Archives of organisation: Documentary and photographic archives of the institution, 1896– . Press cuttings and departmental papers, 1967– . Papers of the Salford Technical and Engineering Association.

Major collections: Walter Greenwood (1903–74): comprehensive collection of MSS and published works, with correspondence, press cuttings and photographs.
Stanley Houghton (1881–1913): MSS of published and unpublished plays, photographs, correspondence.
Bridgewater Collections: archive of Francis Egerton, 3rd Duke of Bridgewater (1736–1803), the pioneer of the great age of canal building in Britain; Bridgewater Estates Company papers, 1895–1950; working papers used by the late Professor F.C. Mather in his study of the Bridgewater Trust, *After the Canal Duke*, covering the period 1825–72.
Lionel Angus-Butterworth papers *re* the history of glassmaking, including a draft of his treatise *The British Glass Industry, 1700–1850*, and company material *re* the family firm, Butterworth Bros., Newton Heath Glass Works, Manchester.
Richard Badnall (*d* 1842): correspondence concerning his proposal for an 'undulating railway'.
William Willink papers: material relating to the Birmingham Canal Company, 1830–1920.
Bartington Hall papers: includes chapel books of Sutton Aston and Aston Grange, Cheshire, 1699–1737; business letters relating to the Antwis family, 1770s; documents relating to the overseers of the poor law etc; ephemera, including some rare items, relating to the canals in the area.
Robert Dockray, civil engineer: correspondence, 1830–60.
Records of English Velvet and Cord Dyers Association Ltd, 1899–1959, and material relating to Oldham & Son Ltd, battery manufacturers, Denton.

Non-manuscript material: British Election Pamphlet Collection, 1949–74: a substantial collection of election leaflets.
Tape-recordings with transcripts of interviews of Salford residents conducted in 1970 by J.M. Goodger for his film *The Changing Face of Salford.*
Original cartoons and other work by Leo Cheney, 1878–1928, first pupil of Percy Bradshaw's cartoon correspondence course.

Finding aids: Lists for most collections. Special card catalogue of Bridgewater Estates papers, with subject index. Published works recorded on library's on-line catalogue. Collections notified to NRA.

Facilities: Photocopying. Microfilm/fiche readers.

Publications: Special Collections (Academic Information Services Leaflet 11).
There are separate leaflets describing the Bridgewater Archives and the British Election Pamphlet Collection.

1094 Working Class Movement Library

Address: Jubilee House, 51 The Crescent, Salford M5 4WX

Telephone: (0161) 736 3601

Fax: (0161) 737 4115

E-mail: enquiries@wcml.org.uk

Website: www.wcml.org.uk

Enquiries: The Librarian, Alain Kahan

Open: Tues, Thurs, Fri: 10.00–5.00; Wed: 10.00–9.00; alternate Sun: 2.00–5.00, by arrangement only.

Access: Generally open to the public, by appointment.

Historical background: The collections were started by Ruth and Edmund Frow *c*1955. Until 1987 the library was housed in their private home in Stretford. It is now administered by the City of Salford, although the collection is owned by trustees. Although Edmund died in 1996, Ruth Frow still plays an active role in acquiring new accessions.

Acquisitions policy: Anything to do with the experience of working people from the 18th century onwards, mostly in Britain, although some international material is acquired.

Major collections: Archives principally of trade unions and political organisations, notably local Labour Party archives (not all complete). These include:

General and Municipal Boiler Makers and Allied Trade Union (GMBATU), print unions (NATSOPA and NGA), Amalgamated Engineering Union (AEU and ASE), Gasworkers and General and Municipal Workers Union, and Furniture Timber and Allied Trades (FTAT), plus unions absorbed into these.

Trades and professions covered include: boilermakers, shipwrights, tailor and garment workers, clerks, foundry workers, cabinet makers, organ makers, bakers, bookbinders, textile workers.

A few papers of individuals, including activists and members of the Communist Party.

Non-manuscript material: Large amount of pamphlet material in archive collections.

Rare books and periodicals, 19th century– ; radical periodicals on microfilm.

Artefacts and books.

Finding aids: Card catalogue. NRA reports: 1008; 31932 (MS collections); 35557 (Salford Trades Council); 35561 (National Association of Powerloom Overlookers); 35562 (Bolton and District Card and Ring-Room Operators); 35565 (Swinton and Pendlebury).

Facilities: Photocopying. Photography by arrangement. Microfilm/fiche reader.

Conservation: Undertaken by City of Salford, and Museums and Art Galleries Service for the North West.

Publications: Library Bulletin (annually, 1989–) [includes information on important recent accessions].

1095   Friends' Provident Archives

Address: Unit 1, Milford Trading Estate, Balkey Road, off Tollgate Road, Salisbury, Wiltshire SP1 2LP

Telephone: (01722) 316928

Website: www.friendsprovident.co.uk

Enquiries: The Stores Supervisor, Colin Horne

Open: Mon–Fri: 9.30–2.45.

Access: Bona fide researchers, by prior arrangement with the Stores Supervisor.

Historical background: The Friends' Provident Institution was established in Bradford, in 1832 under the Friendly Societies Acts to meet the life assurance needs of members of the Society of Friends (Quakers). In 1918 the institution took over the Century Insurance Co Ltd. to form Friends' Provident & Century Life Office, one of the larger composite (life and general insurance) offices, and went on to build extensive interests in North America, Africa and Australasia. In 1974 the Century (general insurance side) was sold to Phoenix Assurance, now part of the Royal & Sun Alliance Group. In 1986 the office merged with United Kingdom Provident Institution to become one of the top ten mutual life offices in the UK. Between 1989 and 1992 the enlarged office entered into a number of arrangements with companies in Europe, culminating in 1992 when Friends' Provident joined with Avero Centraal Beheer Group, now Achmea (Holland), Topdanmark A/S (Denmark) and WASA (Sweden), to establish the pan-European Insurance Group Eureko BV. The consortium was extended in 1994 by Ocidental (Portugal) and in 1996 by Gothaar (Germany). In 1993 Friends' Provident acquired NM UK Group, the UK operation of National Mutual of Australasia, in 1996 it acquired London and Manchester Assurance Co. Ltd, and in 1997 it merged its subsidiary FP Asset Management with Ivory & Sime plc to form Friends' Ivory & Sime plc.

Acquisitions policy: Internal records only.

Archives of organisation: Corporate and other records of the Friends' Provident companies: Friends' Provident Institution, 1832–1918; Friends' Provident & Century Life Office, 1919–73, and Friends' Provident Life Office, 1974– .
Records of UK Provident Institution, 1840–1985 and the UK records of National Mutual Life Association of Australasia, 1897–1993, London and Manchester Assurance Co., and Century Insurance Co Ltd, 1885–1974 (incomplete).

Finding aids: Catalogues for each company. Century Insurance: NRA 18271.

Facilities: Photocopying.

Conservation: Contracted out.

Publications: D. Tregoning and H. Cockerell: *Friends for Life* (1982).

1096 Salisbury and South Wiltshire Museum

Address: The King's House, 65 The Close, Salisbury, Wiltshire SP1 2EN

Telephone: (01722) 332151

Fax: (01722) 325611

E-mail: museum@salisburymuseum.freeserve.co.uk

Enquiries: The Director and Curator

Open: Mon–Sat: 10.0–5.00, by appointment.

Access: Bona fide researchers.

The Museum was founded in 1860. It acquires archives relating to archaeological fieldwork in South Wiltshire and holds minutes and annual reports of its governing body as well as personal papers of General Augustus Lane Fox Pitt Rivers (1827–1900). Photocopying and photography are available by arrangement. There is a microfiche reader.

1097 Salisbury Cathedral Chapter Archives

Address: 6 The Close, Salisbury, Wiltshire SP1 2EF

Telephone: (01722) 555160

Website: www.salisburycathedral.org.uk/pages/index.shtml

Enquiries: The Librarian and Keeper of the Muniments, Miss S.M. Eward

Open: Mon–Fri: 10.00–12.30, 2.15–4.00, by appointment only.

Access: Bona fide researchers, on written application.

The present Salisbury Cathedral was begun in 1220 and has had a continuous history since that date. It has Dean and Chapter archives from the medieval period onwards. There are catalogues in the NRA.

1098 Harrowby Manuscript Trust

Parent organisation: The Earldom of Harrowby

Address: Sandon Hall, Sandon, Staffordshire ST18 0BZ

Telephone: (01889) 508004

Fax: (01889) 508004

E-mail: info@sandonhall.co.uk

Enquiries: The Archivist, Mr M.J. Bosson

Open: By arrangement only.

Access: Scholars and researchers, with a reference and by appointment.

Historical background: A baronetcy was created in the late 18th century for Lord Chief Justice Dudley Ryder. However, he died before his award of a baronetcy could be ratified. His son, Nathaniel Ryder, MP, became a Baron in 1776 and his grandson, Dudley Ryder (Foreign Secretary under Spencer Perceval), was awarded the earldom in 1809. Sandon Hall has always been the seat of the earldom; the present house is the third on this site and dates from the mid-19th century. The collection is principally that of the 5th and 6th Earls and is held in trust for the Bodleian Library (see entry 958).

Acquisitions policy: To maintain and consolidate the records of the Earls of Harrowby and their estates.

Archives of organisation: Estate papers: deeds, correspondence etc relating to administration of estates in Staffordshire, Lincolnshire and Oxfordshire and small subsidiary lands, 12th–20th centuries.

Political correspondence with cabinet ministers, MPs etc, 18th and 19th centuries.

Major collections: Diary series, including those of Lady Mary Wortley Montagu (1689–1762).

Non-manuscript material: Iconographic material, including cartoons and a complete collection of World War I recruiting posters.

Finding aids: Various catalogues, lists, and indexes.

Facilities: Photocopying at nearby office.

Conservation: Contracted out.

1099 Pfizer Central Research Records Management Unit

Parent organisation: Pfizer Ltd

Address: Ramsgate Road, Sandwich, Kent CT13 9NJ

Telephone: (01304) 646040

Fax: (01304) 655650

Enquiries: The Manager, Public Affairs, Alan Murdock

Open: Mon–Fri: 9.30–5.00 by appointment

Access: At the discretion of the company: by application in writing.

Historical background: Pfizer Inc. was founded in Brooklyn, New York, by Charles Pfizer in 1849. Until 1941 Pfizer was purely a US-based fine chemical company, producing primarily citric acid and in 1942 it became the first company to mass produce penicillin. By the end of the war Pfizer had decided to enter the pharmaceutical industry. From 1949 Pfizer began to develop into a multinational company, and in 1952 Pfizer Ltd was established in the UK, moving to Sandwich in 1954 where research and development into human medicinals was undertaken between 1957 and 1964. Commercial expansion into the UK market resulted in a series of take-overs, including Kemball Bishop & Co. Ltd, the British Chemical Company (1958) British Alkaloids (1964), Coty, a perfume company (1963). In 1995 the Animal Health division of SmithKlineBeecham was purchased. Cinematographic film is at the British Medical Association (see entry 562).

Acquisitions policy: Accruals from records management for the Central Research division of Pfizer Ltd.

Archives of organisation: Pfizer Inc.: 1956-, including promotional material.
Pfizer Ltd: site-related records, 1558, 1917–18; company-related records, 1953– ; Kemball Bishop & Co. Ltd, 1877–1966; John Bennet Lawes & Co., 1814–1958; The Cyprus Wine Company, 1951–5; Messrs Crist. Haggipavlu & Sons Ltd, pre-1953; British Alkaloids, 1928–66; Coty, 1924–64; Vitamins Ltd, 1948–56; SmithKlineBeecham Animal Health, 1978–85. Estate papers of Walton Oaks, Walton-upon-the-Hill, Surrey (SKB Animal Health research facility).

Non-manuscript material: Company seals; photographs (Pfizer Ltd and Central Research), 1953– ; videos; slides.

Facilities: Photocopying. Microfilm reader. Photographic image database.

Publications: S. Mines: *Pfizer an Informal History* (1978).
R. Butler: *Richborough Port* (1993).
J. Mantle: *Pfizer at Sandwich. The Story of Pfizer Limited* (1994).
O. Tanner: *25 Years of Innovation: The Story of Pfizer Central Research* (1996).

1100 Royal Society for the Protection of Birds
The Library

Address: The Lodge, Sandy, Bedfordshire SG19 2DL

Telephone: (01767) 680551

Fax: (01767) 692365

E-mail: ian.dawson@rspb.org.uk

Enquiries: The Librarian, I.K. Dawson

Open: Mon–Fri: 9.00–5.15, by arrangement.

Access: Bona fide researchers, by appointment.

Historical background: The RSPB was founded in 1889 to fight the trade in bird plumes used in millinery. It was granted its royal charter in 1904. The work rapidly expanded to cover all fields of bird protection and the society is now the largest conservation organisation in Europe.

Acquisitions policy: To maintain and consolidate the society's archives.

Archives of organisation: Records of the society, including council and other committee minutes, 1898– ; membership and associates registers, 1893–1924; annual reports, 1889– ; watchers' reports and diaries, 1911–1950s; files on legislation and individual reserves, 1930s–1950s; *Bird Notes and News*, 1905– .

Major collections: Papers, correspondence and publications of and relating to William H. Hudson (1864–1922), naturalist and writer, 1890s–1960s.

Finding aids: NRA 24476.

Facilities: Photocopying. Microfiche reader.

1101 Scarborough Library

Parent organisation: North Yorkshire County Council

Address: Vernon Road, Scarborough, North Yorkshire YO11 2NN

Telephone: (01723) 383400/383407

Fax: (01723) 353893

E-mail: scarborough.libraryhq@northyorks.gov.uk

Website: www.northyorks.gov.uk/libraries/branches/scarborough.shtm

Enquiries: The Group Librarian (postal enquiries)
The Information Librarian (telephone)

Open: Mon, Tues, Fri: 9.30–5.30; Wed: 9.30–1.00; Thurs: 9.30–7.00; Sat: 9.30–4.00.

Access: Archive material is generally available to the public, by appointment.

Historical background: The local history collection was founded in 1930. Archives are acquired by deposit, solicited and unsolicited.

Acquisitions policy: To accept deposit of relevant material within accommodation limits and where the donor wishes the material to remain in Scarborough.

Major collections: School log-books, minute books etc, from Scarborough and the immediate area, c1870–c1950 (c120 vols).
Scarborough town rate books, 1837–1900 (c150 vols).
Minutes and accounts of Scarborough Harbour Commissioners, 1752–1904 (20 vols); Scarborough Cliff Bridge Company, 1826–1920; Spa (Scarborough) Ltd, 1920–37.

Minutes and accounts of several local societies, 19th and 20th centuries.
Minor collections of family papers, indentures, property deeds, ships' logs etc.

Non-manuscript material: Prints, topographical, 18th and 19th centuries (c700).
Photographs, topographical and local subjects.

Finding aids: Descriptive typescript catalogues of archive holdings (compiled 1968, not updated).

Facilities: Photocopying. Microfilm/fiche readers/printer.

Publications: Family History in Scarborough Library.

1102 Oates Memorial Library and Museum and Gilbert White Museum

Address: The Wakes, Selborne, Alton, Hampshire GU34 3JH

Telephone: (01420) 511275

Enquiries: The Secretary, Mrs N.E. Mees

Open: By arrangement.

Access: Bona fide researchers, by appointment.

Historical background: The museum is housed in The Wakes, the former home of the Rev. Gilbert White. The house was purchased by the Oates Memorial Trust in 1954 and the dual museums opened in 1955. The Wakes passed out of the White family in 1839 and Gilbert White's possessions were auctioned in the following year. The collection of White's personal items and documents is therefore limited, although a substantial collection, including the *Naturalists' Journal*, is held by the British Library (see entry 561). The bulk of the MS collection is on loan from the Holt-White family. Robert Washington Oates provided the museum with a range of note-books and drawings by members of the Oates family.

Acquisitions policy: To acquire further MSS relevant to Gilbert White and his work and relating to Lawrence Oates, the Antarctic Expedition and Frank Oates in Africa.

Major collections: Gilbert White Collection: original MS of *The Natural History of Selborne*; record of wine and beer brewing, 1771–93; account book, 1758–93, and memoranda; Thomas White's personal copy of the first edition of *The Natural History of Selborne* (reputedly bound in the skin of Gilbert White's dog) and his commonplace book.

Holt-White family documents: including an account book of Gilbert White, 1745–65; sermons; household receipts; various letters to Gilbert White from members of the family. Various White family papers, 1678–1820, including personal letters, legal documents, MS note-books, estate papers, family wills and settlement deeds. Selborne tithes.

Frank Oates (1840–75) Collection: original note-book from the journey in America and Africa together with a small collection of ethnographic items.

Lawrence Oates (1880–1912): original letters and papers from his childhood and early military career in South Africa, Egypt and India. A comprehensive collection of printed material relating to the Scott Polar Expedition and Lawrence Oates's death.

Non-manuscript material: A few items of Gilbert White personalia.

Oates family portraits and paintings by members of the Oates family.

Newspapers relating to the Antarctic Expedition.

Finding aids: Person index and catalogue of the Holt-White collection.

Facilities: Photocopying.

1103 Scottish Borders Archive and Local History Centre

Parent organisation: Scottish Borders Council

Address: St Mary's Mill, Selkirk, Borders TD7 5EW

Telephone: (01750) 20842 ext. 26

Fax: (01750) 22875

E-mail: library1@netcomuk.co.uk

Enquiries: The Study Room Supervisor

Open: Mon–Thurs: 9.00–1.00, 2.00–5.00; Fri: 9.00–1.00, 2.00–3.30.

Access: Generally open to the public; an appointment is necessary to consult records on microfilm.

Historical background: Established in 1984 and housed within the Scottish Borders Library HQ, the Borders Region Archive and Local History Centre developed from a policy to

provide essential sources for the study of local history under one roof. Local Government reorganisation in 1996 renamed the new unitary authority as Scottish Borders Council, covering the same geographical area.

Acquisitions policy: Items of Scottish Borders area interest which can strengthen the collection are added as the opportunity offers and where space permits.

Archives of organisation: Pre-1975 records of the county councils of Berwickshire, Roxburghshire, Peeblesshire and Selkirkshire, including valuation rolls, county council minutes, school board minutes, school log-books and minutes of turnpike trusts.

Major collections: Aimers, McLean & Co. Ltd, machinery manufacturers, 1845–1979. James McCaig & Sons, wool merchants and importers, 1890–1973. Border Union Agricultural Society, 1813–1974. Police records, 1825–1987. River Tweed Commissioners, 1805–1941.

Non-manuscript material: Census returns, 1841–91 and pre-1855 Old Parish records for Roxburghshire, Peeblesshire, Berwickshire and Selkirkshire plus parts of Midlothian now in the Scottish Borders (microfilm). Old Parish records index (microfiche). Usual local history collection of non-manuscript material, including books, maps, postcards and newspapers (many on microfilm).

Finding aids: Lists of collections. Card catalogues for local books and postcard collection. Lists sent to NRAS.

Facilities: Photocopying. Microfilm/fiche readers/printer.

Publications: Free introductory leaflet.

1104 Sevenoaks Branch Archives Office

Parent organisation: Kent County Council Arts & Libraries

Address: Central Library, Buckhurst Lane, Sevenoaks, Kent TN13 1LQ

Telephone: (01732) 453118/452384

Fax: (01732) 742682

Enquiries: The Arts & Heritage Officer, Mr Andrew Lister

Open: Mon–Wed: 9.30–5.30; Thu: 9.30–7.00; Fri: 9.30–5.30; Sat: 9.30–5.00.

Access: Generally open to the public.

Historical background: In the 1930s a muniment room was built at Sevenoaks Library and a considerable quantity of archives deposited; in 1962 the majority of these were transferred to the Kent Archives Office, Maidstone, now the Centre for Kentish Studies (see entry 868), but on the opening of the new library at Sevenoaks in 1986 these documents were returned and now form the basis of the collection, with other material from Sevenoaks Library as well as the records of local authorities superseded by Sevenoaks District Council in 1974.

Acquisitions policy: All material relating to Sevenoaks district.

Archives of organisation: Usual local authority record holdings.

Major collections: Deposited local collections.

Finding aids: Catalogues. Subject, author and place index.

Facilities: Photocopying. Microfilm/fiche readers.

1105 Geographical Association

Address: 160 Solly Street, Sheffield, South Yorkshire S1 4BF

Telephone: (0114) 296 0088

Fax: (0114) 296 7176

E-mail: ga@geography.org.uk

Website: www.geography.org.uk

Enquiries: The Administrator, Miss Julia Legg

Open: By arrangement only.

Access: Academic researchers, subject to prior written application and receipt of written permission.

The association was founded in 1893 'to further the study and teaching of geography', and continues that role today as a forum for teachers of geography at all educational levels. It holds its own archives, although some papers have been deposited with Sheffield Archives (see entry 1107), including minutes of the governing committee and annual meetings, 1893– , and correspondence. There is a complete set of *Geography* (previously *The Geography*

Teacher), 1901– , and a small collection of lantern slides. NRA 24477.

1106 National Centre for English Cultural Tradition

Address: University of Sheffield, Sheffield S10 2TN

Telephone: (0114) 222 6296 (office); (0114) 222 0195 (archive)

E-mail: r.h.wiltshire@sheffield.ac.uk

Website: www.shef.ac.uk/uni/projects/cectal

Enquiries: The Archives Assistant, Robin Wiltshire

Open: Mon–Thurs: 10.00–4.00.

Access: Bona fide scholars, by prior written appointment.

Historical background: The centre was established as the Survey of Language and Folklore in 1964 as part of the English Language Department. It has close links with departments of Folklore, English and Linguistics at the Memorial University of Newfoundland.

Acquisitions policy: The centre relies greatly on voluntary help from local representatives and correspondents in the collection of material: MSS, photographs, tape-recordings, printed books and ephemera relating to folklore, folklife, language and cultural tradition.

Major collections: Dave Bathe Collection covering Derbyshire traditional drama, 1978–85.
Richard and Fairfax Blakeborough MSS *re* North Yorkshire folklore and dialect, 19th century.
Nigel Kelsey Collection of MSS and sound recordings *re* children's folklore in London, 1962–84.
Charlotte Norman Collection: Derbyshire well-dressing customs, 1975–87.
Russell Wortley Collection *re* traditional dance, song, music and drama and calendar custom events, c1870–1979.
Survey response booklets to Survey of English Dialects, c1950, and Linguistic Atlas of Europe, c1970s.
Survey of Language and Folklore, 1966– (12,000 survey cards).

Non-manuscript material: Folklore and language sound records, c1950–1997 (2900); video records, c1930–1998 (230).
Calendar customs, slides, c1960–1995 (8000).

Finding aids: List and indexes to Blakeborough and Wortley Collections.
Card index of student monographs.

Facilities: Photocopying.

Publications: Lore and Language (1969–) [biannual].

1107 Sheffield Archives

Address: 52 Shoreham Street, Sheffield S1 4SP

Telephone: (0114) 203 9395

Fax: (0114) 203 9398

E-mail: sheffield.archives@dial.pipex.com

Enquiries: The Group Manager, Archives and Local Studies, Mrs Margaret Turner

Open: Mon: 10.00–5.30; Tues–Thurs: 9.30–5.30; Sat: 9.00–1.00, 2.00–5.00.

Access: Generally open to the public. A reader's ticket system is in operation. A paid research service is available.

Historical background: The library had acquired a small collection of documents of local interest by 1912; the Jackson Collection was received in the same year and the archive collections have continued to accumulate since then. Until the early 1960s the collections were mainly private, of local families, businesses and solicitors, but since then substantial deposits of parish, public and local authority records have been received. From the beginning, MSS relating to an area within a 30-mile radius of the centre of Sheffield, covering the southern half of the West Riding of Yorkshire and North Derbyshire, were collected, as there was no county record office for the West Riding, or, until 1962, for Derbyshire. Since local government reorganisation in 1974 only MSS relating to the area of the Metropolitan District of Sheffield, or additions to existing collections from outside that area, have normally been accepted. Everything held by South Yorkshire County Record Office up to the abolition of the county council in April 1986 has passed to the office, which also acts as the Diocesan Record Office for the Archdeaconry of Sheffield and for the Roman Catholic Diocese

of Hallam. It is recognised as a place of deposit for public records.

Acquisitions policy: The office is now lead district for archives in South Yorkshire and is responsible for records of county-wide significance, i.e. anything which relates to more than one of the districts. It also collects for Sheffield Metropolitan District.

Archives of organisation: Usual local authority record holdings, including records of South Yorkshire Police, 1831–1975.

Major collections: Deposited collections, of which the following have a wider significance:
Wentworth Woodhouse Muniments, including correspondence and papers of Thomas Wentworth, 1st Earl of Strafford, the 2nd Marquis of Rockingham (1730–82); the 2nd Earl Fitzwilliam (1748–1833); and Edmund Burke (1729–97).
Muniments of Spencer Stanhope of Cannon Hall; Vernon Wentworth of Wentworth Castle; Crewe of Fryston Hall.
Correspondence and papers of Edward Carpenter (1844–1929); H.J. Wilson, Liberal MP, 1885–1912; and John Mendelson, MP for Penistone, c1940–1978.
Arundel Castle MSS: the Duke of Norfolk's Sheffield, Derbyshire and Nottinghamshire estate papers, maps and plans.
Bacon Frank Collection, including papers of the Talbot Earls of Shrewsbury, 1549–1617.
Fairbank Collection: maps and plans of Sheffield and South Yorkshire (1500), with related note-books and surveys, c1736–1848.
Yorkshire Engine Company records, including photographs and plans of arrangement of locomotives, 1865–c1960.
Correspondence relating to Barnsley Canal, 1820–50.
Major holdings of business records, particularly for the steel industry (e.g. Firth Brown); metalware manufacture (e.g. James Dixon & Co.) and coal industry (National Coal Board), 19th–20th centuries.

Non-manuscript material: Early industrial films, late 1920s.
Collection of local architects' plans and drawings, 19th and 20th centuries.

Finding aids: Most pre-1980 deposits fully noted. Personal and place name indexes and subject index available. Most pre-1980 lists sent to NRA.

Facilities: Photocopying. Photography. Microfilming. Microfilm/fiche readers/printer.

Conservation: Full in-house department; outside work is undertaken.

Publications: R. Meredith: *Guide to the Manuscript Collections in the Sheffield City Libraries* (1956; suppl. *Accessions 1956–76*, 1976).
Catalogue of the Arundel Castle Manuscripts (1965).
Catalogue of Business and Industrial Records (1977).
Handlist of Records of Education in Sheffield, 1862–1944 (1978).
Handlist of Records relating to Politics in Sheffield, 1832–1980 (1982).

1108 Sheffield Hallam University Library

Address: Psalter Lane, Sheffield, South Yorkshire S11 8UZ

Telephone: (0114) 225 2721

Fax: (0114) 226 2717

E-mail: c.abson@shu.ac.uk

Website: www.shu.ac.uk/services/lc/people

Enquiries: The Information Specialist, Ms Claire Abson

Open: Term: Mon–Thurs: 8.45–9.00; Fri: 8.45–6.00; Sat: 10.00–5.00; Sun: 1.00–8.00.
Vacation: Mon–Fri: 9.00–5.00.

Access: Generally open to the public, on application to the Campus Librarian.

Historical background: The Psalter Lane site of the Sheffield Hallam University is the present form of the Sheffield School of Art, which was founded as the Government School of Design (Sheffield) in 1843. The library acts as a repository for the records of the School of Art until its amalgamation to form Sheffield Polytechnic in 1969. This polytechnic became a university in 1994.

Acquisitions policy: To acquire any material relating to the Sheffield School of Art.

Archives of organisation: Subscription lists and documents relating to the Sheffield School of Art.

Non-manuscript material: Drawings, sculpture, slides and photographs relating to the School of Art.
Annual reports, prospectuses etc.
Published material on artists connected with the school.

Finding aids: Computer catalogue, index of names of pupils and staff, 1843–1969.

Facilities: Photocopying. Microfilm/fiche readers. Slide projectors.

1109 University of Sheffield Library

Address: Western Bank, Sheffield, South Yorkshire S10 2TN

Telephone: (0114) 222 7230

Fax: (0114) 222 7290

E-mail: l.aspden@sheffield.ac.uk

Website: www.shef.ac.uk/~lib/special/special.htm

Enquiries: The Curator of Special Collections & Library Archives, Mr Lawrence Aspden

Open: Term: Mon–Fri: 9.30–4.30; an appointment is necessary.

Access: Bona fide researchers, preferably by written application. University records are subject to a 30-year closure and certain other records are restricted.

Historical background: Sheffield University received its charter in 1905 and the MS collections have been acquired from 1907 onwards. The official university archives, including the records of the institutions which merged to form the university, date from 1833 and are administered by the university, though the library is responsible for certain older records.

Acquisitions policy: Principally material relating to the university itself and persons and institutions associated with it. Other records are acquired where there is no conflict of interest with the neighbouring local authority repositories. The National Fairground Archive, established in 1994, collects multi-media material recording the history of fairs and show people.

Archives of organisation: Records of Firth College (f. 1879), the Sheffield Medical School (f. 1829), the Sheffield Technical School (f. 1886) and the University of Sheffield, 1905– .

Major collections: Samuel Hartlib (*c*1600–70) MSS: an internationally important collection relating to education, intellectual history, religious movements, agricultural improvements and scientific inventions and including a significant collection of Comenius material, 17th century.

A.J. Mundella (1825–97) papers: correspondence of a Gladstonian Liberal cabinet minister, 1860s–1890s.

W.A. Hewins (1865–1931) papers: correspondence and papers of a leading protectionist economist, founder of the London School of Economics, secretary of the Tariff Commission, Conservative MP and junior minister, 1880s–1930s.

Sir Hans Adolf Krebs (1900–81) papers: Nobel prizewinner, lecturer and professor in biochemistry, Sheffield, 1935–54; Whitley Professor of Biochemistry, Oxford, 1954–67.

Peter Redgrove (*b* 1932) papers: working papers and correspondence of a contemporary poet and dramatist, 1970–89.

Non-manuscript material: Official university archives include a collection of photographs and plans.

Innes-Smith Collection of medical engravings, mainly medical men, 17th–20th centuries.

Finding aids: Lists available of Hartlib, Hewins, Krebs and Mundella collections as well as several of the smaller archives. Partial lists and indexes available for official university archives. Computerised database for all archives in progress. Lists sent to NRA.

Facilities: Photocopying. Photography. Microfilm/fiche reader/printers.

Conservation: Contracted out.

Publications: List of collections available.

1110   Sherborne Castle

Parent organisation: Sherborne Castle Estates

Address: Estate Office, Cheap Street, Sherborne, Dorset DT9 3PY

Telephone: (01935) 813182

Fax: (01935) 816727

Website: www.sherborne.castle.com

Enquiries: The Archivist

Open: By prior arrangement.

Access: Bona fide researchers, by appointment and with the permission of the owner, Mr John Wingfield Digby.

Historical background: Sherborne Castle was built in 1594 and came to the Digby family in 1617. In 1698 the estates of the Digby family in Warwickshire and Ireland were united with those in Dorset, and Sherborne Castle became the principal seat of the family.

Acquisitions policy: To maintain the archive.

Archives of organisation: Estate papers of the Digby and Wingfield Digby families relating to estates in Dorset, Somerset and Warwickshire and in Ireland, 15th century– .

Correspondence of the Earls of Bristol and other members of the Digby family, 1538–1696 (2 vols); and of Henry Fox, 1st Lord Holland, 1753–7 (1 vol.).

Microfilms of the correspondence are available at Dorset Record Office (see entry 285).

Finding aids: Summary list of the Sherborne Castle Estate Archive available at Dorset Record Office. Lists of the Digby MSS available at Birmingham Central Library (see entry 100). Summary list of the Irish estate correspondence in the Wingfield Digby papers available at the Public Record Office of Northern Ireland (entry 81).

Facilities: Photocopying.

1111   Sherborne School

Address: Abbey Road, Sherborne, Dorset DT9 3AP

Telephone: (01935) 812249

Fax: (01935) 810426

Website: www.sherborne.org

Enquiries: The Librarian

Open: Term: Mon–Fri: 8.30–6.00; Sat: 8.30–1.00.
Vacation: Mon–Fri: 8.30–12.00.

Access: Bona fide researchers, by prior appointment only.

Historical background: The school was founded as a monastery school in 705 and refounded after the dissolution by Edward VI in 1550.

Acquisitions policy: To acquire school records (when they cease to have immediate administrative use) and all school publications.

Archives of organisation: Governors' minute books, estate, financial and other records, 1550–.

Some architectural plans.

Shirburnian, 1859– ; school lists, 1869–91, 1898–1904; Shirburnian Society annual reports, 1897– (incomplete).

Major collections: Collections of papers of headmasters and relating to old boys.

Alex Waugh (1898–1981): MS of *Loom of Youth* and his collection of reviews and related correspondence.

Finding aids: Brief handlist.

Facilities: Photocopying.

1112 Shrewsbury School

Address: The Schools, Kingsland, Shrewsbury, Shropshire SY3 7BA

Telephone: (01743) 280526 (Headmaster's office)

Fax: (01743) 340048

E-mail: librarian@shrewsbury.org.uk

Enquiries: The Taylor Librarian and Archivist, J.B. Lawson

Open: Term: by appointment.

Access: Bona fide scholars, on written application.

Historical background: The school was founded by Edward VI in 1552 and the library in 1606. From that time the library has had a continuous policy of acquiring books and MSS.

Acquisitions policy: Current acquisition policy is confined to the history of the school and of old members.

Archives of organisation: Admission registers, accounts, minute books, legal papers, tithe maps, 1552– .

Papers of the clerk to the governing body, 1840– .

Sporting, society and house 'Fasti', c1860– .

Headmasters' and bursars' files, 20th century.

Major collections: Charles Darwin (1809–82), letters.

Samuel Butler (*Erewhon*) (1835–1902), letters and MSS.

Charles Morgan (1894–1958), letters.

Rev. Prof. E. Burton (1794–1836), letters.

Shropshire Local History Collection, including deeds and antiquarian MSS.

Non-manuscript material: Photographic archive, 1860– ; plans and architectural drawings.

Shrewsbury poll books, 19th century.

Large quantity of printed ephemera relating to the school.

Finding aids: MS lists and indexes.

Facilities: Photocopying.

Conservation: Contracted out.

Publications: J.B. Oldham: *History of Shrewsbury School* (1952).

1113 Shropshire Records and Research Centre

Parent organisation: Shropshire County Council

Address: Castle Gates, Shrewsbury, Shropshire SY1 2AQ

Telephone: (01743) 255350

Fax: (01743) 255355

E-mail: research@shropshire-cc.gov.uk

Website: www.shropshire-cc.gov.uk/research.nsf

Enquiries: The Head of Records and Research, Miss Mary Mackenzie

Open: Tues: 10.00–9.00; Wed, Fri: 10.00–5.00; Thurs: 10.00–1.00; Sat: 10.00–4.00.

Access: Generally open to the public. A reader's ticket is required for access to manuscript and some other material (not CARN). A paid research service is available.

Historical background: The centre holds the collection of the former Shropshire Record Office (established in 1946) and the Local Studies Library. The latter's MS collection was acquired by Shrewsbury Public Library, 1882–1974. The centre is a diocesan branch record office for Hereford (Archdeaconry of Ludlow) and Lichfield (Archdeaconry of Salop) and is recognised as a place of deposit for public records. The centre includes the staff of the Shropshire Victoria County History.

Acquisitions policy: Archive and local studies material relating to the county of Shropshire.

Archives of organisation: Records of Shropshire County Council, 1889– , are retained at the Shirehall, Abbey Foregate, Shrewsbury SY2 6ND.

Major collections: Numerous Anglican parish collections and Methodist archives.
Estate collections, including the Attingham, More, Powis and Bridgewater archives.
Local authority collections, including medieval borough archives of Ludlow and Shrewsbury.
Lily F. Chitty Collection: Shropshire archaeology and local history.
King's Shropshire Light Infantry Collection.

Non-manuscript material: Watercolours and drawings by J. Holmes Smith and others, including watercolours of Shropshire churches, 1830–50 (*c*400).
Shropshire Photographic Archive (*c*18,000 prints; 10,000 negatives).

Finding aids: Various lists and indexes. On-line computer index to former local studies MSS. Lists sent to NRA.

Facilities: Photocopying. Photography. Microfilm/fiche readers/printers.

Conservation: In-house facilities. No commercial work is undertaken.

Publications: Family History Guide (1995).
L.F. Chitty Collection Catalogue (1992).

1114   Sid Vale Heritage Centre

Parent organisation: Sid Vale Association

Address: Hope Cottage, Church Street, Sidmouth, Devon EX10 8LY

Telephone: (01395) 516139

Enquiries: The Curator, Mrs Rosalind Whitfield

Open: Easter–Oct: by arrangement.
Closed Mondays.

Access: Bona fide researchers, by written appointment (with SAE) via the Curator. Donations are appreciated.

Historical background: A museum was first established in 1873 and moved to its present site in 1971. The museum is part of the Sid Vale Association, the first civic society (f. 1846). It maintains a local history library, which began as a private collection. The association remains an independent, voluntary institution, now housed in a Grade II building.

Acquisitions policy: To maintain and consolidate the collections relating to the Sid Vale area.

Archives of organisation: Records of the Sid Vale Association, 1846– .

Major collections: Literary MSS of R.F. Delderfield (1912–72).
Collection relating to Holcombe Roman Villa excavations.

Non-manuscript material: Newspapers and print collections.

1115   Skipton Branch Library

Parent organisation: North Yorkshire County Library

Address: High Street, Skipton, North Yorkshire BD23 1JX

Telephone: (01756) 792926

Fax: (01756) 796461

E-mail: skipton.libraryhq@northyorks.gov.uk

Enquiries: The Information Librarian, Miss Helen Parsons

Open: Mon, Wed, Thurs: 9.30–7.00; Fri: 9.30–5.00; Sat: 9.30–12.30.

Access: Open to all serious researchers; an appointment is advisable.

Historical background: The present collection derives from that formed in Skipton urban district council library before it passed to North Yorkshire in 1974.

Acquisitions policy: Accepts donations principally of local historians' papers.

Major collections: Skipton Board of Guardians records, 1873–1930, including smallpox hospital records, 1912–15.
Rowley MSS: history of Skipton, particularly properties in central Skipton.
Raistrick MSS: Yorkshire deeds, overseers papers, enclosure papers, tithes and terriers, lead-mining etc, *c*1600–1930s.
Susan Brooks MSS: mainly concerning her work on the history of Grassington and area.
Serjeantson MSS: relating to Hanlith Hall, estates at Carthorpe, Calton and Hanlith, and Camp Hill (Hall) near Bedale, 1331–1868.
Complementary collections from the same depositors are held in the Craven Museum, Town Hall, High Street, Skipton BD23 1AH.

Non-manuscript material: Maps (*c*400), 1854– .
Photographs covering Craven area, 19th–20th centuries.

Finding aids: Lists. Board of Guardians: NRA 15616; Raistrick MSS: NRA 14065; Skipton

Library Collection: NRA 10242; Serjeantson MSS: NRA 5794.

Facilities: Photocopying. Microfilm/fiche readers (booking essential).

Publications: Family History Guide.

1116   Royal Air Force College Archives

Parent organisation: Ministry of Defence

Address: The Library, Cranwell, Sleaford, Lincolnshire NG34 8HB

Telephone: (01400) 261201 ext. 6329

Fax: (01400) 262532

E-mail: college.library@dial.pipex.com

Enquiries: The College Librarian and Archivist, Mrs J.M. Buckberry

Open: Mon, Tues, Thurs: 8.15–5.00; Wed, Fri: 8.15–4.00.

Access: Bona fide researchers, by prior written appointment.

Historical background: A Royal Naval Air Service Station was established at Cranwell in 1915, and in 1918 RAF Cranwell was formed with the merging of the Royal Naval Air Service and the Royal Flying Corps. The RAF Cadet College, Cranwell, was opened in 1920.

Acquisitions policy: To collect any material relating to the college's history.

Archives of organisation: Records of administration, course syllabuses, programmes, standing orders, student lists, 1920– .

Major collections: Papers and reminiscences of former members of staff and students.

Non-manuscript material: Photographic collection, including staff and student photographs, 1915– .
Videos of graduation parades.
Maps, drawings and plans of the site, 1915– .
Large scrapbooks of newspaper and periodical articles, 1920– .
Journal of the Royal Air Force College (complete set), 1920– .
Piloteer Magazine, 1916–19.

Facilities: Photocopying.

1117   Solihull Library

Parent organisation: Solihull Libraries & Arts

Address: Homer Road, Solihull, West Midlands B91 3RG

Telephone: (0121) 704 6965

Enquiries: The Local Studies Librarian, Mrs S. Bates

Open: Mon–Wed: 9.30–5.30; Thurs, Fri: 9.30–8.00; Sat: 9.30–5.00.

Access: Generally open to the public.

Solihull Metropolitan Borough was created in 1974 from former Solihull County Borough and Meriden Rural District. A local studies collection has existed since then and is designed to provide a general coverage of those areas within the Solihull Metropolitan Borough. It includes maps, photographs, newspapers, books and a few archives, including records of the BSA Small Heath motorcycle factory, Birmingham. However, archives are generally deposited at the County Record Office, Warwick (see entry 1189). A readers' guide to the collection is available and there is a card index. Facilities include photocopying, photography and microfilm/fiche reader/printers. A range of SMBC local history publications is available.

1118   Hopetoun House

Parent   organisation: Hopetoun   House Preservation Trust

Address: South Queensferry, West Lothian EH30 9SL

Telephone: (0131) 331 2451

Fax: (0131) 319 1885

Website: www.hopetounhouse.com

Enquiries: The Archivist, Mrs Patricia Crichton

Open: Papers to be consulted are available at Hopetoun House where research has been approved. A small charge per hour plus VAT is applicable.

Access: Approved academic researchers, on written application to the Secretary, NRA Scotland, PO Box 36, General Register House, Edinburgh EH1 3YY. A copy of all completed research is requested. There is also a charge made for any approved commercial reproduction. Access is not normally granted to material post-1920.

Historical background: The trust is responsible for the private archives of the family and the estate papers.

Acquisitions policy: To maintain the existing archive.

Archives of organisation: Hope family papers, early 17th century–1703.
Earls of Hopetoun, 1703–1902.
Marquesses of Linlithgow, 1902– .

Non-manuscript material: Maps; estate plans; architectural drawings.

Finding aids: Catalogue, NRAS888 the Marquess of Linlithgow, available in Register House, Edinburgh, and at NRA. Catalogue and card index at Hopetoun House.

Facilities: Photocopying at West Register House has to be approved by the Archivist at Hopetoun House. Photocopying available at Hopetoun House for documents (not plans or maps).

Conservation: Contracted out when funds are available.

1119 South Tyneside Central Library
Local History Department

Parent organisation: South Tyneside Borough Council

Address: Prince Georg Square, South Shields, Tyne & Wear NE33 2PE

Telephone: (0191) 427 1818 ext. 2135

Fax: (0191) 455 8085

E-mail: reference.library@s-tyneside.mbc.gov.uk

Website: www.s-tyneside-mbc.gov.uk

Enquiries: The Local History Librarian, Miss D. Johnson

Open: Mon–Thurs: 9.30–7.00; Fri: 9.30–5.00; Sat: 9.30–1.00.

Access: Generally open to the public.

Historical background: South Shields Public Library was opened in 1874 and in 1879 a local history collection was started. On local government reorganisation in 1974 South Shields Public Library became South Tyneside Central Library, which meant that the area was expanded from specifically South Shields to cover Jarrow, Hebburn, the Boldons, Cleadon and Whitburn.

Acquisitions policy: Consolidation of existing holdings and strengthening of the collection in areas not covered before 1974.

Archives of organisation: South Shields Library Committee minutes and annual reports, 1874–1974.

Non-manuscript material: Kelly Collection: posters representing business, industry and entertainment in South Shields, 1790–1880 (*c*2000).
Photographs (*c*3000) and negatives (10,000), including:
Flagg Collection, amateur photographer and historian, *c*1925–*c*1950.
Cleet Collection, professional photographer, slums of South Shields in the 1930s.
Jarrow March Collection, various professional photographers on this event.
Willits Collection, amateur photographer, 1890s and 1900s.
Parry Collection, firm of professional photographers, 1900–50.

Finding aids: Most of the photographs have been catalogued and indexed and work on indexing the posters has begun.

Facilities: Photocopying. Photography. Microfilm/fiche readers/printers.

Conservation: Contracted out.

1120 Ancient Order of Foresters Heritage Trust

Parent organisation: Ancient Order of Foresters

Address: College Place, Southampton SO15 2FE

Telephone: (023) 8022 9655

Fax: (023) 8022 9657

E-mail: audreyfisk@compuserve.com

Enquiries: The Heritage Trust Co-ordinator

Open: Mon–Fri: 9.00–5.00, by appointment.

Access: Approved readers, on written application.

Historical background: The order in its present form dates from 1834 and the Heritage Trust Museum was established in 1992.

Acquisitions policy: To maintain the archives.

Archives of organisation: Executive council reports, journal and annual directories of 'courts' (branches). Collection of 'court' minutes, membership records and accounts.

Non-manuscript material: Photographs.

Finding aids: Lists, sent to NRA.

Facilities: Photography.

Publications: W.G. Cooper: *A History of the Ancient Order of Foresters Friendly Society 1834–1984* (1984).
Index to Archives in Manuscript (1997) [lists the court (branch) minute and membership books in the trust's collection].

1121 Southampton City Archives

Address: Civic Centre, Southampton SO14 7LY

Telephone: (023) 8083 2251

Fax: (023) 8083 2156

E-mail: city.archives@southampton.gov.uk

Enquiries: The Archives Services Manager

Open: Tues–Fri: 9.30–4.30; one evening each month to 9.00pm, by appointment only.

Access: Generally open to the public.

Historical background: The office was established in 1953. It also acts as the Diocesan Record Office for Winchester (Southampton parish records) and is recognised as a place of deposit for public records.

Acquisitions policy: Archives relating to the City of Southampton.

Archives of organisation: Usual local authority record holdings of present and former authorities for Southampton, including records of the borough, 1199– .

Major collections: Deposited collections, of which the following have a wider significance:
Molyneux MSS, including letters on astronomy and scientific experiments, 1681–1713.
Cobb MSS: Smyth and Gee families, including letters from the Duke of Kent, 1808–20, and papers about New Brunswick, Canada, 1820s.
South Coast Engineering and Shipbuilding Employers' Association records, c1902–78.
Charles Napier, family letters from Portugal, Bangalore etc, 1833–40.

John I. Thornycroft MSS: financial, publicity and photographic holdings on ship-building and transport-vehicle manufacturing activities of firm in UK and abroad, c1870s–1967.
Southampton Chamber of Commerce minutes, 1851–1973; Southampton Trades Council minutes and notes, 1929–84.
Garrett and Haysom, monumental masons, records, including accounts and ledgers, c1809–1962; Beeston Funeral directors, 1877–1950.
Southampton Test Conservative Association minutes and files, 1912–80.
Cox and Cawte, bookbindery and family records, 1828–1944.

Non-manuscript material: John H. Isherwood Collection of ships' drawings including Phillips war damage photographs, 1940–50; Atherley Studios, photographs, mid-20th century– .
Lemon and Blizzard, consulting engineers, plans for schools, drainage and others, mainly in Hampshire and Isle of Wight, 19th–20th centuries.
Rawlence and Squarey, chartered surveyors, land and estate agents, includes plans of road improvements, 18th–20th centuries.

Finding aids: Catalogues and indexes; lists sent to NRA.

Facilities: Photocopying. Photography. Microfilm/fiche reader.

Conservation: In-house service.

Publications: Southampton Records, i: A Guide to the Records of Southampton Corporation and Absorbed Authorities (1964).
Sources for Family History (1993).
Hampshire Archivists' Group guides: *Poor Law* (1970); *Transport* (1973); *Education* (1977).
Education Packs — Southampton in the Second World War (1998).

1122 University of Southampton Library
Special Collections

Address: Highfield, Southampton SO17 1BJ

Telephone: (023) 8059 2721/8059 3724

Fax: (023) 8059 3007

E-mail: archives@soton.ac.uk

Website: www.archives.lib.soton.ac.uk

Enquiries: The Archivist and Head of Special Collections, Dr C.M. Woolgar

Open: Mon, Tues, Thurs, Fri: 9.00–5.00; Wed: 10.00–5.00.

Access: Open to all by written appointment.

Historical background: Southampton University received its charter in 1952, having developed from the Hartley Institution (f. 1862), which became a university college of London University in 1902.

Acquisitions policy: Archives of national and international significance having a connection with the university's region or its special collections; papers of individuals associated with the university; archives of Anglo-Jewry.

Archives of organisation: Archives of Hartley Institution, 1862–1902; University College, 1902–52; Southampton University, 1952– .

Major collections: More than 2200 collections, principally of private papers and records of organisations, comprising four groups:

Political, military, diplomatic and official papers, including those of the 1st Marquis Wellesley (1760–1842); 1st Duke of Wellington (1769–1852); 3rd Viscount Palmerston (1784–1865); 7th Earl of Shaftesbury (1801–85); 1st Marquis of Milhaven (1854–1921); and Earl Mountbatten of Burma (1900–79).

Anglo-Jewry archives including papers of Rev. Dr James Parkes (1896–1981); Chief Rabbi J.H. Hertz (1872–1946); Chief Rabbi Sir I. Brodie (1895–1975); Rabbi Dr Solomon Schonfeld (1912–84); Professor E. Heimler (1922–90); S. Rowe (1924–92); M. Fidler (1916–89); J.M. Shaftesley (1901–81); G. Appleton, Archbishop of Jerusalem (1902–93); Anglo-Jewish Association, 1871–1983; Union of Jewish Women, 1902–76; *Jewish Chronicle,* 1841–1990; International and Nuremberg Military Tribunals, 1945–9; Jewish Care, including Board of Guardians for the Relief of the Jewish Poor, the Jewish Association for the Protection of Girls, Women and Children, the Jewish Blind Society and the Home and Hospital for Jewish Incurables, Tottenham, 1757–1989; Council of Christians and Jews, 1940–84; World Congress of Faiths, 1934–92; Women's Campaign for Soviet Jewry, c1970–90; Conscience, 1973–89; International Association for Religious Freedom, 1900–90.

Papers of members of the university, including Professors N.K. Adams (1891–1973), A.A.

Cock (1883–1953), H. Stansfield (1872–1960) and F.W. Wagner (1905–85).

Supporting collections, including Spanish archive material relating to the Peninsular War and the Liberal Triennium, 1805–23; papers of Sir R.H. Kennedy (1772–1840); papers of the Barons Congleton; papers of Sir Khizar Hayat Tiwana (1900–75); papers of Baron Thorneycroft of Dunstant (1909–94); records of National Association of Divisional Executives for Education, 1934–71; Joint Four Secondary Teachers' Associations, 1921–78; literary and musical material, including the papers of N.J. Crisp (*b* 1923) and conducting scores of Gustav Mahler (1860–1911).

Non-manuscript material: Photographs, prints and drawings, especially topographical, relating to Hampshire and the Isle of Wight.

Collections of early recordings of Western orchestral music (30,000 items), including the collection of Norman del Mar (*b* 1919).

Pamphlet collection of the 1st Duke of Wellington.

Parkes Library collections.

Finding aids: Summary and detailed catalogues. Lists sent to NRA. On-line computer databases of the same information, plus databases of surveys of related sources: Jewish archives and senior UK defence personnel, 1793–1970 (the latter jointly with the Liddell Hart Centre, King's College London, see entry 669B). These are accessible via JANET and the Internet; enquiries for on-line access via e-mail to archives@soton.ac.uk.

Facilities: Photocopying. Photography. Microfilming.

Conservation: Full in-house facilities. External work may be undertaken.

Publications: G. Cheffy: *Dr L.F.W. White Memorial Collection of the Records of the National Association of Divisional Executives for Education* (1975) [USL Occasional Paper no.5].

G. Hampson: *Records of the University of Southampton* (1980) [USL Occasional Paper no.7].

C.M. Woolgar: *A Summary Catalogue of the Wellington Papers* (1984) [USL Occasional Paper no.8].

L.M. Mitchell, K.J. Sampson and C. Woolgar: *A Summary Catalogue of the Papers of Earl Mountbatten of Burma* (1991) [USL Occasional Paper no.9].

C.M. Woolgar and K. Robson: *A Guide to the Archive and Manuscript Collections of the Hartley Library, University of Southampton* (1992) [USL Occasional Paper no.11].

K. Robson: *MS 200 Papers of the International Military Tribunal and the Nuremberg Military Tribunals, 1945–9* (1993) [USL Archive Lists, Catalogues and Guides series no.1].

C.M. Woolgar: *MS 173 Archives of Jewish Care, 1757–1989* (1993) [USL Archive Lists, Catalogues and Guides series no.2].

K. Robson: *MS 175 Papers of Chief Rabbi J.H. Hertz (1872–1946), 1853–1949* (1993) [USL Archive Lists, Catalogues and Guides series no.3].

C.M. Woolgar: *MS 225 Archives of the Jewish Chronicle, 1841–1990* (1994) [USL Archive Lists, Catalogues and Guides series no.4].

K. Robson: *MS60 Papers of Revd Dr James William Parkes (1896–1981)* (1997) [USL Archive Lists, Catalogues and Guides series no.5].

——: *MS 220 Papers of Eugene (John) Heimler (1922–90), 1939–93* (1998) [USL Archive Lists, Catalogues and Guides series no.6].

1123   Essex Record Office
Southend Branch

Parent organisation: Essex Record Office, Chelmsford

Address: c/o Central Library, Victoria Avenue, Southend-on-Sea, Essex SS2 6EX

Telephone: (01702) 464278

Fax: (01702) 464253

Website: www.essexcc.gov.uk

Enquiries: The Archivist in Charge

Open: Mon: 10.00–5.15; Tues–Thurs: 9.15–5.15; Fri: 9.15–4.15.

Access: Generally open to the public; an appointment is advisable. The office operates the CARN reader's ticket system. A paid research service is provided at the Chelmsford Office (see entry 228).

Historical background: This branch office of Essex Record Office was established in 1974.

Acquisitions policy: Local government and other archives, including parish, family and estate records, relevant to the area of south-east Essex.

Archives of organisation: Usual local authority record holdings.

Major collections: Deposited local collections.

Finding aids: Indexes and catalogues. Lists sent to NRA.

Facilities: Photocopying. Photography. Microfilm/fiche readers/printers.

Conservation: Full in-house service at Essex Record Office, Chelmsford.

1124   Southport Library
Local History Unit

Parent organisation: Sefton Metropolitan Borough Council

Address: Southport Library, Lord Street, Southport, Merseyside PR8 1DJ

Telephone: (0151) 934 2119

Fax: (0151) 934 2115

Enquiries: The Local History Librarian

Open: Mon, Tues, Fri: 10.00–5.00; Wed: 10.00–8.00; Thurs, Sat: 10.00–1.00.

Access: The local history unit is generally open to the public, but all archives are on application only; an appointment is recommended for detailed research and for microfilm/fiche machines. There is a fee for postal enquiries from all non-residents.

Historical background: Sefton Metropolitan Borough was formed after local government reorganisation in 1974. It combined the areas of Bootle, Crosby and Southport with parts of the West Lancashire District. Material relating to Bootle and Crosby is held at Crosby Library (see entry 523).

Acquisitions policy: There is no active collecting policy but archives are taken in on request.

Archives of organisation: Local government records of Southport County Borough, Formby Urban District and predecessor authorities.

Non-manuscript material: Newspapers, photographs, maps, audio, microfilm/fiche.

Finding aids: Index to maps and newspapers; NRA 2553.

Facilities: Photocopying. Microfilm/fiche readers/printer.

Conservation: Contracted out.

Publications: Assorted local history titles: details on request.

1125 Royal Marines Museum

Address: Southsea, Hampshire PO4 9PX

Telephone: (023) 92819385 exts 224/239

Fax: (023) 92838420

Website: www.royalmarinesmusem.co.uk

Enquiries: The Archivist, Mr Matt Little
The Assistant Curator, Miss Susan Lindsay

Open: Mon–Fri: 10.00–4.30.

Access: Bona fide researchers, by appointment.

Historical background: In 1963 it became necessary to establish a reference library and archive repository for the use of the Royal Marines Historian and Museum, and a certain amount of money was made available for the purchase of items by the Commandant General Royal Marines. This was supplemented by gifts from individuals. In 1965 a number of military and naval reference books were transferred to the museum from the Royal Marines Officers' Mess Library at Plymouth. This was the first of such transfers. Meanwhile the Commandant General's grant continued, which provided the basis for further purchases. In 1988 the museum was designated and is now a registered charity with a board of trustees and a grant-in-aid provided under the terms of the National Heritage Act 1983; it is recognised as a place of deposit for public records.

Acquisitions policy: To strengthen the collection by the acquisition of both modern and antiquarian material, by purchase, donation or bequest.

Archives of organisation: Archives of the Royal Marines Corps, comprising derestricted material from official sources; divisional order books concerning marines administration, organisation and deployment, 1644– .

Major collections: An extensive collection of personal diaries and letters; unofficial logbooks; correspondence; and orders.

Non-manuscript material: Extensive photograph and reference library.
Drawings, maps and plans relating to operations, equipment and barracks.
Navy and Marine Lists.
Oral history tapes (52).

Finding aids: Various card indexes, including name, unit, operation and location. Sections of collection computerised.

Facilities: Photocopying. Photograph copying. Microfilm/fiche reader.

Publications: From Trench and Turret: Letters and Diaries, 1914–18 (RMM, *c*1989).
The Royal Marines Victoria Crosses (RMM, 1987).
The Royal Marines Story (RMM, 1989, 1998).

1126 Southwell Minster Library

Address: Southwell Minster Centre, Church Street, Southwell, Nottinghamshire NG25 0JP

Telephone: (01636) 817810

E-mail: mail@southwellminster.prestel.co.uk

Website: www.southwellminster.org.uk

Enquiries: The Hon. Librarian, Mr L. Craik

Open: Tues: 10.00–4.00; other times by appointment.

Access: Approved readers, students and researchers.

The Minster library dates from the Restoration in 1660. It holds chapter records, 17th century– ; bishops' transcripts for the Diocese of Southwell, 1599–1812; and some local photographs. Local history material and publications relevant to Southwell Minster and the diocese are acquired, and there are catalogues of books and archives.

1127 Lincolnshire Film Archive

Address: 61 Cathedral Drive, Spalding, Lincolnshire PE11 1PG

Telephone: (01775) 725631

E-mail: info@lincsfilm.co.uk

Website: www.lincsfilm.co.uk

Enquiries: The Archivist, Peter Ryde

Open: By appointment only.

Access: Bona fide users, researchers, students of local history etc. Viewing will normally be on video in the first instance. By arrangement (and subject to copyright/donor's restrictions, if any) material can be made available on video for approved uses. Showings on film can be arranged for societies etc, although films themselves are not available on loan to the public.

Historical background: The archive was established in 1986 and operates in association with the Museum of Lincolnshire Life, Lincoln.

Acquisitions policy: To locate, preserve and make accessible film on all aspects of life and work in historic Lincolnshire (Lincolnshire and South Humberside), especially pre-1960, though later items are not refused.

Non-manuscript material: Documentary and non-fiction film illustrating the life and work of the region, 1904–1970s, but principally 1930s and 1940s (430 titles).

Supplementary documentation is available in some cases, including press cuttings, and commentary scripts for local newsreel items. General background information can be supplied for most items.

Finding aids: Full descriptive catalogue. Computer database for search by date, place, region and broad subject area. A detailed subject index is still in preparation, but information on specific subject content is available on application.

1128 Spalding Gentlemen's Society

Address: The Museum, Broad Street, Spalding, Lincolnshire PE11 1TB

Telephone: (01775) 724658

Enquiries: The Hon. Secretary, Mr I. Hutchinson

Open: By appointment.
Closed in August and December.

Access: By arrangement; visitors wishing study facilities will be asked for a reference.

Historical background: One of the oldest learned societies, it was founded by Maurice Johnson, FSA (1688–1755) in 1710, and early members included notable 18th-century figures. Discussion of politics and religion are banned under the founder's ruling. With the exception of the Ashmolean, the museum is the oldest in the UK.

Acquisitions policy: To maintain the collections.

Major collections: Manorial, local government and some monastic records and MSS.
Fens drainage records, 17th–19th centuries.

Non-manuscript material: Portfolios of prints, drawings and plans, early 18th century. Maps.
Society's library, created by purchases and the gift of a volume from every new member.

Finding aids: NRA 4862.

Publications: Annual Report, 1899– .
Various histories, including *Nichol's Bibliotheca Topographica Britannica* (1790) [history of early days of society with list of members and *Literary Anecdotes,* vol. 6 (1812).
W. Moore: *The Gentlemen's Society at Spalding: its Origin and Progress* (London, 1851).
D.M. Owen: *The Minute Books of the Spalding Gentlemen's Society, 1712–1755,* Lincoln Record Society, 73 (1981).

1129 Staffordshire and Stoke-on-Trent Archive Service
Staffordshire Record Office

Parent organisation: Staffordshire County Council and Stoke-on-Trent City Council

Address: Eastgate Street, Stafford ST16 2LZ

Telephone: (01785) 278373 (bookings); 278379 (archive enquiries)

Fax: (01785) 278384

E-mail: staffordshire.record.office@staffordshire.gov.uk

Website: www.staffordshire.gov.uk/archives/

Enquiries: The Head of Archive Services, Mrs Thea Randall
The Principal Archivist, Mr Mark Dorrington

Open: Mon–Thurs: 9.00–5.00; Fri: 9.30–4.30; Sat: 9.00–12.30, by arrangement.

Access: Generally open to the public within the terms of the access policy of Staffordshire and Stoke-on-Trent Archive Service: a reader's ticket is required. A paid research service is available.

Historical background: The record office was established in 1947; before then records were collected by the William Salt Library. The office also acts as the Diocesan Record Office for Lichfield (Archdeaconry of Stafford parish records) and is recognised as a place of deposit for public records. The William Salt Library, Stafford (see entry 1130), Lichfield Record

Office (entry 517), Stoke-on-Trent City Archives (entry 1139) and Burton on Trent Archives (entry 156) are dependent repositories.

Archives of organisation: Usual local authority record holdings.

Major collections: Deposited collections, including the following which have a wider significance:

Dartmouth Family Collection, including papers of the Legge family, who held various government appointments, notably Secretary of State for the Colonies and Admiral of the Fleet, 17th–18th centuries.

Hatherton Collection, including political papers of the 1st Lord Hatherton (1791–1863), Chief Secretary to the Lord Lieutenant of Ireland, 1833–4.

Major business collections include records of Birmingham Rail, Carriage and Wagon Works, with worldwide connections, 19th century.

Non-manuscript material: OS maps for Staffordshire.

Finding aids: Lists and subject, place, personal name and map indexes. Lists sent to NRA.

Facilities: Photocopying. Photography and microfilming by arrangement. Microfilm/fiche readers.

Conservation: Full in-house service.

Publications: Introductory leaflet, general summaries of holdings.
Guide to Parish Registers and Bishops' Transcripts (1999).
Guide to the Contents of Lichfield Record Office (1999).
Guide to Sources, No. 1: Parish Registers and Bishops Transcripts (1999).
Guide to Sources, No. 2: Nonconformist Registers (2000).

1130 Staffordshire and Stoke-on-Trent Archive Service
William Salt Library

Parent organisation: Staffordshire County Council and Stoke-on-Trent City Council

Address: Eastgate Street, Stafford ST16 2LZ

Telephone: (01785) 278372

Fax: (01785) 278414

E-mail:
william.salt.library@staffordshire.gov.uk

Website: www.staffordshire.gov.uk/archives/salt.htm

Enquiries: The Librarian, Mrs Thea Randall

Open: Tues–Thurs: 9.00–1.00, 2.00–5.00;
Fri: 9.00–1.00, 2.00–4.30;
Sat (first in each month): 9.00–1.00.

Access: Generally open to the public. A Staffordshire and Stoke-on-Trent Archive Service reader's ticket is required for restricted-access items.

Historical background: Founded in 1872, the library is based on the manuscript, printed and graphic collections of William Salt (1808–63), a member of a Stafford banking family. It is administered by trustees, but since 1935 its connection with Staffordshire County Council has become close, at first by grant, and since the creation of the Staffordshire Record Office in 1947, also by sharing of staff: the Head of Archive Services also acts as William Salt Librarian. Many manuscript collections, including some of major Staffordshire families deposited with the library early in the 20th century, are now housed in the Staffordshire Record Office (see entry 1129).

Acquisitions policy: Manuscripts are acquired only where they form an integral or additional part of existing collections.

Major collections: William Salt MSS Collection, 9th–20th centuries, reflecting his historical, genealogical and heraldic interests and containing a considerable number of autograph letters, only some of which have Staffordshire connections; also many transcripts of Staffordshire material in the Public Record Office, British Library, College of Heralds, much of which is still unpublished (e.g. the Staffordshire entries in the Thomason Tracts and Dr Burney's newspapers). Notable manuscripts include the Compton Census, 1676.
Papers of the Parker-Jervis family of Meaford.
Anglo-Saxon charters.

Non-manuscript material: William Salt Collection includes printed books, pamphlets, broadsheets, drawings, engravings and other ephemera relating to Staffordshire.
Topographical drawings (3000) and prints; also engraved drawings of personalities.

Finding aids: Manual dictionary index and catalogues of accessions.

Facilities: Photocopying. Photography, by arrangement.

Conservation: Service provided by Staffordshire Record Office and by external contractors.

1131 Tameside Local Studies Library

Parent organisation: Tameside Metropolitan Borough Council

Address: Stalybridge Library, Trinity Street, Stalybridge, Cheshire SK15 2BN

Telephone: (0161) 303 7937/338 2708

Fax: (0161) 303 8289

E-mail: tameside@dial.pipex.com

Website: www.tameside.gov.uk/leisure/new/lh23.htm

Enquiries: The Archivist, Helen Mackie

Open: Mon–Wed, Fri: 9.00–7.30; Sat: 9.00–4.00.

Access: Generally open to the public. An appointment is necessary for the use of microfilm.

Historical background: The Tameside Local Studies Library was set up in Stalybridge in 1976 and took over the local history collections of the libraries of the local authorities which preceded Tameside. It is recognised as a place of deposit for public records.

Acquisitions policy: To locate, acquire and preserve all types of printed, illustrative and archive material related to the Tameside area: Ashton, Audenshaw, Denton, Droylsden, Dukinfield, Hyde, Longdendale, Mossley and Stalybridge.

Archives of organisation: Usual local authority record holdings of the authorities which preceded Tameside.

Major collections: Deposited collections of some local organisations, including churches; schools; trade unions; mechanics' institutes; also some hospitals; local businesses, including mills; families, including Lee family of Park Bridge, and individuals' records.
Archives of the Manchester Regiment.

Non-manuscript material: Maps of the Tameside area, Lancashire and Cheshire, 1577– (c1500).

Photographs, 1860s– (14,500); engravings, pamphlets and broadsides, 1790s– .
Oral history interviews, including those by the former Manchester Studies Unit.
Microfilms of local newspapers, census returns and parish registers.

Finding aids: Catalogues, indexes and typescript guide to the archive collection. Card catalogue of photographs, maps and broadsheets. Indexes of the *North Cheshire Herald* (1895–1972) and *Ashton Reporter* (incomplete). Surname index (incomplete) and street index to the census returns.

Facilities: Photocopying. Photography. Microfilm/fiche readers.

Publications: Guide to the Archives (1994).

1132 John Lewis Partnership plc
Archives Department

Address: Cavendish Road, Stevenage, Hertfordshire SG1 2EH

Telephone: (01438) 312388 ext. 4202

E-mail: judy_faraday@johnlewis.co.uk

Enquiries: The Partnership Archivist, Mrs Judith Faraday

Open: Mon–Thurs: 9.30–3.00.

Access: Bona fide researchers, on written application to the Archivist.

Historical background: John Lewis opened his first shop in 1864; his son, John Spedan Lewis, who joined the business in 1904, developed the partnership trading philosophy which is in operation today. The Peter Jones store in Sloane Square was acquired in 1905, and numerous department stores and store chains were subsequently added, including Waitrose Ltd and Selfridge Provincial Stores. The partnership has also acquired a number of manufacturing units.

Archives of organisation: Records, including ledgers, financial papers and staff records, of the partnership, 1929– .
Records of more than 20 constituent department stores, including Bainbridge, Newcastle, 1838– ; Heelas, Reading, 1854– ; Waitrose foodstores, 1920– ; Stead McAlpin & Co. Ltd, 1835– , Findlater Mackie Todd, wine merchant, 1855– .

Non-manuscript material: House magazine, 1918– ; publicity material; large photographic collection, mainly of retail premises; fabric samples.
Some film, video and audio material.

Finding aids: Computer database. Catalogue and index.

Facilities: Photocopying.

Conservation: Contracted out.

Publications: A. Flanders and others: *Experiment in Industrial Democracy* (1968).
H. Macpherson (ed.): *John Spedan Lewis, 1885–1963* (1985).

1133 Stirling Council Archives Service

Parent organisation: Stirling Council

Address: Unit 6, Burghmuir Industrial Estate, Stirling FK7 7PY

Telephone: (01786) 450745

Fax: (01786) 448285 (prior notification necessary)

E-mail: archives@stirling-council.demon.co.uk

Enquiries: the Council Archivist, Dr John Brims

Open: Wed–Fri: 10.00–12.30, 1.00–4.30.

Access: Generally open to the public; an appointment is advisable.

Historical background: The Stirling Council Archives Service (SCAS) was established in 1996 following the dissolution of the Central Regional Archives Department as a result of the implementation of the Local Government (Scotland) Act, 1994. The previous department held records relating to Falkirk and Clackmannan districts as well as those relating to Stirling District.

Acquisitions policy: Historically important records of Stirling Council and its predecessor authorities, including Stirling County Council, are collected, as well as private records of individuals, families and organisations whose contributions to the community are deemed to be historically significant.

Archives of organisation: Records of Stirling burgh, 14th century–1975, Stirling county and successor authorities.

Records of the burghs of Bridge of Allan, Doune, Dunblane and Callander and of the presbytery of Stirling.

Major collections: Deposited local collections, including MacGregor of MacGregor, 18th–20th centuries, and Murray of Polmaise, 14th–20th centuries.

Non-manuscript material: Stirling *Observer*, 1836–1980; *Stirling Journal*, 1820–1960.

Facilities: Photocopying service. Photography by arrangement. Microfilm/fiche readers.

Conservation: Contracted out.

1134 University of Stirling Library

Address: Stirling FK9 4LA

Telephone: (01786) 673171

Fax: (01786) 466866

E-mail: g.w.willis@stir.ac.uk

Website: www.stir.ac.uk

Enquiries: The Arts Librarian, Mr Gordon Willis
The Associate Librarian, Mrs Carolyn Rowlinson (John Grierson Archive)

Open: Mon–Fri: 9.00–5.00, by appointment.

Access: Generally open to the public. A prior appointment is essential.

Historical background: The university was founded in 1967. The library supervises access to the Leighton Library, Dunblane (see entry 298), in the Rare Books Department of the university library.

Acquisitions policy: Materials for research in film and broadcasting. Material relating to Scottish literature, especially from the 19th century. MSS mostly acquired as gifts or bequests.

Major collections: John Grierson Archive: personal papers, writings on documentary film of John Grierson (1898–1972), with related material, including papers of Norman McLaren, film-maker (1914–87).
Papers of Lindsay Anderson, film-maker (1923–94).
Howietown Fishery (trout farm) records, 1873–1978.
Leighton Library MSS Collection, 16th–20th centuries (c80 MSS).

Collections of Scottish literary interest include MSS of James Hogg, 'the Ettrick Shepherd' (1770–1835); Helen B. Cruickshank (1886–1975); Norman MacCaig (1910–96).

Non-manuscript material: Special collection of early editions of Sir Walter Scott and James Hogg.
W. Tait Collection: minutes of Scottish revolutionary socialist parties, 1883–1943 (microfilm available); also large related collections of newspapers and pamphlets.

Finding aids: Grierson Archive: card index, published list of contents. NRAS lists of other collections. Some material listed in the university library's on-line catalogue.

Facilities: Photocopying. Photography. Microfilm/fiche reader/printer.

Conservation: Contracted out.

Publications: F. Hardy: *John Grierson Archive: List of Contents* (1978).
G. Willis: *The Leighton Library, Dunblane: Catalogue of Manuscripts* (Stirling, 1981).

1135 Stockport Archives

Parent organisation: Stockport Metropolitan Borough

Address: Central Library, Wellington Road South, Stockport, Cheshire SK1 3RS

Telephone: (0161) 474 4530

Fax: (0161) 474 7750

E-mail: stockport.cen.library@dial.pipex.com

Enquiries: The Archivist, Mrs M.J. Myerscough

Open: Mon, Tues, Fri: 10.00–8.00; Wed: 10.00–5.00; Sat: 9.00–4.00.

Access: Generally open to the public; booking should be made in advance. There are restrictions on some records. Contact in advance of a visit is preferable, as some records are outstored.

Historical background: Active collecting, focused on the county borough area, began in the 1960s to supplement documents already held by the library. In 1974 the Archives Service took over the records of the disbanded urban districts included in the new metropolitan borough: Bredbury and Romiley, Cheadle and Gatley, Hazel Grove and Bramhall, and Marple. It is recognised as a place of deposit for public records.

Acquisitions policy: Acquisition of records relating to any aspect of life in the area of the metropolitan borough.

Archives of organisation: Usual local government records for the area of the metropolitan borough.

Major collections: Deposited local collections, including records of Stockport Sunday School, 1784–1970; Christy & Co. Ltd, hat manufacturers, 1773–1969; Bradshaw-Isherwood estate, 1274–1919; R. Greg & Co., 1850–1980.

Finding aids: 16 calendars and indexes for part of the holdings. Lists sent to NRA.

Facilities: Photocopying. Photography. Microfilm readers.

Publications: M.J. Critchlow: *Guide to Calendars, 1–14* (1983).
M.J. Myerscough: *Stockport Archive: a Guide* (1998).

1136 Stockton Museum Service

Parent organisation: Stockton Borough Council

Address: Wynyard House, Queensway, Billingham, Stockton-on-Tees TS23 2LN

Telephone: (01642) 358500

Enquiries: The Museums' Keeper (Local Studies)

Open: Mon–Fri: 10.00–4.00, by appointment.

Access: Generally open to the public.

Historical background: Stockton Museums Service began in 1953, but the holdings have been developed over the last 20 years.

Acquisitions policy: To collect, preserve and maintain records relating to the Stockton Borough area.

Major collections: Minutes of Thornaby Council, 1892–1968; Stockton Council, 1902– .

Non-manuscript material: Photographs, plans, maps, entertainment ephemera, videos, oral history recordings.

Finding aids: Cross-referenced computerised catalogue. Lists.

Facilities: Photocopying. Photography by arrangement. Access to microform readers and material on CD-ROM.

1137 Stockton Reference Library

Parent organisation: Stockton Borough Libraries

Address: Church Road, Stockton-on-Tees TS18 1TU

Telephone: (01642) 393994

Fax: (01642) 393929

Website: www.stockton-be.gov.uk

Enquiries: The Reference Services Officer, Mrs Joyce E. Chesney

Open: Mon–Wed, Fri: 9.30–7.00; Thurs, Sat: 9.30–5.00.

Access: Generally open to the public. An appointment is necessary to use the microfilm/fiche readers.

Historical background: Local historical collection of social history/industrial background of Stockton Borough area, built up over many years.

Acquisitions policy: To identify and acquire material relevant to history of Stockton Borough area.

Major collections: Usual local history collection, mainly of non-MS material, including council minutes, 1903– .

Non-manuscript material: Newspapers, census and parish registers (microfilm); maps, 1859–1990; photographs, late 19th century– .

Finding aids: Card indexes for photographic collection and for weekly newspaper, 1920–60.

Facilities: Photocopying. Microfilm/fiche readers/printer.

Conservation: Contracted out to Teesside Archive (see entry 901).

Publications: Sources for Family Historians in Stockton Reference Library [free leaflet].
Stockton Markets and Fairs [study pack on sale].

1138 Royal Doulton plc

Address: Minton House, London Road, Stoke-on-Trent ST4 7QD

Telephone: (01782) 292292

Fax: (01782) 292099

Website: www.royal-doulton.co.uk

Enquiries: The Royal Doulton Museums Curator, Mrs Joan Jones

Open: By appointment only.

Access: Bona fide researchers. Royal Doulton reserves the right to refuse access.

Historical background: The Minton Archives contain a comprehensive record of the commercial and artistic progress of this premier ceramic manufactory from 1793. In 1968 Minton became part of Royal Doulton.

Acquisitions policy: Acquires items relating to the Minton family, employees and artists; the factory and its productions, including designs and artwork.

Archives of organisation: Minton records, 1793– .

Non-manuscript material: A collection of Minton pottery and porcelain, c1799– .

Publications: A. Giles Jones: *Catalogue of Minton MSS* (2 vols).
J. Jones: *Minton: the First Two Hundred Years of Design and Production* (1993).

1139 Staffordshire and Stoke-on-Trent Archive Services
Stoke-on-Trent City Archives

Parent organisation: Staffordshire County Council and Stoke-on-Trent City Council

Address: Hanley Library, Bethesda Street, Hanley, Stoke-on-Trent ST1 3RS

Telephone: (01782) 238420 (enquiries); 238402 (archivist)

Fax: (01782) 238499/238434

E-mail: stoke.archives@stoke.gov.uk

Website: www.staffordshire.gov.uk/archives/contact.htm

Enquiries: The City Archivist, Mr C.S. Latimer

Open: Wed: 9.30–7.00; Thurs, Fri: 9.30–5.00; Sat: 9.30–1.00.

Access: Generally open to the public within the terms of the access policy of the service. A Staffordshire and Stoke-on-Trent reader's ticket is required. Booking is strongly advised for genealogical enquiries.

Historical background: The City of Stoke-on-Trent was formed in 1910 by the federation of the six local authorities of Tunstall, Burslem, Hanley, Stoke-upon-Trent, Fenton and Longton. From 1974 to 1997 it formed part of Staffordshire County Council, but in 1997 it became a unitary authority. Archives were collected by the library service in consultation with Staffordshire CRO, but with the advent of the unitary authority a more formal arrangement was put in place. Under a joint agreement between the city and the county an archive service and a professional post were established.

Acquisitions policy: Collects material relating to Stoke-on-Trent and the pottery industry.

Archives of organisation: Minute books, and local school board minute books where appropriate, of Burslem borough council and predecessors, 1825–1910; Fenton UDC and predecessors, 1842–1910; Hanley county borough and predecessors, 1847–1910; Longton borough council, 1873–1910; Smallthorne UDC, 1875–1922; Stoke-upon-Trent borough council and predecessors, 1839–1910; Tunstall UDC and predecessors, 1886–1910. School logbooks.

Major collections: Adam Collection: mainly title deeds relating to North Staffordshire, 12th–19th centuries.
Wilkinson/Newport Collection: documents relating to Clarice Cliff, ceramics designer.
Heathcote Collection.
Local Methodist records.

Non-manuscript material: Large local studies collection relating to Stoke-on-Trent and Staffordshire.
Ceramics collection.
Solon Collection of books on ceramics in many European languages.

Finding aids: Lists for some collections; sent to NRA. Various indexes.

Facilities: Photocopying. Microfilm/fiche readers (printouts can be ordered).

Conservation: Undertaken under the joint arrangement of the Archive Service.

1140 Staffordshire University

A Special Collections

Address: Thompson Library, College Road, Stoke-on-Trent ST4 2XS

Telephone: (01782) 294482

Fax: (01782) 295799

E-mail: special.collections@staffs.ac.uk

Website: www.staffs.ac.uk/services/library_and_info/specialcoll.html

Enquiries: The Special Collections Co-ordinator, Sarah Glaccum

Open: Term: Mon–Wed: 9.00–1.00, 2.00–5.00; Thurs–Fri: by appointment.

Access: Approved researchers by prior arrangement; proof of identity is required.

Historical background: North Staffordshire polytechnic was created in 1970, when North Staffordshire College of Technology, Stafford College of Technology and Stoke-on-Trent College of Art merged. In 1988 the polytechnic changed its name to Staffordshire Polytechnic, and in 1992 university status was granted.

Major collections: War Widows' Archive: mostly letters covering the war widows' campaign for pensions.
Dorothy Thompson Collection: working class history collection.
Development Studies Collection: books, periodicals and pamphlets relating to politics and development in Africa.

Non-manuscript material: Slide Library, School of Art and Design: collection of architecture, ceramics, glass, fashion painting, photography and sculpture slides.
Mining Archive: books, journals, government reports, maps.
Design Studies Collection: popular periodicals and small domestic items.
Staffordshire Film Archives: images of Staffordshire and the surrounding area.

Finding aids: Various lists.

Facilities: Photocopying. Microfilm reader/printers.

B Centre for the History of Psychology

Address: School of Sciences, College Road, Stoke-on-Trent ST4 2DE

Telephone: (01782) 294643

E-mail: g.d.richards@staffs.ac.uk

Website: www.staffs.ac.uk/schools/sciences/psychology/chop/chop.html

Enquiries: The Director, Prof. Graham Richards
Sandy Lovie

Open: By prior arrangement.

Historical background: The centre was officially launched in 1999 and is the first research centre in the UK specifically dedicated to the history of psychology. It is proposing to undertake a major survey of archives relating to psychology in Britain. The archives of the British Psychology Society were previously held by the Department of Psychology, University of Liverpool.

Acquisitions policy: Keen to collect relevant material.

Major collections: British Psychological Society archives, including minutes, 1904– .
Child Study Society material, 1891–1939.

1141   Wedgwood Museum

Parent organisation: The Wedgwood Museum Trust

Address: Barlaston, Stoke-on-Trent ST12 9ES

Telephone: (01782) 282818

Fax: (01782) 204222

Website: www.wedgwoodmuseum.org.uk/

Enquiries: The Curator, Miss Gaye Blake Roberts

Open: By arrangement.

Access: Bona fide scholars and researchers, by reader's ticket only on written application.

Historical background: The Wedgwood Museum Trust was founded in 1906 with holdings of ceramics, paintings and manuscripts. The business was established by Josiah Wedgwood (1730–95), who set up his own pottery at Burslem in 1759 and developed a wide range of distinctive ceramic products. The firm was incorporated in 1875 and a new works was developed at Barlaston from 1938 onwards. Other important manufacturers were acquired, 1966–79. The Waterford Glass Group plc acquired Wedgwood in 1986. The Wedgwood Museum Trust was formed in 1906. The archive is an important source for the history of science, the fine arts and the humanitarian movement.

Part of the archive is on temporary deposit at the University of Keele (see entry 476), but apply in the first instance to the museum.

Acquisitions policy: To consolidate relevant holdings of Wedgwood-related material.

Archives of organisation: Records of Josiah Wedgwood and Sons, 1700– . Records, including patterns, of subsidiary companies, notably Mason's Ironstone (f. 1795); Coalport; William Adams (f. 1657); Susie Cooper and George Jones (20th century).
Personal correspondence of Josiah Wedgwood.

Non-manuscript material: Photographs, drawings, paintings and printed ephemera.

Finding aids: Index and full archival list.

Facilities: Microfilm available. Photocopying (on limited items only).

1142   Western Isles Islands Council/Comhairle Nan Eilean Siar

Address: Sandwick Road, Stornoway, Isle of Lewis HS1 2BW

Telephone: (01851) 703773

Fax: (01851) 705349

E-mail: doloan@cne-siar.gov.uk

Website: www.cne-siar.gov.uk

Enquiries: The Director of Corporate Services, Mr David O'Loan

Open: Mon–Fri: 9.00–5.00.

Access: By written application.

Historical background: Comhairle Nan Eilean Siar is a multi-purpose single-tiered local authority (except police and fire) created on local government reorganisation in 1975, combining the Ross and Cromarty and Inverness-shire parts of the Outer Hebrides.

Acquisitions policy: Maintenance of local authority records for the Western Isles.

Archives of organisation: Minute books of the following: Stornoway Town Council, 1863–1975 (under all forms of name); Western Isles lslands Council (Comhairle Nan Eilean), 1974– ; Ross and Cromarty and Inverness-shire District Councils, 1930–70, parochial boards/ parish councils, 1890s–1930, and education district sub-committees, 1927–1970s. Also housing registers, 1931– ; abstracts of accounts (Stornoway Burgh), 1901–60; and valuation rolls (Stornoway Burgh and Lewis parishes), 1947–67.

Major collections: Records of Stornoway Road Trustees, 1866–1901 (also under later form of name); Stornoway Young Men's Mutual Association, 1871–8; Lewis Coffee House Committee, 1878–1910; D.L. Robertson Trust, 1930– ; Dean of Guild Court, 1947–65.

Finding aids: Partial indexes to Stornoway Town Council minutes and Western Isles Islands Council minutes, for internal use.

Facilities: Photocopying.

1143   Western Isles Libraries/ Leabharlainn nan Eilean Siar

Address: 2 Keith Street, Stornoway, Isle of Lewis HS1 2QG

Telephone: (01851) 703064

Fax: (01851) 705657

E-mail: stornoway_library@w-isles.gov.uk

Enquiries: The Chief Librarian, Mr Robert Eaves

Open: Mon–Thurs: 10.00–5.00; Fri: 10.00–7.00; Sat: 10.00–1.00.

Access: Generally open to the public, following written or telephone enquiry.

Historical background: The Town Council Library until 1964, then Ross and Cromarty Branch Library until 1975, the Stornoway library is now the headquarters for the whole of the Western Isles.

Acquisitions policy: Building up local history and Gaelic collections, including archive material.

Major collections: Lewis School Board minute books, 1873–1919. Log-books of closed schools.
Aircraft movement log-books for Stornoway and Benbecula, 1972– .
Barvas parish rent ledgers, 1854–1920.

Non-manuscript material: T.B. Macaulay photographic collection; other miscellaneous photographs, postcards, slides.
Newspapers: *Stornoway Gazette*, 1917– (microfilm), 1940– (bound vols); *West*

Highland Free Press, 1883–1952 (microfilm), 1972– ; *Highland News*, 1883–1952 (microfilm).
Western Isles Islands Council (Comhairle Nan Eilean) agendas and minutes, 1974– (microfilm).

Finding aids: Local history catalogue. Partial subject index being compiled.

Facilities: Photocopying. Microfilm reader.

1144   King Edward VI College

Address: Stourbridge, West Midlands DY8 1TD

Telephone: (01384) 394223

Fax: (01384) 398123

E-mail: office@kec.stourbridge.ac.uk

Website: www.kedst.co.uk

Enquiries: The Keeper of the Archives

Open: Term: Mon–Fri: 9.30–4.00.

Access: Bona fide researchers, by prior appointment only. There are restrictions on certain deposited archives.

King Edward VI College was established in 1976 as a mixed sixth-form college on the site of the former King Edward VI Grammar School for boys. The grammar school had been established in 1552 by royal charter and replaced the school attached to the chantry chapel dating from about 1430. The archives department was set up in 1983 and holds material relating to the history and development of the school and college, including records of governors, property, finance, staff and students. There is a general index. Access is granted by the King Edward VI Foundation Trustees, and application to consult the archives should be made in writing to the Chairman of the Foundation Trustees.

1145   Stowe School

Address: Stowe, Buckinghamshire MK18 1QX

Telephone: (01280) 813164

Fax: (01280) 822769

E-mail: enquiries@stowe.co.uk

Enquiries: The Archivist

Open: Mon–Fri: 9.30–4.30, during term, by appointment.

Access: Bona fide researchers. Written application is necessary.

Historical background: Stowe School was founded in 1923, in the former home of the Dukes of Buckingham and Chandos. The library and archives contain a small amount of material related to Stowe before and after 1923. Nearly all the original family papers were sold in 1921 and many are now in the Huntingdon Library, San Marino, California, USA.

Acquisitions policy: The school welcome donations of relevant material.

Archives of organisation: School records, 1923– .

Major collections: Library: collection of Stowe descriptions by Benton Seeley and others.

Non-manuscript material: Rigaud engravings.
Chatelain/Bickham engravings.
A few J.C. Nates drawings.
J. Mudd & Sons photographs.
Sir Clough Williams-Ellis (1883–1978) plans.
Sale catalogues and descriptions of Stowe.
School magazines.
Plans, drawings, engravings and photographs of Stowe.

Finding aids: Stowe Gardens Resource Centre, Stowe School, contains copies of most of the Seeley descriptions and some articles about Stowe.

Facilities: Photographs of most items can be ordered for purchase.

Publications: M. Bevington: *Stowe: the Garden and the Park*, Chap 24, 'Sources', pp.158–66.

1146 Wigtown District Museums Service

Parent organisation: Dumfries & Galloway Council

Address: Stranraer Museum, 55 George Street, Stranraer, Dumfries and Galloway DG9 7JP

Telephone: (01776) 705088

Fax: (01776) 705835

E-mail: johnpick@dumgal.gov.uk

Enquiries: The Museum Assistant, Mrs N. Goldsworthy

Open: Mon–Fri: 10.00–5.00; Sat: 10.00–1.00, 2.00–5.00.

Access: Generally open to the public, by appointment.

Historical background: Stranraer Museum was founded in 1939.

Acquisitions policy: Material from or relating to places, the environment, people and businesses within the Wigtown District.

Archives of organisation: Burgh archives of Stranraer, Wigtown, Newton Stewart and Whithorn, 16th century– . Some Wigtownshire County Council archives; Machars and Rhins councils administrative records; Commissioners of Police records.

Major collections: Business archives, including protocol books, 17th century– .
Collections of personal papers.

Non-manuscript material: Building warrant plans, late 1800s– .
Photograph collection.

Finding aids: Collections listed by NRAS; National Farmers' Union of Scotland, Wigtown area: NRA 24706.

Facilities: Photocopying.

1147 Shakespeare Birthplace Trust Records Office

Address: Henley Street, Stratford-upon-Avon, Warwickshire CV37 6QW

Telephone: (01789) 204016/201816 (direct line)

Fax: (01789) 296083

E-mail: records@shakespeare.org.uk

Website: www.shakespeare.org.uk

Enquiries: The Senior Archivist, Dr R. Bearman

Open: Mon–Fri: 9.30–1.00, 2.00–5.00;
Sat: (except before bank holidays) 9.30–12.30.

Access: Bona fide researchers.

Historical background: The records office was founded in the early 1860s, primarily as a repository for Shakespearean and allied material, but this limited objective was eclipsed at an early date on the rapid accumulation of documents relating to Stratford-upon-Avon and the surrounding district. It also acts as the Diocesan Record Office for Stratford and Shottery parishes, and is recognised as a place of deposit for public records.

Acquisitions policy: Until about 1945 the record office acted as a repository for any material from the locality which became available for deposit; as a result, not only Stratford-upon-Avon, but most places in Warwickshire and many in the neighbouring counties of Gloucestershire, Worcestershire and Oxfordshire are represented in the collections. Since c1945, with the expansion of neighbouring county offices, most acquisitions relate only to Stratford-upon-Avon and its immediate hinterland.

Major collections: Stratford-upon-Avon borough muniments.
Manorial records.
Warwickshire family collections: Ferrers of Baddesley Clinton; Throckmorton of Coughton Court; Gregory-Hood of Stivichal; Willoughby de Broke of Compton Verney; Leigh of Stoneleigh Abbey; Archer of Umberslade.
Robert Bell Wheler Collection: antiquarian papers, c1800–1820.
Records of Stratford-upon-Avon established and non-conformist churches; businesses and industries; clubs and societies.

Non-manuscript material: Large collection of topographical views (photographs, prints, drawings).
Local history and family history library, with usual reference collection on local history sources, including local newspapers.

Finding aids: Summary list of accessions reproduced by NRA and available in major libraries. Lists and persons, places and subjects indexes.

Facilities: Photocopying. Photography. Microfilm/fiche reader.

Conservation: In-house provision.

Publications: J.O. Halliwell: *A Descriptive Calendar of the Ancient Manuscripts and Records in the Possession of the Corporation of Stratford-upon-Avon* (1863).
L. Fox: 'Shakespeare's Birthplace Library, Stratford-upon-Avon', *Archives*, v/126 (1961), 90.
R. Bearman: *Shakespeare in the Stratford Records* (1994).

1148 Shoe Museum

Parent organisation: C. & J. Clark Ltd

Address: 40 High Street, Street, Somerset BA16 0YA

Telephone: (01458) 842169

Fax: (01458) 843110

E-mail: jean.brook@clarks.com

Enquiries: The Museum Administrator, Jean Brook
The Public Relations Manager, Mr John Keery

Open: Mon–Fri: 10.00–4.45.

Access: Bona fide researchers, by arrangement.

Historical background: Cyrus Clark (1801–66) and his brother James (1811–1906) formed a business partnership in 1833. A fellow Quaker loaned money to help the business in 1863, placing in control William Stephen Clark (1839–1925), who concentrated on footwear. In 1903 C. & J. Clark Ltd was incorporated as a private listed holding company. During the 1930s some retail shoe shops were acquired, including part of the Abbott chain, and the Peter Lord retailing firm was founded. In 1963 C. & J. Clark Ltd became a holding company and Clarks Ltd was set up as the UK manufacturing company. C. & J. Clark remains a private, family-run company.

Acquisitions policy: To maintain the archive, with limited acquisitions of material relating to footwear.

Archives of organisation: Archives of C. & J. Clark Ltd., 1825–1990, includes records of K. Shoes Ltd; Avalon Industries Ltd, 1960–93, and Street Estates/C. & J. Clark Properties, 1934– .

Major collections: Clark family papers, c1800– .

Non-manuscript material: Plans and photographs of company building projects.
Shoes, shoe machinery, shoe buckles.

Finding aids: Descriptive lists; card index.

Facilities: Photocopying. Photography.

Conservation: Contracted out.

Publications: K. Hudson: *Towards Precision Shoe Making* (Newton Abbott, 1968).
G.B. Sutton: *A History of Shoemaking in Street, Somerset: C. & J. Clark, 1833–1903* (York, 1979).

1149 Street Library

Parent organisation: Somerset County Council, Library Service

Address: 1 Leigh Road, Street, Somerset BA16 0HA

Telephone: (01458) 442032

Fax: (01458) 440195

Enquiries: The Area Librarian, Ms Sue Crawley

Open: Mon, Tues, Thurs: 9.30–5.00; Fri: 9.30–7.00; Sat: 9.30–4.00.
Closed Saturday preceding Easter Monday.

Access: Generally open to the public.

Historical background: The library was run privately by C. & J. Clark (shoe manufacturers) until 1959, and much archive material for the town is retained at their HQ, 40 High Street, Street.

Acquisitions policy: Occasional purchase of material on Laurence and Clemence Housman, who lived in the town for 30 years.

Archives of organisation: Stock accession registers, 1900–c1950.

Major collections: Housman Collection: correspondence of Laurence (1865–1959) and Clemence (1861–1955) Housman, brother and sister of A.E. Housman (1859–1936), with Roger and Sarah Clark, 1908–c1930; original sketches and writings; also correspondence with contemporary literary and artistic figures.

Non-manuscript material: First and other editions of publications of Laurence and Clemence Housman.

Finding aids: Catalogue and amendments.

Facilities: Photocopying. Microfilm/fiche readers.

1150 Gainsborough's House

Parent organisation: Gainsborough's House Society

Address: 46 Gainsborough Street, Sudbury, Suffolk CO10 2EU

Telephone: (01787) 372958

Fax: (01787) 376991

E-mail: mail@gainsborough.org

Website: www.gainsborough.org

Enquiries: The Curator, H.G. Belsey

Open: Easter–Oct: Tues–Sat: 10.00–5.00; Sun: 2.00–5.00.

Nov–Easter: Tues–Sat: 10.00–4.00; Sun: 2.00–4.00.

Access: Bona fide researchers, by appointment only.

Historical background: Gainsborough's House Society was founded in 1958 and the house was opened in 1961. It is a small art centre which has collected information about Thomas Gainsborough (1727–88) and his associates over this period.

Acquisitions policy: Material relating to Thomas Gainsborough.

Archives of organisation: Minutes and papers relating to the activities of the society (incomplete).

Major collections: Correspondence and other papers relating to Thomas Gainsborough, including two collections from the Lane Poole family, descendants of Thomas Gainsborough's sister, Susan Gardner.

Non-manuscript material: Photographs of paintings by Gainsborough and material relating to Sudbury.

Finding aids: Calendars and accession registers. NRA 33367.

Facilities: Photocopying. Photography. Microfiche reader.

Conservation: Contracted out.

Publications: *Annual Review* [includes references to new acquisitions].

1151 Sutton Archives and Local Studies

Parent organisation: London Borough of Sutton

Address: Central Library, St Nicholas Way, Sutton, Surrey SM1 1EA

Telephone: (020) 8770 4747

Fax: (020) 8770 4777

E-mail: local.studies@sutton.gov.uk

Website: www.sutton.gov.uk

Enquiries: The Borough Archivist and Local Studies Manager, Ms Kathleen Shawcross

Open: Tues: 2.00–5.00; Thurs: 9.30–7.30; Fri: 9.30–12.30; Sat (1st and 3rd): 9.30–1.00, 2.00–4.45; Sun (1st and 3rd): 2.00–5.00.

Appointments are necessary to view archives and use microform readers.

Access: Generally open to the public; an appointment is necessary and there is a booking system for microfiche readers. Usual restrictions apply to public records. A paid research service is available.

Historical background: The present borough includes the ancient parishes of Beddington and Wallington, Sutton and Cheam, and Carshalton, with small areas of Cuddington and Woodmansterne. The library service began in 1935 and a collection of local history material was started in the 1940s. Following local government reorganisation in 1965 the present local history collection was formed by the amalgamation of the collections for the ancient parishes. The archives are kept separately from the local studies collection and comprise primary source material from the 14th century relating only to the borough, with the exception of Wallington (previously Croydon) Magistrates Court records and copies of Surrey parish registers. The archives service is recognised as a place of deposit for public records, manorial and tithe archives and non-conformist records and is the Diocesan Record Office for the London Borough of Sutton.

Acquisitions policy: To preserve primary documentation relating to the London Borough of Sutton from the earliest times. Material is accepted from within the council as well as from private individuals, organisations and institutions.

Archives of organisation: Records of the London Borough of Sutton, its predecessors and constituent parishes, including rate books, minute books and poor records, 14th century– .

Major collections: Court rolls for the manors of Sutton, 1720–1907; and Carshalton, 1346–1701, 1834–1946; with financial papers, plans and deeds, 19th and 20th centuries.
Carshalton charities records, 1766–1940.
Parish registers, 1538– .
Non-conformist records, including Sutton Congregational Church, 1870–1960.
Phillips Collection relating to the Carew family of Beddington, 15th–17th centuries.
Dr Peatling Collection relating to Carshalton, including notes, pamphlets and cuttings, and transcriptions, 20th century.
River Wandle Collection of deeds relating to fishing rights and milling, 1640–1864.

Royal Female Orphanage, Beddington: minutes, pupil records and records of diphtheria epidemic, 1871–1968.

Non-manuscript material: Croydon Airport Collection, 1915– .
Photographs and glass negatives, 1860– (c20,000); slides (5000).
Microfiche of Surrey parish registers.
Early editions of Surrey maps.
Newspapers, 1863– ; newspapers and census returns (microfilm).
Films and tapes, including Sutton weekly talking newspaper, 1976– .
Oral history interviews and talks.

Finding aids: Catalogue with name, place and subject indexes. Calendar of Phillips papers. Surname indexes to censuses, 1841–81. Lists sent to NRA.

Facilities: Photocopying. Photograph copying. Microfilm/fiche readers/printers.

Conservation: In-house paper conservation with outside work undertaken.

Publications: Guide to Archive & Local Studies Collection.
Guide to Originals and Copies of Surrey Parish Registers Held.

1152 Oscott College Archives

Parent organisation: Archdiocese of Birmingham

Address: St Mary's College, Oscott, Sutton Coldfield, West Midlands B73 5AA

Telephone: (0121) 354 2490

Fax: (0121) 355 3422

Enquiries: The Archivist, Dr Judith Champ

Open: By arrangement.

Access: Bona fide scholars, by written appointment.

Historical background: Founded in 1794 as a joint public school and Catholic theological training college, from 1899 the college has been a seminary for the training of Catholic clergy.

Acquisitions policy: Small accrual of rectors' papers and material produced by students.

Archives of organisation: Administrative records from the college's foundation, although more survives, 1830s– ; includes account books, lecture notes of rectors, note-books of student societies and correspondence.

Non-manuscript material: Pugin plans. Victorian photographs.

Finding aids: Catalogue of early records held at the college. See also NRA 8129.

Facilities: Photocopying.

Publications: J. Champ: *Oscott* (1987) [no. 3 of a series produced by the Archdiocese of Birmingham Historical Commission].

1153 Swansea Museum

Parent organisation: City and County of Swansea

Address: Victoria Road, Swansea, West Glamorgan SA1 1SN

Telephone: (01792) 653763

Fax: (01792) 652585

Website: www.swansea.gov.uk/

Enquiries: The Museums Librarian, Mr Mike Gibbs

Open: By arrangement.

Access: Bona fide researchers, by appointment only.

Historical background: The Royal Institution of South Wales was established in 1835 and moved into its present building in 1841. It is the oldest museum in Wales and was taken over by the City and County of Swansea in 1991.

Acquisitions policy: Local history, and fields covered by the collection.

Archives of organisation: Records of the Royal Institution of South Wales, 1835– .

Major collections: Documents and deeds collected by the antiquarian Lt.-Col. George Grant Francis (1814–82).
Gabriel Powell's Survey of the Lordships of Gower and Kilvey, 1764.
Edward II's marriage contract, 1303.

Non-manuscript material: Photograph collections, including John Dillwyn Llewellyn, late 19th century.

Finding aids: Card index.

Facilities: Photocopying. Microfilm reader.

Conservation: Contracted out.

Publications: Minerva, 1993– [annual journal of the Royal Institution of South Wales].

1154 University of Wales Swansea
Library & Information Services

A Archives

Address: Singleton Park, Swansea, West Glamorgan SA2 8PP

Telephone: (01792) 295021

Fax: (01792) 295851

E-mail: e.bennett@swansea.ac.uk

Website: www.swan.ac.uk/lis/archives.htm

Enquiries: The Archivist, Mrs Elisabeth Bennett

Open: Mon–Fri: 9.15–12.45, 2.00–5.00; Tues evening: 6.00–9.30 (term).

Access: Open to the public; a prior arrangement is essential. Appointments for Tuesday evening must be made by 5p.m. on the previous Friday. Permission is required to use the St David's Priory records.

Historical background: The University College of Swansea was founded in 1920. The library archives department has been built up over the last four decades. In 1969 the South Wales Coalfield Archive was established to preserve the documentary records of the mining community of South Wales. This now forms part of the South Wales Coalfield Collection, which is split between the Archives and the South Wales Miners' Library (see B below).

Acquisitions policy: Documents which relate to existing material in the local collections and the South Wales Coalfield Archive Collection, or to University College Swansea, its research interests and prominent figures associated with it.

Archives of organisation: Minutes of Council, Senate, faculties and main committees, 1920– . Correspondence of Principal and Registrar, 1920–50.

Major collections: South Wales Coalfield Archive: a large number of separate collections, chiefly the records of the National Union of Mineworkers (South Wales area), formerly the South Wales Miners' Federation, and its lodges.

Also records of miners' welfare organisations, co-operative societies, political parties and individuals from all parts of the mining community. Corporation of Swansea medieval charters and administrative records, c1530–c1850.

Family, estate and topographical papers formerly held at the Royal Institution of South Wales, including the Mackworth and Dillwyn-Llewelyn families and George Grant Francis (1814–82), antiquarian.

Industrial records of metallurgical firms in the area.

Mumbles Railway minutes, financial records, parliamentary and legal papers, 1804–1959.

St David's Priory parochial registers and records, 1808–1982.

Swansea and Gower Methodist circuit records, excluding registers, 1859–1984.

Non-manuscript material: Large collection of local printed material. Swansea and Gower census returns, 1841–91 (microfilm).

Finding aids: Lists of collections, sent to NRA. SWCC website (see B below) gives item-level description of manuscripts, audiotapes, videotapes, photographs and banners not in printed guides.

Facilities: Photocopying. Photography. Microfilm/fiche readers.

Conservation: Contracted out.

Publications: D. Bevan: *Guide to the South Wales Coalfield Archive* (1980).

B South Wales Miners' Library

Address: Hendrefoelan House, Sketty, Swansea, West Glamorgan SA2 7NB

Telephone: (01792) 518603

Fax: (01792) 518693

E-mail: miners@swansea.ac.uk

Website: www.swan.ac.uk/lis/swcc

Enquiries: The Librarian, Ms Siân Williams

Open: Term: Mon–Fri: 10.30–1.00, 2.00–5.00. Vacation: Mon–Fri: 9.00–1.00, 2.00–5.00. During term time, the library is normally open some evenings. It is advisable to check on all opening times before visiting.

Access: Open to the public for reference purposes. A prior arrangement is preferred, and is essential for the use of audio-visual material.

Historical background: The South Wales Miners' Library was established in 1973 to house material collected by the Coalfield History Project and is now part of the University of Wales Swansea Library & Information Services. The material collected now forms part of the South Wales Coalfield Collection (SWCC), which is housed in the Archives (see above) and the South Wales Miners' Library.

Major collections: SWCC oral history collection: interviews with people from all parts of community. A wide range of printed material on history of the South Wales Coalfield, including a strong collection of pamphlets relating to the Spanish Civil War.

Finding aids: Lists of audio-visual material on SWCC website.

Facilities: Photocopying. Audio-visual facilities.

Publications: H. Francis: 'The Origins of the South Wales Miners' Library', *History Workshop: Journal of Socialist Historians*, No. 2 (Autumn, 1976).

1155 West Glamorgan Archive Service

Parent organisation: City and County of Swansea/Neath Port Talbot County Borough Council

Address: County Hall, Oystermouth Road, Swansea, West Glamorgan SA1 3SN

Telephone: (01792) 636589

Fax: (01792) 637130

E-mail: archives@swansea.gov.uk

Website: www.swansea.gov.uk/archives

Enquiries: The County Archivist, Miss S.G. Beckley

Open: Swansea: Mon–Thurs: 9.00–5.00; Mon evening: 5.30–7.30, by appointment. Neath: Tues–Fri: 9.00–5.00.

Access: Generally open to the public. Microfilm readers must be reserved in advance and a charge is made for microfilm use.

Historical background: The office was established in 1983 as a branch office of the Glamorgan Archive Service when West Glamorgan County Council built a new County Hall in Swansea. Documents relating to the West Glamorgan area were transferred from Cardiff to form the nucleus of the collection. In 1992 West Glamorgan County Council withdrew from the Glamorgan Joint Archive Service and established an independent county archive service. Since then the manuscript collections at Swansea, Neath and Port Talbot reference libraries have been transferred. The office holds ecclesiastical parish records from the West Glamorgan area of the Diocese of Swansea and Brecon. It is recognised as a place of deposit for public records. In 1996, following local government reorganisation, the office assumed responsibility for the collections of the former Swansea City Archives Office. Service points are operated at Port Talbot Library and at Neath Mechanics' Institute, where professional supervision is also given to Neath Antiquarian Society collections (which will be made available there after cataloguing).

Acquisitions policy: Archival material relating to the area of the county of West Glamorgan.

Archives of organisation: Usual local authority record holdings including records of Swansea City Council and its predecessors, 18th–20th centuries. (Earlier records are held by University of Wales Swansea Archives, see entry 1154A).

Major collections: Deposited local collections, including Neath Abbey Ironworks collection, containing plans, 1792–1892.

Non-manuscript material: Photographic collection relating to the Swansea area, c1850– (c55,000).

Finding aids: Major lists sent to NRA.

Facilities: Photocopying. Microfilm/fiche readers/printer.

Conservation: In-house facilities.

Publications: West Glamorgan Archive Service: a Guide to the Collections (1998).
List of books, booklets, maps and facsimiles available on request.

1156   Bible Society

Address: Stonehill Green, Westlea, Swindon, Wiltshire SN5 7DG

Telephone: (01793) 418100

Fax: (01793) 418118

E-mail: rodericki@bfbs.org.uk

Enquiries: The Senior Information Officer/ Archivist, Mrs Ingrid A. Roderick

Open: Mon–Fri: 9.00–5.00, by prior arrangement with the Senior Information Officer/ Archivist.

Access: Generally open to the public; there is a 75-year closure period.

The British and Foreign Bible Society was formed in 1804 'to encourage a wider circulation of the Holy Scriptures'. It was and remains a non-denominational voluntary society, financed by the donations of its supporters and involved in the translation, publication and distribution of the Bible and related Christian materials throughout the world. It was incorporated by royal charter in 1948. In 1985 the majority of materials predating 1960 were transferred to the Cambridge University Library (see entry 165), where the same access conditions apply. The society continues to accept material directly related to the work and staff of the society. There are manual and automated indexes and photocopying is available. See *Historical Catalogue of Manuscripts in Bible House Library* (1982).

1157   Burmah Castrol Archives Department

Parent organisation: Burmah Castrol plc

Address: Burmah Castrol House, Pipers Way, Swindon, Wiltshire SN3 1RE

Telephone: (01793) 452585/452419

Fax: (01793) 453136/513506

E-mail: vanna_skelley@burmahcastrol.com

Enquiries: The Group Archivist, Miss Vanna Skelley

Open: Mon–Fri: 10.00–4.00, by appointment only.

Access: At the discretion of the company: application should be made in writing to the Group Archivist.

Historical background: The Burmah Oil Company Ltd was incorporated in 1886 to develop the Burmese oilfields, which it left in 1963 when it undertook new exploration elsewhere. As a result of investing in exploration in Iran, it owned 23 per cent of British Petroleum until the 1970s. Rationalisation followed the oil crisis of 1974 and exploration was abandoned in 1986 to focus on lubricants.

Castrol was established in 1899 as C.C. Wakefield & Company Ltd, selling lubricants to a variety of industries. It became a public limited company in 1943 and was renamed Castrol Ltd in 1960. It was acquired by Burmah Oil in 1966.

In 2000 Burmah Castrol was acquired by BP Amoco (see entry 255).

Acquisitions policy: Most accessions result from records management, though outside gifts and deposits are occasionally accepted.

Archives of organisation: Business records of Burmah Oil, 1886-, Anglo-Ecuadorian Oilfields, 1919–75, Asram Oil, 1893–1980, Labitos Oilfields, 1908-, Manchester Oil Refinery (Holdings), 1930s–1970s, Burmese subsidiaries, 1937–63. Business records of C.C. Wakefield & Co. Ltd/Castrol, 1889– , also of acquired companies.

Non-manuscript material: Films, videos and an extensive photograph collection covering the oil industry in the Far East and Castrol's motor sport activity.
Packaging and promotional material.

Finding aids: Computer database, descriptive list, and company, name and subject indexes.

Facilities: Photocopying Photography. Microfilm reader/printer. Video/film viewer.

Publications: T.A.B. Corley: *A History of Burmah Oil Company Ltd*, Vol. 1: *1866–1924* (1983) and Vol. 2: *1924–1966* (1988).
B. Stockfield: 'The Burmah Oil Company Ltd: History and Archives to 1966', *Business Archives*, no. 58 (Nov 1989).

1158 National Monuments Record

Parent organisation: English Heritage

Address: National Monuments Record Centre, Kemble Drive, Swindon SN2 2GZ NMR London Search Room: 55 Blandford Street, London W1H 3AS, Swindon

Telephone: NMRC: (01793) 414600; London Search Room: (020) 7208 8200

Fax: NMRC: (01793) 414606; London Search Room: (020) 7208 8200

E-mail: nmrinfo@english-heritage.org.uk
nmrlondon@english-heritage.org.uk

Website: www.english-heritage.org.uk/ knowledge/nmr

Enquiries: Enquiry and Research Services

Open: Tues–Fri: 9.30–5.00.
Some Sats, please phone for details. Prior arrangement is strongly recommended.

Access: Open to the public. A range of enquiry services is available: see website or contact staff for further details. For more complicated or extensive searches a charged research service is available.

Historical background: Since 1999 the NMR has been the public archive of English Heritage. Under the title of the Historic Buildings and Monuments Commission, English Heritage was established in 1984 with two main responsibilities: the preservation of England's architectural and archaeological heritage; and the management of more than 400 monuments and buildings previously in the care of the Department of the Environment. In 1986 EH took over the conservation work carried out by the Greater London Council Historical Buildings Division, and in 1999 it merged with the Royal Commission on the Historical Monuments of England to form a single lead body for the historic environment.
Before the merger the NMR had been part of the RCHME, which was founded in 1908 'to make an inventory of the Ancient and Historical Monuments and Constructions connected with or illustrative of the contemporary culture, civilisation and conditions of life of the people in England'. The RCHME carried out this brief through its own survey and publication activities and through acquiring external collections which documented the historic environment. In 1963 the National Buildings Record, founded in 1941 to record the nation's architectural heritage, was amalgamated with the RCHME, and in 1983 the commission also took responsibility for the archaeological functions and records of the Ordnance Survey. A significant part of the air photo library of the Department of the Environment was transferred to RCHME in 1985, and in 1986 the Survey of London became part of the organisation.
The current record holdings of English Heritage relate to its own statutory and management responsibilities and are working papers rather than archives. The records relate to scheduled ancient monuments, listed historic buildings, conservation areas and gardens. They

include deeds and research reports in addition to the working files. Access is by prior arrangement as not all material is open to the public. Contact Fiona Sims, Records Management Services (020) 7973 3009. English Heritage is also responsible for the management of the Greater London Sites and Monuments Record. Contact David Eve (020) 7973 3731.

Acquisitions policy: Records in all formats documenting the historic environment of England, including both the architectural and the archaeological heritage.

Archives of organisation: Records of RCHME architectural and archaeological survey work, 1908–99.
Holdings and administrative records of National Buildings Record, 1941–63.
Survey records of Ordnance Survey archaeology section, c1945–83.
Survey of London records, 1894– .
Contents of English Heritage Historic Plans Room, c1740– .

Major collections: NMR contains material in a wide range of formats, but the bulk is photographic and graphical in nature. Material relating to the Greater London area is held at the London branch.

Non-manuscript material: Major architectural photography collections include those of Henry Taunt, c1880–1920; Eric de Mare, 1945–80; York and Son, c1870–1910; Bedford Lemere, c1870–1925; Alfred Newton and Son, 1896–1920; *Country Life*, 1897–1960s; Property Services Agency, 1950–90; Hallam Ashley, c1930–80; Henry Dixon, c1870–1910.
Archaeology collections include OS site records cards, c1945–1983; the archives of the Medieval Village Research Group, and papers of several archaeologists, notably Lily F. Chitty, H. St George Gray and Helen O'Neil.
Vertical air photo collections include full coverage of England, 1946–8, by the RAF; OS aerial photography, 1952–79; and photography, taken by Meridian Airmaps, 1952–84.
Oblique air photo collections include RCHME photography, 1967– , and material taken by a number of independent regional air photographers.
Specialist library for English architecture and archaeology; an extensive collection of microfilms of archaeology archives; digital data sets describing England's archaeological and architectural heritage.

Finding aids: Hard-copy and digital catalogues to some individual collections are available. Indexes are primarily topographical.

Facilities: Photocopying, photography and laser copying services.

Conservation: In-house conservation facilities.

Publications: EH *Annual Report.*
An EH publications catalogue is available on request.

1159 Swindon Library

Address: Regent Circus, Swindon, Wiltshire SN1 1QG

Telephone: (01793) 463240

Fax: (01793) 541319

E-mail: swindonref@swindon.gov.uk

Enquiries: The Reference Librarian

Open: Mon–Thurs: 9.00–8.00; Fri: 9.00–5.00; Sat: 9.00–4.00.

Access: Generally open to the public. Visitors who wish to use microfilm/fiche readers should telephone beforehand.

Historical background: The public library service in Wiltshire comprises (since 1974) the former Wiltshire County Library, Swindon Library (successor to the Great Western Railway Mechanics' Institute Library) and Salisbury City Library. The archaeological sites and monuments record for Wiltshire, with more than 2000 archival aerial photographs of archaeological features, is maintained on computer database at Wiltshire Library and Museum Service HQ, Bythesea Road, Trowbridge, Wilts BA14 8BS. Its use is restricted to bona fide researchers. The collection of Alfred Williams (1877–1930), poet and author, has been transferred to Wiltshire and Swindon Record Office, Trowbridge (see entry 1172). Since local government reorganisation in 1997 Swindon Reference Library is the Swindon location of the Wiltshire and Swindon Record Office. An archivist is in attendance once a month.

Acquisitions policy: Archival material is not now acquired, such material being directed to the Wiltshire and Swindon Record Office.

Major collections: Great Western Railway: administrative and miscellaneous papers relating to the locomotive works and GWR generally (58 items).

Non-manuscript material: Local studies material in various media, including illustrations, maps, ephemera, newspapers and a few sound recordings as well as books and periodicals.
Census enumerators' books, 1841–91; some records, principally minute books, of the Old and New Swindon local boards and UDCs.
Microfiche copies of the parish registers and bishop's transcripts for the parishes which comprise the Borough of Swindon and electoral registers for these parishes, 1832–1900.

Finding aids: A computerised catalogue of local studies holdings.

Facilities: Photocopying. Microfilm/fiche readers/printer.

1160   WH Smith Archive

Parent organisation: WH Smith Archive Trust

Address: Greenbridge   Road,   Swindon, Wiltshire SN3 3LD

Telephone: (01793) 616161

Enquiries: The Consultant Archivist, Mr Tim Baker-Jones

Open: By appointment only.

Access: Bona fide researchers. Thirty-year closure except by special permission. The Trust reserves the right to refuse access.

Historical background: The family business started in London in 1792, and was called WH Smith & Son from 1846 and WH Smith & Son Ltd from 1929. It became the trading subsidiary of a public company, WH Smith & Son (Holdings) Ltd, in 1949. The styles changed to WH Smith Group plc and WH Smith Ltd in 1988. The Trust was established in 1998 when family and business documents were placed with it.

Acquisitions policy: Maintains its own archives only.

Archives of organisation: WH Smith records including retail and wholesale business documents, 1792– .
Smith Estate papers, mainly family deeds of title, in Berkshire, Buckinghamshire, Devon and Suffolk, medieval– .

Major collections: Bowes & Bowes, Cambridge booksellers, records, 1843–1953.

Hambleden Papers, mainly personal/political correspondence of the Rt. Hon. W.H. Smith MP (1825–91).

Non-manuscript material: Photographs and plans.

Finding aids: Lists for Bowes & Bowes records, Hambleden papers, Smith Estate. Papers sent to NRA.
List and index for WH Smith records.

Facilities: Photocopying and photography at discretion of consultant archivist.

Conservation: Contracted out

Publications: H.E. Maxwell: *Life & Times of the Rt. Hon. W.H. Smith MP* (1893).
G.R. Pocklington: *The Story of W.H. Smith & Son* (1921; rev. 1932, 1937, 1949, 1955).
E.A. Ackers-Douglas, 3rd Viscount Chilston: *W.H. Smith* (1965).
B.J. Loasby: *The Swindon Project* (1965)
C.H. Wilson: *First with the News* (1985).
T.W. Baker-Jones: 'The Archives of W.H. Smith & Son Ltd', *Business Archives* No. 54 (November 1987).

1161   Somerset Archive and Record Service

Parent organisation: Somerset County Council

Address: Somerset Record Office, Obridge Road, Taunton, Somerset TA2 7PU

Telephone: (01823) 337600 (appointments only); 278805 (enquiries and staff)

Fax: (01823) 325402

E-mail: somerset_archives@compuserve.com

Website: www.somerset.gov.uk

Enquiries: The County Archivist, Mr Adam Green

Open: Mon: 2.00–4.50; Tues–Thurs: 9.00–4.50; Fri: 9.00–4.20;
Sat (occasional): 9.15–12.15.
Closed for two weeks beginning the last Monday of January.

Access: All but a few restricted classes are available for consultation by the public, by appointment.

Historical background: Archives were first housed in a repository in 1929 and a professional archivist was appointed in 1935. The office acts as the Diocesan Record Office for the Diocese of Bath and Wells and is recognised as a place of deposit for public records. It also houses the document collection of the Somerset Archaeological and Natural History Society.

Acquisitions policy: Archives illustrative of the history and heritage of Somerset, also covering the pre-1974 county (except Bath and North-East Somerset from 1996).

Archives of organisation: Usual local authority holdings: the archives and modern records of Somerset County Council.

Major collections: Deposited collections, including the following which have a wider significance:

Dickinson MSS: merchants' accounts etc relating to Jamaica and trade with the Americas and the Baltic, 18th century.

Tudway MSS concerning the family estate on Antigua, late 17th–20th centuries.

Helyar MSS: Jamaican estate papers, c1660–1713.

Phelips MSS: political papers, mainly of Sir Robert Phelips, early-mid–17th century.

Papers of: William Kirkpatrick relating to India, 1787–1811; John Strachey, historian and scientist, early 18th century; Sir William Joliffe, politician, 1845–66; Edward Lear (1812–88), 1847–86; John Braham (1774–1856), singer, early 19th century; Chichester Fortescue, Lord Carlingford, politician, 1854–90; Hon. Aubrey Herbert, relating to Albania and the Near East, c1900–23.

Non-manuscript material: Oral history recordings.

Finding aids: Catalogues; those of more significant collections sent to NRA. Name, place (including manorial) and subject indexes compiled from catalogues of holdings. Indexes to 1851 census; marriages, 1754–1837; marriage licences, 1765– ; and apprenticeship, settlement and bastardy papers (all in progress).

Facilities: Photocopying. Microfilm/fiche readers.

Conservation: Full in-house paper repair service; outside work undertaken.

Publications: Guide to Sources for Family and House History.

Website is most comprehensive guide.

1162 United Kingdom Hydrographic Office
Data Centre

Parent organisation: Ministry of Defence

Address: Admiralty Way, Taunton, Somerset TA1 2DN

Telephone: (01823) 337900 ext. 3670

Fax: (01823) 284077

E-mail: csm@hdc.hydro.gov.uk

Website: www.ukho.gov.uk

Enquiries: The Research Manager, Hydrographic Data Centre

Open: Mon–Fri: 9.00–5.00, by appointment. Closed for civil service concession days.

Access: Bona fide researchers, on written application. A paid research service is available.

Historical background: The Hydrographic Office was established in 1795 to supply navigational charts to the navy. It is recognised as a place of deposit for public records.

Acquisitions policy: Continual addition of the results of hydrographic surveys and other worldwide hydrographic documents and information.

Archives of organisation: Documents entrusted to the care of the Hydrographic Office by the Admiralty in 1795.

Reports, correspondence and record copies of charts, sailing directions and other Hydrographic Office publications, 1795– .

Non-manuscript material: Charts, plans, maps, coastal views and photographs.

Finding aids: Graphic indexes. Catalogues. Geographical and numerical listings.

Facilities: Photocopying. Photography. Microfilm/fiche readers.

Conservation: In-house service.

Publications: A. Day: *The Admirality Hydrographic Service, 1795–1919.*

R.O. Morris: *Charts and Surveys in Peace and War (The History of the RN Hydrographic Service, 1919–1970).*

1163 Tenby Museum and Art Gallery

Address: Castle Hill, Tenby, Pembrokeshire SA70 7BP

Telephone: (01834) 842809

Fax: (01834) 842809

E-mail: tenbymuseum@hotmail.com

Website: www.virtualtenby.co.uk/museum.htm

Enquiries: The Hon. Curator, John Beynon

Open: Tues–Fri: 10.00–12.30, 2.00–4.00.

Access: Generally open to the public; 7 days' notice is required.

Historical background: Founded in 1878, the museum is still housed in its original building. It is an independent, registered charity, affiliated to the National Galleries & Museums of Wales.

Acquisitions policy: Acquires material relevant to the collections of local interest.

Archives of organisation: Minute books, 1878– .

Major collections: Corporate estates of the Tenby area.
Local archaeology and geology.
Papers of local historians and former Hon. Curator, Arthur Leach, 1940s.

Non-manuscript material: Photograph and postcard collections; supporting library collection.

Finding aids: Card index. NRA 29328 Tenby Borough. NRA 29329 MS collections.

Facilities: Photocopying. Microfilm/fiche readers.

Publications: Guide to Archives in preparation.

1164 Ellen Terry Memorial Museum

Parent organisation: The National Trust

Address: Smallhythe Place, Tenterden, Kent TN30 7NG

Telephone: (01580) 762334

Fax: (01580) 762334

E-mail: ksmxxx@smtp.ntrust.org.uk

Enquiries: The Custodian, Mrs Margaret Weare

Open: Nov–Feb: Mon–Fri: 9.00–5.00, by appointment.

Access: Generally open to the public; a fee is charged.

Historical background: The museum was opened in 1929 and made over to the National Trust by Ellen Terry's daughter, Edith Craig, in 1939. It was the home of the actress Ellen Terry (1847–1928) from 1899 to1928.

Acquisitions policy: Only proven personal items of Ellen Terry and letters to or from her.

Major collections: Correspondence of Ellen Terry and her personal library.

Non-manuscript material: Photographs. Playbills, theatre programmes, c1847–1947.

Finding aids: Catalogue of the correspondence in progress.

Facilities: Photocopying. Photography by arrangement.

Conservation: National Trust conservators.

1165 Ancient House Museum

Parent organisation: Norfolk Museums Service

Address: White Hart Street, Thetford, Norfolk IP24 1AA

Telephone: (01842) 752599

Fax: (01842) 752599

E-mail: oliver.bone.mus@norfolk.gov.uk

Enquiries: The Curator, Mr Oliver Bone

Open: Mon–Fri: 10.00–5.00.

Access: Generally open to the public, by appointment.

Historical background: The Ancient House Museum was founded in 1924 by Thetford Borough Council following the donation to the town of the building by Prince Frederick Duleep Singh (1867–1926). Since 1974 it has been part of the Norfolk Museums Service, a joint district and county council service.

Acquisitions policy: The museum collects material relating to the local history and archaeology of Thetford and surrounding parishes.

Archives of organisation: Accessions registers for the museum and its predecessor Mechanics' Institute, and correspondence with donors, 1924-, minutes of governing body, 1974-, posters relating to events and press cuttings, mainly 1974– .

Major collections: Duleep Singh Collection: manuscripts, personalia, maps, portraits, prints, watercolours.

Non-manuscript material: Plans, drawings, photographs and maps.

Finding aids: Card index. Computerised catalogue in progress.

Facilities: Photocopying. Photography.

Conservation: Paper conservation available in-house; some outside work is undertaken.

1166 Blundell's School

Address: Tiverton, Devon EX16 4DN

Telephone: (01884) 252543

Fax: (01884) 243232

E-mail: info@blundells.org

Enquiries: The Archivist, Mr T.H.C. Noon/Mr Jenkins

Open: School term, by appointment only.

Access: Bona fide researchers, on application to the Archivist.

Historical background: The school was founded in 1604 and its records have accumulated since then. There has been an organised muniment room since before World War II.

Acquisitions policy: We accept anything of local/school importance.

Archives of organisation: Various wills and deeds relating to Peter Blundell (1520–1601), merchant and endower of the school, and the Feoffees of his Good Uses in Tiverton, 1456– . Order books of feoffees, 1660– ; Great Account Book of Peter Blundell's Good Uses, 1610-1847, and three volumes since; register of pupils, 1770– ; register/minutes of old boys, 1775–1850, 1870– ; *Blundellian* (school magazine), 1861–6; 1877– .
Records relating to the 'Case in Chancery', 1839–46.

Non-manuscript material: Collection of watercolour portraits of Tivertonians by George Capron, c1840–50. Various etchings/prints of old school and new school.
Tiverton Gazette, 1890–1939.

Finding aids: The collections are catalogued for the most part.

Facilities: Photocopying. Photography.

1167 Isle of Mull Museum

Address: Columba Buildings, Tobermory, Isle of Mull PA75 6NY

Enquiries: The Librarian, B.B. Whittaker

Open: Easter–mid-Oct: Mon–Fri: 10.00–4.00; Sat: 10.00–1.00.
Mid-Oct–Easter: by arrangement.

Access: Generally open to the public on payment of Museum Association membership fee. An appointment is necessary during the museum closure period.

Acquisitions policy: To collect and keep material of historic interest to the Isle of Mull, adjacent islands and the nearby mainland, particularly Morven and Ardnamurchan.

Major collections: Solicitors' and tradesmen's papers and legal documents relating to Mull, mid-19th century– .
Records of Alexander Crawford Trust, 1854-1911; George Willison (1741–97) Trust, and British Fisheries Society, early-mid-19th century.
Macquarie papers, 1846–86.

Non-manuscript material: Maps, plans and photographic collection.

Finding aids: Subject index.

Facilities: Photography. Photocopying.

Conservation: By Scottish Museum Council.

Publications: Isle of Mull Museum Archive List (1999).

1168 Torquay Museum

Parent organisation: Torquay Natural History Society

Address: 529 Babbacombe Road, Torquay, Devon TQ1 1HG

Telephone: (01803) 293975

Fax: (01803) 294186

Enquiries: The Curator, Ms R.M. Palmer

Open: Mon–Sat: 10.00–4.45; Sun: 1.30–4.45.

Access: Strictly by appointment.

Historical background: The Torquay Natural History Society was founded in 1844 for the study of the natural sciences. Its primary aim was the establishment of a natural history library, but in the following year a museum to illustrate Devonian natural history was also set up.

Acquisitions policy: To acquire material illustrative of natural history, archaeology, anthropology, history, folklore and the industrial and fine arts, especially in relation to the Torquay area.

Archives of organisation: Records of the society, including annual reports, 1845– ; *Journal* and *Transactions*, 1909– .

Major collections: Papers of William Pengelly (1812–94), founder member, honorary secretary and president; and of Father John MacEnery, particularly concerning the study of Kent's Cavern.
Hester Pengelly Collection of autograph letters.

Non-manuscript material: Hambling Collection of photographs (*c*3500).
Torquay Directory, 1846–1948.

Finding aids: Complete index of pictorial records. Catalogue in preparation.

Facilities: Photocopying. Photography by arrangement.

1169 Torquay Reference Library

Parent organisation: Torbay Library Services

Address: Lymington Road, Torquay, Devon TQ1 3DT

Telephone: (01803) 208305

Fax: (01803) 208307

E-mail: reflib@torbay.gov.uk

Enquiries: The Reference and Information Librarian, Anne Howard

Open: Mon, Wed, Fri: 9.30–7.00; Tues: 9.30–5.00; Thurs: 9.30–1.00; Sat: 9.30–4.00.

Access: Generally open to the public; prior enquiry is advisable.

Historical background: Torbay Library Services operated as an independent library authority before local government reorganisation in 1974 when it became part of Devon Library Services. Torbay was established as a Unitary Authority in 1998 and again operates as an independent library authority.

Acquisitions policy: To acquire MSS that reflect the development of the Torbay area. Certain categories of records, such as parish registers and school board records, have been transferred to the Devon Record Office, Exeter (see entry 365).

Major collections: Archives of the predecessor authorities of Torbay District Council, including Torbay, Paignton, Brixham, Churston Ferrers, St Marychurch, Cockington and Tormohun.

Non-manuscript material: A good local studies collection, including illustrations, maps, newspapers and cutting files.

Facilities: Photocopying. Microform reader/printers.

Publications: J.R Pike: *Torquay, Torbay: a Bibliographical Guide* (Torquay, 1973).
Similiar guides to Brixham (1973) and Paignton (1974).

1170 Dartington Hall Records Office

Parent organisation: Dartington Hall Trust

Address: High Cross House, Dartington Hall, Totnes, Devon TQ9 6ED

Telephone: (01803) 864114

Fax: (01803) 867057

E-mail: high.cross.house@dartingtonhall.org.uk

Website: www.dartington.u-net.com/#highcross

Enquiries: The Curator/Archivist, Angie St John Palmer
The Archive Assistant, Yvonne Widger

Open: By arrangement.

Access: Bona fide researchers, by appointment.

Historical background: Dartington was founded in 1925 by Leonard (1893-1974) and Dorothy (*b*1887) Elmhirst, who established a programme of rural regeneration on the estate and funded various pioneering educational and artistic ventures. It received many refugees from Nazi Germany during the 1930s.

Acquisitions policy: To consolidate the archives of the Dartington Hall Trust.

Archives of organisation: Records of the Dartington Hall Trust, including estate documents and plans, 1925– .
Papers of Leonard and Dorothy Elmhirst.

Major collections: Correspondence files of staff, visitors, students and those connected with the arts, including Benjamin Britten (1913–76); Cecil Collins (1908–89); Barbara Hepworth (1903–75); Imogen Holst (1907–84); Aldous Huxley (1894–1963); Rudolph Laban (*d* 1958); Bernard Leach (1887–1979); William Lescaze (1896–1969); Henry Moore (1898–1986); A.S. Neill (1883–1973); Winifred Nicholson (1893–1981); Ben Nicholson (1894–1982); Sean O'Casey (1884–1964); Rabindranath Tagore (1861–1941); Willi Soukop (1907–95); Mark Tobey (1890–1976); Arthur Waley (1889–1966) and H.G. Wells (1866–1946).

Non-manuscript material: Photographs of individuals and of all aspects of the estate; film and video collections; tape-recordings.

Finding aids: Catalogue.

Facilities: Photocopying. Photography.

Conservation: In-house bookbinder; conservation work contracted out.

Publications: M. Young: *The Elmhirsts of Dartington: the Creation of a Utopian Community* (London, 1982).

1171 Treorchy Library

Parent organisation: Rhondda-Cynon-Taff County Borough Council (Education Department)

Address: Station Road, Treorchy CF42 6NN

Telephone: (01443) 773204

Fax: (01443) 777047

E-mail: nick.e.kelland@rhondda-cynon-taff.gov.uk

Website: www.rhondda-cynon-taff.gov.uk

Enquiries: Mr Nick Kelland

Open: Mon–Thurs: 9.30–5.15; Fri: 1.00–8.00; Sat: 9.00–12.00.

Access: Generally open to the public.

Historical background: The Library Acts were adopted in 1933 but the service commenced in 1939. In 1996 the area served by Rhondda Borough Council became part of Rhondda-Cynon-Taff County Borough Council.

Acquisitions policy: To collect any material relating to the Rhondda Valleys.

Major collections: Various MSS and archival collections of local history interest, including Welsh Congregational Church records.

Non-manuscript material: Music scores and literature in the Welsh collection.
Rhondda area OS maps, photographs and census, 1841–91 (microfilm).
Burial registers, 1877– , for municipal cemeteries in Rhondda.
Rhondda Leader, 1897– ; *Western Mail,* 1947– ; and *South Wales Echo,* 1987– (microfilm).

Finding aids: Local history catalogue.

Facilities: Photocopying. Microfilm/fiche readers/printers.

Conservation: Contracted out.

1172 Wiltshire and Swindon Record Office

Parent organisation: Wiltshire County Council in association with Swindon Borough Council

Address: Libraries & Heritage HQ, Bythesea Road, Trowbridge, Wiltshire BA14 8BS

Telephone: (01225) 713709

Fax: (01225) 713993

E-mail: wsro@wiltshire.gov.uk

Website: www.wiltshire.gov.uk/heritage/html/records_archives.html

Enquiries: The Principal, Mr J. N. d'Arcy

Open: Mon, Tues, Thurs, Fri: 9.15–5.00; Wed: 9.15–7.45.
Closed last fortnight in January.

Access: Generally open to the public. The office operates the CARN reader's ticket system.

Historical background: The office was established in 1947. Previously, the Wiltshire Archaeological Society collected material and this was incorporated in 1947. When the Salisbury Diocesan Office was closed in 1980 the great majority of records was transferred to Wiltshire Record Office. Salisbury District Council Muniment Room records were transferred in 1982. Following local government reorganisation the office was renamed and a local service is now provided at Swindon Library (see entry 1159). The office is the Diocesan Record Office for Salisbury and also

Bristol (Wiltshire parish records). It is recognised as a place of deposit for public records.

Acquisitions policy: To maintain archives of the local authority and acquire archival material relating to the area.

Archives of organisation: Usual local authority holdings.

Major collections: Deposited local collections, including records from Wilton House, Salisbury Museum Collection and Wiltshire Archaeological Society.

Facilities: Photocopying. Photography and microfilming by arrangement. Microfilm reader/printer.

Conservation: A full in-house service, including advice to owners of archives.

Publications: M.G. Rathbone: *Guide to the Records in the Custody of the Clerk of the Peace for Wiltshire* (1959).
P.M. Stewart: *Guide to the Records of the Bishop, the Archdeacons of Salisbury and Wiltshire* (1973).

1173 Cornwall County Record Office

Parent organisation: Cornwall County Council

Address: County Hall, Truro, Cornwall TR1 3AY

Telephone: (01872) 323127

Fax: (01872) 270340

E-mail: cro@cornwall.gov.uk

Website: www.cornwall.gov.uk

Enquiries: The County Archivist, Paul Brough

Open: Tues–Thurs: 9.30–5.00; Fri: 9.00–4.30; Sat: 9.00–12.00.
Closed the Saturday preceding every bank holiday; enquire for December stock–taking closure. An appointment is necessary.

Access: Generally open to the public. The office operates the CARN reader's ticket system. Documents may be ordered in advance of a visit.

Historical background: The office was established in 1951. New premises were provided in 1965 and substantially extended in 1988. It also acts as the Diocesan Record Office for Truro and is recognised as a place of deposit for public records.

Acquisitions policy: Historical material relating to the county of Cornwall, with special responsibility for mining records and maps.

Archives of organisation: Usual local authority record holdings.

Major collections: Deposited collections, primarily of local interest, including Truro Cathedral and Arundell archives, mining records and maps; Methodist and Quaker archives; substantial landed estate collections.

Finding aids: Catalogues, indexes; published guides and handbooks. Major catalogues sent to NRA.

Facilities: Photocopying. Photography by arrangement. Microform reader/printer.

Conservation: Full in-house service.

Publications: Series of free information leaflets available (send SAE), including list of publications (no. 3).
Guide to Sources (1995).
List of Accessions (1981/2–) [annual]
Sources for Cornish Family History (rev. 1997).
Guide to Probate Records (rev. 1996).

1174 Courtney Library and Cornish History Archive

Parent organisation: The Royal Institution of Cornwall

Address: River Street, Truro, Cornwall TR1 2SJ

Telephone: (01872) 272205

Fax: (01872) 240514

E-mail: courtney.rcmric@btinternet.com

Website: www.cornwall-online.co.uk/ric

Enquiries: The Librarian, Angela Broome
The Hon. Archivist, H.L. Douch

Open: Mon–Fri: 10.00–1.00, 2.00–5.00.

Access: Generally open to the public; an appointment is recommended. A paid research service is available.

Historical background: Founded in 1818, the institution sponsored a museum from the beginning. The muniment room was added in 1936 and in 1990 its contents were transferred to a modern archive and book store. An additional newly built archive store with computerised environmental control system was completed in 1998. Until 1951 the institution was the official repository for historic documents in Cornwall.

Acquisitions policy: All types of material, including local historians' collections, relating to the history of Cornwall and the culture of its people.

Archives of organisation: Records of the institution, including minutes, 1818– ; letter-books, 1905–38; accession lists, accounts and building plans, 19th and 20th centuries.

Major collections: Charles Henderson Collection: Cornish family estate documents, medieval–17th century.
Couch Family of Polperro and Fowey Collection, 18th and 19th centuries.
Shaw Collection *re* Cornish Methodism.
Hamilton-Jenkin Collection of mine-plans and mine account-books, 18th–19th centuries.
Enys Collection of autographs, many of national importance.
Richard Trevithick and Jonathan Hornblower, correspondence with Davies Gilbert, mainly *re* steam-engines.

Non-manuscript material: Cornish photograph collection, 19th and 20th centuries (*c*40,000).
Heard of Truro, printers, job-work, including posters, 1830s–1840s.
Local newspapers: *Royal Cornwall Gazette,* 1801–1951; *West Briton,* 1810–56.
Microfilms of parish registers, about half the ancient parishes, mainly those in the west.

Finding aids: Catalogues of all collections. Place, name and various subject indexes.

Facilities: Photocopying. Microfilm/fiche readers/printer.

Conservation: Contracted out.

Publications: Annual *Journal* of the Royal Institution of Cornwall.
Newsletter [bi-annual].
Leaflets: *Transcripts and Microfilms of Cornish Parish Registers*; *Sources for Maritime Research*; *Non-Anglican Registers: Cornwall.*

1175 Truro School

Address: Trennick Lane, Truro, Cornwall TR1 1TH

Telephone: (01872) 272763

Fax: (01872) 223431

Website: www.truro-school.cornwall.sch.uk

Enquiries: The Director of Studies, Mr Nigel Baker

Open: Mon–Fri: 9.00–4.30.

Access: Bona fide researchers, by appointment. Records may not always be accessible during school holidays.

Historical background: Founded as the Wesleyan Middle Class School for Boys in 1880, its name was changed to Truro College and then in 1931 to Truro School.

Acquisitions policy: To maintain the school's archives.

Archives of organisation: Minutes of governors' and staff meetings; register of pupils; fee books; accounts, 1880– . School magazine and photographs.

Facilities: Photocopying.

Publications: N.J. Baker (ed.): *Truro School Centenary Booklet* (1980).

1176 Museum of Rugby

Parent organisation: Rugby Football Union

Address: Twickenham Stadium, Twickenham, Middlesex TW1 1DZ

Telephone: (020) 8892 8877

Fax: (020) 8892 2817

E-mail: museum@rfu.com

Website: www.rfu.com

Enquiries: The Curator, Jed Smith
The Librarian, Rex King

Open: Library: Mon–Fri: 10.00–5.00, by arrangement.

Access: Bona fide researchers, by prior appointment.

The English Rugby Football Union is an amateur association founded in 1871 in London. The museum and library were opened in 1984, but memorabilia has been collected throughout the union's existence, and there is the only complete set of *Football Annuals,* 1865– . The archives comprise a fairly complete set of minutes, 1871– , and correspondence. Following major rebuilding the Museum of Rugby opened in 1996, providing a multimedia display environment for the world's largest and most comprehensive collection of Rugby Union memorabilia.

1177 St Mary's Strawberry Hill

Parent organisation: University of Surrey

Address: Information Resources Centre, St Mary's University College, Waldegrave Road, Twickenham, Middlesex TW1 4SX

Telephone: (020) 8240 4309

Fax: (020) 8240 4270

E-mail: lecorea@mailnt.smuc.ac.uk

Enquiries: The College Archives, Adrian LeCore

Open: Mon–Fri: 9.00–5.00, by arrangement only.

Access: Open to members of the public.

Historical background: The college was founded in 1850 to train Catholic teachers for Catholic schools. It removed from Hammersmith to Strawberry Hill in 1925. In 1972 the college diversified and began to provide general degrees in humanities and sciences as well as teaching degrees. Its degrees were originally validated by London University but are now validated by the University of Surrey.

Acquisitions policy: To maintain the collections.

Archives of organisation: Archives of the college.

Major collections: Leigh Bequest: books and MSS on medieval philosophy donated by Dr Yolanthe Leigh, including research papers relating mainly to Duns Scotus.
Anthony West (*d* 1993) Bequest: MSS and research papers, concerned mainly with Irish history and literature.

Facilities: Photocopying. Microfilm reader/printers.

1178 Laurel and Hardy Museum

Address: 4c Upper Brook Street, Ulverston, Cumbria LA12 7LA

Telephone: (01229) 582292

Website: www.geocities.com

Enquiries: The Curator

Open: By appointment.

Access: Generally open to the public.

Since the early 1970s a private collection of material built up by Bill Cubin, the first curator, relating to the film comedians Stan Laurel (1890–1965) and Oliver Hardy (1892–1957) has been built up. This includes personal scrapbooks, letters, films, photographs and audiovisual tapes. The collection is being actively augmented by purchase.

1179 Brunel University Library

Address: Kingston Lane, Uxbridge, Middlesex UB8 3PH

Telephone: (01895) 274000 ext. 2787

Fax: (01895) 203263

E-mail: library@brunel.ac.uk

Website: www.brunel.ac.uk/depts/lib/

Enquiries: The Special Collections Librarian, Mr K.C. Rudd

Open: Term: Mon–Thurs: 9.00–9.00; Fri: 9.00–7.00; Sat: 9.30–1.00; Sun: 2.00–7.00.
Vacation: Mon–Fri: 9.00–5.00.

Access: Bona fide researchers.

Historical background: The university developed from the College of Advanced Technology, Acton, London, and received its royal charter in 1966. See also entry 475.

Archives of organisation: Minutes and other records of the university, *c*1960– .

Major collections: Transport history collections of the following railway historians: Harold Borley (1895–1989), Charles Clinker (1906–83), David Garnett (1909–84), Stuart Leslie Kear and John Palmer.
Working-class autobiographies, 1800–1945 (*c*400).

Non-manuscript material: Railway photographic collections of Charles Clinker, Charles Mowat and Chris Wookey.

Finding aids: Lists of photographs, maps and railway clearing house material.

Facilities: Photocopying. Microfilm/fiche readers.

Publications: Railway Maps and the Railway Clearing House: the David Garnett Collection in Brunel University Library (1986).

1180 Hillingdon Heritage Service

Parent organisation: London Borough of Hillingdon

Address: Central Library, 14–15 High Street, Uxbridge, Middlesex UB8 1HD

Telephone: (01895) 250702

Fax: (01895) 239794, 811164

E-mail: clib@lbhill.gov.uk

Enquiries: The Local Heritage Coordinator, Mrs C Cotton

Open: Mon: 9.30–8.00; Tues–Thurs: 1.00–5.30; Fri: 10.30–5.30; Sat: 9.30–12.00, 1.00–4.00.

Access: Generally open to the public; an appointment is preferred for detailed enquiries.

Historical background: The Uxbridge Collection began in the 1930s when the library opened under the guidance of H.T. Hamson, editor of the *Uxbridge Gazette*. In 1965, with the formation of the present borough, the archives of the constituent authorities (Uxbridge Borough, Ruislip-Northwood, Hayes and Harlington, and Yiewsley-West Drayton UDCs) were acquired. Following internal reorganisation in 1991, the Heritage Service was formed comprising local studies, museum and archives services.

Acquisitions policy: To collect and make available all material relating to the past, present and future of the borough.

Archives of organisation: Records of Uxbridge Board of Health, UDC and Borough, 1856–1965; Ruislip-Northwood and Hayes and Harlington UDCs, 1904–65, Yiewsley-West Drayton UDC, 1911–65, and the London Borough of Hillingdon, 1965– .

Major collections: Charters and other records of the Lords in Trust for the Manor of Uxbridge, 1188–1802.
Minet Family Collection: deeds, maps and plans *re* property in Hayes, 1699–1960s.
Parish records, excluding registers, of St John the Baptist, Hillingdon, 1695–1897.
Records of Providence Congregational Church, Uxbridge, 1789–1962.
W.F. Eves, architects, plans, 1894–1949.

Non-manuscript material: Maps (*c*1000), photographs (*c*10,000), prints and drawings. Cine films (22).

Middlesex Advertiser and Gazette, 1871- (bound vols).

Finding aids: Typescript guide to London Local History Resources: London Borough of Hillingdon (1993). Lists; sent to NRA. Local studies catalogue.

Facilities: Photocopying. Microfilm/fiche readers/printers.

Conservation: Contracted out.

1181 John Goodchild Collection
Local History Studies Centre

Address: The Basement, Drury Lane Library, Drury Lane, Wakefield, West Yorkshire WF1 2TE

Telephone: (01924) 891871

Enquiries: John Goodchild

Open: By prior arrangement.

Access: Generally open to the public, by appointment.

Historical background: The collection is a private one and was opened to the public in 1994. Lectures, talks and guided tours are given.

Acquisitions policy: MSS, books, illustrations and maps, are acquired by gift or purchase. The collection is bequeathed on the death of Mr Goodchild to the local authority.

Major collections: MSS, books, pamphlets, maps and illustrations relating to industry, transport, government, and social, political and religious life in the central part of the West Riding, 12th century– .

Non-manuscript material: Maps, directories and histories.

Finding aids: Card indexes. Advice service.

Facilities: Card indexes. Advice service.

Publications: Numerous publications by John Goodchild.

1182 National Arts Education Archive
Lawrence Batley Centre

Parent organisation: National Arts Education Archive (Trust)

Address: Bretton Hall College of the University of Leeds, Wakefield, West Yorkshire WF4 4LG

Telephone: (01924) 830220 ext. 2308

Fax: (01924) 832108, 832077

E-mail: lbartle@bretton.ac.uk

Enquiries: The Director, Prof. Ron George
The Centre Administrator, Mr Leonard Bartle

Open: Mon–Thurs: 8.45–5.00; Fri: 8.45–4.30; Sat: by appointment.

Access: Scholars, students and members of the general public; an appointment with the Centre Administrator is preferred.

Historical background: The archive was established in 1985 to provide a trace of the developments in art, craft and design education, primarily in the United Kingdom. It has increasingly developed international links and reflects the development of the arts in education. In 1989 a new purpose-designed, environmentally safe centre was built to house the growing collection. The archive is registered with the Museums and Galleries Commission.

Acquisitions policy: Seeks to acquire, by gift, fixed-term loan or purchase, examples of significant material relevant to the purpose of the archive, and to maintain and develop the archive for the advancement of the education of the public in the arts and the promotion of research into the arts.

Archives of organisation: Papers of early discussions and establishment of the NAEA.

Major collections: These are principally non-MSS, illustrating the developments in the child art and basic design movements in art education, in particular the papers of the Society for Education through Art Conference, 1956.
Alexander Barclay-Russell Collection: papers and correspondence relating to his time as Art Master at Charterhouse, as Art Inspector with the London County Council and leading up to the founding of the Society for Education in Art, 1930–60.
Sir Alex Clegg (1909–96), art educationalist: papers, speeches and writings, during his time as Chief Education Officer, West Riding County Council, 1945–74.
National Media Education Archive, 20th century.
The Basic Design Collection papers, letters, catalogues and students' work from the Basic Design Courses, 1950s.

Non-manuscript material: More than 100 collections, including Franz Cizek Collection: paintings by pupils of the Austrian progressive art educationalist, early 20th century.
A.E. Halliwell Collection: graphic and industrial design work by Halliwell and his pupils, 1920–50.
William Johnstone Collection: a selection of his paintings and drawings, 1920–1980.
ILEA collection of child art in London, 20th century.
Don Pavey Collection: art-based games, puzzles and artefacts, 19th and 20th centuries.
John Morley Collection: children's art work, photographs, films and slides relating to his work in art education, including work with Aboriginal children, 20th century.
Brian Allison International Collection, including material relating to world presidents of INSEA, 1948– .
Independent Television Commission Collection: examples of educational television broadcasts with supporting material, 20th century.

Finding aids: Computerised catalogue; printouts available on request. Search facilities are available to visitors.

Facilities: Photocopying. Photography. Audio and visual playback. Slide projector.

Conservation: Contracted out when funding allows.

Publications: List of collections.
Publicity booklet/leaflet.
Series of occasional papers.

1183 Queen Elizabeth Grammar School Archives

Address: 154 Northgate, Wakefield, West Yorkshire WF1 3QY

Telephone: (01924) 373943

Fax: (01924) 378871

E-mail: qegswake@rmplc.co.uk

Enquiries: The Archivist

Open: Term: Thurs: 1.00–4.00, by appointment only.

Access: Generally open to the public. Prior booking is essential.

Historical background: The 'free grammar school of Queen Elizabeth at Wakefield' was founded by royal charter in 1591 at the 'humble suit made unto us by the inhabitants of the town and parish of Wakefield'. Some of the surviving early records, including the Royal Charter and records of governors' meetings, are held by West Yorkshire Archive Service (see entry 1184).

Acquisitions policy: Encourages and welcomes donations and deposits by former pupils and masters, and by friends and acquaintances of the school.

Archives of organisation: Entry registers of pupils, 1860s– .
Reports of examiners and inspectors; documents relating to special occasions; prospectuses; school magazines.

Non-manuscript material: Engravings and photographs of the school.
Newspaper cutting collection.
Books relating to the early history of the school. Books written by or about former pupils including Richard Bentley (1662–1742) and Lord Wolfenden (1906–1985).

Finding aids: Catalogue.

Facilities: Photocopying.

Conservation: Contracted out.

Publications: M.H. Peacock: *The History of Wakfield Grammar School* (1892).
R.B. Chapman: *A history of Queen Elizabeth Grammar School Wakefield* (1912).
J.F. Wilkinson: *For Grammar and Other Good Learning: Glimpses into the History of Queen Elizabeth Grammar School, Wakefield* (1991).

1184 West Yorkshire Archive Service: Wakefield Headquarters

Parent organisation: West Yorkshire Joint Services

Address: Registry of Deeds, Newstead Road, Wakefield, West Yorkshire WF1 2DE

Telephone: (01924) 305980

Fax: (01924) 305983

E-mail: wakefield@wyjs.org.uk

Website: www.archives.wyjs.org.uk

Enquiries: The Principal District Archivist, Mrs Ruth Harris
The County Archivist, Mrs Sylvia Thomas

Open: Mon: 9.30–1.00, 2.00–8.00; Tues, Wed: 9.30–1.00, 2.00–5.00.
Closed on council holidays, for one week in February and for one week in November for stock-taking.

Access: Generally open to the public, by appointment. A paid research service is available.

Historical background: The former West Yorkshire Metropolitan County Council established a county record office in 1974. In 1982–3 the then separate district archive services in Bradford, Calderdale, Kirklees, Leeds and Wakefield were joined with the county's service to form the West Yorkshire Archive Service. When the county council was abolished in 1986 the five districts agreed to continue operating a unified archive service with Wakefield as the lead authority. The joint service accordingly operates record offices in each of the five districts and also administers the archive collections of the Yorkshire Archaeological Society in Leeds (see entry 507). The Wakefield headquarters is recognised as a place of deposit for public records.

Acquisitions policy: Archives relating to Wakefield Metropolitan District, or to existing holdings of county-wide significance.

Archives of organisation: West Riding Quarter Sessions, 1637–1971; West Riding County Council, 1889–1974; West Yorkshire Metropolitan County Council, 1974–86; West Riding Registry of Deeds, 1704–1970; the boroughs, UDCs and RDCs of Altofts, Barnsley, Castleford, Featherstone, Hemsworth, Horbury, Knottingley, Normanton, Ossett, Pontefract, Sandal Magna, Stanley, Wakefield and Whitwood, 1894–1974; Wakefield Metropolitan District Council, 1974– .

Major collections: Wakefield Diocese parishes and cathedral, 1538– , and non-conformist circuits and chapels, 1718– .

West Riding wills, 1858–1941; West Yorkshire valuation offices, petty sessions, coroners, motor taxation offices, prisons and hospitals; Wakefield schools.

Political parties, trade unions, trades councils, transport undertakings (notably British Waterways Board, 1652–1976) and businesses.

Non-manuscript material: OS maps of the West Riding, c1848– .

West Riding electoral registers, 1840– ; national probate calendars, 1858– ; general statutes, 1215– ; local Acts, 1810– ; *Journals* of the Houses of Lords and Commons.

Finding aids: Catalogues sent to NRA. Listed collections indexed at accession level. An increasing proportion of the holdings is summarised and indexed on a computerised county-wide database.

Facilities: Photocopying. Photography. Microfilm/fiche readers.

Conservation: Full in-house archive conservation and binding service. The office participates in the Society of Archivists' conservator training scheme. Some outside work is undertaken.

Publications: B.J. Barber and M.W. Beresford: *The West Riding County Council, 1889–1974: Historical Studies* (1978).
R.W. Unwin: *Search Guide to the English Land Tax* (1982).
B.J. Barber: *Guide to the Quarter Sessions of the West Riding of Yorkshire, 1637–1971 , and other Official Records* (1984).
E. Berry: 'The West Yorkshire Archive Service: the Development of a Unified Service, 1974–1983, and its Work to 1986', *Journal of the Society of Archivists*, viii/4 (1987).
S. Thomas: 'The West Yorkshire Archive Service', *Northern History*, xxiii (1987).
Guide to the West Yorkshire Archive Service for Family Historians (1992).

1185　Walsall Local History Centre

Address: Essex Street, Walsall WS2 7AS

Telephone: (01922) 721305/6

Fax: (01922) 634954

E-mail: localhistorycentre@walsall.gov.uk

Website: www.walsall.gov.uk/cultural_services/lhc/cslhc.htm

Enquiries: The Archivist/Local Studies Officer, Ruth F. Vyse

Open: Tues, Thurs: 9.30–5.30; Wed: 9.30–7.00; Fri: 9.30–5.00; Sat: 9.30–1.00.

Access: Generally open to the public. Booking is necessary for microfilm/fiche readers.

Historical background: The Local Studies Room of Walsall Central Library was established by a local newspaper, the *Walsall Observer*, to mark its centenary in 1968. It housed the Local Studies Library and a collection of miscellaneous MS material acquired over the years by successive librarians. A full archives service, serving the whole of the Metropolitan Borough of Walsall, has been in operation since 1978. In 1986 the service was relocated at a former school which had been specially converted and in 1990 a conservation workshop and photography darkroom were added. It is recognised as a place of deposit for public records.

Acquisitions policy: To locate, collect and preserve archival and local studies material relating to all aspects of life and work in Walsall.

Archives of organisation: Records of Walsall Quarter Sessions, magistrates' and coroners' courts, 19th–20th centuries.

Local government records: Walsall Metropolitan Borough and the superseded urban districts of Aldridge, Brownhills, Darlaston and Willenhall, mainly 19th–20th centuries; Walsall Corporation, 17th–20th centuries.

Major collections: Local non-conformist church records, 18th–20th centuries.
Many important collections of records of local businesses, societies and organisations, mainly 19th–20th centuries.
Walsall Hospital records, 19th–20th centuries.

Non-manuscript material: Photographs (c12,000) and videos of all parts of the borough.
Microfilm copies of local newspapers, 1856– ; census, 1841–91; and church and cemetery registers, 17th–20th centuries.
Large collection of local posters, pamphlets, sale and trade catalogues.
Tape-recordings (c700) of reminiscences of local residents.

Finding aids: Most material is listed and indexed.

Facilities: Photocopying. Photography. Microfilm/fiche reader/printers.

Conservation: In-house service; undertakes outside work.

Publications: Handlist of Accessions [updated annually].
1–2 publications on local history published annually; free list available.

1186 Sandwell Community History and Archives Service

Parent organisation: Sandwell Metropolitan Borough Council

Address: Smethwick Library, High Street, Smethwick, Warley B66 1AB

Telephone: (0121) 558 2561

Fax: (0121) 555 6064

E-mail: archives.service@sandwell.gov.uk

Enquiries: The Borough Archivist and Local History Manager, Miss C.M. Harrington

Open: Mon: 9.30–7.00; Tues: 10.30–6.00; Wed: 9.30–6.00; Fri: 9.30–6.00; Sat: 9.30–4.00.

Access: Generally open to the public. It is advisable to book for use of the microfilm/fiche readers.

Historical background: Libraries in Sandwell have collected archival material since the 19th century. In 1988 the archives and local history material from Oldbury, Rowley Regis, Smethwick, Tipton, Wednesbury and West Bromwich, the predecessor authorities of Sandwell Metropolitan Borough, were brought together in a purpose-adapted centre at Smethwick Community Library. The Community History and Archives Service acts as a Diocesan Record Office for Birmingham (Rural Deanery of Warley) and is recognised as a place of deposit for public records.

Acquisitions policy: To acquire any documents that become available from industry, local government, or any other source relating to the Sandwell area.

Archives of organisation: Records of predecessor local authorities, 1850s–1974.

Major collections: Parish registers, 1539– ; Methodist records, 1832– .
Local government records, mid-19th century– .
Records of Patent Shaft Steel Works, Wednesbury.
Records of T.W. Camm, stained glass studio, Smethwick, 1866–1960.

Non-manuscript material: Maps; local newspapers; photographs (c15,000).

Finding aids: Catalogues and indexes.

Facilities: Photocopying. Photography. Microfilm/fiche readers/printer.

Conservation: Contracted out.

1187 Longleat House

Address: The Estate Office, Longleat, Warminster, Wiltshire BA12 7NN

Telephone: (01985) 844400

Fax: (01985) 844885

E-mail: longleatlibrary@btinternet.com

Enquiries: The Librarian and Archivist, Dr K.D. Harris

Open: Tues–Thurs: 10.00–1.00, 2.15–4.15.

Access: Access is by appointment only and is usually restricted to established scholars and research students. Written application is preferred and a charge is made. Computer catalogue searches are available by post for a fee.

Historical background: The collection is owned by the Marquess of Bath. It has grown up with the house, largely completed in 1580 when the builder, Sir John Thynne, steward to Protector Somerset, died. It reflects the family's land acquisitions, as well as its marital alliances, and the history of the house, its contents and the surrounding parkland.

Acquisitions policy: Limited acquisition of items connected with the existing holdings.

Archives of organisation: Papers of the following families and individuals: Thynne, Devereux, Dudley, Talbot, Coventry, Whitelocke, Granville-Carteret, Portland, Prior, Seymour. Monastic records, e.g. Glastonbury Abbey, Cirencester, Amesbury, Maiden Bradley and Longleat.
Estate papers, mainly for Wiltshire, Somerset, Dorset, Shropshire, Gloucestershire and Herefordshire, and also for Northamptonshire (Norton Hall estate) and lands held in Ireland and North Carolina. The records include manorial court rolls, papers and accounts, 14th–19th centuries, surveys, 14th–19th centuries, and rentals, 17th–20th centuries.
Estate maps and plans, 16th–20th centuries; title deeds, 16th–20th centuries, and enclosure papers, 18th–19th centuries.
Miscellaneous MSS, including household books and accounts, 15th–17th centuries.

Non-manuscript material: A collection of more than 40,000 books is housed in seven libraries. The collection includes medieval codices (c100) and incunabula.

Finding aids: Computer catalogues of estate records and the second series of Thynne papers are in preparation. The named collections all have 19th-century calendars and indexes.

Facilities: Photography. Microfilm reader.

Publications: HMC Reports (1872–1980); see *Guide to the Locations of Collections.*
Microfilm publications: calendars and indexes to the named collections; catalogue (1864) of the MSS collection; catalogue of Miscellaneous MSS; Glastonbury Court and Compotus Rolls.
K. Harris and W. Smith: *Glastonbury Abbey Records at Longleat House,* Somerset Record Society, 81 (1991).

1188 Warrington Library

Parent organisation: Warrington Borough Council

Address: Museum Street, Warrington, Cheshire WA1 1JB

Telephone: (01925) 442889/442890

Fax: (01925) 411395

E-mail: library@warrington.gov.uk

Enquiries: The Area Librarian, Ms Janet Hill

Open: Mon, Tues, Fri: 9.30–7.30; Wed: 9.30–5.00;
Thurs: 9.30–1.00; Sat: 9.00–1.00.

Access: Generally open to the public, on application.

Historical background: Warrington Library claims to be the first rate-supported library. Opened in 1848, it has always concentrated on collecting local material. In 1974 the formerly independent borough library became part of the Cheshire County Library Service. In 1998 it became part of Warrington Borough Council as a unitary authority.

Acquisitions policy: To strengthen existing primary and secondary collections in Warrington history, by purchase, donation or deposit.

Archives of organisation: Town council minutes and rate books, 1847–1974.
Early Poor Law rate and account books, c1729–1834; Police Commissioners' minutes, 1813–47, and borough police records, 1838–1965.

Major collections: Manorial records, 1580–1778.
Quaker records, including Penketh Meeting, 1663–1904.

Rev. E. Sibson papers relating to Ashton in Makerfield, 1588–1847.
Records of some local companies and many local societies, 18th and 19th centuries.
Papers of W.D. Jeans, solicitor, 19th century.

Non-manuscript material: Handbills, engravings, photographs, postcards, posters and other ephemera, mid-18th century– (c19,500).
Warrington Photographic Survey: photographs of streets and buildings, 1973–9 (c2000).
Books and pamphlets, including Lewis Carroll Collection and Eyres Press books (c15,500).
Warrington Parish Church records, 1591–1969, and census returns, 1841–91 (microfilm).
Warrington newspapers, 1853– .
Town maps, 1772– .

Finding aids: Catalogue. Indexes. NRA 9201, 14607.

Facilities: Photocopying. Photography and microfilming, by arrangement.

Conservation: Some work undertaken by Cheshire and Chester Local Studies Service (see entry 236); other work contracted out.

1189 Warwickshire County Record Office

Parent organisation: Warwickshire County Council

Address: Priory Park, Cape Road, Warwick CV34 4JS

Telephone: (01926) 412735

Fax: (01926) 412509

E-mail: warwickshire.archives@dial.pipex.com

Website: www.warwickshire.gov.uk/countyrecordoffice

Enquiries: The Principal Archives Officer, Miss Caroline Sampson

Open: Tues–Thurs: 9.00–5.30; Fri: 9.00–5.00; Sat: 9.00–12.30.

Access: Generally open to the public, by reader's ticket (available on application).

Historical background: The office was established in 1931 and is recognised as a place of deposit for public records. It also acts as the Diocesan Record Office for parish records for Birmingham (non-city parishes) and Coventry.

Acquisitions policy: Archives relating to the historic county, excluding, for most purposes,

Birmingham, Coventry and Stratford-upon-Avon.

Archives of organisation: Usual local authority record holdings, including records of quarter sessions, 1625– .

Major collections: Deposited local collections, of which the following are particularly noteworthy:
Family and landed estates: Greville of Warwick Castle, 12th–20th centuries; Feilding of Newnham Paddox (including Pennant of Downing, Flintshire), 17th–20th centuries; Throckmorton of Coughton, 13th–20th centuries.
Other collections: needle industry records, 19th–20th centuries; canal records (particularly Oxford & Grand Union Canals), 18th–20th centuries; Eagle Engineering.

Non-manuscript material: Large collection of photographs, maps and prints.
Major local history library, including unpublished material.

Finding aids: Catalogues/lists of archival collections; copies sent to NRA. Place, person and subject indexes, some specialized indexes.

Facilities: Photocopying. Photography. Microfilming. Microfilm/fiche readers.

Conservation: In-house service.

Publications: Guide to Parish Registers, Nonconformist Registers and Census Returns in the Warwickshire CRO.

1190   Watford Museum

Parent organisation: Watford Borough Council

Address: 194 High Street, Watford, Hertfordshire WD1 2HG

Telephone: (01923) 232297

Fax: (01923) 224772

E-mail: vicky@artsteam-watford.co.uk

Website: www.hertsmuseums.org.uk/watford/

Enquiries: The Manager, Victoria Barlow

Open: Mon–Fri: 10.00–5.00; Sat: 10.00–1.00, 2.00–5.00, by appointment.

Access: Generally open to the public, by prior arrangement.

The Museum opened in 1981 on the former Benskin Brewery site. It acquires material relating to Watford and surrounding area. Holdings include a large collection relating to Cassiobury House, home to the Earls of Essex, including documents, auction catalogues, books, maps and photographs. There are also maps of Watford town, a large collection of photographs and postcards and prints and drawings by local artists. There is an automated database and photocopying and photography is available by arrangement.

1191   Wells Cathedral Library and Archives

Address: Chain Gate, Cathedral Green, Wells, Somerset BA5 2UE

Telephone: (01749) 674483 (messages)

Fax: (01749) 677360

E-mail: administrator@wellscathedral.co.net

Enquiries: The Archivist, Mrs F.A. Neale

Open: By arrangement only.

Access: Bona fide researchers, on written application and by appointment only.

Historical background: The library is a working library and muniment depository for the Dean and Chapter and has existed since the 13th century. In the 19th century a number of the deeds of former manorial properties were taken over by the Ecclesiastical Commissioners and were eventually transferred to Somerset Archive and Record Service (see entry 1161), which also holds all the episcopal and diocesan material formerly housed in the Bishop's Registry.

Acquisitions policy: Material relating to Wells Cathedral administration.

Archives of organisation: Charters, 958– ; registers, c1240– .
Administrative records of Wells Cathedral, title deeds and administrative records of former estates.
Old Wells Almshouse archives.
Archives of College of Vicars Choral.

Finding aids: Calendar of MSS of Dean and Chapter of Wells Cathedral, HMC (1907, 1914) [2 vols].
Calendars of Vicars Choral archives: *The Earliest Extant Register, 1393–1534; Act Book, 1541–1593,* and *Documents, 1348–1600, of the Vicars Choral of Wells* (1985, 1986).
Calendars of Cathedral and Almshouse archives, plus consolidated index. *Fabric Accounts, 1390–1600, Communars' Accounts,*

1327–1600, and *Escheators' Accounts, 1372–1600* (in English translation with indexes), Friends of Wells Cathedral, Xeroxed typescript (1983, 1984, 1988).

Facilities: Photocopying. Photography.

Conservation: Contracted out.

Publications: Wells Cathedral Miscellany, Somerset Record Society, vol. 56 (1941).
Wells Chapter Act Book, 1666–1683 , HMC, joint publication no. 20 (with Somerset Record Society), vol. 72 (1973).
Wells Cathedral Library (Wells, 1998).

1192 Wells City Record Office

Parent organisation: Wells City Council

Address: Town Hall, Wells, Somerset BA5 2RB

Telephone: (01749) 673091

Fax: (01749) 673098

E-mail: wells.cc@virgin.net

Enquiries: The Archivist, Mr William Smith

Open: By arrangement.

Access: Generally open to the public, by appointment with a week's notice. There are restrictions on some classes of records, e.g. town clerk's files less than 30 years old. Charges may be made for postal enquiries requiring searches.

Historical background: Wells City Council is the lineal descendant of the old corporation, which was formally established by royal charter in 1589. Previously the borough or commonalty (which dates from the second half of the 12th century, when the earliest bishops' charters were issued) was headed by a master supported by common councillors. The first royal charter was issued by King John in 1201 and the latest by Elizabeth II in 1974. The city record office was established in 1979 after discussions with the Somerset Record Office, and was intended primarily as a repository for the archives of the city council, though other material relating to Wells is also acquired from time to time.

Acquisitions policy: Records of the city council, such as minutes, town clerk's files, title deeds and plans. Other acquisitions include material relating to Wells in general, such as photographs and the records of clubs and societies, and small local businesses.

Archives of organisation: Borough charters, granted by bishops and ruling monarchs, late 12th century–1974; convocation (corporation act) books, 1377– c1835, and council and committee minute books, c1835– ; title deeds relating to corporation property, c1240–1696, 18th century– ; sessions books, 1600–1719; receivers' books, 1652–1835; rate books, mainly 18th and 19th centuries; surveys, 1604–5, c1820 and 1848; letter-books, late 19th century–c1970; cash books, ledgers and other accounting records, late 19th century–early 20th century; tithe maps with award, 1837–8; building records, late 18th century–c1960; railway papers, including committee minutes, subscription lists, correspondence, Acts of parliament and other material, c1853–c1865; records relating to public health and sanitation, education, highways, and utilities, 1835–c1920; petty sessions information, c1820–c1900, registers of electors and burgess rolls, 1832–c1900; town clerks' files, c1938– .

Non-manuscript material: Plans relating to the town hall and other corporation property, mainly late 19th and early 20th centuries; maps relating mainly to the borough's sewage system and disposal scheme, 1858-c1910; photographs, mainly pictures of mayors and the corporation, c1870-c1950.

Finding aids: Card index.

Facilities: Limited photocopying. Photography.

Conservation: All conservation work is carried out by the Somerset Archive and Record Service (see entry 1161).

Publications: W. Smith: 'Wells, 1201–2001: 800 years of royal charter', *Archives* (October, 2001).

1193 Holkham Hall

Parent organisation: The Earls of Leicester and the Coke family

Address: The Archivist, c/o Holkham Estate Office, Holkham Hall, Wells-next-the-Sea, Norfolk NR23 1AB

Telephone: (01328) 710510 (limited hours only)/710227

Fax: (01328) 711707

Website: www.holkam.co.uk

Enquiries: The Archivist, Mrs Christine Hiskey

Open: By prior arrangement; limited hours only.

Access: Bona fide academic researchers; a copy of any subsequent publication is requested. A charge is made for access to the archives and also for in-house research. An appointment is necessary. The library and manuscript library is administered separately by the Librarian.

Historical background: Property at Holkham was acquired by Edward Coke (1552–1634), Lord Chief Justice; the hall was built by his descendant Thomas Coke (1697–1759), 1st Earl of Leicester, and passed to Thomas William Coke MP (1754–1842), and hence to the later earls and the present occupant, the 7th Earl.

Acquisitions policy: The archive consists of the records of the family, hall and estate, 17th century– , with deeds, 13th century– . The estate covered many other areas of Norfolk and some outside the county. There are very few external acquisitions.

Archives of organisation: Family papers of Edward Coke and his descendants.

Domestic and building accounts for the hall (including domestic accounts for the old manor house).

Farm and estate accounts, audit books, surveys, letter-books, plans, architectural drawings.

Dungeness lighthouse shipping records; Wells and Fakenham Railway records.

Non-manuscript material: Some photographs and plans.

Finding aids: General catalogue in process (1998); HMC Report (1990) available at NRA and Norfolk Record Office (see entry 939). MS calendars of deeds available at Holkham.

Facilities: Limited photocopying. Photography by arrangement. Some volumes on microfilm.

Conservation: Contracted out.

Publications: A.M.W. Stirling: *Coke of Norfolk and his Friends* (1909).

C.W. James: *Lord Chief Justice Coke and his Descendants* (1929).

R.A.C. Parker: *Coke of Norfolk: a Financial and Agricultural Study* (Oxford, 1975).

S. Wade-Martins: *A Great Estate at Work* (Cambridge, 1980).

1194 Sir Frederic Osborne Archive
Welwyn Garden City Library

Parent organisation: Hertfordshire County Council

Address: Central Library, The Campus, Welwyn Garden City, Hertfordshire AL8 6AJ

Telephone: (01707) 332331

Fax: (01707) 338784

E-mail: wgc.library@hertscc.gov.uk

Enquiries: The Librarian, Angela Eserin

Open: Mon–Wed, Fri: 9.30–8.00; Sat: 9.30–4.00, by appointment.

Access: Bona fide scholars, on written application.

The Osborne Archive is on deposit to Welwyn Garden City Library from the Osborne family. Sir Frederic Osborne (1885–1978) was, with Ebenezer Howard (1850–1928), one of the two most significant and influential figures in the Garden Cities New Town movement. The Osborne archive comprises a large collection of manuscript and printed material amassed by Osborne throughout his life. As well as documenting in great detail the movement in which he played such a central role, there are significant collections on Ebenezer Howard, Letchworth, Welwyn Garden City and the postwar reconstruction movement, as well as papers relating to the planning movement worldwide. No further additions will be made to the archive. A printed catalogue and photocopying are available.

1195 Whitby Literary & Philosophical Society

Address: Pannett Park, Whitby, North Yorkshire YO21 1RE

Telephone: (01947) 602 908

Website: www.durain.demon.co.uk

Enquiries: The Hon. Librarian, Mrs M. Durrans

Open: Oct–Apr: Mon, Wed, Fri: 10.00–12.00; May–Sept: Mon–Fri: 9.30–12.00.

Access: Primarily members, but also open to bona fide researchers.

Historical background: The society was founded in 1825 for the use of members, to support a museum and library, and for promoting the interests of science by other means. In 1887 it received portraits and books from the Whitby Institute and in 1935 part of the Whitby Subscription Library.

Acquisitions policy: Acquires material on any subject concerning Whitby and district, in particular local history, genealogy, geology, ships and shipping, whaling, deeds of property, indentures, iron mining.

Archives of organisation: Annual reports, 1824– . Minutes of finance committee meetings, library sub-committee meetings, budget reports.

Major collections: Local history collection of Percy Burnett (1903–72) (c.200 vols).
St Mary & Michael's Church, registers of births, marriages and deaths.
Shipping records, including muster rolls of Whitby ships, 1708–1835, plus ship logs and ship owners' records, including those of Rev. Daniel Duck, 1788–1824.
George Waddington (1821–98), notebooks of records relating to Whitby, including monumental inscriptions (c39 vols).
Papers and journal, charts and maps of William Scoresby the Younger (1789–1857), whaling captain and explorer.

Non-manuscript material: Photographs by F.M. Sutcliffe, Tom Watson, Varley and others (c600).
Drawings, prints and paintings.
Extensive library relating to geology and palaeontology.

Finding aids: NRA 16822: Cholmely family, baronet of Whitby, muniments.

Facilities: Photocopying. Photography. Microfiche reader.

1196 North Highland Archive

Parent organisation: Highland Council Archives

Address: Wick Library, Sinclair Terrace, Wick, Highland KW1 5AB

Telephone: (01955) 606432

Fax: (01955) 603000

E-mail: brenda.lees@highland.gov.uk

Enquiries: The Archivist, Miss Brenda Lees

Open: Mon, Thurs, Fri: 10.00–1.00, 2.00–5.30; Tues: 10.00–1.00, 2.00–8.00; Wed: 10.00–1.00. By appointment only.

Access: Generally open to the public, subject to statutory closure periods.

Historical background: The archive was opened in 1995 to administer the records of Caithness and Sutherland which were formerly held in the Highland Regional Archives, now Highland Council Archives, Inverness (see entry 465).

Acquisitions policy: To acquire and manage the archives of Caithness and Sutherland.

Archives of organisation: Local authority records, including police and education records covering the burghs of Wick, 1660–1975, Thurso, 1904–65, and Caithness County Council, 1720–1945.

Major collections: Local organisations, clubs and societies including records of Wick Harbour Trust, 1849–1975, and Wick Post Office, 1892–1982.
Papers including the Mowat Collection, 1870–1910, John Mowat (1868–1955); the Keith family, solicitors in Thurso, 1887–1965; Orkney war diaries of Hetty Munro, and Henry Henderson, the 'Bard of Reay'.

Non-manuscript material: Census returns and parish registers on microfilm.
Large-scale OS and inland revenue maps; colour slides of Roy's military survey of Scotland, 1747–55.

Finding aids: Catalogues and lists available for several collections.

Facilities: Photocopying. Photography by arrangement. Microfilm/fiche readers.

Conservation: Contracted out.

Publications: Guide to the North Highland Archive.
Some information in the *Guide to the Highland Council Archive.*

1197 The Gurkha Museum

Address: Peninsular Barracks, Romsey Road, Winchester, Hampshire SO23 8TS

Telephone: (01962) 842832

E-mail: curator@thegurkhamuseum.co.uk

Website: www.thegurkhamuseum.co.uk

Enquiries: The Curator, Brig. (retd) C.J.D. Bullock

Open: By arrangement.

Access: Generally open to the public. A paid research service is available.

Historical background: The museum commemorates the services of the Gurkhas, rifle regiments and three core units, to the British since 1815. It was opened in 1974 and moved to its present site in 1989.

Acquisitions policy: Items and archives relating to Gurkha military history, and the culture, religion and natural history of Nepal.

Archives of organisation: Regimental records, 1815– , including battalion digests; regimental journals; war diaries, 1939– ; casualty lists, 1914–18, 1939–45; registers of honours and gallantry awards.

Major collections: Records relating to the North-West frontier and Nepal.

Non-manuscript material: Operational maps for Burma, World War II, Malayan Emergency and Borneo Confrontation.
Film and audio records covering recruitment, training, service, ceremonials and life in Nepal, 1920s– .
Regimental photograph albums for 2nd, 6th, 7th and 10th Gurkhas.
Library holdings include Indian Army Lists, 1845–1946, and British Army Lists, 1948– .
Memorabilia, medal and badge collection.

Finding aids: Catalogues.

Facilities: Photocopying.

Conservation: Some in-house provision.

Publications: Many booklets published; a full list is available on application.

1198   Hampshire County Council Museums Service

Parent organisation: Hampshire County Council

Address: Chilcomb House, Chilcomb Lane, Winchester, Hampshire SO23 8RD

Telephone: (01962) 846304

Fax: (01962) 869836

E-mail: garnott@hantsmus.demon.co.uk

Website: www.hants.gov.uk

Enquiries: The Librarian, Gill Arnott

Open: Mon–Wed: 8.30–4.00.

Access: Open to members of the public for research only. An appointment is necessary.

Historical background: Much of the collection was acquired with the amalgamation of local museums into the county museum service. The original accession records are still held.

Acquisitions policy: Material is acquired relating to Hampshire history and topography, decorative arts, archaeology, transport, technology and natural science, excluding data relating to the cities of Portsmouth, Southampton and Winchester. The library also holds information that relates to the objects in the museum service collection. Environmental data relating to the archaeology, natural science and geology of Hampshire are collected by keepers of the relevant disciplines.

Major collections: Tasker & Sons of Andover, foundrymen and manufacturers of steam traction engines and trailers: photographs, engineering drawings and some vehicle works registers, together with printed catalogues.
Thornycroft of Basingstoke, motor lorry, bus and coach manufacturer: photographs, some archive material and printed brochures/manuals.
A collection of correspondence and manuscripts relating to William Curtis (1746–99), botanist.
Pattern books for edge tools by Fussells of Mells/Isaac Nash, Belbroughton.

Facilities: Photocopying, microfiche reader.

Publications: Hampshire Museum Papers series.

1199   Hampshire Record Office

Parent organisation: Hampshire County Council

Address: Sussex Street, Winchester, Hampshire SO23 8TH

Telephone: (01962) 846154

Fax: (01962) 878681

E-mail: sadeax@hants.gov.uk

Website: www.hants.gov.uk/record-office

Enquiries: The County Archivist

Open: Mon–Fri: 9.00–7.00; Sat: 9.00–4.00.

Access: Generally open to the public. The office operates the CARN reader's ticket system.

Historical background: The office was established in 1947 and is housed in a purpose-built repository opened in 1993. It acts as the Diocesan Record Office for Winchester Diocese and for two deaneries of Portsmouth Diocese, and is recognised as a place of deposit for public records. Hampshire Archives Trust (f. 1986) acts as a support body for archives in the county, carrying out extensive survey and advisory/liaison work and running the Wessex Film and Sound Archive. For details, contact the Secretary at the above address.

Acquisitions policy: Records relating to Hampshire and Hampshire families, except where the primary connection is with Southampton or Portsmouth.

Archives of organisation: Usual local authority record holdings.

Major collections: Deposited local collections, including the following which have a wider significance:
Winchester Bishopric Estate records, including pipe rolls, 1208/9–1711.
Political correspondence of 1st Baron Bolton (1764–1807); 3rd Baron Calthorpe (1787–1852); 1st Earl of Malmesbury (1746–1820); 3rd Earl of Malmesbury (1807–89); 1st Earl of Normanton (1736–1809); George Tierney senior (1761–1830); William Wickham (1761–1840).
Bonham Carter family papers, 18th–20th centuries, including correspondence with Florence Nightingale.
Literary and political papers of James Harris (1709–80), including correspondence with Henry Fielding, and Handel MSS.
Lemprière family papers relating to the Channel Islands, 19th century.
Shelley-Rolls papers, including papers relating to Percy Bysshe Shelley (1792–1822).

Non-manuscript material: Wessex Film and Sound Archive: film, video and sound recordings.

Finding aids: Increasing number of catalogues available in electronic form. Lists sent to NRA.

Facilities: Photocopying. Photography. Microfilming. Microfilm/fiche readers/printer.

Conservation: Full in-house service.

Publications: Hampshire Record Series. Hampshire Papers.

Portsmouth Record Series.
Various guides to Hampshire Record Office and its collections.

1200 Royal Hampshire Regiment Archives

Parent organisation: Museum of the Royal Hampshire Regiment

Address: Serle's House, Southgate Street, Winchester, Hampshire SO23 9EG

Telephone: (01962) 863658

Fax: (01962) 888302

Enquiries: The Curator or Archivist

Open: Mon–Fri: 10.00–12.30, 2.00–4.00, by appointment

Access: Bona fide researchers, who should first apply in writing.

Historical background: The regiment was established in 1702 and consists of regulars, militia, volunteers and territorials. The Regimental Museum was first opened in 1933. Service records of individuals held by MOD Records.

Acquisitions policy: As part of the general museum policy manuscripts, maps and other documents are acquired which bear upon the history of the regiment.

Archives of organisation: Archives of the regiment, 1702–1992, including war diaries of battalions, casualty lists and a variety of papers and photographs.

Non-manuscript material: Maps and photographs.

Finding aids: Accession register

Facilities: Photocopying. Photography.

Publications: C.T. Atkinson: *History of the Royal Hampshire Regiment* Vol. 1: 1702–1914; Vol. 2: 1914–1918.
D. Scott Daniell: *History of the Royal Hampshire Regiment* Vol. 3: 1918–1954.
B. Pennet: *History of the Royal Hampshire Regiment* Vol. 4: 1945–1992.

1201 Winchester Cathedral Library

Address: The Close, Winchester, Hampshire SO23 9LS

Telephone: (01962) 857200

Fax: (01962) 857701

E-mail: cathedral.office@winchester-cathedral.org.uk

Website: www.winchester-cathedral.org.uk

Enquiries: The Curator, John Hardacre, 5a The Close, Winchester, Hants SO23 9LS

Open: April–Sept: Mon–Sat: 10.30–12.30, 2.30–5.00.
Oct–March: Wed, Sat: 10.30–12.30, 2.30–5.00. (days and times subject to alteration).

Access: Bona fide research students, on written application with references.

The Anglo-Saxon minster was succeeded by a Norman cathedral begun in 1079, and there is a continuous history from that date. Archives, including plans and maps, relate to the priory and the cathedral from the Anglo-Saxon period to the present day. The cathedral has one of the oldest book rooms in Europe, including a fine 17th-century collection; many books were bequeathed by Bishop George Morley (1597–1684).

1202   Winchester College Archives

Address: Winchester College, Winchester, Hampshire SO23 9NA

Enquiries: The Archivist

Open: By written appointment only, during normal school terms.

Access: Approved researchers.

Historical background: Winchester College was founded by William of Wykeham in 1382. His statutes provided for the careful preservation of documents relating to the college's internal administration and to its estates. The oldest documents are still housed in the 14th- century muniment room with its original chests.

Acquisitions policy: To preserve the administrative and educational records of the college.

Archives of organisation: Extensive records of the college's estates, primarily in Hampshire, Wiltshire and Dorset, late 14th century– (some records predate the foundation).
Internal accounts, 1394– (nearly complete).
Assorted educational records, increasingly full from the 18th century– .

Non-manuscript material: Maps and plans of the college's estates.
Photographs of college buildings and portraits.

Finding aids: Various lists and indexes available, especially for pre-1870 records. Copies of the main descriptive list are available at the main university and London libraries, and at relevant county record offices.

Facilities: Limited photocopying. Photography in special cases only.

Publications: J.H. Harvey: 'Winchester College Muniments', *Archives*, v/28 (1962).
S. Himsworth: *Winchester College Muniments* (1976, 1984) [3 vols; descriptive list with indexes by P. Gwyn and others].

1203   Eton College Collections

Address: College Library, Eton College, Windsor, Berkshire SL4 6DB

Telephone: (01753) 671269

Fax: (01753) 801507

E-mail: archivist@etoncollege.org.uk

Enquiries: The College Archivist, Mrs Penny Hatfield

Open: Mon–Fri: 9.30–1.00, 2.00–5.00.

Access: Bona fide researchers, by appointment. Records are closed for 40 years (unless special permission is obtained from the Provost); records identifying individual boys may be closed for 75 years.

Historical background: Eton College was founded in 1440 by Henry VI in a collegiate parish church: the college was soon enlarged to include 70 scholars and 20 commensals (sons of benefactors or friends of the college, paying for board and lodging, but educated free). Commensals were the forerunners of the oppidans, fee-paying boarders of the school, which has grown up around the college and is administered separately. The provost had peculiar jurisdiction from 1443 over the college and parish. Provosts were rectors of Eton until 1875, when a separate vicarage was created, but are still the ordinaries of college and lower (junior boys') chapels. Provosts also had testamentary jurisdiction, which petered out in the 1660s, and the power to issue marriage licences to parishioners. Parish registers were transferred to Buckinghamshire Records and Local Studies Service (see entry 37) after the Parochial

Registers and Records Measure 1978, but microfilms and an index to baptisms and marriages are held.

Acquisitions policy: To maintain archives of the school. Items relating to life at the school, and to the estates, are acquired by gift or very occasionally purchased.

Archives of organisation: Administrative and financial records only of the college (the provost and fellows), 1440– , including estate records, 11th century– .
Records of the school, including house books, society records and sporting annals, *c*1880– .
Enrolled grants of probate and administrations, 1450s–1660s; a few 18th-century marriage licences.

Major collections: Letters, bills, papers and ephemera of boys at the school, 18th–20th century.
Literary manuscripts, including papers of Anne Thackeray Ritchie (1837–1919), 19th and 20th centuries (the responsibility of the College Librarian).

Non-manuscript material: Photographs, maps and plans, printed books.
Museum of Eton Life.
College art collection includes leaving portraits of boys and views of Eton.

Finding aids: Eton College Records, vols 1–65: mainly calendars of estate records to 1871 (sets available in the Public Record Office (see entry 1058) and at the NRA); handlists.

Facilities: Photocopying. Photography.

Publications: H.E. Chetwynd-Stapylton: *The Eton School Lists from 1791–1877* (Eton, 1884).
Eton School Registers, 1841–1918, Old Etonian Association (1903–32) [8 parts].
Etonians who Fought in the Great War (1921).
R.A. Austen-Leigh (ed.): *The Eton College Register,* vols 2 & 3: *1698–1790* (1927; 1921).
W Sterry (ed.): *The Eton College Register,* vol. 1: *1441–1698* (1943).
Etonians who Fought in the World War 1939–1945.
For literary MSS, see D. Sutton (ed.): *Location Register of English Literary MSS* (London, 1988).

1204   Royal Archives

Address: Windsor Castle, Windsor, Berkshire SL4 1NJ

Telephone: (01753) 868286 exts 2260/2465

Fax: (01753) 854910

Enquiries: The Assistant Keeper
The Registrar
The Curator of the Royal Photograph Collection

Open: By arrangement.

Access: Bona fide researchers, on written application and by appointment. Access for students is restricted to postgraduates.

Historical background: The Royal Archives were established in 1912 with the papers of King George III, King George IV, Queen Victoria and King Edward VII, with those of William Augustus, Duke of Cumberland, and the exiled Stuarts. The papers of King George V and King George VI, as well as those of some other members of the royal family, have been added subsequently.

Acquisitions policy: To maintain and consolidate the archive.

Archives of organisation: Official and private archives of the sovereign from King George III to King George VI.

Major collections: Stuart papers: files of the exiled Stuarts, 17th–19th centuries.
Melbourne papers: official correspondence of 2nd Viscount Melbourne (1779–1848).
Cambridge papers: military papers of the 2nd Duke of Cambridge (1819–1904).
Wardrobe accounts, 1660–1749.

Non-manuscript material: Royal Photograph collection, mostly collected by members of the royal family, *c*1842–1990s.

Facilities: Photocopying, photography and microfilming by arrangement. Microfilm reader.

Conservation: In-house paper conservation studio and bindery.

Publications: HMC: *Calendar of the Stuart Papers (to 1718)* (1902–39) [6 vols].
A.C. Benson and Lord Esher (eds): *The Letters of Queen Victoria, 1837–61* (1907) [3 vols].
G.E. Buckle (ed.): *The Letters of Queen Victoria, 1862–1901* (1926–32) [6 vols].
Sir John Fortescue (ed.): *The Correspondence of King George III, 1760–83* (1927–8) [6 vols].
A. Aspinall (ed.): *The Letters of King George IV, 1812–30* (1938) [3 vols].
——: *The Later Correspondence of George III, 1783–1810* (1962–70) [5 vols].

—— : *The Correspondence of George, Prince of Wales, 1770–1812* (1963–71) [8 vols].

R. Fulford (ed.): *Dearest Child, 1858–61*; *Dearest Mama, 1861–64*; *Your Dear Letter, 1865–71*; *Darling Child, 1871–78*; *Beloved Mama, 1878–85* (1964–81); A. Ramm (ed): *Beloved and Darling Child, 1886–1901* [Queen Victoria's correspondence with Victoria, Princess Royal].

F. Dimond and R. Taylor: *Crown and Camera: the Royal Family and Photography* (1987).

F. Dimond: *Presenting an Image* (1995).

Microfilm publications: The Stuart Papers, Cumberland Papers, Melbourne Papers, Peel Correspondence, Cambridge Papers, Cabinet Reports, 1837–1916, Ministerial Correspondence, 1837–1901, Queen Victoria's files on the Eastern question and European foreign affairs, 1840–1900, and a selection from the Royal Photograph Collection.

1205 Royal Borough Musem Collection

Parent organisation: Royal Borough of Windsor and Maidenhead

Address: Museum Store, Royal Borough of Windsor & Maidenhead, Tinkers Lane, Windsor, Berkshire SL4 4LR

Telephone: (01628) 796829

Enquiries: The Hon. Curator, Dr Judith Hunter, 26 Wood Lane, Slough SL1 9EA, tel: (01753) 525547

Open: By arrangement.

Access: Generally open to the public, by appointment only.

From 1951 to 1982 there was a small local history museum in the Guildhall, Windsor. When this was closed the exhibits were moved to the museum store and the collection was renamed. It consists of miscellaneous MSS, maps, photographs, prints, paintings, artefacts, books and printed material relevant to the history of Windsor and the other towns and villages in the borough. The collection has been listed and indexed; photocopying and photography are available. Records from Windsor Muniment Rooms have been transferred to Berkshire Record Office (see entry 1049).

1206 St George's Chapel, Windsor Castle

Address: Archives and Special Collections, The Vicars' Hall Undercroft, The Cloisters, Windsor Castle, Windsor, Berkshire SL4 1NJ

Telephone: (01753) 848688/848725

Fax: (01753) 848763

E-mail: archives@stgeorges-windsor.org

Enquiries: The Archivist, Dr Eileen Scarff

Open: By appointment only.

Access: Approved readers, on written application; there is a 30-year closure rule. A paid research service is available.

Historical background: The College of St George was founded in 1348.

Acquisitions policy: Personal papers of retired or deceased members of the College of St George. Otherwise internal acquisitions only.

Archives of organisation: Records of the Dean and Canons of Windsor, 1348– ; some property deeds predate the foundation, the earliest being of 1140.
Records include chapter acts, accounts, attendance books, estate papers, and some records of the Order of the Garter.

Non-manuscript material: Maps, plans and drawings.
Photographs, printed books, 15th–17th century (c6000).

Finding aids: Catalogue, lists and indexes; lists sent to NRA.

Facilities: Photocopying. Copies of photographs may be obtained. Microfilm readers.

Conservation: Carried out at the Royal Archives (see entry 1204).

Publications: E.H. Fellowes: *The Military Knights of Windsor, 1352–1944* (1944).
—— : *The Vicars or Minor Canons* (1945).
M.F. Bond: *The Inventories of St George's Chapel, Windsor Castle, 1384–1667* (1944).
A.K.B. Evans: *St George's Chapel, Windsor, 1348–1416* (1947).
S.L. Ollard: *The Deans and Canons of St George's Chapel* (1950).
J.N. Dalton: *The Manuscripts of St George's Chapel* (1957).
E.H. Fellowes and E.R. Poyser: *The Baptism, Marriage and Burial Registers of St George's Chapel, Windsor* (1957).

S.M. Bond: *The Monuments of St George's Chapel* (1958).

———: *Windsor Chapter Acts, 1430–1672* (1966).

C. Mould: *The Musical Manuscripts of St George's Chapel* (1973).

E.H. Fellows: *Organists and Masters of the Choristers* (2/1979).

G. Holmes: *The Order of the Garter: its Knights and Stall Plates, 1348–1984* (1984).

1207 Wisbech and Fenland Museum

Address: Museum Square, Wisbech, Cambridgeshire PE13 1ES

Telephone: (01945) 583817

Fax: (01945) 589050

E-mail: wisbechmuseum@beeb.net

Enquiries: The Curator and Librarian, Dr Jane Hubbard

Open: April–Sept: Tues–Sat: 10.00–5.00; Oct–March: Tues–Sat: 10.00–4.00

Access: Generally open to the public, strictly by appointment only. An hourly charge is made for consulting parish registers and there is a limited paid research service.

Historical background: In 1847 the Wisbech Literary Society (f. 1781) and the Wisbech Museum (f. 1835) moved into the present purpose-built premises. The two societies were merged in 1877 after which the library wing was extended. The museum is now a charitable trust. The town library was founded in 1653 and belongs to the town council, but is now housed in the museum.

Acquisitions policy: To maintain and consolidate the collections.

Archives of organisation: Wisbech Museum and Literary Institute collections, including scientific papers.

Major collections: Local archives: records of Wisbech Town Council and its predecessor, the Trinity Gild, 1379– ; Wisbech Hundred Commissioners of Sewers, 1660–1921; Elm enclosure awards; manorial records, 1753–1940; parish registers.
Medieval religious works, including Wycliffe's sermons, 14th century.
Asian palm leaf MSS.
Collections of Rev. Chauncey Hare Townshend (1798–1868), poet: sketchbooks,

literary and other autographs; and of Thomas Clarkson (1760–1846), philanthropist: letters and other material *re* abolition of slavery.
Peckover family papers.
Original MSS of *Great Expectations* by Charles Dickens and *The Monk* by M.G. Lewis (1775–1818).

Non-manuscript material: Maps of the fens, 17th–19th centuries (*c*800).
Photographs by Samuel Smith (1802–92): local scenes, 1852–64; William Ellis: Madagascar, *c*1860–65; Herbert Coates: East Anglian scenes, *c*1920–50; L.G. Annis: fenland drainage, *c*1950.
Collection of local ephemera, newspapers, playbills and posters.
Town library of 16th- and 17th-century books (12,000); museum library of 18th- and 19th-century books.

Finding aids: Lists: NRA 3642, 3944, 9203, 11114, 11115, 19314, 29456.

1208 Surrey History Centre

Parent organisation: Surrey County Council

Address: 130 Goldsworth Road, Woking, Surrey GU21 1ND

Telephone: (01483) 594594

Fax: (01483) 594595

E-mail: shs@surreycc.gov.uk

Website: shs.surreycc.gov.uk

Enquiries: The County Archivist, and Head of Surrey History Service, Dr D Robinson

Open: Tues, Wed, Fri: 9.30–5.00; Thurs: 9.30–7.30; Sat: 9.30–4.00.

Access: Generally open to the public holding Surrey County Library tickets or CARN tickets. Appointments are helpful but not obligatory.

Historical background: The Surrey History Service comprises the former Surrey Record Offices (from County Hall, Kingston, and Guildford Muniment Room) and the County Local Studies Library formerly at Guildford. The centre opened in 1998 in purpose-built premises supported by the Heritage Lottery Fund. It acts as the Diocesan Record Office for Southwark (parts) and Guildford (deaneries of Emly and Epsom) and is recognised as a place of deposit for public records.

Acquisitions policy: Archival and printed materials relating to the history of Surrey.

Archives of organisation: Usual county council and other local authority records.

Major collections: Deposited local collections, of which the following have a wider significance: Broadwood family of Lyne, including John Broadwood & Sons, piano manufacturers, 1800– .

Records of Dennis Bros. of Guildford, motor manufacturers, 20th century; Godalming Navigation, 18th–20th centuries; Royal Philanthropic Society's school, Redhill, 1788–1980; Wey Navigation, 17th–20th centuries.

Goulburn family of Betchworth, including sugar estates in Jamaica, 1795–1858 and correspondence with Sir Robert Peel (1788–1850).

Gertrude Jekyll, watercolours, drawings and photos, late 19th–20th centuries.

More of Losely, including office of the King's Tents 1542–58, and Lieutenancy of the Tower of London, 1615–17.

Onslow estate and family papers, c1232–1968.

Diaries of Henry Peak (1832–1914), architect and Mayor of Guildford.

Williamson local history notebooks and scrapbooks.

Papers of Lewis Carroll (1832–98).

Finding aids: Archive Document Index available on Internet. Archive catalogues on-line. Printed stock catalogued in Surrey Library Catalogue available on Internet. Database for other collections (illustrations, ephemera, sale particulars) in development.

Facilities: Photocopying. Microfilm/fiche readers/printers. Photography. Internet access (no outgoing public e-mailing). CD-ROM access. Sockets for laptops (no scanning allowed). Video players (SEFVA). Education service for schools. Local access service (Surrey). Research service.

Conservation: In-house. Insect eradication service (leaflet available).

Publications: Guide to Parish Registers (updated regularly).

Some lists published in Chadwyck-Healey *National Inventory of Documentary Sources in the UK.*

1209 Wolverhampton Archives & Local Studies

Parent organisation: Wolverhampton Metropolitan Borough Council: Cultural Services Division

Address: 42–50 Snow Hill, Wolverhampton WV2 4AG

Telephone: (01902) 552480

Fax: (01902) 552481

E-mail: wolverhamptonarchives@dial.pipex.com

Website: www.wolverhampton.gov.uk/archives

Enquiries: The Borough Archivist

Open: Mon, Tues, Fri: 10.00–5.00; Wed: 10.00–7.00; Sat (1st and 3rd): 10.00–5.00.
Annual closure in November for one week.
There is limited production of archive materials between 12.00 and 2.00; advance ordering is required for Saturdays.

Access: Generally open to the public.

Historical background: The archives service was founded within the Public Libraries Department of Wolverhampton Borough Council in 1978, although some acquisitions had been made before this date. It moved to new premises, as a discrete service, in 1996. It is recognised as a place of deposit for public records.

Acquisitions policy: The service collects, preserves and makes publicly available records in all media relating to the area managed by Wolverhampton Borough Council.

Archives of organisation: Records of Wolverhampton borough council, 1777– . Records of superseded authorities, i.e. Bilston borough council and Tettenhall and Wednesfield urban district councils, 19th century–1966.

Major collections: Records of Methodist circuits and churches in Wolverhampton, 18th–20th centuries.

Non-manuscript material: Extensive collections of local photographs, printed books, pamphlets and newspapers.

Finding aids: Lists and indexes in hard copy. Automatic cataloguing now in hand, using authority controls. Future lists will be mounted on website. All lists notified to NRA.

Facilities: Photocopying. Photography. Microfilm/fiche readers/printer.

Conservation: In-house paper conservation.

Publications: M. Mills: *Mapping the Past: Wolverhampton, 1577–1986* (1993) [with Teachers Notes].
——: *Town Centre Timeline: National Curriculum History Sources* (1997).

1210 Croome Estate Trust

Address: The Estate Office, High Green, Severn Stoke, Worcester WR8 9JS

Telephone: (01905) 371261

Fax: (01905) 371501

Enquiries: The Archivist, Mrs Jill Tovey

Open: Tues–Wed: 10.00–3.00, by appointment only.
Closed during August.

Access: Academic researchers and genealogical researchers at the discretion of the Archivist. There is no access to private family papers.

The archive holds local estate records of the Coventry family, 14th century– ; papers *re* Croome Court and garden, 18th century; and maps of South Worcestershire area, 17th–20th centuries. There is a card index, and photocopying is available.

1211 Elgar Birthplace Museum

Parent organisation: The Elgar Birthplace Trust

Address: Crown East Lane, Lower Broadheath, Worcester WR2 6RH

Telephone: (01905) 333224

Fax: (01905) 333426

E-mail: birthplace@elgar.org

Website: www.elgar.org

Enquiries: The Joint Curators, Melanie Weatherley and Catherine Sloan

Open: Mon–Sun: 11.00–5.00, by appointment only.
Closed for a month in December.

Access: Access to any person with a relevant enquiry.

Historical background: The Elgar Birthplace Museum and archive was set up in 1936 by Carice Elgar-Blake to honour the life, music and achievements of her father, the composer Sir Edward Elgar (1857–1934).

Acquisitions policy: To collect material relating to Elgar, including musical MSS, correspondence, photographs and memorabilia.

Major collections: Correspondence and musical MSS, both autographs and sketches, by or relating to Sir Edward Elgar.

Non-manuscript material: Photographs. Sound archive of the music of Sir Edward Elgar. Books from the composer's own library.

Finding aids: Partial computerised inventory, indexes to letters and MSS.

Conservation: Contracted out.

1212 King's School, Worcester

Address: 5 College Green, Worcester WR1 2LL

Telephone: (01905) 721700

Fax: (01905) 721710

E-mail: info@ksw.org.uk

Website: www.ksw.org.uk

Enquiries: The Headmaster's Secretary

Open: By written appointment.

Access: Genuine researchers.

The Cathedral College was founded by King Henry VIII in 1541 in place of the cathedral monastery and was governed by the Dean and Chapter. Under the monastery there had been an almonry school and links with Oxford University. Records of the school are integral with those of Worcester Cathedral, held by the cathedral library (see entry 1214), and include King's Scholar's lists, 1545–1820. The school holds pupils' lists, 1820– , governors' minutes, 1828– , and the *Vigornian* school magazine, 1879– . See M. Craze: *King's School, Worcester, 1541–1972.*

1213 Stanbrook Abbey

Address: Callow End, Worcester WR2 4TD

Telephone: (01905) 830209

Fax: (01905) 831737

E-mail: stanbrookabbey@compuserve.com

Enquiries: The Archivist, Dame Margaret Truran

Access: There is no public access to the archives since the abbey is an enclosed religious community. However, the archivist is willing to answer enquiries by post or, if necessary, in the parlour at Stanbrook by appointment.

Historical background: The community was founded in Cambrai in 1625 by English Benedictine monks and remained there until 1793, when the French Revolution forced the nuns to leave. They eventually returned to England in 1795 and finally settled at Stanbrook in 1838 where, as at Cambrai, they continued to run a small school, which was finally closed in 1918. Although the early records were lost to the community, many copies are now held in the archives, which were first organised by the Abbess Lady Gertrude Dubois in 1875.

Acquisitions policy: To maintain and consolidate the records of the community and the nuns.

Archives of organisation: Account books, 1795– ; entry books, 1625–1725, 1838– ; annals of the community, 1623–1907; house journal, 1869– ; papers and letters *re* building of church and monastery, including Pugin's specification, 1860s and 1870s; school records, including list of pupils, 1795–1917.
Abbesses' papers, including correspondence of Lady Gertrude Dubois with a wide range of clerics, 1860s–90s, and of Dame Laurentia McLachlan *re* plain chant and monastic history, 1930s.
Correspondence with foundations in Australia, 1842– , and Brazil, 1911– .
Knight family of Lincolnshire, correspondence *re* life at Cambrai, 1790s.
Papers *re* beatification of Carmelite Martyrs of Compiègne, 1906.

Finding aids: Listing in progress.

Publications: D. Eanswythe Edwards: 'The Archives of Stanbrook Abbey', *Catholic Archives*, no. 2 (1982), 3–11.

1214 Worcester Cathedral Library

Address: c/o 10a College Green, Worcester WR1 2LH

Telephone: (01905) 28854

Fax: (01905) 611139

E-mail: worcestercathedral@compuserve.com

Enquiries: The Librarian, David Morrisson

Open: By arrangement with the librarian.

Access: Approved readers, on written application.

Historical background: Worcester Cathedral has had a continuous history since its foundation as a Benedictine House in 980. The University of Birmingham Library has copied all MS material on microfiche. Positive copies can be obtained on application to the Keeper of Special Collections there (entry 107A).

Acquisitions policy: Apart from the muniments, the only additions to the collection are books relating to the Cathedral and Diocese of Worcester. There is no purchasing fund.

Archives of organisation: Cathedral archive and muniments, including letter-books, deeds, accounts and chapter act books.

Major collections: Medieval MSS, which mainly comprised the working library of the monks (*c*277); some fragments predate the monastic community (the diocese dates from 680).
The Worcester Fragments, a collection of early 13th-century English polyphony.

Non-manuscript material: Church music, 17th–18th centuries.
Maps and plans.
Bishop John Prideaux (1578–1650) collection of books.
Printed books, 16th–18th centuries (*c*4500).

Finding aids: Catalogues of MSS, collections and books. B.S. Benedikz and others: *Worcester Cathedral Catalogue of Muniments* (1977–82) [6 vols; TS], sent to NRA.
New Catalogue of MSS in preparation.

1215 Worcestershire and Sherwood Foresters Regiment

Address: Regimental HQ, RHQ WFR, Norton Barracks, Worcester WR5 2PA

Telephone: (01905) 354359

Fax: (01905) 353871

E-mail: rhq_wfr@lineone.net

Enquiries: The Regimental Secretary

Open: Mon–Fri: 10.00–4.00.

Access: Generally open to the public, on written application. There is no charge, but a donation would be welcomed.

Historical background: Farrington's Regiment of Foot was formed in 1694 and Charlemont's in 1701. These subsequently became the 29th (Worcestershire) and 36th (Herefordshire) regiments of foot and were amalgamated to form the Worcestershire Regiment in 1881. In 1970 the Worcestershire Regiment was amalgamated with the Sherwood Foresters to form the Worcestershire and Sherwood Foresters Regiment.

Acquisitions policy: Acquires material of regimental interest to the Worcestershire Regiment and its antecedent regiments and to the Worcestershire and Sherwood Foresters Regiment.

Archives of organisation: Regimental records, early 18th century– .
Records of service for officers and some soldiers, including 29th Regiment, 1702–1925.

Major collections: Personal papers, including diaries, letters, journals, order books.

Non-manuscript material: Watercolour sketches of uniforms of 29th Regiment, 1742–1890.
Regimental magazine, 1922– .
Photographs, 1872– (2000).
Regimental histories covering period 1694–1950.

Finding aids: Card index. NRA 20951.

Facilities: Photocopying. Photography.

1216 Worcestershire Library & History Centre

Parent organisation: Worcestershire County Council

Address: Trinity Street, Worcester WR1 2PW

Telephone: (01905) 765922

Fax: (01905) 765925

E-mail: wlhc@worcestershire.gov.uk

Website: www.worcestershire.gov.uk/records

Enquiries: The Assistant Archivist

Open: Mon, Fri: 9.30–7.00; Tues–Thurs: 9.30–5.30; Sat: 9.30–4.00.

Access: Generally open to the public.

Opened in 2001, the History Centre holds all the microform family history resources previously held at the Worcester Record Office with a selection of local studies resources from Worcester City Library. All enquiries relating to original documents should be referred to Worcestershire Record Office, see entry 1217. Photocopying is available and there are microfilm/fiche reader/printers. General information sources leaflets, including genealogy and house history, are available.

1217 Worcestershire Record Office

Parent organisation: Worcestershire County Council

Address: County Hall, Spetchley Road, Worcester WR5 2NP

Telephone: (01905) 766351

Fax: (01905) 766363

E-mail: recordoffice@worcestershire.gov.uk

Website: www.worcestershire.gov.uk/records

Enquiries: The County Archivist, Mr A.M. Wherry

Open: Mon: 10.00–4.45; Tues–Thurs: 9.15–4.45; Fri: 9.15–4.00.
Two–week stock-taking closure in November.

Access: Generally open to the public. Prior booking for microfilm/fiche readers is essential. The office operates the CARN reader's ticket system. A paid research service is provided.

Historical background: Worcestershire Record Office was established in 1947. Hereford and Worcester Record Office was created in 1974 following local government reorganisation, and Worcestershire Record Office was established in 1998 following further local government reorganisation. The dependent St Helen's Record Office closed in 2001 and its holdings, including the substantial archive collection from Kidderminster Library, were transferred. The office is recognised as a place of deposit for public records and acts as the Diocesan Record Office for Worcester.

Acquisitions policy: Records of the parent body and its predecessors, public records as appropriate, diocesan records and private records, within the administrative area of the county and its predecessors.

Archives of organisation: Usual local authority record holdings, including Worcestershire County Council records, 1888–1974; Hereford and Worcester County Council, 1974–98; and quarter sessions (Worcestershire and Worcester City), 1600–1973.
Worcester City Council records, 16th century– .
Diocesan records, 12th century– .

Major collections: Local estate and family records, including Vernons of Hanbury, 15th–20th centuries; Russells of Little Malvern, 16th–20th centuries, and Rushouts/Spencer-Churchills of Northwick Park, 14th–20th centuries.
Correspondence of Sir Edward Elgar (1857–1934).

Non-manuscript material: Worcestershire Photographic Survey of the Worcestershire area (*c*70,000).

Finding aids: Inventory lists, indexes and specialised handlists. Some specialised indexes, e.g. wills. Lists sent to NRA.

Facilities: Photocopying. Photography. Microfilming. Microfilm/fiche reader/printers.

1218 Worthing Library

Parent organisation: West Sussex County Council Library Service

Address: Richmond Road, Worthing, West Sussex BN11 1HD

Telephone: (01903) 212060

E-mail: mhayes@westsussex.gov.uk

Enquiries: The Principal Librarian — Local Studies, Mr Martin Hayes

Open: Mon–Fri: 9.30–7.30; Sat: 9.30–5.00, by appointment.

Access: Generally open to the public by prior arrangement.

Historical background: Local history material has been collected since 1896 when the library opened.

Acquisitions policy: Printed material, plus photographs, covering West Sussex. Archival material is now referred to West Sussex Record Office (see entry 241).

Archives of organisation: Copies of: County Council minutes, 1889– ; County Health

Reports, 1874–1974; Worthing Borough Council minutes, 1890– .

Major collections: Usual local history collection including:
Goodman collection of notes, cuttings, ephemera and pictorial material, principally on archaeological and ecclesiastical subjects covering southern England, mainly West Sussex, c.1900–1930s.
Snewin Collection , 1800–1949, of monumental inscriptions 'Worthing Year Books', theatre cuttings (not local) and plays by Peter R. Snewin.

Non-manuscript material: Photographs, prints and original work of art depicting West Sussex (*c*40,000); maps (8500); private press books.

Facilities: Photocopying. Microform reader/printer.

Publications: Local History Mini-Guides to Research: Crawley, East Grinstead, Bognor, Burgess Hill, Shoreham, World War Two, Railways, Family History, Newspapers.
Local Studies source sheets.

1219 Wrexham Archives Services

Parent organisation: Wrexham County Borough Council

Address: Wrexham Museum, County Buildings, Regent Street, Wrexham LL11 1RB

Telephone: (01978) 358916

Fax: (01978) 353882

E-mail: archives@wrexham.gov.uk

Enquiries: The Archivist, Helen Gwerfyl

Open: Mon–Fri: 10.30–5.00, by appointment.

Access: Generally open to the public by prior arrangement.

Wrexham Archives Service was established after Local Government Reorganization in 1996. The area covered by the new authority includes parts of both pre–1974 Denbighshire and Flintshire. Archives relating to these areas already held by the existing record offices at Ruthin (see entry 1070) and Hawarden (entry 434) will remain there at present. An archives service point will be developed within the Local Studies Centre based at Wrexham Museum to provide microforms of records of local interest, and also copies of catalogues, lists and indexes of records of interest to the area, produced by other record offices. The archives service holds minor archival collections, mainly material acquired since its formation in 1996. It is keen to preserve records of historic interest to the area including manuscripts, maps, plans and photographs.

1220   The Bar Convent

Parent organisation: The Institute of the Blessed Virgin Mary

Address: 17 Blossom Street, York YO24 1AQ

Telephone: (01904) 643238

Fax: (01904) 631792

E-mail: info@bar-convent.org.uk

Website: www.bar-convent.org.uk

Enquiries: The Archivist and Librarian, Sr M. Gregory

Open: By appointment only.

Access: Bona fide researchers, by prior arrangement.

Historical background: The Institute of the Blessed Virgin Mary is a religious order for women founded by Mary Ward (*d* 1645) in 1609. The Bar Convent was founded in 1686, and established a boarding school and day school for girls in 1699. The convent has remained on the same site, outside Micklegate Bar, ever since. A museum and gallery has recently been opened.

Acquisitions policy: To maintain the existing archive; to add material relevant to recusant history and to build up the archives of all the IBVM houses in England or founded from England.

Archives of organisation: Administrative records of the Bar Convent, 1686– , including wills of Mother Superiors, vows and account books, 1730– .
Lists of pupils, 1710– .
Pupils' accounts, 1761– .
Lists of nuns.
Archives of the IBVM foundation in Hammersmith, 1667– ; and Cambridge, 1898– .
Archives of the English Province of the Institute of the Blessed Virgin, 1929– .

Major collections: Diaries, journals, memoirs etc of and by those in the convent, including life of Mary Ward, written *c*1645.

Recipe book, 1753.

Non-manuscript material: Portraits of nuns and benefactors.

Finding aids: Handlist 'The 17th and 18th Century Archives of the Bar Convent, York' (TS).

Facilities: Photocopying. Photography.

Publications: History of the Bar Convent [pamphlet].
H.J. Coleridge (ed.): *St Mary's Convent, Micklegate Bar, York* (1887).
Pamphlets, including: The Portraits of the Bar Convent; Education in the Bar Convent in the 18th century; A Recusant Library.

1221   Borthwick Institute of Historical Research

Parent organisation: University of York

Address: St Anthony's Hall, Peasholme Green, York YO1 2PW

Telephone: (01904) 642315

Fax: (01904) 633284

Website: www.york.ac.uk/inst/bihr

Enquiries: The Director, Chris Webb

Open: Mon–Fri: 9.30–12.50, 2.00–4.50, by appointment.

Access: Bona fide researchers. There are restrictions on some modern records. A paid research service is available; details on application to the secretary.

Historical background: The Borthwick Institute was established in 1953 on the initiative of the York Academic Trust, principally to house and make available the York Diocesan Archive. In 1963 it became a research institute of the newly established University of York, specialising in the study of ecclesiastical history, in particular the administrative and legal history of ecclesiastical institutions within the Province of York. Since 1963 the research and teaching duties of the institute have expanded into new subject areas, and its archival holdings have grown to include accessions of political and business archives in addition to the initial core of ecclesiastical material.
The Southern African Archives were collected under a documentation project initially funded by the Leverhulme Trust and the SSRC in the 1970s.

The Institute also houses York Health Archives (see entry 1228).

Acquisitions policy: Principally records of the Church of England in York Diocese, including papers of the archbishops, archdeacons, rural deans, and parishes in the modern archdeaconry of York, and related church material; records of the Methodist District of York and Hull, circuit and chapels records for York; records of the Congregational church in York; records of individuals, families and organisations having a connection with the existing archives; records relating to the research and teaching interests of the university; the records of the University of York.

Archives of organisation: Archives of the University of York, 1963–1980s, and of the predecessor body, the York Academic Trust, 1946–65.

Major collections: Ecclesiastical: York Diocesan records, including administrative records of the archbishops and their subordinate officials, diocesan boards and committees, 13th–20th centuries; records of the diocesan and provincial church courts, 14th–20th centuries, including visitation courts and the northern High Commission court, 1561–1641; records of faculty jurisdiction, 17th–20th centuries; tithe awards and maps for the Diocese of York; York Diocesan Association for Moral Welfare, 1920s–1970s. Probate records for the prerogative, Exchequer and peculiar courts of the Diocese of York, 14th century–1858. Records of the archiepiscopal, dean and chapter and prebendal estates 17th–19th centuries. Records of some individual archbishops and of parishes in the modern archdeaconry of York.

Records of non-conformist churches, including the Catholic Apostolic Church in the West Riding, 19th–20th centuries, York Methodist District, circuit and chapels, 18th–20th centuries, and the Unitarian and Congregational churches in York, 18th–20th centuries.

Records of the Community of the Resurrection at Mirfield and of prominent members, 19th–20th centuries.

Business records: Rowntree plc, its predecessors and associated companies, including Mackintosh, 19th–20th centuries; Vickers Instruments, 19th–20th centuries; Messrs Atkinson and W.H. Brierley, architects, 19th–20th centuries; Grant, Deggens and Rippen, organ builders, 20th century.

Charities: Akroyd Foundation scholarship, including estate papers, 16th–20th centuries; Lady Elizabeth Hastings' charity, 18th–20th centuries; St Stephen's Orphanage, York, 19th–20th centuries; York Children's Trust, 20th century; Hull and East Riding Sheltering Home for Girls, and St Mary's Home charity, 20th century.

Schools: York Blue and Grey Coat Schools, 18th–20th centuries; Ripon Grammar School, 16th–20th centuries; the Mount School (for Quaker girls), York, 18th–20th centuries; Wilberforce School (later Home) for the Blind, 19th–20th centuries; Read School, Drax, 16th–20th centuries.

Hospitals and health: The Retreat, Quaker psychiatric hospital, 18th–20th centuries.

Family and estate: political and personal papers of the Wood family, Earls of Halifax, 18th–20th centuries; Tuke family, Quaker reformers, 18th–19th centuries; Yarburgh family of Heslington; Lords Deramore, family and estate archive, 16th–20th centuries.

Other: Seebohm Rowntree (1871–1954) social survey papers, 20th century; Yorkshire Federation of Women's Institutes, 20th century; York Merchant Taylors Guild, 14th–20th centuries; Mischa Spoliansky, Polish composer, 20th century.

Many small archives covering a wide field, 12th–20th centuries.

Southern Africa: Dennis Brutus (*b* 1924), poet and anti-apartheid campaigner, 1958–70; Capricorn Africa Society, 1958–70s; Tanganyikan papers of Marion, Lady Chesham (1903–73), mainly 1955–65; Rt. Rev. Joost De Blank (1908–68), archbishop of Cape Town, 1941–68; Rt. Hon. Sir Patrick Duncan (1870–1943), noted South African radical, 1928–43; Rev. William D. Grenfell, relating to Angola, and the war of liberation, 1960–77; Dr Franco Nogueira (*b* 1918), Foreign Minister of Portugal, 1961–9, personal and research papers, 1937–69, especially relating to Dr Antonio D'Oliveira Salazar (1889–1970), former Prime Minister of Portugal; Vivian Oury, director of the Mozambique Co.: business papers relating to the company, 1891–1977, including the port of Beira, 1891–1958, and the Zambezi bridge and railway, 1912–35.

Non-manuscript material: Elton Library, the working library of the late Professor Sir Geoffrey Elton, principally covering British and European early modern history.

Gurney Library, principally concerned with ecclesiastical history and archive studies and the periodicals of northern record societies.

Pamphlets relating to spas and water cures from Harrogate Medical Society, 16th–18th centuries.

Large microfilm collection of cartularies of English monastic houses.

Finding aids: Calendars, lists and indexes of the principal areas of the collection, all sent to NRA. Gurney Library catalogue on York University Library on-line catalogue.

Facilities: Photocopying. Photography. Microfilming and microfilm print-outs. Microfilm/fiche readers.

Conservation: In-house paper and parchment conservation, seal repair, binding. Some outside work is undertaken for other repositories.

Publications: D.M. Smith: *Guide to the Archive Collections in the Borthwick Institute* (1973; suppl., 1980).

A. Buchanan: *Guide to Archival Accessions in the Borthwick Institute, 1981–1996* (1997).

C.C. Webb: *Guide to Genealogical Sources in the Borthwick Institute* (3/1996).

——: *Guide to Parish Records in the Borthwick Institute* (1988).

N.K.M. Gurney: *Handlist of Parish Register Transcripts in the Borthwick Institute* (1976).

K.M. Longley: *Ecclesiastical Cause Papers at York*, I: *The Dean and Chapter's Court 1350–1843* (1980).

W.J. Sheils: *Ecclesiastical Cause Papers at York*, II: *Files Transmitted on Appeal 1500–1883* (1983).

D.M. Smith: *Ecclesiastical Cause Papers at York*, III: *The Court of York 1301–1399* (1988).

P. Evans: *Church Fabric in York Diocese 1613–1899: the Records of the Archbishop's Faculty Jurisdiction* (1995).

J. Burg: *Guide to the Rowntree and Mackintosh Company Archives, 1862–1969* (1998).

C.R. Fonge: *Tithe Awards and Maps at the Borthwick Institute* (1994).

A. Ross: *Guide to the Tanganyikan Papers of Marion, Lady Chesham.* (1975).

T. Lodge (comp.), A.V. Akeroyd and C.P. Lunt (eds): *A Guide to the Southern African Archives in the University of York* (1979).

The Institute publishes the following series: Borthwick Texts and Calendars (editions, calendars, handlists of records); Borthwick Lists and Indexes (shorter catalogues, handlists and indexes); Borthwick Studies in History (monographs, essays); Borthwick Papers (studies concerned with the ecclesiastical history of northern England and aspects of the history and historiography of Yorkshire); *Monastic Research Bulletin* (an annual publication on research in progress on British monastic studies); Borthwick Wallets (palaeography teaching wallets).

1222 Castle Howard Archives

Address: Castle Howard, York YO60 7DA

Telephone: (01653) 648444 ext. 43

Fax: (01653) 648462

Website: www.castlehoward.co.uk

Enquiries: The Curator, Dr Christopher Ridgway

Open: Mon–Wed: 10.00–4.00, an hour closure for lunch; by appointment only.

Access: Castle Howard is a private family archive, and all researchers must apply in writing stating clearly their object of study and any qualifications they hold. Access is dependent on the permission of the Howard family and a research fee is charged.

Historical background: The division of the Carlisle Estates in the 1920s resulted in a split archive, of which Castle Howard Archives and the Howard of Naworth papers at Durham University (see entry 311) are the two unequal parts.

Acquisitions policy: To maintain the archives of the Howard family.

Archives of organisation: Documents relating to the building of the house and the Yorkshire estates; and personal papers of the owners of Castle Howard, including the 1st–9th Earls of Carlisle, mainly 18th and 19th centuries.

Some earlier material relating to Howard estates in Cumberland, Northumberland and Yorkshire.

Non-manuscript material: Estate maps and plans, 18th–19th centuries.

Architectural drawings. Small photograph collection.

Finding aids: Catalogue, sent to NRA. Index to personal letters.

1223 Company of Merchant Adventurers of York

Address: Merchant Adventurers' Hall, Fossgate, York, North Yorkshire YO1 9XD

Telephone: (01904) 652243 (Archivist)

Fax: (01904) 654818

E-mail: louise.wheatley@mahall-york.demon.co.uk

Enquiries: The Honorary Archivist, Mrs Louise Wheatley

Open: Mon–Fri: by prior arrangement only.

Access: Bona fide researchers; an appointment is essential.

Historical background: The Fraternity of Our Lord Jesus Christ and the Blessed Virgin Mary was founded in 1357, and its successor, the Guild of Mercers, was incorporated in 1430. The Elizabethan charter of 1581 formally constituted the organisation as the Company of Merchant Adventurers of York.

Acquisitions policy: To acquire, by donation, deposit or purchase, material relevant to the history of the company, and to trade and trading organisations generally in the north-east of England.

Archives of organisation: Archives pertaining to the Company of Merchant Adventurers of York, 1581– , and its precursors, the Fraternity of Our Lord and St Mary, 1357–71, the Hospital of Holy Trinity and St Mary, 1373–1549, and the Guild of Mercers of York, 1430–1580. These consist of royal charters and grants; minute books, copies of acts and ordinances and meetings; Trinity Hospital administration and advowsons; membership records, elections and apprenticeships; correspondence and papers; letters to and from foreign marts, shipping documents, petitions; Corpus Christi pageant records, accounts and indentures; account rolls, 1357–67, 1432–1682; account books, 1728–1937, draft and subsidiary accounts, annual accounts and balance sheets, 1901– ; receipts and vouchers, 1546– ; bonds; cartulary, late 15th century; title deeds, mid-13th century; rental books and rolls, mid-15th century–late 19th century; leases, late 14th century– ; estate plans and tenancy papers; records of repairs, benefactions and building works; records of the York Residence of Merchant Adventurers of England (Hamburg Court Books), the York Residence of Eastland merchants, the Company of Porters of York; annual reports, 1944– ; and some general miscellanea.

Non-manuscript material: Maps, estate plans, architectural drawings.

Portraits of governors, benefactors and families; oil paintings, watercolours, prints and drawings of York and related subjects. Photographs, 1870s– .
Guild ceremonial items; weights and measures; seal matrices.

Publications: D.M. Smith (comp.): *A Guide to the Archives of the Company of Merchant Adventurers of York* (York, 1994).
D.M. Palliser's short history is an in-house publication.

1224 National Railway Museum
Library and Archives

Parent organisation: National Museum of Science & Industry

Address: Leeman Road, York YO26 4XJ

Telephone: (01904) 621261

Fax: (01904) 611112

E-mail: nrm.library@nmsi.ac.uk

Website: www.nmsi.ac.uk/nrm

Enquiries: The Head of Library and Archive Collections Division, Mr D.W. Hopkin
The Curator, Photographic Collections, Mr E. Bartholomew
The Curator, Poster & Pictorial Collections, Miss B. Cole
The Curator, Archive Collections, Mr R. D. Taylor

Open: Jack Simmons Library and Reading Room: Mon–Fri: 10.30–5.00.
Museum: Mon–Sun: 10.00–6.00.

Access: Readers' tickets for both library and archive material are available on written application to the Librarian.

Historical background: The museum was opened in 1975 following the closure of the former British Museum of Transport at Clapham, London, in 1973. The records collected at Clapham, mainly technical papers and engineering drawings, were transferred to York. All the Science Museum's railway collections are now concentrated at the NRM.
The main business archives for the British Railways Board (BRB) and its predecessor companies, including the records formerly held in the British Transport Commission Historical Records Offices in London, York and Edinburgh, are now in the custody of the

Public Record Office (see entry 1058), except for records relating to Scottish railway companies and British Railways Scottish regions, which are held by the National Archives of Scotland (entry 329). BRB and predecessor company records deemed to be of local, rather than national, interest relating to England and Wales have also been deposited by the BRB in designated local government record offices.

As part of the privatization process for the BRB's undertakings between 1994 and 1997, a statutory Railway Heritage Committee was established. This committee has powers to designate, as worthy of preservation, records and artefacts which belong to the companies which have sprung out of the BRB. The committee has further powers to direct companies to offer records and artefacts to specified archives and museums on their disposal. The situation relating to railway company archives remains in a state of flux.

Acquisitions policy: Material, including papers of individuals, organisations and companies, recording the history and development of the railways industry in its widest sense in the British Isles.

Major collections: Technical records and engineering drawings of locomotives and rolling stock from the British Railways Board and its predecessor companies.

Records of the railway rolling stock industry, including Dübs & Co.; Neilson & Co.; Peckett; Charles Roberts & Co.; Sharp Stewart & Co.; Robert Stephenson & Co., and Vulcan Foundry.

Records of Kennedy Henderson & Co., consulting engineers, concerning railways in Africa and South America.

Rugby Locomotive Testing Station records.

Papers of railway officials, historians and enthusiasts, including R.C. Bond, John Click, E.S. Cox, P.C. Dewhurst, Eric Mason and Selwyn Pearce Higgins.

Papers of Tom Purvis, poster artist.

Non-manuscript material: Official glass negatives from British Rail and former railway companies, 1880–1950.

Private negative collections, including P. Ransome Wallis and M.W. Earley.

Extensive collections of paintings, prints, posters, notices, postcards, tickets, labels and ephemera.

Copies of engineering drawings on microfilm.

Finding aids: Catalogues, lists and indexes. Lists sent to NRA.

Facilities: Photocopying. Photography. Microfilm/fiche readers.

Conservation: Contracted out.

Publications: C.P. Atkins: *A Reader's Guide to using the Jack Simmons Library Reading Room* (NRM, 1998).

E. Bartholomew: *Guide to NRM Photographic Collection* (NRM, 1998).

C.P. Atkins: 'The National Railway Museum Library and its Collections', *Journal of the Railway and Canal Historical Society* (July 1986).

D. Jenkinson (ed.): *The National Railway Collection* (Collins, 1988).

C.J. Heap: 'The NRM Photograph Collection', *British Railway Journal*, 34 (Dec. 1990).

1225   Prince of Wales's Own Regiment of Yorkshire

Address: 3 Tower Street, York YO1 9SB

Telephone: (01904) 662790

Fax: (01904) 658824

Website: www.yorkshirevolunteers.org.uk/pwo.htm

Enquiries: Lt. Col. T.C.E. Vines

Open: Mon–Sat: 9.00–4.30, by arrangement.

Access: Generally open to the public, by appointment.

The museum holds the archives of the West Yorkshire Regiment, the East Yorkshire Regiment and the Prince of Wales's Own Regiment of Yorkshire, from formation, 1685– , but not personnel records. Paintings, prints and artefacts are also held.

1226   York Central Library

Parent organisation: City of York Libraries

Address: Library Square, Museum Street, York YO1 7DS

Telephone: (01904) 655631

Fax: (01904) 611025

E-mail: reference.library@york.gov.uk

Enquiries: The Local Studies Librarian

Open: Mon–Wed, Fri: 9.00–8.00; Thurs: 9.00–5.30; Sat: 9.00–4.00.

Access: Archive material is generally available to the public on request in the reference library, subject to satisfactory proof of identity.

Historical background: A record office was established in the library in 1957, when civic records and deposited collections were placed there. Archives were transferred to York City Archives (see entry 1227) in 1980.

Acquisitions policy: Potential donors are advised to discuss the donation with the Local Studies Librarian.

Major collections: Letters of the Thomas Allis (1788–1875) and William Etty (1787–1849) families, and Waterton papers, 1841–65.
Note-books on York subjects.
Records of the Knowles family, stained-glass manufacturers in York, late 19th century.
Calendars of Felons (York Castle), 1785–1851.

Non-manuscript material: Small collection of films of local interest.
Local illustrations (9100) and slides (1000).

Finding aids: Card catalogue and index available in the York Reference Library.

Facilities: Photocopying. Microfilm/fiche readers.

Conservation: Items sent to specialist conservators.

Publications: *Researching Family History in York Reference Library.*

1227   York City Archives

Address: Art Gallery Building, Exhibition Square, York YO1 2EW

Telephone: (01904) 551878/9

Fax: (01904) 551877

Enquiries: The City Archivist

Open: Mon–Fri: 9.00–1.00, 2.00–5.00.

Access: Generally open to the public, by appointment.

Historical background: Civic records and deposited collections were placed in the York Central Library in 1957, when a record office was opened with a full-time archivist. Following reorganisation in 1974 the archives were retained in the administration of the city

and transferred to new premises in the art gallery building.

Acquisitions policy: Non-ecclesiastical records for York and the immediate area.

Archives of organisation: York City council records, 12th century– .

Major collections: Deposited local collections, including the Yorkshire Philosophical Society Collection; York cemetery registers and other records, 1837–1961; the Goodricke-Piggot Astronomical Collection, 1775–1807.

Non-manuscript material: Photograph and glass-negative collection of properties demolished during slum clearance, 20th century. OS maps, 1852– .

Finding aids: Card catalogue and calendars. Some lists at NRA. Yorkshire Philosophical Society: NRA 16393.

Facilities: Photocopying. Photography and microfilming by arrangment. Microfilm reader.

Conservation: Contracted out.

Publications: York City Archives Brief Guide.
Richard III and the City of York [wallet of facsimiles and booklet].
R.J. Green: *York City Archives* (1971).

1228   York Health Archives

Parent organisation: York Health Services NHS Trust

Address: Borthwick Institute of Historical Research, University of York, St Anthony's Hall, Peasholme Green, York YO1 2PW

Telephone: (01904) 642315

Website: www.york.ac.uk/inst/bihr

Enquiries: The Archivist, Dr Katherine Webb (available Mon–Wed)

Open: Mon–Fri: 9.30–12.50, 2.00–4.50, by arrangement.
Closed for a short period at Christmas and Easter.

Access: Bona fide researchers, by appointment. The normal closure period for public records is in operation; staff records are closed for 75 years and patients' records for 100 years. There is a paid research service.

Historical background: York Health Authority established the archives in 1990, with a part-time archivist to catalogue and bring together the archives inherited from its predecessor bodies, which include records of NHS management bodies in York from 1948, and the archives of NHS hospitals and health services in York district. In 1992 York Health Authority became York Health Services NHS Trust. In 1995 York Health Archives moved to the Borthwick Institute.

Acquisitions policy: Archives of NHS hospitals and their predecessors, and of health services and managing bodies in the district, which at present includes York, Easingwold and Selby but previously also included Thirsk.

Archives of organisation: York 'A' Group Hospital Management Committee, 1948–74; York 'B' Group Hospital Management Committee, 1948–74; North Yorkshire Area Health Authority, 1974–82; York Health District, 1974–82; York Health Authority, 1982–92; York Health Services NHS Trust, 1992– .

Major collections: York County Hospital, 1740–1976; Bootham Park Hospital (formerly York Lunatic Asylum), 1777– ; Clifton Hospital (formerly the North Riding Asylum), 1847–1994); some archives for the many other smaller NHS hospitals in York and district, 1948– .

Non-manuscript material: Plans, drawings and photographs of hospitals; annual and special records of the City of York Medical Officer of Health and the School Medical Officer, 1900–72.

Finding aids: Lists for all collections, some in draft; summary guide to collections.

Facilities: Photocopying. Photography. Microfilming and microfilm print-outs. Microfilm/fiche readers.

Conservation: Borthwick Institute Conservation Department.

Publications: K.A. Webb: *Guide to York Health Archives* (2000).

1229 York Minster Archives

Address: York Minster Library, Dean's Park, York, North Yorkshire YO1 2JQ

Telephone: (01904) 611118

Fax: (01904) 611119

E-mail: archives@yorkminster.org

Enquiries: The Archivist, Louise A. Hampson

Open: Mon–Fri: 10.00–5.00.

Access: Open to the public, by appointment; there are some restrictions on modern records.

Historical background: The minster archives were transferred in 1960 from the minster to the minster library. This had been housed in a restored medieval chapel in Dean's Park since 1810. To these archives were then added the Hailstone Collection and a number of smaller accumulations already held by the minster library. The Alcuin Wing, opened in 1998, now houses all the archive holdings as well as a new Archive Reading Room.

Acquisitions policy: Records relating to the minster or complementary existing holdings, by purchase, donation or deposit.

Archives of organisation: Dean and Chapter records, c1150– .
College of Vicars Choral records, 1252–1936.

Major collections: Edward Hailstone collection, comprising deeds and documents relating to Yorkshire (mainly West Riding), 12th–19th centuries.
Private papers of archbishops, deans and canons of York and other accumulations relating to York and Yorkshire.
Additional MSS, 10th–20th centuries.
Music MSS, 16th–20th centuries.
York Wesleyan Methodist records, mainly 19th century.

Non-manuscript material: Pamphlets (especially Civil War tracts); maps and plans (Yorkshire); architectural drawings (York Minster); prints and drawings (Yorkshire, topographical and biographical); photographs (York Minster); newspapers (mainly Yorkshire), 18th and early 19th centuries.
The Evelyn Collection of photographs.

Finding aids: Various lists and card indexes. Database of minster architectural plans, 18th–20th centuries, and topographical prints, 17th–20th centuries, in progress.

Facilities: Photocopying. Photography. Microfilm/fiche reader/printer.

Conservation: In-house service.

Publications: K.M. Longley: *A Guide to the Archives and Manuscript Collections in York Minster Library* (1977) [typescript available locally and at NRA].
The history of the archives is described in K.M. Longley: 'Towards a History of Archive-

keeping in the Church of York', *Borthwick Institute Bulletin* (1976, 1977).

Other lists of Dean and Chapter Archives are given in HMC First Report (1870), 97.

J. Burton: *Monasticon eboracense*, ix (York, 1758).

G. Lawton: *Collectio rerum ecclesiasticarum de diocesi Ebor*, ii (1842).

Many individual documents have been published in various vols of the Surtees Society, Yorkshire Archaeological Society and elsewhere.

1230 York St John College Archives

Parent organisation: Leeds University

Address: Lord Mayor's Walk, York YO31 7EX

Telephone: (01904) 624624

Fax: (01904) 612512

E-mail: r.wolfe@ucrysj.ac.uk

Website: www.yorksj.ac.uk/library/archive.htm

Enquiries: The Archives Development Officer, Mr R.J. Wolfe

Open: Wed, Thurs: 9.00–4.00, or by arrangement.

Access: Bona fide researchers. There is restricted access to the college archives post-1976.

Historical background: St John's College was founded in 1841 as the York Diocesan Training College by the York Diocesan Society for the Education of the Poor in the Principles of the Established Church to meet the demand for teachers. It was renamed St John's when a separate women's college was founded at Ripon in 1862. These two colleges merged again in 1976 to form the University College of Ripon and St John which became a college of Leeds University (see entry 502). The Ripon campus was closed in 2001 when the present name was adopted, and the archives were amalgamated on the York site. See also Yorkshire Film Archive (entry 1231).

Acquisitions policy: To strengthen existing collections on the history of the institution and its background, including relevant biographical material, and to collect material relevant to the history of education, particularly church colleges.

Archives of organisation: York Diocesan Society: archives, 1812–62, including minute books and papers concerning the foundation and early administration of the college.

National Society: correspondence and reports, 1812–62.

St John's College: committee minutes, student and staff records, prospectuses and other assorted material, 1862–1976.

Ripon College: minutes, finance and student records, 1862–1976.

University College of Ripon & York St John: archives, 1976– .

Non-manuscript material: Architects and building plans of the colleges. Photographs of students, college sports teams and building.

Finding aids: Catalogue published on the college webpages, sent to NRA.

Facilities: Photocopying.

1231 Yorkshire Film Archive

Address: York St John College, Lord Mayor's Walk, York YO31 7EZ

Telephone: (01904) 716550

Fax: (01904) 716552

E-mail: yfa@yorksj.ac.uk

Enquiries: The Director, Sue Howard

Open: Mon–Fri: 9.00–5.00, strictly by appointment.

Access: Generally open to the public. Film footage can be viewed on site, or by VHS copies. A research fee is charged.

Historical background: The Yorkshire Film Archive was established in 1986 with a remit to locate, preserve and make accessible moving image material relating to the county of Yorkshire. It moved from Ripon in 2001, to relocate in new, enlarged premises in York in 2003.

Acquisitions policy: Primarily non-fiction film material relating to the county of Yorkshire.

Non-manuscript material: Films, 1897– (3000) reflecting the social, cultural and industrial history of the region.

Yorkshire Video Collection, 1998–2001, the work of members of the Yorkshire Media Consortium.

Finding aids: Database and search facilities.

Facilities: Specialist film viewing facilities.

Appendix I

List, consolidated from editions 2, 3 and 4, of institutions which have transferred their archives

Abbot Hall Art Gallery and Museum, Kendal: Cumbria Record Office (480)

Abingdon Town Council, Abingdon: Berkshire Record Office (1049)

Airdrie Library, Airdrie: North Lanarkshire Archives (269)

Amalgamated Union of Engineering Wsorkers, London: Modern Record Centre (261)

Andover Borough Archives, Andover: Hampshire Record Office (1199)

Anti-Apartheid Movement: Rhodes House Library (994)

Arbroath Library and Art Gallery: Montrose Library Archive (907)

Arbury Hall, Astley: Warwickshire County Record Office (1189)

Arts Council of England: Victoria & Albert Museum (839)

Baillie Library, Glasgow: Mitchell Library (393)

Basingstoke Museum: Hampshire Record Office (1199)

Blenheim Palace: British Library (561A)

Boston Borough Council: Lincolnshire Archives (519)

British Association of Social Workers (BASW): Modern Records Centre (261)

British Athletics: University of Birmingham (107A)

British Council: Public Record Office (1058)

British Ecological Society: Linnean Society (680)

British Theatre Play Library: Theatre Museum (823)

Brixton Reference Library, London: Lambeth Archives Department (672)

Brookes' Club, London: London Metropolitan Archives (688)

Burnley District Library: Lancashire Record Office (1044)

Business Statistics Office Library, Newport: University College London (832); University of Kent at Canterbury (213)

Cardiff Cathedral: National Library of Wales (9)

Carlisle Cathedral Library: Cumbria Record Office (223)

Charity Commission for England and Wales: Public Record Office (1058)

Chartered Society of Physiotherapy: Wellcome Library (844)

Chichester Cathedral Library: West Sussex Record Office (241)

Church Army: Cambridge University Library (165A)

City of London School: Corporation of London Records Office (588)

Clackmannan District Library: Stirling Council Archives Service (1133)

College of St Hilda & St Bede, Durham: Durham County Record Office (309)

Commissioners of Northern Lighthouses, Edinburgh: National Archives of Scotland (329)

Confederation of Health Services Employees (COHSE), Banstead: Modern Records Centre (261)

Cornwall County Library, Truro: Cornwall Studies Library (1056)

Cromwell Museum, Huntingdon: Cambridgeshire Archives Service, Huntingdon (459)

Doncaster Central Library: Doncaster Archives (282)

Dorking County Library: Surrey History Centre (1208)

Down, Connor and Dromore Diocesan Library: Public Record Office of Northern Ireland (81)

Duchy of Lancaster Office, London: Public Record Office (1058)

Dundee Children's Home: Dundee City Archives (301)

Duns Area Library: Scottish Borders Region Archives and Local History Centre (1103)

East Sheen District Library, London: Richmond-upon-Thames Local Studies (1059)

Educational Institute of Scotland: National Archives of Scotland (329)

Electrical, Electronic, Telecommunications and Plumbing Union, Bromley: Modern Records Centre (261)

English National Board for Nursing, Midwifery and Health Visiting: Public Record Office (1058)

English (now British) Organ Archive, Keele: Birmingham City Archives (101)

Essex County Libraries, Local Studies Department, Colchester: Essex Record Office, Colchester (250)

Felsted School: Essex Record Office, Colchester (250)

Film Music Resource Centre: Borthwick Institute of Historical Research (1221)

Forfar Public Library: Montrose Library Archive (907)

General, Municipal, Boilermakers and Allied Trades Union (GMBAT): Working Class Movement Library (1094)

German Lutheran Congregation, London: Westminster City Archives (846); Tower Hamlets Local History Library and Archives (825)

Glasgow Chamber of Commerce: Mitchell Library (393)

Goldsmiths' College, Rachel McMillan Collection: Lewisham Study Centre (676)

Guildford Institute, University of Surrey: Surrey History Centre (1208)

Shropshire Libraries Local Studies Department: Shropshire Records & Research Centre (**1113**)

Sion College Library: Guildhall Library, London (**624**: archives); Lambeth Palace Library (**672**: MS collections)

Society for Psychical Research: Cambridge University Library (**165A**)

Society of Graphical and Allied Trades, Hadleigh: Modern Records Centre (**261**)

Southwark Cathedral: Southwark Local Studies Library (**818**)

Southwark Diocese, London: London Metropolitan Archives (**688**)

Sutton Housing Trust: London Metropolitan Archives (**688**)

Swansea Central Library: West Glamorgan Archive Service (**1155**)

Syon Abbey, South Brent: University of Exeter Library (**368**)

Telford Development Corporation: Ironbridge Gorge Museum Trust (**472**)

Theological College, Edinburgh: National Archives of Scotland (**329**)

Tony Benn Archive: British Library (**561A**)

Trinity House Lighthouse Service: Guildhall Library, London (**624**)

United Bible Societies: Cambridge University Library (**165A**)

Walthamstow Almshouse and General Charities: Waltham Forest Archives (**841**)

Weston Park, Shifnal: Staffordshire and Stoke-on-Trent Archive Service, Stafford (**1129**)

Wigtownshire County Library, Stranraer: Dumfries and Galloway Archives (**294**)

Wye College, Kent: Imperial College London (**643A**)

Appendix II

List of institutions approached for this edition, which reported having no archives

Blackburn College Library, Lancashire
Boston Library, Lincolnshire
Freshwater Biological Association Library,
 Ambleside
German Occupation Museum, Guernsey
Goethe Institute Library, London
Guille-Alles Library, Guernsey
Jewel and Esk Valley College, Edinburgh
Kent Institute of Art and Design, Herbert Read
 Collection, Canterbury
La Société Guernesiaise, Guernsey

Nottinghamshire County Library, Nottingham
Phillips Fine Art Auctioneers, London
Plymouth Proprietary Library, Plymouth
The Railway Club, London
Robert Gordon University, Aberdeen
Tiverton Library, Devon
Tyndale House Library, Cambridge
University of East London, London
Wimbledon Society Museum of Local History,
 London
Yorkshire Museum, York

Appendix III

List, consolidated from editions 2, 3 and 4, of institutions which did not respond; requested not to be included; or supplied insufficient information

4/7 Royal Dragoon Guards, York
Age Concern, London
Airborne Forces Museum, Aldershot
Alexander Keiller Museum, Avebury
Amateur Boxing Association of England, London
Amberley Museum, West Sussex
Ampleforth Abbey, York
Argyll and Sutherland Highlanders Regimental
  Museum, Stirling
Army and Navy Club, London
Arthur Sanderson & Sons Ltd, Uxbridge
Ashburton Museum, Devon
Aston University, Birmingham
Bankfield Museum, Halifax
Bass Museum, Burton upon Trent
Bath Royal Literary and Scientific Institution
Beatle Archive, Liverpool
Bedford Estates, Woburn Abbey, Bedfordshire
Bewdley Museum, West Midlands
Bideford Bridge Trust, Devon
Bilston Branch Library, Wolverhampton
Birmingham Museum of Science and Industry
Body Shop International plc, Littlehampton
Bolton School, Lancashire
Book Trust, London
Booker plc, London
Booth Museum of Natural History, Brighton
Bowes Museum, Barnard Castle, Yorkshire
Bowood House, Calne, Wiltshire
Bradford & Ilkley Community College, Bradford
Brewers and Licensed Retailers Association, London
Bridlington Public Library, Bridlington
Bristol Baptist College
Britannia Royal Naval College, Dartmouth
British College of Optometrists, London
British Federation of Women Graduates, London
Brooklands Museum, Weybridge
Buddhist Society Library, London
Building Societies Association, London
C Hoare and Co, London
Callington Museum, Cornwall
Camberwell School of Arts and Crafts, London
Cambridge School of Education
Cambridge University Botanic Garden
Campbeltown Museum, Scotland
Carlisle Public Library
Cathedral Church of St Mary the Virgin, Glasgow
Catholic Fund for Overseas Development
  (CAFOD), London
Chartered Institution of Building Services Engineers,
  London
Cheltenham Reference Library
Children's International Summer Village, Newcastle
  upon Tyne

Christie's Auctioneers, London
Church of St Mary Magdalene, Newark
Church of St Peter and St Paul, Swaffham
Clifford Chance, London
Coldstream Guards, London
Cosworth Engineering, Northampton
Courtaulds plc, Coventry
Craven Museum, Skipton
Crompton Public Library, Oldham
De Montfort University, Leicester and Bedford
Derry and Raphoe Diocesan Library, Londonderry
Dewsbury Central Library, Yorkshire
Duke of Edinburgh's Royal Regiment Museum,
  Salisbury
Dulwich Picture Gallery, London
Edinburgh Chamber of Commerce, Edinburgh
Faculty of Homoeopathy, Royal London
  Homoeopathic Hospital, London
Fortnum & Mason plc, London
Francis Skaryna Byelorussian Library & Museum,
  London
Friars Minor, English Province Archives, London
Gallery of English Costume, Manchester
Gairloch Heritage Museum, Ross-shire
Geological Survey of Northern Ireland, Belfast
Glaxo Smith Kline, Greenford
Glenalmond College Library, Perth
Great Torrington (Devon) Charities, Great
  Torrington
Greater Manchester Police Museum
Greenalls Group, Warrington
Gwent County Library, Croesyceiliog
Haberdashers' Aske's School, Elstree
Hitchin Museum and Art Gallery, Hertfordshire
Holland & Sherry Ltd, Peebles
Horniman Museum, London
ICI Technology, Middlesborough
Institute of Bankers in Scotland, Edinburgh
Institute of Ismaili Studies, London
Institute of Marine Engineers, London
Institution of Mining and Metallurgy, London
Ipswich Institute
Irish Guards, London
J Sainsbury plc, London
Jaguar Daimler Heritage Trust, Coventry
John Menzies plc, Edinburgh
John Murray Publishers, London
Kelvingrove Art Gallery and Museum, Glasgow
Kingston University, Kingston-upon-Thames
Ladywell Convent, Godalming
Leeds Industrial Museum
Leeds Metropolitan University
Liverpool John Moores University
London Business School

Longholme Library, Scotland
Madresfield Court, Malvern
Manchester Grammar School
Marlborough College, Marlborough
MEPC plc, London
Monmouth Museum, Wales
Morecambe Library, Lancashire
Morton Lodge of Freemasons, Lerwick
Mount Stuart, Rothesay, Isle of Bute
Museum of East Anglian Life, Stowmarket
National Farmers' Union of Scotland, Newbridge,
 Midlothian
Newquay Old Cornwall Society
Normal College, Bangor
Nottingham Central Library
Nottingham City Museums
Nottingham Subscription Library
Nottingham Trent University
Oriental Club, London
Oundle School, Peterborough
Oxford Brookes University
Pearl Group plc, London
Plymouth City Museum and Art Gallery
Prince of Wales's Own Regiment of Yorkshire, York
Quintiles Scotland Ltd
Rationalist Press Association, London
Rexam plc, London
Rochester Diocesan Registry, Kent
Royal Caledonian Curling Club, Newbridge
Royal Cambrian Academy of Art, Conwy
Royal Dragoon Guards, York
Royal Naval Engineering College, Plymouth
Royal Welch Fusiliers Regimental Museum,
 Caernarfon
Royal Society for Asian Affairs Library, London
St Edmund's College Library, Ware
St Dominic's Priory, Library of the Dominican
 Friars, London
St Ives Museum, Cornwall
Scottish Society for Prevention of Cruelty to
 Animals, Edinburgh
Scottish Trades Union Congress, Glasgow

Sea Cadet Association, London
Selfridges, London
Selly Manor Museum, Birmingham
Sheffield City Museum
Shrewsbury Cathedral
Sissinghurst Castle, Kent
Somerset Military Museum, Taunton
Sotheby's Auctioneers, London
South Place Ethical Society, London
Teesside University, Middlesbrough
Torrington Museum, Devon
Travellers' Club, London
Trinitarian Bible Society, London
Tyne and Wear Museums Service, Newcastle upon
 Tyne
Ukrainian Association in Great Britain, London
Union Theological College, Belfast
United Oxford and Cambridge University Club,
 London
University of Abertay, Dundee
University of Glamorgan, Pontypridd
University of Central England in Birmingham
University of Derby
University of Lincoln (formerly University of
 Lincolnshire and Humberside)
University of Luton
University of Sunderland
University of the West of England, Bristol
University of Wolverhampton
Uppingham School, Leicestershire
Ursuline Provincialate, Ilford
Warner Fabrics, Milton Keynes
Watts Gallery, Guildford
Welsh Guards, London
Wesley Historical Society, Irish Branch, Belfast
West Dean College, Chichester
Westminster College, Cambridge
Whitbread, London
Whittlesey Museum, Peterborough
Wilberforce House and Georgian Houses, Hull
Women's Royal Voluntary Service, Abingdon
York College of Arts and Technology Library, York

Main Index

This is a consolidated index to repository titles, plus parent organisations and significant predecessor organisations, where appropriate; organisations listed in the Appendices; and the collections mentioned in each entry.

In general personal names have been given birth and death dates or otherwise identified. Names of businesses have not been inverted e.g. WH Smith appears under W.

Repository titles appear in **bold**.

Hertz, Chief Rabbi J.H. (1872–1946), 1122

Hervey family, Marquisses of Bristol, 158

Hesketh Hubbard Society, 609

Hetherington, Sir Hector (1888–1956), university administrator, 389A

Hewins, W.A. (1865–1931), 1109

Hewison, James King, 351D

Hewitson, W. C. (1806–78), 917

Hewitt, John (1907–87), 253

Hey, Prof. Donald (1904–87), 669A

Hey, John (1734–1815), 203

Heygate, Sir Frederick (*d* 1940), 862

Heythrop College, App.I

Heywood and Middleton Water Board, 444

Heywood Borough, 444

Heywood Library, 444

Heywood of Bolton, 115

Hicks Beach of Coln St Aldwyn, 406

Hickson, J.M., missionary, 64

Higgins, Vera (1892–1968), 766

Higgs and Hill, builders, 688

Higgs, Griffin (1589–1659), 975

High Peak News, 895

Highgate Book Society, 633

Highgate Cemetery, 571

Highgate Dispensary, 633

Highgate Horticultural Society, 633

Highgate Literary and Scientific Institution, 633

Highgate School, 634

Highland Council Archive, 465

Highland Distilleries Co. plc, 389A

Highland Games, 465

Highland Health Board Archives, 466

Highland News, 1143

Highland Park Distillery, 493

Highland Regional Archive see Highland Council Archive, 465

Higson antiquarian collection, 948

Hildyard family of Winestead, 90

Hill and Adamson photographs, 333

Hill Collection, Glasgow sociology, 395

Hill Samuel Group plc, 683

Hill, Adrian (1895–1977), 635

Hill, D.O. (1802–70), photographer, 62, 318, 349, 389B, 1079B

Hill, Henry, paintings, 378

Hill, Howard (1913–80), 458

Hill, James (*d*1727), 440

Hill, Oliver (1887–1968), 768

Hill, Sir Rowland (1795–1879), 299, 726

Hillingdon Heritage Service, 1180

Hillstone preparatory school, 871

Hillyer Bros., trawler owners, 454

Hilton, John (1880–1943), 188

Hilton-Simpson, M.W., anthropologist, 743A, 743B

Hinckley Pint "C" Inquiry, 146

Hindson-Reid Collection, 922

Hinshelwood, Sir Cyril (1897–1967), 777

Hinton, Christopher, nuclear engineer, 661

Hinton, Horsley (1863–1908), 62

Hinton, Paula, 732

Hirst Research Centre Collection, 229

Hirst, Hugo, Collection, 229

Hirst, Thomas Archer (1830–92), 770

Historic Buildings and Monuments Commission, 602

Historic Mortality Data Files, 828

History Club, a society for Oxford women history dons, 971

History of Advertising Trust, 937

History of Technology Research Unit, 1034

Hitchings Collection of Bibles, 405

Hives, Lord, 1016

HM Customs and Excise, App.I

HM Land Registry, 626

HMS Albion disaster, 1898, 718

HMS Victory, 1041

HMS Wildfire RNR RTC (Chatham) Collection, 1062

Hoad & Son, wheelwrights, 1039

Hoare, Sir Richard Colt, antiquary, 279

Hobart of Blickling, 939

Hobart, Robert, Lord, 37

Hobart, Lord Vere Henry, 37

Hobart-Hampden MSS, 37

Hobbes, Thomas (1588–1679), 44

Hockaday MSS Collection, 405

Hodgkin, Thomas (1798–1866), 844

Hodgkin, Thomas (1831–1913), 922

Hodgson, Brian Houghton (1800–94), naturalist, 716, 861

Hodgson, John (1875–1952), 740

Hodgson, Sidney (1879–1973), 821

Hoffman, T., anthropologist, 743B

Hogarth MSS, 501

Hogarth Press, 1053

Hogben, Prof. Lancelot T. (1895–1975), 107A

Hogg MSS, 311

Hogg, Alexander R. (1870–1939), 85

Hogg, James, 'the Ettrick Shepherd' (1770–1835), 1134

Hogg, Brig. O.F.G. (1887–1979), 744

Hogg, Thomas, land agent, 311

Holborn and St Pancras MBC, 571

Holborn College of Law, Languages and Commerce, 835

Holcombe Roman Villa, 1114

Standing Conference on Legal Education, 648
Standish family, 510
Stanford family of Preston Manor, 134
Stanford, Sir Charles Thomas (1858–1932), 134
Stanford, Charles Villiers (1852–1924), 922
Stanger family of Keswick, 414
Stanhope of Chevening MSS, 868
Stanley of Alderley, 236
Stanley, Henry M. (1841–1904), 764
Stannus, Hugh S. (1877–1957), 302
Stansfeld of Fieldhouse Sowerby, 422
Stansfield, H. (1872–1960), 1122
Staple Inn, 673
Stapledon, Olaf, writer, 529
Staples, Leslie (1896–1980), 592
Stapleton, H.E. (1878–1962), 977
Star in the East, 813
Starbuck family of Sherborn, Nantucket Island, Massachusetts, 433
Stationers' and Newspaper Makers' Company, 821
Statistical Society of London, 784
Stawell family, 406
Stead McAlpin & Co Ltd, 1132
Stebbing, William (1831–1926), 720
Steed, Henry Whickam (1871–1956), 720
Steele, Anne (1717- 78), 993
Steele, William (1689–1769), 993
Steichen, Edward (1879–1973), 62
Stein Collection, 561E
Steiner, Rudolf (1861–1925), 539, 615
Stelfox, George (1884–1972), 253
Stencl, A.N. (1897–1983), 799
Stephenson Collection, 239
Stephenson, Elsie (1916–67), 351C
Stephenson, George (1781–1848), 661
Stephenson, Robert (1803–59), 229, 657, 661
Stephenson, Robert Louis (1850–1894), 352
Stepney Metropolitan Borough, 825
Sterling, Sir Louis (*d* 1958) Collection, 833
Stevens Guille Collection, 1088
Stevens, Joan, author, 1084
Stevenson, Bridget (1909–85), 797
Stevenson, H. (1833–88), 940
Stevenson, Joseph (1806–95), 565
Stevenson, R.L. (1850–94), 326
Stewart Bale photographic archive, 528
Stewart of Shambellie, 294
Stewart, James Stuart (1896–1990), 351D
Stewart, Madeau, 986
Stewart, Neil, medical illustrator, 302
Stewart-Meiklejohn family, 1019
Stewart-Murray, Lady Evelyn, Gaelic folktales MSS, 345

Stewartry Burgh, 491
Stewartry District Council, 491
Stewartry Museum, The, 491
Stewarts & Lloyds, 276
Stieglitz, Alfred (1864–1946), 62
Stirling Burgh, 1133
Stirling Council Archives Service, 1133
Stirling County, 1133
Stirling Journal, 1133
Stirling Observer, 1133
Stirling of Keir, 387
Stockport Archives, 1135
Stockport Sunday School, 1135
Stocks, J.W., 36
Stockton and Darlington Railway, 919
Stockton Council, 1136
Stockton Museum Service, 1136
Stockton on Tees borough, 901
Stockton Reference Library, 1137
Stockwell College, 475
Stockwell, Gen. Sir Hugh (1903–86) (B), 669
Stoke Newington borough, 628
Stoke Park, 43
Stoke-on-Trent City Archives, Staffordshire and Stoke-on-Trent Archive Services, 1139
Stoke-on-Trent College of Art, 1140
Stoker, Bram (1847–1912), 502B
Stokes, Sir George (1819–1903), 191
Stoke-upon-Trent Borough Council, 1139
Stone, Darwell (1859–1941), 990
Stone, Sir Benjamin, Collection, 100
Stone's foundry, Deptford, 676
Stonor, Dr, 817
Stonyhurst College Observatory, 165D
Stonyhurst College, 246
Stopes, Marie (1880–1958), 844
Storey Collection, 745
Storey, Gladys (1892–1978), 592
Storey, Very Rev. Robert Herbert (1835–1907), 389A
Stornoway airport, 1143
Stornoway Gazette, 1143
Stornoway Road Trustees, 1142
Stornoway Town Council, 1142
Stornoway Young Men's Mutual Association, 1142
Stow, David, educational pioneer, 401B
Stowe School, 1145
Strachey, James (1887–1967), 566
Strachey, John, historian and scientist, 1161
Strand School, 669A
Strand, 502B
Strange, John (1732–1799), 200
Strangeways oral history, 245

Winterbotham, Strachan and Playne of Minchinhampton, cloth manufacturers, 406

Wintringham, John, solicitor, Grimsby, 418

Wirral Archives, 97

Wisbech and Fenland Museum, 1207

Wisbech Hundred Commissioners of Sewers, 1207

Wisbech Museum & Literary Institute, 1207

Wisbech Town Council, 1207

Wiseman, Cardinal Nicholas (1802–65), 312

Wishaw Burgh, 910

Withering, William (1741–99), 781

Withers, Percy (1867–1945), 1005

Witly, W. Stuart, Collection, 89

Wittets Ltd, Elgin, architects, 356

Wittgenstein, Ludwig (1889–1951), 204

Wm. Baird & Co. (steelworks), 401A

Wm. Beardmore & Co. Ltd, shipbuilders, 383

Wm. Denny & Bros, 474B

Wm. Fife & Sons of Fairlie, 474A

Wm. McEwan & Co. Ltd, Edinburgh, 398

Wm. Younger & Co. Ltd, Edinburgh, 398

Woburn Experimental Station and Fruit Farm, 424

Wodehouse of Kimberley, 939

Wodehouse, P.G (1881–1975) collections, 597

Wolcot, John (Peter Pindar), 311

Wolfenden Report, 497A

Wolley MSS, 895

Wolley, John (1823–1859), 189

Wolseley Collection, Hove Reference Library, 451

Wolseley, car manufacturers, 377

Wolseley, FM Lord (1833–1913), 451

Wolseley, Lady Frances Garnet, 451

Wolstenholme Collection, 109

Wolvercote paper mill, 984

Wolverhampton Archives & Local Studies, 1209

Wolverhampton Borough Council, 1209

Women Artists' Slide Library, 854

Women Graduates Union, Bombay, 1042

Women's Art Library, 854

Women's Campaign for Soviet Jewry, 1122

Women's Co-operative Guild, 458, 550

Women's Engineering Society, 658

Women's International Art Club, 579, 854

Women's International League (Croydon and District Branch), 267

Women's Liberal Federation, 146

Women's Liberation Movement, 855

Women's Library, The, 855

Women's Peace Caravan, 143

Women's Royal Voluntary Service, App.III

Women's Service Library, 855

Women's Social and Political Union Archive, 704

Women's Theatre Collection, 147

Women's Work Exhibition, London,1900, 388

Womens Royal Army Corps, 706

Wood donation, 650

Wood family, Earls of Halifax, 1221

Wood Green borough, 631

Wood, Anthony, historian, 1008

Wood, Charles (1866–1926), 182B

Wood, Christopher (1901–30), 184

Wood, G.H., statistician and social reformer, 452

Wood, Sir Henry (1869–1944), 739

Wood, Robert 'Palmyra' (?1717–71), 650

Wood, Rev. Professor Thomas, 494

Wood, Rev. William (d.1919), 15

Woodall, architects, 527

Woodard Corporation Archives, 856

Woodard schools, 498

Woodbrooke Quaker Study Centre, 108

Woodburn Family of Monckton, 39

Woodcock & Sons, solicitors, 157

Woodforde family, 978

Woodgate, H.A., 990

Woodroffe, Paul (1875–1954), 242

Woods, Percy (1842–1922), 410

Woodside, Burgh of, 3A

Woodthorpe, Col. R.G. (1845–98), 988

Woodward papers, 940A

Woodward, John (1665–1728), 200

Wookey, Chris, railway historian, 1179

Woolf, Leonard, 136A

Woolf, Virginia, 136A, 561A

Woolley Hall estate, 502A

Woolwich Building Society, 872

Woolwich Equitable Benefit Building and Investment Association, 872

Woolwich Ferry Company, 621

Wooton, Barbara (1897–1988), 181

Worcester Cathedral Library, 1214

Worcester City Council, 1217

Worcester College, 1011

Worcester Fragments, 1214

Worcester House, 43

Worcestershire and Sherwood Foresters Regiment, 1215

Worcestershire Library & History Centre, 1216

Worcestershire Photographic Survey, 1217

Worcestershire Record Office, 1217

Wordsworth Library, 414

Wordsworth MSS, 497A

Wordsworth, Christopher (1807–1885), 672

Wordsworth, Dorothy (1771–1855), 414, 758

Wordsworth, William (1770- 1850), 22, 414, 481, 758

Workers' Educational Association, 100, 834, 957

Working Class Movement Library, 1094

Guide to Key Subjects

This list is not intended as an index to collections, but rather as a general guide to repositories with holdings of special relevance in specific subject areas. Where holdings are particularly strong the reference appears in **bold** type.

The list is compiled largely from the checklist of key subject headings returned by repositories, with editorial additions. Coverage of subject terms for local authority record offices and national repositories is selective since to indicate each term ticked would have made this list unduly large.